Aristotle Re-Interpreted

Ancient Commentators on Aristotle

GENERAL EDITORS: Richard Sorabji, Honorary Fellow, Wolfson College, University of Oxford, and Emeritus Professor, King's College London, UK; and Michael Griffin, Assistant Professor, Departments of Philosophy and Classics, University of British Columbia, Canada.

Aristotle Re-Interpreted (edited by Richard Sorabji) is a companion volume to the series, which translates the extant ancient Greek philosophical commentaries on Aristotle. A webpage for the Ancient Commentators Project is maintained at ancientcommentators.org.uk and readers are encouraged to consult the site for details about the series as well as for an updated Bibliography.

Aristotle Re-Interpreted:
New Findings on Seven Hundred Years of the Ancient Commentators

edited by
Richard Sorabji

BLOOMSBURY
LONDON • OXFORD • NEW YORK • NEW DELHI • SYDNEY

BLOOMSBURY ACADEMIC
Bloomsbury Publishing Plc
50 Bedford Square, London, WC1B 3DP, UK
1385 Broadway, New York, NY 10018, USA

BLOOMSBURY, BLOOMSBURY ACADEMIC and the Diana logo are
trademarks of Bloomsbury Publishing Plc

First published in Great Britain 2016
This edition published 2020

Copyright © Richard Sorabji & Contributors, 2020

Richard Sorabji has asserted his right under the Copyright, Designs and Patents Act, 1988,
to be identified as Author of this work.

For legal purposes the Acknowledgements on p. vii constitute an
extension of this copyright page.

Cover design: Terry Woodley
Cover image © The dispute of St Catherine by Masolino da Panicale, 1428–1431
© DEA/V. PIROZZI/Getty

All rights reserved. No part of this publication may be reproduced or transmitted
in any form or by any means, electronic or mechanical, including photocopying,
recording, or any information storage or retrieval system, without prior permission
in writing from the publishers.

Bloomsbury Publishing Plc does not have any control over, or responsibility for, any
third-party websites referred to or in this book. All internet addresses given in this
book were correct at the time of going to press. The author and publisher regret
any inconvenience caused if addresses have changed or sites have ceased to exist,
but can accept no responsibility for any such changes.

A catalogue record for this book is available from the British Library.

A catalog record for this book is available from the Library of Congress.

ISBN: HB: 978-1-4725-9656-7
PB: 978-1-3501-2366-3
ePDF: 978-1-4725-9658-1
eBook: 978-1-4725-9657-4

Typeset by RefineCatch Limited, Bungay, Suffolk

To find out more about our authors and books visit www.bloomsbury.com
and sign up for our newsletters.

Contents

Acknowledgements   vii
List of Contributors   viii

    Introduction: Seven Hundred Years of Commentary and the Sixth Century Diffusion to other Cultures   *Richard Sorabji*   1

1. The Texts of Plato and Aristotle in the First Century BCE: Andronicus' Canon   *Myrto Hatzimichali*   81
2. Boethus' Aristotelian Ontology   *Marwan Rashed*   103
3. The Inadvertent Conception and Late Birth of the Free Will Problem and the Role of Alexander   *Susanne Bobzien*   125
4. Alexander of Aphrodisias on Particulars and the Stoic Criterion of Identity   *Marwan Rashed*   161
5. Themistius and the Problem of Spontaneous Generation   *Devin Henry*   179
6. Spontaneous Generation and its Metaphysics in Themistius' Paraphrase of Aristotle's *Metaphysics* 12   *Yoav Meyrav*   195
7. The Neoplatonic Commentators on 'Spontaneous' Generation   *James Wilberding*   211
8. A Rediscovered *Categories* Commentary: Porphyry(?) with Fragments of Boethus   *Riccardo Chiaradonna, Marwan Rashed, and David Sedley*   231
9. The Purpose of Porphyry's Rational Animals: A Dialectical Attack on the Stoics in *On Abstinence from Animal Food*   *G. Fay Edwards*   263
10. Universals Transformed in the Commentators on Aristotle   *Richard Sorabji*   291
11. Iamblichus' *Noera Theôria* of Aristotle's *Categories*   *John Dillon*   313
12. Proclus' Defence of the *Timaeus* against Aristotle: A Reconstruction of a Lost Polemical Treatise   *Carlos Steel*   327
13. Smoothing over the Differences: Proclus and Ammonius on Plato's *Cratylus* and Aristotle's *De Interpretatione*   *R. M. van den Berg*   353
14. Dating of Philoponus' Commentaries on Aristotle and of his Divergence from his Teacher Ammonius   *Richard Sorabji*   367
15. John Philoponus' Commentary on the Third Book of Aristotle's *De Anima*, Wrongly Attributed to Stephanus   *Pantelis Golitsis*   393

16. Mixture in Philoponus: An Encounter with a Third Kind of Potentiality *Frans A. J. de Haas* — 413
17. *Gnôstikôs* and/or *hulikôs*: Philoponus' Account of the Material Aspects of Sense-Perception *Péter Lautner* — 437
18. The Last Philosophers of Late Antiquity in the Arabic Tradition *Peter Adamson* — 453
19. Alexander of Aphrodisias *versus* John Philoponus in Arabic: A Case of Mistaken Identity *Ahmad Hasnawi* — 477
20. New Arabic Fragments of Philoponus and their Reinterpretation: Does the World Lack a Beginning in Time or Take no Time to Begin? *Marwan Rashed* — 503
21. Simplicius' *Corollary on Place*: Method of Philosophising and Doctrines *Philippe Hoffmann and Pantelis Golitsis* — 531
22. A Philosophical Portrait of Stephanus the Philosopher *Mossman Roueché* — 541
23. Who Were the Real Authors of the *Metaphysics* Commentary Ascribed to Alexander and Ps.-Alexander? *Pantelis Golitsis* — 565

The Ancient Commentators on Aristotle Translations — 589
Bibliography — 595
Index Locorum — 625
General Index — 661

Acknowledgements

The editor would like to thank Christopher Strachan for his translations of Chapters 19 and 21, Jennifer Barnes (with technical advice from Jonathan Barnes), for her translation of Chapter 20, John Sellars for preparing the volume for press, and Alice Wright at Bloomsbury.

This volume was published with the support of The Leventis Foundation and the Canadian Social Sciences and Humanities Research Council.

We are grateful to the publishers mentioned below for permission to reprint the following chapters:

Brepols Publishers	Chapters 16 and 23
Brill	Chapters 3, 4, and 17
Cambridge University Press	Chapters 1, 2, and 19
Fondation Hardt	Chapter 18
Institute of Classical Studies, UCL	Chapter 13
Leuven University Press	Chapter 12
Librairie Philosophique J. Vrin	Chapter 21 extract
Oxford University Press	Chapters 5, 7, and 8
Presses Universitaires de France	Chapter 20
Revue des Études Grecques	Chapter 21
Syllecta Classica	Chapter 11

List of Contributors

Peter Adamson is Professor of Late Ancient and Arabic Philosophy at LMU, Munich, Germany.

R. M. (Bert) van den Berg is a lecturer in ancient philosophy at Leiden University, The Netherlands.

Susanne Bobzien is Professor of Philosophy at the University of Oxford and Senior Research Fellow in Philosophy at All Souls College, Oxford, UK.

Riccardo Chiaradonna is Associate Professor of Ancient Philosophy, Roma Tre University, Rome.

John Dillon is Regius Professor of Greek (Emeritus), Trinity College Dublin, and Director Emeritus of the Dublin Centre for the Study of the Platonic Tradition.

G. Fay Edwards was Assistant Professor of Greek and Roman Philosophy, Washington University in St Louis, Missouri, USA.

Pantelis Golitsis is Lecturer of Ancient and Medieval Philosophy at the Aristotle University of Thessaloniki, Greece.

Frans A. J. de Haas is Professor of Ancient and Medieval Philosophy, and Academic Director, Institute for Philosophy, Leiden University, The Netherlands.

Ahmad Hasnawi is Emeritus Research Director, CNRS/Université Paris Diderot, Paris.

Myrto Hatzimichali is University Lecturer in Classics (Philosophy), University of Cambridge, and Fellow, Homerton College, Cambridge, UK.

Devin Henry is Associate Professor of Philosophy at Western University, Ontario, Canada.

Philippe Hoffmann is Directeur d'études at the École pratique des hautes études, Paris, France.

Péter Lautner is Senior Reader in Philosophy at Pázmány Péter Catholic University, Budapest, Hungary.

List of Contributors

Yoav Meyrav is a Junior Faculty Member at the Department of Philosophy, Tel Aviv University, Israel.

Marwan Rashed is a Professor at the École normale supérieur, Paris, France.

Mossman Roueché is an independent scholar based in London, UK.

David Sedley is Emeritus Laurence Professor of Ancient Philosophy, University of Cambridge, and a Fellow of Christ's College Cambridge, UK.

Richard Sorabji is Emeritus Professor of Philosophy, King's College London, and Honorary Fellow, Wolfson College, University of Oxford, UK.

Carlos Steel is Emeritus Professor of Ancient and Medieval Philosophy, Institute of Philosophy, KU Leuven, Belgium.

James Wilberding is Professor of Ancient and Medieval Philosophy, Ruhr Universität Bochum, Germany.

Introduction: Seven Hundred Years of Commentary and the Sixth Century Diffusion to other Cultures

Richard Sorabji

The Advance in Knowledge

There has been an exponential increase in exploration of the ancient commentators on Aristotle, since 1985 when the translation series Ancient Commentators on Aristotle[1] was funded, since 1987 when the first translation appeared, and since 1990, which saw publication of the series' introduction to Aristotle's commentators, *Aristotle Transformed*.[2] Then there were very few experts on the commentators in the world and the general editor was not one of them. A review of the commentators on Aristotle was included in the introduction to the three-volume sourcebook on the commentators on Aristotle published in 2004, which, however, included little more than the 400 years from 200 to 600 CE, not the present span of nearly 700 years.[3] Over a hundred volumes of commentary have been published in English translation in the series since 1987, some lost in Greek and preserved in Latin, Arabic, or Syriac, and translations are under way from the surviving Hebrew and Arabic and again from Syriac. It is a sign of the geometrical progression in discovery that sixteen of the chapters included here were produced in the last five years, another so fully revised as to be almost a new paper and only six are older than that.

There are areas in which new detective work has been especially active. New fragments have been found or made accessible of the early Boethus of Sidon from the first century BCE,[4] the original advocate and exponent of word by word commentary on Aristotle, who started up a good number of the subsequent controversies. Some of the Boethus fragments are addressed in Chapter 2 and, embedded in a new fragment

---

[1] General Editor Richard Sorabji, Duckworth from 1987, Bloomsbury from 2013.
[2] Edited by Richard Sorabji (London: Duckworth, 1990; 2nd edn Bloomsbury, 2016).
[3] Richard Sorabji, *The Philosophy of the Commentators 200–600 AD: A Sourcebook*, 3 vols (London: Duckworth, 2004; repr. Bloomsbury, 2013).
[4] I use 'BCE', 'CE', referring to the common era, not BC or AD, which refer to Christ, when Islam or faiths other than Christianity are included in the discussion.

of Porphyry, in Chapter 8 below. The Porphyry fragment was invisible to the naked eye but deciphered under multi-spectral lighting, and it is a substantial fragment of what is possibly the most influential commentary of the third century Neoplatonist Porphyry, the lost larger of two commentaries by him on Aristotle's *Categories*. Turning to later Neoplatonism, a lost reply to Aristotle by Proclus in defence of Plato's cosmology is reconstructed in Chapter 12 from the commentators Philoponus, Simplicius, and Proclus himself. New fragments of Proclus' opponent Philoponus, lost in Greek but preserved in Arabic, are discussed in Chapter 19, and the author of that chapter has discovered many more fragments of Greek commentary, nearly all surviving in medieval Arabic,[5] but the most extensive one in Greek, the lost commentary of Alexander on Aristotle's *Physics* Books 4 to 8. It is edited with French commentary and translation in over 600 pages. The vital and transformative study of Arabic has also made it possible in Chapter 19 to reassign Arabic fragments from Alexander to Philoponus.

New fragments expand not only our knowledge of the original Greek texts, but also, when the fragments come from the languages of other cultures, our knowledge of the influence of the Greek texts in those cultures. The spread of Greek philosophy to other cultures is a marked feature of the sixth century CE. One stimulus was the construction by Ammonius in Alexandria of new introductions to philosophy with definitions of philosophy and of philosophical terms and divisions of philosophical fields and of other philosophical items. This became popular as making philosophy more accessible, and there has been work on these introductions and their spread, first in the sixth century to Persian and Syriac,[6] then from the eighth century into Arabic, as described in Chapter 18 and elsewhere[7] and in the seventh and eighth centuries to Fathers of the Greek Church, as described in Chapter 22. That chapter also provides a totally different picture of the Alexandrian philosopher Stephanus, of the spread of his work on definitions and divisions, while Chapter 23 expands the known range of his commentaries. The Ancient Commentators on Aristotle series will match for comparison the translation of an Armenian version of David the Invincible's *Definitions and Divisions of Philosophy* with a translation under way from the surviving Greek version of that same work. The record of conversations on philosophy and science between the sixth century Athenian philosophers and the Persian king who gave them refuge in 531 CE will appear as one of the next translations in the series. The spread of Greek Philosophy into Arabic has been the one most intensely studied of all, particularly in connexion with Philoponus, and is continued in Chapters 18, 19, and 20.

There have been new developments concerning Philoponus, thanks to Pantelis Golitsis, in studying the dating of his commentaries and of their divergence from his teacher Ammonius These are the subject of Chapters 14 and 15. Golitsis also studies in Chapter 23 the twelfth century compilations through Michael of Ephesus of composite

---

[5] See notes 27, 50, 51, 99 for Alexander and Themistius, for Simplicius notes 289, 298, 299, 300, and for Philoponus, note 307 and the new fragments of Philoponus in Rashed's Chapter 20.
[6] See also notes 98, 217, 218, 221, 222, 224, 226, 304–6.
[7] See also notes 228–233.

commentaries with the aid of surviving older commentaries, in order to fill gaps. In both contexts, it has become clearer in what ways later commentators used or re-used the interpretations of Aristotle by their teachers or predecessors.

Many, not all, of the chapters below will focus on one commentator, and some on one or two topics discussed by that commentator. The purpose of the introduction is to provide a setting for these studies by offering a quick, but more rounded, sketch of the commentators involved and of the development of the tradition of commentary as between earlier and later practitioners. Clearly, that does not make it possible to provide comprehensive details about each commentator. But an extra aid is now available in French in Richard Goulet, ed., *Dictionnaire des philosophes antiques* (Paris: CNRS, 1989-). In many cases, if not all, this major work supplies comprehensive available details on the lives and works of Greek philosophers, including, of course, the commentators on Aristotle and, progressing alphabetically, it has published between 1989 and 2016 the volumes up to Tyrsenos. The account in the introduction below offers snapshots only, and fuller details should be sought in these volumes as they progress.[8]

Andronicus: In Athens First Century BCE

Andronicus has been described already by Hans Gottschalk in *Aristotle Transformed*. The main controversy since then has been on what Gottschalk called Andronicus' 'critical edition'. The reputation of Andronicus in Athens in the first century BCE as the man whose edition of Aristotle triggered the commentary movement received a check in the seminal 1997 article of Jonathan Barnes, 'Roman Aristotle'.[9] Andronicus, he rightly said, did not produce a critical edition of Aristotle in the modern sense, one that compares different manuscript copies and emends the text so as to reconstruct as far as possible the original. What he did do, however, is suggested by two pieces of evidence discussed by Barnes. According to Porphyry, who took him as a model for his own later editorial work, Andronicus had assembled separate discussions by Aristotle into the same place.[10] In the same breath Porphyry cited his own practice of establishing a paedagogical order for reading the works being edited, and elsewhere approved putting Aristotle's logic first,[11] a practice followed to this day, and ascribed by Philoponus to Andronicus, in opposition to the preference of Boethus, who is called Andronicus' pupil, for putting Physics first.[12] The other piece of evidence was that he wrote a life of Aristotle and a catalogue describing his works. It is mentioned by Plutarch, but survives only in shortened form in an Arabic version, which refers to at least five

---

[8] I am very grateful to those who commented on parts of this introduction for me: Gillian Clark on Porphyry, John Dillon on Iamblichus, Marwan Rashed on Arabic matters and on what I said about his chapters, Carlos Steel on Proclus, Mossman Roueché on Ammonius and his school.
[9] Jonathan Barnes, 'Roman Aristotle', in Jonathan Barnes and Miriam Griffin, eds, *Philosophia Togata II* (Oxford: Oxford University Press, 1997), pp. 1-69, at pp. 21-44.
[10] Porphyry, *Life of Plotinus* 24.
[11] Porphyry, *in Cat.* 59,21-2.
[12] Philoponus, *in Cat.* 5,15-20.

books.[13] In addition to this, he wrote a 'paraphrase' of Aristotle's *Categories*, which Simplicius treats as something less than his pupil Boethus' 'exegesis' (*in Cat.* 26,17-20; 30,3-5). Andronicus' ideas will have become known from his biography and catalogue, as well as from his paraphrase commentary. He formed a canon of Aristotle's works, as well as arranging them in order, and in this he was largely followed except for two changes. In one, he treated the end of our *Categories* as wrongly amalgamated with the rest; in the other, he rejected as spurious Aristotle's *On Interpretation*, because when its chapter 1 treats spoken sounds as symbols or signs of effects produced in the soul, effects which Andronicus takes to be thoughts (*noêmata*), he cannot find the corresponding passage to which Aristotle refers in his *On the Soul*.[14] Boethus was decisively to reinstate *On Interpretation* as genuine, and to restore the addendum to the *Categories*. In Chapter 1, Myrto Hatzimichali explains why, with one possible exception, he did not engage in textual emendation. This was not because it had not been practised well before the time of Andronicus. Rather, Andronicus' project of canon-formation and arrangement for Aristotle was far more seminal for the commentary movement than any critical edition could have been.

Andronicus added some further impetus still.[15] Michael Griffin has elsewhere given a sense of what Andronicus may have contributed in other ways to the study of the *Categories*. For one thing, he asked about the purpose (*skopos*) of Aristotle's *Categories*. But he also discussed its title and its utility, and why it should be the first to be read of Aristotle's works. These four topics discussed by Andronicus were by the sixth century CE included among the standard topics for discussion in all introductions preceding the commentaries on Aristotle's *Categories*, so Andronicus was already setting the scene for more than 500 years later. In addition, his choice of logic as the starting point prevailed against his younger contemporary Boethus' preference for physics[16] except that by the sixth century a commentary on Porphyry's *Introduction* (*Isagôgê*) tended to precede in the curriculum the commentary on the *Categories*.

Andronicus also wrote a treatise on the division of a genus into species, a favoured ancient (though unsatisfactory) example being the division of animal into rational and

---

[13] Translated in I. Düring, *Aristotle in the Ancient Biographical Tradition* (Göteborg: Elanders, 1957), pp. 221-31, fifth book cited in no. 97, p. 230; supplemented in I. Düring, 'Ptolemy's Vita Aristotelis rediscovered', in R. B. Palmer and R. Hammerton-Kelly, eds, *Philomathes, In Memory of Philip Merlan* (The Hague: Nijhoff, 1971), pp. 264-9.

[14] Ammonius, *in Int.* 5,28.

[15] The classic work on the period of Andronicus and Boethus is Paul Moraux, *Der Aristotelismus bei den Griechen von Andronikos bis Alexander von Aphrodisias: I Die Renaissance des Aristotelismus im I Jh. v. Chr.* (Berlin: De Gruyter, 1973). For recent reinterpretation see Michael Griffin, *Aristotle's Categories in the Early Roman Empire* (Oxford: Oxford University Press, 2015), who supplies a much fuller bibliography at p. 3, n. 23, and his earlier Oxford D.Phil. Dissertation, 2009, *The Reception of Aristotle's Categories c. 80 BC - AD 220*; Tobias Reinhardt, 'Andronicus of Rome and Boethus of Sidon on Aristotle's *Categories*', in Richard Sorabji and Robert W. Sharples, eds, *Greek and Roman Philosophy 100BC- 200 AD*, 2 vols (London: Institute of Classical Studies, 2007), vol. 2, pp. 513-29, and, on Boethus on the category of relative, Concetta Luna, 'Boéthos de Sidon sur les rélatifs', *Studia graeco-arabica* 3 (2013), 1-31. The publications of the important five-year research project, ed. Cristina D'Ancona, are available in print (ISSN 2281-2687) and online at <http://learningroads.cfs.unipi.it/?page_id=111>.

[16] Elias, *in Cat.* 117,17-118,31.

other species. At least he wrote on this, if it is Andronicus to whom Boethius refers by the expression, 'the later sect of Peripatetic wisdom'.[17] Andronicus seems to have insisted on dividing the genus by a genuine differentia, not by a mere accident like paleness, which may or may not belong to humans. In all these ways, Andronicus encouraged the subsequent focus of early Aristotelian commentary on Aristotle's *Categories*. A new fragment on Andronicus' discussion of accidental features is included in the recently discovered fragments of Porphyry in Chapter 8, at 6,9–7,8, and is analysed there.

Andronicus' provocative ideas about the *Categories* were also stimulating to his younger associate in Athens, Boethus. He reorganised Aristotle's ten categories extensively, including them all under Plato's two distinctions of existing in itself or in relation to something else, with the alleged result of reducing their number. He treated Aristotle's category of When, or at-a-time, as subordinate to Time, which he saw as a category of its own, and similarly Aristotle's category of Where, or in-a-place, as subordinate to Place, which he also treated as a category. This last pair of substitutions did not affect the number of categories, but he also placed relation after all the categories as being like a mere sucker or side-shoot. Pamela Huby has suggested the reports would be compatible if he regarded *in itself* and *in relation* as *super-categories*, with time and place as categories falling under *in relation* and quantity as a category that exists *in itself*.[18] He further proposed an emendation of Aristotle's second (and preferred) definition of the category of relatives, apparently to protect it from a charge of circularity.

Boethus of Sidon in Athens First Century BCE

Boethus of Sidon is crucial for the tradition of commentary on Aristotle, in that he is said to have recommended the remarkable project of writing a *word by word* commentary on Aristotle's *Categories* (*exêgoumenos kath' hekastên lexin*),[19] and he did write such a commentary on Aristotle's *Categories*. This was eventually to have a momentous influence on the commentary tradition, although the earliest surviving commentaries after him are not as thorough.[20]

In addition, Boethus, in defending Aristotle's system, seems to have downgraded his key terms, interpreting them as belonging to the lowest available level. This is true of Aristotle's form, of differentia, of universal, and of his first figure of syllogism. In Chapter 2, Marwan Rashed takes up Boethus' downgrading of form as non-substance on the basis of Aristotle's requirement in *Categories* 2a11–13; 3a7–9, that a substance is a *subject* of predicates, and not a predicate, so not *in* a subject. From this, Simplicius

---

[17] Boethius, *De Divisione* 891–2.
[18] Pamela Huby, 'An excerpt from Boethus of Sidon's commentary on the *Categories*?', *Classical Quarterly* 31 (1981), 398–409, citing Simplicius, *in Cat* 63,22; 347,19–21; 134,5; 157,18–21.
[19] Reported by Simplicius, *in Cat*. 30,2.
[20] On the origin of commentaries on Aristotle, see Michael Griffin, *Aristotle's Categories in the Early Roman Empire* (n. 15 above).

tells us,[21] Boethus concluded that, although a compound of matter and form, like Socrates, can be a substance, and so can matter, for example the flesh and bones of Socrates, this is not possible for the *form* of Socrates, his soul. His form cannot be a substance, because form, though not mentioned in Aristotle's *Categories*, is said in his *Physics* 4.3, to be present *in* matter. This exclusion of form was to prove unacceptable more than two hundred years later to Aristotle's greatest defender, Alexander of Aphrodisias, discussed below in Chapters 3 and 4, because in works other than the *Categories*, Aristotle treats soul as substance, even though it is *in* body as a subject (Aristotle, *De Anima (DA)* or *On the Soul* 2.1). Aristotle's *Metaphysics* Book 7 also treats form as a good candidate for being substance, and *Metaphysics* 8 speaks as if a different criterion for substancehood had already been implied in Book 7 (see 7.17): the cause of a thing's being.[22] Alexander himself corrected Boethus[23] by holding that form is a *part* of the compound substance, and a *part* of a substance is a substance.

Rashed in Chapter 2 below cites a treatise in Arabic *On Difference*, existing in two versions, which he argues come from a lost *Question* about differentiae by Alexander.[24] It insists that the differentia of a genus, for example rational as differentiating a species of animal, is *substance* because it is a *part* of a substance, apparently because the differentia (rational) is form and form is *part* of the genus (animal). The *Question* also criticises someone who denies this by again relying on one of the criteria in Aristotle's *Categories* for substancehood (just as Boethus relied on another one in his disqualification of form from substancehood), and this is one of Rashed's reasons for thinking that Alexander's opponent is Boethus. This time, the unsatisfied criterion is that substances receive contrary characteristics. Alexander in the Arabic version replies that it is not differentiae but individual substances that have to receive contraries.

Riccardo Chiaradonna has studied Boethus' downgrading also of universals, again by reference to the *Categories*' definition of substance. On this ground, universals are not even a something (a Stoic category, lower than substance). Simplicius tells us: 'Boethus says first that the universal does not even exist in reality (*einai en hupostasei*), according to Aristotle, and even if it did have any reality, it would not be a *something*. Aristotle rather said it was *in* something.'[25] Chiaradonna concludes from a discussion of a number of passages that Boethus thought of a universal as nothing but a collection of particulars. The recently recovered fragments of Porphyry's lost commentary on the *Categories* in Chapter 8 below, speaking of animal, similarly say 'none of these generic items is a subject'.[26] The text of Porphyry translated and analysed in this chapter

---

[21] Simplicius, *in Cat.* 78,5–20.
[22] Aristotle, *Metaphysics* 8, 1043a2–4; b13–14, after an opening at 1042a3–4 which announces recapitulation and finishing touches (so Christof Rapp in a lecture in Oxford).
[23] Alexander, *DA (On the Soul)* 6,2–6.
[24] Earlier in Marwan Rashed, *L'Essentialisme* (Berlin: De Gruyter, 2007), pp. 63–4 and 76; 'Priorité de l'EIDOS ou du GENOS entre Andronicos et Alexandre: vestiges arabes et grecs inédits', *Arabic Sciences and Philosophy* 14 (2004), 9–63, at 44, cf. 29–30.
[25] Simplicius, *in Cat.* 50,5–8; cf. Dexippus, *in Cat.* 22,32–3. Discussed by Riccardo Chiaradonna, 'Alexander, Boethus and the other Peripatetics: The Theory of Universals in the Aristotelian Commentators', in R. Chiaradonna and G. Galluzzo, eds, *Universals in Ancient Philosophy* (Pisa: Edizioni della Normale, 2013), pp. 299–328.
[26] p. 3, lines 16–26.

includes among others a further new fragment on Boethus' treatment of division by differentia at 14,4–15.

Rashed has drawn attention to yet another way in which Boethus downgrades something of Aristotle's: the priority of Aristotle's first figure of syllogism. Or at least he puts Aristotle's figures all on the same level. The figures are Aristotle's patterns of valid argument concerning all, some, or none of a class of things, and Aristotle thought that certain arguments in the second and third figures had to be proved equivalent to certain arguments in the first, before they could be seen as valid. I shall discuss below the resumption of the debate in the fourth century by the commentator Themistius. Rashed has translated Themistius' text from the superior of two Arabic manuscripts into French.[27] It is to be hoped that Chiaradonna and Rashed, two of the translators of the fragment in Chapter 8, will carry out their plan of compiling the first collection of fragments of Boethus, of which Michael Griffin has already noticed around fifty.[28]

Griffin has again elsewhere provided an important study of Boethus,[29] describing his introduction of the three-part account of the subject matter of Aristotle's *Categories*. In a tradition which Simplicius sees as starting with Boethus and continuing through Herminus, Herminus' pupil Alexander of Aphrodisias, Alexander of Aigai, Porphyry, and Iamblichus, Aristotle's *Categories* is about simple, primary and generic spoken sounds, insofar as they signify things. Simplicius treats the signification as a distinct third element in the account besides spoken sounds and things, for he says in the same breath that, insofar as things are *signified* by spoken sounds, the *Categories* is giving instruction not only about the things signified, but also about *concepts* (*noêmata*).[30] This word is used by Aristotle himself in *On Interpretation* 1, 16a10, which is what suggests the interpretation, and three commentators, starting with Philoponus, report Iamblichus as also having said that Aristotle's *Categories* was about spoken sounds signifying things *through the medium of concepts* (*noêmata*), although not everyone took that conceptual interpretation.[31] Thus Boethus gave rise to a tradition, which in turn encouraged in some a conceptualist interpretation.

In reply to the critical question of the Platonists Lucius, Nicostratus, and Plotinus[32] whether the things signified in the categories include Plato's intelligible Ideas, which Plotinus in *Enneads* 6.1 was to criticise Aristotle for not including, Boethus replied that the *Categories* was not concerned with intelligible substance,[33] and Porphyry said that Boethus was right.[34] Porphyry added that for beginners Aristotle was only discussing

---

[27] *Treatise of Themistius in answer to Maximus and Boethus on the reduction of the second and third figures to the first*. The treatise is translated into French from a better manuscript from Tashkent and discussed in one of Rashed's 2013 Nellie Wallace lectures at the University of Oxford, *Timaeus' Five Worlds: A Study of Plato's Mathematical Ontology*, to be published by Oxford University Press. The inferior manuscript had been translated into French by A. Badawi.

[28] Michael Griffin, *Aristotle's Categories in the Early Roman Empire* (n. 15 above), p. 184, n. 18.

[29] Michael Griffin, op. cit., esp. ch. 6, 'Boethus of Sidon', and chs 4 and 7.

[30] Simplicius, *in Cat.* 13,11–18.

[31] Philoponus, *in Cat.* Prooemium 9,12–15; Olympiodorus, *in Cat.* Prolegomena 18,23–20,12; Elias, *in Cat.* Prooemium 130,14–131,14.

[32] Simplicius, *in Cat.* 73,27–8.

[33] Simplicius, *in Cat.* question: 73,15–76,16; Boethus' reply: 78,4–5.

[34] Porphyry, *in Cat.* 59,17–18.

what names originally signified, which was perceptibles.[35] The implication is that in omitting intelligibles for beginners Aristotle was not denying the existence of intelligible Ideas. But the question bore further fruit, because Plotinus, as Pierre Hadot has stressed,[36] offered Aristotle another pair of possible answers, that Aristotle's application of categories to perceptibles *depends on* their applicability to intelligibles, and that the application to intelligibles can be understood *analogically* from that to perceptibles. Iamblichus accepted versions of these answers and spelled out in detail how they could work.[37]

Griffin cites Boethus as having replied eight times, in Simplicius' reports, to objections raised against Aristotle's *Categories* by Lucius and his followers. He takes Lucius to be a Platonist slightly younger than Boethus, but overlapping with him in the first century BCE.[38] Lucius may have overlapped with the next Platonist critic, Nicostratus in the later first century CE, who replied to Boethus and produced new objections to Aristotle's *Categories*. The fragments drawn from Porphyry's larger *in Cat.* and translated in Chapter 8 reveal that Boethus is responding to unnamed critics of Aristotle even earlier than himself.[39]

A fragment tentatively identified as of Boethus replying to Andronicus was explicated by Pamela Huby far ahead of the present renewal of interest, but Marwan Rashed suggests in Chapter 2 that the text is instead by Porphyry.[40] It is a philosophical analysis, going well beyond Aristotle, of his category of When. The author replies to his opponent that Aristotle treats time and place not as separate categories, nor (even though they are measures) as relatives, but as quantities. Aristotle's categories of When and Where, on the other hand, do not fall under the category of time, but consist of the relationship of a thing to time.

The author further disagrees with Aristotle as well as with his other opponent, criticising Aristotle's view that, because time is defined as countable, it depends on conscious beings. In effect he replies that time has the *capacity* to be counted, but in the absence of conscious beings, there would be no *opportunity* for counting.

Commentators on Aristotle in the First Two Centuries after Boethus

Since the classic work of Paul Moraux[41] and the survey of commentators of the period by Hans Gottschalk and of commentators on Aristotle's *Ethics* by Paul Mercken, both

---

[35] Porphyry, *in Cat.* 57,35–58,7.
[36] Pierre Hadot, 'The Harmony of Plotinus and Aristotle according to Porphyry', in R. Sorabji, ed., *Aristotle Transformed*, ch. 6.
[37] Plotinus, *Enneads* 6.1.3.1–5; 6.3.5.3.
[38] Griffin, op. cit. pp. 180–3; 196.
[39] Chapter 8 below, original pagination 130, 188, concerning an attack on Aristotle's claim about differentiae at *Cat.* 1b16–20.
[40] Pamela Huby, 'An Excerpt from Boethus of Sidon's Commentary on the *Categories*?'; Marwan Rashed, 'Boethus' Ontology' (ch. 2 below), in the original pagination, p. 71, n. 43 and pp. 74–6.
[41] Paul Moraux, *Der Aristotelismus bei den Griechen von Andronikos bis Alexander von Aphrodisias: II im I und II Jh. v. Chr.* (Berlin: De Gruyter, 1984).

in *Aristotle Transformed*,[42] there has been much recent new work on philosophy of the first two centuries after Boethus in general[43] and on the commentators on Aristotle in that period in particular. The latter includes a collection of papers on Aspasius, the teacher of Herminus, who in turn taught Alexander,[44] and Aspasius' commentary on six books of Aristotle's *Ethics* has been translated by David Konstan in two volumes in the series Ancient Commentators on Aristotle. Adrastus was a junior contemporary of Aspasius in the second century CE. His commentaries on Aristotle's *Categories* and *Physics* are lost. He is said to have written a book on Aristotle's *Nicomachean Ethics*, and, although anonymous scholia on books 2 to 4 of Aristotle's *Nicomachean Ethics* are thought to include extracts from him, Paul Moraux identified as fragments from Adrastus only literary and historical questions as being a known interest of his from another book he wrote on that subject. Much better informed are his modifications of Aristotle's astronomy of the planets, which introduce epicycles and eccentrics in place of Aristotle's concentric circlings, in the fragments of his commentary on Plato's *Timaeus*, preserved by someone who may have been Ptolemy's teacher, Theon of Smyrna.[45]

Robert Sharples has discussed the Aristotelians of the period in his sourcebook, *Peripatetic Philosophy, 200 BC to AD 200: An Introduction and Collection of Sources in Translation* (Cambridge: Cambridge University Press, 2010). Griffin's subsequent book, *Aristotle's Categories in the Early Roman Empire*, makes further advances, to be mentioned below. Alexander of Aphrodisias uses several sources from this period: another Alexander coming from Aigai, along with Herminus, and Sosigenes, the last two his teachers. The idea that he had another teacher from the period called Aristotle (or, conjecturally, Aristocles) has been questioned by Jan Opsomer and Bob Sharples, since 'I heard Aristotle' can refer to Alexander's listening to Aristotle being read out.[46]

A sizeable fragment of Herminus' views is translated in Chapter 8 towards the end of the new fragment of Porphyry's lost larger commentary on the *Categories*. Here Herminus discusses the division of a genus into species and disagrees with Boethus, among others. Some of his argument is not recorded elsewhere, either in Alexander's reports of his teacher, or in Simplicius' massive compilation of arguments about the *Categories*, drawn from Porphyry's commentary via Iamblichus.

---

[42] Hans B. Gottschalk, 'The Earliest Aristotelian Commentators'; H. P. F. Mercken, 'The Greek Commentators on Aristotle's *Ethics*', both in Richard Sorabji, ed., *Aristotle Transformed*, chs 3 and 18.
[43] I have to omit here extensive work on Platonists of the period by George Karamanolis, *Plato and Aristotle in Agreement?* (Oxford: Oxford University Press, 2006); George Boys-Stones, *Post-Hellenistic Philosophy: A Study of its Development from the Stoics to Origen* (Oxford: Oxford University Press, 2001); and a series of articles by Riccardo Chiaradonna, including 'Medioplatonismo e Aristotelismo', *Rivista di storia di filosofia* 2 (2015), 426–46.
[44] Antonina Alberti and Robert W. Sharples, eds, *Aspasisus: The Earliest Extant Commentary on Aristotle's Ethics* (Berlin: De Gruyter, 1999).
[45] Richard Sorabji, 'Adrastus: Modifications to Aristotle's Physics of the Heavens by Peripatetics and others, 100 BC to 200 AD', in Richard Sorabji and Robert W. Sharples, eds, *Greek and Roman Philosophy 100 BC-200 AD*, 2 vols (London: Institute of Classical Studies, 2007), vol. 2, pp. 575–94.
[46] J. Opsomer and R. Sharples, 'Alexander of Aphrodisias "De Intellectu" 110,4: "I heard this from Aristotle", A Modest Proposal', *Classical Quarterly* 50 (2000), 252–6.

Alexander of Aphrodisias in Athens (flourished c. 205 CE)

Alexander of Aphrodisias was the greatest defender of Aristotelianism. There has at last been clear confirmation published in 2004 by Angelos Chaniotis that Alexander did indeed around or after 200 CE hold the chair of Aristotelian philosophy in Athens, established a little earlier as one of the Athenian chairs for the four philosophy schools by the Stoic emperor, Marcus Aurelius.[47] There has been intensive study of Alexander, prominently by Paul Moraux, Robert Sharples, and Pierluigi Donini.[48]

Frans de Haas has pointed out[49] that Alexander wanted to bring Aristotelianism up to date to match the rival schools, especially the two most flourishing of Stoicism and Platonism. There were many subjects which Aristotle had not studied at all, he points out. Susanne Bobzien also gives the examples, in her Chapter 3 below, of Fate, Providence, and how to define the idea that something is up to us, so that we are liable to praise or blame for it. Again, Aristotle did not discuss whether causes and effects are bodies or incorporeal. He never solved the puzzles he raised about the reality of time. De Haas cites areas of unclarity in Aristotle, for example on the nature of active intellect. The Stoics had invented a new theory of syllogism based on the relations between complete propositions, not, as with Aristotle, on the relation between terms within propositions.

Alexander had contrasting techniques in his opposition to Stoics. Sometimes he spoke as if Aristotle already knew what they were saying. A striking example is his appropriation of the new Stoic idea of assent (*sunkatathesis*). We shall see that he accepts much of a recent Stoic definition of what is *up to us*, which Aristotle had left undefined, in terms of what we do through the *assent* of reason. Or again, where Aristotle in *On the Soul* 3.3 distinguished belief from mere appearance by reference to the idea of being given reasons (*logos*), Alexander defines the difference between judgement and appearance in terms of our giving *assent* to appearance.

Alexander wrote commentaries, not all surviving, on a large part of Aristotle's corpus. But he also wrote separate treatises, partly because his replies to Galen, and his filling of gaps that Aristotle left, would not easily fit into commentaries on Aristotle. In addition, he wrote *Questions and Solutions* and *Ethical Questions*, which, so Robert

---

[47] Angelos Chaniotis, 'Epigraphic evidence for the philosopher Alexander of Aphrodisias', *Bulletin of the Institute of Classical Studies* 47 (2004), 78–81.

[48] Paul Moraux, *Der Aristotelismus bei den Griechen, von Andronikos bis Alexander von Aphrodias: III Alexander von Aphrodisias* (Berlin: De Gruyter, 2001), completed by Robert Sharples' chapter on Alexander's ethics. Sharples himself provided a massive output on Alexander, as shown by the catalogue of his writings up to 2012 in Peter Adamson, ed., *Ancient Philosophy in Memory of R. W. Sharples* = *Bulletin of the Institute of Classical Studies* 55/1 (2012), Sharples' bibliography at pp. 11–18. Many were on particular issues and texts of Alexander, but an overall survey of Alexander was offered in 'Alexander of Aphrodisias: Scholasticism and Innovation', in W. Haase, ed., *Aufstieg und Niedergang der römischen Welt* II. 36.2 (Berlin: De Gruyter, 1987), pp. 1176–1243. A collection of seven papers on Alexander by Pierluigi Donini was included in a collection of his reprinted papers, with introduction by Bonazzi and Sharples, in Pierluigi Donini, *Commentary and Tradition* (Berlin: De Gruyter, 2011), pp. 87–177.

[49] Frans de Haas, 'The new design of Peripatetic philosophy by Alexander of Aphrodisias', paper heard at the conference in Berlin, 'Aristotle Transferred', 23–4 Oct, 2014, to be published in Proceedings, ed. Gyburg Uhlmann, in preparation.

Sharples argued in *Aristotle Transformed*, reflected classroom teaching, unlike his commentaries on Aristotle, but like the later commentaries of the Neoplatonists. A good number of his lost works have been recovered in Arabic translation, and much, including much of the Arabic, has been translated into English,[50] some into French and a little into Italian.[51] But the very long lists of titles ascribed to him in Arabic bibliography cannot be relied on without investigation.

Two principal subjects from Alexander's huge range are included in Chapters 3 and 4 below. Both discuss Alexander on different aspects of determinism, the first on determinism and moral responsibility, the second on determinism and individuality. But both are concerned with whether the *recurrence* of the same circumstances must have the same outcome. In Chapter 3, Susanne Bobzien homes in on Alexander being the first to deny a certain Stoic principle. The principle is that if in the same circumstances (*periestêkota*) as Alexander puts it in his *On Fate*, or *external* circumstances, as it is more misleadingly put it in the *Mantissa* (*Supplement to On the Soul*),[52] one acted (or chose, as the *Mantissa* adds) now in one way, now in another, there would be a change without any cause, which is impossible.[53] The *Mantissa*'s confinement to *external* circumstances is misleading because the Stoics think one's *internal* psychological state is also relevant to whether one can act otherwise. Bobzien finds no predecessor to Alexander's denial of the Stoic principle, even among Middle Platonist discussions of Aristotle's undetermined sea battle in his *On Interpretation* 9. In her definitive book of the same year, *Determinism and Freedom in Stoic Philosophy*,[54] she throws new light again by pointing out that the name of the second century CE

---

[50] In the Ancient Commentators on Aristotle series: commentaries: *On Aristotle's Metaphysics* 1–5 (4 vols); *On Prior Analytics* 1 (5 vols); *On Topics* 1; *On Aristotle on Sense Perception*; *On Aristotle On Meteorology* 4, from Arabic: *On Aristotle On Coming-to-Be and Perishing* 2. 2–5. Treatises: *On the Soul* (Part 1); *Mantissa* (*Supplement*) *to Aristotle On The Soul*; *Quaestiones* (2 vols); *Ethical Problems*. Translations of treatises elsewhere: by Robert Sharples, *On Fate* (London: Duckworth, 1983); from Latin, with input on Arabic, *On Time, Phronesis* 27 (1982), 58–81; by Robert Todd, *On Mixture* (Leiden, Brill, 1976), by C. Genequand, from Arabic, *On the Cosmos* (Leiden: Brill, 2001); by N. Rescher and M. Marmura, from Arabic, *The Refutation of Galen's Treatise on the Theory of Motion* (Islamabad: Islamic Research Institute, 1965). In ch. 2 below Rashed translates a few extracts from an Arabic use of a lost treatise of Alexander, *Question on the differentia*. Rashed has also translated from Greek into English a passage of Alexander's commentary on *Physics* 6.4, previously lost, in R. Sorabji, ed., *Aristotle and After* (London: Institute of Classical Studies, 1997), pp. 181–95, and repr. as ch. 4 of his *L'Héritage aristotélicien* (Paris: Les Belles Lettres, 2007).
[51] French translations of Alexander include P. Thillet *On Providence* (Lagrasse: Verdier, 2003). Rashed has also translated from Greek into French the substantial remains of Alexander's lost commentary on Aristotle's *Physics* Books 4–8, as well as an Arabic commentary by al-Nawbakhtī on Aristotle's *GC* which uses Alexander's lost commentary as a source and so permits a certain amount of reconstruction. His *L'Héritage aristotélicien* includes three chapters with translations into French from Arabic of fragments of Alexander, lost in Greek, and he has a French translation of Themistius' letter to Julian on Aristotle's syllogistic awaiting publication. There is an Italian translation of Alexander *On the Soul* by Paolo Accatino and Pierluigi Donini (Rome: Laterza, 1996).
[52] Not all passages in the *Mantissa* are necessarily by Alexander, so I will rely on his *On Fate*, but most of the *Mantissa* passages I cite are in agreement with *On Fate*.
[53] Alexander, *On Fate* 15, 185,7–11; *Mantissa* (*Supplement to On the Soul*) § 23, 174,3–7. The authenticity of this part of the *Mantissa* has not been challenged.
[54] Susanne Bobzien, *Determinism and Freedom in Stoic Philosophy* (Oxford: Clarendon Press, 1998), pp. 358–94.

Stoic who pressed this question, Philopator, is given in the late fourth century report of the Christian Nemesius, Bishop of Emesa. It was Philopator's earlier question to which Alexander felt obliged to reply. Nemesius records his argument a third way by saying that with the same *causes as circumstances (aitiôn periestêkotôn)*, it is not possible that the same things happen now one way, now otherwise.[55] I think that Philopator's challenge made Alexander make up his mind how far in advance necessitation would be objectionable. At one point, Alexander tellingly objects to our doing or not doing something having been inevitable before we were born.[56] Many people, but not all, would indeed see inevitability before birth, like Alexander, as particularly threatening to the idea of our moral responsibility, that is, to the idea that we can be justifiably praised or blamed for what we do. Aristotle had been vaguer in the discussion of his sea battle. Various ethical ideas other than responsibility would be jeopardised, he thought, if our acts had been inevitable ten thousand years ago, or for the whole of time. But under pressure from Philopator's question, Alexander goes further. Even in the extreme case, where the same external and internal circumstances have recurred, it still need not be inevitable beforehand how we will act.

The denial of Philopator's principle is one new step by Alexander, but Bobzien rightly argues that he does not take the further step of introducing the idea of will as being free. In her book, she finds the first move of this type in a different tradition marginally earlier in the Christian Justin Martyr (died *c*. 165).

I would draw attention to two small passages of Alexander, mentioned but not discussed in Bobzien's seminal and enlightening treatment, which I think may throw further light on his strategy. In *On Fate* ch. 15 and *Mantissa* (*Supplement to On the Soul*) § 23, he wants to show that even when necessity is absent, a cause can be present, contrary to Philopator's charge from the beginning of each chapter, that that would imply a causeless change. He first argues that the person is the cause, and, in more detail, that the person's deliberation (*boulê*), deliberate choice (*prohairesis*), and judgement (*krisis*) are the cause.[57] That much is intended to establish his first point, that there is a *cause*. To me his most interesting argument for the second point, that there need be no *necessity*, is his observation that we have more than one motive, and he names the noble, the pleasant, and the advantageous.[58] Indeed, we do have different standing motives, and the adherents of Philopator, who introduced the theme of necessity at the beginning of each chapter, would need to show that necessity has to govern which standing motive takes effect. I myself think that that cannot be shown and that Alexander is safe. But it is not whether he is safe that matters for present purposes, but that this is the strategy he intends. He needs such a strategy, if he is to answer Philopator's actual objection, that he has created a change without a cause. The most relevant change in the world is the person's action. The strategy says that whichever standing motive operates provides a perfectly good cause of that action.

---

[55] Nemesius, *On the Nature of Man* 174,3–27 Morani.
[56] Alexander, *On Fate* 17, 188,15.
[57] Alexander, *On Fate* 15, 185,15–16; *Mantissa* § 23, 174,9–10.
[58] Alexander, *On Fate* 15, 185,21–8; *Mantissa* § 23, 174,13–24.

Alexander does not have to worry that from his perspective there is something else that may have no explanation, let alone a necessitating explanation, although that is not necessarily because the motives are incommensurable. There may be no explanation of why this time one standing motive operated, last time another. The objection that this would divorce the agent from his wants or beliefs, or from his character, disposition, or reason does not seem to me convincing.[59] The agent may by character always be equally attracted to two or more incentives, or may be volatile in susceptibilities. It is up to the Stoics to show that there must be an explanation and a determining one of the agent's variability, and this may be difficult. The important point is that the objection Philopator did offer has been answered: the desiderated cause of the action is the operative motive.

Alexander has another related but different strategy that Bobzien mentions. In the *On Fate* version, the wise person does not do what they choose by being necessitated (*katênankasmenôs*), for it might at some time seem reasonable (*eulogon*) to a wise person to refute a prediction of their activity and show the activity's freedom (*eleutheron*), in Alexander's explicated sense, by *not* doing at some time what would [otherwise] have been brought about by that wise person as [also] reasonable (*eulogôs*). In the *Mantissa* version, even if a person chose the same things in the same circumstances, thinking them to be more reasonable, it would not follow that the choosing was necessitated (*katênankasmenôs*), nor that *external* factors were causes of the decisions [sc. which would make the choice forced, *biaion*]. For the power is available (*exesti*) to that person, if they want to show at some time that that their choice is not necessitated (*katênankasmenên*) and want to defeat the prediction, also to chose what they did not [otherwise] think reasonable. Once again, what is being denied here is necessitation, not causation. Their choice depends in either case on what they think reasonable and in one case partly on competitiveness of character. Their normal desires are operating, and the desires correspond to their characters as wise or competitive. The case in *On Fate*, mentioned to show that physiognomic predictions cannot help getting it wrong, is that in which Socrates says that, by the discipline of philosophy, he overcame his *original* nature (*phusis*), which would, as the story is told in other texts, have made him a womaniser.[60] In none of the cases of the ability to refute predictions is the suggestion that wants and beliefs in line with *present* character do not act as *causes*. The point is the entirely different one that the actions are not *necessitated* and in the *Mantissa* are also not *forced* by external factors.

In Chapter 4, Marwan Rashed takes up a very different aspect of determinism, the influence of the stars and the motions of the heavens, which in Alexander's *On Fate* had been mentioned only in two lines, 169,23–5, as the view of unspecified people (possibly Stoics), as if it did not require discussion. This subject is relevant to the possibility of the recurrence of exactly similar *individuals*. It is therefore also a companion to

---

[59] This is mentioned only as a consequence by Bobzien at pp. 134–5, 139, 171, but much more strongly pressed as an objection to Alexander in Michael Frede's posthumous book, *A Free Will* (Berkeley: University of California Press, 2011), pp. 95–101, where his description of Alexander on p. 98 seems to be inspired by Bobzien's.
[60] *On Fate* 6, 171,11–16.

Chapter 10 below, with its discussion of *universals*. Despite the lack of discussion in *On Fate*, Alexander knew, according to Philoponus in his commentary on Aristotle's *GC* 2.11, an objection to Aristotle, that the same individuals would recur, when the same cause recurred through the stars returning to their earlier alignments. For undifferentiated matter would not differentiate them into individuals distinct from the ones produced last time those alignments occurred. Alexander is said to have replied that, even if it were granted that some Socrates would be born one world cycle later, it would not be numerically the same Socrates, because the same *individual* form (*atomon eidos*) will not recur after an interval. I think Alexander will have been drawing on Aristotle saying in *Physics* 5.4 that a walk resumed, or health regained is not the same walking and not the same health. Moreover, in the case of individuals, although celestial bodies remain the same, people return to existence not numerically the same, but the same only in form (not in this case individual form). Alexander had a further reply, according to Averroes, that the heavens cannot return to their earlier alignments, because, so he mistakenly thought, the many circuits were incommensurable – they could not be measured by any unit of length common to all of them. Rashed shows that there were among Alexander's Stoic opponents those who thought that the heavens are causes of the individual. They said that that a uniquely identifying characteristic (*idiôs poion*) was conferred on each infant's soul (regarded as something physical), through its being tempered at birth by the air. Moreover, when the alignment of the heavens recurred a whole world cycle later, the same unique characteristic would be conferred, making the individual unique. There were different Stoic views as to whether this sort of thing happened by necessity, or merely always, although it could not presumably be by some giant coincidence. But the new Socrates would not be born sooner than the next celestial realignment.

I agree with Rashed's view that Alexander likes to answer determinism sometimes by allowing that things are caused, while denying that are therefore *necessitated*. That was the strategy I suggested he used in *On Fate* and in the *Mantissa*, when he argued that we act according to standing *motives* as causes, but it is not necessitated which standing motive will prevail. In the context of celestial motion, however, I would not have expected him to agree with the Stoics insofar as they said that the movement of the heavens is the cause of *individuals*. For in his treatise on Providence, he regards the movements of the heavens providential for existence at the level only of *species*, not of *individuals*. The differences between individuals are accounted for by matter, not by Providence.[61] Hence, when Rashed reports Alexander, according to Averroes' Arabic text, speaking of the heavens as the efficient *cause* (the Greek would be *poioun*) of the *individual*, but with alignments that do not, however, recur, I would expect Alexander to mean that the alignments which his *opponents* call the efficient cause do not recur. This is suggested also by something we shall see below, that although Alexander makes nature depend at some remove on the heavens, he gives a very large role to processes

---

[61] Alexander, *On Providence* 87,5–91,4 Ruland, translated into French from the Arabic in Rashed, *Essentialisme*, p. 253, and 88–92 into English by Robert Sharples in n. 315 to his translation of Alexander, *Quaestiones 1.1–2.15* (London: Duckworth, 1992), p. 98.

started by the male parent and says that the processes are as automatic as marionettes. This would leave room for the parental role to include some factors to play the role of unnecessitated standing motives in his other discussion – Rashed suggests to me the diet that, for various *motives*, the parents have chosen to adopt. But if so much role is given to the parents, I am not sure why Alexander would describe the more remote role of the heavens as the efficient cause of the *individual*.

Rashed argues that Avicenna was able to improve Alexander's argument. His reply to exactly similar individuals recurring was that the *angular velocities* of the celestial circuits are not all commensurable and that therefore the same celestial alignment would never recur. Leibniz, did not believe that there could be exactly similar individuals, and he probably knew, Rashed maintains, the tradition of argument just described. But he had an argument about the limits of our knowledge. Essential propositions can be proved in a finite number of steps. But non-necessary propositions, such as those about individuals and the heavens, would be knowable only through an infinite number of steps and are therefore not knowable in any finite language, but knowable only to God.

Chapter 10 below relates to Alexander's treatment of particulars, discussed by Rashed, when it addresses Alexander's treatment of *universals*. Of these he recognises more than one kind. To a considerable extent, but not entirely, Alexander gives universals a lower status than he gives to the individual enmattered form (Rashed's *atomon eidos*) or nature, for example mortal rational animal. A universal has a lower status if it is the individual form separated by the mind from its material circumstances, so that it exists in thought, not as it really is. Another way for an individual form to be universal is no more than the mere accident of its residing in more than one specimen, in contrast for example, to the form of the sun, which happens to reside only in one. Alexander requires for this last type of universality that the form be *actually* shared by at least two specimens, not merely, as Aristotle required, *shareable*. Alexander allows that biological species are eternal, but only by the *succession* of individual specimens. This may be the first mention of the only kind of eternity that Averroes was later to allow to the human soul. Despite all this downgrading of universals, Alexander was to upgrade them by giving them two important roles. First the common form of, for example, human is what Providence seeks to preserve, not the individual form. Secondly, the common form residing in at least two individuals has the causal role of *bestowing being* on individual and species.

Another topic of Alexander's relevant to the treatment of individuals was his denial that the immortal Active Intellect of Aristotle *On the Soul* 3.5 is a human intellect. Rather it was God, resident in each human only so long as that human existed. So the Active Intellect offered no immortality to individual humans.[62] Themistius was to insist, in common with the majority, that the Active Intellect was meant to be human, but it was only on one interpretation that he supported human immortality.

Concerning the generation of individuals, Alexander supported Aristotle's repeated denial that natural reproduction of offspring requires Platonic Ideas as a model.[63]

---

[62] Alexander, *On the Soul* 89,9–13.
[63] Alexander, *in Metaph.* 103,4–104,18.

Instead, the nature of the individual parent produces the form of the individual offspring by a process as automatic as that of marionettes,[64] although Alexander concedes that nature gets its power from the movements of the divine celestial bodies, and its existence from the divine celestial body.[65] Indeed, the celestial movements also share responsibility for the generation of *inanimate* things, of the four elements, and of compounds generated from them. This goes beyond Aristotle's idea that the sun plays a role in generating things because without its annual approach and retreat the four elements, earth, air, fire, and water, would remain in static, non-interacting layers, and would not turn into each other by vaporising, freezing, smoking, or igniting.[66] We shall see Themistius denying that the supposed generation of grubs out of slime without parents also requires Platonic Ideas, although his reply appeals to principles in nature, not to automatic processes.

Some of Alexander's contributions to the logic and metaphysics of Aristotle's *Categories* were mentioned above under 'Boethus'. He defended form and differentia as being true substance, and disagreed with Boethus' criterion of substancehood, which also failed to accommodate soul as substance. Among his contributions to logic, his prowess is displayed in his less well known controversy against the Stoic idea that 'Socrates is wise' implies Socrates' existence. This led to an exchange of analyses of 'Socrates is dead' that rival the twentieth century discussions of Bertrand Russell.[67]

The view of an earlier leading scholar of Alexander, Paul Moraux, that Alexander's account of the soul was materialistic is now less widespread. I believe that it is mistaken, since Alexander argues against the view of the great doctor-philosopher Galen (129–99 CE) who holds that the soul is a blend of bodily ingredients, and that its capacities simply *follow* from that blend. Instead, Alexander replies that the soul is itself a capacity that *supervenes* (*epiginesthai*) on that bodily blend. 'Supervene' does not here have the meaning of co-variance that it is given in modern analytic philosophy, which would imply that soul is present wherever the right blend occurs, as well as vice versa. Not only in the continuation of the subject by Proclus and Philoponus, but also in Alexander himself, I believe, the soul's supervenience on a blend implies only that that blend is a necessary prerequiste, not that it is a sufficient condition for the presence of soul.[68] One passage in which I have argued that this is Alexander's meaning too is his *On the Soul* 66,6–8, where he says that reason supervenes on perception. He means that bodily beings cannot have reason without perception; by contrast, perception without reason he considers to be the state of all non-human animals, so that perception is far from guaranteeing the presence of reason.

Alexander's treatise *On Time* has been translated into English by Robert Sharples from Gerard of Cremona's twelfth century translation into Latin from an Arabic

---

[64] Alexander *ap.* Simplicius, *in Phys.* 310,25–311,21.
[65] *On Providence* 77,12–79,9; 87,5–91,4 Ruland *Quaest.* 2.3, 49,29–50,7 (the last five Alexander references are translated in Richard Sorabji, *The Philosophy of the Commentators*, vol. 2, ch. 1(b); ch. 4(a)); *On Providence*. 88–92, translated into English by Robort Sharples, n. 315 to his translation of *Quaestiones* 1.1–2.15.
[66] Aristotle, *Metaph.* 7.7, 1033b26–1034a8.
[67] Recorded in Richard Sorabji, *The Philosophy of the Commentators*, vol. 3, ch. 11a.
[68] Richard Sorabji, *Emotion and Peace of Mind* (Oxford: Oxford University Press, 2000), pp. 252–72.

version. He has had it checked against the surviving Arabic, which is later than the Arabic version used by Gerard.[69] It is here that Alexander diverges from Aristotle by saying, as Simplicius also was to report, that time is divided only in thought and is in its own nature a unity. Moreover the instant (or 'now') by which we divide time comes to be only in thought.[70] We shall later see Damascius three hundred years later using similar ideas to maintain his view that the whole of time is present, and to solve Aristotle's puzzles about the reality of time, which depend on time being divided by instants. Although there is an Arabic report that Alexander wrote *Against Galen on Time and Space*, Sharples argues that this is not that treatise. However, Themistius, we shall see, was to continue the tradition of arguing Galen on the subject of time.

Themistius (*fl.* late 340s – 384/5 CE) in Constantinople

Commentator and Civil Servant

Themistius (flourished late 340s – 384/5 CE) requires a little more space because the two sides of his philosophical life are only just beginning to be compared. Philosophers know him best as the author of commentaries on Aristotle which he modestly calls paraphrases, although a later commentator, Philoponus, is said by his modern editor to have drawn on Themistius' treatment of Physics 600 times. Commentaries survive in Greek on three of Aristotle's works (on *On the Soul*, *Physics*, and *Posterior Analytics*), the first two already translated in the Ancient Commentators on Aristotle series, and two in Hebrew and Latin (on *On the Heavens* and *Metaphysics* Book 12).[71] Of these the second is being translated, but study of the first, according to Elisa Coda,[72] requires taking account at least of the Hebrew in Florence MS Biblioteca Nazionale Centrale II. II. 528, which was not available for the CAG (Commentaria in Aristotelem Graeca) edition. Coda points out that Themistius, unlike Simplicius, informs us of Alexander's senses of *genêtos* (created) in his lost commentary on Aristotle's *On the Heavens*, which are based on Aristotle's distinctions in *On the Heavens* 1.11. But they do not include the Platonists' sense of having-a-cause, which Themistius knew, and which Philoponus criticised Proclus for understanding as being-eternally-caused.

Historians know Themistius best as a leading civil servant in the imperial capital of Constantinople, serving six emperors in succession in dangerous times, five of them Christian. His first emperor, Constantius, adlected him to the Senate of Constantinople, later making him President and entrusting him with recruitment to the Senate which expanded from 300 members to 2000, so that Themistius always had influence in the

---

[69] R. W. Sharples, 'Alexander of Aphrodisas *On Time*', *Phronesis* 27 (1982), 58–81.
[70] Sections 11, 28, and 20.
[71] For traces of his writing on Aristotle's *Topics*, translated from Arabic into French, see Ahmad Hasnawi, 'Boèce, Averroès at Abū al-Barakāt al-Baghdādī, témoins des écrits de Thémistius sur les *Topiques* d'Aristote', *Arabic Sciences and Philosophy* 17 (2007), 203–65.
[72] Elisa Coda, 'Un fragment du commentaire perdu au *De Caelo* d'Alexandre d'Aphrodise sur les different sens des termes "engendré" et "inengendré", Thémistius *In De Caelo* p. 43,3–44,17 Landauer', *Studia graeco-arabica* 5 (2015), 13–26.

Senate, however many other posts he accepted or declined.[73] But he not only wrote the commentaries on Aristotle early in his career for his school which prepared people, among other things, for civil service. He also insisted, against strong opposition, on openly advocating the ethics of Plato and Aristotle in public life. So by reading his orations and letters along with his commentaries, we have a rare opportunity of seeing his private philosophy teaching and his public philosophical stance. There are others for whom the mixture of private and public is available: Marcus Aurelius, earlier the Stoic emperor of the Roman world, Boethius, a later civil servant whose *Consolation of Philosophy* describes the political plot that was to terminate his life,[74] and, most relevantly, the pagan emperor in Constantinople, Julian, Themistius' former pupil and later critic when he pointedly told his tutor that he was going to apply the ethics of Plato and Aristotle to imperial life in a very different way.

Harmonisation (i): Spontaneous Generation due not to Platonic Ideas but to Principles (*logoi*) in Nature

With so much ground to cover, it may be surprising that our three chapters on Themistius, 5, 6, and 7, are all on the same theme, and a theme which may seem to be an outdated theory of biology. But in fact this theory, outdated as it is, that living microbes and animals are formed in putrescent matter without parents – the theory of spontaneous generation – was a test case for deciding between the metaphysics of Plato and Aristotle. In the absence of the form which Aristotle thought to be supplied in the male parent's seed, would one need one of Plato's Forms or Ideas, to explain the parentless or spontaneous generation of small animals? The evidence about Themistius' view comes from a commentary by Themistius lost in Greek and preserved only in Hebrew and Arabic, which will before long be more fully available in English translation. This is Themistius' commentary on Aristotle's *Metaphysics* Book 12, and the discussion will be relevant to a current debate on whether Themistius should be seen as an Aristotelian or a Neoplatonist. Because this is debated, I am taking Themistius out of chronological order before the first two Neoplatonists Plotinus and Porphyry in the third century on whom he drew and to whom among others he responded in the fourth.

The contribution of Yoav Meyrav in Chapter 6 argues that what is desiderated in order to explain spontaneous generation should not be translated from Arabic as 'model', which would suggest the Ideas which Plato treated as *models* in his *Timaeus*, but as 'counterpart', and Devin Henry, who takes the story as far as Thomas Aquinas in Chapter 5, is happy to revise the previously available translation, 'model'. The counterpart of the male parent's form need not be a Platonic Idea; it could be something more acceptable both to Platonists and to Aristotelians. The term which Themistius

---

[73] He briefly accepted the chief post of Prefect of the City of Constantinople under Theodosius around 384, but had rejected it earlier, according to his *Orations* 31 and 34, which say at 34.13 that he had been offered it not once or twice but often. The *Suda* thinks he held it under Julian, and it has been argued that he held the equivalent post of Proconsul under Constantius.

[74] Boethius, *Consolation of Philosophy* 1.4,5.

introduces is *logos*, rational principle. There is a rational principle, he says, in the male seed, and spontaneous generation requires its counterpart, a *logos* in nature. As to how it gets into nature, it is breathed into nature, a term explained by James Wilberding in Chapter 7, by the earth soul, a notion found in Platonism in Plotinus *Enneads* 4.4.22.1–46; 4.4.27.1–17 as something that might just be inferred from Plato's *Timaeus*, most plausibly at 77A3-C5, though Plotinus cites a few pages earlier at 40C2-3. This trace of soul, moreover is passed on to plants and these vegetative forms of life are *logoi* (3.8.8.16). Aristotelians might also be accommodated, because the greatest Aristotelian, Alexander of Aphrodisias, posits a creative *logos* as required for spontaneous generation. At least he is either quoted or roughly paraphrased as saying about spontaneous generation, 'Where there is not a creative (*dêmiourgikos*) rational principle (*logos*), generation is impossible without seed (*sperma*)'.[75] In other words, spontaneous generation requires neither a Platonic Idea nor seed, but a *logos*. Thus both Aristotelians and Platonists can be accommodated by Themistius' appeal to counterpart *logoi* in nature, provided that the Neoplatonist view is omitted that such *logoi* would presuppose the existence of the Ideas accepted by Platonists but not Aristotelians.

Harmonisation (ii): World's Eternity Provable from Physics, but also from Overriding Divine Cause not Delaying its Effect

Peter Adamson in Chapter 18 provides another example of Themistius harmonising Aristotle with Platonism. The world can be proved beginningless from considerations of physics supplied by Aristotle in his *Physics* 8.1. But it can also be proved, as by Platonists, from theology. A divine Creator, as overriding cause, cannot be delayed in its effect, so must without beginning have been producing the universe.

No Siding with Aristotelianism or Neoplatonism, Both Sources to be Used

Themistius is more interested in harmonising Plato and Aristotle than in speaking like a committed member of either school. A member of the Aristotelian school could not have gone on, I think, as does the Arabic version of Themistius, to say that Aristotle believed in an earth soul[76] and in its being created by the sun and the oblique path of its transit. In other cases Themistius disagreed with Aristotle, for example on the

---

[75] Asclepius, *in Metaph.* 408,14–15. I owe the reference to Marwan Rashed, *Al-Ḥasan ibn Mūsā al-Nawbakhtī: Commentary on Aristotle De generatione et corruptione* (Berlin: De Gruyter, 2015), p. 323.
[76] The Arabic version of Themistius, I am assured, refers to earth soul, not to Plato's soul of the universe, which carries the stars around us, even though Themistius speaks of spontaneous generation in his commentary on Aristotle *On the Soul* 26,25–30, as making it plausible that the soul of the universe irradiates soul or soul power to bodies, and it would have fitted with Themistius siting his *logoi* within nature, given that Plotinus considers nature to be the inferior part of the World Soul (Luc Brisson, '*Logos* et *logoi* chez Plotin, leur nature et leur rôle', *Les Cahiers Philosophiques de Strasbourg* 8 (1999), 87–108).

dependence of time on conscious beings in *Physics* 4.14,[77] on the relation of productive intellect to self,[78] and on concept formation.[79]

On the other hand, I myself find it hard to think of Themistius as a member of the Neoplatonist school (which he would not yet have recognised as a distinct school when only Plotinus and Porphyry were available). To repeat my introduction to the new edition of *Aristotle Transformed*, he never took the opportunity of making his life under the emperor Julian easier by indicating that he believed in the great powers of theurgy up to a point. He says he had no philosophy teachers other than his father and father-in-law,[80] which would be unusual for a Neoplatonist. He also seems never to have recognised the Neoplatonists' supreme divinity, the One above their Craftsman-God (the Demiurge) who fashioned the physical universe. Ilsetraut Hadot argues that he could have been referring to the One when he comments on Aristotle's application to his God of Homer's line: 'let there be one ruler'. But I think it would be hard for anyone to understand that as an attempt to impose on Aristotle a ruler above Aristotle's God, when Themistius had not mentioned such a higher ruler anywhere else. What Themistius does have in common with the philosophers whom we call Neoplatonists is that he wishes to harmonise Plato and Aristotle wherever possible. But that is not a sufficient condition for being a Neoplatonist: there were harmonisers before Neoplatonism, and Themistius prefers harmony but does not think it his business to argue for harmony at length. It should be less controversial that Themistius did not agree with Iamblichus' version of Neoplatonism. He disagreed with one of the key planks of Iamblichus' philosophy, because he rightly saw that Pseudo-Archytas, whose interpretation of the *Categories* Iamblichus took as Aristotle's model, was spurious.[81] Moreover, his commentaries on Aristotle appealed to at least some Platonists. He tells us in his *Oration* 23 ('The Sophist'), of around 360 CE that his commentaries on Aristotle, though intended only as an aide-mémoire in teaching, accidentally reached a man in Sikyon in Greece, who had been a disciple of Iamblichus, but was not a devotee of that 'new song'. On reading them, he sent his students to consult the oracle of Apollo, who replied that Themistius was indeed the man to go to and he moved his whole school to Themistius in Constantinople.

His Commentaries on Aristotle

In his commentaries, he included original and stimulating ideas in physics about space, time, motion, vacuum, cause, change, and the eternity of the universe. He defended Aristotle from the great philosopher-doctor Galen on the subjects of vacuum and time. Galen's attack on the possibility of vacuum begs the question, because his thought

---

[77] Richard Sorabji, *The Philosophy of the Commentators*, vol. 2, ch. 11(d).
[78] Richard Sorabji, *Self: Ancient and Modern Insights about Individuality, Life, and Death* (Oxford: Clarendon Press, 2006), p. 130.
[79] Richard Sorabji, *The Philosophy of the Commentators*, vol. 1, pp. 174 and 104.
[80] Themistius, *Oration* 21 ('The Examiner' or 'The Philosopher'), 244.
[81] Boethius, *in Cat.* 162A. Themistius is not named when the same suspicion about Pseudo-Archytas is reported and rejected by Simplicius, *in Cat.* 350,10–19.

experiment presupposes its non-existence.[82] As regards time, one of his replies to Galen is that if Aristotle's definition of time is circular, some sort of circularity is required in definitions.[83] But he sided with Boethus in rejecting the idea, which he rightly ascribes to Aristotle, that time requires conscious souls, and criticises Alexander for going beyond Aristotle in calling mankind the maker of time.[84] He opposes a beginning of the universe, we have seen, with the argument that a sufficient cause cannot delay its effect.[85] However, he goes to much greater length on the kinds of intellect in Aristotle *On the Soul* 3.5, in a way that was crucial to the metaphysics of Alexander before him and to Thomas Aquinas' objections to Averroes afterwards. We are said to consist of two intellects: a potential (*dunamei*) intellect, which deposits a storehouse of memory imprints that are potential concepts (*noêmata*) and an intellect which I think is indifferently called actual (*energeiai*) or productive (*poiêtikos*),[86] and which makes the concepts actual and, by becoming one with the potential intellect, enables it to make transitions between concepts, distinguish, combine, and divide them.[87] We are also said to have a passive (*pathêtikos*) or common (*koinos*) intellect, which is involved in the passions of loving and hating and in remembering, and Themistius thinks it is distinct from the potential intellect because the potential intellect is called in its own way impassive.[88] Since the passive intellect, like the potential intellect, is perishable, we do not after death remember our lives. For the productive intellect is the only immortal one, and the productive intellect, being in its fuller way impassive, does not engage in loving, hating, remembering, or discursive thought, but thinks not in time.[89] The active or productive intellect is not me, although it does provide my being or essence.[90]

Active Intellect and Individual Immortality

Themistius disagreed with the view of Alexander of Aphrodisias that the actual or productive intellect is God, because Aristotle claims to be distinguishing intellects within the human soul and when he says that it is the only immortal and eternal thing, he must mean *in us*, because elsewhere, in the heavens there are other immortal entities.[91] For Thomas Aquinas the crucial question was to be whether there is a human intellect that is not only immortal, as Averroes had conceded, but also individual to each human, which Averroes did not concede, since he thought that even the lowest

---

[82] Themistius, *in Phys.* 114,7–21.
[83] Themistius, *in Phys.* 149,4–19.
[84] Themistius, *in Phys.* 163,1–7; 120,17–21.
[85] Themistius, *in Metaph.* 12.6; French translation from Arabic in A. Badawi, *La transmission de la philosophie grecque au monde arabe*, 2nd edn (Paris: Vrin, 1987), pp. 180–94; English translation in preparation by Meyrav and Fraenkel.
[86] Thus we are indifferently said to consist of potential combined with actual (*in DA* 100,18–20; 103,36–8) or productive intellect (100,37–101,1; 101,9–10; 103,16–17; 103,36–8).
[87] Themistius, *in DA* 98,35–99,10.
[88] 101,5–9; 105,22–30.
[89] 101,4–37; 102,16–24; 105,18–27.
[90] 101,13–20; 103,36–8.
[91] 102,36–103,19.

human intellect, which he called material, was immortal only 'by succession', that is, through individual humans always succeeding each other. Themistius' productive intellect would not help Thomas, because Themistius insists that it is single. But Thomas finds comfort in Themistius' claim immediately following, that although the productive intellect is best seen as a single illuminator like the sun, there are intellects which like sunlight are more than one, being both illuminating and illuminated.[92] That, Thomas says, allows individual immortality.

Public Life (i): Freedom of Religion

In public life, Themistius stood for freedom of religion, a certain freedom of speech for the philosopher and a certain view of the philosopher king. On both the last two issues he came into conflict with his pupil the emperor Julian.[93] It is recorded that Themistius persuaded his fifth emperor, the difficult Valens, to commute the death sentence on Christians who were briefly held heretical for supporting the Nicene Creed. Here he is said to have used the argument that God willed there to be different opinions concerning him to enhance reverence because of the difficulty of knowing him.[94] More strikingly, he included in his *Oration* 5 of 364 CE to mark the consulship of his fourth emperor, Jovian, anticipatory praise for the freedom of religion he claimed to expect, citing several grounds for freedom, but among others one unusual in Christian circles, that there are many roads to God. This is different from the much commoner ground that although there is only one road, we cannot be sure which it is. Moreover it might be thought to clash with Christ's saying, 'No man comes to the Father but by me'.[95] Themistius had earlier broached the idea of many roads reaching the same point in connexion not with religion, but with philosophy, in his *On Virtue*, which is being translated into English from Syriac by Alberto Rigoglio for the Ancient Commentators on Aristotle series. In this, Themistius was like his second emperor, Julian, who also made the point about many roads in philosophy.[96] It was probably Themistius who influenced Symmachus to make the many roads argument for freedom of religion in 382 to Themistius' last emperor, Theodosius I.

Public Life (ii) Freedom of Speech, Themistius and Julian

As regards freedom of speech, this was not considered before the seventeenth century something that should be allowed to everyone. Athens, while democracy lasted, was unique in allowing it to all male citizens in good standing, by no means the majority of the population, otherwise to comic poets, and it was widely allowed to individual

---

[92] 103,22–36. This is described in Richard Sorabji, *Self*, pp. 130–6.
[93] A very vivid account is given by Susanna Elm, *Sons of Hellenism, Fathers of the Church* (Berkeley: University of California Press, 2012).
[94] Socrates, *Ecclesiastical History* 4.32.2–4.
[95] John 14:6.
[96] Julian, *Oration* 6 ('To the Uneducated Cynics'), 184C–185A.

philosophers in the Graeco-Roman world at the invitation of individual rulers and at considerable personal risk. Cynic philosophers with their defiance of convention, also claimed it for themselves. In Shakespeare's time, it was permitted to court jesters and King Charles I may have allowed it to confessors advising him on conscionable policy. Themistius in 385 CE had stepped down from the Urban Prefecture given him by Theodosius I, and he defended his holding of office in his *Oration*, 34, 'In reply to those who found fault with him for accepting public office'. As a philosopher, he said, he had admonished and rebuked the earlier emperor Valens, who did not take it badly despite his uneasy manner, while the present emperor Theodosius did not deny him free or frank speech (*parrhêsia*). In *Oration* 26, 'On Speaking or How the Philosopher should Speak', in the late 350s, he insisted against detractors, as he did also in *Oration* 21 of about 355-6 CE and *Oration* 22,[97] that a philosopher must be allowed to promulgate freely in public the ethics of Plato and Aristotle. It is more valuable than medical information, because it benefits not just one person at a time, but people as a whole. A city could reasonably complain that philosophers ought not to confine themselves to their students, except in such technical branches of thought as astronomy or meteorology. A treatise of Themistius survives in Syriac, *On Virtue*.[98] Its translator, Alberto Rigoglio, has pointed out in public discussion its relation to speeches by the emperor Julian in 362 CE, which may fall either side of it. It finishes by describing the kind of free speech that the philosopher should practise. He should rebuke, but without passion, and with humility, after criticising himself severely first. Like the early Cynics Diogenes and Crates, he should love the virtuous, help others to improve, never be angry if insulted, and care nothing for reward, poverty, or power. These sentiments fitted with the emperor Julian's two *Orations* 6 and 7, 'To the Uneducated Cynics' and 'To the Cynic Heraclius', in which Julian argued that a Cynic must *earn* the right to practise frank speech (*parrhêsia*), as did Diogenes and Crates, who got rid of their own passions, honoured the gods, were abstemious, and, in Crates' case, resolved quarrels with grace. The Cynic Diogenes struck with his stick a youth who thought the way to start being a Cynic was to break wind in public. The second of Julian's speeches was an excoriating reply to an equally excoriating satire on him by the Cynic Heraclius. Julian went on in his *Beard-Hater* (*Misopôgôn*) to satirise both himself and the people of Antioch, who had openly ridiculed his wearing the philosopher's beard, his celibate sleeping alone, and abstinence from their own pleasurable activities. He says that since he has now satirised himself, they are free to do that with even greater frankness (*parrhêsia*). He apparently stuck to his rule not to retaliate with punishment, but there is something manic, if forceful, about his replies.

---

[97] *Oration* 26, 313; 320-1; 327-8. Similarly *Oration* 22 ('On Friendship'), 265; *Oration* 21 ('The Examiner' or 'The Philosopher'), 255, which speak of public dislike of philosophers who sit on a couch studying in their room, or whisper words to young men in a corner and avoid the city. Themistius will instead bring speech out into the sunlight and the clamour of the Assembly.
[98] Themistius, *On Virtue*, being translated from Syriac by Alberto Rigoglio.

Public Life (iii): The Philosopher King, Themistius and Julian

The third subject to be taken is the conception of philosopher king. Themistius wrote a lost exhortation to Julian after he had been appointed Caesar in 355, a step on the way, it proved, to his becoming Augustus, or emperor, in 361. In his reply, the *Letter to Themistius*, preserved in and translated from Arabic by Simon Swain,[99] Julian criticised Themistius' comparison of him with Heracles viewed as both philosopher and king using his strength in actions to rid the world of evil. Julian says he knows that Themistius would not attempt flattery, so he is mystified because he has no such special qualities. Referring to Themistius having taught him Plato's *Laws*, Julian reminds Themistius that in the *Laws* it is said that that Cronus set semi-divine *daimones* to rule over humans, because humans are corrupted by absolute power. So Julian cannot be a king in the sense proposed. He then cites Aristotle's *Politics*, 'just to prove I do not completely neglect his works'. This sounds like a reminder of a teacher's suggestion that Julian needed more Aristotle. Themistius thought that Aristotle's logic provided an instrument for argumentation to distinguish what was true from what merely appeared true, and his father thought that Aristotle provided Plato with the defensive wall he needed as being too easily assailable by sophists.[100] But much as he thought that, Themistius cannot reply now Julian is Emperor. Against Themistius' expectations for him as philosopher king, Julian insists that Aristotle says that a king who rules by his own will, instead of by law, hands on the kingship to his children and this is the rule of beasts (the emperor Constantius had killed all rival relatives except Julian). Aristotle prefers the *guardian* of the laws (*nomophulax*) a term that Julian appropriates to describe himself in his *Beard-Hater*, 356, and which was approved in Plato's *Laws* 752D ff. and in Iamblichus' *Letter to Agrippa*.[101] Themistius has misunderstood Aristotle's claim that the happy life consists in activity. This is not political activity, but philosophical thought, thought about society. Here Julian in effect prefers the second best rule of law in Plato's *Laws*, which in his *Statesman* Plato describes as failing to deal with particularities, because it is impractical for the ideal statesman to sit beside everyone and tell them what to do. Aristotle's solution of *Nicomachean Ethics* 5.10 is not mentioned, of allowing to judges discretion or equity (*epieikeia*) to deal with particularities in the application of law. Equity is not contrary to justice, as Plato says in *Laws* 757E, but is a superior kind of justice, contrary only to written law.[102] Themistius had further told Julian to quit indoor philosophy for the philosophy of the public arena.

In response to this last, Julian's reply now takes a new theological turn. He repeats Aristotle's supposed remark to Alexander that any man had as much right to be as proud as Alexander, just so long as he had the right ideas about God.[103] Julian will

---

[99] Simon Swain, *Themistius, Julian, and Greek Political Theory under Rome* (Cambridge: Cambridge University Press, 2013).
[100] Themistius, *Orations* 20 ('A Funeral Oration in Honour of his Father'), 235; 26 ('On Speaking'), 320.
[101] Iamblichus in Stobaeus, *Anth.* 4,223,24–224,17. See Dominic O'Meara, *Platonopolis* (Oxford: Oxford University Press, 2003), p. 100. I follow here an English version of Riccardo Chiaradonna, 'La *Lettera a Temistio* di Giuliano Imperatore e il dibattiyo filosofico nel IV secolo', in Arnaldo Marcone, ed., *L'imperatore Giuliano: Realtà storica e rappresentazione* (Florence: Le Monnier, 2015), pp. 149–71.
[102] Aristotle, *Rhetoric* 1374a27; 1375a29; *Nicomachean Ethics* 1137b8–11; b24; b33–4.
[103] Julian, *Letter to Themistius* 10 in Swain (n. 99 above), based on Plutarch, *On Progress in Virtue* 78D.

entrust all to God, and thank him if he succeeds. Themistius could not yet foresee how far Julian, when he became emperor, would personally carry out as chief pontiff every aspect of sacrificial ritual and divination through entrails more than once a day in his own palace and grounds,[104] and blame the Antiochans in his *Misopôgôn* for neglecting services to the traditional gods. It was only under later emperors around 383–5 CE in *Oration* 31, 352, that Themistius said that he had not chosen the philosophical path concerned with divine matters, but the one concerned with public affairs that was more useful to his audience and in *Oration* 34 of 385 CE that Aristotle's whole philosophy was concerned with the happy life, above all in the whole city, so that he called his philosophy *political*, and said that you cannot do well without doing (*prattein*, 34, 6). These remarks make us regret that we have no trace of Themistius' commentary on Aristotle's *Nicomachean Ethics*, mentioned in Arabic.[105] By accepting office, Themistius' oration continues, he did not *descend* to Plato's cave. Although he was not always above, like Plato, who was becoming like God, nonetheless even when below he was guided by what was above (*Oration* 34, 30). Another thing that Themistius could not foresee was that when Julian decided to turn down a peace offer and make his fatal expedition against the Persians, he would after all compare himself with Heracles in his *Caesars* of 361 CE.

Even on the Syllogism, Julian Prefers Maximus the Miracle-Worker

Themistius had one more philosophical disappointment with Julian when the latter offered to adjudicate two opposed statements about Aristotle's theory of syllogism.[106] Julian's opponent was Maximus of Ephesus, the miracle worker, so-called because he was a master of the priestly ritual or theurgy that was a central part of Iamblichus' philosophy. Maximus was Julian's favourite philosopher and an ever-present guide to him when he became emperor. The question was a technical one, cited above, concerning Aristotle's three figures or patterns of valid syllogistic argument. Was Aristotle right to say that the second and third figures could not be seen to be valid without being reduced to logical equivalents in the first figure? And did that mean that they were imperfect figures? Boethus' contradiction of Aristotle was followed not only by Maximus, but also by Porphyry, Iamblichus, Syrianus, Proclus, Hermeias, and Ammonius, the last of whom gave the reason that no extra term was required to make clear the validity of the other figures. Themistius was on the other side. Themistius' letter to Julian complaining of Maximus' argument has been translated into French from two Arabic manuscripts, cited above in the discussion of Boethus. But it may be guessed who was adjudicated the winner: Maximus, naturally.

---

[104] Libanius, *Oration* 12, 80–2.
[105] Ibn al-Nadīm, *Kitāb al-Fihrist* 252,3 (Flügel); translated in F. E. Peters, *Aristoteles Arabus: The Oriental Translations and Commentaries on the Aristotelian Corpus* (Leiden: Brill, 1968), p. 52.
[106] Ammonius, *in An. Pr.* 31,7–32,7 with Maximus and Themistius at 31,18–21; David, *in An. Pr.* 11.1.

Porphyry of Tyre (232/3 – 309 CE) in Rome and Sicily

Porphyry tells us that his name in Phoenician, Malcus, meant King,[107] but his teacher Longinus called him 'Porphyrios' meaning the royal purple manufactured in his birth place, Tyre. He studied first with Longinus in Athens, then with Plotinus in Rome, who sent him, we shall see, to Sicily. He was also at some time in Carthage, where he tells us that he raised a partridge which spoke to him in sounds adapted to Porphyry's, not with those of a partridge.[108] Among his achievements two were monumental. First, he incorporated Aristotle into Platonism, putting him on the Europaean syllabus ever since, after his teacher Plotinus had mounted a significant attack, saying that Aristotle's *Categories* failed to include Plato's world of intelligible Ideas. Porphyry answered this in his own way in his surviving short commentary on Aristotle's *Categories*, although Plotinus had himself briefly suggested possible remedies. These remedies were developed by Porphyry's younger critic, Iamblichus, and possibly before that in Porphyry's own lost longer and more advanced commentary on Aristotle's *Categories*, of which a newly deciphered fragment is translated in Chapter 8 below. The history of this resuscitation of Aristotle for Platonists was told by Pierre Hadot in *Aristotle Transformed*, with subsequent updates recorded in the Introduction to the new 2016 edition.

Porphyry's second achievement was to edit the writings of Plotinus with a biography of him. The edition took the form of assembling the writings in a coherent order, partly on the model of what Andronicus had done for Aristotle, but in six sets of nine treatises,[109] each set being called an *ennead* or ninesome. The result became canonical and made accessible what we think of in retrospect as the founding texts of a new Platonist school for which the modern name is 'Neoplatonism'.

The introductory biography of Plotinus included also autobiography, so we know much about Porphyry's life and how it related to his work. We have a description of how Plotinus made an already established student, Amelius, read aloud Porphyry's initial essay and then write a criticism to read aloud next time, with a following debate between the two students, until the third time, Porphyry himself understood and accepted the rival view.[110] We can imagine this pattern of teaching centred on student activity, not indeed in Plotinus' Roman classroom, but in the fifth to sixth century classrooms recently excavated from the Neoplatonist school of Alexandria, where the very shape of the rooms lends itself.[111]

Finally, Porphyry wrote extensively on ethics, religion, and soul. His book on *Abstinence from Animals*, that is from killing them, is on all three subjects and is, I

---

[107] Porphyry, *Life of Plotinus* 17.
[108] Porphyry, *On Abstinence from Killing Animals* 3.4.7.
[109] Porphyry, *Life of Plotinus* 24.
[110] Porphyry, *Life of Plotinus* 18.
[111] Richard Sorabji, 'The Alexandrian Classrooms Excavated and Sixth-Century Philosophy Teaching', in Pauliina Remes and Svetla Slaveva-Griffin, eds, *The Routledge Handbook of Neoplatonism* (Abingdon: Routledge, 2014), pp. 30–39, goes beyond the earlier account in the 2nd edn of Richard Sorabji, ed., *Philoponus and the Rejection of Aristotelian Science* (London: Institute of Classical Studies, 2010), pp. 1–10.

believe, one of the most interesting books of late antiquity. Below in Chapter 9 it receives a new interpretation. But I shall start with the work on logic, because his surviving work on Aristotle concerns Aristotle's logic.

Logic

Porphyry wrote an Introduction (*Isagôgê*), which serves in effect as an introduction to Aristotle's logic. Thanks to Ammonius at the end of the fifth century, it became the accepted introduction to the entire Aristotelian syllabus, since Ammonius wrote a commentary or exegesis of it, designed to precede exegesis of the first logical work in the Aristotle syllabus – the *Categories*. The *Isagôgê* discusses five of Aristotle's logical terms: genus and species (discussed in relation to Porphyry and others in Chapter 10 below), the differentiae which distinguish different species within a genus, then properties necessarily co-extensive but not defining, and finally merely coincidental attributes. The earlier history of the status of the differentia is traced by Marwan Rashed in Chapter 2, as explained in the discussion of Boethus above. Boethus denied the differentia could be substance, though he allowed it to be quality or quantity, as did someone cited by the later Christian commentator Boethius (not Boethus).[112] Alexander in reply insisted it must be substance. What is new in Porphyry, Rashed argues in Chapter 2, is to combine the two candidates, and recognise *substantial* qualities and quantities and to classify the differentia under these, although Frans de Haas has shown that Ammonius' school reverted to classifying it under substance.[113]

Porphyry's surviving short commentary on Aristotle's *Categories* introduces the idea that names were originally introduced into language to name perceptible things, and only later was there a second imposition of names, to provide, for example, names of names.[114] That distinction was shown by Sten Ebbesen in *Aristotle Transformed* to have been used by others to answer certain fallacious arguments, e.g. 'Socrates (to use a name) is a human, Human is a species (to use the name of a name), so Socrates is a species'. It was also used by Porphyry, as discussed in the introduction to the new edition of *Aristotle Transformed*, to explain why Aristotle's *Categories*, confining itself for beginners to the names originally introduced and the things they signified, was entitled to omit mention of Plato's intelligible Ideas.

The text offered in Chapter 8 below is argued to be a substantial fragment of Porphyry's lost large commentary on Aristotle's *Categories*. The original contained answers not only to Plotinus, but to all the objections raised against the *Categories*. John Dillon in Chapter 11 infers its great size from its having been compressed in two subsequent commentaries, which were themselves of enormous length, one of them by Simplicius occupying 438 pages of Greek print in the modern edition.[115] The new

---

[112] Boethius, *De Divisione* (*Patrologia Latina* 64), 879B–880A, cited by Rashed, 'Entre Andronicos et Alexandre', *Arabic Sciences and Philosophy* 14 (2004), 29–30.
[113] Frans de Haas, *John Philoponus' New Definition of Prime Matter* (Leiden: Brill, 1997), pp. 222–9.
[114] Porphyry, *in Cat.* 58,4–7.
[115] John Dillon, 'Iamblichus' *noera theôria* of Aristotle's *Categories*', *Syllecta Classica* 8 (1997), 65–77 (repr. as ch. 11 below), citing Simplicius, *in Cat* 2,9–25.

fragment, invisible to the naked eye, was deciphered through the use of multi-spectral lighting. The parchment had been reused and overwritten for a Byzantine prayer book of the twelfth-thirteenth centuries. The fragment includes only 7 folios out of an estimated more than 470. But it names Andronicus and Boethus, described above, from the first century BCE, Nicostratus the somewhat later Platonist critic of Aristotle, and Alexander's teacher Herminus. It also reveals that Boethus is responding to unnamed critics of Aristotle's logic even earlier than himself concerning an attack on Aristotle's claim about differentiae.[116] Boethus' downgrading of universals is also mentioned.

The treatment of universals by Porphyry, among others, is discussed in Chapter 10 below, and I there follow the view of Riccardo Chiaradonna that Porphyry recognises several kinds of universal, but that concepts are recognised as universals not in Porphyry's work on Aristotle's logic, but only in the very different context of his commentary on Ptolemy's *Harmonics*. I believe it was Ammonius over two hundred years later who promulgated the view that Porphyry was talking about conceptual universals in his logical writing.

At the opposite end from universals, Porphyry offered in his *Introduction* to Aristotle's logic an unusual view about individuals, that they are no more than *bundles* of properties, not (as Aristotle would hold) subjects which *possess* properties. He is commonly thought to have taken this view from the Stoics, but I have argued that he and the Stoics could both have derived it from Plato's *Theaetetus*. Porphyry had little reason to introduce Stoicism in an introduction to Aristotle's logic. His motive could be rather that neither he, nor Aristotle in his *Categories*, wants to burden beginners with the Aristotelian notion of matter as opposed to form, and to talk of properties as being *possessed* by a subject would have required Porphyry to introduce Aristotle's matter as what possesses them.[117]

Porphyry's commentary on the next logical work in Aristotle's corpus, *On Interpretation*, is unfortunately lost. But we are told by Boethius of a very interesting interpretation of the opening lines of its chapter 1. For the Aristotelians, he said, there are three kinds of speech and three kinds of verbs and names: written, spoken, and mental.[118] The idea of a mental language, distinct from written and spoken, has been introduced in modern philosophy by Jerry Fodor, and some of the history of the idea has been traced by C. Chiesa.[119] It also relates to how both God and angels communicate.

Ethics

Porphyry's *On Abstinence from Animals* opposes, in four books, the killing of animals for sacrifice to the gods, for eating, or for both. The first book surveys the arguments for

---

[116] R. Chiradonna, M. Rashed, and D. N. Sedley, 'A Rediscovered *Categories* Commentary', *Oxford Studies in Ancient Philosophy* 44 (2013), 129–94 (repr. as ch. 8 below), pp. 130, 188, concerning an attack on Aristotle's claim about differentiae at *Categories* 1b16–20.
[117] Richard Sorabji, *Matter, Space and Motion* (London: Duckworth, 1988), pp. 44–59.
[118] Porphyry *ap.* Boethius, *in Int.*² 29,29–30,10.
[119] C. Chiesa, 'Le problème du langage intérieur chez les Stoiciens', *Revue internationale de philosophie* 45, 178 (1991), 301–21.

and against killing them, more evenly balanced in the ancient world than now. The second book studies the gods, to show that the highest God does not want sacrifice of that sort, but the sacrifice of a pure intellect. The third considers animals, to show that they have the rationality that meets the Stoic criterion for being owed justice like humans. The final book surveys other human communities, to show that a vegetarian diet never did them any harm.

In Chapter 9, G. Fay Edwards argues that the Stoic criterion for being owed justice (rationality) which he uses against them is after all not Porphyry's reason for sparing animals. Nor is the criterion for calling animals rational a criterion of his, but only of theirs. In neither case did he use his own criteria, but he was using the Stoics' criteria against them. His own reason for sparing animals is not only different, but it throws a flood of light on Neoplatonist ethics. He thought that a taste for meat was incompatible with the kind of virtue gained by philosophers who purify themselves from bodily appetites. This is purified virtue, the higher level of virtue that Socrates exemplifies in Plato's *Phaedo*. This, she points out, could explain why it is only philosophers, not ordinary citizens, to whom Porphyry forbids animal sacrifice and meat. Purification would endow one with an *ablabia*, a disposition not to harm, literally a non-harming. This is a form of non-violence, more negative that Gandhi's 'ocean of compassion', but more deliberate than an absent-minded harmlessness. In *On Abstinence* 3.26, the conception is expanded. Escape (*phugê*) from animal food is said to be escape from unjust acts concerned with food – one will not kill animals for that motive. Justice consists in not being harmful to those that are harmless. When passions, appetite, and anger are gone, and reason rules, one enjoys assimilation to God. The reference is to Plato *Theaetetus* 176B, which, using the same words, had said that escape (*phugê*) from evil and assimilation to God is becoming just.

This aspect of *On Abstinence* throws light on how Porphyry would address a puzzle about purified virtue: if one turns away from the life of bodily desires to the purified life of the mind, will one not be neglecting the bodily needs of others, rather than practising justice? Elsewhere in the *Letter to Marcella*[120] he writes to his wife instructing her in acquiring purified virtue, which involves the sobering reminder of what did *not* motivate him when he married her. He says in *Marcella* 14 and 16 that one is assimilated to God only through virtue. If you love the body, you will also love wealth and then you will be unjust to God, to your forefathers, and to other people. The injustice is generalised beyond animals: a meat diet was only one form of love of the body. It also required wealth, but desire for wealth leads to all sorts of other injustices. Porphyry's *Sentences* 32 is a commentary on Plotinus' distinction in *Enneads* 1.2.3 of purified virtue from ordinary social or civic virtue.[121] The purified are no longer motivated by the temptations which fill us with bodily desires, and this is said by Plotinus and by Porphyry's *Sentences* to apply to each of the four main Platonic virtues: wisdom, temperance, courage, and justice. It fits with this that in Plato's *Phaedo* Socrates, when

---

[120] Available in an older English translation by Alice Zimmern.
[121] *The Sentences* is available in English translation by John Dillon, in Luc Brisson, ed., *Porphyre, Sentences* (Paris: Vrin, 2005), vol. 2.

purified from bodily desires, neither feared death nor was tempted to break the law by escaping from prison. Nonetheless, Porphyry's emphasis on *not harming* may seem a conception of justice too *negative* to answer fully the question whether purified people will not neglect the bodily needs of others. Does not justice require one positively to look out for their needs, rather than merely refraining from violating them? Will one even succeed in not violating them, if one does not consider them? Yet Porphyry deliberately rejects the more positive Stoic view of justice, which goes to the opposite extreme, by making justice to others depend on *oikeiôsis*, an extension to all humans of a feeling of kinship such as one feels for oneself and one's nearest. Porphyry complains that that would be philanthropy (*philanthrôpia*, 3.26.9). It would be love rather than justice and it would be directed only to humans. It is true on Porphyry's side that, while justice towards humans would surely be promoted by the Stoic love, nonetheless justice requires one to treat others independently of whether or not one feels akin. But on the other hand, his negative removal of some motives for violation (but not of inattention) does not seem like a guarantee of justice.

Porphyry once contemplated suicide. He tells us in his *Life of Plotinus*[122] that Plotinus noticed, came unexpectedly to his house where he was staying indoors and said that his plan came not from intellect but from a sick bodily humour, and he should take a holiday. So in 368 he went to Sicily, and that is why he did not remain with Plotinus until his death, which was two years later (in 370). It may have been in Sicily that Porphyry wrote *Abstinence*, which unexpectedly does not mention Plotinus. Although some of Plotinus' writings were sent to him in Sicily, he did not edit them or write the *Life* of Plotinus for thirty years, in 301, near the end of his own life. He did write about suicide, however in two places. In *Abstinence*, he twice repeats the argument that the violence of suicide merely thickens the chain attaching one's soul to the body, and he contrasts the effect of a light diet providing only what is necessary.[123] Plotinus had already said that suicide is accompanied by discontent, distress, or anger. Plotinus admitted that even a virtuous person might resort to it, if insanity were coming on, but poison would not promote the soul's welfare, or it might be an escape route if one were taken prisoner in war, but that would not lead to happiness in the next life.[124] One would be in a double-bind, penalised either way. Porphyry says something relevant to suicide again in the *Sentences* or *Starting Points towards the Intelligibles*. These form a condensed interpretation of Plotinus' *Enneads*, which, however, goes beyond Plotinus. In *Sentences* 8 and 9, he says that nature binds the body in soul and later frees it, which is ordinary death, whereas soul first binds *itself* to body and can later free *itself*, but only the souls of philosophers free themselves in this way. The reference is again to the view of philosophy ascribed to Socrates in Plato's *Phaedo* as a preparation for death, in the sense of freeing the soul by purification from attachment to the body.

Two of the ideas discussed by Porphyry as connected with purification – preparation for death and assimilation to God – were to be brought into prominence later as two

---

[122] Porphyry, *Life of Plotinus* 11.
[123] Porphyry, *On Abstinence* 1.38.2; 2.47.1.
[124] Plotinus, *Enneads* 1.9.1–19; 1.4.7.31–3.

out of six or more definitions of Philosophy, when Ammonius introduced a new type of introduction to his commentary on Porphyry's *Isagôgê*. These introductions in Ammonius' school would include discussion of Philosophy and how to define it. It was thought necessary to issue warnings against Cleombrotus, who fatally confused the advocacy of the philosopher's way of freeing soul from body with an exhortation to suicide. Permutations were therefore offered on Porphyry's account of the philosophical way of separating soul and body, so as to present suicide as distinct.

Religion

In matters of religion it is especially relevant that Porphyry was not only a philosopher with his own views, but also a scholar of the history of ideas and a questioner of views in all these spheres: history of ideas, philosophy, and religion. His questions were by no means confined to Christianity, as Gillian Clark has well brought out;[125] he also questioned the ideas and practices of Greek religion and of fellow Platonists. In Book 2 of *Abstinence*, he argued that traditional pagan animal sacrifice only attracted bad demons (*daimônes*, 2.42). The first god needs nothing and the best sacrifice to the gods is a pure intellect and a soul without passion. Such visible gods as the stars can receive sacrifice of non-animals (2.34; 37; 61). In another work, his *Letter to Anebo*, he addresses his critical fellow Platonist, the priestly Iamblichus, writing as if to Anebo, an Egyptian priest. He probes, not disrespectfully of the practices but searchingly, for explanations of how the priestly rituals, or theurgy, favoured by Iamblichus, can work. Why, to take but one example, did they allow erotic festivals to figure in religious worship? Iamblichus' reply (treated below), which incorporates Porphyry's questions, was haughty. It has been called since Marsilio Ficino *On the Mysteries of the Egyptians*.[126] It purported to come from Abammon, an Egyptian name used by Porphyry for the practitioner of the very highest level of virtue he recognises, the paradigmatic virtue of Plato's Ideas or paradigms,[127] a level on top of which Iamblichus was to add priestly virtue.

In a third work, *The Return of the Soul*, Porphyry is reported by the Christian philosopher Augustine[128] as saying that theurgy can purify the imaginative part of the soul to help us to see visions, but not the intellectual part, so it cannot lead us back to God. Augustine may not be the only one to be relieved at this qualification. But it was totally unacceptable to Iamblichus and to the emperor Julian who followed Iamblichus' tradition, to the dismay, as seen above, of Themistius. None of this questioning prevented Porphyry from being the first to write a commentary on the textbook of theurgy, the *Chaldaean Oracles*, composed by an earlier Julian the theurgist in the second century CE, but attributed by him to the ancient Chaldaean gods.

---

[125] Gillian Clark, 'Philosophic Lives and the Philosophic Life: Porphyry and Iamblichus', in T. Hägg and P. Rousseau, eds, *Greek Biography and Panegyric in Late Antiquity* (Berkeley: University of California Press, 2000), pp. 29–51; 'Translate into Greek: Porphyry of Tyre on the New Barbarians', in Miles Richard, ed., *Constructing Identities in Late Antiquity* (London: Routledge, 1999), pp. 112–32.
[126] Iamblichus, *On the Mysteries of the Egyptians*, translated by E. C. Clarke, John Dillon, and J. P. Hershbell (Leiden: Brill, 2003).
[127] Porphyry, *Sentences* 32,94 Brisson (= 31,7 Lamberz).
[128] Augustine, *City of God* 10.9.

In *The Return of the Soul*, as Augustine reports,[129] Porphyry said that in all his searches he had not found a universal road to liberation of the soul, not among the truest of philosophies (Platonism), or the Indians, or the Chaldaeans. Augustine, rightly or wrongly, takes him to mean a road that is for everyone both a necessary and a sufficient route, and he replies that Christianity is exactly that, although he excuses Porphyry for not yet having been able to see, writing as he did before the accession in 312 of the first Christian emperor, Constantine, initially in the West only. He had also witnessed only the persecution of Christians, right up to the end of his life with the emperor Diocletian's purge in 302–3. Even before Themistius, it was a major theme of Porphyry, and not only in *On the Return of the Soul*, that there are many roads (*hodoi*) to God, although this is qualified in *Abstinence*. Even though abstinence from animal sacrifice is required only for philosophers (1.27), and there are different requirements for priests, ordinary citizens, and even for different philosophers (3.2), nonetheless the animal sacrifice permitted to some is not a route to the same destination, because it will not assimilate them to God, but to demons. Nonetheless, Porphyry says to Iamblichus in his *Letter to Anebo*, 'The road to happiness can surely be different', to which Iamblichus replies 'No, it is only in company with us (i.e. priests) and those who secure union with the gods'.[130] Again, the Church historian Eusebius records Porphyry citing in his *Philosophy from Oracles* the oracle of Apollo as saying that there are many paths (*pollai atrapoi*) or roads leading to the gods. He emphasises the relevance to religious tolerance when he says that they were revealed first to non-Greeks, the Egyptians, and then to Phoenicians, Chaldaeans, Lydians, and Hebrews.[131]

It is now doubted that Porphyry wrote a single book of 15 discourses (*logoi*) called *Against the Christians*.[132] He may have written separate treatises on different subjects, and he did compare the four Christian Gospels with each other. He did show, to the satisfaction of modern scholars, that the Book of Daniel cannot have been prophetic, because it was written *after* the events described. He also criticised Christ on a subject he cared about for driving the Gadarene swine over a cliff. He may have been more like his teacher Plotinus, who was not concerned by Christians as such, but by certain Christians in his class, the heretical Gnostics, for their peculiar views.[133] Porphyry was equally interested in exposing as a forgery a work attributed to Zoroaster.[134] The dispassionate, inquiring tone of his *Letter to Anebo* makes me doubt that he can have been the rabid enemy of Christians that many Christians believed him to be. Augustine repeatedly shows respect, and calls him the most learned (*doctissimus*) of the philosophers, though the sharpest (*acerrimus*) enemy of

---

[129] Augustine, *City of God* 10.32.
[130] Iamblichus, *On the Mysteries of the Egyptians* 10.1.
[131] Eusebius, *Praeparatio Evangelica* 9.10.1–5 = fr. 323F, 324F, in A. Smith, *Porphyrii Philosophi Fragmenta* (Stuttgart: Teubner, 1993).
[132] Mark Edwards, 'Porphyry and the Christians', in George Karamanolis and Anne Sheppard, eds, *Studies on Porphyry* (London: Institute of Classical Studies, 2007), pp. 111–26, and, for a wide range of views, Sébastien Morlet, *Le traité de Porphyre contre les Chrétiens: un siècle de recherches, nouvelles questions* (Paris: Études Augustiniennes, 2011).
[133] Gillian Clark, 'Translate into Greek'.
[134] Porphyry, *Life of Plotinus* 16

Introduction 33

the Christians.[135] 'Learned' and 'sharp' surely account for Augustine's paying him so much attention. But another Christian, Eusebius, reacted, in parallel with Iamblichus' haughtiness, with strong hostility. Moreover, Porphyry's discourses labelled *Against the Christians* were burnt under two Christian emperors.

Andrew Smith, to whom we are indebted for editing the fragments of Porphyry,[136] has also challenged another picture of Porphyry as evolving from total commitment to sacrificial rites to the banning of animal sacrifice. It was of course banned in *Abstinence* only for philosophers, or for some philosophers, and Smith adds that the *Letter to Anebo* is only seeking explanations and even in *Philosophy from Oracles*, Porphyry need not be endorsing the sacrificial practices mentioned, although he does consider the oracles cited useful for contemplation and purification.[137]

Porphyry also gave a cautious status to statues of the gods. They merely enable some people to read information about the gods, as if from books.[138] Through gold material the gods leads us to think of their light and purity. Others used black to show their invisibility. White and circular shapes were assigned to the gods in the heavens and circular shape to their eternity. Zeus is represented as seated, to indicate his steadfastness.[139] Porphyry does not say, like Iamblichus, that the gods are received in the statues.[140]

Although Porphyry allowed statues to represent the qualities of gods, he objected to the Christian Origen's subjecting the plain words of Moses to allegorical interpretation. Nonetheless, Porphyry's *Cave of the Nymphs* takes a few lines in Homer as an allegory of the incarnation of the human soul. Perhaps he thought Homer's words were not plain.[141] I turn now to some of Porphyry's other treatments of soul.

Soul

James Wilberding in Chapter 7 explains the theory of reproduction and ensoulment in Porphyry's *To Gaurus On How Embryos are Ensouled*, which he has translated. There

---

[135] Augustine, *City of God* 19.22, emphasised by Gillian Clark, 'Augustine's Porphyry and the universal way of salvation', in George Karamanolis and Anne Sheppard, eds, *Studies on Porphyry* (London: Institute of Classical Studies, 2007), pp. 127–140, at p. 130.
[136] Andrew Smith, *Porphyrii Philosophi Fragmenta* (Stuttgart: Teubner, 1993). Aaron P. Johnson, *Religion and Identity in Porphyry of Tyre* (Cambridge: Cambridge University Press, 2013), provides a catalogue and translation of the most important fragments on this subject.
[137] Andrew Smith, collected papers in *Plotinus, Porphyry, and Iamblichus: Philosophy and Religion in Neoplatonism* (Aldershot: Ashgate, 2011), esp. chs 18 and 19. Eusebius distinguished *Philosophy from Oracles* from the supposed *Against the Christians*, criticising it for its polytheism rather than for being anti-Christian in particular. Some scholars now identify it with *On the Return of the Soul*.
[138] Eusebius, *Preparation for the Gospel* 3.7, = fr. 352F Smith.
[139] Eusebius, *Preparation for the Gospel* 3.9, = fr. 354F Smith.
[140] Eirini Viltanioti draws attention to an attempt in Makarios Magnes, *Apokritikos* 4.28 Goulet, to offer to an opponent ('but if it seems to you'), probably Porphyry, the view that God can even less be incarnate inside Mary than can a Greek God be inside a statue, for in both cases, to different degrees, God would suffer effects, which is impossible for a god: 'Divine statues in Makarios Magnes, Porphyry and Iamblichus', *Journal of Late Antiquity* 10 (2017).
[141] Eusebius, *Ecclesiastical History* 6.19.1–12; Porphyry, *Against the Christians* fr. 39 Harnack.

are rational principles (*logoi*) in the father's seed in an inactive or potential state, but the mother has a role, because once the seed is transferred to her womb, the *logoi* in the seed are actualised by the mother's soul by a process of 'inspiration', or 'breathing in'. It is her soul which actualises these *logoi*, so that they can create not a soul, but a body. It is only after the new body has been created that a pre-existing soul descends from the intelligible world that is suited to that body. Porphyry does not, like Themistius, explain the supposed generation of hornets from the corpse of a horse without parents, but he may contribute to the later account in Themistius the idea of actualising *logoi* by inspiration.

Plato's Myth of Er in his *Republic* at 618A3 and B2 had allowed souls to choose their next life before reincarnation and even to choose whether to be an animal or male or female. At 617E2–5, it is said that you will be joined to your choice by necessity, but the responsibility for what then happens is the chooser's, not God's. Augustine and Nemesius gave incompatible accounts of whether Porphyry allowed such transmigration of a human soul into an animal. But the matter is settled by Porphyry's very short *On What is in our Power*, an interpretation of Plato's Myth of Er, which Wilberding has translated alongside Porphyry's *To Gaurus*. Here we are told that one is given a free first and second choice, and may choose, e.g. to be a dog and a hunting dog, or a human and a woman. But once those two choices are made, the rest is limited. A dog will have much less self-determination than a human. A human male cannot later choose to be a woman. Our previous life also exerts an influence on our choice of life, and our choice of life on our present life. This influence is like the prescription of a law which does not actually force you to do anything, but, like the law, it prescribes and this is what Fate is.

Porphyry's *Against Boethus On the Soul* survives only in fragments, but is probably directed against the Aristotelian Boethus, though it also opposes later Aristotelians, including Alexander of Aphrodisias. The objection is to the Aristotelian view that the soul is mortal, And Boethus may be named as the first of the commentators to uphold Aristotle's view.[142]

Concerning the relation between body and soul, an influential new concept has been ascribed to Porphyry in his *Miscellaneous Researches* (*Summikta Zêtêmata*). Body and soul are unified without fusion (*hênôsthai asunkhutôs*). This concept is found in the fourth century bishop Nemesius in *On the Nature of Man* 40–41 and in the sixth century Athenian Neoplatonist Priscian in his *Answers to King Khosroes* at 51,18; 51,25; 51,30; 52,2–3. These passages are included by H. Dörrie in his reconstruction of Porphyry's *Summikta Zêtêmata* (Munich: Beck, 1959), and Porphyry's work may well have been the source used by Nemesius and Priscian, although John Rist has contested the ascription of this concept to Porphyry.[143] Unification without fusion is a non-spatial relationship, appropriate to soul, because soul is non-corporeal and intelligible not perceptible, and is as a whole unified with every part of the body. Fusion would involve

---

[142] Hans Gottschalk, 'Boethus' psychology and the Neoplatonists', *Phronesis* 31 (1986), 243–57.
[143] John Rist, 'Pseudo-Ammonius and the Soul/Body Problem in Some Platonic Texts of Late Antiquity', *American Journal of Philology* 109 (1988), 402–15.

being destroyed, which is what happens to bodily ingredients which mix in such a way as to perish and turn into another kind of stuff. As a bishop, Nemesius thinks that unfused unification is also a good concept for explaining the union of God and human in Christ, and Jean Pépin has claimed that the idea is also applied by Augustine to the divine Trinity in his *On the Trinity* Book 9, although Rist disputes this. The Christian Claudianus Mamertus (died c. 474) uses the term 'without fusion' (*inconfusibiliter*) of the soul-body relation at *De Statu Animae* 1.15, 59,20–60,16. Augustine also may apply it to the soul-body relation in several works, including the Letter 166 to Jerome, *Corpus Selectorum Ecclesiasticorum Latinorum* 44, where at p. 551,7–12, the soul is said to be extended through the body not by a spatial (*localis*, cf. Porphyry's *topikos*, 41,19–20) diffusion, but by a certain inclination (*intentio*, cf. Porphyry's *rhopê*, 41,17), and to be present as a whole everywhere (cf. 41,6–8).[144]

Finally, there is an argument in Porphyry which I have related to later attempts by Augustine, Avicenna, and Descartes in their arguments from the *Cogito* or from Avicenna's 'Flying Man', to show that body is no part of the soul's essence.[145] In *Sentences* 41, 52,7–53,5 (Lamberz), Porphyry is talking about intellect, not about the soul in general, and he distinguishes intellect from the senses as not owing its essence (*ousiôsthai*) to body, because in turning to itself, it can both know itself and remain intact in separation from body. Perception, by contrast cannot withdraw from body and still know itself, or even remain intact, for it has to perceive bodies and their spatial relation to its own bodily organ.

Work on Aristotle, Pythagoras, and Plato

Porphyry wrote two lost works, both of which presumably maintained the harmony he usually seeks between Plato and Aristotle. They were *On the Unity of the Schools of Plato and Aristotle* and *On the Difference between Plato and Aristotle*. His many commentaries on works by Plato included the two regarded as the most theological, the *Timaeus* and *Parmenides*. They are largely lost, but the fragments on Plato's *Republic* all concern Plato's Myth of Er, and Wilberding has therefore translated them alongside Porphyry's *On What is in our Power*, which is also devoted to the Myth of Er, with the suggestion that they may have belonged to one work. The big question was raised by Pierre Hadot, who identified fragments of an anonymous commentary on Plato's *Parmenides* as being from Porphyry's.[146] Many think this possible, but it is still a matter of controversy.

Porphyry attended also to Pythagoras, on a different scale of course from Plato. His *Life of Pythagoras* is not, like Iamblichus' *Pythagorean Life*, a celebration of a way of life designed to introduce a much longer celebration of the doctrines of a major hero. It is, less ambitiously, the surviving one of four books on the history of philosophy.[147]

---

[144] See Richard Sorabji, *The Philosophy of the Commentators*, vol. 1, ch. 6(b), pp. 204–5.
[145] Sorabji, *Self*, pp. 217–29, with Porphyry at pp. 226–9.
[146] P. Hadot, *Porphyre et Victorinus* (Paris: Études Augustiniennes, 1968), vol. 2, pp. 6–113.
[147] Gillian Clark, 'Translate into Greek'; Mark Edwards, 'Two images of Pythagoras: Iamblichus and Porphyry', in H. J. Blumenthal and E. G. Clark, eds, *The Divine Iamblichus* (London: Duckworth, 1993), pp. 159–72.

Iamblichus (about 245 – before 325 CE) in Apamaea

The commentaries of Iamblichus on Aristotle are lost, but many of his ideas about Aristotle are recorded by Simplicius, especially in his commentary on Aristotle's *Categories*, now translated into English,[148] and in the other two surviving commentaries on Aristotle undisputedly ascribed to Simplicius, the commentaries on the *Physics* and on *On the Heavens*, also virtually all translated.[149] Lost apart from fragments are also his commentaries on most of Plato's *Dialogues*, for which he established a teaching curriculum,[150] and also his commentary on the theurgic text, the *Chaldaean Oracles*. Simplicius on Aristotle's *Categories* says at 2,9-25 that Iamblichus closely copied Porphyry's lost major commentary on the *Categories*, but that he inserted two kinds of addition in almost every section. One addition was the Pythagoreanism of Pseudo-Archytas' scheme of categories, which purported to be an account of categories written by Aristotle's Pythagorean predecessor Archytas and hence to be a source used by Aristotle for his own *Categories*. Only Themistius is known to have seen through this false chronology. Iamblichus' other addition was his so-called 'intellective' theory, which is the subject of John Dillon's classic account in Chapter 11. The theory claimed that Aristotle's categories, including substance, applied to Plato's Ideas, as Plotinus had complained it should have done. The later commentator Elias understood Iamblichus to hold that Aristotle's *Categories* did not therefore criticise, but accepted Plato's theory of Ideas.[151] Ways in which the categories might apply to Ideas are briefly suggested by Plotinus himself, next by Iamblichus in more developed form, as recorded much later by Simplicius, and next by Iamblichus' pupil Dexippus still in the fourth century. In *Aristotle Transformed*, Pierre Hadot argued that Dexippus drew mostly from a development of Plotinus in Porphyry's lost larger commentary on Aristotle's *Categories*. But Concetta Luna has argued that Dexippus drew on Iamblichus' Pythagoreanising distortion of Porphyry's lost commentary. This controversy is recorded in the introduction to the 2016 edition of *Aristotle Transformed*.

One clear example of Iamblichus' intellective theory is provided by his account of Aristotle's category of When (i.e. at-a-time), or for Time itself, even though Time itself is not one of Aristotle's categories, and there is a similar account of the category of Where (i.e. in-a-place) or Place itself. Iamblichus offers an 'intellective' theory of place and time which makes both of them more dynamic than Aristotle had intended. Aristotle's controversial account of a thing's place makes it into the inner surface of a thing's embracing surroundings. Iamblichus makes Aristotle's embrace dynamic, for place stops the dissipation of matter as it departs from the unity of the supreme One, and holds physical things together.[152] Time too is dynamic for Iamblichus. He quotes

---

[148] In 4 volumes of the series Ancient Commentators on Aristotle.
[149] In 12 volumes and 9 volumes respectively of the series Ancient Commentators on Aristotle.
[150] So *Anonymous Prolegomena to the Philosophy of Plato* ch. 26, lines 16-44, ed. Westerink. John Dillon has edited and translated the fragments on Plato's dialogues (Leiden: Brill, 1973). Bert Dalsgard Larsen collected still other fragments on Aristotle in Greek (Aarhus: Universitetsforlaget, 1972).
[151] Elias, *in Cat.* 123,1-3.
[152] Iamblichus *ap.* Simplicius, *in Phys.* 639,22-640,12; *in Cat.* 361,7-362,33, discussed in Richard Sorabji, *Matter, Space and Motion* (London: Duckworth, 1988), pp 204-6.

from Pseudo-Archytas' version of Aristotle's two puzzles in *Physics* 4.10 about the reality of time. The puzzle he tackles argues that no parts of time exist: the past no longer exists, the future does not yet exist, and the present 'now' is not a part of time at all, since it has no size. If you think it has a size, part of that will be past and part future, so in fact it is a sizeless (Archytas says 'lacking parts') boundary between past and future, so not a part. Iamblichus thinks he can instead reply to the puzzle by distinguishing a Platonist essence of time, separate from the cosmos, proceeding from Plato's divine Craftsman or maker of the universe, which gives order to things in the world so that they are temporally separated or simultaneous. It is, as Aristotle says, the number of movement, but the number which causes the movement of Plato's World Soul, not Aristotle's countable aspect of physical movement. This time is indeed indivisible or partless, like other entities in Plato's intelligible sphere, but that creates no problem of non-existence, because it does not flow away into past or future. The time that flows away is time within the world. But that too creates no problem, because the present 'now' in that time is not indivisible or partless, but is an extended present. It cannot be partless, he argues, because anything that changes must have parts and our flowing present 'now' touches with successive parts of itself the transcendent now.[153]

Here Iamblichus goes beyond Pseudo-Archytas, who appears in this passage to surrender to Aristotle's puzzle and allow that the flowing time is both partless (in its present, presumably) and unreal (*anhupostaton*). But Iamblichus does accept Pseudo-Archytas' strange definition of time, part an Aristotelian-sounding number connected with motion, part a Stoic-sounding extension, but in both halves interpreted in a Pythagorean way by Pseudo-Archytas and re-interpreted by Iamblichus.[154]

Iamblichus and Porphyry seem to have known each other, perhaps only too well. For his part, Iamblichus says that he devoted himself (*prostheis heauton*) at one time to Porphyry and that he heard him. Whereas 'heard' can refer in Greek to hearing something read aloud, Saffrey has argued that 'devoted himself' suggests a personal relationship, although it was probably not one of discipleship.[155] They disagreed, among other things, on the role of priestly theurgic practice. Porphyry dedicated to Iamblichus, a work called *Know Thyself*,[156] which stressed what could be achieved by practising philosophy without mentioning priestly ritual or theurgy as necessary. We have seen above that Porphyry is reported as saying that theurgy can purify the imaginative part of the soul but cannot lead us back to God, and that he further wrote to Iamblichus, as if to a minor Egyptian priest Anebo, a set of questions on how his theurgical ritual could work, posing among many other issues why that ritual includes erotic festivals

---

[153] Iamblichus *ap.* Simplicius, *in Cat.* 354,9–26, explained partly in Richard Sorabji, *Time, Creation and the Continuum* (London: Duckworth, 1983), pp. 39–41. But the Platonic nature of Iamblichus' unflowing time is explained by Philippe Hoffmann, 'Jamblique, exégète du Pythagoricien Archytas: trois originalités d'une doctrine du temps', *Les Études philosophiques* 3 (1980), 307–23, esp. 319–23, not by my insouciant pp. 38–9.
[154] Pseudo-Archytas *ap.* Simplicius, *in Phys.* 'Corollary on Time' 786,11–13; *in Cat.* 350,11–12, discussed Hoffmann, op. cit., pp. 308–19.
[155] H. D. Saffrey, 'Pourquoi Porphyre a-t-il édité Plotin?', in Luc Brisson et al., eds, *La vie de Plotin*, 2 vols (Paris: Vrin, 1982–92), vol. 2, pp. 31–64.
[156] Porphyry, fr. 273F-275F Smith.

arousing passion. Iamblichus replied in *On the Mysteries of the Egyptians*[157] as Anebo's superior in the priestly college, Abammon, a figure at the highest level of virtue recognised by Porphyry, although he himself recognises a still higher level of theurgic or priestly virtue.[158] Iamblichus sees the priestly practices called theurgy as essential for obtaining answers to prayers and for achieving mystical union with the gods. The intellectual activity of theoretical philosophers cannot achieve this, as Porphyry thought. It requires acts not to be divulged and unutterable symbols.[159] He defends pagan ritual and sacrifice against Porphyry as if addressing someone who was looking for explanations at too naturalistic a level, and he draws on the theurgic text, the *Chaldaean Oracles*. His replies include possibly the first reference back in 600 years to Aristotle's theory of catharsis in drama. The mild erotic stimulation in religious festivals, he answers Porphyry, does have a value in that, as in Aristotle's account of the value of drama, it provides Aristotelian catharsis *purging* you of such feelings, without increasing them. He also gives his theory about the statues of the gods, which Porphyry had seen as merely representing their characteristics, and declares instead that theurgy constructs them as receptacles (*hupodokhai*) and dwellings (*oikodomêseis*) for the gods.[160]

Iamblichus' conception of statues as receiving gods does not share Porphyry's worry that anything encased in body will be affected by passion. For, quite apart from gods, the purest human souls can avoid that contamination when embodied, according to Iamblichus *On the Soul*.[161] According to this work, the human soul has two essences, one concerned with intelligising, one as an animal soul concerned with nature. Pure human souls which intelligise nonetheless have to descend to reincarnation, like Boddhisatvas, to help impure souls, who can gain the purity needed for intelligising only with the aid of theurgy, which is thereby treated as essential, supplemented by appropriate punishment after death. The pure souls need no such punishment after death, but no human souls can intelligise for ever, since they cannot lose their character of souls and become intellects. So reincarnation will never be escaped. In a letter to a pupil, Macedonius, he speaks of the freedom of the soul, saying that in itself it contains a life that it can make free from fate.[162] But according to the *Mysteries*, this again requires ritual (*hagisteia*) to persuade the gods to free us from fate and allow our souls conjunction (*sunaphê*) with the gods.[163]

Iamblichus sought to include the early Pythagoreans in a unitary Greek tradition, and he wrote a *Pythagorean Life*, not so much a biography as a model of the Pythagorean way of life, as the first of ten books on Pythagoreanism, of which only the first four

---

[157] Iamblichus, *On the Mysteries of the Egyptians* 5.23.
[158] Damascius, *Commentary I on Plato's Phaedo*, para. 144, ed. Westerink.
[159] Iamblichus, *On the Mysteries of the Egyptians* 2.11.
[160] Iamblichus, *On the Mysteries of the Egyptians* 5.3.
[161] Iamblichus, *On the Soul*, ed. and trans. by John Finamore and John Dillon (Leiden: Brill, 2002), § 28, 379.
[162] What survives of 20 letters is edited translated by John Dillon and W. Polleichtner, *Iamblichus of Chalcis, The Letters* (Atlanta: Society of Biblical Literature, 2009); see Letter 8, fr. 2.
[163] Iamblichus, *On the Mysteries of the Egyptians* 8.7.

survive. The *Pythagorean Life*, along with his *Protrepticus*, or *Exhortation to Philosophy* and two mathematical works, formed the first 4 books of an over-arching work on Pythagoreanism.[164] The *Protrepticus* draws on Aristotle's earlier *Protrepticus* by excerpting portions of his lost text. But it presents Aristotle as part of a unified body of wisdom along Pythagorean lines, and prefaces these excerpts by drawing on the Pythagorean *Golden Verses* and proverbs of Pythagoras. Iamblichus' Pythagorean treatment of mathematics, *On the General Science of Mathematics* (*De Communi Mathematica Scientia*) also excerpts Aristotle's *Protrepticus*. The remaining mathematical work in the Pythagorean series is Iamblichus' commentary on the *Introduction to Arithmetic* of Nicomachus of Gerasa.[165]

Iamblichus had established his own school in memory of a previous Apamean Platonist, Numenius, in a beautiful site in Apamea in Syria. Porphyry's fellow student and original interrogator Amelius had already gone there before Iamblichus, and Iamblichus' pupils continued teaching elsewhere maintaining his tradition after Iamblichus' death and the discontinuation of philosophy classes. Not all were faithful, and the emperor Julian, a devotee, in a letter to his Iamblichan associate Priscus, warns against Theodore of Asine, who came to think Iamblichus worldly and self-seeking.[166]

The school continued its other programmes, such as Rhetoric, and it was Julian who in memory of Iamblichus installed in the school the mosaics which I sought to reinterpret in the introduction to *Aristotle Transformed*, as being one for the Philosophy lecture space and one for Rhetoric.[167] Unfortunately, the current war is said to have started with firing from the archaeologists' hut where the mosaics are kept. Since offering my interpretation, I have seen a crude version in Paphos in Cyprus of what I interpreted as the Rhetoric mosaic in Apamea, and there is a different version of it again in Palmyra in Syria, the latter dated to the first century CE.[168] It is highly possible that there was rhetoric teaching in Palmyra, but in the absence of figures labelled as connected with rhetoric, the designers need not have understood the relevance to that subject.[169] We have seen above under 'Themistius' the devotion of Julian to the deceased Iamblichus, and to his follower, Maximus of Ephesus, his Iamblichan extravagances in personal sacrifice of animals and inspection of entrails, and his alienation in scolding the Antiochenes for neglecting these rituals.

There was one side of Iamblichus' views, however, that had a favourable influence on Julian, as shown, for example, in letters excerpted by Stobaeus, some from Iamblichus

---

[164] See Dominic O'Meara, *Pythagoras Revived* (Oxford: Oxford University Press, 1989). *On the Pythagorean Life* has been translated by Gillian Clark (Liverpool: Liverpool University Press, 1989).

[165] Reconstructions of the *Protrepticus* of Iamblichus and of Aristotle are in preparation by D. S. Hutchinson and Monte Ransome Johnson. A draft translation by J. O. Urmson of Iamblichus *On the General Science of Mathematics* has been deposited in the library of the Institute of Classical Studies, University of London, and may be worked up into an annotated translation.

[166] Julian, *Letter* 12 Bidez = 12 Wright.

[167] Richard Sorabji, 'The Ancient Commentators on Aristotle', in *Aristotle Transformed*, pp. 9–10.

[168] Janine Balty, 'Les mosaïques des maisons de Palmyre', *Bibliothèque archéologique et historique* 206 (2011), 1–70.

[169] Ibid.

and some written within a family influenced by Iamblichus.[170] The influence was useful perhaps because of, not in spite of, being about the lowest level of virtue, ordinary civic virtue. The family letter was written by the son, Sopater, of one of Iamblichus' pupils, also called Sopater, to his brother Himerios about ethics in public life.[171] The Iamblichan inspiration for the family can be gauged from Himerios calling his own son Iamblichus. The letter requires that one must exercise providence on behalf of one's subordinates, should remember that wrongdoing is innate, and that punishment may need to be moderated, since it should aim at reform. Julian appears not to have punished those who deliberately insulted him, not, as far as we know, the Cynic Heraclius and not the people of Antioch.

Iamblichus was a clever man, and if I were to choose one idea of his with lasting effect it would be an idea about knowledge. Knowledge need not have the same status as the known; it takes its status from the knower. Thus there can be changeless knowledge of change, timeless knowledge of the temporal or determinate knowledge of the undetermined.[172] This, even if glimpsed in less general terms by earlier philosophers, opens a sea of possibilities, many of which were to be exploited later by Ammonius, Boethius, and others to whom we shall come.

Syrianus (died 437) in Athens

Syrianus succeeded Plutarch of Athens[173] on his death in 432 CE, as head of the Platonist school which Plutarch had re-founded in Athens in his own house. The house has been identified by Alison Franz as one excavated, although now re-buried with markers, south of the Athenian Acropolis. Plutarch will have been born around 350 CE, and certainly while Themistius was still working in Constantinople. Syrianus had started his philosophical studies in Alexandria, perhaps before the troubled period which culminated in the lynching of the female Christian mathematician, Hypatia, by a Christian mob in 415. Later he lived in Plutarch's house in Athens and a fellow student there was Hierocles, who went on to teach in Alexandria and write a commentary on the Pythagorean *Golden Verses*. Syrianus inherited his star pupil, the young Proclus, who had arrived from Alexandria in 430/1, aged perhaps less than 20, depending on his date of birth, and who studied with Plutarch for the last two years of Plutarch's life. Syrianus' most notable other pupil was Hermeias (about 410–450), who returned to teach philosophy in Alexandria around 431/2, and was the father of the great

---

[170] Iamblichus, *Letters* 219, 1-2; 6-7; 223, 14-24; Sopater, *Letter to Himerios*, preserved by Stobaeus *Anth.* 4 (215,12-218,9 for treatment of subordinates), the latter translated with an essay by Simon Swain, *Themistius, Julian, and Greek Political Theory under Rome*, and discussed by Dominic O'Meara, 'A Neoplatonist ethics for high-level officials; Sopatros' Letter to Himerios', in Andrew Smith, ed., *The Philosopher and Society in Late Antiquity* (Swansea: Classical Press of Wales, 2005), pp. 91-100.
[171] Sopater, *Letter to Himerios*, preserved by Stobaeus, *Anth.* 4,215,12-218,9 for treatment of subordinates.
[172] Iamblichus *ap.* Ammonius, *in Int.* 135,14.
[173] Not the more famous Middle Platonist Plutarch of Chaeronea.

Ammonius. Hermeias' commentary on Plato's *Phaedrus*, due to appear in translation in the Ancient Commentators on Aristotle series, is largely a transcription from Syrianus' seminars on the subject, and of comments in the seminar by himself and Proclus, so already gives us some idea of Syrianus' teaching.

There survives, apart from the record of lectures on Plato's *Phaedrus*, Syrianus' commentary on four books of Aristotle's *Metaphysics*, Books 3-4 and 13-14.[174] But a four-page passage of Syrianus is reported also by Asclepius in his commentary on *Metaphysics* Book 7, at a point where Aristotle criticises Plato, so Syrianus seems to have commented on other books.[175] Marinus' *Life of Proclus* 13-14 tells us the teaching course that Syrianus gave to Proclus. Two years were spent on Aristotle's logic, ethics, physics, and theology (the summit of metaphysics), in that order. He then went on to teach what Marinus calls the 'Greater Mysteries' of Plato. Syrianus greatly admired Aristotle's logic, ethics, and physics and regarded him as a 'benefactor of humanity'. But especially in *Metaphysics* 13-14 Aristotle attacked Plato, and for the sake of truth, polemics must be answered, or students might be led to contempt for divine realities and the inspired philosophy of the ancients.[176] He was speaking of the tradition of Pythagoras, Plato, and their followers, probably as assembled by Iamblichus in his ten-part work on Pythagoreanism. Syrianus saw his answers to Aristotle concerning Books 13-14 as applying also to Aristotle's attacks in Book 1,[177] and Aristotle's attacks as calling for an answer again in the excerpt from Book 7. In his commentary on Book 4, he regards Alexander as sufficient for expounding Aristotle,[178] but he still wants to add a commentary, in order to explain the place of theological science, his name for metaphysics, in unifying the study of being.[179] The divine Ideas are the object of the divine Intellect, and give being to all other beings, so that the study of the divine will explains the being of other things. Aristotle's attack on Ideas in Books 13-14, and especially on Idea-numbers, is said to confuse them with the principles, the One, and, below that, the Monad and Dyad.

Syrianus' commentaries on Aristotle's logic are lost, but the fragments have been collected and discussed on the *Categories*, *On Interpretation*, and *Prior Analytics* by R. Loredano Cardullo.[180] Syrianus was different from Porphyry in arguing that Aristotle's claims in logic were meant to apply to metaphysics, and he was therefore more critical, not, however, hostile, but accepting of all that he thought was true. To take Syrianus' treatment just of the *Categories*,[181] he took over and used in his own

---

[174] Translated by John Dillon and Dominic O'Meara (London: Duckworth, 2006-8).
[175] Asclepius, *in Metaph.* 433,9-436,8.
[176] Syrianus, *in Metaph.* 12, 80,4-81,14. I follow here the introductions of John Dillon and Dominic O'Meara to their translations.
[177] *In Metaph.* 13, 195, 101-2.
[178] *In Metaph.* 4, 54,12-15.
[179] *In Metaph.* 4, 57,22 ff.
[180] R. Loredano Cardullo, *Siriano, Esegeta di Aristotele, I Frammenti e Testimonianze dei Commentari all' Organon* (Florence: La Nuova Italia, 1995), esp. pp. 59-65; preliminary report in 'Syrianus' lost commentaries on Aristotle', *Bulletin of the Institute of Classical Studies* 33 (1986), 112-24.
[181] See further Cardullo, pp. 63-4, on his treatment of *On Interpretation*, on which Boethius, the main source, is not very respectful.

metaphysics Aristotle's distinction between what shared a definition (the synonymous) and what shared only a name (the homonymous) and what had their definitions diverse but connected by all relating in different ways to some primary entity (*pros hen*). More speculatively, Syrianus treated the category of quality as united only by a *pros hen* relation to substance. He pointed out that Aristotle's *Categories* intends to distinguish four kinds of beings, not four kinds of expression, when he distinguishes universal and particular substance and accidents. He rightly saw the second definition of relatives in Aristotle's *Categories* as intended to replace the first, and he added that the first was based on language, the second on how things were in reality. He corrected Aristotle's treatment of individuals like Socrates as primary substances, arguing that they are primary only in relation to our knowledge, but not in reality.

I would pick out two important arguments offered by Syrianus against Aristotle. He objected to Aristotle's view that one could learn about geometry by correcting for imperfections in perceived physical shapes. Correction, he reasonably retorted, could not be supplied by sense perception of the imperfect. It would therefore require appeal to the soul's prior possession of perfect Platonic principles (*logoi*) derived from Ideas.[182] Again, rather distorting Aristotle's argument, he complains that Aristotle was also wrong to maintain that the finite bodies of the heavens depend for their infinitely enduring motion on being inspired by their desire for the divine. Aristotle overlooked that the infinite power of the divine Ideas would supply not only infinitely enduring *motion*, but also infinitely enduring *existence*.[183] We shall see Proclus sharpen up this complaint, so as to hoist Aristotle by his own petard, and Ammonius completely defuse it, so as to reinstate the harmony of Aristotle with Plato.

Proclus (412? – 485 CE) in Athens

Proclus took over the headship of the Athenian school when Syrianus died in 437, and held it for nearly 50 years. In Marinus' account, he had with Plutarch read Aristotle's *On the Soul* and Plato's *Phaedo*, and Plutarch told him to write out what was said on the *Phaedo*, saying that if he completed (*sumplêroun*) the notes (*skholia*), they would be treated as commentaries (*hupomnêmata*)[184] by Proclus himself on the *Phaedo*. His much fuller course with Syrianus, covered Aristotle's logic, ethics, politics, physics, and metaphysics, in the first two years before turning to Plato. On this course he wrote out a synopsis with his own judgements (*epikrisis*) of what was said. Syrianus died too soon to teach him the *Chaldaean Oracles* and the Orphics, but he studied Syrianus' notes on the first and Porphyry and Iamblichus on the second and wrote a compendium.[185] He had greater things to do than politics, so although he learnt political virtues from

---

[182] Syrianus, *in Metaph.* 95,29–38.
[183] Syrianus, *in Metaph.* 117,25–118,11.
[184] Proclus' standard word for commentaries, so E. Lamberz, 'Proklos und die Form des philosophischen Kommentars', in Jean Pépin and H. D. Saffrey, eds, *Proclus, lecteur et interprète des anciens* (Paris: CNRS, 1987), pp. 1–20, at pp. 2–3.
[185] Marinus, *The Life of Proclus* 26.

Aristotle's political writings and from Plato's *Laws* and *Republic*, he encouraged Plutarch's grandson to practise politics, so that he himself could avoid the appearance of word without deed.[186] His commentaries on Aristotle's logical works and on Porphyry's *Introduction* to them are lost.[187] But there is a brief summary of Aristotle's principles of motion in physics, the *Elements of Physics*, divided up into short sections, like his *Elements of Theology*. On a large scale, there survive commentaries on Plato, including those on the two culminating and most theological works in the Plato curriculum, Plato's *Timaeus* and *Parmenides*, as well as on Plato's *First Alcibiades* and *Cratylus* and essays on his *Republic*.[188] By his 28th year he had, again according to the same passage in Marinus, written many things, including the *Timaeus* commentary.

What survives about Aristotle is not commentary, but largely criticism. Carlos Steel has earlier drawn attention to the ferocity of Proclus' preference for Plato's *Timaeus* over Aristotle's *Physics*.[189] The young Proclus seems to have taken on the severity of Syrianus' reply to Aristotle's polemics, without the same respect for other aspects of Aristotle. In Chapter 12 below, Steel goes far beyond discussing Proclus' general attitude, when he identifies one of the many things Proclus wrote before the *Timaeus* commentary. Proclus himself says in that commentary that an earlier book of his was an *Examination* (*episkepsis*) *of Aristotle's Objections to Plato's Timaeus*,[190] and Steel reconstructs its arguments. Some are familiar from contexts other than the criticism of Aristotle. Proclus defends Plato from Aristotle by denying that he thinks the soul is something extended. This is surprising because it looks as if Plato thinks the soul, though not tangible or subject to being pushed, is a spatially extended entity which can make spatial movements. In *Timaeus* 43A6–44C2, Plato thinks that babies are prevented from reasoning properly by the physical movements involved in growth and perception interfering with the mathematically calibrated rotations of the rational soul. Proclus' commentary on this, however, is another place in which he goes to great lengths to avoid a spatial interpretation. It is an illusion that the soul is spatially moved. It merely, as it were, sees its reflection disturbed in the waters of the body, and wrongly concludes that it is itself spatially moved.[191] Proclus' denial against Aristotle that Plato accepts human souls being reincarnated within animals follows a line taken by Plotinus. Proclus says that a human soul can be united to an animal only 'from outside and relationally'.[192] Plotinus had said the separable human soul could only be present without being present to animals; it would be a mere image of soul that created the animal body.[193]

---

[186] Marinus, *The Life of Proclus* 12–14.
[187] Introduction to *Cat.*, *in Int.*, *in An. Pr.*, and *in An. Post.*
[188] The *in Crat.* is translated by Brian Duvick, with Harold Tarrant as guest editor (London: Duckworth, 2007).
[189] Carlos Steel, 'Why should we prefer Plato's *Timaeus* to Aristotle's *Physics*? Proclus' critique of Aristotle's causal explanation of the physical world', in Robert W. Sharples and Anne Sheppard, eds, *Ancient Approaches to Plato's Timaeus* (London: Institute of Classical Studies, 2003), pp. 175–88.
[190] Proclus, *in Tim.* 2,279,3–4 Diehl.
[191] Proclus, *in Tim.* 3,330,9–331,1; 3,341,4–342,2.
[192] Proclus, *in Remp.* 334,14.
[193] Plotinus, *Enneads* 1.1.11.9–15.

Other works of Proclus extant in whole or part include a commentary on Euclid's *Elements*, Book 1, and a good number of treatises besides his fragmentary *Examination of Aristotle's Objections to Plato's Timaeus*. There are the *Platonic Theology*, the deductive summary *Elements of Theology*, the *Summary of Astronomical Hypotheses*, and *On the Eternity of the World*, whose 18 arguments against a universe of finite duration are reported by Philoponus. Although Philoponus defends the Christian view in his reply, *Against Proclus on the Eternity of the World*, it has been strongly argued that Proclus explicitly attacks only dissident Platonists like Atticus and elsewhere Plutarch, and could not have used the title 'Against the Christians'.[194] There are also three treatises concerned with providence and evil. They are *On Providence, Ten Problems Concerning Providence* and *On the Existence of Evils*.[195] His work was to have an influential history. An Arabic work excerpted from the *Elements of Theology* was translated into Latin as *The Book on Causes* and taken to be Aristotle's until Thomas Aquinas discovered the Proclean origin. Proclus' *Platonic Theology* and *On the Existence of Evils* were used by the Christian Pseudo-Dionysius in his *On Divine Names* which purported to be the work of St Paul's disciple of more than 400 years earlier, and Ficino's use of Proclus' Plato commentaries in the Italian Renaissance led to Proclus' acceptance as the leading commentator on Plato.

The questions discussed in the three treatises on providence and evil include: why is there evil in a world governed by divine providence? Why are fortunes distributed apparently against deserts to the good and the bad? Can humans be responsible for their conduct, if God has foreknown that conduct for ages? All these questions came to be of interest to Christians, Muslims, and Jews, but all were discussed by other Greek commentators on Aristotle.

The question about evil is answered by Proclus partly by presenting evil as parasitic (a *parhupostasis*) on good, so that it has no independent reality of its own, one of the ideas that was copied by Pseudo-Dionysius and applied to Christianity. It was also answered partly by making evil the effect of coincidence, and coincidences have no explanation, and hence no cause, at least on the construction of Aristotle's *Metaphysics* 6.3, accepted by myself and implied by Alexander, *Mantissa* 171,14, although Syrianus is dismissive of such a view at his *in Metaph.* 14, 194,9–13. The coincidence may in this case be one of individuals not being fit for purpose. But we shall find Boethius below explaining evil by a quite different connexion between Providence and coincidence. God for him is not the cause of evil, nor of the distribution of fortunate and unfortunate lives. The latter is also the conclusion of a different treatment in Plato's Myth of Er in *Republic* Book 10, to which Proclus refers in *On Providence* 39,4–9. It was discussed by Porphyry and again by Proclus in his lectures on the *Republic*. Porphyry, we saw, allows

---

[194] Clemens Scholten, *Johannes Philoponos, De Aeternitate Mundi, Über die Ewigkeit der Welt* (Turnhout: Brepols, 2009), vol. 1, pp. 17–25.

[195] The last four works are translated in the Ancient Commentators on Aristotle series. Philoponus *Against Proclus* is translated by Michael Share and James Wilberding, *On Providence* by Carlos Steel, and the other two by Jan Opsomer and Carlos Steel. All three ethical treatises are lost in the original Greek, were translated into Latin, but badly, by William of Moerbeke by 1280, and all had been plagiarised in Greek in the eleventh to twelfth century by Isaak Sebastokrator. The translations have all benefitted from a retro-translation from Latin into ancient Greek by Benedikt Strobel.

two choices, one of a kind of life and one of its details. Proclus seeks to meet the problem of God's foreknowledge making our conduct inevitable by drawing on Iamblichus' idea that the determinate nature of God's foreknowledge does not make our conduct determined.[196] But more work needs to be done, and would be done by Ammonius and Boethius, in order to meet the problem that if God's knowledge is past, it is irrevocable, and that God's knowledge is infallible, so I cannot act so as to make God mistaken, and it is too late so to act that he foresees something different. Boethius in his *Consolation of Philosophy*, Book 5, was apparently to suggest that God has timeless knowledge of the temporal, and we shall see that this takes us a step further.

In his commentary on Plato's *Cratylus* Proclus devotes a lot of space, in contrast with his pupil Ammonius, to the efficacy of the use in priestly theurgy of divine names. This is relevant to the debate which Plato started on whether there are natural names, or whether, as Aristotle was to say, all names are conventional. The outspoken belief in ritual, which first endeared him to Syrianus, led, so Marinus tells us, to his passing beyond purificatory virtue by such practices as winter sea bathing even in old age, to achieve eventually Iamblichus' highest new level of virtue the theurgic.[197] His public practice may have lain behind his need to take a year's exile in Lydia, possibly because of the hostility of Christians.[198]

Among his influential contributions to philosophy I shall mention two others, one of them explained in Chapter 10 below. It was he who made standard the recognition of three kinds of universals (*katholou*), those that are *before* the many particulars, producing their plurality and enabling them to share in the universal's nature, those that are *in* particulars, associated with Aristotle, and Aristotle's universal concepts that are formed by thought *from* particulars as an *after*-effect (*epigennêmatikê, husterogenôs*) of particulars.[199] But he did not class Plato's Ideas as universal in the way one might have expected. For he denied that a Platonic Idea possesses the very same character as the particulars that fall under it; rather, the particulars have a merely derivative character related to the Form (*pros hen*), without any universal nature being shared with the Form.[200] Even in the text where he speaks of a *universal* before the many particulars, he qualifies that at the same moment by saying that this universal affords to the particulars a *variety* of ways of sharing in itself (*poikilas methexeis*). Proclus' justification for still talking of universality lies in Aristotle's idea, which he cites, of particulars owing their common character to their diverse relations to one single Idea (*pros hen*).

Concerning Aristotle's argument that the finite body of the universe cannot house the infinite power needed to give the universe beginingless and endless motion, so that power must come from something incorporeal – God – Proclus improved on Syrianus'

---

[196] Proclus, *On Providence* 63–5; *Ten Problems*, 2nd problem.
[197] Marinus, *The Life of Proclus* 11, 18, 24–6, 28.
[198] Marinus, *The Life of Proclus* 15.
[199] Proclus, *On Euclid Elements I*, 50,16–51,9, translated in Richard Sorabji, *The Philosophy of the Commentators*, vol. 3, ch. 5(c)3.
[200] Proclus, *On Plato's Parmenides* 880,3–11, translated in Richard Sorabji, *The Philosophy of the Commentators*, vol. 3, ch, 5(a)3.

objection by arguing that Aristotle himself was unwittingly committed to extending his conclusion from God as Mover to God as Creator. For Aristotle's own infinite power argument should have been used to point out that God is needed not just for *motion*, but also to provide the infinite power to give the universe beginningless and endless *being*.[201]

Ammonius of Alexandria (445? – 517/526) and his School

Works and the Organisation of Editions

Ammonius left voluminous records of his teaching, many edited by others 'from his seminars' or 'from his voice'. Commentaries survive on Porphyry's *Introduction* (*Isagôgê*), and on Aristotle's *On Interpretation* and commentaries recorded anonymously from his seminars on the *Categories*, and on *Prior Analytics* Book 1, chapters 1 and part of 2, as well as commentaries edited by Philoponus from Ammonius' seminars on *Prior Analytics 1, Posterior Analytics, On the Soul*, and *On Coming-to-Be and Passing-Away*. Another commentary edited from Ammonius' voice is by Asclepius on *Metaphysics* 1–7, and it is argued by Pantelis Golitsis in Chapter 23 that we have also Asclepius on Books 8–10 in the Pseudo-Alexander commentary assembled by Michael of Ephesus. Nearly five of these works have so far been translated in the Ancient Commentators on Aristotle series. This enormous expansion of commentaries by students based on his seminars goes beyond Proclus' editing of his teachers and beyond his father's recording of Proclus, and suggests deliberate organisation. The anonymously edited commentaries may be left anonymous because the editors made fewer interventions than in the named editions. Ammonius also wrote on Plato's *Gorgias* and twice on his *Phaedo* and lectured on his *Theaetetus*.

Training

Ammonius' father, Hermeias, died early. He had been Proclus' fellow-pupil under Syrianus and was there in 475, when he made a datable astronomical observation with Proclus. He had married Aidesia, Syrianus' relative whom Syrianus had originally intended for Proclus. Aedesia exceptionally managed to retain for her two young sons, Ammonius and his younger brother Heliodorus, the city maintenance (*dêmosia sitêsis*)[202] that had been paid to Hermeias when he taught in Alexandria, and she took them to Athens to study with Proclus after the death of Hermeias.

---

[201] Proclus, *in Tim.* 1,267,16–268,6; and also in his lost *Examination of Aristotle's Objections to Plato's Timaeus, ap.* Philoponus, *Aet.* 238,3–240,9; 297,21–300,2; 626,1–627,20.
[202] Damascius, *Life of Isidore* or *Philosophical History*, fr. 56–57 in P. Athanassiadi, *Damascius, the Philosophical History* (Athens: Apamea, 1999).

Riots and Saving the Philosophy Teaching

When Ammonius was back teaching in Alexandria in 486, a riot broke out between Christian and pagan students over disputed claims about the efficacy of Egyptian priests in restoring the fertility of the wife of a visiting Neoplatonist philosopher. Persecution and torture of Alexandrian teachers, including the Neoplatonist philosophers, followed in 488-9, when Nicomedes was sent from Constantinople to make inquiries.[203] It may have been after this that Ammonius concluded a deal with the Patriarch of Alexandria, a deal which Damascius, who was to bestow on Ammonius his characteristic mixture of praise and blame, described as the agreement of a greedy man (*aiskhrokerdês*) for gain or authorisation (*khrêmatismos*).[204] But the deal kept the Alexandrian school open beyond the end of the following century, whereas the Athenian school's teaching was stopped by the Christian emperor Justinian as early in that century as 529. I suggested in *Aristotle Transformed* that Ammonius' concession was not to parade the worship of the pagan gods, or, as I later said, not the claims of priestly ritual or theurgy. Claims for the powers of Egyptian priests started the riots in 486, and Ammonius did not teach the texts that would require him to discuss theurgy, such as the Platonic dialogues considered theological, the *Timaeus* and *Parmenides*, or the *Chaldaean Oracles* and the Orphics. On their side, the city already provided the magnificent lecture rooms, twenty or more, that have recently been excavated, but it sounds from Damascius as if it also made the continuation of teaching under Ammonius financially possible. I do not think that Ammonius' agreement went against his principles.[205] On the contrary, I agree that there is no trace in Ammonius of a hankering for theurgy. I take him to be like Porphyry who was described above as thinking that theurgy could not achieve all that much, and certainly not union with the divine. This is not to say that Ammonius' successors had no interest in theurgy; indeed, his pupil Olympiodorus did. But he was still teaching in 565 and by then the situation was entirely different. He speaks to his audience as if they were entirely Christian. There were no rowdy pagan students creating a danger of riots. The problem was rather to explain to Christian students the strange beliefs of a pagan Greek philosopher in terms they could understand. There was no question of proselytising. The most interesting example was that of moral conscience, introduced by Olympiodorus in his commentary on Plato's *Gorgias*, in order to explain the idea of Socrates' guardian spirit. In doing so, he drew on recent analyses by Damascius and Philoponus describing moral conscience as one form of a newly identified faculty of self-awareness.[206]

---

[203] *Life of Isidore* or *Philosophical History*, fr. 117-9.
[204] Mossman Roueché suggests this alternative sense to me.
[205] I am sorry to have given a different impression to my friend David Blank, in his 'Ammonius Hermeiou and his school', in Lloyd Gerson, ed., *The Cambridge History of Philosophy in Late Antiquity*, 2 vols (Cambridge: Cambridge University Press, 2010), vol. 2, p. 659, and 'Ammonius', in Edward N. Zalta, ed., *The Stanford Encyclopedia of Philosophy* (Fall 2014 Edition), <http://plato.stanford.edu/archives/fall2014/entries/ammonius/>.
[206] Olympiodorus, *Commentary on Plato's First Alcibiades*, 22,4-23,13 (p. 17 Westerink), cited in Richard Sorabji, *Moral Conscience through the Ages* (Oxford: Oxford University Press, 2014), pp. 41-5.

Teacher of All Leading Neoplatonists

The first, then, of Ammonius' series of achievements was saving the Alexandrian philosophy teaching for another century and a quarter. A second was that he taught all the leading sixth century Neoplatonist philosophers, Damascius and Simplicius, who moved to the Athenian school, and in Alexandria Philoponus, who was to become the most formidable Christian opponent of the Neoplatonist view of the physical world. All three will be described below. Another pupil important for continuing Ammonius' tradition was Olympiodorus, while another, Asclepius, preserved some of Ammonius' teaching on Aristotle's *Metaphysics*.

New Curriculum with up to Six introductions a Mark of the School

As if it was not enough to save the school and to teach so many philosophers, Ammonius inaugurated a new style of six introductions to the study of Aristotle that was to spread to yet others in Alexandria and then to other cultures. There was (1) an introduction to philosophy in general, (2) an introduction to (3) a full commentary[207] on Porphyry's *Isagôgê* (*Introduction* – to Aristotle's logic), (4) Porphyry's *Introduction* itself (5) an introduction to *Aristotle's* philosophy in general, (6) an introduction to the first work of Aristotle in the syllabus, his *Categories*. The ten questions in the introduction to Aristotle's philosophy are said to have been laid down already by Ammonius' teacher Proclus.[208] But Ammonius' new opening introduction (1) about philosophy as a whole was particularly popular. It discussed definitions and subdivisions of Philosophy (as repeated by Elias, David, and Pseudo-Elias) and mentioned questions raised by sceptics (*ephektikoi* – withholders of judgement) about the existence of Philosophy (answered by Elias and David). All of this was unprecedented.[209] Particularly interesting are the definitions of Philosophy, two of which treat Philosophy as a way of life. One definition draws on the claim in Plato's *Theaetetus* 176B1–2 that fleeing from this world is becoming like God as far as possible by becoming just, holy, and wise, and makes it a definition of Philosophy. The other takes up the idea from Plato's *Phaedo* 64A4–6 that Philosophy is a preparation for death, because it enables the soul to ignore the body's appetites. Ammonius (4,15–5,27) picks up Porphyry's ideas on suicide by distinguishing a natural bond of body to soul, broken by a natural death, from a voluntary bond of soul to body, broken by the philosopher's chosen (*prohairetikos*) 'death', a distinction often to be repeated. Cleombrotus, he says, ignored the distinction when he committed suicide by jumping off the town walls, in the belief that this is what the *Phaedo* required. Ammonius' pupil Olympiodorus had an *Introduction to Philosophy*, which is lost, but is

---

[207] Probus' commentary in Syriac is no longer thought to be earlier than the sixth century and hence than Ammonius, thanks to Sebastian Brock, in a series of articles, e.g. 'The Syriac Commentary Tradition' in C. Burnett, ed., *Glosses and Commentaries on Aristotelian Logical Texts* (London: The Warburg Institute, 1993).

[208] David, *in Cat.* 107,24–6.

[209] Porphyry's surviving short commentary on the *Categories* had provided nothing but a very brief version of (5), an introduction to the *Categories*, raising only three of Ammonius' questions about it: its title, subject matter and utility, but the utility only of the opening section.

attested in David's introduction.[210] However, extant is his long discussion of suicide, in his commentary on Plato's *Phaedo*, lecture 1, sections 1–23. He repeated the idea of voluntary freeing only of the voluntary bond, gave three reasons he claimed to be his own against suicide, named five circumstances the Stoics accepted as justifying suicide, found arguments in Plato and Plotinus allowing it in exceptional circumstances, and finished by allowing it only when the body was harming the soul.[211]

This new genre was pursued not only by Olympiodorus, and his followers, Elias (who has all the introductions), David, and Pseudo-Elias, but also by Ammonius' editor Philoponus, Philoponus' pupil Stephanus, and Ammonius' successor Eutocius. All seven could therefore in this respect be considered as belonging to Ammonius' school, and a meticulous comparison of many of them is provided by Mossman Roueché in chapter 22 below. Besides the new definitions of philosophy for beginners, the introductions included definitions of many other philosophical terms as well as divisions between philosophical items. This compact new presentation of philosophy seemed to make it accessible and had wide appeal. It spread into other cultures, in the sixth century into Syriac and Persian, by the seventh to Greek Orthodox fathers of the church, by the tenth century into Arabic, and long before the eleventh century[212] into Armenian. It is Mossman Roueché in Chapter 22 below who quotes from Stephanus' lost introduction to Philosophy the fragment, which he had already cited in 1990,[213] that quotes three definitions of Philosophy and shows that Stephanus had already added to the definition 'preparation for death' Ammonius' warning ... before David and Pseudo-Elias copied it.[214] Roueché further points out that Elias claims as his own Olympiodorus' earlier riposte to the Cleombrotus story, that he himself would have committed suicide if Plato had not taught him otherwise. There is independent evidence for Stephanus and also for Philoponus having written commentaries on Porphyry's *Isagôgê*, and in the case of Philoponus, that he preceded it with a *Prolegomena* about Philosophy. For Philoponus refers to his own *Isagôgê commentary* in his *Physics* commentary,[215] but in his *Categories* commentary, he refers to both his *Isagôgê* commentary and his *Introduction to Philosophy* as well, in what I have labelled (1) and (2) when he says: 'Just as when we started on introductions (*eisagôgôn* – plural), we spoke about (1) things that pertain to the whole of *philosophy* and then (2) defined the aim of the book before us [i.e. Porphyry's *Isagôgê*], let us (5) state the things that pertain to the whole of *Aristotelian* philosophy and then in the same way (6) demarcate the aim of the book before us, *Categories*'.[216] Here four out of six introductions are claimed by Philoponus as his own: introductions to Philosophy, to Porphyry's *Isagôgê*, to

---

[210] David, *Prolegomena philosophiae* 31,34.
[211] Sebastian Gertz, *Death and Immortality in Late Neoplatonism* (Leiden: Brill, 2011), pp. 27–50.
[212] Bridget Kendall and Robert W. Thompson, *Definitions and Divisions of Philosophy by David the Invincible Philosopher* (Chico, CA: Scholars Press, 1983), p. xviii.
[213] Mossman Roueché, 'The Definitions of Philosophy and a New Fragment of Stephanus the Philosopher', *Jahrbuch der Österreichischen Byzantistik* 40 (1990), 107–28.
[214] Ammonius on Porphyry Isagoge 5, 3 and 25. David, *Prolegomena philosophiae* 32,7; Ps.-Elias, *Prolegomena* Lecture 12,1–39.
[215] Philoponus, *in Phys.* 250,28.
[216] Philoponus, *in Cat.* 1,2–6.

Aristotle's philosophy and to his *Categories*. Riin Sirkel, the translator in the Ancient Commentators on Aristotle series, has very acutely raised the complication that Philoponus also uses the plural, 'introductions' at 12,19 when talking about what his listeners have already learnt about the content of Porphyry's *Isagôgê* and at 32,32 about what Porphyry says in introductions. But I now believe that both passages refer to (2) Philoponus' introduction to a commentary on Porphyry's *Isagôgê* and to (4) Porphyry's *Isagôgê* itself, although the second passage will include reference to direct quotations of Porphyry in Philoponus' introduction. Anton Baumstark in 1900 announced a Syriac text which seems to depend on Philoponus' *Introduction to Porphyry's Isagôgê*, via a long chain. It gives biographical incidents about Porphyry appropriate to Philoponus' (2) introduction to a commentary on Porphyry's *Isagôgê*, and Philoponus, whose name means workaholic, seems to be referred to under the name 'lover of toil' as the author of stories about Porphyry.[217] In another Syriac text, again mentioned in Chapter 22 below by Rouéché, Severus bar Shakko (died 1241) names Stephanus as having opposed the idea that logical division can be used to divide a species into individuals, in a context which suggests he did so not in an *introduction*, but in a commentary on Porphyry's *Isagôgê* at level (3).[218]

Eutocius also wrote an introduction to Porphyry's *Isagôgê*, as we learn from a fragment of a commentary by Elias on the *Prior Analytics* and from the Armenian commentary on the same text attributed to David.[219] In addition, a fragment (or paraphrase) from Eutocius' commentary on the *Isagôgê* is also preserved.[220]

Diffusion of New Curriculum to Other Cultures

The tradition of Ammonius' new introductions was not like a modern *Philosophy for Dummies*, but it had something of the same popularity with beginners. Its very accessibility may have helped it to pass to other cultures in different directions. As early as about 570 CE, Paul the Persian addressed two introductions to King Khosroes I of Persia (ruled 531–578), the protector of the Athenian Neoplatonists who fled to him from the Christian emperor Justinian in 531. This and another logical work by Paul, an *Elucidation of Aristotle's On Interpretation*, survive in Syriac, though Paul originally wrote them in Middle Persian. The second, as Hugonnard-Roche explains, was

---

[217] A. Baumstark, *Aristoteles bei den Syrern vom 5. bis 8. Jahrhundert* (Leipzig: Teubner, 1900), pp. 171–9, with the caveats of Christel Hein about not taking the original source of everything to be Philoponus; *Definition und Einteilung der Philosophie: Von der Spätantike Einleitungsliteratur zür arabischen Enzyklopâdie* (Frankfurt: Peter Lang, 1985), p. 37.
[218] A. Baumstark, *Aristoteles bei den Syrern*, pp. 185–7, with the same caveats of Christel Hein, p. 39.
[219] L. G. Westerink, 'Elias on the Prior Analytics', *Mnemosyne* 14 (1961), 126–39, a fragment from the voice of Elias edited by Westerink from Paris suppl. gr. 678, citing Eutocius at p.134, repr. in his *Texts and Studies in Neoplatonism and Byzantine Literature* (Amsterdam: Hakkert, 1980), 59–72; David the Invincible, *Commentary on Aristotle's Prior Analytics*, Lecture III. 1, ed. and trans. from Armenian into English by Aram Topchayan (Leiden: Brill, 2010), pp. 46–7. The first is referred to by Mossman Rouéché in 'The Definitions of Philosophy and a New Fragment of Stephanus the Philosopher'.
[220] In a collection of scholia on the *Isagôgê* attributed to Arethas, and edited by Michael Share (Athens: Academy of Athens, 1994), schol. 36, p. 20,29 ff.

translated into Syriac in the seventh century, and centres on the syllogisms of Aristotle's *Prior Analytics*, seen not as a mere method of argumentation, but as showing why the relations in reality of necessity or impossibility between things and attributes yield different syllogistic conclusions. Aristotle's *On Interpretation, Categories, Topics*, and Porphyry's *Isagôgê* are brought in only as helping to reveal why certain syllogisms reach universally affirmative or negative conclusions.[221] Even this *Elucidation* so Hugonnard-Roche argues,[222] bears some relation to Ammonius, who says that the relations of necessity or impossibility between things and attributes are the very matter (*hulai*) of the propositions in a syllogism.[223] It is, however, Paul's *Introduction to Logic* that gives the Ammonian *divisions* of logic, and, according to Dimitri Gutas,[224] looks very like the then recent discussions in Greek by Elias and David, which suggests that, as in them, it originally formed part of (1) an introduction to Philosophy in general. Moreover, Gutas, following Shlomo Pines, has further made use of a later Arabic work by Miskawayh (died 1029) on the different subject of happiness, which gives the divisions of Philosophy in general for a different purpose, as something to be understood for reaching happiness. Expressed in very similar terms again, Miskawayh's work explicitly refers to Paul having written to Khosroes about the divisions of Philosophy in general. Miskawayh's Arabic text is very like an earlier Arabic text of al-Fārābī (died 950), and Gutas conjectures that both Arabic authors may have been using a translation of Paul from Syriac by Fārābī's Christian teacher Abū Bishr Mattā (died 940). Moreover, Gutas identifies still further work by Paul presupposed by what Miskawayh goes on to say. For Miskawayh next spells out an introduction of type (5), giving the divisions of *Aristotle's* philosophy. If this still reflects Paul's work, it will not reflect his work on Philosophy in *general* but his work on the philosophy of *Aristotle*. Paul, in that case will have written *two* introductions, one of type (1) and one of type (5), both addressed to Khosroes. Furthermore, so, Gutas suggests, Paul may also have written a commentary on Aristotle's *Categories* because that would normally follow an introduction of type (5).

Still earlier than Paul of Persia, Sergius of Resh'aina (died 536), bilingual in Greek and Syriac, is thought to have attended Ammonius' school, and he declared his intention to comment on the whole of Aristotle, but only his Syriac commentary on the *Categories* is extant and that is not edited,[225] although the Prologue and Chapter 1

---

[221] So Henri Hugonnard-Roche, 'Un organon court en syriaque: Paul le Perse vs. Boèce' in Julie Brumberg-Chaumont, ed., *Ad notitiam ignoti* (Turnhout: Brepols, 2013), pp. 193–215. This is now edited with French translation and commentary by Henri Hugonnard-Roche, 'Sur la lecture tardo-antique du *Peri Hermêneias* d'Aristote: Paul le Perse et la Tradition d'Ammonius', *Studia graeco-arabica* 3 (2013), 37–104.

[222] Henri Hugonnard-Roche, 'Un organon court en syriaque'.

[223] Ammonius, *in Int*. 88,17–23.

[224] Dimitri Gutas, 'Paul the Persian on the classification of the parts of Aristotle's philosophy: a milestone between Alexandria and Baghdad', *Der Islam*, 60 (1983), 231–67. Michael Chase points out to me that Philippe Vallat questions the influence of David and Elias on Paul (*Farabi et l'École d'Alexandrie* (Paris: Vrin, 2004), pp. 37 ff.). I think that Ammonius could have been the joint source for both Simplicius and Paul getting their information on introductions (in Paul's case, if not through Elias and David, perhaps through a Persian-speaking student of Ammonius).

[225] John Watt, 'The Syriac Aristotle between Alexandria and Baghdad', *Journal for Late Antique Religion and Culture* 7 (2013), 26–50, at 32.

are translated by Henri Hugonnard-Roche into French and Chapter 2 by John Watt into English.[226]

So far, the spread of Ammonius' tradition of introductions has been to Persia, and into Syriac and Arabic. Among writers in Arabic, Fārābī was a Muslim, but his successors in the Baghdad school were Christian,[227] as was the school's founder Abū Bishr Mattā. The Nestorian Christian Ibn al-Ṭayyib (died 1043) has been called the last significant figure in that Baghdad school.[228] Christel Hein,[229] among others, has brought out his relation to the Ammonian school. He wrote his own commentaries on the *Isagôgê* and *Categories*,[230] and there is an English translation of the introduction to philosophy from the beginning of the prolegomena to his commentary on the *Isagôgê*.[231] His was the most complete Arabic reproduction of the Alexandrian introductions, with discussion of whether Philosophy exists, all six of its definitions with ascription to their authors, discussion of suicide, of the death of what is translated as the 'will' (the wilful) recommended by Socrates, of the areas in which and extent to which Plato thought we could become like God, and of the divisions or branches of Philosophy. He was like Elias, but on suicide closer to David.[232]

The influence of Stephanus in the Ammonian school on the two leading fathers of the Greek Church in the seventh and eighth centuries, Maximus the Confessor and John of Damascus, is documented by Mossman Roueché in Chapter 22 below. Maximus acknowledges Stephanus as his source for Ammonius' definition of Philosophy as preparation for death supplemented by a ban on suicide, and John of Damascus repeats Stephanus' ban on dividing a species into individuals, while both repeat Stephanus' definitions of other philosophical terms, which they may, however, have taken from handbooks.

Finally, David is regarded as an Armenian national hero in Armenia, known as David the Invincible. Whenever his commentaries and introductions were translated

---

[226] H. Hugonnard-Roche, *La logique d'Aristote du grec au syriaque: études sur la transmission des texts de l'Organon et leur interpretation philosphique* (Paris: Vrin, 2004), pp. 143–231, supplementing 'Sergius de Resh'ayna commentaire sur les categories (à Théodore)' on parts of philosophy and divisions of Aristotle's philosophy, *Oriens-Occidens* 1 (1997), 126–35; John Watt, in E. Coda and C.M. Bonadeo, eds, *De l'Antiquité tardive au moyen âge* (Paris: Vrin, 2014).

[227] So Marwan Rashed in Chapter 20 below.

[228] Peter Adamson, 'Knowledge of universals and particulars in the Baghdad school', *Documenti e studi sulla tradizione filosofica medievale* 18 (2007), 141–64.

[229] Christel Hein, *Definition und Einteilung der Philosophie*, pp. 55, 73–4, 81, 83, 85–6, 89–91, 98 (I thank Cristina D'Ancona for drawing my attention to her work); Gerhard Endress, 'Die Wissenschaftliche Literatur', in H. Gätje, ed., *Grundriss der arabischen Philologie II* (Wiesbaden: Reichert, 1987), pp. 400–506; and W. Fischer, ed., *Grundriss der arabischen Philologie III* (Wiesbaden: Reichert, 1992), pp. 3–152.

[230] Cristina D'Ancona, 'Commenting on Aristotle from late antiquity to the Arab Aristotelianism', in Wilhelm Geerlings and Christian Schulze, eds, *Der Kommentar in Antike und Mittelalter* (Leiden: Brill, 2002), pp. 201–51, at pp. 230–2; Gerhard Endress, 'Die wissenschaftliche Literatur'; Christel Hein, *Definition und Einteilung der Philosophie*.

[231] Translated by D. M. Dunlop, 'The Existence and Definition of Philosophy', *Iraq* 13 (1951), 76–94. Dunlop still accepted the attribution to al-Fārābī, which was corrected by S. M. Stern as resulting from Fārābī's name being pasted into an alien book, 'Ibn al-Tayyib's commentary on the *Isagoge*', *Bulletin of the School of Oriental and African Studies* 19 (1957), 419–25.

[232] Hein, *Definition und Einteilung der Philosophie*, pp. 55, 73–4, 81, 83, 85–6, 89–91, 98; Endress, in *Grundriss* vol. 2, pp. 431, 462; vol. 3, pp. 47–8.

into Armenian from Greek, there is an eleventh century reference probably to his *Introduction to Philosophy* in general, in its Armenian version, as already old, as we are told by the translators from Armenian.[233] It has been translated into English from Armenian under the title of *Definitions and Divisions of Philosophy*, and the same text is due to be translated from Greek in the Ancient Commentators on Aristotle series, as already mentioned, along with the corresponding introductions by Ammonius and Elias.

Re-Harmonisation (i) of Aristotle with Neoplatonism: Aristotle's Creator God

Another achievement of Ammonius, after the measured criticisms of Aristotle from Syrianus and the more extravagant ones from Proclus, was to re-harmonise Aristotle with the Neoplatonist view of Plato. Ammonius took up Proclus' objection that Aristotle failed to recognise the implications of his own argument for God as Mover. The acknowledged need for God's infinite power to give the world beginningless and endless motion should have been seen to imply the Neoplatonist view that God's infinite power is needed also as the source of the world's beginningless and endless *existence*. Ammonius wrote a whole book to show that that is precisely what Aristotle intended, so his pupil Simplicius tells us.[234] Simplicius appears to endorse the book and this interpretation of Aristotle is repeated by others in the school, Asclepius and Olympiodorus. Philoponus as a Christian was happy to accept from his teacher that God was Creator as well as Mover, but greatly complicated the argument, in order to establish that the Creation had a beginning.[235]

Re-Harmonisation (ii) Highest Type of Universal not Transcendent Ideas, but in Mind of Creator

In his commentary on Porphyry's *Isagôgê*, Ammonius had learnt from Proclus' three-fold distinction among *universals* (*katholou*), calling it sometimes a distinction among universals or common entities (*katholou, koina*), but also a distinction among forms (*eidê*), or among particular types of universal – genera or differentiae.[236] Ammonius understood that genera and species are something that the divine creator of the world, the demiurge of Plato's *Timaeus* 39E, has beside him (*para*) and in him (*en*), not as his thinking, but as objects of his thought (*noêta*) and as models (*paradeigmata*) for creating the world. It was these universals in God's mind, not transcendent universals

---

[233] Kendall and Thomson, *Definitions and Divisions of Philosophy by David the Invincible Philosopher*, p. xviii.
[234] Simplicius, *in Phys.* 1363,4–12.
[235] Lindsay Judson, 'God or Nature? Philoponus on Generability and Perishability', Richard Sorabji, ed., *Philoponus and the Rejection of Aristotelian Science* (London: Duckworth, 1987), pp. 179–96.
[236] Ammonius, *in Isag.* 41,10–42,26; Philoponus from the voice of Ammonius, *in Cat.* 58,13–59,1; 67,19–24. The distinction is recorded by Ammonius' pupil, Simplicius, as a distinction among common entities (*koina*): Simplicius, *in Cat.* 82,35–83,20, cf. 69,19–71,2.

that Ammonius assigned to the highest of the three levels of universal, putting them *before the many* particulars embedded in matter, rather than *in the many* or *after the many*.[237] Ammonius' threefold distinction recurs in the later commentaries by Elias and David on Porphyry's *Isagôgê*[238] in the Alexandrian school after Ammonius and was promptly transferred into Syriac. In Asclepius' commentary on the *Metaphysics* from the *voice* of Ammonius, Platonic Ideas do not exist as separate realities in their own right (*autai kath' hautas en hupostasei*), but they do exist in other ways, for example (as Ammonius had said) as creative *logoi*, rational principles, which are objects of intellect (*noêtai*) in the mind of the Creator, and as objects of rational thought (*dianoêtai*) in our souls.[239] They also play a role in nature, but not as separated entities (*exêrêmenai*), rather as creative causes. For it is by looking at these rational principles that nature creates things, and it is because of the eternity of the Ideas so conceived, that eternity accrues to the generation of specimens down here.[240] This is very different from the view of Platonic Ideas as transcendent taken in Syrianus' commentary on the *Metaphysics* and it allows some degree of harmonisation with Aristotle, because Aristotle's God was also a thinker with *logoi* in his mind and Aristotle's objection was only to *transcendent* Ideas. Above we saw Themistius attempting a similar compromise when he said that in the supposed spontaneous generation of microbes from decaying matter there are no parents available to supply the right *logoi* but the *logoi* have been put into nature and are actualised by the soul in the earth.[241] There is something extra clever about Ammonius denying that the highest *universals* are transcendent Ideas, because his teacher Proclus would be obliged to agree on the basis of his own very different viewpoint. As seen above under 'Proclus', he denied that the transcendent Ideas of Plato were universals in the sense of natures shared in common with particulars. Rather, they were common or universal only in the sense of being the single model in relation to which (*pros hen*) the particulars that share in them have a variety of different relations and a corresponding variety of characters.

Re-Harmonisation (iii) Mind a Blank Writing Tablet

Another example of Ammonius re-harmonising Plato and Aristotle is given by Frans de Haas in a companion paper to his Chapter 16 below.[242] Aristotle in *On the Soul* 3.4, 429b30–430a2, regards the mind at birth as a blank writing tablet, which appears to clash with Plato's account in the *Phaedo* and *Phaedrus* of how we are born with access

---

[237] Ammonius, *in Isag.* 41,20–42,7; 42,16–20.
[238] Elias, *in Isag.* 48,15–30; David, *in Isag.* 113,11–116,2.
[239] Asclepius, *in Metaph.* 166,30–168,18. See Arthur Madigan S.J., 'Syrianus and Asclepius on Forms and intermediates in Plato and Aristotle', *Journal of the History of Philosophy* 24 (1986), 149–71.
[240] Asclepius, *in Metaph.* 87,25–32. I owe the point to James Wilberding, 'Neoplatonists on Spontaneous Generation', in J. Wilberding and C. Horn, eds, *Neoplatonism and the Philosophy of Nature* (Oxford: Oxford University Press 2012), pp. 197–213.
[241] Themistius, *in Metaph.* 12, in Averroes *in Metaph.* 12, Bouyges III, 1492–4, translated from the Arabic in Sorabji, *The Philosophy of the Commentators*, vol. 2, ch. 1(b)16.
[242] Frans de Haas, 'Recollection and Potentiality in Philoponus', in Maria Kardaun and Joke Spruyt, eds, *The Winged Chariot* (Leiden: Brill, 2000), pp. 165–84.

to knowledge of the Ideas which our souls encountered before birth, so that our minds are not blank at birth, but simply need reminders. Proclus, according to De Haas, thinks Aristotle is simply wrong. But Ammonius makes the best attempt to show that there is no clash: the trauma of reincarnation leaves our knowledge temporarily blanked out as if by drunkenness and requires us to add to Aristotle a new level of potential knowledge: the knowledge of the inebriated. This I argue in Chapter 14 below, though edited by Philoponus in the commentary from the seminars of Ammonius on *On the Soul* 3.4–8, surviving only in Latin, is actually a bit of Ammonius' teaching, not one of Philoponus' interpolations.

Re-Harmonisation (iv) Natural Names in Aristotle?

Robbert van den Berg in Chapter 13 below finds a rather cursory attempt by Ammonius to restore harmony between himself and Proclus on whether Aristotle recognises any names as natural, after having said in the first two chapters of *On Interpretation* that spoken sounds are symbols and signs which signify *by convention* what is in our minds. Proclus had given an elaborate theological theory of a divine name-giver providing *natural* names which matched Ideas, not in their sound but in their meaning, and of expert human name-givers possessing only principles (*logoi*) derived from Ideas and projecting the *logoi* into their imaginations to get a *natural* representation. In the case of naming the gods, the result could be like the statues which accurately represent gods and (in a theory of statues closer to Iamblichus than to Porphyry as described above) receive divine illumination. Ammonius does the minimum to support his teacher's divergence from Aristotle. He connects belief in the efficacy of divine names only with an obscure Egyptian priest, Dousareios, and he qualifies Aristotle's insistence on the conventionality of meaning only to the extent of pointing out that some names have a meaning that is naturally appropriate. Thus *Archelaos*, etymologically 'leader of the people' is naturally appropriate for a kingly person (but apparently *laos*, 'people' is not naturally appropriate for people).

Ammonius' Geometry and Astronomy and his Mathematician Successor

Ammonius impressed one critical pupil with his expertise in other spheres besides philosophy. Damascius said that in geometry and astronomy he would almost say Ammonius surpassed men of all ages,[243] and Simplicius attended a class in which Ammonius used an astrolabe to demonstrate that the star Arcturus had moved one degree from its supposedly fixed position in the last 100 years.[244] This may help to explain why Ammonius' immediate successor for a few years was a mathematician, Eutocius. Philoponus was from early on too opposed to central Neoplatonist doctrines, such as the eternity of the world, to be a dependable teacher of them, and later was

---

[243] Damascius, *Life of Isidore* fr. 57C Athanassiadi; fr. 79 Zintzen, cited by Arnis Ritups, *Aristotle's De Anima III. 6: Essays in the History of its Interpretation*, Ph.D. thesis, (Leuven, 2010), 'Ammonius and his school', pp. 86–100.
[244] Simplicius, *in Cael.* 462,20–31.

more comprehensive in his opposition. Oympiodorus was much too young, although he was to be the next successor. Eutocius had the kind of status in mathematics which Damascius was willing to ascribe to Ammonius. He has been credited with doing more than anyone else to ensure the revival of Archimedes' treatises, by finding copies, writing commentaries on them, and encasing the commentaries with Archimedes' text in codices like the modern hinged book, more capacious than the normal rolls.[245] Three hundred and fifty years later, Thābit Ibn Qurra (died 900), who came from Harrān to Baghdad, was to translate into Arabic two of the same Archimedes texts on which Eutocius had commented. Four of Eutocius' commentaries on mathematics are extant, one of them addressed to Anthemius of Tralles, geometry professor in Constantinople and co-architect of Justinian's church there, Santa Sophia, with its dome a geometrical feat unparalleled in size. Constantinople was not to get a bigger dome for a thousand years. Two of Eutocius' commentaries on Archimedes finish with an inscription purporting to be by a pupil of the other architect, Isidore of Miletus, and naming Isidore as editor. Eutocius also claims to have commented in astronomy on the first book of the *Mathematical Syntaxis*, or *Almagest*, of the astronomer Ptolemy.

Answers to Three Arguments for Determinism

A final example of Ammonius' interest is provided by his answers to three arguments for determinism in his commentary on Aristotle *On Interpretation*. In Chapter 9, Aristotle himself raises only one of the three arguments based on the example of the Sea Battle. Ammonius' other two arguments are The Reaper, which had been told to Zeno, the Stoic, as early as 300 BCE, but of which Ammonius gives the only full discussion extant, and the argument from God's foreknowledge. A volume of the Ancient Commentators on Aristotle series was devoted to comparing the treatments of the Sea Battle in Ammonius and Boethius on Chapter 9.

I believe The Reaper has been underestimated. Among the essays preceding the translations, I construed the determinist as arguing 'There is no perhaps (*takha*) about it', that is about whether someone will reap tomorrow, or whether they will not. I took the determinist to be exploiting an ambiguity in 'Perhaps he will reap'. Does it introduce (1) a *guarded prediction* about the future reaping? Or does it express (2) a commitment to the *present* state of possibilities leaving it open whether he will reap? If the person turns out not to reap tomorrow, that will refute the guarded prediction. But the determinist illicitly takes it to refute the claim that the possibility of reaping had been open yesterday and wrongly concludes that the non-reaping (I here correct a misprint in my original)[246] was already necessary. I do not believe the problem has been successfully diagnosed by Ammonius or in the modern literature.

---

[245] Reviel Netz, in William Noel and Reviel Netz, *The Archimedes Codex* (London: Weidenfeld and Nicolson, 2007), pp. 72–3. The commentary of Eutocius on Archimedes' *On the Sphere and the Cylinder* (in vol. 3 of *Archimedis opera omnia cum commentariis Eutocii*, ed. Heiberg), is translated in Reviel Netz, *The Works of Archimedes*, vol. 1. (Cambridge: Cambridge University Press 2004).

[246] In David Blank and Norman Kretzmann, *Ammonius, On Aristotle On Interpretation 9, with Boethius, On Aristotle On Interpretation 9* (London: Duckworth, 1998), misprinted at p. 14, 16 lines from bottom.

As regards divine foreknowledge, Ammonius credits Iamblichus for his type of answer. Iamblichus, we saw, argued that gods can have definite knowledge (not in the form 'may or may not') of the indefinite (which may or may not happen, there being a genuine possibility of either). But Ammonius goes further by giving the gods timeless knowledge of the temporal future. With the gods, nothing is past or future, because they have no position in time. So with regard to those future events which have a genuine possibility of happening or not happening, the gods know them, but not *as* future. The advantage of this is again not diagnosed, but I believe it to be that if God's knowledge of my future conduct has no position in time, then it is not *past* knowledge and so is not *irrevocable*. Of course, it may be infallible, in which case I cannot so act as to make God wrong. But the important point is that it will not be too *late* for me so to act that his knowledge is (*timelessly, not already*) what it is. Boethius, writing in Latin and independently of Ammonius, gets a little way towards this diagnosis in his *Consolation of Philosophy* Book 5, when he says that God's knowledge is in this respect like the *present* knowledge of someone who sees what you are doing. Present knowledge does not constrain you any more than does timeless knowledge. The determinist's constraint would come only from knowledge that was already past as well as being infallible.

As regards the Sea Battle, Aristotle saw a deterministic threat arising for whatever happens from its *always* having been true in the past that it would happen. Once again, this threat, on one interpretation, turns on irrevocability throughout all past time. One plausible interpretation, among others, of Aristotle's solution is that propositions about whether something will be white have not always been true or false, but only become so near the time, when the circumstances make the matter inevitable. But Ammonius' answer involves more complicated ideas, discussed in the essays cited, about indefinite truth and indefinite division between truth and falsity.

Before moving on to Ammonius' pupil, Philoponus, in the Alexandrian school, and his pupil Stephanus, I shall first turn to Ammonius' two pupils in the Athenian school, Damascius and Simplicius, and first of all to their colleague Priscian, who left a record of what happened to them all in Persia, when they had to abandon the school in Athens after the emperor Justinian stopped the teaching in 529.

Priscian of Lydia and the Move from Athens (531 CE)

The main controversy about Priscian was discussed in *Aristotle Transformed*, namely, whether he is the author of the commentary on Aristotle's *On the Soul* which is ascribed to Simplicius. I have given my own affirmative opinion in the introduction to the new edition of 2016. The commentary on *On the Soul* and Priscian's *Paraphrase of Theophrastus on Sense Perception* were discussed as part of that controversy. Here I shall consider only the third extant work to be translated in the Ancient Commentators on Aristotle series: Priscian's *Answers to King Khosroes*. Priscian was a member of the Athenian Neoplatonist school, when the Christian emperor Justinian put an end to its pagan teaching in 529. Priscian was one of the seven Athenians, including three known philosophers, who accepted the refuge offered at Ctesiphon by King Khosroes I, the king of Persia, in 531, in the first year of his reign (531–578). Priscian recorded the replies given to Khosroes' questions about philosophy and science. The façade of Khosroes' palace at Ctesiphon, a little south of the later city of Baghdad, was still standing at the end of the 2003–2010 invasion of Iraq, although surrounded by military operations. The Greek historian Agathias who records the Athenians' visit was unsympathetic to the Athenian philosophers and contemptuous of Khosroes, including his intellectual ambitions, although Michel Tardieu has collected references in languages other than Greek to a large number of other intellectuals who were welcomed by Khosroes.[247] The religion of the empire, says Agathias, was not pleasing to the Athenians and they were forbidden by law to act in public because they did not conform to the established religion (*Histories* 2.30.3–4). If Khosroes were praised for wanting to get a taste of arguments and to take pleasure in the associated doctrine, he could be regarded as superior to the rest of the barbarians (2.28.5). But how could it be supposed that he had understood Aristotle and Plato's *Phaedo*, *Gorgias*, *Timaeus*, and *Parmenides* translated into an uncultivated (*agrios*) and totally uncivilised (*amousotatos*) language, especially when he had been brought up in the most barbarous way of life which paid attention to battles (2.28.2–4)? Agathias admits Khosroes' brilliant generalship and indomitable spirit in battle (2.32.5), but sets no value whatever on the contrast between Justinian's intolerance of the Athenian philosophers and Khosroes' tolerance of different religions and beliefs. Michel Tardieu has pointed out that in his autobiography, Khosroes said that he had never turned away anyone for being of a different religion or people, and conjectures that his wife may have been Christian. Moreover, Khosroes' own writing shows him keen to learn the laws of other peoples.[248] His dedication to the Athenian philosophers is shown by his remarkably making it a condition of the peace treaty in 532 with Justinian that Justinian allow the Athenian philosophers back to his territory to live the rest of their lives in peace, without fear, and without having to change their traditional religious beliefs (2.31.3). Khosroes, soon after the peace treaty of 532, received another philosopher, Uranius, who got himself into the train of Justinian's ambassador to Persia (2.29.9). The man, declared a charlatan by Agathias, was admittedly a Pyrrhonian sceptic (2.29.7) of the kind that the Athenian Neoplatonists would themselves have considered no philosopher at all, because sceptics of this kind avoided believing in anything, even the existence of philosophy, as noticed above under 'Ammonius', and therefore had the reputation of mere controversialists. But Khosroes for his part arranged inter-religious debates between him and Zoroastrian priests on such substantial subjects as the eternity or otherwise of the universe, the analysis of coming into existence, nature and whether one should posit a single first principle (*arkhê*, 2.29.11), and humbly regarded himself as a pupil (2.32.2). He held other debates too, one between a Nestorian and a monophysite Christian about their disagreements.[249] Another philosopher, Paul of Persia, was described above under

---

[247] Michel Tardieu, 'Chosroes', in R. Goulet, ed., *Dictionnaire des philosophes antiques*, vol. 2, pp. 309–18; see Joel T. Walker, 'The Limits of Late Antiquity: Philosophy between Rome and Iran', *The Ancient World* 33 (2002), 45–69.
[248] Michel Tardieu, 'Chosroes', pp. 311, 312, 317.
[249] Ibid., p. 312.

'Ammonius' as continuing Ammonius' tradition of introductions to Philosophy and Aristotelian logic and as addressing two of them in Middle Persian to Khosroes. His work had enduring influence being translated quickly into Syriac in the sixth century and via Syriac 400 years later in the tenth century into Arabic by Abū Bishr Mattā, influencing the Muslim philosopher al-Fārābī and for a hundred years his Christian successors in the school of Baghdad and the Muslim philosopher Miskawayh. Paul was a Christian at the time he instructed Khosroes in Philosophy, but a thirteenth century Christian Syrian source, Barhebraeus, says that, on failing to become Metropolitan Bishop of Persia, he converted to Zoroastrianism.[250] If that is so, in this cosmopolitan tradition, Abū Bishr Mattā's tenth century translation of Paul the Persian into Arabic was a case of a Christian Syrian translating, for a combined Muslim and Christian readership, the text of a Persian Christian-turned-Zoroastrian, based on a pagan Greek text.

Priscian's record of his answers to Khosroes' questions is fascinating, revealing, but tantalising. The sixth century Greek, from which the Persian translation was presumably made, is lost. What survives is a Latin translation, perhaps of the ninth century, whose translator understood properly neither the Greek nor the philosophy and science. A literal translation into English could only preserve intact the unintelligibility of the Latin. What turned out to be needed was a retro-translation, conjecturing what the original Greek could have been, and a translation into English based at least partly on that. I am indebted to the outstanding scholars who brought their knowledge of Greek, later Latin script and practices, philosophy, and science to bear. The subjects were: the soul, sleep, visions in imagination, the seasons, celestial zones, opposite uses of medicine, tides in the Red Sea, downward movements of fire and air, adaptation of animals and plants to local environment, why only reptiles are poisonous, and the nature of wind. The Athenian philosophers would have been interested enough in the opening topic of the soul, on which Priscian was an expert, if he was the author of the commentary previously attributed to Simplicius on Aristotle *On the Soul*, with its rich Neoplatonist elaborations. But from there the Athenians might have hoped to move upwards to the human and divine intellect, the world of Ideas contemplated by that Intellect and the supreme divinity and source of all things, the One. But Khosroes, that supremely practical ruler wanted to move downwards to the winds, the tides, and animal poisons, subjects on which Priscian had been less well informed, and he lists the large number of scientific books he consulted, although in fact a good many others can be identified as well. Part of the Athenians' desire to move on from Ctesiphon will have been due to the focus on questions about the physical world, which may suggest that they had not had forewarning of the questions. If the questions were not sent to Athens by Khosroes in advance and the answers prepared before they left, or written up after they left, either they will have brought their library with them, or just possibly they will have written up the answers after they left, since we know that Simplicius at least (whether or not Priscian) wrote after that, drawing on some extensive library. Agathias' reasons for their 'all going home and saying goodbye to the barbarian's hospitality' (2.31.2), included his

---

[250] Ibid., p. 315.

not understanding any of the higher (*aiputera*) things because he did not even share their beliefs (*doxa*), presumably about theological matters (3.31.1). For once, Agathias may here have been closer to the mark, but there was much more from him about the supposed immorality of the Persians and their king. And in any case, Khosroes did soon afterwards get Uranius to debate higher matters, about the eternity of the world and a supreme principle, as well as about nature and coming into being, so he was not uninterested. It is not impossible that he had learnt about the higher matters from earlier talks with the Athenians, not included in what Priscian was commissioned to answer.

Damascius up to the Move from Athens (died after 538)

Works

Damascius was the last head of the Athenian Neoplatonist school when its teaching was stopped by the Christian emperor Justinian in 529 and seven Athenians, himself included, accepted refuge in 531 with Khosroes I of Persia. An original thinker, he wrote a considerable number of commentaries on Plato, a major metaphysical treatise *On First Principles*, and he refers to a lecture of his on the priestly *Chaldaean Oracles*. He further wrote a very engaging *Life of Isidore*, surviving only in fragments, about his most admired philosophical colleague and senior, which surveys the history of recent and present Greek Neoplatonist philosophers, awarding them high or low grades for different aspects of their lives as philosophers. Polymnia Athanassiadi, indeed followed the fragments preserved in the Suda by calling her 1999 reconstruction and translation of the fragments *The Philosophical History*. In it, Damascius approves Isidore's view that the study of Plato should be guided by Iamblichus, and he repeatedly pitted himself against the more recent interpretations of Proclus. He wrote very much less on Aristotle, there being only one commentary on Aristotle, well attested by Philoponus, but lost, on Aristotle's *Meteorology*. But there are a few topics on Aristotle and I shall confine myself to these below, after first sketching his career.

Life

We are told that Damascius started as a rhetorician, spending three years in training in Alexandria and then nine years teaching rhetoric.[251] While in Alexandria and still a youth and a student of rhetoric, he gave a funeral eulogy in verse for Ammonius' mother Aidesia. On Athanassiadi's reconstruction, he was caught up in the persecution of pagan teachers in the Alexandrian school, mentioned under 'Ammonius' and targeting both rhetoricians and philosophers, in 488–9, and he and Isidore then fled together. It was also then, on this account, that they had their eight-month tour together, transformative for Damascius, of holy places in Asia and he was converted to an ambition to become a philosopher. At some undetermined time, he did study with

---

[251] Photius, *Bibliotheca* codex 181, 126b40–127a14 (= R. Henry, *Photius, Bibliothèque*, 9 vols (Paris: Les Belles Lettres, 1959–91), vol. 2, p. 192).

Ammonius in Alexandria Plato's philosophy and astronomy, and with Ammonius' brother Heliodorus.[252] It may have been then that he formed his opinion, mentioned under 'Ammonius' that the latter surpassed men of all ages in astronomy and geometry, whereas he regarded Heliodorus as more superficial.[253] His study in Athens was under Proclus' less brilliant successors, involving mathematics with Marinus and philosophy with Zenodotus perhaps in the early 490s. It is not known when he became head of the school at Athens, after failing to persuade Isidore to take up the role more than very briefly. An identification has been offered of the house under the Athenian acropolis where he ran the school,[254] but the identification is still a matter of controversy. The latest date for which there is evidence of his being alive, 538, is given by a dated funerary inscription for a female slave, Zosima, found in Syria from an unknown site, which corresponds to a verse ascribed to 'Damascius the philosopher', this time in the collection of poems of the *Palatine Anthology*.[255] This suggests that Damascius may have returned from Persia to the region of his place of birth, Damascus, and composed the verse which certainly corresponds to his beliefs: 'I, Zosima, who was previously a slave only in body have now found freedom for my body too'.

School to Cover Theology, not Theurgy

Damascius brought to the school a very different view from that of Proclus on the role of theurgy in philosophy. Through his trip to Asian sites with Isidore, he developed a very strong sense of the holy. But what he particularly learnt from Isidore was not theurgic ritual, but *dialectic*. For Isidore, he said, surpassed all of his generation in *logoi*, arguments as I take it but, as has been pointed out,[256] he was thinking of dialectic and argument not just as philosophical debate, but as the use of that debate, within oneself as much as with others, in Plato's *Republic* for reaching understanding of Plato's Idea of the Good, associated by Neoplatonists with their supreme divinity. In other words, Isidore was outstanding at theological reasoning. None of this is to say that Isidore practised theurgic ritual. Indeed, in his commentary on Plato's *Phaedo*, Damascius said that Iamblichus, Syrianus, and Proclus preferred theurgy, while Porphyry and Plotinus preferred philosophy. But Plato preferred that one should stand in the middle as a philosopher, since the philosopher is a Bacchus, the god of wine, that is, he has detached himself from the world of things that come into being.[257] In his *Life of Isidore*, Damascius says that the priestly art and philosophy do not begin from the same starting points. Philosophy descends from the One cause. Theurgy, which is the service (*therapeia*) of the gods, begins from the causes (plural) that surround the cosmos and ties the ropes of salvation onto the level of things that come into being.[258] Again, it does not befit a

---

[252] Photius, loc. cit.
[253] Damascius, *Life of Isidore* fr. 57B Athanassiadi.
[254] Athanassiadi, op. cit.
[255] *Palatine Anthology* 7.553.
[256] See e.g. Ilsetraut Hadot, *Athenian and Alexandrian Neoplatonism* (Leiden: Brill, 2015), p. 11, n. 35.
[257] Damascius, *On Plato's Phaedo* 1, 172 Westerink.
[258] Fr. 4A Athanassiadi.

philosopher to profess divination, or any other priestly science, for the domains of philosophers and priests are completely separate, and yet Patricius drew things in that direction against the rules (*nomos*) of philosophy.[259] Athanassiadi sees here a criticism of Proclus and his follower, Hegias, who may have taken the Athenian chair before Damascius in the early 490s. Damascius says of Hegias, 'We had never heard of philosophy being so despised in Athens as we saw it dishonoured in the time of Hegias'.[260] In another fragment, Isidore is represented as saying to Hegias, 'If, as you say, Hegias, priestly practice is a more divine thing, I too say so. But those who are going to be gods must first become human. This is why Plato too said that no greater good has come to humans than philosophy. But it has come about that nowadays philosophy stands not on a razor's edge, but on the brink of extreme old age'.[261] This is a different type of reservation about theurgy, not the belief in its limitations which I have ascribed to Porphyry and Ammonius, but an acceptance of its divinity, along with warning of the extreme danger of mixing it with philosophy which learns to derive everything from the supreme god, instead of hob-nobbing with lesser gods almost as if one of them. Damascius saw his role in the chair as one of restoring philosophy, and restoring its rational treatment of theology freed from theurgical pretensions.

Three Responses to Aristotle: (i) The Reality of Time

I now return to Damascius' contribution to the study of Aristotle. Independent of mind, he did not hesitate when commenting on Plato, as Gerd van Riel has pointed out, to adopt, for intellectual pleasures, Aristotle's account of pleasure as a completed activity rather than Plato's account of it as a process towards completion.[262]

Attention is given to Aristotle in Damascius' lost work 'On Number, Place, and Time', extensively reported by Simplicius, in his commentary on Aristotle's *Physics*. He follows Iamblichus in giving a dynamic account of place, which he regards as arranging things and keeping them in the right spatial relation to each other, even the parts of organisms. As mentioned above in connexion with Iamblichus' 'intellective' theory of Aristotle's categories, he sees place as embracing things not in Aristotle's inert way, but dynamically, and even giving them, though here Simplicius does not agree, the right size. He compares time as also being dynamic, arranging things and separating them, so that they will not collide.[263] But his account of time is both more original and more directly addressed to Aristotle, since he tries to resolve two puzzles raised by Aristotle in his *Physics* 4.10, but left unanswered, which question the reality of time. I have discussed his treatment of both place and time elsewhere,[264] but I will somewhat revise what I said about Damascius on time.

---

[259] Fr. 88A Athanassiadi. Patricius was a son of the leader of the Goths, whom the Roman emperor Leo treacherously tried to murder, along with his father, after an interpretation of cloud shapes as resembling a lion growing large enough to swallow a Goth.
[260] Fr. 145A Athanassiadi.
[261] Fr. 150 Athanassiadi. Translations of the fragments are adapted from hers.
[262] Damascius, *On Plato's Philebus* 87,1–4; 190. So Gerd van Riel, *Pleasure and the Good Life: Plato, Aristotle and the Neoplatonists* (Leiden: Brill, 2000).
[263] Simplicius, *in Phys.* 625,29; 626,7–9.13–16; 644,33–4.
[264] Place in *Matter, Space and Motion* (London: Duckworth, 1988), pp. 207–8; time in *Time, Creation and the Continuum* (London: Duckworth, 1983), pp. 7–16; 52–63.

According to Aristotle's first puzzle, time does not exist because its parts do not exist, since the past no longer exists and the future does not yet exist. If it is said that at least the present exists, the present is not a *part* of time, because it is a sizeless boundary between past and future. If you think it has a size, you will find that part of that extended present belongs to the past and part to the future. The second puzzle asks when would a sizeless present instant, say, 12 noon today, have ceased to exist? Not while it exists, but also not in the next instant (or 'now' as he calls it), because there is no next now, since between any two sizeless instants or points in a continuum, there are infinitely many others. So it can only have ceased to exist at some *later* instant, say one second after 12. But then, absurdly, it will have continued to exist at the infinitely many instants between 12 and one second past.[265] If on the other hand, you say that a sizeless present instant will never have ceased to exist, we shall be stuck at the same instant as the people of 10,000 years ago.

Damascius' answer to the first puzzle has three parts. First, to resolve the puzzle, we need to look at a different kind of present time over and above Aristotle's sizeless present instant, a present time which he explains both here and in a different context in his commentary on Plato's *Parmenides*.[266] Time, like the motions of the stars which measure it, progresses by discontinuous leaps (*halmata*) of different sizes established by the divine Craftsman or Demiurge who created the world. There are shorter leaps for slower stars and longer leaps for faster ones, so the Demiurge is evidently able to divide leaps into different quantities or measures. But even though the demiurgic leap-like progressions are of variable size, each one is discontinuous, because it is never at a part way point between one position and the next. If we consider the present as an extended demiurgic leap, rather than considering Aristotle's sizeless present instant, the demiurgic *extended* present is not subject to the puzzle's denial that a *sizeless* present instant is not a *part* of time. The sizeless instant will be treated later as existing, but only in our thoughts, not as marked off in actuality.[267] The fact that the leap-present is extended would already solve the first puzzle, but Damascius has a further objection and wants to use it, I believe, in conjunction with the extended leaps.

Damascius' second manoeuvre is drawn from Aristotle *Physics* 3.6, 206a21-8. Time, he says in his own words,[268] as day and night, is not day and night all at once (*athroon*), but has its being (*einai*) in coming to be (*ginesthai*), just like a contest (*agôn* – Aristotle cites the Olympic Games) or dance. These are not all at once, but the contest is present (*parestin*) while being completed part by part (the javelin throwing after the discus event) and the dance is also present (*enestôs*) part by part. He goes on to repeat the formula that time has its being (*einai*) in coming to be (*ginesthai*) and adds that this is

---

[265] Aristotle, *Physics* 4.10, 217b29–218a30.
[266] Damascius, 'On Number, Place, and Time', reported by Simplicius, 'Corollary on Time', *in Phys.* 796,27–797,13; *On Plato's Parmenides* 2, 241,29–242,15 Westerink-Combes.
[267] Ibid.
[268] Damascius 'On Number, Place, and Time', reported by Simplicius, 'Corollary on Time', *in Phys.* 797,36–798,4; 799,14–18. Damascius repeats the formula that time has its being (*einai*) in coming to be (*ginesthai*) and adds that this is its form of reality (*tropos hupostaseôs*).

its form of reality (*tropostês hupostaseôs*). In the same way, Damascius says, the entirety (*sumpas*) of time is at hand (*ephestanai*) by coming into being.[269]

Thirdly, Damascius uses an idea which Alexander had introduced before him to interpret Aristotle: the sizeless divisions of time by which we divide past, present, and future exist as parts of time only in our thoughts, not marked off in actuality, just as does infinite divisibility.[270] It is presumably important for Damascius that the leap-sized progressions in motion and time come into being in reality, unlike the divisions we make merely in thought. For he in his own words, and in Simplicius' report, wants time to have reality (*hupostasis*).[271] If so, the parts that give it reality will also need to be real. So they had better not be only the day and night whose reality he impugns, but the parts corresponding to demiurgic leaps, coming into being one after another. Of course, as well as thinking of day and night as parts of time, we could also imagine periods of time as small as we like, measured by imaginary clocks set to move out of phase with each other by amounts as small as we like, but this would not mean that the demiurgic leap-like progressions were also infinitely divisible, because the time units imagined as being as small as we liked would exist only in our thoughts.

Damascius' younger associate, Simplicius, liked the last two points, but thought he could do without the undivided leaps.[272] In this, I think, he was mistaken, because according to Damascius' second point, a period of time or motion owes its existence to one part coming into being after another. But what has Simplicius supplied that can serve as a *part* and come into being, if he rejects Damascius leaps which do serve as parts of a larger whole and come into being? If he brings forward divisions that we make in our thoughts, such as day and night, these divisions will be subject to the original puzzle. Part of the present day will be past and part future, leaving only a sizeless instant as present. That instant, being sizeless, will not serve as a *part* of time either. Even an infinity of sizeless instants will not serve as a part nor ever constitute a larger whole by mere addition, so he has not found a present that can serve as a part of time. In addition, Simplicius accepts Damascius' idea that sizeless instants, or other divisions we make, exist only in thought, so he has not found a present that exists in reality, which Damascius will need if time is to be real.

Damascius seeks to solve Aristotle's second puzzle, that there is no time at which his sizeless present instant will have ceased to exist, by saying that the puzzle wrongly demands that there be a time of time. But such a regress is not required. Time is a measure and a measure does not stand in need of a measure.[273] But this does not show us how to avoid the second horn of Aristotle's dilemma. If there is no time at which Aristotle's sizeless present instant will have ceased, we will indeed be stuck at the same present instant as the people of 10,000 years ago. Although Aristotle does not state his

---

[269] Damascius, 'On Number, Place, and Time', reported by Simplicius, 'Corollary on Time', *in Phys.* 798,4.
[270] Damascius 'On Number, Place, and Time', reported by Simplicius, 'Corollary on Time', *in Phys.* 799,18–30.
[271] *in Phys.* 799,14–18; 775,31–4.
[272] Simplicius, 'Corollary on Time', *in Phys.* 797,29–36.
[273] Damascius, 'On Number, Place, and Time', reported by Simplicius, 'Corollary on Time', *in Phys.* 799,35–800,16.

solution to either puzzle, I have argued elsewhere, when discussing his two puzzles and answers to them, that his treatment of the continuum gives him an adequate answer.[274] The sizeless present instant will have ceased to exist at any subsequent instant you care to take, however close.

Simplicius is worried by an extra step that Damascius takes in his answer to Aristotle's first problem. In Damascius' own words, the statement is that the *entirety* (*sumpas*) of time is at hand (*ephestanai*) as coming into being, not as being, just as a contest is present (*parestin*) or a dance is present (*enestôs*).[275] Simplicius continues Damascius' own fluidity of language. In his longest protest against what he takes to be Damascius' view, he puts the view as being that the whole of time is present (*enestôs*), or exists all together (*einai hama*),[276] or subsists (*huphestôs*) all together in its infinity,[277] or possesses its always as a whole all together,[278] or the whole exists together (*holon einai hama*).[279] In another place, he says that what Damascius said to him, without convincing him, many times when he was alive was that time exists all together in reality (*einai hama en hupostasei*).[280] Damascius' own fluidity of language and the fact that he was already dead shows that Simplicius' varied formulations were not due to him, but probably to Damascius. Simplicius says he could understand the view if Damascius was referring to the creative eternal principle (*paragôn aïdios logos*) of time in nature coupled with the pre-existing principle (*prohuparkhôn logos*) of time in the soul that always remains numerically the same,[281] but he was not. Even here Simplicius offers further formulations of the idea: time is always present (*parôn*) as a whole and in entirety (*holos, sumpas*); it subsists all together as a whole (*hama holon huphestanai*). But it is useful that we have Simplicius' own confirmation that Damascius was talking about ordinary time.[282] Simplicius' protest, however, overlooks something when he puts his objection 'more clearly'.[283] If the whole of time exists all together, he says, it is a paradox how its parts are not all together. But when Damascius gives the worrying formula in his own words at 797,36–798,4, he uses the examples of a contest or a dance to explain how the whole of time is at hand (*ephestanai*) as coming into being, not as being. So it is clear what he means. If Simplicius had recognised the force of this explanation, he would have realised that Damascius' claim is that what is needed for the whole of time to exist all together is not for the parts to exist all together, but for the parts to have reality. Once again, Simplicius does not satisfy this requirement, because he has rejected Damascius' segments created in reality by the divine Craftsman, leaving himself with only the divisions, such as day and night, that exist merely in our thought.

---

[274] Sorabji, *Time, Creation and the Continuum*, pp. 7–16; 52–63.
[275] Simplicius, *in Phys.* 798,4.
[276] Ibid. 777,8–12.
[277] Ibid. 777,13.
[278] Ibid. 777,15–16.
[279] Ibid. 777,27–31.
[280] Ibid. 775,31–4.
[281] Ibid. 784,2–8.
[282] Ibid. 777,4–33.
[283] Ibid. 777,28–31.

(ii) Infinite Power in a Finite Body

There is another tantalising reference to Aristotle's ideas in Damascius. In his commentary on Plato's *Phaedo*, he refers to Aristotle's argument that the infinite power needed for the infinite duration of celestial motion cannot be housed in the finite body of the universe, but must come from an incorporeal mover, God. We saw Proclus and Syrianus saying that God was needed as the source of infinite existence as well as of infinite motion, and Ammonius replying that that is what Aristotle intended. But here Damascius appears to be removing the original force of Aristotle's argument, which Proclus had exploited. For he says that there *can* be infinite power in a finite body. Sadly however, he says that this was shown elsewhere (*en allois*), probably in his commentary on Plato's *Timaeus*, which is lost.[284]

(iii) The Faculty of Self-knowledge, including Conscience

I come to a final originality in response to Aristotle. Damascius is the older of the two commentators we know of, along with Olympiodorus, who used slightly different language, to endorse a new interpretation of self-knowledge as involving a single faculty of attention (the *prosektikon*), as described by a third commentator, Philoponus.[285] Aristotle had ascribed self-awareness to the common sense, and so still, Philoponus tells us, did the Neoplatonist Plutarch of Athens. But on the new interpretation what is needed is a single faculty at least as high as the operations of which it is aware, and so not sensory as Aristotle had supposed. As a matter of fact, Aristotle once describes our *thinking* as something we perceive,[286] but the new theory would not allow that. This faculty needs to be aware of our rational cognitions, our perceptions and our desires. In its role of making us aware of our desires, it is nothing less than moral conscience. Because Philoponus' terminology is closer to that of Damascius and because Olympiodorus was so much younger, I think Philoponus' 'newer interpreter' is likely to be Damascius. Philoponus takes the new theory to replace Aristotle's common sense, and, even though Priscian, Damascius' colleague, still speaks, as if in Aristotle's way, of the common sense as perceiving that we see, he does so only by a manoeuvre that Aristotle would have rejected, of making the common sense not purely sensory, but rational. He does this in a work whose authorship has been disputed as well as in an undisputed work, adding to the evidence for both being authentically Priscian's.[287]

It need be no surprise that Damascius has thought of a new definition of moral conscience, because conscience was a faculty to which in the *Life of Isidore* he attributed exceptional importance. Speaking of one of the sons of the hopeless philosopher

---

[284] Damascius, *On Plato's Phaedo* II, 36,9–16 Westerink.
[285] Philoponus, *On Aristotle On the Soul 3*, 464,30–465,17, discussed also by Golitsis in ch. 16 below.
[286] Aristotle, *Nicomachean Ethics* 1170a31–2.
[287] Priscian, *On Theophrastus on Sense-Perception* 21,32–22,23; Priscian ('Simplicius'), *On Aristotle On the Soul* 187,27–188,35; 173,3–7.

Hegias, he says,[288] 'Archiadas was particularly concerned with having a clear conscience (*katharon suneidos*), no less than the philosophers. For nothing human is worth as much as a pure (*akeraios*) conscience. A person should live together with his neighbours in a decent manner, and if the true good is contrary to the apparent good, should never prefer the latter, nor give greater importance to anything other than truth – neither the danger of an impending struggle, nor a difficult task from which one turns away in fear, nor the profit gained from undeserved praise, nor the habits of friendship, nor the obligations of family connexions'.

Simplicius (*c.* 480 – *c.* 560) after the Move from Athens

The great importance of the third of the known Athenian philosophers taking refuge in Persia, Simplicius, is that after the Athenians' stay with King Khosroes in Persia, he composed massive commentaries, which preserved more information than any others about the history of Greek commentary on Aristotle, and the history of Greek philosophy more generally, including the fragments of the Presocratics. Preservation may have been a major purpose, since signs of classroom teaching have not been found in his Aristotle commentaries. In the modern editions, the commentary on Aristotle's *Physics* is 1366 pages, that on *On the Heavens* 731 pages, and that on the *Categories* 438, pages, nearly all translated into English in the Ancient Commentators on Aristotle series except for a final 102 pages, which are at the time of writing in draft. He further wrote, among other things, a commentary on the Stoic Epictetus' *Handbook* on ethics, a subject originally chosen as more suitable for beginners than Aristotle's ethics, because it did not presuppose very much logic.[289] There is also an Arabic record of his commentary on the first book of Euclid's *Elements*, with a few excerpts preserved in Arabic and his proof of Euclid's parallels postulate has been discussed with translation.[290]

The value of Simplicius' commentaries as a source of information about Alexander, the greatest commentator in Aristotle's school well over 300 years earlier, was briefly put in doubt, when Marwan Rashed found him distorting Alexander's meaning by leaving out six crucial words from a report on him.[291] But Rashed's subsequent publication of a massive collection of newly discovered fragments from Alexander's commentary on Aristotle's *Physics* reassuringly revealed no other distortions by Simplicius.[292]

I have commented in the introduction to the new edition of *Aristotle Transformed* on the three massive issues raised there in 1990 by Ilsetraut Hadot, who also confirmed

---

[288] Damascius, *Life of Isidore* fr. 146 Athanassiadi.
[289] These are all translated in the Ancient Commentators on Aristotle series.
[290] I. A. Sabra, 'Simplicius' Proof of Euclid's Parallels Postulate', *Journal of the Courtauld and Warburg Institutes* 32 (1969), 1–24.
[291] 'A "New" Text of Alexander on the Soul's Motion', in Richard Sorabji, ed., *Aristotle and After* (London: Institute of Classical Studies, 1997), pp. 181–95; repr. as ch. 4 of his *L'Héritage aristotélien* (Paris: Les Belles Lettres, 2007).
[292] Marwan Rashed, *Alexandre d'Aphrodise, Commentaire perdu à la Physique d'Aristote* (Berlin: De Gruyter, 2011).

the dating of the works, and so I can be briefer here. Where did Simplicius go after the stay with Khosroes at Ctesiphon? Ilsetraut Hadot argued for Tardieu's view that he went to Ḥarrān, just outside the current north border of Syria and inside the border of modern Turkey, and I believe that one of her arguments makes that the most probable place. She further cites the Arabic report that he set up a mathematical school as well as working on Aristotle. If so, he presumably would have been teaching mathematics. It would be interesting if evidence could be found for a continuous school in Ḥarrān right up to the ninth century when the mathematician Thābit Ibn Qurra moved from there to Baghdad, and the tenth century when there is an Arabic report of a Platonist school there and al-Fārābī is said to have moved to Ḥarrān.[293] But continuity, I think, is not necessary: even in Athens the Platonist and Aristotelian schools had disappeared and been re-founded from time to time. But the earlier tradition in a site would recommend it as the site for a refounding, so if Simplicius did set up a school, or use an existing library, his memory could have helped to encourage re-establishment even after discontinuities. To her second question – were the Alexandrian and Athenian Neoplatonist schools united in their viewpoints? – she has reinforced her view in books of 2014 and 2015 that they were,[294] and she has been skilful in finding common beliefs which were shared more or less by all Neoplatonists. Apart from my not including Themistius as a Neoplatonist, this may be compatible with my own opposite emphasis on the individuality of different commentators even within one school, provided that enough latitude is allowed in the more and the less. As regards the third question, whether Simplicius is also the author of a commentary on Aristotle *On the Soul* attributed to him and therefore the author too of a lost commentary on Aristotle's *Metaphysics* mentioned there, I confessed that I had been persuaded by Carlos Steel's case of 2012,[295] that the author of both is Priscian.

In Chapter 21 below, Philippe Hoffman and Pantelis Golitsis throw light on Simplicius' attitude to the progress made in philosophy by Damascius, his master in the Athenian Neoplatonist school. His inability to follow Damascius' argument that the whole of time is present was described under 'Damascius'. But Simplicius also takes up Damascius' treatment of place, briefly mentioned above, and presents it as the culmination of a long tradition of thought. Aristotle's static definition of a thing's place as the inner surface of its surroundings had run in trouble by seeming to deny a place to the outermost heavens, which have no surroundings, and so would not be able to change their place on Aristotle's definition of place, and yet the heavens were taken to rotate. Damascius' definition of place as the measure which positions things in the right way in relation to each other allowed to the heavens a place which repositioned them as they rotated. At the same time, the definition had a theological import, because place bestowed the good order of things in the universe that is ultimately due to the divine One who is the source of goodness.

---

[293] Ibn Khallikan, *Wafayat al a'yan*, ed. Abbas, vol. 5, § 706, pp. 153-7. I owe this reference to Michael Chase.
[294] Ilsetraut Hadot, *Le néoplatonicien Simplicius à la lumière des recherches contemporaines, Un bilan critique* (Sankt Augustin: Academia, 2014); *Athenian and Alexandrian Neoplatonism and the Harmonization of Aristotle and Plato* (Leiden: Brill, 2015).
[295] Carlos Steel, '*Simplicius*', *On Aristotle On the Soul 3.6-13* (London: Bristol Classical Press, 2013).

Two further contributions are made about Simplicius in the chapters below. In Chapter 10, it is argued that Simplicius continued the Neoplatonist tendency to back away from Aristotle's idea that Plato's Ideas were universals.[296] Proclus, we saw, denied that particulars share the character of the Idea; instead they relate to it derivatively (*pros hen*). It was left to Simplicius to clarify that the Idea was common to particulars only as a cause, not as a character common as between Form and particulars. In Chapter 22, Mossman Roueché finds three cases in which Stephanus seems to follow Simplicius, rather than Elias, in fragments from the introduction to his lost commentary on Aristotle's *Categories*, which suggests that somehow Simplicius' introduction had reached Stephanus in Alexandria from Harrān, or wherever Simplicius was writing in the East.

However, despite the value to the Latin-speaking Middle Ages and to us of Simplicius' voluminous commentaries on Aristotle, it has proved hard so far to trace much uptake of his work before that later period. The existence of Simplicius' commentary on the *Categories*, or part of it, is recorded in Arabic. Beyond that it has been argued that in the Arabic-speaking world, Simplicius' commentary on *Physics* Book 8, ch.1, influenced Averroes,[297] that his commentary on the *Categories* or its introduction influenced al-Fārābī,[298] and two papers have found Simplicius' influence in Avicenna.[299] Regarding influence on Fārābī, I have not yet seen discussion of rival claims from others in Ammonius' tradition, apart from the claims of Paul of Persia recorded under 'Ammonius' above. What is certain is that William of Moerbeke translated into Latin in 1266 and 1271 Simplicius' commentaries on Aristotle's *Categories* and *On the Heavens*, and that both were promptly and influentially used by Thomas Aquinas.

Simplicius' commentary on Epictetus' *Handbook*[300] is a very different sort of commentary from the commentaries on Aristotle. In choosing Epictetus, he chose a philosopher unlike Aristotle in his ideal of freedom from emotion, and unlike Plato in his denial of the soul's immortality. The subject of ethics gives Simplicius the opportunity in some of his long digressions to cover topics that Proclus had treated in his three treatises on providence and evil. In commenting on chapter 8, he borrows Proclus' idea that evil is parasitic (a *parhupostasis*) on good, and he discusses moral responsibility and choice (*prohairesis*), a term whose meaning was not the same in Aristotle and Epictetus. Providence was a subject not discussed by Aristotle at all. But

---

[296] See under 'Proclus' above for Sorabji's and Chiaradonna's recording of this tendency in Plotinus, Porphyry, Proclus, and Simplicius, Riin Sirkel's recognition that even earlier Alexander was aware of this Platonist tendency, and the addition of Eustratius below.
[297] Michael Chase, 'Philoponus' cosmology in the Arabic tradition', *Recherches de Théologie et Philosophie mediévale* 79 (2012), 271–306.
[298] Michael Chase, 'The Medieval Posterity of Simplicius' Commentary on the *Categories*: Thomas Aquinas and Al-Fārābī', in L. A. Newton, ed., *Medieval Commentaries on Aristotle's Categories* (Leiden: Brill, 2008), pp. 9–29.
[299] H. Zghal, 'La relation chez Avicenne', *Arabic Sciences and Philosophy* 16 (2006), 237–86, at 257–8; Ahmad Hasnawi, in preparation on Simplicius' replies to newly found fragments of Philoponus *Against Aristotle*.
[300] Translated in the Ancient Commentators on Aristotle series by Tad Brennan and Charles Brittain, 2 vols (London: Duckworth, 2002).

the ideas Simplicius was recording for posterity in this commentary had originally been designed for beginning students, and the aim had been that they should learn something of the Neoplatonist view, rather than that they should become experts on Epictetus or on his differences from Aristotle. The commentary may include references to Simplicius' own situation both in its epilogue about his living in tyrannical times, and in his comments on Epictetus' ch. 24, where he wrote an excursus concerning the philosopher's role in society and Epictetus' idea that power is not needed, but only a life that is trustworthy and of good *conscience* (*pistos, aidîmôn*). Simplicius takes a view about frank speech (*parrhêsia*) under a bad government different from that of Themistius recorded above concerning Constantinople, that the philosopher is free to stay away from the rulers and from coarse (*apeirokalos*) frank speech.

Philoponus (*c*. 490 – 570s) in Alexandria, His Development

I now return from the closed Athenian school to the still flourishing school in Alexandria and to Ammonius' pupil Philoponus. To recall various stages of previous investigation, the work of S. Sambursky and S. Pines on Philoponus' physics was followed by a conference in London in 1983, which also concentrated on Philoponus' physics and resulted in 1987 in the collection called *Philoponus and the Rejection of Aristotelian Science*.[301] At that time, I was particularly interested in three aspects of Philoponus' work. One was Galileo's praise of Philoponus for opposing Aristotle's denial that there could be motion in a vacuum. A second was Thomas Kuhn's description of the introduction into dynamics of impetus theory as a scientific revolution, which, however, he ascribed to the fourteenth century instead of to Philoponus' sixth century disagreement with Aristotle. The third was Philoponus' use of Aristotle's denial of more than finite numbers to attack, on behalf of Christianity, the Aristotelian and Neoplatonist acceptance of an infinite past. In 1990, Koenraad Verrycken offered his new dating and trajectory of Philoponus' career.[302] In 2010 a second edition was published, though it had been completed a year or two earlier, of *Philoponus and the Rejection of Aristotelian Science*, with 40 pages of review and updating of what had been discovered since the 1987 publication. Not least was the archaeological excavation of twenty or more lecture rooms where Philoponus had taught in Alexandria. It would have been hard to foresee in 2008, when the second edition of *Philoponus and the Rejection of Aristotelian Science* was completed, that so much more would have come to light by 2015.

However, in 2008 Pantelis Golitsis offered a new dating and trajectory for Philoponus' career and Marwan Rashed's recovery of works or fragments by the commentators, mostly in Arabic, and of reactions in Arabic to the commentators, had proceeded further. Of the chapters wholly or partly on Philoponus included below by Golitsis, Rashed, Peter Adamson, Ahmad Hasnawi, Péter Lautner, and Frans de Haas, all but two have been written between 2011 and 2015.

---

[301] Richard Sorabji, ed., *Philoponus and the Rejection of Aristotelian Science* (London: Duckworth, 1987).
[302] Koenraad Verrycken, 'The Development of Aristotle's Thought and its Chronology', in R. Sorabji, ed., *Aristotle Transformed*, pp. 233–74.

Golitsis' new evidence for the development of the commentaries of Philoponus is used again in Chapter 15 below. It was the book titles in different manuscripts, not all endorsed in Diels' Berlin edition, stating whether Philoponus' commentaries were taken from the seminars of Ammonius. The aim was not just chronology, but, as with Verrycken earlier, tracing the development of Philoponus away from the thought of his teacher Ammonius. In Chapter 14 below, I tried to see how far that new criterion fitted with other criteria for dating. By and large, it seemed to me that the new criterion did fit with others. At the same time, I was impressed again by the unprecedented research that Verrycken had earlier performed for his different trajectory of Philoponus. Although I had reported in the second edition of *Aristotle Transformed* that Verrycken's account had not on the whole found favour, I realised that any alternative account has to cope with the huge body of evidence that Verrycken assembled. Concerning the new criterion, there were only two qualifying observations that I had to offer. First, I was struck by how very early in his studies under Ammonius, Philoponus started major disagreements with him. The first disagreement was on a subject very central to Christianity, whether the universe had a beginning, and it preceded 517 CE. So in cases where the book titles assure us that Philoponus was drawing from the seminars of Ammonius, and there are other signs that the commentary might be an early one, that does not preclude the interpolations, which are also mentioned in the titles, constituting very major disagreements. The other qualification has bigger consequences and I hope its inclusion will allow readers to make up their own minds between our two views. Golitsis has in forthcoming work[303] made a very good case that when the book titles tell us that a commentary by Philoponus from the seminars of Ammonius has included Philoponus' own *epistaseis*, that Greek word, *epistaseis*, does not mean merely *reflections* of his own, but *critical* reflections, or *objections*, of his own. On the other hand, I think it is important that Philoponus has not yet been found saying that the reflections he includes are *only* critical ones. And indeed, that is not his practice. For example, something has been established by Concetta Luna about a substantial section of Philoponus' commentary (not from Ammonius' seminars) on Aristotle's *Categories*. Philoponus' commentary is very close, often even in wording, to what is standardly called Ammonius' commentary on the *Categories*. In fact, the latter commentary should be described as a commentary taken anonymously from the voice of Ammonius, but the anonymity suggests that the unknown editor saw himself as relatively faithful to Ammonius. Despite Philoponus' closeness on many pages to this commentary faithful to Ammonius, and despite the absence of any warning in the book title, Luna has found Philoponus interpolating his own comments 13 times in 21 pages. But usually the interpolated comments are not objections, even where Ammonius might disagree with them. The editor of Philoponus *in Cat.*, Busse, has indeed found an interpolation which looks Christian, so that Ammonius would not agree with it, and I believe I have found a few more interpolations and one explicit disagreement (*in Cat.* 58,7–59,2) with the faithful anonymous edition of Ammonius.

---

[303] Pantelis Golitsis, '*Meta tinôn idiôn epistaseôn*: John Philoponus as an editor of Ammonius' lectures', in Pantelis Golitsis and Katerina Ierodiakonou, eds, *Aristotle and His Commentators: Studies in Memory of Paraskevi Kotzia* (Berlin: De Gruyter, forthcoming).

So far this is likely to be agreed territory. But when a book title tells us that Philoponus is interpolating objections to Ammonius in what he draws from Ammonius' seminars, does this mean that he is not also including non-critical observations of his own? As I put it in Chapter 14, that would be very surprising, given that he includes a good many non-critical observations in his *Categories* commentary. Why then would he not include non-critical observations elsewhere? I think that the reason why Philoponus' book titles make an announcement when objections are included in a commentary from Ammonius' seminars is not that these are the only interpolations that he makes. Rather, the reason is that it is only right for an editor to dissociate Ammonius from objections, when they are not ones he had raised himself. It is possible also that Philoponus would like to be associated with some objections, but not always. For sometimes he does not put his objection *as* an objection, I believe, and I think it may be that sometimes his authorship of an objection is hidden, and he does not edit the text to make his authorship clear.

If we cannot infer that in Philoponus' commentaries from the seminars of Ammonius the only interpolations will be objections announced in the book title, this will be very relevant to more than one of the chapters below on Philoponus. For the question will arise whether good (non-critical) innovations should be credited to Ammonius or to Philoponus as his editor. Can Philoponus, for example, be credited with any of the non-critical ideas in the commentary on Aristotle *On Coming-to-Be and Passing-Away*, or on *On the Soul*, Books 1 and 2, and, lost in Greek but surviving in Latin, on *On the Soul* 3.4–8 on intellect? This question will arise in Chapter 15 below, where Golitsis favours Ammonius over Philoponus, and in Chapter 17 below, where Péter Lautner makes the reverse ascription to Philoponus, not Ammonius. Lautner does so when he discuses the keen attention to medicine and the brain in Book 2 of Philoponus' commentary on *On the Soul*, and Philip van der Eijk drew the same conclusion in his translation of the same commentary on *On the Soul*, Book 1. The value of Golitsis' challenge is that now we shall have to look and see case by case what points to Ammonius and what points to Philoponus. I have tried to do a little of this in Chapter 14 below in connexion with these same commentaries. But we can no longer assume that nearly all the ideas belong to Philoponus, nor should we, in my view, start assuming that all except objections are by Ammonius.

Golitsis' main aim in Chapter 15 below is to argue that the Greek version of Philoponus on Aristotle *On the Soul* Book 3, is not from the seminars of Ammonius, so, unlike the rest of what survives from Philoponus on *On the Soul*, including the commentary surviving only in Latin on Book 3.4–8, is to be credited entirely to Philoponus. It has been a mistake to ascribe it to Stephanus. The basic ground for ascribing it to someone else was that the commentary surviving in Greek on Book 3 looks unlike any of the rest of the commentary on *On the Soul* that has survived, whether in Greek or in Latin. But Golitsis' plausible explanation is that the rest all belongs together as Philoponus' commentary from the voice of Ammonius, whereas the Greek commentary on Book 3 is a separate commentary by Philoponus himself, and Golitsis provides strong arguments for Philoponus' authorship. This conclusion is all the more striking, when put into relation with Roueché's finding in Chapter 22 below, that Stephanus was Philoponus' pupil, which suggests that a compromise might have been investigated, whether the Greek commentary on Book 3 differed from the rest because it had been edited by Stephanus as Philoponus' pupil. But Golitsis' important conclusion about the Greek on Book 3 implies that no such compromise is needed. The question about the rest of Philoponus' commentary, which is from the voice of Ammonius, as to how far it is therefore simply a record of Ammonius, apart from explicit objections, is a separate question and does not in any way impinge on the new conclusion about the Greek on Book 3.

Frans de Haas' Chapter 16 goes closely with a companion paper on 'drunken potentiality' as describing the state of the newly reincarnated soul. But that has already been discussed above under 'Ammonius'. In Chapter 16 he develops our understanding further, and in a way that is very relevant to the question what is derived from Philoponus and what from Ammonius. He teases out two views on how to defend Aristotle's treatment of chemical mixture. Aristotle wants the ingredients in what he calls a blend neither to perish nor to survive unchanged in the resulting mixture, and he tries to achieve this by saying that the ingredients still exist *potentially*. But Philoponus' commentary from the voice of Ammonius on *On Coming-to-Be and Passing-Away* argues that this must be a different level of potentiality, intermediate between the two levels that Aristotle distinguishes in his classic statement in *On the Soul* 2.5. The ingredients exist potentially in the way that a geometer is only a potentially a geometrical thinker, when he is drunk. All bodies below the heavens, in Aristotle's view are chemical mixtures of the four elements, earth, air, fire, and water. I take it to be Ammonius who supplied the view that in this mixture fire, for example, still exists, but that its drunken level of potentiality means that it is not *pure*. One striking thing is that the text briefly admits that it is worth making an objection (*epistasis*), a favourite word of Philoponus. For elemental fire might be said not to survive in the mixture in impure form, but to have perished utterly, contrary to Aristotle's intention, because fire is defined as having the maximal degree of heat, and any reduction of heat will therefore mean that it no longer exists. Ammonius had a little earlier in the commentary endorsed such a maximal heat argument in a different context. But now that the maximal heat consideration counts against his analysis of elemental fire as existing in an impure state, he shelves further discussion as going beyond what he had proposed to cover. I have been tempted in Chapter 14 to wonder if the objection was raised impromptu by Philoponus himself during the class which the commentary records, and was shelved because the further issue had not been allowed for in the timing of the class. The maximality argument is endorsed by Philoponus in his own person elsewhere.

I have mentioned Péter Lautner as being interested in Chapter 17 in physiology. But this was not for its own sake, but in connexion with a modern controversy about whether Aristotle regarded sense perception as involving a physiological process and whether in particular Aristotle's idea that sense perception involves receiving form without matter was a physiological or a non-physiological idea. The champion of the non-physiological interpretation, Myles Burnyeat, had cited Philoponus as on his side, because Philoponus speaks of the *cognitive* (*gnôstikôs*) reception of form without matter. But what Lautner points out is that Philoponus combines cognitive reception with material (*hulikôs*) reception of form, which is physiological. The physiology has advanced since Aristotle, to whom a theory of vision has been ascribed involving the coloration of the eye-jelly (*korê*). Philoponus knows of the brain and the nerves and something of the structure of the eye, and of the interconnexion between these three, and he treats the *korê* not like Aristotle as an undifferentiated eye jelly, but as the channel of the optic nerve. But he fills the brain and channels up as far as the lens of the eye with *pneuma*, in Aristotle's sense of a physical spirit or gas, giving it the job of registering expansions and contractions.

Philoponus in the Arabic Tradition

The remaining chapters on Philoponus all deal with his subsequent reception in Arabic. So it may help to say a word about the transmission of Philoponus into Syriac and then Arabic. Baumstark reported that all Philoponus' later writings on Christian theology were translated into Syriac, (these include *On the Whole and the Parts*, which has been translated into English)[304] and that according to later Arabic bibliographers, so also were his commentaries on Aristotle's *Prior Analytics*, *Physics*, and *On Coming-to-Be and Passing-Away*.[305] We have also already noticed under 'Ammonius' Baumstark's claim that some Syriac text seems to draw indirectly on biographical reports about Porphyry supplied by a lover of toil (a literal rendering of Philoponus' name), which would have been appropriate to an introduction to a commentary, such as Philoponus says he wrote, on Porphyry's *Isagôgê*.[306] Translations into Arabic, many but not all from Syriac, of various Greek philosophical texts, not at first including Philoponus, came in several waves starting almost two hundred years after Philoponus. The first wave was under the second and third caliphs of Baghdad who ruled between 754 and 785. After a short gap, a second wave started under a caliph who took power in 812. Early in this period the philosopher al-Kindī (*c.* 800 – after 860) organised translations, and he is said to have had indirect knowledge of Philoponus' treatises *Against Aristotle* and *That every body is finite and has finite power*, but certainly not knowledge of Philoponus' *Against Proclus on the Eternity of the World* at any rate as a whole. Later in this period Isḥāq Ibn Hunayn (*c.* 830 – 910/911) translated Philoponus on Aristotle's *Physics* Books 5–8 from which only excerpts survive in the so-called Leiden MS, which has now been translated into English.[307] Marwan Rashed in Chapter 19 cites al-Nawbakhtī (*c.* 850–920) as author of the first surviving Arabic commentary on Aristotle, which was written in paraphrase form on *On Coming-to-Be and Passing-Away*. But al-Nawbakhtī also knew Philoponus' *Against Proclus on the Eternity of the World*, whose translator is unknown, and Rashed supplies three new fragments or reports, two of them lost in Greek, and the other recorded in al-Nawbakhtī. The third wave of translation was from Syriac into Arabic by the Christian Abū Bishr Mattā (died 940), who was discussed

---

[304] By Daniel King, Ancient Commentators on Aristotle series (London: Bloomsbury, 2015).
[305] A. Baumstark, *Aristoteles bei den Syrern*, p. 169.
[306] A. Baumstark, *Aristoteles bei den Syrern*, pp. 171–9, with the caveats of Christel Hein about not taking the original source of everything to be Philoponus (*Definition und Unteilung der Philosophie*, p. 37).
[307] By Paul Lettinck (London: Duckworth, 1994), in the Ancient Commentators on Aristotle series.

above under 'Ammonius and his school' as having possibly translated Paul the Persian and supplied it to his pupil, the major Muslim philosopher al-Fārābī (870–951). Fārābī founded the Baghdad school of philosophy and wrote a commentary on Aristotle's *On Interpretation*, an epitome of all 8 books of Aristotle's logic, including the *Posterior Analytics*, and prefaced them with *Prolegomena to Porphyry's Isagôgê*, including several definitions of Philosophy, and, if the ascription is right, also *Prolegomena to the study of Aristotle's Philosophy*. He is said to have drawn on the prolegomena of Paul of Persia, copying his divisions or branches of Philosophy, and, like Paul, regards the *Posterior Analytics*, with its method of demonstrative proof for science, as the summit. His approach to religion was that of a philosopher using Aristotle's philosophy to provide a rational basis for demonstrating the truth of revealed religion, although he sided with Aristotle against revealed religion in accepting the beginningless eternity of the world. Although he passed on many aspects of Aristotelianism to his successors in the school, they differed from him in being Christians. They were not willing like him to accept Aristotle's belief in the world's eternity.

In Chapter 18, Peter Adamson discusses four of the Greek commentators, Alexander, Themistius, Proclus, and Philoponus, in his account of the use of late Greek philosophers in the Arabic tradition. He distinguishes between philosophers in Greek and in Arabic according to whether they drew conclusions about the eternity or non-eternity of the world on the basis of arguments in physics or arguments in theology. Aristotle in his *Physics* 8.1 argued for the eternity of motion from consideration in physics. Proclus took a theological turn when he construed the word *arkhê* (origin) in Plato as implying not a temporal beginning, but a divine causal origin. Both concluded that the world was eternal, but Philoponus had to use different strategies against them. To Aristotle's arguments from physics he replied that the world cannot be eternal from its own *nature*, because being a finite body, in Aristotle's view, it cannot house the infinite power needed for eternal duration. Against Proclus' theological arguments he responded that a more than finite duration is an absolute impossibility, as the Neoplatonists had accepted from Aristotle, and that absolute impossibilities are impossibilities even for God. Adamson shows that Alexander in his *On the Cosmos* had preceded Philoponus in preferring arguments from nature, but that Philoponus, differing from Alexander in his anti-eternalism, allows God to override the natural destructibility of the world. A preference for theological over physical argument on the duration of the cosmos is found in Arabic in al-Kindī, Thabit Ibn Qurrā, and al-Rāzī, albeit tempered by the theories of early Muslim theologians.

In chapter 19 Ahmad Hasnawi made some important discoveries. Some of the Arabic translations of Greek philosophy made perhaps in al-Kindī's circle in the first half of the ninth century were wrongly ascribed to Alexander. These included the texts known in A. Dietrich's list as D9 and D16. The subject of D16 was forms, but not matter, coming to be out of nothing. I was especially glad to see D16 unmasked, because I had in 1983 expressed disbelief that one of its arguments could be by Alexander.[308] It turns out that the Arabic was an epitome, which is what made the authorship hard to identify.

---

[308] Richard Sorabji, *Time, Creation and the Continuum*, p. 248.

But Hasnawi found that it and D9 were from epitomes of Philoponus *Against Proclus on the Eternity of the World*. This is very relevant to Rashed's Chapter 20 below, because Rashed is asking, among other things, how soon this text of Philoponus was known in Arabic. In Kindī's time, some of the arguments seem to have been known, but not continuous text. That is precisely what would have happened in this case. The arguments would have been known in a chopped version, but mistakenly under the name of Alexander, because the text of Philoponus himself was not available to al-Kindī.

In Chapter 20, Marwan Rashed finds in Arabic and translates two new fragments (the first a report rather than a quotation), lost in Greek, from the beginning of Philoponus' *Against Proclus on the Eternity of the World*.[309] The first fragment reveals that Philoponus called Aristotle the first Greek philosopher to treat the world as eternal, and a comment is added that the Muslim philosopher al-Fārābī followed Aristotle's eternalism. Rashed also finds an excerpt from a known passage of Philoponus *Against Proclus* preserved by al-Nawbakhtī, and shows that al-Nawbakhtī already knew Philoponus' *Against Proclus on the Eternity of the World* as early as the ninth century CE. The fragment in al-Nawbakhtī crucially explains how the Christian Philoponus' discussion of the world being *generated* by God could be attractive to opposite viewpoints, despite Philoponus' insistence on the world having had a beginning. For in Nawbakhtī's excerpt, Philoponus records ambiguities that had been invoked by the Greek Middle Platonist Taurus concerning what Plato meant by calling the world *generated*. According to Taurus, the term 'generated' is ambiguous in several ways. Among other ways, it is ambiguous between the world having been produced by God without any beginning in time (the view of Aristotle and the Neoplatonists including Porphyry and Proclus) and the world's having begun when God made it (as the Christian Philoponus believed and ascribed to Plato), but having taken no time to do so. This last idea of *instantaneous* beginning is a further distinction which Porphyry added to those of Taurus, according to Philoponus, and which was to be used in Muslim theories of instantaneous creation. The beginningless view suited eternalists – the Greek Neoplatonist supporters of Aristotle's eternalism – and was surprisingly accepted also by al-Fārābī, because, despite being Muslim, he accepted Aristotle's eternalist view of the world. The insistence on a beginning suited Fārābī's Christian successors in the Baghdad school, who were supporters of the Christian Philoponus' anti-eternalism and also influenced by the Muslim theological philosophy of the Kalām. They did indeed follow al-Fārābī in accepting Aristotle to a large extent, but *not* in following his eternalism.

Fakhr al-Din al-Rāzī, the twelfth century theologian (not Abū Bakr al-Rāzī the doctor-philosopher), is the thinker who, in a work not published until 2004, *Al-Riyāḍ al-mūniqa*, preserves both the above excerpts from Philoponus' *Against Proclus*: the one

---

[309] For fragments of Philoponus' other treatise, *Against Aristotle*, translated by Rashed into French, see his 'Nouveau fragment arabe du *De aeternitate mundi contra Aristotelem* de Jean Philopon', *Elenchos* 33 (2012), 291–300, and his 'The Problem of the Composition of the Heavens (529–610): A New Fragment of Philoponus and its Readers', in P. Adamson, H. Baltussen, and M. Stone, eds, *Philosophy, Science and Exegesis in Greek, Arabic and Latin Commentaries*, 2 vols (London: Institute of Classical Studies,), vol. 2, pp. 35–58.

to which al-Rāzī adds that Fārābī followed Aristotle's eternalism, and the excerpt from that work of Philoponus in al-Nawbakhtī, which reveals that Taurus' ambiguities of 'generated' were known in Arabic from the ninth century. But al-Rāzī's comment on Fārābī creates a new problem because al-Rāzī elsewhere, like his predecessor Avicenna and like all the manuscripts, credits Fārābī with a famous work about Plato and Aristotle, *On The Harmonisation of the opinions of the Two Sages*. Al-Rāzī therefore tries to present *Harmonisation* as eternalist. But in fact *Harmonisation* exploits the further ambiguity introduced by Porphyry, and says that Aristotle meant the world began, but *instantaneously*, because it did not take time to begin through a gradual process, since there was no time until the world had begun. Rashed has already argued elsewhere that *On the Harmonisation* is not by Fārābī, but by a later Christian member of the school.

Already earlier than the *Harmonisation*, at the turn of the ninth to tenth centuries, al-Kindī's pupils knew enough of Philoponus' report of the ambiguity of 'generated' to have to ward off the eternalist meanings, which Nawbakhtī favoured. But the subsequent plumping for instantaneous creation, though mentioned by Porphyry as a possible meaning of 'generated', was not explicitly endorsed by the Greeks, and may have owed its subsequent popularity more to early ninth century Muslim theologians.

I think it is very striking that as a Muslim Fārābī had the freedom to endorse Aristotle's beginningless universe against the view that was common to Islam and the other Abrahamic religions, that God gave the world a beginning. But Fārābī was a philosopher not only in our sense, but a *faylasūf*: a philosopher who subordinated scriptural revelation to intellectual thought, including Aristotle's. A *faylasūf* does not have to admit the survival of individuals after death, nor a beginning of the universe, nor the unity of God, nor his knowledge of particulars.[310] Nor were the *falāsifa* persecuted for denying these views. The *falāsifa* included Avicenna, Avempace, and Averroes, and they were followed by the Jewish philosophers Maimonides and Gersonides. By contrast, al-Ghazālī, whom we would regard as a very good philosopher, counted as a theologian instead, and he could write against Avicenna *The Destruction of the Philosophers*. But Averroes could write against Ghazālī *The Destruction of the Destruction*. Whatever, persecution there may have been in other spheres, this toleration of philosophical views looks like a model.

The reception of Philoponus in Arabic suggests to me that he came into his own in that milieu. In the philosophy school of Alexandria, he was an odd man out, not suited to doing the job of explaining the pagan Neoplatonist viewpoint faithfully to Christians. Clemens Scholten has pointed out that among Greeks he had to wait 400 years before the Byzantine lexicon called the Suda treated his *Against Proclus* as important.[311] But in Arabic philosophy, the case was different. This had already been illustrated in one way when H. A. Davidson[312] showed how Arabic philosophy preserved and transmitted to

---

[310] These concessions are based on the contents of al-Ghazālī's *Destructio*: S. Stroumsa, *Freethinkers of Medieval Islam*, (Leiden: Brill, 1999) pp. 190-15. Marwan Rashed, *Al-Ḥasan ibn Mūsā al-Nawbakhtī: Commentary on Aristotle De generatione et corruptione* (Berlin: De Gruyter, 2015), pp. 363-5.

[311] Clemens Scholten, *Johannes Philoponos, De Aeternitate Mundi, Über die Ewigkeit der Welt*, vol. 1 (Turnhout: Brepols, 2009), pp. 195-6.

[312] H. A. Davidson, 'John Philoponus as a Source of Mediaeval Islamic and Jewish Proofs of Creation', *Journal of the American Oriental Society* 85 (1965), 318-27.

the Latin Middle Ages the infinity arguments for the world's beginning. But in the school of Baghdad, it turned out that either side of the controversy could benefit from him. His case for the beginning of the universe could be welcomed by the Christians in the Baghdad school, while the founder Fārābī could exploit his record of ambiguities to support a beginningless universe.

Stephanus (*c.* 530 – towards end of sixth century) in Alexandria

Mossman Roueché has transformed our understanding of Stephanus in a series of articles over the years, but now in Chapter 22 with new material and in a form that explains his role in the philosophical milieu of Alexandria. For a start, our Stephanus is not to be identified with a Stephanus who took an appointment away from Alexandria in Constantinople in 610. On the contrary, he was early enough to be the pupil of Philoponus in Alexandria, since it is Philoponus to whom he refers as teacher in the only extant commentary, a commentary from the voice of Stephanus on Aristotle's *On Interpretation*, on which he had presumably heard Philoponus lecture. I don't know whether Stephanus could also have been the recorder and editor of Philoponus own commentary preserved in Greek on Book 3 of the *On the Soul*. He was like Philoponus a Christian, but unlike Philoponus had orthodox views on Christ's dual nature as human and divine, as approved by the emperor Justinian. He can be placed more exactly as following Olympiodorus and Elias in the Alexandrian school, but preceding David and Pseudo-Elias. This is on the basis of his new addition to the definition of Philosophy as preparation for death, which was known to the latter two, but not to the former two Alexandrian philosophers. This addition was discussed above under 'Ammonius', and it included in the definition a warning against suicide. He wrote commentaries, we saw, and introductions to commentaries, for beginners on Porphyry's *Isagôgê* and Aristotle's *Categories*, but his philosophical definitions and divisions from there had exceptional influence. As explained, his definitions were recorded by church fathers, one the expanded definition of Philosophy attributed to him by Maximus the Confessor in the seventh century, and other philosophical definitions (along with a comment on divisions in Philosophy) repeated by John of Damascus in the eighth. We also saw that in the thirteenth century, Severus bar Shakko took indirectly via some Syriac compilation an extract from Stephanus' divisions of Philosophy including the same comment.

A new surprise is that some of Stephanus' definitions appear very close to those in Simplicius' commentary on the *Categories*, written far to the East, possibly in Harrān. This raises the question whether a copy of Simplicius had somehow reached Alexandria. Furthermore, Stephanus is recorded as having, like Simplicius but unlike other Alexandrians, written a commentary on Aristotle *On the Heavens*. Of course this work was of much interest to Stephanus' teacher, Philoponus, and the greater range of Stephanus' writing, as compared with that of his age group, may be due to the influence of the wide-ranging Philoponus. There is evidence for Stephanus' commentaries, lost but recorded, including not only *On the Heavens*, but also all Aristotle's logical works, both his *Sophistical Refutations* and even his work on scientific demonstration, the

Posterior Analytics. In addition, Golitsis suggests in Chapter 23 that Stephanus is the author of both the fragmentary commentary on *Metaphysics* Books 1–2 that is printed in CAG vol. 1 at the foot of the page as an alternative version of Alexander's commentary and of the commentary on *Metaphysics* 6, ascribed to Pseudo-Alexander in the same volume of CAG. His extant commentary on *On Interpretation* is thought, because of parallels, possibly to have influenced Probus, the sixth century commentator in Syriac on, and probably translator of, some of Aristotle's logic. It was also known in Arabic to Ibn al-Ṭayyib in the tenth to eleventh century.

Eustratius and Michael of Ephesus, the Twelfth Century Revival

Robert Browning's case, reprinted in *Aristotle Transformed*, for re-dating Michael of Ephesus by a century to the twelfth century CE continues to make sense of the situation. Eustratius (1050–1120)[313] started writing commentary on Aristotle first, and, unlike Michael's, his commentaries, first on Aristotle's *Posterior Analytics* and then on *Nicomachean Ethics* Books 1 and 6, were Platonist in content. Eustratius' teacher, John Italus, had been thrown out of his job in 1082 for using dialectic to explain Christ's incarnation and his human and divine natures, and his pupils were required to anathematise his doctrines. In 1111, Eustratius was riding high as a court theologian to Alexius I Comnenus in Constantinople. But the period would not tolerate the mixing of logic with religion. By 1114 he was himself suspended for life from divine office for also thinking that we must use dialectic to explain Christ's incarnation and for holding that Christ reasoned in syllogisms. He confessed that he should not syllogise and that the fathers of the church had not done so. It was no accident that the first commentary he chose to write on Aristotle, whether before or after his condemnation, concerned the use of syllogisms to establish universal truths of science. For the second commentary, he was approached, like Michael, by the daughter of the emperor in Constantinople, Alexius I Comnenus, Anna Comnena, who remained in seclusion for many years after her father's death. She is said to have pressured him to write in old age on the *Ethics* for which there had been commentaries by Aristotelians but not by Neoplatonists. Eustratius' commentaries were Platonist in content. In writing on the *Posterior Analytics*, he accepted (195,26–8) Proclus' distinction of three kinds of universal, before in and, as he says 'from' the many particulars. In his *Ethics* commentary (40,22 ff.), referring again to the three universals, he described Plato's followers as holding that Plato's divine Craftsman had in his mind principles (*logoi*), which they also called Ideas and universals, each of which would be a totality within the definition of the particulars which referred to it. He also presented the *Ethics* as favouring moderation, rather than eradication, of emotions, because it was, in Platonist terms, about the elementary level of civic virtue. He backed Plato against Aristotle's view that Good could be not studied

---

[313] I draw here on the accounts by H. P. F. Mercken in *Aristotle Transformed* ('The Greek Commentators on Aristotle's Ethics', pp. 407–43) and A. C. Lloyd, in 'The Aristotelianism of Eustratius of Nicaea', in J. Wiesner, ed., *Aristoteles Werk und Wirkung*, 2 vols (Berlin: De Gruyter, 1987), vol. 2, pp. 341–51.

as one single science, because different things displayed different kinds of goodness, and he supported Plato's view of virtue as knowledge.

Anna asked Michael of Ephesus also to fill gaps in the commentary tradition, and between 1118 and 1138 he compiled a considerable number, with a more strongly Aristotelian viewpoint, using old commentaries by others when available, and not always changing 'I said' to 'he said' when he embedded old texts into his own. As explained by Paul Mercken in *Aristotle Transformed*, to fill gaps in commentary on the *Ethics*, Michael wrote on Books 9 and 10 and used pre-existing anonymous scholia on Book 5 to compile his own separate commentary on that book, additional to the scholia on their own. Eustratius was used for Books 1 and 6 and the anonymous commentary on Book 7 also looks late. The remaining anonymous scholia on Books 2 to 5 were pre-Neoplatonist from the second century CE, as was the commentary of Aspasius which was used for Book 8.

Michael also wrote a commentary on the *Sophistici Elenchi*, edited in CAG as Pseudo-Alexander, of which an earlier version also survives in Latin,[314] commentaries on Aristotle's psycho-physical works, the *Parva Naturalia*, and on four of Aristotle's zoological works. All of these survive and there are a few pages surviving from a commentary on Aristotle's *Politics*.

Much of this was detailed in the introduction to the new edition of *Aristotle Transformed*. But what is entirely new in Chapter 23 is Pantelis Golitsis' reconstruction of authorship in the composite commentary on Aristotle's *Metaphysics* compiled largely by Michael in the twelfth century and ascribed by CAG to Alexander of Aphrodisas from the third century or to Pseudo-Alexander. Alexander is indeed the author of Books 1–5. But Golitsis, we have seen, argues that Stephanus from the sixth century was the author both of Book 6, which is ascribed to Pseudo-Alexander in CAG vol.1, and of the fragmentary commentary on *Metaphysics* Books 1–2 that is printed in the same CAG volume at the foot of the page as an alternative version of Alexander's commentary. For Books 7 to 10, Michael of Ephesus, he suggests, used, but supplemented, the commentary of Asclepius from the voice of Ammonius, also from the sixth century. Asclepius cited Alexander, but not enough, as a marginal comment complained. George Pachymeres was used in the thirteenth century to supplement Michael on Book 9 and in place of Michael on Books 11 to 14. Golitsis leaves for later consideration the access of Michael or Pachymeres to Syrianus on the last two books, 13–14.

---

[314] Sten Ebbesen, *Commentators and Commentaries on Aristotle's Sophistici Elenchi: A Study of Post-Aristotelian Ancient and Medieval Writings on Fallacies*, 3 vols (Leiden: Brill, 1981), vol. 2, pp. 153–99.

1

The Texts of Plato and Aristotle in the First Century BCE: Andronicus' Canon

Myrto Hatzimichali

One of the main developments that characterise first century BCE philosophy is that the detailed study of texts became an autonomous and often central philosophical activity in its own right. For this reason, any investigation of philosophical developments during this period must address questions surrounding the circulation of written texts. In this chapter I will examine the respective fates of the texts of Plato and Aristotle, and the editorial interventions that shaped each tradition. The case of Plato, as well as further evidence on the activity of ancient scholars and editors, will then inform my proposed interpretation of developments in the textual tradition of Aristotle, where the first century BCE holds particular prominence thanks to the well-known sensational stories about the rediscovery of long-lost works. The history of these texts indicates two different and separable types of activity, namely textual criticism and canon-organisation. However, the modern term 'edition' is sometimes used to describe either activity, thus making it more difficult to ascertain what it was that ancient 'editors' actually did. In fact, as Dorandi pointed out, Porphyry is probably the only 'real' ancient editor of a philosophical corpus, having dealt with both aspects of Plotinus' text.[1] Keeping the two activities distinct will help to clarify what happened to Aristotle's text in the first century BCE and inform the eventual value judgement that this period was of paramount importance for the way in which Aristotle has been transmitted to us.

Text-Based Philosophy

In the context of the three revivals of Plato, Aristotle, and Pythagoras it is significant that, as Frede notes, they were connected with the beginnings of classicism as a broader

---

This article first appeared as 'The texts of Plato and Aristotle in the first century BC' by Myrto Hatzimichali in Malcolm Schofield (ed.), *Aristotle, Plato and Pythagoreanism in the First Century BC* (2013), pp. 1–27 © Cambridge University Press 2013, reproduced with permission.

[1] T. Dorandi, '"Editori" antichi di Platone', *Antiquorum Philosophia* 4 (2010), 161–74, at 172.

cultural development calling for a return to the ancients. A principal means available for this return to authors/authorities from many centuries earlier was none other than the systematic study of their texts.[2] Textual exegesis of Plato's and Aristotle's writings was central to the articulation of organised philosophical systems for the two authors, systems that for historical reasons did not develop during the Hellenistic period in the way that the Stoic system did.[3] Matters are more complicated in the case of the Pythagoreans, given the lack of a recognised corpus of writings going back to Pythagoras himself. I will not have much to say about them in the course of this chapter, apart from remarking that the importance of written texts is evident in this movement too, taking the form of a proliferation of pseudepigrapha aimed at supplying the missing texts by several early Pythagoreans.[4] The first century BCE was a pivotal period for this type of activity too: Pseudo-Archytas, who claims paternity of the Aristotelian categories for the fourth-century Pythagorean,[5] as well as 'Timaeus Locrus', *On the nature of the cosmos and of the soul*, a work claiming to be the model for Plato's *Timaeus*, have both been dated to this period.

The increased focus on texts may also be connected to the decentralisation of philosophy from the Athenian schools during the first century BCE, following the growing impact of Rome as a cultural centre and the disruptions of the Mithridatic war. The new peripheral philosophical groups were deprived of the traditional school environment and dialectical interaction and thus focused on books, which eventually became the cohesive element and starting-point in the construction of these groups' philosophical identities. Sedley has pointed out that these developments amount to and 'end for the history of philosophy' in the first century BCE, in the sense that most (even the most innovative and creative) philosophical activity now takes the form of looking back, recovering and interpreting the wisdom of the ancients through their texts.[6]

The precise ways of 'looking back', the tactics and attitudes of individual first-century BCE philosophers towards the texts of the ancients have been taken up by others.[7] In what follows I will focus on the state in which the texts of Plato and Aristotle were made available to anyone who was keen on approaching the original words of the two fourth-century philosophers. Activities that document this keenness on the ancients' original words and are crucial for the circulation of texts include: collecting and distributing copies of books, engaging in textual criticism, defining and maintaining canons (by dealing with questions of authenticity), and writing commentaries or

---

[2] M. Frede, 'Epilogue', in K. Algra et al., eds, *The Cambridge History of Hellenistic Philosophy* (Cambridge: Cambridge University Press, 1999), pp. 771–97, at pp. 783–4.
[3] See P. Donini, 'Testi e commenti, manuali e insegnamento: la forma sistematica e i metodi della filosofia in eta postellenistica', W. Haase, ed., *Aufstieg und Niedergang der römischen Welt* II 36.7 (Berlin: De Gruyter 1994), pp. 5027–100, esp. pp. 5027–35, 5089–94.
[4] The evidence can be found in H. Thesleff, *An Introduction to the Pythagorean Writings of the Hellenistic Period* (Abo: Abo Akedemi, 1961).
[5] See T. A. Szlezák, *Pseudo-Archytas Über die Kategorien* (Berlin: De Gruyter, 1972).
[6] D. N. Sedley, 'Philodemus and the decentralisation of philosophy', *Cronache Ercolanesi* 33 (2003), 31–41, esp. 35–9.
[7] In Malcolm Schofield, ed., *Aristotle, Plato, and Pythagoreans in the First Century BC* (Cambridge: Cambridge University Press, 2013).

producing other forms of exegesis such as translations or monographs on topics arising from particular texts.[8] All of these enterprises flourished in the first century BCE with respect to philosophical texts, marking a philological as well as philosophical revival. It is also pertinent to bring up at this point Strabo's tantalising tale about the loss and rediscovery of Aristotle's books (13.1.54): the most extravagant claim in that story is that the Peripatos declined because its members had almost no access to Aristotle's works, a report that is highly questionable with respect to the Hellenistic period. But the fact that this loss was deemed a satisfactory explanation for the Peripatetic decline does betray very eloquently the importance placed upon original foundational texts in Strabo's own intellectual milieu in the first century BCE.

In order to understand better the ways in which users gained access to these foundational texts, some general remarks on the circulation of books in our period are required by way of introduction. The feature that stands out first of all is the overwhelming centripetal force exercised by Rome and Italy in terms of accumulation of books (alongside other objects of culture such as artefacts, cultic statues, etc.).[9] The first Roman general to have obtained an entire collection of Greek books as war booty was Aemilius Paullus in 168 BCE, when he permitted his sons to carry off the books of king Perseus since they were lovers of learning (Plut. *Aem.* 28.11; Isid. *Etym.* 6.5). Then Sulla famously took from Athens the library of the bibliophile Apellicon of Teos, which contained valuable Aristotelian texts (Str. 13.1.54; Plut. *Sull.* 26). Similarly, Lucullus amassed a very significant collection as war booty from Pontus and Asia Minor (Isid. *op. cit.*). From Cicero's *De Finibus* (3.7–10) we learn that this library contained many Stoic texts as well as Aristotelian *commentarii*.[10]

The Romans also employed gentler ways for the acquisition of Greek books. Cicero's letters to Atticus in 67 BCE contain references to a library (that is, a substantial collection of books) that Atticus had promised to obtain in Greece for Cicero's benefit: 'and please give some thought to how you are to procure a library for us as you have promised' (Cic. *Att.* 1.7). Thus it appears that Greek collections (including philosophical works, presumably among other types of literature) were available for purchase en bloc by Romans who could afford it, especially given economic difficulties in Greece in the aftermath of the Mithridatic war. Finally, with Philodemus we have evidence for the voluntary transportation of a substantial philosophical collection to Italy by a Greek intellectual himself (we know that the collection predates Philodemus' migration because the Herculaneum papyri include several texts written considerably earlier than Philodemus' time).[11]

This concentration and increased availability of books in Italy certainly informs the background to Cicero's philosophical work, but it would doubtless have also benefited the increasing number of Greek philosophers as well as other scholars who pursued a teaching career in Rome (in fact Plutarch is keen to stress that Lucullus' library was

---

[8] H. G. Snyder, *Teachers and Texts in the Ancient World* (London: Routledge, 2000), p. 5.
[9] Strabo 12.5.3; 13.1.19; 14.2.19; 10.2.21.
[10] On Lucullus' library see T. K. Dix, 'The library of Lucullus', *Athenaeum* 2 (2000), 441–64.
[11] See Sedley, 'Philodemus' (n. 6 above), p. 35.

particularly welcoming for Greeks).[12] Meanwhile in the East, we have evidence for the continued flourishing of libraries in Pergamum and Alexandria, and perhaps also Smyrna (Plut. *Ant.* 58; Str. 14.1.37). Strabo (13.1.54) and Posidonius are in agreement about the book-acquisition tactics of Apellicon of Teos in the early decades of the first century, who did not always employ legitimate means, yet his activities offer some indication about the opportunities open to a private bibliophile with philosophical interests and deep pockets.

> He (the tyrant Athenion) sent Apellicon to the island (Delos); he was from Teos but had become an Athenian citizen, and had led a eventful and diverse life. When he developed an interest in Peripatetic philosophy, he purchased both Aristotle's library and many others (for he was very rich); and he acquired by stealth the original copies of the ancient decrees of the Metroon, as well as any other old and rare documents that were to be found in other cities.
> Ath. 5.214D-E = Posidon. fr. 253 Edelstein-Kidd

From this brief survey it emerges that two widespread ways of gaining possession of philosophical books in the first century BCE were war plunder and bloc purchases, the fruits of which could be shared among groups of peers. It is worth noting that our evidence points to private initiatives and networks much more than public or even school collections. But what sorts of texts would these initiatives yield, and how did they develop through scholarly and editorial intervention? This is the main question I will be dealing with in the rest of this chapter, focusing first on the text of Plato and then on that of Aristotle.

Plato's Text

In order to approach the state of play for Plato's text in the first century BCE, one must reconstruct the stage between the Hellenistic period and the organisation of the corpus by Thrasyllus, astrologer to the emperor Tiberius in the first century CE (Tac. *Ann.* 6.20–1). Thrasyllus' arrangement ultimately became canonical, having been universally adopted by modern editions since Burnet.[13] In what follows, I will discuss the main evidence on the history of Plato's text in order to demonstrate the different types of editorial intervention it was subject to, and to show how they resulted in the situation encountered by Thrasyllus.

---

[12] 'He was more keen on the use than the acquisition [of books]; his library was open to everyone, and the promenades and study-rooms surrounding it were without restriction receiving the Greeks, who gathered there as to a nest of the Muses and spent their days in each other's company.' (Plut. *Luc.* 42.1–2)

[13] The Thrasyllan order, however, was far from the norm in editions circulating between the Renaissance and the twentieth century: see M. F. Burnyeat, 'What Was the "Common Arrangement"? An Inquiry into John Stuart Mill's Boyhood Reading of Plato', *Apeiron* 34 (2001), 51–90. For the order of the dialogues in mediaeval manuscripts and its variation from Thrasyllus see H. Alline, *Histoire du Texte de Platon* (Paris: Librairie Ancienne Honoré Champion, 1915), pp. 124, 176–8.

There is good reason to believe that Plato was read widely (and beyond Athens) during the Hellenistic period, not only as a philosopher but also as a literary author. Part of the evidence for this is a group of early Ptolemaic papyri, including those of the *Laches* (*P.Petr.* II 50), *Phaedo* (*P.Petr.* II 5–8) and *Sophist* (*P.Hib.* 228), all going back to the third century BCE. This is precisely the type of evidence that is lacking in the case of Aristotle, making it more difficult to get clear about the circulation of his texts during the Hellenistic period. What makes the Plato papyri listed above particularly significant is that they contain a very large number of variants and deviations from the manuscript tradition, enough to earn the characterisation 'wild' from Turner.[14] The fact that the papyri from our period onwards (first century BCE-first century CE) present a much more normalised text is a phenomenon paralleled in the papyri of Homer. It suggests that some form of editorial activity intervened, probably originating from the scholars of the Alexandrian Museum and Library, where the second century BCE was the most productive period.[15]

Nevertheless, many scholars have been reluctant to credit the Alexandrian librarian Aristophanes of Byzantium with any major influence on the text of Plato and deny any critical edition by him, despite this evidence for a normalisation of the text in the Alexandrian Library.[16] It may be that we have to look to Aristophanes' successor Aristarchus for a more detailed engagement with the minutiae of Plato's text, as indicated by Schironi on the basis of new fragments from what may be a commentary on the *Republic* focusing on linguistic/stylistic aspects.[17] The evidence on Aristophanes of Byzantium is of a different nature, and concerns his view on the arrangement of the dialogues, whereby he opted for five trilogies with the rest of the dialogues in no particular order:

> Some people, one of whom is Aristophanes the grammarian, drag the dialogues into trilogies and place first the one headed by the *Republic* (followed by) *Timaeus* and *Critias*. As a second (trilogy they place) *Sophist, Politicus, Cratylus*; third *Laws, Minos, Epinomis*; fourth *Theaetetus, Euthyphro, Apology*; fifth *Crito, Phaedo, Letters*. The rest follow individually in no particular order.
>
> Diog. Laert. 3.61–2

---

[14] E. G. Turner, *Greek Papyri: An Introduction* (Oxford: Clarendon Press, 1968), p. 108. The *Phaedo* papyrus contains around 70 variants in 4–5 pages of Oxford text, while the *Laches* papyrus offers 40 variants in 3 pages. Burnet adopted 8 and 7 of these variants respectively.

[15] This evidence of course pertains to texts circulating in Egypt and does not permit a parallel assessment of the text(s) used in the Academy. We only know that at the time of Zeno of Citium the works of Plato had recently been made available, and perusal was possible upon payment of a fee to the owners of copies (according to the *Life of Zeno* by Antigonus of Carystus, cited at Diog. Laert. 3.66). J. Barnes, 'The Hellenistic Platos', *Apeiron* 24 (1991), 115–28, at 127–8, is certainly right in pointing out that there was not one 'Hellenistic Plato', and that none of the 'editions' we have information on may be considered as authoritative.

[16] See e.g. R. Pfeiffer, *History of Classical Scholarship* (Oxford: Clarendon Press, 1968), pp. 196–7; *contra* H. Dörrie, *Der Platonismus in der Antike II: Der hellenistische Rahmen des kaiserzeitlichen Platonismus* (Stuttgart: Frommann-Holzboog, 1990), p. 334; Aline (n. 13 above), pp. 84–103. See F. Schironi, 'Plato at Alexandria: Aristophanes, Aristarchus and the 'philological tradition' of a philosopher', *Classical Quarterly* 55 (2005), 423–34, at 431–2, for further references.

[17] Schironi, 'Plato at Alexandria' (see previous note). She brings to attention new fragments from Aristarchus' pronouncements on Platonic expressions occurring at *Resp.* 327B7; 327C6; 414E7; 568A8.

Diogenes or his source (which may be Thrasyllus himself) does not agree with this arrangement, because a critical stance is implied by the verb 'drag' and there is an accusation of randomness in the expression 'in no particular order/ in a disorderly fashion'.

It would appear, then, that the grouping and arrangement of the dialogues was a point of contention for the Platonic corpus in the period up to Thrasyllus. It was probably the dramatic form of the dialogues that encouraged an arrangement following the pattern of the plays performed in the Athenian dramatic festivals. Thrasyllus is explicit about the use of Athenian drama as a prototype and ascribes it to Plato himself:

> Thrasyllus says that he (sc. Plato) published his dialogues following the example of the tragic tetralogy, in the way that they competed with four plays (at the festivals) – at the Dionysia, the Lenaea, the Panathenaea and the Chytroi – of which the fourth was a satyric drama. The four plays together were called a tetralogy.
>
> Diog. Laert. 3.56

It is possible that Aristophanes' trilogies were the result of thinking along the same lines, but opting for the tragic trilogy without the satyric play.[18] Aristophanes could point to dramatic interrelations between the dialogues he grouped together – for example, the connection between *Theaetetus* and *Euthyphro* must be based on direct dramatic sequence since at the end of the *Theaetetus* Socrates leaves to face Meletus' indictment at the king's porch, where he meets Euthyphro.

The evidence on Aristophanes of Byzantium and the fact that all but fifteen dialogues were left by him in no particular arrangement shows that the tetralogical ordering was not the norm in the Hellenistic period, even if it did originate in the Academy (there is no explicit evidence for this apart from Thrasyllus' conviction). Still, Thrasyllus must have found some sort of precedent to legitimise his ascription of the arrangement to Plato, and the only hint we have for such a tetralogical precedent comes from the first century BCE. It consists of a problematic passage in Varro, where a reference to the *Phaedo* is prefaced by what seems to be 'Plato in the fourth', suggesting that for Varro the *Phaedo* came fourth, either in its own tetralogy or in the corpus as a whole: 'Plato in the fourth (?) concerning rivers that are in the underworld names Tartarus as one of them' (*Ling.* 7.37). Doubts have been cast, particularly by Barnes and Tarrant, on the reliability of this reading and the peculiar use of the numeral when one would expect a title.[19] Varro's reference, however, remains our only pointer towards the organisation of the Platonic corpus in the first century BCE, prior to Thrasyllus' intervention.[20]

---

[18] See also Schironi, 'Plato at Alexandria' (n. 16 above), pp. 432–3.
[19] Barnes, 'The Hellenistic Platos' (n. 15 above), p. 127 with n. 50; H. Tarrant, *Thrasyllan Platonism* (Ithaca: Cornell University Press, 1993), pp. 75–6. Tarrant proposes taking the numeral as a cardinal and reading '*in quattuor fluminibus*' rather than '*in quarto de fluminibus*'; he ascribes to Varro the mistake of treating Tartarus as one of the rivers.
[20] The pre-Thrasyllan tetralogical arrangement is sometimes associated with a certain Dercyllides (cf. Alb. *Intr.* 4), but we know nothing about his date, and he may well have been later that Thrasyllus. See Tarrant, *Thrasyllan Platonism* (n. 19 above), p. 73.

From the evidence discussed so far we may already detect two different ways of making an impact on an author's transmission and circulation: firstly, textual criticism and correction, as indicated by the progressive normalisation of Plato's text as we move towards the end of the Hellenistic period and by Aristarchus' possible commentary; and secondly, corpus-organisation, as evidenced by the different pronouncements on the grouping and order of the dialogues. Some additional information on the former type of activity is provided by Diogenes Laertius, who preserves traces of professional philological engagement with the Platonic text. Alongside some comments on Plato's distinctive use of terminology designed to prevent the ignorant from understanding his meaning (Diog. Laert. 3.63–4), we learn about the presence of critical signs in copies of his texts (3.65–6).[21] These critical signs are almost the same as those used by the Alexandrian editors of Homer, with the addition of some more 'philosophically-oriented' signs that may have been developed especially for Plato's text.[22] Thus Plato's text claims a place not too far behind that of Homer as one of the more intensely studied, corrected and annotated in Antiquity, enjoying a rich transmission and provoking interest and debate both within and outside philosophical circles.

A particularly valuable copy of the Platonic text is mentioned alongside equivalent Homeric ones in the recently recovered Galenic treatise *On freedom from grief, Peri Alup(ês)ias*.[23] Galen talks about his lack of grief after a destructive fire in Rome in 192 CE, when many valuable items were lost, including old, 'special editions' going back to eponymous sources. The fire devastated both Galen's own books and those kept at the Palatine libraries:

> So it is not possible to find those texts that are rare and not available anywhere else, or those that are common, but particularly valued due to the accuracy of their readings, 'Callinia' and 'Atticiana' and 'Peducinia' and equally Aristarchean copies consisting of two Homers, and the Plato of Panaetius and many more such things, because there those very writings were preserved, which the men after whom the books are named either wrote or copied (annotated?) in the case of each individual book (Galen, *On freedom from grief* 13[24])

---

[21] A better structured version of this list of critical signs survives in an earlier, second-century CE papyrus from Florence, *PSI* 1488 = *CPF* I.1*** Plato 142T. See Schironi, 'Plato at Alexandria' (n. 16 above), pp. 429–31.

[22] As in the texts of Homer, the *obelos* signifies passages thought to be spurious; the dotted *diple* points to editorial interventions by various scholars, often in a polemical way; the *antisigma* marks transpositions; in addition, the *keraunion* is used to denote passages central to philosophical education (*agôgê tês philosophias*,), and the *asteriskos* to highlight the harmony across Plato's doctrines.

[23] V. Boudon-Millot, 'Un traité perdu de Galien miraculeusement retrouvé, le *Sur l'inutilité de se chagriner*', in V. Boudon-Millot, A. Guardasole, and C. Magdelain, eds, *La science médicale antique: Nouveaux regards* (Paris: Beauchesne, 2007), pp. 73–123, is the *editio princeps*; a new Budé has since appeared (V. Boudon-Millot, J. Jouanna, and A. Pietrobelli, *Galien, Ne pas se chagriner* (Paris: Les Belles Lettres, 2010)); see also J.-B. Gourinat, 'Le Platon de Panétius: à propos d'un témoignage inédit de Galien', *Philosophie Antique* 8 (2008), 139–51.

[24] The text translated here is that of the *editio princeps*, Boudon-Millot (see previous note).

Galen had seen sought-after 'eponymous' copies of both Plato and Homer, as well as other quality copies of unspecified authors from highly esteemed sources. The context in which Panaetius' Plato is mentioned, which includes a reference to Aristarchus' Homer, suggests some degree of textual criticism by the Stoic, enough to ascribe responsibility for the text to him.[25] When an ancient scholar undertook to produce his own text of a particular work, this normally meant using an existing copy as a 'base text' and supplying it with corrections in the form of critical signs (marking atheteseis, transpositions etc.) and/or marginal annotations.[26] So in the case of 'the Plato of Panaetius', I take Galen to refer to a copy of Plato which he knew to be either written out or annotated in the way described above by Panaetius himself.[27] It is not unthinkable that a physical copy that belonged to or was handled by Panaetius could have survived to Galen's time.[28] Galen's evidence is also significant in that it corroborates the beginning of a growing interest in the text of Plato in philosophical circles, already highlighted by Frede with respect to Panaetius.[29]

The same passage from Galen contains a further piece of information that is of relevance to the circulation and state of Plato's text in the first century BCE. It concerns the provenance of the *Atticiana* texts (*Attikiana*) that were lost in the fire: many interpreters now agree that these are to be associated with Titus Pomponius Atticus, Cicero's close associate, who is known to have been involved in the publication process of Cicero's own works and to have employed skilled Greek copyists whose services were much in demand.[30] From Galen's fragmentarily surviving commentary on the *Timaeus* we learn that there was a version of this text from *Atticiana* copies, which at 77C4 (on plants' lack of self-motion) read *huph' heautou* ('by itself'), the transmitted reading of our mediaeval manuscripts, as opposed to the *ex hautou* ('from itself') of some other copies consulted by Galen.[31] It is clear that texts of this provenance were held in high

---

[25] See Gourinat, 'Le Platon de Panétius' (n. 23 above), esp. pp. 147–51. He points to further parallels for Panaetius' philological activity on Plato, including his discovery of alternative openings for the *Republic* (Diog. Laert. 3.37); a controversial athetesis of the *Phaedo* (*Anth. Pal.* 9.358; Elias, *in Cat.* 133); and support for the Attic ending of active pluperfect verb forms in –*ê* in the text of Plato (*enenoêkê*, *epepoiêkê*, Eust. *Ad Od.* 23.220, II.305.31–4 Stallbaum). Panaetius also had views on the books to be ascribed to Aristippus and Aristo, as well as on the authenticity of Socratic dialogues by several authors (Diog. Laert. 2.85; 7.163; 2.64). For a critique of Gourinat see now Dorandi (n. 1 above).

[26] See F. Montanari, 'Zenodotus, Aristarchus and the *ekdosis* of Homer', in G. Most, ed., *Editing Texts – Texte Edieren* (Göttingen: Vandenhoeck & Ruprecht, 1998), pp. 1–21, at pp. 6–10.

[27] The text is unclear and may even be corrupt. It is particularly difficult to ascertain the exact nature of and relationship between the two activities signified by *egrapsan* (from *graphô*, 'to write') and *anegrapsanto* (from *anagraphomai*, 'to inscribe, record') in this context, which is why editors have corrected the latter to *an<t>egrapsanto* ('had copies made'); see Boudon-Millot *et al.* (n. 23 above), pp. 53–4.

[28] See C. Jones, 'Books and libraries in a newly-discovered treatise of Galen', *Journal of Roman Archaeology* 22 (2009), 390–7, at 392; Jones speaks of 'owners or editors' of these texts, at 391.

[29] Frede, 'Epilogue' (n. 2 above), p. 777.

[30] Jones (n. 28 above), pp. 392, and 391–3 for possible identifications of Callinus and Peducaeus; Tarrant (n. 19 above), pp. 193–4; Gourinat, 'Le Platon de Panétius' (n. 23 above), pp. 144–6. R. Winsbury, *The Roman Book* (London: Duckworth, 2009), pp. 53–6, is more sceptical, and warns emphatically against assimilating Atticus' activities to those of a modern publisher. See also Dorandi (n. 1 above), pp. 165–6.

[31] 'I came across this interpretation (sc. 'by itself') based on the published version of the *Atticiana* copies, while in other copies I found "by the motion from itself"' (Gal. *Plat. Tim.* fr. II.107–9 Schröder).

esteem, and it would be appealing to associate their quality with the versions that people like Cicero and Varro were working from. Unfortunately we have no contemporary sources on these texts, as all our information about the *Atticiana* comes from authors of the Second Sophistic (apart from these two references in Galen there are a few more in the lexicographer Harpocration regarding *Atticiana* copies of Demosthenes).[32]

As we sum up with some preliminary results on the fate of Plato's text, it is evident that it had a rich transmission, gaining the attention of philosophers and non-philosophers alike as a mainstream part of Greek cultural heritage, with recognised literary value and high-quality Attic prose. At the same time, the two types of engagement with the text take shape more clearly; on the one side, there are the text-critical and editorial initiatives such as those of Panaetius and Atticus (the producer of the *Atticiana*), that resulted in specific copies and versions of the text becoming renowned for the quality of their readings and sought after by connoisseurs like Galen. Aristarchus' possible commentary on the *Republic* and the critical signs that accompanied some versions of the Platonic text also belong with this text-critical type of activity. On the other side, we have the pronouncements on the arrangement of the corpus and on the titles and sequence of dialogues, exemplified in the activity of Aristophanes of Byzantium and Thrasyllus, the latter reaching increased levels of sophistication with his double titles and generic headings (Diog. Laert. 3.57–8). This is not to say that the two activities cannot be undertaken by the same person or even at the same time (and Porphyry is a case in point as we shall see below), but they are certainly separable, because views on corpus-organisation can be disseminated in separate works and do not require the production of fresh copies of the full texts.[33] In this form they can prove more important and influential than some quality readings on select copies held in a library and menaced by fire.

The Fate of Aristotle's Books

Unlike the case of Plato, where papyrological and other evidence points to an uninterrupted tradition through the Hellenistic period and beyond, in the case of Aristotle's works we have ancient sources speaking explicitly of decisive developments in the course of the first century BCE following a dramatic loss. The story told by Strabo and Plutarch has been interpreted as signifying a momentous rediscovery of long-lost texts in the first century BCE, combined with an epoch-making complete 'edition' of the Aristotelian corpus more or less as we know it by Andronicus of Rhodes. In what follows I will try to take account of the challenge laid down by Barnes in his 'Roman Aristotle',[34] which invites a radical rethinking of developments in the first century BCE and their importance with respect to the state of the corpus before and

---

[32] For the references see Gourinat, 'Le Platon de Panétius' (n. 23 above), pp. 145–6.
[33] We know of a work by Thrasyllus which could be of such a nature, 'Preliminaries to the reading of Democritus' works' (Diog. Laert. 9.4).
[34] J. Barnes, 'Roman Aristotle', in M. Griffin and J. Barnes, eds, *Philosophia Togata II: Plato and Aristotle at Rome* (Oxford: Clarendon Press, 1997), pp. 1–69.

after this period. Barnes' contribution is valuable in that it distinguishes sharply between the actual evidence relayed by ancient sources, and what modern scholars have argued, postulated and speculated on the basis of this evidence. Taking therefore Barnes' distillation of the ancient evidence as a point of departure, I will show that it is possible to draw some less minimalist conclusions than Barnes' own. What is at stake is Andronicus' stature as a figure of great significance in the transmission of Aristotle's texts – could he perhaps be worthy of the libation that Barnes denied him?[35]

Ultimately the controversy over developments in Aristotle's text in the first century BCE is not so much about events (what took place) but about value judgements (how important it was). Even Barnes does not deny that Andronicus of Rhodes had some involvement with the Aristotelian corpus, but he does not regard his role as particularly influential: 'Nothing suggests that the "Roman edition", done by Andronicus of Rhodes, revolutionized Aristotelian studies. His text of Aristotle left little mark on posterity. His work as orderer and arranger of the treatises was not epoch-making'.[36] In fact most of our modern value judgements (positive or negative) concerning Andronicus' work have been based on misplaced expectations about what constituted influential or 'epoch-making' involvement with an author's corpus in ancient times. Andronicus will be found to have fallen short of the canonical, reliable and critical edition he has been credited with in assimilation to modern editors, and so his performance in the text-critical side of things will be disappointing if judged by modern standards. But his achievements in the areas of canon-formation and corpus-organisation can be shown to be of greater significance than Barnes allowed.

The history of Aristotle's corpus is made particularly controversial and complicated by the fact that that several issues are debated at once, when a distinction might be more helpful. One thorny issue is the availability of Aristotle's esoteric works during the Hellenistic period, which is almost impossible to ascertain because familiarity with particular Aristotelian ideas in Hellenistic authors could come from either esoteric or exoteric works.[37] Moreover, different circumstances of transmission and circulation seem to apply to different treatises. Primavesi recently renewed the case for the unavailability of several Aristotelian texts during the Hellenistic period. His grounds was that the texts in our MSS tradition retain the pre-Hellenistic system of book numbering by means of twenty-four plain letters rather than twenty-seven letter-numerals.[38] He takes this to mean that these texts did not pass through the Hellenistic editorial and library-organisational processes and, combining it in turn with the absence of many titles known to us from the Hellenistic catalogue of Aristotle's works preserved by Diogenes Laertius (Diog. Laert. 4.22–7), he concludes that the Aristotelian

---

[35] Barnes, 'Roman Aristotle', pp. 1, 66.
[36] Barnes, 'Roman Aristotle', p. 66.
[37] See Barnes, 'Roman Aristotle', pp. 12–16, for evidence of knowledge of Aristotelian works in the Hellenistic period. F. H. Sandbach, *Aristotle and the Stoics* (Cambridge: Cambridge Philological Society, 1985) argues against any substantial influence by Aristotelian esoteric works on the Stoics on the basis of a lack of any explicit evidence. See also L. Tarán, 'Aristotelianism in the First Century BC', in his *Collected Papers (1962–1999)* (Leiden: Brill, 2001), pp. 479–524 (repr. from *Gnomon* 53 (1981), 721–50), at pp. 482–4.
[38] Thus, for example, the sixth book of the *Physics* is Z rather than ς (see the discussion at Simplicius, *in Phys.* 923,3–7); the eleventh book of the *Metaphysics* (excluding *Alpha Elatton*) is Λ rather than ια.

treatises not listed by Diogenes were inaccessible until the first century BCE.[39] In any case, Andronicus' role in canon formation and corpus organisation was only partially about bringing new works to light, and more about constructing an organic whole out of existing ones, as we will see below.

It is now time to turn to the familiar ancient sources for the fate of Aristotle's works and the activity of Andronicus. The tradition for which Strabo is the earliest extant witness is essentially a tale of loss and rediscovery of the texts of Aristotle and Theophrastus, and we are entitled to turn to it for an explanation of the unavailability of any works in the third and second centuries BCE.[40] Strabo lays special emphasis on the effects of textual provision upon the quality of Peripatetic philosophising. Here we pick up the story in the early first century BCE, when the books of Aristotle and Theophrastus are purchased by Apellicon of Teos, having been hidden at Scepsis for two centuries by the descendants of Neleus, who inherited them from Theophrastus:

> This Apellicon was a bibliophile rather than a philosopher; for this reason, in trying to restore the damage he transcribed the text onto new copies filling the gaps incorrectly, and published the books full of errors. It was the case that the old Peripatetics who came after Theophrastus, not having access to the books at all, apart from a few and mainly the exoteric ones, were not able to produce any real philosophy, but were 'declaiming commonplaces' [LSJ translation of *theseis lêkuthizain*]. The later Peripatetics, however, after these books came to light, philosophised better and were closer to Aristotle's thought, but were forced to speak mainly in conjectures because of the large number of errors. Rome, too, played an important part in this; immediately after the death of Apellicon, Sulla (who conquered Athens) took Apellicon's library. When it came here Tyrannion the grammarian, who was an admirer of Aristotle's, handled it after paying court to the librarian, (as did) some booksellers who used bad scribes and did not collate the texts – the sort of thing that happens also with other books that are copied for selling, both here and in Alexandria.
>
> Str. 13.1.54

Two states of affairs are lamented here by Strabo: firstly, Peripatetics after Theophrastus could do nothing more than engage in rhetorical exercises.[41] This first comment also

---

[39] O. Primavesi, 'Ein Blick in den Stollen von Skepsis: vier Kapitel zur frühen Überlieferung des *Corpus Aristotelicum*', *Philologus* 151 (2007), 51–77, esp. 65–70. He counters Burnyeat's argument ('Aristotelian Revisions: The Case of the *De Sensu*', *Apeiron* 37 (2004), 177–80, at 178–9, n. 3) that the twenty-four letter system excludes any first-century organisation of the corpus (because the twenty-seven letter-numerals were in use at that time) by claiming that Andronicus conservatively followed the system he encountered in the hitherto unavailable texts (p. 68). In normal conditions of transmission and circulation the original pre-Hellenistic system should have been replaced by the letter-numerals.

[40] Primavesi (see previous note), p. 74.

[41] If in fact the reference is not to rhetorical exercises but to genuine philosophical debate and discussion (D. E. Hahm, 'Critolaus and late Hellenistic Peripatetic philosophy', in A. M. Ioppolo and D. Sedley, eds, *Pyrrhonists, Patricians, Platonizers: Hellenistic Philosophy in the Period 155–86 BC* (Naples: Bibliopolis, 2007), pp. 47–101, at pp. 98–101), then R. W. Sharples (*Peripatetic Philosophy 200 BC to AD 200* (Cambridge: Cambridge University Press, 2010), p. 29 is right in saying that Strabo's remark 'verges on the outrageous'.

demonstrates a clear privileging of esoteric over exoteric works (more on this issue below). Secondly, after the appearance of the old books acquired by Apellicon, there was some improvement but it was still felt that Aristotle's true meaning could not be confidently accessed due to faults in the circulated texts. The precarious state of Peripatetic philosophy was jeopardized further by the removal of the books to Rome ('Rome, too, played an important part in this'). The term *aristotelizein* ('to aristotelise', translated above as 'to be close to Aristotle's thought') is unique to Strabo and signifies the type of philosophical investigation that he considered most characteristic of Aristotle, namely the investigation of causes.[42] Strabo's pessimistic attitude towards the later 'Roman' stage of engagement with Aristotle's text is puzzling, given that he claims membership of this group of 'aristotelising' intellectuals as a pupil or fellow student of Boethus.[43] It would seem that he had experienced an inferior and unsatisfactory text: does this mean that Strabo and his fellow Peripatetics read a worse text than we do now? It is possible that these complaints are due to the same genuine difficulties that we still experience with Aristotle's text, only we are happy to accept that this is how Aristotle composed his esoteric works, whereas ancient interpreters felt the need to justify them by appeal to calamities in transmission.[44] Moreover, Strabo was particularly fussy about the quality of his texts and can be suspected of exaggeration here.[45] Thus we may avoid inferring from Strabo's remarks that the books brought to light from Sulla's booty were particularly poor copies, which would diminish the contribution of those involved in bringing them to light.[46] It is, nevertheless, significant that Strabo presents the production of Aristotelian copies as a commercial and thus potentially lucrative activity, meriting the hasty mobilisation of 'some booksellers' – apparently there was a market for these books.

This commercial production took place alongside Tyrannio's work on the Aristotelian manuscripts.[47] Tyrannio came to Rome in the early 60s BCE,[48] but it is not clear exactly when he dealt with the contents of Sulla's library. It is important to examine

---

[42] We can gather as much from Strabo's only other use of the coinage, in reference to Posidonius: 'for his work is full of inquiry into causes (*to aitiologikon*) and Aristotle-style investigation (*to aristotelizon*), which are avoided by the men of our school due to the obscurity of causes' (2.3.8).

[43] See 16.2.24: 'in my time the famous philosophers from Sidon were Boethus, with whom I studied Aristotle, and his brother Diodotus'.

[44] An interesting parallel for elaborately blaming unfortunate editorial interventions for the state of Aristotle's text can be found in Asclepius' commentary on the *Metaphysics*, written from Ammonius' lectures in the sixth century CE, Asclepius, *in Metaph*. 4,4–15. In this passage we find the same key ingredients of Strabo's story: a text is removed from Athens, it remains deliberately hidden, and is belatedly published with faults due to material damage and less-than-expert editing; the alleged consequences did not only affect book-arrangement, but also the continuity of expression (*to sunekhes tês lexeôs*).

[45] When he copied a text (for personal or other use) he required two copies of the original for comparison (*eis antibolên*), cf. 17.1.5. In the passage quoted above he laments commercial booksellers' general failure to do so (*ouk antiballontes*).

[46] Cf. Barnes, 'Roman Aristotle' (n. 34 above), p. 31: 'Andronicus *merely* published copies of corrupt manuscripts' (emphasis added).

[47] There are question marks about the relationship between Tyrannio and the booksellers, see Barnes, 'Roman Aristotle' (n. 34 above), pp. 19–20. I agree that the text might be corrupt and take the connection to be that they both gained access to Sulla's library by 'unofficial' means.

[48] He came to Rome as a captive after the capture of Amisus by Lucullus in 70 BCE, and was subsequently freed by Murena (Plu. *Luc*. 19.7).

what exactly Tyrannio did in this library and under what circumstances. At this point, some more information may be sought in Plutarch's version of the sensational rediscovery, which also introduces Andronicus of Rhodes:

> Having left Ephesus with all the ships, he (sc. Sulla) arrived at Piraeus on the third day; and after his initiation he took for himself the Library of Apellicon of Teos, which included most of Aristotle's and Theophrastus' books: at the time they were not yet well known to most people. It is said that when this Library came to Rome Tyrannion the grammarian arranged most things, and Andronicus of Rhodes through him got access to the copies and prepared the lists that are now in circulation. But the older Peripatetics were clearly elegant and learned in themselves, but did not have access to many or to good copies of Aristotle's and Theophrastus' writings, because the inheritance of Neleus (to whom Theophrastus left the books) fell into the hands unambitious and simple people.
> Plut. Sull. 26

From Cicero's correspondence with Atticus we know that Tyrannio also took charge of rearranging Cicero's own library, very much to Cicero's satisfaction. The words Cicero uses to describe Tyrannio's activity in *Att.* 4.4a and 4.8 are *dissignatio* and *disposuit* ('arrangement' and 'ordering'). This process, as we learn from *Att.* 4.4a, included gluing loose pieces of papyrus together with the help of specialist clerks, and labelling the books. The term 'arranged/prepared' (*enskeuasasthai*) in Plutarch suggests some similar activity for Sulla's library. Tyrannio, therefore, improved the physical state of (some of) the manuscripts that Sulla had brought from Athens.

This does not suggest in any way an 'edition' by Tyrannio; on the contrary, his activity is presented by our sources as distinctly non-public, the result of a private understanding with Sulla's librarian. Apart from his conservation role, Tyrannio also acted as an intermediary, making the texts available to Andronicus, who is credited by Plutarch with making the results of Tyrannio's work public. Andronicus' dependence on Tyrannio is also crucial for the date of his own work on the Aristotelian corpus, which cannot be dated before the early 60s BCE. It is widely accepted that Cicero's failure to mention any of these men's Aristotelian activities, even though he was closely acquainted with Tyrannio, means that these activities took place after Cicero's death in 43 BCE.[49]

This evidence invites further consideration of the relationship between the activity of Tyrannio and Andronicus on the one hand, and the flurry of interest in Aristotelian texts on the other. This surge of activity centred especially on the *Categories*, and can be traced back to the first half of the first century BCE. The Alexandrians Aristo and Eudorus, cited by Simplicius among the 'old interpreters' of the *Categories* are known to have been

---

[49] Moraux was in favour of an earlier date, mainly on the grounds of the revival described below and the report that Andronicus was the eleventh scholarch of the Peripatos (Ammonius, *in Int.* 5,28–9). See P. Moraux, *Der Aristotelismus bei den Griechen von Andronikos bis Alexander von Aphrodisias I* (Berlin: De Gruyter, 1973), pp. 45–58, with Barnes' criticism in 'Roman Aristotle' (n. 34 above), p. 24, n. 108.

active in the earlier part of the first century.[50] Eudorus also knew a text of the first book of the *Metaphysics* (at least), which he treated as fluid or problematic and offered an emendation (*metagrapheisês*) at *Metaph*. 1.6, 988a10–11.[51] The conversion of Aristo and Cratippus from Antiochus' Old Academy to the Peripatos[52] may also be associated with this early revival. But there is no need to date Andronicus' activity before these events, which would require rejecting Plutarch's evidence for his dependence on Tyrannio. Following Frede,[53] we may plausibly connect the early exegetical activity (in which Andronicus himself took part) with the initial publication (*exedôken*) of the Scepsis find by Apellicon. This initiative consisted in making fresh copies (*antigrapha*) with supplements for the damaged parts (an unsatisfactory effort according to Strabo), while the originals remained in Apellicon's library, soon to be carried off by Sulla. We can then treat Andronicus' involvement (i.e. his procuring the books from Tyrannio, making them public and writing the *Pinakes*, on which more below) as an important consequence rather than the cause of first-century surge of interest in Aristotle. Admittedly this takes away from Andronicus the honour of publishing lost works of Aristotle for the first time, but Strabo is quite clear on the fact that Apellicon first produced copies of his prized manuscripts and made them publicly available (*exedôken*).[54] The ancient process of releasing a book to the public is not entirely clear; it could mean placing texts somewhere where they would be available for copying (cf. Diog. Laert. 3.66) and/or a public reading (cf. Diog. Laert. 5.73, where Lyco's books are divided between 'unpublished' and 'read').

Thus far, then, our sources have attributed textual interventions or responsibility for the state of the text to Apellicon (transferring to fresh copies, restoring damages unsuccessfully), the anonymous booksellers (producing commercial copies without proper collation) and perhaps Tyrannio (making some repairs and arrangements). Plutarch does not say that Andronicus engaged in any similar activity, but rather that he made public (*eis meson theinai*) the refurbished texts that he got from Tyrannio and that he wrote up the *Pinakes* that were current in Plutarch's own time. This implies that Plutarch knew or thought that there had been other different *Pinakes*, so he credited Andronicus with some innovation in this respect, but not with building from scratch. If this is all Andronicus did, what of the celebrated Andronican edition?

---

[50] Simplicius, *in Cat*. 159,31–2: 'the old interpreters/commentators of the *Categories* ... Aristo and Andronicus and Eudorus ...'. Aristo had been a pupil of Antiochus of Ascalon since 86 BCE at the latest (Cic. *Luc*. 11–12), and Eudorus was his contemporary (Strabo 17.1.5).

[51] Alexander of Aphrodisias, *in Metaph*. 58,31–59,8; for a discussion see M. Bonazzi, 'Eudoro di Alessandria alle origini del Platonismo imperiale', in M. Bonazzi and V. Celluprica, eds, *L' Eredità Platonica: Studi sul Platonismo da Arcesilao a Proclo* (Naples: Bibliopolis, 2005), pp. 117–60, at pp. 145–9.

[52] The information for this conversion comes from Philodemus' *Syntaxis of the Philosophers*, *Index Ac*. XXXV 10–16.

[53] See Frede, 'Epilogue' (n. 2 above), pp. 773–5, which includes a favourable assessment of Apellicon's activity, avoiding undue influence from Strabo's strictures.

[54] Scholars have denied that Apellicon produced an 'edition', cf. Moraux (n. 49 above), pp. 99–101; Tarán (n. 37 above), p. 484; I. Düring, *Aristotle in the Ancient Biographical Tradition* (Göteborg: Elanders, 1957), p. 393. This is because they take 'edition' to mean production of a 'reliable', critically corrected text. However, the term *ekdosis* (perhaps better translated as 'publication') refers simply to the act of releasing a text to the public.

A lot of the controversy surrounding Andronicus depends upon our understanding of what an edition is supposed to amount to. Scholars have spoken of a 'canonical edition' or an 'authoritative text' by Andronicus, leading one to imagine a newly written out copy of the entire corpus, fresh from Andronicus' hand, in which he opted for readings of the highest quality, destined to become the standard point of reference. As a result of Barnes' sobering remarks, Andronicus' prestige was diminished because his work was found not to have met these high expectations (Barnes himself based his assessment on Andronicus' failure to meet them).[55] But Andronicus should never have been put on such a pedestal to begin with. As we have seen, our sources do not speak of a specifically Andronican text at all, there are no reports of an 'Aristotle of Andronicus' comparable to the 'Plato of Panaetius'. Moreover, Andronicus' name is not mentioned in connection with words implying textual scholarship such as *graphê* ('writing/MS reading'), *diorthôsis* ('correction/edition') or *anagnôsis* ('reading') or with critical signs such as the ones circulating in copies of Plato.[56] Porphyry, who was probably the closest Antiquity has to offer to a modern scholarly edition of a philosophical corpus (see above p. 81), cites Andronicus as an example of his ordering (*diataxis*), not of his correcting/editing (*diorthôsis*) activity (*Plot.* 24.2).

More generally, it is always too much to expect one individual's version of a text to become canonical in an ancient context. In a period when it was practically impossible to produce identical copies because everything was copied by hand, there could be no such thing as a standard stereotypical edition like our OCTs and Teubners. The most successful textual critics of Antiquity were the Alexandrian editors of Homer, who were dealing with a much shorter text than the Aristotelian corpus and were also in control of the Alexandrian library. Even in their case it took centuries to normalise the text by removing the 'wild' divergences (see above p. 85), and still very often they failed to have their readings adopted by the mainstream manuscript tradition.

Andronicus and the Aristotelian Corpus

Does his lack of a distinctly Andronican text mean that Andronicus was inconsequential for Aristotelian studies? On the contrary: the work that he did produce had every chance of being far more influential than the release of a text. This work contained Aristotle's biography, his will, probably some of the spurious letters and a catalogue of Aristotle's works, the *Pinakes* referred to by Plutarch.[57] The evidence for this content

---

[55] See Barnes, 'Roman Aristotle' (n. 34 above), pp. 27–36.
[56] Andronicus is mentioned in connection with an alternative MS reading only at Simplicius, *in Phys.* 440,14–17, which may be taken as Andronicus' attempt to justify his reading in the face of other variants, or as his exegesis of what he took as an uncontroversial text. See Barnes, 'Roman Aristotle' (n. 34 above), p. 30, firmly in favour of the latter option. *Pace* Barnes, Andronicus' text has left some traces in the mediaeval transmission, see Ross' apparatus *ad loc.* (*Phys.* 3.3, 202a14).
[57] It is possible that *Pinakes* was the title of the entire work, following Callimachus's pioneering work in this genre of 'biobliography', see R. Blum, *Kallimachos: The Alexandrian Library and the Origins of Bibliography* (Wisconsin: The University of Wisconsin Press, 1991), pp. 150–60; 233–46. See also below n. 70.

comes from an Arabic translation of a text ascribed to a 'Ptolemy the Unknown', where the author claims to be summarising Andronicus' work on the catalogue of Aristotle's writings.[58] From a reference to the 'fifth book' of this work in the same source[59] we get an indication about its minimum length, which suggests that the catalogue was not a mere list but was accompanied by extensive supporting material. This may have included an explanation and defence of the rationale underlying the catalogue, such as the ordering of the works, problems of authenticity etc.

For more information on what Andronicus did in this work we may turn to the evidence from Porphyry's *Life of Plotinus*:

> First, I judged that I should not leave the books in the chronological order in which they had confusingly been published: rather, I should imitate Apollodorus of Athens and Andronicus the Peripatetic, the former of whom collected Epicharmus the comic poet into ten volumes while the latter divided the works of Aristotle and Theophrastus into treatises, collecting related material into the same place. And so I divided the fifty-four books of Plotinus I possessed into six enneads (I was delighted to hit upon the perfection of the number six and the enneads). And in each ennead I united the related texts, putting first in order the lighter subjects (Porphyry, *Plot.* 24, trans. Barnes).

In this passage Porphyry compares the arrangement activities of three individuals, Apollodorus of Athens, Andronicus and himself, and in all three cases he describes a process of division and collection. Apollodorus gathered all of Epicharmus into ten volumes, while Andronicus and Porphyry divided the works of Aristotle and Plotinus respectively by grouping together material on related subjects. The result of Porphyry's division was the *Enneads*, corresponding to Andronicus' *pragmateiai*. Is then Porphyry crediting Andronicus with the creation of the treatises as we have them out of what were previously separate, disorganised essays? Barnes concludes that 'Porphyry does not hint that Andronicus invented the treatises'. However, by arguing that the *Enneads* correspond to Apollodorus' volumes of Epicharmus and not to any Aristotelian unit, Barnes does not explain the exact sense of the term *pragmateiai* (translated as 'treatises').[60] Porphyry *does* treat this unit as parallel to his own enneads: Andronicus divided into treatises (*eis pragmateias dieile*) and Porphyry divided into six enneads (*dieilon eis hex enneadas*). Elsewhere Porphyry uses the term to refer both to treatises as we understand them, such as the *Metaphysics* or the *Categories*, and more generally to the treatment of particular subjects.[61] The kinds of 'related material' that Porphyry

---

[58] The name is probably due to a misreading of Ptolemaios Khennos ('Ptolemy Chennos', perhaps identifiable with a first-century CE mythographer from Alexandria) as Ptolemaios Xenos ('Ptolemy the stranger'), cf. M. Rashed, *Aristote, De la géneration et la corruption* (Paris: Les Belles Lettres, 2005), p. ccvii. See Barnes, 'Roman Aristotle' (n. 34 above), pp. 25–6; Düring (n. 54 above), p. 213.

[59] No. 97 in Düring (n. 54 above), p. 230.

[60] Barnes, 'Roman Aristotle' (n. 34 above), pp. 39–40.

[61] Porphyry, *Plot.* 14.7: 'Aristotle's "treatise (*pragmateia*)" entitled *Metaphysics*'; cf. *in Cat.* 57,5; but *Intr.* 1,13: 'because this "topic (*pragmateia*)" is very profound'; cf. *VP* 48.1.

goes on to mention with respect to his own groupings are ethics, physics and cosmology, soul, *nous* and forms, and finally metaphysics. Therefore, even if we cannot extract from Porphyry that the units into which Andronicus divided the Aristotelian corpus are the treatises now familiar to us, we can take away at the very least that Andronicus ordered individual works according to subject-matter (*hupothesis* – ethics, physics, soul etc.). In both cases Andronicus emerges as a corpus-organiser rather than as an editor, in a role comparable to that of Aristophanes of Byzantium and Thrasyllus in the case of Plato's works.

This corpus-organisation proved to be a central component of Andronicus' contribution to Aristotelian studies, because it stipulated a specific order for Aristotle's works. Andronicus advocated beginning with logic because this is where demonstration is analysed, and Aristotle uses demonstration in all his other works. This view was opposed by Boethus, who thought physics should come first because it is more 'familiar and knowable' (Philoponus, *in Cat.* 5,15–24 – note that Philoponus reports expository rather than hierarchical criteria for the classifications of both Peripatetics). Andronicus' thematic groupings reveal a tendency to organise Aristotle's philosophy into a system with distinct but interlinked parts and sub-disciplines.[62] In his choice to start with logic Andronicus was in agreement with a number of leading Stoics including Zeno and Chrysippus, while Boethus coincided with Panaetius and Posidonius (see Diog. Laert. 7.40–1). In this case Andronicus' view prevailed and the logical works are still placed at the head of the Aristotelian corpus, starting with the *Categories*. This particular choice had, as Sharples observes, long-term implications for the emphasis that was placed on the problem of universals and the debate on being, knowledge and language.[63]

Andronicus' work also covered questions of authenticity: we get a glimpse into his methods and his criteria when later commentators criticise him for athetising the *De interpretatione* on the basis of what he perceived as an inaccurate reference to the *De anima* (cf. Philoponus, *in DA* 27,21–8). Andronicus' position was also rejected by subsequent commentators in the case of the *Postpraedicamenta*, which he refused to link to the *Categories*. In fact Andronicus believed that he was dealing with an interpolation intended as a 'bridge' between the *Categories* and the *Topics* by those who gave the *Categories* the title *Preliminaries to the Topics* (*ta pro tôn topôn*, cf. Simplicius, *in Cat.* 379,9–12).[64] Barnes discusses Andronicus' (sometimes misguided) choices and compares them to evidence from the catalogue of Aristotle's works found in Ptolemy (see above, pp. 95-6), which claims to follow Andronicus: he points out some discrepancies, but still concludes that Andronicus' canon corresponds more or less to Ptolemy's canon and hence to the modern canon.[65]

Alongside the division into *pragmateiai* according to subject-matter, Andronicus can be credited with one more arrangement of the Aristotelian corpus, this time

---

[62] On Andronicus and logic as an *Organon* see Moraux (n. 49 above), pp. 76–9.
[63] See R. W. Sharples, '*Habent sua fata libelli*: Aristotle's *Categories* in the First Century BC', *Acta Antiqua* 48 (2008), 273–87, at 274.
[64] Adrastus of Aphrodias defended this apparently pre-Andronican placement of *Top.* immediately after *Cat.*, Simplicius, *in Cat.* 15,35–16,16.
[65] Barnes, 'Roman Aristotle' (n. 34 above), pp. 33–7.

according to genre and type of composition. Broadly speaking, there are three sections in Ptolemy's catalogue, corresponding to (i) exoteric works, including the best known dialogues and some miscellaneous writings, nos. 1–28 (ii) the treatises that still form our Aristotelian corpus, nos. 29–56 (iii) collections of problems, constitutions and other such research material, nos. 57–91. They are followed by a brief list of documents and memoranda, including two collections of letters.[66] The Neoplatonist Elias (or David) cites both Ptolemy and Andronicus on the subject of the division of Aristotle's works by genre. The divisions he reports are more complex than the one described above from Ptolemy and they should be traced to the Neoplatonic schools, but it does seem that the Neoplatonists found in Andronicus some precedent for their own elaborate classifications.[67]

It is important to emphasise again that all these pronouncements on authenticity, book-division, grouping and ordering of books etc. must have been found in the treatise containing the *Pinakes* (which was at least five books long as we saw above), and they do not imply the existence of an Andronican copy of the corpus Aristotelicum. Simplicius offers further support for this when he says that he found Andronicus' view about the division of the *Physics* 'in the third book (of his) *On Aristotle's books*' (*in Phys.* 923,10).[68] It would be impossible, in any case, for an ancient edition to convey information on the detailed structure of so large a corpus, because individual books would be contained in separate papyrus scrolls, and an independent catalogue would always be necessary to spell out their order. Andronicus' unfortunate decisions on inauthenticity would then take the form of comments in the context of this general work.[69] This five-volume work had the potential to achieve much wider circulation and thus have a much larger impact than a full-scale edition of the entire corpus. By referring to the incipit and stichometric information provided by Andronicus, users of this work could identify the relevant texts in their own copies, put them in the right order and weed out any spurious material.[70]

We may briefly summarise the results so far on the nature of Andronicus' activity: he made certain texts available to a wider public, which could have included hitherto inaccessible works (or simply neglected ones) and he produced a 'biobibliography' of

---

[66] See Düring (n. 54 above), pp. 221–31.
[67] Elias (David) *in Cat.* 107,11–13; 113,17–20. He mistakenly refers to Ptolemy as 'Ptolemy Philadelphus', 107,13; the exact same words are used with reference to Andronicus at 113,18, which suggests that Elias probably knew of Andronicus indirectly through Ptolemy.
[68] The text here is uncertain; I am reconstructing the title of Andronicus' work as *ta Aristotelous biblia* or <*peri tôn*> *Aristotelous bibliôn*, identifiable with the book known to Plutarch and to Ptolemy.
[69] Barnes, 'Roman Aristotle' (n. 34 above), p. 34, says that 'Andronicus' version of the *Categories* did not contain the pages which conclude our modern editions'. Apart from the fact that this is not how Andronicus conveyed his rejection of the *Postpraedicamenta*, it is not an accurate representation of the practice of ancient editions either. One may compare the view of Aristophanes of Byzantium and Aristarchus that the ending of the *Odyssey* should be at *Od.* 23.296 (cf. Schol. *Od. ad loc.*). The fact that Aristarchus commented on 23.310–43 (Schol. *Od. ad loc.*) means that he kept the suspected one book and a bit in his text.
[70] Ptolemy no. 97 in Düring (n. 54 above), p. 230: 'also *hypomnemata*, whose numbers of lines and incipits you will find in the fifth book of Andronicus' *On the pinax of Aristotle's books*'. Adrastus' comparable work *On the order of Aristotle's writings* used exactly the same methods for identifying texts, cf. Simplicius, *in Cat.* 18,16–21.

Aristotle that included a catalogue of the philosopher's works. Therein he divided and ordered the books according to genre, providing a systematic arrangement by subject matter for the esoteric or 'acroamatic' works that have come down to us, leaving the rest in alphabetical order (at least as far as we can judge from Ptolemy's catalogue).

The Impact of Andronicus' Canon

In order to come to an assessment of Andronicus' impact, we need to combine the evidence discussed above with any available information on the state of the Aristotelian corpus before and after his time, to see if he made any difference. As Barnes demonstrates in detail, there are strong discrepancies between the catalogue of Aristotle's works in Ptolemy and the one appended to Diogenes Laertius' life of Aristotle.[71] The former includes most of the items in the modern canon that emerged from the mediaeval transmission and was eventually formulated by Bekker, whereas in Diogenes' catalogue fewer than ten out of more than one hundred entries can be safely said to correspond to surviving works, with a further fifteen or so partial identifications. Thirty-nine titles point to otherwise unknown works, while seventy-three titles are cited elsewhere but do not form part of our surviving corpus. Barnes cast doubt on Andronicus' claims to the paternity of this radical transformation by arguing that Diogenes' list is not necessarily representative of the pre-Andronican state of affairs because traces of 'Andronican' works can be found earlier than Andronicus.[72]

First of all we need to establish that Diogenes' list is more than a library catalogue and reflects levels of familiarity with Aristotelian philosophy in the Hellenistic period more broadly. This is supported by its correspondence to the doxography that follows it (Diog. Laert. 5.28–34): both the list and the doxography's account of logic ignore the *Categories* and *On Interpretation*, while the doxography ascribes the content of *On Interpretation* to the *Prior Analytics* and in turn that of the *Prior Analytics* to the *Posterior* (Diog. Laert. 5.29).[73] The other indications we have for the pre-Andronican state of affairs are that (i) there was some form of catalogue that was overtaken by Andronicus' (the latter was 'now current' at the time of Plutarch, see above p. 93); (ii) the works were not placed in any particular order or, at least, not in a thematic order (this was Andronicus' contribution according to Porphyry, see above pp. 96–7). As it happens, we know of such a catalogue that lacks thematic order precisely from Diogenes Laertius.

Barnes' main witness for the early availability of 'Andronican' treatises is Cicero. Cicero cites the *Rhetoric* (*Orat.* 114; *De orat.* 2.160), but also reports material on prose rhythm now found in its third book, which is thought not to have been part of the

---

[71] Barnes, 'Roman Aristotle' (n. 34 above), pp. 31–2, 41–4.
[72] Barnes, 'Roman Aristotle' (n. 34 above), pp. 44–63.
[73] On the doxography see Sharples, *Peripatetic Philosophy* (n. 41 above), pp. 31–4. It appears that the *Analytics* suffered especially from a proliferation of pseudepigrapha: Diogenes' list (no. 49) mentions nine books of *Prior Analytics* and later commentators say that forty books of *Analytics* were found in the library of Alexandria, of which only four were genuine (see Philoponus, *in Cat.* 7,26–9).

treatise pre-Andronicus (see Diog. Laert. catalogue, nos. 78, '*Art of Rhetoric*, two books' and 87, '*On Lexis*, two books'). But as Barnes admits, Cicero does not refer to any Aristotelian work in these prose rhythm passages, which means that he could have known a two-volume *Rhetoric* alongside separate collections of material on technical and stylistic matters.[74] Furthermore, Cicero provides evidence that a *Topics* by Aristotle was known before Andronicus, because he professes to translate or report from it in his own *Topica*. The circulation of versions of 'Topics' before Andronicus is confirmed by Diogenes' catalogue (see nos. 55, 60), but the content of Cicero's work bears no resemblance to our *Topics*. The freedom with which Cicero credits his own material to an Aristotelian 'Topics' means that there was no established consensus on what books and what kind of content belonged in that treatise. Thus Andronicus can get credit for arranging the work in its present form. In this case, the changes he effected were more than simply 'enlarging' or 'embellishing'.[75]

Barnes goes on to discuss Andronicus' putative involvement in the construction of the ethical treatises and the *Physics* and *Metaphysics*. Cicero clearly knew two ethical treatises in a form different from that of Diogenes' catalogue and must have been aware of the title *Nicomachean Ethics* which is absent from that catalogue (*Fin.* 5.12).[76] We cannot, therefore, ascribe the title or the construction of our *Nicomachean Ethics* (or Cicero's, if they are different) to Andronicus.[77] Regarding the *Physics*, Barnes shows that scholars misinterpreted the evidence when claiming that Andronicus inserted Book 7, thus 'creating' the treatise. The crucial text here is Simplicius, *in Phys.* 923,3–925,2; what Simplicius in fact says there is that some people, including Andronicus, felt that Aristotle's physical treatise should be divided into two sections, five books of *Physics* and three books of *On motion* respectively. Support for such a division could be found in cross-references within Aristotle's own works (Simplicius, *in Phys.* 923,18–924,13). The grounds for the rather unproductive division after Book 5 (rather than Book 4) must have been that Theophrastus referred to a sentence from Book 5 under the title *Physics*.[78] We can see from this that some decision-making on divisions and book titles by Andronicus (and others?) depended heavily on cross-references and citations, seemingly at the expense of more substantial considerations of content; we may compare this to what happened with *On Interpretation* (see above, p. 97). Finally, on the *Metaphysics* Barnes is right to point out that we have no information linking Andronicus's name with its creation.[79]

---

[74] Barnes, 'Roman Aristotle' (n. 34 above), pp. 51–4. The passages on prose rhythm are *Orat.* 172, 192–3, 214, 228; *De orat.* 3.182.

[75] Cf. Barnes, 'Roman Aristotle' (n. 34 above), pp. 54–7, and especially p. 54 for the disparate works that Andronicus may have assembled into the new *Topics*. It is possible that he excluded some books of the Hellenistic 'Topics' from his version, because they are listed separately in Ptolemy's catalogue (nos. 70 and 71, Düring (n. 54 above), p. 227). For a brief survey and further references on the problems of Cicero's *Topica* see Sharples, *Peripatetic Philosophy* (n. 41 above), p. 39.

[76] The *EN* is absent from Ptolemy's catalogue too, but this has been taken as an error of transmission.

[77] This may prove to be to Andronicus' credit if we follow Barnes, 'Roman Aristotle' (n. 34 above), pp. 58–9: 'our *EN* is an absurdity, surely put together by a desperate scribe or an unscrupulous bookseller'.

[78] See Barnes, 'Roman Aristotle' (n. 34 above), pp. 36, 60, 67–9; the five-plus-three division was also mentioned by Adrastus, Simplicius, *in Phys.* 4,8–16.

[79] Barnes, 'Roman Aristotle' (n. 34 above), pp. 61–3.

As a result, we cannot get any clearer on the pre-Andronican state of affairs on the basis of Cicero or of the compilation of the *Physics* or *Metaphysics*. Our evidence, such as it is, rests on the comparison of Ptolemy's catalogue with the earlier one found in Diogenes Laertius. There can be little doubt that the arrangement of the corpus that was adopted by Andronicus (as seen in Ptolemy) made a lasting impact and defined the way we still read Aristotle. It is likely that some form of Ptolemy's work was known well into the Late Antiquity (because it forms the background of some late antique Lives of Aristotle);[80] therefore editors and scribes could have consulted the catalogue when collecting groups of treatises into large codices. The real point of contention that drives our judgement about Andronicus' importance is whether this canonical arrangement is the result of an active intervention on his behalf or whether what he encountered was already in the shape that we find it in Ptolemy.

Diogenes' catalogue may not represent the exact books available to everyone across the Hellenistic world, but it is nevertheless indicative. It suggests that books from various treatises were circulating individually, many works had different titles and there was no thematic division into groups of works. Therefore Andronicus' impact comes first and foremost from the presentation of a complete, systematic corpus following a rationalised order throughout. Porphyry was of the opinion that the pre-Andronican state of the Aristotelian corpus was one of disorder, comparable to the confused (*phurdên*) initial chronological publication of Plotinus' works. Andronicus' grouping and ordering of Aristotle's books does not need to be undisputed to be considered influential. Its serving as a starting point for further investigation is equally important, for example in the case of Adrastus' work *On the order of Aristotle's works* in the second century CE, which argued for placing the *Topics* immediately following the *Categories* (Simplicius, *in Cat.* 16,2). All later debate on the correct order and the authenticity of the contents of the corpus depends on the awareness of a specific Aristotelian canon: Porphyry and Plutarch tell us that Andronicus organised and disseminated such a canon, and Ptolemy via the Arabic witness confirms that this canon resembled very closely the one that eventually prevailed.

The more evidence we find that this form and organisation of the corpus goes back to Aristotle himself,[81] the more we should value Andronicus for restoring it in the face of the Hellenistic 'disorder' witnessed by the catalogue preserved in Diogenes Laertius. Barnes can be misleading when he says that 'Andronicus cannot have claimed to have invented the treatise (sc. the *Metaphysics*) himself',[82] because this implies that we should expect Andronicus to make such a claim. On the contrary, I suggest that we should expect him to claim the exact opposite, namely that he was restoring Aristotle's original corpus and canon by revealing the philosophical system that was always there, but had become obscured in the course of transmission. We have some indication of the evidence he could have used to support this claim, which pertains to his classification of Aristotelian works by genre. Andronicus quoted some spurious

---

[80] See Düring (n. 54), pp. 105, 116–19.
[81] See Burnyeat, 'Aristotelian Revisions' (n. 39 above), esp. pp. 178–9, n. 3.
[82] Barnes, 'Roman Aristotle' (n. 34 above), p. 63.

correspondence between Aristotle and Alexander attributing the publication of the 'acroamatic' writings to Aristotle himself.[83] The distinction between 'acroamatic' and 'exoteric' works must indeed be very old – there are references to 'exoteric' works in the surviving Aristotelian treatises[84] – but the letters published by Andronicus reinforced the perception that it was the 'acroamatic' writings that contained privileged teaching reserved for devoted disciples. In this way Andronicus could justify as genuinely Aristotelian his separate listing of only esoteric works in thematic/systematic order, and support the claim that this privileged section of his *pinax* was the 'essential Aristotle'.[85] With Andronicus' catalogue to hand, readers and editors could distinguish easily between 'essential' and 'non-essential' texts, and slowly but surely this particular value judgement resulted in the eclipse of all the works that Aristotle had made widely available in his own lifetime.

Conclusion

If we recall at this point the information gathered on the state of Plato's text in the first century BCE, we can see that by comparison the study of Aristotle's text was indeed revolutionised. In the case of the Aristotelian corpus our sources tell a story of true *peripeteia*, with the appearance of new texts or at least new copies with special claims of antiquity and pedigree, and with the standardisation and ordering of the canon in Andronicus' *Pinakes*. A scrutiny of our sources has shown that it was the processes of cataloguing, canon-formation and corpus-organisation that had the greatest impact on the texts we now read, and not the appearance of new 'editions' and text-critical initiatives. If this appears counter-intuitive, we should remember that judgements about the importance or otherwise of ancient editorial activity can be misleading if they are too dependent on modern experiences and expectations.

---

[83] Simplicius, *in Phys.* 8,16–39; Plut. *Alex.* 7.6–8. The explicit connection of Andronicus to these letters comes from Gellius, *NA* 20.5.11–12.
[84] *EE* 1218b34; *EN* 1102a26. Cf. Cic. *Att.* 4.16.2, *Fin.* 5.12.
[85] This sharp distinction escalated, to the extent that Alexander is reported to have treated the content of the dialogues as 'falsehoods' compared to the 'truth' of the acroamatic works, Elias (David), *in Cat.* 115,3–13.

2

Boethus' Aristotelian Ontology*

Marwan Rashed

Boethus is surely one of the most important thinkers of the first century BCE. Though only few testimonies, and no clear fragment, remain, their number and content are sufficient to show how insightful he was in commenting upon Aristotle.[1] It is not just that he was typical of this first generation of commentators who have struck modern historians by their free spirit towards Aristotle's text.[2] Boethus' fragments on substance testify to more than a free attitude towards the Philosopher: it is also possible to recognize, through the many layers of the tradition – Alexander, Porphyry, Iamblichus and Simplicius – a coherent and unitary doctrine. His doctrine, of course, is not un-Aristotelian; it does not even stand somewhere halfway between Aristotle and other thinkers of Antiquity, the Stoics in particular (even if it is obviously inspired by a general Stoic atmosphere). Boethus has consciously built, out of some rare Aristotelian indications, a certain kind of Aristotelianism, among other possible ones.[3] This doctrinal approach is probably both the cause and the effect of a cultural fact: the Peripatos' nearly exclusive focus, in the first century BCE, on the *Categories*.[4] For sure, the treatise of the *Categories*, by itself, does not necessarily produce a definite account of the world. But by contrast with what is the case with other parts of the Aristotelian

---

This article first appeared as 'Boethius' Aristotelian ontology' by Marwan Rashed in Malcolm Schofield (ed.), *Aristotle, Plato and Pythagoreanism in the First Century BC* (2013), pp. 53–77 © Cambridge University Press 2013, reproduced with permission.

* I would like to thank Riccardo Chiaradonna for his invaluable remarks on a previous version of this chapter, as well as Malcolm Schofield and two anonymous reviewers for their very helpful comments. I am very grateful to Richard Sarabji whose numerous remarks and critical comments have allowed me greatly to improve the first version of this chapter. The remaining errors are mine.
[1] Curiously enough, there has been until now no collection of Boethus' fragments. I am currently working, together with Riccardo Chiaradonna and Philippe Hoffmann, on such a project. Our book, to be published by De Gruyter, will include all the fragments (Greek and Arabic), a French translation and a commentary.
[2] See P. Moraux, *Der Aristotelismus bei den Griechen von Andronikos bis Alexander von Aphrodisias I: Die Renaissance des Aristotelismus im I. Jh. v. Chr.*, (Berlin: De Gruyter, 1973), pp. 98–99 and 105–13.
[3] See M. Rashed, *Essentialisme: Alexandre d'Aphrodise entre logique, physique et cosmologie* (Berlin: De Gruyter, 2007), pp. 22–6.
[4] See R. Chiaradonna, 'Platonist Approaches to Aristotle from Antiochus of Ascalon to Eudorus of Alexandria (and beyond)', in Malcolm Schofield, ed., *Aristotle, Plato and Pythagoreanism in the First Century BC*, (Cambridge: Cambridge University Press, 2013), pp. 28–52.

corpus, its basic ontological features seem naturally at home in the framework of a doctrine holding the primacy of the individual material substance.

I. Boethus' Criterion of Substantiality

1. Boethus' theory of substance and predication

It is not just blind following of the tradition – namely, the fact that his knowledge of the Aristotelian corpus would be limited to the *Categories* – if Boethus decided to put matter and the primary substance of the *Categories* at the centre of his ontology. A fragment preserved by Simplicius testifies to the fact that (i) he was aware of the tripartition of *Metaphysics* 7; (ii) he consciously interpreted this tripartition as a *choice* between three possible candidates to the title of substance; and (iii) he opted, against the obvious invitation of *Metaphysics* 7, for what could resemble the first substances of the *Categories*, if one is to follow Aristotle's famous fourfold distinction[5]:

	in a subject	not in a subject
said of a subject	general properties	genera, species and differentiae of primary substances
not said of a subject	particular properties	primary substances

Only matter and the composite of matter and form, so Boethus, will match the criteria for being a (first) substance.[6] Let us translate Simplicius' important testimony:

> It would have been more convenient, <Boethus> says, to mention an extra difficulty, namely that whereas in other writings, after having divided substance in three, he said that substance is said to be in different senses the matter, the form and the composite, he claims here that substance is a unitary category. But what is this category, and how will he subordinate to it these three substances, which are not said according to the same account? Adressing this question, Boethus says that the account of the primary substance is suitable to the matter and the composite. For to both of them belongs the fact of neither being said of a subject nor being in a subject (since none of them is in something else). This being said, the composite, even if it is not in something else, has the form which is in it as something being in something else, namely the matter, whereas the matter does not even have something which would be in something else. They have therefore something common and something different, inasmuch as matter is matter of something *qua* matter, as well as subject, whereas the composite substance is not *of* something. Thus, says Boethus, the matter and the composite will belong to the category of

---

[5] *Cat.* 2, 1a20-b9.
[6] As remarked by R. Chiaradonna in his forthcoming commentary (see above, n. 1), 'in the whole of this argument, Boethus passes directly from the category of substance to primary substance: it is as if secondary substances did not exist in the *Categories*'. R. Chiaradonna devotes a fine analysis to Boethus' critical stance with regard to the universals.

substance, while the form will be outside substance and fall into some other category, either quality or quantity or some other one.[7]

First, or *genuine* substances, must be *genuine* subjects, i.e. things existing *per se*, i.e. things of which everything else is predicated without being themselves possibly predicated of anything. And in an Aristotelian framework, quantities and qualities do not exist *per se*: they need a material subject to inhere in. Hence Boethus' ontological claim: since to be a substance is to be a real subject of predication, it follows that to be a substance is to be a material subject. To be a wordly substance, for Boethus – i.e. to be anything except (perhaps) the Prime Mover –, is to be a concrete and unitary lump of matter. His system, up to this point, seems coherent. Its basic principle is the following:

X is a substance iff X is a subject and X is not in a subject.

As Simplicius' testimony makes it clear, Boethus is conscious of the radical implications of his claim. He knows that if the individual substances of the *Categories* are Aristotle's last ontological word, the claim of the form to substantiality, such as we find expressed in the central books of the *Metaphysics*, becomes very problematic, to say the least.[8] But Boethus is not the kind of commentator to conceal every difficulty in a verbose mess. He is a philosopher, who accepts the consequences of his ontological decisions, even if they appear to contradict Aristotle's authority. That is obviously the reason why he explicitly rejects the substantiality of the form. The form is in a subject, and the form is very unlikely to be a subject.

2. Boethus on inherence

Which kind of texts Boethus might have in mind when claiming that the form was, after all, a predicate or, what for him amounted to the same, something inhering in some material subject, and not itself a subject? A first answer may be that he was simply taking literally the passages of the *Metaphysics* where Aristotle himself spoke of the form as a predicate of the matter.[9] I would of course not reject a possible influence of these texts of the *Metaphysics*. But another piece of evidence suggests another possibility which, in view of the later evolution of the problem, appears to me more promising: the list of the various kinds of *being in something* (*en tini einai*) at *Physics* 4.3, 210a14–24:

> The next step we must take is to see in how many ways one thing is said to be *in* another. In one way, as a finger is in a hand, and generally a part in a whole. In another way, as a whole is in its parts; for there is no whole over and above the parts. Again, as man is in animal, and in general a species in a genus. Again, as the

---

[7] Simplicius, *in Cat.* 78,5–20.
[8] I shall come back on this question below, pp. 115–19.
[9] For a complete list, see J. Brunschwig, 'La forme, prédicat de la matière ?', in P. Aubenque, ed., *Etudes sur la* Métaphysique *d'Aristote* (Paris: Vrin, 1979), pp. 131–66. J. Brunschwig has argued, and I am convinced, that the 'predication' at stake in these passages in not the kind we find in the *Categories*. It is rather a *determination* of the matter by the form, i.e. a kind of relation which does not preclude, as such, the substantiality of the form.

genus is in the species, and in general a part of the species in its definition. Again, as health is in the hot and the cold, and in general the form in the matter. Again, as the affairs of Greece are in the King, and generally events are in in their primary motive agent. Again, as a thing is in its good, and generally in its end, i.e. in that for the sake of which. And most properly of all, as something is in a vessel, and generally in a place.[10]

The first thing to be recalled is that these lines come from Aristotle's treatment of place. We are sure, for at least three reasons, that Boethus read them with some attention. First, we are told by later commentators that Boethus considered physics to be an appropriate starting point for philosophy.[11] The reason was probably that according to him, Aristotle's *Physics* contained a natural description of the world around us, which is necessary before embarking on the study of logic. The second reason is that we find attested, in Themistius' and Simplicius' commentaries on the *Physics*, that Boethus objected to Aristotle's conception of the relation between time and the counting soul.[12] That betrays a fairly good knowledge of *Physics* 4, where our text on the various types of inherence appears. Third, this text *may* have been quoted extensively, and rephrased, at at least one place in Boethus' commentary on the *Categories*. The Byzantine manuscript *Laur.* 71.32 has notoriously preserved interesting fragments from a lost commentary on that work, which has been attributed to Boethus by Pamela Huby.[13] And one of these fragments is an account of the various significations of 'in something' obviously inspired by *Physics* 4.3. Here is the text in question:

(1) 'In something' has eleven uses: as the attribute is *in* the substance (*hôs to sumbebêkos en têi ousiai*), as the parts are *in* the whole, as the whole is *in* the parts, as the form is *in* the matter (*hôs to eidos en têi hulêi*), and further as the genus is *in* the species and the species *in* the genus, and in addition to these the affairs of the subjects are '*in*' [= depend upon] the ruler and those of the ruler '*in*' the subjects, and as being *in* a vessel or *in* place and time. (2) Well, since there are so many uses of 'in something', it is worth asking why it is only in respect of those two relations that categories have been established. We say: some of the other meanings of 'in something' complement each other, like the parts and the whole and the genera and the species and the ruler and the subjects. (3) Others cannot subsist separately, like the form [*eidos*] in the matter and the attribute in the subject, which is also the shape [form, *morphê*] of the subject; for this reason the subject is given a name with reference to it, such as 'white' and 'having increased', and [so] with the other categories that exist in substance. How then in these cases could the one thing be *in* the other in the strict sense, when they do not even exist substantially in the strict sense separated from each other, but only in the thought in which we separate

---

[10] I quote from J. Barnes, ed., *The Complete Works of Aristotle: The Revised Oxford* Translation, 2 vols (Princeton: Princeton University Press, 1984), vol. 1, p. 357.
[11] Philoponus, *in Cat.* 5,16–18; Elias, *in Cat.* 117,21–2.
[12] Simplicius, *in Phys.* 759,18–20, Themistius, *in Phys.* 160,26–8.
[13] Pamela M. Huby, 'An excerpt from Boethus of Sidon's commentary on the *Categories* ?', *Classical Quarterly* 31 (1981), 398–409. I will come back on this ascription below, p. 118, n. 39.

the genera ? (4) For this reason each of the [cases] like this was not judged worthy of a category of its own; but the things that are in time and in place were [judged worthy]. In these alone, since one [thing] contains and the other is contained, each preserving its own nature and neither becoming a part of the other or complementing the other. (5) For in these alone 'in something' becomes a definite nature subsisting in the relation; and for this reason each of them has been judged worthy of a category of its own. For the things that are in time and in place are most clearly different from time and place; that is why things which are numerically identical are at different times in a different place and time.[14]

In the list of the *Physics*, the crucial sentence was '... as health is in the hot and the cold, and in general the form in the matter' (ll. 20–21). Health and, more generally (*holôs*), form, are entities inhering in a subject. The health, even if it is somehow essential to the living body or its part, inheres in them, so that we rightly say: 'Peter is healthy' or 'Peter's heart is healthy'; similarly, the form is inherent in the subject in the sense that it would be impossible for it to exist, were not some matter ready to receive it. The author of the fragment preserved in *Laur.* 71.32, however, does *not* assimilate the inherence of the form in the matter to that of the attribute in the substance. His present aim is to explain why, among the many uses of 'in something', there are only two categories concerned, namely place and time. His answer is that these two categories are the only ones where a *real* (i.e. not merely *in thought*) relation takes place between what contains and what is contained. The other cases are explained away for two main reasons. Some items 'complement each other'. That probably means that there is a sort of circle taking place between them. The author implicitly holds that as soon as the genus is 'in' the species and the species 'in' the genus, neither the genus nor the species is an independent being, characterized by a category *per se*. Other items, on the other hand, 'cannot subsist separately'. Here, we have no circle. The substance is not 'in' its attribute. Only the attribute is in the substance. But the attribute cannot be given a category, since it cannot exist without the substance, nor the substance without it. The reason for this is probably that every *particular* attribute needs a subject to inhere in, and that every subject cannot exist deprived of *any* attribute. The inherence of the form in the matter belongs to this type. But if it does really differ from the inherence of the attribute in the substance, we should probably conclude that the form does not belong to any secondary category. Before discussing this issue below, we cannot but stress, for the time being, that the present fragment remains ambiguous. As such, its formulation might be accepted by someone holding that the form falls in a category other than substance, as well as by someone claiming that the form *is* substance.

Despite this negative result, I think that this text of the *Physics* is crucial for our understanding of why Boethus did not accept the form to be a substance. An interesting clue appears later in Simplicius' commentary, when the discussion focusses on the tenth category, that of *having* (*ekhein*). The Stoics, Boethus tells us, are wrong to rank the *ekhein* among the *pôs ekhein*. They do not grasp that *skhesis* (a noun from *ekhein*)

---

[14] The fragment is edited in T. Waitz, *Aristotelis Organon Graece*, 2 vols (Leipzig: Hahn, 1844–46), vol. 1, pp. 22,28–23,8. I borrow the English translation from R. W. Sharples, *Peripatetic Philosophy 200 BC to AD 200* (Cambridge: Cambridge University Press, 2010), p. 67.

is a homonymous term. For a *skhesis* is either 'of the thing to itself', or 'of the thing to something else', or 'of something else to the subject'.[15] Among these three significations, the first one expresses a *pôs ekhein*, the second a relation (*pros ti*) and the third, so we understand, a 'possession' in the restricted and proper meaning of the term.[16] Then follows a difficult passage, which I translate in its entirety:

> Unless we have, says Boethus, as significations (*sêmainomena*) of *having*, on the one hand what amounts to having anything, either part or field (*khôrion*), which is perhaps also what signifies (*sêmainetai*) the expression taken in itself and, on the other hand, all these other things, in syntactical composition. For if "the field", or "the father", or "the part", is put ahead, it produces the differentia'. To this sense (*sêmasian*) of *having*, he says, is subordinated some other one, which is assigned, in particular, to the case of *possessing*. 'If then someone sets up the category according to its first signification (*kata to prôton sêmainomenon*), he will include into this category *being-wise* (*to phronein*), *being-prudent* (*to sôphronein*) and *being-healthy* (*to hugiainein*) – for *being-wise* amounts to having wisdom –, while we will take apart from it the category of action and passion and it will be separated from the relative (for the man who has acquired will belong to the relative, the fact of having acquired to the *having*, the father to the relative, the fact of being a father inhering itself in that of *having* a son). But if it is according to its second signification (*kata to deuteron* <sc. *sêmainomenon*>), the other significations of having (*ta men alla tou ekhein sêmainomena*) will be included into the other categories, while only the cases of possession of some possessed item will belong to this one'. Such is our account of the considerations of the noble Boethus.[17]

We must be cautious, when interpreting this text, not to be misled by the careless use made by its author of the word *sêmainomenon*. When he employs it in the plural (*sêmainomena*), the author refers to the different significations of the various formulas where the verb *ekhein* appears. He does not speak there of the different significations of the category of *having*. When he alludes to this point, he uses the same word in the singular (*sêmainomenon*). Thus, 'the first *sêmainomenon*' and 'the second *sêmainomenon*' (singular) are not, respectively, the first and the second sense of the *word ekhein*, but the first acception of the *category* itself. Once we have grasped that point, the text is rather plain. Boethus suggested two possible extensions for the category of *ekhein*. According to the first, it includes the second kind of significations (*sêmainomena*), i.e. those where *ekhein* may signify either a possession or more than a simple possession. According to the second, it includes only the first kind, i.e. those significations according to which *ekhein* refers to 'the possession of some possessed item'.

The most remarkable feature of this text, for us, is his readiness to consider *being-healthy* (*hugiainein*) as translatable into *having-health*. The case at stake, in Aristotle's text, was 'having as a state and condition or some other quality (we are said to have

---

[15] Simplicius, *in Cat.* 373,7–18.
[16] Simplicius, ibid.
[17] Simplicius, *in Cat.* 373,18–32.

knowledge and virtue)'.[18] Boethus added a new example, which had no textual basis in the *Categories*. By so doing, he reminded us of our passage of the *Physics*. Thus, if the form *is in* the matter as one of the cases of *en tini*, it is because the matter *has* the form. The matter, then, is clearly the *subject* of the form.

3. A confirmation: 'substance', 'relative' (sic) and 'having' according to Boethus

We must here face a difficulty. In the text just translated, the father is said to be a correlate (*pros ti*), the *being-a-father* a possession (namely, the possession of a son). Similarly, the *possessor* was a correlate, his *possessing* a case of having. But we know from the readers of Alexander's lost commentary on the *Physics* that Boethus drew a distinction between the word 'matter' (*hulê*), which refers to a physical state deprived of form and the word 'subject' (*hupokeimenon*), which designates matter inasmuch as it is envisaged in its connection with a form.[19] If our argument is valid, thus, we should say that what Aristotle calls 'matter' in the passage of the *Physics* is matter as connected with form, i.e. *hulê* as a *hupokeimenon*. Secondly, and more importantly, we should conclude that the subject, by definition (to be a subject is to be a subject *of something*), is a correlate. But in this case, and if we hold that no relative is a substance, the subject will not be a substance, which contradicts the main principle of Boethus' ontology.

The answer is that Boethus seems very keen on distinguishing, for every item, its concrete nature when it is taken in itself from its functional being, which belongs to it insofar as it interacts with other items. The crucial sentence, from this point of view, appears at the end of the text just translated: 'the man who has acquired will belong to the relative, the fact of having acquired to the having, the father to the relative, the fact of being a father inhering itself in that of having a son'. Taken in itself, *father* belongs to the category of relation, because it denotes nothing but the fact of being a relative, i.e. one element in a set of at least two correlated elements. But the relation itself, which links together this relative to its correlative (the son), belongs to the category of having.

Prima facie, we might try to transpose this distinction to the case of the subject and its form. Boethus would have said that the subject taken in itself (i.e. as matter) will belong to the category of substance, the fact of being a subject to the category relation, and the very fact of being the subject of this form to that of having. All the more so, since it is actually more or less what he says, in an apparently similar case, when he adresses the question of the category to which the parts of the body will belong:

> Boethus was right to concede that the hand and the head belong to the relatives inasmuch as they are parts, but not inasmuch as they are hand, i.e. not by the very fact of being a hand or a head – for in such a way, according to him, they are substances. Let us then now consider their being relatives as dictated by their being parts with respect to wholes, and nothing absurd will follow.[20]

---

[18] *Cat.* 15, 15b18–19.
[19] See Themistius, *in Phys.* 26,20 sqq. and Simplicius, *in Phys.* 211,15–18.
[20] Simplicius, *in Cat.* 188,3–7.

Similarly, the subject *qua* subject, i.e. as a correlate of the form, will belong to the category of *pros ti*; its being informed will fall in the category of having: it is because the material subject *has* a form that it is informed; and the subject *qua* matter will be substance, as well as the father *qua* man is substance.

But that would be to forget that according to the fragment in *Laur.* 71.32, which again may have Boethus as its author, the inherence of the form or the accident *as such* is insufficient to produce a category of its own, for the reason that the form and the accident are nothing but 'dependences' of the subject they inhere in. Boethus' answer would therefore have been more radical: we cannot view subject and form as two relatives because a relation, in order to obtain, must link together at least two *subjects*.[21] That is precisely why Boethus adressed this puzzle in the case of the parts and the whole, but not of matter and form.

This discussion sheds some light, by contrast, on an issue which will be important when we address Alexander's position, i.e. that of knowing whether we can consider matter and form as two parts of the composite. For Boethus, the answer is clearly negative. The passage of the *Physics*, by distinguishing the form in the matter from the part in the whole, is enough to exclude, implicitly, the possibility of considering the form as a part of the composite – since the form is dependent upon the matter for its existence. Alexander does not agree. On the contrary, he will not refrain from justifying the form's being a substance by relying on the fact that it is a part of the composite substance.

II. Alexander of Aphrodisias against Boethus on Substance

Alexander's opposition to Boethus allows us to see more clearly in what sense Boethus' ontology is neither a piece of 'Aristotelian orthodoxy' nor un-Aristotelian, but nothing but a possible way of reading Aristotle. The main interest of the commentators is precisely to construct, out of different possible doctrines latent in the Master's corpus, a coherent interpretation. The tensions, and even the contradictions, in Aristotle's writings have given rise to Boethus' interpretation, which identified the substance with the subject of the predication and to Alexander's reading which, as we shall immediately see, tried to substitute Boethus' matter by form at the centre of Aristotle's ontology.

1. The parts of the substance are substances

In a plurality of texts,[22] Alexander holds onto the substantiality of the form by relying on the principle that:

---

[21] More on this below, pp. 119–22.
[22] I have discussed these texts in Rashed, *Essentialisme* (n. 3 above), pp. 35–81.

<PSS> *the parts of the substance are substances.*

The substance in question is obviously the *sunolon*, the parts of which are the matter and the form. In the majority of the texts where he mentions this principle, Alexander formulates it as if it were an analytical rule. The mere fact of being a substance and of having parts would analytically lead to the conclusion that these parts also are substances.

Let us first try to figure out a case where such a rule may obtain. A simple example would be that of two-dimensional figures. Since neither the line nor the point is a part of a figure, we are entitled to say that the parts of any two-dimensional figure are two-dimensional figures. This proposition is true (i.e. the state of affairs it describes obtains) because it is plain, in its case, that being two-dimensional is an analytical condition of being a part of a two-dimensional figure. The case is non problematic because (i) a two-dimensional figure is equivalent to the sum of its two-dimensional parts and, more importantly perhaps, because (ii) any conceivable part of a two-dimensional figure is an *extensive* part of this figure.

The case of biological substance is more difficult, chiefly because we do not know how to define the 'part' of a living body. First, it is not plain that any tri-dimensional part of our constitutive matter is a *part* of our living body. If, for instance, I am cutting an arbitrary slice of a human body, I will extract from it a tri-dimensional cylinder but not a real *part* of this living body. To be a part of a living body is to have some functional unity, as in the case of its external members or internal organs. It is a crucial aspect of Aristotle's biological ontology to claim that the living substance's organs are substances. His reason for this doctrine has probably something to do with the impossibility of giving a satisfactory definition, in terms of form and matter, of the living body as a whole. The pseudo-definition of man as 'rational mortal animal', apart from not being truly Aristotelian, conceals the fact that we would be wholly unable to give a similar definition for any other creature.

Alexander, however, did never accept the 'biological turn' of Aristotle's *De partibus animalium*. This text is even Aristotle's sole major treatise that he does *never* quote. Not only does he make no mention of the physiology of Books 2–4, but, more interestingly, even the methodology of the first book is totally absent from his commentaries and personal monographs. Alexander has tried, again and again, to make the 'real' substance – which corresponds to the biological species – and the definition coincide. That explains that when Alexander claims PSS, he is not primarily thinking of the bodily parts of the living being, but of its parts as a *sunolon*, namely matter and form.

This choice, however, gives rise to still greater difficulties. First, even if they are not solely *extensive* parts, the bodily organs are *also* extensive. Each one is clearly existing, with its own identity and causal distinctiveness – i.e., each one is a relatively independent body which exists as such for the sake of something. There is nothing similar in the case of matter and form, which are distinguishable only on the basis of an analogy between living beings and artifacts. But even this dubious operation is not sufficient to produce a clear idea of each of them. What is really the form of man, as opposed to his matter? The most we can say is that each human being occupies a three-dimensional space characterized by a precise kind of material information. Sublunar matter is organised in this space in such a way that *there* is a man and not, for example, a bronze charioteer or a corpse.

As a consequence, it is hardly possible to interpret PSS as analytical. As soon as we take it this way, it has simply no meaning, because, except in the case of the bodily organs which are precisely *not* at stake here, we have no clear idea of what a part of a substance is – i.e., we have no clear idea of how matter and form can be viewed as *parts* rather than mere *elements* of the *sunolon*.

Another interesting difficulty is that Alexander never uses this principle in order to assess the substantiality of the matter. This fact is in itself a good sign pointing to the polemical context he is engaged in. PSS, which appears for the first time under Alexander's pen (and which I guess he was the first to articulate in this sense),[23] was motivated by the necessity of answering Boethus' theory of substance and predication. In other words, Alexander agrees that matter has some substantiality of its own. What he wants to show is that form is at least as substantial as Boethus' matter.

But if not analytical, and if in practice not even symmetrical, how then to interpret PSS? It seems to me that Alexander does not use it as a scientific rule, but only as a sort of tag, expressing the epistemic fact that we can know, *on some other grounds*, that the form – and, as we shall see, the form more than the matter – is substance and that it is the substantiality of the form which in turn explains the substantiality of the composite – the latter being the only clear substance *we* are acquainted with in the phenomenal world. The sole passage where Alexander gives some explanation in this sense is his monograph *On the Soul*. Probably because he adressed it to a broader audience, he took there the pains to explain away some possible misconception:

> Each of them [sc. form and matter] is, however, substance. For as well as matter, so is form substance. For the parts of substance are substances, or rather, because each of them is subtance, the composite of both is also a substance and a certain unique nature, not like the things stemming from art, which are substances according to the subject and the matter but qualities according to their forms.[24]

This text leaves no doubt as to Alexander's intentions when he relies on PSS. He tries then to articulate, in terms acceptable to Boethus and his eventual followers (i.e. people placing the composite at the centre of their ontology), a truth about the substantiality of the form which they explicitly reject. It remains for us to show how Alexander thinks it possible to interpret the form as a substance.

2. A new theory of inherence

I shall start with a *Quaestio* preserved only in Arabic, where Alexander aims at showing that the differentia of substance falls in the category of substance and not in some other

---

[23] Cf. K. Wurm, *Substanz und Qualität: Ein Beitrag zur Interpretation der plotinischen Traktate VI 1, 2, 3* (Berlin: De Gruyter, 1973), pp. 184–5 and n. 28.
[24] Alexander, *DA* 6,2–6.

category. Roughly speaking, his strategy consists in identifying the differentia (*diaphora*) with the form (*eidos*), to claim the substantiality of the latter by relying on PSS and concluding that the differentia belongs to the category of substance. Let us quote the relevant passage, towards the end of the *Quaestio*:

> The differentiae of the living being, which are not animals, are, however, substance. For the substance, since it is the genus of the living being, retains its nature as it is in the composite beings as well as in each one of the two things out of which the composite has its existence, namely: the form and the matter, the incorporal and the corporal substance.[25]

We find here PSS very crudely expressed. The author makes mention of it in the most possible analytical formulation, so that we may even be tempted to claim that he has deliberately cancelled the real principle at work under the usual tag, in order to make his argument run smoother. But this need not detain us here. What appears more worth of attention, in the vicinity of PSS, are the lines immediately following:

> For the discourse saying that the differentiae of substance are not substances because they do not receive the contraries belongs to someone deprived of understanding. For it is the individuals which are in the substance who receive the contraries, not the genera, the species and the differentiae, since they are all general.[26]

We see that immediately after having dwelt on PSS, Alexander mounts an attack against the *Peripatetic* identification of substantiality with the capacity of receiving the contraries, i.e., obviously, with the fact of being a subject. There is no place I am aware of in the corpus of the Greek commentators where the two criteria are so clearly opposed. Alexander's target here is not the Stoics or some other rival school, but an internal rival interpretation of Aristotle's ontology, put forward, in particular, by Boethus.

In a series of passages, Alexander expressed in nearly the same terms, in the form of a *nota bene* (*sêmeiôteon*), how we are to understand the relation of matter and form.[27] The most complete version appears in Alexander's commentary on the passage of the *Physics* we have already discussed in connection with Boethus.[28] It is transmitted under two forms, first in Simplicius' quotation in his own commentary on the *Physics*, and secondly in a more or less direct quotation from Alexander's commentary in the marginalia of the manuscript *Paris. Suppl. gr.* 643:

> It is to be noted that after having given as an example of 'in a subject' the health in the humours (for health is in them as in a subject), he added 'and in general the

---

[25] See Rashed, *Essentialisme* (n. 3 above), pp. 63–4.
[26] Ibid.
[27] *Mantissa* 5, 120,33–121,7 and Simplicius' quotations: *in Phys.* 270,26–34 and 552,18–24, *in Cael.* 279,5–9.
[28] See above, p. 106.

form in the matter', owing to the fact that the form is in a subject. But also in the second book of his treatise *On the Soul*, after having shown at the beginning that the soul is not a body, he assumed that the soul is 'in a subject' in the body: for what he says there to be 'in a subject' is what is, properly and adequately speaking, a being. He may say then in the *Categories* that no substance is 'in a susbtrate' *among the things* that are said in the *Categories* to be substances, in the same way as he would say that to *that* substance, nothing is contrary. Unless however all things which are subjects are those in which the things which must be in relation to them are 'in a subject', even if they are not in them in the same way as the things of the *Categories* are said to be 'in a subject'.[29]

We do not know whether Boethus himself argued from the inherence of the soul in the body to its non substantial status. We do know, however, that there was a deeply rooted tendency, in the early Peripatos, to consider the soul as a mere quality. It would not be very surprising, in this historical context, if he took the beginning of *De Anima* 2 as implying the qualitative status of the soul taken as the form of the living body.

Be this as it may, Alexander uses the Aristotelian evidence in an opposite direction. That the soul is more a being (*on*) than the body seems obvious for him. So is the fact, stressed in the opening chapter of *De Anima* 2, that the soul is in the body.[30] The conclusion is inescapable, and we have already met it in the Arabic *Quaestio*: the fact of being a subject is not a good criterion for substantiality; the *Categories* cannot be Aristotle's last word in ontological matters.

In the Paris fragment, Alexander suggests two possible ways of getting rid of the narrow normativity of the *Categories*. The first is to assume that the criteria of substantiality put forward in this work are relevant only for a peculiar kind of substances, namely the first substances of the *Categories*. Exactly as in the realm of the elements (*stoikheia*), some substantial forms are contrary to others,[31] we can affirm that some substance may be in a subject, provided that 'subject' is taken in the sense of the *Categories* but 'substance' is not.

An alternative solution is to introduce another sense not only of the word 'subject', but also of the word 'substance'. The subject, according to this proposal, is always dictated by the needs of what it is the subject of. This solution is constantly put forward by Alexander in a similar context. Let us compare the different expressions of the sentence:

- *in Phys.* 2.1, 192b34 sqq. *ap.* Simpl. 270,32–3: 'he now calls "in a substrate" what requires a certain substrate for its being' (*to hupokeimenou tinos pros to einai khrêizon en hupokeimenôi nun legei*).
- *in Phys.* 4.3, 210a20–1: 'All substrates are things in relation to which what is going to exist needs to be "in a substrate"' (*panta [ta] hupokeimena pros ha ta einai deomena en hupokeimenôi esti*).

---

[29] See M. Rashed, *Alexandre d'Aphrodise, Commentaire perdu à la* Physique *d'Aristote (Livres IV-VIII)* (Berlin: De Gruyter, 2011), pp. 191–2.
[30] Alexander is actually simplifying the issue: Aristotle only says that the body as opposed to the soul is subject and matter.
[31] Allusion to *GC* 2.8, 335a3–6.

- *in Cael.* 278b1–3 *ap.* Simpl. 279,7–8: 'by "the form in the underlying matter" he means more generally that which requires a certain substrate' (*to eidos en hupokeimenêi têi hulêi legei koinoteron hôs hupokeimenou tinos deomenon*).
- *Mantissa* 5, 121,6: 'what needs some substrate for its being' (*ho deitai pros to einai hupokeimenou tinos*).

In each of these passages, Alexander argues that in the case of the form, to be in a subject does not amount to being 'received' in some underlying matter already there, but to being in need of some matter to exist *qua* form. It is not just a question of terminology. Alexander obviously wants to stress that we must not envisage the form as passive, ie. as a pure object or state possessed by the (really existing) subject. He claims, on the contrary, that the form is the real active principle, and that the matter is nothing but a condition of exercise of the form. In other terms, the matter is nothing but the concrete, tri-dimensional realisation of the sensible form as it is. It is the form that *has* some matter and not, as postulated by Boethus, the matter that *has* some form. That explains the indefinite adjective *ti* with *hupokeimenon*. A sensible form can be realized by one material disposition only. The word *ti*, here, means a *certain* subject and not *whatever* subject. The human form, for example, can be realized in one and only one material configuration.

We can now understand Alexander's answer to Boethus. To the principle of the substantiality of the subject, we must substitute the principle of the substantiality of the parts of the substance. And to achieve this exegetical turn, we must substitute, to a canonical doctrine of predication (where the matter has the form and the form is predicated of the matter), a non-canonical, or 'deontic', scheme of predication, according to which the form is the subject and the matter what the form needs to have in order for it to exist as a form.

	Fundamental principle of ontology	The couple matter/form and predication
BOETHUS	X is a substance iff X is a subject and X is not in a subject	The form is canonically predicated of the matter. The matter *has* the form.
ALEXANDER	X is a real substance iff X is the part of a phenomenal (= individual) substance, be X a subject or not	The matter is deontically predicated of the form. The form *has* the matter.

III. Boethus Again on the Non Substantiality of the Form

We have seen that Boethus rejected the claim of form to be a substance, and placed it in a category outside substance. But it is easier to deny that it is in the category of substance than to identify *where* else it might be. It should be obvious to anybody that the form is more than a simple quality among others. Even if it is predicated of the matter, the form is much more important to it, so to say, than any other predicated item. The fact that I share in human form is more closely connected to my very nature than the fact that I share in baldness and darkness-of-the-eyes. Alexander's theory had at least the advantage of accounting for this gap between different types of predication.

And Boethus himself could not deny that the secondary substances of the categories were not interpreted by Aristotle as *mere* qualities, quantities or the like.

Moreover, Alexander has a real point in interpreting the form as the dynamic activity explaining that we are entitled to speak of *a* subject. After all, if, as a good Aristotelian, Boethus denied the existence of vacuum in the world, he must have admitted that there is matter *everywhere* in the sublunar (at least). But in that case, how is it possible to speak of this man, or this horse, as *a* subject, without reference to their form? What is it that makes their delimitation *real*, and not purely conventional, as soon as the form is nothing but some kind of inhering accident as, say, wetness or colour?

Even if we must face here the prejudicial lack of textual evidence, I would suggest, in the last part of this paper, that Boethus' answer was twofold. First, he never clearly specified what exactly the form was; and second, he worked with a very relaxed notion of what it is to be an object, which permitted him to bypass the difficulty of having his subjects not substantially constituted by their forms.

1. Boethus on the categories to which form belongs

Let us first recall the end of Simplicius' testimony on Boethus account of substance:[32]

> But thus, says Boethus, the matter and the composite will belong to the category of substance, while the form will be outside substance and fall into some other category, either quality or quantity or some other one.

This sentence is very puzzling. For what is exactly the signification of the 'either ... or ... or ...'? T. Reinhardt writes:

> Boethus' position is either that the form will fall in one and only one non-substance category or that the form will be an aggregate of features classifiable in one or more of the non-substance categories such that normally a plurality of items from the non-substance categories would account for form.[33]

Reinhardt has four reasons to opt for the second solution (which he calls the 'aggregate view').[34] First, because 'some of the non-substance categories make very unlikely candidates for "form" (*sc.* on their own)'. Reinhardt probably means that since quality and quantity are already quoted, it would be absurd to suppose that the 'other one' mentioned in the text could be the single exclusive category to which form belongs. But since at least the relative and the disposition may be alluded to, the argument is perhaps

---

[32] Simplicius, *in Cat.* 78,17–20.
[33] See T. Reinhardt, 'Andronicus of Rhodes and Boethus of Sidon on Aristotle's *Categories*', in R. W. Sharples and R. Sorabji, eds, *Greek and Roman Philosophy 100 BC–200 AD*, 2 vols (London: Institute of Classical Studies, 2007), vol. 2, pp. 513–29, at p. 525.
[34] Reinhardt, ibid.

not entirely conclusive.[35] The second argument is more intricate, and deserves to be quoted at length:

> Second, it seems fairly uncontroversial that quality more than any other non-substance category ought to play a role in the constitution of forms, and to view an aggregate of features would allow Boethus to give a role to the non-substance categories other than quality as he wishes according to [our passage] and yet to accomodate the preeminence of quality by allowing that qualities will normally play a role, a possibility which would not be available on the alternative interpretation, according to which form can fall in one and only one of any of the non-substance categories.[36]

In other words, if I understand rightly, the interpretation in terms of aggregate is preferable because it accounts for the preeminence of quality as well as for Boethus' present *formulation* of the problem, which indeed *does* mention non-substance categories other than quality. But why in this case, did Boethus write '*either ... or ... or ...*'? If I want to say that form is mainly a quality, but that other categories must also be taken into account in its definition, am I not unlikely to write that form 'will fall under *a* category different than substance, *either* quality, *or* quantity, *or* another one'? Someone could reply that all Boethus wants to say is that even if the form taken in itself *is* an aggregate, we can *view* it as a quality, or a quantity, or (perhaps) something else. But first, Boethus does not say that, i.e. he does not introduce *our* view on the form; and second, it would be odd in this case to write '*either*' (*êtoi*) before 'quality'.[37] Even if we were speaking of *our* apprehension of the form, there would be no point in introducing such a sharp disjunction. A sequence 'and ... and ...' (*kai ... kai ...*) would have been more appropriate or, at most, as in Reinhardt's translation,[38] a sequence '... or ... or ...' without 'either'. I leave aside Reinhardt's two last arguments – Porphyry's interpretation of the passage and the overall likelihood of the aggregate interpretation – which seem more confirmative than properly demonstrative. All in all, I would not so easily adopt one of Reinhardt's two solutions. I agree that the exclusive interpretation is as such hardly conceivable, but there are serious difficulties also with the aggregate conception.

The least we can say is that the formulation we are dwelling on betrays some trouble on Boethus' side. If, envisaging the problem from the start, we try to capture what Boethus' sentence could mean, it seems that we can imagine ten basic elucidations, which I shall range from the strongest to the weakest possible claim:

---

[35] We should mention, in this context, that in a *Quaestio* preserved only in Arabic, Alexander tells us that the differentia – which, according to him, belongs to substance – had been put by others under the genus of quality *or of relation*. See Rashed, *Essentialisme* (n. 3 above), p. 57.

[36] Reinhardt (n. 33 above), ibid.

[37] It is by the way significant that Reinhardt (n. 33 above), pp. 524–5, translates: '... and will fall under a different category, quality *or* quantity *or* another one'. Led by his interpretation in terms of aggregate, he naturally skipped the disjunctive particle *êtoi* (*either*).

[38] See the previous note.

(i) Boethus knows to which non-substantial category the form belongs but leaves here the question open because his arguments would be too long and intricate for the present context;
(ii) Boethus thinks that all possible forms must belong to one single category but has not made up his mind as to which of them they belong;
(iii) Boethus thinks that a single form may belong, by its variety of aspects, to different categories he could cite, and in particular to quality, but never to substance;
(iv) Boethus thinks that a single form is a bundle of categories, i.e. is necessarily composed by a plurality of items belonging to different categories he could cite, all other than substances, and likely to include quality (Reinhardt's 'aggregate view');
(v) Boethus thinks that all possible forms do not belong to the same category/ies; different types of forms belong to different categories he could cite, but never to substance.
(vi) Boethus has no idea at all as to the category/ies of the forms; he just claims that arguably, it *is* a category, or some categories, but not the category of substance.
(vii) Boethus thinks that the form, like the point or the instant, somehow exists without belonging to any category.
(viii) Boethus thinks that one and only one of the seven previous theses is correct but that the philosophical business can do without investigating which one;
(ix) Boethus thinks that at least one of the seven first theses is correct but that the philosophical business can do without investigating which one/s;
(x) Boethus thinks that the form is nothing but a *façon de parler*.

I fear that the evidence at hand is not sufficient for allowing us to select one of these options. If I am allowed to resort, in such a severe context, to the tools of rhetorical analysis, I would argue that the way itself in which Boethus evokes the secondary categories tends to show that he did not know what the form exactly was. I am conscious that such a conclusion is rather frustrating. But I cannot succeed in believing that if Boethus had clear ideas about which non-substance category the form falls in, he would have written in the way he did.

Let us however try to better understand his position. Boethus was of course aware of the distinction between species and form. First of all, because one would have to be blind not to see the difference between both usages in Aristotle. Second, because as already stated, he must have been aware of the different meanings of 'in something' listed in *Physics* 4.3.[39] Thus, he knew that the species (*eidos*) is in the genus, while the form (*eidos*) is in the matter. It would be too hasty, then, to attribute to him the view that the form is a quality (*poion*) because Aristotle, in the *Categories*, describes the

---

[39] See above, p. 106. One must however remain cautious about this identification of the author of the passage transmitted in *Laur.* 71.32. First, because Boethus' commentary was surely no more extant in the Palaeologan era (when the scholia have been copied in the margins of *Laur.* 71.32) and, second, because some pages of an anonymous commentary on Aristotle's *Categories* written at the end of the ninth century and preserved in the 'Archimedes palimpsest' have recently revealed that portions of Porphyry's *Ad Gedalium* were still extant in Byzantium in the thirteenth century – when some of its leaves were recycled for the copy of a theological text. (More on the attribution to Porphyry in R. Chiaradonna, D. Sedley and myself, 'A rediscovered *Categories* Commentary', *Oxford Studies in Ancient Philosophy* 44 (2013), and reprinted below as ch. 8). It is a fair conjecture, then, to

species, together with the genus, as a *poion*.⁴⁰ For the species is a *poion* because it is a kind of universal.⁴¹ But then, it includes under its scope also the individual's *matter*, as well as its form.⁴² The species cannot therefore be equated with the individual's hylomorphic form.

Now, as Reinhardt perfectly saw, to be a man or a horse must have amounted for Boethus to having, inherent in some matter, a bundle of items belonging to different non-substance categories. In the famous passage of the *Categories* where he characterises species and genus as *poion*, Aristotle was very careful to distinguish the proper meaning of the term (a *quality*, like 'white') from its extended meaning (a qualification of substance).⁴³ I would suggest, then, that Boethus' vague formulation mirrors the simple fact that he discarded this distinction between quality (*poion*) and qualification of substance (*peri ousian* [...] *poion*), as a dead-end. In other words, Boethus probably did not hold that the form was a bundle of items, but, as a careful reductionist, that it was *nothing but* a bundle of items belonging to different non-substance categories – *poia*, *posa*, etc. – and constituting, all together, the form inhering in the matter. To be a man's form presupposes a nest of interwoven determinations, which are constitutive of the humanity belonging to this particular chunk of matter. If these formal determinations can be considered as 'substantial', it is, at most, because a man cannot exist without them.⁴⁴ To sum up, the import of the 'aggregate view' of the form is that it blocks the temptation to understand the 'qualification of subtance' of the *Categories* as what was to become, among later commentators, a '*substantial* quality'.⁴⁵

2. Boethus on what it is to be a subject as a way of getting rid of Stoic relatively disposed

In the case of Alexander, we know, thanks to some evidence in his commentary on the *Metaphysics* and to the Arabic *Quaestio* already alluded to, that the real 'categorial question' was not that of the three types of substances (matter, form and composite) – since they are all substances – but that of the status of the *differentia*.⁴⁶ It is the

---

suppose that the anonymous fragments preserved in *Laur.* 71.32 come from Porphyry's *Ad Gedalium* (for a parallel case, see S. Ebbesen, 'Boethius as Aristotelian Scholar', in J. Wiesner, ed., *Aristoteles: Werk und Wirkung*, 2 vols (Berlin: De Gruyter, 1987), vol. 2, pp. 286–311, at pp. 309–10 [and repr. as ch. 16 in R. Sorabji, *Aristotle Transformed* (London: Duckworth, 1990)]). Thus, the thesis expounded in these fragments may stem from an author quoted by Porphyry, like Boethus, or belong to Porphyry himself – this second eventuality having not been taken into account by P. Huby.

⁴⁰ *Cat.* 5, 3b13–16.
⁴¹ See *Metaph.* 7.13, 1038b34–1039a2.
⁴² Cf. *Metaph.* 7.11, 1037a5–7.
⁴³ See *Cat.* 5, 3b18–23.
⁴⁴ It is, in a similar context, Andronicus' strategy. See Simplicius, *in Cat.* 54,8–16.
⁴⁵ It is worth noting that we find here something very similar to the double level/signification of the relative admitted by Andronicus, according to Reinhardt's interpretation. See Reinhardt (n. 33 above), pp. 521–2.
⁴⁶ See *in Metaph.* 206,12–207,6 and Rashed, *Essentialisme* (n. 3 above), pp. 56–65. The similarities between these texts had been first noted by P. Moraux, *Der Aristotelismus bei den Griechen III: Alexander von Aphrodisias* (Berlin: De Gruyter, 2001), p. 473, and F. A. J. de Haas, *John Philoponus' New Definition of Prime Matter* (Leiden: Brill, 1997), p. 218, n. 173.

essentialist connection of form and differentia that in turn explains, according to him, that the *differentia* belongs to substance. It is not fortuitous, from this point of view, that we do not find the faintest account of the relationship between form and *differentia specifica* in Boethus' fragments. For the essentialist differentia, as a feature differentiating the very nature of an individual substance, cannot be simply material – since it would need to be finite, and matter is indefinite.

Boethus introduces another account of what it is to be a subject in his attack on the Stoic notion of relation. It appears again in Simplicius' commentary on the *Categories*, in the page immediately following the famous text containing the sole serious account we have of the Stoic doctrine of the relatives.[47] Let us first remark that the whole development comes probably from Boethus' commentary, through Porphyry and Iamblichus. The fact that we owe our only reliable information on the Stoic doctrine to Boethus is already interesting in itself. He is likely to have been one of the rare thinkers of Antiquity to have had a clear grasp of this difficult issue. I shall of course not try to propose a systematic account of what has been said by modern scholars on the Stoic doctrine. Rather, I shall focus on the relevance of this discussion for our understanding of Boethus' doctrine of what it is to be a subject. The context of Boethus' remarks is that of the Stoic distinction between two kinds of relatives, one where the fact of being relative is connected to some 'difference' (*diaphora*) or 'character' (*kharaktêr*) *inside* the substance – the relative (*pros ti*) – and the *relatively disposed* (*pros ti pôs ekhon*) where *no internal* state of the substance has any bearing on the relation. As stressed by M. Mignucci, the criterion for the second class of relative property is furnished by the fact that such a relative is subject to what is nowadays called Cambridge change, that is, if its bearer can acquire or lose the property without undergoing any *intrinsic* alteration, but simply because something *external* has altered.[48] Let us take a stock example of the first class, the sweet taste of a given substance. Its sweetness is a relative (*pros ti*), since to be sweet has no meaning apart from the possibility of being appreciated as sweet by some animal having the organ of taste. Thus, sweetness requires both an internal disposition and an external relation. By contrast, being to the right is not an internal state (since something can change from being to the right as a result of the movement of something *external* to it. Let us now read Boethus' reply:

> That it is necessary also in the case of the relatively disposed (*pros ti pôs ekhonta*) that a <u>character</u> exist in the subjects, has been shown sufficiently by Boethus and is immediately clear. For the relation to something else is not of such a nature that it exists itself by itself, but it is necessary that it exist in the <u>character</u> which is the function of a difference (*en tôi kata diaphoran kharaktêri*). This <u>character</u> is sometimes a quality, as the whiter is such along with colour, sometimes a quantity, as in the more and longer, sometimes a motion, as in the faster, sometimes a time, as in the older, sometimes a place, as in the higher. But the left and the right exist with more than one difference. For they manifest themselves together with place

---

[47] Simplicius, *in Cat.* 165,32–166,29.
[48] M. Mignucci, 'The Stoic Notion of Relatives', in J. Barnes and M. Mignucci, eds, *Matter and Metaphysics* (Naples: Bibliopolis, 1988), pp. 129–221, at p. 149–54.

and with a part of such a kind (namely, it is because we have parts of such a kind that right and left are said, since a stone will not be 'to the right' relatively to a stone if there is nobody to apply it to our right and left parts). Also in the case of the identical, the relative exists, albeit in a startling way: it is not said relatively to something else, but to itself. For what is *fully* similar and not in function of something nor in some qualified way,[49] that is the identical. In this way, the relation exists always together with the <u>characters</u> of the differentia, and these things are not two, contrarily to what these people say, but the composite is one.[50]

Two consequences follow from this.

First, every existential feature must be translatable into physical terms. That means that the *Categories* are supposed to supply us with the list of every well-founded physical being or event. The world is four-dimensional (three spatial dimensions plus time) and material. Every bit of matter has sensible qualities and every object has a configuration and a quantity. Motion and rest are functions of place and time. Relation is just a way to put together everything there is. That means that relation has *always* some physical basis. Let us dwell an instant on the example given by Boethus. I have two stones, S and T, in front of me. I say that S is to the right of T. What does this really mean? According to Boethus, that means that if, while I am standing, I draw a segment between my right eye and S and another segment between my left eye and T, the two segments will not intersect in the space between the vertical plane of the stones and the vertical plane of my eyes.[51] Boethus' intention here is to show how there is no Cambridge change which cannot be reduced to a change affecting items belonging to some categories other than the Stoic relatively disposed.

In an article devoted to the Aristotelian notion of relation, D. Sedley has shown that Aristotle drew a distinction between 'hard-relatives' and 'soft-relatives'.[52] The hard-relatives, which have their very being in a relation, are singled out by the test of cognitive symmetry: if A and B are hard-relatives, we cannot know A without knowing B. Dwelling on the report of the Stoics occurring a page before our passage in Simplicius, Sedley suggested that the Stoics had the same distinction between two kind of relatives, but that they changed the identification criterion of the hard-relatives, which they called relatively disposed: '... hard relativity is now helpfully explicated by a test simpler

---

[49] See the following note.
[50] Simplicius, *in Cat.* 167,2–18. At 167,15–16, *to goun kathapax on, alla mê kata ti mêdepôs* is the manuscripts' unanimous reading according to the CAG editor. The sense is not clear to me. I suggest *to goun kathapax <homoion> on, alla mê kata ti mêde pôs*. It is worth noting that the opposition *kathapax/kata ti* is attested in Hellenistic philosophy, see Philodemus, *Po.* 5.16. The doctor Archigenes, in the second century CE, may have been influenced by Boethus' treatment of the distinction: the quotation in Galen, *Diff. Puls.* 8,626 Kühn seems to be reminiscent of the fragment cited by Simplicius.
[51] Boethus refers implicitly here to the first sense of the right and the left of inanimate beings expounded at *De Caelo* 2.2, 285a3–4. A clear sign that Xenarchus was not the only reader of Aristotle's *De Caelo* in the first century BCE.
[52] That is, if its bearer can acquire and lose the relative property without undergoing any intrinsic alteration, but simply because something external has altered. See D. Sedley, 'Aristotelian Relativities', in M. Canto-Sperber and P. Pellegrin, eds, *Le style de la pensée* (Paris: Les Belles Lettres, 2002), pp. 324–52.

and more effective than Aristotle's 'cognitive symmetry' criterion. A relative property is hard-relative if it is subject to Cambridge change, that is, if its bearer can acquire and lose the relative property without undergoing any intrinsic alteration, but simply because something external has altered'.[53] Superficially, Boethus would agree with this description. But there is an important shift of emphasis, precisely due to the fact that Boethus does his best to alleviate the contrast between the two kinds of relatives. In other words, while Aristotelian users of Cambridge change will underline the fact that one of the relatives will not undergo any internal change, Boethus instead takes the true subject in his example of relatives to be not a single stone, but a *cluster* consisting of two stones and my two sides as I face them. The stone on my right is one element in the cluster which will not cease to be on my right without a change *internal* to the cluster of at least one member, whether of one of the stones or of my sides. We cannot then but conclude that in order to save his materialistic account of relation, Boethus is ready to finesse his views on the subject of predication. For in the case at hand, the subject of the changing characteristics is not a single substance, but a cluster.

Boethus' *having* vs. Stoic *sayable*

Simplicius' report at *in Cat.* 167,2–18, of Boethus' attack on the Stoics' category of relatively disposed has a second interesting feature. It reveals that the Stoics drew some kind of subtle distinction between *diaphora* and *kharaktêr*. The Stoic context is not sufficient to explain the massive presence of the term *kharaktêr* in Boethus' answer. All the less so, since Boethus does *not* use the couple *diaphora–kharaktêr* in the same way as the Stoics did. For in contrast to them, Boethus seems to envisage the *diaphora* as the non-substance *category*, and the *kharaktêr* as the item belonging to it and inhering in the substance. White's *diaphora*, for example, is *quality*, while any realization of the white in the substance is a *kharaktêr*.[54] There is no place for the *fact of somebody having* such or such quality – a *lekton* – which, as we have noted, is probably lurking in the background of the Stoic *diaphora*. The distinction, for the Stoics, was rather straightforward : the qualitative *kharaktêr* was a body, the *diaphora* an incorporeal. For Boethus, the problem was obviously more intricate. Aristotelian qualities being of course incorporeal, it was more difficult, *prima facie*, to draw a sharp distinction between the quality and its *diaphora*. After all, an individual quality *is* a difference of its bearer. However, in suggesting that the *diaphora* was the category to which the quality described as a *kharaktêr* belongs, Boethus was probably *not* alluding to the mere distinction between a genus and one of its particular instantiations. This would have been rather out of place in the framework of his ontology, where universals are drastically downgraded. More probably, Boethus was drawing a distinction between the existential and the predicative aspect of items belonging to the non-substance

---

[53] Sedley, 'Aristotelian Relativities', pp. 339–40.
[54] These considerations are diametrically opposed to Alexander's ontology. For the latter, the only *diaphora* worthy of mention belongs to the category of substance. For Boethus, substance *as such* seems to be indifferentiated; the *diaphora* is always linked to an accidental *kharaktêr* of the subject.

categories. Our sensation is sufficient to assess their existence as *kharaktêres*, even if they are not bodies; their inherence, i.e. the fact that a body *has* them, is sufficient to consider them as *diaphorai*.

As far as we can judge from this text – where the Aristotelian tradition (Porphyry, Iamblichus, and Simplicius), may have left its mark –, I would guess that initially, the *kharaktêr* was counted by the Stoic materialists as a body and the *diaphora* as an incorporeal predicate, i.e. the very fact of having the *kharaktêr*. In other words, the *kharaktêr* must have been the corporeal feature inhering in corporeal subjects, the *diaphora* the incorporeal predicate and the fact of somebody having this *diaphora*, the corresponding *sayable*. At two places in the present paper, we have seen that Boethus was slightly rewriting an Aristotelian doctrine in a way that allowed him to bypass Stoic sayables (*lekta*). First, in his discussion of the category of *having*, Boethus adduced the example of health and rewrote the Stoic sayable of being healthy in terms of the inherence of the accident of health in a subject.[55] And, addressing Aristotle's category of relation, Boethus suppressed from it what could appear as an anticipation of the Stoic *lekton*, in order to explain it as a material affection of a cluster-subject.[56] But Boethus' objection to *having* may rather have been that for him *having* has no genuine consistency nor, if I dare put it that way, any genuine reality comparable to a Stoic *sayable*. The sole function of Boethus' category of *having* is to *say* one thing: it states the inherence of the accident in the substance, or, indifferently, the fact that we can predicate the attribute of the subject.

Conclusion

In conclusion, Boethus' whole enterprise amounted to curtailing the ontological realm as far as he could, by constructing, using the tools of Aristotle's *Categories* alone, a system that did without any kind of shadowy beings – Aristotle's forms, so far from being substances, are nothing but a bundle of items drawn from other categories. The Stoic category of relatively disposed can be replaced by a kind of subject clustered out of several related entities. Stoic sayables (*lekta*) are a superfluous kind of predicate.

---

[55] See above, p. 108.
[56] See above, pp. 120–21.

3

The Inadvertent Conception and Late Birth of the Free-Will Problem and the Role of Alexander

Susanne Bobzien

I. Various Problems of Freedom and Determinism

Let me start with a number of distinctions vital to the subsequent discussion of ancient philosophical theories. These distinctions are kept rough and schematic. They are left deliberately vague in certain respects, because the ancient theories whose understanding they are intended to further are themselves stubbornly vague in those respects. The first distinction is of different kinds of freedom. I distinguish three kinds of indeterminist freedom:

1) *freedom to do otherwise*: I am free to do otherwise if, being the same agent, with the same desires and beliefs, and being in the same circumstances, it is possible for me to do or not to do something in the sense that it is not fully causally determined whether or not I do it.
2) *freedom of decision*: a subtype of freedom to do otherwise. I am free in my decision, if being the same agent, with the same desires and beliefs, and being in the same circumstances, it is possible for me to decide between alternative courses of action in the sense that it is not fully causally determined which way I decide. 1) differs from 2) in that it leaves it undecided in which way it is possible for the agent to do or not to do something.
3) *freedom of the will*: a subtype of freedom of decision. I act from free will, if I am in the possession of a will, i.e. a specific part or faculty of the soul by means of which I can decide between alternative courses of actions independently of my desires and beliefs, in the sense that it is not fully causally determined in which way I decide. 2) differs from 3) in that the latter postulates a specific causally

---

This article first appeared as 'The inadvertent conception and late birth of the free will problem' by Susanne Bobzien in *Phronesis* 43 (1998), pp. 133-75 © Koninklijke BRILL NV 1998, reproduced with permission.

independent faculty or part of the soul which functions as a 'decision making faculty'.

Proponents of any of the kinds of indeterminist freedom may be called indeterminist libertarians. From these three types of indeterminist freedom must be distinguished what I call 'un-predeterminist' freedom.

4) *un-predeterminist freedom*: I have un-predeterminist freedom of action/choice if there are no causes prior to my action/choice which determine whether or not I perform/choose a certain course of action, but in the same circumstances, if I have the same desires and beliefs, I would *always* do/choose the same thing. Un-predeterminist freedom guarantees the agents' autonomy in the sense that nothing except the agents themselves is causally responsible for whether they act, or for which way they decide. Un-predeterminist freedom requires a theory of causation that is not (just) a theory of event-causation (i.e. a theory which considers both causes and effects as events). For instance, un-predeterminist freedom would work with a concept of causality which considers things or objects (material or immaterial) as causes, and events, movements or changes as effects. Such a conception of causation is common in antiquity.

Indeterminist freedom always requires the absence of predetermining causal factors, but in addition allows for different decisions of the same agent in the same circumstances. In the interpretation of ancient texts, indeterminist freedom is often confounded with un-predeterminist freedom. From both these types of freedom must be distinguished the following ones which are compatible with both indeterminism and 'un-predeterminism':

5) *freedom from force and compulsion*: I am free in my actions/choices in this sense, if I am not externally or internally forced or compelled when I act/choose. This does not preclude that my actions/choices may be fully causally determined by external and internal factors.
6) *freedom from determination by external causal factors*: agents are free from external causal factors in their actions/choices if the same external situation or circumstances will not necessarily always elicit the same (re-)action or choice of different agents, or of the same agent but with different desires or beliefs.
7) *freedom from determination by (external and) certain internal causal factors*: I am in my actions/choices free from certain internal factors (e.g. my desires), if having the same such internal factors will not necessarily always elicit in me the same action/choice.

The last two types of freedom (6 and 7) differ from freedom from force, etc. (5), in that the latter only rules out force, compulsion and necessitation, whereas 6) and 7) also rule out full causal determination, e.g. based on nothing but universal regularity of the respective causal factors. The list of types of freedoms 1) to 7) is evidently neither exhaustive nor exclusive.

Note that the only proper Greek term for freedom is *eleutheria*, and that our evidence suggests that *eleutheria* played no role in the discussion of determinism and moral responsibility up to the second century CE. In particular, the term *eleutheria* is *not* involved in the development of the concept of freedom to do otherwise. Rather it is the conceptual development of the phrase *eph' hêmin* that is pertinent here, and which has an altogether different history.[1] It is the notion of autonomous agency (see below) and of not being determined by something else (freedoms type 5–7) which in philosophical discussions in later antiquity becomes connected with *eleutheria*.

Next, there are two categorically different conceptions of moral responsibility, one grounded on autonomy of the agent, the other on the ability of the agent to do otherwise. The first (MR1) considers it a necessary condition for praising or blaming an agent for an action, that it was the agent *and not something else* that was causally responsible for whether the action occurred. The contrast is between self-determination and other-determination to act. Actions or choices can be attributed to the agent because it is in them that the agents, qua rational or moral beings, manifest themselves. Some thinkers consider the un-predeterminedness of an action/choice as a necessary condition for autonomy, and consequently for the attribution of moral appraisal.

The second idea of moral responsibility (MR2) considers it a prerequisite for blaming or praising an agent for an action that the agent could have done otherwise. This idea is often connected with the agents' sentiments or beliefs that they could have done otherwise, as well as the agents' feelings of guilt or regret. Some philosophers consider the indeterminedness of an action/choice as a necessary condition for the guarantee that the agent could have done otherwise. The concepts of indeterminist freedom of an agent (see above) gain importance at the point at which moral appraisal is connected with the idea that at the very same time, the same agent, with the same beliefs and desires, could have done otherwise.

Depending on what conception of moral responsibility an ancient determinist philosopher has, they will encounter different philosophical problems. With an autonomy based concept of moral responsibility, they tend to face the *problem of the compatibility of autonomy and determinism*: how can I, the agent, be held responsible for my actions/choices, if everything, including my actions/choices is determined, predetermined, or necessitated by god, fate, providence, necessity, or various other external and/or internal causal factors? This is the problem which for example the early Stoics faced.

With a concept of moral responsibility based on a concept of freedom to do otherwise, determinists tend to face a very different kind of difficulty: the *problem of the compatibility of freedom to do otherwise and determinism*. In accordance with the threefold distinction of indeterminist freedom, three problems can be distinguished:

---

[1] I have argued the importance of realising the very different philosophical functions of the terms *eleutheria* and *eph' hêmin* in S. Bobzien, 'Stoic Conceptions of Freedom and their Relation to Ethics', in R. Sorabji, ed., *Aristotle and After* (London: Institute of Classical Studies, 1997), pp. 71–89.

- the problem of the compatibility of freedom to do otherwise and determinism
- the problem of the compatibility of freedom of decision and determinism
- the problem of the compatibility of freedom of the will and determinism

All three problems are often referred to as 'the free-will problem', although only the third actually involves a notion of a free will. The label 'free-will problem' is also sometimes used for the problem of the compatibility of autonomy and determinism, namely when the agent is thought to have a faculty of the will, and it is by means of this faculty that the agent decides between different courses of actions. Quite often it is taken to be 'understood', and is hence left completely unclear, what an author means when talking about 'freewill' and 'the free-will problem'. In the following I reserve the expression 'free will' for the kind of freedom I called 'freedom of the will' above. To avoid confusion, I use the phrase 'free-will problem' sparingly, and for the above-mentioned three problems only.

Modern philosophers tend to concentrate on physical or causal determinism based on principles of the kind 'same causes, same effects' or 'like causes, like effects', and the prevalent types of free-will problem are those of the compatibility of universal causal determinism with freedom to do otherwise or freedom of decision. Few philosophers nowadays would postulate a faculty of the will. The earliest unambiguous evidence for the awareness of any kind of 'free-will problem' occurs in Alexander of Aphrodisias. It resembles the problems modern philosophers discuss in that it is concerned with a theory of universal causal determinism which contains a principle of the type 'same causes, same effects', and in that it involves a concept of indeterminist freedom without invoking a concept of the will. It is with the 'discovery' of this kind of problem that I am concerned with primarily in this paper.

The historical treatment of the question of freedom and determinism is exacerbated by the fact that almost all key terms and phrases used to describe the problems involved are hopelessly vague or ambiguous. This is no different in Greek and Latin than in English. Many phrases and statements in philosophical texts before Alexander are – at least at first sight – compatible with an interpretation as concerning indeterminist freedom. However, there is a conspicuous absence of *any* unambiguous account of indeterminist freedom, and of any philosophical problems that would involve such a concept.[2] I have therefore adopted the strategy of denying the awareness of a concept of indeterminist freedom and of the free-will problem (in any of its manifestations) as long as there are neither textual evidence nor philosophical reasons for assuming the opposite.

On the following pages I shall first present the situation as we find it in Alexander; then sketch the development that leads to that state of the discussion; and finally interpret the problems presented by Alexander and some related philosophers in the light of the development that led up to them.

---

[2] Except perhaps the problem in Aristotle, *EN* 3.5 (1114a3–1114b25), but even that is doubtful.

II. The State of the Debate in Alexander

In Alexander's treatise *On Fate* we are presented with a kind of stalemate situation between two philosophical positions: the Stoic compatibilist determinist one and Alexander's Peripatetic and – seemingly – libertarian one. These positions are characterised by their stand (i) on causal determinism and (ii) on that which depends on us (*to eph' hêmin*). The expression 'depending on us' is central to much of the debate: both parties are agreed that moral appraisal for an action presupposes that the action depends on the agent, or is *eph' autôi*.

The Stoic compatibilist position is orthodox and stands in the Chrysippean tradition. Like Chrysippus these later Stoics are concerned with the compatibility of universal causal determinism with moral responsibility based on the idea of autonomy (MR1). They maintain that everything is fated, and define fate in terms of a network of causes. They hold that there is no change without a cause and that every change and every event has preceding causes (*Fat.* 191,30–192,14). The most remarkable element of their determinism is the formulation of a causal principle whose function it is to back up their basic assumption that there is no change without cause (*Fat.* 192,22). This principle is not recorded for any earlier Stoics. It states that in the same circumstances the same cause will necessarily bring about exactly the same effect:

> ... that it is impossible that, when all the same circumstances around the cause and that of which it is a cause are present, things should sometimes *not* happen in a certain way and sometimes should so happen.
>
> Alexander, *Fat.* 192,22–4[3]

Universal causal determinism is thus guaranteed; both in the Stoic sense, in which causes are bodies which actively bring about their incorporeal effects; and in the common modern sense that the same cause in the same circumstances brings about the same effect, where both cause and effect are understood as events. The Stoics in Alexander argue for the compatibility of this physical theory with moral responsibility by means of their concept of what depends on us. They define that which depends on us as that which happens *through us* (*di' hêmôn*), i.e. that which is the result of impulse and assent, and in which the nature of the agent manifests itself.[4] We are thus the main causal factor of our actions and can consequently be held morally responsible for them.

The opposing Peripatetic position which Alexander puts forward is less clear. Instead of a uniform stand, there is a variety of views, alternating, and occasionally fused, a point to which I return later. But there is evidence for a position that proposes freedom to do otherwise and which resembles up to a point modern notions of freedom of decision. For example, we find the account:

---

[3] *To adunaton einai, tôn autôn hapantôn periestêkotôn peri te to aition kai hôi estin aition, hote men dê mê houtôsi pôs sumbainein, hote de houtôs.* Cf. Nemesius, *Nat. hom.* 105.18–21 (Morani), Alexander, *Fat.* 176,21–2; 181,21–5; 185,7–9, *Mant.* 174,2–7; see also Section 8.2 of S. Bobzien, *Determinism and Freedom in Stoic Philosophy* (Oxford: Clarendon Press, 1998).

[4] Cf. Alexander, *Fat.* ch. 13, Nemesius, *Nat. hom.* 105–6 and see below. Despite its simple form, the definition is highly technical. For a detailed discussion see Sections 8.1 and 8.4 of Bobzien, *Determinism and Freedom* (n. 3 above).

'depending on us' is predicated of the things over which we have in us the power of also choosing the opposite.

Alexander, *Fat.* 181,5

and the explicit requirement that this choosing has to be independent of preceding causes:

we have this power of choosing the opposite and not everything that we choose has pre-determining causes, because of which it is not possible for us not to choose this.

Alexander, *Fat.* 180,26–8

Thus universal causal pre-determinism is rejected. Moreover, it seems that the causes that are rejected include not only the external preceding circumstances, but also the agents' disposition or character and reason (*Fat.* 171,11–17; 199,27–200,7): agents can act against their dispositions or character and reason, and are thus causally independent from them. This concept of what depends on us combines two features: the first is that of non-predeterminism, i.e. the freedom from previous states of the world, including those concerning the agent. There are no causes prior to our choosing by which it is predetermined what we choose. The second is the agent's freedom to do (i.e. choose) otherwise.

It should be plain that the positions of the two parties in the debate are incompatible. The Stoics maintain that every change in the world is causally determined by preceding causes. The same cause, under the same circumstances will necessarily bring about the same effect. The Peripatetic claim is that there are some changes in the world that are causally undetermined; and among these are the things that depend on us. In the very same situation, we, the very same causes (causes understood as corporeal entities), could choose one time one way, another time another way, undetermined in our decision by external and internal causal factors. It is essential to see that there is no solution to this conflict: causal determinism and partial causal indeterminism are mutually exclusive.

But although the text implies awareness of a problem of the compatibility of freedom and determinism, the *discussion* seems to have focused on a different problem: the question is not 'which is the correct concept of freedom?' (It is telling that there is no word for 'freedom' used in the debate; whether or what concepts of freedom are involved in the opposed theories has to be inferred from the context. The unfortunate custom of translating the Greek phrase *eph' hêmin* by 'free-will' or cognates of 'free' simply begs the question.) The question of the debate in Alexander is rather: 'which is the right concept of what depends on us?', i.e. 'which concept provides a sufficient condition for the possibility of moral appraisal?' And here two very dissimilar underlying theories collide. To understand the nature of this controversy, we have to realise that the two parties work with two fundamentally different conceptions of what depends on us. For this we need to make explicit the different ways in which the phrase 'depending on someone', or rather the Greek *epi* with dativus personae could be understood. The phrase apparently could denote both what I have named a 'one-sided, causative' concept of what depends on someone, and what I call a 'two-sided, potestative' concept of what depends on someone.

The two-sided, potestative version is well-attested (cf. e.g. LSJ *epi*, I.1g). It refers to a power for alternative kinds of behaviour; it depends on me whether something happens (or will happen). When I call this kind of depending on us 'two-sided', I mean that if something x depends on us, then not x depends on us, too. Thus, in the two-sided, potestative understanding, 'up to us' would be a good translation of the Greek expression: for example, if walking is up to me, so is not walking, and vice versa. In this understanding of 'what depends on us', the class of things that depend on us includes unrealised possibilities. For example, when at a certain time walking depends on me, then not walking depends on me, too. But I will be able only either to walk or not to walk at that time. Hence either one or the other will remain an unrealised possibility.

Note that the two-sided, potestative *eph' hêmin* itself entails neither determinism nor indeterminism. A reading compatible with determinism (and indeterminism) is this: walking depends on me at a certain time if at that time I have *the general two-sided capacity* for walking – even if in the *specific* situation it is fully causally determined that I will (or that I will not) walk.[5]

But, importantly, the two-sided, potestative *eph' hêmin* can also be understood as *indeterminist* in the following way: at a certain time walking depends on me, if at that time it is causally undetermined whether or not I (will) walk, *and* it depends on my free decision whether or not I (will) walk. When the expression is understood as two-sided, potestative in this way, the 'we' ('us') in *eph' hêmin* takes on an interesting role: the 'us' in e.g. 'walking depends on us' is given the status of an active decision-maker. We decide whether or not we walk. Instead of a general capacity had at a certain time, in this case there is a power for undetermined deciding between, and initiating, courses of action. This is a very different kind of capacity. And in this case, if something depends on me, then I have the indeterminist freedom to do and not to do it (cf. Section XI).

Things are quite different again in the case of the one-sided, causative *eph' hêmin*. When I call the phrase 'one-sided', I understand this to entail that if something x depends on us, then not-x does not depend on us; and by 'causative' I refer to the fact that the prepositional phrase in 'x depends on y' refers to that which is the cause or reason of x. In this case a translation like 'attributable to us' may be preferable. If at a certain time my walking is attributable to me, then it is not the case that my not walking is attributable to me, too. For in the assumed situation my not walking does not obtain at all. Here, the natural understanding of 'x depends on us' is that it expresses who has the causal responsibility for the thing or action in question. 'The walking is attributable

---

[5] A related reading compatible with determinism (and indeterminism) is this: walking depends on me at a certain time if at that time I have the general two-sided capacity for walking, and nothing (or nothing external) forces me to walk or prevents me from walking – even if in the specific situation it is fully causally determined whether or not I will walk. This adds to the previous reading my freedom (of type 5 above), i.e. the additional requirement of the agent's being neither hindered from nor forced to follow up either alternative. Still differently, a two-sided potestative concept of *eph' hêmin* that is neutral towards determinism and indeterminism can also be used for action types without reference to a specific time. So walking may be said to be the sort of thing that is generally up to human beings.

to you' translates into 'You are causally responsible for your walking'. The 'we' in *eph' hêmin* now expresses the cause of what happens and depends on us.

The one-sided, causative *eph' hêmin*, too, can be used in the description of an indeterminist as well as a determinist system. However, whereas the two-sided *eph' hêmin* can be used to express an element of underminedness, by implying that we, qua decision-makers, can decide freely between alternative options, the one-sided 'depending on us' cannot be so used. Its function is to help to distinguish between different types of 'causes' of events, not to imply the possibility of freedom to do otherwise.[6] The one-sided, causative concept of what depends on us is not a concept of any kind of freedom, but of a particular kind of causal dependency. However, it presupposes a certain kind of freedom: freedom (type 6) from being externally determined to act; or freedom (type 5) from being in any way forced to act and prevented from acting. Note that these concepts of freedom are not the same as this concept of what depends on us. An action depends on me if (in some way) I bear causal responsibility for it and am in this sense its originator. It is in order for this to be possible that I must not be compelled to act or prevented from acting, i.e. that I must be free from external or from necessitating influences.

Depending on which conception of *eph' hêmin* a philosopher works with, the concept of moral responsibility will differ. In the case of the one-sided, causative *eph' hêmin* moral responsibility is attached to someone if they are – in some sense – the main causal originator and thus autonomous (MR1). This is the position of the Stoics in Alexander. In the case of the *indeterminist* two-sided, potestative *eph' hêmin*, moral responsibility is attached to someone if they are free to do otherwise; if they are *not fully causally determined in their decision between alternative courses of action* (MR2). This appears to be Alexander's own position, according to the passages cited above.

The case which understands the two-sided, potestative *eph' hêmin* as a general capacity, and which is neutral regarding determinism or indeterminism, is usually linked with a concept of moral responsibility based on the agent's autonomy (MR1): moral responsibility is attached to my making use of the two-sided capacity, because it is through the use of this capacity that I, qua rational or moral person, become the originator of the action.

III. The One-Sided Potestative Conception of That Which Depends on Us

Next I shall trace the philosophical development that led up to the antagonistic views in Alexander, with emphasis on the question of how the indeterminist two-sided, potestative concept of what depends on us entered the debate. But let me begin with some remarks on the development of the one-sided, causative concept. This concept

---

[6] Matters are complicated by the fact that when the one-sided causative *eph' hêmin* is employed, it usually refers to the bringing about of something by way of using a general two-sided capacity (see below). Thus the one-sided conception and the two-sided one that expresses a general two-sided capacity come very close, and the context does not always allow one to decide which one is at issue.

has a long history which reaches at least from the third century BCE to the third century CE. However, I have not found a matching philosophical definition or account before the second century CE.[7]

The early Stoics, in particular Chrysippus, clearly did not have an indeterminist two-sided conception of what depends on us.[8] There are reasons internal to the Stoic system which help in explaining this. They regarded the mind as corporeal, and as unitary: a person's character, dispositions, beliefs and desires are all reducible to what impressions a person, or that person's mind, gives assent to. (For the Stoics volitions or desires are a kind of beliefs.) The Stoics operated with a model of a person, or of agency, in which neither a person's character or dispositions, nor a person's volitions can be severed from that person. Rather, they identified the person with the entire nature of the individual's mind, including character, dispositions and all. In this model an action is voluntary, and causally attributable to the person, if it is the result of the mind assenting to impulsive impressions (*phantasiai hormêtikai*), i.e. impressions of something as desirable. Whether or not assent is given to the impressions depends on the agent's individual nature of the mind. What makes an agent morally responsible is that the agent, and not something else causes the action. There is in this model no space for free will (i.e. for a decision making faculty that is causally independent of the mind's individual nature). For the fact that I act in accordance with the overall nature of my mind is considered a prerequisite for attributing the action to me, whereas free will takes the detachment of the decision making faculty from the rest of the person as a necessary condition. The concept of an internally undetermined decision *made by the agent* is thus ill-fitting in the Stoic conceptual framework. And so, accordingly, is the free will problem. It follows that the libertarian condition for the attribution of moral responsibility, that we have freedom to do otherwise, would have made little sense to Chrysippus.

We can see that the Stoic account of that which depends on us in Alexander is an attempt to capture exactly this early Stoic concept of the causal responsibility of rational agents: an action is said to depend on us if it happens through us. The expression 'happens through us' is explicated as happening by (*hupo*) the human being, as a result of impulse and assent, and in accordance with the human being's individual nature (Alexander, *Fat.* ch. 13, esp. 181,18–21, 182,11–16; Nemesius, *Nat. hom.* 105–6).

---

[7] In his discussion of the problem of the compatibility of necessitarianism and fatalism with moral responsibility Epicurus can be shown to have used throughout a one-sided potestative concept of what depends on us. (See S. Bobzien, 'Did Epicurus Discover the Free Will Problem?', *Oxford Studies in Ancient Philosophy* 19 (2000), 287–337.) The standard phrase used by him and his followers is *par' hêmas gignesthai* ('to happen because of us') rather than *eph' hêmin einai* – a linguistic point which is additional support for my claim. Questions of freedom to do otherwise and freedom of decision were, it seems, not discussed.
[8] Cf. Section 6.3.5 of Bobzien, *Determinism and Freedom* (n. 3 above). We do not know with certainty which Greek expressions Chrysippus used, but it is likely that *epi* with dativus personae was among them.

IV. The Two-Sided, Potestative *eph' hêmin*: Aristotle

Things are less straightforward on the side of the indeterminist two-sided, potestative *eph' hêmin*, and with the indeterminist concept of freedom. As I have said above, the first full and unambiguous statement of freedom to do otherwise seems to occur in Alexander's *On Fate*, and in the *Mantissa*. Where then do Alexander's indeterminist concept of what depends on us, and his theory of freedom to do otherwise originate? In the *Mantissa* this theory and concept are attributed to Aristotle.[9] Of course, this must not be taken literally. But it is worthwhile to take up the hint, and to ask: where in Aristotle's extant writings do we find his view on that which depends on s.o. (*epi* with dativus personae)? The answer is: in the *Nicomachean Ethics* 3.2 and 3.3, on deliberation and deliberate choice (*prohairesis*), and 3.5, on the question of whether we are morally responsible for our actions and our virtues and vices; and in the parallel sections in the *Eudemian Ethics* 2.6 (1223a1–9) and 2.10.

In *EN* 3.3 Aristotle argues that deliberate choice is deliberate desire of those things that depend on us (*EN* 1113a10–11). The things that depend on us are the things that we can bring about, as opposed to events brought about by nature, necessity, or chance, and also as opposed to those things only people other than us could bring about (*EN* 1112a21–33). They are in the first instance actions (*EN* 1112a31, 34). In 3.5 we learn that besides actions, virtues and vices depend on us (*EN* 1113b3–1115a3). Note the relation between deliberate choice and the things that depend on us: deliberate choice is choice of the things that depend on us, i.e. in the first instance of actions (*EN* 1113a10–11). That is, we deliberate about and choose between possible courses of actions. The choice we make (*prohairesis*) is itself not one of the things that depend on us, and the idea that it was would have been quite alien to Aristotle's thinking.

There is however one factor in Aristotle's concept of what depends on us which we also have in Alexander: its 'two-sidedness'. In *EN* 3.5 we learn that if doing something depends on us, then not doing that same thing also depends on us, and vice versa (*EN* 1113b7–8, cf. *EE* 1226a27–8), and this relational property of the concept is preserved in later Peripatetic philosophy. But Aristotle's concept of what depends us does not entail indeterminism. We have no reason to assume that he has anything more in mind than that the things that depends on us are those which on a generic level it is possible for us to do and not to do, given that we are not externally prevented from doing them. In the two *Ethics*, all the concept of what depends on us does is give *the general range of courses of action* from which we can choose. The concept is independent of (and prior to) Aristotle's concept of deliberate choice, and of any mental capacity we have. It is taken as a basic concept, undefined and generally understood, by means of which the scope of the objects of deliberate choice is determined.

Thus Aristotle's remarks on that which depends on us are a far shot from Alexander's definitions. In none of the passages does Aristotle give a philosophical definition of that which depends on us; nor is he concerned with fate or causal determinism; and

---

[9] Cf. the titles of chs 22 and 23; see also Alexander, *Fat.* ch. 39.

certainly there is no mention of freedom to act or choose otherwise, circumstances and agent being the same.

V. Early Commentaries on the *Nicomachean Ethics*

Let us consider next the extant early commentaries on the *Nicomachean Ethics*, i.e. the commentary by Aspasius (who wrote in the first half of the second century CE) and the Anonymous on Books 2 to 5 (who presumably wrote in the second half of the second century).[10] The first thing to notice is that both commentators introduce the topic of fate where they comment on the Aristotle passage that states that deliberate choice is of the things that depend on us, and in which Aristotle lists the types of causes necessity, nature and chance.[11] Aspasius contrasts a thing's being fated and a thing's being determined by necessity with its depending on us (*in EN* 74,10–13) and a little later contrasts 'depending on us' with 'being necessitated' (*katênagkastai, in EN* 76,11–14).[12] This suggests that he understands something's depending on us as presupposing freedom from force or compulsion – just like Aristotle and the Stoics. The Anonymous has a different concept of fate: fate is subordinated to nature, and it is not untransgressable (*aparabatos*). He thus expressly rejects a property commonly linked with fate by the Stoics and many others, and his view of fate closely resembles that of Alexander (cf. *Fat.* ch. 6 and *Mant.* 186).

A second point of interest is that both commentators introduce into the present context the idea of something's being able to be or happen otherwise: Aspasius presents the Aristotelian account of what is necessary as what cannot be otherwise (*anagkaion gar legetai to mê endekhomenon allôs ekhein*, Aspas. *in EN* 71,25–7). The Anonymous writes that the actions we deliberate about (and that is, the things that depend on us) are things which can be done in this way and otherwise (*alla <bouleuometha> peri toutôn ha kai allôs kai houtôs endekhetai prakhthênai, in EN* 149,34–5). Again, the Anonymous is one step ahead, talking about *acting* otherwise. The formulations, especially that of the Anonymous, lend themselves in principle to an indeterminist concept of freedom to do otherwise as we found it in Alexander. But there are no signs that either commentator took them that way.

As in Aristotle, there is no philosophical account of that which depends on us. As in Aristotle, too, deliberate choice is not one of the things that depend on us, but is *of* the things that depend on us. The things that depend on us are actions and virtues and vices. And finally, it depends on us to do and not to do things, not to *choose and not to*

---

[10] Cf. P. Moraux, *Der Aristotelismus bei den Griechen von Andronikos bis Alexander von Aphrodisias II: Der Aristotelismus im I und II Jh. V. Chr.* (Berlin: De Gruyter, 1984), pp. 226–7, 324–7; or perhaps later? See R. W. Sharples, *Alexander of Aphrodisias, Ethical Problems* (London: Duckworth, 1990), introduction.
[11] Aspasius, *in EN* 74,10–14; Anon. *in EN* 150,1–4. It may have been Theophrastus who introduced fate into this context; cf. Stobaeus, *Ecl.* 1,89,2–5. The earliest clearly two-sided concept of *eph' hêmin in the fate debate* that I have found so far is in Josephus, *Ant.* 13.172. I have been unable to trace any connection between Josephus and the positions discussed in this paper.
[12] This is the standard Stoic contrast, as we usually find it in Epictetus.

choose things, as Alexander has it. You may say, well, that was to be expected; after all this is what Aristotle says, and we are here dealing with commentaries on Aristotle. This is true. However, in the *Paraphrase* of Book 3 of the *Nicomachean Ethics*, ascribed variously to some Heliodorus and others, in at least one place we have '*helesthai kai mê*' instead of Aristotle's original '*prattein kai mê*' (52,25–7); and in the *Mantissa* ch. 22 we read, marked out as Aristotle's view, that deliberate choice depends on us (*eph' hêmin hê prohairesis, Mant.* 169,38). So at some point Aristotle's remarks on the things that depend on us must have been understood as being primarily about choice and only secondarily about actions (cf. also Ammonius, *in Int.* 242,24–5 and below, Section X). We do not know when the *Paraphrase* was written, but it is very likely to date after Alexander.

Thus, in both commentators the concept of what depends on us seems wholly compatible with both causal determinism and causal indeterminism. They both include elements which we find in the same context in Alexander but not in Aristotle. They both introduce formulations of the 'it could be/happen otherwise' kind and they both connect Aristotle's *EN* 3.3, on deliberate choice and what depends on us, with fate – something Alexander did as well (e.g. *Fat.* 180).

VI. Middle-Platonists on Contingency and That Which Depends on Us

For a closer connection between Aristotle's works and Alexander, concerning that which depends on us, we need to look elsewhere: viz. at the texts of the Middle Platonists.[13] The Middle Platonists – like virtually all philosophical schools, sects and currents in the first and second century CE – had developed their own position on fate and that which depends on us. Their theory of fate is based on a handful of passages from Plato, and is influenced in many aspects by the Stoics. We find variants of the theory e.g. in Alcinous' *Handbook of Platonism*, in the treatise *On Fate* by [Plutarch], in Nemesius' *On Human Nature* and in Calcidius' commentary on Plato's *Timaeus*.[14] [Plutarch], Calcidius, and Nemesius – although at variance in many details – go back to some elaborate Platonist theory of fate which *may* stem from the first half of the second century,[15] but which should in any event at least in part precede Alexander. This common source encompassed first a part on fate in which – among other things – a distinction was drawn between things that are *included* (*periekhein*) in fate, which are all things, and those things that are *fated*, or *in accordance with fate* (*kath' heimarmenên*),

---

[13] I use the term 'Middle-Platonist' to refer to those Platonists commonly classified in this way, but do not maintain that there was any unified Middle-Platonist school.
[14] Alcinous, *Didasc.* ch. 26, Nemesius, *Nat. hom.* e.g. 110, 125–6, Calcidius, *Tim.* 142–187, [Plutarch] *Fat.* passim, Apuleius, *Plat.* 1.12, perhaps an echo in Alexander, *Mant.* ch. 25, 183.
[15] So Moraux, *Der Aristotelismus bei den Griechen II* (n. 10 above), pp. 495–6, following Gercke and others. There is a problem in that the texts that provide reports of this theory are either clearly later (Nemesius, Calcidius) or cannot be dated with any certainty (Alcinous, [Plutarch]). It is also clear that over time the theory underwent extensive step-by-step development, and many elements of the theory as reported by Calcidius and Nemesius are certainly later than the second century.

which are all those things that are necessary. In addition, it contained a section on the things included in fate but not fated; a section on providence; a critique of Stoic doctrine of fate; and a discussion of fallacies concerned with determinism.

For my present purposes the section on things included in fate but not fated is relevant. In all three sources this section differs from the rest of the Middle-Platonist theory in that (i) the only traces from Plato are a couple of examples tacked on in the section on chance; (ii) the passage is clearly based on a whole range of texts from Aristotle, which all dealt with 'that which is not necessary'.[16] It looks as if someone has taken a list of types of things that are not necessary, perhaps from Aristotle *EN* 3.3 1112a31–3, perhaps from some later, 'updated', list,[17] and then has worked his way through the works of Aristotle, picking out and systematising the relevant sections. The passage draws from Aristotle's *Physics, Metaphysics, Nicomachean Ethics, De Interpretatione* and perhaps from the *Categories*. The list of things not necessary is of interest for two reasons: first, it includes that which depends on us (*to eph' hêmin*). Second, we do not simply have a presentation or co-ordination of bits from Aristotle, but a *systematisation*, in which at that a couple of distinctions and terms are added which we do not find, or do not find used in that way, in Aristotle.

Regarding the origin of this passage, we may assume that it was compiled in the second century CE at the latest. It may well be earlier. As I said above, the only bits from Plato in it are two examples tacked on to the section on chance. There is thus no reason to think that the author of the common source of the Middle-Platonist doctrine of fate is the originator of the passage. The rest of the Middle-Platonist fate theory stands without it, and vice versa. The original author of this bit of 'Middle-Platonist' theory could be equally well a Peripatetic or a Platonist – if indeed such a distinction made sense at the time. We may say the author was an Aristotle scholar.

The passage appears to have employed the following classificatory scheme: the most general term is the possible (*to dunaton*). It encompasses both the necessary (*to anagkaion*) and the contingent (*to endekhomenon*): the necessary is determined as the possible the opposite of which is impossible; the contingent as the possible the opposite of which is possible, too (*dunaton hou kai to antikeimenon dunaton*).[18] This is the distinction of one-sided and two-sided possibility as we find it in Aristotle's *De Interpretatione* 12 and 13 (*Int.* 22b36 ff.; 23a15–16), although Aristotle did not consistently use the term 'contingent' (*endekhomenon*) for two-sided possibility in the way our source seems to have done. That which depends on us is then characterised as a subclass of the contingent.[19] That is, the section connects explicitly a distinction and an account from Aristotle's modal theory (that of two-sided possibility), with the question of moral responsibility, as it comes up in Aristotle's ethics.

Is not all this a bit far-fetched? you may object. Surely the Stoics and the Megarics or Dialecticians had already connected the problem of determinism with modal logic,

---

[16] Nemesius, *Nat. hom.* 103–4, [Plutarch] *Fat.* 570F–572F, Calcidius, *Tim.* 155–6.
[17] See e.g. Theophrastus in Stobaeus, *Ecl.* 1,89,2–5, Alexander, *Fat.* 211,1–4, *Mant.* ch. 25, Nemesius, *Nat. hom.* 112,13–15 for such lists.
[18] Nemesius, *Nat. hom.* 103.20–1, [Plutarch] *Fat.* 571B.
[19] [Plutarch] *Fat.* 571C–D, Nemesius, *Nat. hom.* 114.21–4.

for instance in the Mower Argument and the Master Argument.[20] This is true, and given that the same Middle-Platonist source discussed these very fallacies and criticised the Stoic theory of fate,[21] the trigger for connecting Aristotelian modal theory and Aristotelian ethics may well have come from there. You may also object that the connection between the concept of contingency, qua two-sided possibility, and of what depends on us is just a commonplace. However, for instance the early Stoics, it seems, had neither a definition of what depends on us nor a term for contingency: they talked about two-sided possibility in terms of what is true but not-necessary and what is false but possible.[22] Moreover, the Stoics had a one-sided concept of what depends on us and they were by far not the only ones (see Section XII).

But be that as it may. The best way to find out whether Aristotle's *De Interpretatione* 12 and 13 were used for the development of a concept of what depends on us is to look at the passages and the ancient commentaries on them. In *De Interpretatione* 13 Aristotle connects the concept of capacity (*dunamis*) with that of two-sided possibility, stating that not all capacities are two-sided, or capacities of opposites (*antikeimena*), although rational capacities are, like that of human beings for actions, e.g. walking (*Int.* 13, 22b36–23a6; cf. *Metaph.* 9, 1046b1–2, 4–7; 1048a2–3, 8–9; 1050b30–4). Thus here Aristotle links the concept of two-sided possibility with the capacities for opposites, and draws the connection to human rational capacities. All the signs are that what Aristotle has in mind is a general capacity, and not a capacity involving freedom to do otherwise. (For instance, he mentions the fact that there are non-rational capacities for opposites, e.g. *Int.* 13, 23a3–4: *enia mentoi dunatai kai tôn kata tas alogous dunameis hama ta antikeimena*.)

Ammonius, in his commentary on this very passage of the *De Interpretatione*, states that in the case of us human beings, whose rational capacities are two-sided (*in Int.* 242,19–20),

> we are master ... of our deliberate choice, and it depends on us to do or not to do any of the things that happen in accordance with deliberate choice.
>
> Ammonius, *in Int.* 242,24–7

Ammonius here connects that which depends on us with Aristotle's two-sided possibility (the contingent), via the rational capacities of which Aristotle speaks, interpreting these in particular as power of deliberate choices.[23] But deliberate choice and that which depends on us were the topic of *EN* 3.3.

---

[20] For the Mower Argument see e.g. Diog. Laert. 7.25; Ammonius, *in Int.* 131,25–32; for the Master Argument Epictetus, *Diss.* 2.19.
[21] [Plutarch] *Fat.* 574E, Calcidius, *Tim.* 160–1. Note also that Ammonius discusses the Mower Argument in his commentary on *De Interpretatione*, see previous note.
[22] Cf. Cicero, *Fat.* 13, Plutarch, *Stoic. Rep.* 1055E.
[23] Aristotle himself introduced deliberate choice (but not that which depends on us) into this context in *Metaph.* 9, 1048a10–15, but in a very different way than Ammonius: his point is that circumstances permitting we will necessarily realise that side of our two-sided capacities for which we have a desire resulting from deliberate choice.

The next line of our passage (*in Int.* 242,27–8) is also of interest: there the question is raised whether the capacities of the gods correspond to one-sided or two-sided possibility. And then we learn: Alexander asked himself the same question. Now, if Alexander asked himself that question, it seems very likely indeed that what led up to the question, i.e. the above-quoted passage in the commentary just beforehand, stems also from Alexander, that is – presumably – from *his* (lost) commentary on the *De Interpretatione*.[24] Thus it appears that both our Aristotle scholar from the Middle-Platonist common source and Alexander connected that which depends on us with a passage on modal logic from Aristotle's *De Interpretatione* 13.

But let us return to our Aristotle scholar and the subordination of that which depends on us to the contingent in the Middle-Platonist common source. There we find three types of the contingent: one part of the contingent is 'for the most part', one 'for the lesser part' and one 'in equal parts'.[25] Those for the most part and for the lesser part are characterised as opposites. For example, if for the most part the weather is hot in August, it is cold, or not-hot, in August for the lesser part.[26] On the other hand, the 'in equal parts' is that which depends on us, as for instance walking and not walking, and in general acting and not acting.[27]

In Aristotle we find neither this threefold distinction of the contingent, nor the category of what is 'in equal parts'. However, there can be no doubt that this third category is derived from Aristotle's *Int.* 9, 18a39-b9, and is meant to pick up what Aristotle calls 'as it happens' (*hopoter' etukhen*) there.[28] In chapter 9 of the *De Interpretatione* Aristotle investigates whether or in what way the Principle of Bivalence holds for future propositions. One of his problems is that, if all propositions that state something about the future are already true or false now, this fact could somehow entail that all future events are predetermined already now.[29] Aristotle contrasts the 'as it happens' with necessity and explains it as 'it is no more thus than not thus (*ouden mallon*), nor will it be' (*Int.* 18b9, cf. 19a18), and it is about these (the things 'as it happens') that one deliberates (*Int.* 18b31, cf. 19a9).

Hence, I assume, our Aristotle scholar – or some earlier Aristotle exegete – simply reasoned as follows: the 'as it happens' must be part of the contingent, since according to Aristotle it is not necessary. An expression, parallel to 'for the most part' was then coined for this subtype of contingent, namely 'in equal parts', based on Aristotle's phrase 'no more thus than not thus'. Since Aristotle says that the 'as it happens' is concerned with deliberation and action, and this is – according to Aristotle himself – the sphere of that which depends on us, the Aristotle scholar concluded that the 'as it happens'

---

[24] See Moraux, *Der Aristotelismus bei den Griechen II* (n. 10 above), p. 363.
[25] *Epi to polu, ep' elatton, ep' ison*; Nemesius, *Nat. hom.* 104,1–2, [Plutarch] *Fat.* 571C, cf. Calcidius, *Tim.* 156.
[26] Nemesius, *Nat. hom.* 104,2–4, [Plutarch] *Fat.* 571C. [Plutarch] maintains that both are subordinated to nature (ibid.).
[27] [Plutarch] *Fat.* 571C–D, Nemesius, *Nat. hom.* 104,4–5 in connection with 114,19–22.
[28] Cf. e.g. [Plutarch] *Fat.* 571C: *to de hôs episês kai hopoteron etukhen*. See also Ammonius, *in Int.* 143,1–7, Alexander, *in An. Pr.* 163,21–9, *Fat.* 174,30–175,4.
[29] For the controversy among scholars over this passage see e.g. D. Frede, 'The Sea-Battle Reconsidered', *Oxford Studies in Ancient Philosophy* 3 (1985), 31–87.

must be that which depends on us. This identification of the 'in equal parts' with that which depends on us suggests that, unlike the 'for the most part' and the 'for the lesser part', the 'in equal parts' was not given a statistical interpretation. The phrases 'for the most part' and 'for the lesser part' express probability in the sense that if it is, say, hot in August 95% of all years (of all days?), then it is 'for the most part hot' in August. But our Aristotle scholar cannot have understood the statement 'walking is "in equal parts"' to mean 'people walk 50% of the time; or 50% of the time relevant to walking'. Rather, the idea must have been that in any situation of possible walking it is no more likely that the person walks than not – quite independently of how much people statistically actually walk.

In Nemesius we are twice given a definition of the 'in equal parts'; it is 'that of which we are capable of <doing> both it and its opposite'. (*auto te dunametha kai to antikeimenon autôi*, Nemesius, *Nat. hom.* 104,6–7; 114,21–2). In the second passage this definition is followed by the explicit identification of the 'in equal parts' with what depends on us, and it is illustrated with examples (*Nat. hom.* 114,24–115,2). Note the similarity of the definition with on the one hand Aristotle's things that 'are at the same time capable of opposites' (*dunatai hama ta antikeimena*) from *De Interpretatione* 13 (23a3–4, see above), and with Alexander's definition of that which depends on us as 'that of which we have the power of choosing also its opposite' (*hôn en hêmin hê exousia tou helesthai kai ta antikeimena, Fat.* 181,5–6) on the other (see above Section II).

As an interim result we can state: we have in this Middle-Platonist common source a concept of what depends on us which seems to be the outcome of bringing together and systematising three bits of Aristotelian doctrine:

- the things that depend on us, as those we deliberate about and from which we choose, from *Nicomachean Ethics* 3.3;
- the concept of two-sided possibility, or the contingent, and its relation to the two-sided capacities of rational beings from *De Interpretatione* 13 and *Metaphysics* 9; and
- the problem of future contingents, and the idea of things that can equally happen and not happen from *De Interpretatione* 9.

The resulting concept is captured in the account of what is 'in equal parts' – which is identified with what depends on us – as: 'that of which we are capable of <doing> both it and its opposite'.[30]

VII. The Philosophical Relevance of the Link between the *Nicomachean Ethics* and the *De Interpretatione*

Why have I spent so much time on the development of a concept of what depends on us in the context of Aristotle's *De Interpretatione*? The reason is this: my above question

---

[30] We do not know who first brought together the *Nicomachean Ethics* and the *De Interpretatione* in this context. We do know that Aspasius wrote a commentary not only on the former, but also on the latter, which is however lost; cf. Moraux, *Der Aristotelismus bei den Griechen II* (n. 10 above), p. 231.

was when and where that concept was first understood as indeterminist, and as implying the possibility that the same person, with the same beliefs and desires, in the same circumstances does otherwise. The obvious question now is whether the *eph' hêmin* of our Aristotle scholar was taken to imply indeterminist freedom. The definition 'that of which we are capable of <doing> both it and its opposite' itself is of no help: it is just as ambiguous in this respect as were Aristotle's original phrases 'what depends on him to do and not to' (cf. *EE* 1223a7–8, 1226b30–1) and 'being at the same time capable of opposites' (*Int.* 23a3–4). Take walking as an example: walking depends on me because I am capable of both walking and <doing> the opposite, i.e. not walking. This can mean that I have the general two-sided capacity of walking and of not walking – which would be compatible with determinism. Alternatively, it can be understood as implying that there are no *pre*ceding causes which sufficiently determine that I walk, or determine that I do not walk. This understanding would be incompatible with pre-determinism. Or it can be understood as implying that it is causally undetermined whether or not I walk. This would be incompatible with determinism.

Perhaps the Middle-Platonist identification of what depends on us with what happens 'in equal parts' was a step in the direction of undetermined choice. For if the 'in equal parts' is understood as tied to individual situations such that e.g. in every situation of possible walking it is no more likely than not that I walk (see above), then the capacity expressed in the account 'capable of <doing> both it and its opposite' will also be tied to an individual situation. That is, something depends on us at a certain time if at that time we are capable of doing both it and its opposite. But this is still ambiguous between (i) having at that time a general capacity to walk and being at that time (ii) un-predetermined or (iii) causally undetermined in our walking.[31]

The vagueness in the definition of that which depends on us seems to be resolved in favour of an un-predeterministic or indeterministic concept, once the connection of that which depends on us with the problem of the truth-values of future propositions is fully taken into account. For in *De Interpretatione* 9 the problem of truth-values of future propositions is connected with the question of the undeterminedness of the future, more precisely, the undeterminedness of whether something will happen at a particular future time: it is not yet determined *now* whether there will be a sea-battle *tomorrow*. Here pairs of propositions about the occurring of future events are at issue, and the occurring is tagged to a particular time in the future: the occurring of a sea battle tomorrow versus the absence of the occurring of a sea battle tomorrow. Plainly the question here is not whether a sea battle (or anything else) has a *general capacity* of occurring, and whether it has that capacity now. The question is whether tomorrow a sea-battle will or will not take place. That is, starting out from one and the same situation, viz. the present one, it is assumed that something could or could not obtain at some later time; and it is at present undetermined whether or not it will obtain.

Thus here we have expressly one necessary condition for indeterminist freedom to do otherwise: exactly the same antecedent situation is combined with the possibility of

---

[31] The same ambiguity is connected with *hama* in Aristotle's phrase *dunatai hama ta antikeimena* from *De Interpretatione* 13, 23a3–4.

two opposed states of affairs obtaining in some later situation in such a way that the antecedent situation leaves it undetermined which of the later states will obtain. However, in Aristotle's *De Interpretatione* this is merely a matter of logic: Aristotle does not consider whether the present situation is *causally* responsible for what happens in the future. A fortiori, he does not ask whether definite truth-bivalence of future propositions would entail that human decisions are causally predetermined.

VIII. Alcinous and Ammonius

Did our Aristotle scholar, or the Middle-Platonists – when drawing on *De Interpretatione* 9 and identifying what depends on us with what happens 'to equal parts' – make this step from the logical undeterminedness of the future by the present to the causal undeterminedness of human decisions and/or actions? We do not know. However, remnants of such a thought can perhaps be detected in chapter 26, on fate, possibility, and that which depends on us, in the *Handbook of Platonism* of the Middle-Platonist Alcinous. This passage displays many similarities to those in Nemesius, Calcidius, and [Plutarch], but is sufficiently distinct to suggest that it belonged to a slightly different tradition.[32] Alcinous works with a two-sided, potestative concept of what depends on us which in its formulation is closer to Aristotle than the one in Nemesius. Thus he writes: *adespoton oun hê psukhê kai ep' autêi men to praxai ê mê* (*Didasc.* 179.10–11; cf. Aristotle, *EE* 1226b30–1). Of interest to us now is what we find shortly afterwards:

> The nature of the possible falls somehow between the true and the false, and being by nature undetermined, that which depends on us uses it (i.e. the possible) as a vehicle. Whatever happens as a result of our choosing will be either true or false.[33]
>
> *Didasc.* 179.20–3

and then again:

> The possible ... is undetermined, and it takes on truth or not depending on the inclining in either direction of that which depends on us.[34]
>
> *Didasc.* 179,31–3

This can be read as the abbreviated version of an argument in which the idea of undeterminedness as found in *De Interpretatione* 9 is applied to the concept of what

---

[32] Cf. e.g. J. Dillon, *Alcinous, The Handbook of Platonism* (Oxford: Clarendon Press, 1993), pp. 160–4. Alcinous flourished some time between the first and third century CE. I assume the second half of the second century or the early third century as a likely date; but he may be even later: cf. T. Göransson, *Albinus, Alcinous, Arius Didymus* (Göteborg: Acta Universitatis Gothoburgensis, 1995).

[33] *Hê de tou dunatou phusis peptôke men pôs metaxu tou te alêthous kai tou pseudous, aoristôi de onti autôi têi phusei hôsper epokheitai to eph' hêmin. Ho d' an helomenôn hêmôn genêtai, touto estai ê alêthes ê pseudos.*

[34] *To de dunaton ... aoristainon de tôi eph' hêmin kata tên eph' hopoteron rhopên lambanei to alêtheuein ê mê.* As J. Whittaker (in his comments in the Budé edition, *Alcinoos, Enseignement des doctrines de Platon* (Paris: Les Belles Lettres, 1990), p. 134, n. 424) has pointed out, the whole section reflects Aristotelian thought and terminology.

depends on us. The link with the *De Interpretatione* is suggested by the repeated reference to truth and falsehood, which is entirely absent in the relevant chapters of the *Nicomachean* and *Eudemian Ethics*. The argument could have run like this: future contingents are not yet true or false now. It is so far undetermined whether the event announced in them will or will not happen. If we choose that it happens, it will happen. If we choose that it does not happen, it will not happen. Once we have chosen, circumstances permitting, the corresponding propositions will be either true or false. This implies that at least up to the point of the decision it is not predetermined which way we choose.[35]

A similar thought can be detected in Ammonius at the beginning of his comments on *De Interpretatione* 9. There he maintains that the logical principle that states the indefiniteness of the truth-values of contrary pairs of propositions about the future is necessary for ethics. It is needed, so that it can depend on us whether we choose or do not choose and perform or do not perform certain actions. Ammonius' argumentation in this passage implies that prior to our decision it is not yet fully determined which way we decide (see Ammonius, *in Int.* 130,23–33, quoted below).

So two passages, one of them presumably earlier than Alexander, suggest that an indeterminist two-sided concept of what depends on us was developed in the context of the exegesis of Aristotle's *De Interpretatione* 9. However, two things should be noted: first, in both passages no mention is made of causation: that is, we do not know whether the indeterminedness was understood as absence of *causal* factors – as opposed to the 'necessitation' of the future by logical determinism which leaves it open *in which way* the future is determined by the past or the present. However, we know that some Stoics, presumably from the second century, discussed Aristotle's *De Interpretatione* 9.[36] Since in Stoic philosophy the connection was drawn between logical and causal determinism, it is thus likely that the link with causation was made at least by some philosophers in the second century. Second, even if there is no *pre*determination (causal or otherwise) of a human choice or action, within the context of ancient theory of causation which allows for objects to be causes this need not imply that the choice or action is causally *un*determined (That is, it could be freedom of type 4.) For example, if the assumption is that there is a core of personality or moral character in each person, then even if the decision is not *pre*determined, it may be determined *at the time of the decision* by the fact that the person is such and such a person. That is, the person would still in identical circumstances always go for the same action.

IX. From the Middle-Platonists to Alexander of Aphrodisias

I leave it open whether the Middle-Platonists understood their two-sided concept of *eph' hêmin* as implying undeterminedness or non-*pre*determination by causal factors.

---

[35] The two passages quoted are most remarkable also for the fact that in them *eph' hêmin* does not refer to the things that depend on us, but to some kind of decision making faculty.

[36] Cf. Alexander, *Fat.* 177,7–14; Boethius, *in Int.*² 208,1–3. In the Alexander passage the example of the sea-battle draws the link to *De Interpretatione* 9 and the terminology and theory is Stoic, although presumably not early Stoic, and Alexander connects the argument with the theory of fate.

My concern is rather whether Alexander was familiar with the second century theory of *eph' hêmin* as found in some of the Middle Platonist texts on fate, and whether it is likely that his concepts (which I sketched in Section II) could have developed from it. There is some evidence that this was so.

To begin with, although we do not have the distinction of things contingent into 'for the most part', 'for the lesser part', and 'in equal parts' in his treatise *On Fate*, we do find it in his commentaries on the *Prior Analytics* and the *Topics*, and in the *Mantissa* ch. 22. In his comments on Aristotle, *Top.* 112b1 the threefold distinction occurs preceded by the distinction between necessity and contingency (Alexander, *in Top.* 177,19-27), just as in Nemesius (*Nat. hom.* 103–4) and [Plutarch] *Fat.* 571B-D. In his comments on Aristotle, *An. Pr.* 32b8 the threefold distinction is introduced by 'one meaning of the "contingent" is the following; to this belong also the things that come to be in accordance with deliberate choice' (Alexander, *in An. Pr.* 162,31-2). So Alexander, too, connects the threefold distinction with Aristotle's concept of deliberate choice. However, unlike our Aristotle scholar from the Middle-Platonist texts he does not equate things that happen in accordance with deliberate choice with the things 'in equal parts'. Rather, he classifies them among things for the most part (*to epi to pleiston*, cf. also Alexander, *in An. Pr.* 169,6–9; 270,23–5). For things 'in equal parts' we obtain the example of Socrates' taking a walk in the evening, and his talking to some particular person. This fact, together with the absence of the threefold distinction in his *On Fate*, and of that which depends on us in his commentaries, suggests to me (i) that Alexander draws not from the Middle-Platonist texts, but from a source they, like him, drew from,[37] and (ii) that he did not connect the threefold distinction with the question of determinism and freedom at all. In the above passages on things for the most part he is not concerned with acts of choice, but with the relation between one's choices and their realisation:[38] far more often than not one actually does what one has chosen to do. Alexander's two examples for what happens 'in equal parts' on the other hand invite a statistical interpretation. They are both cases where one cannot easily say that Socrates does them more often than not, or less often than not.[39]

Thus Alexander, though acquainted with the concept of the 'in equal parts' seems not to have made the connection between it and that which depends on us. Nonetheless, it seems likely that he knew the account of what depends on us which in Nemesius was identified with that of the 'in equal parts'; that he understood it as implying indeterminism; and that it was a precursor of his own concept. If we trust Alexander's

---

[37] On this point I agree with Bob Sharples; see R. W. Sharples in P. Moraux, *Der Aristotelismus bei den Griechen von Andronikos bis Alexander von Aphrodisias III: Alexander von Aphrodisias* (Berlin: De Gruyter, 2001).

[38] See also Sharples, ibid.

[39] The story undergoes still a different twist in the *Mantissa* ch. 22, which seems not to present Alexander's own view as held in *On Fate*, but an alternative Peripatetic one. Here a twofold distinction of what happens for the most part and what happens for the lesser part comes up in the context of the discussion of that which depends on us. The things in accordance with deliberate choice are partly subordinated to what happens for the most part (when one acts 'in character', as it were), partly to what happens for the lesser part, and each is connected with its own type of *eph' hêmin* (see also below Section XII). This time the connection is between one's character, etc. and one's choices, not between one's choices and one's actions.

own words, in his *On Fate* ch. 26 (196,24 ff.) he presents one of a number of arguments of his opponents which were meant to criticise 'that that which depends on us is such as the common conception of human beings believes it to be'. The main point of the argument is the claim that a two-sided *eph' hêmin* would preclude virtues and vices depending on us, since at the time when we are virtuous we are not capable of acting viciously, and vice versa. The argument begins:

> If, they say, those things depend on us of which we are capable of <doing> also the opposites ...[40]

This is almost exactly the definition of what depends on us as we find it in the Middle-Platonist texts. What shall we make of this? It seems to me that the most natural conjecture would run somewhat like this:

These critics of the 'Middle-Platonist' two-sided concept of what depends on us were most probably the Stoics Alexander criticises most in his book, i.e. orthodox Stoics who in the second century CE held a theory of fate similar to Chrysippus'. We know that the Stoic doctrine of fate had been the subject of criticism by the Middle-Platonists in their treatise(s) on fate.[41] These Middle-Platonist critics, as we have seen, had adopted a two-sided, potestative concept of what depends on us, based on Aristotle's writings- although this was not the only one they had (see below Section XII). So it is likely that some second century Stoics in turn criticised this two-sided concept; and that this is what we find in the Alexander passage. We can however not rule out with certainty that Alexander's opponents in this chapter are not Stoics but 'dissident' Peripatetics.

If the argument Alexander presents is Stoic, we can infer that the concept of *eph' hêmin* was at least un-*pre*determinist, if not indeterminist. For only then is it incompatible with the Stoic theory of fate, and would give the Stoics reasonable grounds to reject it. In that case would be evidence that before Alexander an un-predeterminist two-sided concept of what depends on us was discussed among Middle-Platonists (or Peripatetics) and Stoics. If the argument was part of a dispute internal to the Peripatetic school, the criticism of the two-sided, potestative *eph' hêmin* need not have had anything to do with the question of determinism. It could merely have been a way of pointing out that the definition does not harmonise with Aristotle's own claim that virtues and vices depend on us.

In any event we can be reasonably certain that *Alexander* understood the criticised account of what depends on us as not only un-predeterminist, but indeterminist. For his criticism of the argument (which extends to ch. 29 of his *On Fate*) is one of the passages where he undoubtedly defends an indeterminist concept of what depends on us (*Fat*. ch. 29, 199,29–200,7, see Section XII).[42]

---

[40] *Ei, phasin, tauta estin eph' hêmin, hôn kai ta antikeimena dunametha ...*
[41] [Plutarch] *Fat.* 574E–F, Calcidius, *Tim.* 160–1.
[42] Could Nemesius' source have taken this account from Alexander, rather than the other way about? This is chronologically possible, but unlikely. For in Nemesius the account occurs twice as account of the 'in equal parts' (which suggests it was a technical definition), and in one of these cases what happens 'in equal parts' is then *equated* with what depends on us. Moreover, it would be rather odd if the *one* account of what depends on us which Nemesius picked from Alexander is taken from an argument by Alexander's *opponents*.

Thus Alexander interpreted the 'Middle-Platonist' concept of what depends on us as indeterminist. However, in Alexander's standard accounts of what depends on us there are two additional elements that are absent in the 'Middle-Platonist' account:

> 'depending on us' is predicated of the things over which we have in us the power of also choosing the opposite.
>
> Fat. 181,5

Thus, the two new features are: (i) the element of choosing or not choosing (*helesthai*) to perform an action, instead of simply acting and not acting; (ii) the introduction of a power (*exousia*) which the individual on whom something depends possesses.[43] Both features are significant in that they reflect important developments of the understanding of moral responsibility and its relation to freedom in later antiquity.

X. The Element of Choice in the Accounts of What Depends on Us

The first important innovation in the account, which we witness not only in Alexander but also in some later authors, is that from action to choice. In Alexander's accounts it manifests itself in the change from 'the power of *doing* opposites' to 'the power of *choosing* opposites'. We find variations of the formulation with 'to choose' (usually *haireisthai*) many times over in his *On Fate*.[44] We also find such formulations in chapters 22 and 23 of the *Mantissa*.[45] Similar accounts are preserved in Ammonius' *On De Interpretatione* (130,30–2, on Aristotle, *Int.* 9, quoted below), in Boethius' *On De Interpretatione*[2] (203, on Aristotle, *Int.* 9),[46] in the later paraphrase of the *Nicomachean Ethics* 52,25–7, a passage to which I referred earlier, and in Nemesius, *Nat. hom.* 115,22–7, a passage whose origin I assume to be later than Alexander's *On Fate*. A comparable explanation is preserved in Calcidius, *Tim.* 151.

There were three main philosophical theories concerned with human choice available to second and third century philosophers, all of which are possible influence factors, one deriving from Aristotle, another from Epictetus, a third from Plato.

---

[43] As far as I am aware, in Alexander the two-sided 'Middle-Platonist' account of what depends on us (i.e. the simple account, without reference to choosing and/or power) occurs only in the opponents' argument in ch. 26. Of the four closest passages one contains *exousia* (*Fat.* 180,2), one the verb 'to choose' (*Mant.* 174,32); the remaining two (*Mant.* 170,1; 171,24) are from ch. 22 of the *Mantissa* which in any event presents a position quite different from Alexander's in his *On Fate* and *Mantissa* ch. 23; of these *Mant.* 171,24 does not provide an account either. However, the fact that the two first-mentioned passages are so close to the 'Middle-Platonist' one, and each only adds one of Alexander's additional features, makes it the more likely that Alexander's accounts are a development of the more basic 'Middle-Platonist' one that resulted from Aristotle exegesis.

[44] See e.g. *Fat.* 180,26–8; 181,5–6.13–14; 184,18–19.

[45] In ch. 23, which seems to present Alexander's view, there is no definition of that which depends on us with 'to choose', but choosing plays a major role passim; e.g. *Mant.* 174,9–12; 175,23–5. In ch. 22 *prohaireisthai* is used instead of *haireisthai* (*Mant.* 171,22–4; 172,10–12).

[46] Ex libero arbitrio, ut quod possum et *velle et non velle*, an velim hoc antequam fiat incertum est.

I suspect that a combination of them is responsible for the introduction of 'choice' into the accounts of what depends on us. None of the three positions was originally concerned with freedom of decision or indeterminist freedom in general.

First, I have traced above the adaptation of Aristotle's theory of deliberate choice (*prohairesis*) from his ethics into the debate over fate: his concept of deliberate choice was connected with that which depends on us by the commentators, in [Plutarch]'s *On Fate* (571D), by Nemesius, by Alexander (e.g. in *Fat.* ch. 12, *Mant.* ch. 22). For Aristotle, deliberate choice is what distinguishes human, rational agency from animal action. Its characteristic feature is that it is a certain appetitive state of the soul which results from deliberation about possible courses of action. Whether we deliberate well, and what the outcome of our deliberation is depends on our character or settled dispositions. There is no evidence that Aristotle maintained that the same agent in the same circumstances could come up with a different choice (*prohairesis*). Moral responsibility is grounded on the fact that the agents are the beginning (*arkhê*) of their actions (and dispositions).

Second, Epictetus, spelling out parts of early Stoic philosophy, restricts that which depends on us to certain 'mental events' or movements of the soul. Only the use of our impressions, that is giving assent to them or withholding it, depends on us, since these are the only things not subordinate to external force or hindrances. Assenting to impulsive impressions (*phantasiai hormêtikai*), i.e. impressions of something as desirable or to be avoided, *is* choosing a course of action. The realisation of what we have chosen to do does not depend on us, insofar as it is always possible that it is thwarted by external hindrances. The stress in Epictetus is on the points that it is oneself who chooses, and that one is not necessitated (*katênagkasthai*) in one's choice. To what impressions we give assent depends on our dispositions (or *prohairesis*, see Section XI). The question of whether the same person in the same circumstances could choose otherwise is not addressed. I believe that – in harmony with the orthodox Stoic view – Epictetus' answer would have been 'no'.[47] If a person wants to act in a different manner than they do, they have to change their disposition or *prohairesis*, i.e. that factor on the basis of which they make individual choices. Epictetus emphasises that moral accountability is – primarily – connected with the use of our impressions (e.g. *Diss.* 1.12.34) rather than with our actions. We are morally responsible because it is in our assenting and choosing that our character and dispositions are reflected (MR1). The influence of Epictetus on philosophers and intellectuals in later antiquity was immense, and at the beginning of the third century various elements of his philosophy had been absorbed into the general philosophical discussion, including Christian and Platonist thought.[48]

Third, Plato may have provided a further motive for the change from action to choice. As I mentioned above, the Middle-Platonist philosophers arranged their doctrine of fate around a number of passages from Plato. One of them comes from the Myth of Er in Book 10 of the *Republic*. There the souls, before they are born again, have

---

[47] I argue this point more fully in Bobzien, *Determinism and Freedom* (n. 3 above), Section 7.1.
[48] Epictetus' philosophy was known e.g. to Dio Chrysostom, Philostratus, Lucian, Celsus, Marcus Aurelius, Gellius, Galen, Origen, Gregory of Nazianzus, and Augustine.

to *choose* a life, and in that context they are told that the consequences of their choice, whether good or bad, will be their responsibility, and that they cannot blame god: *aitia helomenou: theos anaitios* (*Rep.* 617E). For Plato, in this passage, the question was not one of freedom of decision. His concern was that the human soul *and not someone else* – in particular not god – is responsible for the choice (MR1). From the second century onwards, mainly in Platonist texts, the above quote from Plato occurs so regularly that we can infer that it, and with it parts of the Myth of Er, were a central element of the Platonist theory of fate.[49]

In some texts that present the Middle-Platonist theory of hypothetical fate,[50] Plato's theory undergoes a significant development. In Alcinous (*Didasc.* ch. 26, 179,8–13) Plato's formerly 'pre-natal' choice of a life is presented as including the choice of individual *actions* in one's life, and it has become dependent on the soul whether or not to act. In Nemesius the term *prohairesis* has entered the interpretation of Plato's statement: now the individual choices (*prohairesis*) and some of the actions in accordance with choice (*kata prohairesin*) depend on us (*Nat. hom.* 110,5–9; cf. 109). Neither text suggests that *prohairesis* or *haireisthai* refers to freedom of decision. Rather, the importance of the introduction of individual choices lies in the fact that it is in their choices that people manifest themselves qua rational or moral beings: my choices, since determined by nothing but myself, reflect *who I am*. This is why I am morally responsible for what I choose (MR1). It is in order to ensure this that choices have been exempted from the *predetermination* by fate (freedom of type 4). In the parallel passage in Calcidius (*Tim.* 151) on the other hand we find in this context a statement that connects that which depends on us with the motions of the soul only, and which invokes a notion that comes close to that of freedom of decision: in it the fact that the choice between opposite motions of the soul is in our power is used to explain why these motions depend on us. Still – as in Plato – the choice is one of good or bad.[51] The Middle-Platonist interpretations of Plato with their focus on individual choices of actions are likely to reflect the general focus on choices and mental events which seems to have started at the time of Epictetus or a little earlier.[52]

---

[49] Cf. e.g. Calcidius, *Tim.* 154, Hippolytus, *Ref.* 19.19 (*Doxogr. Graec.* 569,19–22), Nemesius, *Nat. hom.* 110,7–9, Maximus of Tyre 41.5a, Justin, *Apol.* 44, Porphyry *apud* Stobaeus, *Ecl.* 2,164; see also Tacitus, *Ann.* 6.22.

[50] This theory, the earliest traces of which are preserved in Tacitus, *Ann.* 6.22 and Plutarch, *Quaest. Conv.* 740C, maintains that certain human activities are not fated but caused by the person, whereas the consequences of these activities are fated. Cf. e.g. J. Den Boeft, *Calcidius on Fate: His Doctrines and Sources* (Leiden: Brill, 1970), pp. 28–34.

[51] Collocati autem in alterutram partem (i.e. good or bad) meriti praecessio animarum nostrarum motus est iudiciumque et consensus earum et appetitus vel declinatio, quae sunt in nobis posita, quoniam tam horum quam eorum quae his contraria sunt optio penes nos est.

[52] On the one hand, from the second century onwards sources that discuss determinism seem generally to concentrate more on mental activities like thinking, deliberating, assenting and choosing. For instance, the Chaldaeans listed such mental states and events among the things they claimed were predetermined by the stars (e.g. Gellius, *NA* 14.1.23, cf. Nemesius, *Nat. hom.* 104,18–21). These explicit mentions of the predetermination of the motions of the soul may have triggered their explicit exemption from external causal predetermination or force on the side of the 'libertarians'. On the other hand, there is the importance of the problem of choice (*prohairesis*) between good and evil in early Christian theory, Platonism, and Gnosticism, in particular in the context of the question of the origin of evil.

Returning to Alexander and the other authors that add choice into the account of that which depends on us, we can note two things: first, the introduction of choice appears to result from a combination of the three possible influence factors, Plato, Aristotle and Epictetus. Second, the motivation for adding choice into the account appears not to have been the attempt to express freedom of decision.

Alexander knows and uses both a concept of *prohairesis* of the Epictetan/Platonic type, as moral choice (*Fat.* 169,12), and the Aristotelian one of deliberate choice (in the majority of places, e.g. *Fat.* 180; 194–5; 212). How exactly Alexander thought these concepts of choice to link up with 'to choose' in his account 'power to choose opposites' is uncertain.[53] Mostly the expressions appear to be understood as non-moral and as the result of deliberation, i.e. in the Aristotelian sense.

However, there seems to have also been a distinctly non-Aristotelian element involved in the introduction of choosing into the accounts of what depends on us. In Alexander, the accounts containing the verb 'to choose' (*haireisthai*) are apparently not regarded as a substitute for those containing the verb 'to act' (*prattein*), but rather as a supplement. Not only do we find both kinds of accounts several times, we also regularly find choosing and acting co-ordinated in one phrase or account.[54] We find the same juxtaposition in Nemesius (*Nat. hom.* 115,22–8; 116,3–5) and in Ammonius (*in Int.* 130,30–2). These latter authors provide a reason why action as well as choice are considered: action presupposes choice, and praise and blame concern both action and choice: both are culpable (Nemesius, *Nat. hom.* 115,27–8, Ammonius, *in Int.* 130,32–3); moreover, sometimes we are prevented from realising our choices (Nemesius, *Nat. hom.* 116,3–5). This suggests that the switch from action to choice, or rather the addition of choice to action, was motivated by a change of focus regarding what is of primary moral relevance: choices rather than actions. Here Stoic, and in particular Epictetan, thought appears to have been influential, possibly via the Middle-Platonist re-interpretation of Plato's Myth of Er. This may be the most promising conjecture of why in Alexander the account of *eph' hêmin* so frequently includes the term 'choice'. Alexander states, for instance, in a similar vein, 'the assessment of morally right action is made not only from the things that are done, but much rather from the disposition and capacity from which it is done' (Alexander, *Fat.* 206,16–18). Thus it seems that the origin of the term 'to choose' in the account of *eph' hêmin* is non-Peripatetic, although Alexander then generally interprets it in the Aristotelian sense, as choice that is the result of deliberation, and not as fundamental moral choice.

Taking the various points together, it seems that the initial grounds for the inclusion of choice in the accounts of what depends on us in Alexander, Ammonius, Boethius, Heliodorus, and Nemesius are unlikely to have been the quest for an indeterminist concept of freedom of decision (as opposed to freedom of action), or the question of whether people are causally indetermined in their choices between alternatives. Rather it is the recognition of choice as the specific activity through which human rational

---

[53] The terms in the accounts are *hairesis* / *haireisthai*, not *prohairesis* / *prohaireisthai*, but Alexander also uses *haireisthai* to refer to Aristotle's deliberate choice (*Fat.* ch. 11).
[54] *Fat.* 181,14: *exousian tês haireseôs te kai praxeôs tôn antikeimenôn*; cf. *Fat.* 179,3.11; 189,10–11; *Mant.* 174,4; 175,24–5; 180,28–31.

beings can have an influence in the world, and accordingly, to which moral appraisal is to be attached. (The issue was autonomy rather than freedom to do otherwise.) This is perhaps further corroborated by the fact that in several of the passages in Alexander that are most clearly indeterminist (see next section) the version of the account with 'to act', and not the one with 'to choose' occurs.

XI. The Term *exousia* in the Accounts of What Depends on Us

On the other hand, the second change in Alexander's account – from 'being capable of doing and not doing something' to 'having the power (*exousia*) of doing and not doing something' – appears to be pertinent to the development of a concept of freedom of decision. Formulations of the account with *exousia* occur as standard in Alexander's *On Fate* (33 instances according to Thillet's index) and in *Mantissa* ch. 23, and there can thus be little doubt that the use is philosophically motivated. Alexander seems to be the first – of whom we know – to use the term *exousia* in this kind of account of what depends on us.[55] It further occurs in *Quaestio* 3.13 of the *Quaestiones* ascribed to Alexander; in Nemesius (*Nat. hom.* 112,10; 115,25) in a passage I believe to be later than his reports from the Middle-Platonist theory of fate, in Ammonius (*in Int.* 148,14.23); and in slightly different wordings in Iamblichus (Stobaeus, *Ecl.* 2,173,21) and Simplicius (*in Ench.* 20). How can we explain the appearance of *exousia* in the accounts? On this question, I can only offer conjecture.

First, since the term *exousia* seems to have replaced the verb *dunasthai* in the account, and this verb was linked with Aristotle's two-sided *dunamis*, *exousia* may have been meant to stand in for Aristotle's two-sided, rational capacity from *Int.* 13 and *Metaph.* 9 (see Section VI). Second, in Alexander *exousia tês haireseôs / exousia tou haireisthai* could take the place filled in other late second and third century authors by the phrase *prohairetikê dunamis*.[56] This phrase in turn seems to be a descendant of *prohairesis* in the Epictetan sense and which Epictetus himself already used in place of *prohairesis* throughout in *Diss.* 2.23. (But it also experiences an Aristotelian interpretation, cf. e.g. Nemesius, *Nat. hom.* 119,11.) For Epictetus *prohairesis* does not refer to a person's particular choice in a certain situation. First and foremost he uses the term to denote a disposition of the human mind which determines a person's individual choices. The exertion of this disposition is the only thing that is never necessitated by external circumstances. What we choose thus depends on us.[57] If this is where *exousia* in the accounts comes from, it may refer to a specifically human disposition for making choices. Third, Alexander uses *exousian* (*en hêmin*) *ekhein tou* ... as virtually synonymous with (*hêmeis*) *kurioi tou* .... The latter formulation occurs about a dozen

---

[55] We do not find *exousia* in this context in Aspasius, the Anonymous on the *Nicomachean Ethics*, Alcinous, [Plutarch] *On Fate*, (nor in Justin and Tatian) nor in *Mantissa* ch. 22 and Alexander's commentaries on the *Topics* and *Prior Analytics*.

[56] Clement, *Strom.* 6.135.4 (500,20–1 Staehlin); cf. Nemesius, *Nat. hom.* 119,4–5.11.

[57] Epictetus' *prohairesis* can perhaps be described as a precursor of a concept of the will. However, it is *neither* a separate faculty or part of the mind (i.e. one that can be in conflict with other faculties or parts of the mind), *nor* is it free in the sense of being causally independent in its choices.

times in this context. This fact may provide another link to Aristotle's *Ethics* (see Alexander, *Fat.* 178,26–8; 180,9–12), but formulations with *kurioi* for *eph' hêmin* are standard in practically all schools. There could also be a link between Alexander's use of *ekhein exousian* to Epictetus, who uses it to say whether we or some external influences have control over certain things. Fourth, the Middle-Platonist Maximus of Tyre uses *exousia* twice in his 41st speech, in the context of explaining how vice entered the world: it is this power of the soul (*exousia tês psukhês*) which enables us to do bad things (*Orat.* 41.5a and g).

More important than where exactly the use of the term *exousia* originates is the particular way in which the various influences are combined. It is the synonymy with *kurios* which best shows the significance of the replacement of *dunasthai* by *exousia*. *Ekhein tên exousian tou prattein* (*haireisthai*) *kai mê prattein* (*haireisthai*) can be understood in two different ways. Compare the sentences

1) the king has the power (authority, control) over living and dying (life and death)
2) the king has the power (ability, capacity) to live and to die

Similarly, the above sentence can be understood as

1) we have the power (authority, control) over acting/choosing and not acting/choosing
2) we have the power (two-sided ability, capacity) to act/choose and not to act/choose.

In the cases of type (1), with *genitivus obiectivus*, where someone has the power, authority, or control over certain things, we can separate the person who has the power from the things over which they have the power in a way that cannot be done in cases of type (2). The king's power over living and dying can be concerned with *other people's* lives. The king's power to live and die is concerned with his own condition. In case (1), the agent becomes a 'decision maker', in case (2) this is not so. The synonymity of 'having the *exousia*' and 'being *kurios*' over something in Alexander suggests that we have case (1) in his accounts of what depends on us. Something depends on us if we are in control over doing/choosing and not doing/choosing it. This is noticeably different from the earlier formulation with *dunasthai*: there clearly a two-sided *capacity* was at issue.

But owing to the introduction of 'doing/choosing something *or its opposite*', *kurios* and *exousia* do not function in the same way anymore as they did in Aristotle and Epictetus: in the latter authors it was the fact that nothing hindered us from doing or choosing something that made us have control over them. In Alexander's account, the terms are (at least at times)[58] understood differently: what makes us have control over things is the fact that we are causally undetermined in our decision and thus can freely decide between doing/choosing or not doing/choosing them. The element of free decision in Alexander's account thus lies not in the addition of the phrase 'choosing or not choosing', but in the introduction of the term '*exousia*'. We can thus see that the

---

[58] See the next section. Note that the phrase *exousia tou prattein kai mê prattein* itself can also be understood as 'not being hindered either way by external or internal factors'; and also as 'having a general two-sided capacity to act'. In neither case would freedom of decision need to be involved.

change to *exousia* in the account may have been of great significance, since it provided a way to express that the agent is a causally undetermined decision maker. The introduction of the term into this context is then also one further step towards the concept of a free will, since such a concept requires an independent faculty of decision making.

It may also be worth considering in this context the relation between the expressions *exousia* and *autexousion*. A link between them, although in a deterministic setting, can be observed already in Epictetus.[59] Something is in my own power (*autexousion*) if I have power (*exousia*) over it in the sense that nothing can prevent me from doing it. Epictetus clearly contrasts *autexousios* with someone else's *exousia* over oneself. *Autexousios* indicates that something is outside the sphere of influence of others, and because of that in the sphere of my power. I suggest that a similar relation was assumed by Alexander and other authors who favoured an indeterminist concept of *eph' hêmin*: for from the late second century onwards *autexousion* became more and more common as a philosophical term used instead of *eph' hêmin*, and at Nemesius' time seems to have superseded it. Alexander uses it very rarely, but in one place he states that *autexousion* is what is actually meant by *eph' hêmin* and that his opponents miss this meaning of the term (*Fat.* 182,22–4; cf. 189,9–11). Thus something may have been considered as in someone's own power (*autexousion*), and as truly *eph' hêmin*, precisely if that person has the *exousia* over doing/choosing it or its opposite. *Autexousion* may then have been understood by some as implying indeterminist freedom of the agent.

XII. The Volatility of the Concept of Freedom to Do Otherwise

Thus it seems that in Alexander's accounts of what depends on us it was rather the expression *exousia* than *haireisthai* that served to express the element of freedom of decision. We saw at the beginning that Alexander had a concept of freedom to do otherwise. We have now seen how this concept developed, absorbing both Stoic and Aristotelian and perhaps Platonic elements on its way. However, we would be quite wrong to assume that at the turn of the second century a general awareness of the problem of causal determinism and freedom to do otherwise had arisen, and that it had become part of the philosophical standard repertory of the time. There are several points that suggest that at his time Alexander is almost an isolated case, and that concepts of freedom to do otherwise are a rather marginal phenomenon without a clear philosophical context.

First, it is noteworthy that the one-sided, causative conception of what depends on us was by no means peculiar to the Stoic system, nor generally seen as a feeble attempt of the Stoics to nominally save moral responsibility – even if Alexander wants to make us believe this (*Fat.* ch. 13). On the contrary, it seems to have been regarded as a serious alternative or as a complement to the two-sided, potestative conception in second and third century Middle-Platonist and Peripatetic writings. We find non-Stoic accounts of

---

[59] Cf. *Diss.* 1.25.2; 4.1.62; 4.1.68; 4.7.16; 4.12.8; see also Bobzien, 'Stoic Conceptions of Freedom' (n. 1 above), p. 82 with n. 48; p. 86, n. 59.

such concepts in [Plutarch] *On Fate* ('That which depends on us is that part of the contingent which is already happening in accordance with our impulse'),[60] in the *Mantissa*, and in Nemesius. Had the general concern at the time been to preserve freedom to do otherwise as a prerequisite for moral accountability, this repeated approbation of a one-sided, causative *eph' hêmin* would be decidedly odd. On the other hand, if we assume that the two-sided, potestative concept was considered to express a two-sided general capacity which provides the vehicle through which rational or moral agents manifest themselves in their actions, this fact is far less startling. For in that case both the one-sided concepts and the two-sided one serve to ensure that the agent is causally – and hence morally – responsible for the action, if in slightly different ways. (Remember that the one-sided concepts seem to have assumed a two-sided general capacity through which the agent causes the action.) On this assumption it is also not surprising to find that the Neoplatonist conception of what depends on us is one-sided and causative (cf. Plotinus, *Enn.* 3.1.9–10; 3.2.10; 6.8.7), and that this fact seems not to have outraged anyone at the time.

The philosophical origins of the non-Stoic accounts of a one-sided, causative *eph' hêmin* are nowhere explicitly stated. The accounts in Nemesius and in the *Mantissa* show a striking resemblance to the later Stoic one which defines that which depends on us as that which happens through us (*di' hêmôn*, see above Sections II and III). Thus Nemesius writes:

> We say that, generically, all things that are done voluntarily through us depend on us....[61]

and the *Mantissa* has:

> For those choices of which the cause is nature or upbringing or habit are said to depend on us in the sense that they happen *through us*.[62]

However, I surmise that these accounts – and the above-quoted one in [Plutarch]'s *On Fate* – originate from (incorrect) Aristotle exegesis, presumably from an interpretation of the *Nicomachean Ethics* Book 3, from passages like the following:

> We deliberate about the things that depend on us and that can be done; ... All groups of human beings deliberate about the things that can be done *through them* ... we deliberate about those things which come to be *through us* and not always in the same manner.[63]

---

[60] *to de eph' hêmin thateron meros tou endekhomenou, to kata tên hêmeteran hormên êdê ginomenon*, [Plutarch] *Fat.* 571D-E.
[61] *legomen toinun genikôs panta ta di' hêmôn ekousiôs prattomena eph' hêmin einai* ..., Nemesius, *Nat. hom.* 114,15–16, cf. 102.
[62] *hôn gar proaireseôn hê phusis ê agôgai kai ethê estin aitia, hautai houtôs eph' hêmin legontai hôs di' hêmôn gignomenai*, *Mant.* ch. 22, 172,7–9.
[63] *bouleuometha de peri tôn eph' hêmin kai praktôn ... Tôn d' anthrôpôn hekastoi bouleuontai peri tôn di' hautôn praktôn ... hosa ginetai di' hêmôn, mê hôsautôs d' aei, peri toutôn bouleuometha*, Aristotle, *EN* 1112a30-b4 (italics mine); cf. also 1112b27; 1111b23–4, 26.

Thus where Aristotle argues on the generic level of (possible) actions, the passages from [Plutarch] and *Mantissa* ch. 22 talk about individual happenings. (Nemesius is ambiguous here.)

The unfamiliarity of second or early third century thinkers with an indeterminist concept of freedom to do otherwise is also beautifully illustrated by the awkward way in which it is handled in ch. 22 of the *Mantissa*, which seems to present a presumably Peripatetic alternative to Alexander's position. Its charming solution to the problem of Stoic fashion determinism lies in the introduction of 'that which is not' (*to mê on*) as an influence factor.[64] The argumentation runs roughly like this:

> If everything is caused, and the same causes have the same effects, and our choices are determined by a combination of our nature, habit, and education, then our choices do not depend on us. But choice does depend on us, and accordingly not everything is caused. The reason for this is that a little bit of 'not-being' is mixed in with the earthly things. In particular it can be detected in the things responsible for that which happens for the lesser part. This 'not-being' weakens the things or causes in which it exists, and thus weakens the continuity of causes. In things external to us this fact leads to chance events. In the causes in us, i.e. in our nature and habit, it leads to that which depends on us in the proper sense (*kuriôs*). Whenever the 'not-being' in us is responsible for a choice of ours, then that choice depends on us in the proper sense.

It is hard to see how in this theory moral responsibility is to be attached to the choices that depend on us. Their causal undeterminedness appears to render them some sort of random motions. Perhaps wisely, moral responsibility is not mentioned in the whole chapter. What is more, since the choices that depend on us in the proper sense result from a weakness or lack of tension of our nature and habit, something's depending on us in the proper sense can hardly have been judged as a positive thing.[65]

A third point that shows that a concept of freedom to do otherwise was far from being securely established, is that not only is there no unambiguous evidence for it before Alexander, but also in Alexander's *On Fate* and in the *Mantissa* there is a steady vacillation between various concepts of what depends on us, some advocating freedom to do otherwise, others implying only the absence of any *pre*determination by external and/or internal causal factors, and still others that are clearly compatible with determinism.[66]

We have seen above that Alexander's phrases of the kind 'having the power to do/choose opposites' are ambiguous between determinist, un-predeterminist and indeterminist readings. In this context Alexander's encounter with the second century

---

[64] This is reminiscent of Plato' struggle with not-being, e.g. in the *Sophist*; cf. also Cicero, *Fat.* 18; Augustine, *Lib. arb.* 201–5.

[65] This is very different e.g. in Cicero's *On Fate* 11 and Alexander's *On Fate* ch. 6, where the agents are envisaged as overcoming their nature or habit.

[66] This point has been discussed in R. W. Sharples, 'Responsibility, Chance, and Not-Being in Alexander of Aphrodisias *Mantissa* 169–172', *Bulletin of the Institute of Classical Studies* 22 (1975), 37–63.

CE orthodox Stoic theory of fate becomes crucial: it is only where the two-sided, potestative *eph' hêmin* meets with the Stoic causal principle (that in the same circumstances the same causes necessarily bring about the same effect, see above Section II) that the phrases are disambiguated, and that a concept of freedom to do otherwise is uncontroversially in play. Generally, wherever Alexander considers the possibility that the same person in the same circumstances acts or chooses otherwise than they do, phrases like 'having the power to do/choose opposites' seem to acquire an indeterminist meaning.

In particular, indeterminist freedom is almost certainly at issue in the important passages in which Alexander depicts the fictitious situation of someone who acts against their character, or against what seems reasonable to them, in order to show that determinism is wrong (*Fat.* chs 6 and 29, *Mant.* 174,33–5). Equally, the passage in which Alexander argues that our regret shows that we have the power to choose opposites suggests a concept of freedom to do otherwise. He says

> For it is on the grounds that it was possible for us also not to have chosen and not to have done this that we feel regret and blame ourselves for our neglect of deliberation.
>
> *Fat.* 180,29–31, trans. Sharples[67]

Here the concept of freedom of decision appears finally – to be connected with a conception of moral responsibility based on the agent's ability to do otherwise (MR2). A third important argument is that the same circumstances do not necessarily lead the same agent to the same actions/choices, because there are several – incommensurable – ends looking towards which we decide and choose (*Fat.* ch. 15, *Mant.* 174,17–24). All these arguments strike one as thoroughly modern, and as easy to grasp within a framework of today's discussions of the 'free-will problem'.

Contrasted with these are the many Alexander passages with arguments which, for someone who expects a defence of freedom to do otherwise, simply seem to beg the question. However, most arguments make perfect sense as soon as one understands them as concerned not with indeterminist freedom but with different philosophical questions. There are first those passages in which Alexander basically contents himself with paraphrasing Aristotle, for instance where he describes the agent as causally responsible, or as a beginning (*arkhê*) of action (*Fat.* chs 15, 20; *Mant.* 173,10–21); similarly where he opens up the vexed questions of character determination and of one's responsibility for the formation of one's character (*Mant.* 175,9–32, *Fat.* ch. 27). Here Alexander does not go beyond Aristotle, leaving it open whether, when we *begin* forming our character, we are 'free' or our dispositions predetermined. Moreover, the whole question of one's responsibility for forming one's character makes most sense on the assumption that (at least in some situations) what one does *is* fully determined by what character one has. Finally, determinist reasoning, quite

---

[67] Similarly, but not as clear, *Fat.* ch. 19 on pardon and blame, where Alexander plainly goes beyond Aristotle, *EN* 3.1, and *Fat.* ch. 16.

similar to Chrysippus' position (cf. Cicero, *Fat.* 7–9, 41–3) can be found in *Mantissa* ch. 23 (174,35–9). It suggests that if at different times the same person chooses similar things, the reason is not that the circumstances are similar (and function hence as external necessitating causes), but because the person's dispositions are similar each time.

These remarks may suffice as an illustration that Alexander is by no means clear and consistent about whether his phrases like 'having the power to do/choose opposites' are to be understood as indeterminist.[68] This may be partly explained by the fact that Alexander does not have a fully-fledged concept of a faculty of a will, and a fortiori not one of a will that is free in that it can operate independently of the agent's beliefs and desires. This is so despite the fact that he has collected all the ingredients required for a notion of acting from free-will: he has endowed human beings with a two-sided power (*exousia*) of decision making, which

- is not necessitated by external or internal influence factors;
- is exercised as the result of a process of deliberation;
- is envisaged as separable from the agent's character, disposition, or nature;
- is envisaged – it seems – as separable from the agent's reason: we can decide against what appears to us as the most reasonable course of action;
- leads to decisions that are not causally predetermined by internal or external factors, so that it is possible that the same agent, with the same desires and beliefs, in the same circumstances, chooses differently.

But all these points do not add up to 'choosing and acting from free-will', since for Alexander the human soul is not separable from the body and in principle susceptible to causal impacts. It remains unclear what the independent decision making faculty would be which has the power over choosing opposites: it can hardly be one of the non-rational parts of the soul. But if it is a, or the, rational part, the difficulty arises how it can – as Alexander suggests – decide against the course of action that appears as the *most reasonable* one to the agent: either this was not the most reasonable course of action after all, or it is not a super-ordinate *rational* part of the soul that decides. Thus even if a decision is not necessitated, predetermined or externally determined, there seems to be no suitable place for an independent decision making faculty in Alexander's conception of the soul.

A full concept of acting from free-will, and a full awareness of the free-will problem in the narrowest sense are not developed in the context of the Stoic-Peripatetic debate over the compatibility of universal causal determinism and freedom to do otherwise. Neither the Stoics nor the Peripatetics experience *within* their systems *any* of the free-will problems listed at the beginning. The Stoics did not require a concept of free-will, since they did not connect moral responsibility with freedom to do otherwise. As a

---

[68] Note also the strange restriction on indeterminism when he writes: 'we have this power of choosing the opposite and *not everything* that we choose has predetermining causes because of which it is not possible for us not to choose this' (*Fat.* 180,26–8, my emphasis). Calling to mind the above-discussed argument from *Mant.* ch. 22, this suggests that it is sufficient if in *some* of our choices there are no predetermining causes.

The Inadvertent Conception and Late Birth of the Free-Will Problem 157

consequence, they had no reasons to concern themselves with any free-will problem. Theirs is the problem of the compatibility of autonomous agency and causal determinism. On the Peripatetic side, Alexander had no free-will *problem* either. It is true, at least at times he seems to regard a concept of freedom to do otherwise as a prerequisite for moral responsibility. But he secures such freedom by simply denying *pre-*determination of human actions. Unlike Stoics and Platonists, he can do so, because he does not believe in universal divine providence. A free-will problem (in the wider sense) thus arises only *in the confrontation of the two philosophical systems*, when later Stoic causal determinism meets late Peripatetic freedom to do otherwise – with such freedom understood as a necessary condition for moral responsibility.

If we want to find philosophers who are troubled by a free-will problem *within* their system, we need to turn to Platonists and Christian thinkers. In their theory of hypothetical fate the Middle Platonists had severed the Stoic chain of causes at the point of human choices and actions (see above Section VI). This was made possible by the fact that they proposed an immaterial human soul which can initiate action in the material world.[69] In this way they had gained un-predeterminist freedom, thus guaranteeing the agent's autonomy. However, as the Middle Platonists also advocated the universal impact of divine providence, the severance of the chain of causes did not solve all their difficulties. For human actions and choices, even if not the result of the network of causes, are still in accordance with divine providence. The problem of determinism is thus no longer that of predetermination by a chain of corporeal causes, but of predetermination by god's providence, even if this does not work through the network of material causes. In particular the problem became dominant, how to bring into agreement the evil choices and actions of human beings with god's providence, given that god is by definition good. Early Christian thinkers struggled with a similar question, despite considerable differences in their 'metaphysics'; and they, too, had the advantage of an immaterial soul which made it possible that human action became independent of the network of material causes.

It is in this context that finally a faculty of the will is introduced (no doubt influenced again by Epictetus' concept of *prohairesis*), to warrant the independence of human evil deeds from god's providence or creation. In which way this will was considered as free varies and is often hard to determine: indeterminist freedom of decision, un-predeterminist freedom, and freedom from force or compulsion (voluntariness) seem to alternate in our sources. Since the problem is no longer the independence from preceding material causes (this has simply been postulated), formulations of determinism of the kind 'same (corporeal) causes, same effects' are no longer fitting. As a consequence, an unambiguous description of the freedom involved in the various theories, whether indeterminist, un-predeterminist, or neither, becomes hard to find. Accordingly, it is seldom clear what kind of problem of 'freedom' of the will the philosophers were dealing with. After Alexander, the problem of determinism

---

[69] Cf. e.g. Alcinous, *Didasc.* 153,4–5 hê de praxis psukhês logikês energeia dia sômatos ginomenê.

and freedom to do otherwise is most clearly present in the commentaries on Aristotle's *De Interpretatione*, where – if I am right – lay one vital element of its coming into existence.

XIII. Results

The problem of the compatibility of causal determinism and freedom to do otherwise appears to have been formulated only in the second century CE. This seems to have been the result of a confrontation of a refined Stoic universal causal determinism on the one hand, with a two-sided, potestative concept of what depends on us (is *eph' hêmin*), based on Aristotle's ethics, on the other. Presumably in the early second century, and as a consequence of combining Aristotle's theory of deliberate choice with his modal theory and with his theory regarding the truth-values of future propositions, this concept was interpreted as implying freedom to do otherwise. Who exactly was responsible for this new indeterminist understanding of that which depends on us is unclear, but it seems to have been accepted thereafter both by some Peripatetics and by some Middle-Platonists. Alexander's accounts, and some later ones, of that which depends on us display two further developments of this indeterminist concept of freedom. First, the addition of choice (*hairesis*) to action in the accounts reflects a refinement of theory of action and moral responsibility, which focuses more on intra-psychic events, and in particular on the choice of good or bad, and the culpability of that choice. Here Stoic and Platonist impacts become apparent. Second, the replacement in the account of 'being capable of' by 'having the power or authority (*exousia*) over' introduces a decision making faculty, and thus leads to a concept of free decision – the result probably of a fusion of Epictetan and Aristotelian elements. Alexander stops short of a concept of free will, due it seems in part to the fact that he believes the human soul to be inseparable from the corporeal item of which it is the form. The need of a free will becomes pressing in Platonist and Christian philosophy, in the context of the problems of how vice entered the world, and how god's providence and foreknowledge of the future is compatible with human responsibility. But this is no longer in the context of a physical theory of *universal causal* determinism, characterised by principles of the kind 'like causes, like effects'. Rather the determinism is now teleological only, and the context theological.

From the third century onwards, physical causal determinism was, it seems, no longer considered an attractive or plausible theory, let alone a threat. Overall, the problem of causal determinism and freedom to do otherwise, appears not to have been a very prominent topic in antiquity. There is a certain likelihood of an awareness of it for some second century Stoics who were confronted with the Peripatetic or Middle-Platonist indeterminist concept of what depends on us; and for those Peripatetics and perhaps Middle-Platonists who in turn criticised Stoic determinism. There is good evidence of it in certain passages of Alexander's *On Fate* and in the *Mantissa*. Origen may have been aware of it. And it lingers on in later commentaries on Aristotle's *De Interpretatione*.

It is then presumably only a slight overstatement when I conclude with saying: the problem of physical causal determinism and freedom of decision entered the scene in the second century CE, by a chance encounter of Stoic physics and the fruits of early Aristotle exegesis, with the contemporary focus on the culpability of mental events and the introduction of a power of decision making as catalysts – and it was not part of the philosophical repertoire for long.[70]

---

[70] This is the revised version of a paper I gave to a seminar of the Institute of Classical Studies of the University of London in 1994, and I would like to thank the audience for helpful criticism in the discussion. I am especially grateful to Bob Sharples, who not only put me on to the topic and invited me to give the paper, but also generously sent me several pages of detailed comments.

4

Alexander of Aphrodisias on Particulars and the Stoic Criterion of Identity[1]

Marwan Rashed

One could claim that for an Aristotelian philosopher, particulars are not a philosophical problem – at least not an epistemological one. For an Aristotelian philosopher daily confronted with Stoic theories of Providence and individuation, however, this was a haunting question. After all, what did Aristotle have to say on the status of the particulars not *qua* belonging to a species, but *qua* pure singularities taking place within the world? I would like to show that even if Alexander is too much of an Aristotelian to have a real theory of the particular, his reaction to his historical context leads him to new insights on this topic. These insights, in turn, constitute a starting point out of which Avicenna and Leibniz developed their ideas about how fatalism could be avoided without giving up the principle that the entire effect corresponds to its full cause. I will try to sketch, in the following pages, the main phases of this long and intricate story.

1. Some Preliminaries: Dexippus on the Peculiarly Qualified (*idiôs poion*)

The problem of the particulars in the Aristotelian tradition seems to me best understood if we start with a strange passage taken from Porphyry's *Isagôgê* (7,16–19). I quote Jonathan Barnes' recent translation:

> ... a most general item is said of everything under it – genera and species and individuals; a genus which comes before a most special item is said of all the most

---

This article first appeared as 'Alexander of Aphrodisias on particulars and the Stoic criterion of identity' by Marwan Rashed in Robert W. Sharples (ed.), *Particulars in Greek Philosophy* (2010), pp. 157-79 © Koninklijke BRILL NV 2010, reproduced with permission.

[1] All my thanks to R. W. Sharples, who invited me to present this paper at the Seventh Keeling Colloquium, and to Peter Adamson, Riccardo Chiaradonna, Richard Sorabji, and Kevin Tracy for helpful discussions on different aspects of it. The errors are mine.

special items and of the individuals; an item which is only a species is said of all the individuals; and an individual is said of one only of the particulars.[2]

In the translation, 'individual' stands for *to atomon* and 'particular' for *to kata meros*. The doctrine expressed here has already struck readers as un-Aristotelian. I should mention in particular A. C. Lloyd, R. Chiaradonna, and R. Sorabji:[3] how is it possible to explain that contrary to the strict separation between primary and secondary substance we find in the *Categories*, and to the fact that the individual cannot be an object of predication, Porphyry applies the structure of predication until the last ontological level? Why does he not respect the boundary between the general and the particular so clearly drawn by Aristotle himself?

It is not my purpose today to scrutinize all the intricacies of Porphyry's doctrine of predication. I only want to lend emphasis to the distinction he draws, at the lowest level, between the individual, which in this sense is to be assimilated to some sort of predicate, and the particular which represents the logico-ontological subject of the ultimate predication. Or, more exactly, Porphyry seems to envisage the individual under a double aspect, first its sensible existence, which is a simple and obvious fact (which is much more problematic for Plotinus) and secondly its verbal formulation. By this, I mean its formulation as a particular individual, and not as a member of a species or a genus. I think that Chiaradonna has definitely shown that this text must be understood in the light of a declaration of Dexippus, in his commentary on the *Categories* (30,20-6), about the possibility of differentiating between some particulars belonging to the same species. Let us quote this text in the translation of Long and Sedley:

> But if form is that which is predicated in the category of essence of a plurality of numerically different things, in what does single individual differ from single individual, seeing that each is numerically single? Those who solve this difficulty on the basis of the peculiarly qualified – that one individual is distinguished, say, by hookedness of the nose, by blondness, or by some other combination of qualities (*sundromêi poiotêtôn*), another by snubness, baldness, or greyness of the eyes, and again another by other qualities – do not seem to me to solve it well.[4]

Two points must be noted here: first, Dexippus does not mention by their name the people whom he is criticising for having admitted such a theory of the *idiôs poion*. It is

---

[2] J. Barnes, *Porphyry, Introduction* (Oxford: Clarendon Press, 2003), p. 8.
[3] Cf. A. C. Lloyd, 'Neoplatonic and Aristotelian Logic', *Phronesis* 1 (1956), 146–60; R. Chiaradonna, 'La teoria dell'individuo in Porfirio e l'*idiôs poion* stoico', *Elenchos* 21 (2000), 303–31; and R. Sorabji, *The Philosophy of the Commentators, 200–600 AD: A Sourcebook*, 3 vols (London: Duckworth, 2004), vol. 3, pp. 165–8. According to Sorabji, Porphyry borrows from the *Theaetetus* (209C), not some Stoics, the idea that an individual person is a quality or a bundle of qualities. His reason would be to spare beginners the details of matter and form, which he omits only for pedagogical reasons. Be this as it may, that commits him to what will interest us here, that the individual person, being qualities, can be predicated of something else, See also R. Sorabji, *Self: Ancient and Modern Insights about Individuality, Life, and Death* (Oxford: Clarendon Press, 2006), pp. 137–53.
[4] A. A. Long and D. N. Sedley, *The Hellenistic Philosophers*, 2 vols (Cambridge: Cambridge University Press, 1987), vol. 1, p. 169 (text 28J).

not obvious at all, therefore, that we have to identify them with the Stoics, nor even with some authors having misinterpreted their doctrine. Secondly, the problem faced by Dexippus is, in a sense, purely Aristotelian: for if (1) the form (*eidos*) constitutes the lowest level we can express through discursive language, and (2) for an Aristotelian, what is real can be seized through a formula, how are we to conceive of the individuals manner of existence? I follow then Chiaradonna's proposal to understand this text as directed primarily against Porphyry (and not some Stoics). It is Porphyry's doctrine of the particular substance which is at stake, i.e. the claim made by the commentator that the individual can be, if not defined, at least described, by a collection of characteristics. In other words, we have to identify the 'individual' in the text already quoted, which was predicated there of the 'particular', with the famous *athroisma idiotêtôn* of the *Isagôgê*.

At this stage, we must contrast this doctrine, which seems genuinely Porphyrian, with another one already to be found in Alexander: in view of his Aristotelian doctrine of the immanent form, Alexander is ready – at some level of generality, and leaving the cosmological conditions of the problem out of consideration;[5] to admit that some genus may include only one species, or some species only one individual. The two cases have in fact almost nothing in common: according to Alexander's point, there would be no impossibility, in the case of species with some unique token (such as the species 'sun' or 'world', for instance), that there be more.[6] There would be no logical contradiction if there were more than one sun, or even more than one world. On the contrary, according to the vertical structure (from top to bottom) of Porphyry's doctrine, it is as impossible to find two particulars having the same individual formula as to find two species having the same definition. However, precisely this tenet raises a problem. Nearly every formula (more on this restriction later), be it a canonic definition by genus and differentia or a simple description, because it is composed out of common nouns, can be applied, precisely, in common, to many particulars. If 'snub' or 'bald' are more than proper names but there are always two or more particulars to whom these adjectives can be truly attributed, then it is no help to consider a collection of such terms instead of only one of them.

That is why Dexippus replies, in the lines immediately following his exposition of the argument, by saying (Dexippus, *in Cat.* 30,26–30):

> For it is not the conjunction of qualities which makes them differ numerically, but, if anything, quality as such. We should rather reply to the problem as follows, that things that are numerically distinct do not differ from each other in nature and essence, but their distinctness resides in their countability. They are different, then, in being countable; for it is in the process of each being counted one by one that number arises.

Dexippus rejects every differentiation of the particular which would treat it as a nature or essence. Whereas a difference between two genera, or two species, can be understood

---

[5] See M. Rashed, *Essentialisme: Alexandre d'Aphrodise entre logique, physique et cosmologie* (Berlin: De Gruyter, 2007), pp. 254–7.
[6] On this problem, see in particular Simplicius, *in Cat.* 55,24–56,15.

on the basis of two different formulas, this approach becomes inadequate in the case of two co-specific particulars. Their difference is only to be explained by their being countable (*kata to arithmeisthai*). By saying this, Dexippus seems to stress the etymological validity of the Aristotelian terminology. When the Aristotelians say that the particular substance is one in number (*arithmôi*), they mean that it is a distinct element belonging to some set of homospecific elements, this set having some cardinal. A particular apple is such only because it belongs to a countable set of apples, a particular man to a countable set of men, etc. Even if Dexippus does not state it explicitly, it seems that we can go a step further and hold that according to him, this theory allows for the possibility of two individual substances being in their constitution entirely identical. This identity does not threaten the fact that we *can* distinguish between them, just by counting them.

2. Alexander's Criticism of the Eternal Return

It seems likely that the main tenets of Dexippus' deflationist reply to Porphyry's *Isagoge* go back to some piece of orthodox Peripateticism. For the idea that the distinction between two individuals of the same species is a simple fact, irreducible to any conceptual (classificatory) formulation, is genuinely Aristotelian. There is however a question that Dexippus does not address – for he does not need to address it in the context of a commentary on the *Categories* –, namely that of the explanation, for two homospecific individuals, not so much of their mere discernibility (which indeed simply occurs *kata to arithmeisthai*) as of their eventual idiosyncrasy In other terms, even if the spatial and temporal conditions of existence of any physical substance are sufficient to explain why any two such substances are not one and the same object, Dexippus tells us nothing about the *corporeal* features of these substances. As soon as one tackles this question, however, it appears that Porphyry's curious doctrine expresses a serious difficulty in the Aristotelian ontology of the sensible world.

At the end of chapter 2.11 of *On Coming-to-Be and Passing-Away* [*GC*] (which is also the end of the treatise), Aristotle affirms (338b5–19) that the return of numerically the same individual sublunar substances is impossible. The only form of eternal return pertains to the species. The species is eternal, but no individual is such, neither as sempiternal (for it is doomed to corruption), nor as reappearing periodically. If the first option seems uncontroversial to everybody in antiquity, the second one is much more difficult. Let us assume, in effect, that everything that is created can be totally explained by the presence of some undifferentiated matter on the one hand, and of some efficient causality produced by the disposition of the cosmos on the other. Then, matter being always the same, the coming again of some given configuration will be necessary and sufficient for the coming again of some individual compound, hence of some individual substance. It is exactly the doubt expressed by some philosophers, according to Alexander quoted by Philoponus in his commentary:[7]

---

[7] Philoponus, *in GC* 314,9–16.

Someone might, as Alexander says, raise a difficulty against Aristotle. For if matter always persists as the same, and the efficient cause is always the same, what would be the reason for there not coming to be again, over some longer period of time, the same things from the same matter, produced by the same [causes]? Some indeed say that this happens during the rebirth (*palingensia*) and the Great Year, in which there happens the restoration of all things as the same. This being the case, there could also be the rebirth and recurrence in number of particular individuals whose substance is perishable.

To this objection, Alexander replies in the following terms:[8]

> To this it should be replied that even if it is granted that Socrates is reborn, the Socrates who came to be later will not be one and the same in number with the Socrates who had come to be earlier. For that which is one and the same in number cannot have intervals: for one in number comes about not on account of being from the same things, but on account of persisting as the same, when being earlier and later. Therefore the sun is the same in number, but Socrates, as he said, is not the same in number; for the individual form (*atomon eidos*) does not persist, even though matter persists (*hê hulê menei*).

Alexander's answer, it is worth being noted, does not reject the idea of the individual being materially the same. He thinks rather that even if Socrates-2 has exactly the same physical composition as Socrates-1, this is not sufficient for holding that Socrates-1 and -2 are identical. For an individual substance to be identical is to *remain* identical over some period of time. Alexander does not explain here what he means by this temporal identity He does not envisage all the puzzles that one can raise against the idea of a material continuity, as soon as we hold matter to be fluid, something he dwells upon elsewhere.[9] He just states that some break in the temporal existence of the individual substance makes every self-identity impossible.

Thus, an important question remains: even if it is *possible* for two substances to have the same physical constitution, does this situation really happen in the history of the world? Philoponus remains silent on this issue, but we are lucky enough to be taught by Averroes' *Epitome* of *GC*, that Alexander denied this eventuality: exactly the same physical constitution does never repeat itself in the world. Here is a translation of this text:[10]

> Alexander believes that the state and disposition of the spheres at any given time never recur individually. He maintains that if we assume all of the stars to be at a

---

[8] Ibid. 314,16–22. I adapt this translation from I. Kupreeva, *Philoponus, On Aristotle On Coming-to-Be and Perishing 2.5–11* (London: Duckworth, 2005), p. 109.
[9] See I. Kupreeva, 'Alexander of Aphrodisias on Mixture and Growth', *Oxford Studies in Ancient Philosophy* 27 (2004), 297–334.
[10] For the Arabic text, see Ibn Rusd, *Jawāmi' al-kawn wa al-fasād*, ed. A. al-Taftāzānī and A. S. Zāyid (Cairo: Société générale égyptienne d'édition, 1991), 35,10–36,9. I adapt the present English translation from S. Kurland, *Averroes, On Aristotle's De Generatione et Corruptione Middle Commentary and Epitome* (Cambridge, MA: Mediaeval Academy of America, 1958), pp. 137–8.

particular point in the sphere of the constellations, for example in the Ram, and then all of them, both the fast and the slow ones, begin to move, they need not necessarily all of them revert to the exact same point from which they began their movement, but the revolutions of some will be proportionate to those of others, so that, for example, when the sun completes one revolution the moon will have completed twelve. And there will be a similar relationship between the revolution of the sun and of each one of the stars. Then it should be possible for all of them to return to any one place, to any place you may postulate. But we find the exact opposite to take place. For the sun traverses its sphere in 365 ¼ days and the moon traverses its sphere in 27 ½ days. When 27 ½ days are multiplied [by twelve], they do not yield 365 ¼ days. Since this is so, and the efficient cause does not return upon itself numerically, and neither can the material cause do so, it becomes evident that it is impossible in any way whatsoever for the individual to recur. Now that is what we set out to prove.

We might add to what we have already said that even though the revolution of the moon is not commensurate with that of the sun in days, it does not follow that they are not commensurate with one another at all. For it is possible that their common unit of measurement is a shorter time. But if that were so, the common measure could be one quarter of a day. To ascertain whether these revolutions of the stars are commensurable or not is most difficult or well nigh impossible, for that would have to be based upon a knowledge of the time of a single revolution in the case of each star as it is in truth. That is impossible because of the limited and approximated nature of our observation of these things. What we can ascertain in this matter is that they are approximately commensurate to one another, as the astronomers believe. Whatever the case may be, it is impossible for the individual to recur.

It seems that with the help of both testimonies, we can reconstruct in its entirety Alexander's answer to the upholders of the eternal return of individuals. For it is often the case that in such polemical contexts, Alexander divides his response into two parts.[11] The first move is called by him the 'so what?' reply (*antiparastasis*), the second objection *enstasis*. The *antiparastasis* consists in admitting, for the sake of the argument, the opponent's first assumption, on the basis of which he tries to destroy Aristotle's theory, and to show that this assumption does not lead to that result. The *enstasis*, on its side, attacks directly the opponent's assumption by showing that and how it is false. A clear example of this way of proceeding is furnished by Simplicius' commentary on the *De Caelo*, where Alexander's response to one of Xenarchus' objections is presented under this double form.[12] Xenarchus' argument was directed against Aristotle's claim that there are only two kinds of simple lines, the straight one and the circular, hence only two kinds of simple motions, Apollonius has shown, says Xenarchus, that the

---

[11] See M. Rashed, 'Priorité de l'*eidos* ou du *genos* entre Andronicos et Alexandre: vestiges arabes et grecs inedits', *Arabic Sciences and Philosophy* 14 (2004), 9–63, at 25–6 [repr. in M. Rashed, *L'héritage aristotélicien: Textes inédits de l'Antiquité* (Paris: Les Belles Lettres, 2007), pp. 29–83, at pp. 45–6].
[12] See Simplicius, *in Cael.* 13,22–14,29.

helicoidal line is simple as well. Therefore, it is impossible to prove by following this path that there are only two – and not, after all, three – simple motions. Alexander replies first 'so what?' (*kat' antiparastasin*): even if we concede to Xenarchus that the helicoidal line is simple, it does not follow that the simple motions are not two. For Aristotle was not saying that the different kinds of simple lines are *efficient causes* (13,31, *poiêtika aitia*) for the different kinds of simple motions. There may perfectly well be some simple line to which no simple motion corresponds. The task of the 'so what?' reply being thus completed, Alexander can now respond with the objection *kat' enstasin*: it is false that the helicoidal line is simple, because it is generated by two simultaneous motions one straight on the surface of a cylinder parallel to its axis and the other circular (the rotation of the cylinder around its axis).

I propose then to interpret our two testimonies in the same manner. Philoponus would have preserved Alexander's *antiparastasis* ('even if we concede the return of the same physical constitution produced by the same astral configuration, it does not follow that its two instantiations are *numerically* identical to one another') and Averroes his *enstasis* ('it is false that the same astral configuration – and, by way of consequence, the same physical constitution – occurs twice in the world history').

We have reached so far the conclusion that Dexippus' reply to Porphyry only superficially agrees with the main tenets of Alexander's ontology. For sure, Alexander would have objected to the thesis of the collection of individuating features that it cancels the important distinction between the species and the individual; that only a species can be adequately expressed through a formula; that a particular, on the contrary, is simultaneously too wide and too narrow for this approach.[13] But Alexander, unlike Dexippus, since he is engaged in a polemic against the Stoics, must explain why two individuals must be not only distinct, but also, in the eternity of time intrinsically different *and*, to some extent, unpredictable. What then is Alexander's solution?

3. Three Disconnected Claims in Alexander: Matter as Non-Being, Free-Will, and Astral Singularities

A first answer consists in underlining the role of matter. Form, as is well-known, is according to Aristotle unable to master the matter entirely. There are always 'material circumstances' which explain that the form never realises itself in exactly the same way. This answer is not unknown to Alexander.[14] However, this solution to our problem is not entirely satisfactory. For matter as such, or *prima materia,* is pure indifferentiation. It is only through some formal activity – already at the lowest level of the supposedly uniform homoeomerous parts like flesh and bone – that we are confronted with some differentiation. We do not see therefore why the matter would account for the

---

[13] Too wide, because its particular features are probably infinite, and surely indefinite, so that they cannot be grasped by a formula, as extended as it may be; too narrow, because for every formula composed of common nouns, it is always possible to find two particulars to which this 'individual' formula – to use Porphyry's terminology – may be applied.

[14] See for example Alexander, *DA* 87,13–14.

differentation of the particular. As such, matter is as perfectly regular and undifferentiated as the void. If we have only form and matter in the world, it would be more plausible to attribute to some formal principle, and not to the matter, the existence of *different* particulars. In this sense, Porphyry's attempt at giving a version of the peculiarly qualified in terms of form was not absurd.

Alexander, in the passage from his commentary on the end of *GC*, was very probably responding to some people holding, at least by way of hypothesis, the everlasting recurrence of astral configurations. It is striking that in the fragment quoted in translation by Averroes, reference is made to the eternal return of the *individual* configuration (cf. 35,11 and 36,9: *bi-al-sahs*). I think we can interpret this allusion, on the face of it, in two different ways, one more akin to astral fatalism (everything that happens is produced by the stars), the other to astral determinism (everything that happens is ultimately produced by the stars, except what stems out of our (free) will).

In their chapter on Stoic everlasting recurrence, Long and Sedley rightly individuate four distinct claims on this issue:[15]

a. Socrates-1 and -2 are numerically identical;
b. They are indiscernible tokens of the same type;
c. They are numerically identical but inessentially discernible;
d. They are slightly discernible tokens of the same type.

According to (a), we have one and only one Socrates. It is even misleading to speak of Socrates- 1 and -2, According to (b), the fact that they are separated by some period of time where they do not exist makes them numerically different. However, their physical constitution and. their relations to the other items and events of their respective world is the same. According to (c), we would have the curious thesis that though numerically identical, Socrates- 1 and -2 would be discernible 'with respect to certain external accidents'. Since this report is made only by Alexander, I shall come back to it shortly. Finally, (d) presents itself explicitly as a revision of the original doctrine. It is feeble and does not need to retain us longer here.

On all this, Alexander is our most important evidence: For (a) is attested almost exclusively by him (directly or through Simplicius), and (c) by him only.[16] Moreover, we owe the mention of Chrysippus' *On the World,* in this context, to his commentary on the *An. Pr.* (180,36). In other words, Alexander is our sole evidence – perhaps, although less clearly, together with Nemesius – attributing to the Stoics the thesis of the numerical identity of Socrates-1 and -2. Alexander's 'so what?' reply in Philoponus confirms this remark. Alexander was objecting to his adversary that even if the celestial return was conceded, such a fact would not imply by itself the numerical identity of Socrates-1 and -2 (i.e. Long and Sedley's thesis [a]) but only their being indiscernible tokens of the same type (Long and Sedley's [b]), This dialectical move obviously implies

---

[15] Long and Sedley (n. 4 above), vol. 1, p. 312.
[16] See, respectively, Alexander, *in An. Pr.* 180,33–6; 181,25–31 (= Long and Sedley 52F), Simplicius, *in Phys.* 886,12–16 (= Long and Sedley 52E).

that the thesis of Alexander's adversaries, as interpreted by him at least, consisted in (a) rather than in (b). This being said, it is remarkable that (b) is presented explicitly as a revision of (a) by its unique exponent, Origen.[17] I think, then, that Philoponus' quotation confirms the suggestion expressed by Long and Sedley that (a) represents the original doctrine of the Stoics on this issues, (b) (c) (d) being revisions made to render the claim of everlasting recurrence more acceptable by laymen. Alexander was perfectly right on this issue.

In the light of the evidence produced so far, it would. seem possible that the Stoics, rather that some astrologers, were Alexander's target in the commentary on *GC*. Even if they are not named and even if Averroes designates them only as 'partisans of the returns', it was certainly the Stoic, and even Chrysippus' doctrine of the numerical identity of Socrates-1 and -2, which Alexander aimed at. This being so, how are we to understand astral determinism, as opposed to fatalism, according to the Stoics?

A comparison with Chrysippus' ideas on divination might here give some insight into the question. Chrysippus, who wants to save divination as well as to avoid necessitarianism, attempts rewriting this conditional as a negated conjunction, in a well-known and much disputed text *(De fato* § 15), Cicero writes the following: '... At this point Chrysippus loses his cool. He hopes that the Chaldeans and other seers can be cheated, and that they will so use connectives as not to put their theorems in the form 'If someone was born at the rising of the Dogstar, he will not die at sea' but rather to use a *material* not a *strict* conditional 'Not both: someone was born at the rising of the Dogstar, and he will die at sea'. What hilarious self-indulgence! To avoid collapsing into Diodorus' position, he teaches the Chaldeans how they should express their theorems!'"[18] Would Chrysippus have expressed himself in the same way with regard to the mere existence of the individual, as to say; 'not both: x is born at the date t and he will not display the uniquely qualifying character i'? I think that answer to this question must be negative, for the two cases under consideration are different. From this point of view, a sentence introducing Averroes' report must be recalled. The Commentator says that 'the partisans of the returns ... say that when the position which belonged to all the parts of the heavens when Zayd was existing comes back again, then Zayd comes back one and the same again'. It is noteworthy that Alexander – if (as I assume) he is Averroes' source here – employs a conditional. Of course, it would be very unlikely that even if his adversary had formulated this case according to the pattern set forth by Chrysippus for divination, Alexander would have bothered himself with such a refined hairsplitting. But despite this restriction, it seems probable that the adversary would not have disagreed with the formulation by means of a material conditional 'Not *both*: the cosmic configuration at the place and time of Socrates' birth is such *and* Socrates lacks this uniquely identifying character.' This implies that the configuration carries with it the uniquely identifying character of Socrates, but not by way of *strict* conditional. I think that this represents the tenor of §§ 7–8 of Cicero's *De fato* passage in which we find attributed to Chrysippus the idea of a difference of nature *(natura)* due to the general environment. I am very tempted to interpret the word *natura*, here,

---

[17] Cf. Origen, *Contra Celsum* 4.68 (= Long and Sedley 52G).
[18] Translation borrowed from Long and Sedley (n. 4 above), vol. 1, pp. 232–3.

as referring to the different uniquely identifying character and I must confess that I do not even see what other candidate could be suitable.[19] Cicero, on my view, would have neglected, for polemical reasons or because he misunderstood it, the fact that a distinction had to be drawn between our uniquely identifying character being cast at the instant of our birth and the series of all our actions, my being on this chair rather than on that, etc.

To return to the proposition about the cosmic configuration, it is obvious that it can be temporally expanded so as to become perfectly general. By 'general', I do not intend here some Aristotelian universal, but the extensive and historical sum of all world-events. If we take the ordered series of all celestial configurations and the Ordered series of all sublunar births, we would be allowed to say: 'not *both*: the first *and* those born lack these uniquely identifying characters'. Further, if it can be proved that the series of all configurations possesses some necessity of itself, we have to admit, at the level of the constitution of the uniquely identifying character – but only at that level, if we reject Cicero's testimony on this point – necessitarianism as true.

Thus, Philoponus would give us a clue – unnoticed as such until now – for our understanding of the Stoic uniquely identifying character.[20] The three basic premises are the following:

a. there never happens to be, between two successive conflagrations, the same astral configuration;
b. the uniquely identifying character is tempered in the air, like a steel in some liquid, at the instant of birth; as such, it is closely connected with soul;
c. the air, as part of the atmosphere, is directly influenced by the position of the stars.

Of these three premises, only the second one is attested in the ancient sources. It appears in von Arnim's collection under the headline *anima refrigeratione orta* as a general Stoic doctrine (*SVF* 2.804–8). It is plain, however, that we can attribute it to Chrysippus in particular with some confidence, for von Arnim has simply overlooked the fragment, to be found in *Ad Gaurum* 14.4, where the author (probably Porphyry) mentions 'the air which, according to Chrysippus, has swooped down on the nature at the instant of the exit from the throes of the birth (*ex ôdinôn prohodos*)'.[21] From the Homeric age, the Greeks knew that when a metal is being tempered in water or oil, it acquires some extra virtues of resistance and solidity.[22] The metaphor, in a Stoic context, was appealing. When the foetus is still kept in the mother's womb, it has no real individuality but, as Roman theoricians of law will express this situation later, it is only

---

[19] See also Cicero, *De officiis* 1.109: *innumerabiles* [= *anarithmêtoi*] ... *dissimilitudines naturae morumque*. On this text, see C. Gill, 'Particulars, Selves and Individuals in Stoic Philosophy', in R. W. Sharples, ed., *Particulars in Greek Philosophy* (Leiden: Brill, 2009), pp. 127–46.
[20] For previous reconstructions of this doctrine, see Sorabji (n. 3 above), vol. 3, pp. 173–4, with further bibliographical indications.
[21] See also the annotated French translation of the entire treatise in A.-J. Festugière, *La Révélation d'Hermès Trismégiste*, 4 vols (Paris: Gabalda, 1944–54), vol. 3, p. 293, for our passage.
[22] Cf. C. Daremberg and E. Saglio, *Dictionnaire des Antiquités grecques et romaines*, vol. 2.2 (Paris: Hachette, 1896), art. 'Ferrum', pp. 1093–4.

part of the belly of the mother – exactly as a fruit in the tree is part of the tree.[23] At the very instant when the offspring sees the light, it becomes independent from its mother – being no more necessarily nourished by her, by contrast with its previous vegetative life in the womb – and, so to say, 'cast' and 'tempered' in the air under the form of a real human individual. I suggest, then, that there is a very close connection between the uniquely identifying character of individual animals, the soul as a connate physical *pneuma*, and the air in which we are tempered when we come to birth.

The two other premisses, even if they are not attested in our sources, are not extravagant. The first one may very well be implicit in the doctrine criticised by Alexander *ap.* Philoponus, and the third one is a minimal meteorological claim. If I am not entirely mistaken, the fact that any two astral configurations within a world cycle cannot be identical with each other assures us that any two uniquely identifying characters cannot be identical.

On the other side, this cosmological structure presents the advantage of explaining why, provided that the astral trajectories follow the same course in each repetition of the world cycle, individuals with the same uniquely identifying character reappear from world to world. An objection could be that such a cosmos would be too mechanical, making Providence unnecessary. But this is not necessarily the case. A text from Philo, *On the sacrifice of animals* (= *SVF* 2.695) alludes to the fact that the seasons take place for the sake of the preservation of the sublunary world: 'for winter and summer, spring and autumn, seasons which come back every year and, which are beneficial to life, are affections of the air, which is made changing for the sake of the preservation of the things which come after the Moon'. The different aspects of the sky in one cycle, being regular as well as each time different, would thus account for the perpetuation of similar individuals as well as for some principle of plenitude in the production of the uniquely identifying character. Thus, I guess that there was an important difference, for Chrysippus, between two types of top-bottom relations. The first type concerned the casting of the uniquely identifying character. In this case, we must postulate a rather direct and mechanical efficiency: our uniquely identifying character is tempered by the cosmic configuration at the very instant of our birth. But Chrysippus is not Leibniz, the fact that Caesar will cross the Rubicon is no part of his uniquely identifying character. The fact that Caesar would cross the Rubicon was predictable on a consideration of his astral theme,[24] but it was not materially and *presently* inlayed into Caesar's substance when his nature, at his birth, was tempered as a soul – we can only affirm that his person must have been endowed, then, with a set of natural properties which had *everything* to make him cross the Rubicon – but which would not have prevented him from being annihilated by a Gallic army before having crossed the Rubicon. It is, I guess, only in the case of correlations belonging to the

---

[23] Cf. Aetius, *Plac.* 5.15.2 (= *SVF* 2.756). Cf. J.-B. Gourinat, *Le Stoïcisme* (Paris: Presses Universitaires de France, 2007), p. 75.

[24] Anna Maria Ioppolo, in her review of A. A. Long's *From Epicurus to Epictetus: Studies in Hellenistic and Roman Philosophy* (Oxford: Clarendon Press, 2006), published in *Elenchos* 27 (2006), 502–10, in particular 506–9, provides compelling arguments against Long's view (expressed in his 'Astrology: Arguments pro and contra', in J. Barnes, J. Brunschwig *et al.*, eds, *Science and Speculation: Studies in Hellenistic Theory and Practice* (Cambridge: Cambridge University Press, 1977), pp. 165–92) that, given his dates, Chrysippus is not likely to have been aware of any practice of astral divination.

second type and not to the first that Chrysippus changed the conditional into the negation of the conjunction.[25]

Let us consider Alexander's commentary on *GC* again. As already said, the 'so what?' reply was the following: even if the same celestial configuration comes back again, Socrates-1 and -2 are not numerically identical; and the objection: the same celestial configuration will never come back again. We notice a hidden premiss in the 'so what?' reply, namely the direct connection between supralunar and sublunar world, Unfortunately, Alexander does not tell us whether he recognizes such a thesis as valid also within the framework of his own ontology. The answer to that question cannot be that he entirely dismisses it: his Zeitgeist was deeply influenced by astral determinism and, more decisively, Aristotelian passages such as *Physics* 8.2, 253a7–20 seemed to explain every internal impulsion in the living body as determined by its external surroundings. This context explains why, in the objection, Alexander described the heavens as the efficient cause (*al-fā'il* = *to poioun*) of the individual. Thus, Alexander must have faced a problem which was not entirely dissimilar to that of Chrysippus. For even if Alexander objects to the Stoic position that in the case we posit an eternal return, Socrates-1 and -2 would not be *numerically* identical, this argument is of no great value if one's concern is above all to get rid of determinism. As soon as we posit astral determinism, be I intrinsically unique in the eternity of time (Alexander) or only in this repetition of the world cycle but indiscernible from my counterparts in the past and future worlds (Chrysippus), that does not seem to make any real difference with respect to the eventual autonomy of my choices. If, in the infinity of past and future worlds, I have ever given and shall ever give the same talk under the same circumstances, it seems at least very unlikely that there is anything like a free choice in my decision to deliver it.

The crucial problem, for Alexander, is finally to explain in what sense there can be something undetermined in the sensible, although everything which happens happens in virtue of a cause. And we must confess that each time Alexander is urged to specify what he has in mind, he appears much embarrassed. In his treatise *On fate*, he tries to argue against determinism by referring to our internal experience of choice and free-will[26] – which seems simply to beg the question: how to be sure that this appearance of

---

[25] I tend to be convinced, on this thorny topic, by the interpretation of Chrysippean modalities put forward by M. Mignucci and J. Vuillemin. See M. Mignucci, 'Sur la logique modale des Stoïciens', in J. Brunschwig, ed., *Les Stoïciens et leur logique*, 2nd edn (Paris: Vrin, 2006), pp. 303–32; J. Vuillemin, 'Le carré chrysippéen des modalités', *Dialectica* 37 (1983), 235–47; and J. Vuillemin, *Nécessité ou contingence: L'aporie de Diodore et les systèmes philosophiques* (Paris: Éditions de Minuit, 1984), in particular pp. 129–46, with the corrections published in J. Vuillemin, 'Nouvelles réflexions sur l'argument dominateur: une double référence au temps dans la seconde prémisse', *Philosophie* 55 (1997), 14–30.

[26] See for example Alexander, *Fat.* 12, 180,8–12: '... for choice is the impulse with desire towards what has been preferred as a result of deliberation. And for this reason choice does not apply to the things that come to be necessarily, nor to those that do so not necessarily but not through us, nor even in the case of all the things that do so through us; but in the case of those things that come to be through us over which we have control both to do and not to do them' (translation by R. W. Sharples, *Alexander of Aphrodisias on Fate* (London: Duckworth, 1983), p. 57, who notes in his commentary, p. 142, 'The definition of choice at 180.8f. is based on Aristotle's at *eth. Nic.* 3.3 1113a10, but cast in terminology borrowed from the Stoics'). On this text, see also D. Lefebvre, 'Alexandre d'Aphrodise, Supplément au traité de l'âme (extrait)', in J. Laurent and C. Romano, eds, *Le néant: Contribution à l'histoire du non-être dans la philosophie occidentale* (Paris: Presses Universitaires de France, 2006), pp. 103–17, at p. 105.

deliberation is not a mere illusion, a collateral effect in our phantasy of every action taking place 'in us' under the influence of some external principle? By contrast, in the *Mantissa*, Alexander points to 'matter', which he assimilates to 'not-being', in order to explain that everything in nature is not causally determined.[27] As already said, it seems difficult not to consider this appeal to matter as a piece of wishful thinking. As we have previously remarked, matter as such is perfectly indifferentiated, so that it seems hardly possible to attribute to it any resistance to the efficient principle, which would account for some autonomy at the level of the particulars.

I stop here my account of Alexander, noting how the three aspects of his defence of the singularity of the particular remain disconnected from one another: there are always singular configurations in the heavens, but their presence is only allusively brought into relation with the particular animals on earth; these are singular because of 'matter'; in the case of human beings, their capacity of choosing each one of the two branches of any dilemma attempts to introduce another breach in the edifice of determinism, and may be another cause for the fact that the sublunar as a whole does not repeat itself in *exactly* the same way. Human deliberation introduces some perturbation on earth, however tenuous it may be as compared to the cosmos as a whole. Thus, we still do not have a coherent and embracing theory of the particular. This flaw in Alexander's doctrine is likely to have a deep philosophical ground. Very simply put, Alexander attempts to refute determinism without giving up the principle that everything that happens happens in virtue of some cause. Matter, thus, plays for the particular the role both of a cause and of a protection against other causes, like the astral principles, which would be 'more' a cause, so to say, than itself.

4. Avicenna and Leibniz

a. *Avicenna*

In order to have a coherent theory of the particular, in this neo-Aristotelian context, one of the two fundamental premisses had to be given up: either by accepting that the sublunar particular be entirely determined by the supralunar world, or by assuming that something can happen without a cause.

For various reasons, in particular some tenets of his Neoplatonist creed, Avicenna is a convinced determinist. Everything in the world happens because of some causes of higher status. The sublunar world, including what pertains to our choices and volitions, is totally determined by astral positions, themselves dictated by a finite number of superior intellects subordinated to one another. Avicenna had surely access to Alexander's commentary on *GC* – known, as we have seen, to Averroes in the Muslim far West a century later – and makes use of it in his own treatise devoted to generation

---

[27] See now the edition of the Greek text by R. W. Sharples, *Alexander Aphrodisiensis, De anima libri mantissa* (Berlin: De Gruyter, 2008), pp. 118–22 and his commentary, pp. 225–7. On this solution, see Lefebvre (previous note), pp. 106–11.

and corruption.[28] Avicenna's position, then, represents a kind of compromise, urged by some Neoplatonist principles, between Alexander and the Stoic position he criticizes.

If our previous reconstruction is correct, Avicenna has thus read, in Alexander's response to the anonymous Stoics, the 'so what?' reply *and* the objection. In the first move, Alexander was implicitly accepting the influence of the supralunar on the sublunar and explicitly denying that the two particulars determined by two identical astral configurations were numerically identical; in the second move, Alexander was denying that some astral configuration might come back again, but committed a strange mistake, spotted by Averroes: he inferred from the fact that the lunar and solar period are not commensurable in full days the erroneous conclusion that they are not commensurable at all. Of course, as remarked by Averroes, what is not commensurable in full days can nevertheless be commensurable, provided that we can find some smaller common unit.[29]

Avicenna had thus all the necessary ingredients for a new theory of the particular. I want first to sketch its main tenets.[30]

There is nothing to say about matter, apart from the fact that it is there. As soon as we try to attribute to it some resistance to the informative action of some agent, we credit it with a physical property which contradicts the fact that it has, *per se*, no property at all. The only intrinsic property it has is the fact that it occupies a tridimensional continuous space. Avicenna's idea is thus the following: it is sufficient, if we want to avoid the case of indiscernible tokens of the same type, to interpret their difference as the result of some spatial variation in the disposition of matter, as small as we wish. Socrates will be different from his counterpart, for example, because of some minimal variation in the disposition of matter when he was conceived or in his subsequent history. But how to explain the possibility, in a determinist account, that there will always be some difference in the disposition of matter? The answer lies in the postulate of the relative incommensurability of the angular velocity of the different astral periods. The ratios between these periods being irrational, it is impossible to have twice exactly the same configuration. For the same reason, we shall never find exactly the same sublunar events repeating themselves. Human history, in particular, will not repeat itself. Every particular is intrinsically singular.[31]

---

[28] Ibn Sīnā, *Kitāb al-Sifā, al-Tabī'iyyāt*, 3 *Al-Kawn wa al-fasād*, ed. M. Qāsim (Cairo: Dar 'al-kātib 'al-'arabī, 1969), pp. 195–200. The Latin medieval translation has been edited: cf. Avicenna, *Liber Tertius Naturalium De Generatione et Corruptione*, édition critique de la traduction latine médiévale par S. Van Riet, Introduction doctrinale par G. Verbeke (Leuven: Peeters, 1987), pp. 148–51, for our passage.

[29] Ibn Rushd (n. 10 above), 36,3–6.

[30] For more details and a French translation of the Arabic, see M. Rashed, 'Théodicée et approximation: Avicenne', *Arabic Sciences and Philosophy* 10 (2000), 223–57.

[31] Let us quote the Latin medieval version (Avicenna (n. 28 above), pp. 149–50): 'For example, if the number of one of the circuits was five, of another seven, and of a third ten, they would come together in one number and seventy will be the number numerically shared by those numbers. For when the star which accomplishes its cycle in five years will be back back after fourteen periods and the star which accomplishes its cycle in ten years will be back after seven periods, they will be all together; and then, figures similar to those which have occurred will be counted in equal times. And if the comparison of times in the circuits is not number to number, and that can be because times are continuous, not discrete, and it is not impossible that a continuum should differ from a continuum as to whether it be straight or curved, for that reason the relation of one time to another will not be one of number to number. And now that is verified in quantities, it will doubtless therefore be verified in motions and times, and it is impossible that any aggregate should be found in which they

Accordingly, there is a real gap between the superior and the inferior levels of emanation. The superior levels can be treated with the help of a discrete calculus. For, the principles being finite in number, their relationships are also finite in number and can be calculated. This fact gave rise to the invention of combinatorics by al-Tūsī, mathematician, astronomer, and commentator of Avicenna.[32] By contrast, the inferior levels – which correspond to the sensible world, including the supralunar spheres – fall under the jurisdiction of the continuum and the geometrical irrational. One notices immediately, in the context of divine providence, how interesting this distinction can be. For even if we assume that God knows the decimal development of an irrational number, we cannot claim that this knowledge, for Him, is exactly of the same type as his knowledge of a rational number. There is a difference pertaining to the thing itself, and not just to our way of apprehending it. Then, if there is a way to 'apply' this difference between discrete and continuous quantities or, which amounts to the same, between natural and irrational numbers, to the problem of Providence, we could have the formalization of the problem Alexander was in search of, What Alexander was calling 'matter' becomes now irrationality Incommensurability in the ratios between the angular velocities of the planets creates some third way between pure determinism and the radical autonomy of the sublunar realm with respect to higher cosmic principles.

I would like here to draw a hermeneutical distinction between the general intuition of this theory and its historical context. Its context is that of the cosmology of the Neoplatonists, which divides the world into the divine realm, where we have to posit the different types of Intellects, the supralunar world, where we find extension and circular motion, and the sublunar world, whose material items are subject to generation and decay. It is obvious that Avicenna's reflexion attempts primarily at explaining how, in this determinist context, there can be some space for a certain kind of indetermination. But we may also look at his solution in a more general way, and ask ourselves whether it may have some validity outside its original context. I think it has, and that Leibniz has been sensitive to its theoretical richness.

b. *Leibniz*

Let us start with a relatively late text of Leibniz (written in 1715), which has been recently edited by M. Fichant.[33] Suggestively enough, it is entitled, *in Greek, Apokatastasis pantôn, Restitution of all things*. In the Greek cosmological context, the word had two significations, meaning either the Stoic everlasting recurrence or, in Origen, precisely against this Stoic doctrine, man's blessed afterlife. Even if it is beyond any doubt that Leibniz was well aware of Origen's doctrine – through his interest in Pedersen in

---

all share. And, after it has been confirmed in the science of geometry that quantities that match any quantity are equal to each other, while those that differ and are not shared do not match any one quantity, no shared quantity is found to contain all. And since it would not be found, it will be impossible for the same configuration to recur.'

[32] R. Rashed, 'Combinatoire et métaphysique: Ibn Sina, al-Tusi et al-Halabi', in R. Rashed, ed., *Les doctrines de la science de l'antiquité à l'âge classique* (Leuven: Peeters, 1999), pp. 61–86.
[33] G. W. Leibniz, *De l'horizon de la doctrine humaine, Apokatastasis pantôn (La Restitution Universelle)*, Textes inédits, traduits et annotés par M. Fichant (Paris: Vrin, 1991).

particular[34] – his project, in the *Apokatastasis* is to vindicate some sort of everlasting recurrence. The method, however, is new: Leibniz attempts to apply combinatorics to the question of the eternal return. His basic idea is the following. Every world can be subject to a verbal description. But every verbal description is composed of sentences, which do not exceed a certain length, and these sentences are composed out of words; these words, in their turn, are composed out of the letters of the alphabet. Thus, if we assume that the annals of the world may be adequately captured by our language, whose elements are discrete, we are forced to recognize that the world cannot encompass events which the language would be unable to describe. But since the set of all the combinations with permutations of a finite set of elements is necessarily finite, the annals cannot be indefinitely extended. Consequently, in some infinite period of time, such as the world history, the sequence of letters constituting the annals must repeat itself. At this stage, however, Leibniz introduces an important *caveat*:

> However, even if some prior century comes back again with respect to the sensible things, i.e. with respect to the things that can be described by books, it is not true that it will come back again with respect to everything: For there will always be some distinctions, even if they are imperceptible and cannot be described by any book. For the continuum is divided in parts which are infinite in number, so that in any part of matter, there is a world of an infinite number of creatures, which cannot be described by any book, whatever be its length. True, if bodies were constituted out of atoms, all things would come back again exactly in the same collection of atoms, provided that new atoms do not aggregate themselves from outside; as if we were to suppose Epicurus' world, separated from others by some interworlds. But in this case, the world would be a machine of which some creature of limited perfection would have a perfect knowledge, which is not the case in the true world.[35]

We understand, on the basis of some other Leibnizian texts, the deep significance of such a distinction between countability and continuity. It is the actual infinity of the divisions of the continuum which allows, if perhaps not a real escape from determinism, at least the possibility of distinguishing between the necessary and the contingent. According to the *General Inquiries about the Analysis of Concepts and Truth* of 1686, the essential propositions are demonstrable by the resolution of their terms, which leads, in a finite number of steps to an identity A = A. By opposition, existential, i.e. contingent, propositions, when analyzed, lead to an infinite regress, which can be grasped *a priori* only by the infinite Mind:

> A true contingent proposition cannot be reduced to equivalent propositions. But it is proved by showing, in a further and further developed resolution, that it for ever approaches equivalent propositions, but without ever reaching them. Hence it is open only to God, who embraces in his mind the whole infinity, to know

---

[34] Leibniz (previous note), pp. 20–4.
[35] Leibniz (n. 33 above), p. 72.

the certainty of all contingent truths. Hence the distinction between necessary truths and contingent ones is the same as that between lines that meet and lines that approach each other asymptotically, or between commensurable and incommensurable numbers.[36]

I could stop here. We have seen how some disconnected elements in Alexander's reply to the Stoics were put together and elaborated by Avicenna, and how this new approach of the question of determinism is not unsimilar to Leibniz' treatment of the problem. However, I would like to say a last word on the probability of a historical connexion between Avicenna and Leibniz. Avicenna's doctrine was well-known during the Middle Ages. It was assimilated by Scotus, Nicole Oresme, and many others during the Renaissance.[37] One of these authors was Christopher Clavius, who writes, in his commentary on the *De sphaera* of John of Sacrobosco, the following words:

> It follows from these considerations that it completes its whole course through the Zodiac in approximately 49,000 years. For if we want to express ourselves with precision, in such an interval of time, the ninth sphere, according to the above-mentioned tables, accomplishes actually a little more than an entire circle, going through 360 degrees, 5 thirds, and 31 fourths. This interval of time, i.e. the 49,000 years, is usually called the 'Platonic Year'. For it is in this interval that, they say, all stars will come back to the same position again. And according to some people, everything in the world will then have to be at the very place in which it is seen today. But this is a bold affirmation. For since, according to the majority of people, the motions of the heavens are mutually incommensurable, it cannot happen that all the stars may one day reach the very position and place that they have today or had in the past.[38]

Since Leibniz, in his *Dissertatio de arte combinatoria* (1666) quotes this commentary of Clavius, we can be sure that already as a young student, he was acquainted with Avicenna's reformulation of Alexander's reply to the Stoics. It seems likely that Alexander's objection against the Stoics contained the seminal idea out of which a whole subsequent tradition – but, paradoxically enough, not Alexander himself – tried to escape fatalism without renouncing the thesis that everything that happens in the world happens in virtue of a cause.

---

[36] G. W. Leibniz, *Generales inquisitiones de analysi notionum et veritatum*, in *Recherches générales sur l'analyse des notions et des vérités*, introduction et notes par J.-B. Rauzy (Paris: Presses Universitaires de France, 1998), p. 276.
[37] Many of then have been traced back by E. Grant, *Nicole Oresme and the Kinematics of Circular Motion* (Madison: University of Wisconsin Press, 1971).
[38] C. Clavius, *In Sphaeram Ioannis de Sacro Bosco commentarius* (Geneva: Samuel Crispinus, 1608), pp. 55–6.

5

Themistius and the Problem of Spontaneous Generation[1]

Devin Henry

At the outset of *Generation of Animals* [*GA*] Aristotle endorses the common belief that some living things come into being, not from other organisms of the same kind, but spontaneously (*apo tautomatou*) from putrefying matter:

> Of animals, some come to be from the union of female and male (in those kinds that have sexes; for not all them do, but in the blooded animals, outside of a few exceptions, when the individual has been completed it is either male or female), whereas among the bloodless animals, while some species have sexes so that they generate offspring of the same kind (*ta homogenê gennan*), others generate, but what they produce at any rate is not something of the same kind. This includes all those animals that do not come to be from the union of animals but from decaying earth and residues.[2] (*GA* 1.1, 725a18–26; cf. Plato, *Politicus* 270C-272B)

Aristotle offers his own account of the phenomenon in *GA* 3.11, where he attempts to set out the causal mechanisms responsible for the process (762a8–31).[3] The first

---

This article is a substantially revised version of 'Themistius and Spontaneous Generation in Aristotle's *Metaphysics*' by Devin Henry in *Oxford Studies in Ancient Philosophy* 24 (2003), pp. 183–208. By permission of Oxford University Press.

---

[1] I wish to thank Richard Sorabji for giving me the opportunity to revise my *OSAP* paper and, especially, to Yoav Meyrav whose important contribution to this volume was the impetus for the revisions. In many ways his paper supplants the arguments of my original paper.
[2] Unless otherwise specified, all translations are my own.
[3] By referring to this mode of generation as "spontaneous" (*apo tautomatou*) Aristotle is not using the concept in the technical sense from *Physics* 2.4-6. First, as we shall see, Aristotle offers a causal account of spontaneous generation in *GA* 3.11 that identifies very determinate factors that are responsible for the phenomenon. By contrast, one of the marks of "spontaneous" events in the *Physics* sense is that they are causally indeterminate and therefore unaccountable (*Physics* 197a8–24). For this reason Aristotle thinks we cannot acquire scientific knowledge of *Physics*-style spontaneous events (*Metaph.* 11.8). Yet, that is precisely what *GA* 3.11 seeks to provide. Second, the *Physics* classifies spontaneous events as chance events in the sphere of nature. And chance is *by definition* something infrequent; it is outside (*para*) what happens always or for the most part (*Physics* 196b10–22). The mode of generation under investigation in *GA* 3.11 is far too regular, in

commentator to notice the implications that this had for Aristotle's broader metaphysics was the fourth Century CE commentator, Themistius. Themistius had noticed that the existence of spontaneous generation did not sit well with Aristotle's own attack on Plato's the theory of Ideas. In this paper I want to explore Themistius' worry and how Aristotle (unbeknownst to Themistius) had tried to resolve it.

In *Metaphysics* 7.7 Aristotle argues that each particular thing comes into being by the agency of something (the moving cause), out of something (the matter), and comes to be something (i.e. acquires a substantial form). One of the central messages of *Metaphysics* 7.7–9 is that particulars always come to be from other particulars, which renders Platonic Ideas superfluous:

> It is clear, then, that the cause that consists of the Ideas (if they are treated as something alongside the particulars as some speak of them) is of no use, at least in relation to being and coming-to-be. Nor, at any rate, could they exist as self-subsistent entities. In the case of some things it is even obvious that the generator is such as to be like the thing generated, not, however, identical with it, nor one in number, but one in form, as in the case of natural things (for a human generates a human).... Therefore, it is clear that it is not necessary to set up Ideas as paradigms. For we should have looked for Ideas especially in these cases, since these are substances most of all. But the particular generator is sufficient to produce and be the cause of the form that comes to be in the matter.
>
> *Metaph.* 7.8, 1033b26–1034a5[4]

Aristotle's target here is the account of generation put forward in Plato's *Timaeus*. Plato agrees with Aristotle that everything that comes into being must come to be by the agency of some cause (*hup' aitiou tinos*), since nothing can come into being without a cause. On Plato's model, however, generation also requires a paradigm or model (*paradeigma*) that the generator must look to when bringing something into being. This role is played by separately-existing Ideas (*Timaeus* 27D5–28B4). For Aristotle there is no need to appeal to Ideas because in every case the particular generator is sufficient to explain how the form comes to be in the matter.[5]

Aristotle's view, to qualify as chance in his sense. Aristotle thinks that entire classes of animals (e.g. the so-called *ostrakoderma*) come into being spontaneously. Indeed, it is this kind of regularity that makes it possible for him to offer a causal account of the proess. For a further defense of this point see D. Balme, 'Development of Biology in Aristotle and Theophrastus: Theory of Spontaneous Generation', *Phronesis* 7 (1962), 91–104; A. Gotthelf, 'Teleology and Spontaneous Generation in Aristotle: A Discussion', *Apeiron* 22 (1989), 181–93; G. E. R. Lloyd, *Aristotelian Explorations* (Cambridge: Cambridge University Press, 1996). For an alternative (and in my opinion unsuccessful) interpretation that attempts to locate spontaneous generation within the context of *Physics* 2.4–6 see J. Lennox, 'Teleology, Chance, and Aristotle's Theory of Spontaneous Generation', *Journal of the History of Philosophy* 20 (1982), 19–38 (repr. in J. Lennox, ed., *Aristotle's Philosophy of Biology* (Cambridge: Cambrudge University Press, 2001), pp. 229–49). See also Thomas Aquinas, below.

[4] Themistius' objection (which I examine below) is targeting a condensed version of this conclusion at *Metaphysics* 12.3, 1070a27–30.

[5] Aristotle need not be committed to the claim that the particular generator supplies a paradigm or model for the thing that comes into being. Even if he does mean that (see *Physics* 2.3, 194b26), he certainly does not think the nature in the seed generates the offspring *by looking to* the parent's form in the way that a craftsman looks to her model.

What Themistius had noticed was that this argument ignored spontaneously generated organisms, which do not come to be from other particulars of the same kind but from putrefying matter:

> This argument is persuasive as a refutation of the Ideas, but its author [sc. Aristotle] overlooked the many animals that are not born from their likes, in spite of their great numbers. For we see that a kind of hornet is born from the bodies of dead horses, bees from dead cows, frogs from putrescence when it becomes sour. We see that nature does not generate these things from their likes in form, and yet we are convinced that in the semen and seed of each kind of animal and plant there is a formative principle (*logos*) by which is begotten these animals and plants that are begotten from it specifically and not from another (so that a horse is not generated from the semen of a human nor a human from the semen of a horse, nor a plant from the seed of another plant). So where are the counterparts[6] of these formative principles in that from which these <spontaneously generated> animals are born? Unless a suitable formative principle (*logos*) had already been put into nature previously, ready to create any possible species of animal and having found a proper material for creating a certain animal from it, the individual would not have been brought into actuality.
>
> Themistius, *in Metaph.* 12 ap. Averroes, *Long Commentary on the* Metaphysics, iii. 1492-4[7]

In the first line Themistius refers to Aristotle's argument against the Ideas as 'persuasive'.[8] And what is persuasive (at least in the rhetorical sense) can be looked at as untrue and deceptive. What Themistius is saying, then, is that Aristotle's argument may be forceful enough to persuade his audience but is not sufficient to establish its conclusion.[9] In particular, it is vulnerable to objections about spontaneous generation, which is precisely what Themistius goes on to say.

It is easy to see why Themistius thinks spontaneous generation poses a problem for Aristotle's argument. The reason Aristotle thinks Platonic Ideas are unnecessary is that in each case the particular generator is competent (*hikanon*) on its own to produce and

---

[6] Accepting Meyrav's translation of the Arabic *naẓīr*. On the importance of this term see the next note.
[7] My translation combines Genquand's original text with insights from Yoav Meyrav's new translation (this volume). In my original paper I used Genequand's translation, which had Themistius asking: 'Where are *the models* of these proportions (*logoi*) in that from which these animals are born?' And I had read this in the context of the *Timaeus*' insistence that generation requires Ideas to serve as models after which the generator patterns its movements (27D5–28B4). Hence I naturally took Themistius to be defending the need for Platonic Ideas against Aristotle's criticism. However Meyrav's new translation corrects 'models' to 'counterparts', which I have adopted here. On his translation, Themistius is not (at least not explicitly) saying that we must have recourse to Platonic Ideas as models but only *logoi* in the earth that serve as the analogues for the form-carrying principles at work in the seeds of parents in sexual reproduction (see below). Meyrav argues that Themistius is ultimately trying to make room for some sort of transcendent origin of the natural world and spontaneous generation helps him with that. As Themistius goes on to say, those formative principles that are latent in the earth must have been put there by 'higher causes'.
[8] Averroes' Arabic corresponds to the Greek *pithanos* here.
[9] I owe this insight to Richard Sorabji (personal communication).

be a cause of the form that comes to be in the matter (1034a4–6). In cases of natural generation— generation that proceeds from an internal principle of change—this role is played by the male parent whose semen transmits a species-specific form to the materials provided by the female (*Metaph.* 1032a12–5, 1071a20–3; *PA* 640a23–6; *GA* 734b34–735a4, 743a27–36, 765b10–14, 768a5–21). Spontaneous generation looks like an obvious counter-example because these organisms come to be, not from conspecifics, but from putrefying matter. What, in these cases, explains the form that comes to be in the matter? Themistius thinks that we must posit special formative principles, or *logoi*, latent in the earth that code for the forms of spontaneously generated organisms and are the analogues of those transmitted in the seeds of sexually-reproducing organisms. Themistius goes on to argue that these formative principles must have a transcendental origin, since they could not have come from any particular generator that bears the form in actuality: 'This shows you that these *logoi* have already been inspired by a cause nobler, worthier, and higher in rank than themselves, i.e. the soul in the earth which Plato thought had been created by the secondary gods,[10] and Aristotle thought had been created by the sun and the ecliptic.'[11]

In the remainder of this paper I want to take a closer look at Themistius' claim that spontaneous generation undermines Aristotle's argument against the Ideas. As we shall see, Aristotle did not overlook the philosophical implications that spontaneous generation had for his argument. He had already anticipated such an objection in *Metaphysics* 7.9.

Themistius' objection seems to acquire its force from a certain reading of Aristotle's argument. According to this interpretation, one of the central principles underlying Aristotle's model of generation is what Bodnar calls 'the principle of causational synonymy', which says that causes have to be synonymous with (i.e. bear the same name and definition as) the effects they bring about.[12] And the way this is typically understood is that cause and effect must be the same in form (as when man begets man).[13] It is for this reason, the interpretation goes, that Ideas are superfluous in the context of generation. For Aristotle insists that particulars always come to be from other particulars that already bear the form in actuality.

When the argument is read in this way Themistius' objection has bite, since cases of spontaneous generation are not instances of formal replication. However this line of interpretation faces a problem. After arguing that generation does not require Ideas in chapter 8, Aristotle immediately turns to spontaneous generation in chapter 9. So

---

[10] See *Statesman* 271A ff., where Plato associates the so-called earthborn races during the time of Kronos with 'souls planted in the earth like seeds' by the secondary gods.

[11] I owe this revised interpretation to Yoav Meyrav. For a more thorough analysis of Themistius' position see his contribution to this volume.

[12] I. Bodnar, 'Aristotle's Natural Philosophy', in E. N. Zalta, ed., *The Stanford Encyclopedia of Philosophy* (Spring 2012 Edition), <http://plato.stanford.edu/archives/spr2012/entries/aristotle-natphil/>, Section 3.

[13] J. Lennox, 'Are Aristotelian Species Eternal?', in J. Lennox, ed., *Aristotle's Philosophy of Biology* (Cambridge: Cambridge University Press, 2001), pp. 131–59, at pp. 151–3, calls this model where particulars come to be the sorts of things they are by becoming like their generator in form 'formal replication'.

Aristotle not only anticipated Themistius objection, he thought he could disarm it by showing how the argument of chapter 8 extends to spontaneous generation. This places constraints on how we interpret the argument against Ideas. In particular it should rule out any reading that makes it dependent on formal replication. With this in mind, I want to offer a different interpretation of the final argument in *Metaphysics* 7.8.

In *Metaphysics* 7.7 we are told that in cases of natural generation the efficient cause (that *by which* the substance comes into being) is the organism's formal nature (*hê kata to eidos phusis*), which is derived from another individual that already bears the form in actuality (1032a12–5). But this is not the feature of natural generation that Aristotle thinks allows us to dispense with Ideas.[14] If it were, then spontaneous generation would clearly undermine his reasoning there. Instead Aristotle argues that Ideas are unnecessary because in every case of generation 'the particular generator is sufficient to produce and be the cause of the form that comes to be in the matter'. Natural generation is simply offered as a case where this fact is obvious: he says that 'in some case' (*epi men dê tinôn*), namely 'in the case of natural substances' (*en tois phusikois*), it is 'obvious' (*phaneron*) that there is no need to appeal to separately-existing Ideas because *in those* cases (e.g. when a human generates a human) we can see the form right there in the particular generator.[15] Spontaneous generation is problematic, then, not because it fails to exhibit the pattern of formal replication (as Themistius supposes), but because it is simply not obvious that in those cases the source of the product's form pre-exists in any particular substance. And yet the fact that Aristotle immediately turns to spontaneous generation in chapter 9 suggests that even in those cases we do not need Platonic Ideas. As we shall see, the upshot of Aristotle's account is that the particular material causes surrounding a spontaneous generation are sufficient on their own to produce the organism that comes to be from them. This not only renders Ideas superfluous, it also obviates the need to posit special *logoi* of a supernatural origin that serve as the counter-part of the form-carrying motions in the father's semen.

After concluding in *Metaphysics* 7.8 that generation does not require Platonic Ideas Aristotle immediately raises the following aporia in 7.9:

> But someone might raise a puzzle as to why some things can come to be both through craft and of their own accord (*apo tautomatou*), for example health, while others cannot [sc. they come to be only in the first way], for example houses.

What is responsible (*aition*) for this, Aristotle says, is that in the former case 'the matter that forms the starting-point of coming-to-be' (*hê hulê hê arkhousa tês geneseôs*) is such that it can 'move itself' (*kineisthai huph' hautês*) in the particular way that the craft moves it, whereas those materials that cannot do this need the craft to impose the form on them. And so the latter products cannot exist apart from the craft (1034a14–19). Aristotle extends this idea to nature toward the end of the chapter:

---

[14] *Pace* Lennox.
[15] Aristotle makes a similar point at *GC* 2.9, 335b20–4.

> It is the same with things that are formed by nature. For the *sperma* produces things just as those that come to be from the craft (for it contains the form potentially, and that from which the *sperma* comes in a way shares the same name as the product).... And, just like the formation of craft products, those things are spontaneously generated whose matter is capable of moving itself with the same motion that the *sperma* initiates, while those whose matter is not like this cannot be generated in any other way than from others <formally> like themselves.
>
> 1034a33-b7

According to Aristotle's theory of natural generation, the *sperma* of each species contains a power (or *dunamis*) that is suitable to produce the form that comes to be in the offspring (*PA* 640a23–33, *GA* 729b5–7, 743a26–36, 766b12–14, 767b20–768a2). It is in this sense, I take it, that the father's semen contains the offspring's form potentially, not as a latent (unactualized) form that is deposited in the matter supplied by the female, but as a causal power that is suitable to impose that form on the matter. In this respect natural generation is similar to craft production:

> Heat and cold soften and harden the iron, but they do not produce the sword [the whole product]. This is accomplished by the movement of the tools the craftsman employs, which contains the *logos* of his craft. For the craft (*tekhnê*) is the principle and form (*arkhê kai eidos*) of the product, though it is located in another, whereas the motion of nature is located in the thing that is generated and is derived from another natural substance that possess the form in actuality.
>
> *GA* 734b37–735a4; cf. 730a14–15, 740b29–741a3

What Aristotle appears to be saying in *Metaphysics* 7.9 is that, in cases of spontaneous generation, the matter involved in the process is itself capable of effecting the same kinds of changes that the form-carrying seed initiates in natural generation. This is why some living things can come into being of their own accord in the absence of *sperma*.

This idea is perfectly in line with what Aristotle says about spontaneous generation in the biological works. The main discussion is found in *GA* 3.11, which concerns the generation of the so-called *ostrakoderma* (the class of hard-shelled animals that includes whelks, sea-urchins, and limpets).[16] It is important to keep in mind that, to Aristotle, these are rather simple life forms, essentially just blobs of flesh living inside a hard shell. And while he is interested in how these animals acquire their characteristic structures, his primary concern in *GA* 3.11 is how the living thing inside the shell originally comes into being (the counter-part of fertilization in sexual generation). At

---

[16] Aristotle recognizes two primary modes of generation proper to the kind, both of which occur in the absence of *sperma*: budding (761b24–762a8); and spontaneous generation from putrefying materials (762a8–26). Here I focus on the latter. At 761a16–18 Aristotle says in *one* way it appears as though the ostrakoderms are generated from *sperma* and from themselves, though in *another* way they are spontaneously generated. I take it that by saying that some appear to be generated 'from *sperma* and from themselves' he has in mind those that reproduce by budding (e.g. mussels). With this method the new organism comes into being out of a slimy fluid substance that is emitted from the parent organism. However, Aristotle denies that this is *sperma* (semen) in the proper sense (761b33–5).

GA 762a35-b6 Aristotle tells us what will count as a proper explanation of the phenomena:

> Anyone who wishes to investigate the phenomenon properly must inquire into what, with respect to the thing being formed, is the material principle (*to kata tên hulikên arkhên sunistamenon*) in these sorts of cases. In <sexually reproducing> females this is a certain residue of the animal that is potentially the same sort of thing as that from which it came and is provided alongside the motive principle of the male, which turns it into the animal. What, in the case of spontaneous generation, should we say corresponds to that? And what corresponds to the principle of motion from the male, and whence does it come?

This conforms to Aristotle's standard account of scientific explanation. For any phenomenon *P* we can be said to have explained *P* when we have identified its proper causes. In the case of spontaneous generation, this requires identifying its material and efficient causes. We will thus *have explained* the phenomenon when we have identified these two principles.[17] It is clear from the rest of the passage that Aristotle seeks to model his account of spontaneous generation on the more general theory of sexual reproduction set out in the first three books. According to that model, an embryo is formed when the heat in the father's semen comes into contact with the menstrual fluid and initiates a chemical reaction that causes the small bits of spermatic residue in it to fuse together into a unified mass (*GA* 729a9-13, 739b20-33; cf. 771b22-4). Here the menstrual fluid (or the spermatic residue it contains) is the material source of the embryo (it provides the matter that gets formed into the embryo), while the seminal heat is the principle of motion (it fashions the menstrual fluid into an embryo and catalyses its development).

Aristotle compares all of this to the coagulation of milk. Experience shows that if you store milk in a bag made from the stomach of a young ruminant, the rennet will transform the milk into solid curds and liquid whey. The Greeks figure out that the same effect could be produced by other active ingredients such as fig-juice. The causal interaction between rennet (or fig juice) and milk provided the empirical model for understanding how semen imposes form on the menstrual fluid during fertilization. In both cases the product of this chemical reaction is an unorganized, amorphous mass: an embryo (*kuêma*) in the one case, and a curd in the other (724b18). This method of reasoning by analogy — where we study the dynamics of an observable phenomenon that is familiar from everyday experience (the action of rennet on milk) and then extrapolate to the unobservable phenomenon we are trying to explain (the action of semen on menstrual fluid) to identify a causal mechanism — is a particularly good example of an argument that moves from 'what is more familiar to us' to 'what is more familiar by nature'. What Aristotle is attempting to do in our passage is extend this

---

[17] Notice that Aristotle does not ask, in addition, for its final (or formal) causes. I take it this is because he does not think spontaneous generation is a teleological process. The form that the organism eventually acquires does not serve as the end for the sake of which its development takes place; there simply is no final cause (*pace* Thomas Aquinas below). Instead material-efficient causation is sufficient to necessitate the end that results independently of final causation.

explanatory model to spontaneous generation by identifying the appropriate analogues: What is the material principle that becomes the embryo (the analogue of menstrual fluid)? What is the active ingredient that imposes form on that matter (the analogue of seminal heat)? And how do these factors causally interact to produce a spontaneous organism? As we shall see, Aristotle believes that life can emerge spontaneously when you have a sugar-rich medium[18] that is acted upon by some kind of heat. These correspond to the material and efficient causes, respectively.

Aristotle sets out his theory of spontaneous generation in two difficult passages from *GA* 3.11:

> [T1] Animals and plants come to be in the earth and in water because there is water in earth and *pneuma* in water, and in all *pneuma* there is soul-heat (thus, in a way, everything is full of soul). This is why it forms quickly whenever it gets enclosed. It gets enclosed when the corporeal fluids are heated and something like a foamy blister forms. And the thing that takes shape differs in kind as being more or less valuable depending on the inclusion wherein the principle of soul resides, while the places and type of corporeal substance that gets enclosed are responsible (*aitioi*) for this.
>
> *GA* 3.11, 762a18–27

> [T2] We must grasp that even in the case of those animals that reproduce, it is the heat in the animal that makes the residue (the <material> principle of the embryo) out of the incoming nutriment by separating off <the sweet substance> and concocting it.... What the heat in <sexually reproducing> animals works up from their nutriment, <in spontaneous generation> the heat in the surrounding atmosphere puts together and amalgamates by concoction out of sea-water and earth. And the principle of soul that is enclosed and separated off in the *pneuma* makes the embryo and imparts motion to it.
>
> *GA* 3.11, 762b6–18

Text T1 appears to be doing two things. First, Aristotle gives a brief sketch of how a living thing comes into being spontaneously: as 'the corporeal fluids' (*tôn sômatikôn hugrôn*)[19] are heated they bubble (the 'foamy blister'), which encloses some *pneuma* and soul-heat.[20] This heat-infused bubble becomes the embryo that forms the starting-

---

[18] This is what Aristotle calls 'the sweet' (*to glukos*). *De sensu* refers to this as a useful residue extracted from the nutriment in the normal process of digestion by the heat in the animal (441b24–442a10, a26–30. As we shall see, it is what serves as the material cause of an embryo in both sexual reproduction (*GA* 762b6–8) and spontaneous generation (762a12–13).

[19] The fluid in question either refers to the putrefying ooze or to the sugar ('the sweet') that arises in connection with putrefaction (cf. 762a12–14). As we shall see, the latter is what provides the raw material out of which the living thing develops.

[20] The image here seems to be the following. As the fluid putrefies bubbles arise that trap bits of *pneuma* containing soul-heat. These *pneuma*-infused bubbles then crust over and solidify which, I take it, forms the beginning of the living organism itself (the creature inside the shell). Aristotle fills this picture out in *Meteorologica* 4 (see below).

point of the new animal (as we learn from T2). The second half of the passage tells us that different species of ostrakoderms differ from one another according to differences in their respective 'inclusions' (= shells, casings, etc.). These differences are in turn determined by two factors: (i) the place where the creature develops (e.g. under the earth), which can act as a kind of mould; and (ii) the type of materials that get enclosed with the *pneuma* (e.g. sea water, mud, etc., as Aristotle goes on to say: 762a27–32). A particularly good example of this is afforded by Aristotle's explanation of how the spines of sea-urchins are formed.

At *PA* 679b15–31 Aristotle tells us that the sea urchin has the best defence system of all the hard-shelled animals because 'it has a good, thick shell all around it fortified by a palisade of spines'. In *GA* 5.3 he tells us how these parts are formed by referring their structure to various material-level causes surrounding their development, including their relative lack of natural heat and the congealing effects of the surrounding water:

> Thus, with wild animals the reason they have hard hair is that they live outdoors in the open air, but in other cases it is the environment's being of such a kind that is responsible for this (*aition . . . ho topos toioutos ôn*). This is shown by what occurs in the case of the sea urchins, which are used as a remedy for cases of strangury. These creatures, because the sea water in which they live is cold on account of its depth (60 fathoms or even more is the depth at which they are found), although they are themselves small, are covered by long, hard spines: *long*, because the growth of the body is diverted there (for as they possess but little heat and do not properly concoct their nourishment they contain a great deal of residue, and it is out of residue that spines and hair and things of that sort are formed); *hard and petrified*, because of the cold and its congealing effect.
>
> *GA* 5.3, 783a18–29 (translated after Peck)

With naturally generated organisms, the embryo's own internal heat is responsible for concocting the incoming nutriment during the formation of its bodily structures. A sea-urchin lacks the requisite degree of natural heat and so is unable to impose limits on its nutriment as it streams from its body. Its characteristic spines are formed as these streams of nutriment come into contact with the cold sea water, which congeals them into long hard spikes.[21] In this case the same (internal) limit and structure that would otherwise have been imposed on the growth of the embryo by the heat transmitted in the parent's seed is supplied by the congealing powers of the cold sea water.

T2 follows on the methodological passage above where Aristotle says that what we are seeking are the analogues of menstrual blood and seminal heat (the material and efficient causes of an embryo). The first part of T2 describes the formation of the material principle. Aristotle reminds us that in sexual reproduction it is the female's

---

[21] More specifically, the lack of natural heat explains the length of the spines (the animal cannot impose its own internal limit on their growth), while their hardness is explained by the congealing effects of the cold water (the streams of nutriment are ossified by it).

own natural heat that makes the matter out of the food she consumes by separating out the useful (sweet) nutriment and working it up into *sperma*.[22] In the case of spontaneous generation this role is taken up by 'the heat in the surrounding atmosphere' (*hê tês hôras ên tôi periekhonti thermotês*, cf. 743a35–6). The result serves as the matter out of which the embryo is formed (the material cause). The second part of T2 identifies the source of the heat that provides the efficient cause of the process. In the case of sexual reproduction this role is played by the heat in the father's semen, which forms the menstrual blood into an embryo by fusing it together and then catalyzes its development. In spontaneous generation this agency is provided by 'the principle of soul that is enclosed and separated off in the *pneuma*'. This, I take it, refers back to the heat-infused *pneuma* from T1 that gets trapped inside 'the foamy blisters'.

According to the *GA* theory, then, the matter of the embryo — the analogue of menstrual blood — is a 'sweet' substance that has been extracted from putrefying seawater or mud and worked up by the heat from the surrounding environment. This material is then formed into an embryo and set in motion by the bit of soul-heat that gets trapped together with *pneuma*.[23] Since the conditions necessary for this to take place are said to occur in connection with putrefaction (762a8–18), we need to say a word about this process. For that we can turn to *Meteorologica* 4.

Aristotle treats putrefaction (*hê sêpsis*) as a special type of destruction in which an organic body undergoes a process of becoming increasingly dry until eventually ending up as soil or dung (379a8–9, 22–3; cf. *HA* 569a10–15, 570a7–12). What explains this process, he says, is the fact that when a living body decomposes its internal (soul) heat gets expelled, which in turn causes its natural moisture to evaporate along with it (379a23–4). And since there is nothing left to draw in any new moisture (attracting moisture and drawing it in being a function of a body's internal heat, 379a25–6), the putrefying thing eventually dries out. It is this loss of heat and moisture that comes to form the basis of putrefaction. However, Aristotle is careful to point out in *GA* 3.11 that it is not so much the putrefaction of the body itself that is crucial for spontaneous

---

[22] The question of whether or not Aristotle recognised female *sperma* has confused commentators because Aristotle uses the term in different ways, including (1) for an organism's reproductive material generally (including plant seeds), (2) for male semen (technically *gonê*: e.g. 727b34), and (3) for the immediate product of fertilisation (technically *kuêma*: e.g. 724b14–18, 728b34–5; cf. 731a2–4). While it is true that in some places Aristotle denies that females contribute *sperma* (e.g. 727a26–30), in those passages he almost certainly means (2) semen. Female *sperma* is explicitly mentioned in several places in the *GA* (e.g. 728a26–7, b23, 750b4–5, 767b16–17, 771b20, b22–3). Indeed, Aristotle thinks that it is because the female produces *sperma* that she is also a principle of generation (716a11–13). Nevertheless Aristotle stresses that what she produces is not the same kind of *sperma* as the male "as some allege"; she produces menstrual fluid, which is colder and less-thoroughly concocted than male semen on account of which it lacks the ability to transmit form (727b6–7, 728a27–31; cf. 726b31–727a2, 738a12–15, a34-b2, 765b16–35). Instead female *sperma* plays the role of matter. On the female's contribution to generation see D. Henry, 'Understanding Aristotle's Reproductive Hylomorphism', *Apeiron* 39 (2006), 269–300; 'How Sexist is Aristotle's Developmental Biology?', *Phronesis* 52 (2007), 251–69; 'Generation of Animals', in G. Anagnostopoulos, ed., *A Companion to Aristotle* (Chichester: Wiley-Blackwell, 2009), pp. 368–83.

[23] By 'soul-heat' here Aristotle presumably means the natural or inborn heat of the decaying animal corpse that escapes from it as a result of putrefaction. See below.

generation; putrefaction and the thing putrefied are only a by-product of that (762a13–15). What is important is the interaction between the heat and moisture as they are released into the atmosphere, which happens in connection with putrefaction. It is here, outside the putrefying ooze, that Aristotle thinks the real action takes place. At *Meteor.* 379b7–9 we are told that living things are generated spontaneously whenever 'the natural heat that is expelled <from the putrefying matter> fuses together (*sunistanai*) the substance that is being thrown off along with it'.[24] It is the amalgamation or fusion of the putrefying thing's natural moisture (the passive factor) by its natural heat (the active factor) as they are released together into the atmosphere that forms the starting-point of a spontaneous generation.

When we combine this with the canonical account of spontaneous generation in *GA* 3.11 the following picture emerges. At *GA* 762a9–13 Aristotle says that all things formed by spontaneous generation come into being 'in connection with putrefaction (*meta sêpseôs*) and a mixture of rain [or sea] water' and that as 'the sweet (*tou glukeos*) is separated out' from the putrefying body it gets diverted 'to the principle that is being constituted' (i.e. the embryo). The *Meteorologica* gives us an expanded version of that account. The water mixing with the dead matter, on the one hand, and the heat from the surrounding environment, on the other, combine to initiate putrefaction. The process that ensues (the thing that happens 'in connection with putrefaction') then includes two important events: (i) evaporation, whereby 'the sweet' (the useful material) is extracted from the putrefying body in the form of a moist vapour (*GA* 762a12–13); and (ii) recombination, whereby the sugar-rich material is immediately concocted as it is thrown off from the putrefying body by the (soul) heat being expelled along with it (*Meteor.* 379b7–9, *GA* 743a35–6, 762a12–13, b14–16). I submit that (i) is the counterpart of the process by which menstrual blood is formed in the mother (762b6–9), while (ii) is analogous to the way the heat in the father's semen extracts the small bits of spermatic residue in the menstrual fluid and fuses them together into an embryo (*GA* 729a9–13, 739b20–33, 771b22–4; cf. Lloyd, *Aristotelian Explorations*, pp. 116–17). This is another example (or so I contend) of Aristotle's claim in *Metaphysics* 7.9 that the material-level forces at work in spontaneous generation have the power to bring about by themselves the same changes that the form-carrying seed brings about in sexual reproduction.[25]

Of course this is not the only way to interpret Aristotle's account of spontaneous generation in the works on natural science. Freudenthal, for example, outright rejects this reading saying that 'in Aristotle there is no 'necessitation from below': Aristotle's matter does not organize itself spontaneously into structured substances such as living

---

[24] The material being thrown off here is the body's natural moisture. Presumably this moisture (the corporeal fluid from T1?) contains the sugar that forms the material principle of the embryo (*GA* 762a12–14).

[25] See also J. Wilberding, *Neoplatonism and the Philosophy of Nature* (Oxford: Oxford University Press, 2012), p. 199: 'Aristotle looks to material causes as the source of the abiogenetic living thing's form, though he stops short of saying that the forms themselves are actually present in the matter. Rather, this matter 'can bring about by itself the kind of change which the seed brings about'. Without diving into the details, we might say that the form results from the goings-on in matter without any teleological guidance by a formal principle.'

beings'. Instead he takes Aristotle to be committed to a form of vitalism where the heat at work in spontaneous generation has its own special powers to organize matter on a par with those carried by the heat in male semen.[26] On this reading, it is not the matter itself that effects change in spontaneous generation but the *pneuma* and vital heat contained therein.[27]

One of the virtues of the vitalist reading is that Aristotle can be seen as anticipating Themistius' theory thereby removing the bite of his objection. (It is also very close to the reading offered by Thomas Aquinas: see below.) Aristotle agrees, on this reading, that spontaneous generation requires special formative principles, or *logoi*, that code for the forms of the species in question and that these are the 'counterparts' of those principles transmitted in the semen of sexually-reproducing males. These form-carrying principles are already present in the earth (as Aristotle could be taken to say in T1) ready to produce any species that might come to be from it. The major disadvantage of this reading, however, is that it conflicts with the spirit of *Metaphysics* 7.9. According to that account some things come into being of their own accord because the matter involved is capable of moving itself (*kineisthai huph' hautês*) with the same kinds of motions that would otherwise come from certain form-inducing principles (the craft in the craftsman or the nature in the seed). If Aristotle meant to say that the matter of a spontaneous generation has this ability only because it is endowed with special vital principles, we would have expected him to make that crucial point here.

For my part I favour the more naturalistic reading of Aristotle's theory. On this reading the heat at work in spontaneous generation is not some mysterious substance that has the power to bring matter magically to life. Soul-heat is just the ordinary heat of a living organism that is generated (Aristotle thinks) by various internal metabolic processes. And while it is true that he makes a point of saying that this heat is not the heat of fire (*GA* 2.3, 737a1–4), in doing so he is simply making the claim that there are two kinds of heat that have different causal powers: the heat of fire, which burns and destroys; and the heat of animals, which can generate and foster life.[28] Aristotle was well-aware that the heat from the sun can also foster life (737a4–5), as any gardner will tell you. This is why he says in T1 that in a way everything is full of soul. As I read

---

[26] See G. Freudenthal, *Aristotle's Theory of Material Substance* (Oxford: Clarendon Press, 1995), pp. 1 and 25–7.

[27] Gotthelf offers a similarly vitalistic interpretation of Aristotle's theory of spontaneous generation. On Gotthelf's reading, the heat at work in spontaneous generation carries what he calls an 'undifferentiated potential for life' (A. Gotthelf, *Teleology, First Principles, and Scientific Method in Aristotle's Biology* (Oxford: Oxford University Press, 2012), pp. 142–50, esp. p. 149). This interpretation strikes me as *ad hoc*. Aristotle never invokes a *dunamis* for life. Rather, Gotthelf brings in this concept as a way to save his interpretation of Aristotelian teleology from certain criticisms raised by Lennox, 'Teleology, Chance, and Aristotle's Theory of Spontaneous Generation', (n. 3 above).

[28] By calling this 'soul-heat' Aristotle means, not that it carries soul, but that it is the heat that is involved in executing the basic soul-activities including, most importantly, the metabolizing of food, which is due to concoction, and all concoction, Aristotle says, is the work of heat (*GA* 765b16). On my reading the soul-heat that plays the role of efficient cause in *GA* 3.11 is the internal heat that is released into the atmosphere from a decaying corpse during putrefaction. Alternatively, Aristotle may be thinking of this as heat that originally comes from the sun and gets trapped in the 'foamy blister' that becomes the living organism (which then becomes that organism's own soul-heat).

GA 3.11 Aristotle does not need to endow *pneuma* and soul-heat with special vitalistic powers that infuse matter with life. His primary interest in that chapter is at the very rudimentary level of explaining how life can emerge spontaneously from putrefying matter in the absence of *sperma*. And there is little evidence that Aristotle saw life as a scientifically mysterious phenomenon that required special kinds of vital principles to explain.[29]

So what of the so-called principle of causational synonymy? As we have seen, scholars tend to interpret this principle in the strong sense as the claim that in every case of generation the form of the product must pre-exist in the producer. However, in *Metaphysics* 7.7–9 Aristotle only insists on the much weaker claim that generation would be impossible unless *some part* of the product pre-existed. And he is explicit that this condition is satisfied at the level of material causes (1032b31–3). In cases of natural generation (e.g. man begets man) the product comes to be from another particular bearing the same name (*ex homônumou*, 1034a22) and definition as itself. Here it is both the form and matter together that pre-exist in the particular. In the crafts Aristotle says that the product comes to be only from something that bears the same name *as a part* of itself (*ek merous homônumou*, 1034a23), namely the form, which he identifies with the craft in the builder's soul (cf. *GA* 730b12–19; cf. 734b34–735a4, 74025–9). 'Therefore,' he says, 'it follows that *in a sense* health comes from health and a house comes from a house, that which has matter from that which has not; for the medical craft is the form of health <in the doctor> and the building craft is the form of the house <in the builder>' (1032b11–14). With spontaneous generation there is still an important sense in which the product comes to be from some pre-existing part of itself. However, in this case it is not the form but the matter that pre-exists in that from which it comes to be. And the matter, Aristotle says, is just as much a part of the product as the form (1032b32–1033a1). So in spontaneous generation there is causational synonymy at the level of material causes. Part of what Aristotle is trying to do in *GA* 3.11 is make good on this claim (761a14–762a7, 762a27–32).

Returning to Themistius' objection, whatever Aristotle means at *Metaphysics* 1034b4–7 by saying that in cases of spontaneous generation the matter is capable of initiating the same sorts of changes that *sperma* initiates, one thing is clear. Contrary to what Themistius claims, instances of spontaneous generation do not show that Aristotle's theory of generation is inadequate. All spontaneous generation shows is that in some cases the source of form is not the form of another organism of the same kind. But it doesn't follow from this that there must be formative principles or *logoi* latent in the earth and put there by 'higher causes'. For Aristotle, plants and animals that are generated spontaneously derive their forms from their material causes, which may equally be considered a pre-existing part of the product itself.

---

[29] This is especially true for spontaneous generation. As I go on to say, the simplicity of spontaneous life is the key to understanding why Aristotle thinks that in their case the matter is sufficient to explain its emergence. Aristotle is ambivalent about whether or not to classify spontaneously generated organisms as plants or animals because he thinks that, for the most part, they lack the higher capacities of soul. To explain the emergence of spontaneous life, then, is simply to explain how matter can come to acquire rudimentary nutritive capacities (absorbing nutrients and transforming them into more of itself).

To close this paper, I would like to offer what is (as far as I know) the only other attempt to reconcile Aristotle's belief in spontaneous generation with his broader metaphysics, that of Aquinas. As we shall see, Aquinas ascribes to Aristotle something close to the view put forth by Themistius.

In his commentary on *Metaphysics* 7 Aquinas discusses an objection raised by an unnamed source who likewise appeals to the existence of spontaneously generated animals to expose a flaw in Aristotle's attack on the Ideas:

> Now it must be observed from what has been said here that it is possible to solve the problems facing those who claim that the forms generated in these lower bodies do not derive their being from natural generators but from Ideas that exist apart from matter. For they seem to maintain this position chiefly because of those living things that are generated from decay, whose forms do not seem to come from anything similar to them in form. ... Nor does it seem (to them) that the argument that the Philosopher used against those who posited separate exemplars, viz., that the forms in things causing generation are sufficient to account for the likeness of form in the things that are generated, holds in all cases.
>
> Thomas Aquinas, *in Metaph.* 7.12.8, § 1455, trans. Rowan, slightly modified[30]

The anonymous objection resembles the one put forward by Themistius insofar as they both claim that Aristotle's argument against Ideas is inadequate since it does not cover cases of spontaneous generation. In those cases (the objection goes) the particular generator is not sufficient to account for the form that comes to be in the matter because it does not already bear that form in actuality. The current version of the objection goes further by claiming that spontaneous generation actually requires an appeal to separately existing Ideas in order to serve as models or paradigms after which the organism comes to be. Aquinas thinks this objection can be overcome without recourse to Platonic Ideas by appealing to a view closely resembling that of Themistius.

Aquinas' response begins with an attempt to reconcile the *Physics* doctrine of spontaneity with the fact that spontaneously generated animals do not come to be by chance but through definite and tractable causes (§ 1402).[31] The way he does this is by arguing that spontaneously generated animals are in one sense accidental and in another sense for the sake of something. When the cause is referred to particulars operating in the sublunary world, e.g. heat and cold, the outcome can be considered the result of chance and not the end for the sake of which the process takes place. For 'the heat that causes decay is not inclined to have as its goal the generation of this or that particular animal that results from decay, as the power in the seed has as its goal the generation of something of a particular type' (§ 1403). But when the cause is referred to 'the powers of the heavens' (by which Aquinas presumably means the rotation of the sun and moon) we say that spontaneous generation comes to pass for the sake of what

---

[30] Thomas Aquinas, *Commentary on the* Metaphysics *of Aristotle*, trans. J. P. Rowan, 2 vols (Chicago: Henry Regnery Company, 1961). All translations of Aquinas are from Rowan.

[31] See n. 3 above.

results. For in that case the animal that comes into being is not considered accidental but 'directly aimed at', since it is the goal of the celestial rotation that 'all forms existing potentially in matter should be brought to actuality' (§ 1403).

At the level of particular sublunary causes Aquinas agrees with Themistius insofar as he thinks there must be some kind of formative power already present in the earth corresponding to the active principle in the father's semen. In natural generation this form-generating power comes from the father *and* from the celestial body, whereas in spontaneous generation it derives from the celestial body alone:

> Now in the matter of those things that are generated from decay there also exists a principle that is similar to the active power in the seed, by which the soul of such animals is caused. And just as the power in the seed comes from the complete soul of the animal and from the power of a celestial body, in a similar fashion the power of generating an animal that exists in decayed matter is from a celestial body alone in which all forms of things that are generated are present virtually as in their active principle.
>
> § 1457

In attributing this position to Aristotle Aquinas could be thinking of his claim that humans are generated by humans 'and by the sun' (*Physics* 2.2, 194b14). However, what Aristotle has in mind there is simply the fact that the stages of an animal's life-cycle are causally dependent on the motions of the sun and moon (*GA* 4.10, 777b16–778a9; *GC* 2.10, 336a33-b16; *GC* 2.11, 338b3–5). While he does think this same phenomenon can be given a teleological explanation, it is not in the sense that the cosmic cycles occur for the sake of regulating the animal's life. Rather, he thinks the natures of animals use those cycles to regulate their life-cycles. And being 'used for the sake of something' is a form of teleological explanation.

Nor does Aristotle need to appeal to transcendental causes in order to accommodate spontaneous generation within his system. If my interpretation is correct, Aristotle is quite prepared to argue that the particular material causes (including the place where the organism develops) are adequate by themselves to generate the offspring that comes to be from them — as we saw, for example, in his explanation of how sea urchins come to acquire their protective spines. But this raises a new problem. If the necessary interactions between material-level forces are sufficient to account for the forms of spontaneously generated organisms, does that not render formal and final causes superfluous in the core cases? What of the significance of Aristotelian teleology and the central role it affords to (immanent) forms in determining the pattern of changes in natural generation? If some living things can come into being in the absence of such causes, why should we think they play any role at all?

As I read Aristotle there is a distinction to be made here between those cases that require teleological explanation and those where material necessity alone is capable of bringing about the effect. Spontaneous generation is an example of the latter. But how exactly does Aristotle intend to draw this distinction? *PA* 641b23–8 suggests that he thinks it is, at least in some cases, empirically obvious when final causes are at work: 'In every case we say that *this* is for the sake of *that* whenever it is apparent (*phainêtai*) that there is some end towards which the change progresses if nothing impedes it.' Like many biologists in history Aristotle may be relying on certain features or signs that indicate that some process is goal-directed. The process might exhibit a high degree of regularity in the face of minor perturbations; or it might involve a lot of complicated, well-choreographed changes; or the result might be too complex or make too obvious a contribution to the survival of the animal to be the result of blind mechanical forces. Consider the omentum, which Aristotle is happy to attribute to material necessity alone (*PA* 4.3, 677b21–8). While the formation of this part exhibits regularity, it is just a simple membrane which does not exhibit the sort of functional complexity that cries out for a teleological explanation. Unlike the heart or eye it is not made up of several components carefully adjusted to one another so that they execute a complex function. Its production is no more complicated than the formation of skin on the surface of cooling broth. The fact that spontaneous generation typically only produces very simple organisms (fleas, gnats, limpets, whelks, etc.) with very little by way of complex adaptations (ostrakoderms are all essentially blobs of flesh enclosed in a rather simple shell) may have suggested to Aristotle that final causation is simply not required in these cases. Teleology only enters the picture in the case of the more 'honourable' organisms that are equipped with the sort of complex adaptations that (he thinks) could never result from blind necessity. These organisms can only come to be from other organisms whose seeds contain formative powers that have as their end the forms of the offspring that come to be from them (*PA* 1.1, 640a19–27; *GA* 5.1, 778b4–11).

6

Spontaneous Generation and its Metaphysics in Themistius' Paraphrase of Aristotle's *Metaphysics* 12

Yoav Meyrav[1]

Themistius' Paraphrase of Aristotle's *Metaphysics* 12 has received little attention in scholarly literature despite its unique place in the history of philosophy as the only complete surviving work on *Metaphysics* 12 from antiquity.[2] The Paraphrase's ill fate in modern scholarship is mostly due to the sorry fact that the original Greek text is lost. Fragments of Isḥāq ibn Ḥunayn's ninth Century Arabic translation of the work survive

---

[1] I would like to thank Richard Sorabji for generously opening the door for this publication and for his effective and thought provoking oversight of the various stages of its composition, as well as his countless invaluable remarks and suggestions. I would also like to warmly thank Carlos Fraenkel, whose attentive reading of the various drafts of my paper and penetrating comments – always relevant and to the point – contributed much needed coherence and lucidity to my argument. The extremely fruitful correspondence with Devin Henry and James Wilberding – together and separately – produced some happy surprises, and I would like to thank them for a stimulating encounter and educational experience. I can only hope it was as advantageous for them as it was for me. I am also grateful to Chiara Ferella for some very helpful advice. An early draft of this paper was presented in the graduate seminar at Tel Aviv University on 19th November 2014, organized by Ofra Rechter. I would like to thank the participants for their intelligent questions and suggestions, as well as the Department of Philosophy and School of Philosophy for ongoing financial and moral support. Special thanks are due to Orna Harari, forever my Greek teacher, whose coffee breaks I kept hijacking for the sake of discussing the ideas in this paper. This paper is dedicated to my mentor, Ilai Alon, in endless gratitude for, well, everything. The best way I can begin repaying my debt is by offering a publication worthy of his approval.

[2] To the best of my knowledge, the first modern paper written about it was the classical piece by Shlomo Pines, who offered a dazzling account of Themistius' reworking of Aristotle's theology. Pines thought Themistius' lasting influence could be extended as far as to Hegel. See S. Pines, 'Some Distinctive Metaphysical Conceptions in Themistius' Commentary on Book Lambda and their Place in the History of Philosophy', in J. Wiesner, ed., *Aristoteles: Werk und Wirkung*, 2 vols (Berlin: De Gruyter, 1987), vol. 2, pp. 177–204 (repr. in *The Collected Works of Shlomo Pines*, ed. S. Stroumsa (Jerusalem: Magnes Press, 1996), vol. 3, pp. 267–304). Pines' paper opened so many opportunities for future scholarship, and it's baffling that almost no one continued the promising leads he had offered. A happy notable exception is Carlos Fraenkel, who took Pines' lead to show how Themistius' revision of Aristotle's theology is reflected in Maimonides, and through Maimonides – in Spinoza. See C. Fraenkel, 'Maimonides' God and Spinoza's *Deus sive Natura*', *Journal of the History of Philosophy* 44 (2006), 169–215.

in different forms, most of which have been published in one way or another.[3] Luckily, we possess the complete Hebrew translation (from the Arabic), made by the accomplished translator and philosopher Moses Ibn Tibbon in 1255.[4]

This paper revisits Themistius' discussion of spontaneous generation with an attempt to contextualize it within his Paraphrase of *Metaphysics* 12, explore its metaphysical considerations, and offer a revised understanding of some of its key points based on a philological analysis of the text. The importance of Themistius' account of spontaneous generation has been asserted by the ground breaking and valuable work of Devin Henry, whose analysis of Themistius' challenge to Aristotelian biology, as well as the response he offers on Aristotle's behalf, has become a standard point of reference, and is integrated in subsequent studies on spontaneous generation in Ancient and Medieval philosophy.[5] However, Themistius' discussion was never

---

[3] The beginning of the original complete Arabic translation, which comprises the paraphrase of chapter 1 and the beginning of chapter 2, is preserved in MS Ẓāhiriyya (Damascus) 4871, 38r–38v; an abridged version of the Arabic translation of the paraphrase of chapters 6–9 survives in MS Ḥikma 6 of the Dār al-Kutub Library in Cairo. I have consulted photocopies of these manuscripts (thanks to, respectively, Jamil Ragep and Alexander Treiger), both of which have been edited in Badawi, *Arisṭū ʿinda al-ʿArab* (Cairo, 1947), pp. 12–21, 229–33. Until a new critical edition appears, it is important to use Badawi's problematic edition in consultation with D. Frank, 'Some Textual Notes on the Oriental Versions of Themistius' Paraphrase of Book I [sic] of the *Metaphysics*', *Cahiers de Byrsa* 8 (1958/9), 215–30. Although the Arabic bio-bibliographical literature isn't conclusive about Isḥāq being the translator, there is scholarly consensus that the translator is indeed Isḥāq (Badawi, *Arisṭū*, 17; Frank, 'Textual Notes', p. 215, n. 2; Pines, 'Metaphysical Conceptions', p. 287, n. 3; C. Genequand, *Ibn Rushd's Metaphysics* (Leiden: Brill, 1984), pp. 9–10), and this is in tune with the title in MS Ẓāhiriyya 4871 and the testimony of the Hebrew manuscripts (some of which plausibly maintain that the translation was revised by the polymath Thābit Ibn Qurra; 826–901).

[4] This translation was published by Samuel Landauer in 1903 as part of the Commentaria in Aristotelem Graeca (CAG 5.5) series, along with Landauer's revision of a Latin translation of questionable quality, made from the Hebrew by the otherwise unknown Moses Finzi, and published as late as 1558. Themistius' Paraphrase wasn't translated into a modern Western language until the appearance of a French edition by R. Brague, *Themistius: Paraphrase de La* Métaphysique *D'Aristote (Livre Lamda)* (Paris: Vrin, 1999), which also surveys other surviving fragments in Arabic and Hebrew. The Institute of Microfilmed Hebrew Manuscripts (IMHM) in Jerusalem holds microfilms of 10 extant manuscripts of Themistius' Paraphrase, 6 of which are important for reconstructing Moses ibn Tibbon's Hebrew translation and have been consulted here: Paris – Bibliothèque Nationale heb. 894, 41r–47v (IMHM catalogue entry F30349; F31526; listed as D in Landauer's critical apparatus); Muenchen – Bayerische Staatsbibliothek, Cod. hebr. 234, 175v–204r (F 1185; A in Landauer); Muenchen – Bayerische Staatsbibliothek, Cod. hebr. 108, 80r–90v (F 1623; B in Landauer); Leipzig – Universitaetsbibliothek B.H.fol.14, 234v–247t (F 30745; C in Landauer); Torino – Biblioteca Nazionale Universitaria Cod. AI 14, 560r–567v (F 34308; unavailable to Landauer); Moscow – Russian State Library, MS Guenzburg 271, 63r–77v (F47889; unavailable to Landauer). References to Themistius' text are given according to the pages and line numbers of Landauer's edition, accompanied with references to the appropriate Arabic fragment when applicable. I have revised Landauer's edition in several places according to a new critical edition that is currently in preparation. As this is not the focus of the paper, I will not justify my revisions, except in a few crucial points.

[5] D. Henry, 'Themistius and Spontaneous Generation in Aristotle's Metaphysics', *Oxford Studies in Ancient Philosophy* 24 (2003), 183–207. A revised and updated version of Henry's paper is included in this volume (ch. 5 above). For subsequent discussions see for example D. N. Hasse, 'Spontaneous Generation and the Ontology of Forms in Greek, Arabic, and Medieval Latin Sources', in P. Adamson, ed., *Classical Arabic Philosophy: Sources and Reception* (London: Warburg Institute, 2007), pp. 150–75; J. Wilberding, 'Neoplatonists on 'Spontaneous' Generation', in J. Wilberding and C. Horn, eds, *Neoplatonism and the Philosophy of Nature* (Oxford: Oxford University Press, 2012), pp. 196–213, also in this volume (ch. 7 below). Genequand's discussion of Themistius' fragments in Averroes' *Long*

studied in face of the actual critique he is addressing. Henry's analysis, as well as the scholarly discussions that followed, is based on a lengthy quotation of the Arabic translation of Themistius, supplied by (a very unsympathetic) Averroes in his *Long Commentary on Aristotle's Metaphysics*.[6] Although the passage is rich, Averroes quotes it removed from its original context within Themistius' *Paraphrase*, which is essential for a complete understanding of his argument. What's more, a systematic philological analysis of all of the surviving evidence in Arabic and Hebrew points to a refined reading of some key points of the text which have significant bearings on the understanding of it.[7]

The present paper is divided into 3 sections. In section 1, I present Themistius' reconstruction of Aristotle's argument against the existence of Platonic Ideas in *Metaphysics* 12.3 and show how it lays the foundations for a concept of coming to be that excludes the parent from being an active agent in the process of begetting. In section 2, I offer a fresh analysis of Themistius' discussion of spontaneous generation in light of the argument against the Ideas he brings forth on Aristotle's behalf and suggest a reinterpretation of some of its key arguments. In section 3, which is an appendix of sorts, I offer some of Themistius' remarks concerning Aristotle's discussion of God as intellect and ask whether they perhaps reflect a harmonization between Plato's Ideas and Aristotle's notion of forms in the intellect.

Before I continue, it is important to note that unlike the more 'traditional' commentary genre (e.g. Alexander of Aphrodisias and Simplicius), which consists of a quotation of a passage from Aristotle's text followed by a commentary on it, Themistius' activity within the framework of a 'paraphrase'[8] poses much difficulty for the scholar, since his text ceaselessly shifts between any of the following: exact quotations from Aristotle, rewording of his text, reordering of the text, glosses, casual remarks, extensive remarks, and lengthy independent digressions. Accordingly, more often than not it is difficult to determine Themistius' position toward the text he is paraphrasing: whether he is simply presenting Aristotle's view, adopts it, interprets it on its own terms, defends it, offers tentative critical remarks, revises it, or voices his own (with or without

---

Commentary on Aristotle's Metaphysics is an important early contribution, especially with regard to spontaneous generation. Genequand was the first to flesh out the explosive implications of Themistius' treatment and its reverberation in Averroes and other Arabic philosophers. See Genequand, *Ibn Rushd's Metaphysics*, esp. pp. 27–9.

[6] See Averroes, *Tafsīr Mā Ba'd al-Ṭabī'a*, ed. M. Bouyges (Beyrut, 1948), vol. 3, pp. 1492,3–1494,14. I have also consulted a photocopy of the original Arabic Manuscript (Leiden, Universiteitsbibliotheek, Or. 2074, kindly supplied by Amos Bertolacci), as well as two versions of the Medieval Hebrew translation of Averroes (see below, n. 12). An English translation of the fragment originally appeared in Genequand, *Ibn Rushd's Metaphysics*, pp. 105–7, and was later revised in R. Sorabji, *The Philosophy of the Commentators: A Sourcebook*, 3 vols (London: Duckworth, 2004), vol. 2, pp. 42–3. Alongside Brague's French translation of Themistius' Paraphrase, there is another French translation of this fragment in A. Martin, *Grand commentaire de la Métaphysique d'Aristote: Tafsīr Mā ba'd aṭ-ṭabī'at. Livre lam-lambda* (Liège, 1984), pp. 128–30.

[7] In this manner my paper has a focus different from that of Henry's contribution to this volume, which offers a critical discussion of the relationship between Themistius' argument and Aristotle's biology.

[8] For the 'paraphrase' genre in Themistius see R. B. Todd, *Themistius, On Aristotle On the Soul* (London: Duckworth, 1996), pp. 2–4, and further references there.

agreement with Aristotle). In other words, it is fundamentally difficult to establish what Themistius' opinion actually is, and this should be kept in mind when reading this paper and others about Themistius' paraphrases. The reader should also keep in mind that while my discussion is devoted to sections of the text where Themistius' voice is dominant, there are plenty of places within the paraphrase in which he stays very close to Aristotle's text and keeps his remarks and interpretations to the minimum (e.g. the paraphrases of chapters 4, 5, and 8), and this might result in contradictory elements within the paraphrase.

1. Themistius' Reconstruction of Aristotle's Critique of the Platonic Ideas

Metaphysics 12.3 concludes with a condensed argument that supposedly rejects the need for Platonic Ideas in coming to be, as Aristotle already believes that there are sufficient principles to explain coming to be without them:

> Evidently then there is no necessity, on this ground at least,[9] for the existence of the Ideas. For man is begotten by man, a given man by an individual father; and similarly in the arts; for the medical art is the formal cause of health (1070a26–30).

Themistius replaces this brief outline with a much more detailed argument, which is based on Aristotle's elaborate discussions in *Metaphysics* 7.7-9.[10] It is extremely important to analyze this argument, since *this* – rather than Aristotle's original brief remarks – is the argument that Themistius directly responds to in the fragment found in Averroes quotes, which as I've mentioned is the starting point of all modern scholarship on Themistius' view. Here is a translation of the argument Themistius supplies on behalf of Aristotle, which I break into sections for the sake of convenience:

> [1] But if the form that had existed prior [to its successor] is the agent for the formation of that [i.e., the posterior] form – so that man is indeed created from man, and a horse is indeed created from a horse, and in every case the particular from a particular (for the universal does not beget and is not begotten, but that which begets and is begotten is indeed a 'this' and a 'that'), what need do we have, then, in [the context of] coming to be, for the Idea Plato had talked about? (7,17–21)
>
> [2] And what need does the begetting form have for the other form [i.e., the Platonic Idea] as a model for it, given that it itself is a model for what is created from it? For the name and the definition will be common to both, and their form

---

[9] It is not entirely clear what these grounds in fact are. Judson suggests that the expression rolls back to 1070a4–5: 'each substance comes into being out of something synonymous' (L. Judson, 'Metaphysics Λ 3', in M. Frede and D. Charles, eds, *Aristotle's Metaphysics Lambda* (Oxford: Clarendon Press, 2000), pp. 111–35, at p. 135). Elders writes that this is 'typically Aristotelian' terminology, summing up the argument of the chapter (L. Elders, *Aristotle's Theology* (Assen, 1972), p. 112).

[10] See Henry's contribution to this volume for a detailed discussion of Aristotle's arguments and further references.

is one, and it is of the nature of the begetting form that it beget another form just like it (7,20-3).

[3] And we find that art does not need a [separate] form to be set up as a model for it in anything it does, so that, for example, when it aims to make a chair, it would not be able to make it without the aid of a model; for art in itself is the model for the chair, because the form of the chair stands in the mind of the carpenter who makes it, just as medicine is the form of health, and masonry is the form of the house (7,23-7).[11]

As a critique of the Platonic Ideas, this seems compelling, and Themistius sets up for himself a challenge considerably more serious than Aristotle's laconic closing statements of chapter 3. Looking at the argument, we can see that each of its parts addresses a different function of the Platonic Ideas and shows that we can supply it without them. Parts 1 and 2 deal with natural coming to be, while part 3 deals with artificial things. Part 1 criticizes Platonic Ideas as active principles, while parts 2 and 3 criticize Platonic Ideas as external models according to which things come to be. Part 1 addresses the possibility of the Platonic Idea as the active principle in the process of begetting of living things, and shows that there is no need for them assuming that the parent already occupies this function. Part 2 denies the need for Platonic Ideas as external models according to which living things are begotten, since the shared definition of maker and made (and, obviously, shared form) are sufficient to show that the individual form is its own model. Part 3 denies the need for Platonic Ideas as models according to which the arts do their work, since artisans act according to the form of the product (chair; health; house) already present in their mind.

Themistius does not respond to the argument in its entirety. He offers no defence against part 3 of the argument, and replies only to some of part 2. Some of his attention is devoted to the Aristotelian claim that an individual form (e.g. the form of 'this man') serves as a model for its offspring – also claimed in part 2 – by introducing spontaneous generation as a counter-example which proves that sameness of definition (man begets man) and a shared form are not necessary conditions for coming to be. Finally, Themistius completely rejects the premise of part 1, which is not accidentally constructed as a conditional statement. He will try to show that the prior existing individual form (e.g. 'this man') is not – and cannot be – the active formative principle in the coming to be of its offspring, because the act of reproduction is simply an act of one body upon another, and this interaction by itself is insufficient for determining the form of its outcome. The result of Themistius' defence will not be a reinstating of Plato's Ideas, but rather a corroboration of the need to appeal to a principle beyond the individual parent, as well as to a cause higher than nature, in order to provide an acceptable account of coming to be. The question whether something of the original Platonic Ideas remains in Themistius will be discussed briefly in section 3 but mostly remain open.

---

[11] All of the translations from Themistius' paraphrase are my own, and I must confess that I've sacrificed elegance for the sake of literalness, given the complexities of the source material.

2. From Ideas to *Logoi* via Spontaneous Generation: Themistius' Reply to Aristotle's Critique

Themistius opens his discussion by providing a counter-example to Aristotle's argument, enumerating types of animals that do not come to be from their co-species:

> This argument is persuasive (*maspīq/muqniʿ*)[12] for denying the [Platonic] Ideas, but its author neglected the plurality of animals that are created by [things] different from their like [i.e., their co-species], in spite of their great number. For we see a species of hornets that is begotten from the bodies of dead horses; and we see bees begotten from the bodies of dead cattle; and we see frogs begotten from putrescence; and we see the mosquitoes – which is a kind of a small-bodied fly – begotten from wine after it is spoiled.[13] And we do not find nature originate these things from their likes in form (7,27–8,2; Averroes 1492,3–9).

As Wilberding has already pointed out, Themistius describes 'certain correspondences between species of corpses and species of abiogenetic life-forms.'[14] The introduction of spontaneous generation to the discussion is not meant merely to show the reader that there are instances when animals come to be from things other than their co-species. If that were all he was saying, that would hardly amount to a refutation of Aristotle's critique, as it could be said that spontaneous generation is a result of chance, namely spontaneity in its narrow sense, which Themistius himself would agree is the product

---

[12] Unlike Genequand's choice, 'sufficient', I am translating the Arabic term *muqniʿ* as 'persuasive' (Brague translates *convaincant* – 'convincing' – while Martin's *suffire* sides with Genequand). *Muqniʿ* by itself can go either way in Arabic, but here it is most likely a translation of the Greek *pithanon*, as can be gathered from the Arabic translation of Themistius' Paraphrase of Aristotle's *De Anima*, which was also the work of Isḥāq ibn Ḥunayn (M. C. Lyons, *An Arabic Translation of Themistius' Commentary on Aristoteles De Anima* (Norfolk: Cassirer, 1973); see e.g. Themistius *in DA* 61,24 = 95,2 in the Arabic edition). As Richard Sorabji remarked in a private communication, a 'persuasive' argument is not necessarily true. Other legitimate options would be 'convincing' and 'plausible'. It is worth noting that three different Hebrew translators of the present passage understood *muqniʿ* as a rhetorical term. Moses ibn Tibbon's *maspīq* (which finds support in Hebrew Ms D and a corrective hand in Ms C and should be preferred over Landauer's choice *pōseq* – 'ends' – which does not reflect the Arabic) is a technical term which marks statements that are third in the line of power after demonstrative statements and generally accepted (dialectical) statements. This choice is shared by the fourteenth century reviser of the Hebrew translation of Averroes' *Long Commentary on the Aristotle's Metaphysics* (see, for example, Paris – Bibliotheque Nationale heb. 889, 234v20), who most likely consulted Moses ibn Tibbon's translation of Themistius' Paraphrase when revising the translation. The original Hebrew version of Averroes' *Long Commentary* translated *muqniʿ* as *heletziyī*, a technical term whose precise meaning is 'rhetorical' (MS Vatican Heb. 336, 183r1). For an elegant discussion of the different Hebrew versions of Averroes' *Long Commentary* see Yehuda Halper, 'Revision and Standardization of Hebrew Philosophical Terminology in the Fourteenth Century: The Example of Averroes's Long Commentary on Aristotle's Metaphysics Δ', *Aleph: Historical Studies in Science and Judaism* 13 (2013), 95–137, esp. 95–100.

[13] For discussions of other Medieval examples for these cases see R. Kruk, 'A Frothy Bubble: Spontaneous Generation in the Medieval Islamic Tradition', *Journal of Semitic Studies* 35 (1990), 265–82; M. Van der Lugt, *Le ver, le démon et la vierge: Les théories médiévales de la génération extraordinaire* (Paris: Les Belles Lettres, 2004), pp. 131–87.

[14] Wilberding, ch. 7 below, p. 225, and for further examples and references, n. 47.

of a privation of a principle, rather than a real positive principle of coming to be.[15] The orderly nature of the phenomena Themistius is describing is important because it shows that spontaneous generation is an integral part of the course of nature, and therefore every account of generation which aspires to be complete must take it into consideration. That's why spontaneous generation is a serious challenge for Aristotle's critique. Moreover, the correspondence between cause and effect in each class of spontaneous generation will soon play an important part in the fundamental underlying distinction between the formative principle and the physical interaction upon which Themistius' own concept of coming to be will build. But for the moment, it will suffice to say that Themistius is describing a natural and regular – rather than accidental – phenomenon. He continues:

> And we know that in the sperm and the seed of every single animal and plant there is a *logos* (*yaḥas/nisba*) proper to it by which are begotten these animals and plants which are begotten from it specifically and not from another, so that neither does a horse come to be from the sperm of a man, nor a man from the sperm of a horse, nor a plant from the seed of another plant (8,2–5; Averroes 1492,2–12).

Here Themistius introduces to the discussion a notion of *logos*, which is undefined but seems to be a principle according to which biological reproduction proceeds, as it ensures a correspondence within species between the parent's seed and its offspring.[16] Themistius characterizes the *logos* as something that makes sure that nature doesn't get things wrong. In other words, Themistius is trying to show that the *logos* has something to do with the uniformity of nature, as a proper correspondence between a given material cause and a given substantial effect. Each of these *logoi* is proper to a certain species. As Henry has already observed, this is an explanation which is in tune with Aristotle's biology.[17] Themistius' strategy, then, will be to show that even if we start with a biological point of view that is in accord with Aristotle, we'll still have no choice but to appeal to a principle beyond the individual parent to account for coming to be.[18]

Themistius proceeds to search for the *logos* within the process of spontaneous generation:

---

[15] For this, see Henry's remarks in ch. 5 above, n. 3.

[16] Themistius' account of *logoi* doesn't seem to relate easily to any known account of *logoi* that survives from the Platonic and Neoplatonic traditions (see Sorabji's discussion in this volume, pp. 293-4, for the various options). Granted, he's exempt from the criticism Middle Platonic philosophers suffered for confusing *logoi* with Ideas, and he seems to share Plotinus' distinction between them, but the distinction isn't spelled out, and what can be gathered is different from Plotinus' view. One must keep in mind that, as Todd puts it, 'Themistius' relationship to the twin pillars of the ancient philosophical tradition [i.e., Neoplatonism and Peripatetics] is [...] unusually free from scholasticism. In this we can perhaps detect the intellectual independence of an aristocrat whose involvement with teaching was a relatively brief prelude to a public career and not a lifelong professional commitment' (F. M. Schroeder and R. B. Todd, *Two Greek Aristotelian Commentators on the Intellect: The De Intellectu Attributed to Alexander of Aphrodisias, and Themistius' Paraphrase of Aristotle De Anima, 3.4-8* (Toronto: Pontifical Institute of Medieval Studies, 1990), p. 34).

[17] See Henry, 'Themistius and Spontaneous Generation', p. 187.

[18] Earlier in the paraphrase, Themistius remarks that matter has 'fundamentally in nature an *alternating logos* (*yaḥas mithalef*)' (5,9).

> Where are the counterparts (*dimyōney/nazā'ir*)[19] of these *logoi* [i.e., the *logoi* in the sperm and the seed] in that from which this [i.e., the spontaneously generated] animal is begotten? Unless a suitable *logos* had been put in nature previously, ready to create any possible animal species, having found proper matter (*ḥomer/'unṣur*)[20] for creating a certain animal from it, it [i.e., the spontaneously generated animal] wouldn't have been brought into actuality[21] (8,5-7; Averroes 1492,13-1493,2).

The question Themistius is asking here can only make sense if we fully realize that in spontaneous generation the relation between cause and effect is not accidental. Assuming that we do not have two distinct systems of coming to be within nature (which would be opposed to the idea of nature), the fact that putrescence begets frogs rather than hornets should be awarded the same explanation as the fact that human sperm begets human beings rather than horses. In other words, Themistius widens the scope of the *logoi* so as to include all possible cases of coming to be in the natural world, suggesting that they are prior to the individuals and 'had been put in nature previously.' The *logos* is the formative agent that determines what species of animals the matter will be fashioned into once it is organized in a certain manner. So, just as animals that are begotten by their co-species come to be according to a specific *logos* inhering in the seed or sperm that ensures that they are of the same species as their parent, spontaneously generated animals which are begotten by specific material causes in nature must also come to be according to a specific *logos*, inhering in nature, that ensures that they, rather than a different species, are begotten from it. But if this is the case, one must relinquish the idea promoted in part 2 of the argument Themistius puts forth on Aristotle's behalf, namely that shared definition and shared form (man begets man) are sufficient to exhibit the causal role of the parent in determining the form of its offspring. This can no longer be maintained, not only because there are cases in which the begetter has nothing in common with the begotten, but also, as we shall soon see, because the parent has no causal role in determining the form of its offspring.

---

[19] The understanding of Themistius' argument here has been affected by Genequand's mistranslation of *nazā'ir* as 'models', which creates the impression that Themistius is advocating an orthodox notion of Platonic Forms. *Naẓīr* (in the singular) is the Arabic term that Isḥāq (the Arabic translator of Themistius' Paraphrase) uses for translating the Greek *analogos* in his translation of Themistius' Paraphrase of *de Anima* (See the glossary in Lyons, *Themistius*), so we can establish a direct connection to the Greek. As for internal evidence, the Arabic *naẓīr* is employed a few times in the surviving Arabic of the Metaphysics Paraphrase in other, less problematic contexts, and Isḥāq is usually consistent in his translations. Martin's French 'equivalents' (Martin, *Grand commentaire*, p. 129) is also a good option. Moses Ibn Tibbon's Hebrew translation, incidentally, may be part of the problem, because he translated both *mithāl* ('model; paradigm') and *naẓīr* ('counterpart') as *dimyōn*.

[20] Note the echo of Themistius' remark about matter having a fundamental alternating *logos* in its nature (above, n. 18). Genequand's translation of the present passage omits the important use of 'matter' here, probably because *'unṣur* by Averroes' time has become a less frequent option for translating the Greek *hule* than other alternatives like *mādda* and *hayūlā*.

[21] The final words of this sentence ('wouldn't have been brought into actuality'; Heb. *lo' haya yōtze' el ha-po'al*) are omitted from Averroes' Arabic quotation, and subsequently from Genequand's English translation of the text. Restoring them makes a very big difference because it enables us to understand differently the syntax of the sentence, and it proves that for Themistius the *logos*, rather than the parent, is the agent that actualizes the offspring.

Themistius then takes a dramatic step forward and claims that scientific explanation of coming to be should actually *start* with spontaneous generation, employing an analogy with artistry to clarify his point:

> Do not be deceived by contempt for these animals, but reflect that they fill us with admiration toward the Artisan; the skill He exhibits by making something out of clay is greater than the skill He exhibits by making something out of gold and ivory. If you examine carefully what happens with animals bigger than that [i.e., than spontaneously generated animals], you will find that nature proceeds there exactly in the same way (8,7–10; Averroes 1493,2–6).

More than a passing remark or a poetic statement, Themistius is actually offering a restatement – 'with a theological twist,' to borrow Ahuva Gaziel's term – of Aristotle's justification for the study of inferior animals in his *Parts of Animals*:

> For even in the study of animals disagreeable to perception, the nature that crafted them likewise provides extraordinary pleasures to those who are able to know their causes and are by nature philosophers [...]. For this reason we should not be childishly disgusted at the examination of the less valuable animals. For in all natural things there is something marvellous.[22]

Instead of Aristotle's philosophical pleasure of examining the marvel of natural phenomena, Themistius offers admiration of the Artisan's skill.[23] Now since this skill is more greatly exhibited in spontaneously generated animals, an examination of them will actually provide us with *better* understanding of coming to be. From the point of

---

[22] Aristotle, PA 1.5, 645a7–10, 15–17 (trans. Lennox). Ahuva Gaziel identifies this connection in a passage from Averroes' *Book of Animals*. Averroes relocates it to the Aristotelian passage it echoes, but its source should be pushed back to Themistius' passage under discussion here, Averroes of course having known it. See Ahuva Gaziel, 'Spontaneous Generation in Medieval Jewish Philosophy and Theology', *History and Philosophy of Life Sciences* 34 (2012), 461–80, at 470. Averroes' reference to this passage does not address spontaneous generation, but as Gaziel shows, the Spanish Jewish Philosopher Joseph Albo (c. 1380 – 1444) does. In fact, Albo combines Aristotle, Themistius, and Averroes to form an elaborate approach: 'The excellence of an artificer can be seen in his work in two ways. It may show that he has made a wonderful piece of work out of excellent material [...] Or the artificer may have made beautiful vessels with fine engravings out of inferior material. A goldsmith, for example, made beautiful vessels with beautiful engravings out of iron. This surely shows the artificer's great skill and perfection, since he was able to make such beautiful figures and engravings on iron, which is an unyielding material that resists the work of the engraver. [...] Aristotle says that there is more reason for studying the inferior animals produced by putrefaction than the others, not because of the animals themselves, for they are very low and composed of very inferior material, being produced from putrefaction, but by reason of the divine power contained in them. For it shows the excellence and perfection of the producer, who infused the power of life into such inferior material, so that from putrefaction and without the union of male and female there arises an animal being similar to that which is born of the union of male and female. It thus redounds to the credit of the artificer' (Albo 1929–30, ii: 6–8; quoted in Gaziel, 471).

[23] While beyond the scope of this paper, I hope to show elsewhere, through the study of the analogy of the artisan in the *Metaphysics* 12 paraphrase, that Themistius in fact has a more general cosmogonic framework which assumes a Divine Creator who has moulded cosmogenic matter according to a plurality of forms.

view of natural inquiry, Themistius is implying that Aristotle had it the wrong way around: instead of devising a theory about coming to be based on co-specific begetting, and then seeing how (if at all) spontaneous generation fits within it, one should start with spontaneous generation, which requires more 'skill', and only then proceed to easier examples. In other words, 'man begets man' camouflages what is actually going on.

Themistius proceeds to explain exactly how co-specific coming to be is analogous to spontaneous generation, demonstrating that ultimately the father who begets his son has no causal advantage over the dead cattle from which bees are begotten, effectively rejecting part 1 of the argument he presented on behalf of Aristotle and necessitating an appeal to pre-existing forms:

> It is necessary for there to exist *logoi* and forms[24] that had been put into nature, upon which it works its work. For even if man is indeed begotten by man, the father exerts no artistry in his composition of this, which cannot be in another state better than the state he is in. He arrives at this state because the *logoi* and forms had been put into the nature of each of the substances; not by means of artistry on the part of the father, but from the *logoi*. The body doesn't work on [another] body, except only on its surface, whereas nature works on the corporeality of the body (*be-gūf ha-geshem/juthat al-jism*) in its entirety (8,10–16; Averroes 1493,6–1494,1).

For Themistius, the fact that man begets man does not mean that man is the formative agent of his offspring. First, it is obvious that there is no artistry involved here, because man proceeds from man naturally, regardless of what the parent has in mind (this is of course obvious in any other animal). Second, the 'man begets man' example actually exhibits the shortcoming of co-specific generation when compared to spontaneous generation; in the former case, the offspring is just like the parent, while in the latter case, the effect (e.g. frog) is *better* than the cause (e.g. putrescence). Spontaneous generation also shows us that the individual form cannot serve as the model for its offspring, because in spontaneous generation the 'parent' and the 'offspring' are completely different. We have to appeal to a different formative agent, which is the *logos*. It is important to note that this agent is immanent in nature, not transcendent. It is prior to the individual, but still exists in the natural world. It has been *put* in nature.

But Themistius goes even further than that. In the final sentence of the above quotation he seems to be saying that an appeal to prior *logoi* would have been necessary even if *all* coming into being were co-specific. This is reflected by his assertion that 'the body doesn't work on [another] body, except only on its surface, whereas nature works on the corporeality of the body in its entirety.' The bodily interactions that result in the generation of a new living being cannot by themselves determine its form, because the form has to do with the entire body, whereas physical interaction is limited to the body's external surface. Some other principle should be responsible for the form of the

---

[24] I take the 'and' in the formula '*logoi* and forms' – here and in its other occurrences in the text – to reflect an epexegetic *kai*, although the forms here need not be understood in the Platonic sense.

product of this interaction, and it can only come from nature, whose action upon the body is comprehensive. Therefore, there must be in nature *logoi* which are in a way prior to the individual substances; the form cannot be simply transmitted from one individual to another, but co-specific generation renders this more difficult to uncover. If we return to the original argument Themistius advanced against the Ideas on Aristotle's behalf, we can take these remarks to object to part 1 of the argument ('the form that had existed prior [to its successor] is the agent for the formation of that [i.e. the posterior] form').

Having affirmed the existence of *logoi* in nature that are prior to the individuals although not transcendent, it is time to ask how they work. Themistius writes:

And no wonder that nature does not understand the movement of its work toward the end aimed at, since it does not know and does not think about the work it does. This shows you that these *logoi* have been inspired[25] by a cause nobler, worthier, and higher in rank than themselves, i.e. the soul in the earth (*ha-nefesh asher ba-aretz/al-nafs al-latī fī al-'arḍ*)[26] which Plato thought had been created by the secondary gods, and Aristotle thought had been created by the sun and the ecliptic.[27] Therefore, it [i.e., nature] does its work and advances toward the end

[25] Literally: 'have been inspired with an inspiration' (*ulhimat ilhām*).
[26] This is probably a translation of the Greek *hē psukhē en tē gē*. Themistius' matter-of-fact statement connecting the soul in the Earth to Plato's secondary gods perhaps suggests an appeal to some established tradition, although nothing of the sort can be found explicitly in Plato. The earliest known advocate of a 'soul in the earth' was Plotinus, who also connects it to spontaneous generation: 'since many living creatures are seen to come from the earth too, what stops us from claiming that it is a living creature as well?' (*Enn.* 4.4.22; trans. B. Fleet in R. Sorabji, *The Philosophy of the Commentators* (n. 6 above), vol. 1, pp. 256-7; see further discussion in J. Wilberding, 'Neoplatonists on the Causes of Vegetative Life', in A. Marmodoro and B. D. Prince, *Causation and Creation in Late Antiquity* (Cambridge: Cambridge University Press, 2015), pp. 171-85, at pp. 174-6). Plotinus, it seems, attempts to connect this idea with Plato's *Timaeus* 77A3-C5, especially when Plato refers to a soul which is 'wholly passive and does not turn within itself around itself, repelling motion from without and using its own native motion, it is not endowed by its original constitution with a natural capacity for discerning or reflecting upon any of its own experiences. Wherefore it lives indeed and is not other than a living creature, but it remains stationary and rooted down owing to its being deprived of the power of self-movement' (Plato, *Timaeus*, 77B-C; Plato is referring to a kind of lower soul in humans, which is seated 'between the midriff and the navel', but perhaps its description can be expanded to plants and earth itself). Plotinus is very unsure about this and suggests that perhaps the idea of the soul of the Earth is implicated through Plato's assertion that Earth is 'the first and oldest of the gods within the heavens' (*Timaeus*, 40C), 'for how could it be a god if it did not have this sort of soul?' If Themistius is following Plotinus here, he is doing so very superficially, or perhaps through some intermediate, less refined source which mixes up Plotinus' soul in the earth and his world soul. Plotinus cannot maintain the position that the soul in the earth inspires the *logoi*, because for him *logoi* are rational principles in Nature, which is the inferior part of the World Soul. For a recent discussion of the role of *logos* in Plotinus, see P. Kalligas, 'The Structure of Appearances: Plotinus on the Constitution of Sensible Objects', *Philosophical Quarterly* 61 (2011), 762-82.
[27] This is a rather ambitious interpretation of Aristotle's claim at *Metaph.* 12.5, 1071a13-17: '[T]he cause of man is both its elements, fire and earth as matter, and the distinctive form, and furthermore some other external thing, i.e. its father, and beyond these the sun and its oblique course, which are neither matter, nor form, nor privation, nor the same in form, but rather are movers' (trans. in A. Code, 'Some Remarks on Metaphysics Λ 5', in M. Frede and D. Charles, eds, *Aristotle's Metaphysics Lambda* (Oxford: Clarendon Press, 2000), pp. 161-79, at pp. 171-2). One of Aristotle's points is that the Sun's motion along the ecliptic course provides for the circularity of seasons that secures the ceaseless process of generation and consequently the permanence of species. In this respect the Sun

without understanding the end, just as inspired people talk and foretell the future without understanding themselves what they say (8,16–23; Averroes 1494,1–9).[28]

Themistius explains that although it is within nature's power to act upon a body as a whole, we cannot see it as the cause that actualizes the *logoi* which have been put in it, since nature is an unconscious agent and cannot determine the end toward which it acts. The cause that directs the *logoi* toward the end aimed at is the 'soul of the earth', by means of some sort of 'inspiration', which Themistius does not take the trouble to explain, but – following the lead offered by James Wilberding – I would like to suggest means an instance of actualizing the *logoi* and setting them to motion.[29] This would

---

can be seen as a principle of life, but there's a long way to go from this to claiming that the Sun and the ecliptic create 'the soul in the earth', a concept which is absent from Aristotle (but see next note). Themistius' own remarks on this passage in his Paraphrase shed no new light on the matter. He states: 'The proximate cause is like the father, the sun is a remoter cause, and [a cause] remoter than the sun is the ecliptic. These things are not causes for the created thing by way of matter, nor are they [causes] by way of form and privation; but they are movers – not proximate and of shared form like the father, but they are remoter and stronger, [being always] in actuality. For they are the principles of the proximate causes as well' (10,32–11,4). It is interesting to note that among the various changes Themistius makes to Aristotle's original argument, he treats the Sun and the ecliptic as different causes with different causal power.

[28] I believe that Themistius is engaged in a rather irresponsible syncretism between the soul in the earth ascribed to Plato and a universal soul that he ascribes to Aristotle. In Themistius' Paraphrase of *De Anima* there is a short discussion where spontaneous generation is introduced in the context of Themistius' entertainment of the idea of the existence of a single 'soul of the universe' (*hê tou pantos psukhê*), which is undeveloped there, but for Themistius does not affect Aristotle's discussion in the *De Anima*. Themistius seems to assume that Aristotle held some notion of a 'single' soul: 'Whatever [soul] it is, it will make no difference to Aristotle's theory at least. For he says that in the present work he is not inquiring into that soul that is single, nor is he defining it, but he is inquiring into the [soul] of a human being, and that of a horse and a cow [...] in defining the soul he says that he is not defining the [soul] that is from without and single (*tên exôthen kai mian*), but the entelechy that comes from that [soul] onto bodies that have organs, while perhaps being able to define that [external soul] too in the same way' (Themistius, *in DA* 26,7–11.15–18; trans. Todd). See Todd's notes to his translation for the inherent difficulties in Themistius' view here. Themistius views favorably the option that the soul of the universe 'irradiates' (*ellampein*) soul or 'ensoulment' (*empsukhia*) to bodies, and cites the phenomenon of spontaneous generation as evidence for the plausibility of this (Themistius, *in DA* 26,27–30; see the next note for this passage). Although Themistius is discussing individuals' souls, not individuals' forms, the strategy is the same: using the example of spontaneous generation as a means to appeal to an exterior principle beyond the individuals.

[29] Wilberding, ch. 7 below, p. 227. Wilberding finds similarity between what Themistius is describing here and a process described in Porphyry's *Ad Gaurum*, where the verb *empnein* ('to inspire') is used to describe 'the mother's actualization of the *logoi* in the seed-embryo'. Wilberding suggests that if we accept an analogy between the soul in the Earth and the mother, *empnein* 'would mean to actualize them [i.e., the *logoi*] and set them in motion'. Is Themistius using the same technical term for 'inspiration' in the present discussion as well? I think this hypothesis can be defended, but needs some justification which I'll try to offer here.

In a private communication, Wilberding pointed to the use of *empneitai* in this technical sense in Themistius' *De Anima* Paraphrase, with regard to Themistius' discussion of spontaneous generated animals (see n. 28), 'which simultaneously with the [coming to be] of the blending immediately receive inspiration, are alive and are self-moved' (Themistius, *in DA* 26,28–9, re-translating, according to Wilberding's suggestions, the Greek *ha tê toiade krasei tou sômatos hama euthus empneitai kai zê kai keneitai ex heauton*). Wilberding reads *empneitai* for the printed *empnei te*, an option available in the critical apparatus in Heinze's edition, and his reading is in agreement with Isḥāq's Arabic translation of Themistius' *in DA* (at 15,9), if we read *mutanaffasa* (literally: recipient of breath/soul).

clarify Themistius' earlier description of their function as 'ready to create any possible animal species, having found proper matter for creating a certain animal from it.' The soul of the earth itself, as a moving principle and a final cause, is the product of an even higher cause, of whose origin Plato and Aristotle offer different explanations. Plato thinks that the secondary gods are responsible for it, while Aristotle ascribes it to the Sun and the ecliptic.

While Themistius' explanation here leaves much to be desired and keeps us in the dark regarding his immediate philosophical sources, there are three important things that can be gathered from the text. First, Themistius stresses on more than one occasion that the *logoi* have been 'put into nature', and this implies that although they exist in the sperm and in the seed, in a way their existence can be seen as independent from the individual substances. This is why recourse to spontaneous generation is important, and ultimately what makes the difference between Themistius' explanation and Aristotle's standard account. Second, Themistius' appeal to the soul in the earth, a higher principle than nature, shows that for him nature's unconsciousness renders it unfit to be the source of its own teleological activity.[30] The *telos* should be supplied from without, and the ontological link between the soul in the earth and the metaphysical realm perhaps suggests some sort of divine involvement, which is hinted at but never explained. And finally, Themistius' insistence on ascribing the soul in the earth to Aristotle as well as to Plato suggests that he is advocating harmony between the two instead of simply defending Plato and rejecting Aristotle. Themistius concludes:

> Now although the Arabic of the paraphrase of *Metaphysics* 12 employs a different term, *ulhimat*, I would like to suggest that *empneitai* is still a good candidate, owing to the analogy with inspiring foretelling of the future offered by Themistius. Hypothetically, if for the 'inspiration' of the *logoi* Isḥāq would have chosen the proper Arabic conjugation of *tanaffus*, he would've had a problem with the translation of the foretelling aspect, and the analogy would have fallen apart. So perhaps he worked the other way around, beginning with prophetic inspiration and working back to the inspiration of the *logoi*. This would work with *empneisthai*, because it can be used in a 'divinely inspired' sense, similarly to *enthousiazein* (see for instance Themistius, Oration 13, 165D6–166A1: *aisthanomai emautou empneomenou ēdē kai enthousiōntos* – 'I feel myself inspired and enthused'). The choice of the Arabic *ulhimat* echoes the Islamic philosophical and theological tradition, where one finds a distinction between two sorts of divine influence: *waḥy* and *ilhām*. Very roughly speaking, *waḥy* was the higher form of revelation, saved for true prophets (e.g. Muhammad), who received universal divine messages which were to be communicated to mankind, while *ilhām* was a specific, lower form of divine inspiration which was given to individuals, and actually brought rise to many theological debates concerning its legitimacy as a verifiable source of knowledge (for useful discussions see D. B. MacDonald, 'Ilhām', *Encyclopaedia of Islam*, 2nd edn, Brill Online, 2015. Accessed 31 March 2015 <http://referenceworks.brillonline.com/ entries/encyclopaedia-of-islam-2/ ilha-m-SIM_3533>; D. Lobel, *Between Mysticism and Philosophy: Sufi Language of Religious Experience in Judah Ha-Levi's Kuzari* (Albany: SUNY Press, 2000), pp. 121–5). In short, *ilhām*, as an instance of divine inspiration aimed at a specific individual, serves as a rather adequate analogy to Wilberding's understanding of *empneisthai* as a specific instance of actualizing the *logoi* and setting them to motion.

[30] For the tension (or lack thereof) between nature's unconsciousness and teleological activity in Aristotle see J. M. Rist, 'Some Aspects of Aristotelian Teleology', *Transactions and Proceedings of the American Philological Association* 96 (1965), 337–49.

In short, it is impossible for there *not* to exist in nature *logoi* and forms, since [otherwise] a thing would need its like in order to be begotten, and not everything that is begotten has a like from which it is begotten. But when we inquire into[31] a certain [individual] form, from which a certain actuality arises, we know that it [i.e., the actuality] is not created only by it [i.e., the individual form].[32] This form [i.e., the actualized form], then, is created as if it had been latent in something else, and it is truly latent in the begetting nature (8,23–7; Averroes 1494,9–14).

Themistius believes that he has shown that the existence of *logoi* is absolutely necessary and he seems to equate them with forms (although he doesn't explain how but somewhat clumsily reverts the terminology of the discussion back from *logoi* to forms). The counter-example of spontaneous generated animals can be expanded to the totality of living beings, the reproduction of which is impossible to explain without positing *logoi* as formative principles immanent in nature that supply the proper formal component to the causal interaction between bodies which leads to coming to be of new individuals. Each instance of this process is actualized by an inspiration from the soul in the earth, a final cause that is ontologically linked to the metaphysical realm.

3. An Open Question: What Happened to Plato's Ideas?

Having discussed Themistius' presentation of Aristotle's critique of the Platonic Ideas and his own critical response to it, we find ourselves in a somewhat awkward position. Granted, Themistius introduces a concept of *logoi* that have somehow been put into unconscious nature and are actualized ('inspired') by the soul in the earth, itself a product either of the 'secondary gods' (Plato), or the 'Sun and the ecliptic' (Aristotle). But after all, assuming that Themistius' defence against Aristotle's critique is successful, we are left with just that – an appeal to *logoi* and to a higher final cause in coming to be. Nothing is actually said about Plato's transcendent Ideas, which were the reason for the discussion in the first place. The metaphysical framework that Themistius offers stops with the soul in the earth as the agent of *logoi*, and after a few concluding remarks he returns to straightforward paraphrasing, starting afresh with *Metaphysics* 12.4.

But perhaps we should look elsewhere in the text for the Platonic Ideas? As Pines has already shown, throughout Themistius' discussions of Aristotle's God, he takes

---

[31] Genequand has 'we need' for *iḥtajnā ilā*, which is possible, and this is also how ibn Tibbon understood the Arabic, but 'we inquire into' makes more sense, and the Arabic could be translating the Greek *zētoumen* (this is what Isḥāq does, e.g., in his Arabic translation of Theophrastus' *On First Principles* 7b6; see D. Gutas, *Theophrastus, On First Principles (known as his Metaphysics)* (Leiden: Brill, 2010), pp. 132, 192).

[32] My translation of this sentence is very different than Genequand's, who has: 'But when we need any form, we act is such a way that we know that this form cannot be produced by this act alone.' Genequand's translation is a good reflection of the Arabic published in Bouyges' *Tafsīr* (1494,11–13), but the text there needs revision since it makes little sense, and Ibn Tibbon's Hebrew doesn't do us any favors either. I have therefore reconstructed it by combining the original Arabic MS (Leiden, Universiteitsbibliotheek, Or. 2074, 158r13–15) with the early Hebrew translation of Averroes (MS Vatican Heb. 336r21–2).

many liberties with the text.[33] One of Themistius' most noteworthy interpretative moves is understanding Aristotle's assertion that God intellects Himself as meaning that God intellects all of the intelligibles. This, for Themistius, implies a fundamental identity between God and the existents.[34] But in the following passage Themistius seems to go further and equate the intelligibles with forms:

> [The Divine Intellect is] intellect and intelligible at once. Unlike the sense – which is not the same as the sensible when its [i.e., the latter's] form is imprinted, while its substance remains outside – the state of the Intellect with the intelligibles is [such that] they belong to Him substantially. For *He carries all of the forms*, with no substance that is mixed with matter kept outside, for there is no matter there, but [rather] an abstract form that is unmixed with matter, which is attached to that which intellects it or thinks it, without being divided or having some of it[s parts] drawn away from each other, as [is the case of] the sensibles with regards to the sense, for it is grounded (*taqū'a*) in the intellect ... The First Divine Intellect [...] intellects the intelligibles that are existents in Him and *assumes their forms (metzuyyar lahem)* (20,17-22; 25-6 partially quoted in Arabic abridgement: 17,10-13; emphases added).

It is tempting to understand this remark as effectively adopting a somewhat simplified version of the Middle Platonic notion of 'Ideas as thoughts of God'. However, one can just as well maintain that Themistius is putting to practise Aristotle's characterization of the intellect as the form for forms in *De Anima* 3.8.[35] So is Themistius referring to Plato's Ideas, or Aristotle's forms? If one is insistent upon finding some completion on Themistius' behalf in the form of a remnant of the Ideas he defended earlier against Aristotle's critique, this is probably the place one should look for them. Alternatively, one could relinquish the attempt to fill this lacuna in Themistius' text and settle for Themistius being a good Aristotelian here. But perhaps we don't have to decide. Whatever he originally meant, Themistius would most likely allow the reader to take either side – or even both – following the footsteps of Eugenius, his father and teacher, who was no stranger to harmonizing Plato and Aristotle:

---

[33] Pines explored Themistius' reinterpretation of Aristotle's assertion that God intellects only Himself as meaning that God intellects all of the intelligibles, as Themistius assumes a fundamental identity between God and the existents, which he takes to be ontologically dependent on Him (See Pines, 'Metaphysical Conceptions', p. 186, and the references there); Pines also presents Themistius' threefold interpretation of the notion of God as *arche*, namely God as the formal cause, the final cause, and the '*arche* of motion" (ibid. p. 188). He then proceeds to show that for Themistius, God is the *nomos* of the cosmos, which obeys Him as a principle of rightness and order (ibid. pp. 188–9).

[34] This is most obvious in the statement 'that which is them is He, and that which is He is His intelligibles' (20,25–6; partially quoted in Arabic abridgement: 17,14–15).

[35] 'It is necessary that [knowledge and perception] are identical either with the things themselves or with their forms. With the things themselves not, for it is not the stone that is in the soul, but its form. So the soul is like a hand, for indeed the hand is the tool for tools and the intellect the form for forms and perception the form for perceptible' (Aristotle, *DA* 3.8, 431b28–432a3). I would like to thank Richard Sorabji for this point.

When passing from the Academy to the Lyceum, he did not change his clothes; he would often first make a sacrifice to Aristotle and then end by worshipping Plato. He always got angry at those who actually tried to build a dividing wall between the two [sacred] enclosures and to separate them.[36]

---

[36] Themistius, *Oration* 20, 235C8-D3 (trans. in R. J. Penella, *The Private Orations of Themistius* (Berkeley: University of California Press, 1999), p. 54). Themistius ostensibly denies any originality of his paraphrases, in which he 'deposited and stored the legacy that I have received from my forefathers' (*Oration* 23, 294D1-3; trans. Penella, p. 121. See Penella's n. 24 for a short discussion of this passage alongside further references to the debate surrounding it).

7

The Neoplatonic Commentators on 'Spontaneous' Generation

James Wilberding

In 1864 during a lecture at the Sorbonne Louis Pasteur pronounced the theory of spontaneous generation dead with the triumphant statement: 'Never will the doctrine of spontaneous generation recover from the mortal blow struck by this simple experiment'.[1] With this Pasteur summed up the results of a series of tests involving fluids contained in flasks that prevented any outside particles from entering. What the experiment showed is that purportedly spontaneously generated organisms were actually being generated by microbes coming in through the air. Prior to Pasteur spontaneous generation had certainly had its critics, but it is worth lingering on the fact that the theory survived in some form for as long as it did – over two millennia.

Nevertheless, throughout its history spontaneous generation – which, for reasons that will be made clear immediately below, I shall also be referring to as 'extraordinary' generation – presented a challenge to those interested in explaining the world. After all, all biological generation involves two major *explananda* – the generation of a species form and the generation of a soul – and while cases of normal biological generation at least offer some obvious starting points for explaining them, namely the parents, who possess both the form and souls of the relevant type, these starting points are notoriously absent in the case of spontaneous generation, or at least in some cases. It has now become common to distinguish between two kinds of spontaneous generation: *abiogenesis*, in which a living thing arises out of lifeless matter, and *heterogenesis*, in which a living thing of one kind arises out of the matter of a living thing of some other kind. (Accordingly, ordinary biological reproduction may be characterized as *homogenetic biogenesis*.) Although this distinction has been called

---

This article first appeared as 'Neoplatonists on "Spontaneous" Generation' by James Wilberding in James Wilberding and Christoph Horn (eds), *Neoplatonism and the Philosophy of Nature* (2012), pp. 197–213. By permission of Oxford University Press.

[1] L. Pasteur, 'Jamais la doctrine de la génération spontanée ne se relèvera du coup mortel que cette simple expérience lui porte', in Pasteur Vallery-Radot, ed., *Oeuvres de Pasteur*, 2 vols (Paris: Masson, 1922), vol. 2, p. 342.

'modern',[2] it should help us to navigate through some of the features of the discussions of spontaneous generation in antiquity and late antiquity. That said, by the end of this chapter, it should be clear why from a Neoplatonic perspective none of these terms – 'spontaneous', 'abiogenesis', or 'heterogenesis' – is actually well suited to describe the phenomena in question. For now, however, let us avail ourselves of the traditional terminology.

The heritage of the problem of spontaneous generation is often traced back to Aristotle, and rightly so. For, although one can find discussions of the phenomenon of extraordinary generation in earlier sources, prior to Aristotle such cases were not described as 'spontaneous' nor were they seen as particularly problematic. A brief look at one earlier theory, such as that found in the Hippocratic texts *On Generation, On the Nature of the Child*, and *Diseases 4*[3] should do to make this point plain. What we find here is a theory of ordinary seminal generation that can easily be applied to extraordinary generation on account of a combination of three features: it is non-teleological; it assumes the pre-existence of forms in nature; and it is not particularly concerned with the generation of soul. The author of these texts advances a theory of pangenesis, according to which the seed is drawn from all parts of both parents, and this allows him to maintain a firm hold on the principle that nothing is coming to be out of nothing, since the form or substance of each of the offspring's relevant parts can be accounted for by tracing its origin to a like form or substance in one or both of the parents. The rest of the embryological story is told by appealing to common physical principles such as like moving to like and predominance – the details need not concern us here; it is simply important to note that the principles involved are not teleological. And this absence of teleology allows this same basic model to be applied to, e.g., the extraordinary generation of plants. For to each kind of plant there corresponds a particular juice or humour (*khumos*) in the soil which accounts for the substance of that kind of plant, and whereas in seminal generation seeds grow into mature plants by drawing in these juices – again, like going to like –, extraordinary generation can be explained simply by saying that these juices come together on their own.[4] In this way,

---

[2] C. E. Dinsmore, 'Premodern Theories of Generation', in Gary B. Ferngren, ed., *The History of Science and Religion in the Western Tradition* (New York: Garland, 2000), pp. 541–8, at p. 546. In fact, ordinarily abiogenesis and heterogenesis are distinguished in terms of whether the source-matter in question is organic (heterogenesis) or inorganic (abiogenesis). I have rendered the distinction in a slightly modified form to suit the vocabulary of ancient discussions of life and generation better.

[3] I am following Lonie in taking these treatises to be the work of a single author, though he does dispute the widely held view that *Diseases 4* is simply a continuation of the previous two treatises. (He does, however, agree that *On Generation* and *On the Nature of the Child* form a continuous whole.) See I. Lonie, *The Hippocratic Treatises 'On Generation', 'On the Nature of the Child', and 'On Diseases IV'* (Berlin: De Gruyter, 1981), pp. 43–51.

[4] *Diseases 4* § 34. Here the author addresses the problem of why certain plants cannot be grown in certain regions, whereas other regions 'grow them spontaneously (*automaton*). (Here we must, however, bear in mind that this term cannot quite have its Aristotelian sense, as explained above.) The theory can easily account for the extraordinary generation of plants. Further, when the author ultimately comes to discuss the extraordinary generation of worms in the foetus, what is most striking is his utter lack of wonder at and curiosity in the phenomenon: 'A large number of worms are produced ... in the following way. A burning pus is formed from the milk – which is itself formed from an excess of blood which has putrefied in consequence of its sweetness – and a living creature is engendered in it' (*Diseases 4* § 54).

even in the latter case, no new forms are coming to be, nor need there be a problem in these Hippocratic treatises regarding the second *explanandum*, namely the coming to be of a soul, though for a rather different reason, since soul just does not figure into this Hippocratic account. The author offers no discussion of how the powers of growth and nourishment arise in plants, nor does he seem to view the arrival of higher powers in human offspring as particularly problematic.[5] In both cases he seems content with the idea that whatever powers do arise in the wholes are to be accounted for in terms of the natural behaviour of their parts.

With Aristotle things change, primarily because with him ordinary reproduction becomes a teleological process, and since the teleological nature of ordinary reproduction is a pre-condition of the very possibility of 'spontaneous' generation – 'spontaneity' is by definition a process that *appears* teleological without actually *being* so[6] – Aristotle can now characterize extraordinary generation as *spontaneous* generation.[7] An in-depth look at Aristotle's remarks on spontaneous generation would carry us too far afield,[8] but the following points should strike most readers as more or less uncontroversial. Aristotle, too, must account for the coming-to-be of the form and the soul of the generated thing. Like our Hippocratic author above, Aristotle looks to material causes[9] as the source of the emerging living thing's form, though he stops short of saying that the forms themselves are actually present in the matter. Rather, this matter 'can bring about by itself the kind of change which the seed brings about.'[10] Without diving into the details, we might say that the form results from the goings-on in matter without any teleological guidance by a formal principle. For example, mud, when warmed by the sun, might produce a *pneuma* which in turn produces some movement that ultimately – and *entirely ateleologically* – results in the form of a living thing such as a worm. Once the form of the emerging living thing is accounted for, explaining the coming-to-be of its soul is rather straightforward, since Aristotle defines the (non-rational) soul as the first actuality of the organic body.[11] Thus, we might say

---

[5] Cp. the rather incurious 'The embryo starts to move once the extremities of the body have branched'. In what follows the author discusses when and how the articulation of the body occurs, but does not come back to address the topic of the origin of motion. Other Hippocratic treatises do employ the terminology of *psychê* in the embryological contexts, notably *On Regimen* and *Fleshes*. For a comparison of these accounts, see B. Gundert, 'Soma and Psyche in Hippocratic Medicine', in J. P. Wright and P. Potter, eds, *Psyche and Soma: Physicians and Metaphysicians on the Mind-Body Problem from Antiquity to the Enlightenment* (Oxford: Oxford University Press, 2000), pp. 13–35.

[6] *Phys.* 197b14–37.

[7] See e.g. *HA* 539a21–5; 546b15–548a24; 550b32–551a13; 569a10–70a24; *PA* 640a27–34; *GA* 759a8–63b16.

[8] Important studies on spontaneous generation in Aristotle include D. M. Balme, 'Development in Biology in Aristotle and Theophrastus: Theory of Spontaneous Generation', *Phronesis* 7 (1962), 91–104; J. G. Lennox, 'Teleology, Chance and Aristotle's Theory of Spontaneous Generation', in *Journal of the History of Philosophy* 20 (1982), 219–38; A. Gotthelf, 'Teleology and Spontaneous Generation in Aristotle: A Discussion', in R. Kraut and T. Penner, eds, *Nature, Knowledge and Virtue: Essays in Memory of Joan Kung* = *Aperion* 22/4 (1989), 181–93; and Henry's and Meyrav's contributions to this volume.

[9] This is meant to include not just the material substance from which it originates but also certain environmental factors. Cp. *HA* 550b32–551a13.

[10] *Metaph.* 1034b5–6.

[11] *DA* 412a27–8.

that for Aristotle the appropriate soul simply emerges once a body characterized by a form of a certain sort is completed.

In some sense, then, Aristotle has more to explain than our Hippocratic author, though this is partly to his credit. He must account for the coming-to-be of soul, a stone that our Hippocratic author left unturned, as well as for the genesis of forms, which our Hippocratic author simply posited as pre-existing in matter. And it is an often noted fact that Aristotle's account of the phenomenon of spontaneous generation struggles even on Peripatetic terms, since various kinds of living things would appear to arise with a certain regularity under certain conditions, yet regularity is supposed to be a result of *nature*'s teleological agency and not of chance or spontaneity.[12] Each of these problems becomes even more pressing once placed within a Neoplatonic framework. The genesis of form becomes particularly problematic for Neoplatonic commentators because forms of natural kinds derive from principles situated in the intelligible world and are not the sort of thing that could result from the chance movements of matter, and so their presence in the sensible world must be accounted for in some way. Under ordinary biogenetic conditions, the soul of the progenitor is there to provide this intelligible formal principle, but in cases of extraordinary generation it is not obvious that there is a soul to fulfil this role. One Platonic attempt to deal with this problem can be found, albeit in a somewhat inchoate form, in Augustine.

In *De Trinitate* (3.8 [13]) Augustine seeks to explain the 'miracles' performed by the Egyptian magicians in *Exodus* 7:12 who throw down their staffs and have them change into serpents.[13] As he explains, it was not the magicians who created the serpents:

> But, in truth, some hidden seeds of all things that are born corporeally and visibly, are concealed in the corporeal elements of this world. For we must distinguish between the seeds of fruit and living things that are visible to our eyes and the hidden seeds of these visible seeds, from which, at the bidding of the Creator, the water produced the first swimming creatures and fowl, and the earth the first buds after their kind, and the first living creatures after their kind. For neither at that time were those seeds so drawn forth into products of their several kinds, as that the power of production was exhausted in those products; but oftentimes, suitable combinations of circumstances are wanting, whereby they may be enabled to burst forth and complete their species. For, consider, the very least shoot is a seed; for, if fitly consigned to the earth, it produces a tree. But of this shoot there is a yet more subtle seed in some grain of the same species, and this is visible even to us. But of this grain also there is further still a seed, which, although we are unable to see it with our eyes, yet we can conjecture its existence from our reason; because, except there were some such power in those elements, there would not so frequently be produced from the earth things which had not been sown there; nor yet so many animals, without any previous commixture of male and female; whether on the

---

[12] Cp. e.g. *Phys.* 2.8, 198b34–6.
[13] This 'miracle' is particularly problematic for Augustine, since the magicians in question are battling against God's servants Moses and Aaron.

land, or in the water, which yet grow, and by commingling bring forth others, while themselves sprang up without any union of parents. And certainly bees do not conceive the seeds of their young by commixture, but gather them as they lie scattered over the earth with their mouth. For the Creator of these invisible seeds is the Creator of all things Himself; since whatever comes forth to our sight by being born, receives the first beginnings of its course from hidden seeds, and takes the successive increments of its proper size and its distinctive forms from these, as it were, original rules.[14]

Here we can witness Augustine struggling with a Christian version of the Platonic problem concerning the generation of forms. Forms of living things in the sensible world must all be provided by a higher principle – in this Christian context, from God – and cannot be said simply to arise by chance. The solution that Augustine is advancing here[15] remains rather murky, but its main lines can be made out. Whereas Aristotle has the forms deriving from a kind of matter that allows itself to be changed in a *seed-like* manner – and thus to be produced spontaneously since the process is merely *like* a teleological process – Augustine posits *actual seeds* of all natural species of living things in matter.[16] Let us call this the 'seminal theory' of extraordinary generation. We might see the seminal theory as a return to the Hippocratic (or even Anaxagorean) account of extraordinary generation, which posited the pre-existence of the forms in the matter, but by embracing the language of 'seeds', Augustine both allows for a certain degree[17] of teleology in such cases of generation and puts himself in a position to explain how these forms are ultimately derived from an intelligible (and divine) source.

While the seminal theory is well equipped to account for the intelligible origin of the forms, explaining the origin of the soul presents certain problems. For Neoplatonists could not allow the soul to arise from a seed.[18] Both Porphyry and Plotinus make this

---

[14] Trans. Rev. Arthur West Haddan, B.D., slightly revised.
[15] And cp. *De Genesi ad litteram* 3.12 (19); *Questiones in Heptateuchum libri vii*, q. 2.
[16] More precisely he says that the seeds are 'concealed in the corporeal elements of this world (*in istis corporeis mundi hujus elementis latent*)'. Augustine might well mean that every kind of seed is somehow contained in every element, but I suspect that he might have something like the correspondence theory between elements and living beings – that there are four classes of living beings that correspond to the four elements [see Plato, *Tim.* 39E-40B. As Olympiodorus points out (*in Meteor.* 310,16–25) Aristotle opposes this correspondence theory at 382a6–9 but in *GA* 761a16–32 one does find something resembling this theory. See also Plotinus 2.1.6.54 and my commentary *ad loc.* in J. Wilberding, *Plotinus' Cosmology: A Study of Ennead* II.1 *(40)* (Oxford: Oxford University Press, 2006)] – in which case the element of water would contain the seeds of all aquatic organisms, while the other elements would contain the seeds of their respective organisms. This seems to capture the theory behind his examples – that water produced the first aquatic creatures, while earth produced the first terrestrial ones. Such an account would raise a number of questions, e.g., how would he deal with elemental transformation, and how exactly do these seeds grow into full-grown organisms? Cp. M. van der Lugt, *Le ver, le demon et la vierge* (Paris: Les Belles Lettres, 2004), pp. 135–9.
[17] The 'completion of the species', however, is still dependant on 'suitable combinations of circumstances' arising in nature, which might often be due to chance. But when these preconditions are met, teleological principles take over.
[18] See e.g. Plotinus 3.1.8.7–8; Proclus, *in Tim.* 3,332,24–6; Michael Psellus *Opuscula psychologica, theologica, daemonologica* 142,13–16 O'Meara. Longinus appears to have thought otherwise (Porphyry, *in Tim.* fr. 6 [4,9–12 Sodano = Proclus, *in Tim.* 1,51,9–13 Diels] and cp. Porphyry, *AG* 2.2 with my notes *ad loc.*), but his philosophical abilities were not held in high regard (Porphyry, *VP* 14,19–20).

assertion in conscious opposition to what they took to be the Stoic view, according to which the soul develops out of a seminal state:

> Yes, they say, but just as the seed has the form-principle for teeth which [the offspring] develops after its delivery, and similarly for beards and seed and *menses*, so too are there form-principles of impulse, representation and sensation in [the seed], though their development [takes place] only after birth (Porphyry, *AG* 14.1)

To see why Neoplatonists find this Stoic version of the seminal theory objectionable, we must consider their own views on the metaphysics of seeds.[19] A seed is a composite of *logoi* and moist corporeal matter,[20] where the *logoi* are immaterial and without mass and extend throughout the seed in such a way that every material portion of the seed contains all the *logoi*.[21] In sexual reproduction the father is the sole producer of seed; more specifically, it is the father's lowest level of soul, the vegetative soul, that is the producer. The fact that the seed is generated by the father's vegetative soul carries important consequences both for the mechanics of family resemblance and for the seed's own psychological status. Regarding the former, the *logoi* in the seed will be replicas of the father's own and thus account for the formation of the various parts and features of the offspring, with any maternal resemblance being due to factors external to the seed itself. As for the latter, the seed's origin determines its place in the Neoplatonic ontological hierarchy. For one of the fundamental principles of Neoplatonic metaphysics is that a product or offspring is always inferior to its producer or generator.[22] Thus, the psychological status of the seed must be in some way inferior to that of the vegetative soul, and this is sometimes expressed by saying that the *logoi* in the seed are in a state of potentiality.[23] We should understand this to mean that the seed in and of itself lacks the activity characteristic of the vegetative soul, though it may acquire this activity by re-inserting itself into the ontological hierarchy. That is to say, conception on this Neoplatonic view occurs when the seed reverts back to the vegetative soul, though since it is now in the womb the object of its reversion is the *mother's* vegetative soul rather than the father's. By means of this reversion the seed – though we might now better characterize it as an embryo – is brought from a state of potentiality to actuality and comes to be in full possession of a vegetative soul, which then begins the process of forming the body. At the same time, the mother's role in

---

[19] For a more in-depth account of what follows, see J. Wilberding, 'Porphyry and Plotinus on the Seed', *Phronesis* 53 (2008), 406–32, on Porphyry and 'The Revolutionary Embryology of the Neoplatonists', *Oxford Studies in Ancient Philosophy* 49 (2015), 321–60, for later Neoplatonic commentators.

[20] 5.1.5.11–13; 5.9.6.15–20.

[21] 5.1.5.11–13; Porphyry *Sent.* 37.33–41; Porphyry, *in Tim.* fr. 51 [38,30 ff.] Sodano (= Proclus, *in Tim.* 1,396,10–26). Those unfamiliar with the Neoplatonic doctrine of *logoi* are referred to L. Brisson, 'Logos et *logoi* chez Plotin. Leur nature et leur rôle', *Les Cahiers Philosophiques de Strasbourg* 8 (1999), 87–108. For present purposes we might just describe them as rational formal principles that guide psychic activity in matter.

[22] 4.7.8.9–11; 3.8.5.24–5; 5.1.6.37–39; 5.1.7.47–8; 5.5.13.37–8; 5.8.1.19–21; 6.7.17.4–6. Porphyry, *Sent.* 13; Proclus, *ET* § 7; Philoponus, *in Phys.* 191,24–5; *et al.* And see A. C. Lloyd, 'The Principle that the Cause is greater than its Effect', *Phronesis* 21 (1976), 146–56.

[23] See e.g. Porphyry, *AG* 14.3 (54,12–13 Kalbfleisch) and Proclus, *in Parm.* 792,7–8 Steel.

reversion provides the necessary explanatory foothold for the possibility of maternal resemblance in the absence of female seed.

This brief look at the metaphysics of seeds should suffice to show why the souls of offspring cannot be thought to have arisen from seeds. For the principle of the inferiority of the product together with the fact that the seed is produced by a vegetative soul rules out the possibility of a sensitive soul already being present in the seed.[24]

The seminal theory's inability to account fully for the coming-to-be of the generated living thing's soul should help us appreciate the appeal of an alternative theory, which has both the forms and souls coming in from an external source. Avicenna provides us with an illustration of this approach to extraordinary generation, which has already been examined by others so that here a brief general outline of his approach will suffice.[25] Avicenna has both the form and the soul of the creatures in question being delivered automatically from the so-called Giver of Forms, which he identifies with the lowest of the celestial intelligences, when a suitable receptacle comes to be in the sensible world, where the suitability is defined in terms of the *krasis* of a body's constituent parts. Importantly, seeds play no role in Avicenna's account. The suitability of the receptacle body arises not because seminal form-principles are there directing its creation, though neither is it entirely left to chance, as it was in Aristotle. Rather, even this aspect of abiogenesis is directed, at least in part, by outside influences, namely from emanations stemming from the celestial bodies.[26] Let us call this the 'reception theory', which has both forms and souls coming in from the outside.

---

[24] To those seeking to salvage the seminal theory by maintaining that the sensitive soul is present *potentially* in the seed, Porphyry offers the following response: For the sensitive soul to be present potentially can mean one of two things. Either the soul's presence in the seed amounts to a first potentiality, and this would simply mean that the seed is the kind of thing that can eventually receive a sensitive soul, which is unobjectionable, since it concedes that the soul is not already in the seed; or else it means that the potential presence is meant in the sense of a second potentiality, which would mean that the sensitive soul is actually in the seed but remains inactive. But this again would transgress the principle of the inferiority of the product (see AG 1,1–2,4 and 14,2–4). This argument is buttressed by another that we will discuss in greater detail below, namely that a soul can only be present in an underlying body that is suitably organized to accommodate the activities of that soul (AG 13).

[25] Those interested in a more detailed discussion of Avicenna's views on spontaneous generation are referred to D. Hasse, 'Spontaneous Generation and the Ontology of Forms in Greek, Arabic, and Medieval Latin Sources', in P. Adamson, ed., *Classical Arabic Philosophy: Sources and Reception* (London: The Warburg Institute, 2007), pp. 150–75, esp. pp. 155–8, and M. van der Lugt, *Le ver, le demon et la vierge* (n. 11 above).

[26] Cp. Avicenna *The Directives and Remarks (Al-Isharat wa-'l-tanbihat)*: 'Là se trouvent les formes des éléments, et en ceux-ci, selon leur rapports dus aux corps célestes et à ce qu'ils envoient, sont nécessités des mélanges de préparations variées, opérées par certaines forces qui les disposent. Et là, les âmes végétales, animales et raisonnables débordent de la substance intellectuelle qui est proche de ce monde' (trans. A.-M. Goichon, *Ibn Sīnā (Avicenna) Livre des Directives et Remarques: Traduction avec Introduction et Notes* (Beruit: Commission internationale pour la traduction des chefs d'oeuvre / Paris: Vrin, 1951), pp. 423–3). It is worth noting here that Avicenna, in contradistinction to Plotinus, does not hold that souls pre-exist and then descend into their receptacle bodies. Rather, they are brought into existence at the moment that the receptacle is made suitable. On this aspect of Avicenna's thought, see P. Adamson, 'Correcting Plotinus: Soul's Relationship to Body in Avicenna's Commentary on the Theology of Aristotle', in P. Adamson, H. Baltussen, and M. W. F. Stone, eds, *Philosophy, Science, and Exegesis in Greek, Arabic, and Latin Commentaries* (London: Institute of Classical Studies, 2004), pp. 59–75, esp. pp. 64–7.

What we have here, then, are two different approaches to explaining how the intelligible forms and souls come to be in the living things resulting from extraordinary generation, and to the extent that they both share this common aim, both might generally be characterized as Neoplatonic. In the next section we shall see that there was an alternative theory, intermediate between these two extremes, that bears similarities to the seminal theory by positing pre-existing form-principles in the matter that teleologically guide the formation of the body, but also integrates the reception theory by having the forms and souls automatically come in from the outside once the receptacle has been made suitable.

* * *

Porphyry's *Ad Gaurum* offers us the best starting point for our examination, not because the *Ad Gaurum* contains an extensive discussion of extraordinary generation, but rather because it discusses the metaphysics of ordinary reproduction in greater detail than any other Neoplatonic treatise, and this detailed account of ordinary reproduction together with the remarks that he does make on extraordinary generation can be brought together to give us a fairly good idea of how he understood the latter. Thus, we must first get clear on some of the basic details of Porphyry's theory of reproduction. In order to simplify things somewhat, I am going to focus in what follows on the more difficult case, namely the generation of *animals* as opposed to plants, since only this case allows us to examine the problem of the coming-to-be of a sensitive soul.[27]

In animals, homogenetic biogenesis begins with the production of a seed. As we saw above, a seed occupies a specific place in the Neoplatonic ontological hierarchy, which places certain restrictions on it. As the product of a vegetative soul, it cannot in and of itself be on a par with a vegetative soul, nor can it contain or generate a sensitive soul, since this would also violate the principle of the inferiority of the product. What it can do is revert to and 'blend' with the mother's soul and thereby raise itself back up to the level of vegetative soul. In this way the *logoi* within it, which up until this point of conception were utterly inactive, are set in motion thanks to 'inspiration'[28] deriving from the mother's soul and begin to create in turn. Here again, of course, the principle of the inferiority of the product must be observed – production is always directed downward. Thus, the *logoi* are not working upwards towards the production of a sensitive soul but downwards towards the production of a body that conforms to these *logoi*.

How, then, does the offspring gain a soul? It already has a vegetative soul, as this was supplied (albeit in a state of potentiality) by the father and brought to activity by the mother. But the animal soul, which contains the powers of sensation and impulse, and in the case of human beings the rational soul, must be supplied from an external source,

---

[27] Porphyry follows Aristotle by taking the powers of sensation and impulse as the two defining characteristics of animals that distinguish them from plants (*AG* 1.1).

[28] See below n. 50.

and Porphyry employs a version of the reception theory to explain how that can happen:

> For there are things that are mastered but in no spatial manner and are held together but in no bodily manner, rather they form a natural unity (*sumphuomena*) through the suitability and likeness of the things on the receiving side (*tôn dekhomenôn*). And it is neither place nor time nor any other force that holds these things together. Rather, it is lack of suitability (*anepitêdeiotês*) that obstructs and dissolves [their unity], and suitability (*epitêdeiotês*) that brings them together, masters them, and holds them together for however long the harmony between them exists (*AG* 12.3)

As Porphyry emphasizes throughout *Ad Gaurum*, it is the suitability of the matter that determines the presence or absence of soul, and he likens this manner of bond to that obtaining between fire and wood. Like the soul, fire is in some sense trying to move up and away from its body (that is to say from the wood that the fire is consuming) and yet it remains bound to the wood on account of its suitability to the fire. Once this body has been reduced to ashes, it is no longer suitable and the fire departs.[29] In the case of sensitive soul this means that the organs of sensation must be completed for it to be present. Moreover, the degree of suitability appears to be more specific than this:

> In the same way, the instrumental animal that is well-fitted for a suitable soul immediately possesses in sympathy the soul that will use it. And the soul's sympathy for this [body] but not that [body] is granted by its previous existence or even by the rotation of the universe that leads like to like.
>
> *AG* 11.4

I do not want to get bogged down here in questions concerning Porphyry's theory of transmigration, his reading of the myth of Er,[30] or even his cosmology. All that is important here for our immediate purposes is that different kinds of bodies will be suited to receive different kinds of souls. When a human body is formed, a rational soul (including the powers of sensation and impulse) descends automatically from the intelligible region to be present to that body. When bodies of other species, e.g., of dogs or horses, are generated, they too receive soul, but of a different kind. Porphyry might even mean to say that different individual bodies are suited to different individual souls.

We might sum up Porphyry's account of homogenetic biogenesis by pointing to two critical moments: First, *logoi* in the seed are responsible for producing a suitable receptacle-body, and here we would do well to bear in mind that these *logoi* are themselves first in a state of potentiality and then brought to their creative activity; Then, a soul – and

---

[29] *AG* 14.4.
[30] On this, see J. Wilberding, 'The Myth of Er and the Problem of Constitutive Luck', in A. Sheppard, ed., *Ancient Approaches to Plato's Republic* (London: Institute of Classical Studies, 2013), pp. 87–105.

perhaps the form (Porphyry is silent on the issue) – is delivered from outside. Here we have, then, aspects of the seminal and reception theories briefly examined above united into a single theory of homogenetic biogenesis, and this theory – in broad outline, at least – can be found again in many other Neoplatonic authors and as such has a claim to being the orthodox Neoplatonic theory of biogenesis.[31]

When we now turn to consider Neoplatonic theories of extraordinary generation,[32] we discover these same two moments again. To begin with the integration of the reception theory, we may witness Neoplatonic commentators invoking it to explain animation. A passage drawn from Philoponus may serve to illustrate this invocation of receptivity in the Neoplatonic theory:

> Perhaps, then, just as the genesis of spontaneous animals and plants does not arise from succession from a soul that is present before, but the matter having become suitable, there are sent into it by the whole of creation (*ek tês holês dêmiourgias*) the forms (*ta eidê*) of herbs and animals and the psychical powers in them, so too it happens with the non-rational soul in all animals from the whole of creation when they subsist. The power, then, that is generative of the non-rational soul is not in the particular nature but in the universal nature, which is the cause of the forms of soul.[33]

Here I would like to relegate Philoponus' remark about 'forms' being delivered to a footnote,[34] in order to focus on the role that the reception theory plays in the animation of the living things resulting from extraordinary generation. In this and other passages,[35] Philoponus identifies 'the whole of creation' as the source of animation.

---

[31] See now Wilberding, 'The Revolutionary Embryology' (n. 19 above). For Plotinus, see *Enn.* 5.7 *passim* for the role of *logoi* in embryology, and for the reception theory, see 4.3.8.49–50 and 12.35–9; 1.1.12.28–9; 1.9.1.6–7. Plotinus usually limits his remarks on suitability to species, that is to say that a certain *kind* of matter is required for a certain *kind* of soul (e.g., 3.3.4.37–41; 4.3.12.35–9). Nevertheless, his remarks on the relation of the individual souls' descents to universal providence make clear that this doctrine of suitability is also at work on an individual level (cp. 4.3.13.8–10 and 23–5; 6.4.15.6–8).

[32] Since Neoplatonic commentators tend to focus on cases of heterogenesis, our discussion will also be focused on these cases.

[33] Philoponus, *in DA* 268,31–37 (trans. W. Charlton with some revisions). The text at 268,36–8 is corrupt but may be reconstructed from Sophonias, *in DA* 57,14–17. Note that Sophonias, *in DA* 57,4–9 = Philoponus, *in DA* 268,9–14 and Sophonias, *in DA* 57,9–14 = Philoponus, *in DA* 268,31–6. Sophonias simply skips over Philoponus, *in DA* 268,14–31. The translation above reflects this reconstruction.

[34] Here and elsewhere (see *in GC* 169,6 ff.; *in Phys* 191,9–29 and 403,19–31) Philoponus describes 'forms' as opposed to *logoi* as being derived from the whole of creation (but cf. *in DA* 52,13–25, where he does problematically say this about *logoi*). His claim here about the 'forms' (*eidê*) being delivered from the World-Soul is in no way in conflict with his claim (to be discussed below) that the *logoi* of the bodies are derived from the vegetative souls of the deceased. The *logoi* are responsible for making the body a suitable receptacle for the form, at which point the form is automatically supplied. The *logoi* are thus comparable to the sculptor, who simply makes the matter suitable. See *in GC* 283,27–284,7 and *in DA* 198,10–12.

[35] See Philoponus *in GC* 169,6 ff.; *in Phys* 191,9–29 and 403,19–31. Themistius *in DA* 26,25–9 (where *empneitai* should be read with PQ for Heinze's *empnei te* at lines 28–9) also identifies the World-Soul as the source of animation for spontaneously generated creatures.

Despite the regrettable murkiness of this phrase,[36] Philoponus' intended meaning comes out in the final line: it is the nature of the universe, that is, the World-Soul, from which the souls of these creatures are derived.[37] The invocation of the reception theory should come as no surprise in light of the reasons set out above: Neoplatonic metaphysics refuses to allow that a higher-order entity such as a soul could emerge out of a lower-order entity such as a body or seed. Hence, the Neoplatonic commentators have the soul-powers delivered to the respective bodies, once these bodies have become suitable receptacles.

It remains to investigate how the bodies were thought to become suitable receptacles, and this is where the nod to seminal theory is on view. Neoplatonic commentators make *logoi* responsible for constructing the bodies of these heterogenetic creatures, just as in normal reproduction. The inclusion of form-principles in a theory of extraordinary generation might seem *prima facie* anomalous, since seminal form-principles would seem to have an exclusive role in *homogenetic biogenesis*. Yet some such teleological principles must have seemed necessary to them to account for the fact that under certain conditions certain kinds of receptacles are produced with a striking regularity. As we have seen, Aristotle sought to account for this regularity by pointing to the different kinds of matter from which the spontaneous creatures were thought to arise, e.g., some emerging from dung, others from timber, others from the flesh or from hair of certain animals.[38] In this way Aristotle comes very close to saying that seed-principles of these creatures are pre-contained in the matter out of which they arise, but he stops short of this conclusion, saying rather that the matter can be moved in a seed-*like* manner (*Metaph.* 1034b5–6). But it is a short step from here to saying that seminal principles are contained in the matter, and this is precisely how the Neoplatonic commentator Asclepius understands Aristotle's remarks when he comes to this passage of the *Metaphysics*:

> Thus [Aristotle] says that in the case of those natural creatures possessing matter that possesses the demiurgic *logos* and imitates seed (*ekhousin hulên ekhousan logon dêmiourgikon kai mimoume nên to sperma*), they come to be spontaneously (whereas it is impossible for those without such matter to come to be without a seed).[39]

---

[36] R. B. Todd, 'Some Concepts in Physical Theory in John Philoponus' Aristotelian Commentaries', *Archiv für Begriffsgeschichte* 24 (1980), 151–70, has suggested that this phrase is drawn from Proclus. See Proclus, *in Tim.* 3,53,6–13. Cp. *in Tim.* 1,446,1–7 and Damascius, *in Phd.* 1,3 Westerink.

[37] See Sophonias, *in DA* 57,14–17 with n. 33 above.

[38] *HA* 550b32–551a13.

[39] Ascelpius, *in Metaph.* 411,9–12. At 408,7–10 Asclepius states that the corpse of a bull contains the same *logos* to create a drone that a drone-seed has. This exegesis should be compared to that of Michael of Ephesus (*in Metaph.* 501,1–10), who in this case simply repeats Aristotle's views without any Neoplatonic contamination in terms of form-principles pre-existing in the matter. For similar claims about the role of *logoi* in accounting for extraordinary generation, see e.g. Philoponus, *in GC* 84,8–12; Syrianus, *in Metaph.* 186,4–5; Simplicius, *in Phys.* 162,29–31 (within a discussion of Anaxagoras) and 1293,3–5; and the passages discussed below.

This view of pre-existing form-principles being responsible for the generation of the receptacle-bodies of abiogenetically and heterogenetically generated creatures is not to be found in Porphyry's *Ad Gaurum*, which simply remains silent on this issue, but it is compatible with the little about extraordinary generation that one does find there, and it is clearly formulated by Themistius, Philoponus and Proclus (in addition to there being some indications, which I shall discuss below, that Plotinus might have been thinking along these lines).[40]

This appeal to *logoi* in cases of extraordinary generation has significant consequences. First of all, it is no longer fitting to refer to these processes as cases of 'spontaneous' generation, since these *logoi* are teleological principles.[41] Secondly, heterogenesis is no longer really *hetero*-genesis, since the *logos* posited to be in the matter is a *logos* of the creature being generated, so it actually is a case of like producing like.[42] Finally, since *logoi* in matter may be fairly characterized as rational channels of soul-activity, the pre-existence of *logoi* in matter requires the pre-existence of a soul, to which these *logoi* belong. Hence, what might appear to be a case of abiogenesis, it not really *a*-biogenesis, since there is a soul at work.

This raises the question of the exact origins of these *logoi*: which soul is responsible for supplying these *logoi*? And there is another, related question, which we might best approach by calling to mind one of Aristotle's arguments for the spontaneous generation of oysters. He describes how the people of Chios transported oysters from Pyrrha to Lesbos, and found that although they increased greatly in size, from which one might conclude that the new environment suited them, the number of oysters did not increase.[43] From this we are supposed to conclude not only that oysters do not reproduce but also that the spontaneous generation of oysters only occurs in certain places. Thus the following question must be posed to the Neoplatonists: If extraordinary generation is to be explained by positing a soul that supplies *logoi* that create the receptacle-bodies of the creatures in question, how are we to explain the selectivity involved? That is to say, how are we to account for the fact that the *logoi* of such-and-such a creature are supplied in this case but of some other creature in that case?

Some Neoplatonists appear to have come up with a single response to both of these questions, at least for cases of heterogenesis, by pointing to the organism being putrefied. Plotinus, for example, indicates in the following passage describing a case of heterogenesis that it is the 'soul which leaves', i.e., the individual soul of the dying plant or animal, that is said to 'give before it goes':

---

[40] Themistius, *ad Metaph.* 12, 1070a26-8 (cited and discussed below); Philoponus, *in DA* 52,4-21 and *in GC* 84,8-12; Proclus, *in Tim.* 1,2,19-26 and *in Parm.* 793,4 ff. Steel; cp. [Simplicius], *in DA* 63,15-17.

[41] This is not to say that the Neoplatonists do not themselves at times continue to refer to these phenomena as 'spontaneous.' They do, but the term has now lost its original meaning. At times one finds Neoplatonists pointing this out. Syrianus, for example, speaks casually of spontaneously generated living things at *in Metaph.* 186,4 but then in 186,12-14 points out that 'the spontaneous' is not an acceptable explanation for these cases. Cf. Proclus, *in Tim.* 1,2,19-31 and 1,262,5-12.

[42] Syrianus, for example, makes this point at *in Metaph.* 186,7.

[43] Aristotle, *GA* 763a33-b4.

And sometimes the soul remains in the same living thing and gives, like the soul in plants; but sometimes when it goes away it gives before it goes, as with plants which have been pulled up or dead animals, when from their putrefaction many are generated from one. And the soul-power from the universe co-operates, the kind of power which is the same here, too.[44]

The question here is: What is the soul of the deceased giving? It cannot be giving soul *per se*. For as we have seen, Plotinus explains the presence and absence of soul simply in terms of the suitability of the body: Soul is everywhere and is present to that which is suited to receive it. Moreover, it would go against the now familiar principle that the product of generation cannot be ontologically superior to the producer, since one of the common explananda is the generation of worms (which have some degree of sensation and impulse) from decaying plants (which do not). It must rather be that the souls of the deceased are somehow responsible for generating suitable receptacles for soul. If so, then in order to do this it would seem that the vegetative soul must remain in the body after death for a time. The idea is that once the body of, e.g., a bull is no longer a suitable receptacle of a sensitive soul, its sensitive soul departs while its generative soul remains and continues to work with the corpse, part of this work being the formation of the bodies of the creatures generated heterogenetically from it.

Indeed, Plotinus explicitly acknowledges the lingering of the generative soul in the body after death as a consequence of his metaphysical psychology in which the action of higher substances on lower substances is explained in terms of the doctrine of

---

[44] *Enn.* 3.4.6.40–45; Armstrong's translation, slightly revised. The exact sense of the last line is impossible to determine with any certainty, but it is important because it shows the extent to which Plotinus is willing to consider the soul power of the individual plant or animal as a distinct agent in causal explanations. *sunergein* and its cognate *sunergon* are technical terms in the *Enneads* that are regularly distinguished from proper causes in a manner that closely resembles the Stoic distinction between *sunektika* causes and *sunerga* causes. The clearest illustration of this distinction can be found in a brief discussion of natural generation in 3.1.6.1–4, where Plotinus sets out to distinguish the role that parents play in generation from that of the universe and the stars. It is a horse that is responsible for generating a horse, and a man that is responsible for generating a man. The main causal role (*to polu*) must be attributed to the parents, while the rotation of the universe is only a *sunergon*. In fact, this is in keeping with a large number of statements regarding the causal role of the universe in individuals, in which he routinely refers to the universe, the heavenly circuit, the celestial bodies and place as being *sunerga* of various sublunar phenomena and states of affairs. (The universe is described as a contributing cause in 2.3.14.15–17; 3.1.5.21–2; 4.4.31.3 ff.; 4.9.2.28–33; the heavenly circuit in 2.3.10.7–10; 3.1.6.3–5; the celestial bodies in 2.3.8.6–8, 12.1–11, 14.4–7; 2.9.13.14–18; 4.4.6.15–16, 30.1–16, 31.8–12, 38.22–3; place in 2.3.14.4–7 and 16; 3.1.5.24–7). This has recently been taken as a reference to the World-Soul (by Matthieu Guyot in L. Brisson and J.-F. Pradeau, eds, *Plotin, Traités*, 8 vols (Paris: GF-Flammarion, 2002–10), vol. 1, *ad loc.*), and this might be right, but Plotinus' usual manner of referring to the World-Soul is *hê tou pantos*, *hê tou holou* or *hê holê* (4.3.1.26; 2.3.18.9; 2.9.7.5; 3.1.8.5; 1.1.11.13–15; etc.). He does often refer to soul powers coming from the All (2.3.15.13; 4.3.27.1–3; 4.4.37.13; 4.9.3.23; etc.) but it seems odd to describe the World-Soul itself as being a power that comes from the All. If it is the World-Soul here, then we have a clear statement that it is not the World-Soul that is primarily responsible for the products of spontaneous generation. This might possibly be a nod to the view explored above that the *logoi* need to be set in motion and actualized by another soul that possesses them actually, but it might also just refer to the influence of environmental forces that contribute to the process.

double activity. According to this doctrine,[45] a substance is identified with its so-called 'internal activity' and is distinguished from its so-called 'external activity' that it gives off from itself as a necessary by-product and which is, as it were, a trace or image of the internal one. The most common illustration of this doctrine is fire: If we identify fire with its (internal) activity of burning, then the heat that it necessarily gives off will be its external activity. The heat is an image of fire insofar as it too is hot, but *qua* hot it is surely inferior to fire itself. As the fire example makes clear, nothing prevents the external activity from lingering on in the environment even after the fire itself has been extinguished. If we think of the relationship between the soul and the body of a living organism as analogous to that of a fire and a hearth, then we see that just as the hearth stays warm for a while even after the fire has been extinguished, so too may the body retain a trace of soul even after the soul has departed.

> Why, then, supposing that the body is like something warmed, but not like something illuminated, does it not have any trace of life when the other soul has gone out of it? It does have it for a short time, but it fades quickly, just as the things which are warmed when they go away from the fire. There is evidence for this in the growth of hair on corpses, and the growth of their nails, and the living creatures which move for a long time after they have been cut in two; for this is probably the trace of life still present in them.
>
> 4.4.29.1–8, trans. Armstrong

Plotinus, then, does think that a 'trace' of soul remains in the body after the death of an animal, and that this trace is responsible for generative activities such as growing nails and hair. This, in my view, makes it very likely that he thought the 'giving' in *Ennead* 3.4.6 is also being done by this trace of soul, which is beginning to look like the vegetative soul. In fact, this is exactly what Philoponus will say three centuries later:

> After the departure of the soul they [viz. the faculties of the vegetative soul] evidently remain for a short time in the relevant body, for nails and hair will also grow on corpses. But if even after death there is still clearly a trace of the faculty of growth in the body, it is necessary that there will also be a trace of the faculty of nutrition; for nutrition is for the sake of growth. From this, therefore, it is clear that these faculties have their essence in this <body>; and if they do, of necessity the faculty of generation will do so, too; for it belongs to the same series, for where the former two are, there of necessity the third also appears. One might say that there is a trace even of this in a dead body because of the living beings that come into being from corpses, such as wasps, bees, grubs, etc.[46]

---

[45] On the doctrine of double-activity, see the classic study by C. Rutten, 'La doctrine des deux actes dans la philosophie de Plotin', *Revue philosophique* 81 (1956), 100–6, and now G. Aubry, *Dieu sans la puissance: Dunamis et energeia chez Aristote et chez Plotin* (Paris: Vrin, 2006), pp. 222–39, and E. K. Emilsson, *Plotinus on Intellect* (Oxford: Oxford University Press, 2007), pp. 22–68.

[46] *in DA* 17,9–19 (trans. van der Eijk).

This appeal to the nature of the deceased organism not only provides a credible source for the *logoi*, it also goes some way towards explaining why certain circumstances give rise to certain kinds of creatures. For there appears to have been a fairly common view that there were certain correspondences between species of corpses and species of heterogenetic life-forms, with the connections between hornets and horses and between bees and cows being most commonly mentioned, though one also frequently finds mention of others, including snakes being generated from human corpses.[47] This correspondence theory allows Neoplatonists to maintain that the *logoi* contained in the nature of a certain species of animal accounted not only for its own features but also for the organisms that come to be from it after it dies. The nature of a bull, for example, would contain some *logoi* that would administer the formation of its limbs and organs during gestation, other *logoi* that would account for the development of its more mature features such as horns, and still other *logoi* that would be responsible for constructing the bodies of the bees that arise out of its corpse. The virtue of this suggestion is that it basically reduces the extraordinary phenomena of heterogenesis to the more familiar and less problematic phenomenon of the appearance in maturity of species-specific features such as horns and beards.

The appeal to the soul of the deceased organism, then, goes some way towards explaining extraordinary generation, but it does leave some questions unanswered. First, we saw that in the Neoplatonic theory of homogenetic biogenesis, there were two steps involved in the supplying of creative *logoi*: first, *logoi* are supplied in the male seed in a state of potentiality, and then these *logoi* are brought to actuality by an external agent (the mother). So are the *logoi* supplied by the deceased organism similarly in need of actualization? Further, there is the question of where the soul of the emerging creature comes from. It cannot be from the same source as the *logoi*. For a vegetative soul cannot supply the 'higher' power of sensation. Finally, an appeal to the soul of the deceased is possible only for cases of heterogenesis, so how are we to explain the presence of *logoi* in cases of abiogenesis, that is, in cases of extraordinary generation from matter that is not derived from some other living thing?

Let us consider each of these questions, beginning with the first. On the one hand, actualization would seem to be required by general principles of Neoplatonic metaphysics. If the *logoi* in question are a creation of a vegetative soul, then they should be inferior to the vegetative soul; that is, they should be in a state of potentiality and

---

[47] Philoponus, *in Phys.* 105,14 ff. and 179,5 ff.: hornets from horses and bees from cows/bulls; Asclepius, *in Metaph.* 408,2 ff.: bees from bulls; snakes from humans (according to Alexander); scorpions from basil under a moistened brick; Michael Psellus, *Oratio Minora* 28,27 ff.: dung-beatles from donkeys; hornets from horses; bees from cows/bulls; gnats from putrid water; Olympiodorus *in Meteor.* 278,9–10: hornets from horses; bees from cows/bulls; Photius, *Bibliotheca* 400a: bees from cows; hornets from horses; dung-beatles from donkeys; snakes from human beings; Plutarch, *Agis* 60.5 (identical to Photius); Pseudo-Galen, *Ei zôon to kata gastros* 175,6 ff.: worms from plants; hornets and bees from horses and cows; Simplicius, *in DC* 98,6 ff. and *in Phys.* 239,18 ff.: bees from cows; hornets from horses; various worms from various animals and plants. On the generation of snakes from human corpses see also L. Brisson, *et al.*, *Porphyre, La Vie de Plotin*, 2 vols (Paris: Vrin, 1982–92), vol. 2, p. 204. For some occurrences of these correlations in medieval philosophy, see van der Lugt, *Le ver, le demon et la vierge* (n. 11 above), pp. 137–8 and p. 167, n. 173.

thus in need of actualization by some external cause. On the other hand, the textual evidence we possess is not nearly as explicit about the Neoplatonic commentators envisioning an actualization of *logoi* in the case of extraordinary generation as is the case with ordinary reproduction,[48] and they might well have thought that actualization by an external cause is necessary only in cases of *seminal* reproduction. For as we saw above, it is only the *logoi* in the seed that are said to be in a state of potentiality and consequently in need of actualization. If, then, the account above is correct and the *logoi* of heterogenetic creatures are supplied not seminally but *directly* by the vegetative souls of the deceased; if, indeed, the vegetative souls of the deceased are themselves the agents responsible for the creation of these creatures' bodies by means of these *logoi*, as Philoponus suggests, then it would seem that the *logoi* in question never slip into a state of potentiality in the first place so that no actualization is necessary.

With this question in mind, let us examine two further passages on heterogenesis, both of which invoke another agent of creation, beginning with a passage from Themistius' commentary on Aristotle's *Metaphysics*, which in its entirety has only survived in a Hebrew translation of an Arabic translation of the original Greek, though the passage we are interested in has also been preserved in Arabic in Averroes' Long commentary on the *Metaphysics*. Here Themistius offers a Platonic objection to Aristotle's claim that Platonic Forms are superfluous in developmental biology, since a human being's form will always be provided by the father (*Meta.* 1070a26–8), by pointing to the phenomena of heterogenesis, in which there is no father to account for a transmission of form:

> This argument is persuasive for denying the [Platonic] Ideas, but its author neglected the plurality of animals that are created by [things] different from their like [i.e., their co-species], in spite of their great number. For we see a species of hornets that is begotten from the bodies of dead horses; and we see bees begotten from the bodies of dead cattle; and we see frogs begotten from putrescence; and we see the mosquitoes – which is a kind of a small-bodied fly – begotten from wine after it is spoiled. And we do not find nature originating these things from their likes in form.
>
> And we know that in the sperm and the seed of every single animal and plant there is a *logos* proper to it by which are begotten these animals and plants which are begotten from it specifically and not from another, so that neither does a horse come to be from the sperm of a man, nor a man from the sperm of a horse, nor a plant from the seed of another plant. Where are the counterparts of these *logoi* in that from which this [i.e., the spontaneously generated] animal is begotten? Unless a suitable *logos* had been put in nature previously, ready to create any possible animal species, having found proper matter for creating a certain animal from it, it [i.e., the spontaneously generated animal] wouldn't have been brought into actuality. [...] It is necessary for there to exist *logoi* and forms which have already

---

[48] See, again, Wilberding, 'Porphyry and Plotinus on the Seed', on Porphyry and 'The Revolutionary Embryology' on later Neoplatonic commmentators (both n. 19 above).

been put into nature, upon which it works its work. [...] these *logoi* have been inspired by a cause nobler, worthier, and higher in rank than themselves, i.e. the soul in the earth which Plato thought had been created by the secondary gods, and Aristotle thought had been created by the sun and the ecliptic.[49]

Here we can easily see Themistius agreeing with the theory set out above on two central points. First, Themistius is casually accepting the correspondence theory as empirical fact. Secondly, he understands seminal *logoi* to be an important part of any explanation of ordinary reproduction, and he insists that there must be comparable *logoi* at work in heterogenesis. It is equally clear that Themistius is invoking the soul of the Earth as part of his explanation, though the precise role it is supposed to play is less clear. It is possible that he intends the soul of the Earth to be replacing the vegetative soul of the deceased as the agent *supplying* the *logoi*. Yet there are several reasons to think that for Themistius the soul of the Earth functions to *actualize* the *logoi* rather than merely supplying them. First, Themistius himself signals in this passage that the change from potentiality to actuality demands some explanation. Secondly, Themistius describes the relationship between the form-principles and the soul of the Earth in terms of the latter 'inspiring' the former. This is striking because in Porphyry's *Ad Gaurum* the term 'to inspire' (*empnein*) is used only twice – each time in a very technical sense, namely of the mother's actualization of the *logoi* in the seed-embryo. Recall that the *logoi* in the seed-embryo are supplied by the father but they need to be actualized and set in motion by the mother's soul, and it is precisely this activity that Porphyry describes as 'inspiration'.[50] Moreover, the soul of the Earth is invoked by Neoplatonists as the actualizer of the *logoi* in other contexts, namely in explanation of the generation of plants and trees. Simplicius' commentary on Aristotle's *Physics* offers a fine example of this: 'the form pre-exists in actuality [...] in the form-principles established in actuality within the earth, by which what is in a state of potentiality is led to actuality.'[51] Thus, Themistius would simply be extending this theory to cover cases of extraordinary generation. And finally, there is a certain parallel to a comparable invocation of the soul of the Earth in Proclus.

---

[49] I would like to thank Yoav Meyrav for providing me with his revised translation of this passage. Readers are advised to see his contribution to this volume for a translation of the passage in its entirety and for more discussion.

[50] *AG* 10.6: 'The fathers, when this vegetative power is with them, only fortify it towards its task, whereas the mother's external soul, by inspiring (*empneousa*) it, fortifies it toward its task, just as the fathers did, *and* steers the task'. The sense of this passage is difficult, and I refer readers to my note *ad loc*. in J. Wilberding, *Porphyry, To Gaurus On How Embryos are Ensouled and On What is in Our Power* (London: Bristol Classical Press, 2011) for a discussion of this and other possible translations. Also *AG* 16.4: 'For what is lacking to the [offspring's] nature, which always needs to be 'inspired' (*empneisthai*) from the perceptive power because it is, as we said [a reference to *AG* 6.3], an offspring of the sensitive desire and obedient to sensation (although it has no part in sensation, just as the irrational part of soul is brought into order by reason, although it is not able to engage in rational activity), this comes from the mother'.

[51] Simplicius, *in Phys*. 313,11–13. For more detailed discussion of this and other related texts, see J. Wilberding, 'Neoplatonists on the Causes of Vegetative Life', in A. Marmodoro and B. Prince, eds, *Causation and Creation in Late Antiquity* (Cambridge: Cambridge University Press, 2015), pp. 171–85.

The passage in question, from Proclus' commentary on Plato's *Parmenides*, also invokes the 'nature' or soul of the Earth to help explain cases of heterogenesis:

> And finally let us ascend to that single nature that is in the earth which generates alike 'All things that breathe or creep upon the earth' (Homer *Od.* 18.131). Must we not say that this nature contains in advance the *logoi* of the creatures that grow upon it? Or how explain the cases that we see of generation coming about other than from like, such as the creatures produced by putrefaction? What is the source of generation in these cases? And how is it that in the same region sometimes certain plants grow and at other times others, without human design? Clearly because [the earth's] nature as a whole has in herself the reason-principles and capacities for creating them all.[52]

Like Themistius, Proclus not only subscribes to the standard Neoplatonic view that *logoi* must be posited to account for cases of heterogenesis but also connects these *logoi* to the soul (or nature, as he calls it) of the Earth. And once again it is not immediately clear whether the Earth is meant to be supplying these *logoi* or actualizing them, but two things would seem to speak for the latter. First, as the beginning of this passage shows, Proclus seems to think that the nature of the Earth is involved in the generation not just of heterogenetic creatures but of *all* earthly creatures, and this would make little sense if Proclus were envisioning the Earth as supplying *logoi*, since in homogenetic biogenesis the *logoi* are supplied by a seed. Secondly, this appeal to the soul of the Earth is embedded in a larger discussion of actualizing principles that begins with the female nature of the mother (see *in Parm.* 792,9–15 Steel). In this discussion it appears that Proclus is proposing that various natures are nested within one another, such that higher-level natures contain the form-principles of all the creatures belonging to lower-level natures and contribute to their actualization without being proximate suppliers of these *logoi*. This suggests that the Earth's nature, like the mother's nature, must contain all the relevant *logoi* in actuality not in order to supply them but in order to help bring them to actuality.[53]

Conclusion

We began by briefly outlining two attempts at making Aristotle's theory of spontaneous generation more compatible with the demands of the Platonic metaphysics of intelligible principles. What I termed the 'seminal theory' sought to account for both the forms and souls by pointing to internal principles in matter, while the 'reception theory' had both form and soul being delivered from an outside source. This has been an attempt at a synthetic reconstruction of a general Neoplatonic theory of

---

[52] Proclus, *in Parm.* 793,4–11 Steel (trans. Dillon and Morrow slightly revised).
[53] For a longer discussion of this passage, see Wilberding, 'The Revolutionary Embryology' (n. 19 above), pp. 336–42.

extraordinary generation that takes the middle path. On this theory, there are indeed seminal principles in the matter, but these are only responsible for the formation of a receptacle-body; once this receptacle-body is complete, the soul (along with the form)[54] is delivered from the outside. I have furthermore attempted to show that there is some evidence that suggests that in cases of heterogenesis these form-principles are provided by the vegetative soul of the deceased animal rather than directly by the World-Soul.[55] These form-principles may need to be brought into actualization by a soul that possesses them actually (just like the *logoi* in a seed), and the nesting-relation of souls would account for this by positing the same *logoi* in the soul of the Earth so that the Earth can take on the role analogous to the mother.

Along the way it has become clear that there is certainly a sense in which the Neoplatonic commentators share Louis Pasteur's aspiration to rid natural science of 'spontaneous' generation, even if their approaches to doing so are very different. There is a mutual commitment to the view that an adequate explanation of the phenomena cannot allow that life simply emerge from lifeless matter. Indeed, it would seem that the Neoplatonic commentators were in their own way – by theory rather than by experiment – looking to deliver their own 'mortal blow' to the doctrine of spontaneous generation.

---

[54] See above n. 34.

[55] The determination of the respective roles of the soul of the deceased and the World-Soul is surely the most controversial aspect of this reconstruction, but I think it makes the best sense both of the passages examined and of the fact that the cases of extraordinary generation that Neoplatonists make reference to seem always to involve decaying matter. That said, I am not convinced that both souls are necessarily involved in all cases for all authors. In the Philoponus passage examined above (*in DA* 17,9–19), for example, it appears that the deceased is giving not just *logoi* but vegetative soul itself, so that no actualization by the soul of the Earth would be necessary. And perhaps there were also cases of abiogenesis (as opposed to heterogenesis), in which the soul of the Earth supplies the *logoi* itself.

8

A Rediscovered *Categories* Commentary: Porphyry(?) with Fragments of Boethus

Riccardo Chiaradonna, Marwan Rashed, and David Sedley

The celebrated Archimedes Palimpsest[1] has turned out to include not only seminal works of Archimedes, but also two speeches by Hyperides and – identified as recently as 2005 – fourteen pages of an otherwise unknown commentary on Aristotle's *Categories*,[2] in a copy written around 900 CE.[3]

This article first appeared as 'A rediscovered *Categories* commentary' by Riccardo Chiaradonna, Marwan Rashed, and David Sedley, with a palaeographical appendix by Natalie Tchernetska, in *Oxford Studies in Ancient Philosophy* 44 (2013), pp. 129–94. It reappears here by permission of Oxford University Press. The Greek text can be found in the original publication in *Oxford Studies in Ancient Philosophy*.

---

[1] See R. Netz, W. Noel, N. Tchernetska, and N. Wilson, *The Archimedes Palimpsest* [*Archimedes*] 2 vols (Cambridge: Cambridge University Press, 2011). The discovery of the new *Categories* commentary was made by Nigel Wilson. Reviel Netz's partial transcription of some folios then launched the project, which gained early momentum from a lively email exchange led by Bob Sharples, Stephen Menn, and others, and from a meeting hosted by the British Academy. The slow and laborious work of systematic transcription was carried out by Marwan Rashed, David Sedley, Bob Sharples, Natalie Tchernetska, and Nigel Wilson in a series of workshops in London, Cambridge, and Paris. Thanks are due to the Institute of Classical Studies, to University College London, to the Faculty of Classics at the University of Cambridge, and to the École Normale Supérieure, Paris, for supporting the workshops. We thank the imaging team directed by Roger Easton; the manager of the Archimedes Project, William Noel, for providing the images and much practical support; Sibylle Nalezinski and Steve Kimberley for the generous amount of time they put into the technical facilitation of (respectively) the London and Cambridge workshops; Alex Lee for technical help with the transcription; Brad Inwood and John Magee for valuable comments on a first draft of the present article; and Jonathan Barnes for an extensive and characteristically probing set of notes on the second draft, many of which can be fully taken into account only in the comprehensive edition that is eventually envisaged for this text. During the collaborative work on this text Bob Sharples fell ill and died. He had played a key role in the process of decipherment and interpretation, and we dedicate this article to his memory.

[2] Transcription and images of the *Categories* commentary can be found in Netz et al., *Archimedes*, vol. 2, pp. 311–39. Codicological information can be found in vol. 1, along with a sketch of the issues of content (253–7) discussed more fully in the present introduction.

[3] See Netz et al., *Archimedes*, vol. 1, pp. 253–7 (description of text); vol. 2, pp. 311–N39 (images and transcription).

Even if it contained nothing else, the citations that this last manuscript preserves from named earlier commentators – Andronicus, Boethus, Nicostratus, and Herminus – would be enough to make it an important addition to our knowledge of the *Categories* tradition. Its new evidence on the first-century BCE Aristotelian Boethus is especially significant. Two of the three citations from him (3,19–22; 14,4–12) probably embody his words more or less verbatim, to judge from the combination of direct speech and peculiarly crabbed language, very unlike the author's usual style. In addition, the author mentions a group of anonymous commentators already criticized by Boethus, thus giving further unexpected insights into the early reception of Aristotle's work.

But the author's own contributions are rich and fascinating too. If his date and identity could be established, the new text would make an even greater impact on our present state of understanding. In this article it will be argued that the new fragment is, to all appearances, a remnant of the most important of all the ancient *Categories* commentaries, Porphyry's lost *Ad Gedalium*.

The grounds for such an attribution will be set out in this introduction. There will then follow a translation of the passage, and finally a commentary on the commentary. Our aim is not, in the space of a single article, to settle all the interpretative questions, but on the contrary to initiate discussion, to develop our proposal regarding authorship, and, above all, to bring the already published text to the attention of interested scholars in the field of ancient philosophy.

The commentary consists of seven consecutive folios, recto and verso, each with thirty lines per side and around forty letters per line. For ease of reference, we have renumbered the sides into a simple consecutive run, 1–14.

Despite its severely damaged state, it has proved possible to decipher much the greater part of the text on these fourteen pages. In what follows, we start with a brief description, then turn to the question of authorship.

The entire fourteen pages deal, incompletely, with just two consecutive lemmata from the *Categories*. The passage already under discussion when the text opens is 1a20-b15, a strikingly long lemma, especially given that the same passage is divided into three lemmata by Ammonius, and into five by Simplicius. The commentator has by this point already dealt, presumably at some length, with Aristotle's well-known distinction there between properties that are 'said of a subject' and those that are 'in a subject'. As the text opens, he is discussing the later part of the lemma, 1b10-15, where Aristotle explains a principle of transitivity according to which when predicate B is said of subject A, and predicate C is said of subject B, then predicate C is said of subject A. Various aspects of this theorem, and problems arising from it, occupy the commentator from 1,1 to 7,8. But he then returns (7,8–9,30) to the opening part of the main lemma, its fourfold division of predicates (1a20-b9), which he presents as applying a neglected Aristotelian method of division, one that can also, as he proceeds to illustrate, be used effectively in the doxographical mapping out of philosophical theories.[4]

---

[4] Similar fourfold doxographical schemata occur in earlier writers, e.g. Philo, *Opif.* 99, Sextus Empiricus, *Adv. Math.* 9.210, but without specific discussion of the methodology. The author's complaint about his predecessors' neglect of the method (7,17–19) supports the assumption that the analysis is his own, or his immediate source's, contribution to the *Categories* tradition.

At 9,30–10,12 we encounter the transition to a new lemma, *Categories* 1b16–24, where Aristotle explains his thesis that any two different genera, such as animal and knowledge, which are not subordinated one to the other will normally be divided by two specifically (*tôi eidei*) different sets of differentiae. The commentator takes the opportunity here to explain the basic vocabulary of genus, species, and differentia, as befits the opening pages of a work that was itself placed first in the Aristotelian corpus. Otherwise his discussion, as for the preceding lemma, is largely taken up with resolution of the exegetical problems raised by his predecessors.

The *Categories* was the earliest Aristotelian treatise to attract commentaries and critiques, from the first century BCE onwards. The numerous exegetes, of whose work only a small proportion has survived, included not only Aristotelians, but also Platonists, Stoics, and others of uncertain philosophical allegiance. The surviving commentaries are in fact all the work of Neoplatonists, starting with the short question-and-answer commentary by Porphyry (third century CE), but they contain plentiful reports of the views of earlier commentators and critics.[5]

Since our commentary repeatedly cites previous commentators from the first century BCE to the second century CE, but none later than that, we can be confident that it was written in the Roman imperial era, not earlier than the time of Alexander of Aphrodisias (*c.* 200), whose teacher Herminus is the latest commentator cited, and probably not very much later either.[6] This enables us to set about searching for its author's identity systematically, since we are fortunate, in the case of this particular Aristotelian treatise, to have from Simplicius (*in Cat.* 1,9–2,29 Kalbfleisch)[7] a detailed survey of the commentary tradition down to the beginning of the sixth century.[8]

---

[5] A convenient survey can be found in P. Moraux, *Der Aristotelismus bei den Griechen von Andronikos bis Alexander von Aphrodisias*, 3 vols (Berlin: De Gruyter, 1973–2001). Michael Griffin, *Aristotle's Categories in the Early Roman Empire* (Oxford: Oxford University Press, 2015), provides an updated survey of the debates on the *Categories*.

[6] The logical terminology in our commentary is common and widely paralleled in ancient and late ancient sources: e.g. *periektikos / periekhôn / periekhomenos* (3,11; 4,28; 13,1), *eidikôtatos* (5,1–2). Parallels for these and others of the commentator's terms can be found in J. Barnes, *Porphyry: Introduction* (Oxford, 2003), pp. 106, 114, 161–2, and *passim*.

[7] *Simplicii in Aristotelis Categorias commentarium*, ed. K. Kalbfleisch, CAG 8 (Berlin: Reimer, 1907). Simplicius and the other Aristotelian commentators cited below are quoted from the CAG edition.

[8] Simplicius' full list is: Themistius' paraphrase; Porphyry's question-and-answer commentary; Alexander, Herminus, and others, who touched 'to a moderate degree' (*metriôs*) on specific questions; Maximus, a Neoplatonist who almost entirely followed Alexander; Boethus; Lucius and Nicostratus, systematic critics of the *Categories*; Plotinus' critique of the *Categories* at *Enn.* 6.1–3; Porphyry's *Ad Gedalium*; Iamblichus; Dexippus; and Simplicius himself. This list is not meant to be exhaustive: for example, it omits the names of early exegetes and critics (Andronicus, Eudorus, Ariston, Athenodorus) whom Simplicius himself recalls elsewhere (e.g. *in Cat.* 159,32), and also Aspasius and Galen (cf. n. 18 below), who certainly both wrote on the *Categories*. Yet it is extremely unlikely that Simplicius omitted the author of a hugely extensive and late (as least as late as Alexander) commentary such as the one in the Palimpsest. As regards the Arabic tradition of the *Categories*, the bibliographer al-Nadīm, writing in tenth-century Baghdad, is not aware of any commentary on the *Categories* between Herminus and Simplicius beyond those mentioned by the latter: 'Among those who explained [the *Categories*] and wrote commentaries about it there were Porphyry, Stephanus the Alexandrian, Illinus [a mysterious 6th-century Alexandrian commentator], John the Grammarian, Ammonius, Theophrastus, and Simplicius .... There is a fragment ascribed to Iamblichus.... Shaykh Abū Sulaymān said that Abū Zakariyā' worked over the translation of this book with the commentary of Alexander of Aphrodisias; [it amounted to] about three hundred leaves' (trans. B. Dodge, *The Fihrist of al-Nadīm: A Tenth-Century Survey of Muslim Culture*, 2 vols (New York: Columbia University Press, 1970), vol. 2, pp. 598–9, slightly modified).

The first of the three most important lost commentaries is that of Alexander of Aphrodisias, the greatest of the ancient Peripatetic commentators and a seminal influence on his Neoplatonist successors. Neither Alexander himself nor any commentator later than him is named, yet the author cites the following predecessors: Andronicus (Peripatetic, first century BCE), Boethus (Peripatetic, first century BCE), Nicostratus (probably a Platonist of the mid-second century CE),[9] and Herminus (Peripatetic, mid-second century CE).[10] Thus he takes into account a series of predominantly Peripatetic authors, up to and including Alexander's own teacher Herminus, but stopping short of Alexander himself. And he once, differently from all his other citations, speaks of Herminus in the imperfect tense (14,16), in a clause which might be translated 'Herminus too used to raise the same sort of doubt'. Such language would be well suited to reminiscences of one's own teacher, and *prima facie* favours Alexander's authorship.

However, Porphyry's surviving short commentary on the *Categories*, probably written after the mid-third century, likewise names more or less this same set of commentators, again with no mention of Alexander himself, one reason almost certainly being that he is frequently following Alexander's commentary, and naming the commentators whom Alexander himself cited.[11] Our text is certainly not identifiable with Porphyry's short commentary, but corresponds to it closely in content. An attractive alternative to Alexander's authorship is therefore that we have here part of Porphyry's hitherto lost large commentary on the *Categories*, the *Ad Gedalium*. This is the second option to consider.

Alexander was an Aristotelian, Porphyry an Aristotelianizing Platonist. There are competing signs favouring both attributions. In support of the former, it can be observed that the author at least once shows a degree of detachment from Platonism that would be unusual in a Platonist. When it comes to the most contentious of all issues among Platonists of the imperial era, whether Plato thinks the world to be eternal or created, he simply lists both interpretations of Plato as being advocated by 'some' (8,13–15), without a hint at Porphyry's own strong commitment to the eternalist option. This interpretative openness towards Plato's *Timaeus* is more typical of the Peripatetic tradition.

On the other hand, at 3,23–6 the author appears to compare the metaphysical status of Aristotelian species at *Categories* 1b10–15 to that of Platonic Forms, a rapprochement likelier to come from the pen of a Platonist than of a Peripatetic. Also, at 5,14–19 he cites as if familiar to his audience a technical distinction, between the 'unallocated' (*akatatakton*) and the 'allocated' (*katatetagmenon*), which is unattested for any author before Porphyry, Alexander and Plotinus included, whereas Simplicius (*in Cat.* 53,7–9; 79,28–9) closely associates its authorship with Porphyry.

---

[9] See A. Gioè, *Filosofi medioplatonici del II secolo d.c.: testimonianze e frammenti. Gaio, Albino, Lucio, Nicostrato, Tauro, Severo, Arpocrazione* (Naples: Bibliopolis, 2002), pp. 155–219.

[10] Herminus was probably Galen's contemporary: see N. Rescher and M. Marmura, *The Refutation by Alexander of Aphrodisias of Galen's Treatise on the Theory of Motion* (Islamabad: Islamic Research Institute, 1965), pp. 79–80 (Arabic text), 18–19 (English translation). This incidentally adds a further obstacle to identifying Galen as the author of our text (see n. 18 below).

[11] On Porphyry's authorities in the short commentary see R. Bodéüs, *Porphyre, Commentaire aux Catégories d'Aristote* (Paris: Vrin, 2008), pp. 28–32.

In addition, there are a number of passages which correspond nearly verbatim to passages of Porphyry's surviving short commentary. They do not prove single authorship, since *Categories* commentators regularly copied material from each other, but they fit the hypothesis very comfortably.

Finally, our commentary shows a particular interest in comparing Stoic doctrines (12,13–14),[12] a feature of Porphyry's *Ad Gedalium* on which Simplicius (*in Cat.* 2,8–9) takes the trouble to remark.

The balance of probabilities therefore already favours Porphyry.[13] It would be harder to account for the presence of Platonist-sounding material in Alexander than for that of Peripatetic-sounding material in Porphyry, who in the preface to his *Isagôgê* openly declares his debt to the Peripatetics in this general area, and who anyway tends to wear his Platonism very lightly in his Aristotelian works.

One intriguing complication lies in the fact that at 7,19–20 the author of the *Categories* is referred to simply as 'the Philosopher'. This reverential designation of Aristotle became standard among Platonist commentators, whereas it was never used by Peripatetics as far we know. To that extent the usage again favours Porphyry over Alexander. However, its application to Aristotle has proved hard to trace back earlier than Themistius, writing a full generation after Porphyry.[14]

At 14,23–30 the author's solution to a puzzle about the differentia raised by earlier commentators corresponds closely to Porphyry's own solution as reported by Simplicius (*in Cat.* 58,7–12), while differing from what we know of Alexander's solution. That solution of Porphyry's does not occur in his short commentary, and it has already been inferred by Kalbfleisch (in app.) and others that it must instead have been in the *Ad Gedalium*.

A really vital criterion is length. The commentary before us was an exceptionally long one, to judge from the seven surviving folios: *c.* 3,000 words, which are just one part of the exegesis of a mere thirty-four lines of the Aristotelian text. For example, the doxographical illustration of the fourfold division method (7,24–8,28) is a substantial excursus with no equivalent in the other *Categories* commentaries.[15] And the portion of commentary from the start of the text down to 7,8, totalling around 1,500 words, is just part of the commentary on *Categories* 1b10–15. We cannot know how much is lost at the beginning, but when the text starts the author is already replying to a criticism of Aristotle, and before that there must have been some initial exegesis of the lines. So it is unlikely that the full commentary on this passage was less than 1,700 words in length. The same passage is covered by Simplicius in around 1,000 words (51,26–54,21).

---

[12] The references to the Stoics at 8,11–12 and probably 8,28 are less significant, because they are parts of two cosmological doxographies, not directly related to the theme of the *Categories*.

[13] So far as the choice between Porphyry and Alexander is concerned, there is independent evidence (edited in S. Ebbesen, 'Boethius as an Aristotelian Scholar', in J. Wiesner, ed., *Aristoteles: Werk und Wirkung*, 2 vols (Berlin: De Gruyter, 1986), vol. 2, pp. 286–311, at pp. 309–11) that the *Ad Gedalium* survived into the thirteenth century, when our manuscript was recycled as part of a palimpsest, whereas there is no corresponding evidence for the survival of Alexander's commentary. There is no hint that a manuscript from late antiquity containing Alexander's commentary – like, for example, the copy available to the Syriac translator (see n. 8) – was ever transliterated in Byzantium.

[14] See n. 35, p. 241 below. [Correction: we have now found an instance in Alexander, *Mixt.* 228,10.]

[15] Cf. n. 4 above.

Extrapolating from this sample, we may suspect that the entire commentary was likewise a good deal longer than that of Simplicius, which itself is the longest *Categories* commentary to come down to us, running to 170,000 words. Thus even on a conservative estimate our commentary is likely to have been well over 200,000 words in length, filling more than 470 folios, of which we have just seven.

Porphyry's *Ad Gedalium* was likewise an enormous work, reported to have run to seven volumes,[16] and to have been a comprehensive commentary (Simpl. *in Cat.* 2,5-9). Its great size was partly due to its lengthy replies to the objections that had been raised against the *Categories* (ibid. 2,6–7, cf. 12–13), an unmissable feature of our text too, where, for example, a complex response to Nicostratus' anti-Aristotelian puzzle alone takes up most of the first four pages.

Alexander's commentary, by contrast, was comparatively cursory in scope (Simpl. *in Cat.* 1,13–14: he touched 'to a moderate degree' on specific questions). In the Arabic copy available to Shaykh Abū Sulaymān and Abū Zakariyā' in the tenth century it is reported to have been 300 folios in length.[17] The Greek manuscript in which our commentary is preserved, dated around 900 CE, will have consisted, according to the above calculations, of nearer to 500 folios. Assuming even approximate correspondence between the amounts of Greek and Arabic text per folio, this again counts against identifying the two works.

There is one more option still to consider. We hear of only one other commentary that may have come close to challenging Porphyry's in size and scope,[18] that of his contemporary Iamblichus. According to Simplicius (*in Cat.* 2,9–15), Iamblichus' commentary too was long (*polustikhon*), and largely based on Porphyry's, sometimes following it verbatim. Simplicius adds that Iamblichus nevertheless severely condensed Porphyry's replies to the various objections, a parsimony hardly visible in our text. Nor are there signs of the Pythagorean motifs one could expect in Iamblichus' commentary (see Simpl. *in Cat.* 2,13–25). Most important, on two issues where Iamblichus is reported as diverging from Porphyry – a particular application of the *akatatakton/*

---

[16] Would a work of over 200,000 words, such as we have seen our commentary probably to be, be likely to be divided into seven volumes or books, as the *Ad Gedalium* was? By the third century, when the codex was starting to supersede the scroll, the size of a single 'book' was no longer likely to be determined by the amount of text that could conveniently be contained in one complete volume. What could be expected was rather that, if a work was divided into books, these would be of broadly similar length to each other. Thus on the one hand Porphyry's *De abstinentia* is divided into four rather short books, averaging around 9,000 words each, on the other his commentary on Ptolemy's *Harmonics* runs to 58,000 words without any division into books. But that a seven-book division was at least plausible for our text is suggested by the parallel of Proclus' commentary on Plato's *Parmenides*, of which seven books survive, totalling over 180,000 words (177,000, plus the lost portion at the end of book 7).

[17] See n. 8 above. Shaykh Abū Sulaymān and Abū Zakariyā' were very serious Aristotelian scholars, and there is good reason to trust their figure.

[18] Another option is worth noting. Galen, a near contemporary of Alexander, is known to have written a commentary on the *Categories*, in four books, which has not survived in the very substantial corpus of his writings (see *Lib. prop.* 19,42 and 47 Kühn, ed. Boudon-Millot (Paris: Les Belles Lettres, 2007), pp. 166–7 and 171). But it is never cited by the later *Categories* commentators, and we may doubt whether it entered general circulation. In any case, at least some of the terminology used in the commentary, e.g. *akatatakton / katatetagmenon*, is foreign to Galen's usage in his voluminous surviving works. See further n. 10 above.

katatetagmenon distinction (Simpl. *in Cat.* 53,6–14), and the view that the differentia is said of a plurality of species only for the most part (Simpl. *in Cat.* 56,6–8) – our author can clearly be seen taking Porphyry's position (5,14–25 and 11,12–17 respectively, see commentary ad locc.). Finally, unlike other predecessors, Porphyry is never named in our text, despite the fact that Iamblichus is known to have expressed numerous disagreements with him regarding the *Categories*.[19]

The three major lost *Categories* commentaries are those of Alexander, Porphyry, and Iamblichus. Our text has significant discrepancies with the first and third of these, but a near-perfect match with the second, Porphyry's. The case for identifying the monumental *Categories* commentary preserved in the palimpsest with Porphyry's *Ad Gedalium* is therefore a very strong one.

The case does not of course amount to proof, since we cannot altogether exclude the hypothesis that another similarly massive *Categories* commentary, closely dependent on Porphyry's, remained unrecorded in the main ancient tradition but somehow survived well into the Byzantine era. Further consideration of the authorship question may have to bring in such additional criteria as stylistic analysis and the evaluation of philosophical quality. To prepare the ground for that later stage, our aim in the present study has been to work towards the most faithful possible reconstruction of the text and its contents.

We have for the same reason kept to a minimum our interventions in the text, while recognizing that (as Jonathan Barnes in particular has urged upon us) more passages than so far acknowledged may well contain corruptions.

Note on Parallel Passages

In footnotes at the end of the relevant paragraph we note parallel passages, normally given by author's abbreviated name only, and indicating that author's *Categories* commentary (*in Cat.*): Porphyry, Dexippus, Ammonius, Boethius, Simplicius, Philoponus, Olympiodorus, and Elias/David. There is also reference to the anonymous *Paraphrasis Categoriarum*, and to an Armenian fragment of Alexander's lost *Categories* commentary. Comparable passages in other works are not listed here, although some are noted in the ensuing commentary.

Note on Presentation of the Text

Because of the extraordinarily problematic state of the codex, in which the erased text has been restored to some degree of visibility by a variety of imaging techniques, it has been necessary to adopt a hybrid system of symbols, based mainly on the Leiden System usually used for papyrological editions. As in that system, letters with sublinear dots indicate letters read by the editors with less than certainty, and letters inside square brackets are those conjecturally supplied by the editors. However, free-standing sublinear dots outside square brackets represent letters unread by the editors, without distinction between illegible and altogether missing ones.

---

[19] See D. P. Taormina, *Jamblique, critique de Plotin et de Porphyre* (Paris: Vrin, 1999).

For alternative manuscript readings see the critical apparatus included in the original publication (*Oxford Studies in Ancient Philosophy* 44 (2013), 129–94). Here the Greek text and critical apparatus are omitted.

Anonymi in Aristotelis Categorias Commentarium

[1]...] only, but also of all the things predicated [...]. For since [...] of the things [...] of a subject [...] under 'What is it?' in a subject [...] to be predicated of all the things that fall under this. But if this is so, it is necessarily the case that, since something is being predicated of something as a subject, and other things are being predicated of that which is predicated, these too are said of a subject; but these will be said both of the first thing chosen and of a subject.[20] For example, man is predicated of Socrates as of a subject. For under 'What is Socrates?' we will say that he is a man, and man will be common to all particular men under 'What is it?'. And also, in turn, animal is predicated of man as of a subject. For under 'What is man?' we say that he is an animal, and animal is predicated of every man under 'What is it?'. Therefore animal is validly predicated of Socrates as of a subject. For Socrates too is an animal, and animal could be said of all particular men. Hence we understand '*as* of a subject'[21] as *apo koinou*. For he means neither when one thing is predicated[22] of another as of a subject, nor again all those things that are in just *any* way predicated of that which is predicated, but all those things that are predicated *as* of a subject of that which is predicated. For it is when things are thus that, as it is put, 'they all will be said of <the> subject too'.[23]

[1,26] Against this, Nicostratus,[24] citing a much-discussed puzzle, writes as follows: 'But on this basis someone could raise the puzzle that some are in the habit of raising, that, at least so far as what has been said is concerned, it will turn out as follows: Aristarchus is grammatical, [2] and [grammar is knowledge, therefore] Aristarchus too [is knowledge. And again,] white is a colour, the cloak is white, therefore the cloak is a colour.

[2,4] 'But Aristotle has taken "white" in two senses, because he did not speak simply of the things that are predicated, but added "as of a subject" because [...] do not have [...] used [?] for the subject, [... neither] "Aristarchus is grammatical" [nor] "The cloak is white" is for the thing used [?] among the things said of a subject, but something that is in a subject. For white is in the cloak *qua* cloak, and grammar is in Aristarchus' soul as subject.'

---

[20] It seems likely (cf. 9–19) that lines 4–9 contain another restatement of the transitivity principle, but their exact construal has proved particularly difficult to establish.
[21] The citation is of *Cat.* 1b10–11. In English *katêgoreisthai tinos kath' hupokeimenou* and *katêgoreisthai tinos hôs kath' hupokeimenou* are both naturally rendered 'to be predicated of something as of a subject'. To distinguish the latter formula, which is importantly different in this text, we print 'as' in italics.
[22] The grammatically irregular construction in 21–2, *hotan* + indicative, can easily be normalized by emendation, but is in fact attested in the commentators, e.g. Simpl. *in Phys.* 186,32–4.
[23] *Cat.* 1b11–12.
[24] The first four letters of this name are missing, but Nicostratus is the only known commentator on, or critic of, the *Categories* whose name fits the traces.

[2,13] 'But species', Nicostratus says in rectifying the argument, 'is a term that applies to the things that *are* said of a subject, as in the following example: "Socrates is a man, man is a species, therefore Socrates is a species." [For man] is predicated of Socrates as of a subject, [and species] is likewise predicated of man as of a subject; and Aristotle himself says[25] that what is predicated is a subject. Hence when man is predicated of Socrates, species is said of Socrates. For the species predicated of the man which is predicated of Socrates, the universal man himself, is predicated [of Socrates....] For [...] the other [...]. For it was said [...] of a subject [...] is predicated [...] is predicated of the subject [...] subject [...] has an account [...] [3] is predicated.'[26]

[3,1] But to say that man is a species in this sense (for he is a kind of animal) – that is not something that they do under 'What is it?' by the act of predication. For in 'What is a man?' we would not say a species, but an animal. Nor in 'What is an animal?' would we say a genus, but an animate substance. By calling man a species, or animal a genus, we are speaking in a different sense, predicating a certain accident, and not indicating some reality that belongs to the subject. It is the commonality and the common relation that we call a species; and the commonality is an accident in man, in so far as it ranges inclusively over a plurality, but is not predicated under 'What is it?'. For man is not a commonality. And again, that man has animal as its genus we indicate on the basis of its common relation, because we say that the genus covers differentiae which are under it. Hence when we say that animal is a genus and man a species, we are predicating an accident.[27]

[3,16] But [animal is not similarly predicated of man as an accident. For it] is [...], and is among the things predicated of a subject. For it is not appropriate to respond to the examples cited by saying what Boethus says, namely: 'Animal is predicated of man *as if* of a subject; for none of these generic items is a subject.' For one should say that [Aristotle] is using ['said of a subject' in the most precise possible sense], since he is now speaking about things which are themselves real and existent, not having their reality in something else, but as Plato and others characterized the Forms.

[3.27] 'Man is a species' is a false proposition, and so is 'Animal is a genus'. For with regard to things predicated of a subject, one should always take as premiss the definite predications, such as the universal taken universally, 'Every man [4] is an animal'. But 'Every man is a species' and 'Every animal is a genus' are false. Hence the indefinite propositions 'Animal is a genus' and 'Man is a species' are not true either. For if they were, one of the two definite propositions would have to be true, since that is the reason for the indefinite proposition being true too. For both are false: both 'Every animal is a genus' (because the individual man is an animal but not a genus) and 'Some animal is a genus' (for the same reason: for the individual man is some animal). Similarly, both 'Every man is a species' and 'Some man is a species' are false. For the individual man,

---

[25] Cf. *Cat.* 2b17–21; 3a13–14.
[26] Passages parallel to 2,13–3,1: Porph. 80,29–81,2; Dexip. 26,13–16; Ammon. 30,2–5; Simpl. 52,9–11; Olymp. 50,12–22.
[27] Passages parallel to 3,1–5: Porph. 81,3–14; Dexip. 26,27–31; Simpl. 52,11–18. Passages parallel to 3,5–16: Alexander (in E. G. Schmidt, 'Alexander von Aphrodisias in einem altarmenischen Kategorien-Kommentar' ['Alexander'], *Philologus* 110 (1966), 277–86, at 280–2); Porph. 81,14–22; Ammon. 31,9–12.

being a man, is not a species. Which propositions are like these is explained in the *De interpretatione*.[28] [29]

[4.12] Hence, since the first predication is said of all of the predicated item as of a subject, necessarily it is predicated of all of the subject item too. For whatever things are said of all of the predicated item will be said of the subject too.

[4.17] But why is it that species is not said of every man, but is said of man? Is man not said of every particular man? Yes, but *qua* commonality. For it is in so far as man is a commonality that he is called a species.

[4.21] But, they say, 'aquatic', 'winged', and 'four-footed' are predicated of animal, yet none of these is also predicated of man. Those who raise this puzzle[30] seem unaware of what that which is 'said of a subject' is. For four-footed and the other ones mentioned are predicated of animal not as of a subject, but as included by it, and they are specificatory of animal. Things predicated of a subject must be broader than it, given that [genera] are more generic [5] than species, which themselves are either indivisible *qua* most specific, [or ...].

[5,2] [Some people criticize 'predicated of something different'.[31] ...] For they say that things predicated of a subject are not predicated of something different from themselves, but of the same thing. For animal is predicated according to the conception of man, not *as* animal, and animal is predicated not *as* animal of horse. Again, colour too is predicated of white as of a colour, and likewise all the genera are predicated as of themselves. And it would not be in accordance with some *other* conception that they were said to be predicated of something else, because of the subject's admitting the same definition as that which is predicated of it;[32] for since it admits the same definition, it is the same in species. In what way is one thing being predicated of another?

[5,14] In reply to this, we say that even if animal is predicated of man as of animal, one must nevertheless see the difference between the unallocated and the allocated. The unallocated is presumably different from the allocated. For that which has been allocated is smaller than the unallocated. Nor are rational and mortal additions to animal, but two divisions of it [...] and allocations of it to certain things of which it itself can be predicated, in the way that animal can be predicated of man, the unallocated of the allocated [...] having become different [...] having been allocated [...] predicated [...] of a subject [... [6]...] for a name to be said of a subject [...] a significant sound concerning certain significations [...] the names which

---

[28] Cf. *Int.* ch. 7. Although the plural *tois* is strictly incorrect for citation of a single-book work, there are enough parallels for the loose usage to discourage emendation (the earliest is admittedly from the fourth century CE, Didymus Caecus, *Comm. in Eccl.* 80,2, *apo tôn Peri hermêneias*). If one were to emend, the choice would lie between *en tôi Peri hermêneias* and *en tois eis to Peri hermêneias*, the latter meaning 'in our commentary on the *De interpretatione*'.

[29] Passages parallel to 3,27–4,12: Alexander (in Schmidt, 'Alexander', p. 281); Dexip. 26,23–8; Simpl. 52,11–13.

[30] A correction to the original transcription helpfully suggested by I. Polemis, '*Philologikes paratêrêseis se anônumo upomnêma stis 'Katêgories' tou Aristotelê*', *Parekbolai* [online journal] 2 (2012), 23–6, has been confirmed upon reinspection of the images.

[31] *Cat.* 1b10.

[32] Cf. *Cat.* 2a19–27.

signify certain things [...] will have the same capacity [...] predicated of certain things.[33]

[6,9] We should not overlook the fact that Andronicus and others thought that it is not only the things predicated under 'What is it?' that are predicated of a subject, but others too, in the way that musical is predicated of Aristoxenus as subject, grammatical of Aristarchus, and Athenian of Socrates. Perhaps, then, all these should be included too. For all [
...] to be said of a subject under 'What is it?', but if also [...] to be said of a subject [...] that all the things that we say of something by way of predication are what that thing is. For we say that Socrates is Athenian, that Aristoxenus is musical, and that Aristarchus is grammatical, but do not add that to walk and to sleep is what they are. Again, all the things that are predicated of these, when we say that these are those, will also be said of the subject: for example, Aristarchus is grammatical, and one who is grammatical is knowledgeable, and grammatical [...] is predicated [of Aristarchus] as of a subject, [therefore] knowledgeable will be said of Aristarchus too [...], [7] and similarly for everyone who is grammatical and everyone who is musical.[34]

[7,2] However, when the body is called white, we will say that white has two meanings: (*a*) the colour, and (*b*) the coloured. It is not whiteness that is predicated of the body, because the body is not whiteness, but the qualification derived from this, homonymously called white. Nor can colour be predicated of the body, but coloured can be.

[7,8] Now that these points have been completed, and that 'of a subject' and 'in a subject' have been clarified, and how they differ from each other, the appropriate sequel would be to display the method by which he has made his division so as to encompass all beings. [We should] point out that, there having been two divisions – (1) the method of division into four (and potentially into fewer), and (2) the method of division into ten [(and potentially into more)] – about the division into ten a great deal [has been said by commentators, whereas about] the division into four, which is more scientific in form, they have not enquired. In some cases this was because they did not understand the Philosopher's[35] intention when he makes a division, after determining that a double method has been created: (1) the method of division into few, fewest, or fewer, and (2) the method of division into the most possible, many, or more.

[7,24] Hence if we ourselves are asking what sorts of thing are, in a division, inherent in the necessity of the thing, we will say that there is a dialectical method that goes as follows: when two things are predicated of one thing, and again [...] concerning that thing, and two also turn out true, and [it is] clear [that...] the truth is seen.[36] For this

---

[33] Passage parallel to 5,2–30: Simpl. 53,4–18.
[34] Passage parallel to 6,9–7,2: Simpl. 54,8–21.
[35] This honorific reference to Aristotle as 'the Philosopher' (i.e. the philosopher *par excellence*) is poorly attested before Themistius (*in DA* 30,37 and 68,28) in the mid-fourth century, but comes to be a standard usage among Platonist commentators on Aristotle. See above, p. 235.
[36] If one adopted the conjectural restoration noted in the critical apparatus for 27–30, the translation might be 'When two things have been predicated of one thing, and also denied of that thing, on the basis of them two predicates also turn out true; and clearly when three pairs have been eliminated, the truth is seen.'

[8] is the method. And when different people pick out different positions, the propositions too must turn out true in a variety of ways.

[8,3] What I am saying will be clearer if we take an example, that of the world, of which certain people say 'subject to generation' and 'subject to destruction'. For because two terms, 'subject to generation' and 'subject to destruction', are predicated of the world, there have been four propositions, and four questions, about the world. Of these one is true, but because different people have championed different ones all have appeared to some people to be true, and again all to be false. For it is either subject to generation and subject to destruction, as the followers of Zeno thought; or neither subject to generation nor subject to destruction, as Aristotle thought, and Plato too in some people's opinion; or subject to generation but not subject to destruction, as some of the Pythagoreans hold (and some people think that Plato too goes this way); or not subject to generation but subject to destruction. For even if no one has championed this last position, the proposition nevertheless exists, and therefore there are four of them in all.

[8,18] The same result occurs also when one thing is predicated of two: in this way too four propositions are formed. For given that void is held to be place deprived of body, if we take that which is outside the world and that which is inside the world as two subjects, we will say that, since void is one thing applied to two, the division yields four propositions: that either there is void outside and inside the world, as Democritus and Epicurus held; or neither inside nor outside, as Aristotle and Plato held; or outside but not inside, <as the followers of Zeno held, or inside but not outside>,[37] as Strato thought.

[8,28] Since then this principle [yields the same result as] the previous one [...] into a division [...]. [9] For whenever predication occurs along these lines, and [you have found] four propositions, you have included everything in those four. For when things are being predicated of that-which-is as of a subject, and in a subject, he says that everything that is is either said of some subject and in a subject; or neither said of some subject nor in a subject; or in a subject but said of no subject; or said of a subject but in no subject. For whatever existing thing you take, by setting down the propositions it will be possible to state the truth about it. And this is how these things are included in the four propositions.

[9,11] So much for the method. The reason why nothing has escaped it is that some things have been adduced negatively, and especially the one proposition according to which he says that some things are neither said of a subject nor in a subject. For just as if he had said that, of all the things that are, some are horses, [some not, ...] he would have included everything by assigning some to their proper species, and negating others, so too by assigning some to a genus, and negating others, he does not leave the four kinds in the same genus. This would become clear if you divided all the things that

---

[37] The missing words, omitted through a scribal haplography, are restored by R. W. Sharples, 'Strato of Lampsacus: The Sources, Texts and Translations', in M.-L. Desclos and W. W. Fortenbaugh, eds, *Strato of Lampsacus: Text, Translation, and Discussion* (New Brunswick: Transaction Publishers, 2011), pp. 5–229, at p. 72 = fr. 26C, where this sentence is cited.

are either by species or by genus. For you would find nothing that is not in accordance with such a division.[38]

[9,23] One should not on the basis of this division suppose that what-is is being divided as a genus into species, nor is[39] 'things that are' a plural noun, but rather a collective one. Hence when he says 'Of the things that are some are of this kind, some of that',[40] he is like someone pointing to the plurality of men and saying 'Of these, those ones are Spartans, those ones Argives', [...] he established in many places from [...] plurality [...[41] [42]

[9.30] Having filled out the division, and [...] [10] he has introduced the topic of 'in a subject' and 'of a subject', introducing the theorem as to what the difference between these is [...] again. And [now he proceeds[43]] into the *Categories* proper, writing:

[10,4] *Of things which are different in genus and not ranked under each other, the differentiae too are different in species, for example those of animal and knowledge. For the differentiae of animal are, for example, footed, winged, and two-footed, but none of these is a differentia of knowledge. For knowledge does not differ from knowledge by being two-footed. But nothing prevents genera which are ranked under one another from having the same differentiae. For the higher ones are predicated of the genera under them, so that all the differentiae of the thing predicated will also belong to the subject.*

1b16–24

[10,13] Genus, species, and differentia being said in many ways, to list all the several senses, as Boethus has done, [would be] a long [task, ... but] it is necessary [at least] to indicate [what sort of thing is in the *Categories*] called genus, what sort of thing [is called] species, and what a differentia is.

[10,18] Genus, then, is what we call that which is predicated, under 'What is it?', of a plurality of things which differ in species.[44] For example, animal will be a genus predicated under 'What is it?' of winged, footed, and aquatic, each of which differs in species. For in characterizing what each of them is, we will appropriately say 'animal'.

[10,23] Species is that which is predicated, under 'What is it?', of a plurality of numerically different things. For example, man is said of a plurality of things, namely individual countable men, who differ only numerically. And countable is that which has [..., such as ... and] Socrates. And each of these [...] we characterize [...] by way [11] of characterizing them we will say man.

---

[38] Passages parallel to 9,11–22: Ammon. 26,3–10; Philop. 30,1–24; Olymp. 44,1–22.
[39] On the first emendation canvassed in the critical apparatus to line 24, the translation of 24–5 would be 'for "things that are" is not a plural noun but ...'; on the second (prompted by Jonathan Barnes's questions), it would be 'nor that "things that are" is not a plural noun but ...'.
[40] *Cat.* 1a20 ff.
[41] If the reconstruction tentatively suggested in the critical apparatus were accepted, the meaning of 28–30 might be 'For he used a method of this kind in many places, when enumerating a given plurality.'
[42] Passages parallel to 9,23–30: Porph. 86,7–13; Simpl. 45,30–2.
[43] The missing verb may be *erkhetai*; cf. Elias/David, quoted in the commentary ad loc.
[44] Cf. *Top.* 102a31–2.

[11,1] But since many species which are the same in genus are different, a differentia is said to be as follows: that which is predicated of a plurality of different things under 'What sort of thing is it?'. For example, winged is predicated of a plurality of species – swan and crow. For each one indicates some sort of animal. For the differentia is indicative of the quality of a genus.[45]

[11,7] Since, then, there is a series of ten primary genera – the ones which are going to be explained – in whichever one of these some genus is found, that is the one in which every species of this genus will be, and also the differentia which defines the quality of the genus. For the differentia does most to validate the [ ],[46] if that which validates it is also in that primary genus.[47]

[11,12] However, that the differentia is said of a plurality of species is the case only for the most part. For there are also some differentiae that are equal in number with the species. [...] of bird.[48]

[11,17] It also needs stating that those genera are under one another of which one is under the other, as, for example, winged and animal are under one another, and those are not under one another of which neither is under the other, as, for example, animal and knowledge are both genera but neither is predicated of the other. Since, then, of universals some are genera, some are species, and some are differentiae, and of the species and genera some are only species, whose division yields particulars, others only genera, than which there is no [higher genus], [...] [12] animal [...]. For the genus bird is also a species of animal, and these are under each other, but not in the sense of each under each. For that is impossible, since in that way the same thing will be both species and genus of the same thing; [so he means, not] this, but that one is under the other. [...

[12,6] But if] neither were a species [of the other, they would not be] under one another, for example, animal and knowledge. For each of these is a genus, and neither is knowledge a species of animal, nor is animal a species of knowledge. For this reason, then, these are not under one another. Given, then, that there are also other genera, those between that which is only a species and that which is only a genus, and that in addition there are the highest and primary ones, when he says[49] 'different in genus' [1b16] we should take him to mean at any rate the primary genera, which are genera only. But if someone says that there is only one genus of all beings, as is held by the Stoics, with whom Aristotle disagrees in many places [...][50]

[12,18] One must make the distinction that of genera that are different from each other some are under one another, some not under one another. It is of those that are not under one another that he says the differentiae are different, and that it is not the

---

[45] Passage parallel to 10,13–11,5: Porph. 82,5–22. Passage parallel to 11,6–7: Porph. 82,23–4.
[46] The conjectures listed in the critical apparatus might if adopted have the following respective meanings: 'the species ..', 'its [i.e. the species'] being a substance', 'the being of this [i.e. the species]'.
[47] Passages parallel to 11,7–11: Porph. 82,23–8; Simpl. 56,16–18.
[48] Passages parallel to 11,12–17: Porph. 82,29–32; Simpl. 56,6–8; Anon., *Paraphrasis Categoriarum* 8,10–22.
[49] A correction to the original transcription helpfully suggested by Polemis, '*Philologikes paratêrêseis*', has been confirmed upon reinspection of the images.
[50] Passages parallel to 11,17–12,13: Porph. 83,14–24; Simpl. 56,18–57,1.

same ones that each divides.⁵¹ For one set are those of animal, the others those of knowledge. But of the genera that are under one another it is possible for some differentiae (he does not think it is possible for all) to be the same. For animal and bird are genera under one another; and winged, footed and two-footed are differentiae of animal, but not differentiae of bird. But some other differentiae are the same in number for animal as for bird: for of animals some are herbivorous, some seed-eating, some carnivorous, and there are the same differentiae of birds. [Animal] is predicated [of bird], as the containing genus is predicated [13] of the genus which it contains. For bird is an animal. Their not being the same differentiae means neither of their two genera falling under the other.⁵²

[13,3] It was not casually that he said 'different in species' [1b16-17], since it is possible for them, owing to speech and homonymy, sometimes to appear to be the same, like animal and furniture. For these are different genera and not under one another, yet just as 'with feet' and 'without feet' are differentiae of animal, so too they are differentiae of furniture. For of pieces of furniture too some are with feet, some without: with feet, for example, a couch, without feet, for example, all the other ones, which do not possess feet. But obviously here they are homonymous. For just as foot is homonymous with regard to animal and couch, so too are 'with feet' and 'without feet'. Hence when he says 'in species' here he means 'in definition'. For even if it sometimes chances that the differentiae of genera which are different and not under one another are indicated by the same name, nevertheless they are not the same in definition. This is his usage also in book 1 of the *Topics*, in the division of multiple meanings, where he puts it as follows: 'Sometimes, then, both by name and in the actual fact of the matter they conflict altogether in species, i.e. in definition.'⁵³ ⁵⁴

[13,20] But Herminus understands 'other genera' as simply equivalent to 'of which one is not under the other', even if both are under some genus, in the way that winged is animal and footed is animal, and says that they have the same differentiae. For footed differs from footed by the one being two-footed, the other four-footed, and winged from winged likewise.⁵⁵ Hence, he says, the addition that the differentiae must be 'different in species', and not merely 'different'. For, he says, the above differentiae, although not different but the same, are not the same in species, but in genus. He says this in ignorance of the fact that Aristotle counts as genera which are different from each other and not under one another not merely those of which one is not under the other, but which are not both under a single genus either, [14] as will be clear: for he supplied examples indicating his belief that 'other genera' are like this. For he spoke of

---

⁵¹ With an emendation such as suggested by Barnes, the translation of 20-1 would be, more credibly, 'not the same ones that divide each'.
⁵² Passages parallel to 12,1-13,3: Porph. 83,35-84,20; Elias/David 158,11-14. Passages parallel to 12,18-13,3: Dexip. 28,16-27; Boethius 178B-C; Simpl. 57,11-13, 59,13-19.
⁵³ The citation is reminiscent of *Top.* 1.15, esp. 106a9-13, but is not in the transmitted text of the work, and its meaning is far from clear. It is also uncertain whether 'i.e. in definition' is meant as part of the quotation, or as the author's own gloss. Cf. Dexip. *in Cat.* 29,31-30,2: '*eidei* in the sense of *logôi*, just as in the *Topics* too he is in the habit of interchanging them'.
⁵⁴ Passages parallel to 13,3-19: Dexip. 29,31-30,2; Ammon. 31,25-30; Simpl. 57,13-21; Philop. 41,22-42,9; Olymp. 51,25-36; Anon., *Paraphrasis Categoriarum* 8,4-10.
⁵⁵ See Simpl. *in Cat.* 57,26-7: Herminus gave gryphon and sphinx as examples of winged tetrapods.

knowledge and animal, two genera of which neither is akin to the other and which are not ranked under some one common genus.[56]

[14,4] Boethus says that in another way too the conception of 'different in genus' is like this. For the things 'different in genus' are *some* things different in genus; and the things that are different in genus must be contrary to the things that are the same in genus. So just as under that genus there are beings the same in genus, so too beings different in genus are different genera. Hence, says Boethus, those who consider the universal statement to be false, because there are some genera which are different and not under one another, but which have the same differentiae, for example triangle and quadrilateral. For of both triangles and quadrilaterals some are equal-sided, some unequal-sided; and of vices and virtues some are rational, some irrational.

[14,16] Herminus too used to raise[57] the same sort of doubt. But he says that all such people have completely missed the meaning of what is being said, because of not having determined [that these too are][58] genera that are different (for the doubt he raises is not about these) and not under one another, but both under another. For both triangles and quadrilaterals are straight-sided figures, and, prior even to that, shapes. And likewise both virtues and vices have disposition as their common genus.[59]

[14,23] But it is better to say that genera that are not under one another but different have differentiae which are different in species, in the sense that to the species of each of the different genera different differentiae belong. For let there be different genera, e.g. animal and knowledge, and let their species be the subjects of these – man the subject of animal, music the subject of knowledge. The species which are their subjects, namely man and music, have different differentiae: that of man [...[60]

Commentary

Section A: The Transitivity Principle (1,1–6,8)

The Aristotelian lemma already under discussion when the text opens appears to be the entire passage *Categories* 1a20-b15, a surprisingly long lemma, straddling the boundary between what since the Renaissance have been called chapters 2 and 3 of the treatise:

> [1a20] Of the things that are, (*a*) some are said of a subject but are not in any subject. For example, man is said of a subject, the individual man, but is not in any subject. (*b*) Some are in a subject but are not said of any subject. (By 'in a subject'

---

[56] Passage parallel to 13,20–14,4: Simpl. 57,22–58,12.
[57] On the possible significance of the imperfect tense here, see p. 234 above.
[58] At 14.18 the translation in square brackets assumes the completion [*einai kai tau*]|*ta*. Alternative completions include [*mē einai all' at*]|*ta* ('because of not having determined [that there are no other] things that are different genera'), and [*einai eniot' at*]|*ta* ('because of not having determined [that sometimes certain] things are different genera').
[59] Passage parallel to 14,16–20: Simpl. 58,19–21.
[60] Passage parallel to 14,20–6: Dexip. 28,6–29,15. Passage parallel to 14,23–30: Simpl. 58,7–12.

I mean what is in something, not as a part, and cannot exist separately from what it is in.) For example, individual grammar is in a subject, the soul, but is not said of any subject; and individual white is in a subject, the body (for all colour is in a body), but is not said of any subject. (*c*) Some are both said of a subject and in a subject. For example, knowledge is in a subject, the soul, and is also said of a subject, grammar. (*d*) Some are neither in a subject nor said of a subject, for example, the individual man or the individual horse – for nothing of this sort is either in a subject or said of a subject. Things that are individual and numerically one are, without exception, not said of any subject, but there is nothing to prevent some of them from being in a subject – individual grammar is one of the things in a subject.

[1b10] Whenever one thing is predicated of another as of a subject, all things said of what is predicated will be said of the subject also. For example, man is predicated of the individual man, and animal of man; so animal will be predicated of the individual man also – for the individual man is both a man and an animal.

trans. J. L. Ackrill modified

The commentator has by this point already dealt, presumably at some length, with Aristotle's well-known distinction at the beginning of the lemma between properties that are 'said of a subject' and those that are 'in a subject'. In Simplicius' shorter surviving commentary the meaning of these terms takes up eight pages of the CAG volume (44-51), so we may assume the missing commentary on the present lemma to be in excess of that.

The reason for thinking that a single long lemma is presupposed is that some pages later (7,8-13) the commentator will announce that he has only now finished explaining the difference between 'said of a subject' and 'in a subject', and will thereupon return to the fourfold division set out in the early part of the passage, still without indicating any change of lemma. The choice of so long a lemma, we may conjecture, was motivated by the wish to examine together all the evidence for the 'said of a subject' relation (see Porph. *in Cat.* 79,35-80,2).

However, as our text opens the author is discussing the later part of the lemma, 1b10-15, where Aristotle explains a principle of transitivity: when predicate B is said of subject A, and predicate C is said of predicate B, then predicate C is said of subject A. Various aspects of this theorem, and problems arising from it, occupy the commentator from 1,1 to 7,2.

1,1-26. It is at first sight unclear whether here the author is still engaged in his own initial exegesis of 1b10-15, or is already dealing with an alleged difficulty to which it gives rise (but see further below, introductory note on 1,26-2,13). Either way, his concern appears to be the following. Aristotle has said: when B is predicated of A '*as* of a subject' (*hôs kath' hupokeimenou*), everything that is said of B will also be said of A. What kinds of predication are included? In lines 1-19 the commentator is apparently explaining the principle's application to cases of genuine essential predication, where B is predicated of subject A and B is part of a true answer to the question 'What is A?' (so that, for reasons we will encounter shortly, no 'as' (*hôs*) is needed: note the systematic omission of 'as' (*hôs*) in 4-10, 13-14, 16-18). We may assume that, prior to this, he discussed another set of predications, which are, more weakly, '*as*' of a subject. One example of these will be encountered at 6,9-7,2, where our author indicates some sympathy for Andronicus' suggestion that professional or toponymic identifiers, such as 'grammatical/grammarian' used of Aristarchus and 'Athenian' used of Socrates, fall within the transitivity principle.

By hypothesizing that such a distinction underlay the text down to 19, we can begin to see the point of 20-6. According to the commentator, it was precisely in order to include both these essential and these quasi-essential predications under the transitivity rule that Aristotle added 'as'. The locution 'as of a subject' is broad enough to include not only predications that are actually 'of' a subject but also those that mimic them without conveying essence; it is, on the other hand, not so broad as to include absolutely all predications (1,21-4).

However, in order to understand the text this way, we must assume that the transitivity rule is formulated entirely in terms of 'predicated *as of*'. This is not strictly what it says: 'Whenever one thing is predicated of another *as of* a subject, all things said *of* what is predicated will be said *of* the subject also.' The commentator's solution (20-1) is that 'as of a subject' is, by an *apo koinou* construction, to be supplied throughout Aristotle's formulation of the transitivity principle. (On this 'as of' locution, see further on 3,16-22.)

1,26-2,13. An objection to what precedes (*pros ... tauta*, 1,26) is now noted and discussed. It seems likely that the following sequence has occurred. Before page 1, an objection to Aristotle's transitivity principle had been cited: Aristotle should not have restricted it to cases of essential predication (as indicated by the 'predicated as of a subject' locution), since it works in many cases of non-essential predication too. Our author then replied (down to 1,26) that Aristotle's '*as* of a subject' was designed precisely to allow such cases to be included. The new objection is that, once the principle is loosened in this way, it legitimates faulty inferences such as 'Aristarchus is a grammarian/grammatical [*grammatikos*]; grammar [*grammatikê*] is knowledge; therefore Aristarchus is knowledge.'

Nicostratus (see p. 234 above), although a well-known critic of the *Categories*, is not in our other sources associated with this puzzle in either of the two versions that follow, both of which are usually reported without attribution. Correspondingly, with regard to at any rate the puzzle's initial formulation, our author likewise does not speak of Nicostratus as the originator, but as citing an already familiar puzzle. According to Simplicius (*in Cat.* 1,18-2,2), Nicostratus raised puzzles against virtually every tenet of the *Categories*, making it unsurprising if he often had to fall back on an existing repertoire.

The familiar, more developed form of the puzzle is that, by applying Aristotle's transitivity principle, we get absurd inferences such as 'Socrates is a man, man is a species, therefore Socrates is a species', and 'Man is an animal, animal is a genus, therefore man is a genus'. But Nicostratus himself starts with a feebler version (1,27-2,14), followed by a refutation (2,4-13), after which he replaces it with the stronger and more familiar version (2,13-3,1). Only after that does our commentator clearly introduce his own reply on behalf of Aristotle (3,1-4,17).

The initial, weak version of the puzzle seems (in a badly damaged stretch of text) to be as follows: 'Aristarchus is grammatical, and [grammar is knowledge, therefore] Aristarchus too [is knowledge. And again,] white is a colour, the cloak is white, therefore the cloak is a colour.' As either the commentator or, more likely (see next note), Nicostratus himself immediately points out, 'grammatical' and 'white' are in this very context (*Cat.* 1a25-9) identified by Aristotle as items that are 'in' a subject, as opposed to being 'said of' it. The transitivity principle was therefore clearly never meant to apply to them (2,4-13).

2,13-3,1. Although it is not explicit in whose voice the above refutation of the initial puzzle has been expressed, it seems likely that it is still Nicostratus speaking. For when Nicostratus resumes at 2,13-15 he is 'rectifying' (*euthunôn*) the argument, which shows that he had himself first noted its weaknesses, whether these were initially pointed out by him or by someone else.

Very significantly, Nicostratus' new version corresponds to the classic form of the puzzle cited above, e.g. 'Socrates is a man, man is a species, therefore Socrates is a species'. The text is too badly damaged for much more than this to emerge. Our passage is, nevertheless, sufficient to establish two crucial points.

First, it was to all appearances Nicostratus himself who, to remedy the previous weak version of the puzzle, created the version which was to become standard thereafter. Second, in his revised version, Nicostratus argues that the *universal* (*katholo*[*u*, 2,24) man is predicated of Socrates. This latter remark may have encouraged Alexander to distinguish between the nature 'man' and the same nature as *universal*. Alexander's view on universals is (with slight changes in terminology) presupposed in our author's response to Nicostratus. See further the following note.

3,1-16. We now meet the first part of the author's own solution to the reformulated puzzle, more or less identical to the solution articulated by Porphyry, *in Cat.* (his short commentary) 81,3-22. The transitivity principle applies to essential predications, but calling man a species and animal a genus is on the contrary an accidental predication. To say this of them is not to state their essences (i.e. to state a 'thing', *pragma*, that belongs to them), but to indicate that they are called 'man' and 'animal' respectively in virtue of a 'commonality' (*koinotês*) or of a 'common relation' (*koinê skhesis*), i.e. the 'accidental' sharing of a property in so far as they range over a plurality. It is, in this sense, 'accidental' that each kind has plural members. As emerges from an Armenian fragment of Alexander's lost commentary on the *Categories* (see Schmidt, 'Alexander'), Alexander developed an argument like this in exactly the same context, namely when replying to the 'Socrates is a species' puzzle. Furthermore, the view according to which 'what is universal' (*to katholou*) is merely an accident of the definable nature is well attested in Alexander's extant works (*Quaest.* 1.3, 8,12-17; 1.11a, 21,21-22,6; 1.11b, 23,22-24,8; *in Top.* 355,18-24; see the survey in R. Sorabji, *The Philosophy of the Commentators 200-600 AD: A Sourcebook, 3. Logic and Metaphysics* [*Commentators*] (London: Duckworth, 2004), pp. 149-56). We can plausibly infer that Alexander developed his celebrated theory about 'the universal as an accident' when replying to Nicostratus and rejecting the latter's improved version of this transitivity puzzle.

Whereas the theory in our commentary and in Porphyry's short *in Cat.* closely corresponds to that of Alexander, the terminology is not exactly the same. The terms *skhesis* (3.9 and 13) and *koinotês* (3,8–10, 12; Porph. *in Cat.* 81,16, 20) do not occur in Alexander's extant versions of the 'universal as accident' theory. The word *skhesis* is common in imperial philosophy, but it is worth noting that Porphyry was particularly fond of it: see H. Dörrie, *Porphyrios' Symmikta Zetemata: Ihre Stellung in System und Geschichte des Neuplatonismus nebst einem Kommentar zu den Fragmenten* (Munich: Beck, 1959), pp. 87–8.

3,16–22. The author now contrasts his own solution to the transitivity puzzle with an alternative propounded by Boethus. We have already seen above (on 1,1–26) how the author himself appears to explain Aristotle's expression 'predicated *as of* a subject' (*hôs kath' hupokeimenou*): the *hôs* locution is in his eyes designed to allow the transitivity principle to apply to terms which, although not strictly predicated of a subject, are predicated *similarly to* items which are. Boethus, it turns out, interprets the same 'as' differently: in the counterfactual sense 'as if' (*hôsan*). As an Aristotelian who famously rejected universals, he denies that a species like man could be a proper subject of predication at all. So when the transitivity principle says that since man is predicated of an individual *as of* (*hôs*) a subject, and animal is predicated of man as subject, animal is predicated of the individual as subject, Boethus' distinctive move is to understand 'as of' to mean 'as if of'. 'Man is an animal' is a mere quasi-*kath' hupokeimenou* predication, because the universal man is not a genuine subject.

Now Aristotle's 'as' might be thought to occur at the wrong point in the sentence to make this interpretation possible, since in Boethus' eyes it is unproblematic for an individual to be the genuine subject of the predicate man, so no 'as if' is needed. The 'as if' locution should have been saved for modifying the predication relation between animal and man. Yet this latter relation is in fact expressed without the modifier. To understand how Boethus has performed his trick, we should recall that the commentator himself (1,20–1) has told us that the 'predicated as of' locution is used *apo koinou*, i.e. that it is to be supplied equally with the other 'predicated of' locutions in the same sentence. We may suppose that Boethus had already before him favoured that same extension. Thus Boethus' reading of the transitivity principle is probably as follows. Animal is predicated of Socrates *as of* a subject, because it is predicated of man *as of* a subject, and man is predicated of Socrates *as of* a subject. Here 'as of' is broad enough to cover both strict *kath' hupokeimenou* predications (as probably in the first and third cases) and quasi-*kath' hupokeimenou* predications (as at least in the second).

Cf. Simpl. *in Cat.* 50,6–9, where Boethus (speaking of 'universal time') is reported to claim that what is universal does not even exist and, even if it did exist, is not 'something': hence it cannot in any way be a subject of inherence according to the 'in a subject' relation. (See further M. Rashed, 'Boethus' Aristotelian Ontology', in M. Schofield, ed., *Aristotle, Plato and Pythagoreanism in the First Century BC* (Cambridge: Cambridge University Press, 2013), pp. 53–77.)

The question remains, why Boethus' reading of the transitivity principle could, as the text seems to imply, be thought to offer an alternative answer to Nicostratus' puzzle. The relative chronology means that Boethus could not himself have been answering

Nicostratus. Nevertheless, his theory could have been thought to offer the following alternative reply to Nicostratus' puzzle. Our author himself has apparently concluded his own solution (3,16–19) by insisting that genus is merely an accident of animal, although animal is an essential predicate of man, thus locating the fallacy in the premiss, 'Animal is a genus', now exposed as not being a genuine predication. Theoretically an alternative solution could be to locate the fallacy in the other premiss, by denying that 'Man is an animal' is a genuine *kath' hupokeimenou* predication. Since only Boethus interprets the transitivity principle in such a way as to secure this result, the opportunity is taken to discount his interpretation.

3,23–6. The author now adds his reason for rejecting Boethus' revised reading of the transitivity passage. Aristotle, he insists, is here talking about real entities: not things that have their being in something else – in the way that Boethus presumably thinks that genera and species have their being in individuals – but with the kind of independent existence enjoyed by Platonic Forms. We know from Syrianus (*in Metaph.* 106,5–7) that Boethus equated the status of Plato's Forms with that of 'universals' (*genika*), presumably in so far as both Forms and universals are not real entities. Our author apparently provides an *ad hominem* reply to Boethus and argues that, contrary to what Boethus says, both Aristotle's secondary substances and Plato's Forms are real entities that do not exist 'in something else'. Here the author seems to combine Aristotle's criterion for establishing what has substantial existence in the *Categories* (substances are not 'in something else', i.e. in a subject) with Plato's remark in the *Timaeus* (52C) that the images of the real Forms come to be 'in something else' (*en heterôi tini*), i.e. in the receptacle, whereas the separated Forms themselves do not share this condition. Platonist philosophers regarded this criterion drawn from the *Timaeus* as a hallmark of the substantial status of separate Forms, which as such remain in themselves and are not in something else (see e.g. Plot. 6.5.3.5–8). This may in turn explain why our author refers to 'Plato *and others*'.

The overt rapprochement between Aristotle and Plato suggests that our author was an Aristotelianizing Platonist rather than a Peripatetic. He does not, however, conflate Plato's Forms with Aristotle's secondary substances, but more cautiously suggests that both kinds of entity satisfy the same criterion for substantial existence – the fact of not being 'in something else'. His attitude contrasts with Iamblichus' thoroughgoing Platonization of Aristotle's *Categories* (see Simpl. *in Cat.* 2,13, and Elias/David, *in Cat.* 123,2–3), and fits well with Porphyry's nuanced attitude to the harmony of Plato and Aristotle. See R. Chiaradonna, 'Porphyry and Iamblichus on Universals and Synonymous Predication' ['Porphyry and Iamblichus'], *Documenti e studi sulla tradizione filosofica medievale*, 18 (2007), 123–40, and the general discussion in G. Karamanolis, *Plato and Aristotle in Agreement? Platonists on Aristotle from Antiochus to Porphyry* (Oxford: Clarendon Press, 2006), pp. 243–330.

3,27–4,12. The author now offers the second part of his reply to Nicostratus' puzzle, demonstrating that by Aristotelian principles 'Man is a species' and 'Animal is a genus' are false propositions. As 3,18 shows, however, this should not be taken to mean that man is not a species, but that a proposition such as 'Man is a species' is false according to the criteria that make genuine *kath' hupokeimenou* predications true or false. (This is perfectly compatible with 3,7–8, 12–16, 4,20–1, where our author distinguishes 'Man is a species' from *kath' hupokeimenou* predications and takes 'Man is a species' to mean 'Man happens to be common'). The author calls upon an Aristotelian distinction between three kinds of proposition: universal, particular, and indefinite. An indefinite proposition, e.g. 'Man is an animal', cannot be true unless a corresponding definite proposition – the universal 'Every man is an animal', or the particular 'Some man is an animal' – is true. In the case of 'Man is a species', however, neither of the corresponding definite propositions is true: neither, that is, 'Every man is a species', nor 'Some man is a species'. Therefore the objectors' syllogism rests on a false premiss.

In addition to the parallels for this response listed under the translation ad loc., cf. Philop. *in An. Pr.* 325,27–33. The likelihood that the response, originating from Alexander, was transmitted to the later commentators through Porphyry's *Ad Gedalium* has already been noted by C. Luna, 'Commentaire', in P. Hoffmann and C. Luna, *Simplicius: Commentaire sur les Catégories d'Aristote. Chapitres 2–4* (Paris: Les Belles Lettres, 2001), pp. 416–17.

4,12–21. This passage purports to be a new exegetical paraphrase of the transitivity principle, clarifying why species is not, in the appropriate sense, predicated of animal as subject. The 'first predication' at 4,12–14 is said to be that whereby we predicate a general item (e.g. the genus animal) of 'all of the predicated item' (*kata tou katêgoroumenou pantos*, 4,13–14, 16), e.g. 'man'). Our author means that here the more generic predicate A is said of all of the subject B, which is itself a predicated item ('Man' is predicated of all particular men). The transitivity rule holds for this kind of predication, and the more generic predicate will be predicated of every subject item too. At 4,17–21 the author remarks that species is predicated of man, and that man is said of every particular man, but that (unlike animal) species is not said of every particular man. As he explains here, man is said of every particular man 'as commonality' (see 3,8). Presumably, this remark means that when we say 'Man is a species' we do not consider man as a predicate said *kath' hupokeimenou* of every subject item under it, but only in so far as man has a common relation (see 3,13) with every subject item of which it is predicated, i.e. in so far as man happens to be instantiated by the *many* individuals under it (and not in so far as every individual man shares the name and the definition of man). Cf. Porph. *in Cat.* 81,9–16.

4,21–5,2. Nicostratus' puzzle is finally left behind, and a different, anonymous objection to the transitivity principle quoted: animal is predicated of man; the differentiae aquatic, winged, and four-footed are predicated of animal; yet those same differentiae are not predicated of man.

Our author has an easy reply: these differentiae are not predicated of the genus animal 'as of a subject' (they are contained by the genus but are not part of its definition). Hence, as he remarks at 4,24–6, the critics are not aware what 'said of a subject' means.

5,2–6,8. The commentator now moves to a rather more serious point. Some critics react against Aristotle's view that the transitivity principle holds for cases in which predicate and subject are *different* items (*Cat.* 1b10–11). Against Aristotle, these critics argue that genera are actually predicated as of themselves. For when we predicate a genus of the items under it (e.g. when we predicate animal of man or of horse, or when we predicate colour of white) we take the genus only in so far as it is the genus of *that* species, and we take the species only in so far as it is included in the higher genus (not in so far as it contains further features that differentiate it from the genus): colour is predicated of white as of a colour. Thus, 'animal is predicated of horse' and 'colour is predicated of white' can be equated, respectively, with 'animal is predicated of a (specific) animal' and 'colour is predicated of a (specific) colour'. In such predications the subject and the predicate admit the same definition: hence, according to these opponents, we can take them to be the same in species (5,12–13).

In answering this puzzle, our author adopts the distinction between the genus *taken in itself* and the genus in so far as it is associated with (or distributed among) its species. Even if it is the same genus, the author remarks, the genus is taken in two different senses ('The unallocated is presumably different from the allocated', 5,17–18). In consequence of this fact, the subject and the predicate can be seen as different. Our author repeatedly describes these two different senses of the genus with the expressions *akatatakton* (5,17–19, 23) and *katatetagmenon* or *katatachthen* (5,17–19, 23–5).

Significantly, the strategy is virtually identical to Porphyry's response to the same puzzle as reported by Simplicius, *in Cat.* 53,6–9 = Porph. 56F Smith: 'Porphyry says that the concept of animal is twofold: one is of the allocated (*katatetagmenon*) animal, and the other of the unallocated (*akatatakton*). Thus the unallocated is predicated of the allocated, and thereby it is different.' (Cf. Simpl. *in Cat.* 79,24–30 = Porph. 59F Smith, for attribution of the same distinction to Porphyry in a different context.)

There has been an extensive debate about the meanings of Porphyry's pair of terms. Our commentary does not suggest that the *akatatakton* is a Platonic separate genus (*status quaestionis* in Chiaradonna, 'Porphyry and Iamblichus'). The translations 'allocated' and 'unallocated' are those proposed by A. C. Lloyd, *The Anatomy of Neoplatonism* (Oxford: Clarendon Press, 1990), pp. 62–8.

For the present discussion it is worth noting three further points. First, these terms do not occur in Porphyry's short commentary, and Simplicius' citations of them from Porphyry undoubtedly refer to the *Ad Gedalium*. Second, to the best of our knowledge they do not pre-date Porphyry. Plotinus 6.3.5.18–23 contains an argument which is very close to that of Porphyry as reported by Simplicius, *in Cat.* 79,24–30, but without using this pair of terms. Nor are they found in any of Alexander's extant works. Third, Iamblichus, as reported by Simplicius, *in Cat.* 53,8–18, modified Porphyry's reponse to the present puzzle in some crucial respects; he was not completely happy with Porphyry's distinction between the *akatatakton* and the *katatetagmenon* (further details in Chiaradonna, 'Porphyry and Iamblichus'). The fact that our text carries Porphyry's precise solution, with no trace of Iamblichus' criticism of it, is further strong support for its identification with Porphyry's *Ad Gedalium*.

It is very difficult to make sense of the badly damaged 6,1–8. The allusions to 'signifying words' at 6.5–6 might suggest that our author is referring to the theory of homonyms: Simplicius (*in Cat.* 27,23–33) informs us that the *akatatakton/katatetagmenon* distinction was used in that context.

6,9–7,2. The author moves to an issue raised by Andronicus 'and others'. Andronicus' proposal, which our author seems tentatively to endorse (6,14–15), consists in allowing an extension of the transitivity principle to predicates which do not fall under 'What is it?', i.e. to non-essential predicates. This holds for qualities such as musical, grammatical, and Athenian, which are predicated of individual substances. Accordingly, the genera and differentiae of these non-essential predicates can be predicated of the subject items too: respectively Aristoxenus, Aristarchus, Socrates. As Andronicus specifies at 6,23–4, however, this does not hold for *every* non-essential predicate: predicates such as 'to walk' (*peripatein*) and 'to sleep' (*katheudein*) do not satisfy the transitivity principle.

Our text is closely paralleled in Simplicius, *in Cat.* 54,8–16. See Luna, 'Commentaire', pp. 436–47, and for discussion (and criticism) of Andronicus' puzzle, see Barnes, *Porphyry*, pp. 360–1.

7,2–8. Here, at the very end of his long discussion of the transitivity principle, the author returns to a version of the puzzle that was quoted by Nicostratus at 2,3–4 and answered immediately at 2,4–13: the cloak is white, white is a colour, therefore the cloak is a colour. The earlier solution, apparently offered by Nicostratus, was that according to Aristotle at *Cat.* 1a25–9 white is 'in' a thing rather than 'said of it as subject'. Now our commentator opts for a different view: 'white' is homonymous between (*a*) the colour white, and (*b*) coloured white.

Presumably the disadvantage of accepting Nicostratus' solution would have been that 'grammatical', also said by Aristotle in the same passage to be 'in' someone's soul and not said of a subject, would have thereby been excluded too, as indeed Nicostratus had pointed out (2,4–13). The new solution, by dismissing the 'white' puzzle as founded on a homonymy and not on any mistake about the 'said of' relation, allows 'grammatical' to be treated differently, *as if* said of a subject, and thus to conform to the transitivity principle, in accordance with Andronicus' proposal, which our author has tentatively endorsed at 6,9–7,2.

Alternatively, or additionally, these lines may express a supplementary point whereby our author aims to make Andronicus' view more precise. As noted above, Andronicus distinguishes two classes of accidental predicates: (*a*) those which satisfy the transitivity principle (e.g. musical, Athenian, grammatical), and (*b*) those which do not satisfy it (e.g. to walk, to sleep). The present lines consider a third class, (*c*) those accidental predicates which are homonymous and satisfy the transitivity principle according to one of their meanings, but not according to the other—as white satisfies it in so far as it means 'coloured', i.e. the qualification derived from the colour, but not in so far as it means 'whiteness', i.e. the colour itself.

In this reprise the subject is no longer 'the cloak' but simply 'the body'. This may show that our author is thinking less of the puzzle itself than of Aristotle's formulation in the current lemma (1a25–9), 'For example individual grammar is in a subject, the soul, but is not said of any subject; and individual white is in a subject, *the body* (for all colour is in a body), but is not said of any subject.'

Here the topic is presented as continuing directly from Andronicus' broadening of the transitivity principle at 6,9–7,2, and the identical transition occurs in Simplicius, *in Cat.* 55,8–20 (see Luna, 'Commentaire', pp. 438–9).

Section B: The Fourfold Division (7,8–9,30)

7,8-13. This sentence marks a major transition in the commentary, albeit still with regard to the same lemma. We are invited to return to the first part of it, and to consider the principle by which Aristotle arrived at the fourfold division of beings at *Cat.* 1a20-b9: 'Of the things that are, (*a*) some are said of some subject but not in any subject; ... (*b*) Some are in a subject, but not said of any subject; ... (*c*) Some are both said of a subject and in a subject; ... (*d*) Some are neither in a subject nor said of a subject ...'

7,13-26. The author starts by distinguishing the current fourfold division from Aristotle's tenfold division of the categories themselves, which will be set out at the start of chapter 4. He then maps onto this a second distinction: that between (1) the most economical division, judged by the fewness of the classes, and (2) the fullest division, where there is always merit in finding further classes to add. The awkward wording ('division into few, fewest, or fewer, and ... into the most possible, many, or more', 22-4) is perhaps designed to allow that, depending on context, the two methods need not necessarily aim for the absolute minimum and absolute maximum of divisions. Hence our author is careful to say (14-15) that a type-1 division might be into fewer than four, or a type-2 division into more than ten (as our translation conjectures for the lost line 17). He may also be alluding to the fact that some interpreters had proposed a type-1 division into fewer than four categories (e.g. Andronicus, who endorsed the Xenocratean minimal division into *per se* and relative), whereas other exegetes criticized Aristotle's type-2 division for being incomplete on the ground that it left out items such as conjunctions (Athenodorus, Lucius). In the corresponding passage of Porphyry's short commentary, *in Cat.* 71,16-26, the fourfold and the tenfold divisions are simply called 'smallest' and 'largest' respectively, but even so he concedes (71,28-9) that, from a certain point of view, the most basic division is twofold, namely into substance and accident.

7,16-17: 'about the division into ten a great deal [has been said by commentators]'. This refers to the numerous recorded debates (for a conspectus see Sorabji, *Commentators*, pp. 62-7) as to the legitimacy of, and the principles underlying, Aristotle's tenfold list of categories in *Categories* chapter 4. An alternative title of the treatise was *On the Ten Genera* (see Porph. *in Cat.* 56,31).

7,26-8,3. The 'dialectical method' now invoked is meant to be diagnostic of the fourfold division, as the author explains. The text at 7,27-8,3 is badly damaged, but the general combinatoric point seems as follows. Take any pair of attributes, *F* and *G*, and some subject *x* of which they can in principle be either affirmed or denied: *x* must be either both *F* and *G*, or neither *F* nor *G*, or *F* but not *G*, or *G* but not *F*: there are no further permutations beyond these four. Call this version 1 of the dialectical method.

8,3-18. Version 1 is now illustrated with a doxographical example (see further n. 4 above), where *x* = the world, *F* = subject to generation, and *G* = subject to destruction.

The four permutations are mutually exclusive and jointly exhaustive, which guarantees that precisely one of them must be true. Three of them have had proponents, the author notes, and the fact that the fourth – that the world is not subject to generation but subject to destruction – has never been championed does not prevent it from making up the combinatoric set, which is itself a logical rather than a doxographical construct. Cf. Carneades, whose sixfold division claimed to collect all actual and all possible positions on the supreme good (Cic. *Fin.* 5.16, 21–2).

It is remarkable that the two famously competing interpretations of Plato's *Timaeus* are here both listed: the one favoured by most Platonists, that the world is eternal (12–13), and the one favoured by Plato's critics, including Aristotle, but by only a minority of Platonists, that the world was generated at a past time, but will endure for ever (13–15). The author's open-handedness on this classic issue at one stage struck the original editorial team as an obstacle to identifying him with a Platonist such as Porphyry. But Porphyry's Platonism is not prominently displayed in his Aristotelian works (note the equally remarkable 'of the Ideas, *if* [*eiper*] *the Ideas exist*', Porph. *in Cat.* 91,16), and the overriding concern in the present context is to ensure that each of the first three positions is (even if the fourth cannot be) well populated with adherents.

Two further facts should be mentioned. (*a*) This combinatorial doxography on the generation of the world was closely paralleled in Alexander's lost *Commentary on Aristotle's* Physics (fr. 539 Rashed: see M. Rashed, *Alexandre d'Aphrodise: Commentaire perdu à la Physique d'Aristote (Livres IV–VIII). Les Scholies byzantines* (Berlin: De Gruyter, 2011), pp. 487–91). (*b*) By contrast, no trace of this excursus can be found in the Neoplatonist commentaries on the *Categories*. Simplicius (*in Cat.* 44,3–11; 45,8–18) does not provide any parallel to our section, but includes a Pythagoreanizing development on the relation between the tetrad and the decad, and sets out a numerical combinatorial rule by which one can calculate the number of different combinations for any given number of things (see Luna, 'Commentaire', pp. 159–61, and, for further parallels and discussion, M. Asztalos, 'Boethius as a Transmitter of Greek Logic to the Latin West: The *Categories*', *Harvard Studies in Classical Philology* 95 (1993), 367–407, esp. 368–9). If our author is Porphyry, we find here a further confirmation of his overall attitude: he basically incorporates Alexander's exegesis, which he regards as the standard interpretation of the *Categories*, and his Platonist commitment does not come to the forefront. It would not be surprising that Iamblichus (Simplicius' immediate source) should have rewritten this part of his predecessor's work and suppressed the doxographical excursus.

8,18–20. Version 2 of the dialectical method is now added: take a single attribute, F, and a pair of subjects, x and y, of which F might be either affirmed or denied: either x and y are both F; or neither x nor y is F; or x is F but y is not; or y is F but x is not. Thus, version 1 works with one subject and two predicates, version 2 with two subjects and one predicate.

8,20–7. The void example adduced to illustrate version 2 of the dialectical method has the merit that all four positions have adherents. To fit version 2, void or 'empty' is treated as a predicate which can be affirmed or denied of two regions: the interior of the world, and the region outside it.

8,28–9,11. The author now returns to the fourfold division set out in the Aristotelian lemma, which, he may be saying in some particularly damaged lines, matches both versions of the dialectical method. He does not tell us which version it resembles more closely, but its primary affinity is clearly to version 1: one subject (things-that-are) and two predicates (said of a subject, in a subject). A difference from both versions, however, lies in the fact that it does not list four theses exactly one of which can be true, but four predication relations only one of which can obtain *in any given case*.

9,11–22. The author explains how it is the method's use of pairs of contradictories, rather than contraries, that ensures its exhaustiveness. Also, see Simplicius *in Cat.* 44,26–45,7 and the commentary of Luna, 'Commentaire', pp. 144–59.

9,23–30. Finally under this lemma, the author resists a reading of Aristotle's 'Of the things that are, some are said of a subject ...' as amounting to division of a genus, namely being, into its species. For Aristotle, famously, denies that being is a genus (*Post. An.* 92b14; *Metaph.* 3.3, 998b22). Hence the author's riposte is that the division of 'beings' really is, as the very grammar suggests, the division of a plurality, not of a generic unity called 'being'. This may be an implicit critique of the Stoic genus 'being' (*to on*): cf. 12,13–15 and note on 12,6–18.

Section C: Genus, Species, and Differentia (9,30–14,30)

9,30–10,12. We now encounter the one new lemma to appear in the fourteen preserved pages. As is sometimes done by Alexander, Porphyry, and other commentators, the lemma is not set apart as a heading, but is incorporated into the discourse as a verbatim quotation. We have no way of telling whether such was the regular practice in this particular commentary.

The text of the lemmatized passage, 1b16–24, contains no significant variants on the transmitted text of Aristotle. Both it and the ensuing exegesis endorse the transmitted reading *heterogenôn* (1b16), where a number of ancient commentators advocated *heterôn genôn* (see Simpl. *in Cat.* 57,21–2). However, at 13,5 and 13,20 one sees signs either of the influence of the latter reading, or alternatively of interpretative considerations that would in due course lead to that reading's introduction. Porphyry in his short commentary likewise adopts *heterogenôn* (Porph. *in Cat.* 81,26 (lemma); 83,7; 84,4).

10,3: '... into the *Categories* proper' (*eis autas tas Katêgorias*). This locution – whether or not one prints, as we have done, an initial capital – contrasts the central core of the work with the preliminary chapters, later known as the *Antepraedicamenta* – at the very least chapter 1 on homonymy etc. – and the material from chapter 9 onwards which came to be known as an appendix to the work, the *Postpraedicamenta*. For the distinction see Elias/David, *in Cat.* 144,31–145,4, 'After homonyms, synonyms, and paronyms ... Aristotle comes to the categories themselves. But before the instruction on them, he divides things that are *said* and that *are*.' That is, the *Categories* proper starts at the beginning of chapter 2, but not immediately! We may then suspect that Elias/David was in agreement with our author on the point, starting the treatise proper right here, at 1b16. Porphyry in his short commentary (59,34–60,10) likewise holds that the *Categories* proper starts somewhere after chapter 1, but does not specify where.

10,13–18. The author uses this new lemma as an opportunity to introduce the concepts of genus, differentia, and species. In the interests of brevity (not, one would have thought, his own primary concern!), he declines to follow Boethus in supplying a list of the various non-philosophical senses of *genos, diaphora,* and *eidos* in Greek. For some idea of what these would have included, see Porph. *Isag.* 1,18–2,10; 3,22–4,1; 8,8–15. The fact that Porphyry did there opt to include this wider range of meanings does not militate against the conjectural identification of our present text as his *Ad Gedalium*; for Simplicius (*in Cat.* 54,24–5) specifically cites the *Isagoge* as the text where Porphyry does so, without mention of the *Ad Gedalium*.

10,18–23. This definition of genus is traditional and comes from Aristotle, *Top.* 102a31–2. It occurs in Porph. *Isag.* 2,15–17; *in Cat.* 82,5–10. For further parallels and discussion see Barnes, *Porphyry*, pp. 63–4.

10,23–11,1. The definition of species is traditional too and is modelled on that of genus, with 'numerically different' (*kat' arithmon*) replacing 'differ in species' (*tôi eidei*). See Alex. Aphr. *in Top.* 47,10–11; 123,24–6; Porph. *Isag.* 4,11–12; *in Cat.* 82,10–11. Discussion in Barnes, *Porphyry*, pp. 97–9.

11,1–7. Again, the definition of differentia is modelled on that of genus, with 'what sort of thing is it?' (*poion ti*) replacing 'what is it?' (*ti*). Very close parallels can be found in Porph. *in Cat.* 82,14–15, 17–22, and *Isag.* 11,7–8, and the account is common in later texts. Discussion and parallels in Barnes, *Porphyry*, pp. 191–3.

11,7–12. Our commentator argues that differentiae belong to the same primary genus, i.e. category, as their genus (for example, the differentia of man will be a substance, that of red a quality, etc.). This passage is closely paralleled at Porph. *in Cat.* 82,25–9, and the same view is extensively developed in the second part of Alexander's treatise *On the Specific Differentia* (surviving in two different Arabic versions): see Alex. Aphr. *De diff. II* [10/10']-[11/11'] Rashed. On Alexander's essay see M. Rashed, *Essentialisme: Alexandre d'Aphrodise entre logique, physique et cosmologie* (Berlin: De Gruyter, 2007), pp. 53–79 ('La Quaestio *De la différence* II', with translation and commentary), esp. pp. 63–4 and 73–9; see also Barnes, *Porphyry*, pp. 352–3.

11,12–17. Our author argues that differentiae are said of a plurality of species only 'for the most part' (11,13, *hôs epi to polu*), some differentiae being equal in number to the species. The same view is found at Porph. *in Cat.* 82,29–32. Simplicius, *in Cat.* 56,6–10, reports that Iamblichus disagreed with Porphyry on this point (see Barnes, *Porphyry*,

p. 193). Our commentary does not bear any trace of Iamblichus' position (cf. commentary on 5,2–6,8 above).

11,17–12,6. Our author clarifies what subaltern genera are, i.e. genera of which one is under the other, but not of course in the sense of each under the other. The parallel in Porphyry's short commentary is again very close (*in Cat.* 83,35–84,4), and these lines set out the structure of Porphyry's tree (*Isag.* 4,14–32). For discussion and parallels see Barnes, *Porphyry*, pp. 104–12.

12,6–18. After defining subaltern genera, our author clarifies the concept of genera that are not one under another, e.g. animal and knowledge (these examples come from *Cat.* 1b16–20, and their choice plays an important part in the following discussion). At 12,9–13 he distinguishes between two kinds of 'different genera': those which are intermediate (*metaxu*) between indivisible species and highest genera, and the highest and primary genera (i.e. the ten categories) themselves. As he explains at 12,12–13, we should take 'different in genus' at *Cat.* 1b16 to refer 'at any rate' to the primary genera, which are only ten. This indeterminacy as to the range of genera that might be included under the rule is paralleled at Porph. *in Cat.* 84,4–9, where Aristotle's 'things different in genus' (*heterogenê*) are identified as entirely disjoint (*ap' allêlôn pantê diestôta*) genera, *such as* (*hoion*) the different categories. Different highest genera are no doubt the clearest possible example of 'things different in genus' whose differentiae must be different (hence, possibly, the use of 'at any rate'), but Aristotle's 'things different in genus' certainly include subordinate genera ranked under different categories (e.g. animal and knowledge). It is hard to see how in the author's view they can extend below these, to any genera in the same category (e.g. animal/stone, knowledge/slave), since at 13,28–14,4 he appears to restrict Aristotle's 'different genera' to genera which do not fall under *any* common genus.

In the badly damaged lines 12,13–18 our author is clearly denying that 'being' is itself a genus, a denial also emphasized at Porph. *Isag.* 6,5–7: 'For the existent is not a single genus common to everything, nor are all things co-generic in virtue of some single highest genus – as Aristotle says. Rather, let the ten first genera be posited, as in the *Categories*, as ten first principles (*arkhai*)'. Unsurprisingly, our author contrasts this view with that of the Stoics, on which see especially J. Brunschwig, 'La théorie stoïcienne du genre suprême', in J. Barnes and M. Mignucci, eds, *Matter and Metaphysics* (Naples: Bibliopolis, 1988), pp. 19–127.

12,18–13,3. The author now turns to Aristotle's rule that any two different genera, such as animal and knowledge, which are not subordinated one to the other will normally be divided into species by two specifically (*tôi eidei*) different sets of differentiae (*Cat.* 1b16–20). He first distinguishes between subaltern and non-subaltern genera and paraphrases Aristotle's remark that it is only in the case of the latter (e.g. animal and knowledge) that the differentiae must be different (12,18–22). He then returns to subaltern genera (e.g. animal and bird), offering an illustrative paraphrase of Aristotle's remark that nothing prevents such genera from sharing some of their differentiae (12,22–13,5). It is likely that he returned to the exegesis of this remark shortly after our manuscript breaks off, in a passage corresponding to Simpl. *in Cat.* 59,13–19.

13,3–19. He now focuses on the meaning of 'in species' or 'specifically' (*tôi eidei*) at *Cat.* 1b17. Why should differentiae in different non-subaltern genera be said to be different in *eidos*? By way of answer, he cites the problematic case of animal and furniture. These are different and non-subaltern genera, which should therefore fall under Aristotle's rule (granted the further assumption that they do not belong to the same category, substance; Elias/David, *in Cat.* 158,10–11, classes furniture as a relative). In that case, their differentiae too should be different. Yet 'with feet' and 'without feet' are differentiae of both. This is not a real counter-example to Aristotle's rule, the author replies, because the terms are homonymous: the 'foot' of an animal and the 'foot' of a couch are alike in name but different in meaning. His proposal is that Aristotle's addition of *tôi eidei* refers to precisely this fact, namely that differentiae in different and non-subaltern genera must have different *definitions*, even if their name happens to be the same. Accordingly, *eidos* here should be understood as equivalent to *logos*, and our author refers to Aristotle's use of *eidos* synonymously with *logos* in *Top.* 1.15 (see n. 53 above).

13,20–14,4. The author rejects Herminus' rival interpretation. According to Herminus, Aristotle's rule applies to genera which are 'different' merely in the sense that they are not one under the other, even if (13,19: *kan*) both happen to be under some higher common genus: for example, winged and footed, both of which are under animal. Now genera of this latter kind may well have the *same* differentiae, for example two-footed and four-footed (Herminus' examples are taken from Arist. *Top.* 6.6, 114b20–5, where the *Cat.* 3 rule is in fact partly rectified). This to all appearances conflicts with Aristotle's rule, according to which different genera are divided by *different* differentiae. According to Herminus, however, *tôi eidei* in *Cat.* 1b17 should be understood in its literal meaning, 'in species'. On such an interpretation, different genera which fall under the same higher genus are divided by differentiae which are not completely different, but different *in species*, although they are one in genus. This means that such genera are divided by differentiae which differ from each other in species, e.g. two-footed and four-footed (*a*) as differentiae of winged animals and (*b*) as differentiae of footed animals, but which are the same in so far as they belong to the higher genus, e.g. two-footed and four-footed as differentiae of animal (cf. Simpl. *in Cat.* 57,22–58,1 with Luna, 'Commentaire', pp. 473–4).

A later passage (14,16–23) will clarify how Herminus came to hold this view, by rejecting some previous interpretations of Aristotle's rule.

At 13,28–14,4 our author replies to Herminus that his interpretation is too restricted, because, by taking 'different genera' to mean merely genera not in a genus-species relation to each other, he has overlooked the fact that Aristotle illustrated his point with two genera, animal and knowledge, which are 'different' in a much more radical sense than that, a sense which in any case amounts to a more natural meaning of 'different'. Animal and knowledge differ not merely in the sense that they are not in a genus-species relation to each other, but (*pace* Herminus) in the sense that they cannot be ranked under any common genus (see 'not merely ... but', 13,30).

Our author's solution is the same as that found in Porph. *in Cat.* 83,4–10. And his position is very close to Alexander's view as stated in the first part of the essay *On the Specific Differentia*, where Alexander refers to his commentary on the *Categories*: see

Alex. Aphr. *De diff. I* [1] Rashed; and *in Top.* 112,14–24. Interestingly, Alexander's essay is likely to be directed against Herminus' view on differentiae: see Rashed, *Essentialisme*, pp. 104–22; also Barnes, *Porphyry*, pp. 348–50.

14,4-15. The author now moves to Boethus' interpretation of Aristotle's rule. As emerges from 14,9–15, Boethus had developed his view in the course of responding to a group of critics who argued that Aristotle's universal rule about things different in genus is false ('Those who consider the universal statement to be false': here *to katholou* means 'the universal statement', cf. Gal. *PHP* 2.5.85 and 91 = v. 259–60 K. = CMG 5.4.1.2, 144–6; Greg. Nyss. *De vita Mosis* 2.65.10; id., *In illud: 'tunc et ipse filius'* 12.17–18). They noted that Aristotle's universal rule in *Cat.* 1b16–20 is falsified by a subset ('some': 14,10) of 'things different in genus and not under one another', namely those whose differentiae (contrary to *Cat.* 1b16–20) are the same. The examples given are (1) triangles and quadrilaterals, two genera which are both divided by the differentiae equal-sided or unequal-sided; and (2) vices and virtues, which share the differentiae rational and irrational.

Boethus apparently concedes the exception that the critics have pointed out, but uses it constructively (as Aristotle himself does at *Top.* 144b20–5), to restrict the intended scope of the rule, rather than to falsify it. Aristotle's 'different in genus', he maintains, cannot have been meant to include genera that are 'akin' to each other (cf. 14,2–6), such as triangle/quadrilateral or virtue/vice. That is, he was using 'different in genus' as the *contrary* of 'the same in genus' (14,6–7), and therefore intended it to be understood as applying only to completely disjoint genera. It seems to follow that in Boethus' view, as apparently in our author's, the rule does not apply to syncategorematic genera. .

14,16-23. The author now resumes his exposition of Herminus' own interpretation. When Herminus is reported as saying that 'all such people' (14,16–17) have misunderstood Aristotle's rule, we must take him to be referring not just to Boethus but at the same time to the anonymous critics whom Boethus had quoted. What these predecessors all had in common was their belief that Aristotle's rule could not be successfully applied to genera that are akin, such as triangle and quadrilateral. In view of Herminus' own interpretation of the rule (13,20–8), we already know his main reply to these predecessors: contrary to their view, non-subaltern pairs of genera in a single category, and even in a single domain, such as triangle and quadrilateral, do fall under the rule, and their differentiae do differ, although not generically but only specifically. Our author does not bother to repeat that interpretative stance, but quotes the reply to Boethus that Herminus based upon it. That reply, at 14,16–20, is highly condensed, and is further obscured by a lacuna at a key point (see n. 58 above for some alternative completions), but one possible expansion of it might be as follows.

(1) 'Herminus too used to raise the same sort of doubt' [that is, he too used to ask how genera such as triangle and rectangle are meant to fit Aristotle's rule].
(2) 'But he says that all such people have completely missed the meaning of what is being said' [that is, both the anonymous critics and Boethus have misunderstood Aristotle],

(3) 'because of not having determined that these too' [i.e. co-ordinate genera such as triangle and quadrilateral, in addition to the more radically disjoint genera cited by Aristotle, such as animal and knowledge]
(4) 'are genera that are different' [that is, count as different genera under Aristotle's rule]
(5) '(for the doubt he raises is not about these)' [that is, cases such as triangle/quadrilateral are not among those on which Aristotle casts doubt at 1b20-4, where as possible exceptions to the 'different differentiae' principle he mentions only subaltern genera, and *not* co-ordinate subgenera]
(6) 'and not under one another, but both under another' [that is, co-ordinate subgenera are not under one another, being instead both under another genus; therefore they do after all conform to Aristotle's rule, which excludes only genera that are under one another].

What then follows at 20-3 is merely a completion of step 6 above, spelling out *what* genus triangle and quadrilateral are under, and likewise for vice and virtue.

The exchange recorded at 14,4-23 provides significant new evidence about post-Hellenistic debate on the *Categories*. It has no parallel in Simplicius. If our author is Porphyry, it is possible that Simplicius' direct source Iamblichus suppressed this development when rearranging the *Ad Gedalium* material.

14,23-30. The final reply to Herminus provides crucial evidence in support of Porphyry's authorship. For the author's proposed modification is virtually identical to Porphyry's thesis as paraphrased by Simplicius, *in Cat.* 57,22-58,14 (= 57F Smith), undoubtedly drawing it from the *Ad Gedalium*, since it has no parallel in Porphyry's short commentary. Nor is it paralleled in Alexander's extant works. Apparently our author aims to combine the merits of his previous solution at 13,3-14,4 (most probably that of Alexander's lost *in Cat.*), which takes full account of Aristotle's examples in the *Categories*, with those of Herminus' solution (13,20-8), which gave a more satisfying account of *tôi eidei*.

Both interpretations turn on Aristotle's specification that different genera must have differentiae that differ 'in species', but they understand it in different ways. For Herminus, the reference is to different species *of* differentia, for our author it is to the differentiae of different (e.g. animal) species: on the latter view, Aristotle's point is that the differentiae of the various species of knowledge, e.g. music and grammar, are different from the differentiae of the various species of animal, e.g. man, horse. Our author thus connects 'species' (*eidos*) at *Cat.* 1b17 with 'differentiae', rather than with 'different' (see Luna, 'Commentaire', pp. 497-8). It is unclear whether he raised the problem of how this explanation of *eidos* is compatible with his previous one (*eidos* = *logos*, 13,12-19). Possibly he sought to reconcile the two readings in the immediately following – and now lost – part of his work.

The Purpose of Porphyry's Rational Animals: A Dialectical Attack on the Stoics in *On Abstinence from Animal Food*[1]

G. Fay Edwards

In his treatise, *On Abstinence from Animal Food*, Porphyry argues at length in favour of the view that philosophers should be vegetarian. One of his central arguments, in Book 3 of the work, is that animals are rational like humans, and that this makes it unjust to kill them for food. According to popular scholarly consensus, this argument accurately reflects Porphyry's own psychological and ethical commitments regarding animals.

In this paper, however, I argue that Book 3 does *not* reflect Porphyry's own commitments. Instead, I suggest, it constitutes a dialectical attack on the Stoic position, arguing that the *Stoics* ought to believe that animals are rational, given their theory of rationality, and that, because of this, the *Stoics* ought to believe that it is unjust for humans to eat animals, given their theory of justice. In other words, Porphyry's argument is that, contrary to what the Stoics themselves believe, their own theories of rationality and justice entail vegetarianism.

Since Porphyry's own theories of rationality and justice differ, however, from their Stoic counterparts, I argue that Porphyry himself believes that it is unjust for philosophers to eat meat without believing that animals are rational. If I am right, then this will have enormous implications for scholarship on Porphyry, which regularly assumes the interpretation that I am rejecting.

The paper is split into three parts: In Part 1: The Consensus Interpretation, I outline the scholarly consensus on Book 3 alongside its *prima facie* plausibility. In Part 2: Theories of Justice, I distinguish between the Stoic and Porphyrian theories of justice, and argue that animal rationality has ethical implications only for the Stoic theory. Finally, in Part 3: Theories of Rationality, I distinguish between the Stoic and Porphyrian theories of rationality, and argue that Porphyry's evidence of animal capacities is only intended to make animals rational according to the Stoic account.

---

[1] Many thanks to Richard Sorabji, Peter Adamson, Julia Staffel, Ryan Platte, and Roshan Abraham for their help in completing this paper.

Part 1: The Consensus Interpretation

In Book 3 of *On Abstinence*, Porphyry argues that animals possess capacities for perception (*aisthêsis*),[2] memory (*mnêmê*),[3] pleasure (*hêdonê*),[4] pain (*lupê*; *algêdôn*),[5] the passions (*pathê*) more generally[6] (e.g. emotions and illness), and significant vocal utterance (*phônê sêmantikê*).[7] According to most scholars, he does so because he thinks that the presence of these capacities in animals proves the psychological thesis that:

PT: All animals are rational.

That is, that animals possess reason (*logos*) or have rational souls (*logikê psukhê*)[8] like humans (albeit to a lesser degree[9]).

Notice that, understood in this way, Porphyry rejects the standard Aristotelian line that humans alone are rational, and all other animals irrational.[10] This is apparently news to him, however, since he actually insists throughout Book 3 that Aristotle agrees with him.[11]

Porphyry argues in favour of **PT**, again, according to most scholars, because he thinks that the rationality of a creature has implications for ethics, endorsing an ethical thesis something like the following:

ET: If and only if X is rational, it is unjust for other rational beings to kill X for food.[12]

---

[2] 3.1.4, 3.8, 3.19.2, 3.21.4, 3.25.3. Where a text is not named in a reference, the reference is always to *On Abstinence*.
[3] 3.1.4, 3.10.3, 3.21.6, 3.22.2, 3.24.5.
[4] 3.22.4–5.
[5] 3.22.3. Cf. 3.21.7.
[6] 3.8.1, 3.19.2, 3.22.3–5, 3.7.2–7.
[7] 3.3–3.6. This list is not intended to be exhaustive, but to name the capacities that are most prevalent in Porphyry's Book 3 argument. He also appeals to the presence of virtue and vice (3.10–13, 3.22.8, 3.23.3–4) and skill (3.15) in animals.
[8] These three formulations are treated as equivalent in our texts and will thus be treated as such in this paper.
[9] Porphyry apparently supposes that rationality is not all-or-nothing, but a matter of 'more and less' (*mallon kai hêtton*; 3.7.1, 3.8.7). To my knowledge, there is no detailed account in the literature of precisely what it would mean for animals to be rational/possess rational soul to a lesser degree than humans, on Porphyry's understanding.
[10] Among other things, Aristotle denies animals reason (*logos*; *DA* 427b13, *Pol*. 1332b4–5, *DA* 428a23–4, cf. *EE* 1224a27) thought (*to phronein*; *DA* 427b7–9) intellect/intellection/an intellectual part (*nous*; *noêsis*; *to noêtikon*; *DA*, 429a5–8, 433a11–2, 414b18–9, *PA* 641b7), calculation (*logismos*; *DA* 433a11–2), and discursive thought (*dianoia*; *PA* 641b7, cf. *DA* 415a7–12).
[11] Aristotle is named in support of Porphyry's position on six occasions in Book 3 (3.6.5, 3.6.7, 3.7.1, 3.8.6, 3.9.5, 3.12.4) and appears nowhere else in *On Abstinence*. Indeed, even when not mentioned by name, his influence is evident – for example, compare 3.7.4–5 with *HA* 602a30-b5 and 631b19–32a14, and 3.2.2 with *Int*. 16a5–7.
[12] 'For food' because Porphyry seems to think that there are some circumstances under which it is permissible to kill animals e.g. in self-defence (2.4.2, 3.26.3).

Porphyry, then, is taken to believe that philosophers ought to be vegetarian because he believes that all animals are rational (**PT**), and that the killing of rational beings for food by other rational beings (such as humans) is unjust (**ET**).[13]

Notice that, understood in this way, Porphyry ought to believe that *all* humans should be vegetarian. This, however, is not what he maintains. Instead, he insists throughout *On Abstinence* that vegetarianism is only necessary for philosophers.[14]

Many scholars understand Book 3 in this way and take Porphyry to be committed to both **PT** and **ET** (or something like it[15]). Among them are Richard Sorabji,[16] Catherine Rowett,[17] Gillian Clark,[18] Stephen Newmyer,[19] Gary Steiner,[20] John Passmore,[21] Kerry Walters, and Lisa Portmess.[22] Since it is accepted by the majority of scholars, I refer to this reading as 'the consensus interpretation'.

The prevalence of the consensus interpretation is not hard to explain, for, at least at first glance, it seems well-supported by the text. For instance, in Book 3, Porphyry claims that his arguments 'demonstrate' (*epideiknusthai*; *deiknutai*) that 'animals are rational' (*logika onta ta zôia*)[23] and have 'rational souls',[24] and says that it is 'true' (*alêthês*) that reason (*logos*) can 'be seen in absolutely all animals'.[25] He also asserts that animals have been 'allocated the same soul' as humans,[26] and that they differ from us not in 'essence' (*ousia*), but only in the degree (*mallon kai hêtton*) to which they possess reason.[27] All of this speaks in favour of taking him to be committed to **PT**.

---

[13] Porphyry believes that PT and ET ought to make philosophers entirely vegetarian because he believes that all meat-eating involves the killing of an animal. He points out that no-one eats animals that have died naturally or savage animals that might justly be killed (3.18.2; 3.26.4).

[14] 1.27–28, 2.3.1, 2.4.3–4, 1.37.3, 4.18.8, 1.48.1–2, 1.52.2, 1.56.2, 4.6.1.

[15] It is rare for scholars to spell out, in the literature, exactly what they take Porphyry's commitments to be. However, they generally take him to believe that the rationality of animals makes it unjust for humans to kill them for food, which is, at least, very close to **ET**.

[16] Richard Sorabji, *Animal Minds and Human Morals* (London: Duckworth, 1993), p. 182.

[17] Catherine Rowett (formerly Osborne), *Dumb Beasts and Dead Philosophers: Humanity and the Humane in Ancient Philosophy and Literature* (Oxford: Oxford University Press, 2007), p. 228.

[18] Gillian Clark, *Porphyry, On Abstinence from Killing Animals* (London: Duckworth, 2000), p. 3; Gillian Clark, 'Animal Passions', *Greece & Rome* 47 (2000), 88–93, at 91.

[19] Stephen Newmyer, *Animals in Greek and Roman Thought: A Sourcebook* (London: Routledge, 2011), p. 108.

[20] Gary Steiner, 'Animal Rights and the Default of Postmodernism', in E. D. Protopapadakis, ed., *Animal Ethics* (Berlin: Logos Verlag, 2012), pp. 151–62, at p. 154, and Gary Steiner, *Anthropocentrism and Its Discontents: The Moral Status of Animals in the History of Western Philosophy* (Pittsburgh: University of Pittsburgh Press, 2005), pp. 104–11.

[21] John Passmore, 'Treatment of Animals', *Journal of History of Ideas* 36 (1975), 195–218, at 211.

[22] Kerry Walters and Lisa Portmess, *Ethical Vegetarianism: From Pythagoras to Peter Singer* (Albany: State University of New York Press, 1999), p. 36; Jonathan Barnes, *Porphyry, Introduction* (Oxford: Clarendon Press, 2003), p. 111; George. E. Karamanolis, *Plato and Aristotle in Agreement? Platonists on Aristotle from Antiochus to Porphyry* (Oxford: Clarendon Press, 2006), p. 268; Daniel A. Dombrowski, *Vegetarianism: The Philosophy Behind the Ethical Diet* (Amherst: University of Massachussetts Press, 1984), p. 116, all attribute **PT** to Porphyry, but do not comment on whether they take him to be committed to **ET** as well.

[23] 3.18.1. All translations of *On Abstinence* are Clark's, except where otherwise noted.

[24] 3.1.4. Cf. 3.7.1, 3.9.1, 3.23.2.

[25] 3.2.4.

[26] 3.26.1, 3.7.1. Cf. 3.8.8, 3.23.7–8, 3.23.3.

[27] 3.7.1, 3.8.7.

Furthermore, Porphyry says of animal rationality that 'once that is proved, we can reasonably ... extend justice to every animal,'[28] which, he seems to think, entails not killing them for food.[29] Conversely, he justifies the killing of plants for food by appeal to their *irrationality*.[30] Taking Porphyry to be committed to an ethical thesis like **ET** also makes good sense of why he argues for the rationality of animals (**PT**) in *On Abstinence* – for, in combination with **ET**, a psychological thesis like **PT** has vegetarian implications. All of this speaks in favour of taking Porphyry to be committed to **ET** also.

Despite its *prima facie* textual support, however, I shall argue that the consensus interpretation is incorrect on both counts. Porphyry, I shall argue, is committed neither to **ET** nor to **PT**, in that order.

Part 2: Theories of Justice

In order to understand the purpose of Porphyry's Book 3 argument correctly, it is important to recognise that it provides a response to an earlier Stoic argument,[31] reported by Porphyry in 1.4–6. This Stoic argument, in short, is that meat-eating is not unjust because animals are irrational. In reply, Porphyry appears to argue, in Book 3, that meat-eating *is* unjust because animals are *rational*. Since Book 3 constitutes a reply to the Stoics, let us begin by reviewing the Stoic position as Porphyry presents it.

The Stoic Theory of Justice

According to Porphyry, the Stoics maintain that justice 'includes' (*teinein*; *parateinein*) rational beings (*to logikon*) and excludes irrational beings (*to alogon*).[32] Since they also maintain that, as a matter of fact, all human beings are rational[33] and all non-human animals irrational,[34] their view is that justice includes all human beings and excludes all non-human animals.

Furthermore, Porphyry takes the Stoics to believe that rational beings are included in justice *because* they are rational (rather than because they possess another characteristic that is co-extensive with, or dependent upon, rationality), and irrational beings excluded *because* they are irrational. This is indicated in the opening passages of Book 3, where Porphyry says:

---

[28] 3.1.4. Cf. 3.18.1, 3.13.1.
[29] 3.26.4–5.
[30] 3.18.2.
[31] Porphyry actually identifies the argument as belonging to 'the Stoics and Peripatetics,' making no attempt to distinguish the two schools (1.6.3, cf. 3.24.6). Despite this, it is Stoic views that dominate the discussion, and that shall, therefore, be our primary focus.
[32] 1.4.1–2. Cf. 3.18.1; 3.12.1; 3.13.1; 3.22.7.
[33] Notoriously, human children are also irrational according to the Stoics, but are distinguished from animals by appeal to their *potential* for rationality.
[34] 1.4.2.

Since our opponents [i.e. the Stoics] say that justice includes (*parateinein*) only those beings that are like us and must therefore (*dia touto*) exclude animals that are irrational, let us ... demonstrate (*epideiknuntai*) that every soul is rational ... once that is proved, we can reasonably, even according to our opponents (*kai kata toutous*), extend justice to every animal.[35]

In this passage, Porphyry's claim that the Stoics think justice includes a creature only if it is *like* human beings in the relevant respect, and thus that it must exclude *irrational* animals, shows us that the requisite sense of likeness is the possession of rationality. This means that, as Porphyry understands the Stoic theory, a creature is included in justice *only if* it is rational (a necessary condition).

Furthermore, Porphyry's claim that a proof of animal rationality would, according to the Stoics, result in the inclusion of animals in justice, shows that he also takes them to believe that a creature is included *if* it is rational (a sufficient condition). Thus, Porphyry takes the Stoics to believe that a creature is included in justice if and only if it is rational (a necessary and sufficient condition).

If Porphyry succeeds in proving that animals are rational, then, he will also succeed in proving that, at least according to the Stoic theory, they must be included in justice. Thus, our next question is: What would it mean for animals to be included in justice, on the Stoic view?

Informative here is the Stoic *reductio ad absurdum* of the view that justice includes animals, as reported by Porphyry in 1.4–6. The argument goes: If justice included animals, and animals were treated as if they were 'appropriate' (*oikeios*) to humans,[36] then humans would have to 'spare' (*pheidesthai*)[37] and 'not harm' (*mê blaptein*; *diakeômetha ablabôs*) animals,[38] as with other human beings (i.e. other creatures that are included in justice). Were this the case, then it would be unjust for humans to make use of animals *for food*,[39] for labour on the land,[40] and in craft.[41] Since human life *qua* human *requires* that humans make use of animals in these ways, however, including animals in justice leads to the absurd consequence of making human life either impossible or necessarily unjust.[42] Therefore, justice must, instead, *exclude* animals,

---

[35] 3.1.4. trans. Clark slightly modified.
[36] 1.4.2.
[37] 1.4.3.
[38] 1.4.3; 1.5.2. The way the view is presented suggests that animals *can* be harmed by humans, but that this harm is permissible (as opposed to animals being *incapable* of being harmed due to their irrationality).
[39] 1.4.2. Since the Stoics maintain that death is not bad but 'indifferent' (Diog. Laert. 7.102 = A. A. Long and D. N. Sedley, *The Hellenistic Philosophers*, 2 vols (Cambridge: Cambridge University Press, 1987), hereafter LS, 58A4), it might seem puzzling for them to suppose that killing animals for food could 'harm' animals. Yet, since the Stoics also believe that bad things (e.g. injustice) harm (Diog. Laert. 7.103 = LS 58A5), this may not be so bizarre – all they need is a way of understanding harm that does not require viewing indifferents as bad.
[40] 1.4.2; 1.5.2; 1.6.2. Notice that this appears to make human slavery unjust. Cf. Diog. Laert. 7.121–2.
[41] 1.5.2.
[42] Humans would either justly 'live the life of beasts' (1.4.4), or they would unjustly live as humans (1.5.3). Both are absurd because a just human life must be possible due to the teleological ordering of nature.

which are 'inappropriate' (*allotrios*)[43] to human beings, and such actions towards animals are not, and cannot be, unjust.

Although the text is compressed, the argument, as I understand it, suggests that for a creature to be included in justice is for it to be an appropriate object of moral concern for (in Stoic terminology, for it to be *oikeios* to) other creatures that are included in justice, such that these others are required not to harm, but rather to respect its welfare in their actions (and *vice versa*). This *oikeios* nature of other individuals is recognised, according to the Stoics, in a process called *oikeiôsis*.[44] Now, the existence of such a requirement is what makes it *possible* for actions between these individuals to be just or unjust, on the Stoic view. In particular, it makes certain actions between them, such as the killing and eating of one individual by another, *unjust*.

Conversely, for a creature to be excluded from justice is for it not to be an appropriate object of moral concern for (in Stoic terminology, for it to be *allotrios* to) creatures that are included in justice, such that *there is no requirement* for these others not to harm, but rather to respect its welfare in their actions, and *vice versa*. This makes it *impossible* for any action between these individuals to be either just or unjust, on the Stoic view. In particular, the killing and eating of the excluded individual by one that is included in justice is not (and cannot be) unjust.

The Stoic claim that justice includes all human beings and excludes all non-human animals means, then, that it is possible for humans to act justly or unjustly only towards other human beings, and not towards non-human animals (and *vice versa*[45]). In particular, humans can kill and eat non-human animals without being unjust, on the Stoic view.[46]

With this in mind, we can see that were justice, instead, to *include* non-human animals, then animals *would* be appropriate objects of moral concern for human beings, on the Stoic view. If this were the case, then not only would it be *possible* for humans to act justly or unjustly towards animals, but it would be positively *unjust* for humans to *make use of animals for food*, according to the Stoics.

Putting this together with our earlier observation that, for the Stoics, a creature is included in justice if and only if it is rational,[47] we can see that, for them, it will be unjust for humans to kill and eat animals if and only if animals are rational – that is, at least as Porphyry presents them, the Stoics are committed to **ET**. Thus, should Porphyry succeed in proving to the Stoics that all animals are rational (**PT**), then he will also succeed in forcing them to conclude that the human use of animals for food is *unjust*, and that all humans ought to be vegetarian, according to their very own theory of justice.

---

[43] 1.4.3.
[44] Plutarch, *On Stoic Contradictions* 1038B. This is why Porphyry claims that 'the followers of Zeno make *oikeiôsis* the origin of justice' (3.19.2). Cf. 3.22.6–7 and 3.26.9.
[45] That is, animals can behave justly or unjustly towards humans either. Notice that the Stoic position does not seem to allow for one-sided relationships, such that one party is an appropriate object of moral concern for the other, *but not the other way around*. Cf. 1.6.1.
[46] Of course, human actions towards animals can be unjust *towards other human beings* e.g. when a man kills another's ox for fun.
[47] This suggests that, at least as the view is presented by Porphyry, there is a fact of the matter about whether a creature is *oikeios* or *allotrios* to humans – *oikeios* if rational, *allotrios* if not.

Porphyry's Theory of Justice

The pertinent question, of course, is whether Porphyry endorses a theory of justice similar enough to that of the Stoics to make him committed to a principle like **ET** himself. Yet, this is not something that can simply be assumed, since different ancient schools adopt different theories of justice, and, in non-Stoic theories, rationality does not always play the same central role.

Take, for example, the Epicurean theory, as reported by Porphyry in 1.7-12. This theory holds that a creature is included (*exagein*) in justice if and only if it has *made a contract* with us not to harm, or be harmed by, us.[48] The Epicureans, like the Stoics, maintain that it is morally permissible for humans to kill and eat animals,[49] but, for them, this is because they believe that animals *have not made a contract* of mutual non-harm with us, and not simply because they lack rationality.[50]

In order to convince the Epicureans that it is unjust for humans to kill and eat animals, then, it would need to be shown, not simply that animals are rational (**PT**), but that they have made a contract of mutual non-harm with us, which is violated when we kill them for food. The Epicureans, in other words, are *not* committed to **ET**. The question is, is Porphyry?

Interestingly enough, whenever Porphyry speaks of rationality as the criterion for inclusion in justice, he is careful to identify this as the *Stoic* position. Recall, for example, his words at the beginning of Book 3, where he says only that it is *according to our opponents* that animal irrationality excludes, and animal rationality includes, animals in justice.[51] The same disclaimer appears again later in the book, when Porphyry asks:

'If, *as our opponents say*, justice includes (*parateinein*) rational beings, why should justice ... not also include animals?'[52]

Indeed, nowhere in *On Abstinence*, nor in any of his other works, does Porphyry endorse the view that a creature is included in justice if and only if it is rational.

Instead, in the closing sections of Book 3 of *On Abstinence*, Porphyry is openly critical of the Stoic theory of justice, and endorses, in its place, a Platonic theory. He says:

Those who have thought to derive justice from the *oikeiôsis* of human beings have, it seems, failed to recognise the peculiar character of justice: for ... justice lies in restraint and harmlessness towards everything that does not do harm. *This is how* (*outôs*) the just man thinks, *not that other way* (*ouk ekeinôs*); so justice, since it lies in harmlessness, extends as far as *animate* beings (*hôs diateinein tên diakiosunên*

---

[48] 1.12.5. Cf. Epicurus, *Key Doctrines* 32-3 = Diog. Laert. 10.150-1 and Lucretius 5.1011-27 = LS 22K.
[49] 1.12.1 (Eating animals); 1.11.2-3 and 1.12.6 (killing animals).
[50] The Epicurean position, in *On Abstinence*, is that rationality is *necessary* for contractual agreements (1.12.6), but not sufficient, since human beings can be excluded from justice despite their rationality (1.10.3; Cf. 3.13.1, and Epicurus, *Key Doctrines* 32 = Diog. Laert. 10.150).
[51] 3.1.4.
[52] 3.18.1 (trans. Clark slightly modified. My italics.)

kai akhri tôn empsukôn keimenên en tôi ablabei). That is why (*dio*) the essence (*ousia*) of justice is that the rational rules (*en tôi to logikon arkhein*) over the irrational, and the irrational follows (*hepesthai de to alogon*). For when the rational rules and the irrational follows it is absolutely necessary (*pasa anankê*) for a human being to be harmless (*ablabê*) towards anything whatever. When the passions ... have withered (*marainesthai*), and the rational part exercises the rule that is appropriate for it, assimilation (*homoiôsis*) to the Greater follows at once.[53]

In this passage, Porphyry tells us that the Stoic theory of justice – identified by reference to the doctrine of *oikeiôsis* among human beings – is incorrect. Rather than requiring harmlessness towards *rational* beings (that is, beings with rational souls i.e. humans), as on the Stoic view, Porphyry claims that justice, in fact, requires harmlessness towards *animate* beings (that is, beings with sensitive souls i.e. humans and animals) – at least, towards those animate beings that do us no harm.[54]

This tells us two important things about Porphyry's position: First, Porphyry rejects *rationality* as the criterion for inclusion in justice, and supposes, instead, that justice includes *animate* beings, whether or not they are rational. Thus, being just, for Porphyry, requires not harming harmless *animate* beings – that is, beings with a sensitive soul – rather than not harming only *rational* beings, as on the Stoic theory; second, it tells us that Porphyry *does* believe that justice requires vegetarianism, for, on his view, eating meat *entails* harming harmless animate beings,[55] which he clearly rejects as unjust. Porphyry's position, then, seems to be that eating animals is unjust, but apparently not because animals are *rational*.

Yet, Porphyry's account of his own theory does not end there. Instead, he goes on to clarify that, on his view, justice is not, in *essence*, harmlessness towards harmless animate beings, but is itself a *state of soul*[56] in which the rational part 'rules over' the irrational part.[57] This is, not coincidentally, precisely the definition of justice that Porphyry endorses in the *Sentences*[58] – the only other place in his extant works where he discusses justice at any length.

What, then, we might wonder, is the relationship between actions and soul states, according to Porphyry? As I understand it, Porphyry's position is that those actions

---

[53] 3.26.9–11.
[54] Notice that harmlessness is the common thread in all three theories of justice that appear in *On Abstinence*. For the Stoics, justice requires harmlessness towards rational beings; for the Epicureans, towards those beings who are part of our contractual community; and for Porphyry, towards those animate beings that do not do us harm.
[55] Porphyry tells us that killing animals harms them by depriving them of soul (2.12.3), and that only harmless animals are killed for food (3.12.5, 3.26.4).
[56] Although one might initially suppose that Porphyry's claim is that justice consists in rational *beings* (i.e. humans and gods) ruling over irrational *beings* (i.e. the non-human animals), the final sentence of this quotation and the passages that follow make clear that he has in mind the relationship between different parts of the same individual soul.
[57] Both ideas derive from Book 4 of Plato's *Republic*, where justice is defined as the rule of the rational over the irrational parts of the soul (*Rep.* 441E), and the just man is said never to do harm (*Rep.* 335D-E).
[58] *Sent.* 32.13–14; 32.28–9. Cf. 40.75–7. All translations of the *Sentences* are John Dillon's, taken from L. Brisson, ed., *Porphyre, Sentences*, 2 vols (Paris: Vrin, 2005), unless otherwise noted.

which necessarily result from[59] a just state of soul are just, while those which result from an unjust state of soul are unjust.[60] This is what I believe he means to indicate by declaring that harmlessness is 'absolutely necessary' when one's soul is correctly ordered. If this is right, then it means that the justice of an action is determined by reference to the *internal psychic state of the agent* – and not, as the Stoics would have it, by reference to psychological facts about the patient.[61] Harmlessness towards harmless creatures – and its accompanying vegetarianism – is *just*, then, for Porphyry, because it is an action that *results from* the possession of a just state of soul, and has nothing to do with the nature of animals as rational beings. That is, Porphyry himself is not committed to ET.

Understanding Porphyry's theory of justice in this way allows us to lay to rest a worry that troubles advocates of the consensus interpretation, such as Gary Steiner,[62] Johannes Haussleiter,[63] and Richard Sorabji.[64] The worry is that, if Porphyry believes that it is unjust for humans to kill animals for food because animals are rational (ET) – that is, that there is something *about the animals* that makes eating them morally wrong – then he ought to think it necessary for *all human beings* to be vegetarian.[65] Yet, as noted earlier, this is not what Porphyry maintains. Instead, he insists throughout On Abstinence that *only philosophers* need to be vegetarian,[66] and says that other individuals, be they 'athletes of the body ... soldiers ... sailors ... orators ... [or] those who have chosen the life of public affairs',[67] can go on eating meat.[68] Indeed, Porphyry even explains why the ancient lawgivers did not make meat eating illegal,[69] by appealing to

---

[59] In fact, this is a simplification of Porphyry's position, since, as I understand it, actions which *result in* a just soul state are also just, for Porphyry. For our purposes, however, this is unimportant.

[60] For a similar understanding of justice in Plotinus see E. K. Emilsson, 'Plotinus and Plato on Soul and Action', in R. Barney, T. Brennan, and C. Brittain, eds, *Plato and the Divided Self* (Cambridge: Cambridge University Press, 2012), pp. 350–67, at pp. 355–7. Notice that it is, in principle, possible for an individual to be vegetarian without being just (e.g. if meat were unaffordable), on this understanding of Porphyry's position.

[61] Notice that, unlike the Stoics, Porphyry's theory makes one-sided relationships possible, such that human actions can be just or unjust towards animals *without* animal actions towards humans being capable of the same (e.g. if animals were to lack a rational part, and thus incapable of possessing a just/unjust soul state). This could allow Porphyry to respect the Platonic and Aristotelian claims that animals do not partake of justice (Plato, *Protagoras* 322C, 323C-D, 324A, 325A, 351B; Aristotle, *Pol.* 1253a15), whilst allowing that human actions towards animals can, nevertheless, be unjust.

[62] Steiner, *Anthropocentrism*, p. 105.

[63] Johannes Haussleiter, *Der Vegetarismus in der Antike* (Berlin: Töpelmann, 1935), p. 326.

[64] Sorabji, *Animal Minds*, p. 182.

[65] Notice that the same problem would exist if Porphyry's position were that it is unjust to eat animals because they are *animate*. We only escape this difficulty once we recognise that, for him, justice is determined primarily by the soul state of the agent.

[66] *Supra* 14.

[67] 1.27.1. The exemption of athletes and soldiers, in particular, is repeated at 2.4.3. This is Porphyry's attempt to incorporate into a single, coherent system Pythagoras' recommendation that athletes eat meat (1.26.3 and Porphyry's *Life of Pythagoras* 15) and Plato's tolerance of meat in the city (*Rep.* 373C) and recommendation that soldiers be fed meat (*Rep.* 404A-D).

[68] Sorabji, *Animal Minds*, p. 182, tries to solve this problem by making the unattractive move of suggesting that Porphyry is simply not serious about restricting this diet to philosophers.

[69] This is a response to an earlier anti-vegetarian argument offered by the Epicureans, which argues that ancient lawgivers allowed the eating of (certain) animate creatures because this was advantageous (1.12.1). Cf. 2.3.2.

the fact that they were making laws for ordinary individuals on how to live 'according to nature' (*kata phusin*), rather than for the philosopher on how to live the superior, godly life.[70]

By recognising that Porphyry's own theory of justice does *not* commit him to ET, however, and realising that, for him, it is not the nature of the animals being eaten, but the soul state of the agent doing the eating, that makes eating meat unjust, we can easily and consistently explain his restriction of a vegetarian diet to philosophers.[71] All we need do is recognise that, according to Porphyry, there is *more than one* just soul-state.

In the *Sentences*, Porphyry recognises two different kinds of just soul-state – viz. 'civic' (*politikai*) and 'purificatory' (*kathartikai*) justice.[72] Though both are defined as a soul state in which the rational part rules over the irrational,[73] civic justice is said to involve only 'assigning measures to the irrational part (*hê alogia*) and bringing about a moderation of the passions (*metriopatheia*)',[74] whereas purificatory justice is said to go further and to bring about a complete *absence* of passion (*apatheia*).[75] The difference, it seems, is in the degree to which the rational part is in control of the irrational part. The soul state that is civic justice, Porphyry explains, enables 'the performance of actions that are in accordance with nature (*kata phusin*)',[76] and leads to *harmlessness* towards one's neighbours (*ablabê tôn plêsion*),[77] but only purificatory justice leads to 'assimilation (*homoiôsis*) to god'.[78] Of the two, it is purificatory justice which is characteristic of the philosopher.[79]

This doctrine of different levels of justice opens up the possibility of the same action being just at the civic level of ordinary human beings, but unjust at the purificatory level of the philosopher, when it results from a soul state in which there is only moderation, rather than absence, of the passions.

This all fits well with *On Abstinence*. In particular it explains why, in the closing passages of Book 3, Porphyry distinguishes between not merely two kinds of individual (viz. the just and unjust), but *three*.[80] The first individual is one in whom the irrational part overpowers the rational (*to alogon kratounta*) and who is motivated solely by his passions.[81] As a result, he is harmless towards his children and spouse, but harmful

---

[70] 1.28.3–4. For a similar contrast between what is in accordance with nature (and suitable for ordinary people), and what is divine (and suitable for philosophers) see both 1.28.3–4 and Porphyry, *Letter to Marcella* 25.1–6. Cf. *de Antro* 35.

[71] Notice, too, that Porphyry's theory of justice, when combined with his belief that animals are irrational/lack a rational soul-part, allows him to respect Platonic and Aristotelian claims that animals do not partake of justice (Plato, *Protagoras* 322C, 323C-D, 324A, 325A, 351B; Aristotle, *Pol.* 1253a15), whilst maintaining that actions involving animals can, nonetheless, be unjust.

[72] There are actually *four* levels of virtue in *Sent.* 32, but the latter two are inaccessible to embodied human souls (*Sent.* 32.95–7). For a similar doctrine of levels of virtue in Plotinus, see *Ennead* 1.2.

[73] *Sent.* 32.13–14 (civic justice) and *Sent.* 32.28–9 (purificatory justice).

[74] *Sent.* 32.77 (my italics). Cf. 32.6; 32.29–30.

[75] *Sent.* 32.75.

[76] 32.84–5 (trans. Dillon slightly modified).

[77] *Sent.* 32.7–9.

[78] *Sent.* 32.32–3.

[79] *Sent.* 32.15.

[80] 3.27.2.

[81] Cf. 1.43.3.

towards all others. The second individual is one in whom the rational part controls the irrational and keeps its passions in check. As a result, he is harmless not only towards his close relatives, but also to 'fellow-citizens ... strangers and all human beings'.[82] Finally, the third individual is one in whom the rational part dominates the irrational to such an extreme degree that the passions of the irrational part wither away altogether.[83] As a result, he is harmless not simply to all human beings, but to all harmless animals, i.e. he is vegetarian.[84] This last individual is the most like god,[85] since he most closely approximates god's complete harmlessness.[86]

Understood in light of the distinctions in the *Sentences*, we can see that, in these passages, Porphyry is describing unjust, civically just, and purificatorily just individuals, respectively, who, due to differences in their soul states, also exhibit different behaviours. Notice, in particular, that, although the civically just person extends his harmlessness further than the unjust individual, he does not extend it beyond human beings to other animals. In other words, civic justice, as a soul state in which the passions are merely moderated, does not result in vegetarianism. On the other hand, purificatorily just individuals – i.e. philosophers – do extend their harmlessness to non-human animals, and purificatory justice, as a soul state in which the passions are absent, *does* result in vegetarianism. What Porphyry tells us about the ancient lawgivers, then, is that, when they permitted the consumption of meat, they were making laws which promoted civic, as opposed to purificatory, justice.

In sum, then, Porphyry's theory of justice has it that the justice of an action is determined solely by reference to the soul state of the agent, with just actions resulting from just soul states and unjust actions from unjust soul states.[87] This theory, combined with Porphyry's belief that there is more than one just soul state, allows him to maintain that the very same action can be just at one level and unjust at another. In particular, it allows him to maintain that civic justice is perfectly compatible with being a meat-eater, while purificatory justice (i.e. that of the philosopher) entails vegetarianism.[88]

---

[82] 3.26.11.
[83] Cf. 1.44.1 and *Sent.* 32.138–9.
[84] 3.26.10. Porphyry seems undecided as to whether this individual harms plants, however – sometimes he suggests that plants, unlike animals, are not harmed when used for food (3.18.2, 3.27.2; Cf. 2.12.3, 2.24.2), sometimes that, though plants *are* harmed, this harm is necessary and, therefore, permissible (3.18.3, 3.27.3).
[85] Becoming like god is, of course, the philosophic ideal in Plato's *Theaetetus* (176B).
[86] 3.26.11. He is also more like god than the others, according to Porphyry, because he needs less than they do, and god needs nothing (3.27.3–4, 3.26.11).
[87] Notice that this makes it possible for an individual to be vegetarian, but not just, if their vegetarianism does not result from the correct state of soul.
[88] I often think that Porphyry believes the Stoics get many things right *at the lower level*, and that their major mistake is not to recognise the existence of the higher levels in his Platonist system. In this case, Porphyry's civic justice is similar to Stoic justice in that both require harmlessness towards all and only human beings. The Stoic mistake, however, is to fail to recognise the existence of a higher level of justice which requires more of the philosopher.

Justice: Conclusions

In this section, we have seen that, according to the Stoic theory of justice as Porphyry presents it, meat-eating will be unjust for human beings if and only if animals are rational (**ET**). Yet, we have also seen that Porphyry's own theory of justice differs from that of the Stoics, such that meat-eating is unjust for philosophers, on his view, simply because of the soul state from which it results, and has nothing to do with the rationality of animals. In short, Porphyry takes the *Stoics* to be committed to **ET**, but is not himself so committed.

Porphyry, then, does not argue for the rationality of animals (**PT**) in *On Abstinence* because of what it would mean *for him*, but because of what it would mean *for the Stoics*.[89] This is why he claims, at the start of Book 3, only that proof of animal rationality would result in the inclusion of animals in justice 'according to our opponents'.[90]

Part 3: Theories of Rationality

Of course, Porphyry could still believe that all animals are rational – that is, possess reason, or have rational souls – despite himself believing that animal rationality has no implications for ethics. In other words, he could be committed to **PT**, without being committed to **ET**, and the consensus interpretation could still be half correct.

To determine whether this is, in fact, the case, let us begin by briefly surveying the evidence that Porphyry presents in Book 3. We will then be in a position to consider what *exactly* this evidence is supposed to show.

Porphyry's Evidence

As mentioned earlier, Porphyry's evidence, in Book 3, takes the form of arguments purporting to demonstrate the presence of various capacities in animals. Although not an exhaustive list,[91] the capacities with which he is mostly concerned are perception (*aisthêsis*), memory (*mnêmê*), and the passions (*pathê*) – e.g. pleasure, pain, illness, and emotions such as anger, fear, envy, and distress[92] – as well as the capacity for significant vocal utterance (*phônê sêmantikê*). Important to Porphyry's argument is the claim that animals possess *exactly the same* capacities for these things as are present in human beings, and not just mere analogues of the human capacities,[93] and he appeals both to

---

[89] So too, Porphyry does not claim that it is permissible to eat plants 'because they appear to be quite incompatible with reason', (3.18.2) because this reflects his own view, but instead to answer the Stoic worry from 1.6.3, that any criterion for including animals in justice would also include plants (and thus, absurdly, leave nothing for humans to eat). Porphyry's point is that, the Stoic commitment to **ET** can be used to commit them to excluding only meat from their diet.

[90] *Supra* 35.

[91] Space denies a full exposition and examination of all of Porphyry's arguments, which are extensive. Instead, I limit myself to tackling the capacities which are most prevalent in Book 3.

[92] 3.19.2, 3.22.3–5.

[93] See especially 3.22.5. Cf. 3.8.6–7.

empirical observation and to the expert testimony of Aristotle to convince his audience that this is the case.[94]

Regarding perception, memory, and the passions, for example, at the start of Book 3, Porphyry speaks of his intention to show that 'every soul is rational in that it shares in *perception* and *memory*',[95] and, throughout the book, repeatedly claims that animals and humans are genuinely alike in both their 'perceptions' and 'the passions of the soul'.[96] In an attempt to establish that animals perceive in exactly the same way that humans do, he argues that 'it is not the case that humans alone taste flavours and see colours, that their sense of smell perceives scents, their hearing perceives sounds, and their sense of touch perceives hot and cold and whatever else is tactile, as if animals do not do likewise'.[97] As part of his argument, Porphyry appeals to the similarities between animal and human bodies (they have similar sense organs and flesh, he says, as well as similar bodily fluids[98]) which, he thinks, makes them apt to experience the same affections.[99] Differences in animal and human bodies, Porphyry argues, may make them more or less difficult to affect, but do not make the affection of an entirely different character.[100] So too, Porphyry argues that animals really do become pleased, pained, angry, afraid, and distressed in the same way as humans – to believe otherwise, he says, is quite simply 'contrary to the obvious'.[101]

Porphyry also argues that animals possess the capacity for significant utterance, which he defines as 'voice signifying with the tongue the internal passions, that is, those in the soul (*phônê dia glôttês sêmantikê tôn endon kai*[102] *kata psukhên pathôn*)'[103] – a definition which is clearly intended to recall Aristotle's *On Interpretation*.[104] As evidence of this animal capacity, he points to the fact that 'animals are heard to speak (*phthengesthai*) differently when they are afraid, when they are calling, when they are asking to be fed . . .',[105] and that experienced animal handlers can tell when an animal is 'hungry or thirsty or tired or in heat', that it is searching for something, has found something, or is calling to its young.[106] He tells us that 'the lion shows (*dêloi*) by roaring that it is threatening, the wolf shows by howling that it is suffering, and the bleating of

---

[94] For Porphyry's appeals to Aristotle see *supra* 11.
[95] 3.1.4.
[96] 3.8.1. Cf. 3.8.6, 3.8.8.
[97] 3.8.1.
[98] 3.7.2, 3.25.3.
[99] 3.7.3–7. Particularly peculiar is Porphyry's appeal to the fact that animals experience the same illnesses as humans, and respond in the same way under the same physical conditions (e.g. both human females and mares miscarry when they smell a light that has been snuffed out!). How this is supposed to demonstrate animal rationality is somewhat perplexing.
[100] 3.8.6–7. Porphyry uses the phrase *mallon kai hêtton* for the difference in of degree of bodily affection. Cf. *supra* 9.
[101] 3.21.6–7, 3.22.3–5.
[102] I modify Clark's translation, taking *kai* to be epexegetic, and bringing out Porphyry's use of *pathê*.
[103] 3.3.2. Cf. 2.34.2.
[104] Aristotle, *Int.* 16a4: 'Spoken sounds (*ta en têi phônêi*) are symbols of passions (*pathêmata*) in the soul.'
[105] 3.4.2. Cf. Aristotle's claim that 'all animals have a special cry for mating' (*HA* 536a14).
[106] 3.5.6.

the sheep alerts the shepherd to what they need'.[107] Animals, he says, can also understand when human voices are 'angry or friendly or calling ... hunting or wanting something or giving something' and can respond appropriately in each case.[108]

With this survey of Porphyry's evidence in mind, our next question is: What *exactly* is this evidence supposed to show?

The Stoic Theory of Rationality

Clearly Porphyry's evidence is supposed to show that animals are rational in some sense – after all, Porphyry claims that his arguments 'demonstrate' that 'animals are rational',[109] as we saw earlier (Part 1). Yet, just as different ancient schools have different theories of justice, they also have different theories of *rationality* – that is, they adopt different positions on what it means to be rational or have a rational soul. This means that evidence that makes animals rational according to one theory, may not make them so according to another. Let us begin, then, by considering whose theory of rationality is at play in Book 3.

Interestingly enough, before Porphyry presents his evidence of animal capacities, he first outlines the *Stoic* position on reason, in a passage which runs as follows:

> According to the Stoics (*kata tous apo tês stoas*) there are two kinds of reason (*logos*), the internal (*endiathetos*) and expressive (*prophorikos*), and again correct (*katôrthômenos*) and faulty (*hêmartêmenos*) reason. So it is proper to state exactly which of these animals lack. Is it only correct reason, and not reason altogether (*haplôs*)? Or is it reason in all respects (*pantelôs*), both the internal and that which proceeds to the outside? They [i.e. the Stoics] appear to predicate complete deprivation (*sterêsis*) of reason, not just of correct reason, for in the latter case even animals would not be irrational but rational, in the same way as, according to them (*kat' autous*), almost all human beings are. For, according to them (*kat' autous*), there have been one or even two wise men, in whom reason is correct, and the rest are all bad ... even though all alike are rational ... [The Stoics] say that all the other animals without exception are irrational, meaning by 'irrationality' complete deprivation of reason.[110]

---

[107] 3.5.7.
[108] 3.6.1. Porphyry does offer examples of more impressive, Dr. Doolittle-style conversations between humans and animals (e.g. 3.3.6–7), but apparently does not believe them, saying: 'Let us pass over these stories because of our natural trait of incredulity' (3.4.1). He also mentions the ability of certain animals, e.g. parrot and hyenas, to repeat human words (3.4.4–5), which is a common anti-Stoic example (cf. Sextus Empiricus, *Adv. Math.* 8.274), but does not appear to demonstrate an ability to signify their internal state in the same way as these other examples. Cf. Philo, *On Animals* 98, Philoponus, *in DA* 495,5–27.
[109] *Supra* 23.
[110] 3.2.1–4.

In this passage, Porphyry tells us that the Stoics distinguish between internal and expressive reason,[111] and between the sage's correct and the non-sage's faulty reason, and that they deny all of these to animals. Although he does not explain the relationship between the divisions, it seems best to think of correct and faulty reason as two ways in which internal and expressive reason can *manifest* in humans, such that non-sages possess internal and expressive reason *of a faulty sort*, sages of a correct sort.[112]

Porphyry apparently relates the Stoic position, at the beginning of Book 3, in order to be clear about what he needs to show to make animals rational like humans according to the *Stoic* theory,[113] and he is keen to point out that he does not need to demonstrate the presence of the more demanding 'correct' reason in animals in order to make them rational like ordinary humans, on the Stoic view. Porphyry is so empathic that these are *Stoic* views that he is expounding, however, that we might already wonder whether what would need to be true of animals to make them rational like humans *on his own view* is different.

Unfortunately for us, this short passage is everything that Porphyry tells us about the Stoic theory of reason. To generate a richer picture of their theory, then, I turn briefly to other sources.

According to numerous ancient authors, the Stoics are empiricists about reason. They believe that human infants begin life with completely irrational souls which are later transformed into completely rational souls (that is, souls without any irrational parts)[114] by means of perceptual experience.[115] Transformation occurs when repeated perceptual exposure to instances of the kinds in the world (e.g. 'white', 'human', 'dog') leads the human soul to acquire 'conceptions' (*ennoiai*; *prolêpseis*) – i.e. generic grasps – of these kinds.[116] So, for example, a conception of 'human' may be something like 'two-legged, upright, mortal animal,' of dog 'four-legged, barking, mortal animal.'[117] According to our sources, it is a set of conceptions like these which constitutes reason,

---

[111] Sextus, by contrast, reports that the Stoics grant certain animals, e.g. parrots, expressive reason (*prophorikos logos*) and claim that these animals differ from humans because they lack internal reason (*endiathetos logos*) alone (*Adv. Math.* 8.274-6). However, most other sources agree with Porphyry that the Stoics deny expressive reason to all animals (e.g. Seneca, *De Ira* 1.3.8, Philo, *On Animals* 98-99, Varro, *LL* 6.56 = *FDS* 512, cited in Barnes, *Introduction*, p. 57, Herodianus, *Reliquiae GG* 3.1.108, 9-16 Lentz = *FDS* 671).

[112] This would explain why Porphyry goes on to argue, *contra* the Stoics, that expressive reason (3.3.1) and internal reason (3.7.1 onwards) are both present in animals, but does not present a separate argument in favour of their possession of faulty reason.

[113] This is unsurprising, since it is only if he convinces the Stoics that animals are rational, that he will commit them to including animals in justice.

[114] Galen, *PHP* 4.3.2-5 (= LS 65K), 5.6.34-7 (= LS 65I), 7.1.12-5 (= LS 29E), Plutarch, *On Moral Virtue* 446F-447A (= LS 65G). Galen recognises Posidonius as an exception, since he divides the soul into rational and irrational parts.

[115] Augustine, *City of God* 8.7 (= LS 32F), Cicero, *On the Laws* 1.30; *Acad.* 2.21 (= LS 39C); 2.30 (= LS 40N). Porphyry seems to have something like this notion of rationality in mind when he says, in Book 3, that 'memory ... is of prime importance in the acquisition of reasoning (*logismos*)' (3.10.3).

[116] Diog. Laert. 7.54.

[117] For more on Stoic conceptions, see Michael Frede, 'The Stoic Conception of Reason', in K. Boudouris ed., *Hellenistic Philosophy* (Athens: International Association for Greek Philosophy, 1994), vol. 2, pp. 50-63, and H. Dyson, *Prolepsis and Ennoia in the Early Stoa* (Berlin: De Gruyter, 2009), esp. pp. 118-120.

for the Stoics,[118] and the possession of such a set which makes the human soul rational. Presumably, something like this is what is meant by the 'internal' reason of *On Abstinence*.

The difference between the rationality of the Stoic sage ('correct' reason) versus that of non-sage human beings ('faulty' reason) seems to be in the accuracy and technical detail of the conceptions that are present in the soul. Only the sage, it seems, possesses truly accurate technical understandings of each kind's essence, while ordinary human beings possess under-developed and inaccurate versions of the same.[119]

Once the human soul is rational, the Stoics maintain that *all* of its experiences – even its perceptions, memories and passions – are also rational (i.e. belong to the rational soul).[120] Such experiences are rational, it seems, in that they exhibit conceptual structure and propositional content. Thus, human perceptions are rational because they have contents such as 'this is a human being', or 'that dog is white', which is made possible by the possession of the corresponding conceptions, 'human', 'dog', and 'white' – and the same goes for all other human experiences. It is this structuring of human experiences that makes it possible for them to be expressed in language,[121] on the Stoic view – the 'expressive' reason of *On Abstinence* – that is, the Stoics believe that internal reason is necessary for expressive reason.

Importantly, in *On Abstinence*, the Stoics actually *define* the capacities for perception, memory and the passions as *rational* capacities, which require conceptual and propositional content (i.e. internal reason).[122] So, for example, they define memory as the 'comprehension of a proposition (*axiôma*) in the past of which the present tense was comprehended by perception',[123] and the passions as 'bad judgements (*kriseis*) and beliefs (*doxai*)'.[124] This makes perception, memory and the passions *impossible* for irrational beings.

Non-human animals are, of course, irrational, for the Stoics. Given their theory of reason, this means that animals *lack* conceptions (internal reason) – even the under-developed and inaccurate kind (faulty reason). Consequently, all animal experiences are

---

[118] Plutarch, *On Common Conceptions* 1058E-F, Galen, *PHP* 5.3.1 (= LS 53V), Aetius, 4.11.4 (= LS 39E4), Iamblichus *ap.* Stobaeus, *Ecl.* 1,318,1–4 (= *SVF* 1.149). Although it might seem strange for reason to consist in something like a body of information about the world, Frede, in 'The Stoic Conception of Reason', suggests that conceptions grant their possessor inferential capacities more akin to what we might think of as rationality, e.g. a conception of human enables its possessor to posit premises such as 'if x is a human, then x is mortal'.

[119] This is Dyson's interpretation (*Prolepsis and Ennoia*, pp. 48, 64–5).

[120] Diog. Laert. 7.51 (= LS 39A6); Stobaeus, *Ecl.* 2.86.17 (= *SVF* 3.169); Plutarch, *On Moral Virtue* 446F (= LS 65G1); Galen, *PHP* 5.6.37 (= LS 65I4).

[121] Sextus, *Adv. Math.* 8.70 (= LS 33C); Galen, *PHP* 2.5.11–13 (= LS 53U). For a competing interpretation of the Stoic position see Richard Sorabji, 'Perceptual Content in the Stoics', *Phronesis* 35 (1990), 307–14.

[122] Notice that this makes the pre-rational "perception" of children not really perception at all.

[123] 3.22.2.

[124] 3.22.3. Cf. Andronicus, *On Passions* 1 (= LS 65B), Galen, *PHP* 4.2.10–18 (= LS 65D), Plutarch, *On Moral Virtue* 446F-447A (= LS 65G).

irrational (i.e. lack conceptual and propositional content),[125] and cannot be expressed in language (expressive reason). This latter is why the Stoics deny animals the ability to speak, in *On Abstinence*, and say, instead, that they can only *quasi*-speak.[126] So too, putting this together with the Stoic decision to *define* the capacities for perception, memory, and the passions as *rational* capacities (i.e. capacities which exhibit conceptual and propositional content), leads them to claim that animals cannot really perceive, remember and emote, but that they only *quasi*-perceive, *quasi*-remember, and *quasi*-emote.[127]

Now that we have a clearer picture of the Stoic theory of rationality, our next question is: How similar is the Stoic theory to Porphyry's own?

Porphyry's Theory of Rationality

The answer, in short, is *completely dissimilar*. To begin with, Platonists like Porphyry are *innatists* about reason. Unlike the Stoics, they divide the soul into rational and irrational parts, and claim that all human beings begin life in possession of both parts – although the rational part only becomes accessible to them later in life. Thus, Iamblichus reports the canonical Platonist position as follows:

> The followers of Plato and Pythagoras say that reason (*logos*) is present in the newly-born but is obscured by external influences.[128]

This he contrasts with the Stoic position, saying that:

> The Stoics claim that we are not immediately born with reason, but that reason is gathered together from perceptions and impressions.[129]

Porphyry, unsurprisingly, adopts the standard Platonist line on the matter, claiming that 'the rational soul (*to logikon*) exists in a way even in babies',[130] and that 'although the human race in the first stage of life is held down in an irrational condition (*en*

---

[125] Frede, 'The Stoic Conception of Reason'; Charles Brittain, 'Common Sense: Concepts, Definition and Meaning in and Out of the Stoa', in D. Frede and B. Inwood, eds, *Language and Learning* (Cambridge: Cambridge University Press, 2005), pp. 164–209; Brad Inwood, *Ethics and Human Action in Early Stoicism* (Oxford: Clarendon Press, 1985); Julia Annas, *Hellenistic Philosophy of Mind* (Berkeley: University of California Press, 1992), all adopt this sort of interpretation of the Stoic view. Though see Charles Brittain, 'Non-Rational perception in the Stoics and Augustine', *Oxford Studies in Ancient Philosophy* 22 (2002), 253–308, for the suggestion that the Stoics may have allowed *quasi*-conceptions to animals to account for the complexity of animal behaviour. Cf. Seneca, *De Ira* 1.3.6–7.

[126] 3.22.5.

[127] 3.22.5. Other sources also record this Stoic position. e.g. Seneca says that animals do not possess memory proper (*Ep.* 124.16), Philo that animals can only *quasi*-cheat because cheating is rational (*On Animals* 83), Varro that animals cannot speak (*loqui*), but only quasi-speak (*ut loqui*; LL 6.56 = FDS 512, cited in Barnes, *Introduction*, p. 57), and Galen says that 'Chrysippus... takes passions away from the irrational animals' precisely because he thinks that the passionate part of the soul is the same as the rational part (*PHP* 5.6.37 = LS 65I4).

[128] Iamblichus, *DA* 15 *ap.* Stobaeus, *Ecl.* 1,317,20.

[129] Iamblichus *ap.* Stobaeus, *Ecl.* 1,318,1–4 (= *SVF* 1.149).

[130] *Ad Gaurum* 12.5.2–4. Cf. *Ad Gaurum* 12.1.3–12.3.2.

alogiai... katiskhêmenos)... this race was believed to be rational from the beginning'.[131] The rational soul, Porphyry believes, is present in humans from the start, but only becomes accessible to them later on.[132]

It is possible for human infants to possess reason from birth, on Platonist conceptions, precisely because, unlike the Stoics, they maintain that reason does *not* develop from perceptual experience.[133] In fact, according to Porphyry, it is *impossible* for reason to develop from perception – thus, he complains in *Ad Gaurum*:

> 'The ignorant... Stoics... have turned things upside-down and dared to generate the better from the worse... they make... the soul responsible for perception and impulse the offspring of nature, and again the rational [soul] (*hê logikê*) the offspring of these.'[134]

Porphyry's complaint is that the Stoic position – characterised as one in which the rational soul is generated by the perceptual soul – is impossible because the rational soul is *better* than the perceptual soul, and what is generated must be *worse* than its generator (a standard Neo-Platonic principle).[135] For Porphyry, the rational soul must, instead, generate the perceptual soul,[136] and not the other way around.

Indeed, Porphyry apparently supposes that reason and perception have completely opposite activities, and that the former is completely independent of the latter. Thus, in his *Commentary on Ptolemy's Harmonics*, he says:

> Perception (*hê aisthêsis*) apprehends things approximately (*holoskherôs*) and to the extent that the sense object makes an impression (*tupôsêi*) upon it... while reason (*ho logos*)... is found to have obtained a prior grasp of the whole of what is being judged (*proeilêphôs heurisketai hapan to krinomenon*) and to be such as to possess accurately within itself the form (*ekhôn to eidos par' heautôi akribôs*) of what is investigated – more accurately than when it is observed among sensible objects. And so reason actually supplies what is missing from it [viz. the form supplied by perception] and corrects the fault (*to hêmartêmenon euthunei*).[137]

Although this passage is difficult, the stark contrast between reason and perception is clear. Reason is presented as something which possesses complete and perfect knowledge of the forms that are imperfectly encountered in perception,[138] *before* they

---

[131] Porphyry, *Against Boethus, ap.* Eusebius, *Preparation for the Gospel* 11.28.2–3 (= fr. 242F Smith).
[132] *Supra* 130.
[133] This is despite the fact that perception plays a role in 'rousing the rational part to actuality' (*Ad Gaurum* 12.5.1–4) – clearly an attempt to incorporate Plato's theory of recollection into the Neo-Platonic system.
[134] *Ad Gaurum* 14.3.1–7.
[135] *Ad Gaurum* 14.3.8. Cf. *Sent.* 13.1–2.
[136] See *Abst.* 1.29–30, where this is exactly what Porphyry maintains.
[137] Porphyry, *in Ptol. Harm.* 14,31–15,5 translated by H. Tarrant, *Thrasyllan Platonism* (Cornell: University Press, 1993), slightly modified. Cf. Porphyry, *in Ptol. Harm.* 15,10–20 (trans. Tarrant, p. 138).
[138] For more on Porphyry's doctrine of immanent forms see Riccardo Chiaradonna, 'Porphyry's Views on the Immanent Incorporeals', in G. Karamanolis and A. Sheppard, eds, *Studies on Porphyry* (London: Institute of Classical Studies, 2007), pp. 35–49.

are so encountered. As a result, it is capable of correcting the inadequate grasp of the forms that is achieved by perception. This is made possible, it seems, by reason's direct access to non-perceptual versions of the forms, which it contains 'within itself',[139] while perception has only indirect access to inferior sensible forms, which are external to it.[140]

As I understand it, Porphyry's view is that reason accurately grasps the *essences* of the kinds it encounters in the sensible world (e.g. human, dog, white), because it has direct access to the Platonic forms, viewed as pure essences of kinds which embody no accidental features. By contrast, perception has only indirect access to sensible forms which necessarily embody both essential *and* accidental features.[141] This means that perception itself cannot distinguish essential from accidental features. Instead, it is because reason has access to, for example, a pure human (the Platonic form) that we can recognise that laughter is not part of the essence of human, even though all and only sensible humans laugh.[142]

If this is correct, it looks as if possessing reason, or a rational soul, for Porphyry, involves possessing complete and accurate knowledge of the Platonic forms – i.e. the essences of kinds – and that humans are rational insofar as they all possess such knowledge (although such knowledge may remain latent in some human beings[143]). This makes Porphyry's account of human reason look more akin to Stoic *correct* reason, and as if what makes humans rational *for Porphyry* is more demanding than what makes humans (at least non-sage humans) rational for the Stoics.[144]

Porphyry's Platonist division of the soul into distinct parts also marks a great point of divergence from Stoic theory. For, whereas the Stoics suppose that the human soul is entirely rational, for Porphyry, the human soul is divided into rational and irrational parts, which are responsible for different activities.[145] This has the effect of making some activities rational, others irrational, for Porphyry, even in human beings.

In particular, while the rational part of the soul is responsible for contemplation of the Platonic forms, on Porphyry's view, and remains 'pure from all perception and unreason' even whilst embodied,[146] the *irrational* part (*hê alogia*; *to alogon*[147]), animates the body and is responsible for all of the living capacities (*dunameis*) that require

---

[139] This is Porphyry's adoption of the Plotinian doctrine that for a subject to obtain complete and unerring cognition of its object, it must contain (i.e. be identical with) its object. For more on this see E. K. Emilsson, *Plotinus on Sense Perception* (Cambridge: Cambridge University Press, 1988).
[140] Cf. *Sent.* 43.14–45.
[141] e.g. Blackness is always present in sensible ravens, but is not part of the essence of a raven (Porphyry, *Introduction* 19,18–20).
[142] Porphyry, *Introduction* 12,17–9.
[143] *Ad Gaurum* 12.2.3–12.3.2.
[144] Plotinus uses *orthos logos* to refer to 'that very highest in us' i.e. the rational soul, as opposed to the lower soul (*Enn.* 4.4.17.22).
[145] See esp. 1.30.
[146] 1.30.6.
[147] *hê alogia*: 1.30.7, 1.31.2, 1.33.3, 1.34.3, 1.43.2–3, 1.44.1, 3.27.2, 3.27.7, *Sent.* 32.77, *Ad Gaurum* 6.2.9, 6.3.1. Cf. *Enn.* 3.2.2.34, *Enn.* 1.1.4.3–4; *to alogon*: *Abst.* 1.34.1, 1.45.2, 3.27.2, *Sent.* 32.129, *Ad Gaurum* 16.4.7. Cf. *Enn.* 4.4.28.64, *Enn.* 4.4.43.7.

bodily organs in order to function.[148] These capacities include perception (*aisthêsis*),[149] perceptual impressions (*phantasiai*), memories (*mnêmai*), and opinions (*doxai*),[150] as well as passions (*pathê*)[151] such as pleasure,[152] pain,[153] illness, fear, desire, anger, love, grief, and envy.[154] For Porphyry, then, in contrast with the Stoics, these capacities are irrational – that is, belong to the *irrational* soul – even in human beings.[155]

Despite his thoroughly negative view of perception and what it can accomplish, Porphyry maintains, in his *Commentary on Ptolemy's Harmonics*, that 'conceptions' (*ennoiai*) of kinds (presumably, imperfect and inaccurate grasps of forms) *can* be acquired by means of perceptual experience, as the Stoics maintain (faulty reason).[156] The difference is that, for Porphyry, these are formed by Aristotelian *imagination* (*phantasia*) – which is, for him, a lower soul capacity – and are not constitutive of reason. This could, I think, explain his complaint, in the *Sentences*, that the Stoics downgrade reason to the level of imagination.[157] If Porphyry thinks that conceptions are the province of imagination, however, then it seems possible that he might think, *contra* the Stoics, that conceptual and propositional content is *not* the mark of rationality, but is possible in beings which possess imagination alone.

It should be clear from the preceding discussion that the Stoic and Porphyrian theories of rationality differ radically from one another. While the Stoics believe that reason can be empirically acquired, and consists in a set of under-developed conceptions of kinds (faulty reason), Porphyry believes that such conceptions are the province of imagination alone, and that genuine reason, which is innate, consists in complete and accurate knowledge of essences of kinds (something more akin to Stoic correct reason). Again, whereas, for the Stoics, the entire human soul and all of its

---

[148] Porphyry is very clear that this lower soul-part, in itself, *lacks* reason. Thus, he tells us that, though it may be 'brought into order by reason (*hupo logou rhuthmizetai*)' and is an 'offspring of reason,' the irrational part is not itself 'able to engage in rational activity (*logikôs* ... [*en*]*ergein*)' (*Ad Gaurum* 16.4.7–5.1). Indeed, it cannot have 'rational thoughts (*logismoi*),' and is 'in its own essence (*kata tên oike*[*ian*] *ousian*) unable to move rationally (*logikôs kineisthai*)' (*Ad Gaurum* 6.2.9–3.1).

[149] 1.30.7, 1.31.1, 1.33.3, 1.38.4, 1.39.2, 1.41.5. Cf. *Enn.* 6.7.3.26–8, *Enn.* 1.1.4.1–13.

[150] 1.32.3, 1.34.7. Note that Plotinus recognises memory in both the higher and lower soul to allow for memories of both perceptual and intelligible phenomena. For this doctrine see *Enn.* 4.3.27.

[151] 1.30.1, 1.31.1, 1.33.4, 1.34.4, 1.36.2.

[152] 1.33.2.

[153] 1.33.2.

[154] 1.34.7. Similar lists feature in Porphyry's *Sentences* and *Ad Gaurum*. For example, in the *Sentences*, the passions are said to belong to the irrational soul (32.77), and perception (32.107), pleasure (32.113), pain (32.115), anger (32.117), fear (32.120), and desire (32.124), are all named as things which are not part of our nature as rational souls. Cf. *Ad Gaurum* 12.3.12–12.4.1, 12.7.1–12.7.8, as well as Iamblichus' report that Plotinus 'removes from the soul the irrational powers (*hai alogoi dunameis*): those of perception (*hai aisthêseis*), impression (*hai phantasiai*), memory (*hai mnêmai*), and reasoning (*hoi logismoi*). He includes only pure reason (*ho katharos logos*) in the pure essence (*ousia*) of soul,' Iamblichus, *DA* 13 ap. Stobaeus, *Ecl.* 1,369,20–3 (trans. Finamore and Dillon slightly modified).

[155] Porphyry is incredibly negative about such capacities in *On Abstinence*, e.g. 1.30.7, 1.33.3, 1.38.4.

[156] Porphyry, *in Ptol. Harm.* 14,10 (trans. Tarrant, *Thrasyllan Platonism*, p. 120).

[157] Porphyry complains that, for the Stoics, 'the status of intellect (*nous*) [i.e. human reason or rational soul] and imagination (*phantasia*) [was] one of name only; for the imaginative faculty in a rational animal was, in their view, intellection (*noêsis*) ... it was logical for them, seeing as they made everything depend on matter and the nature of body, to make intellect depend on these also,' (*Sent.* 43.36–40; trans. Dillon slightly modified).

experiences are rational, Porphyry divides the human soul and its experiences into the rational and irrational. In particular, whereas, for the Stoics, perception, memory and the passions proper are rational capacities (i.e. belong to the rational soul), for Porphyry, they are irrational capacities (i.e. belong to the irrational soul).

Now that we have an idea of how the Stoic and Porphyrian theories of rationality compare, let us turn back to Porphyry's evidence, in Book 3 of *On Abstinence*, to determine what exactly this evidence is supposed to show.

Porphyry's Evidence Revisited

Central to Porphyry's Book 3 argument, remember, is his claim that animals possess *exactly the same* capacities for perception, memory, and the passions as are present in human beings. As we have seen, however, for Porphyry, such capacities are *irrational* – that is, belong to the *irrational* soul – even in human beings. Thus, it seems extremely unlikely that the presence of such capacities in animals would commit Porphyry himself to thinking that all animals are rational (**PT**).[158]

Instead, I suggest, Porphyry intends this evidence to prove that all animals are rational (**PT**) according to the *Stoic* theory of rationality. His argument, as I understand it, goes something like this:

Premise 1: Perception, memory, and the passions are rational (viz. belong to the rational soul), according to *Stoic* theory.

Premise 2: Animals possess perception, memory and the passions (as per empirical evidence and the expert testimony of Aristotle[159]).

Conclusion: Animals are rational, i.e. have rational souls (**PT**).

Since Porphyry himself does *not* agree with the Stoics that perception, memory and the passions are rational (i.e. belong to the rational soul), however, he himself can grant these capacities to animals, *without* supposing that animals are rational. That is, he can endorse **premise 2** without endorsing the argument's **conclusion**. As before, Porphryy does not offer such an argument because of what it would mean *for him*, but because of what it would mean *for the Stoics*.

There are dialectical-sounding passages, in Book 3, which suggest that something like this is, indeed, what Porphyry intends. For example, he says:

---

[158] Indeed, Porphyry frequently claims, in his logical works, that animals are *irrational*. For more on this, see G. Fay Edwards, 'Irrational Animals in Porphyry's Logical Works: A Problem for the Consensus Interpretation of *On Abstinence*', *Phronesis* 59 (2014), 22–43.

[159] Aristotle says that all animals experience pleasure, pain and desire (*epithumia; orexis*; *DA* 414b3–6. Cf. *DA* 432b6–7), and that some have imagination (*DA* 428a23–4) and memory (*Mem.* 450a13–14). In *Sense and Sensibilia*, he tells us that 'the most important attributes of animals ... are, manifestly, attributes of soul and body in conjunction, e.g. perception, memory, passion, appetite and desire in general, and, in addition, pleasure and pain. For these ... belong to all animals' (436a7–10). Cf. *Post. An.* 99b35–6 and *Metaph.* 980a27, where perception is granted to all, and memory to some, animals.

> Since every animate creature is perceptive by nature (*hoti pan empsukhon empsukhon aisthêtikon euthus einai pephuken*) ... it is not plausible to require that animate nature should have a rational (*logikon*) and an irrational (*alogon*) aspect – not when one is debating with people who think that nothing shares in perception unless it also shares in understanding (*pros anthrôpous dialegomenos mêthen oiomenous aisthêseôs metekhein ho mê kai suneseôs*).[160]

That is, since animals are perceptive by definition (as per Aristotle[161]), and since perception is a rational capacity (requires 'understanding'), according to the Stoics, the Stoics must admit that all animals are rational (**PT**) – or, in the language of the passage, that 'animate nature' has only a 'rational aspect'.

In another passage with a similar dialectical feel, Porphyry tells us that:

> Our opponents [i.e. the Stoics] grind this out every time in their Introductions, defining a project as an indication of completion ... memory as comprehension of a proposition in the past of which the present tense was comprehended by perception ... There is none of these that is not rational, and all exist in animals.[162]

The point here, I take it, is that the *Stoics* define these capacities in such a way as to make them rational, and thus that, since these capacities really *do* exist in animals, the *Stoics* ought to admit that animals are rational (**PT**). The same sort of move is made with the passions, at 3.22.3–5, which are rational according to *Stoic* theory, and which Porphyry maintains really *do* exist in animals.[163]

Although more research is needed in this area, I would suggest that Porphyry can *agree* with the Stoics that these capacities have conceptual and propositional content (Stoic internal reason),[164] whilst *disagreeing* that such content makes these capacities rational – his belief that it is *imagination* which forms conceptions opens the way for this position. If this is the case, then his disagreement with the Stoics is not just a matter of terminology, but a real difference in doctrine – for Porphyry supposes that animal experiences have the conceptual and propositional content that the Stoics deny, but does not believe that this makes those experiences *rational*. What would make them rational, on Porphyry's view as I understand it, would be something like their being informed by the innate knowledge of the Platonic forms which is possessed by reason.

Turning next to Porphyry's evidence of significant vocal utterance in animals, this is clearly designed to show that animals possess the expressive reason that is denied to

---

[160] 3.21.3–4 (trans. Clark slightly modified).
[161] *Sens.* 436b11–13, *Metaph.* 980a27, *DA* 427b7–8; 433b27–30; 434a30-b1.
[162] 3.22.2.
[163] Cf. the argument from Strato that, since we can sometimes see and hear things that we do not notice, thought (*phronein*) or intellection (*noein*) is necessary for perception (3.21.8–9). This is swiftly followed with the comment: 'But let us suppose that perception does not need intellect (*nous*) to do its job' (3.22.1).
[164] We might think that Porphyry's treatment of perception as a *krisis* (*in. Ptol. Harm.* 16,16–19) or *doxa* (*Ad Gaurum*, 4.9.4–5) supports something like this view. Cf. Plotinus, *Enn.* 3.6.1.2, 4.3.3.23, 4.3.26.8, 4.4.22.30–3, 4.4.23.37–43, 4.6.2.17, 4.9.3.26–7, 4.4.6.14.

them by the Stoics, and to make them rational according to the Stoic theory. Notice, however, that the vast majority of Porphyry's examples of animal communication are of a rather rudimentary sort. Generally, animals are not presented as having human-like *conversations*, but, instead, to be capable of signifying that, say, they are pained by something, as when a dog whimpers over a thorn in its paw, or that they are afraid of something, as when the same dog barks gruffly at a stranger. Yet, it is difficult to see how this sort of rudimentary ability to signify 'the passions of the soul' would require reason, as *Porphyry* understands it.

In fact, Porphyry grants exactly the same kind of basic communication to new born humans in *Ad Gaurum* (notice that the very same verb – *phthengesthai* – is used of both),[165] where he says:

> The infant utters sounds (*phthengesthai*) without signs (*asêma*)[166] … but nevertheless signifies (*episêmainein*) what causes it pain (*ta lupounta*) through gestures (*phantasiai*) and crying.[167]

This passage is striking because Porphyry, as we have seen, holds that the rational soul of human infants does not become accessible to them until later in life, which means that this sort of basic communication does *not* require access to a rational soul, on Porphyry's view.[168]

Nor is Porphyry alone in granting this sort of rudimentary communicative ability to animals – Boethius and Ammonius, in their commentaries on Aristotle's *On Interpretation*, both do the same. Boethius, for example, says that:

> Dumb animals, too, utter some spoken sounds which signify. The barking of dogs signifies their anger, another softer sound indicates their pleasure.[169]

And Ammonius, likewise, grants animals the ability to signify the 'passions and dispositions of the soul',[170] saying that:

> A dog by his bark signifies the presence of a stranger.[171]

---

[165] e.g. 3.3.7, 3.4.2, 3.4.5. Cf. Aristotle, who uses the verb *phthengesthai* to describe the songs of birds (*HA* 618a5, 632b17), and the cry of a baby (*HA* 587a27).
[166] I take the point here to be that babies do not use *words*, which are, in Aristotle's language, 'significant by convention'.
[167] *Ad Gaurum* 12.4.7–10 (trans. Wilberding).
[168] Once more, it seems as if, on Porphyry's view, the capacity for this sort of significant utterance might be explained by the possession of imagination. See, for example, 3.5.1–2, where the ability to respond when called seems to be attributed to *phantasia*, and *Ad Gaurum* 6.3.5–7, where it is implied that animals are receptive to the farmer's voice due to their possession of *phantasia*. Notice, also, that the human infant's communicative ability (*supra* 163) is linked to *phantasiai*, although Wilberding translates 'gestures'.
[169] Boethius, *in Int.* 54,21–5. Another example he gives is that 'the neighing of a horse reveals a searching for a companion horse,' *in Int.* 59,14.
[170] Ammonius, *in Int.* 31,2.
[171] Ammonius, *in Int.* 30,23.

Strikingly, both authors compare these significant animal sounds to the tears, shouts, groans, and lamentations of human beings,[172] which, they maintain, are similarly apt to signify pleasure or displeasure, shock or surprise. Indeed, Ammonius even compares them to noises made by children who have not yet learnt to speak, saying that 'the vocal sounds of irrational animals resemble these in being uttered by them now excitedly, now gently and with a certain peaceful disposition',[173] which is rather striking given the passage in Porphyry's *Ad Gaurum*.

That these two authors consider this kind of capacity for communication limited, however, is shown by the fact that they distinguish it from the ability to use *words* (*onomata*), which, they say, belongs to humans alone. The difference, both Ammonius and Boethius maintain, is that words are significant 'by convention', animal noises and the sorts of human noises just mentioned, significant only 'by nature'.[174] The higher-level capacity for genuine conversation is, on their view, inaccessible to the non-human animals.

Porphyry's evidence for significant vocalisation in animals is then, I suggest – just like his evidence of animal perception, memory, and passions – intended to commit the *Stoics*, and not Porphyry himself, to the belief that animals are rational (**PT**). His argument, it seems, proceeds in something like the following way:

Premise 1: Voice significant of the passions of the soul (Stoic expressive reason) is rational (viz. requires a rational soul), according to *Stoic* theory.

Premise 2: Animals possess voice significant of the passions of the soul (as per empirical evidence and the expert testimony of Aristotle).

Conclusion: Animals are rational, i.e. have rational souls (**PT**).

Since Porphyry himself does *not* believe that the kind of significant vocal utterance in question requires a rational soul, however, he himself can grant this capacity to animals, *without* supposing that animals are rational.

Now, some scholars, such as Gillian Clark[175] and George Karamanolis,[176] have accused Porphyry of departing from Aristotle in granting significant vocal utterance to animals in *On Abstinence*, despite his claims to the contrary. Yet, once we recognise that Porphyry is granting only a very limited capacity for communication to animals, we can see why he takes Aristotle to be in perfect agreement with him. After all, Aristotle tells us, in the *Politics*, that voice, as a signifier (*sêmeion*) of pleasure or pain, is present in non-human animals,[177] and, in *On Interpretation*, that both animal and human sounds 'reveal something' (*dêlousi ti*).[178] As long as Porphyry is not intending to grant

---

[172] Boethius, *in Int.* 54,1–2.16–21, Ammonius, *in Int.* 31,24.
[173] Ammonius, *in Int.* 30,25–30.
[174] Boethius, *in Int.* 56,18–20, Ammonius, *in Int.* 31,1–2.
[175] Clark, *On Abstinence*, n. 381, suggests that Porphyry is too keen to focus on Aristotelian texts that are 'unusually sympathetic' to animals.
[176] Karamanolis, *Plato and Aristotle in Agreement?*, p. 268, says that 'Aristotle ... clearly denies language in animals, and Porphyry is misleading when he implies the opposite'.
[177] *Pol.* 1253a10–14.
[178] *Int.* 16a28.

animals the ability to use *words* and have *conversations* in the same way that humans do, there is no reason to suppose that he is granting animals a more advanced capacity than is granted to them by Aristotle.

Although somewhat speculative, I would suggest that Porphyry adopts a similar position to Boethius and Ammonius concerning the difference between animal and human communicative abilities. Boethius, after all, tells us that his own commentary on *On Interpretation* closely follows Porphyry's own commentary on the same,[179] which is clearly being recalled in the early passages of Book 3 of *On Abstinence* when Porphyry defines expressive reason. If I am correct, then Porphyry's position will be that, although animals and humans both possess the ability to signify the passions of their souls using naturally significant sounds, only humans have the more advanced ability of using *words* significant by convention (which seems to require knowledge of the forms, on Porphyry's account[180]). Porphyry, I would suggest, thinks that this option, which is available to him,[181] is unavailable to the Stoics, who were of the opinion that even human words were *naturally* significant,[182] and who denied the existence of the Platonic forms.[183] That is, Porphyry supposes that the Stoics have no way of distinguishing between the rudimentary communicative abilities of animals, and the genuine language of human beings.

In sum, none of Porphyry's evidence, in Book 3, seems anywhere near advanced enough to show that animals possess the sort of innate knowledge of the Platonic forms that looks to be constitutive of reason, on Porphyry's view. What we have here is an insistence that lowly and limited capacities for perception, memory, and the passions, alongside a rudimentary ability to signify the passions of one's soul, somehow requires a rational soul in animals. This looks bizarre for a Platonist with such a high bar for what constitutes rationality. However, once we recognise that Porphyry takes the Stoics to *downgrade* reason to the level of imagination, we can see why he supposes that evidence which makes animals rational according to *Stoic* theory need not make them rational according to his own.

If I am right, of course, the question arises concerning what we are supposed to make of Porphyry's claims, encountered in Part 1 of this paper, that his arguments 'demonstrate' that 'animals are rational'[184] have 'rational souls',[185] and possess reason,[186] and that they have been 'allocated the same soul' as humans.[187]

---

[179] Boethius, *in Int.* 7,5–6.
[180] 'When the voice takes over the soul's image (*eikôn*) for articulation in speech and brings it into accord with both the archetypal forms themselves and the forms in matter that participate in them. And thus the image of reality is again produced from the intelligible in a form accessible to sensation – through hearing', Porphyry, *in Ptol. Harm.* 14,24–27 (trans. Tarrant, *Thrasyllan Platonism*, p. 135). Cf. Aristotle's claim, in *Politics* 1253a14–19, that only human language 'reveals (*dêloun*) . . . the just and unjust', and Plato's denial that animals can speak like humans in *Phaedrus* 249B because it requires knowledge of the Platonic forms.
[181] Porphyry apparently endorses a conventional link between 'words' and what they signify (*Letter to Anebo, ap.* Iamblichus, *de Myst.* 7.5.1–6).
[182] Origen = LS 32J. Philo, *De opif. mundi* 148, and *Quaest. in Genes* 1.20; Origen, *Contra Celsum* 1.24.
[183] *Sent.* 42.18–20.
[184] 3.18.1.
[185] 3.1.4. Cf. 3.7.1, 3.9.1, 3.23.2.
[186] 3.2.4.
[187] 3.26.1, 3.7.1. Cf. 3.8.8; 3.23.7–8; 3.23.3.

On my view, in these passages, Porphyry is saying something a little more nuanced than it might, at first, seem. He is saying that his arguments demonstrate that animals are rational, have rational souls, or possess reason, in exactly the same way as humans do, *when reason is understood as the Stoics understand it*. This is why he clarifies the Stoic position on reason at the beginning of Book 3. Since Porphyry believes, however, that the Stoics are wrong about what reason consists in, he supposes that evidence that makes animals rational according to the *Stoic* theory, fails to make them rational according to his own. Finally, animals have been 'allocated the same soul' as humans, for Porphyry, insofar as they possess the same *irrational* soul – which is to say that they possess exactly same capacities for affection (perception, memory and the passions) as humans do.

Rationality: Conclusions

In this section, we have seen that the Stoic and Porphyrian theories of rationality differ from one another in significant respects, and that Porphyry's evidence looks designed to show that animals are rational only according to the *Stoic*, and not according to his own, more demanding theory. That is, Porphyry's argument looks like a dialectical attack on the *Stoic* position, which attempts to commit the *Stoics* to **PT**, even though Porphyry is not himself so committed.

Conclusion

In this paper, I have argued that the consensus interpretation of Book 3 of *On Abstinence* is incorrect. On my understanding, Porphyry believes neither that the rationality of animals is what makes it unjust for philosophers to kill animals for food (**ET**), nor that all animals are rational (**PT**). Instead, the purpose of his argument, in Book 3, is to prove that all animals are rational, according to the *Stoic* theory of rationality, and that this makes it unjust to kill animals for food, according to the *Stoic* theory of justice. In other words, Porphyry's argument is a dialectical attack on the Stoic position, which attempts to establish that *Stoic* theories of rationality and justice require vegetarianism.

Much more remains, of course, to be said about the topics that are raised in this paper. More of an explanation is needed, for instance, concerning why Porphyry himself believes that philosophers should be vegetarian, if this belief has no basis whatsoever in the rationality of animals.[188] So too, Porphyry's views concerning the various capacities that appear in Book 3 – viz. perception, memory, the passions, and significant utterance – needs more in-depth discussion, along with a detailed study of how Porphyry's evidence affects the Stoic position – if it does at all. Finally, since much of Book 3 is inspired by other authors, such as Plutarch, it may be fruitful to ask how

---

[188] This is a question that I attempt to answer in G. Fay Edwards, 'Food for Thought', in Peter Adamson and G. Fay Edwards, eds, *Animals* (Oxford: Oxford University Press, forthcoming).

innovative Porphyry is really being when he attacks the Stoic position in the way suggested.

In other words, our work on Porphyry's *On Abstinence* has only just begun. This paper should be viewed, then, not as a final word on the matter, but as a first attempt at clarifying Porphyry's own commitments and style of argument in this intriguing text, which opens the matter up for further debate.

10

Universals Transformed in the Commentators on Aristotle[1]

Richard Sorabji

Are Plato's Ideas Universals?

Aristotle regarded Plato's supreme substances, his Ideas or Forms, as being universals, as opposed to particulars, whereas he himself treated universals as only secondary substances, or as not deserving the title of substances at all. I shall start with his treatment of Plato's Ideas. He says that Plato's postulation of Ideas grew out of Socrates' search for definitions which provided not mere instances of some kind of thing, but a formula which applied universally to every instance of the kind.[2] He added that Platonists made Plato's Ideas universal (*katholou*).[3] One of his objections to Plato's Ideas was that they were meant to explain the coming into being of things. But to explain coming into being, you need a trigger (*to kinêson*), whereas Ideas were meant to be unchanging, so as to serve as objects of definition, and so are not suitable as triggers.[4]

If we skip from Aristotle (384–322 BCE) to three of the late Neoplatonists, Syrianus (died 437 CE), Proclus (*c.* 411–85 CE) and Simplicius (wrote after 529 CE). Simplicius says that the Platonic Idea is common (i.e. universal) as a cause, not as a common nature. Before him, Syrianus and his pupil Proclus had explained further why the Idea is not some nature common to and shared with the particulars that fall under it. The particulars do not have merely a name in common with each other, so that they are 'homonymous', or ambiguous, like river bank and money bank in English. Nor at the opposite extreme do they have name and definition in common, so that they are in Aristotle's terms 'synonymous'.

---

[1] This paper revises my Introduction to the translation of Philoponus, *in Cat.* by Riin Sirkel, Martin Tweedale, and John Harris (London: Bloomsbury, 2015), which in turn superseded my 'Universals Transformed: The First Thousand Years after Plato', in P. F. Strawson and Arindam Chakrabarti, eds, *Universals, Concepts and Qualities* (Aldershot: Ashgate, 2006), pp. 105–25. I am very grateful to Riccardo Chiaradonna for giving me comments based on his extensive knowledge of the subject.
[2] Aristotle, *Metaph.* 1.9, 991b3–7.
[3] Aristotle, *Metaph.* 8.1, 1042a15; 13.9, 1086a32–3.
[4] Aristotle, *Metaph.* 1.9, 991b3–7.

As Syrianus puts it first,[5] Ideas are not synonymous with (do not share the same definition as) things down here. Nor are they homonymous with them in any chance sense, but only in the way that a model and cause is related to an image of itself. Proclus puts this by saying that particulars are related to the relevant Idea *aph' henos* and *pros hen*, that is, by being derived from and related to a single thing.[6] A simple example from Aristotle of this relationship is that a medical man and a medical instrument are both related to the art of medicine, but are defined differently, one being defined as a practitioner of, and one as a tool for practising, the art. And neither is defined as being the art of medicine, nor is it defined in the same way as the art of medicine. Thus they are neither synonymous at one extreme, nor fully homonymous like 'bank' and 'bank' at the other. The intermediate option is that their meanings are associated by *diverse* relations to and derivations from a single thing (*pros hen* or *aph' henos*), the medical art.[7] Proclus applied this distinction of Aristotle's to how particulars relate to Ideas. Something remarkable has happened here. The sharpest Neoplatonist critic of Aristotle, Proclus, refutes Aristotle's complaint that Plato's Ideas are universals, only by invoking Aristotle's innovative distinction of a type of ambiguity in which things are variously related to or derived from a single entity. He has to use Aristotle against Aristotle, in order to defend Plato. This is typical of the Neoplatonist commentary tradition in which, even for an opponent of Aristotle, Plato and Aristotle are intertwined.

Elsewhere, Proclus makes it explicit that although the particulars have it in common that they are all related to the Idea in which they share, they have *diverse* ways of sharing in it (*poikilas methexeis*).[8] For Proclus, then, there is no common nature here. So we may be startled when in this last passage, Proclus speaks of universals and says that universals are found at three levels. Every universal is either *before* the many particulars, or *in* them, or formed by reflection (in the mind) *after* and derivatively from the particulars. Why is the Platonic Idea called a *universal* before the many particulars? Proclus has explained already: the Idea is universal in the sense of being the single thing to which all the particulars under it *relate*, albeit by *diverse* relationships. As Simplicius puts it, it is not a common nature, but common as the *cause* which makes the particulars what they are. These arguments are very explicit, but already we do not find, as far as I know, the earlier Neoplatonists Plotinus, Porphyry, or Iamblichus calling Plato's Ideas without qualification universals. Indeed, Riccardo Chiaradonna has argued that they do not believe that they are without qualification universal.[9]

---

[5] Syrianus, *in Metaph.* 114,35–115,3. I am indebted to Riccardo Chiaradonna for pointing out to me that Proclus was explaining his teacher's view, not innovating it.
[6] Simplicius, *in Cat.* 82,35–83,20. This and the next reference were analysed in Richard Sorabji, *The Philosophy of the Commentators, 200–600 AD: A Sourcebook*, 3 vols (London: Duckworth, 2004), vol. 3, ch. 5(b)2–3.
[7] G. E. L. Owen called this focal meaning and supplied the references, 'Logic and Metaphysics in Some Early Works of Aristotle', in I. Düring and G. E. L. Owen, eds, *Aristotle and Plato in the Mid-Fourth Century* (Göteborg: Almqvist & Wiksell, 1960), pp. 163–90; repr. as ch. 10 in his collected papers, *Logic, Science, and Dialectic* (London: Duckworth, 1986), pp. 180–99.
[8] Proclus, *On Euclid's Elements* I, 50,15–51,9 at 51,3.
[9] R. Chiaradonna, 'Universali e intelligibili in Plotino', in V. Celluprica and C. D'Ancona, eds, *Aristotele e i suoi esegetici neoplatonici* (Naples: Elenchos, 2004), pp. 1–35; id. 'Porphyry and Iamblichus on Universals and Synonymous Predication', *Documenti e studi sulla tradizione filosofica medievale* 18 (2007), 123–40.

The transformation of Platonic Ideas into not being universal did not happen immediately. Plutarch and Atticus, Middle Platonists of the first and second centuries AD, are said to have still been calling Platonic Ideas universal, albeit universal rational principles (*logoi*) in human souls, and for that they were to be criticised by Proclus' Neoplatonist teacher Syrianus (died *c*. 437) for confusing such principles in human souls with paradigmatic Ideas separated from matter and with the creative thoughts of the divine Demiurge.[10] Aristotle's greatest defender, Alexander of Aphrodisias, head of the Aristotelian school in Athens after 200 CE, denies that Ideas are the sort of universal found in particulars,[11] but in doing so in his commentary on Aristotle's *Metaphysics*, he does not deny that they are universals at all. However, Gyburg Uhlmann has pointed out that the 'alternative' recension' to Alexander's commentary, printed by the modern editor Hayduck at the bottom of the page, but ascribed by Pantelis Golitsis in Chapter 23 below not to Alexander but to Stephanus, goes further and does deny that Ideas are universal.[12] The difference from Alexander is explicable, given the authorship of Stephanus in the sixth century CE, since this commentary will have been written up in the light of later Neoplatonist denials of universality.[13]

The rebuke to the Middle Platonists Plutarch and Atticus for confusing rational principles (*logoi*) in human souls with Platonic Ideas needs explanation. It was the founder of Neoplatonism, Plotinus, who first distinguished *logos* in the Intellect as still being Platonic Ideas from the derivative *logoi* in various levels of soul: soul as a *hypostasis* or level of being, the World Soul, Nature as an organising principle, which on one interpretation of Plotinus is the inferior part of the World Soul, and individual souls. In soul at any of these levels, the *logoi* are no longer a unified totality, but are separated, and are for Plotinus merely an expression (*hermêneus*) or imitation (*mimêma*) of Platonic Ideas, 1.2.3.28 and 30. And the *logoi* transmitted by soul to create bodies are a further image (*eidôlon*), 4.3.10.39.

Plotinus' distinction between *logoi* and Platonic Ideas may already have been followed in the fourth century by Themistius in Constantinople, even though he was not, in my view, a Neoplatonist, but an independent exponent of Aristotle making respectful use of Plato. Yoav Meyrav translates in Chapter 6 of this volume the only surviving versions of Themistius' text from the Arabic of Averroes and from Hebrew,[14] which speak of a soul in the earth. This idea is not to be found in Aristotle, but seems rather to echo Plotinus, who not only believes that there is a soul, or rather a trace (*ikhnos*) of soul, in the earth, and that this trace of soul is passed on to plants (4.4.22.1–46; 4.4.27, 1–17), but also says that though these vegetative forms of life are lowly, they are nonetheless rational principles (*logoi*, 3.8.8, 16). If Plotinus says that the traces of

---

[10] Syrianus, *in Metaph*. 105,36–106,2.
[11] Alexander, *in Metaph*. 1,50,7–15, cited by Riin Sirkel, 'Alexander of Aphrodisias' Account of Universals and its Problems', *Journal of the History of Philosophy* 49 (2011), 297–314, at 305.
[12] Gyburg Uhlmann (n. 16 below), referring to *altera recensio*, page 82, numbered 11.12.
[13] Riccardo Chiaradonna, however, cites earlier texts in which universality is silently omitted from the characteristics of Plato's Ideas: Seneca, *Letters* 58.16; Cicero, *Topics* 31. See his 'Porphyry and Iamblichus on Universals and Synonymous Predication' (n. 9 above).
[14] Themistius, *in Metaph*. 12, in Averroes, *in Metaph*. 12, Bouyges III, 1292–4, translated by Yoav Meyrav, ch. 6 in this volume.

soul in the earth are *logoi*, Themistius' view seems very close, that there are *logoi in* the earth soul. It is noticeable that Themistius, like Plotinus, does not call the *logoi* Platonic Ideas. The case is clearer with Plotinus' Athenian Neoplatonist successors: Syrianus insisted (*loc. cit.*) in the fifth century that *logoi* were distinct from Ideas, as did his pupil Proclus, who made *intellect* possess Ideas, whereas *soul* possesses only *logoi* as the reflections (*emphaseis*), copies (*eikones*), and projections (*probolai*) of Ideas, (*Elements of Theology* 194, *On Plato's Parmenides* 4, 896,25; 897,15–16; 22–3; 896,23–7; 982,4–9), and in the Athenian school Simplicius agreed *in Cat.* 12,16–25.[15] Plotinus' distinction of *logoi* in the soul as mere images of Platonic Ideas thus became Neolatonic orthodoxy for some time, although in the late Neoplatonist school in Alexandria, Ammonius *in Isag.* 41,21–42,7, and probably his pupil Philoponus (*in DA* 38,13–15; 58,9; *in Phys.* 133,27–8; 193,1–4; possibly 241,20–3) tended to remain silent about the distinction. Keen to harmonise Aristotle with Plato, Ammonius treated *logoi* in the divine Creator's mind as constituting the highest level of entities distinguished by his teacher Proclus, those 'before' or prior to the many particulars, and avoided Proclus' mention of Ideas distinct from them, in the hope of producing a view acceptable to both Plato and Aristotle.

To return to Proclus' argument against the universality of Plato's Ideas, it drew on Aristotle's distinction among types of ambiguity. That distinction had had a history of its own among the commentators before Proclus. Aristotle's distinction of being related to or derived from a single thing was transferred to Neoplatonism partly through the Aristotelian Alexander in his commentary on Aristotle *Metaphysics* 4.2, 1003a33, at his 240,31–241,21 (cf. 263,25–36), and then by Proclus' teacher Syrianus in his commentary on the same passage, at his 56,13–57,21. But Syrianus, as Gyburg Uhlmann has made clear,[16] had rested content with Aristotle's idea of homonymy, saying that the Idea and the particulars that share in it have only a name, not a definition in common. Proclus thus innovated in using instead Aristotle's different distinction and saying that the particulars are related in different ways to the one Idea, so that they are *neither* synonymous with it, *nor* fully homonymous.

As regards synonymy and homonymy, Alexander had made a small transformation of his own. In two places in his commentary on Aristotle's *Metaphysics*,[17] he supposes that someone might accept that individuals are not homonymously human, or homonymously equal, and he endorses this in one of his two texts, *in Metaph.* 51,18 and 24–5, saying that individual humans *do* share with the Platonist Idea the same definition of human and so are 'synonymous', because 'rational mortal animal' (the definition of human) applies to the Idea and to individual humans alike. Even so, this, he says, is not in the *proper* or *true* sense (*kuriôs, alêthôs*). He further explains in this text that he means the definition is not properly their *definition*, and this is presumably

---

[15] See Carlos Steel, 'Breathing Thought: Proclus on the Innate Knowledge of the Soul', in J. J. Cleary, ed., *The Perennial Tradition of Neoplatonism* (Leuven: Leuven University Press, 1997), pp. 293–309; Robbert van den Berg, 'Smoothing over the Differences', ch. 13 in this volume.

[16] Gyburg Uhlmann, draft working paper, 'On the function of Platonic doctrines in late antique commentaries on *Metaphysics* A9, A6, M 4 – an example of late antique knowledge transfer', presented at her conference in Berlin, 2014 entitled 'Aristotle Transferred'.

[17] Alexander, *in Metaph.* 83,12–17; *in Metaph.* 51,18 and 24–5.

because individuals are not definable for Aristotle, *Metaphysics* 7.15, but he thinks that for Platonists (although Syrianus and Proclus would later deny this),[18] Ideas are definable.[19] In a third text, the later alternative edition, cited by Uhlmann, he makes a *different* point, that the *Equal itself* is not properly predicated of particular pairs of equal things. In both cases, he allows that things may be synonymous, sharing both name and definition, yet not *properly*. This 'synonymous, but not proper' is a small transformation of Aristotle's usage, even though the term 'proper', like the term 'synonymous' is an Aristotelian term.

Are Plato's Ideas what we define, or is that something else?

Proclus also disagreed with Aristotle's claim that Platonic Ideas are something that can be *defined*. As Carlos Steel has spelled out, they are too unitary and simple to be articulated in a definition.[20] Instead, we define what is common (*koinon*) in particular things, and we can do so because we have in our souls not the Idea, but a rational principle (*logos*) or form (*eidos*), of which what is common in the particulars is an image.[21]

The denial that Platonic Ideas were definable also did not happen immediately. Alexander of Aphrodisias had still held that for Plato Ideas were intended by Plato to be objects of definition,[22] though for Alexander himself we shall see the thing we define was form residing in matter, regardless of whether it was universal. Nor did Proclus' alternative account of what is definable remain unchanged after him. Ammonius was Proclus' pupil, but he subjected Proclus' account to a certain transformation. He agreed that what we define is a thing (*pragma*) like the genus human which exists in particulars, and that we do so by means of what is in our souls. But he does not give Proclus' honorific names to what is in our souls, 'rational principle (*logos*)' and 'form (*eidos*)', which suggest that they are eventually derived from *Ideas*. Instead he says that we define human in accordance with a merely conceptual genus (*ennoêmatikon*) and our own concept (*ennoia*) and thought (*dianoia*), and following that analogy, says that human is a mortal rational animal.[23] Riccardo Chiaradonna has thrown light on conceptual definition (*ennoêmatikos logos*) in Porphyry and Galen. In Porphyry, it still has some status and is not based on any old concept, but on the common conceptions of all humans, which are taken to be correct as far as they go. But the conceptual definition need not be consciously articulated, and it does not yet tell us, or even try to

---

[18] I am grateful to Riccardo Chiaradonna for again pointing out that Syrianus anticipates Proclus at *in Metaph.* 115,19-26.

[19] I do not take Alexander's 'synonymous but not proper' to be a reference to the *pros hen* and *aph' henos* relation that medical men and medical instruments bear to the medical art, because I do not take the instances of medical to be 'synonymous', that is to have the same definition.

[20] Proclus, *Commentary on Plato's Parmenides* 939,10-22; 986,10-14; Book 7 (Latin) 513,32-3.

[21] Proclus, *Commentary on Plato's Parmenides* 980,29-33; 980,6-981,3. Carlos Steel, 'Definitions and Ideas: Aristotle, Proclus and the Socrates of the *Parmenides*', *Proceedings of the Boston Area Colloquium in Ancient Philosophy* 19 (2003), 103-21.

[22] Alexander, *in Metaph.* 50,7-15.

[23] Ammonius, *in Isag.* 68,25-69,11.

tell us, the *essence* of what is defined.[24] Nonetheless, at least in Galen, it puts a constraint on the essential definition (*ousiôdês logos*), because that must conform to the conceptual one. I shall return to Ammonius' passage and we shall see that it enables Ammonius' pupil Philoponus in turn to go still further and say that what we define is not a genus in accordance with our concept, but simply our concept. This topic will be ongoing.

Universals Downgraded: Aristotle, Boethus, Stoics

I turn now to the other half of Aristotle's treatment of universals. Not only should they not be upgraded to the level of Plato's Ideas, as if they were the supreme substances, but in his *Categories* chapter 5 Aristotle downgrades the universals he is discussing there, genera and species, as only *secondary* substances, and contrasts them with individuals, which are primary substances, on the grounds that individuals are subjects, never predicates. Later in his *Metaphysics* 7.13, 1038b34–1039a3, he goes further and makes the case for the genus or universal not being a substance at all. There are some doubts briefly expressed about this in *Metaphysics* 7.13, 1039a17–20, but they are not repeated in the retrospect at 8.1, 1042a31.[25] Aristotle also discusses universal propositions or concepts, in *Posterior Analytics* 1.5 and 2.19. Relevant to the latter passage would be the proposition that a human is a rational mortal animal or the concept of a human as a rational mortal animal. But Aristotle does not, like some later thinkers, treat this kind of universal as if it were a different grade on the same scale as the universals that reside in particulars in the world.

Of later followers of Aristotle, Boethus in the late first century BCE, the founder of line-by-line commentaries on Aristotle, is reported as saying that the universal is not even an existent (*en hupostasei*) according to Aristotle,[26] and not a genuine *subject* of predication.[27] Being a subject of predication was the criterion for substancehood in Aristotle's *Categories*, even if he later required substance to be explanatory. Because Boethus followed the *Categories* criterion, he also denied that form was substance and

---

[24] Porphyry *ap.* Simplicius, *in Cat.* 213,8–28: Aristotle's *account* of the category of quality in his elementary *Categories* is a conceptual account (*logos ennoêmatikos*), the essential (*ousiôdês*) account being reserved for his *Metaphysics*. I have benefited here from Riccardo Chiaradonna showing me his 'Galen and Middle Platonists on Dialectic and Knowledge', *Proceedings of the Thirteenth Symposium Hellenisticum*, forthcoming.

[25] I do not regard the phrase 'nothing or posterior' at Aristotle *On the Soul* 1.1, 402b5–8 as attempting to downgrade universals in general. It only gives a warning about a non-unitary genus. Thus we must take care about the genus soul as to whether there is a single definition of it, just as we need to take care whether there is [*not* just as there is] of living being, or whether there is a different definition for each soul, that of horse, dog, human, god, while living being, the universal, is either nothing or posterior. Such downgrading would not apply to a unitary genus, much less to a species like human.

[26] Simplicius, *in Cat.* 50,5–8, cf. Dexippus, *in Cat.* 22,32–3, discussed by R. Chiaradonna, 'Alexander, Boethus and the other Peripatetics: The Theory of Universals in the Aristotelian Commentators', in Riccardo Chiaradonna and Gabriele Galuzzo, eds, *Universals in Ancient Philosophy* (Pisa: Edizioni della Normale, 2013), pp. 299–328.

[27] *Anonymi in Aristotelis Categorias Commentarium*, p. 3, lines 16–26, edited, translated, and discussed by R. Chiaradonna, M. Rashed, and D. Sedley, 'A Rediscovered Categories Commentary', *Oxford Studies in Ancient Philosophy* 44 (2013), 129–94, and reprinted as ch. 8 above; Chiaradonna (previous note).

gave that honorific title instead to matter and the compound of matter and form, because he saw these as subjects, but form as something predicated of a subject.[28] Alexander was to reply to Boethus' views on both universal and form.

It should be mentioned that another school also downgraded universals, the Stoics. On one view, the founder in Athens in 300 BCE, Zeno of Citium, treated universals as mere concepts, not in the sense of Boethus' thinkings (*noêseis*), but in the sense of concepts thought (*ennoêmata*).[29] But (again on one view), the third head of the Stoic school changed to treating them as sayables, *lekta*, that is as *predicates* which serve as the *contents* of thoughts. On this account, they are below physical objects which have being (*onta*), but they are allowed the intermediate status of somethings (*tina*), unlike Plato's Forms which are not-somethings, or nothings (*outina*). But the texts are confusing as to whether universals are spared relegation to this outer darkness.[30]

Alexander: Multigrade Universals and a Few Causal Roles

I once thought that Alexander continued to downgrade universals, and it has been argued on the other side that he reinstated them.[31] But I am now inclined to think that he recognised different grades of universal, some downgraded, but not for Boethus' reasons, others somewhat upgraded. He treats one grade of universal as something mind-dependent, when he speaks as if an enmattered form or nature (*eidos*, *phusis*), which is not in reality (*en hupostasei*) or in its own nature (*kata tên hautou phusin*) universal (*katholou*) or (equivalently) common (*koina*), can *become* (*ginesthai*) common and universal by being thought or constructed (*suntithenai*) by a conceptual separation (*têi epinoiai khôrismos*).[32] The separation seems to be from the material circumstances of the enmattered form or nature. Examples of these enmattered forms or natures in individual humans, or in individual animals, are *rational mortal animal*, and *animate being with sensation*.[33] Alexander says that when the nature is thought of separately from the things with which it exists (*huphistanai*), it is thought of *not* as it exists.[34] As Riin Sirkel has pointed out, Boethius in the sixth century CE (not Boethus

---

[28] Marwan Rashed, 'Priorité de l'*eidos* ou du *genos* entre Andronicos et Alexandre: vestiges arabes et grecs inedits', *Arabic Sciences and Philosophy* 14 (2004), 9–63, at 19–24 (repr. in his *L'héritage aristotélicien: Textes inédits de l'Antiquité* (Paris: Les Belles Lettres, 2007), pp. 29–83, at pp. 39–44); 'Boethus' Aristotelian ontology', in Malcolm Schofield, ed., *Aristotle, Plato and Pythagoreanism in the First Century BC* (Cambridge: Cambridge University Press, 2013), pp. 53–77.

[29] A. A. Long and D. N. Sedley, *The Hellenistic Philosophers*, 2 vols (Cambridge: Cambridge University Press, 1987), vol. 1, ch. 30.

[30] V. Caston, 'Something and Nothing: The Stoics on Concepts and Universals', *Oxford Studies in Ancient Philosophy* 17 (1999), 145–213; sketched in Sorabji, 'Universals Transformed', pp. 106–8.

[31] R. Chiaradonna, 'The Theory of Universals in the Aristotelian Commentators', pp. 299–328; Sorabji 'Universals Transformed' (n. 1 above); R. Sorabji, *The Philosophy of the Commentators* (n. 6 above), vol. 3, ch. 5(e), where translations are assembled.

[32] See Alexander, *On the Soul* 90,2–11 (cf. *Quaestio* 1.3, 8,3–4); *Quaestio* 1.3, 8,17–22; *Quaestio* 2.28, 79,16–18; *Quaestio* 2.28, 78,18–20.

[33] Another example is footed biped animal, and I take it that the *essence* of bronze residing in a piece of bronze is another example of form or nature in Alexander, *On the Soul* 87,8–16.

[34] Alexander, *Quaestio* 1.3, 8,19–20.

the Aristotelian) expanded this point, when he interpreted Alexander as meaning that the thought of a form or nature as universal is not of the form or nature as it really *is*, because the material circumstances have been ignored, but it is still a useful thought. Boethius compares how a line cannot exist apart from matter, but it is still useful that mathematical thought considers it in abstraction from body.[35]

The other, higher grade of universal exists independently of the mind in particulars. But here something must be noticed about form or nature. As existing independently of the mind, the form or nature seems to exist in two different ways, only *one* of which is universal. In relation to the material circumstances of a single individual like Socrates (or to the material circumstances of a unique individual like the sun) it is non-universal. Marwan Rashed points out in Chapter 4 that Philoponus reports Alexander as speaking of an individual form (*atomon eidos*) of Socrates.[36] He says that even if, as some think, the heavenly bodies returned to the same configuration and the same matter with the same efficient cause produced the same things, it would not be the same Socrates that came into being, because after the time gap, his *individual form* would not remain (*ou gar menei to atomon eidos*). I take it that this is in line with Aristotle *Phys.* 5.6, which denies that we would have the same walking or the same health after an interruption. Alexander is reported elsewhere as saying that such a form is perishable in number, by which he means that numerically the same form cannot recur, but that, on the other hand, it is imperishable in species (*eidei*),[37] and this last points to his further view that in relation to the material circumstances of *all* the humans there are over the whole of time, the form (*eidos*) is common or universal.

For a form's universality outside the mind Alexander makes a stronger requirement than Aristotle, that it be not only shareable, but actually *shared* by more than one individual. Alexander makes the requirement especially when he is thinking of a universal as a genus or species. For animal or human to be universal, or a genus or species, is for there to be *more than one* species under the genus, or specimen under the species, which has the appropriate form or nature. In the natural world, there is usually more than one specimen, but there is only one sun, and it is accidental to the particular form or nature whether there is more than one.[38] Aristotle's more modest requirement, that a universal need only be of a *nature* to be shared (*pephuke katêgoreisthai*), is expressed in *Int.* 17a39–40. Alexander's stronger requirement recurs frequently in contexts where he is arguing that an individual can exist without having a genus or species under which it falls. It can do so if, like the sun, it is the only specimen of its kind, so that its form is not shared by at least two specimens. By contrast, on this view, a genus cannot exist if there is not more than one species, or specimen under

---

[35] Boethius, *Second Commentary on Porphyry Isagôgê*, in *Patrologia Latina*, ed. Migne, vol. 64, cols 84B-85A, cited by Sirkel, 'Alexander of Aphrodisias' Account of Universals and its Problems' (n. 11 above), p. 311.

[36] Alexander *ap.* Philoponus, *in GC* 314,16–22, cited by M. Rashed, 'Alexander of Aphrodisias on Particulars', in R. W. Sharples, ed., *Particulars in Greek Philosophy* (Leiden: Brill, 2010), pp. 157–79, at p. 162 (reprinted as ch. 4 above, p. 165).

[37] Alexander *ap.* Simplicius, *in Phys.* 234,13–19, cited by Rashed, *Essentialisme*, p. 237.

[38] Alexander, *Quaestio* 1.11, 23,25–31; *in Top.* 355,18–24.

it.[39] The individual's priority in being able to enjoy independent existence from a universal genus is a different kind of priority, of course, from an *explanatory* priority such as the form or nature is said to have over the individual.

Universality turns out not even to be essential to *definition*. For definitions are not of what is common *qua* common, but of the form or nature to which it is an *accident* to be common. If there were only one human, the definition of human would still be of the nature or form. Of course this does not happen, but it shows that although definitions are of the form or nature that is common, they are not of it because (*hoti*) of the commonness.[40] It is true that intellect contemplates not a particular piece of bronze, but the essence or form of bronze, which is said by Alexander in another passage to be universal, but in view of the present passage, I take it that it need not contemplate the form of bronze *qua* universal, if universality is taken in the sense that requires more than one instance.

There may seem to be clashes between the idea of universals as dependent on abstraction by the mind and universals as forms or natures existent in reality in more than one particular, and Alexander's two conceptions were already seen in Martin Tweedale's pioneering article as clashing.[41] First, why does Alexander twice say that what is universal or common *becomes* common or universal when it is thought?[42] The word 'becomes' may seem to imply that it is never common outside of the mind, but we know that it is common accidentally when there is more than one instance. I suggest it will reconcile the two conceptions if what Alexander means instead is that the form abstracted by the mind becomes *non-accidentally* common or universal.

The second potential clash arises from the *appearance* that in On the Soul 90,2–8, Alexander implies that universals exist *only* in thought, whereas we know this is not true of universals in particulars. The text moves from saying that the things that are universal and common have their being in the enmattered particulars to saying that *if their being lies in being thought*, they *perish* when separated from the intellect, and that if they are not thought, they *are no longer*. This initially startling conclusion depends on the italicised 'if'-clause which is itself a re-phrasing of the more qualified 'if'-clause earlier in the same six lines: 'if their being *intelligibles* has its being in their being

---

[39] Alexander concerning the sun, *ap.* Simplicius, *in Cat.* 85,13–17; Elias, *in Cat.* 167,1–2; Alexander, *Refutation of Xenocrates*, trans. from surviving Arabic by S. Pines in his *Collected Works*, vol. 2, p. 10; Alexander, *Quaestio* 1.3, 8,8–17; *Quaestio* 1.11, 21,22–9; 22,6–9; 24,8–16, and in order to explain why Aristotelians make individuals like Socrates primary substances and genera secondary substances, Dexippus, *in Cat.* 45,19–22; Simplicius, *in Cat.* 82,26–8, although Riccardo Chiaradonna, 'The Theory of Universals in the Aristotelian Commentators', pp. 299–328, would differentiate Alexander from Boethus. Robert Sharples suggests that Alexander occasionally forgets his requirement of more than one, because in the natural world 'singletons', as Sharples dubs them, are very much the exception (see his 'Alexander of Aphrodisias on Universals: Two Problematic Texts', *Phronesis* 50 (2005), 43–55).

[40] Alexander, *Quaestio* 1.3, 8,7–17. It is true that intellect contemplates not a particular piece of bronze, but the essence or form of bronze, which is said by Alexander in another passage to be universal, Alexander, *On the Soul* 87,16, but in view of the present passage, I take it that it need not contemplate the form of bronze *qua* universal, if universality is taken in the sense that requires more than one instance.

[41] M. Tweedale, 'Alexander of Aphrodisias' Views on Universals', *Phronesis* 29 (1984), 279–303.

[42] Alexander, *Quaestio* 1.3, 7,28–8,5; *On the Soul* 90,5–6.

thought'. That had meant that it was not they, but their *intelligibility*, that depended on thought. I presume the stronger formulation is used because Alexander is now thinking only of the lower grade of universal, the one abstracted by the mind. The lower grading of abstracted universals is due not only to their mind-dependence, but also, we have seen, to their not representing universals as they exist in reality.

At one point Alexander might be thought, wrongly, to be downgrading universals further. In distinguishing genus from matter, he says that matter is a thing and, for each of the things it underlies, it contributes to that thing being a this something, whereas the genus *taken as genus* is not an underlying thing, but a mere name, and possesses its common character in being thought, not in any reality (*en hupostasei tini*).[43] But I think the qualification 'taken as genus' is relevant here. Alexander is not saying of any given genus, such as animal, that it is a mere name. Part of what Alexander says reminds me of the objection raised against Aristotle by Nicostratus, the Platonist of the mid-second century CE, and discussed by Alexander in his commentary on Aristotle's *Categories* (preserved only in Armenian), then by Porphyry and later by Dexippus.[44] The objection is that, even if we can say that man is an animal, and animal is a genus, we cannot say that man is a genus. Dexippus and later Boethius both solve the problem by drawing on a distinction of Porphyry's. The name 'genus' is what Porphyry calls a name 'of *second imposition*', merely the name of a name. At any rate Dexippus and Boethius, who both draw on Porphyry, use this solution.[45] Part of what Alexander is saying about genus, *taken as genus*, is similar. To call e.g. animal a genus does not tell us about animals, but classifies the name 'animal'. He also reminds of something further: the universality of genus, *taken as genus*, has to do not with there being more than one specimen, but with our having removed in our thoughts the form's being embedded in particulars at all.

At certain points, however, Alexander does upgrade non-mental universals by giving them certain explanatory roles. In its capacity as common, a given form or nature is required not only to be the same in many particulars but also to be eternal and to *bestow likeness* on the particulars. Perhaps it bestows likeness on the different particular things, because it is itself alike in each of them. This is an issue again brought into prominence, with extra texts, by Marwan Rashed, and I shall cite the texts he brings in evidence.[46] Alexander puts his view in two ways. Sometimes he insists that

---

[43] Alexander, *Quaestio* 2.28, 78,16–20.
[44] Alexander's discussion recorded in German by E. G. Schmidt, in 'Alexander von Aphrodisias in einem alt-armenischen Kategorien-Kommentar', *Philologus* 110 (1966), 277–86, at 280–2, as noted by Chiaradonna, Rashed, and Sedley, 'A Rediscovered *Categories* Commentary', pp. 145, 176 (pp. 239–42, 251–2 above). Nicostratus' earlier objection and one of Porphyry's discussions are in (Porphyry?) *Anonymi in Aristotelis Categorias Commentarium*, 2,13–4,12, ed. and tr. with comments, Chiaradonna, Rashed, and Sedley, 'A Rediscovered Categories Commentary', pp. 129–94 (pp. 231–62 above); Porphyry discusses the issue also in his shorter *in Cat.* 81,3–22; Dexippus in his *in Cat.* 26,13–27,2. Porphyry in Sorabji, *The Philosophy of the Commentators*, vol. 3, p. 237.
[45] Dexippus, *in Cat.* 26,23–27,2, and Boethius, *in Cat.* 176D–177A Brandt. (See Ebbesen, 'Porphyry's Legacy to Logic', p. 383 and, without reference, 'Philoponus, "Alexander" and the Origins of Medieval Logic', in R. Sorabji, ed., *Aristotle Transformed* (London: Duckworth, 1990), pp. 445–61, at p. 457.) For second imposition see Porphyry in Sorabji, *The Philosophy of the Commentators*, vol. 3, p. 237.
[46] Rashed, *Essentialisme*, pp. 102, 237–60. Rashed recognises Alexander's two different kinds of genus and species in 'Priorité de l'*eidos* ou du *genos* entre Andronicus et Alexandre' (n. 28 above), p. 34.

natural forms or natures are eternal and imperishable, sometimes that they are common or universal. The form is perishable in number, as each individual perishes and loses its form, but it is not perishable in species (*eidei*).[47] Form is a *substance* and an eternal, unitary (*aïdios, monadikê*) substance.[48] Aristotle is said to take it rightly that, as matter is eternal, there must also be some form that is eternal. It is not the form that comes into being in matter that has to be this, but rather the productive (*poiêtikon*) form, which, if it is to be like the form being produced, will need to pre-exist it in a way.[49] In this passage, the form is again said to be eternal, although it is not clear whether the productive form that pre-exists in a way is the eternal one, or the particular parental form.[50] But even the particular form in the father is allowed by Alexander elsewhere to produce something similar in *species* to *itself*, i.e. something human,[51] and so it ought to be regarded as the same in *species* as other human forms.

Whether or not it was the eternal form that was called productive, Alexander does think in terms of productivity when he speaks of what makes things similar to *each other*. In Alexander Quaestio 1.3, features that are common (*koina*) and correspond with each other (*pros allêla*) and that are common in things and invariable (*adiaphora*) in their own nature are said to be *causes* (*aitia*) in all the things that have them of their being *similar* (*homoia*) and of the same nature. The common features are what remain similar and the same in the coming into being of all the particulars,[52] and they evidently cause similarity amongst particulars, even though on the next page he says, probably thinking of biological species, that the common things owe their imperishability throughout eternity to something else: to the succession of the particulars in which they are.[53] Could it be that the supposed eternal succession of the human species is due to the biological form or nature, *qua* common or shared? The same context recurs in another text which says that nature and divine providence are directed to the generation of the substance of things down here, to their differentiation and to the *form* in them.[54] So the ultimate aim of nature is not to produce individuals, but apparently their (common) form. Insofar as Alexander allows that common features cause similarity, he is giving them the very same role that Proclus later says calls for a Platonic Idea. An Idea is needed, Proclus says, to explain why the same form exists in different individuals, despite their continual flux.[55]

It appears that Alexander sometimes offers another explanatory role to the form or nature insofar as it is specifically the same in different individuals. At any rate, Simplicius reports an explanatory role which he thinks inconsistent in Alexander. Alexander is said to claim that 'individuals are *constituted* (*huphestanai ek*) out of the common

---

[47] Alexander *ap.* Simplicius, *in Phys.* 234,17–18.
[48] Alexander, *in Metaph.* 214,27–9.
[49] Alexander, *in Metaph.* 215,16–18.
[50] Particular parental has been suggested to me by Tomasz Tiuryn.
[51] Alexander *ap.* Simplicius, *in Phys.* 311,12–17.
[52] Alexander, *Quaestio* 1.3, 7,31–2.
[53] Alexander, *Quaestio* 1.3, 8,22–3.
[54] Alexander, *On Providence*, translated into French from the Arabic by Rashed, *Essentialisme*, p. 253.
[55] Proclus, *Commentary on Plato's Parmenides* 883,37–885,3, cited by Steel, op. cit.

feature (*to koinon*) and the differences.⁵⁶ Some such role is also suggested by a passage which I had previously agreed with A. C. Lloyd to reject the as inauthentic.⁵⁷ I had come to think of it as an addition made at the end of a text by someone in the tradition of Porphyry, the first of the Neoplatonist commentators on Aristotle, for whom what is common may be a 'completive' part of the individual. This passage was already emphasised by Tweedale. It comes in the last two lines of Alexander's *Quaestio* 1.11, at 24,21-2. The first half of 1.11 reports what Alexander had said in his *commentary* on Aristotle's *On the Soul*, which unlike his *own* treatise *On the Soul*, is lost. The second half of 1.11 is a reprise which looks like a *revised* report of what Alexander's commentary had said. The last two lines take it to have said that what falls under (*hupo*) what is common depends for its existence on what is common, and that its *being consists in* (*to einai en*) possessing what is common in itself. The claim about what its being *consists in* was absent from the first half. The term 'under' suggests that the common or universal is being considered as a genus or species. The desiderated universal evidently needs to have enough reality to bestow *being* on what falls under it. Marwan Rashed has found a text which he calls T2, surviving in Arabic, in which Alexander says that the genus is *in* the species, which he takes to mean that it helps to constitute the species.⁵⁸ This type of explanatory role does not seem to fit very well with Alexander's idea that what bestows *being* on Socrates is the *particular* enmattered form or nature, rational mortal animal, rather than a genus or a species *under* which the particular falls. But perhaps the idea of bestowing being needs to be differentiated further than Alexander differentiates it. It would be possible that the genus or species explains Socrates being the kind of *substance* that he is, but his father's particular form *generates* him, while his mother supplies the matter that differentiates him as the *individual* that he is.

Alexander appears, then, to have offered to certain universals an explanatory priority, in that they either *create similarity* amongst individuals or help to *constitute* them and to provide what they *consist of*. He also sometimes ascribes a different kind of priority when he uses the test of whether genera could exist without species or individuals, or individuals without genera or species. But these tests of ontological priority give different results according to what background assumptions are being made, as we shall find in Porphyry, who repeated Alexander's tests. So they are not as significant as the *explanatory* priorities which Alexander finds, and I shall leave them until we encounter them again in Porphyry.

Insofar as Alexander's universals depend for their existence on the mind, or exist through the mere accident that, unlike the sun, they have more than one instance, their status remains comparatively low. It is the form or nature, whether it happens to be universal

---

[56] Alexander *ap.* Simplicius, *in Cat.* 83,16-20, cited in Sorabji, *The Philosophy of the Commentators*, vol. 3, ch. 6(b)2. Marwan Rashed takes Alexander to claim similarly that the genus helps to constitute the species, when he says that the genus is *in* the species in the text of Alexander surviving in Arabic that he calls T2 ('Priorité de l'eidos ou du genos entre Andronicus et Alexandre' (n. 28 above), p. 15).

[57] A. C. Lloyd, *Form and Universal in Aristotle* (Liverpool: Francis Cairns, 1981), p. 51. Paul Moraux had earlier rejected the entire reprise in the second half of 1.11 as the work of a student; see his *Alexandre d'Aphrodise: Exégète de la noétique d'Aristote* (Liège and Paris: Faculté de Philosophie et Lettres de l'Université de Liège, 1942), pp. 22, 53.

[58] Marwan Rashed, 'Priorité de l'eidos ou du genos entre Andronicus et Alexandre' (n. 28 above), p. 15.

or not, to which Alexander assigns the higher status. But he does restore importance to universals outside the mind, to the extent that he offers them the above explanatory roles.

Porphyry: Universals Multigrade, not Concepts only and not Ideas

Porphyry (232 – c. 309 CE) was the pupil and editor of Plotinus in Rome. His discussion of universals is often couched in terms of genera. Genera and species are universals, not particulars, and Aristotle's ten categories (*katêgoriai*) are genera that can be predicated (*katêgoreisthai*) of the species or individuals below them. In a tradition which is described as starting as early as the commentator Boethus (not Boethius) in the first century CE, Simplicius says that many commentators took Aristotle's *Categories* to be concerned with three matters: (1) simple, primary and generic spoken sounds, (2) insofar as they signify (3) things, and Porphyry is listed as one who agreed. Indeed, Porphyry does say in his surviving shorter commentary on Aristotle's *Categories* that Aristotle's book is about spoken sounds insofar as they signify things.[59] Moreover, the infinity of beings and of expressions that signify them, or vocal sounds that indicate them, are included under ten genera.[60] Although this misses the opportunity of mentioning concepts, three commentators, starting with Philoponus, report *Iamblichus*, who drew closely on Porphyry's lost major commentary on the *Categories*,[61] as saying that Aristotle's *Categories* was about spoken sounds signifying things *through the medium of concepts* (*noêmata*).[62] This kind of formulation is approved by Simplicius, who by way of glossing the idea of signification, says that the *Categories* is giving instruction not only about the things signified, but also about *concepts* (*noêmata*).[63] Simplicius also connects the categories with genera, when he says that the *Categories* is about the ten most comprehensive (*holikôtata*) genera and that what the spoken sounds signify is the most generic (*genikôtata*) of beings.[64] There are of course some variations in the tradition about who took what to be the subject matter of Aristotle's *Categories*.[65]

---

[59] Porphyry, *in Cat.* 58,4–7.
[60] Porphyry, *in Cat.* 58,12–15.
[61] Simplicius, *in Cat.* 2,9–25.
[62] Philoponus, *in Cat.* Prooemium 9,12–15; Olympiodorus, *in Cat.* Prolegomena 18,23–20,12; Elias, *in Cat.* Prooemium 130,14–131,14.
[63] Simplicius, *in Cat.* 13,11–18.
[64] Simplicius, *in Cat.* 9,7; 13,20.
[65] One pupil of Ammonius, Simplicius, reports Boethus as saying that for the past masters of his time (*arkhaioi*), including Aristotle, the only things signified were thoughts (*noêseis*), Simplicius, *in Cat.* 41,28- 42,2, which would reduce the subject matter of the *Categories* to words and thoughts. Ammonius' next successor but one in the chair at Alexandria, Olympiodorus, gave a much fuller account, but contradicted Simplicius' claim of uniform agreement, and switched the purely conceptual interpretation to Alexander of Aphrodisias, while assigning Porphyry to the camp which made Aristotle's *Categories* to be only about spoken sounds, so that he would be a nominalist rather than a conceptualist, Olympiodorus *in Cat.* Prolegomena 18,23–20,12. In Olympiodorus' school, Elias restored Porphyry to the camp of *concepts* and Alexander to that of *things*, Elias, *in Cat.* Prooemium 129,10–130,13. For a further variation, see below on the anonymous edition of Ammonius' lectures on Aristotle's *Categories*.

Among the ancient commentators Ammonius seems to have started the tradition of interpreting Porphyry as treating Aristotle's genera in his logical works as *concepts*. Yet the evidence Ammonius actually cites is weak. Thus when Porphyry says in *Isagôgê* 3,19, that he has given a sketch of the *concept* (*ennoia*) of the genus, Ammonius by a dubious but influential interpretation, takes this to mean a sketch of the *conceptual* genus (*ennoêmatikon genos*).[66] But Porphyry in this passage does not speak of conceptual definition, nor of the companion idea of the common conceptions of all people. Simplicius tells us that Ammonius' pupil Philoponus also follows some conceptual interpretation of Porphyry, saying that Porphyry thought Aristotle's treatment in his *Categories* of the ten genera was only about genera in our thought (*dianoia*), hence about *concepts* (*noêmata*), not about words or things. He supposed Porphyry was confused by Aristotle saying at *Categories* 11b15 that he had spoken enough about the genera when he had only talked (for beginners) about *conceptual* genera (*genê ennoêmatika*).[67]

What evidence is there that Porphyry did construe Aristotle as treating genera and other universals too in his logical works as concepts?[68] Some of the evidence cited is no stronger than that of Ammonius. It is not strong evidence that Porphyry, in the surviving shorter of his two commentaries on Aristotle's *Categories*, says that it is beyond the preparation of introductory students (*eisagomenoi* is connected with his other title, *Isagôgê* or *Eisagôgê*) to recognise that whereas certain other things have being (*estin*), for something to be (reading: *to*) designated universal (*katholou*) is not a description of reality (*en huparxei*), but is a designation that goes as far as the level of our *conception* (*epinoia*).[69] I think this is not saying that universals are concepts, but that to call something universal is to employ a second-order concept, or in Porphyry's terminology a term of second imposition. In other words, we are not discussing the universals, but only our mode of characterising them. In a second passage Porphyry says, addressing beginners in his Introduction (*Isagôgê*), which on one view is an introduction to Aristotelian logic, that for them he will not discuss the issues about genera and species themselves, but only how the past masters, especially the Aristotelians, treated genera and species in a logical way.[70] But it is not safe to interpret 'logical' as meaning that genera will be treated as concepts. Again, Porphyry says that it is from all of the particular humans that is *conceived* (*epinoeisthai*) the human that is predicated (*katêgoroumenon*) in common, and from all the particular animals that we *think* (*noein*) the animal that is predicated in common.[71] None of this is very strong evidence for Ammonius' view that Porphyry treats genera as concepts on his logical works. Nor, I think, is the report cited by Chiaradonna on Porphyry in Simplicius *in*

---

[66] Ammonius, *in Isag.* 68,25–69,11.
[67] Philoponus, *in Cat.* Prooemium 9,3–12.
[68] This subject is discussed by Riccardo Chiaradonna, 'Porphyry and Iamblichus on Universals and Synonymous Predication', *Documenti e studi sulla tradizione filosofica medievale* 18 (2007), 123–40; id. 'What is Porphyry's Isagôgê?', *Documenti e studi sulla tradizione filosofica medievale* 19 (2008), 1–30.
[69] Porphyry, *in Cat.* 75,25–9.
[70] Porphyry, *Isag.* 1,9–16.
[71] Porphyry, *in Cat.* 90,33–91,3.

Cat. 213,8-28, that Aristotle's *account* of the category of quality in his elementary *Categories* is a conceptual definition (*logos ennoêmatikos*), the essential (*ousiôdês*) account being reserved for his *Metaphysics*. For that does not imply that the *category* of quality is a concept, but only that Aristotle's *account* of it is a conceptual definition.

We have seen that the subject matter of Aristotle's *Categories* was said by Porphyry to include the things which spoken words signify and that *Iamblichus*, though evidently not Porphyry, said this meant that the subject mater included *concepts*. A number of commentators drew on the fact that Aristotle himself speaks of concepts in a different work, his *On Interpretation*. Sten Ebbesen has drawn attention to Iamblichus' pupil Dexippus as putting even more premium on concepts as being what spoken sounds *primarily* signify,[72] and he reminds us that that Dexippus will have been partly influenced, via Iamblichus, by Porphyry's lost larger commentary on the *Categories*. He concedes that Porphyry's surviving short commentary on Aristotle's *Categories* does not contain the word 'concept' (*noêma*).[73] As it is, Ebbesen finds only two possible references by Porphyry to concepts as the things signified. Both references are in reports on Porphyry by Boethius. Ebbesen finds Porphyry talking of *mental* discourse, which is probably a reference to Aristotle *On Interpretation* 16a3-4 and 10. That is where Aristotle takes spoken sounds to be symbols or signs of effects in the soul, identified as concepts (*noêmata*). Porphyry's gloss is that the effects in the soul are names and verbs composed in the mind and are something different in kind from the verbs or names spoken or written.[74] For a second time, however, he foregoes the opportunity of calling them concepts, although Ammonius later does in a similar passage, and Aristotle himself had so called them.[75] In Boethius' other report, Porphyry is interested in the hearer waiting for a concept (*intellectus* in Latin, standing for Greek *noêmata*), when the speaker attends to one thing (*res*), and hearer and speaker eventually agree on the same concept.[76] Here reference to concepts and things alternates, so Porphyry is not consciously stressing concepts as opposed to things. In the absence of Porphyry's lost major commentary on the *Categories*, the other texts look more like ones which could have inspired a stress on concepts, rather than themselves providing one.

To turn to the other side of the case, it has recently been argued by Riccardo Chiaradonna and Christophe Erismann that Porphyry recognises other grades of universal different from concepts. These grades of universal would not include Platonic Forms, insofar as the Neoplatonists do not endorse without qualification Aristotle's view of Platonic Forms as universals. But there would, on this view, be grades of universal other than the conceptual. According to Chiaradonna,[77] even in his

---

[72] Dexippus, *in Cat.* 7,1-2; 9,22-10,10, discussed by Sten Ebbesen, 'Porphyry's Legacy to Logic: A Reconstruction', in R. Sorabji, ed., *Aristotle Transformed* (London: Duckworth, 1990), pp. 141-71.
[73] Ebbesen, 'Porphyry's Legacy to Logic', p. 147, and his 'Boethius as an Aristotelian Commentator', in R. Sorabji, ed., *Aristotle Transformed* (London: Duckworth, 1990), pp. 373-91, at p. 382.
[74] Boethius, *in Int.²* 29,29-30,10 Meiser, apparently alluded to in Ebbesen, 'Porphyry's Legacy to Logic', pp. 142-3.
[75] Ammonius, *in Int.* 22,14.
[76] Boethius, *in Int.²* 40,9-28 Meiser, cited ibid., p. 162.
[77] 'Porphyry and Iamblichus on universals and synonymous predication'.

introductory works on Aristotle's logic, Porphyry evinces belief in levels of genus not dependent on the mind. One context in which he does so is in discussions of what is prior, or naturally prior, to what, as between individuals, species and genera. The priority relations discussed are not applicable to concepts. In his commentary on Aristotle's *Categories* 90,12–91,12, Porphyry discusses priority when he addresses the concern why Aristotle's treatment of substances in his *Categories* took individuals like Socrates as *primary* substances and species and genera as only *secondary* substances. He replies that since Aristotle is there talking about significant expressions and these apply primarily to perceptible things, Aristotle was right to claim that individuals are prior to species. For the human species would not exist if there were no individual humans. This is not to deny that the human species can survive the loss of any one individual like Socrates. Porphyry goes on to discuss a still higher level of priority and ask why Plato's intelligible Ideas and God are not called the primary substances. The answer recognises Plato's Ideas, but says that although these are indeed prior by nature or in relation to nature (91,24–5), they are once again not the present topic of discussion. Here Porphyry seems to recognise two further levels of reality beyond concepts. One is the species, which is in one way prior to the individual, and so is surely a species different from the concept, since that depends on abstraction from individuals. The other is the Platonic Idea, which, however, he declares not a subject for the beginner. Of these three levels of reality the Idea is already not regarded as universal, on Chiaradonna's interpretation of Porphyry. But two of Proclus' three levels of universal will have been recognised, even if not by the names 'in the many' and 'after the many': namely, universal concepts and the universals prior to individuals. That there are such genera and species prior by *nature* to individual substances is recognised by Porphyry again in his *Isagôgê* 17,8–10. Erismann adds to these passages cited by Chiaradonna some further texts where Porphyry emphasises a perspective that seems opposite to Aristotle's.[78] Genus, he says, is prior to species and genus and species to individual, and prior in nature,[79] because individual humans could not exist if there were no human genus or species. These priority tests are tests of what could exist without what, and had also been used by Alexander, but the test produces different results according to whether one thinks of genera as requiring at least two particulars and so being dependent on them or as being merely *capable* of belonging to more than one particular. It also matters whether genera are being compared with the totality of species or individuals falling under them, or with a smaller selection, and it matters again whether genera are thought of as *making* individuals what they are, and so having them as dependents. This last priority test is not merely ontological, but invokes *explanatory* priorities, asking what explains the existence of what.

In this last connexion, Porphyry's *Isagôgê* appeals to the idea of an origin (*arkhê*), which is sometimes applied to Plato's Ideas in their role as the causal origin of things in the perceptible world, although, as Chiaradonna stresses, he is not here talking about the level of intelligible Ideas. He nonetheless says that the genus is the *origin* of species

---

[78] C. Erismann, *L'homme commun: La genèse du réalisme ontologique durant le haut Moyen Âge* (Paris: Vrin, 2011), pp. 96, 98, 103, citing *Isag.* 14,10–12; 15,12–13; 15,18–19; 17,9–10.
[79] *Isag.* 17,9–10.

and individuals below it, perhaps because it makes them what they are,[80] since the human, both common and particular, is *constituted* (*sunestêken*) of genus and differentia.[81] This talk of the genus as *origin* and as *constitutive* seems even more clearly removed from a discussion of the relations between concepts.

Chiaradonna accepts that Porphyry also has a conceptual account of universals, but he looks for it in a different direction, not to his logical works but to the treatment of abstraction in his *Commentary on Ptolemy's Harmonics*.[82] The text in Düring's edition is difficult because it seems to give at least two different explanations, and because some of the time Porphyry is following a much earlier Platonist, Thrasyllus. At Düring 13,21-14,6, sections 24-9 in Harold Tarrant's translation,[83] Porphyry speaks in a more Aristotelian way of the form being disengaged in our soul from its material embodiment. The result is a concept (*ennoia*, repeated), and when the concept is confirmed, we have knowledge (*epistêmê*). At Düring 14,6-30 (Tarrant sections 30-9), the soul uses imagination (*phantasia*) to get a more detailed and accurate picture of the form, and then via the concept passes to the *universal* (*to katholou*, mentioned only here) and the form is stored free from material embodiment. By a further act of concentration (*epibolê*) the knowledge (*epistêmê*) is supplemented by understanding (*nous*). And now we hear for the first time that the concept is a concept of, or is accompanied by understanding of, the immaterial Platonic Idea (*eidos*) which had in the first place endowed matter with form, like the impress from a signet ring (Tarrant sections 30-5). What the soul has done is to make the form disembodied again, and when your voice articulates in speech the image (*eikôn*) that the soul contains, it makes that image conform both to the archetypal Idea and to the embodied form (Tarrant sections 36-9). No comment is made on whether or not the Platonic Idea is universal, although the soul has acquired a universal and the image it has acquired agrees with the Idea.

Ammonius: Multigrade Genera, the Highest being Non-Universal *logoi* in the Mind of Aristotle's Supposed Creator God

Ammonius (between 435/45 - between 517/26), head of the philosophy school in Alexandria, had learnt from his teacher Proclus' threefold distinction between universals before the many, in the many and after the many particulars.[84] In two commentaries, one anonymously edited 'from Ammonius' voice', Ammonius, and his own pupil Philoponus in a further commentary, call it a distinction among universals (*katholou*), common entities (*koina*), genera (*genê*), species (*eidê*), or forms (the same word *eidê* again), and another pupil, Simplicius, speaks the same

---

[80] *Isag.* 2,7-13; 5,9-12; 6,6-7.
[81] *Isag.* 11,15-17.
[82] R. Chiaradonna, 'Porphyry's Views on the Immanent Incorporeals', in G. Karamanolis and A. Sheppard, eds, *Studies on Porphyry* (London: Institute of Classical Studies, 2007), pp. 35-49, at pp. 45-8.
[83] H. Tarrant, *Thrasyllan Platonism* (Ithaca, NY: Cornell University Press, 1993), ch. 5.
[84] Proclus, *in Eucl.* 1,50,15-51,9.

way.[85] But Ammonius transformed Proclus' *first* level 'before the many'. Proclus, we saw, had heavily qualified the claim of this level to be universal, and Ammonius does not call it universal, but actually denies that it is universal.[86] But what he does do is to transform it into a level that would be acceptable to Aristotle. What we find at the level 'before' the many particulars are not Plato's transcendent Ideas, existing outside the mind,[87] but *logoi*, rational concepts, in the mind of Plato's Demiurge or Creator God.[88] This already goes a good way towards harmonising Plato with Aristotle, because Aristotle's God was also a thinker with *logoi* in his mind. In Ammonius, or rather in another commentary from the voice of Ammonius edited by Asclepius on the *Metaphysics*, Platonic Ideas are said not to exist as separate realities in their own right (*autai kath' hautas en hupostasei*), but they do exist in other ways, for example (as Ammonius had said) as creative *logoi*, rational principles, which are objects of intellect (*noêtai*) in the mind of the Creator, and as objects of rational thought (*dianoêtai*) in our souls.[89] There is something extra clever about Ammonius denying that the highest universals are transcendent Ideas, because his teacher Proclus would be obliged to agree on the basis of his own quite different view, that the Ideas of Plato are not universals in the sense of natures shared in common with particulars. Rather, they are common or universal only in the sense of being the single model in relation to which (*pros hen*) the particulars that share in them have a variety of *different* relations.

The *second* set of genera, species or forms is *in the many* and is universal. Ammonius, as anonymously reported, says that the Aristotelians speak about this kind.[90] He explains that it is these universals in the many that depend (as Alexander had said) on there being more than one particular, but he finds a new reason, which Philoponus will later contradict, in Aristotle's *Categories* 2a36-b6. They depend on more than one particular in order to have something of which to be predicated (*katêgoreisthai*). This requirement of more than one, Ammonius is reported as saying, does not apply to the intelligibles *before the many*, for these are not universals at all. And now the anonymous reporter of Ammonius' lectures seems to explain why Ammonius adds this last point, that the discussion is not about intelligibles before the many, and in doing so, to make a mistake in the opposite directions from Ammonius.[91] He takes it that Ammonius is thinking about Porphyry *Isagôgê* 15,18, and he wrongly takes Porphyry to say there that in principle a genus could exist even on the hypothesis that there were *no* species, when in fact all Porphyry means is that the genus would survive the loss of any *one* species. But having made this first mistake, the anonymous reporter makes another

---

[85] Ammonius, *in Isag.* 41,2–42,26; 68,25–69,11; 104,28–31; Commentary *in Cat.* anonymously edited from Ammonius' voice (henceforth: Ammonius, *in Cat.* Anon.) 41,3–11; Philoponus, *in Cat.* 58,13–59,1; 67,19–24. The distinction is recorded by Ammonius' pupil, Simplicius, as a distinction among common entities (*koina*), Simplicius, *in Cat.* 82,35–83,20, cf. 69,19–71,2.
[86] Ammonius, *in Cat.* Anon. 41,5–6.
[87] Plato, *Parmenides* 132B-C.
[88] Ammonius, *in Isag.* 41,21–42,7.
[89] Asclepius, *in Metaph.* 166,30–168,18. See Arthur Madigan SJ, 'Syrianus and Asclepius on Forms and Intermediates in Plato and Aristotle', *Journal of the History of Philosophy* 24 (1986), 149–71.
[90] Ammonius, *in Cat.* Anon. 41,3–11.
[91] Ammonius, *in Cat.* Anon. 41,6–11.

and assumes that Porphyry must have been talking about intelligible genera prior to the many, since they are the only non-universal type of genus and could exist without any species, and that Ammonius is correcting Porphyry. In fact Ammonius himself, we saw above, had interpreted Porphyry's discussion on rather thin grounds as being addressed in the opposite direction, neither to intelligibles before the many nor to the universals in the many, but downwards to mere human concepts derived from the many. This gives us a warning that whoever the anonymous editor was of Ammonius' seminars on Aristotle's *Categories*, he does not always interpret Ammonius accurately. I have therefore suggested giving an abbreviated reference to him in case of ambiguity as Ammonius *in Cat.* Anon. instead of Ammonius *in Cat.*, as has been the universal practice including my own, since that practice suggests that we have unadulterated Ammonius.

The *third* of Ammonius' levels is merely in our soul. Such genera are conceptual (*ennoêmatika*) as being in our thought (*dianoia*). This is where Ammonius interprets Porphyry's 'sketch of the concept (*ennoia*) of the genus' rather dubiously as a sketch of the *conceptual* genus. What we do is define a thing like human in accordance with our own concept (*ennoia*) and thought (*dianoia*), and following that analogy, say that human is a mortal rational animal.[92] On this topic too we shall see Ammonius' pupil Philoponus correcting him, because he does not agree that what we define is things like human, and to Philoponus I shall now turn.

Philoponus' Commentaries on Aristotle: Ammonius' Multigrade Universals, but with Concepts given Extra Roles

Ammonius' pupil Philoponus was eventually in his theological works to take a very startling new view of universals. But in his commentaries on Aristotle, he recognises all three of Ammonius' levels, and uses the nomenclature of their being 'before', 'in', or 'after' the many particulars. But even here there are some differences from Ammonius and from Ammonius as anonymously reported, and some of these differences, we shall see, already give concepts a slightly greater importance.

Philoponus twice speaks of the idea sponsored by Ammonius that there are creative principles (*dêmiourgikoi logoi*) separated from matter in the mind of the divine Creator, and he calls them, like Ammonius, genera (though not universals) 'before the many'.[93] In one of these passages he is commenting on Aristotle's saying that we must ask whether there is a single definition of soul corresponding to a single definition of living being or of any other common items predicated (*katêgoreisthai*), or whether there is a different one for horse, dog, etc, so that the universal living being is either nothing or posterior. Philoponus' comment is that the universal which Aristotle is here downgrading is not the genus *before* the many particulars, such as the creative principles, because those cannot be defined. Rather, Aristotle's talk of what has a

[92] Ammonius, *in Isag.* 68,25–69,11.
[93] Philoponus, *in DA* 38,13–15; 58,9.

definition must refer to *conceptual* entities (*ennoêmatika*) which are posterior, since what we define is the *concept* (*ennoia*) that we have of things.[94] Here Philoponus' claim that we define the *concept* goes beyond Alexander, who thought that we define a *form* such as mortal rational animal, and beyond Ammonius, who thought that we define *human* as mortal rational animal in *accordance* with our concept.[95]

There are three other commentaries in which Philoponus compares two levels of universals, the conceptual and those in particulars, with each other and with particulars. In one text he says that the existence of universals is in particulars, but when the universals are *taken as* universals, they come to be in the soul.[96] In another, he says that nature never makes what is common and indiscriminate, but only what is particular and articulated, and universals arise only then out of the collection of particulars, whereas we, unlike nature, start by applying indiscriminate universals.[97] In a third commentary Philoponus discusses whether universals or particular individuals are prior. He expresses, like Ammonius, a firm view on this in his *in Cat*. In nature, genera, species, and universals are prior and particulars depend on them.[98] But like Porphyry and Ammonius before him, he also presents a defence of the opposite priority, not based on nature, which appears in Aristotle's *Categories*. Aristotle there makes individual substances such as Socrates prior to universals like human or living being. Talking of universal substances, Philoponus defends Aristotle partly by saying that universals and common items like animal in the many particulars do indeed depend on the particulars, because if there were no such thing as a human being, or Plato (and similarly for other species), there would be no such thing as animal. This, however, is the place where he criticises the particular way of defending Aristotle that we found in the anonymous edition of Ammonius' lectures on Aristotle's *Categories*, which makes the universal or common item animal depend on particulars in order to have something of which they can be *predicated*.[99] Philoponus disagrees with Ammonius as here reported, by saying that what is *predicated* of individuals is not the common items existing *in* the many particulars but *concepts* and the *conceptual* which are *after* the particulars. Nonetheless, he says, Aristotle is still right, because there would be neither the animal in particular animals, nor animal as a *concept*, if there were not individual animals.[100]

Philoponus' Theology: Universals Transformed into Concepts Only

There are, then, already two differences from Ammonius on the role of concepts. But in later works of Christian theology Philoponus makes a far more radical break with Ammonius and with the tradition by downgrading the status of universals to being

---

[94] Philoponus, *in DA* 38,13–17 on Aristotle, *De Anima* 1.1, 402b5–9.
[95] Ammonius, *in Isag.* 68,25–69,11.
[96] Philoponus, *in DA* 307,33–4.
[97] Philoponus, *in Phys.* 14,3–17; 15,20–4.
[98] Philoponus, *in Cat.* 50,6–9; 53,11–13; 53,28–9.
[99] Ammonius, *in Cat.* Anon. 40,19–21.
[100] Philoponus, *in Cat.* 58,7–59,2.

only concepts. In his theological work *Arbiter* (or *Diaitêtês*) of or just before 553, Philoponus insists that in particulars, *natures* are not common or universal, but particular (*idia*), and further accepts universals *only* in the mind. The relevant passage survives not only in Syriac, but in excerpts from the original Greek in John of Damascus in his *On Heresies*, and it has been highlighted by Ebied, van Roey and Wickham and by Erismann.[101] Here Philoponus refers to Alexander's common nature of man, rational mortal animal, but says twice that, as it exists in particular men, it is *not* common: 'Now, this *common nature* of man, in which no one man differs from any other, when it comes into being in any one of the individuals, then comes into being particular (*idia*) to that one and *not common* (*koinê*) to any other individual, as we set forth in chapter four. Thus that rational mortal animal which is in me is *common to no other* animal'.[102] And again a few lines further: 'Thus that rational mortal animal which is in me is *not common* to any of the other humans. Nor would the nature of animal in this horse come into being in any other, as we have just shown'.[103] These two unqualified statements claim that each nature, as it exists in an individual, is *unique* like the individual form (*atomon eidos*) which Philoponus in his commentaries ascribes to Alexander,[104] and not common or universal. This goes closely as part of a single view with Philoponus still treating, like Alexander as interpreted above, a nature like mortal rational animal as common or universal in the *mind*. And this is where he insists it is universal *only* in the mind. To see this, we need to look at his statement sandwiched in between the two particularising statements cited by Erismann. The sandwiched passage issues a warning that there are two perspectives and he starts by talking about the universal in the mind. 'Therefore each nature is said to be what it is, not in one way but in two: in one way when we consider the common account (*logos*) of each nature by itself, for example the common nature of human or of horse coming into being in *none* of the individuals.' Here Philoponus recognises a universal perspective, because he distinguishes the nature as abstracted by the *mind* from any of the individuals, and so as truly common or universal. In returning, however, to what is outside the mind in particulars, he reverts to his individualistic perspective. Philoponus' idea that a universal exists only in the mind reaches its climax in later theological works, when he argues for the heresy for which he was condemned, that the Christian Trinity is not three persons, but three substances, and even godheads. In the biggest transformation of all that we have seen, he says that if these three godheads constitute a single God, that one God must be a mere universal existing only in our *minds*.[105]

---

[101] R. Y. Ebied, A. Van Roey, and L. R. Wickham, *Peter of Callinicum, Anti-Tritheist Dossier*, Orientalia Lovanensis Analecta 10 (Leuven: Peeters, 1981), p. 26; Erismann, 'John Philoponus on Individuality and Particularity', pp. 143–59, from John of Damascus *On Heresies*, in *Patrologia Graeca*, ed. Migne, vol. 94, col. 748A; cf. col. 744C.
[102] Philoponus, *Arbiter* 7 = John of Damascus *Book on Heresies* 83.52–5 (Kotter).
[103] Philoponus, *Arbiter* 7 = John of Damascus *Book on Heresies* 83.59–68 (Kotter).
[104] Philoponus, *in GC* 313,16–22.
[105] Philoponus, *Against Themistius*, and two other texts, fragments translated from Syriac in Ebied, van Roey and Wickham, op. cit., pp. 51,5–9, 31–2; *On Theology*, translated into Latin from Syriac by A. van Roey, 'Les fragments trithéites de Jean Philopon', *Orientalia Lovaniensia Periodica* 11 (1980), 135–63. I have benefited from discussion with Mossman Rouéché in treating the theological works.

Eustratius

By way of postscript, I should say that Eustratius (1050–1120) after a five hundred year gap, produced a variant on Proclus' three types of genus and species, in his commentary on Aristotle's *Posterior Analytics* at 195,5–196,16. He called the lowest type 'from the many' rather than 'after the many'. It is only this last type that he calls conceptual (*ennoêmatika*, 196,9). He says that in thought (*kat' ennoian*) such a genus is from the various species and such a species from the particulars, 195,16–18. It is a collection (*athroisma*) put together (*suntetheimenon*) from its parts, 195,34–6, and they are what embrace and are *predicated* (*katêgoreisthai*) of what falls under them, 196,3–12, in contrast to the genera which are *in* the species or species which are *in* the particulars.[106]

Universals Transformed

Let me survey what transformations we have noticed in the idea of universals in the tradition of ancient commentary on Aristotle. Boethus downgraded them. Alexander multiplied grades, going beyond Aristotle by including as a grade on the same scale conceptual universals, but ameliorated the low status of both grades by giving the non-conceptual ones certain explanatory roles. He also innovated in discussing Aristotle's rejection of Plato's Ideas by saying that even if Ideas and particulars were synonymous, sharing both name and definition, yet the definition might not be *properly* shared by the particular. Porphyry followed Alexander by accepting multigrade universals, but Ammonius influenced posterity by associating Porphyry with the idea that only concepts are universals. Proclus and Simplicius drew from Aristotle's concepts in Alexander when they gave reasons why Aristotle was wrong on both counts about Plato's Ideas: Ideas were not universals, except in a qualified sense, but they were causes. Proclus accepted three levels of reality: Ideas before the many particulars and two grades of universal, one in the many particulars and a conceptual one modelled after the many particulars. His pupil Ammonius accepted three levels, but transformed the highest one into non-universal concepts in the mind of Plato's Creator God. This was the first of two steps in presenting Aristotle as agreeing with Plato, contrary to the complaints of Proclus, because Aristotle's God was a thinker who entertained concepts in his mind. Ammonius' harmonisation of Aristotle with Plato was completed by rejecting the claim of Proclus, and of Proclus' teacher Syrianus, that Aristotle did not recognise his own arguments as implying that God was a Creator, just as Plato thought. Philoponus diverged from Ammonius, and from Ammonius' anonymous editor, by giving to concepts the role of being what we define and predicate. But only in his theological work did he reach the final transformation of making concepts into the only universals, thus concluding that the Christian Trinity consisted of three godheads having no unity except as a universal Godhead existing only in our minds.

---

[106] This is described, and equipped with paraphrases rather than translations, by A. C. Lloyd, 'The Aristotelianism of Eustratius of Nicaea', in Jürgen Wiesner, ed., *Aristoteles Werk und Wirkung*, 2 vols (Berlin: De Gruyter, 1987), vol. 2, pp. 341–51.

11

Iamblichus' *Noera Theôria* of Aristotle's *Categories*[1]

John M. Dillon

In the preface to his commentary on Aristotle's *Categories,* Simplicius, in the course of reviewing his predecessors in the field, has this to say about Iamblichus:

> Following on him (*sc.* Porphyry), the divine Iamblichus has also himself composed a lengthy commentary on this work, for the most part following the work of Porphyry even to the extent of *verbatim* borrowing, but in some cases criticizing and more clearly elucidating him (*diarthrôn akribesteron*), while at the same time compressing his lecture-style longwindedness in the refutation of objections, *and throughout his work superimposing upon more or less every section the intellectual interpretation (noera theôria) of the subject-matter,* as well as adding to the work another element over and above these that is useful: for, seeing that Archytas the Pythagorean, even prior to Aristotle, had made the division into the ten primary genera in his work *On the Universe* (*Peri tou pantos*),[2] he incorporated it into his commentary, and where Archytas had set out clearly by means of examples the distinguishing marks of each of them, and explained their order in relation to each other, the specific differentiae of each, and their common and particular properties, he produces in the appropriate places Archytas' contributions, shows their agreement with Aristotle's doctrine, and, in cases where there is discrepancy (of which there are just a few), he has brought these to the attention of scholars, not neglecting, either, to explain in each case the cause of the discrepancy–and

---

This article first appeared as 'Iamblichus' *Noera Theoria* of Aristotle's Categories' by John Dillon in *Syllecta Classica* VIII (1997), pp. 65–77. © Syllecta Classica in Association with Project Muse.

[1] Earlier versions of this talk have previously been delivered to audiences at the Institute of Classical Studies in London (February 1986), and in Princeton (December 1987), and have profited much from discussion and criticism at those venues. I am particularly indebted to Prof. S. Strange, at the latter venue, for a penetrating written response, from which I have derived much profit.

[2] Also entitled, in the *Codex Ambrosianus* and elsewhere, 'On the Basic Principles of Discourse, or On the Ten Categories'. This has been most recently edited, in both its Doric and its Koine versions, by T. A. Szlezák, *Pseudo-Archytas Über die Kategorien*, Peripatoi 4 (Berlin: De Gruyter, 1972). It is most plausibly dated to the first century CE, and seems to incorporate the results of the first generation of criticism of the *Categories*, by such men as Andronicus, Ariston, and Eudorus. Iamblichus, of course, took it as genuine.

reasonably so, because it is clear all through the work that Aristotle is intending to follow the lead of Archytas.

Simplicius, *in Cat.* 2,9 ff.

What can we gather from this account? First, surely, that Iamblichus based his commentary for the most part fairly closely on that of Porphyry. What was the nature of Porphyry's large commentary (which is lost)[3] we shall see in a moment. To this capacious framework Iamblichus added (1) certain criticisms or modifications of Porphyry, such as Simplicius periodically reports;[4] (2) the adducing of the relevant passages of Archytas, which Simplicius tells us that he was the first commentator to do;[5] and (3) some 'higher criticism', or, as Simplicius terms it, 'intellectual interpretation' (*noera theôria*) of nearly all sections of the work. It is this last aspect of Iamblichus' commentary to which I would like to devote some consideration on this occasion.

First of all, though, let us consider the nature of Porphyry's large commentary. Simplicius gives us a description of it just before discussing Iamblichus:

> After these (*sc.* Plotinus and earlier critics of the work), Porphyry, to whom we are indebted for all that is good, composed with great industry a comprehensive commentary on the book, along with solutions to all the objections proposed, in seven books, that is, the commentary addressed to Gedalius, including also many details concerning Stoic doctrine, according as they are relevant at each point.

Simplicius, *in Cat.* 2,5–9

Porphyry, then, we may gather, is ultimately responsible for the setting out of, and the responses to, all the *aporiai* concocted by the line of critics of the *Categories* in the Middle Platonic period, mainly Lucius and Nicostratus, but also Eudorus before them and Atticus after them, as well as Stoics such as Cornutus and Athenodorus, and following on all of them, Plotinus, in *Enneades* 6.1–3 (and possibly in oral communications as well). This is frequently obvious from Simplicius' account in the course of his commentary, but on the basis of this testimony we may take it to be the case even when no explicit reference to Porphyry is provided. It would seem also reasonable, by the same token, to credit Porphyry with such references to Stoic doctrines as we find in the course of the commentary. And all this is doubtless then to be included in that part of Iamblichus' commentary which he took over from Porphyry virtually unchanged – merely, perhaps, 'compressing his lecture-style long-windedness in the refutation of objections'.[6]

---

[3] Porphyry's short commentary, in question and answer format, is of course extant (edited by A. Busse in CAG 4.1), and has now received an excellent translation, with introduction and commentary, in the Ancient Commentators on Aristotle series by S. Strange (London: Duckworth, 1992). The bulk of Porphyry's large commentary can, in fact, be recovered with a fair degree of certainty from Simplicius.

[4] e.g. 129,1; 155,15; 160,10–11; 302,25–6.

[5] This should imply that all of the references to Archytas in Simplicius' commentary may be attributed to Iamblichus. Simplicius doubtless had access himself to the work of 'Archytas', but he is not the sort of man to do again what had been perfectly well done before him.

[6] *Sustellôn tên hôs en skholais pros tas enstaseis makrologian.* Presumably this is the meaning of *en skholais*. If so, it is an interesting judgement on the nature of Porphyry's discursiveness.

When all this has been added up, and subtracted from the total of Simplicius' commentary, what have we left? Simplicius himself is very modest, and quite explicit, as to what his own contribution is. I quote from slightly further on in the preface:

> My aim in this work has been, on the one hand, to derive from the text, as far as I could, a more accurate understanding of what is being said, and on the other to make clearer and more harmonious the profound thought of the author, inaccessible as it is to the majority of people; and thirdly, to compress somehow into smaller compass the vast and varied mass of previous commentaries – not, as did the great philosopher Syrianus, to the minimum possible, but as far as possible so as to leave out nothing essential.
>
> Simplicius, *in Cat.* 13,4 ff.

So then, Simplicius is trying as far as possible to compress his material, even as he has told us above that Iamblichus compressed the longwindedness of Porphyry, as well as clarifying some of his formulations. It is plain that posterity has been spared some truly monstrous works. What, then, if anything, does Simplicius feel that he is adding to this great tradition?

> If I have been able to add anything at all, for this I give thanks, after the Gods, to these men, under whose guidance it is that I have raised any points worthy of acceptance or contributed any elucidations worthy of note. I would, however, urge all those who take up this book never to disregard the writings of Iamblichus and Porphyry in favour of these annotations of mine, but to use my work, if at all, merely as an introduction and practice exercise for the more accurate understanding of their utterances.
>
> Simplicius, *in Cat.* 3,10–17

One cannot help but like Simplicius. We are unable, alas, to take his advice, so we must do the best we can with what he has transmitted to us.

I am not concerned here with the larger question of how much of Iamblichus' commentary we can recover from Simplicius, and from a comparison of his commentary with the surviving portion of the short commentary, in dialogue form, of Iamblichus' pupil Dexippus.[7] On the present occasion I am only concerned with the securely attested passages of Iamblichus' commentary (such as do not in fact figure in that of

---

[7] The daunting problem of recovering all that could be recovered of Iamblichus' commentary from the the pages of Simplicius is brought home to one by the fact that many sections of Dexippus' commentary appear more or less word for word in Simplicius without any attribution to Iamblichus, where, in effect, Simplicius has no dispute with or demurral from what Iamblichus is saying. Any notion that Simplicius is taking these passages from Dexippus himself, though he does know of his commentary (cf. Simplicius, *in Cat.* 2,9 ff.), should be dispelled by the circumstance that at least seven passages closely similar or identical to Dexippus are explicitly attributed by Simplicius to Iamblichus (see list provided on page 11, note 14 of my translation of Dexippus). To such passages may also presumably be added all references to Archytas, whom Simplicius tells us Iamblichus was the first authority to make use of.

Dexippus), which are sufficient to make clear his rather bizarre approach to the subject matter of the *Categories*. These passages have been adequately collected (though not, in my opinion, adequately commented on), by the Danish scholar B. Dalsgaard Larsen,[8] and I shall use his numeration, along with the references to Simplicius' commentary.

Iamblichus' techniques of allegorical exegesis of Plato's dialogues, which form the basis for the allegorical method of the later Athenian School, notably Syrianus and Proclus (but also, of course, Simplicius himself, and his mentor Damascius) are reasonably well known by now.[9] What is less widely appreciated, perhaps, is that he manages to apply much the same method to the rather less amenable subject matter of Aristotle's *Categories*.[10] Certainly, he concerns himself as well with all the traditional subjects of controversy and debate on the work, but in most of this he is content to follow Porphyry, and is therefore not distinguished from him by Simplicius. It is only in the application of *noera theôria* to the subject matter that he really comes into his own.[11]

Let us first examine some characteristic passages, and then, on the basis of these, try to derive a picture of Iamblichus' method as a whole.

The first issue arising, as we should expect from what we know of Iamblichus' method of commentary,[12] is the definition of the *skopos,* or essential subject matter, of the treatise. In the case of the *Categories,* Iamblichus had before him a long history of controversy as to the subject matter, in the course of which there had been been champions of all three possible subject matters for the *Categories* to wit, words, things, and concepts.[13] It seems to have been Herminus, the teacher of Alexander of Aphrodisias, who first came up with the solution that in a way the subject matter concerns all three classes of entity, and this solution was refined variously by Alexander and later by Porphyry.

---

[8] *Iamblique de Chalcis, Exégète et Philosophe* (Aarhus: Universitetsforlaget, 1972). Vol. 1 contains the introduction and commentary, vol. 2 contains the actual fragments. Dalsgaard Larsen, however, though making many useful observations, is curiously uninterested in the details of Neoplatonic philosophy, and treats Iamblichus primarily as an exegete, rather than a man who is doing philosophy in the mode of exegesis. He makes no effort to reclaim the passages from Dexippus, though he is quite well aware of them, or to incorporate those that concern Archytas.

[9] First discussed by K. Praechter, 'Richtungen und Schulen im Neuplatonismus', *Genethliakon für Karl Robert* (Berlin: Weidmann, 1910), pp. 105–6; but see also my remarks in the introduction to *Iamblichi Chalcidensis: in Platonis Dialogos Commentariorum Fragmenta,* ed. J. M. Dillon (Leiden: Brill, 1973), pp. 54–66.

[10] His few surviving comments on the *Prior Analytics* (fr. 137–45) seem, by contrast, to be strictly practical. The subject matter there, presumably, defied all transcendental interpretation.

[11] It sounds as if Porphyry did not envisage a 'higher' interpretation of the *Categories* at all. The contrast, then, between his exegetical principles and those of Iamblichus would be that much starker than in the case of their respective *Timaeus* commentaries, where Proclus makes a distinction between the 'more piecemeal' (*merikôteron*) commentary of Porphyry and the 'more epoptic' (*epoptikôteron*) approach of Iamblichus *(In Platonis Timaeum Commentarii* 1,204,24 ff.), this latter epithet presumably denoting both a more holistic and a more transcendental approach to the subject matter.

[12] See my commentary on *In Phaedrum,* fr. 1, and *In Timaeum,* fr. 1 in *Iamblichi Chalcidensis: in Platonis Dialogos Fragmenta* (n. 9 above), pp. 248–9 and 264–5.

[13] *Phônai, pragmata, noêmata.* Simplicius gives these anonymously at *in Cat.* 9,4–10,8. Interestingly, Dexippus presents a dialectical survey of all three positions by Sosigenes, one of the teachers of Alexander of Aphrodisias *(in Cat.* 7,4–9,24), which one would expect, therefore, to have figured at least in Iamblichus' commentary, but of which no clear record survives in that of Simplicius.

Porphyry's definition of the *skopos* is as follows: 'It is about the objects of predication (*ta katêgoroumena*); these are simple words significatory of things, *insofar as they are significatory*, but not insofar as they are simply utterances (*lexeis*).' Porphyry is quoted by Simplicius *(in Cat.* 10,20 ff.) in terms which make it sound as if he is emending Alexander's definition (which was 'concerning the simple and most generic parts of speech, signifying simple entities (*pragmata*), and the simple thoughts (*noêmata*) relative to those simple entities'), but it is not easy to see what substantial matter they are in dispute about, and Simplicius himself says just below *(in Cat.* 13,15 ff.) that a somewhat amplified version of this formula is the view of a whole chorus of authorities, comprising 'both Alexanders (*sc.* Alexander of Aigai as well), Herminus, Boethus, and Porphyry', and that this is assented to by Iamblichus and Syrianus and 'my own masters' (*sc.* Ammonius and Damascius).

On the other hand, a tradition stemming from Olympiodorus *(in Cat.* 19,36 ff.)[14] presents Iamblichus as reconciling from a rather lofty perspective the imperfect and partial views of his predecessors, as if he was the first to come up with this portmanteau definition. If this is not complete fantasy, it may indicate that Iamblichus in his commentary tried to pretend that he was being somewhat more original than he in fact is. As far as we can see, at any rate, Iamblichus in his definition of the *skopos* is not deviating in any substantial way from that of Alexander, as retooled by Porphyry.

The definition of the *skopos* cannot, therefore, really count as part of Iamblichus' distinctive *noera theôria*, but it is worth mentioning at the outset, I think, as an indication of the attitude which Iamblichus may have taken up to his predecessors, even when he did not have much to quarrel with them about. For what it is worth, I give the final version of the *skopos,* as presented by Simplicius, as it may be substantially that of Iamblichus:[15]

> (It concerns) simple and primary and generic words, insofar as they are significatory of realities (*onta*), and it instructs us at all events also about the things signified by them, and about the concepts in accordance with which things are signified by words.
>
> Simplicius, *in Cat.* 13,13–16

Leaving aside the *skopos,* then, let us turn to examine some examples of the *noera theôria* in action. We may begin with a question of perennial interest to ancient commentators, whether Aristotle's definition of substance in chapter 5 of the *Categories* (4a10), 'that which, being numerically one and the same, is able to receive contraries', really identifies an essential attribute of substance, or simply an accidental one. For one thing, is it applicable to intelligible as well as to sensible matter? For another, is it even applicable to the substances of the heavenly regions, or to such substances as fire or

---

[14] Taken up later by Elias, *in Cat.* 130,14 ff.

[15] Simplicius does, after all, make an interesting distinction between the first group of authorities, from the Alexanders to Porphyry, saying that Iamblichus 'assents' to them (*epipsêphizei*), and Syrianus 'clarifies' (*saphênizei*) – either all his predecessors, or just Iamblichus. What we may have here, then, is the Iamblichean definition, as 'clarified' by Syrianus.

snow? This latter objection, at least, probably goes back to Lucius and Nicostratus,[16] while Plotinus is cast by Simplicius *(in Cat.* 115,24–116,10),[17] and presumably by Iamblichus himself before him,[18] as the protagonist of the former. The particular point made by Plotinus (in *Enneades* 6.1.2.15–18) to which Iamblichus is replying here is that, even if 'being, while numerically one and the same, receptive of contraries' identifies a *characteristic* of substance, it does not describe its essence, its *ti estin*.

The first line of response to this, relayed by Dexippus (57,18–59,8), and so presumably adopted by Iamblichus as at least a preliminary defence,[19] is that Aristotle is only here concerned with sublunary, physical substance, and should not be held to be defining the essence of eternal, simple substances as well. Further, as regards the heavenly bodies, and fire and snow, such characteristics as circular motion, or heat cannot count as one of a pair of contrary qualities in these cases, as they are essential to the composition of those bodies.[20]

However, Iamblichus does not stop there, but takes the offensive, proceeding, as Simplicius says, *Puthagorikôteron* – on more Pythagorean lines (116,25 ff. = fr. 33).[21] He professes, by the employment of analogical reasoning (*di' analogian*),[22] to discern the co-existence of contraries at the level of intelligible substance as well – to wit, Motion and Rest, Sameness and Otherness, the very *megista genê* of the *Sophist* which Plotinus in *Ennead* 6.2 adopted as the 'categories' of the intelligible world. The only difference, Iamblichus maintains, is that on the intelligible plane the contraries are present, not successively, but simultaneously.[23] He goes on to discern the coexistence of contraries also in the substance of the heavenly bodies, the distinction from the intelligible realm being that there the contraries coexist in a simple entity, while in the celestial realm they exist in different parts at different times *(in Cat.* 117,27–30).[24] At the lowest level, which is the physical, the opposites can be present only alternately.

[16] It is anonymous in Simplicius, *in Cat.* 114,21 ff.
[17] Though also anonymously, for whatever reason (*phasin*), but he represents *Enneades* 6.1.2.15–18 pretty closely.
[18] Dexippus (5,20 ff.) presents this as an *aporia* of Plotinus, which would seem to clinch the matter.
[19] Dexippus is, of course, quite capable of drawing directly on Porphyry as well, but since Dexippus' arguments here (especially at 58,24 ff.) go beyond what is to be found in Porphyry's short commentary (99,1–100,8), I would take it that Iamblichus took over and elaborated Porphyry's arguments.
[20] This is an ingenious point, but it does not quite solve the problem, it seems to me, since we are not given an example of what would be a pair of contrary qualities to which the sun, or fire, would be hospitable.
[21] He prefaces this, as so often, by adducing Archytas (*in Cat.* 116,11–24), whose formulation he finds superior to Aristotle's, both because he adds *diamenoisan* to *tôn enantiôn dektikan*, as it eliminates the secondary substances from consideration (since they do not 'outlast' changes in qualities), and because he adds *ou kata ton auton de khronon*, thus eliminating the non-temporal level of substance from consideration. Archytas is thus praised, once again, for superior clarity. It is almost as if Iamblichus recognised with half his mind that 'Archytas' was later than Aristotle, and thus able to 'improve' on him. Why, otherwise, except through weakness of intellect, would Aristotle fail to follow his lead?
[22] One may see a connection here with his procedure in the *Timaeus Commentary*, where he discerns the conflict (*enantiôsis*) between Atlantis and Athens as being reflected analogously at all levels of being, right up to the dyad that follows immediately upon the One (Proclus, *In Platonis Timaeum Commentarii* 1,77,24 ff. = *In Timaeum*, fr. 7).
[23] *in Cat.* 116,29: *ou para meros all' hama*.
[24] In this connection he shows quite a detailed acquaintance with the technical terminology of astronomy/astrology, bandying about such terms as *apoklima*, *antimesouranêma*, and *antiperistasis*.

This passage is a good example, I think, of the *noera theôria* at work. Iamblichus' focus of interest is ontological rather than logical, and he delights in seeing the same feature – in this case, the ability to receive contraries – manifested analogically at varous levels of reality: 'this property of substance is common to every (level of) substance' (*to idiôma touto tês ousias koinon kata pasan ousian*) as he says *(in Cat.* 118,2).

To turn now to the category of Quantity, his argument in favour of weight (*rhopê*) being classed as a third type of quantity,[25] along with *megethos* and *plêthos* (representing continuous and discrete quantity respectively) is another interesting example of his method *(apud* Simplicius, *in Cat.* 128,16–129,7 = fr. 36). First of all, he claims Archytas (25,1–3) as his authority for this triadic division (against Porphyry, Comutus, and probably Alexander).[26] Then he straightway relates this to ontology by seeing a distinction between weighted and weightless quantities at various levels of reality: the four elements having relative weight and lightness, as against the heaven, which is weightless; among types of motion, the rectilinear ones, involving weight, as against the circular, which is weightless; and then, rising to the level of immaterial essence, the Soul, which has an inclination (*rhopê*) towards what is below it or above it, as against Intellect, which is unaffected by such inclinations, and thus *arrepes*.

A little further on *(apud* Simplicius, 135,8–28 = fr. 37), Iamblichus gives us an 'intellectual' explanation[27] of the fact that 'of quantities, some are discrete, others continuous':

> Since the power of the One, from which all quantity derives, extends alike through all things, and demarcates each thing in its procession from itself, insofar as it penetrates totally indivisibly through all things, it generates the continuous, and insofar as it performs a single and indivisible procession without interval; whereas insofar as it halts in its procession at each of the forms and defines each and makes each of them one, in this aspect it produces the discrete; so in virtue of being the single dominant causal principle of these two activities it produces the two types of quantity.
>
> Simplicius, *in Cat.* 135,10–17

He continues this line of thought for some while longer, linking the two classes of quantity in the universe in various ways with the processive and static aspects of the One, ending with the following interesting remark: 'For the potency of the

---

[25] That is, one can have measurements of weight, such a mina or a talent, as well as those of size or number.

[26] In this connection, we may note that Athenodorus of Tarsus is recorded (*in Cat.* 128,8) as 'agreeing with' Archytas in proposing *rhopê* as a third class of quantity, which can be taken, I think, as a pretty good argument for dating Pseudo-Archytas later than Athenodorus (late first century BCE), and is so taken by Szlezák (n. 2 above, p. 121) – though, as Szlezák also points out (p. 120), the triad of number, size, and weight is perfectly common in the Classical period, and is employed at various points in the dialogues by Plato (e.g. *Euthyphro* 7B-C, *Respublica* 602D, *Philebus* 55E), which would add Platonic authority to this amplification.

[27] Simplicius actually speaks of him here as 'exhibiting his *theôrêtikê epistêmês*'.

intelligible measurements comprises at the same time both the remaining and the processive elements in one and the same entity; for which reason, if one attributes just one or the other of these to the intelligible and divine measurement, in the case of assigning the unmoving ones alone, one becomes deceived by the errors of the Peripatetics, and in the case of the processive ones, by those of the Stoics.' He thus satisfactorily puts both of the chief rivals of Platonism in their place, criticising on the one hand the Peripatetic Unmoved Mover, and on the other the dynamic Active Principle of the Stoics.

The *noera theôria* here, then, consists in identifying the characteristics of being discrete or continuous as aspects of the power of the One, active at every level of reality, and thus gives a metaphysical underpinning to the rather bald and unpretentious text of Aristotle. It also furthers another constant aim of Iamblichus in his exegesis, which is to emphasise the unity underlying each category – something that was frequently challenged by hostile critics.

We may turn next to a long passage (*apud* Simplicius, *in Cat.* 216,6–219,35 = fr. 65), in which Iamblichus presents an account of 'the more intellectual causal principles' (*noerôterai aitiai*) of Quality. His aim here is to establish the substantial existence of qualities as objectively existent *logoi* in the universe – as against the criticism, voiced by Plotinus among others (*Enneades* 6.1.10.54 ff.), that 'quality is a kind of non-substantial characteristic' (*kharaktêr tis ouk ousiôdês*). With this aim in view, he turns first to a critique of those who hold various unsound views about quality. In quite an elaborate doxography, he isolates five classes of thinker who offend in this way, beginning with the Eretrian School, Dicaearchus and Theopompus, who deny any substantial existence to qualities, and proceeding through a second, anonymous group, to the Atomists and Epicureans, Academics,[28] and finally Stoics (who take all qualities as material states of *pneuma*), all of whom had in one way or another an inadequate grasp of the concept of Quality.

He then turns (*in Cat.* 218,5 ff.) to the commendation of Aristotle's own doctrine, which he describes as 'admirable' (*thaumasia*), since he declares qualities to be immaterial *logoi*. How he can possibly derive this message from chapter 8 of the *Categories* is explained by the fact that he is able to adduce the corresponding section of the *Metaphysics* (4.14, 1020a33 ff.) where Quality is discussed from a somewhat different angle. Porphyry had already remarked (*apud* Simplicius 213,10 ff. = fr. 70) that the account of Quality in the *Categories* is *ennoêmatikos* (by which he seems to mean something like 'subjective', or 'reflecting people's concepts'), as opposed to that given in the *Metaphysics,* which is *ousiôdês*, 'objective', or 'reflecting substantial reality'.

---

[28] Presumably members of the New Academy (later Platonists should be referred to, one would think, as *Platônikoi*), but if so, this is a little strange. They are commended for introducing the concept of *hekta*, or 'possessions', as a term for qualities of all sorts, both permanent states, such as wisdom, and temporary conditions, such as walking or sitting. The reason that this terminology seems hardly suited to Academic sceptics is that he goes on, after commending them for identifying these *hekta* with the Forms, to criticize at least some of them (*in Cat.* 217,24 ff.) for saying both that the Forms are 'possessed' (*ekhesthai*) and are 'separate' (*khôrista*). They should have distinguished more clearly between 'forms-in-matter' or *logoi*, which is what these *hekta* really are, and transcendent Forms. But one does not have the impression that the New Academy concerned itself with such questions.

For Iamblichus, it would seem, both expositions of Quality are concordant, and *ousiôdês*. He takes Aristotle's formulation, 'a quality is that in virtue of which things are said to be qualified (*poioi*)', as a recognition that qualities are *logoi* which impose form on (*eidopoiousin*) qualified things (*in Cat.* 218,8-9), and he links this with Aristotle's first definition of quality in *Metaphysics* 5 as 'the *differentia* (*diaphora*) of primary being'. It is the peculiarity of qualities both to possess real existence (*hupostasis*) and to exercise that existence inseparably from the matter they are qualifying. They are thus immanent *logoi*, not transcendent Forms.

On the other hand, he distinguishes qualities from what he calls 'the reason-principle inherent in the shape' (*ho kata tên morphên logos, in Cat.* 219,10), which he characterizes as something lifeless and devoid of activity (*apsukhos kai anenergêtos*). I presume that by this he means simply the structural proportions or other visible features of an object, which supervene on the imposition of quality by the *logos* in question. He only mentions this latter entity because, although Aristotle, he claims, distinguishes these senses of *logos*, many people confuse them.

Again, at *in Cat.* 271,6 ff. we are given what Simplicius calls Iamblichus' *theôretikôterai epistaseis*, his 'more theoretical interpretation', of the fourth class of qualities, that is, 'shape and the external form of each thing' (*skhêma te kai hê peri hekaston huparkhousa morphê*), set out by Aristotle at 10a11-26. Here Iamblichus takes his start from the observation that Plato in the *Timaeus* (55D ff.) postulates *skhêmata*,[29] that is, the primary shapes formed by combinations of triangles, as the causal principles of the differences between bodies, deriving all qualitative *differentiae* from the differences between the basic *skhêmata*. Plato, however, says Iamblichus, would distinguish between purely mathematical *skhêmata*, which would serve as the transcendent causes of the physical shapes of bodies, and the immanent *skhêmata*, which are material and physical and involved in motion. Aristotle, Iamblichus has to admit, does not here recognise immaterial or mathematical *skhêmata* as causal principles,[30] but only immanent, enmattered (*enula*) ones, which come into being with bodies, and define and shape their surfaces. On the other hand, he maintains, Aristotle is not declaring the shapes actually to *be* bodies, as do the Stoics, because Aristotle classes bodies under Quantity, not under Quality.

Aristotle's doctrine, then, says Iamblichus (*in Cat.* 271,23 ff.), is median between that of Plato, which takes shapes as being entirely immaterial, and that of the Stoics, which holds them to be material. But Iamblichus plainly feels that Aristotle is not expressing himself here with sufficient clarity, and he adduces the formulation of Archytas to throw light on what Aristotle really means.[31] Archytas declares that this species of Quality does not consist in *shape* (*en skhêmati*), but rather in *shaping* (*en*

---

[29] In fact, Plato does not happen to use the term *skhêmata* to describe the basic shapes anywhere in the passage 55D-57D, but merely *sômata* or *eidê*. This, however, does not disturb Iamblichus.

[30] In fact, as we know, Aristotle was particularly sarcastic about the efficacy of the basic triangles, cf. *De Caelo* 3.7-8, 305b27 ff. We may note, incidentally, that, though Plato nowhere uses the term *skhêmata* to describe the primary bodies, Aristotle in this passage does.

[31] This passage is of particular interest, as being one of the comparatively few places where a degree of criticism of Aristotle is evident. Plainly if Aristotle is deviating in doctrine from the divine Plato, he cannot be correct. It is not his business to 'mediate' between Plato and the Stoics!

skhêmatismôi),[32] indicating a distinction between the constitution of the shapes and the actual shapes in bodies. Even so, however, the shapes being dealt with here are not the original *logoi*, which would be analogous to the Platonic 'primary bodies', but those shapes which supervene upon the shaped bodies.

Time forbids the examination of much more of Iamblichus' exegesis on the present occasion,[33] but I feel that, in conclusion, I should not neglect a topic on which Iamblichus has a good deal to say that is interesting, that of Time itself. R. Sorabji has subjected Iamblichus' doctrine of Time to a fascinating examination in chapter 3 of his major synoptic study, *Time, Creation and the Continuum*,[34] but I think that there is still something to be said on the subject from a Neoplatonic perspective.

The question of the nature and status of Time arises, of course, in connection with the discussion of the category 'when', which is passed over in very summary fashion by Aristotle (if, indeed, it is Aristotle at all) at *Categories* 11b10. The fact that Aristotle has nothing to say on the subject in the *Categories* gives commentators a free hand, which they exercise with the help of his discussion of Time in the *Physics*. Iamblichus applies to the subject the same *noera theôria* which he employs for the rest of the work. In all cases he is concerned with discerning the real *ousia* behind the physical manifestations, employing for this purpose, as is his policy, the insights of 'Archytas'. Since 'Archytas' had the benefit, in all probability (as I remarked earlier), of at least the first generation of commentary on the *Categories*, his treatment of all the categories, including Time, is more structured than that of Aristotle, and is further influenced by the Stoic theory of categories, which presented them unequivocally as modes of *being*. 'The "when"', says Archytas (*in Cat*. 352,24 ff. = 29,11 ff.), 'and Time in general, contain as a characterizing property (*idion*) the indivisible and the insubstantial (*to ameres kai to anupostaton*)'. He defines it as 'a kind of number of movement and in general the interval (*diastama*) of the nature of the universe'.

Iamblichus fastens on this characterization of time as both *ameres* and *anupostaton*. The same thing, he says (*in Cat*. 353,19 ff. = fr. 110), cannot be both, since partlessness is a characteristic of real being, which is an hypostasis. Archytas must therefore in fact be talking about two levels of time,[35] and this gives Iamblichus the opportunity to

---

[32] Iamblichus is here getting a good deal of mileage out of Pseudo-Archytas' bald statement (*in Cat*. 24,19): *kai tês poiotêtos diaphorai tessares· to men gar autês estin en pathei, to de en hexei, to de en dunamei, to de en skhêmatismôi*. It is highly unlikely that he intends here any such contrast with *skhêma* as Iamblichus is attributing to him. Indeed, this constitutes a good example of Iamblichus' creative use of Archytas to buttress his imaginative interpretation of Aristotle.

[33] There are interesting passages of *noera theôria* also at *in Cat*. 146,22 ff., where Simplicius describes Iamblichus as 'advancing doctrines of a more theoretical nature' about Quantity (*theôrêtikôteron . . . epiballôn*); at 327,7 ff., where we get what he refers to as a *theôrêtikôtera tekhnologia* of Iamblichus about action and affection; and at 374,7 ff. we are given Iamblichus' *noera theôria* of 'having'. All of these passages exhibit the same features as those we have discussed.

[34] (London: Duckworth, 1983), pp. 33–45.

[35] Archytas, of course, is talking about nothing of the sort, any more than he was making a distinction between *skhêma* and *skhêmatismos* earlier (cf. above, n. 32). The two epithets are for him virtual synonyms, and refer to exactly the same sort of time. This is just another nice example of the creative interpretation of Archytas. On Iamblichus' use of Archytas here, see P. Hoffmann, 'Iamblique exégète du pythagoricien Archytas: trois originalités d'une doctrine du temps', *Les Études Philosophiques* (1980), 302–23.

introduce his theory of intellectual time, as archetype of the time that we experience in the physical world.[36]

As in the case of Quality, or any of the other categories, Iamblichus wants to take Time, as manifested in this realm, to be an emanation of an intellectual archetype, or Form, of Time. This entity is not, as Plotinus would have it (in *Enneades* 3.7.11), identical with the life of the Soul, but is rather the ordering principle of the psychic realm, 'which measures becoming (*genesis*), first that of the Soul, and secondly the becoming proceeding from it' (Simplicius, *in Phys.* 793). It is only at this latter stage that time becomes insubstantial, a continuous flow of evanescent 'nows'. Strictly speaking, it is not even the lower, or participated time, that flows, but the things which participate in it.

'Where', he asks, 'should we think that the flow and shifting (*ekstasis*) of Time occurs? We shall say, in the things which participate in Time. For these are always coming into being and cannot take on the stable nature (*ousia*) of Time without changing, but touch that nature with ever different parts of themselves' (*apud* Simplicius, *in Phys.* 787,17–20 = fr. 107,37–43).[37] Iamblichus is thus able to accept previous definitions of Time as 'the measure of motion', or 'the circuit of the heavens', or whatever, as describing, if anything, the lower level of time, while he is primarily concerned with intellectual Time, as causal principle of this lower time.

It was Sambursky[38] who seems to have first made the suggestion that there is a 'strong resemblance' between Iamblichus' concept of the two levels of Time and the analysis of Time by J. E. McTaggart, as set out in his article, 'The Unreality of Time'.[39] Sambursky suggests, specifically, that McTaggart's 'B-series' of temporal expressions, which express simply an order of events, such as 'before', 'after', 'simultaneous with', or conventional dating expressions, such as 'Sept. 8, 1995', can be compared with Iamblichus' notion of intellectual time.

I must confess that I do not see this at all. McTaggart is surely concerned with distinguishing two ways of looking at time as manifested in the physical world, and his distinction derives whatever validity it has from its efficiency in doing that. Iamblichus, on the contrary, is concerned with this very curious entity, the intellectual monad of Time (which he also discusses in his *Timaeus Commentary*, à propos *Timaeus* 37D),[40] the characteristic of which is to comprehend as a whole, statically, and from above in the intellectual realm, all the flux of physical events. It might be described as 'sempiternity', in contrast to eternity. Indeed, Iamblichus is at pains to distinguish it from eternity, of which it is in fact the primary image. What may have induced

---

[36] This exegesis of Iamblichus is also preserved by Simplicius in his *Commentary on the Physics* 792,20–793,23 (= fr. 108). All these texts are conveniently collected, with translation and comment, in S. Sambursky and S. Pines, *The Concept of Time in Late Neoplatonism* (Jerusalem: Israel Academy of Sciences and Humanities, 1971).

[37] Translation Sorabji (n. 34 above), p. 38.

[38] Sambursky (n. 36 above), p. 21 n.

[39] In *Mind* 17 (1908), 457–74 (revised and reprinted in *The Nature of Existence*, 2 vols (Cambridge: Cambridge University Press, 1921–27)).

[40] Of which *verbatim* extracts are preserved by Simplicius in his *Physics Commentary*, 792,20–795,3, as well as near-*verbatim* reports by Proclus in his *Timaeus Commentary* 3,30,30–32,6 and 33,1–30 (= Iamblichus, *in Timaeum* fr. 64).

Sambursky to think of McTaggart is something that Iamblichus says in the course of *In Platonis Timaeum Commentarii*, fr. 63 (from Simplicius):

> We too agree that there is an order of time – not, however, an order which is ordered, but one which orders, nor one which follows upon principles which lead it, but which is a leader of, and senior to, the things brought to completion by it. Nor do we believe it to be that order which is parcelled out individually in reason-principles or motions or other distinct powers, but that which is preserved complete in its entirety in accordance with the productions of the demiurge as a whole. *The notion of 'before' and 'after' in this order we do not understand in the sense of changes involving movements, nor in any other such sense, but we define it as the sequence of causes, and the continuous concatenation of creations and the primary activity and the power which brings motions to fulfilment, and all things of this sort.*

However, it can readily be seen, I think, that the purposes and thought-worlds of McTaggart and Iamblichus are very far apart, despite the interesting point of comparison in the matter of redefining 'before' and 'after'.

It is worth bearing in mind that Iamblichus gives us a similar treatment of Place (which, again, Simplicius characterizes as *noera theôria*, at *in Cat.* 361,7). As in the case of Time (and indeed as in the case of Quality), we must see Place not just as a mere limit of bodies, but rather as an active principle descending from above, both keeping separate bodies distinct and holding individual bodies together, 'a corporeal power which supports bodies and forces them apart and gathers them up when they fall and collects them together when they are scattered, at once bringing them to completion and encompassing them on all sides', to quote the rather turgid phraseology of his *Timaeus Commentary*.[41] We must see Place, then, as an entity operative at every level of the universe, up as far as the intelligible realm (Intellect is the 'place' of the Forms), if not even to the level of the One itself (if that is what we may assume from Simplicius' expression at *in Cat.* 364,3: *ep' ekeinon ton theion topon*).

These, then, I think, constitute a set of useful examples of the *noera theôria* in action. It will be seen that it is Iamblichus' purpose to salvage Aristotle, reconciling him both with his perceived doctrine elsewhere (as, for example, in the *Metaphysics* and the *Physics*), and with that of Plato and the Pythagoreans. The aim is to establish a metaphysical framework for the interpretation of the *Categories*, revealing the hidden levels of truth inherent in it. This is achieved, of course, at the cost of ignoring what seems to us the essentially anti-metaphysical, as well as tentative and exploratory, nature of the *Categories*, but it would be somewhat anachronistic to condemn Iamblichus too severely for that. The text of the *Categories* had been a battleground for at least three hundred years before his time, from the period of Andronicus, Ariston and Eudorus of Alexandria, and the Stoic Apollodorus of Tarsus, in the first century BCE, through that of the Platonists Lucius and Nicostratus, and then Atticus, and the

---

[41] fr. 90 (*apud* Simplicius, *in Phys.* 639,23–640,11).

Stoic Cornutus, and lastly Alexander of Aphrodisias, in the first and second centuries CE, down to Plotinus and Porphyry in his own day, with every phrase and word of the text liable to challenge and requiring defence. Iamblichus' distinctive contribution is to take the *Categories* as a coherent description of reality in the Neoplatonic sense, and that, bizarre as it may seem to us, is not really all that more perverse than many of the various ways in which the work had been treated in the centuries before him.

12

Proclus' Defence of the *Timaeus* against Aristotle: A Reconstruction of a Lost Polemical Treatise[1]

Carlos Steel

1. Aristotle: First Reader and Critic of the *Timaeus*

The first reader and first interpreter of Plato's *Timaeus*, Aristotle, is also its most severe critic. Aristotle quotes the dialogue sixteen times and often discusses its doctrine.[2] There are explicit references to the *Timaeus* in the *De Anima, De Caelo, De Generatione et Corruptione, Physica, De Sensu*, and *De Respiratione*. Moreover, there are many indirect allusions to doctrines put forward in the *Timaeus*. Aristotle criticises in particular the role of the demiurge and the paradigm, the temporal generation of the everlasting world (which contradicts the principle that whatever is generated must be perishable), the disorderly motions of the elements before the formation of the universe, the composition of the world soul out of circles in rotation, the status of the receptacle (matter or place or both), the construction of the four elementary bodies out of regular solids composed of triangles, the transformation of the elements, the rejection of absolute lightness and weight, the suggestion of a movement of the earth around its axis, the explanation of sight, the explanation of breathing. If one brings together all those scattered remarks, one must conclude that Aristotle had studied the dialogue intensively. According to Simplicius, he even made a summary of the

---

This article is a substantially revised version of 'Proclus' Defence of the *Timaeus* against Aristotle's objections. A reconstruction of a lost polemical treatise' by Carlos Steel in Thomas Leinkauf and Carlos Steel (eds), *Plato's* Timaeus *and the Foundations of Cosmology in Late Antiquity, the Middle Ages and Renaissance* (2005; Ancient and Medieval Philosophy, Series I, 34), pp. 163–93 © Leuven University Press 2005, reproduced with permission.

---

[1] For the revision of this paper which originally appeared in 2005 I have profited from the new translations in the Ancient Commentators on Aristotle series, in particular Michael Share's *Philoponus, Against Proclus On the Eternity of the World 1–5* (London: Duckworth, 2004); *Philoponus, Against Proclus On the Eternity of the World 6–8* (London: Duckworth, 2005), and Ian Mueller's *Simplicius, On Aristotle on the Heavens 3.1–7* (London: Duckworth, 2009); *Simplicius, On Aristotle on the Heavens 3.7–4.6* (London: Duckworth, 2009).

[2] On Aristotle's critique of the *Timaeus*, see H. Bonitz, *Index Aristotelicus* (Berlin: Reimer, 1870), 598a-b; H. Cherniss, *Aristotle's Criticism of Plato and the Academy* (Baltimore: The Johns Hopkins Press, 1944); G. Claghorn, *Aristotle's Criticism of Plato's Timaeus* (The Hague: Nijhoff, 1954).

dialogue,[3] which again shows how much this work fascinated him, probably because Plato dealt here with physical and biological problems, which were dear to him. Notwithstanding his great interest in the *Timaeus*, Aristotle is very critical about its arguments: all his comments are negative. To the despair of the Platonic reader, Aristotle never seems to consider the peculiar literary genre of the *Timaeus*, a plausible account about the generation of the world, mixing argument and narrative. Throughout the tradition, Platonists of all kinds tried to refute Aristotle's criticism or they attempted to show that Aristotle did not mean to attack the doctrine of Plato, but only his particular mode of exposition. The first position is characteristic of Atticus and of most of the Platonists in the first centuries CE; the latter is the perspective of the commentators on Aristotle at the end of the fifth and the early sixth century. As Simplicius explains, there is no contradiction between Aristotle and Plato in doctrinal matters. When Aristotle seems to attack his master, his critique only concerns the manner in which Plato expresses his views. For Plato often uses a narrative form and a metaphorical language, which may lead his readers to erroneous views, if taken literally.[4] To defend the harmony of Plato and Aristotle was for Simplicius also of great strategic importance in his controversy with the Christian John Philoponus, who, as we shall see, liked to exploit the oppositions within the pagan philosophical tradition so as to undermine it.

Ammonius Saccas, the master of Plotinus, seems to have been the first to defend this concordance of Plato and Aristotle as a general hermeneutic principle.[5] 'This man [...] was the first to behold clearly the teachings of both Plato and Aristotle, and to bring them into one and the same view and to hand on a philosophy free from factions to all his students, particularly to the best of them, Plotinus, Origen and their successors.'[6] This testimony on Ammonius comes from Hierocles, who became professor of philosophy in Alexandria in the mid-fifth century, after having studied in Athens with Plutarch. In his treatise *On Providence* (preserved in Photius' summary), he condemns 'all those who try to break up the unanimity of Plato and Aristotle as "trivial thinkers"'. They are to be avoided: 'they have corrupted many of the Platonic arguments, and yet they claim Plato as their teacher, just as is the case with the writings of Aristotle among those who confess to honour his school; their machinations have no other purpose than to make the Stagirite clash with Ariston's son [Plato]'.[7] Thanks to Ammonius, however, another approach has prevailed in the Platonic school and

---

[3] See *in Cael.*, 296,16–18; 379,16–18.
[4] On this hermeneutic strategy, see C. Steel, 'Surface Reading and Deeper Meaning: On Aristotle Reading Plato and Platonists reading Aristotle', in Michael Erler and Jan Erik Hessle, eds, *Argument und literarische Form in antiker Philosophie* (Berlin: De Gruyter, 2013), pp. 469–94.
[5] On the harmony of Plato and Aristotle there is a vast secondary literature see *inter multos*: Lloyd P. Gerson, *Aristotle and Other Platonists* (Ithaca: Cornell University Press, 2005); George E. Karamanolis, *Plato and Aristotle in Agreement? Platonists on Aristotle From Antiochus to Porphyry* (Oxford: Clarendon Press, 2006).
[6] See Hierocles, *On Providence* (summarized by Photius, codex 251), 461a; translation (with some changes) from H. Schibli, *Hierocles of Alexandria* (Oxford: Oxford University Press, 2002), p. 338 (see also pp. 329, 330, 335–6). For a discussion of the harmony of Plato and Aristotle in the Platonic school, see also Schibli's introduction, pp. 26–30.
[7] See Hierocles (in Photius' summary), 173a, translation of Schibli, pp. 335–6.

Hierocles is pleased to situate his own philosophy in that tradition, in which he was initiated through Plutarch, 'his own guide'. This hermeneutical tradition will be continued in Alexandria by Ammonius and will find its magnificent expression in the great commentaries on Aristotle of Simplicius. In Athens, however, another direction was taken, it seems, with the succession of Syrianus as head of the school.[8] In his Commentary on the *Metaphysics* Syrianus is often extremely critical of Aristotle and does not make an attempt to harmonise his doctrine with that of Plato.[9] In his preface to Books 13 and 14 he clarifies his position: he does not belong to those people who find pleasure in polemics with Aristotle, on the contrary, he gratefully acknowledges the great contribution of Aristotle to humanity in logic, ethics and natural philosophy, even in theology. But Aristotle's attack on the doctrine of the first principles of Pythagoras and Plato (i.e. the doctrine of the Ideas) is so unfair and shows so much misunderstanding that one must show in defence of the truth the invalidity of his arguments. This preface, however, does not prevent him from engaging in often personal invectives against Aristotle in the commentary.[10]

Syrianus' successor, Proclus was about nineteen when he arrived in Athens around 430. He took some classes with Plutarch – already an old man – and read with him Aristotle's *On the Soul* and Plato's *Phaedo*. After Plutarch died in 432 Proclus continued his philosophical education under the guidance of Syrianus. 'In less than two years Proclus read with him all of Aristotle's treatises on logic, ethics, politics, physics, and the theological science which surpasses them all. When Proclus was suitably educated through those studies which, so to speak, are a kind of preparatory initiation, or lesser mysteries, Syrianus led Proclus to Plato's mystagogy' (*Vita Procli* § 13). The young Proclus, then, was well trained in Aristotle's philosophy, but he learned from his masters in Athens that only Plato revealed the ultimate truth on the first principles of all things. Proclus' first publications show that he had adopted Syrianus' critical attitude to Aristotle. Thus, in his commentary on the *Timaeus* he does not miss an occasion to counterattack Aristotle, whenever a doctrine had been subject to Aristotle's criticism. Simplicius, who had great admiration for Proclus, may have been embarrassed to notice how polemical Proclus' attitude to Aristotle often was. In his commentary on the *De caelo*, he confronts Alexander of Aphrodisias, who was always biased against what Plato says, with some of his own predecessors, who were as much prejudiced against Aristotle. 'Alexander', he writes, 'seems to be from the outset prejudiced against the arguments of Plato, just as some people who lived a short time before us (*oligon pro hêmôn*) were against the arguments of Aristotle'.[11] Who were those predecessors?

---

[8] I. Hadot denies that there was a fundamental difference in the approach to Aristotle and Plato in Alexandria and Athens. See her *Le problème du néoplatonisme Alexandrin, Hiéroclès et Simplicius* (Paris: Études Augustiniennes, 1978) and recently *Athenian and Alexandrian Neoplatonism and the Harmonization of Aristotle* (Leiden: Brill, 2015). See, however, the critical review of C. d'Ancona in *Studia Graeco-arabica* 5 (2015), 375–84.

[9] On Syrianus' attitude to Aristotle, see H. D. Saffrey, 'Comment Syrianus, le maître de l'école néoplatonicienne d'Athènes, considérait-il Aristote?', in his *Recherches sur le Néoplatonisme après Plotin* (Paris: Vrin, 2000), pp. 131–40, and recently C. Helmig, *Forms and Concepts: Concept Formation in the Platonic Tradition* (Berlin: De Gruyter, 2012), pp. 205 ff.

[10] See *in Metaph.* 80,4–81,14.

[11] See *in Cael.* 297,1–5.

Could they be Philoponus? This supposition is not likely: Philoponus is a contemporary of Simplicius and he is as much critical of Plato as of Aristotle; besides, Simplicius would have introduced him in less subtle, even insulting terms. The reference must be to Proclus. As a matter of fact, Simplicius uses the same phrase 'a short time before us' later in his commentary to introduce Proclus: 'Proclus of Lycia, who had become Plato's successor a short time before me, wrote a book to dissolve the objections made by Aristotle here [i.e. in *De Caelo* 3]'.[12] Proclus' treatise in defence of the *Timaeus* against Aristotle got lost in late antiquity, but its content can be partially reconstructed from three sources: Proclus himself in his Commentary on the *Timaeus*, Philoponus, and Simplicius. I shall examine their testimonies in the three following sections.

2. Proclus' Defence of the *Timaeus* against Aristotle

When comparing Plato and Aristotle, even commentators with sympathy for Plato will admit that, in the explanation of physical and biological matters, Aristotle surpasses his master, who is more intent on the intelligible realm. This is not, however, Proclus' opinion. From the very beginning of his commentary on the *Timaeus* he makes it clear that he is not impressed by Aristotle's physics. When compared with the *Timaeus*, the entire project of Aristotle seems to be nothing but the work of a disciple trying to emulate the teaching of his master. Aristotle's originality is only found in a more detailed – and often useless – explanation of some particular phenomena.[13] The fact that Aristotle so often criticises the *Timaeus* shows that he felt the need to distance himself from this work, which had a deep influence on his own philosophy of nature. Whenever Proclus comes upon a doctrine that was subject to Aristotle's critique, he attempts to solve Aristotle's objections, which, in his view, all stem from a misunderstanding of Plato's argument. For this refutation of Aristotle Proclus exploited arguments he had already developed in an earlier treatise:

> Since I know both Aristotle's objections to the generation of the soul and the solutions the Platonists have adduced in response to them, I do not think that it is necessary to waste more effort on them, in particular since these polemics risk bringing us astray. For the soul is not a circle like a magnitude, and the one [sc. Aristotle] who has refuted this hypothesis [namely that the soul is a circle like a magnitude] should not believe that he has thereby laid hold on Plato's doctrine.[14]

---

[12] See *in Cael.* 640,24–5 and the discussion below on p. 346.
[13] See C. Steel, 'Why should we prefer Plato's *Timaeus* to Aristotle's *Physics*? Proclus' critique of Aristotle's causal explanation of the physical world', in R. W. Sharples and A. Sheppard, eds, *Ancient Approaches to Plato's Timaeus* (London: Institute of Classical Studies, 2003), pp. 175–87.
[14] *in Tim.* 2,278,32–279,1: *oude edei tautēn elegxanta tēn hupothesin oiesthai kathaptesthai tēs Platōnikēs theōrias.* Baltzly translates: 'neither is it necessary when this supposition has been refuted to think that you have thereby accepted the theory of Plato', which is the very contrary of what Proclus says! The expression *kathaptesthai tēs Platōnikēs theōrias* means 'to lay hold upon Plato's doctrine'. Proclus says: One should not believe that by attacking an hypothesis, which is not Plato's, but Aristotle's false interpretation of it, on may thereby lay hold on Plato's doctrine itself. For a nice parallel, see Sextus Empiricus, *Adv. Math.* 11.14.2: *hē enstasis phainetai mē kathaptesthai tou Xenokratous.*

Therefore, I think that I will leave this polemics aside. For I have published, as I know, a special treatise, which offers an examination of Aristotle's objections against the *Timaeus*. In that book, there is ample discussion about these matters and it is argued that Aristotle is not right when he ascribes the belief that the soul has magnitude to the *Timaeus* and demonstrates from there that it cannot know by means of magnitude, which is divisible, intelligible objects, which are indivisible, as neither can what is indivisible fit what is divisible. It is also argued that, according to the teaching of the *Timaeus*, the movements of the heaven are not identical with movements of the soul, but owe their existence to the soul and that it is not impossible [contrary to what Aristotle says] to think many times the same thing with the same faculty; on the contrary, it is necessary in discursive thinking, if it is the case both that the intelligible objects are limited and that thinking is circular. All these questions, I think, I can now leave aside since they have been discussed in greater detail in that book.[15]

As we learn from this testimony, before composing his commentary on the *Timaeus*, Proclus had written a polemical treatise in which he defended the doctrine Plato put forward in this dialogue against the objections of Aristotle: *tôn pros ton Timaion Aristotelous antirrêseôn episkepsis*. Philoponus, as we will see, quotes the same work under the title *episkepsis tôn pros ton Platônos Timaion hupo Aristotelous anteirêmenôn*. This is probably the authentic title, as it corresponds to the title of another polemical treatise of Proclus against Aristotle, his 'Examination of the objections raised by Aristotle in the second book of the *Politics* against the *Republic* of Plato' (*episkepsis tôn hup' Aristotelous en deuterôi tôn Politikôn pros ton Platônos Polteians anteirêmenôn*). The latter treatise, which only has partially survived, is attached as an appendix to the series of essays which constitute the present commentary on the *Republic*. We know from Marinus that Proclus had already composed his commentary on the *Timaeus* at the age of 27/8. The defence of the *Timaeus* against Aristotle was published before that commentary, probably some years earlier, for the way Proclus refers to it indicates that it is not a recent work. It seems, then, that this treatise and maybe also the parallel treatise in defence of the *Republic* belong to the early scholarly productions of Proclus. This makes our attempt to reconstruct this lost treatise even more interesting. For we see that Proclus, from the beginning of his scholarly activity, felt the need to defend the *Timaeus* against Aristotle. As is evident from the title and from the quotations, this treatise was not a general attack on Aristotle – after all, even Proclus would accept many doctrines of Aristotle that are in perfect harmony with Plato –, but a counterattack against Aristotle's critique on the *Timaeus*.

In the above quoted text Proclus summarises the arguments he had put forward in his defence of Plato's explanation of the generation of the soul in the *Timaeus* against Aristotle's objections in *On the Soul*, 1.3, 406b25–407b25. Proclus discusses four of Aristotle's objections: (1) If Timaeus constructs the soul out of circles, it must be a magnitude. Proclus replies that Aristotle is right when he attacks the view that the soul

---

[15] *in Tim.* 2,278,27–279,16.

is a magnitude, but wrong in attributing such a view to Plato, for whom the soul is an incorporeal substance. (2) 'How will the soul think, if it is a magnitude?' (407a10) Aristotle asks. Rightly again, for the divisible can never grasp indivisible intelligible objects. But this objection cannot touch Plato, since he made a similar argument before Aristotle. (3) Aristotle attributed to Plato the claim 'that the motions of the soul are the motions of heaven' (407a2). This again is false, since the motions of the heavens proceed from the motions of the soul, which are incorporeal activities without any extension. (4) If the rotation of the soul is everlasting and occurs many times, the soul will have to think of the same thing many times (407a31). But, as Proclus replies, this is not impossible, given the fact that the intelligible objects are limited and the rotation eternal. To think of the same again and again is even necessary for those souls that engage in discursive thinking.[16]

Besides the above quoted text Proclus refers probably to the same lost treatise also in the first book of his commentary, when comparing Plato's and Aristotle's views on the intellect. Proclus criticizes Aristotle for having adopted Plato's doctrine of the intellect only partially. In fact, whereas Plato clearly distinguishes the unparticipated intellect of the divine Demiurge from the participated intellect, Aristotle has abandoned in his cosmology the unparticipated intellect. The divine intellect, as Aristotle understands it, is not absolutely transcendent, as is the demiurgic intellect in the *Timaeus*. In fact, Aristotle's first intellect is the intellect that merely moves the first sphere of the fixed stars. Moreover, Aristotle eliminates the world soul, as he connects the intellect with the cosmic organism without the mediation of the soul. Concerning all those issues, Proclus concludes: 'Against Aristotle also [a book] has been written specifically on these topics'.[17] Although Proclus does not say that he himself has written this work, it is plausible that he refers to his own 'Examination of Aristotle's objections'. Where, however, did he find Aristotle's objections against Plato's doctrine of the intellect in the *Timaeus*? It may have been Aristotle's rejection of a demiurgic intellect in the *Metaphysics* and in *De Caelo*. Regarding the elimination of the world soul, Proclus may have had in mind the comment Aristotle makes in *De Caelo* 2.1, 284a27–35: 'it is impossible that the heaven should persist eternally by the necessitation of a soul'. Aristotle observes that a soul eternally linked to the celestial body would have 'an Ixion's lot without end and respite'. Though Plato is not mentioned, this critique of Aristotle aims at *Tim.* 36E where the world soul is said to be 'interwoven' with the body.[18] Proclus must have noticed that Aristotle is here attacking Plato's view.[19] In his commentary on the *De Caelo* Simplicius propounds an interpretation of this passage that makes Aristotle concordant with Plato: both accepted the animation of the world.[20]

Throughout the commentary on the *Timaeus* we find passages where Proclus defends Plato's doctrine against Aristotle's criticism. Thus, Proclus defends the view

---

[16] See *in Tim.* 2,278,27–279,16; one finds a similar critique of Aristotle's objections at 2,250,8–14.
[17] See *in Tim.* 1,404,7–21.
[18] Aristotle makes a similar critique at *DA* 1.3, 407b2–3 where the *Timaeus* is explicitly mentioned.
[19] See *Theol. Plat.* 1,75,16 ff.
[20] See *in Cael.* 376,28 ff., and G. Guldentops, 'Plato's *Timaeus* in Simplicius *In De Caelo*', in T. Leinkauf and C. Steel, eds, *Plato's Timaeus and the Foundations of Cosmology in Late Antiquity, the Middle Ages and Renaissance* (Leuven: Leuven University Press, 2005), pp. 195–212, at pp. 206–9.

that the world is generated against Aristotle's critique in *De Caelo* 1.10. As a corporeal being, the universe cannot produce itself nor maintain itself in being. The physical world depends for its existence on another superior cause and in that sense it is generated and perishable. This does not prevent it from existing for an infinite time. One must, however, distinguish between what is eternal in an absolute sense (the intelligible realm) and what is eternal because it continues to exist for the whole time. As Proclus shows, Aristotle himself accepted this distinction between eternal being and eternal duration in time. Moreover, at the end of the *Physics*, Aristotle formulates a remarkable argument to demonstrate that no body can possess from itself an unlimited power to exist. If the world exists eternally – and on this hypothesis Proclus fully supports Aristotle –, it must have this power from an incorporeal principle.[21] The discussion of the generated status of the world probably carries on the arguments Proclus had developed in his earlier treatise against Aristotle.[22] This supposition is strengthened by the fact that similar arguments occur in the texts quoted by Philoponus from this treatise (cf. infra). It is also interesting to compare Proclus' defence of the generated status of the world with Simplicius' harmonising explanation of the *Timaeus* against the critique of the Peripatetics (mainly Alexander).[23] Whereas Proclus uses arguments taken from Aristotle to counter Aristotle's critique against Plato's *Timaeus*, Simplicius elaborates the same arguments (for example, the principle 'that no body can have an unlimited power') to show that Aristotle is not really disputing with Plato, but is in concordance with his master on this important question. Aristotle's polemic was only concerned with the discourse of Plato, which, when read superficially, could give rise to false opinions and make people accept a temporal origin of the world. To be sure, Proclus also admits that there is no conflict between Plato and Aristotle on the essential question, whether or not the world exists from all eternity. But they have divergent views on how this eternity should be understood:

> In this respect at least [the two] men do not contradict each other, but they do differ, in that Plato says that the substance of the heaven is stretched out along the whole of time, whereas Aristotle simply supposes that it always exists [*Cael.* 1.12, 291b25], even if he too is compelled through many arguments to reduce it to temporal infinity, calling 'eternity' a infinite stable power [*Cael.* 1.9, 279a25-8]. He also demonstrates that an infinite power cannot belong to a finite body. It follows, then, that the world, as a corporeal entity, must always be receiving the infinite power and never has it as a whole, because it is finite. It is thus only true to say of the world that it becomes infinite in power, not that it is such. [...] Therefore, Aristotle is also compelled to agree that the world is somehow in the process of being generated. Besides both also say that the world is numerically the same, but the latter [Aristotle] says that it *is* the same, the former [Plato] that it *becomes* the

---

[21] See *in Tim.* 1,251,11-254,18 (with excellent notes in the French translation of A. J. Festugière (Paris: Vrin, 1966-68), vol 2, pp. 90-3) see also 279,9-29; 293,6-296,12; 395,1-10.
[22] The discussion of the ambivalent meaning of the term *genêton* in *in Tim.* 1,223-264,3 is also found in a passage from the *Episkepsis* quoted by Philoponus, *Aet.* 138,19-28.
[23] See Guldentops (n. 20 above), pp. 199-206.

same. This is in accordance with their principles. For the one [Plato] has posited an efficient cause prior to the universe and from which the universe has its existence, whereas the other [Aristotle] does not admit an efficient cause for any of the eternal beings. And the one [Plato] engendered time together with the substance of the heaven, [Aristotle] together with its movement: for he says that time is the 'number of movement' [*Phys.* 4.11, 219b1–2].[24]

Two times Proclus uses in this text the verb *anagkazetai*, which indicates that Aristotle is 'compelled', 'forced', as an opponent in a debate, to admit reluctantly the truth of Plato's view if he wants to remain consistent with his own principles.[25] The difference between Plato and Aristotle not only concerns their different modes of expression. It is ultimately due to a different view about the first principles of all things. Aristotle refuses the hypothesis of the Ideas and therefore cannot admit a really efficient or creative cause of the universe. Efficient causality only concerns the sublunary world. The celestial bodies and the world as a whole have no efficient cause of their being, but only a final cause.[26] From this misunderstanding about the first principles follow all the other views that distinguish Aristotle from Plato. One gets the impression, Proclus says, that Aristotle, because he could not grasp the first principle of all things – the One – has always to find an explanation of things on a lower level.

> Whatever Plato attributes to the One, Aristotle attributes to the intellect: that it is without multiplicity, that it is object of desire, that it does not think of secondary things. Whatever Plato attributes to the intellect of the divine Demiurge, Aristotle attributes to the heaven and the celestial gods. For, in his view, creation and providence come from them. Whatever Plato attributes to the substance of heavens [namely, time], Aristotle attributes to their circular movement, taking distance from theological principles and occupying himself with physical explanations beyond what is needed.[27]

3. Philoponus using Proclus against Aristotle

3.1. Philoponus' Quotations from Proclus' Lost Treatise

So far I have reconstructed Proclus' lost *Episkepsis* from passages in his commentary on the *Timaeus* wherein he attempts to dissolve Aristotle's objections to Plato. Such a reconstruction remains of course hypothetical, as there are no literal quotations. Fortunately, we can confirm and complement Proclus' own information by the testimony of one of his fiercest opponents in the next generation of Neoplatonic

---

[24] *in Tim.* 1,294,28–295,19.
[25] Simplicius uses the verb *anagkazetai* two times, but in a polemic with Alexander: see *in Cael.* 444,11 and *in Phys.* 871,2.
[26] See C. Steel, 'Proclus et Aristote sur la causalité efficiente de l'intellect divin', in J. Pépin and H. D. Saffrey, eds, *Proclus, lecteur et interprète des anciens* (Paris: CNRS, 1987), pp. 213–25.
[27] *in Tim.* 1,295,20–7.

scholars, John Philoponus. This former student of Ammonius in Alexandria composed a refutation of a Proclus' arguments on the eternity of the world and a treatise against Aristotle on the same subject. In his Refutation of Proclus he quotes extensively from Proclus' own treatise against Aristotle and mentions explicitly the first, the third and the fourteenth *kephalaion* of that work. This is the list of quotations:

31,7-32,10 (from the first chapter): Aristotle's opposition to Plato, in particular on the Ideas.

82,12-25: on the eternity of the world; if god is always creator, the world itself must always exist as his effect.

95,2-12: continuation of the same argument.

95,27-96,18: continuation (see also 99,1-8 = 96,6-14).

138,19-139,3: in what sense do we have to understand the term *genêton* when applied to the world (see also 148,1-7).

166,26-168,2: the world is generated because it depends for its existence on a superior cause (on 167,17-20 recapitulation of text quoted in 96,7-11).

224,18-225,10: the world is eternal as image of an eternal model.

238,3-242,15 (from the 13th chapter): the world is both generated and eternal; its eternity is not connatural, but received from a higher cause; the world cannot possess an infinite power of existence. (See also 297,5-300,2 = 238,3-240,9; 300,22-6 = 239,25-240,4).

318,19-319,2 (from the 14th chapter): discussion of five errors of Plato in physical questions.

482, 21-483,6: rejection of a fifth element.

523,12-524,8: Proclus defends Plato's view on the composition of the heavens against Aristotle's assumption of a fifth element.

581,26-582, 5: the world has past, present, and future.

626,1-627,20: same argument as in 238,3 ff. and 297,5 ff. with one additional quotation.

The reason why Philoponus finds it important to adduce so many quotations from Proclus' treatise is obvious. His aim is to refute the claim that the world is eternal, a doctrine which in his view cannot be reconciled with the belief that the world is created. To his astonishment Proclus and all later commentators (including Philoponus in his earlier works when reporting the lectures of Ammonius) subscribe to Aristotle's view, though Plato himself had given strong arguments for the temporal generation of the world. On this issue, however, most Platonists attempted to minimise the opposition between the two philosophers, except, it seems, Proclus in his earlier work. What then could be a better refutation of Proclus' defence of the eternity of the world than using his own arguments against him?

Whereas Philoponus in his early works defended – as all other members of Ammonius' school in Alexandria – a harmonising interpretation, in his treatise *Against*

Proclus he finds pleasure in pointing to the differences between the two major thinkers of the pagan tradition. It is absurd to claim, he says, as do some of the recent philosophers, that Aristotle is not attacking the doctrine of Plato, but only those who misinterpret that doctrine.

> Aristotle's refutations of Plato are not directed at people who have misunderstood the words of Plato, as some of the recent authors imagine out of embarrassment at the disagreement between the philosophers, but they contradict the views of Plato himself.[28]

3.2. The Dispute on the Ideas

To justify his claim that Plato and Aristotle are in fundamental disagreement, Philoponus quotes a passage from Proclus' treatise against Aristotle. The quotation comes from the first chapter of the treatise and illustrates the general perspective from which Proclus confronts Aristotle. From the beginning of the treatise Proclus straightforwardly points out the discordance between Plato and Aristotle. As Proclus says, this disagreement can be seen on many occasions and in particular in Aristotle's obstinate refusal to admit the hypothesis of the Ideas. It seems as if Aristotle has a real disgust for this theory: he cannot even stand the term 'paradigm' calling it metaphorical and empty talk (cf. *Metaph.* 991a20–2). One finds this disapproval of the doctrine of the Ideas in all works of Aristotle. Thus in his logic (i.e. *An. Post.* 83a33) he calls the Ideas just a 'twittering' of sounds (*teretismata*).[29] In his *Ethics* (*EN* 1.6, 1096a11–1097a14) he criticizes the doctrine of the Idea of the Good. In his physical works he finds it inappropriate to refer to the Ideas in the explanation of processes of generation (see *GC* 335b9–24). The most explicit and articulate attack on the doctrine of the Ideas is to be found in the *Metaphysics*: 'since Aristotle deals here with the first causes and develops lengthy accusations against the Ideas, in the first books, in the middle and in the last'. Even in his dialogues Aristotle makes it clear that he has no sympathy for this Platonic doctrine,[30] so that some may believe that he opposed the doctrine primarily because he liked to quarrel with his master and not for some philosophical reason. All this is of course grist to Philoponus' mill. After the quotation from Proclus he is pleased to conclude:

> Thus, even Proclus explicitly conceded the disagreement between the [two] philosophers; or rather, demonstrated it from Aristotle's own [writing]. This being

---

[28] Philoponus, *Aet.* 29,3–8. In his commentary on the *Second Analytics* (243,16–19) Philoponus criticises in almost the same terms those who attempt to minimize the opposition between Plato and Aristotle on the Ideas. In the commentary on the *De Anima*, on the contrary, he defends a harmonising interpretation. On the radical shift in position in the work of Philoponus, see the contribution of P. Golitsis in this volume, ch. 15.

[29] The expression was considered as an insult by Platonists: for a fierce attack on Aristotle' criticism of the Platonic Ideas, see Atticus, fr. 9, pp. 67–9 ed. E. des Places.

[30] See *Aet.* 32,5–8. It is improbable that Proclus still had access to dialogues of Aristotle. He probably got this information from Plutarch, *Against Colotes* 1115B-C.

so, one might well be amazed at the gross effrontery of those who have tried to show that Aristotle and Plato are in agreement even on this point.[31]

3.3. On the Eternity of the World

The discordance between Plato and Aristotle is also manifest in the question of the eternity of the world, which constitutes the main focus of Philoponus' treatise. Against Aristotle's arguments for the eternity of the world Philoponus adduces Plato's *Timaeus* which defends the view that the corporeal world is generated and has a temporal beginning. To his astonishment, however, Platonic commentators on the *Timaeus* tend to obliterate the differences between Plato and Aristotle on this issue. According to Philoponus, Proclus takes an ambivalent position. On the one hand, he defends with Plato against Aristotle the generation of the world; on the other hand he shares with Aristotle the belief in the eternity of the world and offers many arguments in defence of this thesis. Philoponus strategically exploits arguments from Proclus' earlier work to demonstrate how inconsistent he is in his acceptance of Aristotle' belief in the eternity of the world. As there is already a massive scholarly literature about the discussion on the eternity of the world, I pass to the next question.[32]

3.4. On the Fifth Element

Related to the eternity of the world is the question about the nature of the celestial body. Aristotle argues in *De Caelo* 1.2 that the celestial bodies, which move with a natural circular motion, must be made of a simple substance different from the four sublunary simple bodies (whose natural movements are in a straight line: up or down). This fifth substance, which is by nature imperishable, is the ether. With this explanation Aristotle opposes the view Plato defends in *Timaeus* where it is said that the Demiurge made the divine celestial bodies 'mostly out of fire' (40A2-4). Philoponus rejects Aristotle's view emphatically: the celestial bodies are composed of the same materials as the sublunary and are therefore equally perishable.[33] He finds for his view an important ally in Plato and his commentators.[34] Philoponus is pleased to exploit their arguments in his refutation of the doctrine of the eternity of the world. If it can be shown that even the celestial bodies are perishable, it follows *a fortiori* that the whole world is perishable. To his anger, however, he notices that Proclus, in his 13th chapter of his treatise *On the Eternity of the World*, uses Aristotle's arguments about the eternal

---

[31] *Aet.* 32,8-13 (trans. M. Chase).
[32] See M. Baltes, *Die Weltenstehung des Platonischen Timaios nach den antiken Interpreten*, 2 vols (Leiden: Brill, 1976-78) and the comprehensive study of the discussion in the Platonic tradition in H. Dörrie and M. Baltes, *Der Platonismus in der Antike V* (Stuttgart: Frommann-Holzboog, 1998), pp. 84-180; 374-535.
[33] See on this issue C. Wildberg, *John Philoponus' Criticism of Aristotle's Theory of Aether* (Berlin: De Gruyter, 1988).
[34] On the debate about the fifth element between Platonists and Aristotelians, see Dörrie and Baltes (n. 32 above), pp. 190-211; pp. 558-88.

circular motion of heaven. With this argument, he writes, Proclus not only contradicts Plato, who never accepted a fifth element, but also contradicts himself. For in his other writings and in particular in his *An Examination of Aristotle's objections against Plato's Timaeus*, he rejected Aristotle's doctrine.

> In the treatise we have mentioned many times, *An Examination of Aristotle's objections against Plato's Timaeus*, he strongly stands by Plato's view and establishes that the nature of the heavens is not alien to the elements here below, as Aristotle claims, but is itself composed out of them. [35]

This is indeed the view Proclus put forward in his commentary on the *Timaeus*.

> The whole heaven is composed out of a preponderance of fire, but it includes in a causal manner the powers of the other elements – for instance, the solidity and stability of the earth; the adhesive and unifying quality of water; the tenuousness and transparency of air.[36]

Going through all the arguments of Proclus, one does not have the impression that he contradicts himself, as Philoponus claims. For Proclus always insists that the fire and the other elements are not present in the celestial bodies in the same mode as they exist in the sublunary bodies. In this sense Aristotle is right when he considers the heavens to be a fifth nature besides the four elements. 'For in the heavens the elements are not the same as they are here, but are rather the supreme parts of them'.[37] Proclus defends the same view, though in a more polemical way, in the treatise against Aristotle, as quoted by Philoponus: 'the celestial fire is not destructive ('burning'), but life giving, as is the heat innate in us. [...] The whole heaven is made of this fire; the stars have most of this element, but have also the supreme parts of the other elements'.[38] Yet the celestial bodies keep a kinship (*suggeneia*) with the elements below so that there is nothing absolutely 'alien' in the universe.[39]

Philoponus is particularly pleased to notice that Proclus uses the expression 'not an alien nature' (*xenên phusin*) for the heaven.[40] He quotes it also in 483,1, 523,5, 524,9, and 526,20. One finds the same phrase again in Philoponus' lost *Against Aristotle On the Eternity of the World*. Quotations and summaries of this lost polemical work (which was written after the *Against Proclus*) are preserved in Simplicius' *Commentary on De Caelo*. At the end of the second book Philoponus expresses his anger, Simplicius says, with those who introduce into the celestial bodies 'an alien and strange nature with no

---

[35] *Aet.* 523,1–7.
[36] *in Tim.* 2,43,21–6. I quote the text in the translation of D. Baltzly in his article 'What Goes Up: Proclus against Aristotle on the Fifth Element', *Australasian Journal of Philosophy* 80 (2002), 261–87, esp. 273. Baltzly only discusses the arguments in the Commentary on the *Timaeus*.
[37] See *in Tim.* 2,49,19–29, and the discussion in Baltzly, 'What Goes Up', pp. 284–5.
[38] See the text quoted in *Aet.* 523,11–18.
[39] See *Aet.* 524,2–8.
[40] Proclus never uses the expression in his extant works.

communication with the other elements', whereas all important philosophers believe that the heaven is composed out of the four elements.[41] Simplicius, however, accuses Philoponus of misunderstanding and perverting blasphemously the view of the Platonists he is quoting. As he is accustomed, in this question too Simplicius defends the fundamental harmony between Aristotelians and Platonists. Those who say that the heaven is composed out of the four elements, do not want to make it of the same nature as the sublunary realm; whereas those who consider the heaven as a fifth substance, do not make it for that reason alien and foreign in the universe without communication with the rest.

Already before Simplicius Proclus made an attempt to reconcile Aristotle and Plato in that sense.[42] If one counts the whole heaven composed out of the best of the elements as one thing and adds to it the four sublunary elements, we may speak of five natures altogether, he says. He also points to the discussion of the five regular solids. As is well known, Timaeus attributes four of those solids to the four sublunary elements, whereas the fifth figure (dodecahedron) is assigned 'to the whole' (55C). In this cryptic phrase Proclus recognizes a reference to the celestial body. As he says in the prologue of his commentary: in attributing to the heavens a fifth substance Aristotle follows Plato 'for it makes no difference to call it a fifth element or a fifth world or fifth figure, as Plato called it'.[43]

Simplicius uses the same argument to demonstrate the concordance between Aristotle and Plato on the fifth essence.[44] As one may expect, Philoponus considers such an interpretation a perversion of the authentic meaning of Plato's text.[45] After a brief summary of the doctrine of the regular solids (which he interprets 'symbolically') he attacks Proclus' interpretation of *Tim.* 55C in sharp terms. 'Some who are always intent to conclude what their own opinion is and not the truth, say that through the figure of the dodecahedron Plato indicates the nature of the fifth element, from which the celestial bodies come forth. Hence, Plato, they say, knew before Aristotle the fifth element'.[46] Philoponus, however, convincingly shows that the passage in the *Timaeus* has another meaning. The figure of the dodecahedron does not correspond to the nature of the heavenly body, but indicates symbolically the nature of the whole universe, which encompasses all things.[47]

3.5 A List of Errors in Plato's *Timaeus*

Philoponus' testimony about Proclus' lost treatise against Aristotle is precious, but it is also biased and limited. He only quotes those passages from Proclus' early treatise which are of some interest for his own polemics against the doctrine of the eternity of the world. Therefore he is mainly interested in two questions: the eternity or temporal

---

[41] See *in Cael.* 90,21–5.
[42] See *in Tim.* 2,49,19–29, and the commentary of Baltzly, 'What Goes Up', pp. 284–5.
[43] See *in Tim.* 1,6,30–7,2.
[44] See *in Cael.* 12,16–28; 87,1–21, and *in Phys.* 1165,28–33.
[45] See *Aet.* 531,13.
[46] See *Aet.* 532,15–20.
[47] See *Aet.* 532,20–537,21.

origin of the world and the question of the fifth element. Proclus, however, must have discussed many more topics in his defence of the *Timaeus* against Aristotle, as we can infer from a long text (*Aet.* 318,13–319,14) in which Philoponus enumerates five blatantly erroneous views that can be extracted from the *Timaeus*. With these examples Philoponus wants to convince his readers how foolish it is to rely on Plato as if he were an unquestionable authority. Plato is undoubtedly a great philosopher, but not a divine genius: he makes many errors, as is clear from the numerous objections against his doctrine in the following generations.

> Would it be so strange that Plato, who was after all only human, is wide of the truth at some points. That this happened to him in many areas and in particular in his doctrine about physical matters – not to mention his views about God –, is shown from the countless objections directed at him by, amongst others, Aristotle, and perhaps it will not be a bad thing if we too mention a few of them in the present context.[48]

Philoponus enumerates five examples of obvious errors that Plato makes in the *Timaeus*: (1) his view on the position of the sun; (2) the transmigration of rational souls into animals; (3) the denial of a force of attraction in bodies, (4) the comparison of the female womb with an animal; (5) the attribution of perception to plants. In case the reader is not yet convinced, Philoponus next launches a violent critique of the immoral proposals Plato makes in the *Republic* (such as the community of women). I shall not enter in that discussion here. For our purpose, however, the list of five errors in Plato is of great importance. In fact, they are all based on arguments in the *Timaeus* and they were all subject to Aristotle's critique. More importantly, Philoponus informs us that he found a discussion of those doctrines in the treatise of Proclus against Aristotle of which he quoted already so many passages. This reference is made explicit for the discussion of Plato's view on metempsychosis: 'in the fourteenth chapter of the treatise that we often quoted, in which he defends *Timaeus* against Aristotle'. Moreover, as is evident from Philoponus' concluding sentence, not only this, but also the four other topics were discussed by Proclus: 'If we would not fall outside the scope of our proposed subject, I could have set out each of the errors with the defences of Proclus and could have demonstrated, if it is not coarse to say, that they contain no truth.'[49] I shall examine in detail each of the five errors, using all relevant information to reconstruct Proclus' defence of the *Timaeus* against Aristotle.

> (1) The most celebrated experts in astronomical sciences have demonstrated that the sun occupies the middle sphere among the planets and this has also been the view of all who have come after them. Plato, on the contrary, declares in the *Timaeus* that the sun occupies the rank next after the moon. That he is wrong on this point, nobody with expertise in mathematics will deny.[50]

---

[48] *Aet.* 318,5–12 (trans. Chase slightly modified).
[49] *Aet.* 319,10–15.
[50] *Aet.* 318,13–18.

According to Timaeus' exposition the sun is situated in the second celestial sphere after the sphere of the moon: 'He (i.e. the demiurge) set the Moon in the first circle, around the earth, and the Sun in the second' (38D1-2). If one follows, however, the views of the most respected astronomers, like Ptolemy, the sun must be placed in the middle of the seven spheres, i.e. between, on the one hand, the Moon, Mercury and Venus, and, on the other hand, Mars, Jupiter, and Saturnus. Platonic philosophers made various attempts to reconcile Plato's view in the *Timaeus* with the alternative astronomical theory, which had become dominant since Hellenism.[51] Proclus discusses the problem in two important digressions, one in his commentary on the *Timaeus* (3,60,31–63,30) and another in his commentary on the myth or Er in the *Republic* (2,219,20–221,26). In the commentary on the *Timaeus*, Proclus challenges the scientific truth of mathematical astronomy.[52] He reminds those people who too easily rely on the mathematicians in defence of the middle position of the sun, that even the scientists who use mathematics in astronomy, cannot make absolutely certain demonstrations in this case, but only adduce plausible arguments. He quotes Ptolemy who in the *Syntaxis* admits that the middle position of the sun is only the most probable hypothesis explaining planetary movements. 'One shouldn't thus pay too much attention to the mathematicians, as they only use probable arguments' (2,63,20–1). However, there is also the authority of the *Chaldean Oracles* where it is said that the demiurge 'intercalated the fire of the sun' between the six zones.[53] Proclus does not attempt to find an agreement between both systems, but explains why Plato defended his position. Because he wanted to associate the moon with the sun with which it is closely affiliated, he let them appear in conjunction in the universe. Besides, Plato stands not alone with this view; even Anaxagoras is said to have held it. The commentary on the *Timaeus* is an early work of Proclus. If one turns to the commentary on the myth of Er, which is probably one of Proclus' latest works, one can see that he makes a stand, without hesitation, for the Chaldean order of the planets. They hold that the sun is set in the middle of the seven zones 'having heard from the gods themselves that the solar fire "was established at the site of the heart"'.[54] As he says, he will follow in this question the revelation of the gods. To explain Plato's discordant position, he notices that Plato adopts the astronomical view of his time. For Aristotle, following Callipus and the astronomers of his time, defends the same position (cf. *Metaph.* 12.8, 1073b32 ff.). It seems that Proclus in his later work definitively abandons the Platonic explanation of the order of planets in favour of the Chaldean order (which also corresponds to the Ptolemaic order). In his commentary on the *Timaeus* he still leaves the question open.

---

[51] Thus, the Platonic philosopher Theon of Smyrna (second century CE) attempted to reconcile the Platonic position with the Pythagorean view that attributed a central place to the sun. For a defence of the Platonic order of the planets, see also Macrobius, *In somnium Scipionis* 1,19, §§ 14–17 with an excellent survey of the history of this debate in the recent edition by Armisen-Marchetti (Paris: Collection des Universités de France, 2001).

[52] See also the annotated translation of A. J. Festugière, *Proclus, Commentaire sur le Timée*, 5 vols (Paris: Vrin, 1966–68), vol. 4, pp. 83–8; *Proclus, Commentaire sur la République*, 3 vols (Paris: Vrin, 1969–70), vol. 3, pp. 172–3.

[53] See fr. 200* in the edition of R. Majercik, *The Chaldean Oracles* (Leiden: Brill, 1989).

[54] See *in Remp.* 2,220,11–18 (fr. 58 in the edition of R. Majercik).

One may doubt whether Proclus discussed this question also in his *Episkepsis*. After all, on this point, Aristotle never criticized Plato's *Timaeus*. However, later Peripatetics may have put forward this objection against the *Timaeus*. Therefore Proclus felt obliged to defend Plato in this issue.

> (2) Following Pythagorean myths Plato makes rational souls transmigrate into the bodies of irrational animals. Like many other philosophers Proclus too claims to agree and in the fourteenth chapter of the treatise we have often mentioned, in which he wrote a defence of the *Timaeus* against Aristotle, he clearly demonstrates that this was Plato's own view and not an opinion of some other, and he attempts to dissolve Aristotle's objection to this doctrine, but not rightly, as it seems to me.[55]

In the appendix at the end of the *Timaeus* (91D-92C) one finds a description of the formation of the lower animals (birds, land animals, and fishes) into which the perverted rational souls transmigrate as a punishment for their degradation. This punishment was announced by the demiurge at the first creation of the rational souls: 'according to the character of his depravation, a man should constantly be changed into some beast of a nature resembling the formation of that character' (42C). One finds a similar doctrine expressed in other dialogues (*Phaedo* 81E-82B; *Phaedr.* 249B; *Rep.* 617D-620D). Aristotle ridicules this doctrine in his *De Anima* 1.3, 407b22-5: 'as if it were possible, as in the Pythagorean myths, that any soul could be clothed in any body – an absurd view, for each body seems to have a form and shape of its own. It is just like saying that the art of carpentry could be embodied into flutes.' Platonic philosophers were often embarrassed with this doctrine and they developed different arguments to render it less awkward.[56] Plato, one could say, is using Pythagorean myths: this is not his own view. We should not take the stories about the transmigration into irrational animals literally: they have a metaphorical meaning and are supposed to warn us: those who live a life of passions will end up living as brute beasts.[57] But Proclus, as Philoponus informs us, did not follow this common strategy in his defence of Plato against Aristotle. He insisted that Plato defended the transmigration into beasts as his own view and that it is not just a myth with a moral message.

Proclus' Commentary on the last section of the *Timaeus* is lost, but we may reconstruct his interpretation of the transmigration from his commentary on the *Republic* in which he recapitulates the arguments he had developed in his earlier work on the *Timaeus*.[58] In the final myth of the *Republic*, Socrates mentions the possibility of transmigration into irrational animals (618A). This passage offers for Proclus the

---

[55] *Aet.* 318,19–319,2.
[56] For a survey, see R. Sorabji, *The Philosophy of the Commentators, 200–600 AD: A Sourcebook*, 3 vols (London: Duckworth, 2004), vol. 1, pp. 213–16.
[57] On the debate about the transmigration of the soul in the Platonic tradition, see H. Dörrie and M. Baltes, *Der Platonismus in der Antike* VI.2 (Stuttgart: Frommann-Holzboog, 2002), pp. 96–110, 334–82.
[58] See *in Remp.* 2,335,19–20. Later in the discussion Proclus refers to another (now lost) work (A commentary on the *Palinody* of the *Phaedrus*) in which he had argued against Aristotle on the interpretation of the transmigration of the souls: see *in Remp.* 2,339,15–16.

occasion for a long digression on various problems about metempsychosis. Proclus has no problems in accepting Aristotle's argument that 'not any soul can enter any body' (*DA* 1.3, 407b22). What Aristotle says, is not so original. According to Proclus, Aristotle adopted a principle that Plato had already formulated in the *Phaedrus* (249B): 'only the soul that has contemplated the truth may enter into this our human form', that is, only rational souls can be embodied in human bodies.[59] Besides, even Aristotle could not refuse to accept the transmigration of the souls, at least from one human being to another. For if he admits that both the world and the souls are eternal, but the latter limited in number, the conclusion is unavoidable: the souls must enter new human bodies to make the ensoulment possible for eternity.

But what, then, do we have to make of the many texts in which Plato seems to accept that the human soul enters the body of a beast? Proclus answers that the human soul may reside in an irrational animal as a punishment, not, however, in such a way as to constitute the animal 'being united with it substantially'; the human soul can only be united to the animal body 'from outside and relationally'. One has to distinguish in fact two modes of animation of irrational animals: the animation by their own irrational soul and a supplementary animation by the human soul present in them without being its constitutive form. In the *Timaeus* Plato only discusses the last mode of animation. It was not, however, his intention to show that this was the only mode of animation of the animals. For how could the world be perfect, if the three types of animals (in the air, in water, on earth) of which there is an intelligible paradigm, only come into existence because of the moral failures of human animals? Therefore, we have to conclude that the human souls that are sent into an animal for punishment enter an animal that already possesses its own irrational soul. The lion has a lion soul, but may have, supplementary, a human soul attached to it for punishment. Philoponus' quotation confirms that Proclus had set out similar arguments already in his *Episkepsis*.

(3) Plato denies that there is a force of attraction (*helktikên*) in bodies, even though medical doctors have as it were demonstrated through perception that such a force is inherent in us.[60]

At *Timaeus* 80B-C it is said that there is no special force of attraction in bodies such as there is in the loadstone. All apparent pulling can be reduced to pushing. This view goes against the standard explanation of physical causality where pulling and pushing are opposed forces, and was therefore often challenged. The Aristotelian Strato refers to it in his discussion on the vacuum.[61] As Philoponus comments, Plato's view is contradicted by the observation of doctors. Galen indeed often discusses the force of attraction, as do other medical authors such as Oribasius. Nemesius mentions the *helktikê* as one of the four powers of the vegetative soul.[62] In his own commentary on the *Timaeus* Galen

---

[59] See *in Remp.* 2,334,11–13.
[60] *Aet.* 319,2–5.
[61] See Simplicius, *in Phys.* 663,6 (fr. 62 Wehrli).
[62] See Nemesius, *Nat. Hom.* 83,2; see also Simplicius, *in Phys.* 1190,21 ff.

even expresses his amazement at Plato's position, who disagrees on this point with Hippocrates.[63] We do not know what Proclus had to say about this topic in the lost part of his commentary, but he probably discussed it, as we can infer indirectly from a later source. In his commentary on the *Meteorology*, Olympiodorus discusses why some Egyptian potsherds attract humidity when touching some damp on the edge in a pit. As he informs us, Aclepiodotus, a disciple of Proclus, had examined that question in his commentary on the *Timaeus*, asking whether those potsherds attracted humidity by some 'attractive force' or not. If Asclepiodotus examined the question, he was probably following Proclus' commentary.[64]

(4) Plato thought that the matrix is a living being, what is false, as has been sufficiently demonstrated by Galen in his *Diagnostics*.[65]

When discussing the formation of the sexual organs in the human body Plato ascertains that the matrix of women functions in their body as a semi-independent small animal with an innate urge to procreate (91C1–2). Philoponus supposes that Aristotle is indirectly hinting at this doctrine in *De generatione animalium* 1.18, 724a14–726a25 and he quotes in his commentary *ad locum* the relevant texts from the *Timaeus*. In the present text he refers to Galen for having sufficiently demonstrated in his *Diagnostics* that this explanation is not true. In Book 6, chapter 5 of *De locis affectis* (which was known in Antiquity as 'Diagnostics'), Galen discusses the diseases related to the uterus. In this context he quotes indeed the text from the *Timaeus* where the womb is compared to 'an animal anxious to procreate'. Though he does not add any critical comment on Plato, it seems from what follows that he does not adopt this view.[66] Already in antiquity there was a controversy among the commentators on to what Galen really believed. Interesting is the comment of Stephanus of Alexandria: 'starting from this text some attempt to say that Galen himself seems to believe that the matrix is an animal and they say that he contradicts himself. For everywhere he rejects this doctrine'.[67] We have no comments in the extant works of Proclus on this curious doctrine.

(5) Plato says that also plants share in sense-perception: this is not what Aristotle believes and those who honour Plato cannot demonstrate it to us.[68]

Timaeus argues that the plants not only have vegetative life, but also a 'pleasurable and painful perception with desires'.[69] This view again was for later Platonists an

---

[63] See Galen, *in Tim.* fr. 19.
[64] See Olympiodorus, *in Meteor.* 321,26–9.
[65] Aet. 319,5–8.
[66] See *De locis affectis*, 6.5, 425,4–14 (and also *De semine* 525,13–17, after a sharp attack on the views of some contemporary Aristotelians). On the discussion on the womb in Antiquity, see H. King, *Hippocrates' Woman: Reading the Female Body in Ancient Greece* (London: Routledge, 1998), pp. 222–5.
[67] Stephanus, *Scholia in Hippocratem* (Königsberg, 1834), vol. 1, p. 328,5–8.
[68] Aet. 319,9–10.
[69] See *Tim.* 77B6–7. That plants have some form of perception is also presupposed in the arguments of *Phil.* 22B5 and *Theaet.* 167B-C.

embarrassment. Aristotle seems to have defended a more plausible opinion: plants only have vegetative life; sense-perception is a characteristic of animals.[70] Plotinus follows the standard Peripatetic view (4.4.22.33; 4.9.3.21), but in 3.4.2.12 he admits a sluggish form of perception in the plants. Proclus comments on the question in several passages of his work, and always defends the Platonic view against the Peripatetics who make sense perception a distinctive faculty of animals.[71] The section in the Commentary explaining *Tim.* 77B is lost, but Proclus' argument can be reconstructed from a discussion in 2,83,15 ff. Proclus discusses in this text in what sense we can attribute perception to the world soul and the world as a whole. In his answer he distinguishes four grades of perception, the last of which is the kind of perception that exists in plants: 'the ultimate form of perception is that in which there is a very faint knowledge and much passivity and close to natural sympathy: it cannot know the forms of the sensible things, for example that the agent is hot or cold, but only perceives that what occurs is pleasurable or painful; such is the perception of the plants, as Timaeus further will explain to us: it is only a perception of the pleasurable and painful that comes from the sensible objects'.[72] Proclus' view is adopted by Damascius and Priscian (Ps.-Simplicius).[73]

The short summary of Philoponus has given us some insight in the other matters that Proclus discussed in his *Contra Aristotelem* besides the eternity of the world and the fifth element. Another important Platonic doctrine from the *Timaeus* severely criticised by Aristotle was the geometrical composition elements. We know from Simplicius how Proclus defended this doctrine against Aristotle.

4. Simplicius and Proclus in Defence of Plato's Geometrical Doctrine of the Elements

The explanation of the elementary bodies as regular solids composed out of triangles (*Tim.* 53C-57D) is undoubtedly one of the most splendid and original ideas of Plato, but also one of the most problematic.[74] Aristotle severely criticizes this doctrine in the third book of his treatise *On the Heavens*. The third book is devoted to the study of the simple bodies or elements, their generation and change. As usual, Aristotle first presents the views of his predecessors. Some denied that there is generation at all: there is one underlying substance out of which all things develop. Others claimed that all simple bodies are generated, their ultimate elements being plane planes. The last theory (defended by Plato) is criticized in detail at 3.1, 299a1–300a19. In the last chapters

---

[70] See *DA* 410b22–3; 424a32–b3; *De somno* 454a11–19.
[71] See *in Tim.* 2,82,20–23; 85,5–7; 3,196,3–4; 329,2–6; *In Remp.* 1,232,25; 2,12,13–15, *Theol. Plat.* 3,24,9.
[72] See *in Tim.* 2,83,30–84, 5.
[73] See Damascius, *in Phil.,* § 6, 6,5–6; 35,3–4; 163,4–5; Damascius, *De princ.,* 2, p. 154,2; *in Parm.* 3, p. 43,7–9. Pseudo-Simplicius calls the perception in plants 'a weaker and as it were sleeping perception' (*in DA* 317,12–14). See C. Steel, *'Simplicius', On Aristotle On the Soul 3.6-13* (London: Bristol Classical Press, 2013), p. 188, n. 499.
[74] For a recent evaluation, see J. Opsomer, 'In defence of geometric atomism: Explaining elemental properties', in J. Wilberding and C. Horn, eds, *Neoplatonism and the Philosophy of Nature* (Oxford: Oxford University Press, 2012), pp. 147–73 (with reference to previous studies).

(3.7-8) Aristotle discusses how generation takes place and criticizes again previous views, and in particular the Platonic theory of the generation from triangular planes (306a1-307b19), which is, in his view, a mathematical *a priori* speculation not based upon any natural experience. His conclusion is that the elements differ primarily not in shapes but in qualities and functions and powers. Aristotle puts forward no less than fifteen arguments against Plato's explanation. One may wonder why he felt the need to discuss that theory at length. Alexander supposes that he did so because it was an original and novel theory.[75]

The most extensive commentary on the *De Caelo* we have from Antiquity is that of Simplicius. When dealing with Aristotle's polemics against Plato, Simplicius is not at ease. He knows of course the *Timaeus* and quotes large sections of the text. One gets the impression, however, that he has not much sympathy for this extravagant mathematical speculation of Plato. On the other hand, he could not leave Plato without a defence against the often strident arguments of Aristotle. Fortunately, he could rely upon the work of his predecessors, and in particular on Proclus:

> As some other Platonist philosophers have [already] responded to the objections put forward [by Aristotle] against the proposed generation of bodies from planes, and in particular Proclus of Lycia, who had become Plato's successor a short time before me, wrote a book to dissolve the objections made by Aristotle here, I thought that it would be good to put, as concisely as possible, these solutions after the objections.[76]

In the following pages of his commentary Simplicius quotes *verbatim* Proclus' solutions for all fifteen objections of Aristotle. Though Simplicius does not give the title of Proclus' work, the quotations in which Proclus defends the *Timaeus* argument against Aristotle come most probably from the *Episkepsis*. As we have seen, the critique of Plato's geometrical explanation was an essential part of Aristotle's attack on the physics of the *Timaeus*, and it is impossible that Proclus would not have dealt with this critique in his refutation of Aristotle. Besides, the problem of the fifth solid was certainly discussed in the *Episkepsis*, as we have learned from Philoponus.

Proclus was not the first Platonist to defend Plato's geometrical explanation of the elements against Aristotle, as Simplicius observes and he probably relied on his predecessors in his defence of Plato. This is what Proclus himself admits, as we have seen.[77] Simplicius occasionally discusses views of other Platonists on this issue. Some claimed that not the physical bodies themselves are composed out of planes, but their incorporeal *eidos* which must be distinguished from the forms in matter.[78] Alexander

---

[75] See Simplicius, *in Cael.* 562,1-2. For a reconstruction of the interpretation of Alexander, see P. Moraux, *Der Aristotelismus bei den Griechen von Andronikos bis Alexander von Aphrodisias* III: *Alexander von Aphrodisas* (Berlin: De Gruyter, 2001), pp. 181-241.
[76] *in Cael.* 640,21-7.
[77] See *in Tim.* 2,278,29-30 quoted above, p. 330.
[78] See *in Cael.* 578,20-6.

of Aphrodisias discusses in his *Questions* a similar view defended by Platonists.[79] He forces them into the dilemma: the geometrical structures either belong to matter or to form. Both suppositions are impossible. Other Platonists, Simplicius informs us, proposed a symbolical interpretation of the geometrical figures, as did Iamblichus in his commentary on the *Timaeus*. The 'recent Platonists', however, Simplicius says, try to explain the text 'as it stands in its literal meaning'.[80] Proclus adopts in his response to Aristotle's objections such a 'realistic' interpretation: the geometrical explanation of *Timaeus* gives us insight in the basic structure of the physical bodies.[81] As Proclus' commentary on the last part of the *Timaeus* is lost, the extensive quotations in Simplicius allow us to reconstruct his interpretation of *Tim.* 53C-57D. All together they constitute a unique document on Proclus natural philosophy.

Before we turn to Proclus' arguments some comments must be made on the general perspective from which Simplicius understands this passage. Otherwise we run the risk of attributing to Proclus some views that are characteristic of Simplicius. In fact, as we have said, Simplicius does not share Proclus' anti-Aristotelian stance. After having quoted from the 'diadochos' himself Simplicius will always add his own comments, thereby qualifying Proclus' statements. Whenever he can, he will try to make Proclus' critique less virulent and search for a philosophical compromise so that also the point of view of Aristotle gets its due. At the beginning of the discussion, Simplicius formulates again the fundamental principle of his exegesis, namely the harmony between Plato and Aristotle. That he feels the need to express this harmony view at the start may be a way to take distance from the views Proclus had expressed at the beginning of his *Investigation*, namely that Aristotle often contradicts Plato.

> Here again there is an opportunity to say what I often use to say, namely that there is no real disagreement between the [two] philosophers. If Aristotle seems to contradict Plato it is because, out of consideration for those who understand Plato superficially, he frequently focuses on the apparent meaning of the argument, which can also be understood wrongly. One can see this clearly also in the present text, I think, in which Plato has reported the views of Timaeus the Pythagorean.[82]

---

[79] See *Quaestiones* 2.13, 58,1 ff. and the annotated translation of R. W. Sharples, *Alexander of Aphrodisias, Quaestiones 1.1–2.15* (London: Duckworth, 1992), pp. 112–14: 'Against the Platonists who say that it is the shapes and forms of the bodies that are put together from the triangles, not the bodies themselves.'

[80] See *in Cael.* 564,10–14. In my 2005 version of this paper I considered the 'recent Platonists' to be a reference to Proclus himself. Ian Mueller (*Simplicius, On Aristotle. On the Heavens 3.1–7* (London: Duckworth, 2009), p. 126, n. 61) rejected this identification and suggested that it may be a reference to Pericles of Lydia, a disciple of Proclus. Textual basis is too limited to confirm this identification. Mueller, however, is right that what follows is not Proclus' view, but an Aristotelianizing interpretation. Opsomer (n. 74 above), pp. 156–8, distinguishes among the 'recent Platonists' two different views: 'the second is branded as 'Pythagorean', and is in fact the one that forms the background of Proclus' and Simplicius' refutation of Aristotle's objections'.

[81] Proclus follows here again his master Syrianus: see *in Metaph.* 85,38–86,2: 'Plato indicates with mathematical names the efficient and creative powers of nature'. Interestingly, Philoponus understands the geometrical composition of the elements 'symbolically': see *Aet.* 533,21 and 534,15.

[82] *in Cael.* 640,27–641,5.

In his attempt to harmonise Plato and Aristotle Simplicius applies the following principles which he explains in his introduction:[83]

1. Plato follows in this dialogue the Pythagorean tradition. We should not take the mathematical explanation as a description of what the things really are. It is an *endeixis*, an indication, a suggestion, helping us to understand and explain the physical phenomena, just as the mathematical hypotheses of Ptolemy (epicycles and eccentric movements) are not to be taken as physical realities, but help us to make the planetary movements intelligible. Simplicius also insists that the geometrical forms in the *Timaeus* are not purely mathematical structures, but indicate quantitative structures of the physical bodies.
2. The Platonic explanation does not force us to give up the basic Aristotelian distinction between matter and form. Simplicius quotes a passage from the treatise of Timaeus of Locri *On Nature* where it is said that all physical bodies are composed out of matter and form. The author of this treatise summarised the cosmological argument of Plato's dialogue, but integrated in its some Aristotelian material, such as the matter-form distinction.[84] This treatise is a pseudo-Pythagorean fraud from the imperial period, but it was considered authentic by Proclus and Simplicius. The latter had no problem in using it for an interpretation of the *Timaeus*. Simplicius finds in the *Timaeus* the Aristotelian' doctrine of matter. He distinguishes, however, between prime matter, which has no property whatsoever, and what he calls the second substrate, matter without qualities, but already having quantitative dimensions (what the Stoics called *to apoion sôma*).[85] In his view, the four regular solids provide the different dimensional structures for matter, making it an appropriate substrate for the reception of the qualities. As Simplicius repeatedly says, in our search for an ultimate explanation of physical phenomenona, we cannot stand still at the qualitative features (hot, cold, dry, and wet). We have also to indicate the causes of the qualities and thus we will find the quantitative figuration of matter, which is more fundamental that the qualitative differences.

But let us now turn to the objections. As we have said, in *De Caelo* 3.7–8, Aristotle develops fifteen arguments against the geometrical explanation Timaeus gives of the generation and mutual transformation of the elementary bodies. For each of them Simplicius quotes the answer of Proclus, with his own comments. In his *Aristotle's*

---

[83] See *in Cael.* 563,26–566,20; see *in Phys.* 228 ss. On these hermeneutical principles see Opsomer (n. 74 above) and I. Mueller, 'Aristotelian Objections and Post-Aristotelian Responses to Plato's Elemental Theory', in J. Wilberding and C. Horn, eds, *Neoplatonism and the Philosophy of Nature* (Oxford: Oxford University Press, 2012), pp. 129–46.

[84] See on this issue A. Ulacco and J. Opsomer, 'Elements and elemental properties in Timaeus Locrus', *Rheinisches Museum für Philologie* 157 (2014), 154–206.

[85] On the distinction between prime matter and the 'second substrate' (or 'non qualified body'), see Simplicius, *in Cael.* 134,10; 565,3 and 6; 599,5; *in Phys.* 514,9 and *in Cat.* 140,27; Philoponus, *in Cat.* 65,18; 83,17; *in Phys.* 156,16; *Aet.* 426,22; on *apoion sôma* see also F. A. J. De Haas, *John Philoponus' New Definition of Prime Matter* (Leiden: Brill, 1997).

Criticism of Plato and the Academy, H. Cherniss discusses all of Aristotle's arguments and how Proclus and Simplicius attempt to counter them.[86] Recently (2012) Ian Mueller and Jan Opsomer carefully examined where Simplicius agrees with Proclus and where he disagrees. There is no reason to do it all again. To illustrate Proclus' reply to Aristotle, I will limit myself to some comments on the first two objections, which deal with the special status of the element earth. Following Timaeus' exposition not all elements can interchange, for the earth is not constructed out of the same basic triangles as the other three elements. Only the earth is constituted out of isosceles triangles, whereas the regular solids that constitute the three other elements are made out of triangles with unequal sides. 'Hence it is not possible for all of them to pass into one another by resolution' (54C). Thus, when earth is dissolved into parts in the encounter with fire, those parts cannot enter into the composition of the other elements. Earth drifts about 'until its own parts somewhere encounter one another, are fitted together, and again become earth; for they can never pass into any other kind' (56D).

To exclude earth from the interchange of elements is, as Aristotle objects, both 'unreasonable' and against empirical evidence, since we see that all elements interchange. 'Those philosophers make statements about the phenomena which do not agree with the phenomena.' They have indeed a wrong conception of the first principles and absolutely try to reduce all phenomena to their predetermined views. Instead of searching for sensible principles for sensible things, they apply a priori geometrical principles to explain physical change. 'They behave like speakers who defend a thesis in a debate, because they are attached to some principles. They stand on the truth of their principles against all the facts, not admitting that there are principles which ought to be judged from their consequences and in particular from the end.'[87] In physics, the final criterion of truth is the sensible phenomenon. 'Aristotle, in short, is complaining that Plato does not even "save the phenomena"; that his exclusion of earth from the interchange of bodies was forced upon him by the nature of the principles he had chosen beforehand (i.e. in this case the triangles out of which the corpuscles are constructed).'[88]

One might expect Proclus to reply to Aristotle with a defence of the intelligible principles that explain the phenomena. This is not the case, however. On the contrary, Proclus answers the challenge with the defence that Plato's view is much more in accordance with the phenomena than Aristotle's. Aristotle criticizes Plato's neglect of experience in his speculative doctrine. However, as Proclus replies, upon a more accurate examination of experience, one has to conclude that Plato has the right view, and not Aristotle: as experience teaches, the earth is never transformed into any of the other elements nor any of the other into earth.

---

[86] See Cherniss (n. 2 above), pp. 148–63; A. E. Taylor, *A Commentary on Plato's Timaeus* (Oxford: Clarendon Press, 1928), pp. 403–9; excellent comments in S. Sambursky, *The Physical World of late Antiquity* (London: Routledge & Kegan Paul, 1962), pp. 50–61; for a recent appraisal, see L. Siorvanes, *Proclus: Neo-Platonic Philosophy and Science* (New Haven: Yale University Press, 1996), pp. 215–32.
[87] See *Cael.* 3.7, 306a12–16 (trans. Guthrie modified).
[88] See Cherniss (n. 2 above), p. 150.

Against this objection Proclus says the following: we should say the contrary, namely that those who make earth change and move what cannot be moved,[89] are not following the phenomena; for nowhere can one see earth [itself] changing into the other [elements], but earthen things change, insofar as they are filled with air or water, whereas all earth is unchangeable when it is only earth, for instance when it has become ash and dust. For in metalworking the humid parts are entirely consumed, whereas the ashy parts remain unaffected. This does not mean that earth would remain itself absolutely unaffected by the other [elements]: for it is divided by the other when they fall upon it; but its parts remain until they again encounter one another and make again of themselves some unity. If, however, someone were to say that earth changes into the other [elements] according to its qualities, as it is cold and dry, then it would sooner change into fire than water does: yet, we can see that water is entirely burned up, whereas earth, taken in itself, is never burned up. And heaven, he says, is neither divisible nor changeable, earth, which is 'the most venerable of the things within the heaven' is divisible but not changeable, whereas the intermediate elements [i.e. fire, air, water] are both divided and changing.[90]

This long quotation is in itself sufficient proof of the manner of Proclus' refutation. Particularly surprising is his appeal to experimental data, such as the metallurgical practices in which metals are transformed. All this may suffice to silence the hardcore Peripatetic. At the end, however, he comes with a metaphysical argument, which is very characteristic for his thought: the need of intermediaries in the procession from one extreme term to another. If in the universe the heaven is without any change and division and the sublunary elements entirely subject to change and division, there must be one of the elements mediating and holding the universe together: this is earth, which is divisible as the other elements yet not changeable.

Proclus develops this view on the special position of the element earth further in his reply to Aristotle's *second* objection. If earth is outside the cycle of transformation, Aristotle argues, earth alone is imperishable and cannot be dissolved into any other body. It can be dissolved, but only in the triangles from which it is itself composed, whereas each of the other three elements is dissolved into triangles from which the two others can also be composed. So strictly speaking only earth has the right to be called 'element', if it is proper to elements to be imperishable.[91]

In his reply quoted by Simplicius (645,15–28), Proclus again insists that earth has a special status among the elements as it does not change into the three other elements. He quotes again Plato's praise of the earth in *Tim.* 40B-C: 'the first and oldest of things within the heaven'. To confirm the special status of earth among the elements Proclus also refers to the cosmological myth at the end of the *Phaedo* where Socrates gives a description of the true earth (108C-110B). This earth, which reaches into the starred heaven and is as pure as it, has all around 'many hollow places into which water and

---

[89] *kinein ta akinêta*, almost idiomatic since Plato's *Laws* 684E1 and 913B9.
[90] See *in Cael.* 643,13–27.
[91] See *Cael.* 3.7, 306a17–21, with Simplicius' explanation.

mist and air have collected' (109B).[92] One should not, however, conclude from its privileged status that the earth does no longer interact with the other elements, as Aristotle objects. Like all other elements the earth can be dissolved into the parts out of which it has been constructed and be reconstructed again. 'And if earth too is affected by being divided by the other and also acts on them by compressing and contracting them and consequently breaking them up, it is rightly coordinated in opposition to the things by which it is affected and on which it acts according to a same affection.'

One finds an extended version of Proclus' argument quoted by Simplicius in Proclus' own commentary on the *Timaeus*, precisely in the section where lemma 40B-C on the status of the earth is explained.[93] As Proclus says, those who are used to look at the material, heavy, opaque character of the earth may wonder why Timaeus called the earth 'the first and oldest of the things within the heaven'. We should consider, however, also the properties of earth by which it excels the other elements: its stability in the centre of the universe, its productive character (as manifested in whatever grows from earth), its correspondence to the heaven. In this text too Proclus refers the Plato's doctrines on the earth as one can find them in the myth of the *Phaedo*.

In the same section of his commentary, Proclus also defends Plato against Aristotle's critique that made the earth move around its axis. It is reasonable to suppose that Proclus had developed a similar argument in his lost *Episkepsis* and that Simplicius may have been influenced by him in his own treatment of this difficult question.[94]

Although Simplicius quotes large extracts from Proclus' work to counter Aristotle's objections, he was apparently not at ease with Proclus' polemical approach. For after having quoted Proclus' replies to Aristotle, he always attempts to diminish the opposition of Aristotle to Plato. If we admit with Aristotle that earth, like all other elementary bodies, is ultimately composed from prime matter, the mutual transformation of all elements (including earth) remains possible, even if this transformation is excluded on the level of the composing triangles.

> In order that Plato may not seem to disagree with himself nor Aristotle to disagree with Plato, [one should consider that] according to Plato, earth too changes into the other [elements] and from them, insofar as it composed of the same prime matter [as the other elements], but insofar as it is composed directly of the isosceles triangle, it is unchangeable. For as long as the triangles keep their own specificity, earth cannot come to be from the half-triangle nor the other [elements] from the isosceles triangle.[95]

---

[92] On the interpretation of these 'hollows' see C. Steel, 'The divine Earth. Proclus on Timaeus 40BC', in R. Chiaradonna and F. Trabatonni, eds, *Physics and Philosophy of Nature in Greek Neoplatonism* (Leiden: Brill, 2009), pp. 259–81. On the Neoplatonic interpretation of the final myth of the *Phaedo* see 'Plato's geography: Damascius' interpretation of the *Phaedo* myth', in J. Wilberding and C. Horn, eds, *Neoplatonism and the Philosophy of Nature* (Oxford: Oxford University Press, 2012), pp. 174–96.
[93] See *in Tim.* 3,141,1–144,22.
[94] See *Cael.* 2.13, 293b30–2. On Simplicius' interpretation of this text, see *in Cael.* 517,1–519,11 and Guldentops (n. 20 above), pp. 209–11.
[95] *in Cael.* 644,7–13.

Only when the triangles are broken up and resolved down to prime matter, can what was first earth then take the form of another element. Simplicius finds a confirmation of this interpretation in a passage from the *Timaeus* (50B10-C6), where the *chôra* is described as 'what is always receiving all things [...]; by nature it lies as a molding-stuff for everything, being changed and marked by the entering [figures]'. Simplicius adopts the same concordist interpretation in his comments on the second objection.[96] Proclus, however, would never have accepted that the triangles could be broken up.

Conclusion

In this paper I attempted to reconstruct a lost treatise of Proclus in which he critically examined Aristotle's objections against Plato's *Timaeus*. Simplicius, Philoponus and Proclus himself have been our sources. Proclus develops the arguments of his earlier treatise in his great commentary on the *Timaeus*. Philoponus fully exploits Proclus' treatise against Proclus himself, in particular to refute his views on the eternity of the world. On this question and on many other issues, Philoponus believes, Plato and Aristotle are radically opposed. Proclus does not dissimulate their disagreement, but, to Philoponus' anger, he does not distance himself from Aristotle's interpretation of the *Timaeus* in the discussion about the eternity of the world. Instead of sincerely accepting with Plato that the world is generated and temporal, he defects to the Aristotelian view and thus comes in contradiction with his earlier work, as Philoponus demonstrates. Simplicius also read Proclus' early treatise and he quotes large extracts from it in his commentary on the *De Caelo*. Simplicius, who is the great advocate of the harmony of Plato and Aristotle, is often embarrassed by Proclus' polemics. Whenever Proclus quotes a text from Aristotle to convince the philosopher that he too is 'compelled' to admit the truth of the Platonic principles, Simplicius makes of it an argument to demonstrate that Aristotle is fundamentally in agreement with Plato. How different their ultimate goal may have been in this polemic, both ideological opponents, Philoponus and Simplicius, offer us valuable information on a lost work of Proclus, in which he attacked Aristotle with youthful zeal in defence of the *Timaeus*. The treatise witnesses both his admiration for the *Timaeus* and his irritation for Aristotle's unfair treatment of its doctrine.

---

[96] *in Cael.* 645,28–646,3.

13

Smoothing over the Differences: Proclus and Ammonius on Plato's *Cratylus* and Aristotle's *De Interpretatione*

R. M. van den Berg

I. Introduction

Ammonius, the son of Hermeias († between 517 and 526), was not a prolific author, unlike his teacher Proclus (412-85). Whereas the latter wrote up to seven hundred lines a day, the only large work that Ammonius ever wrote was his commentary on Aristotle's *De Interpretatione*.[1] Remarkably enough, for someone whose entire reputation rests on his study of Aristotle, he does not claim any credit for its content. His work, he writes at the beginning, is a record of the interpretations of his divine teacher Proclus. If he too is able to add anything to the clarification of the book, he 'owes a great thanks to the god of eloquence'.[2] How much did the god of eloquence allow Ammonius to add? No other sources of Proclus' course on the *Int.* survive. Yet in one case we are able to study Ammonius' originality or the lack of it: his discussion of Aristotle's views on *onomata*, a group of words that corresponds roughly speaking to our nouns and which I shall refer to as 'names' in this paper.

One of the major issues in Greek linguistic thought throughout Antiquity was the relation between names and their objects. Does there exist some sort of natural relation between names and their objects or are names just a matter of convention? Plato had discussed the question in his *Cratylus*, in which he had made a certain Hermogenes the spokesman of the conventionalist position and the eponymous character Cratylus an

---

This article first appeared as 'Smoothing over the differences: Proclus and Ammonius on Plato's *Cratylus* and Aristotle's *De Interpretatione*' by Robbert van den Berg in *BICS* supp 83, 1 (2004), pp. 191-201. Reproduced with permission.

[1] On Proclus' love for hard work (*philoponia*), see Marinus, *Proclus* § 22, 29-37 ed. Saffrey-Segonds. On Ammonius and his writings, see L. G. Westerink, 'The Alexandrian Commentators and the Introductions to Their Commentaries', in R. Sorabji, ed., *Aristotle Transformed: The Ancient Commentators and Their Influence* (London: Duckworth, 1990), pp. 325-48, at pp. 325-8, and D. Blank, *Ammonius, On Aristotle On Interpretation 1-8* (London: Duckworth, 1996), pp. 1-6.
[2] Ammonius, *in Int.* 1,6-11.

adherent of the naturalist position. In the end, Socrates forces both Hermogenes and Cratylus to admit that names are partly by nature and partly by convention, hence that they are both right and wrong. Many scholars, both ancient and modern, believe that in the first chapters of *Int*. Aristotle responded at least in part to the views expressed in the *Cratylus*. As it so happens, an excerpt of Proclus' lecture notes on that Platonic dialogue has survived. A first reading of the two commentaries seems indeed to suggest that there is a substantial overlap between them on the relevant issue, even though Proclus may at times be critical of Aristotle. As we shall see, this apparent correspondence has even inspired an attempt to emend Proclus' text at one point on the basis of Ammonius' commentary.[3]

In this paper I will argue that in fact Ammonius' concept of *onoma* is significantly different from that of Proclus'. As Proclus had observed, but as Ammonius tried to downplay, Aristotle had been arguing *against* Plato. For Proclus this did not pose any particular problem. Like all Neoplatonists, Ammonius included, he was convinced that the divinely inspired Plato had to be right. If Aristotle chose to deviate from Plato and the truth, that was his problem.[4] Proclus sets Socrates up as a judge (*in Crat*. § 10, p. 4,12) between the conventionalist Hermogenes and the naturalist Cratylus, a judge who shows that they are both right and wrong. Aristotle is explicitly counted among the partisans of Hermogenes.[5] On the whole, one can say that Proclus is very critical of Aristotle in *in Crat*.[6]

Ammonius, on the other hand, wanted to show that Plato and Aristotle were in complete harmony with each other, even where this is not evident. He too presents Socrates as a mediator between Hermogenes and Cratylus (*in Int*. 37,1), but this time Aristotle is not grouped together with Hermogenes, but presented as being of the same

---

[3] On this correspondence, see A. Sheppard, 'Proclus' Philosophical Method of Exegesis: The Use of Aristotle and the Stoics in the *Commentary on the Cratylus*', in J. Pépin and H. D. Saffrey, eds, *Proclus lecteur et interprète des anciens* (Paris: CNRS, 1987), pp. 137–51; I. Hadot, 'La vie et l'œuvre de Simplicius d'après des sources grecques et arabes', in I. Hadot, ed., *Simplicius: sa vie, son œuvre, sa survie* (Berlin: De Gruyter, 1987), pp. 3–39, at p. 6, and Blank (n. 1 above), pp. 5–6; for the emendation proposed by Sheppard, see the discussion of **T. 8** below.

[4] On the attitude of Proclus and his teacher Syrianus towards Aristotle, see H. D. Saffrey, 'How Did Syrianus Regard Aristotle?', in Sorabji, *Aristotle Transformed* (see n. 1 above), pp. 173–9, at p. 175: 'Proclus, even more than his teacher, will note the divergence between Aristotle and Plato, since he will pass the same global judgement on the *Physics* that Syrianus passed on the *Metaphysics*, and will even go so far as to say: "As for the great Aristotle, it is my opinion that he arranged as much as possible his treatise on nature in a spirit of rivalry with the teachings of Plato" (Proclus, *in Tim*. 1,6,21–4 and its whole development until 7,16), and his commentary on the *Timaeus* will at every opportunity establish the priority of Plato over Aristotle'.

[5] Proclus, *in Crat*. § 16, p. 5,28.

[6] Aristotle's Peripatetic dialectical methods are childish play in comparison to that of Plato's (§ 2); Aristotle believes that there are a single rhetorical and a single dialectical technique, whereas Plato more accurately says that there are two rhetorical and two dialectical techniques (§ 4); Plato has arrived at a fuller understanding of the concept of 'truth' than Aristotle has (§ 36); Aristotle contradicts himself when he maintains that names are conventional symbols but argues at the same time that assertoric statements are receptive of truth and falsity (§ 47); Aristotle wrongly claims that speech does not signify as an instrument but conventionally (§ 49); Aristotle's syllogism to prove the fact that names are conventional is flawed (§ 58). In short, Proclus clearly sees the conflict between Aristotle's position and that of Plato, and he is only too happy to point out where Aristotle goes wrong.

mind as Socrates. As we shall see, Ammonius, when discussing the nature of names, takes his point of departure from Aristotle. Since Aristotle's idea of what a name is differs from Plato's, Ammonius will arrive at a concept of name that is fundamentally different from that of Proclus, who takes Plato as his starting point. On the assumption that Proclus, who for the most part appears to be quite consistent throughout his enormous œuvre, did not radically change his views when lecturing on *Int.*, we may thus infer from this that Ammonius was not slavishly following Proclus. This becomes all the more apparent in the case of Ammonius' interpretation of Cratylus' position in the dialogue. In order to harmonize Plato with Aristotle, Ammonius offers a rather original, albeit not very convincing reading of that position.

Once we have established the fundamental difference between the two of them, we will be better able to explain a phenomenon to which Richard Sorabji has recently drawn attention: the absence of any interest in divine names in Ammonius' commentary. Finally, this case study will allow us to make a more general observation about the relation between the Athenian and Alexandrian commentators.

II. Plato and Aristotle on Names

Before turning to Proclus' and Ammonius' ideas about names, let us first see what Plato and Aristotle themselves have to say on this issue in the *Cratylus* and *Int*. It is, of course, always risky to assume we find Plato's own view presented unproblematically in any Platonic dialogue. But if we take Socrates to be Plato's mouth-piece, as Proclus does in his commentary on the *Cratylus*, it appears that for Plato an *onoma* is, or at least should be, a likeness, an image (*eikôn*), of the thing it represents. In this way it is natural. It is not clear how exactly a word is supposed to imitate its object. At one stage, Socrates suggests that the meaning of a word (its *dunamis*) should be in harmony with its object.

It does not really matter what sounds are used to express this meaning. The English 'pocket-book' and French 'livre du poche' may sound different but they are both equally apt expressions of the type of book that is such that one can easily carry it around in the pockets of one's coat.[7] From this, both Proclus and Ammonius conclude that for Plato the sound of a word is conventional, unlike its meaning. Not unimportant for what follows is that Socrates furthermore argues that a word must be like its object since it is a tool (*organon*) for giving instruction and dividing being.

Aristotle, on the other hand, equates names with spoken sounds. About these spoken sounds he writes:

T. 1 Now spoken sounds are symbols of affections in the soul and written marks symbols of spoken sounds. And just as written marks are not the same for all men, neither are spoken sounds. But what these are in the first place signs of – affections

---

[7] Later on in the dialogue (426C-427D), Socrates will, rather surprisingly in the light of this description, argue that sounds too imitate the nature of a thing, the 'l' sound for example suggests smoothness and softness. Despite this, Proclus and Ammonius especially focus on the model which opposes a natural meaning to a conventional sound.

of the soul – are the same for all. And what these affections are likenesses of – actual things – are also the same. These matters have been discussed in the work on the soul and do not belong to the present subject.

Int. 16a3–9, trans. Ackrill

Aristotle here opts for the view that names are purely a matter of convention. Whereas thoughts are likenesses (*homoiômata*) of their objects, and hence in a way natural, names are merely symbols (*sumbola*) of these thoughts, since they are conventional. Any articulated sound may express any given thought. There is good reason to believe with many modern scholars that Aristotle takes issue with the *Cratylus* here, especially when he writes that 'every sentence (*logos*) is significant, not as a tool (*organon*) but by convention' (*Int.* 16b33 f.).

III. Proclus and Ammonius on Names

III.1 What Does a Name Consist In?

For Proclus a name consists in form and matter (*in Crat.* § 10, p. 4,16–18). He derives this idea directly from the *Cratylus* (390A) where it is said that the name-giver embodies the *eidos* of a word in syllables. These syllables, which act like the matter of a name, may differ, just as a blacksmith may put the form of a certain tool like a drill in this piece of iron or in that one. The shared *eidos* explains why words that mean the same thing sound differently in various languages, e.g. *hippos* and 'horse'. What is more, Proclus does not believe that the material component of a name, i.e. sound, is essential to it. He believes in the existence of a superior type of names on the level of the divine Intellect, hence above the material realm, from which many of our names originate.[8] This prompts of course the question of how the gods use these names. According to Proclus, they can as it were read each other's thoughts: they know these intellectually (*noêtikôs*) not perceptually (*aisthêtikôs*).[9] By the same token, when they hear our prayers, they do not perceive them as sound from without, but they already know what we are going to ask.[10]

Aristotle on the other hand, had defined a name as a spoken sound (cf. **T. 1**). Ammonius follows him in this, although he has to concede to Proclus that names[11]

> **T. 2** . . . are not simply vocal sounds, but vocal sounds shaped and formed . . . by linguistic imagination and accepted as symbols of thoughts in the soul (Ammonius, *in Int.* 22,33–23,2, trans. Blank).

As we shall see below, Proclus wants names to be as much like their objects as possible. By claiming that there is a certain *eidos* present in the matter of the syllables, it becomes

---

[8] *in Crat.* § 51, pp. 29,21–32,4.
[9] *in Crat.* § 77, p. 37,3–5.
[10] *in Crat.* § 35, p. 35,25–6.
[11] Hence for Aristotle (*Cat.* 4b32) as for Ammonius (*in Int.* 16,28–30) speech is a quantity of sound.

possible to study that *eidos* through its name. For Proclus names are windows to a higher metaphysical world. Ammonius on the other hand does not want names to be too much like their objects. For, although he tries to show that for Aristotle too names are natural in a sense, he must take into account that Aristotle presents them first and foremost as symbols.

III.2 What Does a Name Refer To?

Aristotle, in a famous passage in the first book of the *Metaphysics* (987a29-b10), tells us how in his youth Plato became first acquainted with Cratylus and his Heraclitean notion that the whole sensible world is always in a state of flux. Under the influence of Socrates' moral philosophy, he subsequently arrived at his celebrated theory of unchanging Forms after which all sensible things are named. He spells out what is at least suggested by Socrates at the end of the *Cratylus* (439A-440D), viz. that the names are primarily names of the Forms. Proclus likewise assumes that the name-giver 'should perform his function when looking to the Forms of the things that are being named'.[12] However, a human name-giver cannot contemplate the Forms directly, but only to the extent that they are present in us. For, according to Proclus the human soul consists of *logoi*, emanations of the Forms. When the soul wants to study these, it projects these on the imagination (*phantasia*) 'as on a mirror', which receives them as images (*in Euclid.* 141,2-9). Names, so Proclus contends, are produced by this imaginative faculty as copies of the projected *logoi*.[13] In other words, names are remote images of the Forms themselves.

Ammonius, by contrast, claims on the authority of Aristotle that names refer to our thoughts of actual, material things (cf. **T. 1**). Ammonius, *in Int.* 6,4-14, in a discussion of what Aristotle means by 'affections in the soul' which are likenesses of the actual things (**T. 1**), he explains that the imagination (*phantasia*) takes an imprint of the very same external things that sense perception knows. Elsewhere, Ammonius' position becomes even more evident. In a discussion of how the name-givers attributed the appropriate gender to each name, Ammonius explains that they applied the same principles not only in the case of seas and rivers and the like, but also with regard to the gods themselves. To the extent that these gods were heavenly bodies, like the sun and the moon, these name-givers determined the genders of their names in accordance with astronomical, empirical observations. They even did so in the case of the hypercosmic entities, 'seeing with the eyes by which these things were naturally seen, ... even if from far off'.[14] These hypercosmic entities are no doubt a type of superior

---

[12] *in Crat.* § 81, p. 37,26-7.
[13] On these *logoi*, see C. Steel, 'Breathing Thought: Proclus on the Innate Knowledge of the Soul', in J. J. Cleary, ed., *The Perennial Tradition of Neoplatonism* (Leuven: Leuven University Press, 1997), pp. 293-309. On the relation between these and names, see *in Crat.* § 16, pp. 5,25-6,19, where Proclus ascribes a comparable theory to Pythagoras; *in Crat.* § 53, p. 23,24-5. On this issue see further R. M. van den Berg, 'What's in a Divine Name? Proclus on Plato's *Cratylus*', in J. H. D. Scourfield, ed., *Texts & Cultures in Late Antiquity: Inheritance, Authority, and Change* (Swansea: The Classical Press of Wales, 2007), pp. 261-77.
[14] Ammonius, *in Int.* 36,13 f.

gods, who are immaterial and hence can not be studied by the senses. Yet Ammonius persists in presenting them as external objects far removed from us, which we study by a sort of sixth sense (the Platonic 'eye of the soul'). Compare this to Proclus' description of how we construct divine names:

> **T. 3** [human name-givers] work either under divine inspiration or in an intellectual fashion when they produce moving images of their internal visions (Proclus, *Theol. Plat.* 1.29, p. 124,9–11).

The gods too belong to the metaphysical world, so their names are produced in a like manner. To the extent that these names have not been revealed to us by the gods themselves, they are images based on internal visions of a higher world, not on (some sort of) sense perception of external objects.

The imaginative faculty, then, that produces names is the same for Ammonius and Proclus, but the models after which this faculty produces the names are different.

III.3 How Does a Name Resemble its Object?

Both Proclus and Ammonius explain the fact that names are not just a matter of convention, but also natural, by claiming that names resemble their objects along the lines that had been suggested by Plato in the *Cratylus* (see § II above). Let us now see how Proclus and Ammonius describe the resemblance between names and their objects. As we have seen above (§ III.1), Proclus believes that names refer especially to metaphysical entities as they are present in us. Names are a kind of portrait-like images of these entities. This becomes especially clear in the case of divine names. Since names resemble these metaphysical divine beings, Proclus, like many other Neoplatonists,[15] considers them as statues (*agalmata*) in sound of the gods:

> **T. 4** And as the telestic art ... fashions statues suitable for the reception of divine illumination, so too by the same power of assimilation the art of legislation institutes names as statues (*agalmata*) of their objects, when it *images* (*apeikonizomenê*) through echoes of this sort or that the nature of real beings (*in Crat.* § 51, p. 19,12–17).

Proclus compares names to statues because he wants names to be as much like their objects as possible. As we shall see when we discuss the function of names according to Proclus and Ammonius (§ III.4), Proclus believes that one can derive knowledge about the entities in the metaphysical world, especially about the divine beings, from the etymologies of their names, precisely because names resemble their objects so closely.

---

[15] On the idea of divine names as statues Neoplatonism, see M. Hirschle, *Sprachphilosophie und Namenmagie im Neuplatonismus: Mit einem Exkurs zu 'Demokrit' B 142* (Meisenheim am Glan: Hain, 1979), pp. 39–61.

Ammonius, on the other hand, is reluctant to admit that names are simply statues of their objects, because in that case he would then run into trouble with Aristotle's statement that names are symbols, not likenesses of their objects:

T. 5 Likeness differs from symbol in that it wants to image (*apeikonizesthai*; cf. **T. 4**) the very nature of a thing as far as possible and it is not in our power to change it (for if the painted likeness of Socrates in a picture does not have baldness, snub nose and bulging eyes, it would not be called his likeness), while a symbol or a sign (the Philosopher calls it both) is entirely up to us, given that it arises from our invention alone (Ammonius, *in Int.* 20,1–8, trans. Blank).

The fact that it is indeed in our power to change names, Ammonius observes with Aristotle (cf. **T. 1**), is among other things evident from the fact that various languages may refer to the same thing by means of different sounds.

It comes as a surprise to the reader to be told a couple of pages further down that names nevertheless *are* likenesses comparable to painted portraits. Ammonius has to rethink the issue because now he tries to show that Plato and Aristotle are in concord; since according to Plato names are images of their objects, names have to be likenesses of some sort. In his attempt to show that Plato and Aristotle are in harmony, Ammonius argues as follows: we should distinguish between natural likenesses and artificial likenesses. Natural likenesses are the product of nature, like shadows and reflections, whereas artificial likenesses (*homoiôma tekhnêton*) are the product of a human art (*tekhnê*). Ammonius denies that names are natural likenesses, for names consist in arbitrary sounds to which convention has assigned a certain meaning. In this way, Aristotle is right to call them symbols rather than likenesses. On the other hand, it cannot be denied that names, however arbitrary their sounds, may be appropriate to the nature of their object. To return to our previous example of the 'pocket-book' and the 'livre du poche' (§ II), the sounds are completely arbitrary and yet these words are equally fit descriptions of the thing they refer to. These words are not formed at random, but have been constructed on purpose to fit their objects. Hence they are artificial likenesses. Ammonius draws attention to the fact that Aristotle too apparently believes that names are descriptive, as is evident from the fact that he presented etymologies in the same way as Plato had done in the *Cratylus* in order to uncover ancient opinions about the matters under discussion. Ammonius concludes from this that both Plato and Aristotle believe that names are by nature in this sense.[16] When Aristotle calls a name a 'symbol' rather than a 'likeness' he means that a name is not a *natural* likeness.

But what about the argument that any given portrait of Socrates must resemble any other given portrait of Socrates? Ammonius offers the following suggestion:

---

[16] Ammonius, *in Int.* 37,15–27; cf. D. Sedley, 'The Etymologies in Plato's *Cratylus*', *Journal of Hellenic Studies* 118 (1998), 140–54, at 143, who makes a comparable observation that the attitude of Aristotle towards etymologies is in general not that different from that of Plato in the *Cratylus*, although of course Aristotle does not claim, as does Ammonius, that all names are like their objects.

> **T. 6** Others say names are 'by nature' since they fit the nature of the things named by them ... And they too say that names resemble images – not natural ones, but those by the art of painting (*hê zôgraphikê tekhnê*), which makes different likenesses of different models and still strives to copy as well as possible the form (*eidos*) ... (Ammonius, *in Int.* 35,1–9, trans. Blank).

From the example that Ammonius gives, he has something like this in mind: a king, a leader, and a commander are not entirely the same. Yet they all share the same *eidos* in that they have a mind fit for ruling. So if one wants to give an appropriate name to someone with such a mind, one may call such a person either 'Basiliskos' (Kinglet), 'Agesilaos' (Leader of the people), or 'Archidamos' (Commander of the people). Ammonius probably got his idea from *Crat.* 393A-B, where Socrates explains that the names 'Hector' and 'Astyanax' signify more or less the same thing, since both are names fit for a king.[17] It is hard to see how this theory might work. It may be that when Chinese formulate a word for 'man' they are looking at a slightly different model than Greek name-givers, but what about fire? In this case the model is the same for all, so if name-givers resemble painters (**T. 6**), and if all portraits of the same person have to look the same (**T. 5**), it necessarily follows that the Chinese and Greek words for 'fire' are similar, which, of course, they are not.

As has been pointed out, the idea that names are conventional as far as their matter is concerned but natural to the extent that they resemble their objects, is familiar from Proclus and indeed from Plato. Yet the opposition of natural to artificial likeness seems to be a device of Ammonius' own making, designed to harmonize Plato with Aristotle. This distinction influences his interpretation of the *Cratylus*, for he advances the claim that his distinction can indeed be traced back to the dialogue. Whereas Socrates considers names as artificial likenesses, Cratylus himself, Ammonius argues, is a representative of the view that names are natural likenesses:

> **T. 7** Some of those who think that names are by nature say 'by nature' opining that they are the products of nature, as Cratylus the Heraclitean thought when he said that a fitting name had been assigned by nature to each thing ... For he said that names resemble the natural images of visible things, like shadows and what usually appears in water or mirrors, but not the artificial ones (*in Int.* 34,22–8, trans. Blank, adapted).

It is a pity for Ammonius, though, that nowhere in the *Cratylus* does Cratylus suggest that nature produces names as likenesses of things like shadows and reflections.[18] What

---

[17] This passage also seems to echo a Neoplatonic doctrine of art, famously expressed by Plotinus in *Enn.* 5.8.1.32–40 (*On Intelligible Beauty*) who says to those who (like Plato) despise the arts (*tekhnai*) since they merely copy material things which are already themselves copies that they should take account of the fact that the arts do not simply imitate what they see, but that they run back up to the forming principles (*logoi*) of their models.

[18] Cf. Blank (n. 1 above), p. 149 n. 160, who points out that Cratylus actually says that the primal names had been assigned by a more than human power, viz. a god or a daimon.

is more, neither does Proclus in his commentary on the *Cratylus*. It can even be shown that this is not how Proclus interprets Cratylus' position. About the ways in which something can be called 'natural', Proclus writes:

> T. 8 [t]he term 'natural' can be understood in four ways: (1) as both the whole essences of the animals and plants and their parts; (2) as their activities and powers, like the lightness of fire and its heat; (3) as the shadows and reflections in mirrors; or (4) as fabricated images which are similar to their archetypes. Adopting the *fourth* [MSS: second; Sheppard: third] sense, Cratylus says that the name of each thing is proper, because it was appropriately put by those who first put names skilfully and knowledgeably (Proclus, *in Crat.* § 17, pp. 7,18–8,4, trans. Duvick).

There is a problem with the text as it has been transmitted. The question is whether Cratylus adopts the third sense or the fourth sense of 'natural'. According to the MSS he adopts the second sense, but as already noted by Usener, that cannot be correct. He then suggested the fourth sense. Anne Sheppard[19] suggested that, given Ammonius' remarks about Cratylus' position, we should assume that Cratylus adopts the third position. However, according to Proclus, Cratylus believes that this first name-givers *posited* the names *skilfully* (*entekhnôs*). Hence, he believes that names are in the words of Ammonius 'artificial likenesses'.[20] Ammonius' reading, then, did not originate with Proclus. In fact the latter has some textual support for his interpretation of Cratylus' position. When asked whether there is a craft (*tekhnê*) for name-giving and whether there are craftsmen who practice it (*Crat.* 428E6–7), Cratylus agrees whole-heartedly (*panu ge*).

III.4 What is the Function of a Name?

It should be clear by now that Proclus and Ammonius differ significantly over what a name is. It will not come as a surprise that they ascribe different functions to the analysis of names as part of doing philosophy. Plato had described names as a didactic instrument (*organon*, see § II): they are a source of knowledge. Proclus too believes that it is possible to reach things themselves through the mediation of names. These include such entities like the Beautiful, and Soul, to cite two examples from Proclus, but also the gods, who for Proclus coincide with abstract metaphysical entities. Whether or not this is consistent with Plato's intentions, Proclus is especially interested in names as a source of theological wisdom.[21] As we have seen (§ III.2), Proclus believes that names depend on our innate *logoi* which in turn depend on the divine Forms. The study of these names is supposed to activate the innate knowledge of the metaphysical world which we possess thanks to these *logoi*, in an unarticulated, passive way. This activation

---

[19] Sheppard (n. 3 above), pp. 147–9.
[20] The reason why Proclus brings up the third sense of 'being natural' is probably that for him names are vocalised copies of projections on our imagination of the *logoi* in our souls. These projections are compared to mirror images, on which see § III.2 above.
[21] On this see van den Berg (n. 13 above).

is described in terms of the Platonic doctrine of recollection (*anamnêsis*). The fact that names are like statues is a great help. Our souls are incapable of grasping the metaphysical realities in an unmediated form, and it is only through images such as names that we can contemplate them.[22]

If names are so constructed as to allow us a glimpse of the metaphysical realm, name-giving should be a task entrusted to expert metaphysicians. As Plato's Socrates had observed in the *Cratylus* (389A2) the human name-giver is the 'rarest of craftsmen' (*dêmiourgos*). Proclus connects this craftsman with the Craftsman from the *Timaeus*. For him, the primal name-giver is the demiurgical Nous who contemplates the Forms. The human name-giver likewise contemplates the Forms present in himself as *logoi*.[23]

For Aristotle, names are only a means for communicating our thoughts to others. Ammonius follows him in this:

> **T. 9** Vocal sounds are enunciative of thoughts and therefore are given to us by nature so as to indicate through them the concepts of our soul, so that we can share with one another and be part of the same society, man being a social animal (Ammonius, *in Int.* 18,30–3, trans Blank).

It goes without saying that for Ammonius names can never be the source of metaphysical and theological wisdom that they are for Proclus. After all, they refer to particular things in the outside world that cause likenesses in the soul. There is no divine name-giver in whose footsteps we follow. What is more, there is no guarantee that names can be trusted to be correct. Take the names of the gods that are heavenly bodies which we mentioned earlier on (§ III.2). Ammonius believes that the gender of a name should depend on the object named. He blames the Egyptians for calling the moon masculine. The Greeks did better because they claim that it is mascufeminine.[24]

The fact that Ammonius' concept of name is so significantly different from Proclus' may help us to explain a recent observation by Richard Sorabji in regard to Ammonius' commentary on *De Interpretatione*.[25] Whereas the discussion of divine names takes up a good deal of Proclus' commentary on the *Cratylus*, Ammonius is nearly completely silent about them, although one would expect Ammonius to discuss them. The fact that divine names were effective in rituals was taken to be proof that they were of a divine origin, and hence in a sense natural. The reason for this silence cannot be that Ammonius was afraid to run into trouble with the Christian authorities on whom the Alexandrian school depended for its survival, for Ammonius does not hide the fact that he is pagan. We have already seen, for instance, that at the beginning of his

---

[22] For names as a means to reach the things themselves, see *in Crat.* § 9, p. 3,17–24. For names as source of knowledge of the divine, see e.g. *Theol. Plat.* 1.5, p. 25,18–23; on the fact that we can only contemplate the divine through images, see *in Crat.* § 135, p. 178,13–22; on this topic further see further van den Berg (n. 13 above).

[23] For the Demiurge as first name-giver, see Proclus *in Crat.* § 51, pp. 19,22–20,21; *Theol. Plat.* 1.29, p. 124,12–20.

[24] Ammonius, *in Int.* 35,33–36,2.

[25] See R. Sorabji, 'Divine Names and Sordid Deals in Ammonius's Alexandria', in A. Smith, ed., *The Philosopher and Society in Late Antiquity* (Swansea: The Classical Press of Wales, 2005), pp. 203–13.

commentary he invokes the god of eloquence (§ I) and that he considers the heavenly bodies to be gods (§ III.2). Furthermore, he explicitly mentions one of the most important deities of the Neoplatonic pantheon, King Helios (*in Int.* 39,6). His reluctance is rather explained, I think, by the fact that he does not believe that divine names are a source of profound theological information, as Proclus believed them to be. Remarkably, when Ammonius briefly discusses the question whether the fact that names are effective in rituals shows that they are natural, he associates this position, as Richard Sorabji observes, not with his Athenian teacher Proclus, but with some otherwise unknown priest from Petra, a certain Dousareios (*in Int.* 38,23–8). This, it seems to me, was a matter of courtesy towards Proclus. Ammonius' Aristotelian conception of names did not allow him to believe in the existence of a privileged class of divine names. Since he did not want to be seen turning against his own master, he took aim at the poor unknown priest from Petra instead, thus smoothing over the differences between Proclus and himself.

IV. Concluding Remark: Two Ways of Reading

Since the aim of these proceedings is not just to study the content of the ancient commentators, but also their methods, let me try to conclude this paper with a more general conclusion, however tentative, about the methods of the so-called Athenian and Alexandrian schools. As is well known, K. Praechter in his seminal paper *Richtungen und Schulen im Neuplatonismus* argued that the Athenian school of Syrianus, Proclus and Damascius was distinctively different from the Alexandrian school of Ammonius and his students. The Alexandrians, weary of the exotic speculations about Plato's metaphysics which were the hallmark of the Athenians, concentrated on sober commentaries on Aristotle. These days there is a contrary tendency to smooth over the differences between the Alexandrians and the Athenians.[26] As an example of this, let me cite Ilsetraut Hadot's introduction to the proceedings of the conference on Simplicius held in Paris in 1985, later included in an English translation in Richard Sorabji's *Aristotle Transformed*, where she explicitly takes issue with Praechter.[27] Simplicius, it should be noted, was considered by Praechter as belonging to the Athenian school rather than to the Alexandrian school of Ammonius and his followers. Mme Hadot starts by pointing out that the commentaries on Aristotle's *Metaphysics*, written in part by the Athenian Syrianus and in part by the Alexandrians Ammonius and Asclepius, are extremely similar. She then continues with two further arguments which bear directly on the material that I have been discussing in this paper. She points

---

[26] For a dissident voice, see H. J. Blumenthal, 'Alexandria as a Centre of Greek Philosophy in Later Classical Antiquity', *Illinois Classical Studies* 18 (1993), 307–25, esp. 315–25 (p. 323: '[s]hould we also accept that there were no differences between the philosophical views of the Athenians and Alexandrians? I think the answer is "no", but let me say that at the start that this is one of the many areas in the study of late Neoplatonism that requires further work before it can be answered definitely.').

[27] Hadot (n. 3 above), 3–7 (= 'The Life and Work of Simplicius in Greek and Arabic Sources', in Sorabji, *Aristotle Transformed* (see n. 1 above), pp. 275–303, at pp. 275–8).

to Anne Sheppard's paper, mentioned above, on the relation between the commentaries of Proclus and Ammonius (§ III.3). As I have tried to show, contrary to the claim advanced in that paper, Proclus and Ammonius' views on names were distinct. Hence an examination of this issue does not support the thesis that there were no fundamental differences between the two institutions, rather the opposite.

Furthermore, Hadot points to the various commentaries on Aristotle's *Categories*. Contrary to what one would expect, she, Philippe Hoffmann, and Pierre Hadot, having worked through the first forty pages of Simplicius' commentary, did not encounter 'a single piece of evidence' which favoured Praechter's thesis. They were unable to find any difference between the interpretive tendency of Simplicius' commentary on the one hand, and of the commentaries of Ammonius, Philoponus, Olympiodorus, and David on the other. Now Philippe Hoffmann, however, was able to do so in a richly documented contribution to these same proceedings on Simplicius on categories and language.[28] He observes that none of the Alexandrian commentators ever explains the relations between the things, our notions of them and the names by which we communicate these (the three elements involved in speech, discussed by Aristotle at the beginning of *Int.*, see **T. 1**).[29] Simplicius, by contrast, sketches what we may now identify as a Proclean model of these relations: the human soul contains the Forms in a secondary way as *logoi*, from which it derives notions as images of them. Words activate our innate knowledge of the Forms by means of recollection (*anamnêsis*) and put us on the way towards the divine.[30] Simplicius' commentary, then, betrays the influence of reflections on language as current in the Athenian school but not in Alexandria. The case of Simplicius may also serve as an argument against the possible objection that the differences between Proclus and Ammonius are due to the context, i.e. that Ammonius is commenting on Aristotle, for so is after all Simplicius.

Let me end by stressing that these different theories about language probably originate from two different ways of dealing with texts by Plato and Aristotle. In the case of Proclus, it is, I think, evident that he orientates his interpretation of the *Cratylus* toward his main preoccupation: extracting a theology from Plato's dialogues. His interpretation of names as images of the metaphysical world is motivated by this concern. The names of the gods are like statues of them, and a source of knowledge about them. He does not care whether this conception of names squares with Aristotle or not. But Ammonius starts off from Aristotle, and his immediate concern is with the correct interpretation of Aristotle. Still, he feels the need to harmonize Aristotle with Plato as the ultimate point of reference. He reads Plato through an Aristotelian lens which makes him see things in Plato which simply are not there (e.g. Cratylus' natural likenesses). This would never have happened to an Athenian Neoplatonist like Proclus, for he starts from Plato and then compares him to Aristotle if possible, quite happy

---

[28] P. Hoffmann, 'Catégories et language selon Simplicius – La question du «skopos» du traité aristotélicien des «Catégories»', in I. Hadot, ed., *Simplicius: sa vie, son œuvre, sa survie* (Berlin: De Gruyter, 1987), pp. 61–90.
[29] Hoffmann (n. 28 above), pp. 83–4.
[30] Simplicius, *in Cat.* 12,16–13,32.

simply to note the differences without developing a strategy to harmonize the tensions between the two. Hence we have here two different ways of reading Plato in connection with Aristotle, and they *do* influence the outcome. Praechter's old thesis of opposites obscured the connections between the two schools. The now popular thesis of similarity may well blind us to the differences.[31]

---

[31] This paper has benefited from various discussions and especially from the detailed criticism of Francesco Ademollo (Florence). It was written with the financial support of the Netherlands Organization for Scientific Research.

14

Dating of Philoponus' Commentaries on Aristotle and of his Divergence from his Teacher Ammonius

Richard Sorabji

Two Major Hypotheses on the Dating

There have been two major hypotheses since 1990, and much valuable discussion concerning the dating of Philoponus' commentaries on Aristotle and of his divergence from Ammonius. In 1990 Koenraad Verrycken summarised in *Aristotle Transformed* his new datings for Philoponus' work, drawing on apparent contradictions in his statements about the eternity or coming-into-being of the universe and its contents, about the nature of place, and about the possibility of vacuum and of motion in a vacuum. His earlier dissertation of 1985 included also Philoponus' changing treatment of Aristotle's prime matter.[1] He suggested solving these problems by postulating a phase around 517 CE in which Philoponus accepted his teacher Ammonius' Neoplatonism and interpretation of Aristotle as agreeing with Plato and with Neoplatonism, and a later phase in which he reverted to his Christian origins on the level of doctrine and repudiated the Neoplatonist and Aristotelian ideas, especially where, as with eternity or the Creation of the universe, they contradicted Christian ideas. This called for a second edition of some earlier commentaries on Aristotle after 529 CE. Verrycken was aware that his particular dating might not be accepted, and even that the appearance of a Neoplatonist or Aristotelian view might sometimes be due to the expository nature of commentary on Aristotle.[2] This and other explanations have since been proffered, and the particular dating has received widespread criticism,

---

[1] Koenraad Verrycken, 'The development of Philoponus' thought and its chronology', in Richard Sorabji, ed., *Aristotle Transformed* (London: Duckworth, 1990), pp. 233–74. I shall not take up the refinements in Koenraad Verrycken, 'John Philoponus', in Lloyd Gerson, ed., *The Cambridge History of Philosophy in Late Antiquity*, 2 vols (Cambridge: Cambridge University Press, 2010), vol. 2, pp. 733–55. Philoponus' treatment of prime matter, reviewed by Frans de Haas, *John Philoponus' New Definition of Prime Matter* (Leiden: Brill, 1997), pp. 31–6, was interpreted by Verrycken, *God en wereld in der wijsbegeerte van Ioannes Philoponus. De overgang van een Alexandrijns-Neoplatonische naar een christelijk scheppingsleer*, I-III, PhD dissertation (Leuven, 1985).
[2] Ibid. pp. 244, 273.

which I have summarized elsewhere.[3] Nonetheless, even if Philoponus does not juxtapose as often as suggested different viewpoints of his own, Verrycken's citations establish that he does develop different viewpoints across a wide range of texts and topics, so that it remains necessary to consider his evidence in formulating any alternative dating.

The second major hypothesis was offered in 2008, by Pantelis Golitsis who exploited an under-used source of evidence that bears on several questions. He has also been kind enough to discuss at two workshops his further work in preparation.[4] I shall, however, refer to his 2008 publication, except where explicitly stated. Philoponus' seven commentaries on Aristotle are divided into books, and four commentaries are, or at least some books in four commentaries are, described in their titles as being Philoponus' commentarial (*skholastikai*) notes (*aposêmeiôseis*) from the meetings (*sunousiai*), i.e. seminar sessions, of Ammonius (his teacher), with Philoponus' name or other designation coming first. The four are *in An. Pr., in An. Post, in DA*, and *in GC*. The last three of these four are described as containing further (critical) reflections (more below on the meaning of *epistaseis*) of his own (*idiôn*) by Philoponus. The remaining three of Philoponus' commentaries on Aristotle are *not* ascribed to the seminars of Ammonius. Philoponus also refers twice to a commentary, now lost, on Porphyry's Introduction (*Isagôgê*), his introduction that is, on one interpretation, to Aristotle's logic.[5] All this could have several important implications. First, although the titles of his commentaries were written in by successive scribes, Golitsis has sought out the best manuscripts and has taken them to represent Philoponus' own description, and from this he has inferred quite a precise timetable for Philoponus' commentaries on Aristotle. The commentaries whose book titles refer to Ammonius' seminars were written first and commissioned as editions of *Ammonius*' lectures as they were delivered in the order of the standard curriculum between 510 and 515. Philoponus' commentary on Aristotle's *Physics*, which contains a lecture dated to 517, is not connected in its book titles with Ammonius' lectures in the modern edition of Vitelli under the general editorship of Diels, and moreover it contains open disagreement with Ammonius. If that is right, the commentary will reflect courses that Philoponus *himself* was giving. However, Golitsis allows me to mention that in further work he will now be taking seriously Trincavelli's earlier alternative reading of the manuscript title, which does at

---

[3] Summarised in R. Sorabji, 'Introduction', in R. Sorabji, ed., *Philoponus and the Rejection of Aristotelian Science*, 2nd edn (London: Institute of Classical Studies, 2010), pp. 1–40, at pp. 14–18. But I regret that I omitted an important discussion by Clemens Scholten, *Antike Naturphilosophie und christliche Kosmologie in der Schrift "De Opificio Mundi" des Johannes Philoponos* (Berlin: De Gruyter, 1996), and misascribed to Christian Wildberg the views he was reporting from Scholten, *Johannes Philoponos, De Aeternitate Mundi I* (Turnhout: Brepols, 2009). Scholten's two books raise as theoretical possibilities many alternatives to Verrycken's interpretation of apparent contradictions, without however making the case for one rather than another. But the negative conclusion is drawn that a satisfactory dating is not in sight (*Antike Naturphilosophie*, p. 121).

[4] Pantelis Golitsis, *Les commentaires de Simplicius et de Jean Philopon à la Physique d'Aristote* (Berlin: De Gruyter, 2008), pp. 23–7. His further work presented in Oxford workshops in 2013–4, 'John Philoponus' commentary on the third book of Aristotle's *De anima*, wrongly attributed to Stephanus', is in this volume. I am grateful to Anna Marmodoro for organising one workshop and co-organising the other.

[5] References at Philoponus, *in Phys.* 250,28; *in Cat.* 1,2.

the beginning of the commentary on *Physics Book One* mention both Ammonius' seminars and Philoponus' (critical) reflections, and he will be explaining the transformative consequences. Philoponus' editions of Ammonius' lectures will have included, again, Golitsis suggests, in the order of the standard curriculum: on Porphyry's *Isagôgê*, and on Aristotle's *Categories*, then on the eighth book of his *Physics*, which precedes the lecture of 517 on the *Physics*, whether or not the series includes more on the *Physics*. So far, Golitsis' conclusion rightly observes the standard view that most commentaries on Aristotle reflect teaching classes. But, by way of exception, the commentary on Aristotle's *Meteorology* is not connected by any titles to Ammonius and Golitsis argues it does not appear to reflect teaching either, so was written after Philoponus had stopped teaching courses on Aristotle. The task now, as I see it, is to consider how far the new considerations about titles, combined with many others, including some highlighted by Verrycken, can enable us to confirm or disconfirm the details of dating and divergence and provide a modified picture.

Some Initial Qualifications on Evidence from Titles

Golitsis' new attention to titles is so important that I shall try to form a view on what we can infer from them. There is *independent* reason for thinking that up to a point the titles do provide useful pointers on dating. So, before looking at particular commentaries, I will suggest a mixture of such positive pointers along with some qualifications. As a first pointer, one would expect that while still a beginning student Philoponus would, in writing his commentaries, follow Ammonius to a considerable extent, but would later diverge after further reflection. Again, another inference drawn from the titles chimes with independent data: the gradual increase in Philoponus' divergence from Aristotle, and hence from Ammonius' accommodation of Aristotle. For we have a late date, 529 CE, for his far more extensive disagreement on behalf of Christianity with the pagan Neoplatonists, in his non-commentary treatise, *Against Proclus on the Eternity of the World*, while his *Against Aristotle on the Eternity of the World* is shown by cross references to be later still.[6]

But the titles might suggest other things too, because Philoponus or his scribes not only refer in three cases out of four to Philoponus' addition of his own (critical) reflections, but also always put his name *first*, before that of Ammonius in the titles. This could suggest that Philoponus was never an editor in the sense of one who *confined* himself to recording Ammonius, but that his reflections might not at first be objections. Indeed, we shall find that in some texts his identifiable reflections avoid outright criticism. We shall, however, find that things are not so tidy, because objections do start in commentaries which must be considered early.

I must now mention Golitsis' new suggestion that the word *epistaseis* in Philoponus and Simplicius means not just reflections, but *critical* reflections or objections.[7] Liddell

---

[6] Richard Sorabji, 'John Philoponus', in *Philoponus and the Rejection of Aristotelian Science* (n. 3 above), section entitled 'Chronology of Philoponus' Writings'.
[7] Presented in the 2013–4 workshops and in the further work forthcoming.

and Scott claim that reflecting and opposing are two distinct meanings of the corresponding verb, *ephistanai* and *ephistasthai*. If they are right, *epistaseis* may sometimes not merely *include* instances of criticism, but will also have criticism as one of its *meanings*. Golitsis has indeed found cases in which criticism *has* to be the meaning and in others it could be, although this sometimes needs argument.[8] Important as Golitsis' point is, it will not affect what I want to say. If Philoponus' book titles, some of them, announce the addition only of criticisms, that does not of itself mean that Philoponus was adding no non-critical reflections of his own. That needs to be independently investigated, and I shall below present evidence from Philoponus *in Cat.* that he was. There could be more than one reason for Philoponus, or his scribe, to announce in the book titles only the *critical* reflections. It need not be, or not solely, that Philoponus took more pride in them; he will for fairness and accuracy not have wanted to present the critical reflections as ones which Ammonius would endorse.

A further inference might be drawn from the one title, that of Philoponus on Aristotle's *Prior Analytics*, that refers to Ammonius' seminars, *without* referring to Philoponus' (critical) reflections. Does that suggest that this commentary on Aristotle is earlier than the others and is a bare record containing no (critical) reflections? But we shall find evidence that Philoponus *in An. Pr.* is *later* than his *in Cat.*, and in any case why does the title put Philoponus' name first, instead of doing what we find in certain *other* commentaries from Ammonius' 'voice', namely that the reporter is left *anonymous*? There are commentaries on Aristotle *Categories* and *Prior Analytics* anonymously drawn, according to their titles, from the voice of Ammonius. The anonymity might be taken as a much clearer sign of a commentary being a close student record of Ammonius with very little independent reflection. Yet even this is not an absolutely sure sign. I shall mention below a case of an added reflection in the commentary on Aristotle's *Categories* anonymously drawn from the voice of Ammonius, which I shall abbreviate as 'Ammonius *in Cat.* Anon'. Golitsis avoids the inference that Philoponus *in An. Pr.* is his earliest commentary on Aristotle, because he takes it that Philoponus would have written commentaries in the order of the student curriculum, and the *Prior Analytics* comes *after* the *Categories* in that curriculum. But is the order of the student curriculum a reliable guide?

Golitsis is surely right that we could expect that divergence would increase still further, once Philoponus was invited to give seminars himself, since they would lead him to further reflection. Moreover, there is a further independent reason to agree with Golitsis again that Philoponus would be invited before long to give seminars, because the task of teaching the entire Aristotle syllabus, and even the task of teaching the whole of Aristotle's *Physics*, could not be accomplished by Ammonius or anyone else on his own in a single year, and we shall find evidence that Philoponus did not attempt that either. That is unsurprising, given that the surviving first four books of Philoponus'

---

[8] Marwan Rashed has in discussion cited for the meaning of reflection: Philoponus, *in GC* 271,25–6. In this passage, the word *ekeino* makes a reference forward to something which is itself ambiguously conceived either as a view or as a criticism. We are told two things about it, first that we should know it (*isteon*), and secondly that it is worthy of *epistasis*. Does *epistasis* here mean criticism or reflection? The view in question deserves to be *criticised*, but the forthcoming criticism deserves only to be *reflected* on.

Physics commentary, ignoring the last four which survive only in fragments, already take up 786 pages in Diels' edition. Moreover, the requisite task would have been even more daunting, because in each single year, students of different intakes or years would need seminars, some on more elementary, some on less elementary works of Aristotle. It would not be easy for one person to teach all the logical works of Aristotle, which were the introductory ones, in a single year, let alone his more advanced works in the same year. The Greek commentary on Aristotle's *De Anima* Book 3, whose ascription to Philoponus is controversial, though backed by Golitsis in Chapter 15, divides the text into *praxeis*, which look like individual sessions, no doubt with time for discussion, varying in length between 6 and 12 pages of Diels' text. Ammonius would from early on have had every incentive to entrust some of the teaching to his best students.

This complexity, however, would in turn mean that it would be difficult to predict the order in which Philoponus would hear Ammonius. When he first arrived, Ammonius might be lecturing on the end of the *Physics*, that is on Book 8. When Philoponus was asked to take over some teaching, the need in a given year might be for introductory texts of Aristotle or for more advanced ones. When Eutocius, succeeded Ammonius in the chair, we have reason to think his lectures on Aristotle were confined to the logic, so there would be more need for Philoponus to teach more advanced texts. The standard order for students to study the Aristotle curriculum would not therefore necessarily be a guide to the order of Philoponus' commentaries, and I shall try to show below that there was not always a correspondence.

There is a further question. As pointed out by Marwan Rashed, Philoponus says in the *Corollary on Place* within his commentary on Aristotle's *Physics* 4 that he had expressed his disagreement in Ammonius' presence while he was still alive and Ammonius used to state (*elegen*) a defence.[9] The verb *elegen* is in the imperfect tense, and this reference to a past habit rather than a past occasion suggests that Ammonius was no longer alive. Golitsis has found similar evidence that *in DA* 3 was written after Ammonius' death.[10] But the fact that Ammonius had discussed Philoponus' disagreement is evidence that Philoponus' disagreement on central issues cannot be taken as a sign of its being later than Ammonius' death. At least he was alive when Philoponus started formulating the disagreement on place. Nonetheless, the omission of Ammonius' name from the title is not always a sign of such divergence from Ammonius, because Ammonius' name is omitted from the title of the commentary on Philoponus' *Categories* where, I shall argue, Philoponus' reflections are frequent but, with one exception, *not* critical.

Despite these complications, the evidence of titles is still relevant to dating, and it is relevant to much more besides. It forces us also to think constantly about a further question: which ideas in Philoponus' commentaries should be attributed to Ammonius

---

[9] Philoponus' Corollary on Place, *in Phys.* 583,13–14, cited by Marwan Rashed, 'Alexandre d'Aphrodise et la "Magna Quaestio"', *Les Études classiques* 63 (1995), 295–351; reprinted in his *L'Héritage aristotélicien* (Paris: Les Belles Lettres, 2007), citation at p. 117. Cf Philoponus Aet. 359, 14ff.

[10] Golitsis has pointed out that Ammonius was also no longer alive at the time of Philoponus, *in DA* 2.7, where it has to be conjectured what Ammonius *might* say in reply, 335,7. It can be added that there is another imperfect tense about what he *used to* say (*ephaske*), 334,38.

and which to Philoponus? It has occasionally been held in the past that Philoponus' commentaries are merely reporting Ammonius' seminars on Aristotle as his editor,[11] and that much of the credit in certain commentaries should be switched to Ammonius.[12] I do not believe that a stage has been found at which Philoponus was only reporting Ammonius as editor, although that would have would have supplied a different answer to Verrycken's question why Philoponus sometimes appears to speak as a convinced Neoplatonist. An initial caution might be drawn from the acknowledgement that Ammonius makes to his own predecessor Proclus, as discussed by Robbert van den Berg in this volume. After he claims only to be recording (*apomnêmoneuein*) the exegeses of his divine teacher Proclus, to which he is able to add nothing more than eloquence,[13] he in fact diverges very widely, even though there is also much in common. Of course Ammonius' respectful motivation was very different from Philoponus'. But it is a warning that as with Ammonius so with Philoponus, a formal announcement of debt to a teacher entitles us to expect some similarity, but does not entitle us to expect no divergences. The announcements in Philoponus' titles do indeed require us to think afresh about assigning credit, but we shall still have to look for evidence case by case, and I shall come back to that.

Ammonius' acknowledgement of debt is relevant to another important question, the relation of student to teacher in sixth century Alexandria. Ammonius' own teacher in fifth century CE Athens, Proclus, had in his turn been told by *his* teacher, Plutarch of Athens, to write out what had been said in their discussions of Plato's *Phaedo*, so that if the notes (*skholiai*) were completed, there would also be a treatise (*hupomnêmata*) on the *Phaedo* by Proclus himself.[14] The titles of Philoponus' commentaries may well give us further evidence on the relation of student to teacher in sixth century Alexandria. But we might expect the relation of the combative Philoponus to his teacher, to be still more divergent than that of Proclus to Plutarch or of Ammonius to Proclus.

I shall now try to substantiate a modified view about the dating of Philoponus' commentaries on Aristotle and divergence from Ammonius. It will differ not only from that of Verrycken and to some extent of Golitsis, but also from the chronology I gave for Philoponus' commentaries on Aristotle on pp. 37–40 of *Aristotle and the Rejection of Aristotelian Science* (London: Duckworth, 1987), which antedated Verrycken and which reflected interpretations of that time. I shall start with Philoponus' commentary

---

[11] H. D. Saffrey, 'Le chrétien Jean Philopon et la survivance de l'école d'Alexandrie au VIe siècle', *Revue des études grecques* 67 (1954), 408, repeated by Muhsin Mahdi, 'Alfarabi against Philoponus', *Journal of Near Eastern Studies* 26 (1967), 234–5, denied by Verrycken (n. 1 above), pp 238–9. Clemens Scholten, without backing the hypothesis, said that Philoponus' commentary on Aristotle's *De Anima* might be (for all we know) wholly, or at any rate wide-rangingly, Ammonius, p. 178.

[12] Arnis Ritups, *Aristotle De Anima III. 6: Essays in the history of its interpretation*, PhD dissertation (Leuven, 2010) offers at pp. 100–1 four general criteria any one of which would be sufficient for crediting Ammonius.

[13] Ammonius, *in Int.* 1,6–11. He goes on to steer closer to Aristotle than he believes Proclus would on the central issue of the artificiality of names, and he virtually omits Proclus' star example of the names of gods as natural names, as proved by their efficacy in ritual, whether for my reason that propaganda for pagan ritual was the one agreed taboo on pagan teaching, or for Robbert van den Berg's that he didn't share Proclus' view of divine names, but concealed this out of courtesy, or for both reasons.

[14] Marinus, *Life of Proclus* ch. 12.

on Aristotle's *Physics* and the date 517 CE, which has been taken to be that of Philoponus writing the commentary on Aristotle's *Physics*, or, by Verrycken, as the date of writing in progress on the first edition of that commentary. Philoponus' commentary is intact only for Books 1–4 of the *Physics*, the rest being preserved only in fragments. After that I shall consider Philoponus' commentary on Aristotle's *Categories*, another commentary for which there is independent evidence on the relative order. Neither commentary, I believe, conforms, or conforms wholly, to the expectations that might be created by the titles, although the evidence of titles will still be useful where it coheres with other evidence. After that again, I shall consider how far Philoponus' other commentaries on Aristotle can be arranged in order around these two more dateable ones.

Proposals on Dating: Does 517 date Philoponus' whole *Physics* Commentary, or only Book 4.10–14?

It has been thought that the date 517 in Philoponus' commentary on *Physics* 4.10 dates the whole *Physics* commentary, but I shall question this. In 517 Philoponus may not have been studying philosophy with Ammonius for very long, and Ammonius, assuming he was still alive, would probably have been in his 70s.[15] Philoponus himself was still alive in the 570s, but Verrycken points out that in his early days he had probably been studying, and perhaps writing, 'grammar', that is philology, before turning to Ammonius for philosophy. This is inferred from Simplicius' sneer that when Philoponus came 'to us' from (the works of) the grammarian Herodian, that he was not in a position to criticise Aristotle's physics, and that in philosophy, he was a late-learner.[16] Philoponus' date of birth has been estimated as 490 and his arrival with Ammonius as 510,[17] but estimates depend partly on other dating issues to be discussed below.

What I wish to point out is that Philoponus' commentary on Aristotle's *Physics* Book 4 is not unitary. It contains three sets of chapters, which discuss in turn place, then vacuum and dynamics and finally time. As between these three sets of chapters, we find strong disagreement with Aristotle alternating with very little disagreement, as the subject changes within the same book, and we find different practices about whether to separate disagreement into an appendix or 'corollary'. To illustrate, it has been shown by Keimpe Algra, one of the two translators of Philoponus' commentary on the first five chapters of Book 4, that these chapters, which concern *place*, already have discreetly in mind the disagreement with Aristotle, as Marwan Rashed had already noticed for 4.5, although the explicit disagreement is separated off into the appendix or *Corollary on Place*. But they deliberately postpone expounding the disagreement until the Corollary

---

[15] H. D. Saffrey puts his birth at about 440, in *Dictionnaire des philosophes antiques*, vol. 1 (Paris: CNRS, 1989), p. 168, perhaps following L. G. Westerink, *Anonymous Prolegomena to Platonic Philosophy* (Amsterdam: North Holland Publishing, 1962), p. x, which estimates a birth between 435 and 445. I have suggested in the Introduction above not much earlier than 445.

[16] Simplicius, *in Cael.* 26,21–3; 159,3.7; *in Phys.* 1133,10, cited by Verrycken, p. 238, n. 25, and p. 250, n. 103.

[17] H. D. Saffrey, 'Le chrétien Jean Philopon', p. 403.

is reached in the fourth chapter.[18] This separation off of disagreements into an appendix was recommended by Philoponus himself in the Prooemium to his commentary on the *Categories* at 6,30–5.[19] In discussing the next chapters on vacuum, by contrast, *Physics* 4.6–9, Philoponus explicitly ridicules Aristotle's dynamics in a vacuum. He does so within the commentary proper, not waiting for the appendix, and introduces his rival theory of impetus as the requisite dynamic force, applying it to the motion of projectiles and comets. He also denies Aristotle's view that motion would be impossible in a vacuum. This is all the more surprising, in that he wrote a *Corollary on Vacuum*, yet evidently did not feel able to save up his objections for that, as he had done in the immediately preceding chapters on the topic of *place*.

Philoponus' commentary on the final five chapters of Book 4 on *time, Physics* 4.10–14, provides another contrast again. There is very little criticism of Aristotle at all. More surprising is the brevity and flimsiness of Philoponus' discussion in his comments on Book 4.14 at 770,19–21, of another major issue about time, whether Aristotle's definition of time as the countable aspect of change makes time depend on the *actual* existence of souls, on the supposition that countability requires the *opportunity* to be counted, as opposed to the mere capability of being counted.[20] Aristotle's answer in *Physics* 4.14, 223a21–9 that it does call for the actual existence of souls had been attacked by Boethus and Themistius and, on one interpretation[21] possibly by Galen, while being defended by Alexander. Philoponus, disappointingly, does not join this controversy, but concedes Aristotle's claim that time as countable will not exist if there are no souls to count it. But, again avoiding naming himself, he says on the other side that someone will ask: what if time is not something countable, but actually is number? This anonymous query is also disappointingly treated, for Aristotle had already denied

---

[18] Keimpe Algra, Introduction to his and Jan Ophuijsen's translation of *Philoponus, On Aristotle Physics 4.1–5* (London: Bristol Classical Press, 2012). Marwan Rashed, 'Alexandre d'Aphrodise et la "Magna Quaestio"' (n. 9 above), n. 56. I contrast the three sections of commentary on Book 4, translated between 2011 and 2013, in my introduction to Sarah Broadie's translation of 4.10–14. In the actual commentary on 4.1–5, Algra points out, Philoponus confines his hint of disagreement to remarking at 587,22–30, that on one point those who say that place is extension may have a more reasonable way of saving the idea that a thing's place is equal in size to it. But on the other hand, at 552,10–14, he alerts the reader that he will expound after going through the text what could be said by proponents of the view that place is extension, as if he had already got the Corollary on place ready, but was simply postponing it until after the current bit of commentary proper. Algra thinks that for these chapters commentary and corollary were prepared at the same time and that the moderation of Philoponus in the commentary proper does not mean that the commentary was written earlier than the corollary. The corollary itself reveals at 583,13–15, that Philoponus had already raised objections in Ammonius' class and received a defence of Aristotle from Ammonius. Algra sees a few extra hints that in the commentary on 4.1–5, Philoponus already had the rival view of place but was holding it back for the corollary, namely that by accident, and without critical intent, he lets slip wording that fits his own view but not Aristotle's: e.g. 'place as a whole', 541,6–7; a place can be taken up and occupied, 597,32–598,2; 'force of the void', 600,6.

[19] As Pantelis Golitsis points out in *Simplicius et Jean Philopon à la Physique d'Aristote* (Berlin: De Gruyter, 2008).

[20] The dispute is described in R. Sorabji, *The Philosophy of the Commentators 200–600 AD*, 3 vols (London: Duckworth, 2004), vol. 2, ch. 11(d). I thank Pantelis Golitsis for greatly improving my treatment of Philoponus' scanty criticisms.

[21] Peter Adamson, 'Galen and Al-Rāzī on time', in Rotraud Hansberger, M. Afifi al-Akiti, and Charles Burnett, eds, *Medieval Arabic Thought: Essays in Honour of Fritz Zimmermann* (London: The Warburg Institute, 2012), p. 9.

at *Physics* 4.11, 219b5-8 that time is (the number) by which we count, and Philoponus does not explain why Aristotle was wrong to rule that out. He certainly seems keen not to criticise Aristotle openly, as he was to do in commenting on Aristotle's treatment of vacuum in the adjacent chapters, *Physics* 4.6-9. To that extent he is closer to his procedure in discussing Aristotle's view of place in *Physics* 4.1-5, but there there was the different motive that objections were being saved up for a corollary or appendix. This shortage of discussion might be explained by supposing that Philoponus' class on Aristotle's account of time was for a more elementary group of students. But his hesitation about open criticism, and the flimsiness of such criticism as he does give suggest that in commenting on *Physics* 4.10-14, he is at an early stage of working out his own position on some issues and of challenging Aristotle, or his teacher Ammonius' defence of Aristotle. The reference to the early date 517 CE as the date at which he is writing comes from the commentary on 4.10, that is, from the same bit of commentary which so far looks early, at 703,16-20. In that case, we should no longer take it as dating the whole *Physics* commentary, or work on some first edition of it, which Verrycken thinks may possibly have covered all eight books.[22] Rather, it will date only the bit of commentary on 4.10-14 which there are *independent* reasons to think of as early.

We should now recall some of the initial qualifications about the use of evidence for dating. Given the colossal size of Philoponus' commentary on just the first four books of Aristotle's *Physics*, 517 could not have been the date of writing more than a part of it, quite possibly a part covering less than Aristotle's *Physics* Book 4.[23] We know that any students studying the whole of Aristotle (to leave Plato aside) would need instruction for well over two years, because we know that two years was an astonishing record set by the brilliant Proclus when he received dedicated private tuition on Aristotle from Plutarch of Athens.[24] Nor, given the demands of the huge teaching curriculum for successive intakes of students which overlapped at the same time, can we entertain presuppositions about the order in which Philoponus might hear, teach or compose commentary. The order of commentary need not have corresponded to the order of the books in Aristotle's *Physics*. So it need be no surprise that the commentary on *Physics* 4.10-14 was written before that on *Physics* 4.1-9. Nor, we shall see, need it be any surprise that a commentary on Physics 8.1 was written before that again.[25] It is just as likely that a series of seminars might have been spent on a sufficiently distinct part of a book like *Physics* 8.1 on eternal motion or *Physics* 4.10-14 on time, and that these were taken in succession because of their related subject matter.

We should also recall that Philoponus' disagreements with Ammonius or Aristotle, though significant when truculently expressed or sufficiently extensive, are not on their own a reliable indication of lateness. For example, if the disagreements on eternity started *before* 517 in a commentary on *Physics* 8 – and this must still be discussed – we

---

[22] Verrycken (n. 1 above), pp. 248-9.
[23] I must correct my earlier statement that *much of it* was written in 517 (*Matter, Space, and Motion* (London: Duckworth, 1989), p. 24), or more accurately that it *was being* written in 517 (Introduction to A. R. Lacey, *Philoponus, On Aristotle Physics 2* (London: Duckworth, 1993)).
[24] Marinus, *Life of Proclus* 13.
[25] Doubts on the commentary being written a book at a time in the order of Aristotle's books have also been raised by Clemens Scholten, *Antike Naturphilosophie* (n. 3 above), p. 137.

must acknowledge how *soon* the disagreements began. It would be fewer than 7 years after Philoponus coming to study with Ammonius, if the highly conjectural date of 510 for his arrival is accepted. Even in the commentary on Aristotle's treatment of place in *Physics* 4.1–5 and its *Corollary*, the very strong disagreement with Aristotle and Ammonius about the nature of place need not be *all that* late for the reason already noticed, that Philoponus had expressed his disagreement in Ammonius' presence while he was still alive.[26] This is evidence that Philoponus' disagreement on central issues cannot be taken as a sign of its being later than Ammonius' death. That the commentary on 4.1–10 is not *all that* late, is shown also by its accepting Aristotle's account of qualitiless prime matter, so Frans de Haas has argued against Verrycken, and its not yet having switched to Philoponus' later substitution in his treatise *Against Proclus* of 529 CE of three-dimensions as the basic subject, instead of Aristotle's qualitiless prime matter.[27]

If I am right that the commentary on *Physics* 4.10–14 is comparatively *early*, the book titles, at least in Diels' edition, are not in this case a safe guide, since they give no hint of that earliness. For they do not mention Ammonius, and so do not alert us that Philoponus on 4.10–14 will still be following Ammonius' seminars relatively closely. But this is for a simple reason, that needs to be added to the considerations mentioned so far, that the book titles in Diels' edition are supplied at the *beginning* of each of Books 1 to 4, and there is no separate title for the commentary on the last part of Book 4. This is not to deny that it is *by and large* true of the four books that Philoponus writes more independently of Ammonius with substantial disagreements which Verrycken has emphasised and that occasionally he offers even ridicule. We shall find below that the book title of Philoponus' commentary on Aristotle's *Categories*, also fails to indicate its comparative earliness, but for a different reason.

Is Philoponus' Commentary on *Physics* 8.1 still earlier than 517?

Is Philoponus' commentary on *Physics* 8.1, lost except for a few fragments, still earlier than the commentary on 4.10–14? We seem to learn this when Philoponus points out in his commentary on 4.13 at 762,7–9, that he had raised criticisms earlier (now mostly lost) in a commentary (*skholai*)[28] on Book 8, evidently on 8.1. In that book Aristotle

---

[26] Philoponus, *Corollary on Place, in Phys.* 583,13–14.
[27] Frans de Haas, *John Philoponus' New Definition* (n. 1 above), pp. 31–6. Similarly, Pantelis Golitsis, *Les commentaries de Simplicius et de Jean Philopon* (n. 4 above), p. 32.
[28] The other occurrence of the word *skholai* in Philoponus is to his commentary on the *Meteorology*, and refers back from his second commentary on Nicomachus' *Introduction to Arithmetic*, 2.7.19–20. The kindred word *skholia* is used for Philoponus' commentaries based on Ammonius. Erich Lamberz has suggested that the term *skholia* refers back to commentaries taken from the voice or seminars of one's own teacher: 'Proklos und die Form des philosophischen Kommentar', in J. Pépin and H. D. Saffrey, eds, *Proclus, lecteur et interprète des anciens* (Paris: CNRS, 1987), pp. 1–20, especially pp. 4–7. Lamberz records the following examples. Amelius wrote 100 *skholia* from the seminars of Plotinus. Proclus, according to Marinus, *Life of Proclus* ch 12, initially wrote *skholia* recording the seminars of Plutarch on Plato's *Phaedo*. We have extracts from Proclus' *skholia* on Plato's *Cratylus*. *Skholia* is used for Hermeias' commentary on Plato's *Phaedrus* based on the seminars of Proclus. For Philoponus' reprises of Ammonius the term *skholia* is often used, and also *skholika aposêmeiôseis*, and this includes Philoponus' commentary on Aristotle's *Categories*.

tried to prove the eternity of *motion*, but Philoponus claims that he (Philoponus) had proved in his comments that Aristotle showed anything but that. In discussing 4.13, Philoponus also states very briefly at 762,2–3, presumably again as something discussed before, his objection to Aristotle's argument in *Physics* 8.1, 251b19–26 for the eternity of *time*. About that argument he confines himself here to saying that someone who did not want time to be eternal (and he carefully avoids naming himself) would not concede Aristotle's ground for its eternity, that every instant is both the beginning and end of some period. That objection is preserved also in a single Arabic sentence surviving from Philoponus' commentary on Book 8.[29] Verrycken performed a most valuable service in drawing attention to this back reference and to two back references elsewhere to a commentary on Book 8.[30] It appears, then, although we shall see this was not Verrycken's conclusion, that Philoponus had already *before* commenting on 4.13, and hence before 517, challenged Aristotle on the subject that would be most obviously opposed to his Christian belief in God having brought the universe into being from non-being. Philoponus' criticism of Aristotle, then, seems to have started earlier than 517, probably before the death of Ammonius, but so far only concerning the most central stumbling block for a Christian.

Verrycken, however, has challenged this claim by postulating two editions of Philoponus' commentary on Books 4 and 8 of Aristotle's *Physics*. He accepts that the commentary on *Physics* Book 4, as we have it, refers to earlier dissent, in the commentary on 8, from the view of Aristotle and Ammonius on eternity (and in one reference on place). But he proposes that Philoponus will have written this version of his commentary on 8 as a late second edition, after his *Against Proclus* in 529 CE. Indeed, Verrycken gives reasons [31] for thinking that Philoponus will have written this second edition well on into the 530s after his *Against Aristotle*. That requires Verrycken to postulate another second edition also: Philoponus' commentary on *Physics* 4.13 refers back to disagreements with Aristotle in the commentary on Book 8, and so will also need to have been added as a still later second edition, and although a version was being written before 517,[32] this version will not yet have contained reference to past disagreements. Further, he argues some surviving fragments of the commentary on Book 8 (not including the fragments of 8.1, which are very few) can be interpreted as still siding with Ammonius and Aristotle and as *accepting* the eternity of the world, so that they would thus represent traces of the earlier pre-517 viewpoint, thus supporting the need to postulate a later second edition.[33] However we shall see in connexion with Philoponus' commentaries on *Physics* Books 1–3 and on *Posterior Analytics* that it is often hard to decide whether Philoponus is endorsing or merely reporting Aristotle's view, so that this last argument calls for more discussion than I shall give here. Certainly, as Verrycken points out, Simplicius preserves Philoponus' dissenting arguments against

---

[29] Philoponus' commentary on Books 5–7 is available in English translation by Paul Lettinck from the surviving Arabic, with two fragments of Book 8 (London: Duckworth, 1994). The reference at 762,2–5 is anticipated in the comments on Book 8 at 251b10–28, p. 135 in Lettinck's translation.
[30] From Philoponus, *in Phys* 3.5, 458,30 and 4.8, 639,7–9, so Verrycken (n. 1 above), p. 244, n. 57.
[31] Verrycken, p.252.
[32] Verrycken, pp. 244, 248–9.
[33] Verrycken, pp. 245–6, nn. 64–7.

Aristotle's eternalism from Philoponus' much *later* work, *Against Aristotle*.[34] But it is only if we have already accepted Verrycken's belief in a late revised commentary on *Physics* 8 that we could infer its content from that of the late *Against Aristotle*. Verrycken's biography of Philoponus is evidently a more complex one. He explains it by suggesting that under Ammonius' influence Philoponus drifted away from his Christian origins to become Neoplatonist, but that 529 represented a return to Christianity on the level of doctrine. He suspects, although he does not commit himself, that this was in turn motivated by opportunism rather than by sincere conviction.[35] My preferred reconstruction supposes instead that, after Ammonius' death, as his tutelage receded, there would be not a sudden second stage of reversion, but an increased re-thinking and greater outspokenness, tempered by many other possible motivations. This would expand the disagreements if they had already started on the subject of eternity even before 517, while Ammonius is likely to have been alive.

Philoponus' Commentary on *Physics* 4.1–10: Composed Last?

So far I have concluded that Philoponus' commentary on *Physics* Book 8, with its disagreement on eternity seems to have been early. The commentary on *Physics* 4.10–14 seems to be next, because it offers no further disagreement, but refers back only to that one. There are reasons for thinking the commentaries on Book 4.1–10 are the last to be composed of those that have survived intact on the *Physics*, partly because of the strength of disagreement on place, vacuum and the possibility of motion in a vacuum. This, we saw, is expressed not only in the Corollaries inserted as appendixes, but also in the commentary on Aristotle's chapters on vacuum, and discreetly by anticipation in the commentary on Aristotle's chapters on place. Admittedly, we have seen that Philoponus had already expressed his disagreement with Aristotle about place while Ammonius was alive. But in Philoponus' commentary on *Physics* 4.1–10, disagreement is expressed very fully in the Corollary on Place, and quite truculently in the commentary and Corollary on Vacuum.

Philoponus' Commentary on *Physics* Books 1–3

I turn now to Philoponus' commentary on Books 1–3 of Aristotle's *Physics*. This can reasonably be seen as having been written before that on Book 4.1–10. It has received close study from Catherine Osborne (now Rowett) in the introductions to her two-volume translation of it.[36] Disagreements with Aristotle are not expressed so strongly

---

[34] Verrycken, p. 252, citing Simplicius *in Phys.* 8, 1130,7–1131,7; 1133,17–1135,15; 1147,10–1149,4; 1171,30–1175,26; 1157,6–1159,4; 1164,11–30; 1166,37–1167,16.
[35] Verrycken, pp. 240–1. The much later Arabic ascription of opportunism has been discredited by Sarah Stroumsa, 'Al-Farabi and Maimonides on the Christian philosophical tradition: a re-evaluation', *Der Islam* 68 (1991), 107–24.
[36] Catherine Osborne (now Rowett), Introductions to *Philoponus, On Aristotle's Physics 1.1–3* (London: Duckworth, 2006) and *Philoponus On Aristotle's Physics 1.4–9* (London: Duckworth, 2009).

as in the commentary on 4.1–10. But a number of the features Osborne picks out show Philoponus speaking independently of, or in opposition to, Aristotle or Ammonius or both. Thus Philoponus goes beyond Aristotle when he uses grammar to flesh out the character that Aristotle assigns to the privation that precedes possession, when something comes into being. The grammatical points are likely to be Philoponus' own contribution as grammarian, rather than repeated from his teacher Ammonius.[37] Philoponus reveals disagreements between Aristotle and Plato that Ammonius had wished to interpret away, in order to support his belief in the harmony of the Greek philosophical tradition. Philoponus, by contrast, says that Aristotle disagrees that there are Platonic Ideas at a level prior to that of particulars, although in a later back reference the opposite seems to be said.[38] Philoponus uses the first person singular, 'But I say', to make a point against other interpreters, and introduces a personal argument (*idion epikheirêma*) against Aristotle, to show that Aristotle's opponent could have been refuted more easily.[39] The disharmonious first person intervention does not look like a repetition of the pacific Ammonius. Philoponus defines body differently from Aristotle as the three-dimensional, without including reference to Aristotle's prime matter.[40] Speaking, unlike Ammonius, against Aristotle, he allows as one possible option that the world or body came into being from non-being, and he may be referring back to his commentary on *Physics* 8, when he adds that he has adequately rehearsed the case for that elsewhere.[41] He insists on a related point against Aristotle about coming into existence from non-being: Aristotle must grant that *forms* can arise without having existed before in any way whatsoever, by supervening (*sunginesthai*) in Aristotle's special sense which means that, like the attunement of a lyre or the soul or life of an animal, they can arise from the bodily mixture making the body merely *suitable* to receive them. 'Supervene' does not have the sense of the modern term in analytic philosophy, which would imply co-variation between a given form and a given bodily mixture. On the contrary, as the idea of being merely *suitable* (*epitêdeios*) implies, the right bodily mixture is a mere *necessary prerequisite* of a given form, life or attunement arising, and, as Philoponus says in related passages, the form does not *follow* from the bodily mixture. It is not made (*poiein*) by the mixture and cannot be explained as a *result* (*apotelesma*) of it. Nor is the mixture a material cause (*hulikon aition*) of it.[42] There are a good many critical reflections here, even if the others are not as major as those on the world's eternity, on which disagreement had started much earlier.

Philoponus' commentary on *Physics* Book 2 again shows independence of mind in criticising Aristotle (though not Ammonius) concerning his definition of nature, and his statement that every product of nature is produced for a purpose.[43] Verrycken is right that it does not yet challenge Aristotle on the central doctrines he has highlighted,

---

[37] Philoponus, *in Phys.* 1.5, 119,14–120,18.
[38] Philoponus, *in Phys.* 1.6, 133,27–8; 1.9, 193,1–4.
[39] Philoponus, *in Phys.* 1.1, 12,2; 1.3, 86,12.
[40] Philoponus, *in Phys.* 1.2, 39,7–8.
[41] Philoponus, *in Phys.* 1.3, 55,22–4.
[42] Philoponus, *in Phys.* 1.9, 191,10–25. I have analysed related passages in R. Sorabji, *Emotion and Peace of Mind* (Oxford: Oxford University Press, 2000), pp. 266–70.
[43] Philoponus, *in Phys.* 197,30–198,1; 309,9–310,15.

but I am not convinced that it actually *accepts* Aristotle's belief in eternity. Of four texts that Verrycken cites, one explicitly says that it is telling Aristotle's view, and I think the others are likely to be doing the same.[44]

As regards Philoponus' commentary on *Physics* Book 3, it is the topic of infinity that makes it relevant for Philoponus to challenge Aristotle's belief in eternity. He does so clearly in two passages[45] and in a third refers back to his challenge to eternal motion in his early commentary on *Physics* Book 8.[46] I do not see any opposite trend in Philoponus' commentary on *Physics* 3, for example his still adhering to eternity in other passages, or to other views of Aristotle which he will go on to criticise in his commentary on Book 4. Verrycken does see an opposite trend juxtaposed. But he concedes that the other passages he cites do not *accept* Aristotle's belief in eternity, and I believe the fact that they do not *challenge* that belief every time it is mentioned in an exposition, is not significant.[47] Philoponus does not seem to me to be *endorsing* Aristotle's denial of vacuum, when he points forward to the next Book, *Physics* 4, and says that Aristotle will *show* there is none. This looks to me like no more than an announcement of Aristotle's programme.[48] The passages where Verrycken takes Aristotle to be endorsing Aristotle's conception of place seem also to me to be merely expository.[49]

The picture I have of Philoponus' *Physics* commentary, then, is that there was an early challenge before 517 CE on eternity in Philoponus' largely lost commentary on Book 8. The commentary on 4.10–14 refers back to that challenge, but as yet has no further challenge, and little reflection, to add. The commentary on Books 1–3 shows much more independence, and that on Book 4.1–10 is actually very critical of central doctrines of Aristotle. Most of this fits perfectly well with what the scribal titles might suggest, but the surviving titles naturally do not inform us about commentary on particular groups of chapters like *Physics* 4.10–14, nor about fragmentary commentary like that on *Physics* 8.1. So they would not have revealed the earliness of those bits of commentary and would not have hinted at the early divergence from Aristotle on a central subject – eternity.

Philoponus' Commentary on Aristotle's *Categories*

There is another commentary whose title also omits reference to Ammonius and so gives no warning of what I believe to be its earliness, and here too the earliness is compatible with quite extensive, though in this case non-critical, additions. This is Philoponus' commentary on Aristotle's *Categories*. I believe there are signs of earliness in Philoponus *in Cat.*, as I have argued elsewhere.[50] For one thing, over long stretches

---

[44] Verrycken (n. 1 above), p. 244, citing Philoponus, *in Phys.* 236,29–237,4; 298,6–12; 303,1–5; 303, 18–25.
[45] Philoponus, *in Phys.* 428,23–430,10; 467,1–468,4.
[46] Philoponus, *in Phys.* 456,17–458,31.
[47] Verrycken (n. 1 above), p. 245, nn. 60–3, cites *in Phys.* 405,3–7; 410,21–4; 438,5–6; 484,15–19.
[48] Verrycken, p. 247, n. 85, cites Philoponus, *in Phys.* 440,16–17.
[49] Verrycken, pp. 246–7, cites Philoponus, *in Phys.* 444,5–6; 447,18–20; 448,20–1; 464,23–4; 463,3–4.
[50] Originally published as the Introduction to *Philoponus, On Aristotle's Categories 1–5*, translated by Riin Sirkel, Martin Tweedale, and John Harris (London: Bloomsbury, 2015).

it is extremely close, even in wording, to Ammonius *in Cat.* Anon., which it appears to have copied. But this observation needs to be tempered, since Philoponus' commentary *in Cat.* (as possibly also Asclepius from the voice of Ammonius *in Metaph.*) includes a substantial number of *additions* to that earlier commentary.[51]

I have argued in the earlier work cited that Philoponus *in Cat.* innovated over Ammonius *in Cat.* Anon. by giving *concepts* a larger role. I would now add that he openly disagrees with Aristotle as Ammonius' editor interprets him. He does so at *in Cat.* 58,7-59,2 in the course of criticising an argument which is ascribed to Aristotle in Ammonius *in Cat.* Anon. 40,19-21. The argument is that universals need particulars in order to be *said* of them. In Philoponus' version of the cited argument, they need particulars in order to be *predicated* of them. And Philoponus *replies* that what we predicate are only concepts.[52]

Philoponus also avoids a mistake made by the anonymous editor of Ammonius *in Cat.* Anon. At *in Cat.* 9,3-12, Philoponus follows Ammonius *in Isag.* 69,2-11, in what I believe to be a first mistake of ascribing to Porphyry the view that the only universals are at the lowly level of concepts. But the anonymous editor of Ammonius *in Cat.* Anon. 41,7-12 contradicts Ammonius' interpretation of Porphyry and makes the *opposite* mistake of taking Porphyry *Isag.* 15,18 to be talking about intelligible universals at the highest level of Platonic Ideas furthest removed from human concepts. The anonymous editor only does so, because he misreads *Isag.* 15,18, as saying that a genus could survive *all* its species being destroyed, when *Isag.* itself means only that it could survive any *one* of its species being destroyed. In one respect, the anonymous editor is right to differ from Ammonius, because it is true that the discussion in *Isag.* 15,18, is not about what human *concepts* can survive. But this is because it is about genera and species embedded in individuals in the world.

Further divergences were ascribed to Philoponus *in Cat.* by Adolf Busse in the preface to his edition of the anonymously edited commentary. He suggests three places at which Philoponus *in Cat.* added Christian ideas, which the anonymously edited version omitted. The most plausible is at 169,19, where Philoponus qualifies the denial in Ammonius *in Cat.* Anon. that a blind person could see again, by adding, presumably in reference to Christ's healing the blind, 'unless by divine power'.[53] I think that Philoponus, as a Christian addressing pagans, would have had a good motive for adding the qualification in reference to Christ's healing the blind, whereas for a pagan like Ammonius, it would have been pointless or even provocative to lengthen the

---

[51] Additions to Ammonius' lectures are possible also in Asclepius' *Commentary from the voice of Ammonius on Aristotle's Metaphysics*. That commentary includes 252 extracts from Alexander's commentary and plenty from Syrianus, according to Concetta Luna, *Trois études sur la tradition des commentaires anciens à la Métaphysique d'Aristote* (Leiden: Brill, 2001), Appendix 6 for Alexander, pp. 142-86 for Syrianus. This is a higher rate of extract than we find in the one commentary (on *On Interpretation*) that was apparently written out by Ammonius himself, judging from the editor Busse's index of Ammonius' cross-references to other commentators. On the other hand, for Ammonius being cited by Simplicius, *in Phys.* 192,22-3; 193,4-5, as making the same point on a certain issue as Alexander, see Golitsis, *Les Commentaires de Simplicius et de Jean Philopon* (n. 4 above), p. 61, n. 82.

[52] Philoponus, *in Cat.* 58,13-21.

[53] I agree with Marwan Rashed, who kindly explained his doubts about Busse's other examples.

account by referring to pagan divine powers, and against the grain to acknowledge Christ's.

Concetta Luna has found Philoponus making a much larger number of additions, 13 by my count, to the earlier Ammonius *in Cat.* Anon. in a mere 21 pages,[54] none of them presented as objections. Apart from an opening section missing from Ammonius (25,27–27,9), the 13 additions in Philoponus' commentary are:

1. It gives extra explanations (27,11–27).
2. It adds an excursus on what types of contrary will make an exhaustive division (29,22–30,24).
3 and 4. It twice offers a solution different from that of Ammonius *in Cat.* Anon. (33,20–31; 34,16–35,8).
5. It inserts an extra problem and solution (33,32–34,7).
6. It replaces a 2-fold division in Ammonius *in Cat.* Anon. with a four-fold division (31,19–26).
7. It gives a different account of what is being divided in another pair of divisions (43,3–9).
8. It adds extra evidence (36,6–11).
9. It gives a distinction with three examples absent from Ammonius *in Cat.* Anon., separates it from the Anonymous' context of solving an objection to Aristotle, and extends the discussion to grammarian's items: disyllable and trisyllable (38,28–39,15).
10. It adds a section explaining things said (*legomena*), and includes, unlike any other commentary, grammarian's items: conjunctions, prepositions and articles (43,17–44,2).
11. It substitutes a list of items of interest to Philoponus as omitted from the *Categories*, viz.: point, instant, monad, privations, negations, movements, changes, in place of Ammonius *in Cat.* Anon.'s list of point, privation, matter, form (46,14–48,27).
12. It gives the right reference to Aristotle, when Ammonius *in Cat.* Anon. makes a further mistake and does not (27,27–31).
13. It includes a Christian reference, shortening Ammonius *in Cat.* Anon.'s 'divine substances' to 'the divine substance' (29,14–27).

Luna infers from the closeness in wording in other passages to the anonymously recorded version that someone, and this surely must be Philoponus,[55] was making additions to a *written* version (her p. 354), the only known written version being the

---

[54] C. Luna, *Commentaire sur les Catégories d'Aristote. Chapitres 2–4* (Paris: Les Belles Lettres, 2001), pp. 147–8, 151–3, 186, 208, 219–25, 280–5, 288–9, 332–58; 422–3, 545–51, 847–57.

[55] The alternative that the someone who made additions was not Philoponus, but Ammonius, as recorded in some *unknown* record subsequently used by Philoponus, seems to me to run into many difficulties. Not only does it multiply hypothetical records beyond necessity, but also the additions 9, 10, 11, 13, and the other Christian references supplied by Busse all smack of Philoponus. Another addition is traced by Luna (p. 345) to Porphyry and Iamblichus, and could have reached Ammonius, she thinks, at best only orally from Proclus.

anonymous recording, in one or other of its manuscripts.[56] It is striking that the additions by Philoponus turn out, except for the first one about the predication of concepts, to be non-critical reflections, not objections, and this will be true of other additions cited below. I think this has implications for other commentaries which, unlike this one, Philoponus draws from the seminars of Ammonius with (critical) reflections of his own. If Golitsis is right that in these commentaries Philoponus feels free to add criticisms of his own, he will *a fortiori* have felt free to add non-critical reflections. Given the large number of non-critical reflections that he adds to his *in Cat.*, he would be most unlikely to confine himself elsewhere to critical objections.

We may have a further contribution of Philoponus' own, when at *in Cat.* 133,1–4, he comments on Aristotle's recommendation to explore puzzles. At any rate, the sentiment expressed looks much closer to his own attitude than to Ammonius' harmonising of disagreements, when he says that Aristotle recommends such exploration because he wants us not to rest content with his own (Aristotle's) words, but ourselves to investigate such things as self-propelling agents.

Despite this evidence for Philoponus' additions, there are further signs of the comparative earliness. Another of Philoponus' commentaries, that on Aristotle's *De Anima*, has the putatively early hallmark of being drawn from the seminars of Ammonius, albeit with (critical) reflections of Philoponus' own. But it refers back at 391,32 to, and improves on, a theory given in Philoponus' own commentary on Aristotle's *Categories* as if Philoponus *in Cat.* were *earlier still*. It makes no difference to the comparative earliness whether the improvement was a reflection added by Philoponus or recorded by him from Ammonius. Philoponus' own commentary in *Cat.* had required an apple's fragrance to be inseparable from (bits of) it, and so it allowed the bits, and hence the substance of the apple, to reach all the way to the organ of smell. But in reflecting on *On the Soul*'s requirement that the sense of smell should act at a *distance* from what is perceived, Philoponus, or Philoponus reporting Ammonius, later offered a different view and said at 391,32 ff. that what needs to reach the organ of smell is not the fragrance after all, but the activity (*energeia*) of the fragrance. This meets the requirement of logic that the fragrance does not get separated from the bits of apple, and also the requirement of psychology that the bits act at a *distance* from the organ of smell. The reference back suggests that Philoponus *in Cat.* was written earlier than the comparatively early Philoponus from the seminars of Ammonius *in DA*.

There is also reason to think that Philoponus *in Cat.* 1 is earlier than his commentary from the seminars of Ammonius on *An. Pr.* The reason is possible references back to his own *in Cat.* 8,23–7 and 15,13–14 from his *in An. Pr.* 1 from the seminars of Ammonius at 1,5 and 273,1.[57] Of course, cross references are no more decisive on their own than scribal titles, since it is in principle possible for cross references to be added

---

[56] The manuscript M is fuller than F and suggests to Luna that it may represent another written version besides that of manuscript F, but its extra information was not used by Philoponus, so is not an alternative source for him. So Luna, pp. 355–6, 422–3.

[57] So R. Sorabji, 'John Philoponus', in his, ed., *Philoponus and the Rejection of Aristotelian Science* (London: Duckworth, 1987), p. 38, n. 263.

in at a later date. But each piece of evidence needs to be considered. It would also be no good pleading that Philoponus' second reference back might be to *Aristotle's* discussion of the many meanings of 'being', not to his own, because Aristotle discusses that not in his *Categories* but elsewhere, notably in *Metaphysics* 4.2.

My conclusion both for Philoponus *in Cat.* and for certain parts of his *in Phys.* is that both are early, but that in these two works Philoponus had already begun to add his own reflections early and already even objections. If so, the presence of some objections in Philoponus *in Cat.* is not on its own reliable evidence of lateness, although elsewhere the extent of the objections and the vehemence of expression may be.

There is a further important question. When a book title tells us that Philoponus is interpolating objections to Ammonius in what he draws from Ammonius' seminars, does this mean that he is not also including non-critical observations of his own? That would be very surprising, as I have indicated, given that he includes a good many non-critical observations in his *Categories* commentary. Why then would he not include non-critical observations elsewhere? I think that the reason why Philoponus' book titles make an announcement when objections are included in a commentary from Ammonius' seminars is not that these are the only interpolations that he makes. Rather, the reason is that it is only right for an editor to dissociate Ammonius from objections, when they are not ones he had raised himself. It is possible also that Philoponus would like to be associated with some objections, but not always. For sometimes he does not put his objection *as* an objection, I believe, and I think it may be that sometimes his authorship of an objection is hidden, and he does not edit the text to make his authorship clear.

If we cannot infer that in Philoponus' commentaries from the seminars of Ammonius the only interpolations will be objections announced in the book title, this will be very relevant to more than one of the chapters below on Philoponus. For the question will arise whether good (non-critical) innovations should be credited to Ammonius or to Philoponus as his editor. Can Philoponus, for example, be credited with any of the non-critical ideas in the commentary on Aristotle *On Coming-to-Be and Passing-Away,* or on *On the Soul,* Books 1 and 2, and, lost in Greek but surviving in Latin, on *On the Soul* 3.4–8 on intellect? This question will arise in Chapter 15 below, where Golitsis favours Ammonius over Philoponus,[58] and in Chapter 17 below, where Péter Lautner makes the reverse ascription to Philoponus, not Ammonius, when he discusses the keen attention to medicine and the brain in Book 2 of Philoponus' commentary on *On the Soul,* as did Philip van der Eijk in his translation of the same commentary on *On the Soul,* Book 1. The value of Golitsis' challenge is that now we shall have to look and see case by case what points to Ammonius and what points to Philoponus. I have tried to do a little of this below in connexion with these same commentaries. But we can no longer assume that nearly all the ideas belong to Philoponus, nor, in my view, should we start assuming that all except objections are by Ammonius.

---

[58] The same prioritation of Ammonius was proposed in a Leuven University PhD dissertation of 2010 by Arnis Ritups, but for Philoponus on *On the Soul* Book 3, chapter 6, a book which Golitsis now credits to Philoponus.

Philoponus' other Commentaries on Aristotle: On *De Anima*

With two little parts of Philoponus' *Physics* commentary assigned to 517 CE and to before 517 CE, and his *Categories* commentary marked as early, how far can his other commentaries on Aristotle be dated in relation to these fixed points?

As regards Philoponus' commentary on Aristotle's *De Anima*, or *On the Soul*, which we have just taken to be later than his commentary on the *Categories*, the authorship of the commentary on Book 3 has been disputed, although Golitsis has now made a strong argument for Philoponus as author, and not merely as recorder of Ammonius.[59] He has added that we find open disagreement in one of the (critical) reflections at *in DA* 2.7, 334,40, where Ammonius' view is called puzzling and strange. At the same time he has pointed out that this commentary refers back at 528,34–529,4, to *in Phys.* 3, 414,20–7,[60] so may be later than that commentary too.

The commentaries on the other two books of *De Anima* do not necessarily have the same late date, nor does the commentary surviving in Latin translation on Book 3 chapters 4–8 on the intellect, which has been argued to be closely related. Marcel de Corte used twenty seven to twenty eight arguments to show this, and William Charlton added others.[61] The commentary on Book 1 is described in its title as from the seminars of Ammonius with added (critical) reflections. This reference to the seminars of Ammonius, though not repeated, is unanimously taken to apply to the commentary on Book 2 as well, and judging from the similarities invoked, it is likely to apply also to the lost Greek of the Latin translation commenting on *On the Soul* 3.4–8.

This still leaves Golitsis' question how much of the rest of Philoponus' *De Anima* commentary is to be attributed to Ammonius: certainly a good amount. But in particular, whose are the many (non-critical) reflections on brain, nerves and other medical matters? Where (as here) the title tells us that Philoponus draws from the seminars of Ammonius and warns of Philoponus' own *epistaseis*, or *critical* reflections, I did not conclude that all the rest is by Ammonius. On the contrary, I offered above reason to think that if Philoponus offered some critical reflections, he is likely to have included many more *non-critical* reflections. Insofar as there is any independent evidence about scientific interest, Ammonius is tentatively called by his pupil Damascius the greatest geometer and astronomer of all time,[62] and we are told by another student, Simplicius, of an impressive demonstration in astronomy.[63]

---

[59] I agree with Golitsis that the new theory of a faculty of self-awareness of psychological acts, including acts of conscience, at 464,30–465,31, is not likely to be reportage of Ammonius, if, as seems likely, the newer interpreter is Damascius, not the much later Olympiodorus, who used slightly different language anyhow, since Ammonius would not be likely to refer to his old friend and eventual pupil Damascius merely as a newer interpreter.

[60] Pantelis Golitsis, 'John Philoponus' Commentary on the Third Book of Aristotle's *De Anima*, Wrongly Attributed to Stephanus', ch. 15 in this volume.

[61] Marcel de Corte, ed., *Le Commentaire de Jean Philopon sur le Troisème Livre du 'Traité de l'Ame' d'Aristote*, (Liège: Bibliothèque de la Faculté de Philosophie et Lettres de l'Université de Liège, 1934), pp. ix-xv; William Charlton, *Philoponus, On Aristotle On the Intellect* (London: Duckworth, 1991), pp. 5–6.

[62] Damascius, *Life of Isidore* fr. 57C in P. Athanassiadi, *Damascius, the Philosophical History* (Athens: Apamea, 1999).

[63] Simplicius, *in Cael.* 462,12–31.

But Asnmonius is not particularly associated with medicine, Rather, it was Gessius, Ammonius' 'senior student', who held a chair of medical philosophy according to Ammonius' proselytising Christian student Zacharias.[64] Gessius is mentioned as a second target of Zacharias' proselytising, not as deriving his medicine from Ammonius and in the school of Alexandria, Gessius could have learnt his medicine from any of the doctors. Thus Philoponus too could have learnt his medicine from Gessius or other doctors there. I think Golitsis' evidence from titles is important for alerting us that we can no longer take it for granted where Philoponus got his medical information, and need to see if there is further evidence. But I do not at present know any evidence that he is simply offering a record of Ammonius' medical comments. It has to be settled case by case whether there are signs pointing to Ammonius or to Philoponus' interpolations, and this has not been done for the medical interests.

I think we can do this to some extent for other subjects, however. First, there are signs of Philoponus' interpolations in the commentary on *On the Soul* Book 1 when it diverges from Ammonius in giving to concepts yet another role, besides the one recognised in his *Categories* commentary. The new role concerns *definition*: what we define is the *concept* (*ennoia*) that we have of things.[65] Ammonius had stayed much closer to Alexander by saying that we define human as mortal, rational animal (i.e. by its form), and added only that we do so in *accordance* with our concept.[66] Philoponus has here not merely supplemented Ammonius, but also silently disagreed with him.

On the other hand, there are clear signs of Ammonius' original seminar, when we look at the treatment in Latin of a theme in *On Intellect*, that is, *On the Soul* 3.4-8, which has been very ably discussed by Frans de Haas in a companion paper to his Chapter 21.[67] Aristotle says in *On the Soul* 3.4, 429b30-430a2, 'the mind is in a way potentially the things it thinks, but potentially in this way: as with a writing tablet on which nothing is written in actuality'. The blank tablet clashes with Plato's account in the *Phaedo* and *Phaedrus* of how we are born with access to knowledge of the Ideas which our souls encountered before birth before the present incarnation, or periodically after a number of incarnations, so that our minds are not blank at birth, but simply need reminders. Proclus thinks Aristotle is simply wrong, according to de Haas, but, Iamblichus, Priscian (published as 'Simplicius') and Damascius harmonise Plato with Aristotle by saying that the trauma of reincarnation makes it *as if* our mind were a blank writing tablet. We do have principles (*logoi*) derived from the Ideas hidden in our potential intellect, but until the active intellect brings them to light, the descent of the soul to a low level (*huphesis*) and separation (*khôrismos*) from the Ideas makes the soul flow outwards away from its own essence (*ousia*), until it can revert (*epistrephein*) to the *logoi* within it. Philoponus on 3.4-8, from the seminars of Ammonius, preserved in Latin, takes the subject further.[68] To describe the state of the soul after birth, we need to

---

[64] Zacharias of Mytilene, *Ammonius* 362-5 Colonna.
[65] Philoponus, *in DA* 38,13-17 on Aristotle *De Anima* 1.1, 402b5-9.
[66] Ammonius *in Isag.* 68,25-69,11.
[67] Frans de Haas, 'Recollection and potentiality in Philoponus', in Maria Kardaun and Joke Spruyt, eds, *The Winged Chariot* (Leiden: Brill, 2000), pp. 165-84.
[68] Ed. Verbeke, 39,27-40,43; 62,6-63,18.

distinguish an extra level of potentiality between the two that Aristotle distinguishes in *On the Soul* 2.5. There a little child potentially has grammatical knowledge, a trained adult has it at a higher level of potentiality even when asleep, only the person using it has it in full actuality. Between the first two potentialities we need another level, like that of a person not capable of functioning (Latin: *non est operari*) when he wants because, when the intellect descends (*descendens*), non-rational life imposes the fog of a swoon (*in nubilo; alienatio*), or drunkenness (*in ebrietatibus*). Plato himself in the *Phaedo* compared the soul that investigates through the senses to someone who is drunk.[69] The harmonisation of Plato with Aristotle that De Haas here illuminates, based on a non-Christian belief in reincarnation, is not something that the Christian Philoponus would have wanted to interpolate, if it had not been in Ammonius, but is clearly Ammonius' work. The analogy with drunkenness is applied to another context in the next commentary of Philoponus, but there we shall find that although Ammonius introduces the analogy, he has to consider a type of critical objection (*epistasis*) which, I believe, although I am not sure, could be one directed by Philoponus' against Ammonius.

On *De Generatione et Corruptione*

Philoponus' commentary on Aristotle's *De Generatione et Corruptione* from the seminars of Ammonius with (critical) reflections of his own is regarded by Verrycken as earlier than 517 CE, on the grounds that he finds no juxtaposed later layers, and that in places where it is relevant to discuss Aristotle's belief in the eternity of motion and the world, Philoponus appears to go along with it.[70] I would only say in reply that the beginnings of his later denial of eternity may be here. For at *in GC* 169,7, Philoponus argues that forms arise in a suitable blend of matter as a necessary (not sufficient) condition and do so from outside the whole creation (*ek tês holes dêmiourgias*), i.e., on one interpretation, without having existed beforehand. Philoponus was later, in his commentary on *Physics* Book 1, in a passage already mentioned, to use the arising of forms out of nothing and *ek tês holês dêmiourgias*, in order to argue that the world itself could have been created out of nothing.[71] In fact, on another translation of the Greek phrase, *in GC* 169,7 will already have ascribed to the divine Creator the creation of forms out of nothing.[72]

Frans de Haas in Chapter 16 of the present book[73] has drawn attention to Philoponus from the seminars of Ammonius *in GC* 271,16–272,24, which discusses Aristotle *GC* 2.7 and defends Aristotle with a solution to a puzzle brought against him. Pure fire is admittedly hot in the extreme. But in a compound with the three other elements, air,

---

[69] Plato, *Phaedo* 79C1–8.
[70] Verrycken (n. 1 above), esp. p. 255.
[71] Philoponus, *in Phys.* 191,1–33.
[72] Catherine Rowett (formerly Osborne) may be right, however, to reject my former translation of the Greek phrase as 'from the Demiurge's universal creation' (n. 31 to the introduction of her translation of Philoponus, *in Phys.* 1.1–3 and n. 286 to her translation of Philoponus, *in Phys.* 1.4–6).
[73] Frans de Haas, 'Mixture in Philoponus'.

water, and earth, fire cannot be hot in the extreme, so cannot be pure fire. It is probably Ammonius in reply who refers back indirectly to the kind of potentiality for geometry found in the drunken geometer, which he had invoked at 188,16–26 in commenting on *GC* 1.10, and certainly in on *On the Soul* 3.4–8, surviving only in Latin. But he refers to the drunken potentiality not directly, but by emphasising that Aristotle himself in *Physics* Book 7 recognised a distinct sense of potentiality. Indeed Aristotle there invokes drunkenness, saying that someone who has knowledge does not have to acquire knowledge all over again, on recovering from drunkenness which prevented him from using it.[74] Ammonius emphasises that there is a whole range (*platos*) of intermediate kinds of potentiality. However, at 271,25–272,12, Ammonius recognises that there is still a critical objection (*epistasis* – Philoponus' preferred word) worth making against his defence that it is only *pure* hot, and hence only *pure* fire, that has been destroyed. The objection is that *fire qua fire* is hot in the extreme, so since *extreme* heat gets destroyed in a mixture, so does fire qua fire, even though heat allows of different degrees and so *heat* has not been destroyed qua heat. Ammonius does not answer, saying only that the objection went beyond the proposed discussion. Indeed, if the maximalist objection was raised impromptu by Philoponus himself during the class which the commentary records, it could have been shelved because the further issue had not been allowed for in the timing of the class. Ammonius returns to the subject at 276,18–23, but only to repeat his first solution and without addressing the further *epistasis*. Elemental fire in a compound, he says, has *something* of its form, and though destroyed in its *pure* state, is not completely destroyed qua fire, but only qua *pure* fire. It is potentially fire in the special sense explained in terms of drunkenness.

There is something strange about Ammonius cutting off discussion of the maximality objection, because the point it makes is one he seems to have endorsed for a different purpose in a slightly earlier context at 245,18–246,1. If he there endorsed it, surely he needs to consider whether it now counts against him. The earlier topic was this: Aristotle denies that elemental fire, for example, can be an *unchanged* ultimate source of all other things, *GC* 332b5–10. Rather, anything will be changed when it turns into something else, for if fire could be an unchanged source of all else, all other things would be fire. Ammonius weighed up a reply in terms of *purity*, like the one he was soon to favour in a different context, that when fire generated air, the fire might not be destroyed, but only lose its *purity*. But in the present context, instead of accepting this answer, he rejects it in favour of the *maximality* view, that elemental fire is dry in the *maximal* degree, and therefore cannot persist at all when it turns into elemental air, which is moist in the maximal degree. This is the very view that he was to decline to discuss, when he recognised it as counting against his purity view in the other discussion. Could it be that his later lecture, as recorded by Philoponus, had not allowed for his earlier endorsement of the maximality view to be turned against him by some bright spark, so that he postponed discussion until after the lecture? And could the proponent of the maximality view have been Philoponus on the second occasion, or even on both? That the insistence on maximal dryness and heat for fire is a view

---

[74] Aristotle, *Physics* 7, 247b13–248a6.

Philoponus accepted is suggested by his using the same sort of principle again in non-commentary, works, both to oppose, as here, allowing earth to enter unchanged into compounds and against Christian treatments of the mingling of unchanged divine and human natures in Christ.[75] If Philoponus' intervention can be so hidden, it will not be a quick job to decide where his interventions occur in the commentaries he takes from Ammonius' seminars. Philoponus *in Phys.* 4 is much more outspoken in its objections, and if it too draws on Ammonius' seminars, this may indicate that it comes from a later phase than *in GC*.

On *Prior Analytics*

Philoponus' commentary from the seminars of Ammonius on Aristotle's *Prior Analytics*, though apparently referring back to Philoponus' own *Categories* commentary, shows signs of earliness. The title still calls Philoponus a grammarian, and it mentions no (critical) reflections added by Philoponus. This is the only one of Philoponus' commentaries on Aristotle not yet translated or in the course of being translated into English with annotation and discussion. More may be learnt from translating its opening part alongside the commentary drawn anonymously from the voice of Ammonius on *Prior Analytics* 1.1-2 for comparison. Sten Ebbesen has denied the attribution to Philoponus of the commentary on Book 2 and called it a Byzantine collection of scholia.[76] I shall leave it out of my tentative table below of Philoponus' commentaries.

On *Posterior Analytics*

Philoponus' commentary from the seminars of Ammonius on Aristotle's *Posterior Analytics*, with his own (critical) reflections added, was regarded by Verrycken as having in its present form juxtaposed late views in a second edition with those of an earlier edition which still accepted eternity. I think the references to eternity may be merely expounding Aristotle. But a sign of being somewhat later is that Philoponus openly denies what Ammonius implied, that Plato and Aristotle agree that Ideas exist only in the mind of the Creator.[77] Verrycken cites five further passages where Philoponus openly disagrees on other matters with Ammonius by name.[78] On the other hand, these other disagreements are not on major doctrines.

The attribution to Philoponus of the commentary on *Posterior Analytics* Book 2 is doubtful. It is pitched at more elementary students than the commentary on Book 1.

---

[75] De Haas cites Philoponus, *Against Proclus* 11.14, and *On Parts and Wholes*, ch. 4, now translated from Syriac by Daniel King in the Ancient Commentators on Aristotle series (London: Bloomsbury, 2015).

[76] Sten Ebbesen, 'Analyzing syllogisms or *Anonymous Aurelianensis III* – the (presumably) earliest extant Latin commentary on the *Prior Analytics*, and its Greek model', *Cahiers de l'institut du moyen-âge grec et latin* 37 (1981), 9-11. I owe this and the next Ebbesen reference to Nikos Agiotis.

[77] Philoponus, *in An Post*, 242,14-243,25.

[78] Verrycken, n. 31.

On our subject of the level of entities *before* the many, it endorses the view we know to be that of Proclus that these entities are Platonic Ideas,[79] whereas in his later commentary on Aristotle's *De Anima* Book 1 Philoponus twice endorses Ammonius' view that the genera *before* the many are creative principles (*dêmiourgikoi logoi*) separated from matter in the mind of the divine Creator,[80] and in *in Phys*. 1, we saw, Philoponus even denies that Aristotle wanted there to be Ideas before the many, although he goes on to waver on that.[81] There have been many suggestions about authorship, but Sten Ebbesen regards it as a thirteenth century work by Leo Magentinus.[82] I shall leave it too out of my table below of Philoponus' commentaries.

On *Meteorology*

Philoponus' commentary on Aristotle's *Meteorology* has been dated to well after 529 CE, both because of the lack, mentioned above, of signs that it reflects teaching, and because it shares with Philoponus' late treatise *Against Aristotle on the Eternity of the World* an attack on Aristotle's eternal fifth celestial element. Instead, the sun is made of fire. Moreover, there appear to be cross references between the two works, either forwards from the *Meteorology* (Étienne Évrard), or backwards to the *Meteorology* (Christian Wildeberg).[83]

On Porphyry's *Introduction* (*Isagôgê*)

An eighth lost commentary is not on Aristotle, but on Porphyry's *Introduction* (*Isagôgê*), that is, on one interpretation, his introduction to Aristotle's logic. There is a reference back to it from Philoponus *in Phys*. 2.3, 250,28. But there is a more significant probable reference back from an early work, Philoponus *in Cat*. 1.2, suggesting that it is earlier still. Here Philoponus says 'when we were starting on the *Introductions*'. Riin Sirkel has pointed out that Philoponus twice again uses the plural, *Introductions*, some pages later, in order to name what we refer to in the singular as Porphyry's *Isagôgê* (*Introduction*) at *in Cat*. 12,19 and 32,32.[84] This suggests, as I point out above in the introduction to

---

[79] Philoponus (?), *in An. Post*. 2, 435,25–30.
[80] Philoponus, *in DA* 38,13–15; 58,9.
[81] Philoponus, *in Phys* 1.6, 133,27–8; 1.9, 193,1–4.
[82] Sten Ebbesen, Review in *Aestimatio* 9 (2012), at p. 363, of Frans de Haas, Mariska Leunissen, and Marije Martijn, eds, *Interpreting Aristotle's Posterior Analytics in Late Antiquity*. See the earlier Preface and Introduction to Owen Goldin's translation of *Philoponus (?), On Posterior Analytics 2* (London: Duckworth, 2009), where, however, my suggestion of a revision of Asclepius by Philoponus was clearly wrong.
[83] É. Évrard, 'Les convictions religieuses de Jean Philopon et la date de son commentaire aux Météorologiques', *Bulletin de l'Académie royale de Belgique* 39 (1953), 299–357, at 340, citing *in Meteor*. 16,31. Christian Wildberg, 'Prolegomena to the study of Philoponus' *Contra Aristotelem*', in Richard Sorabji, ed., *Philoponus and the Rejection of Aristotelian Science* (London: Duckworth, 1987), pp 197–209, at pp. 202–8, citing *in Meteor*. 24,38–25,2; 91,18–20, 97,16.
[84] Riin Sirkel, n. 1 to *Philoponus, On Aristotle's Categories 1–5*, translated by Riin Sirkel, Martin Tweedale, and John Harris (London: Bloomsbury, 2015).

this book, that Philoponus wrote a number of the six types of introduction introduced for beginning students by his teacher Ammonius.

A Possible Order of Commentaries and Rate of Divergence from Ammonius

The evidence adduced so far can suggest only a very tentative possible order of the commentaries discussed, all the more so because Golitsis is currently working on his own conclusions, of which he has been kind enough to show me an early draft. But just on the basis of the evidence assembled here a tentative order would be:

in Isag. from 510 onwards
in Cat.
in An. Pr. 1
in An. Post. 1
in GC
in Phys. 8
in Phys 4.10–14 in the year 517 CE, with Ammonius quite possibly alive
in DA 1 and 2, Ammonius no longer alive, but used to say and might say things about vision, with *in DA* 3, chs 4–8 *On Intellect*, surviving in Latin
in Phys 1–3
in DA 3 in Greek (Golitsis shows it referring back to *in Phys* 3)[85]
in Phys. 4, Ammonius no longer alive, but he used to disagree about place
in Meteor. after 529

This order would have the interesting result that Golitsis' conjecture was correct that Philoponus was following the order of the student curriculum, in the four comparatively early commentaries on Aristotle's logic. These four naturally skip any commentary on Aristotle's De *Interpretatione*, which would have come in the second place, because Ammonius himself had written a commentary on that. I cited actual evidence based on cross references for the order of the first three, so I would not be relying on the assumption, which I challenged above, that the curricular order would be the obvious order. Rather, the cross references provide *independent* evidence that, for the more introductory logical works, the curricular order was followed. Since the order could easily have been more haphazard, this suggests that Ammonius might indeed have exercised some supervision, assigning the writing, and the order of writing, of a version of the introductory student seminars on logic, though not as a bare record without any reflections. The remaining commentaries come from the area of physics, which for Aristotle included psychology, and the difference from strict curricular order could support Golitsis' idea that Philoponus was by then recording his own lectures. The breaking up of the *Physics* commentary would correspond to the fact that it was too

---

[85] Pantelis Golitsis, 'John Philoponus' Commentary on the Third Book of Aristotle's *De Anima*', ch. 15 in this volume.

large and complex a work to teach as a whole, as the more introductory logical texts might have been.

As for divergence from Ammonius, I do not know of any commentary where Philoponus made a bare record of Ammonius. Already in *in Cat.* he was adding his own reflections, and there already I detected one case of open disagreement with Aristotle as described by Ammonius' anonymous editor, on the role of concepts in predication. The *in An. Pr.*, also early, needs further study, but the extent of disagreement is greater in *in An. Post.* with six disagreements, one quite important. I detected Philoponus *in DA* 2 revising the earlier theory of *in Cat.* on fragrance and *in DA* 1 silently disagreeing with Ammonius about objects of definition. Philoponus *in GC* may already have bordered on the denial of the world's eternity, if it was discussing a Demiurgic creation of forms out of nothing. But the first really major disagreement on that subject, and one much recalled by Philoponus later, concerned the Christian denial of eternity, and that was first announced in *in Phys.* 8. This would have been Philoponus' seventh commentary in the hypothetical order above, since it was written before 517, and if he started in 510, he would have written seven commentaries in seven years. The parts of the *Physics* commentary, some of it reflecting a more advanced student audience and requiring a high degree of originality, would have taken a long time. The disagreement on eternity started before 517 and the disagreement on place was debated with Ammonius while he was alive. Philoponus wrote down the disagreement on place along with that on vacuum and dynamics *in Phys.* 4.1–10. These disagreements are on a new scale and of a new importance. I have spoken of them as the foundation of a completely different perspective providing an alternative to Aristotelian science. If all this is right, we have not found a stage at which Philoponus was a mere recorder of Ammonius. He added his own reflections at least from the time of the early *Categories* commentary. But the scientific revolution, to borrow a name,[86] began in the earliest of the *Physics* commentaries, that on Book 8.

---

[86] Thomas Kuhn's name for the introduction of impetus theory in dynamics, which, however, he assigned to the fourteenth century, and which was only one part of Philoponus' change of scientific perspective.

15

John Philoponus' Commentary on the Third Book of Aristotle's *De Anima*, Wrongly Attributed to Stephanus[1]

Pantelis Golitsis

It is generally agreed that the commentary on the third book of Aristotle's *On the Soul* or *De Anima*, published by Michael Hayduck in 1897, is not by John Philoponus.[2] Although all three books of this commentary were attributed to Philoponus in 1535 by Vittore Trincavelli (the editor of the *editio princeps*),[3] Hayduck was sceptical about the

---

[1] I wish to especially thank Valérie Cordonier, Börje Bydén, and Richard Sorabji for inviting me to present this paper at various audiences in Paris, Göteborg, and Oxford. I am grateful to all participants for their stimulus and fruitful comments.

[2] M. Hayduck, ed., *Ioannis Philoponi in Aristotelis De anima libros commentaria*, CAG 15 (Berlin: Reimer, 1897). See e.g. H. J. Blumenthal, *Aristotle and Neoplatonism in Late Antiquity. Interpretations of the De anima* (Ithaca: Cornell University Press, 1996), pp. 62–5 and 196–7, and W. Charlton, *Philoponus, On Aristotle on the Intellect* (London: Duckworth, 1991), pp. 1–12, for arguments that seek to rule out the possibility that Philoponus is the author of the Greek commentary on Book 3; W. Charlton, '*Philoponus' On Aristotle On the Soul 3.1–8* (London: Duckworth, 2000), pp. 1–12, repr. in W. Chalrton, '*Philoponus' On Aristotle On the Soul 3.9–13, with Stephanus, On Aristotle On intepretation* (London: Duckworth 2000), for arguments that seek to attribute the commentary to Stephanus. Lately, Christian Tornau, 'Bemerkungen zu Stephanos von Alexandria, Plotin und Plutarch von Athen', *Elenchos* 28 (2007), 105–27, has most interestingly provided a further argument, based on a parallel text, for attributing the commentary to Stephanus; his thesis fundamentally rests on the assumption that a comment on assertion and denial is unique in its formulation to 'Ps.-Philoponus' (*in DA* 3, 546, 1–6) and Stephanus (*in Int.* 6,23–5), since in Ammonius, *in Int.* 27,1–3, only denial is dealt with. Mossman Roueché has pointed out to me, however, that this very comment is also found in Ammonius' commentary on the *Prior Analytics* (*in An. Pr.* 22,34–23,8), where is attributed to Alexander of Aphrodisias (cf. Alexander, *in An. Pr.* 15,4–11). It could, therefore, be made by anyone familiar with Alexander's commentary or with Ammonius' teachings on logic. Two scholars have resisted so far to the general tendency: W. Bernard, 'Philoponus on self-awareness', in R. Sorabji, ed., *Philoponus and the Rejection of Aristotelian Science* (London: Duckworth, 1987), p. 154, n. 3 (2nd edn, 2010, p. 195, n. 3), according to whom 'several collections of his [i.e. Philoponus'] comments existed side by side in his day', and P. Lautner, 'Philoponus, in *De anima* 3: Quest for an author', *Classical Quarterly* 42 (1992), 510–22, especially 514–5, where he asserts that 'the *in De anima* 3 might be nothing other than the detailed lecture notes of a disciple or disciples [of Philoponus]'; this is also my opinion, albeit argued in a different way. A. Ritups, in his unpublished dissertation *Aristotle De Anima* III. 6: *Essays in the history of its interpretation* (Leuven, 2010), also opts for Philoponus. R. Sorabji, 'New findings on Philoponus: Part 2 – Recent studies', in R. Sorabji, ed., *Philoponus and the Rejection of Aristotelian Science*, 2nd edn, pp. 11–40, especially p. 29, prudently speaks of the 'disputed Greek commentary on book 3'.

[3] The title describes it as a *hupomnêma* of John the Grammarian on the books of Aristotle's *De Anima*.

attribution of Book 3. He claimed that there are important stylistic differences between the first two books and the third book.[4] This is undoubtedly true but it only proves, as Hayduck himself noted, that what we read in his (and in Trincavelli's) edition is a composite commentary: one author is responsible for the commentary on Books 1 and 2, while some other author is responsible for the commentary on Book 3. I will claim in this paper that the first author is Ammonius, whereas the second is Philoponus.

Hayduck would disagree with my claim, since he had a second argument, which he felt to be more decisive: in two Byzantine manuscripts, he says, namely the *Parisinus gr.* 1914, which is the oldest surviving manuscript of the commentary, and the *Mutinensis* III. F. 8, the third book is introduced as *biblion triton apo phonês Stephanou* ('Book 3 from the voice of Stephanus'). In fact, six out of thirteen manuscripts that contain the composite commentary on the *De Anima* ascribe the third book to Stephanos.[5] We should be aware, however, that in good philology numbers do not count. A partial collation quickly shows that the five manuscripts, dating from the fifteenth and the sixteenth centuries, are direct or indirect copies of the sixth, namely the *Parisinus gr.* 1914, that is, Hayduck's codex D, which is traditionally dated to the twelfth century.[6] D originally had no titles for Books 2 and 3, which ought to be added in red ink, just like the general title of the commentary, which is written in red at the beginning of Book 1. The missing titles have been provided some decades later by two correctors, D^2 and D^3, who collated a second manuscript and either restored portions of text that had been omitted by D^1 or deleted portions of text that had been repeated by D^1.[7] D^2 added the title 'commentary on the second book of *On the Soul*' (*exêgêsis tou deuterou peri psukhês*) at the beginning of Book 2, whereas D^3 added the words 'Book 3 from the voice of Stephanus' (*biblion triton apo phônês stephanou*) at the beginning of Book 3. Unless it can be proved that D^3's addition was copied onto *Parisinus* from another manuscript, the attribution to Stephanus has no value. Quite tellingly, the addition of these words was D^3's last intervention, since he did not go on with his collation into Book 3. He must have stopped because the manuscript he used for his collation did not contain the commentary on Book 3 that D did; it contained, in all probability, a different commentary, which is nowadays lost in the Greek original but is known to have been used by Sophonias in the late thirteenth century.[8] The attribution to Stephanus might well have been a reasonable guess by D^3, who was unable to make sense of the fact that the *apo phonês* commentary contained in D was not the same as the (not *apo phonês*) commentary attributed to Philoponus in the manuscript he used for his collation; thus, being familiar with Stephanus' *apo phonês* commentary on the *De interpretatione*, he attributed it to him.

---

[4] Hayduck, op. cit., p. v, says the first two books show verbose industry, the third a meagre brevity of interpretation.
[5] Apart from the *Parisinus gr.* 1914 and the *Mutinensis* III. F. 8, these manuscripts are: *Leidensis Voss.* F 61, *Oxoniensis Laud. gr.* 48, *Angelicus gr.* 104, and *Marcianus gr.* 232.
[6] According to my palaeographical judgement, this manuscript is older and should be dated to the eleventh century.
[7] See e.g. f. 4ᵛ, 94ʳ, and 94ᵛ.
[8] See S. Van Riet, 'Fragments de l'original grec du « De intellectu » de Philopon dans une compilation de Sophonias', *Revue philosophique de Louvain* 63 (1965), 5–40.

A substantial part of the commentary used by Sophonias is preserved in Latin, since it was translated by William of Moerbeke in 1268. It is misleadingly known as Philoponus' *On the Intellect* (*De intellectu*) thanks to its first editor Marcel De Corte, who took Moerbeke's colophon literally (cf. *De intellectu*, 119,62–4 Verbeke: 'Here ends the commentary of John the Grammarian or Philoponus or the Alexandrian on Aristotle's chapter on the Intellect in the book *On the Soul*'). The 'chapter on the intellect', of which the colophon speaks, corresponds to our chapters 4–8 of the third book of the *De Anima*, but Philoponus' alleged commentary on it, as translated by Moerbeke, is very different in content and style from the surviving Greek commentary on Book 3. It is, however, very similar to the surviving Greek commentary on Books 1 and 2.[9] This similarity led De Corte to infer that the authentic Philoponan commentary on Book 3 has been replaced at some time in the Greek tradition by the commentary of another author.[10]

De Corte was right about the unity of the Latin commentary on Book 3 with the Greek commentary on Books 1 and 2 but he was wrong about its authorship. It escaped his notice that in most and in the best manuscripts the commentary bears the title 'Notes taken after the manner of schools[11] (*skholikai aposiemeiôseis*) by John the Alexandrian on Aristotle's discourse [Greek *scil.*: *logon*][12] On the Soul from the courses (*sunousiai*) of Ammonius, son of Hermeias, with some (*tinôn*) critical observations (*epistaseis*) of his own'. Such a long title, of course, could not be repeated at the beginning

---

[9] M. De Corte, ed., *Le Commentaire de Jean Philopon sur le Troisieme Livre du « Traité de l'Ame » d'Aristote*, (Liège : Bibliothèque de la Faculté de Philosophie et Lettres de l'Université de Liège, 1934). De Corte gives twenty-eight arguments of style and content (pp. ix–xv) that unite the commentary translated into Latin with the Greek commentary on Books 1 and 2, which De Corte attributes without qualification to Philoponus. Although we will be seeing that this author is not really Philoponus, the homogeneity of the work cannot be doubted. It suffices to recall with De Corte a self-reference made by the author in *De intellectu* 2,7–11 De Corte = 2,27–31 Verbeke, which refers back to *in DA* 2, 266,4–6). Further arguments have been supplied by Charlton, *Philoponus On Aristotle on the Intellect*, pp. 5–6. We can add some further parallels: cf. *in DA* 1, 70,19–25: 'Likewise the soul, too, when it appears in its own light shows what mode of being it has, i.e. a divine, incorporeal and impassive mode of being, yet if it appears in the dark, i.e. in the body and in the affections, we shall see it, as Plato says (cf. *Republic*, 611C7-D7), just as those observing Glaucus the sea-god, observing not his true being as such but seeing the seaweed around him as if it were he himself. I mean the affections or the body and we will believe that the soul is some of those' with *De intellectu*, 53,62–6 Verbeke: 'This is how Plato also taught us to think of the human soul. He says: "We seem to have been seeing it here as some people see the sea-god Glaucus." They do not see its substance, but the things which have grown into its appearance from outside'; and *De intellectu*, 38,99–39,3 Verbeke : 'But to this it may be replied that we ought to interpret what Aristotle says here carefully and thoughtfully with regard to his whole thought and to what he says everywhere about the intellect. If we have shown a thousand times over, quoting Arristotelian texts, that he wants the rational soul to be separate and immortal ...', with *in DA* 2, 246,24–7: 'But we ought to look to the whole idea of the Philosopher and recall the things said about the intellect before. So if he everywhere declares the intellect separable and immortal, we should understand the soul here to be both the vegetative and the non-rational.'

[10] Cf. De Corte, *Le Commentaire de Jean Philopon*, p. ix: 'Our intention is to demonstrate that [...] only the Graeco-Latin translation edited by us corresponds to Philoponus' original Greek lost to this day, and that consequently the Greek text of the Berlin edition is to be attributed to a pseudo-Philoponus'.

[11] *skholikai*, meaning that the notes correspond to the way Aristotle is taught at class, that is, through commenting on successive passages of Aristotle's text.

[12] Hayduck erroneously edits *eis tên Peri Psukhês*, which is not attested in any manuscript. Some manuscripts have mutated *ton*, i.e. *logon*, to *to*.

of each book of the commentary. Indeed, in a manuscript older than Moerbeke's translation, namely the *Meteora, Monê Metamorphôseôs* 536, which has unfortunately lost a great deal of its first and its last quires, we read an abridged title for Book 2: 'school notes and (*skholia kai*) notes (*aposêmeiôseis*) of John of the school of Alexandria on book 2 of Aristotle's On the Soul'. *Skholia kai* is manifestly a corruption of *skholikai*, but the *aposiemeiôseis*, of which the title speaks, must clearly be notes of something, that is, of Ammonius' lectures, which were undoubtedly mentioned in the general title of the commentary in Book 1, nowadays lost. If we conceive of a similar title for book 3 (viz. 'school notes of John of the school of Alexandria on book 3 of Aristotle's On the Soul'), we can easily explain how Moerbeke was led to ascribe his *De intellectu* to Philoponus without any further qualification.

The authenticity of the general title of the commentary, as is testified in the Greek manuscript tradition, cannot be doubted, since it is fully consistent with the titles of other commentaries: Philoponus' commentaries on the *Posterior Analytics* and on *On Coming-to-Be and Perishing* are precisely described in the manuscripts, just as the commentary on the *De Anima*, as 'Notes taken after the manner of schools from the courses of Ammonius, son of Hermeias, with some critical observations of his own.' Therefore, we are forced to admit that in these commentaries Philoponus' *own* thinking is only to *some* extent represented, since these commentaries are explicitly said to contain just *some* critical observations by him. Therefore, Gerard Verbeke, whose edition of the *De intellectu* replaced that of the De Corte, could hardly be right when he decided to enrich his introduction with a chapter on Philoponus' *psychologie et noétique*, a chapter starting as follows:

> The exposition which follows is based on the Prologue and on the two first books of the Greek commentary of Philoponus, and will eventually make it possible to interpret the theory of intellect expounded in the Latin version of Book 3.[13]

It is quite likely that the theory of intellect which Verbeke describes in his book is not Philoponus' own theory but the theory of Philoponus' teacher Ammonius. Indeed, it is not without perplexity that a few pages later Verbeke notes:

> One finds in this commentary an Aristotle much more spiritualist than he was in fact, an Aristotle who foreshadows the philosophy of Plotinus and the Neoplatonists, and in basic agreement with them.[14]

This must be, we may surmise, the Aristotle of the Neoplatonist Ammonius. He further asks:

---

[13] G. Verbeke, *Jean Philopon, Le Commentaire sur le De anima d'Aristote, Traduction de Guillaume de Moerbeke* (Louvain: Publications Universiatires de Louvain / Paris: Éditions Béatrice-Nauwelaerts, 1966), p. xx.
[14] Ibid., p. lxx.

Are there genuinely Christian elements in the doctrine of Philoponus? We have hardly found any such. Insofar as Philoponus allows the doctrine of the pre-existence of the soul and of reincarnation, we should rather ask whether these doctrines were compatible in his mind with Christian faith.

But there is no need to go that far. Insofar as such doctrines are globally accepted by a pagan Platonist, it suffices to simply trust the title of the commentary: what we read in this commentary does not in the main reflect Philoponus' own beliefs but it reflects the beliefs of his teacher Ammonius. Had this commentary been a proper work by Philoponus, it surely would not have been qualified by Philoponus himself as 'notes taken at the courses of Ammonius, son of Hermias'.

We can also adduce the testimony of his other commentaries. In Philoponus' commentary on Aristotle's *Meteorologica*, which is not described as *aposêmeiôseis* and, therefore, is not supposed to reflect Ammonius' lectures, Philoponus refers to his *own* commentary on the fourth book of Aristotle's *Physics* as 'our own writings (*sungrammata*) after the manner of schools on the fourth book of the *Physics*'.[15] Both the commentary on the *Meteorologica* and the commentary on the fourth book of the *Physics* are well known for containing some of the most original thinking of Philoponus.

We have seen so far, just by giving due attention to the testimony of the manuscripts, that the commentary on Books 1 and 2, as well as the part of Book 3 that has been translated into Latin by William of Moerbeke, is not composed by Philoponus in the proper sense but by Philoponus' teacher Ammonius. With the exception of his *epistaseis*, Philoponus' task consisted in editing for publication the notes he had taken at Ammonius' courses.[16] I shall now go on to examine not the titles but the contents of the composite commentary edited by Hayduck. Select examples will suffice to establish three things: (i) that Philoponus published an oral commentary by Ammonius on the *De Anima*, (ii) that he enriched this commentary with critical observations of his own, and (iii) that he himself later commented on book 3 of the *De Anima*.

I. Ammonius' (Oral) Commentary on the *De Anima*

In the commentary on Book 1, the author rejects twice a claim made by Andronicus of Rhodes about *De Interpretatione*'s being spurious because it contains in its very beginning a blind reference to the *De Anima*. While commenting on *De Anima*, the author of the commentary spots two passages to which the alleged blind reference corresponds, as precisely does Ammonius in his commentary on the *De Interpretation*,[17] the unique commentary known to have been published by Ammonius himself.

---

[15] Philoponus, *in Meteor.* 35,18–19.
[16] I discuss in more details Philoponus' role as an editor of Ammonius in a paper given at a conference held at the University of Thessaloniki: *Aristotle and His Commentators: Studies in Memory of Paraskevi Kotzia* (publication forthcoming).
[17] Cf. *in DA* 27,21–9: 'On the basis of this passage we can refute Andronicus of Rhodes, who declared *On Interpretation* spurious: since Aristotle there says that thoughts are passions of the soul, as it is said in *On the Soul*, Andronicus says that this is nowhere stated in *On the Soul*, so that either *On the*

Moreover, the author of the commentary on Books 1 and 2 insists on the harmony between Plato and Aristotle, which is a well known feature of Ammonian exegesis. Compare, for instance, the following passages:

> These are the things that serve to show that even according to Aristotle himself the soul is subject to movement and that Plato was not wrong in assigning self-movement to it. And for a grateful arbitrator of these arguments no battle will be found to exist between these philosophers, except in the words alone. As Aristotle is used to do in many places when he is refuting the apparent meaning [of Plato's sayings], he does so here, too.
>
> *in DA* 95,7–12; trans. van der Eijk modified

> Therefore, Empedocles spoke well about love and strife, and the Pythagoreans about numbers, meaning by that the intelligibles, as did the Platonists speaking about forms. And we have shown that Aristotle openly represents the same things. It is therefore as to the appearance that Aristotle battled against these philosophers, so that we do not accept their doctrines by trusting their appearance.
>
> *in Metaph.* 233,36–40

Soul or *On Interpretation* must be spurious; but *On the Soul* has been agreed to be by Aristotle; therefore, *On Interpretation* is spurious. We reply that in this passage by "*passions peculiar to the soul*" [1.1, 402a9] Aristotle means nothing else than thoughts, so that this is what he referred to in *On Interpretation*' (trans. van der Eijk, adapted), and 45,8–14: 'Look, he has again called thinking a passion. This relates to Andronicus of Rhodes, who declared *On Interpretation* spurious because there Aristotle says that thoughts are passions of the soul, as has been said in *On the Soul*, yet evidently nowhere in *On the Soul* has he called thoughts passions, Andronicus believed. In that case look just at this text, where he says "*Thinking in particular seems to be something peculiar*" [1.1, 403a8], i.e. a peculiar passion. If, then, he says, the soul has a passion peculiar to it, it is thinking' (trans. van der Eijk, adapted), with Ammonius, *in Int.* 5,24–6,33: 'As for the book's being a genuine work of the Philosopher, none of those who studied the writings of Aristotle wished to cast doubt on it, in view of the persuasiveness of its content, the technical character of the observations it transmits (a character quite usual for the Philosopher) and the agreement <of our treatise> with his other courses – except for Andronicus of Rhodes, who was eleventh in succession from Aristotle. When Aristotle heard Aristotle in the prooemium of this book calling thoughts "passions of the soul" and adding "these have been discussed in *On the Soul*", he failed to understand where in the course *On the Soul* the Philosopher called thoughts "passions of the soul" and, thinking it necessary for one of the two courses, this one and *On the Soul*, to be shown to be a counterfeit work of Aristotle, he considered he had to reject this one as spurious, rather than *On the Soul*. It must, however, be understood that often in *On the Soul* the imagination is called a "passive intelligence" by the Philosopher [...]. And he also clearly extends to all the activities of the soul in common the name "passion"; at any rate, he says there that the passions of the soul pose a dilemma as to "whether they are all shared by the one who has them, or whether there is one which is peculiar to the soul itself" [1.1, 403a3–5]. In solving this dilemma he adds: "Of most things [the soul] seems to suffer or to do none without the body, for example becoming angry, taking heart, desiring, sensing in general. But *thinking in particular seems to be something peculiar* (reading *idiôi* with manuscripts GM); and, if it too is an imagination or is not without imagination, not even this could exist without body" [1.1, 403a5–10]. Even before this, in the prooemium of the same course, he says: "We also seek to investigate and to know both the soul's nature and its being, and then all its accidents, of which some seem to be the *passions peculiar to the soul*, while other seem to belong in common to the animals too, because of the soul" [1.1, 402a7–10]' (trans. Blank, adapted).

Now since Plato says that all activity without further qualification is motion, whereas Aristotle says that only the natural activities are motions, it comes out that both the account that says according to Plato that the soul is subject to motion and the account that says according to Aristotle that the soul is not subject to motion are true; their disagreement lies only in the words.

in DA 95,22-6; trans. van der Eijk, modified

It should be noted that the same rationale as to the differentiated use of the word *kinêsis* in Plato and Aristotle is also found, with a similar wording, in Ammonius' pagan student Simplicius.[18] It would be strange indeed to ascribe this rationale not to Ammonius but to Philoponus.

While commenting on Book 2.3, 415a11 ('we shall speak about the theoretical *nous* elsewhere') the commentator explains that Aristotle does not mean the divine *nous* that exists in heavenly bodies, as Alexander of Aphrodisias had believed, but he means the theoretical intellect, as opposed to the practical intellect, of human beings. He considers this statement to be linked to what Aristotle has said in the previous chapter, namely that 'about the intellect and its theoretical power nothing yet has been made clear, but it seems that the intellect is a different kind of soul, a kind that alone (that is, among the parts or powers of soul) can by nature be separated <from the body>, as the eternal is separated from the perishable'.[19] The divine *nous* of the heavenly bodies, however, is not separable in such a way, since heavenly bodies are eternal.[20] It is plain that such an account does not fit into a Christian or creationist account of the universe, as one would expect from Philoponus.

The author of the commentary approves of Aristotle's postponing the examination of the theoretical intellect, because this intellect is a separate form and speaking about separate forms is the task of the theologian:

For as I have said many times, he himself says in the *De partibus animalium* (1.1, 641a32-b10) and in book *Epsilon* of the *Metaphysics* (6.1, 1026a5-6) that it belongs to the student of nature to speak not about all soul but about its parts that are not without matter. Since, then, the theoretical intellect is separate, he reasonably says that there is another account concerning it; for it belongs to the theologian to speak about separate forms. But still, as is his custom, just as towards the end of the *Physics* he brought himself up to the separate cause of natural things and discussed

---

[18] Cf. Simplicius, *in Phys.* 821,20-1: 'The apparent difference of their accounts being of this extent, I wonder whether their disagreement lies only in the names [they use]'. Other concordist passages in the *DA* commentary are the following: 37,18-32; 114,24-8; 116,26-8; 165,28-32.

[19] *DA* 2.2, 413b24-7.

[20] *in DA* 261,10-18: 'Here again he is clearly to be seen separating the intellect and not reckoning it with the other powers of the soul. And here again Alexander says, he is speaking about the divine intellect which is in eternal things. Yet not far off is what he said about it when he said "But concerning the intellect and the power to contemplate nothing is yet evident. But it looks as if it is a different kind of soul, and this alone is capable of being separated." He says the very same thing here too: there he said "nothing is yet evident", and here "another account". But no one would say that those things were said about the divine intellect. For it is not separated from those bodies, since they *are* eternal' (trans. Charlton, very lightly modified).

the unmoved cause,[21] so here too after discussing the other things he will bring himself up to the intellect too.

in DA 261, 27–35; trans. Charlton, modified

Let me first note that, in this case too, the author's reference to the *Physics* is also found with a similar wording in Simplicius:

> But, of course, Aristotle too (i.e. not only Plato) did not stop at nature as being the first or principally productive <cause>, but he himself (i.e. just like Plato) went up to the unmoved cause that moves all things, and he attached all moving things to this cause towards the end of the treatise.
>
> Simplicius, *in Phys.* 8,6–9

The appeal to the specific task of the *phusikos* as a means for resolving exegetical problems is precisely ascribed to Ammonius by Philoponus in the latter's commentary on the fourth book of the *Physics*. Philoponus says in his commentary that Ammonius, who is labelled as 'the philosopher',[22] discarded his idea of the *kenon diastêma* as what *topos* really is on the grounds that such an empty extension is not natural, because it does not have in itself the principle of motion and rest (as any natural thing must have, according to Aristotle's definition of nature); and not being natural, it does not concern the physicist, which is precisely the task assumed by Aristotle in the *Physics*:

> Nevertheless, when we made these points against what Aristotle said about place, the following defence was put forward by the Philosopher (*sc.* Ammonius): being a philosopher of nature, Aristotle discusses those things which exist and are governed by nature; but nature is a principle of motion and rest: so if that is what nature is, whatever things are natural have in themselves a principle of motion and rest. So whatever things do not have in themselves a principle of motion and rest are not natural; and so the physicist will not discuss them. Now, extension of the kind we describe, having no principle of motion and rest in itself (for it does not grow or change or move in place, and does not come into being nor perish), cannot be a natural thing. Therefore, since Aristotle's discourse is concerned with natural things, he now inquires what is the place of natural things, being obviously itself natural. It is reasonable, then, that he denies that an extension such as we describe is the place of natural bodies, whether it exists or not (for it is not natural), and that the only natural place for bodies that he finds among natural things is the boundary of the container according to which it contains the contents.
>
> Philoponus, *in Phys.* 583,13–29; trans. Furley, modified

---

[21] Cf. also *in DA* 20,31–21,7.
[22] Cf. also Philoponus, *in An. Post.* 111,31–112,1: 'The philosopher (*sc.* Ammonius) said that his teacher Proclus objected to Alexander's explanation . . .'.

Philoponus goes on to explain that this is nonsense.[23] There is of course nothing strange in Philoponus' being critical of Ammonius in a commentary which is properly ascribed to him. Philoponus is equally critical of Proclus and of Aristotle in his *Contra Proclum* and *Contra Aristotelem*. But there would be something strange in his being critical of Ammonius in a commentary which is said to reproduce Ammonius' lectures, as is the commentary on the *De Anima*. It is the announced presence of the *epistaseis* that allows us to do away with such a strangeness.

II. Philoponus' *epistaseis* on Ammonius' Commentary on the *De Anima*

What is an *epistasis* and how is it demarcated? It is usually translated as 'observation' but in a commentarial context it properly means 'critical observation' or 'criticism'. That this is the technical sense given to the term by Philoponus can be seen through his use of the related verb *ephistanein* in a passage that gives a first instance of his criticisms of Aristotle's doctrine of place (which are subsequently more fully developed in his so-called Corollary on place):

> It should be pointed out as a criticism to him (*ekeinôi epistateon*, i.e. to Aristotle)[24] that, on the basis of these considerations (212a24–8) as well, it is shown that place is not the limit of the container.
>
> Philoponus, *in Phys.* 592,16–17

The same sense can also be deduced from the following statement of Simplicius:

> The commentator's judgement must be impartial, so that he may neither mischievously seek to prove something well said to be unsatisfactory, nor, if some point should require criticism (*ei ti deoito epistaseôs*), should he be so obstinate as to try to demonstrate that Aristotle is always and everywhere infallible, as if he had enrolled himself in the Philosopher's school.[25]
>
> Simplicius, *in Cat.* 7,26–9; trans. Chase, modified

Despite this statement, Simplicius is nowhere critical of Aristotle. Philoponus, on the contrary, is repeatedly critical not only of Aristotle but also of his fellows and

---

[23] Cf. Philoponus, *in Phys.* 583,30–585,4; see especially 584,1–4: 'But since Aristotle explicitly and continually, both here and in his discussion of the void, attempts to show that there is no extension other than body-extensions, the Philosopher's defense of Aristotle is shown to be fictitious.' (trans. Furley)

[24] K. Algra and J. van Ophuijsen, *Philoponus, On Aristotle Physics 4.1–5* (London: Bristol Classical Press, 2012), wrongly take *ekeinôi* to refer to one of two alternatives interpretations and translate *epistateon* as if it were *sêmeiôteon*: 'With regard to the former alternative it should be noted that ...'.

[25] Cf. also Simplicius, *in Phys.* 791, 32–3: 'Damascius objects to Plotinus (*ephistanei autôi*) that in his teaching he substitutes eternal intellect for eternity' (trans. Urmson) and 795,15–17: 'Damascius, through his love of labour and his sympathy with Iamblichus, did not hesitate to reject many of Proclus' doctrines (*tôn Proklon dogmatôn ephistanein*)'.

predecessors. While publishing Ammonius' lectures on the *Posterior Analytics*, he adds a critical observation, which takes in this case the form of an identifiable textual unity inside the commentary through the contradistinction of *kai phasi ge ... emoi de dokei ...* ('They claim ... I think ...'), about Aristotle's famous dictum 'so goodbye to the Ideas':[26]

> They claim wishing to defend these words of Aristotle that Aristotle himself explicitly proclaims on every occasion that the demiurgic principles (*logoi*) of things are Ideas. For it is he who in the *Metaphysics* says that just as the order[ly arrangement] in a camp does not arise spontaneously, but from the order within the commander, so the order in the cosmos does not arise spontaneously but from the order in the Demiurge (cf. 12.10, 1075a14–15). And <...> that in the doctor who is ill. And it is he himself who says that the demiurgic intellect sees all things when it sees itself, and that intellect insofar as it is a plenitude of forms is also a form (*DA* 3.8, 432a2). Further, he says in *On the Soul* 'those who say that the soul is the place of forms speak rightly' (3.4, 429a27–8) but, they say, it is in regard to those who misunderstand the doctrines concerning the Ideas and think that whiteness subsists by itself and not in the demiurgic *logos*, or think this of a bodiless humanity, as if it had nose and feet and hands and such things, that he was always wont to rebuke the argument about such Ideas. But I think that such a defence is thoroughly unconvincing; for if Plato had posited the Forms as demiurgic *logoi* existing within the Demiurge, Aristotle himself, who everywhere says the same things, would have never objected to this; and he would have pointed out that Plato meant the Ideas to be such, but others misunderstood him. But this is not what Aristotle is up to, here. Rather, it is obvious that he is always doing battle against the doctrine of Forms and not against those who conceive of it incorrectly. For in the *Metaphysics* (cf. 1.9; 10.3, 4–5) he draws out many long refutations of the doctrine. It is related that even while Plato was alive Aristotle directed against him with great courage his refutations of this doctrine.
>
> *in An. Post.* 242,26–243,21; trans. Goldin and Martijn, modified

Philoponus rejects even more straightforwardly the thesis that Aristotle's criticisms of the Platonic doctrine of Ideas are addressed to those who misunderstand it some years later in his *De Aeternitate Mundi Contra Proclum*.[27] But the contrary thesis that Aristotle

---

[26] *An. Post.* 1.22, 83a32: *ta gar eidē khairetōsan*. Not making a distinction between proper commentary of Ammonius and added *epistasis* of Philoponus, K. Verrycken, 'The Development of Philoponus' Thought and its Chronology', in R. Sorabji, ed., *Aristotle Transformed: The Ancient Commentators and Their Influence* (London: Duckworth, 1990), pp. 233–74, especially p. 257, believes that this passage is sign of a partial revision of Philoponus' own commentary on the *Posterior Analytics*.

[27] Philoponus, *Aet.* 29,2–13: 'From these passages we can most certainly see that Aristotle's refutations of Plato are not directed at people who have wrongly understood Plato, which is a fiction created by some more recent commentators out of fear at the disagreement between the [two] philosophers, but rather constitute a rebuttal of the notions of Plato himself. For, if Aristotle had not been attacking Plato's own doctrine on the Forms but, as these commentators claim, that of people who have misunderstood him, he would have specified precisely this at the outset and not have refuted the doctrine of the Forms generally and without qualification' (trans. Share, lightly modified).

was indeed a partisan of the doctrine of Ideas is precisely put forward on the basis of the very same passages in the commentary on the first book of the *De Anima*:

> Some have thought that here he speaks of the Forms, alluding to Plato. But this is not the case. For Aristotle, too, thinks that the genera and species exist prior to the plurality [of individual instances]. At any rate, in the *Metaphysics* he says that, just as the order[ly arrangement] is twofold, the one being in the commander, the other in the soldiers, and that the orderly arrangement in the soldiers is derived from that of the commander (cf. 12.10, 1075a14–15), and health, too, is twofold, the one being in the doctor, the other in the body that is being restored to health, and the health that is in the doctor is productive of that of the body (cf. 11.3, 1061a5–7), likewise the orderly arrangement in the universe has come into being as a result of the orderly arrangement in the Craftsman. Consequently, he also knows the transcendent formal principles of things. Again, in the present treatise he says: 'The active intellect is the things' (cf. 3.5, 430a14–15), and 'those who say that the soul is the place of forms speak rightly' (3.4, 429a27–28). Again, in the *Metaphysics*, when discussing the divine intellect, he says that the forms of all things are present in it; at any rate, he says that when seeing itself it sees all things, and when seeing all things it sees itself. And there are numerous other statements by him that one could quote, which all express the same thought. Therefore the discussion here is not about the forms that are prior to the many, but about the things that come into being later.
>
> in DA 37,18–32; trans. van der Eijk, modified

We need not posit a volte-face of Philoponus, as Koenraad Verrycken once did,[28] in order to account for these contradictory passages. It simply suffices to trust the titles of the manuscripts and ascribe these two passages to different units of the commentaries: whereas the second passage is what Ammonius said in his lectures on *On the Soul*, the first passage is an *epistasis* added by Philoponus to Ammonius' lectures on the *Posterior Analytics*. And since the *epistasis* is made in the commentary on the *Posterior Analytics* and not in the commentary on the *De Anima*, we may conclude that the latter commentary has been published by Philoponus earlier than the former.

Philoponus' emphasis on Aristotle's contradicting Plato with great courage (*karterôtata*) even when Plato was still alive, might even be an indication of his failing to do so, when he was a pupil of Ammonius. This seems to be equally suggested by the incident related by Philoponus in his commentary on the *Physics*, where Ammonius' response to his objection seems to have led him to acquiescence.[29] This would imply in its turn that Ammonius was not alive, when Philoponus published Ammonius' lectures. It would be strange, indeed, if the famous Ammonius, the holder of the chair of philosophy in Alexandria, entitled his pupil to publish commentaries that were in

---

[28] See Verrycken (n. 26 above).
[29] See the passage quoted above, p. 400. Philoponus expressed to Ammonius only his objection and his response to Ammonius' response was not made until he himself lectured on Book 4 of the *Physics*.

places overtly critical of him. At any rate, Ammonius was certainly dead when Asclepius published his master's lectures on the *Metaphysics* under the title 'Comments on Aristotle's *Metaphysics* made by Asclepius from the voice of Ammonius son of Hermeias': Ammonius is called by Asclepius *hêrôs*, a word which praisingly qualifies a dead person.[30] This provides us with a simple but perfectly sufficient explanation of why these commentaries, contrary to those published by other pupils anonymously,[31] mention in their titles the names of the *reportatores*: Asclepius and Philoponus, who were presumably Ammonius' assistants and best pupils, were asked to produce reliable publications of their dead master's teachings.

As specified in its title, the commentary on the *De Anima* also contains some *epistaseis* by Philoponus. We can readily spot one such passage in the commentary on book 2, where Philoponus speaks anew of an explication put forward by 'the philosopher', that is, Ammonius:

> Let that be our arbitration on that. But someone might plausibly raise this difficulty, that if seeing does not occur by the emission of sight-streams, but the activities of the objects of sight travel to the eye, how do we get to know the distances between us and the things seen? For if the activities travel as far as the eye, both things near and things far should be seen in the same way; if, however, we get to know the distances of the objects of sight, clearly the images, that is, the activities of the objects of sight do not travel to us. And how could one even imagine activities of shapes and colours travelling through the air? But to this the Philosopher said that the activities do not travel as far as the eye but, in a word, all the air is filled with all objects of sight. But this is even more difficult and more absurd. For in the first place the same difficulty still remains. For if the air generally is filled with the presentations of objects of sight, how do we get to know their distances? What is extremely far and what is near should appear in the same way. And not even the furthest things should escape perception if the air is filled with all presentations. But perhaps to this he could have replied that, just as those who suppose sight-streams say that they are weaker as they proceed further, and that is why they do not see what is far off, we suppose the same about the activities, that they are weaker when they proceed a long way. But what could he have replied to this? If all the air is filled with presentations, what need is there to make the supposition that the activities go in a straight line? For we ought to see those that are not far from us and, in a word, we ought to see all that we are able to see, wherever we look, if

---

[30] Asclepius, *in Metaph.* 92,29–31: 'The hero Ammonius, who was the pupil of Proclus and the teacher of me Asclepius, said that the Pythagoreans called the ideas numbers in a symbolic way.' On the rank of 'hero' within the pagan pantheon, see L. Brisson, 'Le commentaire comme prière destinée à assurer le salut de l'âme', in M.-O. Goulet-Cazé, ed., *Le commentaire entre tradition et innovation* (Paris: Vrin, 2000), pp. 329–53. A 'hero' is an intelligible soul that has been freed from the human body. That these commentaries were posthumously published is equally suggested by the use of past tense, which can be compared with the use of present tense in Ammonius' anonymously published commentary (see next note) on *An. Pr.* 23,8–9: 'This is Alexander's explication; the great philosopher (i.e. Ammonius), who explicates the passage in a deeper and more precise way, says (*legei*) that …'.

[31] As is Ammonius' commentaries on the *Categories* (CAG 4.4) and on the *Prior Analytics* (CAG 4.6).

the air is filled with presentations. Why, then, do we not see the heavens and every
object of sight without gazing at them?

in DA 334,30–335,12; trans. Charlton, lightly modified

This passage is part of a quite long *epistasis* about vision (334,30–355,11). Ammonius contended that, when seeing, the air is filled with the images of the objects of sight. Philoponus finds this contention strange and claims that the activities of the objects of sight move through the air without its being affected and they imprint the colours and shapes of the sight-objects on the sense-organ.[32] What is important for our present purpose is to point out that Philoponus uses conditionals (*phêseien an*) to describe Ammonius' *possible* answers to his queries: his questions that were never really put to Ammonius. This indicates anew that Ammonius was not alive when Philoponus published his lectures adding some critical observations of his own.

We may, then, suggest the following evolution in Philoponus. A qualified grammarian and a skilful pupil, Philoponus was assigned by Ammonius the task of transcribing his lectures. When Ammonius died, Philoponus was commissioned (as Asclepius wascommissioned too), possibly by some authorities or by Ammonius' relatives, to produce reliable publications of Ammonius' teachings. By then a teacher of philosophy himself, Philoponus occasionally added to these publications some *epistaseis* of his own, that is, critical observations on Ammonius' lectures. It has not been noted that, in all probability, this very type of enriched commentary is an invention of Philoponus. The commentaries on the *On the Soul* (survived partly in Greek, partly in Latin), the commentary on the *Posterior Analytics*, the commentary on the *On Coming-to-Be and Perishing* and, as I try to show elsewhere,[33] the commentary on the *Prior Analytics* and the commentary on the first two books of the *Physics* precisely consist in publications of Ammonius' lectures enriched with some *epistaseis* by Philoponus. It is reasonable to assume that it was his gradual distanciation from Ammonius' authority and the latter's defence of Aristotle that progressively led Philoponus to his criticisms of Aristotle. For Philoponus was about to conceive of a further innovation: he would, of course, freely use what was well said by Ammonius and by other commentators on what Aristotle meant and, when they failed to do so, he, as a good commentator, would explain what Aristotle really meant; but, when Aristotle failed to explain how things really are, Philoponus would moreover express his own judgment.[34] This new methodology is programmatically stated in his *own* commentary on the *Categories*:

The commentator should neither, on account of good will, try to make sense of what is badly said as though receiving it from a tripod, nor should he, on account of hatred, take in a bad sense what is said beautifully. He should rather try to be a

---

[32] Cf. *in DA* 335,12–30.
[33] See my paper mentioned in n. 16.
[34] I offer a more detailed account of this passage in P. Golitsis, *Les Commentaires de Simplicius et de Jean Philopon à la Physique d'Aristote: Tradition et innovation* (Berlin: De Gruyter, 2008), pp. 197–200.

dispassionate judge of what is said and he should first explain the meaning of the ancient text and interpret the doctrines of Aristotle, and then go on to express his own judgement [on how things are].

Philoponus, *in Cat.* 6,30–5

The most prominent examples of Philoponus' methodology are the so-called Corollaries on place and on void of the commentary on the fourth book of the *Physics*, as well as the refutation of Aristotle's fifth element in his commentary on the *Meteorology*. But we may now return to the disputed Greek commentary on the third book of the *On the Soul*, so as to point to an eloquent exemplification of someone's being, as Philoponus wants it, a 'dispassionate judge' (*kritês apathês*) of Aristotle.

III. Philoponus' Commentary on the Third Book of the *De Anima*

The disputed author of the commentary on Book 3 overtly criticizes Aristotle as to what it is that perceives the activities of the senses: it is the 'attentive part' of the rational soul, he says, and not the particular senses themselves, as Aristotle believed:

> So Aristotle does not speak rightly but, as we said, it belongs to the attentive part of the soul to get to know the activities of the senses. And that this is so can be seen from the things themselves. For when reason is engrossed with something, even if sight sees, we do not know that it has seen because reason is engrossed. And later, when reason comes to itself and, though not seeing the friend, even now says that it has seen him, it is as if it were retaining a small imprint of the thing seen and, though it was engrossed, now having recovered it said that it saw. So it belongs to reason to say 'I saw'.
>
> *in DA* 466,27–35; trans. Charlton, lightly modified

At the end of his exposition, the commentator utters a verdict:

> We are not paying our nursling's dues to Aristotle (*tropheia ouk apodidomen Aristotelei*) but declare that his account is false.
>
> *in DA* 467,4–5

Some pages earlier, however, while discussing an argument put forward by Themistius about the number of the senses, the commentator had given the opposite verdict:

> Paying our nursling's dues to Aristotle (*tropheia tôi Aristotelei nemontes*) we shall show that this proof too belongs to him.
>
> *in DA* 450,20

Now, the classicizing expression *tropheia apodidonai tini*, which is first found in Hesiod as *threptêria apodidonai tois tokeusi* (meaning 'paying our dues to our parents for bringing us up'),[35] stems from the classical rhetoric tradition and in particular from Isocrates, who used it to remind the Athenians of their debt towards their fatherland.[36] Quite tellingly, however, it is found in a philosophical context only in the disputed commentary on the third book of the *De Anima* and in Olympiodorus' commentary on the *Meteorologica*:

> But the great philosopher, our own ancestor, paying his nursling's dues to Aristotle (*tropheia aponemôn Aristotelei*), he frees him from this absurdity.
> Olympiodorus, *in Meteor.* 175,14-15

'This absurdity' is connected with the claim, made by Alexander of Aphrodisias, that for Aristotle all winds move according to the rotation of the universe, that is, from east to west, and 'the ancestor and great philosopher' who rescues Aristotle from the absurd idea to want to make all winds east winds, can be no other but Ammonius. Since it is impossible that Olympiodorus is the Christian author of the commentary on the *DA* 3, and it is rather implausible that he took the expression *tropheia apodidonai tôi Aristotelei* from the latter, granted that the commentary on *DA* 3 is addressed to Christian students,[37] we may ascribe the expression to Ammonius himself, who used it to mean 'pay our dues to Aristotle by setting him free from accusations made against him'.[38] Following the example of his great ancestor and master, Olympiodorus pays his dues to Aristotle twice in his commentary on the *Meteorologica*.[39] The author of the disputed commentary, however, differentiating himself from the tradition of 'the great philosopher', who is dispassionately called by him *Ammônois ho philosophpos*,[40] once pays his dues to Aristotle and once not; he acts, we may say, as a 'dispassionate judge'.[41]

Let us now call the testimony of a cross-reference, which has been left unnoticed and which points to Philoponus' being the above 'dispassionate judge'. It concerns the distinction between the formal cause of being something, i.e. its essence, and the being of something, i.e. the compound of matter and form, which are respectively expressed through the use of dative and accusative case-inflections construed with *einai*. As the author of the disputed commentary has repeatedly explained, there is no difference between using the dative or the accusative, when it comes to immaterial beings:

---

[35] Cf. Hesiod, *Opera et dies* 188.
[36] Cf. Isocrates, *Archidamus* 108,1. Cf. also Lysias, *Epitaphius* 70,5.
[37] As is suggested by a tacit quotation of the *Genesis* in *in DA* 547,8-14. In *in DA* 527,30-1, the author equally refers to the 'pious doctrines' (*ta eusebê dogmata*), meaning the doctrines of the Scriptures.
[38] There is, of course, the possibility that Olympiodorus was the first to use this expression and that the author of the *in DA* 3 was somehow familiar with Olympiodorus' exegetical rhetoric. If so, his use of the expression has also a tone of irony, which would hardly be surprising for Philoponus.
[39] Cf. Olympiodorus, *in Meteor* 5,19-23 and 239,14-28.
[40] *in DA* 473,10.
[41] Cf. also *in DA* 544,26-31, where Philoponus points dispassionately to an internal contradiction in Aristotle's work. I thank Carlos Steel for drawing my attention to this passage.

It has been said both in [our teaching of] the *Categories* and [of] the *Physics*[42] that 'being this' (*tode*) is one thing and 'to be this' (*tôide*) is another. 'Being this' signifies the two together, that which is form with matter, such as water or a magnitude, whereas 'to be this' signifies the form alone without the matter, such as the being of water, the being of a magnitude. In the case of things that are in matter there is this <double> way of signifying, but in the case of things that are immaterial, 'being this' and 'to be this' are the same, for example in the case of God or a mathematical point or the like: both case-inflections signify the same thing.

in DA 528,34–529,4; trans. Charlton, modified

This explication of the Aristotelian use of accusative and dative case inflections construed with *einai*, which might seem banal, seems to have originated in Ammonius' lectures: it is found without the formalization made through the demonstratives *tode* and *tôide* in Ammonius' commentary on the *Categories* (as published by an anonymous pupil), in his commentary on the *Metaphysics* (as published by Asclepius), where the most relevant discussion is made by Aristotle, as well as in the *De intellectu*:

And why didn't he say 'being an animal' (*zôion*) but he said 'to be an animal' (*zôiôi*)? We reply that the things are characterized either from their matter or from their form or from their composite, that is, from their matter and their form; if, then, he had said 'being an animal', he would have signified the matter and the form, but having said 'to be an animal' he signified that in virtue of which a thing is characterized, that is, the form.

Ammonius, *in Cat.* 21,9–15

Having said that, he further asks whether saying 'being an animal' and 'to be an animal', or saying 'being good' and 'to be good', or saying 'being a soul' and 'to be a soul' is the same thing (cf. Aristotle, *Metaph.* 7.6, 1031a31-b3). And generally, as has been said in [our teaching of] the *Categories*, when applied to simple things, 'being an animal' and 'to be an animal' is the same, that is, when applied to simple substances, and 'being a soul' and 'to be a soul' is the same. But when applied to the

---

[42] It might not be unnecessary to point out that it is not the *Categories* (or the *Physics*) itself but a teaching of the *Categories* (and of the *Physics*) that is here meant. For a self-evident case see Philoponus, *in Phys.* 705,20–4: 'He says "exoteric arguments" in order to contrast the demonstrative arguments presented to academic audiences with the ones based on received opinions and plausible considerations. It has also been stated in [our teaching of] the *Categories* that those arguments are exoteric that are not demonstrative, and are addressed not to the real [philosophers] in the audience but to ordinary people, and are based on plausible considerations' (trans. Broadie, completed), which matches perfectly Philoponus, *in Cat.* 4,15–22. Ammonius, for his part, speaks of 'those who understand superficially'; cf. Ammonius, *in Cat.* 4,22–7: 'They are called popular because Aristotle wrote [them] for those who understand superficially. The philosopher deliberately used a clearer style in these works and his proofs are not so much demonstrative as they are plausible, [deriving] from received opinions. The others are called school [works], since they would have to be listened to attentively by one who is serious and in fact a genuine lover of philosophy' (trans. Marc Cohen and Matthews).

human being, it is not the same any more, because the human being is constituted by matter and form, so that it is not the same thing to say 'being a human being' and 'to be a human being'.

Asclepius [Ammonius], *in Metaph.* 389,26–33

He spoke similarly in the *Categories* (cf. *Cat.* 1a5), because animal is one thing, what it is to be animal another, and man is one thing, what it is to be man another.

Philoponus [Ammonius], *De intellectu*, 23,28 Verbeke[43]

It is also found in Philoponus' own commentary on the *Categories*:

This is why Aristotle, here too, wishing to give the definition in terms of form, did not say 'what being an animal (*zôion*) is for each of them' (for this signifies the composite, i.e. the matter and the form) but he said 'what it is to be an animal (*zôiôi*) for each of them', i.e. what it is in virtue of which each of them is an animal, so as to make it clear that the definition is of form; for they are animals in virtue of this.

Philoponus, *in Cat.* 23,8–13

And, quite revealingly, the distinction between dative and accusative case-inflections is explicated and put forward by Philoponus in his commentary on the *Physics* too, where it helps to illustrate Aristotle's argument that if the infinite is a substance and a single principle, as some people hold, then it must be simple, and if it is simple, then 'infinite' and 'being infinite' will be the same thing, which means that each part of the infinite will be itself infinite, which is tantamount to the absurdity that one infinite is many infinities:

For in each of the compounds 'being this' (*tode*) is one thing and 'to be this' (*tôide*) is another, as has been said also in [our teaching of] the *Categories* (for 'being this' signifies the compound, as when I say 'being an animal', but 'to be an animal' signifies the form in virtue of which the being is present to the animal); but in the case of simple entities it is the same thing to say 'being a soul' and 'to be a soul' (for not even in its definition can it be divided into more), and to say 'being an intellect' and 'to be an intellect'. If, then, the nature of the infinite is such that 'being infinite' is for it the same as 'to be infinite', every part of it will be infinite ...

Philoponus, *in Phys.* 414,20–7; trans. Edwards, modified

---

[43] Verbeke, unlike De Corte, seems to miss the causal sense of *quia* (*hoti*) and wrongly takes 'aliud est ... homini esse' to by a quotation of Aristotle. The Greek should be rendered as following: *houtôs ephê kai en Katêgoriais, hoti allo esti to zôion kai allo esti to zôiôi einai kai anthrôpon einai kai anthrôpôi einai*. The very same content is found in Elias (David), *in Cat.* 144,20–1: *Allo estin eipein zôiôi einai kai zôion einai kai anthrôpôi einai kai anthrôpon einai*. I thank Mossman Roueché for drawing my attention to these passages.

Let us recapitulate. The author of the commentary on the third book of the *De Anima* tells us that he has explained twice, once in his teaching of the *Categories* and once in his teachings of the *Physics*, that 'being' construed with the accusative case and 'being' construed with the dative case mean different things, when they are applied to material or compound realities. Philoponus explains *both* in his teaching of the *Categories* and in his teaching of the *Physics* that being construed with the accusative case and being construed with the dative case mean different things, when they are applied to compound realities. A sceptic might neglect the formalization made through the use of the demonstratives *tode* and *tôide*, which is only found in the disputed commentary on the *DA* 3 and in Philoponus' commentary on the *Physics*, and not accept Philoponus' authorship for the former on the assumption that such an explication could be made by any philosopher who was familiar with Ammonius' teaching. But the same sceptic will have to accept that this philosopher, just like Philoponus, made this explication in the same terms while explicating the same two texts. That such a *persona duplicata* is unnecessary is shown by Simplicius, who was a pupil of Ammonius but who does not say a word about this distinction in his commentary on the *Categories* and who, even more significantly, in his commentary on the *Physics* articulates Aristotle's argument against the infinite's being a substance in the same way as Philoponus does, stating that *apeiron einai* and *apeirôi einai* will be the same thing but without explicating the difference between the use of accusative and dative case-inflections.[44] This suggests that the two commentators made use of the same source for reconstructing Aristotle's argument, apparently Ammonius' lectures on the *Physics*, and that Philoponus explicated anew for his own audience the difference between *tode einai* and *tôide einai* out of his own initiative. Later, while lecturing on the third book of the *De Anima*, he recalled having made the same distinction twice, namely in his lectures on the *Categories* and on the third book of the *Physics*. We do not know whether he also lectured on the first two books of the *De Anima*. But the possibility that he only lectured on Book 3, which I think is true, should come as no surprise; we know that he also commented separately (and selectively) on different books of the *Physics*.[45]

We may now return to the doctrine of the attentive part of the soul and properly grasp the irony that emerges from the following passage of the commentary on *DA* 3:

> But more recent interpreters neither tremble (*kataidesthentes*) at Alexander's frown nor pay heed to Plutarch, but pushing away even Aristotle himself they have devised a newer interpretation: they say that it belongs to the attentive part of the rational soul to lay hold of the activities of the senses.
>
> *in DA* 464,30–4; trans. Charlton, lightly modified

---

[44] Cf. Simplicius, *in Phys.* 473,11–24.
[45] Philoponus, *in Phys.* 3, 458,30–1, and *in Phys.* 4, 639,7–9 and 762,7–9, refer back to Philoponus' (lost) commentary on *Phys.* 8.

At first, it sounds as if the author of the commentary was a traditionalist, who condemned novelty[46] and criticized the modern interpreters.[47] In reality, however, he sides with them:

> We agree with these interpreters that there is not a sixth sense which gets to know [that we see and hear]. Not, however, because the same sense sees and knows that it sees, but because this belongs to the rational part of the soul, and of this, to the attentive.
>
> *in DA* 465,31–4; trans. Charlton

The apparent criticism put forward in the first passage is in reality a fake criticism and makes a fine intertextual play with a statement made by Philoponus in his commentary on the *Physics*, as is to be seen through the parallel use of the participle (*kat*)*aidesthentes*:

> Up to this point Aristotle's argument proceeds from the inequality of the speed of moving things compared with that through which their movement occurs, arguing that it would not be possible, if there were a void, for motion to occur through it; but anyone who has the goal of arriving at the truth in all cases, let him gather all his power, lest through the harshness and obscurity of Aristotle's arguments he misses his goal. It is better perhaps first to go through the whole argument about the void, and then take up each of the arguments from the beginning and enquire what truth or falsity is in it, not fearing anything (*aidesthentas*),[48] and not putting the reputation of this man before the truth.
>
> Philoponus, *in Phys.* 650,27–651,4; trans. Huby, modified

Indeed, Aristotle's authority is repudiated more than once in the commentary on the *DA* 3:

> But we say to this: 'You argue badly, Aristotle'!
>
> *in DA* 464,13–14

> We, however, say on Homer's behalf: 'O Aristotle, you have understood the distich ill'!
>
> *in DA* 486,22–23

Such apostrophes match perfectly well with Philoponus' spirit, who has admirably written in his *De Aeternitae Mundi Contra Proclum*:

---

[46] Novelty (*kainoprepeia*) was an exegetical 'sin' for Simplicius; see P. Hoffmann, 'Simplicius' Polemics', in R. Sorabji, ed., *Philoponus and the Rejection of the Aristotelian Science* (London: Duckworth, 1987), pp. 57–83.
[47] According to Lautner, 'Philoponus, in *De anima* 3: Quest for an author', p. 516, such a recent commentator was Damascius.
[48] Cf. also Philoponus, *contra Proclum* 29,5–6: '... which is a fiction created by some more recent commentators out of fear (*aidesthentes*) at the disagreement between the [two] philosophers'.

> So the hypothesis regarding an incorporeal and formless matter has been shown to be a baseless fiction and unproven assumption, even if ten thousand Platos and the rest of the roll-call of the ancients had advanced this view regarding it. Indeed, we shall decline to believe anything that lacks rational proof: 'if you don't hear yourself saying something', says Plato (*Alc. I* 114E7–9), 'you should never believe someone else when they say it'.
>
> Philoponus, Aet. 445,7–14; trans. Share

Philoponus' denial of the existence of unformed matter in his *Contra Proclum*, composed in 529, allows us to date the commentary on *DA* 3 before the *Contra Proclum*, since the existence of unformed matter is accepted in the former work.[49]

To conclude: we should discard Stephanus as a possible author of the *in DA* 3, which is an attribution depending on a Byzantine addition onto a manuscript with no title, and reascribe this commentary to Philoponus on grounds of a self-reference, exegetical attitude, and general style.[50] This commentary, possibly through the initiative of a pupil who recorded it, replaced Ammonius' commentary on Book 3, as previously published by Philoponus, thus allowing two different editions to reach Byzantium: Philoponus' edition of Ammonius lectures and the composite edition in which Ammonius' lectures on Book 3 was replaced by those of Philoponus. The second edition was that copied by D¹, whereas D³, who added the words '*biblion triton apo phônes stephanou*', had only access to the first edition.

---

[49] Cf. *in DA* 543,29–31: 'For this thing, magnitude, is the first form that comes along before all other forms to formless matter: first it is made quantitative and then after that it is made qualitative.' (trans. Charlton)

[50] We should be aware, of course, that questions of style when dealing with commentaries depend very much on the type of commentary; *in DA* 3 is, as it seems, the only commentary *apo phonês Philoponou*.

16

Mixture in Philoponus: An Encounter with a Third Kind of Potentiality[1]

Frans A. J. de Haas

From Antiquity onwards readers of Aristotle's *De Generatione et Corruptione* (*GC*) have struggled with the notion of potentiality that is the foundation of Aristotle's theory of mixture. In *GC* 1.10, 327b22–31 Aristotle claims that ingredients somehow remain present in the resulting mixture in potentiality (*dunamei*). Only in this way, he explains, is it possible to extract the ingredients from the mixture and to restore them to their previous being in actuality (*energeiai*). But what does it mean for ingredients to exist in potentiality if a mixture (*mixis*) is a genuine unity sharply to be distinguished from a mere aggregate (*sunthesis*) as Aristotle stipulates in the same chapter? Do the ingredients not simply perish, so that Aristotle has recourse to a mysterious kind of potentiality only to meet his requirement that the ingredients can be extracted from the mixture again? The problem gains momentum when we realise that Aristotle's theory of mixture is crucial to his view of the constitution of the physical world. According to Aristotle each and every composite in the sublunary realm is a mixture of all four elements.[2] The homeomerous materials, such as blood, bile, bone, and flesh consist in such a mixture; they in turn make up the anhomeomerous parts of sublunary substances, such as face and hands. Without the theory of mixture, therefore, the material composition of every entity over and above the elements would remain completely unaccounted for.

This article first appeared as 'Mixture in Philoponus. An encounter with a third kind of potentiality' by Frans A. J. de Haas in J.M.M.H. Thijssen and H.A.G. Braakhuis (eds), *The Commentary Tradition on Aristotle's* De Generatione et Corruptione, *Ancient, Medieval and Early Modern* (1999), pp. 21-46 © Brepols Publishers, Turnhout, Belgium, 1999, reproduced with permission.

[1] This paper has much profited from discussions with audiences at the Universities of Amsterdam and Groningen, as well as from the insightful comments of Richard Sorabji, Sylvia Berryman, and my colleagues at the Utrecht University Department of Philosophy: Jaap Mansfeld, Keimpe Algra, Cees Leijenhorst, and Irma Croese. Over the past three years my research was supported in turn by the Foundation for Research in the Fields of Philosophy and Theology (SFT), subsidised by the Netherlands Organisation for Scientific Research (NWO); The Niels Stensen Foundation; and at present the Royal Netherlands Academy of Arts and Sciences.
[2] See Aristotle, *GC* 2.7, 334b16–18; 2.8 *passim*.

In a rather neglected Renaissance study of this problem, Jacopo Zabarella's *De mistione*,³ we find a neat classification of the solutions its author has found in his sources:

1. the substantial forms of the elements are preserved integrally, but the basic qualities are reduced (cap. II: Avicenna),⁴
2. both the forms and the qualities are preserved in reduced actuality, which explains in what sense the elements cease to be in favour of the *forma misti* (cap. III: Averroes),⁵
3. both the forms and the qualities perish in the mixture and a new form and a new quality are generated, which exhibit only a degree of similarity with the original forms and qualities (cap. IV: Duns Scotus),⁶
4. the forms perish entirely, but the qualities are preserved in reduced actuality, which is apparent from the fact that their potencies (*vires* or *virtutes*) are found in the mixture (cap. V: Marsilius of Inghen,⁷ Thomas Aquinas,⁸ Aegidius Romanus,⁹ Ludovicus Buccaferreus,¹⁰ etc.).

---

³ The *De mistione* is contained in Jacobus Zabarella, *De rebus naturalibus libri XXX. In Aristotelis libros De anima* (Frankfurt, 1606-7; repr. Frankfurt, 1966).
⁴ Cf. Avicenna, *Liber tertius naturalium de generatione et corruptione* (ed. Van Riet), cap. 7: *Capitulum de destructione cuiusdam novae opinionis in mixtione elementorum*. The action and passion of the elementary qualities presupposes the actual presence of the elements themselves, whose essences should not be identified with the activities they give rise to.
⁵ Cf. Averroes, *Commentarium medium in Aristotelis GC* (contained in *Aristotelis opera cum Averrois commentaria* (Venice, 1562-74; repr. Frankfurt, 1962), vol. 5) comm. 82-90 (pp. 86-94); cf. the *Paraphrasis*, pp. 392-3, and *in Cael.* Comm. 67 (pp. 227-8).
⁶ Cf. Duns Scotus, *Reportata Parisiensia Super Sententiis* lib. 2, dist. 15, q. un. (ed. Vivès, vol. 23): *Utrum maneant elementa in mixto*. Here Scotus explicitly opposes both Avicenna and Averroes by insisting that pluralities are never to be posited unnecessarily, *numquam sunt plura ponenda sine necessitate*: there is only a single *forma mixti* present in the compound. The forms of the elements merely exist *in virtute* in the sense in which any higher order form (e.g. rational soul) subsumes lesser forms (e.g. vegetative and sensitive soul) in a new unity, with the lesser forms surviving neither integrally (Avicenna) nor in reduced actuality (Averroes).
⁷ Cf. Marsilius, *Quaestiones in libros de generatione et corruptione* (Venice, 1505; repr. Frankfurt, 1970), lib. 1, q. 22 *Utrum elementa maneant formaliter in mixto*, esp. p. 95ʳᵃ. Cf. in the same volume Albert of Saxony, *Quaestiones in libros de generatione et corruptione* lib. 1, q. 19, esp. p. 145ᵛ.
⁸ Cf. Thomas Aquinas, *De mixtione elementorum*, in vol. 43 of the Leonine edition (Rome, 1976).
⁹ Cf. Aegidius Romanus, *Commentaria in libros de generatione et corruptione* (Venice, 1505; repr. Frankfurt, 1970), esp. comm. 90. This line of argument can also be found in Boethius of Dacia, *Quaestiones de generatione et corruptione*, ed. Sajó (Hauniae, 1972), vol. 5, pars I, q. 52b.
¹⁰ Cf. Ludovicus Buccaferreus, *In duos libros de generatione & corruptione Aristotelis commentarius* (Venice, 1571), textus 82 ff., pp. 122 ff., see esp. p. 124 for the potency which is called an intermediate potency, *potentia quadam quae dicitur potentia media* being explicitly attributed to 'Johannes' sc. Philoponus with whom Buccaferreus claims he is going to dissent. He deals with the question *An elementa remaneant in mixtione secundum eorum substantiam* on pp. 132b ff. with his own opinion on pp. 141v-142r. Buccaferreus defends the opinion that in a mixture all forms, both substantial and accidental, perish. The elements remain only with respect to their primary qualities in a single *complexio*. Rather indiscriminately, he sides with almost every predecessor who stated that the elements remain not *formaliter* but merely *virtualiter* in any sense of the term. All in all Buccaferreus seems to have had a different approach to our problem from Zabarella and therefore he distributes his ancient and medieval predecessors differently. This is not the place to compare their accounts of mixture in more detail.

As it turns out, the second view is the one Zabarella himself supports. Hence this view is most elaborately discussed and defended in chapters 7–13 of the *De mistione*. In chapter 10 Zabarella claims that his view is supported by 'the Greek commentators', to wit Alexander's *De mixtione*[11] and Philoponus' *in GC*.[12] As we shall see, Zabarella's presentation of his sources is not to be trusted entirely. Even if we assume he had access to the original sources the wish to produce ancient authorities for his own position may have influenced his judgement.

A first glance at the four positions reveals that unlike Aristotle they all distinguish between the *forms* of the ingredients and their *qualities*. Moreover, they speak of 'reduction' or 'reduced actuality' of forms and/or qualities where Aristotle used the term 'in potentiality' to describe how the ingredients are preserved in the mixture. This paper will focus on the background of these two characteristics of Zabarella's classification. Why and how did the distinction between forms and qualities become relevant to the problem of mixture, and what does it mean for a form or quality to be preserved in 'reduced actuality'?

Zabarella points to Alexander (fl. 205 CE) and Philoponus (± 485–570 CE) as his ancient sources for the view he favours. Here I shall focus mainly on Philoponus' *in GC*, which is still influential in modern times,[13] with a brief look at Alexander as a source of inspiration for Philoponus, and a more elaborate look at Proclus and Simplicius who provide a Neoplatonic alternative to Philoponus' view of mixture. First, however, a survey of the relevant statements in Aristotle is called for.

---

[11] Alexander's *De mixtione* (ed. I. Bruns, Supplementum Aristotelicum 2.2 (Berlin: Reimer, 1892), pp. 213-38) is an independent treatise attacking the Stoic theory of mixture and defending Alexander's own Peripatetically inspired concept of mixture. For a translation and commentary see R. B. Todd, *Alexander of Aphrodisias on Stoic Physics: A Study of the De mixtione with Preliminary Essays, Text, Translation, and Commentary* (Leiden: Brill, 1976).

[12] Eiteded by H. Vitelli (CAG 14.2). Zabarella (1533–89) may have had access to the Aldine edition of the Greek text of this commentary (Venice, 1527, with a preface by Andreas Ausulanus), which was reprinted with slight variations. In the Aldine edition Philoponus' commentary is conveniently combined with Alexander's *De mixtione* in a single volume: *Ioannes grammaticus in libros de generatione et interitu. Alexander Aphrodisiensis in meteorologica. Idem de mixtione*. According to Vitelli, p. x, this edition was perhaps based on (a descendant of) the inferior manuscript Marcianus Ven. 232 (= T) dating from the fourteenth century. Zabarella may also have used the Latin translation of Philoponus' commentary by Hieronymus Bagolinus of Verona (Venice, 1549 and reprints), which closely follows the Aldine text. However, Zabarella's Latin technical vocabulary is entirely different from Bagolini's. For example, for *eilikrinôs* Zabarella has *perfecte* throughout, whereas Bagolini prefers *syncere*; for *kekolasmenos* Zabarella has *obfuscatus, impuratus, incompletus, imperfectus* where Bagolini prefers *temperatum, castigatum*; for *tas huperbolas kolazei monon* Zabarella has *frangere mutuo excellentias suas* where Bagolini translates *excessus domet solum*. Hence, it seems likely that Zabarella gives his own rendering of the Greek text – whether he knew the Bagolini translation or not.

[13] Cf. H. H. Joachim, *Aristotle On Coming-to-Be and Passing-Away* (Oxford: Clarendon Press, 1922), p. ix: 'The commentary of Philoponos is very valuable as an aid to the interpretation of Aristotle's treatise, and I have used it freely in my notes'; C. J. F. Williams, *Aristotle's De Generatione et Corruptione* (Oxford: Clarendon Press, 1982), index s.v. 'Philoponus'.

Aristotle

How and *why* did Aristotle introduce the potentiality of mixed ingredients?[14] It serves as the solution to a problem raised at the beginning of chapter 1.10 of the *De Generatione et Corruptione*, 327a34-b6. Aristotle tells us that some people[15] claim that mixture does not exist. In the sample case[16] of a mixture of two ingredients

1. either the two ingredients are preserved unaltered (*Preservation*), or
2. one of the two perishes because it is overcome by the other (*Domination*), or
3. both perish (*Corruption*).

The opponents point out that in the case of Preservation it makes no sense to speak of a *mixture* of the ingredients because this state is indistinguishable from the unmixed state. The case of Domination is a case of generation & corruption instead of mixture, and violates the principle that all mixed ingredients should be on an equal footing in the mixture. In the case of Corruption it makes no sense to speak of a mixture *of these ingredients* since both of them have perished in the process. Hence mixture does not exist.

If Aristotle wants to hold onto the notion of mixture (which he does), it seems fair to assume that he will try to show *both* (I) that mixture does not collapse into generation and/or corruption, neither in part (against 2) nor in whole (against 3), *and* (II) that mixture consists in a genuine change of the mixables (against 1). Indeed, in *GC* 1.10, 327b6-10 Aristotle announces that the problem set out earlier can be solved when two differences are brought to light, the first between mixture and generation & corruption, the second between what is mixable (*mikton*) and what is generable & corruptible (*gennêton, phtharton*). These two differences are the topic of the remainder of *GC* 1.10,

---

[14] The literature on Aristotle's theory of mixture is extensive. Apart from the classics H. H. Joachim, 'Aristotle's Conception of Chemical Combination', *Journal of Philology* 29 (1904), 72–86; Joachim (n. 13 above); W. J. Verdenius and J. H. Waszink, *Aristotle on Coming-to-Be and Passing-Away: Some Comments*, 2nd edn (Leiden: Brill, 1966), and Williams (n. 13 above), I have found most useful the exchange between R. Sorabji, 'The Greek Origins of the Idea of Chemical Combination: Can Two Bodies be in the Same Place?', *Proceedings of the Boston Area Colloquium in Ancient Philosophy* 4 (1988), 35–63 and J. G. Lennox, 'Commentary on Sorabji', *Proceedings of the Boston Area Colloquium in Ancient Philosophy* 4 (1988), 64–75; R. Sorabji, *Matter, Space, and Motion: Theories in Antiquity and Their Sequel* (London: Duckworth, 1988), ch. 5; A. Code, 'Potentiality in Aristotle's Science and Metaphysics', in F. A. Lewis and R. Bolton, eds, *Form, Matter, and Mixture in Aristotle* (Oxford: Blackwell, 1996), pp. 217–30; and E. Lewis, *Alexander of Aphrodisias, On Aristotle Meteorology 4* (London: Duckworth, 1996), esp. pp. 42–4. On potentiality in Aristotle and his interpreters see also E. McMullin, 'Four Senses of Potency', in E. McMullin, ed., *The Concept of Matter* (Notre Dame: University of Notre Dame Press, 1965), pp. 295–315.

[15] In view of the Zenonian structure of the argument R. Kent Sprague, 'An Anonymous Argument against Mixture', *Mnemosyne* 26 (1973), 230–3, has suggested that the argument derives from neo-Eleatic sophistical contemporaries of Aristotle's. However, since she is not convinced by Aristotle's solution she tends to overestimate the power of the argument and believes that Aristotle's theory is actually defeated by it. Cf. also Verdenius and Waszink (n. 14 above), pp. 47–8.

[16] For simplicity's sake the argument is confined to the case of a mixture of two ingredients, whereas Aristotle's more considered view is that each sublunary mixture contains all four elements, cf. *GC* 2.8.

327b10–31. In my view Aristotle only aims to achieve (I) in *GC* 1.10. For a discussion of (II) we have to wait until *GC* 2.7.[17]

In order to establish a difference between mixture and generation & corruption Aristotle has to defuse the radical distinction between being and not-being on which the argument of his opponents turns. He achieves this by introducing the famous distinction between actual and potential being. Here is how Aristotle introduces the potentiality of mixed ingredients:[18]

> Since, however, some things that are, are in potentiality, and some in actuality, it is possible for things that have been mixed, in some way to be and not to be. For that which has come to be from them [i.e. the mixture] is something else in actuality, whereas each [of them] is still in potentiality what they were before they were mixed, i.e. has not been destroyed[19] – which the previous aporetic argument tried to show.[20] Moreover, it is manifest that things that are mixed come together from having formerly been separate, and are capable of being separated again. So neither do they both remain in actuality like the body and its whiteness,[21] nor do they perish – either of them or both – because their potentiality is preserved.
>
> *GC* 1.10, 327b22–31, trans. after Williams

The actuality-potentiality distinction clearly addresses the distinction between separation and the specific type of unification found in a mixture, i.e. a unification of things that have formerly been separate. The previous analysis of the problem yields that if mixture is to exist next to generation & corruption the ingredients cannot have

---

[17] Contrary to later interpretations, I do not believe that *GC* 327b30–1 'their *dunamis* is preserved', refers to the powers of the elementary qualities hot, cold, moist, and dry for the simple reason that Aristotle has not yet introduced these powers at this stage. Instead, I take it that after rejecting Preservation, Domination and Corruption in 327b29–30 Aristotle uses 'their *dunamis*' to pick up the *dunamei* of 327b25; 'their potentiality' is equivalent to 'their potential existence'. For the alternation between *dunamis* and *dunamei* in this sense cf. e.g. *Metaph.* 9.6, 1048a25–35; 13.10, 1087a16.

[18] Aristotle, *GC* 1.10, 327b22–31.

[19] It is difficult to decide whether this tantalizing sentence allots the potential being to the ingredients, or the mixture. Keimpe Algra suggested to me the following alternative translation: let 327b25–6 *hekaterou* be the subject complement on a par with 327b25 *heterou*, and *tou gegonotos ex autôn* the grammatical subject throughout: 'For that which has come to be from them [i.e. the mixture] is something else in actuality, whereas *it* [i.e. the mixture] is still in potentiality each [of the things] that were before the mixture occurred, and have not been destroyed.' Cf. Philoponus, *in GC* 191,16–17. Although it seems that neither alternative can be ruled out, I have a slight preference for the translation adopted in the text because it keeps the grammatical focus on things that have been mixed (*ta mikhthenta*) rather than shifting to the mixture and reverting to things that are mixed (*ta mignumena*) again in the sequel 327b27 ff. Cf. H. H. Joachim in J. Barnes, ed., *The Complete Works of Aristotle: The Revised Oxford Translation*, 2 vols (Princeton: Princeton University Press, 1984), vol. 1, p. 536.

[20] Cf. H. H. Joachim in J. Barnes (see previous note), p. 536: 'This was the difficulty that emerged in the previous argument'. Contrast Williams (n. 13 above), p. 34: 'This is the solution to the problem raised by the previous argument', which seems too much for the imperfect of *diaporein*. I suggest that the imperfect is intended to underline that the previous argument was still incomplete, and awaited Aristotle to bring out the implication just stated.

[21] From 327b15–17 it is clear that the union of body and whiteness and other affections and dispositions is not a mixture because this is an example of Preservation: their union leaves them untouched.

been destroyed. *Ipso facto* they must be capable of regaining their previous separate existence, as everyday examples such as the mixture of wine and water testify.[22] Judging from this text potential existence consists in this separability.[23]

In view of later interpretations it is important to note that Aristotle nowhere suggests that he attributes this potentiality to the primary qualities hot, cold, dry, and moist. As a properly dialectical argument GC 1.10 operates entirely within the confines of the initial problem and the obvious fact that mixture is opposed to separation. The latter gives rise to an analysis of separation and union from which mixture emerges as a specific kind of union *on these very terms*: it is a union of items all of which existed separately before they were united. Needless to say, the primary qualities are not such items. It is paramount to insist on the limited scope of GC 1.10, and, in consequence, the limited scope of the well-defined notion of potentiality introduced in it.

So far, Aristotle has shown how we may conceive of the mode of being of the ingredients of a mixture. However, we have not been presented with an account of the change the mixables undergo in order to be unified in a mixture, other than the suggestion that its beginning and end terms are separation and lack of separation. The concise closing statement of GC 1.10 that 'mixture is the unification of things altered' affirms that Aristotle is still aware that some kind of alteration is needed to escape the objection that mixture makes no difference (against 1). Yet, he has not given the slightest indication as to the nature of this alteration, in spite of the contrast between the sense of the term 'alteration' in the initial statement of the problem and in GC 1.4.[24]

---

[22] According to Stobaeus, *Ecl.* 1.17, 1,54,8–11 W (= *SVF* 2, p. 153,21–3) water and wine can be separated by means of an oil-drenched sponge; see Todd (n. 11 above), p. 241 *ad* 232,2–5 with S. Sambursky, 'On Some References to Experience in Stoic Physics', *Isis* 49 (1958), 331–5, at 332–3. Cf. Nemesius, *Nat. Hom.* 3, c. 128–9 (Moriani, p. 39c) where this example serves to illustrate the preservation of constituents in a blend below the level of perception, a theory attributed to Democritus by Alexander at *Mixt.* 2, 214,18–28 and similarly *Mixt.* 15, 232,18–20: 'such an alteration in these bodies entails that they be held capable of dissociation, because the body that was affected by them originally came to be from their mixture' (trans. Todd). Philoponus, *in GC* 191,29–31 explains that when a mixture of wine and water is pressed through water-lettuce only the water is drawn up, especially when the wine is thick. In commenting on Aristotle's claim that ingredients can be separated again Philoponus, *in GC* 191,31–192,4 carefully adds that even if there are no means to neatly separate the ingredients they should still be regarded as separable because they are capable of existing independently (*kath' heauta hupostênai*) insofar as depends on them (*hoson eph' heautois*). The tools fail to oblige the theory, not the ingredients.

[23] Here I have no space to elaborate on how precisely this separation is supposed to take place (but see Richard Sorabji, *Matter, Space and Motion* (n. 14 above), p. 103, n. 101). Cf. Joachim (n. 14 above), 81–6, stressing the importance of Aristotle, *Meteor.* 4.1. Most recently Lewis (n. 14 above), pp. 3–15, has convincingly defended the authenticity and importance of *Meteor.* 4 in the introduction to his translation of Alexander, *in Meteor.* 4.

[24] G. Morrow, 'Qualitative Change in Aristotle's *Physics*', in I. Düring, ed., *Naturphilosophie bei Aristoteles und Theophrast* (Heidelberg: Lothar Stiehm Verlag, 1969), pp. 154–67, provides a thoroughly Platonic interpretation of alteration in Aristotle. He believes that Aristotle does not succeed in upholding the distinction between alteration and generation (Morrow ignores the difference between change in form and change in the whole of both matter and form, Aristotle, GC 1.2, 317a23–7). Morrow aims at showing that in spite of Aristotle's claims to the contrary (*Phys.* 5) alteration is not in fact a primary kind of change in Aristotle's physics. The qualitative changes surrounding the transformation of the elements and mixture are a case in point (pp. 159–61, 164–5). As I hope to show elsewhere this interpretation shows a remarkable affinity with the ancient Neoplatonic approach to Aristotle's physics.

We have to wait until *GC* 2.7 before more is revealed about the alteration of the mixables. In *GC* 2.1–6 Aristotle has developed a sophisticated theory of the nature and role of the primary qualities hot, cold, moist, and dry in the constitution and change of the elements 'out of' each other. In *GC* 2.7 Aristotle points out that if we want to say that homeomerous materials like flesh and marrow are 'out of' the elements, a different understanding of the phrase 'out of' is needed. If flesh is constituted 'out of' e.g. fire and earth, we seem to have two options:

i. fire and earth both perish so that flesh is neither (which conflicts with the notion that flesh consists of *the elements*), or
ii. fire and earth are preserved which means that flesh is a mere combination (which conflicts with the notion of homeomereity).

This dilemma is similar to the argument against mixture discussed above, so it is not surprising that here the alternative of mixture comes in:

> [1.] Is there a possible solution along these lines, taking into account the fact that things can be more or less hot and cold? When one exists *simpliciter* in actuality, the other exists in potentiality; when, however, it is not completely so, but one is cold *qua* hot, the other hot *qua* cold, because in being mixed things destroy each other's excesses, then what will exist is neither their matter nor either of the contraries existing *simpliciter* in actuality, but something intermediate, which, in so far as it is in potentiality more hot than cold or vice versa, is proportionately twice as hot in potentiality as cold, or three times, or in some other similar way.
>
> [2.] It is as a result of the contraries, or rather the elements,[25] having been mixed that the other things [*sc*. the homeomerous compounds] will exist, and the elements from them [*sc*. the compounds], which are in some way <the elements>[26] in potentiality, not in the same way as matter but in the way we have explained.[27] In this way what comes to be is a mixture, in that way it is matter.
>
> [3.] Since the contraries are also acted upon as stated in the definition in Book I – for the actually hot is cold in potentiality and the actually cold hot in potentiality,

---

[25] Cf. Verdenius and Waszink (n. 14 above), pp. 62–3.
[26] Joachim (n. 13 above), p. 243, and Verdenius and Waszink (n. 14 above), p. 62, read 'and the elements, which are in some way <the contraries> in potentiality, will come to be from [the contraries].' However, with G. A. Seeck, *Über die Elemente in der Kosmologie des Aristoteles: Untersuchungen zu "de generatione et corruptione" und "de caelo"* (Munich: Beck, 1964), p. 60, n. 1, they take 'or rather the elements' as an epexegetical addition to 'the contraries' (see previous note). Accordingly, we should take Aristotle as continuing with the elements (334b18, rather than the contraries) as the complement of the compounds. On this interpretation the structure 'the compounds out of the elements and vice versa' is set against 'one element out of another and vice versa' in order to bring out a different sense of 'out of' and a different sense of potentiality (see next note). Cf. also Philoponus *in GC* 275,31 ff. discussed below.
[27] i.e. as explained above in *GC* 1.10. Joachim refers to both 1.10, 327b22–31 and 2.7, 334b8–16 as if the same kind of potentiality were involved throughout. Verdenius and Waszink, in line with their understanding of the previous sentence, mistakenly refer to the theory of the reciprocal action of contraries in *GC* 1.7.

so that unless they are in balance they change one into the other, and the same holds in the case of the other contraries – first, the elements change in this way; but flesh and bones and suchlike come from these <elements>, the hot becoming cold and the cold hot when they approach the mean, for here they are neither one thing nor the other, and the mean is large and not an indivisible point. Similarly dry and wet and suchlike produce flesh and bone and the rest in the middle range.

Aristotle, GC 2.7, 334b7–30, trans. Williams, modified

Aristotle distinguishes between two kinds of potentiality rooted in the primary qualities. *Qua* opposites, they are potentially their opposites; *qua* contraries with latitude between them,[28] they are potentially any intermediate stage on the way towards their opposite. The realisation of these potentialities gives rise to two different changes, which affect the elements in two different ways. When primary qualities change into their opposite the elements suffer substantial change: they perish and are transformed into another element. When primary qualities change into an intermediate stage on their scale under the influence of mutual interaction, i.e. when 'they'[29] destroy each other's excesses', the elements are mixed. The presence or absence of a certain balance between the primary qualities (on the same range) determines whether transformation or mixture occurs, as we already saw in the account of mixture. In short, both the transformation and the mixture of the elements depend on changes of the primary qualities.

At the same time the important distinction between mixture and generation & corruption is maintained because they are caused by different kinds of change of the primary qualities. What is more, since we are dealing with qualitative changes, mixture consists in a genuine change (against 1) which is not fatal to the nature of the mixables (against 2 and 3).[30] Since by definition mixture occurs when the qualitative changes are such as not to cause a transformation of the elements, the elements are preserved in the mixture. Finally, though in the initial argument of *GC* 1.10 the term 'alteration' remained ambiguous, it now turns out that the final statement 'mixture is the unification of mixables when altered' can be evaluated on Aristotle's terms: the mixables are unified as the result of a particular kind of *qualitative* change.[31]

Apart from the potentialities of the qualities to change into either their opposites or an intermediate degree, Aristotle seems to refer to the kind of potentiality he discussed

---

[28] Cf. *Cat.* 10, 12a9–25; *Metaph.* 10.7. These are the *emmesa enantia* of the later tradition.

[29] 'They' here refers to two qualities on the same scale, e.g. the hotness in fire and in air, or the hotness in fire and the coldness in earth. When fire and air, or fire and earth combine a mean is reached between the different degrees of temperature. Note that for Aristotle the difference between these opposites is relative to our sense of touch (*DA* 2.11, 424a2–7). In reality there is one range of temperature.

[30] It is a burning question whether it is convincing to regard a change in constitutive qualities as a merely qualitative change, but an exploration of this problem in Aristotle's view exceeds the limits of this paper. Here I am only concerned to show how Aristotle may have conceived of his solution judging from the two major texts used by the later tradition.

[31] The question how Aristotle could believe that such qualitative changes caused the unification and separation of mixables will have to remain open here.

in *GC* 1.10. Moreover, he claims that the homeomerous mixture is in potentiality the elements in this sense. Apparently, he does not feel the need to distinguish between this kind of potentiality as a mode of being of the ingredients in the mixture, and the potentiality of the mixture to yield the ingredients when analysed.[32]

We may conclude that the distinction between the forms and the qualities of the ingredients that we found in Zabarella has a basis in Aristotle's two-tiered discussion of mixture in *GC* 1.10 and *GC* 2.7. The problem of how to connect the two accounts raises a plethora of questions. Does Aristotle *reduce* mixture to the mutual blunting of the elementary qualities, and, hence, does he *reduce* the potentiality of the ingredients to the potentiality of the elementary qualities? If so, does this apply in all cases, or merely when the elements are concerned as in *GC* 2.7? Does the potentiality of the *ingredients* consist in the potentiality of their *forms*, although Aristotle does not mention them even once? If so, is the potentiality of the ingredients to be explained in terms of their being "blunted" as in the case of the qualities? Are the qualities of the elements *constitutive* of their essence and form? These and other questions Aristotle left for his commentators to ponder.

Philoponus[33]

In his introduction to the first part of *GC* 1.10 Philoponus duly summarises the problem Aristotle has to face: in a mixture either both ingredients are preserved, or they both perish, or one is preserved while the other perishes. As Philoponus will note further on in his textual commentary (*in GC* 189,10–17), this aporia demands a proper distinction between generation & corruption, and mixture. He states that Aristotle solves the problem by means of the distinction between potentiality and actuality (*in GC* 188,14–15) which he goes on to explain in the following way:

> [1.] In mixed wine both the water and the wine exist in potentiality. This is neither according to the first sense [of potentiality], i.e. in terms of suitability (*epitêdeiotês*) as water is air in potentiality; nor according to the second sense without qualification, i.e. in terms of mere disposition (*hexis*), like the sleeping geometer.
>
> [2.] But both the water and the wine are disposed in the mixture in the way in which a geometer who is drunk and trying to do geometry is in actuality with respect to disposition, though not purely. For each is actual in the mixture in a

---

[32] Cf. n. 19 above.
[33] Philoponus' main comments on mixture were already translated into German by W. Böhm, *Johannes Philoponos, Grammatikos von Alexandrien: Ausgewählte Schriften* (Munich: Schöningh, 1967), pp. 283–99, with extensive notes on their influence in Arabic and Medieval thought, pp. 450–4, which in effect summarise the pioneering results of A. Maier, *An der Grenze von Scholastik und Naturwissenschaft: Die Struktur der materiellen Substanz, Das Problem der Gravitation, Die Mathematik der Formlatituden*, 2nd edn (Rome: Edizioni di Storia e Letteratura, 1952), Part I: 'Die Struktur der materiellen Substanz'. There is a full English translation with notes of Philoponus' *in GC* by C. J. F. Williams (2 vols, 1999) and Inna Kupreeva (2005) in the series Ancient Commentaries on Aristotle, edited by Richard Sorabji.

tempered mode (*kekolasmenôs energei*). So in this way both are preserved in potentiality though neither is preserved in actuality as it was originally. For their pure actuality has been tempered, and is not as it was before they were mixed.

[3.] In this way, then, we shall escape all difficulties.

Philoponus, *in GC* 188,16–26

In an attempt to locate the relevant kind of potentiality in Aristotle's philosophy Philoponus resorts to a comparison with the two kinds of potentiality that Aristotle distinguished in *De Anima* 2.5 in relation to both sense perception and knowledge.[34] A human being has *first* potentiality for knowledge when he is born, simply because as a human being he has a soul which is naturally disposed to acquire knowledge.[35] Aristotle notes that we say that someone can see or hear even when he is asleep (*DA* 417a11). Apparently, the potentiality is preserved even when physical causes prohibit its actualisation. In the physical context of mixture Philoponus uses the example of the transformation of water into air to illustrate first potentiality: water may turn into air (§1).

A human being who has acquired knowledge of a particular field (which is first actuality or disposition, *hexis*), e.g. a geometer or a grammarian, has *second* potentiality for knowledge. He is able to use the knowledge he possesses and to apply it to a particular case whenever he wishes, external circumstances permitting. A sleeping geometer does not lose his knowledge; he is merely incapable of using it until he wakes up.[36]

Philoponus claims that the potentiality of mixed ingredients is different from both first and second potentiality (§2). For although mixed ingredients retain their actuality (*hexis*) in the mixture, they do so in a reduced or tempered mode (*kekolasmenôs*).[37] This reduced actuality constitutes a separate type of potentiality,[38] viz. the potentiality to recover the previous purity of actuality. In the sequel Philoponus explains what actuality he has in mind: it is the actuality of the essential form of the ingredients.[39] Water and wine do not perish but continue to exist, and hence their actuality or form

---

[34] More detail is provided in a parallel passage in the *theoria* to *GC* 2.7 (271,1–24), to which I refer in the following notes and p. 423 ff.

[35] Cf. *An. Post.* 2.19, 100a13–14.

[36] Cf. *Phys.* 7.3, 247b13–16. Philoponus also regards sleep as an impediment, see *in GC* 271,7–10; however, contrary to Aristotle he seems to identify second potentiality with the state of a sleeping builder, or a builder who cannot apply his knowledge because he does not have the proper building materials.

[37] Cf. 198,26–7: 'it does not totally destroy, but only tempers (*kolazei*) the extremes'. See also 198,21–3: 'if a drop of wine is mixed with an increasing amount of water, first the quality is blunted (*amblunêtai*), and finally it changes completely (*pantelôs metaballei*)'. For the quality see also 202,12–13 and below p. 424.

[38] Here Philoponus seems to speak of a qualified instance of the second type, whereas in 271,14.16 he considers it as an independent meaning (*sêmainomenon*) of the term 'in potentiality', which is to be located between first and second potentiality (271,18); see below p. 423.

[39] Cf. 191,26–8: '... [Aristotle] means that mixed ingredients are naturally disposed to wholly recover their own form (*eidos*) by means of certain separating (cf. *diakritikon* at Alexander, *On mixture* 232,25) tools that cause alteration, because they have not lost their complete (*teleion*) form but only its purity (*eilikrines*)'; cf. 192,11–14, esp. 12: 'the forms themselves tempered'.

is not lost. Nevertheless, the mixture does affect them in that their actuality or form is somehow tempered.[40]

The example of the drunken geometer (§2) explains the character of this third kind of potentiality.[41] Unlike the sleeping geometer (§1), a drunken geometer may still try to use the knowledge he possesses. However, the intoxication affects the disposition of the geometer and keeps him from reaching full second actuality (i.e. a successful application of geometrical knowledge). This example concerning *second* actuality (188,21-3) serves to introduce the notion of tempering which Philoponus then applies to the *first* actuality (188,23-6) by which the ingredients exist in a mixture. For in a later passage Philoponus locates the corresponding type of potentiality on a range *between first and second potentiality* (271,14-24, see below). This location seems to rule out that the tempered second actuality of the drunk geometer, which is to be located between second potentiality and second actuality, is itself an illustration of the mode of being of the ingredients in a mixture. As the later passage makes clear (271,11-14), their mode of being is conceived as a kind of *potentiality* between existence and non-existence, not between degrees of second *actuality*.

This solution meets all requirements of the argument in GC 1.10: generation & corruption are avoided; mixing somehow affects the ingredients; the mixed ingredients have an equal status in the mixture; they both exist 'in potentiality'. Hence Philoponus triumphantly concludes that hesitation concerning the obvious reality of mixture is removed and plain experience is vindicated (188,30-3).

In the *theoria* to GC 2.7 Philoponus provides further details concerning his third type of potentiality (271,14-24). It should be regarded as a range between first and second potentiality as its extremes. He compares it with the ontological status of a house in the process of being built: it is not a house in potentiality as are the bricks and wood (i.e. first potentiality), nor – we should add – a complete house ready to serve as shelter (second potentiality). Again, sperm is a human being in potentiality in a different sense from an embryo that is being formed. Again, a newborn baby is a grammarian in a different sense from a child that has the proper age to learn grammar, or a child that is being taught grammar. There is a wide range (*platos polu*) in these cases because one state is closer to the form, another further away from it. This intermediate range of potentiality constitutes the third sense of 'in potentiality'.[42]

---

[40] Here we encounter the famous issue of the latitude of forms which I have to leave aside here. In discussing the fourteenth century Oxford Calculators E. D. Sylla, 'Medieval Concepts of the Latitude of Forms: The Oxford Calculators', *Archives d'Histoire doctrinale et littéraire du Moyen Age* 48 (1974), 223-83, at 227, n. 10, already noted the presence of this theory in Philoponus *in GC* 170,12 but it is widely spread in both Philoponus and other Neoplatonists. See further I. Croese, *Simplicius on Continuous and Instantaneous Change* (Utrecht: Faculteit Wijsbegeerte, 1998), pp. 82-4.

[41] Philoponus uses the same kind of potentiality and the same example to explain Platonic recollection in Aristotelian terms in *De intellectu* 39,1-20 (ed. Verbeke). For this and other applications of the third type of potentiality see F. A. J. De Haas, 'Recollection and Potentiality in Philoponus', in M. Kardaun and J. Spruyt, eds, *The Winged Chariot* (Leiden: Brill, 2000), pp. 165-84.

[42] Of course this range is to be distinguished from the range of the hot, cold, wet, and dry mentioned by Aristotle GC 2.7, 334b28, which explains how different kinds of mixture can arise from a mixture of the same four elements in different ratios. For Philoponus' comments on *this* range, see the *theoria*, 272,12-33, and the textual commentary, 274,21 ff.

Unlike Aristotle, Philoponus already brings the qualities of the ingredients into play in the context of *GC* 1.10. He implies that the process of mixing consists in a blunting of the *quality* (198,22–3); he states that mixing occurs because the mixables act and are acted on with respect to *quality* (202,12–13). Finally, he seems to reduce the potential existence of the *ingredients* to the tempered mode of their characteristic *qualities*. Likewise, each ingredient needs an addition (*prosthêkê*) with respect to its own quality in order to become in actuality what it was beforehand – which, we are told, is not a full-scale change entailing generation & corruption (202,21–5).[43]

When commenting on the final sentence of *GC* 1.10, Aristotle's definition of mixture, Philoponus makes a careful attempt to connect *GC* 1.10 and 2.7 into a single description of mixture:

> This can be the definition of mixture, 'unification of the mixables through alteration', because the things mixed are preserved in one way but perish in another. For, as was said, they are not such-and-such in actuality, but having been tempered they appear to have perished, and they no longer preserve the perfection of such-and-such a form. On the other hand they remain and are preserved in this way that their qualities have not changed entirely but their unity remains.
>
> Philoponus, *in GC* 203,10–16

The ingredients appear to have perished because their *form* has lost its perfection in that it is reduced to a tempered mode of being. In reality, the ingredients remain because their distinctive *qualities* have not changed entirely but continue to exist in a unified mode.

It is to be noted that this interpretation is reflected in a slight though perhaps significant change in the wording of Aristotle's definition. 'Mixture is the unification of mixables *that have been altered (alloiôthentôn)*' in the lemma (203,8) is rephrased as 'mixture is the unification of the mixables *through alteration (di' alloiôseôs)*' in the commentary (203,11). The latter phrase leaves open the possibility of distinguishing between a non-qualitative change of the ingredients as such (i.e. the loss of perfection of their essential form) and a concomitant change of their qualities (i.e. their 'blunting' so as to form a new unity). Moreover, the latter phrase more clearly distinguishes mixture from alteration, which may be a necessary part of, or preparation for mixture, but not all that the process of mixing consists in. Mixture is to be distinguished from mere alteration as much as from generation & corruption.[44]

So far we may conclude that our commentator sees the need to combine *GC* 1.10 and 2.7. He reduces the potentiality of the ingredients to a reduced status of their forms, which explains their apparent corruption. At the same time the qualities of the ingredients are blunted so as to constitute a new unity. In this way the ingredients are preserved.

---

[43] The vocabulary of this passage is very close to Alexander, *Mixt.* 231,16–22, see below pp. 429–30. These lemmata may be indebted to Alexander, *in GC* 1.10 even though he is not mentioned explicitly.
[44] For the need to distinguish mixture from alteration cf. Philoponus, *in GC* 327b14, 190,15–21; 327b27, 192,4–8. On the status of alteration as a necessary part of a different kind of change see *Phys.* 7.3 and Croese (n. 40 above), ch. 6 for its reception by Simplicius.

However, this is not Philoponus' final word on the issue. In the footsteps of Aristotle he returns to the topic of mixture in his *theoria* and commentary on GC 2.7. In this context the ingredients are the four elements, which constitute the primary mixtures, i.e. homeomerous substances like bile, blood, bone, and flesh. Philoponus identifies Aristotle's solution to the problem of GC 2.7 as the solution of GC 1.10, (270,16–18) which he describes at length in its application to fire and the four elementary qualities (270,18–271,2). As the form of fire is not preserved in purity, so the highest degree of each quality is lost in the composite. As the pure form of fire remains in potentiality, so does the highest degree of each quality.[45] Then he lists the three senses of 'potentiality' discussed above (271,2–24, see pp. 422–23). So far, so good.

At this point, however, Philoponus draws attention to the essential relation between fire and the highest degree of hotness, which implies that the preservation of fire and the reduction of hotness are irreconcilable.

> [1.] So this [i.e. the account summarised above] is obvious, but one must know the following which is worth critical reflection. For someone will say that if we say that the purely hot has not perished qua hot but it has perished qua *purely* hot, we can no longer say that fire too has perished qua *pure* fire but not qua fire as such. For if fire insofar as it is fire is seen as maximally and purely hot (fire qua fire is not hot in relation to one thing and cold to another but maximally hot) – if, then, you say that the maximally hot qua maximally hot has perished, and fire qua fire is maximally hot, it is clear that fire insofar as it is fire has perished in the compound. Moreover, it will be true to say that fire insofar as it is fire has *completely* perished, but the hot qua hot has not perished *without qualification*, but [only] qua *maximally* hot.
>
> [2.] And this is reasonable. For it is not the same to say 'hot' and 'fire', since it is not the case that if something is hot, it is fire, but if something is *maximally* hot, it is fire, and if something is fire, it is *maximally* hot. If fire qua fire has completely perished, it is clear that the compound is fire in potentiality according to the first sense of 'in potentiality', according to which we also say that matter is fire in potentiality. The compound does not possess anything of fire in virtue of which [fire] is fire.
>
> [3.] However, what has been stated earlier remains true of the hot. Since it has perished qua maximally hot but not qua hot without qualification, it is reasonable that the compound is not called maximally hot in potentiality according to the first sense of 'in potentiality', but it will be called thus according to the distinctions made above.
>
> Philoponus, *in GC* 271,25–272,10

Philoponus makes perfectly clear that if the elements are essentially characterised by hot, cold, moist, and dry *to the highest degree*, they cease to exist the moment a change

---

[45] From *in GC* 277,27–278,2 it is clear that this description applies to all qualities whether constitutive of substances or not.

of degree in these qualities occurs.[46] If the compound no longer possesses anything distinctive of fire, it is no longer fire in potentiality in the third sense of potentiality; first potentiality now suffices. Yet, the third sense of potentiality still applies to the qualities themselves inasmuch as they may regain their highest degree once it is lost.

How are we now to interpret the commentary on *GC* 1.10? Is it perhaps an earlier stratum of the commentary, to be overruled by this later insight which was prompted by an objection not envisaged before?[47] I believe not: in the textual commentary on *GC* 2.7, 334b18 ff. it becomes clear that the commentary on *GC* 1.10 should be regarded as a faithful account of what Philoponus believes to be *Aristotle's* theory of mixture,[48] although *Philoponus* himself wishes to restrict the application of third potentiality to qualities alone.

In *GC* 2.7, 334b18–19 Aristotle stated that the compounds are 'in some way <the elements> in potentiality, not in the same way as matter but in the way we have explained' (translated above p. 419). We already saw that this passage takes up the notion of potentiality used in *GC* 1.10. Philoponus provides two explanations of the difference this sentence indicates. The second is most interesting for our present concerns. He explains the difference in terms of the different senses of 'in potentiality':

> [1.] However, perhaps one will provide a more natural interpretation of the phrase 'the compound is not the simple [elements] in potentiality in the same way as matter is' when one points to that difference between the senses that we have also mentioned above in the *theoria*. The difference is this: matter is said to be the simple [elements] in potentiality without possessing any trace of their form, which is the first sense of 'in potentiality', but not so the compound. For it already has something of the form of the simple [elements] even though their purity has perished. This cannot be the case according to the first sense of 'in potentiality'.
>
> [2.] Moreover one must point out the following, viz. that if Aristotle says that matter and compounds are not said to be the simple [elements] in potentiality in

---

[46] Aegidius Romanus, *Comm. in GC* comm. 90 (n. 9 above) uses the same argument to the same effect. However, Averroes, *Comm. in Cael.* comm. 67 (n. 4 above) uses the argument to defend why it cannot be said that the elements remain *perfectly* in the mixture. He goes as far as to compare their ontological status to an intermediate state between substance and accident: the substantial forms of those elements are reduced from perfect substantial forms and their being (*esse*) is as if intermediate between forms and accidents.

[47] A further complication is that Philoponus' *in GC* is a report of Ammonius' teachings 'together with a number of critical reflections (*epistaseis*) of his own' (*in GC* 1,1–5). It is conceivable that Ammonius relied on Alexander for most of his account, and that Philoponus added this criticism as a consideration of his own. The passage Philoponus, *in GC* 271,26 ff. is emphatically introduced as 'a worthwhile remark someone might make'.

[48] In the next section we shall see that it was probably Alexander who introduced the reduction of the forms of the ingredients in the explanation of mixture. If so, Philoponus' restriction is a correction of Alexander's view rather than Aristotle's. In *Aet.* 13.14, 518,17–18 Philoponus also speaks of 'tempering the excess of fire' (not heat) in an argument designed to ridicule Aristotle's criticism of Plato's *Timaeus* in *Meteor.* 1.3, 340a1; here we would indeed expect Philoponus to argue on Aristotle's terms.

the same sense, he necessarily believes that fire and the other [elements] have not perished completely qua fire in the compound, but qua *pure* fire, and that tempered fire is identical with relative hotness.

Philoponus, *in GC* 276,11–23

From the first paragraph it is clear that Philoponus believes that this interpretation does more justice to Aristotle's allusion to a difference in potentiality. Moreover, from the second paragraph it appears that he believes that Aristotle here alluded to the difference between first and third potentiality. If so, Philoponus is right to bring out the implication that Aristotle must have believed the elements to be present in the compound in a tempered mode. We have already seen that Philoponus agreed with an anonymous objection against Aristotle that fire is only convertible with *the highest degree* of hotness (271,25–272,10, see above). Hence we may infer that he knowingly disagrees with (what he believes to be) Aristotle's view.

This interpretation of Philoponus can be confirmed from *in GC* 2.5, 245,18–246,1 and from later writings. At *in GC* 2.5, 245,18–246,1 Philoponus discusses a rather curious interpretation of the statement 'Everything comes to be from fire; hence everything is fire'. Some people suggested that everything is fire because while changing into the other elements fire is not destroyed but only loses its purity (245,18–25). Philoponus replies that partial loss of the nature of the elements in terms of their qualities (*sic*) is relevant only to the generation of a composite, not to the generation of the simple elements out of each other. For each of the elements has its qualities to the highest degree, unmixed, and untempered. Dry fire cannot remain medium dry after turning into moist air for air is moist *to the highest degree* as fire is dry *to the highest degree*. To avoid the attribution of sheer contradictory qualities the entire nature of fire must change in order to become air (245,25–246,1).

In later writings Philoponus holds on to the view of mixture defended in *in GC* 2.7. In *Contra Proclum* 11.14 Philoponus aims at showing that Plato's philosophy is full of contradictions. One of these is that according to *Timaeus* 54B1-D2 the element earth cannot change into any of the other three, whereas from *Timaeus* 42E8–43A2 it follows that all four elements are combined in creating the visible world. Such a composite must be a homeomerous fusion of the elements. Hence, Philoponus concludes, 'if none of the elements is present in the composite in actuality, but the form (*idea*) of each has perished when they have been mixed and some other form (*eidos*) has supervened upon their mixture and fusion (e.g. the form of flesh or blood), I believe it is clear to everyone that in the composite earth too has changed' (*Aet.* 462,9–15). Finally, in the *Tractatus de totalitate et partibus* Philoponus stipulates once again that the elements remain potentially in the mixture only in the sense that they may reappear as specifically (not numerically) the same elements when the mixture falls apart, whereas only the qualities of the elements remain in reduced purity.[49]

---

[49] Philoponus, *Tractatus de totalitate et partibus ad Sergium presbyterum* cap. 4, pp. 130–1 (ed. and Latin translation from the Syriac in A. Šanda, *Opuscula monophysitica Iohannis Philoponi* (Beirut: Typographia Catholica PP. Soc. Jesu., 1930); German in Böhm (n. 33 above), pp. 297–8; English in D. King, *Philoponus, A Treatise Concerning the Whole and the Parts* [publ. with *Philoponus, On*

We have seen that Zabarella refers to Philoponus in support of the view that both the forms and the qualities of the ingredients are preserved in reduced actuality. Now we can say that Zabarella was wrong.[50] It seems likely that he only consulted Philoponus' comments on *GC* 1.10 without taking into account the correction Philoponus added in his commentary on *GC* 2.7. Indeed, Zabarella focuses on Philoponus' commentary on *GC* 1.10 for the 'third intermediate mode' (472A *tertio modo medio*) of potentiality with respect to the forms of the elements.[51] He does not mention any statement contained in Philop. *in GC* 2.7! Hence it passed unnoticed that Philoponus himself adhered to the fourth view Zabarella listed, which was to be defended by e.g. Thomas Aquinas: the forms perish but the qualities are preserved in reduced actuality.[52]

Alexander of Aphrodisias: A Source of Inspiration?

Zabarella mentions Philoponus together with Alexander, and we have seen that the interpretation of Aristotle that Philoponus provides in his comments on *GC* 1.10 contains some echoes of Alexander's *De Mixtione*. Hence Alexander deserves closer inspection.

As Todd already noted,[53] Philoponus' commentary is our principal source for Alexander's lost commentary on *De Generatione et Corruptione* with which our

---

Aristotle Categories 1–5] (London: Bloomsbury, 2015), pp. 199–200): 'So of these parts and elements, there are some that are in the whole in potentiality, others in actuality. Examples of the former are the four elements, viz. water, air, earth and fire, in a body. The substances of these [elements] are destroyed, for water is not in actuality [present] in corporeal composites and neither is earth, air or fire; rather, it is [present] only in potentiality and it is so in such a way that the composite entity could be dissolved into its individual [parts], each in accordance with its own species, yet without their being numerically identical with those from which it was originally composed. For how could things that had just been destroyed come back into being? Their qualities, namely heat, coldness, dryness and wetness, persist through confusion and mixture within the composite, and therefore their purity decreases.... Therefore the integrity of qualities that are in opposites is destroyed and the elements thus exist merely in potentiality within composites, since it is possible that sometimes one of the opposed qualities will overcome [the other] and it will again become very cold or hot, as it had been originally. This is especially evident when the composite is dissolved.' Cf. cap. 7, pp. 134–5 Šanda. In the context of Philoponus' monophysitism it is useful to have mixture as an example of how a new unity may come to be from different elements: so did the unique nature of Christ come to be out of its divine and human components.

[50] Böhm (n. 33 above), p. 452, made the same mistake. In the case of Zabarella this mistake cannot be attributed to the inferiority of the manuscript on which the Aldine edition and its descendants was based (see n. 12). The text of the relevant passages is virtually the same as that of our Berlin edition. In the 1527 Aldine edition, see for *GC* 1.10 p. 42ab and for *GC* 2.7 p. 60ab, 61b; in the 1549 Bagolinus translation, see for *GC* 1.10 contextus 82 ff. pp. 29a ff.

[51] Zabarella, *De mistione* c. 10, 471F-472C paraphrases Philoponus, *in GC* 188,17–25 = contextus 82, containing the contrast between the sleeping and drunken geometer, 191,26–7 = contextus 84, and 198,24–30 = contextus 89; see above p. 415.

[52] Among recent commentators Lewis (n. 14 above), pp. 42–4, also understands Aristotle in this way: 'The *potential* existence of a constituent in a compound is grounded by the *actual* existence of the chemical powers which constitute the constituents' (p. 44). To him Aristotle's motive was: 'If [the elements] existed actually they would actually move towards their natural places, yielding the dissolution of the compound. So they exist, but potentially' (p. 43).

[53] Todd (n. 11 above), pp. 251–2.

commentator was plainly familiar.[54] Alexander's *De Mixtione* chs 13–15 is a restatement of Aristotle's theory of mixture that may derive from the lost commentary although it has been restructured to fit the purpose of the anti-Stoic treatise. At *Mixt.* 15, 232,24–32 Alexander explains that the ingredients of a proper mixture do not remain the same in form as they do in apparent mixtures:

> [1.] In these cases [i.e. apparent mixtures] the residue after the dissociation stays the same in form as before and is only decreased in quantity, but with the bodies that have been blended the difference is that each of the things in potentiality in the body produced from the blend is separated out, changing into the perfection (*teleiotês*) of which it was deprived through the process of balanced reciprocal interaction; and because of this characteristic 'being separated' (*khôrizesthai*) is also predicated of these bodies.
>
> [2.] So if it is reasonable to describe the bodies perfected (*teleioumena*) by such a change not as 'coming to be' but as 'being separated', and if the other statements made about the process of blending follow our basic principles, are consonant with how bodies change and come to be, and preserve the common preconceptions about blending, only Aristotle will have propounded the true theory of blending.
>
> trans. Todd, modified

For Alexander, blending and separation become a special kind of change 'between' generation and alteration. As such, it is a rather awkward intermediate between a change in substance and a change in quality. According to Alexander separation of the ingredients of a mixture is the result of restoring the perfection that was lost through qualitative interaction during the process of mixing. Earlier at *Mixt.* 15, 231,16–22 Alexander had couched the same change in terms of the preservation of the ingredients in potentiality, with a corresponding loss of actuality. To restore them to their perfection requires 'just slight assistance', and 'some addition' which is not a full generation or change.[55] All in all this account compares well with the form's loss of purity and

---

[54] Philoponus often refers to Alexander *in GC*, otherwise lost in Greek. E. Gannagé, 'Alexandre d'Aphrodise *In De generatione et corruptione apud* Gabir b. Hayyan, *K. al-Tasrif*, *Documenti e studi sulla tradizione filosofica medievale* 9 (1998), 35–86, has published fragments of Alex. *in GC* 2.2–5 in Arabic, embedded in an extensive commentary on Aristotle's *GC* 2.2–6 transmitted under the name of the eight century Arabic alchimist Gabir ben Hayyan but probably dating from the ninth-tenth century CE (translated into English in E. Gannagé, *Alexander of Aphrodisias, On Coming-to-Be and Perishing 2.2–5* (London: Duckworth, 2005)). In the context of mixture an indication of Alexander's influence is Philoponus' tendency to restrict the phenomenon of mixture to particular kinds of liquids: compare Alex. *Mixt.* 8 *passim* (see Todd (n. 11 above), p. 204), 13, 228,36–229,3; 14, 230,34–231,4, 231,12–13 with Philoponus, *in GC* 200,19–23; 200,30–201,5; 202,16–18; only at 200,25–7 does Philoponus preserve Aristotle's perspective (328a33-b5) that liquids mix *most easily*. In the context of Alexander's polemic against Stoicism a denial of the universality of mixture served to deny the universal validity of the Stoic theory of blending. For Alexander's introduction of the reduction of the form see the main text.

[55] Alexander, *Mixt.* 15, 231,22–9 also makes the important point that the recovered ingredients are only specifically, not numerically, identical with the original ingredients. In *Mixt.* 15, 231,30–232,18 Alexander describes a number of illustrations of his theory. Philoponus mentions specific recovery only in the *Tractatus de totalitate et partibus ad Sergium presbyterum* 130-1 Šanda (German in Böhm, p. 297; English in King, p. 199), quoted in n. 49 above.

actuality as described by Philoponus in his comments on *GC* 1.10,[56] although we have seen that he is more explicit about the ontological status of the ingredients in the mixture than Alexander.[57] The conclusion seems warranted that the view Philoponus sets out and later rejects is at least partly due to Alexander. Although he was surely aware of this debt to Alexander, he considers the commentator as a faithful expounder of Aristotle to such extent that he presents his (implied) rejection of the view that forms persist in reduced actuality as a rejection of Aristotle's, not Alexander's, view (cf. 276,18–23).

A Neoplatonic Alternative to Philoponus: Proclus and Simplicius

Philoponus' view of Aristotle's theory of mixture is relatively moderate when compared to his fellow Neoplatonists Proclus and Simplicius. Both Proclus and Simplicius revive a neo-Aristotelian interpretation of *GC* 1.10 already mentioned (not supported) in Galen, Stobaeus, and Plotinus.[58] On this interpretation of mixture the bodies of the ingredients remain juxtaposed, while only the qualities mix. With this interpretation in hand Proclus and Simplicius reject Aristotle's notion of mixture as part of the defence of Plato's theory of triangles of the *Timaeus* against Aristotle's attack in *De Caelo* 306a1–307b24 which they read in the interpretation of Alexander. Let us study this complex situation somewhat further.

One of Aristotle's fifteen arguments against Plato's theory of triangles aimed at showing that combinations (*suntheseis*) of atomic triangles or Democritean atoms fail to constitute the continuous wholes that homeomerous bodies like flesh and bone are believed to be, because mere contact does not constitute continuity. Combination may suffice to constitute the elements, but not continuous bodies; hence generation, which is generation of bodies, is abolished (*Cael.* 306b22–9).[59] Simplicius reports that Alexander went even further and emphasised that there will always be void between adjacent particles of the elements.[60]

---

[56] A similar terminology with regard to the mixing of qualities is found in Plotinus, *Enn.* 2.7.2.22–5: 'When quality comes together with quality it is not that quality which it was before, but is associated with another, and, because in that association it is not pure, it is no longer perfectly what it was, but is dimmed (*ēmaurôtai*)' (trans. Armstrong). The verb *amaurô* is a hapax in Plotinus.

[57] On Alexander's reticence in this respect see Todd (n. 11 above), p. 240, who refers to Philoponus' drunken geometer as an improvement on Alexander.

[58] Galen, *In Hipp. de Nat. Hom.* vol. 15, p. 32,1–11 Kühn (= *SVF* 2.463); Arius Didymus *Epitome* fr. phys. 4 (= *Dox.gr.* 449,1–3 = Stobaeus *Ecl.* 1.17.2,1–4); cf. Plotinus, *Enn.* 2.7.1.8–9; 2.10–11, without attribution. Cf. Sorabji (*Matter, Space, and Motion*, n. 14 above), p. 72.

[59] In Arabic and Latin medieval commentaries on the *De Caelo* this passage often provides the occasion for a discussion of mixture; see e.g. Avicenna *De caelo* III summa VIII cap. 3, Averroes *De caelo* III comm. 67, Albertus Magnus *De caelo et mundo* III tr. 2 c. 1.

[60] In Alex. *Mixt.* 2,215,22–7 a theory of mixture that employs the juxtaposition of surfaces is mentioned and dismissed without further discussion. Simplicius reports Alexander as having claimed that, even if we allow the triangles to constitute the elements, they do not constitute bodies, so that every atomic theory does away with generation altogether (Simplicius, *in Cael.* 659,33–660,3).

In his *De Caelo* commentary (640,20–672,23) Simplicius sets out to refute each of Aristotle's fifteen arguments on the basis of Proclus' otherwise lost treatise *Investigation of the Objections of Aristotle to Plato's Timaeus*.[61] Here we also find a discussion of mixture (659,11–661,14). Simplicius reports that Proclus gave an adequate reply to Alexander (660,4–14). Proclus' second argument is most striking: 'No wonder if there is juxtaposition, not union. For [the ingredients] also had to be separable from each other' (660,7–8). Proclus simply constructs a contradiction between Aristotle's requirements that the elements in a mixture are separable again and that the mixture is a unity: if the former, not the latter. Exit Aristotle's theory of mixture! The thrust of his argument is not unlike the Eleatic argument Aristotle set out to overcome in *GC* 1.10.

Simplicius develops Proclus' idea (660,19 ff.) and suggests that even the four elements are merely juxtaposed in small particles. He explains that the appearance of unity and continuity is caused by the unity of the form of flesh or bone that supervenes, just as robes made of threads of different colours give the impression of one mixed colour. The same applies to the four elements:

[1.] So even when the four elements, juxtaposed to each other, exchange qualities and in some way alter each other towards themselves, even so their bodies themselves neither pervade one another nor are they unified with each other nor do they change into each other completely. This is evident from the fact that the elements are separated again in the case of corruption, and each of them moves towards its own wholeness because they inhered in actuality.

[2.] For if each lost its own form during composition, how does it receive it again on the corruption of the composite? For even if during the composition they change towards each other and the water in us is made watery and the air blazes up, even so their bodies hold together by contact, and generally constitute an analogue to glue used in the arts. The glue does not make things continuous either, because the limits of the things glued together do not disappear.

[3.] It is rather as when a number of torches come together and all their flames mix and appear to be one, but when the torches are separated each torch's own flame and the light it spreads are drawn apart with them. In this way too the conglomerate of the four elements displays a single appearance while their bodies are adjacent to each other and mutually alter each other by means of their qualities. In the same way a song composed of different sounds mixed by juxtaposition in small parts also appears to be a unity. Some such thing the so-called blend is too: a common alteration of bodies adjacent to each other, as long as they are adjacent.

Simplicius, in Cael. 660,26–661,14

---

[61] Cf. Proclus, *in Tim.* 1,404,20–1; 2,279,2–4 for the existence of this work.

This is a view of mixture that agrees for the most part with the atomistic spirit of Plato's *Timaeus*. Mixture is merely apparent, because against the Stoics it must be held that the elements can never pervade each other *qua* bodies.[62] Moreover, complete blending cannot explain the increase of volume of the mixture.[63] At the same time the absence of pervasion explains why the elements can be separated again. Hence Simplicius believes, against Aristotle, that the elements remain present in the mixture in actuality (§1) – he has no need for the potentiality that Aristotle brings into play.[64] The elements remain discontinuous, only held together by contact as if they are glued together (§2).[65]

When dealing with the shape of squeezed elementary particles (*in Cael.* 657,2–9) Simplicius is willing to allow some loss of purity although *pace* Philoponus that does not result in corruption. Although the particles have lost their pure shape (*to skhêma eilikrines*) they should not be called 'out of elements': 'they are elements but somewhat unnaturally disposed'. He makes a rhetorical appeal to the fact that 'to some people' a similar anomaly of the elements is acceptable in mixtures and various changes. Here he is in clear opposition to Philoponus who only allows preservation of the elements when the purity of the qualities is preserved.

On the other hand (§3), since the bodies are adjacent to each other the immaterial qualities that inhere in them may mutually affect each other, much as Aristotle described. Here, as in Aristotle, contact is a necessary requirement for the 'mixture' to occur. A bundle of torches is a vivid image of this conception (§3): the flame and the light it spreads appear to be a new single item (like the form of the mixture) but when the torches are separated it becomes clear that there was no such thing as a new unity.

Simplicius' distinction between separation *qua* body and mutual interaction *qua* qualities seems to be a conscious answer to Alexander, with whom he shared the rejection of Stoic blending. However, Alexander clearly stated that in the case of mixture 'a single body comes to be *both* with respect to the substrate *and* with respect to the quality'.[66] He subscribed to Aristotle's definition of mixture as 'the unification of mixables when altered', which he glosses in a way that contains much of the vocabulary Simplicius used: 'The unification through action and passion of bodies adjacent to each other through change, without corruption of any of them'.[67] Simplicius' definition is phrased as a rival definition: 'A common alteration of bodies adjacent to each other as long as they are adjacent'.[68]

As we may expect from a Neoplatonist, the supervenience of the form on a mixture is not the same as the unity of form and matter in Aristotle. True unity must remain the prerogative of the intelligible realm, for which the interweaving of forms in

---

[62] See e.g. *in Phys.* 530,9–531,10. Cf. Sorabji (*Matter, Space, and Motion*, n. 14 above), ch. 5.
[63] For this issue see Sorabji (ibid.), p. 72, cf. Plotinus, *Enn.* 2.7.1.15–20.
[64] For Simplicius' reservations about the potentiality of mixed ingredients see esp. *in Cat.* 281,4–6.
[65] This seems to be a clear reminiscence of *Tim.* 42E-43A, esp. 43A2: *sunekollôn*.
[66] Alexander, *Mixt.* 15, 231,15–16.
[67] Alexander, *Mixt.* 14, 231,10–12.
[68] Simplicius, *in Cael.* 661,13–14.

Plato's *Sophist* is an important precedent.[69] Simplicius regards the lack of union at the corporeal level as a manifestation of the dispersion and scattering that distinguishes the physical realm from the intelligible.[70] Elsewhere he also questions the blending of physical qualities. At *in Cat.* 281,2-31 he reports that Plotinus' view of *krasis* as the blending of extremities which produces another quality (not substance) from the blend, was not accepted wholesale by later philosophers. They did accept that the intermediate quality was different from the extremities, but not as the result of blending or composition, for these are corporeal processes inappropriate to immaterial qualities. The superior view is that physical mixture does not occur at all since each so-called intermediate quality is caused directly by its own intelligible *logos*.[71] It is clear that in this framework the unity and continuity of a mixture that was so dear to Aristotle cannot survive.[72]

How does Philoponus' position compare? Between Aristotle's text, Alexander's authoritative interpretation, and the rival Stoic theory of blending Philoponus finds a different route than Simplicius. Against Proclus and Simplicius and with Alexander, Philoponus accepts the notion of mixture. He even elaborates on the notion of potentiality involved. With Proclus and Simplicius but against Alexander, Philoponus limits mixture to the level of qualities, although like Alexander he opposes qualities to forms rather than bodies. Unlike Proclus and Simplicius he seems to question neither the unity of the mixture nor the possibility of regaining the ingredients from it.

Philoponus' acceptance of mixture and the type of potentiality involved leads him to interesting speculations on a third sense of 'potentiality'. For Philoponus this third sense of 'potentiality' is not restricted to the explanation of mixture: his examples show that the range between first and second potentiality is exhibited in all areas where its extremities are found. More specifically, the third type of potentiality also features in Philoponus' explanation of recollection in an Aristotelian framework, where it has parallels in Simplicius.[73] More research is needed to see how

---

[69] Cf. *in Phys.* 100,1-22, esp. 15-18.

[70] A concise statement to this effect is Simplicius, *in Phys.* 531,5-7: 'So perhaps sublunary [bodies] do not pervade each other because they are most material and resistant and by nature scattered from each other (hence, too, mixed entities constitute something larger), but the heavenly bodies are different.' Cf. more elaborately *in Ench.* 38, 361-99 Hadot (= 99,50-100,45 Dübner). For Simplicius the scattering is caused by indefinite three-dimensional prime matter, see Sorabji (*Matter, Space, and Motion*, n. 14 above), pp. 7-18; F. A. J. De Haas, *John Philoponus' New Definition of Prime Matter: Aspects of its Background in Neoplatonism and the Ancient Commentary Tradition* (Leiden: Brill, 1997), pp. 120 ff.

[71] At *in Cat.* 281,7-15 Simplicius (Iamblichus?) argues against colours as proper mixtures of the opposites white and black, drawing on Aristotle, *Sens.* 439b17-440b24 in support for the view that juxtaposition of extremes, or overlay, or some greater distance is what we are dealing with in this case. However, in that passage Aristotle argues that these alternatives are to be rejected in favour of the mixture view!

[72] In the tentative discussion at *in Cael.* 306,1-16 Simplicius is close to attributing a theory of combination, not mixture, to Aristotle. See further Simplicius, *in DA* 52,19-22.

[73] See my paper 'Recollection and potentiality in Philoponus' (n. 41 above).

this particular range or latitude is connected to Neoplatonic physics and metaphysics in general.

Conclusion

In this study I have tried to show that Philoponus' commentary on Aristotle's account of mixture has to be understood against the background of a discussion between three views of mixture that dominated the Aristotelian tradition as a whole. The starting point was Zabarella's classification of solutions to the main problem of mixture: how to interpret Aristotle's claim that the ingredients are preserved in the mixture in potentiality. If we correct and supplement Zabarella's classification on the basis of our findings, the following table is the result.

		Forms	Qualities
1	Early neo-Aristotelians – Proclus – Simplicius – Avicenna	preserved in actuality	preserved in reduced actuality
2	Alexander – Averroes – Zabarella	preserved in reduced actuality	preserved in reduced actuality
3	Duns Scotus	perish	perish
4	Philoponus – Marsilius, Thomas, Aegidius – Buccaferreus	perish	preserved in reduced actuality

In a sense Proclus and Simplicius belong with Avicenna because they accept the preservation of the elements in actuality, along with reduced actuality and interaction in the realm of qualities. However, since they reject Aristotelian mixture and discuss the problem in terms of body vs. qualities rather than forms vs. qualities they are best regarded as belonging to a different school altogether. Alexander is probably the main source of the influential account of Averroes. Philoponus belongs with the fourth group due to his criticism of Aristotle (or rather Alexander). He accepts the corruption of the ingredients while only their qualities are preserved in reduced actuality. It remains to see whether his influence on the medieval authors that subscribe to a similar view can be established.

Zabarella's reports on his sources should be handled with care. His summaries of Alexander are inadequate, his understanding of Philoponus is wrong. He himself claims that his 'true' interpretation of Averroes was not followed by any Averroist (see e.g. 465A, 466B) which should give us pause as well. Moreover, I fail to see how he can believe that his complicated interpretation of Averroes can be backed up by his interpretation of Alexander and Philoponus: they seem to represent three quite different doctrines indeed. Although a quick glance at Zabarella's other medieval sources seems to confirm his classification of them it cannot be ruled out that closer inspection will yield some surprises as it did with Philoponus. The details of Zabarella's own theory of mixture still await further investigation.

To conclude on a more general note: in charting the commentary tradition on Aristotle's work from Late Antiquity through Arabic, Latin Medieval, and Renaissance authors it is tempting to assume we are dealing with a single line of tradition. However, it is still far from clear which ancient commentaries were available (in Greek or in Arabic, Syrian, or Latin translation) at what date.[74] But even if this can be established we cannot be sure that a particular commentator actually used his predecessors' commentaries, even when he refers to them by name: perhaps he merely copied a reference from another commentary. In this way Zabarella's mistake may have arisen. More importantly, every commentator who analyses the problem of the potentiality of the ingredients in a mixture as it is presented in Aristotle's texts in *On Generation and Corruption* is faced with a limited number of possible solutions. Every commentator, then, is perfectly capable of re-inventing the wheel. However, the application of the third kind of potentiality in the context of mixture seems to have been invented for the first time by John Philoponus.

---

[74] But see now M. Rashed, *Al-Ḥasan ibn Mūsā al-Nawbakhtī: Commentary on Aristotle De generatione et corruptione* (Berlin: De Gruyter, 2015).

17

Gnôstikôs and/or *hulikôs*: Philoponus' Account of the Material Aspects of Sense-Perception

Péter Lautner

I

Nowadays, a major divide in the interpretation of Aristotle's theory of sense-perception is between the so-called literalists and spiritualists. The former claim that in perceiving a perceptible quality the perceiver takes on the quality in the relevant organ in the strict sense: the eyes, or more precisely the eye-jelly (*korê*), turn red when apprehending the red of a poppy.[1] By contrast, the spiritualists reject the idea that in sense-perception the activity of a sense-organ requires any alteration in its material set-up. The capacity for sense-perception is a basic, irreducible capacity of the sense-organ. The eyes do not see in virtue of undergoing any other change – rather they see just because their capacity for vision is activated by an object to be seen. The perceiving subject becomes aware of the perceptible object without any underlying physiological process.[2] The spiritualists also appeal to John Philoponus as an authority for the thesis that the colour cannot be

---

This article first appeared as 'Hulikôs and/or phusikôs: Philoponus' Account of the Material Aspects of Sense-Perception' by Péter Lautner in *Phronesis* 58 (2013), pp. 378–400 © Koninklijke BRILL NV 2013, reproduced with permission.

[1] R. Sorabji, 'Body and Soul in Aristotle', *Philosophy* 49 (1974), 42–64; 'From Aristotle to Brentano: The Development of the Concept of Intentionality', in H. Blumenthal and H. Robinson, eds, *Aristotle and the Later Tradition* (Oxford: Clarendon Press, 1991), pp. 227–60; 'Aristotle on Sensory Processes and Intentionality: A Reply to Myles Burnyeat', in D. Perler, ed., *Ancient and Medieval Theories of Intentionality* (Leiden: Brill, 2001), pp. 49–63; S. Everson *Aristotle on Perception* (Oxford: Clarendon Press, 1997).
[2] M. F. Burnyeat, 'Is an Aristotelian Philosophy Of Mind Still Credible? (A Draft)', in M. C. Nussbaum and A. O. Rorty, eds, *Essays on Aristotle's De anima* (Oxford: Clarendon Press, 1992), pp. 15–26; 'Aquinas on "Spiritual Change" in Perception', in D. Perler, ed., *Ancient and Medieval Theories of Intentionality* (Leiden: Brill, 2001), pp. 129–55; '*De Anima* II 5', *Phronesis* 47 (2002), 28–91; T. K. Johansen, *Aristotle on the Sense-Organs* (Cambridge: Cambridge University Press, 1998). For a list of pros and contras, see V. Caston, 'The Spirit and the Letter: Aristotle on Perception', in R. Salles, ed., *Metaphysics, Soul, and Ethics in Ancient Thought: Themes from the Work of Richard Sorabji* (Oxford: Clarendon Press, 2005), pp. 245–321, and H. Lorenz, 'The Assimilation of Sense to Sense-Object in Aristotle', *Oxford Studies in Ancient Philosophy* 33 (2007), 179–220. Both are arguing, with different arguments and results, that such a strict dichotomy – either literalist or spiritualist – is wholly unjustified.

taken on by the eye-jelly literally.[3] On their account, the sixth-century commentator dematerializes the perceptual process. To take the example of sight: the medium is not affected, but simply lets through the activity of the colour seen. Furthermore, on their view Philoponus interprets Aristotle's dictum that the sense receives the form of the sense-objects without their matter to mean that the sense is affected by the form in a cognitive way (*gnôstikôs*).

This characterization of Philoponus has also been accepted by those who favour the literalist interpretation: they think that he explained the sensory activity in terms of immaterial activities.[4] It seems, however, that the picture is more complex than has been described hitherto. My aim is to show that Philoponus' approach cannot be characterized as supporting the spiritualist case unambiguously. I hope to show that his explanation is somewhere in between the extremes of the two positions.[5] In itself, the claim is not new, but I aim to furnish it with new evidence.[6]

First, however, let us see the aspects of his theory of sense-perception that have been taken to support the spiritualist case. Philoponus says many times that the particular senses work in a cognitive way (*gnôstikôs*), which is supposed to mean that they do not undergo material change of any kind (*in DA* 309,15–29):[7]

> For it is not by being affected (*pathon*) in any way or by changing (*metaballon*) from the contrary state that it is made like it, but by receiving its form (*eidos*), not by coming to be as matter to it. For the sense (*aisthêsis*) does not become white when it has received the form of the sense-object (which is why it is not properly (*kuriôs*) said to be affected or to be altered (*alloiousthai*)) but it receives the regular feature (*logos*) of the form in a cognitive way (*gnôstikôs*) in itself. For just as we say that the wax is in potentiality (*dunamei*) what the ring is, because when it is affected by it it becomes what the latter is in act (*energeiai*), not having received its matter but only the form, so too sense, when it is affected by the sense-objects, takes the impression of (*ekmattesthai*) their form in a non-corporeal way (*asômatôs*). But there is the difference that the wax itself becomes the matter of the

---

[3] Burnyeat, 'Aristotelian Philosophy of Mind', p. 18; 'Aquinas', p. 130 (n. 2 above).
[4] Sorabji, 'From Aristotle to Brentano' (n. 1 above), pp. 232–3. C. Rapp, 'Intentionalität und *Phantasia* bei Aristoteles', in D. Perler, ed., *Ancient and Medieval Theories of Intentionality* (Leiden: Brill, 2001), pp. 63–97, at p. 76, modifies the claim by saying that touch and taste can be subject to material change, unlike the other senses that can undergo cognitive change alone.
[5] Philoponus endorsed many important features of Aristotle's theory. He did not question the formal aspects of the sensory process, and accepted its complexity and richness (in which it could be contrasted with Plato's account), which involves different types of perceptibles and a complex overall process which includes, e.g., the common sense. Interestingly enough, he also accepted certain elements of the hylomorphic scheme insofar as he thought that perceptual processes are accompanied by physiological changes. His views were incorporated in commentaries, and on the genre see, in general, R. Sorabji, 'The Ancient Commentators on Aristotle', in R. Sorabji, ed., *Aristotle Transformed: The Ancient Commentators and Their Influence* (London: Duckworth, 1990), pp. 1–31; I. Hadot, 'Le commentaire philosophique continu dans l'Antiquité', *Antiquité Tardive* 5 (1997), 169–76; and, especially on the *De Anima* commentaries, H. J. Blumenthal, 'Neoplatonic Elements in the *De Anima* Commentaries', *Phronesis* 21 (1976), 64–87.
[6] To the best of my knowledge, the claim has been made only by Caston (n. 2 above), p. 290.
[7] Translations from the *De Anima* commentary are from W. Charlton, *Philoponus, On Aristotle On the Soul 2.1–6* (London: Duckworth, 2005), sometimes lightly modified.

form that is in the ring, whereas the sense does not become the matter of the sense-object, but takes the impression of the *idea* of it in a cognitive way. And sense has something more beyond the wax. For the wax, even if it becomes the matter of the form in the ring, still does not receive the form through the whole of itself, but on the surface, whereas the perceiving power (*aisthêtikê dunamis*), the whole of it through the whole of itself, takes the impression of the *ideas* (*ideai*) of the sense-objects in a vital fashion (*zôtikôs*).

See also 438,6–15:

> Sense is not affected by the combination of matter and form, but only by the form, as wax is affected by the seal. Nor is it affected as a combination, for the organ does not become coloured or odorous, but is affected only in respect of its form, I mean the perceiving power itself. The body suffers the effect of heat, and the sense of touch suffers, but not the same effect. The sense is affected cognitively, and only by the form of the hot thing, whereas the organ, the flesh, as matter, is affected as a combination (*kata to sunamphoteron*), becoming the subject for the heat to inhere in, and being affected as a whole by the heating agent as a whole.

Again, to mention the working of another sense-organ, he goes against common assumptions (but thinks that he sides with Aristotle) in taking the pupil (*korê*) to be, not the aperture of the iris membrane, but the channel of the optic nerve, through which the optic *pneuma* goes out: 366,11–13. Moreover, visual perception requires the transparency of the lens (336,33–7):

> We say, then, that in reality the optic *pneuma* descends from the brain through the optic nerves (*optika neura*), and goes on until it reaches the lens (*krustalloeidos*), and its terminations are in that. That is why the discernments (*kriseis*) also of the visible objects are there. And that is why it [the lens] too is transparent so that the activities of the visible objects may be transmitted through it to the optic *pneuma*.

The lens is part of visual sense-organ and has to be transparent. This implies that it works like a medium, which cannot be coloured either. It has the task of allowing the activities of the visible objects to pass through to the optic *pneuma*. Furthermore, the *korê* is filled not with liquid but with *pneuma* and, as it will become clear later, *pneuma* is not a kind of bodily substance especially designed for receiving colours.[8] In such circumstances, there is no chance for the sense-organ to take on the quality of the perceptible object.

In the following, first, I shall be concentrating on two issues: the possible involvement of material processes in the operations of the particular senses, and the character of *pneuma*. Then I shall try to formulate some thoughts about the meaning of *gnôstikôs*.

---

[8] It is a kind of air, transparent by nature, and the seat of the soul: see 158,12–24; 162,2–15.

II

Even if we accept that by and large Philoponus supported the spiritualist case, the theory he puts forward contains elements that may make us cautious about crediting him with such a position without qualification. It has already been noted that, on his view, the operations of the particular senses vary in respect of their connection to bodily processes.[9] For example, the senses of smell and touch are tied to bodily processes especially closely. As the general problems of smell have been relatively extensively discussed by others, let it suffice to summarize the main points only.[10] Certain fine-textured effluences are produced by bodies which emit a smell, and at the same time the media of smell, the water or the air, have a smell-conveying power (*diosmos dunamis*) by the aid of which odours are transmitted incorporeally to the sense-organ.[11] Odours travel though the medium without affecting it. Effluence theory can account for certain facts about fragrances, such as the problem of why one odour can overpower another. However, it cannot explain perception of them, although effluences must contribute to the cognitive process.

Philoponus does not discuss the process of perceptual activity here, but he spent much time in discussing the flesh as the material cause of olfactory perception.[12] The material conditions of smell are provided by the organ which is situated at the front of the brain; more precisely, it is the mastoid outgrowth of the brain.[13] The organ itself does not take part in the perceptual process formally, since functional determination comes with the imposition of form. The material cause is embraced and determined by the form (282,23-5).

---

[9] Sorabji, 'From Aristotle to Brentano' (n. 1 above), pp. 233-4. The commentator's emphasis on the connection between cognitive and physiological processes may be due to his general interest in medical matters. The connection between his philosophical stance and medical interest has been discussed by R. B. Todd, 'Philosophy and Medicine in John Philoponus' Commentary on Aristotle's "De Anima"', *Dumbarton Oaks Papers* 38 (1984), 103-10. For a more general assessment of the interaction between philosophy and medicine, see R. B. Todd, 'Galenic Medical Ideas in the Greek Aristotelian Commentators', *Symbolae Osloenses* 52 (1977), 117-34.

[10] See J. Ellis, 'The Trouble with Fragrance', *Phronesis* 35 (1990), 290-302, at pp. 295-9; Sorabji, 'From Aristotle to Brentano' (n. 1 above), pp. 233-4.

[11] For *diosmos dunamis*, see 353,12-13.20-1; 354,10; 390,30; 391,4-6; 393,13.26; 394,12.

[12] The point has been generalized in 388,23-8 where flesh is considered as a material cause for the motions of the soul. It is even a contributory cause (*sunaition*) of intelligence, for the soul is tied to body, its motions disposed along with the motions mixtures of the body. The way the soul acts is linked to the state of this mixture, although its motions are not motions of the mixture.

[13] *Mastoeidēs apophusis tou egkephalou*. See 353,29-30; 392,32; 433,33. In 395,15-16, we read that the sense-organ is in the ethmoid bone, which separates the nasal cavity from the brain, while in 392,32 it is put after the ethmoid bone inside. The term *apophusis* is used by Galen in the same sense (see, e.g., *De usu partium* 12.7, ii. 198,11.14-15; 199,10; 201,16.20.28 Helmreich). Moreover, Galen's explanation of olfactory perception (see *De usu partium* 8.6-7; *De instrumento odoratus*) resembles the one we find in Philoponus. Galen uses the term in both treatises: *De usu partium* 8.6, i. 463,25-464,1 Helmreich, and *De instrumento odoratus* 30,13-14; 36,4-5 Kollesch. In the latter text he claims explicitly that olfactory affections come about, not in the lower parts of the nose (*en tois katô tês rhinos moriois*), but in the outgrowths of the front-ventricles of the brain (*en de tais apophusesi tôn prosthiôn egkephalou koiliôn*, 30,13-14). In her notes, J. Kollesch, *Galen über das Riechorgan* (Berlin: Akademie-Verlag, 1964), p. 71, mentions that the meaning of the term is not clear; it might refer to the *bulbus olfactorius*.

Touch is more connected to matter and is more corporeal in form (417,37); it is the coarsest-grained of all the particular senses.[14] What is the nature of its connection to bodily processes? In order to answer the question, we have to see, first, that there is a clear distinction between the medium and the sense-organ (*aisthêtêrion*, 418,13) on the one hand and the *sense* (*aisthêsis*) on the other. Whereas the medium is acted on and becomes matter for the various tactile qualities, the sense receives the activities of the sense-objects. By contrast, the sense-organ undergoes physical change. What is the sense and what is the sense-organ? How shall we separate and localize them? It seems that Philoponus' answer is that the sense and the sense-organ are different aspects of the same bodily entity, the flesh. Perhaps, for example he thinks that the sense is a *hexis* of the suitably-constituted flesh, whereas the sense-organ is the flesh suitably constituted. To come to that conclusion we have to get grips with a problem.[15] At one point he says that the flesh itself does not become like those qualities it apprehends.[16] It does not become heavy or light, viscous or friable, rough or smooth. Rather, it receives the forms of these things in a peculiar, 'cognitive' way. This seems to be an appropriate description of the operation of the senses. Later on, however, he claims that this same flesh can take on tactile qualities, such as heat, moistness, cold and dryness.[17] To get rid of the apparent difficulty, we have to turn to the passage in between, where we are told that the same bodily structure, the flesh, has a double function (433,1-4):

> But since, as has often been said, every body consists of a mixture together of moist and wet and hot and cold, for this reason also whenever it is affected by them, as a sense it apprehends and gets to know them, but as a natural body it is affected in a material way by them.

As a sense, then, the flesh apprehends and gets to know the tactile qualities in a cognitive way; as a body, however, it is affected in a material way by them, which means that it takes on these qualities. The distinction may also serve to elucidate the difference between a change in the sense-organ which is accompanied by sense-perception and a change which is not like this. The flesh can grow warm without the person's being

---

[14] See 416,23: *pakhumesterê*. It is called so because the flesh is more solid than the air or the various liquids attached to the other senses.

[15] The solution may be a development of Alexander's critique of Galen's view in *Quod animi mores* 3 (32,1-13; 37,16-24 Müller), that the sense is the blend of the body. Alexander responds in *De anima* 26,21-2 that it is a *hexis* based on that blend. As he says, soul in general is a *hexis*, *dunamis*, or *eidos* that supervenes (*epiginesthai*) on the blend of the body (see also 25,4-9). Philoponus is familiar with the Galenic theory (see *in DA* 51,13-52,1). For an analysis of the issue, see R. Sorabji, 'The Mind-Body Relation in the Wake of Plato's *Timaeus*', in G. Reydams-Schils, ed., *Plato's Timaeus as Cultural Icon* (Notre Dame: University of Notre Dame Press, 2003), pp. 152-62, at pp. 156-7; see also his *Emotion and Peace of Mind* (Oxford: Oxford University Press, 2000), pp. 261-3, 267-70, and, on ancient versus modern senses of 'supervene', *Perception, Conscience, and Will* (Aldershot: Ashgate, 2013), pp. viii-ix.

[16] 433,36-434,1.

[17] 433,7-11. This is how the flesh can grow warm without being perceived. Philoponus has to explain certain bodily changes that do not involve sense-perception. These changes are of the same type as those that involve sense-perception. The flesh can grow warm, which may or may not result in sense-perception. The problem, however, may be restricted to touch and, to a lesser extent, taste.

aware of it.[18] But that does not imply that the sense can work without appropriate changes in the sense-organ. In the case of touch (and taste as well) the connection is especially strong since, depending on the aspect under which we consider it, the flesh can work either as the sense or as the sense-organ.

On the basis of this latter assumption, we may be in a position to qualify the claim Philoponus made elsewhere that there is no sense-perception without sense-organ. In an Aristotelian context, such a claim seems fairly banal, but Philoponus formulates it in a peculiar way. He makes a clear distinction between the activities of touch and taste on the one hand, and those of the other three senses on the other. In the former case, the relation of the cognitive activity of the sense to the material activity of the sense-organ is quite intimate. Material and cognitive processes are simultaneous and their substrate is numerically the same. We cannot say that tactile perception is only a cognitive process, since both the activity of the sense and the process in the sense-organ are related to the same bodily structure, the flesh. It seems that the cognitive process requires certain material processes in the very same body, although we cannot prove the thesis that, once the flesh takes on the tactile qualities in a material way, it also receives the forms or activities in a cognitive way. Nonetheless we are entitled to say that the sense and the sense-organ are the same in substrate (even if that does not mean that they are also the same either functionally or conceptually). And if this is the case, Philoponus' claim is not only that sense-perception requires a specific physical and physiological set-up, but also that certain physical and physiological processes necessarily accompany sense-perception. Thus, in order to give an account of sense-perception we have to possess a proper description of the material process (getting cold or wet, for instance) that underlies sense-perception.

This is not to say, of course, that these physical and physiological processes are responsible for sense-perception as efficient causes. They are material causes.

Since the sense of taste works as a special case of touch, much of what can be said of the one applies to the other as well: perhaps this is the reason why Philoponus does not dwell on the sense of taste so much. But the other three senses function in a slightly different way. As has already been mentioned, the sense of smell receives the odours transmitted by the smell-conveying power of the medium incorporeally. Furthermore, the medium of hearing has a sound-conveying power to transmit sounds to the sense.[19] The medium of sight also transmits the specific activities of coloured objects in the same way. This means that the sense and the sense-organ are exposed to perceptual impacts even if they received them in a different way.

As for the sense-organs in these cases, they are clearly different from the senses. The eyes (or the vitreous liquid and choroid or corneal membrane therein), the sense-organ of smell at the front of the brain (its mastoid outgrowth) and the acoustic membrane are distinctly different from the respective senses. The mechanism of hearing offers a

---

[18] This presupposes that awareness is essential for actual sense-perception. On Aristotle's account, taking on the perceptual form without the matter is identical with the perceiver's awareness of colour or sound: see De Anima 3.2, 425b26–426a19. In general, perceptual awareness is inevitably linked to first-order perception (see again De Anima 3.2). This has been accepted by Ps.-Simplicius (sc. Priscianus?), Philoponus' colleague in Athens (e.g. in DA 109,25–7, to mention but one example).

[19] See *diêkhês dunamis* in 340,33–6; 341,6–7; 353,12–13.20–1; 354,10; 357,15–16.19.22; 358,3; 364,22.

good example. Just like other senses, the sense of hearing originates in the brain and proceeds through the nerves to the roots of the ear, called membranes. The nerve proceeding from the brain is furnished with a channel where the acoustic *pneuma* resides. For this reason, there must be some air which is enclosed in the cavity of the sense-organ and inherent to the membranes and the drumskin, the outer membrane of the drum. It receives the sound transmitted by the air outside and, in virtue of having a power to convey sounds, transmits the sounds to the (acoustic) membranes.[20] Philoponus never says that the particular sense-organs of these three particular senses would be the same in substrate as the senses themselves. Their relationship is more complex. Nevertheless, he stresses that that the sense-organs have a crucial role in sense-perception. He points out that the physiological conditions and processes contribute to the perceptual activity a great deal: they can promote or hinder the activity of the senses. To take the example of smell: those animals that have a covering over the sense-organ of smell need to breathe in so as to dilate the olfactory nerve. With a dilated nerve they are able to receive the activities (*energeiai*) of the objects of smell in a pure way (*katharôs*).[21] As a consequence, we can say that there must be some bodily changes in the sense-organ in order that the sense can function properly. The sense is not affected in the way the sense-organ is, but the proper affection in the sense-organ is necessary for the sense to function.

Even though he agreed to the important role of the sense-organ in sense-perception, Philoponus was not committed to the assumption that the sense will be affected in the perceptual process literally. He believes that he gets support for this view in Aristotle's text. In interpreting *De Anima* 2.5, 417b12–16, he makes two distinctions between different ways of being affected (304,29–305,2). The first distinction is between, on the one hand, changes that proceed from a state (*hexis*) to its contrary, which involves a kind of destruction of the initial state by the agency of something contrary, and, on the other, changes in which a state turns into activity.[22] (The change from a state to its contrary involves the changing thing having existed in potentiality from the relevant point of view: turning black to white implies that the black thing was potentially white at the beginning.)

The second distinction that he emphasizes is one *within* the changes that proceed from contrary state to contrary. The core of the argument involves a further distinction within the case of being in potentiality. On the one hand, a thing can change into a lack of that state, which is a genuine alteration and affection. On the other hand, a thing can also change to a state from a lack of that state, which is neither an affection nor an alteration. This is a change to perfection and nature. By 'change to nature', Philoponus

---

[20] 364,16–365,2. The processes of sight and hearing are similar in many respects. Here Philoponus emphasizes that both require something transparent in the sense-organ itself, a liquid in the eyes and an inborn air in the cavity of the sense-organ of hearing. The other analogy concerns the role of membranes. The eye contains the choroid or the corneal membrane, whereas the sense-organ of hearing contains a kind of membrane which must have something to do with what we call now eardrum (368,5–7).
[21] 395,13–14. By *katharôs* the commentator may mean a way of reception similar to what is termed *gnôstikôs* or *asômatôs*. In 392,1 he uses *asômatôs* in the same context.
[22] Philoponus makes the first distinction with reference to 417b2–7.

means a change to that which the thing is by nature and at which its nature aims (304,24–6).[23] He takes the example of acquiring knowledge. This kind of change happens when what is receptive of knowledge gets so far as to receive knowledge. Neoplatonically speaking, this is a kind of progress to itself. For this reason, it is a change from a lack of nature to a state appropriate to nature.

It seems, therefore, that the relation between sense and sense-organ is quite intimate in the case of every sense. On discussing the Pythagorean theory that the soul is an attunement of bodily parts in 439,33–440,3, Philoponus claims that the soul supervenes (*epiginomenon*) on some composition and proportionality.[24] To put this in the context of sense-perception, the attunement of the strings differs from the perceptual power which resides in the proportionality (*summetria*) of the sense-organ. The sense is a power inherent in the particular proportionality characteristic to each sense-organ. Hence it is not the same as the proportionality, although it perishes if the proportionality is destroyed. This means that the sense depends on the sense-organ as a necessary prerequisite.[25]

But how can the sense-organ as a necessary prerequisite contribute to the process of sense-perception? In order to see this more precisely, we have to discuss the nature and function of the *pneuma*.

III

The role and importance of *pneuma* reaches far beyond the confines of visual perception. Generally speaking, *pneuma* is the primary sense-organ for sight, hearing and smelling (433,25–30). This is not to say that the eyes (the liquid and the choroid membrane therein) or the membrane or the organ of smell at the front of the brain are not sense-organs. They are, but not the primary ones. It may be better to call them *particular* sense-organs. Touch and taste are not exceptions either. In their case, the primary sense-organ is inside the flesh.[26]

Pneuma is also called the common sense-organ for all:[27] it is what ensures the unity of sense-perception at the level of bodily ingredients and processes (and cf. 19,35–6). It is reasonable, then, that the so-called 'common sense' resides in the flesh with the *pneuma* as its substrate (433,35). Thus it seems that *pneuma* is the physiological counterpart of the common character of the perceptual system, the 'common sense'.

---

[23] For another analysis of the twofold distinction, see Burnyeat, 'De Anima II 5' (n. 2 above), p. 63, and Lorenz (n. 2 above), pp. 183–5. It is agreed that, if acquiring knowledge is a change at all, it should be char-acterized as developing or perfecting the nature one already has.

[24] See also *in Phys.* 191,11–16 and *in GC* 169,4–27. I owe the references to Sorabji (n. 15 above), p. 158.

[25] Hence the sense supervenes on the sense-organ not in the modern sense of 'co-varying' with it. I owe this point to Richard Sorabji.

[26] 433.33–4.

[27] From this point of view, Philoponus credits *pneuma* with a role which Aristotle seems to assign, not to the *sumphuton pneuma* in *De motu*, but to the blood (with the heart) which triggers the principle of perceptual system in a physical way (*De insomniis* 3, 461b11). Here I dissent from W. Charlton, *Philoponus, On Aristotle on the Intellect* (London: Duckworth, 1991), p. 112, n. 45.

Furthermore, the sensitive faculty related to each sense exists in the *pneuma*, not in the body.[28] Philoponus discusses acoustic *pneuma* in particular, but his most detailed analysis is devoted to the optic one.[29] What can we say about its role in visual perception?[30] To begin with, we must notice that visual perception is treated holistically, for the functioning of the eye cannot be separated from the visual apparatus. To be an eye requires the co-operation of the brain, the optic nerves and the *pneuma*. One can say that the activity of the eye is peculiar in relation to other parts of the body, but not peculiar in relation to the whole: to be a substance with definite function it requires the whole.[31] As I mentioned earlier, in most cases Philoponus interprets the *korê* in Aristotle's text to mean, neither the aperture of the iris membrane, nor the eye-jelly, but the channel of the optic nerve, through which the optic *pneuma* goes out to the lens.[32] The channel of the optic nerve is thus filled with *pneuma* that is not a proper vehicle for receiving colour, which might give the impression that visual perception occurs without the involvement of bodily processes. The point might be generalized, since Philoponus makes the general claim that the senses start from the brain and proceed through the nerves to the special sense-organs. (In the case of hearing, for example, he says that the nerves are filled with acoustic *pneuma*: 364,16–17.) This suggests two questions: what is the nature of the *pneuma* and what kind of change or alteration does it undergo?

In general, *pneuma* is inseparably connected to the non-rational soul.[33] It possesses a kind of bodily structure: presumably it is made up of a sort of humid air; it contains vapours (239,5–15), and is subject to bodily changes.[34] To take but two examples: as a result of a vicious mode of life it is thickened by its vapours; and healthy (i.e. light and dry) diet can make it lighter and less solid (19,27–8). *Pneuma* is the common sense-organ for all, and the optic *pneuma*, for example, as the primary sense-organ of sight, is a spatially determinable part of the general *pneuma*-stuff, which is homogeneous. Its distinguishing feature lies in its being exposed to influences coming from the eyes. As far as its specific spatial position is concerned, the optic *pneuma*

---

[28] 161.20–1. For this reason, the sense itself is not damaged when the specific sense-organ goes wrong.
[29] On acoustic *pneuma*, see 364,15.19–20; on optic *pneuma*, 336,17.20.33.37; 337,6.14.32; 348,37; 350,25.31; 364,36; 365,30; 366,13; *De intellectu* 99,49.
[30] In what follows, I shall deal with the conditions in the perceiving body and leave the processes in the medium for future considerations. In her discussion of the role of the medium, S. Berryman, '"It Makes No Difference": Optics and Natural Philosophy in Late Antiquity', *Apeiron* 45 (2012), 201–20, (referring to *in DA* 331,13–15) points out that for Philoponus both light and colour are supposed to be present through the medium as incorporeal actualities, and yet to have localized effects. See also R. Sorabji, 'Introduction', in R. Sorabji, ed., *Philoponus and the Rejection of Aristotelian Science*, 2nd edn (London: Institute of Classical Studies, 2010), pp. 1–40.
[31] 47,20–6. I suppose that the thesis applies to the other sense-organs as well.
[32] Exceptions are in 423,15–19 and *De intellectu* 99,48, where the term is taken to refer to the whole eye – membranes plus liquid – and in 368,1–3 where it refers to the aperture of the membrane, which is in conformity with common usage.
[33] See 12,18; 15,11; 18,35. This is linked to the problem of pneumatic vehicle of the soul (18,26–8; 19,21–3), much discussed in Neoplatonic circles in late antiquity. Non-rational soul resides in this *pneuma* and perishes together with it (164,4). On the problem in Philoponus, see P. van der Eijk, *Philoponus, On Aristotle On the Soul 1.1–2* (London: Duckworth, 2005), p. 123, n. 183.
[34] The *pneuma* seems to be a certain kind of air: see 364,20.

descends from the brain through the optic nerves, and goes on until it reaches the lens, which is where its terminations are.[35] The liquid and the membranes in the eye are, in relation to *pneuma*, a medium, although in relation to the air and other things they constitute a sense-organ (418,20–2). It is clear that *pneuma* is not coloured in the process of sense-perception, but that does not rule out the possibility that it undergoes some change. In fact optic *pneuma* is altered in the process of seeing: as a primary sense-organ of sight, the *pneuma* undergoes some alteration, even if it is not colouration.

Actually, there is a succession of processes between the particular sense-organs and the *pneuma*. In the *De Intellectu*, a medieval Latin translation of Philoponus' lost commentary on Aristotle, *De Anima* 3.4–8, we read a short causal story: in vision for example the air, the medium, is altered by colours, it alters the pupil, and the pupil alters the optic *pneuma*.[36] We are now in a position to supplement this story. Each particular sense-organ undergoes *two* types of bodily change. As bodies, they are exposed to certain general impacts, such as heat; as sense-organs, however, they receive specific kinds of impacts to which they can give specific physiological responses. As a specific sense-organ, then, the eyes, for example (or more properly, the liquid and the choroid membrane therein) are affected when they are compressed or expanded (*sunkrinesthai, diakrinesthai*) by the activity of colours.[37] It is important to note that the eyes undergo such physical change not in virtue of the motion of the medium, the air. Their change is due to the activity of colours. Compression and expansion are the bodily processes underlying the perception of colours. (The same holds true of smelling, since the sense-organ of smell, the mastoid outgrowth at the front of the head, does not become foul-smelling or sweet-smelling either; rather, it is made to expand or contract by the specific activity of the sense object: 396,15–16.)

Optic *pneuma* contacts the eye at the lens and is affected by the compressions or expansions of the liquid and the membrane in the eye. It can be affected in this way since it contains vapours. The optic *pneuma*, as we know from the Latin *De Intellectu* again, is part and parcel of the central sense-organ, the *pneuma*, for the *pneuma* is one and the same in substrate, although many in account (*ratio*), since it is capable of receiving many kinds of affections. The text runs as follows (99,49–57 Verbeke):[38]

---

[35] 336,34–6; 364,35–365,2; 365,33. Optic *pneuma* receives the affections (*ti peponthenai*) which come from visible objects: 161,25–6.

[36] 98,47–99,50: 'In vision the air is altered by colours, it alters the *pupilla* (I mean the eye itself), the *pupilla* something else (say the visual *pneuma*)' (trans. Charlton, slightly modified).

[37] 439.18–20. The material change of the sense-organ of sight has also been stressed by Caston (n. 2 above), p. 290.

[38] Translation from Charlton (n. 27 above), slightly modified. In translating *sensitivis* (99,50) as 'sensitive powers' I am following Richard Sorabji's suggestion. Bossier (in Charlton (n. 27 above), p. 113, n. 46) understands *sensiterium* in 99,51, 52, and 54 for the MSS' reading of *sensitivum*. (See also the critical apparatus in G. Verbeke, *Jean Philopon, Commentaire sur le De anima d'Aristote, Traduction de Guillaume de Moerbeke: Édition critique avec un introduction sur la psychologie de Philopon* (Louvain: Publications Universiatires de Louvain & Paris: Éditions Béatrice-Nauwelaerts, 1966).) Even if one does not accept his understanding of the term itself, it is clear on the basis of texts from Philoponus *in DA* 2 discussed above that sense-organ and *sensitivum* are aspects of the same thing: they are the same in substrate.

But the last thing altered is one single thing, the power of sight which judges the forms (*species*) of visible things; and it is the same with hearing and other sensitive powers; each sense-organ through some affection produced in it serves the power to perceive, and there is a final thing at which the affection ceases in each sense-organ; it is a single thing without parts, the power to perceive which he also, as often, calls a 'mean' (*medietas*). This power is one and without parts as a subject but many in account because it is receptive of many affections.

This seems to be the bodily mechanism underlying visual perception. The change in question is just as bodily as cognitive since, as has been stated in *De Intellectu* 18,2–3, the whole *pneuma* can be expanded or contracted (cf. 20,3–4). Since the description also applies to every other sense-organ, one might think that in sense-perception they undergo similar bodily change: i.e., the parts of *pneuma* that are the primary sense-organs for each particular sense can also change in this way.

Furthermore, it is the particular senses that 'judge' (*krisin poiein*) the incoming data – even if this is not a judgement properly speaking, only a discrimination of different perceptual experiences of the same modality. Such judgement takes place in the lens, which may be due to the homogeneity of the *pneuma*.[39] As soon as the impact from the visual sense reaches it, it starts performing its particular task. The cognitive impacts (and the physical impacts along with them) do not have to reach the brain, which is the origin of the particular senses (and the nerves filled with *pneuma*), in order to be discriminated. Further discrimination, now of perceptual experiences of different modalities, takes place in the *pneuma*, which is the central sense-organ in the brain.

As mentioned above, Philoponus also claims that the 'common sense' resides in the *pneuma* (433,35). So in what sense can we talk about the 'common sense' as a power additional to the particular senses?[40] Philoponus gives a clear answer to this, for he attributes specific functions to the 'common sense'. It distinguishes between the visible and the audible, and is also capable of perceiving that the different visible things are one.[41] This might sound a little bit strange, although Philoponus may only want to say that it is capable of forming a unique shape out of the various colour impressions, which enables us to say that this particular set of colours constitutes the shape of the visible object. Consequently, another function of the 'common sense' is to grasp the so-called common objects of sense-perception (shape, size, motion, rest and number). But perhaps

---

[39] See 350,31–3. In 350,25–6 he says, however, that optic *pneuma* discerns the sight-objects in the vitreous humour (*to krustalloeides hugron*), not in the lens (*to krustalloeides*). On the presence of the judgemental and perceptive capacity in the *pneuma*, see also 158,11–12 and 161,20–1.

[40] See W. Charlton, *Philoponus, On Aristotle On the Soul 2.7–12* (London: Duckworth, 2005), p. 158, n. 418.

[41] *De Intellectu* 99,63–5. This might be an indirect reference to Aristotle, *De Sensu* 7, 447b24–448a1. To tell whether sweet and white belong to one and the same thing, we have to know whether we are perceiving sweet and white simultaneously. Simultaneous perception of them may indicate that they originated from the same external thing. This can be connected to the view that in order to know that there is a world of bodies endowed with multiple properties we have to be aware of ourselves as single perceivers of those properties. See R. Sorabji, 'Self-awareness', in M. M. McCabe and M. Textor, eds, *Perspectives on Perception* (Fankfurt: Ontos Verlag, 2007), pp. 131–42, at p. 138.

we can tell the difference between the various levels of our perceptual faculty on the basis of physiology as well. To take the example of sight, again, we must consider the following factors. The (vitreous) liquid and the choroid membrane in the eyes constitute the specific sense-organ, whereas the optic *pneuma* is the primary sense-organ of sight.

This point leads us to the *pneuma* as a whole which acts as the common sense-organ. At first glance, we may be allowed to make a distinction between particular and common sense-organ. To take the example of sight, again, we may draw a distinction between the (vitreous) liquid and the choroid membrane in the eyes on the one hand and the *pneuma* on the other. The problem with the distinction is twofold. First, we cannot make any qualitative distinction within the spatially different parts of the homogeneous *pneuma*: this applies to the relationship between *pneuma* and optic *pneuma* as well (the latter being the part of the former which descends from the brain through the optic nerves, and goes on until it reaches the lens). Secondly, optic *pneuma* also serves as the primary sense-organ of sight, which means that one part of the *pneuma* is involved in the very process of seeing.[42] It seems, then, as if sight is based on the activities of two sense-organs: the liquid and the choroid membrane in the eyes, and the optic *pneuma*. It also seems that they underlie different stages of the visual process, since the optic *pneuma* alone is credited with the process underlying the process of judging (*krinein*), while the specific sense-organ takes on the particular sense-objects in the form of contractions and expansions.

If we realize, however, that the optic *pneuma* is an integral part of the *pneuma* as a whole then we are no longer entitled to claim that there is a clear-cut difference between the physiological bases of, respectively, the particular senses and the 'common sense'. For Philoponus, processes in the *pneuma* may well accompany such higher order perceptual activities as the recognition of common sensibles or the distinction between different types of particular sense objects, but certain processes go along with the working of the particular senses.[43] This is all the more reasonable since the senses and the sense-organs are the same in substrate. It seems, therefore, that at the level of physiology there is no sharp limit between the particular senses and the rest of the perceptual system. Whereas we can make a clear distinction between a particular sense and the 'common sense' we cannot make exactly the same distinction in their physiological set-up. Rather, it might be better to sketch a threefold scheme here: (1) the special sense-organs are exposed directly to external influences, which results in their contraction or expansion; (2) this is the way they made an impact on the part of the *pneuma* connected to them, which as a result also gets contracted or expanded; finally, (3) the impact in the optic/acoustic *pneuma* extends over the 'inner' areas of the *pneuma* as well. For this reason, the *pneuma* conceived of as the seat of 'common sense' cannot be separated qualitatively from the individual *pneumata* which are the primary sense-organs for each sense-modality.

---

[42] Philoponus explicitly says that it is the optic *pneuma*, not *pneuma* as a whole, which discriminates at the level of sight: 350,25–6.31–2.

[43] Note that, in this way, Philoponus clearly assigns *krisis* to the particular sense, while at the same time separating it from the reception of the particular sensibles. Moreover, he can do this with reference to the different physiological processes accompanying them: that is, the contraction or expansion of the vitreous liquid and the choroid membrane on the one hand, and the changes of the optic *pneuma* on the other.

The causal chain extending from the external sense object to the common sense-organ may also deserve attention. Even if there is no evidence for a causal interaction between the change in the sense-organ and the activity of the sense in terms of efficient causality, there is one point where we can see such an interaction. The sense-organ is influenced by external sensibles. The organ of sight is affected by the colours in a physical way, even if the medium, the air, does not change in the same way in transmitting colours. Colours make the eyes compact or extend; brighter colours make the eyes more compact.[44] It seems therefore that colours affect the special sense-organ 'materially', *hulikôs*, and the change produced thereby extends through the primary sense-organ, the optic *pneuma*, to the common sense-organ. This is a physical change triggered by a specific sense-object. It is unclear whether the cognitive activity of the sense is due to the same causation or to a parallel one, though the description of tactile perception with the flesh serving both as sense-organ and sense may point to a single line of causation initiating different mechanisms or, to put it more precisely, different aspects of the same change. Thus it seems that purely physical processes from without are not efficient causes of the processes of either the sense or the sense-organ.

IV

On the basis of this description, then, we can hope to clarify the meaning of *gnôstikôs*. A sense is affected in a 'cognitive' way by the activities of the particular sense-objects. What kind of activity is this, over and above the obvious fact that we cognize particular sense-objects through the specific affections of the senses? The first thing to note is that *gnôstikôs* goes along with *zôtikôs*, 'in a vital fashion' (see again *in DA* 309,15–29, as quoted above). It is also clear that the *zôtikôs* way of functioning is somewhere in between the *hulikôs* and the *gnôstikôs* ways. By *hulikôs* the commentator refers to purely material changes. In psychological explanations, the term is used to denote affective changes in the body (cf. 187,25; 416,30).

The relation between *zôtikôs* and *gnôstikôs* is more intricate since both terms refer to the activity of the sense: we must be cautious, since Philoponus uses two terms, *aisthêsis* (sense) and *aisthêtikê dunamis* (perceiving power), and connects *gnôstikôs* to the former, and *zôtikôs* to the latter.[45] He also says that the perceiving power is a kind of life (326,30–1). What is the meaning of *zôtikôs*, then? My suggestion is that the term refers to an aspect of the perceptual process which involves an emphasis, not on awareness, but on the importance of the process for the life of the animal. Philoponus makes an important distinction in his commentary on Aristotle, *Physics* 2 (*in Phys.* 241,20–3):

---

[44] See 316,35–317,2, where Philoponus gives a parallel description of the mechanism in the case of touch as well: hot makes the flesh compact.

[45] Philoponus mentions sense (*aisthêsis*) and perceiving power (*aisthêtikê dunamis*) separately, as if they were separate entities. As the distinction seems to be consistent (we find it both in 309,28–9 and in 438,10), one might assume that *aisthêtikê dunamis* (see also 19,35; 140,25; 292,15–18; 293,7; 326,30–2; 338,31) refers to the perceptual faculty as a whole, whereas *aisthêsis* denotes a particular sense. The problem is that in 140,25 Philoponus uses the term *aisthêtikê dunamis* in the plural, so the root of the distinction must be elsewhere.

For nature does not produce by looking at the paradigm (*paradeigma*). For even if it contains the reason-principles (*logoi*) of things that come about, it does not contain them cognitively as the carpenter does, but only vitally since it has been made in accordance with them.

From this passage it is clear that, by distinguishing vital and cognitive activities, Philoponus is trying to explain the creative activity of nature without attributing to it any kind of foresight.[46] Vital activities do not involve any planning or intention. They can be specific and, unlike the material ones, productive activities of an organic unity; nature can produce all sorts of natural things out of itself without any intention. Furthermore, when he is discussing the transmission of sounds to the sense of hearing, Philoponus says that the inborn (*sumphuês*) air, located in the ears, moves (*kineisthai*) not in respect of place, but 'in a vital way'.[47] This means that the air transmits the sound to the sense. Moving 'in a vital way' is thus nothing but fulfilling a specific function. The specific impact to which the senses are subjected is the reception of sensible forms. And, of course, this is the function of the senses.

To sum up, it seems that the term *zôtikôs* refers to an aspect of the sensory process which is neither physiological nor involving awareness. The perceptual process can be called vital in the sense that it is inevitable for the animal to exist. That explains the meaning of *gnôstikôs* too, since receiving influences in a cognitive way is the specific function of the senses.

But, still, there is a puzzle here, since Philoponus seems to waver as to what is received by the senses exactly. In one passage (309,19) he talks about reception of the '*logos* of the form' (*ton logon tou eidous*), in another about reception of the forms as a reception of 'pure' (*katharoi*) *logoi* of the sense-objects (437,11).[48] Furthermore, in 309,25 and 29 (quoted above), he mentions that sense-perception is a reception of the *idea* of the sensible things (*tôn aisthêtôn*).[49] What is the relation between *logos tou eidous*, *katharos logos tôn aisthêtôn*, and *idea tôn aisthêtôn*?

---

[46] We find similar distinctions in Proclus' *Elements of Theology* (39), revised in Damascius, *De principiis* 79. Proclus claims that, unlike cognitive activities (specifically those which are connected to reversion), vital activities do not involve any kind of knowledge. (For a list of the different levels, see Syrianus, *in Metaph*. 81,32–5) Consequently, vital activities do not contain any kind of awareness either. That does not rule out, however, the possibility that they can be cognized by the soul. In his commentary on Aristotle's *De Anima*, Ps.-Philoponus claims that we can be aware of our vital activities (465,10–16), but the source of awareness is the attentive power (*to prosektikon*) which belongs to the rational faculties. Ps.-Simplicius (Priscianus?) also notes that the medium must also be affected vitally in order better to stimulate the sense-organ (*in DA* 161,11–12; 162,28). Working *vitally* characterizes the functioning of the medium, but that does not mean that it works *cognitively*.

[47] See 369,4–6: 'it is possible to say 'in a vital way', meaning by 'movement' the transmission of sounds to the sense'.

[48] The text runs as follows (437,8–11): 'This, he says, is how the sense comes to be what the sense-object is: it does not become white or sweet but it receives the form (*eidos*) of the sense-object without the matter, that is, it takes impressions of the pure *logoi* of them (*autôn*) in a cognitive way'. Much hinges on the reference of *autôn*, which seems to be to *aisthêtôn*. If we want to reconcile the use of *logos* here and in 309,19 with *ton logon tou eidous* then we may say that the term *aisthêton* refers to sensible qualities, which are perceived primarily, and not to the external things having these qualities. The emphasis on purity may indicate that Philoponus takes *logoi* to mean the structural (i.e. formal) elements of the external thing.

[49] See 309,24–9 (part of the text quoted p. 438 above).

It is interesting to see how Philoponus makes use of the Platonic term *idea*. Except for clear references to the doctrines of Plato or his followers,[50] he only once uses the term to denote an abstract entity which is not accessible via sense-perception.[51] Elsewhere he employs it to refer to either structure or appearance.[52] It might be strange, however, to claim that sense-perception is the reception of the *structure* of the sensible object, whatever that might be. The sense will not possess the whole structure of the sensible object. Hence the only possibility for understanding the term here is to say that perception of colour, which is a feature of the surface of a thing, may be better considered the reception of an *appearance*. To put it otherwise, perception is a reception of a sensible form. Colours are not structural elements and they can only, at best, *indicate* the structure. For this reason, since there seems to be an ambiguity here, my suggestion is that the term *idea* is used to mean appearance in the broad sense (not restricted, that is, to visual experiences), whereas the expression *logos tou eidous* has a more precise meaning, referring to the reception of the form as a specific *ratio*. For the specific sense-organ and the *pneuma* receive the sensible forms as particular ratios, something that corresponds to the different degrees of the compression or expansion of the matter of the sense-organ.[53] In discussing Aristotle's notion of the sense as a mean in De Anima 2.11, 424a4, Philoponus aims to support the thesis that the sense is capable of receiving the form of either sensible quality contrary to one another (435,27–8).[54] We can only speculate as to how to account for the individual and specific differences between the various sense-impressions, but theoretically the various ratios allow for such differences. What is clear is that, on his account, as sense-organs they exist in a certain proportionality and mean state (439,9–10):[55] in fact, it is due to their existence as a mean state that they are capable of grasping the sense objects.

---

[50] There are quite a few: see 37,18; 63,4.12; 77,6; 78,27; 79,16; 80,23.
[51] *De Intellectu* 15,50. This meaning can be ruled out in the context discussed above.
[52] I suppose he uses it to refer to 'appearance' in 55,22–4 (on the physiognomists' theories based on appearance) and 397,10 (on the many forms of odours), and to 'structures' in 369,13 (on the elemental change).
[53] This is reinforced by the remark in 440,1–2 that the sense is in a certain proportionality (*summetria*) in the sense-organ. The proportionality of the specific sense-organ characterizes the blend of this organ as a mixture of different kinds of particle. The specific organ, like the eye, can contract or expand without any change of the proportion of its ingredients. By contrast, the proportionality in the *pneuma* as a primary and common sense-organ can-not be the feature of such a mixture since the *pneuma* is homogeneous. Instead, it might exclusively characterize the contractions and expansions of this humid air in the nerves.
[54] See the text of the *De Intellectu* quoted above, and *in DA* 435,25–7; 435,34–436,6; 439,5–10.31; 440,9.17–18. This kind of mean state has something to do with non-rationality, although not to the extent we ourselves (with our desires and passions) are non-rational: see 255,10–11. Sometimes, Philoponus talks about the sense-organ as a mean, and my guess is that he is able to do this because of the supposed identity of sense-organ and sense in substrate.
[55] Alexander thinks that in order to compare and distinguish the reports of the five individual senses the sense must be indivisible, spatially and numerically alike. Otherwise it would be one perceiving subject apprehending one thing, and another subject another; but this does not permit comparisons and distinctions to be made; but if something is numerically and spatially indivisible, how can it be affected by black and white simultaneously? This is the 'contraries problem' (see Sorabji, 'From Aristotle to Brentano' (n. 1 above), p. 229). Philoponus does not seem to extend it to the sense: he is talking about the medium only (*in DA* 329,14–20).

V

To sum up, it seems that Philoponus considered sense-perception as something that involves both bodily and non-bodily changes. As a consequence, we cannot say that his analysis offers clear-cut support for either the literalist or the spiritualist interpretation. Rather, he elaborates a theory that contains elements of both positions. On the one hand he claims that sense-perception necessarily involves bodily processes, either in the particular sense-organs, such as the acoustic membrane or the tongue, or in the primary sense-organ, the *pneuma*. In the case of touch and taste, the special sense-organ, the flesh, does seem to take on the relevant tactile and gustatory qualities literally: it does become hot or cold during the perception of these qualities by the sense. But Philoponus rejects the possibility that the primary sense-organ can take on any of the qualities perceived by the senses. Moreover, the sense-organ of sight cannot turn red either, since the only physical change it undergoes as a sense-organ is compression and expansion. The same applies to the sense-organs of hearing and smell as well.

On the other hand, we cannot say either that the activities of the senses are to be reduced to bodily activities. Bodily and cognitive changes are changes of the same substrate from different perspectives, and we cannot establish a primacy between them in terms of efficient causality. Efficient causality can only be established in the way the external objects affect the specific sense-organs. Colours do not only initiate cognitive changes in the sense of sight: they merely move the eyes *hulikôs* by compressing or expanding them.[56]

---

[56] An earlier version of this paper was read at the tenth ISNS Annual Conference held in Cagliari in June, 2012, and I am indebted to the audience, especially to John Dillon for questions and helpful remarks. I am also grateful to George Boys-Stones and Richard Sorabji who read the penultimate version and suggested many revisions, and to the anonymous referee for pointing out many infelicities and proposing important points to discuss and improve. My study was supported by the Hungarian Research Fund (OTKA), project number 104574.

18

The Last Philosophers of Late Antiquity in the Arabic Tradition

Peter Adamson

The classical texts of Greek philosophy reached the Islamic world through a double filter. One filter was the Syriac tradition: Christian authors produced translations of and treatises inspired by Greek works, which formed a partial basis for the later Arabic translation movement.[1] A second filter was provided by late antique Greek authors immediately preceding, and in some cases contemporaneous with, the scholars who produced a philosophical literature in Syriac.[2] One could point to a similar historical continuity in the case of Latin medieval philosophy, where late ancient authors like Boethius and Augustine exercised enormous influence for many centuries. But at least some of the differences between early Arabic and early Latin philosophy can be ascribed to the very different fortunes of the late antique philosophical corpus in the Latin- and Arabic-speaking worlds. Whereas the output of the Greek commentators was largely unknown in Latin, it was to an amazingly large extent retained in Arabic. This was thanks to the translation movement of the ʿAbbāsid era. Without going into great detail about the translation movement in general, I will begin this paper by recalling a few basic and well-known points about the reception of the commentators. I will then focus on two topics which display how late antique philosophy was received in the Islamic world: the question of how logic relates to philosophy, and the dispute over the world's eternity. In both cases, I will not only highlight the decisive influence of late ancient philosophy on authors writing in Arabic. I will also try to show how these authors reacted to contemporary cultural pressures by reshaping, extending, and departing from their Graeco-Arabic sources.

This article first appeared as 'The last philosophers of late antiquity in the Arabic tradition' by Peter Adamson in *Entre Orient et Occident: la philosophie et la science gréco-romaine* (2011; Entretiens 57), pp. 1–38 © Fondation Hardt 2011, reproduced with permission.

---

[1] For an overview see H. Daiber, 'Die syrische Tradition in frühislamischer Zeit', in U. Rudolph, ed., *Grundriss der Geschichte der Philosophie: Philosophie in der islamischen Welt 1. 8.-10. Jahrhundert* (Basel: Schwabe, 2012), pp. 40–54.
[2] Consider that Sergius of Reshʿaynā died in 536 CE, only 7 years after the closure of the Platonic school in Athens.

The Commentators in Arabic

The *Commentaria in Aristotelem Graeca* (CAG), a monumental edition of the commentators produced in Germany over a century ago, was read rather sparingly until relatively recently. A renewed interest in this corpus has represented one of the biggest shifts in the study of ancient philosophy over the past 30 years. Largely this has been instigated by the Ancient Commentators on Aristotle Project led by Richard Sorabji. As a result, now in the early twenty first century we can say that we have just about caught up with, and perhaps even surpassed, the knowledge of late antique philosophy that was achieved in Baghdad in the tenth century CE. Not coincidentally both endeavors involved a huge effort of translation, as well as thoughtful analysis of the commentators' ideas. If we consider the fruits of the Graeco-Arabic translation movement, we can see immediately how keen was the interest taken in Greek commentaries under the 'Abbāsids.[3] Medieval book lists, above all the invaluable *Fihrist* of Ibn al-Nadīm, tell us of numerous translations of commentaries by Alexander of Aphrodisias, Themistius, Porphyry, and members of the Alexandrian school like Ammonius, Simplicius, Philoponus, and Olympiodorus.

A smaller number of commentaries and works by Greek commentators are preserved, wholly or partially, in their Arabic versions. Completely preserved commentaries are rare; here a prominent example would be the paraphrase of the *De Anima* by Themistius. We also have him on *Metaphysics* Book Lambda, as I will discuss later on. More common are commentaries known partially or as fragments. For instance we have large parts of the Arabic version of Philoponus' commentary on the *Physics*. Also extant are Arabic fragments of some of Alexander's commentaries, for instance those on the *Physics*, *Metaphysics* and *On Generation and Corruption*. In some cases these supplement what can be known from the Greek tradition. There are surviving Arabic versions of independent treatises from some of the same authors, especially Alexander.

In addition we can, even in the absence of Arabic versions of the commentaries, observe the direct influence of commentators on Arabic philosophy. The works of al-Kindī, the first Hellenizing philosopher to write in the Islamic world, already betray extensive influence from Greek commentators from the Alexandrian school, as well as from earlier authors like Alexander.[4] But the influence of the Alexandrian commentators

---

[3] See the very useful table provided by D. Gutas, 'Greek Philosophical Works Translated into Arabic', in R. Pasnau, ed., *The Cambridge History of Medieval Philosophy*, 2 vols (Cambridge: Cambridge University Press, 2010), vol. 2, pp. 802–14. See also C. D'Ancona, 'Greek into Arabic: Neoplatonism in Translation', in P. Adamson and R. C. Taylor, eds, *The Cambridge Companion to Arabic Philosophy* (Cambridge: Cambridge University Press, 2005), pp. 10–31, with a table at pp. 22–3 focusing specifically on Neoplatonists; and further id., 'Greek Sources in Arabic and Islamic Philosophy', in the online *Stanford Encyclopedia of Philosophy*, ed. E. N. Zalta: <http://plato.stanford.edu/entries/arabic-islamic-greek>.

[4] For a good example see S. Fazzo and H. Wiesner, 'Alexander of Aphrodisias in the Kindī Circle and in al-Kindī's Cosmology', *Arabic Sciences and Philosophy* 3 (1993), 119–53. The influence on al-Kindī from the Alexandrian tradition is clear from his use of Philoponus in treating the world's eternity (see below), and from his discussion of the nature of philosophy at the beginning of *On First Philosophy*. As detailed by A. Ivry, *Al-Kindī's Metaphysics* (Albany: State University of New York Press, 1974), 115–8, this passage and the related definitions of philosophy in al-Kindī's *On the Definitions and Descriptions of Things* extensively parallel authors like Ammonius, Elias and David. His works are available in translation in P. Adamson and P. E. Pormann, *The Philosophical Works of al-Kindī* (Karachi: Oxford University Press, 2012). See also P. Adamson, *Al-Kindī* (New York: Oxford University Press, 2007).

peaks in the tenth-eleventh centuries with the so called 'Baghdad Peripatetics', a group of mostly Christian Aristotelian philosophers who produced their own commentaries and treatises based on Aristotle. They often imitate the very form of the commentaries, as well as reproducing the comments made by their Greek forebears – sometimes verbatim. Among the Baghdad Peripatetics, the author who follows the Alexandrians most closely is the last representative of the school, Abū l-Faraj ibn al-Ṭayyib. We have extant commentaries from his pen on Porphyry's *Isagôgê* and Aristotle's *Categories*.[5] Other members of the school also engaged extensively with the Greek commentators. This includes not only the famous Muslim thinker al-Fārābī, but also a number of Christian Peripatetics such as Yaḥyā ibn ʿAdī.[6] As we will see in a moment, the logical writings of these authors provide eloquent testimony of the impact of the commentary tradition. Another fine example is the so-called 'Baghdad *Physics*', which incorporates comments by numerous members of the Baghdad school, including Ibn ʿAdī, as well as excerpts from Alexander's and Philoponus' commentary in Arabic translation.[7] Also worth noting is Ibn ʿAdī's commentary on *Metaphysics* Alpha Elatton, which seems to imitate the Greek commentaries by first treating the doctrine (*theoria*) of each passage, before moving on to the wording (*lexis*).[8]

There are, then, a large number of texts displaying the impact of the Greek commentators on philosophy in Arabic in the ninth-eleventh centuries CE. To some extent, their influence wanes thereafter, as philosophical commentary tends to be directed towards Avicenna rather than Aristotle. Of course the revival of Aristotelianism in Andalusia, above all in the commentaries of Averroes, constitutes a major exception. Averroes in fact preserves for us some of the fragments mentioned above, for authors like Alexander. But in what follows here I will be focusing on the early period. Before delving into specific topics, I'd like to note three points of continuity between the Greek commentary tradition and the early Arabic tradition of Hellenizing philosophy (*falsafa*). These are not novel points, but well worth repeating.

First, the Arabic tradition carries on Greek attitudes towards the prospects of reconciling Aristotle with Platonism. This is not to say that all authors take a harmonizing attitude, but rather that a harmonizing attitude is the norm, yet admits of

---

[5] For the former see K. Gyekye, *Ibn al-Ṭayyib's Commentary on Porphyry's Eisagoge* (Beirut: Dar el-Machreq, 1975); trans. in K. Gyekye, *Arabic Logic: Ibn al-Ṭayyib's Commentary on Porphyry's Eisagoge* (Albany: State University of New York Press, 1979). For the latter, see C. Ferrari, *Die Kategorienkommentar von Abū l-Faraj ʿAbdallāh ibn aṭ-Ṭayyib* (Leiden: Brill, 2006).

[6] His works are edited in S. Khalifat, *Yaḥyā ibn ʿAdī: the Philosophical Treatises* (Amman: Publications of University of Jordan, 1988). See further G. Endress, *The Works of Yaḥyā ibn ʿAdī: an Analytical Inventory* (Weisbaden: Reichert, 1977).

[7] See the edition in A. Badawī, *Arisṭūṭālīs: al-Ṭabīʿa*, 2 vols (Cairo, 1964–65). The commentary's contents are summarized in P. Lettinck, *Aristotle's Physics and its Reception in the Arabic World* (Leiden Brill, 1994). See further several studies by E. Giannakis: *Philoponus in the Arabic Tradition of Aristotle's Physics*, D. Phil. Thesis (Oxford, 1992); id., 'The Structure of Abū l-Ḥusayn al-Baṣrī's Copy of Aristotle's *Physics*', *Zeitschrift für Geschichte der arabisch-islamischen Wissenschaften* 8 (1993), 251–8; id., 'Fragments from Alexander's lost Commentary on Aristotle's *Physics*', *Zeitschrift für Geschichte der arabisch-islamischen Wissenschaften* 10 (1995–96), 157–87.

[8] P. Adamson, 'Yaḥyā ibn ʿAdī and Averroes on *Metaphysics* Alpha Elatton', *Documenti e Studi sulla Tradizione Filosofica Medievale* 21 (2010), 343–74. See also C. Martini Bonadeo, 'Un commento ad alpha elatton "sicut litterae sonant" nella Baghdād del X secolo', *Medioevo* 28 (2003), 69–96.

exceptions. Good examples of harmonization (not without nuance) can be found on the Greek side in authors like Porphyry and Simplicius, and on the Arabic side in al-Kindī and the author of the work *On the Harmony of the Two Sages*, whose ascription to al-Fārābī has recently been a matter of dispute.[9] Other authors are less optimistic about the prospects for a consistent Platonic Aristotelianism. Here one might think of Alexander or Syrianus on the Greek side, and al-Rāzī on the Arabic side.

Second, the Greek tradition already involves the passing of Platonism and Aristotelianism – more or less fused into a single tradition, as just mentioned – from pagans to Christians. The last philosophers of Greek antiquity were mostly pagans, but the *very* last philosophers of Greek antiquity were often Christians. Most prominent here is of course John Philoponus, but one thinks also of the associates of Olympiodorus, Elias and David – who are often among the closest models for the commentaries of Ibn al-Ṭayyib. On the Arabic side, it's already been mentioned that the Baghdad Aristotelians were almost all Christians, and the central role of Christians in the translation movement hardly needs emphasis. Indeed *falsafa* was an admirably ecumenical enterprise. Not only do we find devout Muslims like al-Kindī working together with the Christian translators and scholars who were so indispensable to the translation movement, but we find Christian authors like Ibn ʿAdī engaging politely with Jews in philosophical exchanges.[10]

Third, authors writing in Arabic took over from late antique authors not only philosophical ideas, but a philosophical curriculum. In the case of Porphyry's *Isagôgê*, a work by a Neoplatonist had actually been added to the standard Aristotelian curriculum pursued at Alexandria.[11] It became such a standard part of philosophical education that al-Kindī uses it as a basis to refute the Trinity because, he says, it is well known to his Christian opponents.[12] More generally and more fundamentally, the late ancient ordering of Aristotle's works and of the philosophical sciences (which of course go hand-in-hand) penetrated deeply into Arabic philosophy.[13] This question of how

---

[9] For a sceptical view see M. Rashed, 'On the Authorship of the Treatise on the Harmonization of the Opinions of the Two Sages Attributed to Al-Fārābī', *Arabic Sciences and Philosophy* 19 (2009), 43–82, following the lead of J. Lameer, *Al-Fārābī and Aristotelian Syllogistics. Greek Theory and Islamic Practice* (Leiden: Brill, 1994), pp. 30–39. See also Rashed, ch. 20 in this volume. On the topic of harmonization see further C. D'Ancona, 'The Topic of the 'Harmony Between Plato and Aristotle': Some Examples in Early Arabic Philosophy', in A. Speer, ed., *Wissen über Grenzen. Arabisches Wissen und lateinisches Mittelalter* (Berlin: De Gruyter, 2006), pp. 379–405; A. Bertolacci, 'Different Attitudes to Aristotle's Authority in the Arabic Medieval Commentaries on the *Metaphysics*', *Antiquorum Philosophia* 3 (2009), 145–63.

[10] See S. Pines, 'A Tenth Century Philosophical Correspondence', *Proceedings of the American Society for Jewish Research* 23 (1954), 103–36.

[11] Whether the *Isagôgê* itself is a Neoplatonic work is less clear; for an affirmative answer see R. Chiaradonna, 'What is Porphyry's *Isagoge*?', *Documenti e Studi sulla tradizione filosofica medievale* 19 (2008), 1–30.

[12] See A. Périer, 'Un traité de Yaḥyā ben ʿAdī. Défense du dogme de la Trinité contre les objections d'al-Kindī', *Revue de l'orient christian* 3rd series, 22 (1920–1), 3–21. Al-Kindī's arguments, without the response of Ibn ʿAdī, are translated in R. Rashed and J. Jolivet, *Oeuvres Philosophiques & Scientifiques d'al-Kindī: Volume 2, Métaphysique et cosmologie* (Leiden: Brill, 1998) and in Adamson and Pormann (n. 4 above).

[13] See G. Endress, ed., *Organizing Knowledge: Encyclopaedic Activities in the Pre-eighteenth Century Islamic World* (Leiden: Brill, 2006); D. Gutas, 'The 'Alexandria to Baghdad' complex of narratives. A contribution to the study of philosophical and medical historiography among the Arabs', *Documenti e Studi sulla Tradizione Filosofica Medievale* 10 (1999), 155–93; P. Adamson, 'The Kindian Tradition: the Structure of Philosophy in Arabic Neoplatonism', in C. D'Ancona, ed., *Libraries of the Neoplatonists* (Leiden: Brill, 2007), pp. 351–70.

philosophical disciplines relate to one another provides a common link between the two topics I will be discussing in the remainder of this paper.

Logic as an Instrument of Philosophy

In Greek commentaries on the works of the *Organon* – Porphyry's *Isagôgê* plus Aristotle's 'logical' works – it became standard to discuss the question whether logic is a part or an instrument of philosophy.[14] The very term *organon* (instrument) shows which way the Aristotelians were inclined to see the issue. For them, logic was not strictly speaking a philosophical science, but rather a discipline or art (*tekhnê*) which contributes instrumentally to philosophy. They developed this view in opposition to the Stoics. For the Stoics, logic constituted one of the three parts of philosophy, alongside ethics and physics. Alexander of Aphrodisias objected to this, on the grounds that logic has a different subject-matter (*hupokeimenon*) and goal (*telos*) from philosophy.[15] Its subject-matter is 'statements and propositions (*axiômata kai protaseis*)', and its goal is 'to prove that, when propositions are compounded with one another in certain ways, something may be deduced by necessity from what is posited or conceded'.[16] Elsewhere in the same commentary, Alexander develops the idea that logic studies argument *forms*, that is, syllogistic forms, to which terms stand as matter. This is why a certain syllogism can be represented schematically (indeed Alexander uses the word *skhêma*), with letters instead of terms (e.g. 'All A is B, all B is C, therefore all A is C'). As has been pointed out, Alexander here seems to be taking a step towards what we might call 'formal' logic.[17] Better, one might instead say that he is acutely observing the significance of Aristotle's own steps towards treating logic schematically and 'formally'.

However, things are not so simple. One reason Alexander and other commentators disagree with the Stoic view is that for them logic is *defined* by its instrumental role, in that the study of logic (when done properly) ignores 'useless' yet valid inferences. It is not germane to point out that 'If A, then A; A; therefore A' is a valid inference. Rather the serious logician is interested in argument forms that can be used to advance philosophical science.[18] This differentiates the Aristotelian outlook from the modern understanding of logic as the study of purely formal systems (since trivial inferences belong to the system just as much as 'useful' inferences). To put it another way, the

---

[14] For the issue a good place to start is R. Sorabji, ed., *The Philosophy of the Commentators 200–600 AD: A Sourcebook*, 3 vols (London: Duckworth, 2004), vol. 3, ch. 1(b). See further K. Ierodiakonou, 'Aristotle's Logic: an Instrument, Not a Part of Philosophy', in N. Avgelis and F. Peonidis, eds, *Aristotle on Logic, Language and Science* (Thessaloniki: Sakkoulas, 1997), pp. 33–53; T.-S. Lee, *Griechische Tradition der aristotelischen Syllogistik in der Spätantike* (Göttingen: Vandenhoeck & Ruprecht, 1984), ch. 2; A. C. Lloyd, *The Anatomy of Neoplatonism* (Oxford: Clarendon Press, 1990), pp. 17–21.

[15] Alexander, *in An. Pr.* 1,18–2,2.

[16] Translation from J. Barnes *et al.*, *Alexander of Aphrodisias, On Aristotle Prior Analytics 1.1–7* (London: Duckworth, 1991).

[17] Lee, *op. cit.*, pp. 38–9, citing Alexander, *in Pr. An.* 53–4 for the form/matter idea and the importance of substituting letters for terms.

[18] Thus Lee, *op. cit.*, pp. 49–50 speaks of Alexander envisioning a 'working logic.' Cf. Ierodiakonou, *op. cit.*, p. 36. She also points out (p. 38) that the Periapetetics underestimated the Stoics' own stress on the utility of logic. See also Lloyd, *op. cit.*, pp. 18–19.

commentators seem to be interested more by soundness than by validity. This becomes clear when they say, in a phrase that will reappear frequently in the Arabic tradition, that the role of logic is to 'distinguish the true from the false and the good from the evil'.

Actually, if we look at the formulation in a preserved excerpt from Elias on the *Prior Analytics*, we see that he is a bit more nuanced than this. What he says is that 'philosophy uses logic (*kekhrêtai tê logikê*) to show, in the theoretical domain, what is true and what false, and in the practical domain what is good and what is bad'.[19] Note that logic does not establish the true, false, good, and bad. Rather it is *used* to establish these things. This is an important qualification, because the commentators need to hold on to the idea that logic is merely instrumental, even if it is an indispensable instrument. The goal is to devise arguments which establish truth. And logic is merely necessary, not sufficient, for the grasp of truth. As Katerina Ierodiakonou has argued, the commentators would have a principled reason for insisting on this point. Logic studies the expression (*phônê*), not the thing itself (*pragma*). But each philosophical science has some range of objects – real things out in the world – which it studies. For instance, physics studies things subject to motion and rest. Since logic deals with the words which refer to things rather than the things referred to, logic is not a proper philosophical science.[20]

This is, of course, consistent with its merely necessary and non-sufficient character – logic as such is pre-philosophical, precisely because it does not by itself establish truth. Even commentators with more ambitious views of logic acknowledge this. Here I am thinking particularly of Ammonius, who endorses what he identifies as the Platonic valorization of logic as both part *and* instrument of philosophy. This is because he wants to bring Aristotelian logic into close relation with Platonic dialectic (as described in the middle books of the *Republic*, for instance), which is clearly much more than an instrument.[21] But Ammonius is able to distinguish 'mere' logic from truth-yielding dialectic by using Alexander's idea of syllogistic form which needs to be filled in by matter. Logic is a mere instrument because the form is 'empty', but once the arguments (*logoi*) are 'taken together with real things' logic becomes a part of philosophy.[22] Ammonius might as well have said that, once applied to the real things, logic is simply *identical* to philosophy, insofar as philosophy consists of demonstrations with a logical form.

In any case, the 'non-scientific' status of logic did not prevent it from being every student's introduction to philosophy in the late ancient teaching curriculum. And for good reason: as we've seen, logic is merely instrumental, but it is an indispensable or necessary instrument. One can no more do philosophy without logic than one can do carpentry without tools. This attitude passed into the Arabic tradition along with the textual tradition of commentary on the *Organon*. As has been noted by numerous scholars – notably Gerhard Endress in his study of the standing of logic in Arabic

---

[19] In L. G. Westerink, 'Elias on the *Prior Analytics*', *Mnemosyne* 14 (1961), 126–39, at 134,23–4.
[20] Ierodiakonou, *op. cit.*, p. 46.
[21] See P. Hadot, 'La logique, partie ou instrument de la philosophie?', in I. Hadot, ed., *Simplicius, Commentaire sur les Catégories, fasc. 1: Introduction* (Leiden: Brill, 1990), pp. 183–8, who connects Ammonius' view to the treatment of dialectic in Plotinus, *Enneads* 1.3.
[22] Ammonius, *in An. Pr.* 10,38–11,3. For him the Platonic view is the reasonable middle ground between the extreme positions of the Stoics and Peripatetics. Cf. also Lee, *op. cit.*, p. 40.

culture – several Arabic texts repeat, even verbatim, the commentators' remarks about logic's instrumentality.[23] As usual Ibn al-Ṭayyib adheres closely to the Alexandrian commentators here, remarking for instance that logic is 'the instrument for philosophy (adā li-l-falsafa); without the instrument, the agent can do nothing'.[24] Various members of the Baghdad school also classify logic as an art in terms of its subject-matter and goal, and they reproduce Greek ideas about this, saying for instance that its subject-matter is expressions (alfāẓ).[25]

The Arabic commentators, however, are in a rather different dialectical situation than the one faced by their Greek predecessors. The latter were opposing a Stoic (and Platonic) tradition which gave too much weight to logic, by making it a full-blown part of philosophy. The former, by contrast, are defending the merits of logic against detractors who argue that it is worthless. In particular, they are confronted by the rival claim of grammar to be the fully adequate study of expressions.[26] So famous as hardly to need mention is the debate before the vizier Ibn al-Furāt, between the grammarian al-Sīrāfī and the father figure of the Baghdad school, the Christian Abū Bishr Mattā. This event, and related criticisms, provoked several responses from members of the Baghdad school. Al-Fārābī thematizes the relationship between logic and grammar in his *Enumeration of the Sciences* (Iḥṣā' al-'ulūm), and Ibn 'Adī wrote a treatise *On the Difference between Logic and Grammar* which expounds the subject-matter and goal criteria for demarcating each art.[27]

Because the aim of these philosophers is to extol the importance of logic, they understandably give a rather different impression of logic's status than the Greek commentators, who focus on its mere instrumentality. Admittedly, the members of the school do faithfully repeat that logic is an instrument. Abū Bishr, for instance, is quoted

---

[23] See G. Endress, 'Grammatik und Logik. Arabische Philologie und griechische Philosophie im Widerstreit', in B. Mojsisch, ed., *Sprachphilosophie in Antike und Mittelalter* (Amsterdam: Grüner, 1986), pp. 163–299. For a useful overview of the relevant sources see also C. Hein, *Definition und Einteilung der Philosophie* (Frankfurt: Peter Lang, 1985), pp. 153–62.

[24] *in. Cat.*, ed. Ferrari, *op. cit.*, 10,25.

[25] As Endress, 'Grammatik und Logik', p. 207, points out, *lafẓ* renders *phônê* in Isḥāq b. Ḥunayn's Arabic translation of *On Interpretation*. Al-Kindī shows less awareness of the Greek treatment of this issue. In his *On the Quantity of Aristotle's Books*, he unblinkingly makes logic one of four broad areas of the Aristotelian corpus, without mentioning its merely instrumental status. He does, however, implicitly set logic apart in much the way suggested by Ierodiakonou, in that he names types of entities studied by physics, intermediate science (which he here identifies as psychology, elsewhere as mathematics), and metaphysics. Logic has no type of entity assigned to it. See M. Guidi and R. Walzer, *Uno Scritto Introduttivo allo Studio di Aristotele* (Rome: Bardi, 1940), § II.2.

[26] On the grammar vs. logic debate see Endress, 'Grammatik und Logik'; id. 'La controverse entre la logique philosophique et la grammaire arabe au temps des khalifs', *Journal for the History of Arabic Science* 1 (1977), 339–51; A. Elamrani-Jamal, *Logique aristotélicienne et grammaire arabe: étude et documents* (Paris: Vrin, 1983). The account of the debate from al-Tawḥīdī is edited and translated into English in D. S. Margouliath, 'The Discussion Between Abu Bishr Matta and Abu Saʿid al-Sirafi on the Merits of Logic and Grammar', *Journal of the Royal Asiatic Society* (1905), 79–129.

[27] Ed. Khalifat, *op. cit.*, pp. 414–24. Trans. in A. Elamrani-Jamal, 'Grammaire et logique d'après le philosophe arabe chrétien Yaḥyā b. ʿAdī (280–364 H/893–974)', *Arabica* 29 (1982), 1–15. Endress, 'Grammatik und Logik', provides annotated translation of the debate as recounted by al-Tawḥīdī and Ibn ʿAdī's treatise, at p. 238–96. See also P. Adamson and A. Key, 'Philosophy of Language in the Medieval Arabic Tradition', in M. Cameron and R. Stainton, eds, *Linguistic Content: New Essays in the History of the Philosophy of Language* (Oxford: Oxford University Press, 2015), pp. 74–99.

in the report of the debate as saying that logic is 'one of the instruments (ālāt) by which one knows correct from faulty speech, and unsound from sound concept (maʿnā) – like a balance (mīzān), with which I may know the more from the less'.[28] But formulations like this might easily leave one with the impression that logic sorts out the true from the false on its own. This can be seen from Ibn al-Furāt's purported characterization of Abū Bishr's view when introducing the debate. According to the vizier, Abū Bishr claims that 'there is no way to knowledge of the true and false (lā sabīl ilā maʿrifat al-ḥaqq wa-l-bāṭil), the right and wrong, or the good and bad, apart from logic'. This is the sentiment we found in Elias' commentary on the *Prior Analytics*, but stripped of its nuance: now logic is *the way* to know truth, goodness and so on, rather than something that is *used by philosophy* to know these same things.

Of course we can hardly rely on Ibn al-Furāt (or those who are reporting the debate to us) to capture Abū Bishr's view accurately. But an almost identical statement is given by Ibn ʿAdī's student Ibn Zurʿa in his own defense of logic: 'it is clear and obvious, to anyone who knows about logic or follows what its adherents have said, that logic is an art whose goal (gharaḍ) comprises the sorting out (takhlīṣ) of true from false in speech, and the discrimination (tamyīz) of good from evil in action'.[29] This is in at least superficial disagreement with Ibn al-Ṭayyib, who following a different strand of the Greek tradition (found in Ammonius, Elias and others), says that the end (ghāya) of logic is demonstration (burhān).[30] Ibn ʿAdī's *On the Difference between Logic and Grammar* also makes demonstration the definitive end of logic. Logic's subject-matter is 'expressions insofar as they refer to universal things (al-umūr al-kulliyya)',[31] and the reason the things in question must be universal is that the goal is demonstration. For demonstration concerns itself only with universals, not particulars.[32] A demonstration is, more precisely, a composition of universal referring expressions into a syllogism which is (necessarily) in accord with the way things really are. Ibn ʿAdī thus goes on to give the following overall definition of logic: 'the art which is concerned with expressions which refer to universal things for the sake of composing [those expressions] in a way that agrees with the things to which they refer'.[33]

Again, one could be forgiven for thinking that someone who has perfectly mastered logic can dispense with the rest of philosophy. If I am already in possession of syllogisms that confer universal knowledge of how things are, what else remains to be done? Alternatively, to put it in terms of the formulation used by Ibn al-Furāt and Ibn Zurʿa,

---

[28] Margouliath, *op. cit.*, p. 93.
[29] N. Rescher, 'A Tenth-Century Arab-Christian Apologia for Logic', *Islamic Studies* 2 (1963), 167a9–11. Ibn Zurʿa is arguing against unnamed opponents who accuse logic of undermining religion rather than of being superfluous. He takes the rather surprising line that logic instead lends an important support to religion, because it distinguishes the possible from the impossible. This allows us to define a miracle as that which is (naturally) impossible; hence without logic there can be no concept of miracles!
[30] K. Gyekye, *op. cit.*, § 52.
[31] Khalifat, *op. cit.*, p. 422. Of course Ibn ʿAdī is thinking here of Porphyry's understanding of the *Categories* as studying words insofar as they signify things.
[32] On this see P. Adamson, 'Knowledge of Universals and Particulars in the Baghdad School', *Documenti e Studi sulla Tradizione Filosofica Medievale* 18 (2007), 141–64.
[33] Khalifat, *op. cit.*, p. 423.

if logic tells me the difference between true and false, good and evil, isn't it *sufficient* for philosophical wisdom, rather than a mere necessary instrument? As I say, it is natural that the philosophers might give this impression, given their need to stress the value of logic. But in fact, the defense of logic requires them only to show that it is a necessary and not sufficient means of reaching truth. Whereas the Greek commentators needed to emphasize, against the Stoics, that logic is only an instrument, the Baghdad school needs to emphasize, against al-Sīrāfī and his ilk, that it is an instrument one cannot do without.

Thus our philosophers owe us an account of why logic is a necessary tool for reaching the goals they mention – discerning truth from falsehood and good from evil, producing demonstrations – without being by itself capable of reaching those goals. To my knowledge the first adequate answer to the question in the Arabic tradition is suggested by al-Fārābī, and further taken up by Ibn ʿAdī. For al-Fārābī the key text is found in his *Enumeration of the Sciences*:

> Among the objects of the intellect, there are some things about which the intellect cannot err at all. These are the things man perceives by himself as if he were naturally endowed with knowledge of them and certainty regarding them – for example that the whole is greater than the part, and that every three is an odd number. About other things it is possible to err, and to deviate from truth to untruth. These are the things which are such as to be grasped with ratiocination (*fikr*) and consideration (*taʾammul*), by argument and proof. So regarding these, but not regarding the things [known immediately], the man who seeks to arrive at certain truth about what he is inquiring into needs the canons (*qawānīn*) of logic.[34]

Al-Fārābī unfortunately omits to explain further, proceeding instead to a comparison between logic and grammar which is rather unflattering to grammar (logic deals with objects of the intellect, grammar with linguistic expressions).

But for greater illumination, we can turn to Ibn ʿAdī – not his study of logic in relation to grammar, but the more rarely studied *On the Four Scientific Questions Regarding the Art of Logic*.[35] This little treatise implicitly raises the issue of logic's necessity (that is, instrumentality) as opposed to its sufficiency, and gives a persuasive account of why it is merely necessary. Ibn ʿAdī defines logic in now-familiar terms as 'an instrumental art by which one discriminates between truth and falsehood in theoretical science, and between good and evil in practical science' (98,19–20). He then explains each term in the definition, one by one, in a manner reminiscent of his somewhat pedantic approach to commenting on lemmata in Aristotelian texts. His

---

[34] Al-Fārābī, *Catálogo de las Ciencias*, ed. and trans. A. Gonzalez Palencia (Madrid: CSIC, 1953), p. 22,5–14 in the Arabic text.
[35] M. Türker, 'Yaḥyā ibn ʿAdī ve Nesredilmemis, bir Risalesi', *Ankara Üniversitesi Dil ve Tarih-Cografya Fakültesi dergisi* 14 (1956), 87–102, Arabic edition at 98–102. Trans. in N. Rescher and F. Shehadi, 'Yaḥyā Ibn ʿAdī's Treatise 'On the Four Scientific Questions Regarding the Art of Logic'', *Journal of the History of Ideas* 25 (1964), 572–8. I quote from the Rescher and Shehadi translation, with some modifications, giving the page and line number from the Türker edition.

explanation of the term 'instrument (*āla*)' is that it is something intermediary (*mutawassiṭa*) between the artisan and his subject (99,1–2). This is reprised in the next paragraph, in which Ibn ʿAdī stresses the absolute need for logic (99,11–13):

> The good obtained through [logic] and apprehended by the intermediary [of logic] (*bi-tawassuṭihā*) is beyond any parallel, since it [sc. this good] is complete happiness. There is no happiness more complete for theory than belief in the truth, and it is through it [sc. logic] that this is apprehended; and in action no [happiness] more complete than acquiring the good, which without it cannot be possessed.

As with other passages we've examined, this could give the impression that logic is all one needs in life, whether in theory or in practice. But a more careful reading shows that Ibn ʿAdī is careful to describe it as an instrument and intermediary to the end of happiness. Again, the question is how exactly it serves to bring us to truth and the good, without doing all the work itself.

His answer is given shortly thereafter (99,14–100,7), and has a clear relationship to what we have seen in al-Fārābī. The relevant passage is too long to quote in its entirety, so I summarize: whatever is known (*maʿrūf*) is known either with no need for proof, because it is self-evident, or known by means of proof. Things known without proof are either sensible forms (which may be essential or accidental), or immaterial and grasped directly by the intellect. Of the latter, there are simple things known by stipulation (*waḍʿ*) and definition, and there are composed things we know as 'immediate premises (*muqaddimāt ghayr ḏawāt awsāṭ*)' (99,25). As for that which is known by proof, knowledge 'is obtained by resorting to [logic] from a knowledge of things other than it, with a need for prior, antecedent knowledge in making it known. This type of knowledge-acquisition is called proof, argument, and demonstration' (99,27–9). He illustrates the point by referring to the way mathematicians derive previously unknown essential truths from the properties of things like lines and numbers.

Ibn ʿAdī's explanation of logic's instrumental role must be understood in the context of the foundationalist epistemology of Aristotle's *Posterior Analytics*. As explained there, two kinds of knowledge are involved in science. First, there are the things we know by proving them – Aristotle calls these things objects of 'demonstrative knowledge (*epistêmê*)' (2.19, 99b15–17). But we cannot demonstrate everything, because this would lead to an infinite regress (see *Post. An.* 1.3, 72b18–25). Thus there must be some things known immediately – in *Post. An.* 2.19 the state of knowing such things is not called *epistêmê* but rather *nous*.[36] Ibn ʿAdī, making more explicit what is surely already implicit in the passage from al-Fārābī's *Enumeration*, says that logic enables us to extend our immediate knowledge so as to produce demonstrations. I take it that he means something like this: I have immediate knowledge that man is animal.

---

[36] On this chapter see P. Adamson, 'Posterior Analytics II.19: a Dialogue with Plato?', in V. Harte, M. M. McCabe, R. W. Sharples, and A. Sheppard, eds, *Aristotle and the Stoics Reading Plato* (London: Institute of Classical Studies, 2010), pp. 1–19.

I also know immediately that every animal is mortal.[37] I then use a logical scheme (All A is B; All B is C; Therefore All A is C) to infer that man is mortal. Without the logical scheme I would be unable to extend my knowledge any further than what I know immediately. Recall that Ibn ʿAdī has defined 'instrument' as an intermediary, and now it is clear why: logic is instrumental because it is the intermediary used to arrive at mediated knowledge.

Notice that on this account, we can in fact have certain knowledge of many things without using logic. (So Ibn al-Ṭayyib is exaggerating when he says, as we saw him saying above, that the philosopher can do *nothing* without logic – unless he holds, rather implausibly, that immediate knowledge is not part of 'philosophy'.[38]) The indispensability of logic does not consist in its supplying us with the principles of knowledge, but with *completing* our knowledge and thus conferring total happiness, that is, the fulfillment of our rational capacity. Obviously this raises further questions. For instance, we might be willing to admit that logic, when added to immediate knowledge of principles, could in theory lead us to theoretical perfection. But to say the same about practical perfection would imply a highly rationalist account of ethics, in which we reach the practical good simply by reasoning correctly from first practical principles.[39]

Leaving this aside, it is worth asking whether Ibn ʿAdī and like-minded philosophers genuinely adhere to a purely instrumental vision of logic, in which it does nothing but to extend knowledge from what is grasped immediately. The answer depends on what we understand as falling under 'logic'. The logic Ibn ʿAdī has in mind is basically syllogistic, so that his account applies primarily to logic as we find it in the *Prior Analytics*. It could certainly be adapted to explain the need for texts like the *Topics* and *Sophistical Refutations* as well, since these help us avoid invalid, and valid but non-demonstrative, inferences. But the *Organon* touches on many themes other than validity and the criteria required for demonstration. The *Categories* commits Aristotle to a division, at least, of words into ten types – and for the post-Porphyrian tradition, this division has ontological significance insofar as the *Categories* studies 'words as they refer to things'. Even restricting ourselves to the criteria for demonstration, consider a claim Ibn ʿAdī highlights in *On the Difference between Logic and Grammar*: that

---

[37] Of course there is a puzzle about how such things could be known 'immediately', unlike al-Fārābī's examples ('the whole is greater than the part'). But Ibn ʿAdī has made a place for principles like this by mentioning items of knowledge grasped directly through sensation, and in this he is true to the account in *Post. An.* 2.19. Note that 'immediately' should not be taken to mean something like 'instantly' or 'from the beginning', as al-Fārābī suggests in the case of fundamental rules of reasons. Rather, it means without any antecedent premises. This is consistent with the idea that a first principle might be grasped only after a lengthy process of induction based on sensation.

[38] Incidentally it is worth noting an echo of Ibn ʿAdī's account in Ibn al-Ṭayyib. In the *Categories* commentary (ed. Ferrari, *op. cit.*, 18,21 ff.), he contrasts things grasped without error and immediately by sensation, as well as things grasped as principles by the intellect, with those that are grasped only by prior knowledge. His examples of the former are more like al-Fārābī's: that equal things are equal to the same thing and that the whole is greater than the part. But since other things do stand in need of proof, 'this logical art is intended precisely to give us a way (*ṭarīq*) and method by which we may adequately reach hidden things by means of evident things: namely demonstration' (19,15–17).

[39] Indeed this sort of view is put forth by al-Fārābī in other contexts, as I have pointed out in Adamson, 'Knowledge of Universals', p. 149.

demonstrative knowledge is always of universals. This notion is put to use in such robustly non-logical contexts as Avicenna's proof of the immateriality of soul and his discussion of God's knowledge of particulars.[40] In short, Aristotle's *organon* may include some metaphysics and certainly includes what we would call epistemology. So even if Aristotle's Greek and Arabic interpreters manage to show that logic is an instrument, not a part, of philosophy, they have little hope of showing that the *Organon* is instrumental for, rather than part of, Aristotelian philosophy.

Physics or Theology? Arguments for and against the World's Eternity

Consider the following two ancient Greek arguments for the eternity of the world:

> Assume there is a first motion. Then what is potentially moved either (a) comes into existence at some moment, or (b) is potentially moved for an eternity before actually moving. In either case, a prior motion is required: in the case of (a), to make the movable exist, or in (b) to actualize the movable's potentiality for motion. Thus the supposedly first motion is not after all first, which shows that the assumption of a first motion is incoherent. Similarly, motion cannot end, because whatever destroyed the last mover would itself need to be destroyed.
>
> The maker of the cosmos is eternally generous, and creates through his generosity; therefore the cosmos that he creates is eternal. Furthermore, if he went from not creating to creating or vice-versa, he would change, but the maker of the cosmos is immutable.

The first summarizes Aristotle's argument in *Physics* 8.1 (251a9-b10; 251b28-252a6), the second Proclus' opening argument in his *On the Eternity of the World*.[41] Both arguments attempt to prove the same conclusion, namely that the physical cosmos is eternal *ex parte ante* and *ex parte post*. Despite this they are importantly different in strategy.

Aristotle's argument is presented alongside other proofs of the world's eternity given in *Physics* 8. For instance, he argues that there cannot be a first moment of time,

---

[40] I have discussed these issues in P. Adamson, 'Correcting Plotinus: Soul's Relationship to Body in Avicenna's Commentary on the *Theology of Aristotle*', in P. Adamson, H. Baltussen, and M. W. F. Stone, eds, *Philosophy, Science and Exegesis in Greek, Arabic and Latin Commentaries*, 2 vols (London: Institute of Classical Studies, 2004), vol. 2, pp. 59-75; id., 'On Knowledge of Particulars', *Proceedings of the Aristotelian Society* 105 (2005), 273-94.

[41] H. S. Lang and A. D. Macro, *Proclus, On the Eternity of the World* (Berkeley: University of California Press, 2001). This argument is preserved only in Arabic, and is translated in the volume by J. McGinnis. For the Arabic text see also A. Badawī, *Neoplatonici apud arabes* (Cairo, 1955), 34,4-35,8. For a French translation see G. C. Anawati, 'Un fragment perdu du *De Aeternitate Mundi* de Proclus', in *Mélanges de Philosophie Grecque offerts à Mgr. Diès* (Paris: Vrin, 1956), pp. 23-5. For a German translation by P. Heine see M. Baltes, *Die Weltentstehung des platonischen Timaios nach den antiken Interpreten*, vol. 2 (Leiden: Brill, 1976), pp. 134-6. The extant Greek portions of Proclus' text may be found in John Philoponus, *On the Eternity of the World Against Proclus*, ed. H. Rabe (Leipzig: Teubner, 1899).

because this is incoherent (251b10-251b28), and that since heavenly motion is circular, it can be beginningless and endless, having no contrary (264b9-265a12; cf. *De Caelo* 1.3). These arguments all turn on Aristotle's conception of motion: either motion in general, or time which measures motion, or the motion of the heavens. This is no accident, for physics is the study of motion. These are, then, properly *physical* arguments for the eternity of the world. While Aristotle believes that the eternal motion of the cosmos does require an explanatory principle that is itself unmoving, a 'first mover', this principle is not first in the order of discovery. What we grasp first is the nature of motion; then we grasp that motion must be eternal; and only then do we argue from the eternity of motion to an eternal cause of that motion.

Proclus uses a very different strategy, proving the eternity of the cosmos by appealing to the eternity and generosity of its maker, which he simply assumes (he is of course thinking of the Demiurge in Plato's *Timaeus*). A number of Proclus' arguments in *On the Eternity of the World* have this structure, which as we will see is representative of Proclus' way of understanding the world's eternity. For him the world is not eternal in its own right, so to speak, but rather because it is the effect of an eternally active cause. Thus the most appropriate way to understand or demonstrate the world's eternity would be by reasoning from the nature of its cause. We could call this a *theological* approach.

The purpose of this second section of my paper is to trace these two contrasting approaches to the question of the world's eternity through some authors of late Greek and early Arabic philosophy. The issue is whether the question of the world's eternity is properly answered by physics or by metaphysics. Here 'metaphysics' is understood to mean the study of the ultimate causes of things. This terminology is perhaps anachronistic for some of the Greek authors discussed below (and certainly for Aristotle, who of course does not use the word or title 'metaphysics'). But it captures the way that early Arabic philosophical works tend to treat physics and metaphysics. For instance Abū Sulaymān al-Sijistānī, a student of Ibn ʿAdī, says:

> Inquiry concerning the conjunction of effects with causes has two aspects: the first, insofar as it ascends through their connections to their cause; the second, insofar as the power of the cause pervades its effects. Inquiry in the first mode belongs to the physicist; in the second, to the science of metaphysics.[42]

Applying this contrast to the problem of the world's eternity, the 'physical' approach means arguing for or against eternity from what we actually observe about the world, especially about motion and things that are in motion, since for Aristotle this is the subject-matter of physics. We may then, following Aristotle, use the eternity of the world and its motion to argue that the world must have an eternal moving cause. The 'metaphysical' or 'theological' approach, by contrast, answers the same question by appealing to necessary truths governing the causation excercised by world's principle(s).

---

[42] The passage appears in *On the First Mover*, translation from J. Kraemer, *Philosophy in the Renaissance of Islam: Abū Sulaymān al-Sijistānī and his Circle* (Leiden: Brill, 1986), p. 291.

To understand the Peripatetic treatment of these problems one can do no better than to turn once again to Alexander. As it happens one of the most important texts for establishing his thought on the eternity of the world is not preserved in Greek, but only in Syriac and Arabic translations: this is the treatise known as *On the Principles of the Cosmos*.[43] After an introductory section, the *Principles* begins by explaining (§4) that 'natural' bodies are bodies that have principles of motion. Indeed an internal (*fī ḏātihi*) principle of motion is what we mean by 'nature' (*ṭabīʻa*). The heavens have such a principle, and are thus natural bodies. Furthermore, as Alexander remarks, discussions elsewhere have shown that the heavenly bodies are 'divine, ungenerated and imperishable' (§4).

Thus at the very outset of the work, Alexander has indicated his adherence to what I have called the physical approach to the question of the world's eternity. The heavens are natural, despite their divinity, and their nature ensures their eternity (see further §46, §57). Other arguments for eternity in the *Principles* are taken from the *Physics*. Alexander uses Aristotle's argument against the possibility of a first motion (§66–69), and also rehearses the argument that there cannot be a first instant of time (§70–71), since any instant has time both before and after it – an allusion to the Aristotelian doctrine that the 'now' or instant is not a part of time, but is without extension, a division between past and future.[44] Recognizing the eternity of motion allows us to establish the eternity of an unmoved mover. Alexander says both on his own behalf and on that of Aristotle that we know the first cause is eternal because we know its effects are eternal, rather than vice-versa (§49, §89; compare Aristotle, *Physics* 259a6–7).

Another passage in the *Principles* likewise reveals Alexander's commitment to the physical approach. He has just pointed out that sublunar bodies constantly change into one another, and are thus generable and perishable. He then continues:

> This kind of perishability existing in the universe is not something happening to it by the will and resolution of some other being, I mean by that the divine things, but it is something inherent in its proper nature. For it does not fit the divine nature to will that which is not possible, just as it is not possible either, according to the opinion of those who profess the doctrine of creation, that perishability should attach to what has not been generated at all.[45]

Even though the divine causes (the first cause and the heavens) do bring about change in the sublunar world, the proper nature of sublunar bodies is in a sense independent of those causes. What is possible for the sublunar bodies is determined by their nature, and the same is true for the heavens: since they are *not* generable, they must also be

---

[43] C. Genequand, *Alexander of Aphrodisias on the Cosmos* (Leiden: Brill, 2001). Citations are to Genequand's section numbers. See further G. Endress, 'Alexander Arabus on the First Cause: Aristotle's First Mover in an Arabic Treatise attributed to Alexander of Aphrodisias', in C. D'Ancona and G. Serra, eds, *Aristotele e Alessandro di Afrodisia nella tradizione araba* (Padua: Il Poligrafo, 2002), pp. 19–74.

[44] See also R. W. Sharples, 'Alexander of Aphrodisias, *On Time*', *Phronesis* 27 (1982), 58–81. This notion of the instant is affirmed in the passage translated as § 11–13, at pp. 62–3.

[45] § 139–40, translation from Genequand, *op. cit.*

incorruptible.[46] Alexander believes we can come to know the corruptibility of sublunar bodies and the eternity of the heavens (and thus of the cosmos as a whole) by studying their natures, that is, by understanding the intrinsic principles of their motions. This is the case even though, as he says elsewhere, the eternal motion of the heavens has the prime mover as an extrinsic final cause (§52).

This should be compared to one of Alexander's *Quaestiones* (1.18), where Alexander argues 'that it is not possible for the world to be incorruptible through the will of God, if it is corruptible by its own nature'.[47] This *quaestio* has attracted attention for its discussion of modal notions: Alexander holds that it is impossible for S to be P when S is prevented from being P, or when S has no natural disposition towards being P.[48] In light of this, Alexander is able to refute the Platonist position that 'according to its own nature', the world is disposed towards corruption and not eternity, but that the world nevertheless possesses an eternal existence given to it extrinsically by God (as we will see below, this is roughly the position that will be taken up by Proclus). Employing his notion of impossibility, Alexander argues (31,25–32,3) that if the world has no innate disposition towards eternity, it cannot possibly be eternal. Even God cannot make such a thing eternal, since, as he says, 'what is impossible in this way, since it is impossible for all, is impossible even for the gods' (32,3–4). The Platonists' position is, he might say, like holding that water has no innate disposition to be dry, but could be made dry by the gods. Alexander's own view is of course that the Platonists are exactly wrong: the nature of the world is such that it has only a disposition to be *eternal*, not to be corrupted. Thus it is impossible – purely because of the world's nature – that the world be generated or corrupted.[49]

Things look a bit different in the works of Themistius. His views on the world's eternity are again largely faithful to those of Aristotle, as may be gleaned not only from his paraphrases of the *Physics* and *De Caelo*,[50] but also from his paraphrase of *Metaphysics* Book *Lambda*, which is preserved in Arabic, Hebrew and Latin.[51] In Book

---

[46] For this commonly held principle in Greek thought, see L. Judson, 'God or Nature? Philoponus on Generability and Perishability', R. Sorabji, ed., *Philoponus and the Rejection of Aristotelian Science* (London: Duckworth, 1987), pp. 179–96.

[47] Alexander of Aphrodisias, *Quaestiones* 30,23–4.

[48] See the citations provided in R. W. Sharples, *Alexander of Aphrodisias, Quaestiones* 1.1–2.15 (London: Duckworth, 1992), pp. 66–70.

[49] Admittedly Alexander does also use arguments that are not straightforwardly 'physical'. For example, he alludes repeatedly in the *Principles* (e.g. at § 23) to the fact that the heavens 'imitate' the eternity of the first cause.

[50] In his paraphrase of *Physics* 8.1, for example, Themistius follows Aristotle closely in arguing for the impossibility of a beginning of motion (210,3 ff.) or time (211,34 ff., concluding with the point that 'if time is eternal, then so is motion', 212,8), and for the impossibility of an end to motion (212,10 ff.). Like Aristotle and Alexander he says that the eternity of the first mover follows from the eternity of motion (233,14–17). For the *Physics* paraphrase see the edition of H. Schenkl, CAG 5.2 (Berlin: Reimer, 1900); for the extant Latin version of the *De Caelo* paraphrase see the edition of S. Landauer, CAG 5.4 (Berlin: Reimer, 1902).

[51] Arabic edition in A. Badawī, *Arisṭū ʿinda l-ʿarab* (Cairo, 1947). Latin and Hebrew editions by S. Landauer, CAG 5.5 (Berlin: Reimer, 1903). Badawī's Arabic text must be read alongside the textual variants supplied in R.M. Frank, 'Some Textual Notes on the Oriental Versions of Themistius' Paraphrase of Book I [sic] of the *Metaphysics*', *Cahiers de Byrsa* 8 (1958–59), 214–30. French translation in R. Brague, *Thémistius, Paraphrase de la Métaphysique d'Aristote (livre Lambda)* (Paris: Vrin, 1999). On this text see also S. Pines, 'Some Distinctive Metaphysical Conceptions in Themistius' Commentary on Book *Lambda* and Their Place in the History of Philosophy', in his *Collected Works III* (Jerusalem: The Magnes Press, 1996), pp. 267–94.

Lambda, chapter five, Aristotle had appealed to the eternity of the world as a premise for proving the existence and nature of the first cause. He did not, however, attempt to prove here that the physical world is eternal – as we would expect, if it is right to say that he sees this as a matter for physics. In his paraphrase of this chapter Themistius mostly confines himself to expanding on allusions to the world's eternity by inserting versions of the *Physics* 8 arguments, e.g. on time (at 12,13 ff.) and the impossibility of a first motion (13,5 'there is no origination of motion except through [another] motion').

So far, so Peripatetic: he merely makes explicit the physical arguments that Aristotle has given elsewhere. But consider the following:

> We say that motion cannot cease or come to be. If it were originated, then its mover would be prior to it. But how can we imagine that it has a mover, which is eternal (*azalī*), but that it does not come to be from it for all of eternity (*dahr*)? There is nothing to prevent its coming to be from it. And there is nothing that begins to be in a state, such that by being in this state it would originate [the motion], since all that originates only originates from [the first mover], but there is nothing other than [the first mover] that could hinder it or awaken its desire. Nor is it possible for us to say that it was first incapable of bringing its effect about, and then capable, [or that it first did not will and then willed, or did not know and then knew,][52] because this would require change, which would in turn require that there be something else that changes it [sc. the first mover]. But if we say that there is something that prevents it [from causing the motion], then it would follow that there is some other cause more powerful than it.[53]

At the beginning of the passage Themistius is alluding to the argument of *Physics* 8.1 with which we began this section. But he soon veers off into an argument that is more reminiscent of Proclus': the first cause is immutable, unique, and cannot be made to act by anything else. Thus it is the nature of the *cause* that determines the eternity of its effect. So in this passage, at least, we can see Themistius going further than Alexander in a Platonizing direction, using metaphysical argumentation in the midst of a generally physical treatment of the world's eternity.

Let us turn now to Proclus, whose discussion of the eternity of the world in his *Commentary on the Timaeus* is among the most clear and detailed expositions of the problem from a Neoplatonic point of view.[54] The fact that this exposition is found in the context of interpreting the *Timaeus* is no accident. Just as the decisive texts on the world's eternity were, for the Peripatetics, two unambiguously physical works from Aristotle's corpus (the *Physics* and *De Caelo*), so for the Platonists the question of the

---

[52] This phrase in brackets appears in the version reported by Sharastānī: see Frank, *op. cit.*, p. 220, n. 73.
[53] Badawī, *Arisṭū* 12,18–13,5; cf. 14,21–32 in the Latin version.
[54] Proclus, *in Tim.* 1,276,8–296,12. See further J. F. Phillips, 'Neoplatonic Exegeses of Plato's Cosmogony (*Timaeus* 27C-28C)', *Journal of the History of Philosophy* 35 (1977), 173–97; R. Sorabji, *Time, Creation and the Continuum* (London: Duckworth, 1983), chs 13–15; G. Verbeke, 'Some Late Neoplatonic Views on Divine Creation and the Eternity of the World', in D. O'Meara, ed., *Neoplatonism and Christian Thought* (Albany: State University of New York Press, 1982), pp. 45–53.

world's eternity arises in the context of discussing the *Timaeus*.[55] Since Platonists saw the *Timaeus* as the dialogue in which Plato sets out his views on the physical world,[56] we might initially expect Proclus to pursue exclusively physical arguments in his *Commentary*. And in fact, in this very section on the world's eternity, Proclus reproaches his predecessor Severus for 'bringing mythic obscurities into natural philosophy' (1,289,14–15), going on to add, 'these exegetical points, being unrelated to physics, must not be admitted' (1,290,2–3). However, matters are complicated by the fact that for Proclus, the *Timaeus* is also a work of theology, insofar as the dialogue sets out how the physical cosmos is fashioned by a demiurge.[57] Thus it is as a practitioner of 'natural philosophy' in a rather different sense than Aristotle's that Proclus addresses himself to the infamous interpretive difficulty raised by Plato's claim, at *Timaeus* 28b, that the physical world 'has been generated, beginning from some starting-point (*gegonen, ap' arkhês tinos arxamenos*)'.

An earlier Platonist reading of this passage, associated with Atticus and Plutarch, understands Plato to be saying that the world has a beginning (*arkhê*) in time, and takes *gegonen* to be a reference to that temporal beginning. Proclus rejects this, arguing that *gegonen* instead echoes the immediately preceding contrast (*Timaeus* 27D-28A) between the realm of becoming (*to gignomenon*) and the intelligible world of being (*to on*). The cosmos, holds Proclus, is perpetually in a state of coming-to-be, and thus it may be said always to be undergoing generation. As for the word *arkhê* at 28b, it refers not to a temporal beginning but to an 'external cause', namely the Demiurge himself (see *in Tim.* 1,279,23–5). Proclus praises his Neoplatonic predecessors Plotinus, Porphyry, and Iamblichus for likewise seeing the passage as a reference to the fact that the world has an external cause, rather than a beginning in time (1,277,11–14).

Proclus gives a series of arguments against the idea that the world has a temporal beginning. Most of them are textual; that is, Proclus tries to establish Plato's meaning by citing other passages in the *Timaeus* and beyond. For our purposes his final two arguments (1,288,14 ff.) are more interesting. These proceed, like the first argument of his *On the Eternity of the World*, from the nature of the Demiurge. Unlike the cosmos the Demiurge belongs to the realm of being, and thus he must always be doing whatever he does. But, 'if he always makes (*dêmiourgei*), what is made always exists too' (1,288,16–17). On the other hand, the eternity (*aidiotês*) possessed by the world is not the same as

---

[55] As Lang and Macro, *op. cit.*, remark, p. 21, 'for the Platonists the problem of the eternity of the world is indistinguishable textually from Plato's *Timaeus* and its account of how the world, or cosmos, is made'.

[56] Proclus himself announces at the beginning of his commentary (1,1,17–18) that the topic of the dialogue is the philosophy of nature. On this see M. Martijn, *Proclus on Nature* (Leiden: Brill, 2010).

[57] This becomes clear especially from Proclus' use of the *Timaeus* in his *Platonic Theology*. See Proclus, *Théologie Platonicienne*, vol. 1, ed. and trans. H. D. Saffrey and L. G. Westerink (Paris: Les Belles Lettres, 1968), e.g. at 19,6–8 (the *Timaeus* is one of the dialogues that studies 'divine things' from a mathematical, ethical, or physical point of view); 24,17 (it is one of the most important dialogues for Plato's theology); 25,8–11 (it deals specifically with the intellectual gods, the demiurgic monad, and the encosmic gods, see further 27,17–18); 29,24–30,3 (the *Timaeus* is about physics, but 'for the sake of natural philosophy' must also deal with the noetic gods, since one knows images through their paradigms). See also the use of the *Timaeus* at *Platonic Theology* 5.15–20.

the timeless eternity (*aiôn*) of the realm of being; rather the world is eternal in the sense of lasting for infinite time. And it is preserved eternally only by the constant renewal of its existence by its cause (1,278,19–21). So the generation of the world is not the generation of something that comes to be and later passes away, or that begins moving and later completes its motion. It is not, that is, the sort of generation studied in physics.[58] To Proclus' mind, it is a sign of Plato's superiority over Aristotle that he grasps the need to ground the world's continued existence in theological, rather than physical, principles (1,295,22–7).

In arguing that the question of the world's eternity is decided above all by its relationship to an external cause, Proclus opens the door for anti-eternity arguments that belong to the same theological or metaphysical arena. The opening was exploited by John Philoponus in his works on the eternity of the world. We are in possession of fragments of a work rebutting Aristotle's arguments for the eternity of the world in *De Caelo* and the *Physics* (*Against Aristotle*),[59] and a monumental treatise which repeats, and then refutes, Proclus' arguments in *On the Eternity of the World* (*Against Proclus*).[60] Philoponus seems also to have written an independent treatise arguing that the world cannot be eternal because it does not possess infinite power; this work was known in the Arabic tradition.[61] Philoponus uses different strategies in responding to Aristotle's physical arguments and Proclus' theological arguments. Against Aristotle, he argues that since the heavens are finite (by virtue of the fact that they are bodies), they cannot move for an infinite period of time by their very nature.[62] Instead – and here Philoponus could find some common ground with Proclus – if the heavens move eternally they can do so only by receiving the infinite power required to do so from an external cause. There is no possibility, then, of a physical proof of the heavens' eternity. Similarly, in refuting the arguments given by Aristotle in *Physics* 8, Philoponus argues that Aristotle has illegitimately assumed that the production of the world must be like the production of anything in nature. But this is false, because the world is created by God, and God's creative act need not obey the laws of nature.[63]

When arguing against Proclus, Philoponus must of course take a different tack. Here it will not be sufficient simply to say that the physical world's nature is compatible with a beginning in time. He must dispute Proclus' claims about the way in which God, or the Demiurge, in fact creates the world. Only this will tell us whether the world is

---

[58] See the remark of Phillips, *op. cit.*, p. 178, that '*to aei gignomenon* means for Proclus that which comes to be by a cause external to it (*in Tim.* 1,279,24 f.) . . . this relationship to its higher cause makes the cosmos a special sort of *genêton* to which the concepts of the natural sciences do not apply.'

[59] Preserved in Simplicius' commentaries on *De caelo* and the *Physics*; see C. Wildberg, *Philoponus, Against Aristotle on the Eternity of the World* (London: Duckworth, 1987).

[60] Edited by H. Rabe (Leipzig: Teubner, 1899).

[61] See S. Pines, 'An Arabic Summary of a Lost Work of John Philoponus', *Israel Oriental Studies* 2 (1972), 320–52; repr. in vol. 2 of his *Studies in Arabic Versions of Greek Texts and in Medieval Science* (Jerusalem: The Magnes Press, 1986). This may or may not be the same as the work discussed by Simplicius at *in Phys.* 1326–36. See D. Furley and C. Wildberg, *Philoponus and Simplicius, Place, Void, and Eternity* (London: Duckworth, 1991), pp. 107–28.

[62] Simplicius, *in Cael.* 79,2–8; Fragment II.49 in Philoponus, *Against Aristotle*. Translation by Wildberg, *op. cit.*

[63] Simplicius, *in Phys.* 1141,12–16; Fragment VI.115 in Philoponus, *Against Aristotle*. Translation by Wildberg, *op. cit.*

eternal or not. As I have pointed out elsewhere, Philoponus seems to be aware that his task is to show that even the Demiurge cannot create an eternal cosmos.[64] For instance, an eternal world would require there to be an actual infinity, which is impossible, as Aristotle and Proclus both admit. Likewise, an eternal world would be equal to its Creator in eternity, but this is impossible, for what is brought into being must be lesser than its cause. These are not physical impossiblities, that have to do with the nature of the created cosmos: rather they are absolute impossibilities, which limit the possible outcome of God's creative power and generosity. Philoponus recognizes that he and Proclus in a sense agree, insofar as both accept that the world's temporal duration is determined by God, not by its nature: 'if Proclus agrees with Plato about these doctrines [sc. that the world acquires its being from an external cause, is in itself generable and corruptible, and is finite], then he makes it clear that the world is corruptible by its nature, while incorruptibility belongs to it from above nature, supplied by some superior power' (§29, 240,19–23).

Recent scholarship has suggested that the Arabic tradition continues this trend towards discussion the world's eternity by using theological or metaphysical arguments, rather than physical ones. As we might expect given Philoponus' influence on him, al-Kindī is a good example.[65] In fact al-Kindī seems even happier than Philoponus to assume that physical considerations are not decisive in settling the matter. He enthusiastically endorses Aristotle's cosmology, according to which the heavens consist of an ungenerable and indestructible fifth element – but adds that, of course, the heavens can only exist for as long as God wills.[66] He thus casually discards as irrelevant the entire debate between Philoponus and Aristotle. And reasonably so, if physical considerations are in any case overriden by theological ones. Similarly, a study by Marwan Rashed showed that al-Fārābī saw Aristotelian arguments for the world's eternity drawn from physics as falling short of demonstrative status.[67] Some such arguments are merely dialectical. Others can be used to prove the *fact* that the world is eternal, without attaining a demonstration, because a proper demonstration argues from cause to effect (in this case, from God to the world). Thus only a theological argument can be demonstrative.[68]

I have elsewhere suggested that al-Kindī was motivated to disprove the world's eternity because he adhered to the contemporary theological contrast (as seen most prominently in the controversy over the nature of the Qur'ān) between the eternal and the created.[69] He does not consider the possibility that something could be both created *and* eternal. This uncritical acceptance of the created-eternal dichotomy could not last

---

[64] See Adamson, *Al-Kindī* (n. 4 above), pp. 84–5.
[65] Or so I have argued in *Al-Kindī*, p. 88.
[66] See his *On the Nature of the Celestial Sphere*, in M. Abū Rīda, ed., *Rasā'il al-Kindī al-falsafiyya*, 2 vols (Cairo 1950–53), vol. 2, pp. 40–46: 46, and §13 in Adamson and Pormann, *op.cit.*
[67] M. Rashed, 'Al-Fārābī's Lost Treatise *On Changing Beings* and the Possibility of a Demonstration of the Eternity of the World', *Arabic Sciences and Philosophy* 18 (2008), 19–58: 21 for Maimonides' distinction between natural and theological proofs.
[68] Ibid., 44. Such proofs would proceed, for instance, from the eternity and unchanging activity of God to the eternity of His effect, namely the world.
[69] See Adamson, *Al-Kindī*, pp. 98–105.

for long, and indeed it was already rejected by al-Kindī's contemporary Thābit Ibn Qurra. His short treatise explaining Aristotle's *Metaphysics* has been edited and translated by David C. Reisman and Amos Bertolacci.[70] It deals with, among other things, the manner in which God bestows existence on *things* in the physical cosmos. Thābit sees divine causation of motion as tantamount to divine causation of existence:

> The First Mover is the cause of the form that gives subsistence to the substance of all the things that are properly in motion. Thus the subsistence of the substance of each one of them does not belong to it in itself, but rather is from something that is the first ground (*sabab*) for its motion ... The First Mover, then, is the principle and cause for the existence (*wujūd*) and perdurance of the forms of all corporeal substances. For, when we imagine the removal of the existence of natural motion [from corporeal substances] ... their substance undoubtedly corrupts.[71]

For Thābit's Aristotle, the first mover does not merely cause the motion of a cosmos whose existence is taken for granted, but rather causes the cosmos to exist precisely by making it move. The argument proceeds by supposing that for any natural object to exist is for it to have a form, and for it to have a form is for it to have a proper motion.

Thābit's Aristotle does not however say that God is an *efficient* cause of that existence, only that He is a final cause: God causes motion as an object of desire (*shawq*). Thābit nonetheless ascribes to Aristotle the view that God's relationship to the world is one of 'willful making (*ṣanʿirādī*)' (§6). In light of this it is still unclear what sort of proof should be given regarding the world's eternity. Thābit's Aristotle may still want to say that the eternity of motion is implied by the intrinsic nature of the heavens or of bodies in general. In that case the final causality exercised by God will be only a necessary condition for the persistence and motion of these bodies. As it turns out, though, Thābit's Aristotle makes no appeal to the nature of the physical cosmos when proving the world's eternity:

> *Treatise*, §4: What Aristotle says is that the most excellent [state] for the First Principle is that in which it is the cause from eternity of the existence of everything that exists ... without having become like that only at some time, after not being like that ... So this is more excellent than that the First Cause is the cause of the existence of the universe at some time.[72]

This has nothing to do with the impossibility of a first motion or moment of time. Rather, the argument is that for God to be most excellent (*afḍal*), He must have an eternal, rather than changing, relationship with the cosmos. And of course this could

---

[70] D. C. Reisman and A. Bertolacci, 'Thābit ibn Qurra's *Concise Exposition of Aristotle's Metaphysics*: Text, Translation and Commentary', in R. Rashed, ed., *Thābit ibn Qurra: Science and Philosophy in Ninth-Century Baghdad* (Berlin: De Gruyter, 2009), pp. 715–76. I am grateful to the authors for allowing me to see this important study in pre-print form. Their translations, with some minor modifications.
[71] Reisman and Bertolacci, *op. cit.*, § 2.
[72] Ibid., § 4.

only be the case if the cosmos is itself eternal. Thābit's Aristotle continues by observing that, if God went from not being a cause of existence to being a cause of existence, there would have to be some second, further cause to explain this change. But this is impossible, since there is nothing else that could either assist or hinder God in bringing existence to the world.

We have seen this sort of argument before. It is very like Themistius' argument from the paraphrase of *Lambda*, altered so as to make God a cause of existence, as well as motion.[73] But unlike Themistius, Thābit gives *only* this theological argument for the eternity of the world, proceeding then to deal with possible objections. The first objection is that if the world is eternal, then it has no cause – in other words, al-Kindī's assumption that the eternal and created are exhaustive and mutually exclusive. Thābit rejects this in his own voice (§5), and goes on to ascribe to Aristotle a rebuttal, which again relies on the idea that the first cause cannot change so as to start bringing the world into existence. The second objection is that if the world is eternal then God can have no will (or at the very least that He *need* not have a will, since He can serve as a final cause without actually doing anything at all). This is refuted by reverting to the claim that God must be as perfect as possible – thus God does have will, but does not have desire, since causing without will or out of desire would both imply imperfection. Thābit's discussion of the eternity of the world is thus strikingly theological in character. This is despite the fact that Thābit's *Treatise* is to be located much more in the Peripatetic than the Neoplatonic tradition.

The theological approach can also be discerned in early Arabic writings that are overtly hostile to the Aristotelian tradition. One example is a work of uncertain authorship entitled *On Metaphysics*. It was discovered by Paul Kraus in an Istanbul manuscript, where it is ascribed to the famous philosopher and physician Abū Bakr al-Rāzī. Despite his suspicions about its authenticity, Kraus included it in his edition of the works of al-Rāzī.[74] The work has since found its supporters and detractors as an authentic Razian document.[75] I myself am increasingly convinced that it is authentic. One reason is that the treatment of the world's eternity chimes well with remarks on the same topic in al-Rāzī's certainly authentic *Doubts About Galen*, which I will mention below. *On Metaphysics* is only partially extant and has a rather disjointed structure, with no smooth transitions between the three main sections of the extant work.[76] These three sections are: a general attack on philosophers' claims that 'nature' explains motion

---

[73] Reisman and Bertolacci, *op. cit.*, demonstrate Thābit's reliance on the paraphrase of Themistius in their commentary on the text, though they do not cite Themistius as a source for this particular passage.

[74] Al-Rāzī, *Rasā'il falsafiyya*, ed. P. Kraus (Cairo, 1939), pp. 116–34.

[75] See A. Badawī's chapter on al-Rāzī in M. M. Sharif, ed., *A History of Muslim Philosophy* (Wiesbaden: Otto Harrassowitz, 1963), at pp. 440–41. He cites previous views, mostly noncommittal (to this group may be added the remarks in A. Bausani, *Un filosofo 'laico' del medioevo musulmano: Abū Bakr Muḥammad ben Zakiryya Rāzī* (Rome: Istituto di studi islamici, 1981), at p. 14). The most significant study of the work accepts its authenticity: G. A. Lucchetta, *La natura e la sfera: la scienza antica e le sue metafore nella critica di Rāzī* (Lecce: Milella, 1987).

[76] It ends abruptly in the midst of a discussion of whether the cosmos must be of finite size. There are also internal references, which may be to other sections of the same work; if so the original text could have been quite extensive. (See especially the reference at 120,11 to a 'section on the soul (*bāb al-nafs*)'; and also 124,5–6; 128,16–17; 129,11–12.)

and operates teleologically (116,2–124,6), a section disputing philosophical theories of how the human fetus is generated (124,7–128,2), and a cosmological section, dealing *inter alia* with the eternity of the world, the possibility of multiple worlds, and the question of whether the world is infinitely large (128,3–134,11).

The author's discussion of the eternity of the world follows on from the attack on teleology. So it is no surprise that he finds unconvincing the physical arguments that have been adduced in favor of the world's eternity. He repeats (128,3–8) Aristotle's argument in *Physics* 8.1 against the possibility of a first motion, and then says rather dismissively (128,8–9):

> What we say is that the body and the motion are originated together, and we have undermined [the above argument] already, by saying that the Creator, the great and exalted, possesses an act that operates without His having changed.

Interestingly, the response seems designed to anticipate and rebut even the revised version of Aristotle's argument, as it appears in Themistius and Thābit, in which the argument is supposed to turn on the immutability of God as an agent, rather than on the conceptual impossibility of a first motion.[77] For the author insists that God could create body and motion *de novo* without Himself changing. In responding to Aristotle's argument from the nature of time,[78] by contrast, the author is willing to meet the philosophers on their own ground. He interprets the Aristotelian view (correctly) as follows: there cannot be a first instant of time, because there must be a time before and after every instant. But, he argues (128,17–129,5), if this is taken to imply that no period of time can actually begin or end, then neither could there be a first moment of Sunday or last moment of Saturday! Furthermore, time is analogous to space,[79] so if there is a time before and after every time, then there must be a spatial extension beyond every spatial extension, and therefore the world is infinitely large, contrary to what the philosophers believe (129,6–9).

Because of the author's dialectical strategy he is happy to confront specific arguments of the upholders of eternity (*ahl al-dahr*)[80] on the empirical level of physics, when it

---

[77] This is despite the fact that the argument is not set out that way by the author: 'Aristotle gives several proofs that the world's motions are eternal. In one of these he assumes that the world has always existed (*anna al-ʿālam qadīm*). What he says is that if motion began in time, then the body [of the cosmos] stayed unmoving for an infinite time, and then moves. If [the body of the cosmos] has a mover that has always existed, which moves it, then either it changes or the body that it moves changes. Whichever of the two moves, there was a motion before that motion' (128,3–6).

[78] Paraphrased at 128,11–16, and said to appear not in the *Physics*, but in *Metaphysics* book *Lambda*. This fact and the aforementioned response to the argument from motion suggest that the author may, like Thābit, have consulted the Arabic version of Themistius' paraphrase of *Lambda*. Tantalizingly, the author says he has elsewhere responded to a similar argument in a refutation of Proclus.

[79] For this assumption see also 132,5–7, and compare al-Ghazālī, *The Incoherence of the Philosophers*, ed. and trans. M. Marmura (Provo: Brigham Young University Press, 1997), p. 33.

[80] The expression first appears at 125,1 in the context of the argument over the formation of the embryo; at this stage *ahl al-dahr* is perhaps used as a general term for those who pay insufficient reverence to the divine as cause of the world (e.g. materialists). But it may also suggest the continuity of the author's polemic: just as his opponents think that nature is a sufficient cause of human formation, so they believe it is self-sufficient and in no need of a creator, and therefore eternal.

suits him. But the dominant feature of his treatise is an impatience with appeals to 'nature', whether this be to explain apparent intelligent design in the world or the formation of human embryos, or to undergird the opponents' chosen cosmology. An appeal to nature cannot settle any of these issues, because nature is subordinated to divine action. The author's philosophically astute scepticism about natural philosophy comes out most strongly in passages where he attacks the Aristotelians' use of induction from sense-experience. When one group of opponents attempt such an argument (the world is infinitely large, because we never see a body without another body beyond it), he responds by pointing out the weakness of such inductive inferences (127,17–128,2). Is an African who has only met black people entitled to think all people are black? Or is someone from a landlocked area entitled to think that all land is surrounded by further land? Our polemicist is on to something here. He realizes that counter-examples[81] carry a weight that positive generalizations made from experience cannot, since such generalizations could always be falsified with the discovery of a counter-example in the future. Here the author moves beyond rejecting physical arguments for the opponents' various cosmological claims, and suggests the ultimate inefficacy of Aristotelian physics as a whole.[82]

Let us now turn briefly to al-Rāzī's *Doubts About Galen*, which also contains a discussion of the world's eternity.[83] This is provoked by Galen's treatment of the issue in the lost *On Demonstration*, where it was argued that such things as the heavens and oceans have never been known to change from their state (*'an ḥālihi*). Since these large-scale features of the cosmos are unchanging over time, we can infer that the cosmos as a whole is eternal (3,18–21). Al-Rāzī contrasts this passage unfavorably to the more agnostic treatment of the same topic in other Galenic works, and exposes certain weaknesses in the argument. Particularly interesting for us is his point that things can be destroyed without displaying change or decay over time. For instance, a glass vessel might persist as it is for some time, then suddenly be struck by a rock (4,23). Could the same sort of thing happen to the cosmos? Yes, at least according to some: 'it is in this way that the world is destroyed, according to those religious believers (*mutadayyinīn*) who speak of the world's destruction' (5,2–3). Al-Rāzī need not be endorsing this suggestion. Rather, he's pointing out that it is a possibility which is not

---

[81] Such as he presents elsewhere in the text, e.g. when he says that semen cannot be a sufficient cause of pregnancy, because if it were women would conceive a child whenever it were present (125,3–6).

[82] He is similarly scathing about Aristotle's appeals to common opinions, or *endoxa*, which represent another important starting-point for the Peripatetics. In response to Aristotle's claim 'that there is no need to give a proof (*dalīl*) of nature, owing to its obviousness, and the fact that everyone recognizes it and grants its existence' (116,3–4), he says, 'something is not true just because everyone grants it, just as something is not wrong just because everyone denies it ... Proof is unnecessary only for immediately evident things (*al-ashyā' al-mushāhada*), and for the intellectual first principles of demonstrations; but nature is not grasped by the senses, nor is the knowledge of it a principle in the intellect' (116,9–10.14–16).

[83] For an edition of the work see Al-Rāzī, *Kitāb al-Shukūk 'alā Jālīnūs*, ed. M. Mohaghegh (Tehran, 1993). The relevant section is translated in J. McGinnis and D. C. Reisman, *Classical Arabic Philosophy: An Anthology of Sources* (Indianapolis: Hackett, 2007), pp. 51–3. Regarding its treatment of the eternity of the world, see P. Koetschet, 'Galien, al-Rāzī, et l'éternité du monde. Les fragment du traité *Sur la Démonstration* IV, dans les *Doutes sur Galien*', *Arabic Sciences and Philosophy* 25 (2015), 167–98.

eliminated by Galen's inductive argument. This is reminiscent of *On Metaphysics*, especially a passage (which I take to be dialectical in just the same way) where the author proposes that the phenomena explained as 'natural' by philosophers could just be the result of direct divine action.[84] In both contexts, natural experience is shown to be non-demonstrative once the possibility of divine action is considered.

Conclusion

I have here examined two topics which display the continuity of late antique and early Arabic philosophy. This continuity is hardly surprising, given how closely the first philosophers of the Arabic tradition engaged with the last philosophers of antiquity. On the other hand, we should always be mindful of the context of that engagement. With respect to the instrumental status of logic, we saw that members of the Baghdad School retained the commitments of their Greek authorities while also formulating a response to the attack of contemporary critics. On the topic of the world's eternity, slightly earlier authors like al-Kindī, Thābit and al-Rāzī carry on the late ancient process by which physical arguments are shown to be inadequate to determine whether the world is eternal or not. Their discussions must also be read in contemporary context, in this case provided by *kalām* authors who strictly opposed an eternal God to created things, and proposed occasionalist views on which God acts directly in the world, obviating the need for stable natures.[85] Such developments threw into doubt the apodeictic pretensions of Greek science. Then again, subtle reflection on the epistemic status of logic, physics, and other philosophical disciplines had always been a part of Greek science itself. Aristotle taught al-Fārābī the difference between the demonstrative and the merely dialectical; Galen taught al-Rāzī the difference between the certain and the merely probable.[86] Such distinctions invited authors writing in Arabic to stand in judgement over their favorite authorities, and to decide not only what should be retained from the antique tradition – but also where there was room for improvement.

---

[84] Al-Rāzī, *Rasā 'il* 116,17–18: 'on what basis do you deny that God, great and exalted, is all by Himself (*bi-ḏātihī*) the one who necessitates the powers of all other acts, and the natures of things?'

[85] For more discussion of the relation between *kalām* and the first generations of philosophy in Arabic, see P. Adamson, 'Arabic Philosophy: *Falsafa* and the *Kalām* Tradition before Avicenna', in J. Marenbon, ed., *The Oxford Handbook of Medieval Philosophy* (New York: Oxford University Press, 2012), pp. 58–82. I should perhaps clarify that in speaking of a 'theological' approach to the eternity debate I do not mean a *kalām* approach, but rather an approach proceeding from premises about God and His relation to the world. In this sense 'theology' is simply the part of philosophy dealing with God.

[86] See also R. Chiaradonna, 'Galen on What is Persuasive (*Pithanon*) and What Approximates to Truth', in P. Adamson, R. Hansberger, and J. Wilberding, eds, *Philosophical Themes in Galen* (London: Institute of Classical Studies, 2014), pp. 61–88.

19

Alexander of Aphrodisias *versus* John Philoponus in Arabic: A Case of Mistaken Identity[1]

Ahmad Hasnawi

In 1947 'Abdarraḥmān Badawī published the medieval Arabic translations of ten short treatises by Alexander of Aphrodisias.[2] Since that time a number of studies have appeared that shed new light on the transmission from Greek into Arabic of these works as well as others published later. The treatises attributed to Alexander preserved in Arabic include some for which no Greek counterpart has yet been found.[3] It is in relation to three of these (D.8a, D.9, and D.16)[4] that I wish to advance new evidence. As regards D.8a, I shall show that it is another version of *Quaestio* 1.21, alongside what has already been recognised as a translation of the same *Quaestio* (D.2b). On the other hand, as to D.9 and D.16, I shall show that these are not treatises by Alexander but adapted versions of extracts from the *On the Eternity of the World Against Proclus*, a work composed by the Christian author John Philoponus[5] in order to refute Proclus' eighteen arguments for the eternity of the universe. One of the most fruitful aspects of research on Alexander of Aphrodisias in Arabic has proved to be the work that has gone into identifying and extracting from this 'Alexander' the *disjecta membra* of a

---

This is an abridged version of an article that first appeared in French as 'Alexandre d'Aphrodise vs Jean Philopon: notes sur quelques traités d'Alexandre "perdus" en grec, conservés en arabes' by Ahmad Hasnawi in *Arabic Sciences and Philosophy* 4(1) (1994), pp. 53–109 © Cambridge University Press, translated and reproduced with permission.

[1] Translated by Christopher Strachan.
[2] 'A. Badawī, *Arisṭū 'inda al-'Arab*, Dirāsa wa-nuṣūṣ ġayr manšūra, al-ǧuz' al-awwal (Cairo, 1947), pp. 253–308.
[3] These works are listed in M Aouad and R. Goulet, 'Alexandros d'Aphrodisias', in R. Goulet, ed., *Dictionnaire des philosophes antiques* (Paris: CNRS 1989), vol. 1, pp. 125–39, on pp. 135–7.
[4] The treatises will be hereafter designated by the numbers assigned to them in the list of Alexander's works in Arabic in A. Dietrich, 'Die arabische Version einer unbekannten Schrift des Alexander von Aphrodisias über die Differentia specifica', *Nachrichten der Akademie der Wissenschaften in Göttingen: Philologisch-historisch Klasse* 2 (1964), 93–100. Under D.2 and again under D.8, Dietrich includes two separate treatises. In the case of D.2, I refer to the second treatise as D.2b, and in the case of D.8, to the first treatise as D.8a.
[5] John Philoponus, *De Aeternitate Mundi contra Proclum*, ed. H. Rabe (Leipzig: Teubner, 1899).

'Proclus arabus'.[6] This last, it is true, already incorporated, here or there, propositions which came originally from Philoponus.[7] From now on, it is proper to recognise the existence of a 'Philoponus arabus' *directly* presented in the guise of Alexander. As it happens, in so doing we are recovering, as far as I know for the first time, significant fragments of *On the Eternity of the World Against Proclus* in Arabic translation.[8]

The three texts which I shall be discussing share the common feature of being anonymous translations and of originating, to judge from their vocabulary and 'phraseology', as well as their free style of translation, in what it has been suggested should be called 'Al-Kindī's circle'.[9]

1

D.8a entitled: *Maqālatu al-Iskandari fī al-ṣūrati wa-annahā tamāmu al-ḥarakati wa-kamāluhā 'alā ra'yi Arisṭū* [Alexander's Treatise on form, that it is the completion of movement and its fulfilment in Aristotle's opinion (hereafter *FCM*)[10]] is in fact an

---

[6] Cf. G. Endress, *Proclus Arabus: Zwanzig Abschnitte aus der Institutio Theologica in arabischer Übersetzung* (Beirut: Orient-Institut der Deutschen, 1973); in the Preface, pp. 7–8, the author provides an account of the various stages in this process; see also F. Zimmermann, 'Proclus arabus rides again', *Arabic Sciences and Philosophy* 4 (1994), 9–51.

[7] Endress, *Proclus Arabus*, index p. 314, under 'Johannes Philoponos,' and esp. pp. 229–31.

[8] Apart from the very short fragments quoted by al-Bīrūnī in his book on India, *Taḥqīq mā li-al-Hind* [*Al-Bîrûnî's India*, ed. by E. Sachau (London, 1887)]. On the knowledge the Arabs had of the *De Aeternitate Mundi contra Proclum*, see Endress, *Proclus Arabus*, pp. 17–18, which contains the bibliography.

[9] See Endress, *Proclus Arabus*, pp. 192 and 242. G. Endress talks about a group of translators with Al-Kindī as their *spiritus rector*. F. Zimmermann refers to 'the Kindi workshop', more commonly, 'the Kindi circle', cf. 'The Origins of the so-called *Theology of Aristotle*', in J. Kraye, W. Ryan, and C. Schmitt, eds, *Pseudo-Aristotle in the Middle Ages* (London: The Warburg Institute, 1986), pp. 110–240, esp. p. 112 and App. II, p. 136. *Proclus Arabus* has useful material on the vocabulary used by this group of translators, pp. 76–153; on translation technique (in particular their periphrastic method of translation) and certain stylistic features, pp. 153–84, more specifically on 'phraseology', pp. 171–84.

These analyses are conducted by G. Endress on a *corpus* of texts, taken as terms of comparison with the 'Proclus arabus', that is to say here the twenty propositions of Proclus' *Elements of Theology* translated into Arabic, edited by Endress. The composition of this *corpus* is described on pp. 63–76; it comprises thirteen treatises by Alexander of Aphrodisias, including four preserved only in Arabic, *cf.* pp. 64–7. (In reality, account is taken also of the 'trilogy', on which see below n. 11). D.8a is taken into account, but not D.9, nor D.16, despite the author's assertion to the contrary [p. 66, k] as regards the latter. The text in question is in fact D.27g (on which see below, n. 48) which presents arguments partly parallel to those of D.16. One has only to consult the lexical entries and the phraseology presented as characteristic of the versions in the *corpus* to be convinced of the relationship between our treatises and the texts comprised in it. It is right to lay emphasis, as Endress does, on the variability of the degree of relationship between the texts of the *corpus* and what in this case serves as the term of reference, namely the 'Proclus arabus', and consequently on the variations among these texts themselves. A concomitant idea is that there are differences that are due to the personalities of individual translators within the group; cf. pp. 185–93.

[10] I reproduce here an English version of the excellent translation that M. Aouad and R. Goulet offer of this title, which, moreover, the Arab biobibliographers do not mention. The treatise was published by 'A. Badawī in *Arisṭū*, pp. 289–90, and translated by him in *La transmission de la philosophie grecque au monde arabe*, 2nd edn (Paris: Vrin, 1987), pp. 165–6. Dietrich does not identify it as a version of any Greek work of Alexander's; neither does R. W. Sharples, 'Alexander of Aphrodisias: Scholasticism and Innovation', in W. Haase, ed., *Aufstieg und Niedergang der römischen Welt II 36.2* (Berlin: De Gruyter, 1987), pp. 1176–1243, on pp. 1192–3, and M. Aouad and R. Goulet in *Dictionnaire des philosophes antiques I* (Paris: CNRS, 1989), p. 137, no. 32.

adapted version of *Quaest*. 1.21. Another translation of this treatise has already been identified, albeit buried, so to speak, in the course of a text consisting of the mingled contents of three of Alexander's *Quaestiones*,[11] but no one has gone so far as to recognise D.8a as a second version of this same *Quaest*. 1.21.[12] However, the following comparison between the text of D.8a and *Quaestio* 1.21 demonstrates that this is the case.[13]

Quaestio 1.21. In what category movement [belongs]. (34,30–35,15 Bruns; trans. R. W. Sharples)	*Alexander's treatise on form as the completion of movement and its fulfilment in Aristotle's opinion* (D.8a: Bad. 289–290)
If someone did not accept that movement was in quantities because it is not placed in quantities in the *Categories*, it would be said to be relative to something. But, whatever thing movement is that possesses the property of being relative to something, it will be an affection.	
	Alexander said: Aristotle mentioned in his book that is called *Book of the Lectures on Physics* that form is the completion <of movement> and its fulfilment. Consequently we wish to explain the Philosopher's doctrine as regards movement and form and clarify it. Accordingly we say:
For if to be moved is to be affected in some respect, and it is by the presence of affection that what is affected is affected, and what is moved is moved through the presence of movement, movement will be an affection.	movement is a certain affection, and what is affected is affected in virtue of an affection and what is moved is moved in virtue of a movement. If that is the case, then movement is a certain affection.

[11] Badawī, *Aristū*, pp. 278–80. These three *Quaestiones* have been grouped under the title, *kalām al-Iskandar al-Afrūdīsī, naql Saʿīd b. Yaʿqūb al-Dimašqī* [Treatises by Alexander of Aphrodisias, translation by Saʿīd b. Yaʿqūb al-Dimašqī]. H. Gätje, 'Zur arabischen Überlieferung des Alexander von Aphrodisias,' *Zeitschrift der Deutschen Morgenländischen Gesellschaft* 116 (1966), 255–78, at 262, is the first, it appears, to isolate the translation of *Quaest*. 1.21 effectively from what he called a 'trilogy' (*Quaest*. 1.22 = Bad. 278–9, 5; *Quaest*. 1.21 = Bad. 279, 5–16; *Quaest*. 1.11a = Bad. 279, 16–280). On p. 261 he includes an account of the history of this progressive disentanglement.

[12] See now, however, F. Zimmermann, 'Proclus arabus rides again', pp. 25–9.

[13] Alexander of Aphrodisias, *Quaestiones, De Fato, De Mixtione*, ed. I. Bruns, Supplementum Aristotelicum 2.2 (Berlin: Reimer, 1892), pp. 34–5. Here I shall use the English translation by R. W. Sharples in *Alexander of Aphrodisias, Quaestiones 1.1–2.15* (London; Duckworth, 1992), pp. 74–5. For the Arabic version, the translation I offer here follows ʿA. Badawī's edition, corrected where necessary from a copy of the Damas Ẓāhiriyya ʿāmm 4871 manuscript (Z).

The words or passages of the Greek original which correspond to the translation in D.8a are underlined in Sharples' translation, as they are also in my translation of the Arabic text. It is clear that though it is possible in the majority of cases to establish these 'correspondences', this is, however, not always so (see, for example, in D8a, Bad. 289, 16–17). The asterisks surrounding suspension points indicate a word or words illegible in my copy.

But affection is quality; for qualities involving affection, and affections, are the third species of qualities.

So incomplete activity, being an affection, will be quality; but what will complete activity be, and under what category?
Or rather: if such activity and actuality is form,

and of forms some are natural and others produced by art, and the natural forms are substances while those produced by art are qualities, this difference will apply to the actualities too.
But there are also qualities of natural forms, which do not contribute to the being of the underlying things, but to their being of a certain sort ...

What then must one say light is, since it too itself is the actuality of the transparent (*diaphanês*) qua transparent? Or if light is not by nature the form of the transparent, nor yet its being in some [sense] (for it does not exist along with the transparent, nor is it in its being, but it comes to be through the presence of something in it and according to the relation of one thing to another), it will itself too be some affection which comes to be according to the relation and presence of something in what is transparent, being analogous to colour, as Aristotle

Now the Philosopher had asserted in his book that is called *Book of the categories* that affection is the third species of the species of quality.

We now resume the argument and say: movement is either incomplete, or completed. Incomplete movement is affection, – I mean the accidental quality of something. As for completed movement, that is form – I mean the completion of something and its fulfilment, and that is what the Philosopher names *anṭālāšyā* in his book which is called *Book of the Lectures on Physics*. What this name signifies is the disappearance of potentiality and of the possibility of [moving] towards the completion and the fulfilment, which is the form of the thing.

We also say in regard to form that it is of two kinds: one natural, the other a product of art. Natural forms are substances; as for forms that are products of art, these are qualities. He [*sc.* Alexander] says at this point: sometimes a natural form may be a quality, when the form is not there to complete the substance of the thing, but serves to distinguish it from the rest of things. A thing is, in fact, such if it is in a particular state whereby it is separated from the rest of things.

If someone objects: if this is the case, light will be the form of the transparent and its fulfilment, we shall answer him that light is not a natural form of the transparent, for it is not produced always at the same time as the transparent nor is it in its substance, but it is produced at the same time as the coming of something else along with the transparent – I mean that light is produced from the fact of the arrival of a particular thing in something else capable of receiving this first thing. If this is the case, light will be some affection in the transparent body. The Philosopher has asserted that light is the colour of the transparent and an affection in it.

also said: for he says that light is like the colour of the transparent.   It is thus clear that light is not the form of the transparent, but that it is an affection and a colour; it is also proved correct and it is clear that a natural form is completed movement, that it is the completion of the thing and its fulfilment and that it is a substance – according to the Philosopher's doctrine.

I have three observations to make on why the bringing to light of the new version of *Quaest.* 1.21 is of interest:

1. This version, anonymous as it is, displays the characteristic features of the translations of Greek works that were carried out in what it has been proposed to call 'al-Kindī's circle'.
One of these features consists in the presence of additions and omissions.[14] If we look at D.8a, the omissions are, to all appearances, the result of an intention to simplify.[15] Thus, saying that affection is a third species of quality presupposes the proposition that affection is a quality. In this way the translator-adaptor avoids a needless repetition; likewise if he avoids mentioning affective qualities, it may be because they seem to him to have no bearing on the essential purpose of this detailed treatment of movement. The same wish for simplification and pruning would account for the other cases of omission. In 35,10-11, the statement 'nor yet its being', which is omitted, may seem to replicate what will come in 11-12: 'nor is it in its being'. The shade of meaning, if any, that differentiates the first formulation from the second is thus certainly lost. In lines 13-14 of the same page, 'which comes to be according to the relation and presence of something', which is omitted, might in the eyes of our adaptor appear as a superfluous repetition of 'it comes to be through the presence of something in it and according to the relation of one thing to another' which stated the proof supposed to lead to the conclusion to the effect that light is an affection. There was then no point in including it for a second time in the conclusion itself. The same observation applies to the suppression of 'analogous to colour' in line 14, since this statement occurs again in the 'quotation' from Aristotle, though with the loss of *hoion*, we pass from an analogy (light is to the transparent as colour is to bodies capable of receiving it) to an identification (light is the colour of the transparent). The suppression of 'this difference will apply to the actualities too' (Bruns 35,6-7) would be explainable by the following situation: the adaptor was guilty of a serious inaccuracy in translating *energeia* in lines 3 and 4 by *ḥaraka* (movement)[16] and

---

[14] On the additions, explanations and lacunae characteristic of these versions in general, see Endress, *Proclus Arabus*, pp. 194-5 and his analyses of those peculiar to 'Proclus arabus', pp. 195-241.

[15] This however does not apply to omissions that can be explained as lacunae in the manuscript copy used by the translator-adaptor of D.8a, viz. the missing beginning of *Quaestio* 1.21 (Bruns 34,31-3) and a lacuna of 15 words (Bruns 35,4-5) explainable as the result of homoeoteleuton.

[16] The contrast between a movement that is complete (*teleios*) and a movement that is incomplete (*atelês*) is to be found in Aristotle in *Physics* 5.4, 228b11-15, in the discussion on *the unity* of movement. Complete movement possesses unity, while incomplete movement does so only if it is continuous. Isḥāq b. Ḥunayn's Arabic translation contrasts *ḥaraka tāmma* and *ḥaraka ġayr tāmma*, see *Arisṭūṭālīs: al-Ṭabīʿa*, ed. ʿA. Badawī, 2 vols (Cairo, 1964-5), vol. 2, p. 566,11-15.

would thereafter have been somewhat loath to transfer the same distinction that has just been applied to forms to *energeiai* pure and simple, not qualified as 'completed' (i.e. to what, for him, are movements).

2. No less important than the omissions are the additions. In the case of D.8a as in general for the other translations of Alexander's treatises to emanate from 'al-Kindī's circle', these additions consist of an introduction, a conclusion and explanatory comments. The introduction makes reference to a doctrine of Aristotle's taken from one of his works duly mentioned by name. This is followed either by the statement of a puzzle that is to be resolved or, as in D.8a, of the avowed wish to explain, to provide an exegesis (*talḫīṣ*) of the Aristotelean doctrine in question. The conclusion follows a standard formula in introducing a summary restatement of the doctrine discussed.[17] The explanatory comments relate to various individual assertions. The doctrinal content of these often enables us to pinpoint the philosophic context inhabited by the adaptor and his readers. The wording of the title given to the treatise is also a valuable indication of the philosophic provenance.

The title of D.8a, 'that form is the completion of movement and its fulfilment' is brought into the introduction added by the adaptor as a proposition taken from Aristotle's *Physics*. K. Deichgräber suggests that this may be seen as an allusion to *Physics* 3.2, 202a7 f. This association, though relevant, is so only indirectly.[18] As the quotation is in any case not *verbatim* we cannot rule out the possibility that what we are dealing with is not a reference to a passage of Aristotle as such, but to an interpretation of Aristotle.[19] To my mind, there is a precise context, one in which the Greek commentators on Aristotle's *Physics*, in their wish to explain his definition of movement (*Physics* 3.1, 201a10–11: 'the actualisation of what is potentially, as such, is movement'), bring into play the notion of a double entelechy: on the one hand that of something that is in possession of its completed form, cut off from all potentiality; on the other, that of something that, starting from potentiality, heads towards the form while at the same time preserving that potentiality. This last is the entelechy

---

In a quite different context, Proclus employs the expression 'complete movement' to designate the activity of *Nous*, and this 'complete movement' is identifiable as an activity (*energeia*) in the sense in which it is opposed to movement (*kinêsis*) in Aristotle, for example in *Metaph.* 9.6. See J. Christensen de Groot, 'Philoponus on *De Anima* II, 5, *Physics* III, 3 and the propagation of light', *Phronesis*, 28 (1983), 177–96, on pp. 192–3.

[17] These are listed in Endress, *Proclus arabus*, pp. 180–3; pp. 181–2 are concerned with the occurrence of these formulae in Arabic translations of Alexander.

[18] See Deichgräber's contribution in Dietrich, 'Über die Differentia specifica,' p. 95. One can only say that the idea of the form's being transmitted *from the mover to the moved* which is put forward in the Aristotelean *Physics* passage does not play a major part in *FCM*.

[19] Some idea of how such interpretations of Aristotle are cited may be gained from a quotation from Ǧābir b. Ḥayyān, who mentions *FCM* itself next to the *Paraphrase* of the *Physics* by Themistius. 'fa-aqūlu inna Arisṭūṭālīsa yaqūlu fī kitābihi fī al-Samāʿi al-ṭabīʿiyyi inna al-ṣūrata hiyya tamāmu al-ḥarakati wa-kamāluhā. Wa-qad ḥakā ḏālika ʿanhu al-Iskandaru fī risālatihi wa-ḥakā ḏālika Ṯāmisṭiūs fī tafsīri kitābi Arisṭāṭālīsa fī al-Samāʿi al-ṭabīʿiyyi.' K. al-Baḥṯ, quoted by P. Kraus, *Jābir ibn Ḥayyān: Contribution à l'histoire des idées scientifiques dans l'Islam II: Jābir and Greek science* (Cairo, 1942; repr. Paris, 1986), p. 321, n. 2: 'Aristotle states in his book of the *Physics* that the form is the completion of movement and its actualisation. Alexander reports this in his treatise and Themistius reports it in his paraphrase of the book of the *Physics*.'

characteristic of a thing in a state of movement (the actualisation of that which is potentially, as such); the first is the entelechy characteristic of the terminal state of things resulting from movement.[20] Our version of Alexander's treatise shows signs of the notion of double entelechy: its *leitmotiv* (form as completion of movement) refers to the final state of movement; but the gloss on the word *anṭālāšyā* explains it as denoting the entelechy proper to the state of movement.[21]

3. By bringing this context into view, the adapted version of *Quaestio* 1.21 at one and the same time restores to us the Greek context of this *Quaestio* itself, which is reflected in the discussions the Greek commentators offer of *Physics* 3.1, in which the definition of movement is set out, and in particular of 3.1, 200b32–201a3.[22] The question raised

---

[20] The notion of double entelechy is set out in Themistius' *Paraphrase* of the *Physics*, ed. Schenkl, CAG 5.2 (Berlin: Reimer, 1900), p. 69,9–20 and in Philoponus, *in Phys.* 342,17–343,12 which reproduces Themistius virtually unaltered. This passage from Philoponus' commentary is paraphrased in the scholia dating from the tenth-eleventh century, which accompany the school edition of the Arabic translation, by Isḥāq b. Ḥunayn (d. 910/911), of Aristotle's *Physics*. See *al-Ṭabīʿa*, pp. 171,8–13; 176,6–9 where Themistius is cited in Philoponus' version. We know from *al-Fihrist* by al-Nadīm (completed in 988) that the translation of Philoponus' commentary on the first four books of the *Physics* is due to Qusṭā b. Lūqā (d. c. 912). See *al-Fihrist*, ed. R. Tağaddud, 3rd edn (n.p., 1988), p. 311,1–3. It is perhaps not without interest that the translation of the last four books of this commentary on the *Physics* is attributed by al-Nadīm to Ibn Nāʿima al-Ḥimṣī, the very same man who translated Aristotle's *Theology* for al-Kindī. The scholia concerned with these books, such as they have come down to us, were probably brought in line, from the point of view of terminology and style, with the normal practice of the Baghdad 'school'.

The scholia relating to double entelechy are cited below. These passages are no more than a reflection, and certainly a later one, of the context I am referring to, which could have been transmitted earlier through other channels, a fact to which *FCM* justly bears witness.

– 'By actualisation he (*sc.* Aristotle) refers in this case (i.e. in the definition of movement) to the starting off of what exists potentially towards activity, not completion – so that that which is potentially would be cancelled and that which is in activity would be actualised –, but rather [actualisation] so that the potentiality, while remaining stable, lasting and essential is in activity. It is then in fact that movement occurs. (*Al-Ṭabīʿa*, p. 171,8–10.)

– 'The actualisation is double: first and last. The last is the actualising of that which is potentially, the first is the approach towards the last actualisation, potentiality being preserved while the approach continues; and it is in this that movement consists.' (ibid. 11–13)

– 'And Themistius ... considers that the last actualisation is the actualisation of the form in the event of which potentiality comes to rest and is cancelled. The first actualisation is the progression towards this actualisation.' (176,6–10)

[21] This explanatory gloss comes just after one that relates to the word 'form'. These two glosses (or these two parts of the same gloss) do not quite fit together. In the first, form is identified with actualisation; while in the second, actualisation is defined as the passage of potentiality towards actualisation which is, it goes on to clarify, form. Is it to be concluded from this that the gloss on *anṭālāšyā* is a subsequent addition, a sort of gloss on a gloss? We may well think so. But even if this is the case, the philosophic context I have been talking about still remains as the background to the text under discussion.

[22] In saying this I appear to be assigning a single theme to *Quaest.* 1.21. Sharples, *Quaestiones 1.1–2.15*, p. 74, n. 220, refers to 'the apparent diversity of topics' that characterise it. He points out that the title only fits the first part (cf. p. 3 and n. 11, his remarks on the titles of the *Quaestiones* in general, of which certain, like that of *Quaest.* 1.21 are described as 'inept and unhelpful'), and suggests, following Bruns, that 'it may be that something has been lost from the text after 35,8'. I should emphasise that the two Arabic versions would be in the same situation as the transmitted Greek text.

To tell the truth, it is not only the transition between the first and the second part of this *Quaest.* that is a problem. The purpose of the discussion on light in the second part is not easy to make out, but the result to which it appears to lead, namely that light is an affection, would point to its being a

by this passage is whether, given that there are several types of movement falling into different categories, the notion of movement is still essentially single, or, on the other hand, a homonymous (equivocal) concept.[23] What interests me here is what the medieval Muslim philosophers may have taken to be Alexander's position on this question. In fact if Alexander appears to assert in this treatise that movement is an affection, and therefore a quality, John Philoponus' *Commentary on Aristotle's Physics* revealed to them that Alexander held that movement was a homonymous term and not a genus.[24] We cannot answer this question with certainty nor even be sure, in the present state of our knowledge, that the Muslim philosophers perceived this divergence in the way that we believe that we do. To return to our Arabic version D.8a, we might describe the shift of emphasis that it causes *Quaest.* 1.21 to undergo, in the following way: while this text (or rather the first part of it) would, in my opinion, come in at the stage of the presentation of the third proposition (called by Philoponus *axiôma*, *lemma* by Simplicius) aimed at preparing for the definition of movement, the Arabic version, for its part, situates it later on, at the point when the elucidation proper of the definition of movement takes place. The 'official' theme of *Quaest.* 1.21, 'Under what category should movement be subsumed?' is, so to speak, buried underneath that of form as completion of movement.

    matter of determining its category status on the understanding that it is not by nature the form of the transparent (see however on this point *Quaest.* 1.2, 7,3–4 = Sharples, p. 23). In this instance, light would have the same category status as movement. The transition between the part in which the conclusion is drawn that movement is an affection and the question, 'into which category does completed activity fall?', is not easy to grasp either. Is the implication here that complete activity is the form-result of movement? But in that case, why is the division of forms that are complete activities limited to substances (natural forms) and qualities (forms established by art)? Finally, there seems to be an ambiguity as regards the notion of quality that applies on the one hand, to the qualities that are forms produced by art, on the other to the quality that makes a natural form what it is. In a way, we can read this *Quaest.* as being about the category status of light. But it is perhaps not without some interest that it could have been understood as directed mainly at the question of what category movement falls under.

[23] See Themistius, *Paraphrase* of the *Physics*, 68,16–30; Philoponus, *in Phys.* 343,22–344,7; Simplicius, *in Phys.* 402,9–406,16. This lies at the root of the discussion that was to lead, in the natural philosophy of the Latin Middle Ages, to the distinction between movement as *forma fluens* and movement as *fluxus formae*. See on this discussion A. Maier, *Die Vorläufer Galileis im 14. Jahrhundert* (Rome: Edizioni di Storia e Letteratura, 1949), pp. 9–25, and *Zwischen Philosophie und Mechanik* (Rome: Edizioni di Storia e Letteratura, 1958), pp. 61–143. The Greek background to this set of problems is not touched upon in the studies bearing on the medieval context. On this point I take the liberty of referring the reader to my essay: 'Le statut catégorial du mouvement chez Avicenne : contexte grec et postérité médiévale latine', in R. Morelon and A. Hasnawi, eds, *De Zénon d'Élée à Poincaré* (Louvain: Peeters, 2004), pp. 607–22.

[24] Cf. *in Phys.* 349,5–6, which finds an echo in one of the scholia on the Arabic translation of the *Physics*: 'Wa-laysat (ay: al-ḥarakatu) isman muštarakan kamā ḏāhaba ilayhi al-Iskandaru.' *Al-Ṭabīʿa*, p. 176,4–5: '[Movement] is not as Alexander has claimed a homonymous (equivocal) noun.' We should note that the reference to Alexander here comes from Philoponus' *Commentary*.

    Alexander's position on this question appears more complex in Simplicius' account, *in Phys.* 403,13–23 [the greater part of this passage 403,13–19 is translated by C. Luna in *Simplicius, Commentaire sur les Catégories: Fasc. III* (Leiden: Brill, 1990), p. 75 and see p. 76]. There Alexander maintains that entities may well fall under the same genus and yet be homonymous. Thus the different types of movement fall under a single genus, that of relation; but as *movements occurring in different categories* (substance, quality, quantity, place), they are homonymous. In other words whether movement is characterised as univocal or equivocal depends on the heading under which it is considered.

2

The two following treatises whose Greek source we are in the process of identifying are not by Alexander of Aphrodisias, but are, both of them, extracts from *On the Eternity of the World Against Proclus* by John Philoponus. The first, *Maqālatu al-Iskandarī fī anna al-fiʻla aʻammu mina al-ḥarakati ʻalā raʼyi Arisṭū*, [Treatise by Alexander: that activity is more general than movement in the opinion of Aristotle (D.9)[25]] has aroused no suspicion among the experts as to its authenticity. K. Deichgräber has supplied the following as the likely Greek title of this treatise: 'Concerning making being wider than causing movement according to Aristotle' and thinks that it refers to a passage from the *De Generatione et Corruptione* 1.6, 323a15–20, while at the same time recognising that the conclusion of the passage says the opposite 'causing movement is wider than making'.[26] We are now in a position to restore the true 'title' of this 'treatise', *epipleon hē energeia tēs kinēseōs, hōs Aristotelei dokei*, which is none other than the opening sentence of the account taken from *Against Proclus* 4.4–6. We can also follow the epitomizer's way of working. As in the versions of the other pieces based on authentic treatises by Alexander, the account corresponding to Philoponus' text is preceded by an introduction and followed by a conclusion. This does no more than reaffirm the thesis put forward in the treatise and repeat that such is Aristotle's doctrine. The introduction confers on the treatise the canonical form of the other pieces of Alexander issued by 'al-Kindī's circle': a reminder of a proposition of Aristotle's supposedly taken from one of his works, a statement of a puzzle and an assertion of the wish to resolve it. There is a degree of clumsiness in the statement of the puzzle. The Aristotelean theses between which an incompatibility would arise, would be two propositions: 'All movement produces an activity and all activity arises from a movement' on one hand, and the proposition, 'Activity is more general than movement' on the other. In fact, Philoponus has just shown, in sections 1–3 of *Against Proclus* 4, against Proclus' fourth argument,[27] that, for God, the transition from non-creation (of the Universe) to creation is comparable to the actualisation of a capacity or a disposition (*hexis*) and by the same token is neither a change (*metabolē*) nor a movement (*kinēsis*). His purpose is now to establish, in sections 4 to 6, to which D.9 corresponds, the following two points: 1) it is not necessary for the act of creation, the divine making (*poiēsis*) and more generally activity (*energeia*), to be a movement (*kinēsis*). There are in fact two sorts of *energeia* that must be distinguished from each other, the incomplete *energeia* that is movement and the complete *energeia* that constitutes activities like the appearance of light, visual perception or intellection. 2) Even in the case of movement, that is, incomplete *energeia*, it is in what is acted upon that it resides, as Aristotle recognises, and not in the agent. The implication here is that even if we supposed that divine making were a movement, the movement would be in the object of the making and not in God. In the sixth section, Philoponus cites the testimony of Aristotle as support for this last thesis.

The epitomizer of D.9 omitted some parts and modified others in Philoponus' text. Some of his eliminations are 'innocent'. Thus it was no doubt his desire to abridge that

---

[25] Published in Badawī, *Arisṭū*, pp. 293–4. This treatise was not mentioned by the Arab biobibliographers.
[26] Cf. Dietrich, 'Über die Differentia specifica', p. 95.
[27] Set out in *Aet.* 55,25–56,26.

led him to omit the quotations from Aristotle and the explanations that go with them (67,3–68,3). On the other hand the elimination of passages relating to God (65,24–6; 66,25–7; 68,20–3, a passage not reproduced in my double-columned presentation)[28] manifestly stems from intention. Philoponus' argument covering the three sections of chapter 4 is 'decontextualised'. Although the intention to generalise is already present in Philoponus – whose aim is to turn Aristotle's teaching against Proclus – the epitomizer, by leaving out the references that bring in God, purges the text of its polemical context and turns it into a didactic account of a neutral Aristotelean doctrine.

There can be little doubt that it was this 'decontextualisation' that removed all suspicion concerning the attribution of the text to Alexander of Aphrodisias – a suspicion, moreover, that would have been all the harder to justify given that the theories contained in the treatise could be claimed by Alexander. Accordingly, we shall find in Alexander the three examples illustrating the notion of complete *energeia* that appear in D.9.[29] The second part of D.9 (even in the case of an incomplete *energeia*, viz. movement, the movement resides in what is acted upon, not in the agent) could

---

[28] Apart from those just noticed, there are certain omissions that can no doubt be put down to a wish to simplify. This is evident in Rabe 65,8–10 where the qualification *hêi toiouton* is omitted in the definition of movement, an omission which is reminiscent of the parallel omission, in D.8a, of *hêi diaphanes* in the definition of light (Bruns 35,10); and Rabe 65,20–2.

Other omissions may concern words or phrases that refer back to earlier arguments. So at 65,5–6 *prôtou* ('first') is omitted and *hexin* ('disposition') replaced by *al-fi'li*. Philoponus is referring to the first of two sorts of transition that he had distinguished earlier (cf. Rabe 61,23–62,11), the transition from the first potentiality (*protera dunamis*) to the *hexis*, and the transition from the latter, called second potentiality (*deutera dunamis*) or first actuality (*prôtê energeia*) to the second actuality (*deutera energeia*). Perhaps the same observation should be made about the omission of 66,20–2, where the word *diathesis* ('condition') figures.

Apart from the stereotyped formulae used for transitions and conclusions, we shall take note of three important additions aimed at providing explanation in the body of the text, *i.e.* not counting the added introduction and the sentence embodying the conclusion. A comment, however, about the concluding formulae, *fa-(qad) istabāna/tabayyana (al-āna) (wa-ṣaḥḥa) (ayḍan)*. Of the four occurrences we encounter (Bad. 293, 10; 16; 294, 14; 15), two correspond to the Greek phrases *dedeiktai ara* ('So it has been shown') (Rabe 68,15 ≈ Bad. 294,14), and *houtô men oun* ('Thus, then,') (Rabe 65,10 ≈ Bad. 293,10). The same observation applies to the references to Aristotle: if we leave out of account the reference in the added introduction, of the three other references to the *Physics* scattered throughout the text, two are also found in Philoponus (Rabe 65,7–8 ≈ Bad. 293,8–9; Rabe 67,2 ≈ Bad. 294,8, the Arabic reference does not directly mention the title but alludes to it as 'the book we have just named' and does not specify what part of the *Physics* is involved).

[29] The passages in question belong to the piece called *How seeing comes about according to Aristotle* (Alexander, *De anima liber cum mantissa*, ed. I. Bruns, Suppl. Arist. 2.1 (Berlin: Reimer, 1887), pp. 141–7), which was translated into Arabic by Isḥāq b. Ḥunayn under the title *Maqālatu al-Iskandari al-Afrūdīsī fī kayfa yakūnu al-ibṣāru 'alā madhabi Arisṭāṭālīs* (D. 13). This translation is then later than that of D.9. It was edited and translated by H. Gätje in *Studien zur Überlieferung der aristotelischen Psychologie im Islam* (Heidelberg: Winter, 1971), pp. 146–63.

– Light and colours are generated suddenly (*athroôs = duf'atan*), Bruns 143,21 = Gätje 151,55.
– Light and the forms of visible objects are generated suddenly, Bruns 143,26–7 = Gätje 151,59–60.
– Aristotle shows that sight is generated without taking time (*akhronôs = bi-lā-zamānin*), Bruns 143,29–30 = Gätje 153,62.
– Comparison between intellectual grasp and the sudden illumination (and coloration) of the potentially transparent in the presence of a source of light, Bruns 144,36–145,3 = Gätje 155,100–157,1.

On the relations between Philoponus and Alexander of Aphrodisias, in regard to the appearance and propagation of light and in regard to perception, see J. Christensen de Groot, 'Philoponus on *De Anima* II, 5, *Physics* III, 3 and the propagation of light', *Phronesis* 28 (1983), 177–96, at 180–2.

perfectly well be taken as a repetition of the theory put forward by Aristotle in *Physics* 3.3, a theory that was adopted by Alexander himself.[30]

The double-columned presentation below follows the same lines as that used for *Quaest.* 1.21. In the left-hand column is M. Share's translation of Philoponus' text and in the right-hand column is my own translation of D.9.[31]

Philoponus, *Against Proclus*: 65,1–68,17 Rabe	Alexander's Treatise, that activity is more general than movement (D.9: Bad. 293–4)
4. ... for activity is, according to Aristotle, wider than movement.	Alexander said: Aristotle mentioned in his book which is called *Book of the lectures on Physics* that activity is more general than movement. A difficulty as to this has been raised by saying: if to every movement there belongs an actvity,[32] and if every activity occurs only on account of a movement, why then does Aristotle say that activity is more general than movement? We wish then to resolve this difficulty and expound it.

---

[30] See for example *Quaest.* 3.7, 93,2–9. In *Aet.* 4.4 (= D.9, Bad. 293,7–15), Philoponus adopts an argument from his *in DA* 2.5 (ad 417a14). The title of our treatise D.9 appears in this argument in two forms:
– p. 296,22–3: 'activity is more general than movement [movement than being affected]'. We may note in passing that the bracketed phrase recalls, except for the substitution of *paskhein* for *poiein*, the sentence in *GC* to which K. Deichgräber referred, cf. above n. 26.
– p. 297,27: 'activity is wider than movement'.
The contrast between movement as incomplete activity on the one hand, and complete activity as the instantaneous expression of the disposition on the other, reappears in practically the same terms as in *Aet.*; cf. *in DA* 296,25–6 (with cross-reference to the *Physics*) and 297,1–3). Finally, the three examples of complete *energeia* are also to be found there: the appearance of light, p. 297,4–6 (but excluding the mention of fire and sun as examples of light-sources); sense-perception not, as in *Aet.* 65,18–19, restricted to sight; more significantly, the complex treatment of movement or activity in relation to thought, p. 297,12–26, is replaced in *Aet.* 65,22–4, by a shorter discussion concerning intellect.
I first encountered the *in DA* in my research on the source of D.9 when my attention was directed towards the exegetic literature bearing on *De Anima* 2.5.

[31] M. Share, *Philoponus, Against Proclus On the Eternity of the World 1–5* (London: Duckworth, 2004). Also worthy of mention is the translation of D 9 by 'A. Badawī, *La Transmission*, pp. 167–8.

[32] *Fi'l* has been translated uniformly by 'activity' which may here be preferable to 'actuality', and matches Share's rendering of *energeia*. *Fi'l* retains the ambiguity of the word *energeia* between actuality and activity. In the remainder of the text, *energoun* ('being active'), which is opposed to *paskhon* ('being affected') is translated by *fā'il* ou *fa'āl* (Rabe 66,1 = Bad. 293,18; and 66,20 = 294,4), which is opposed to *maf'ūl bihi* ou *maf'ūl* (Rabe 66,2 = Bad. 293,19; 66,19 = 294,3). On the other hand, *poiēsis* and *poioun* ('making', noun and verb) are rendered by *'amal* and *'āmil* (Rabe 68,16 = Bad. 294,15; *ginomenon* ('coming into being') opposite *poioun* ('making') is translated by *ma'mūl*). The vocabulary Philoponus uses here is that of *Physics* 3.3.

For he says that activity is of two kinds, complete and incomplete. Incomplete activity is, he says, movement. For, according to him, movement is change from first potentiality to capacity. This is how he defines it in book three of the *Physics*: 'movement is the realisation of what potentially is, *qua* such'. By 'realisation' he means the actual (*autên*) activation and fulfilment of the potential. So movement is incomplete activity. By complete activity, on the other hand, he means instantaneous production from a capacity without the capacity becoming in any way different. Instantaneous production is production that does not proceed with the passage (*kinêsei*) of time but happens in an instant, like the emanation of light from a source of illumination; for as soon as a source of illumination such as a fire or the sun is visible, everything capable of it is instantaneously illuminated. Of this kind too is the activity of seeing; we instantaneously perceive sensible objects the moment we look at them.

It is for this reason that Aristotle denies that the senses are in movement during the perception of sensible objects.

And nor is the activity of the mind movement; it grasps the objects of thought (*ta noêta*) instantaneously and without any interval.
If, then, the activity of these is instantaneous, and on that account complete and not movement, how could he have the effrontery to say that the activity of God is movement?

We say then that activity is of two kinds, one incomplete, the other complete. In regard to incomplete activity, the Sage has said that it is movement, for movement, according to him, is the transition from potentiality to activity; and that is how he defined movement in the third treatise of his book which is called *Lectures on Physics*, viz. that movement is the realisation of potentiality and possibility. It is now clear and shown to be true that movement is incomplete activity. As to complete activity, it is the sudden manifestation of the state of something without its state's changing in any way. By sudden manifestation of the state of something, I mean only the state that is manifested without any time, such as the appearance of light <from its source> such as a fire or the sun; for, as soon as one of these two sources appears, it illuminates all at once, everything suited to accepting its light. And this is how the activity of seeing occurs; for the moment we open our eyes, we see together all the sensible objects in our field of vision in the same way.

We also say: intellectual activity is not a movement, for the intellect grasps intelligibles, suddenly, without there being any separation between them.

It is thus clear and shown to be true that activity is more general than movement, as the Sage has asserted; for all movement is activity and all activity is not movement, as we have shown and made clear.

5. But Aristotle does not think it right to call even activities which are incomplete and take place in time movements of the active parties but [thinks that they should] rather [be described as movements] of the things that are acted on. A mind that is skilled in building or in teaching does not itself undergo any alteration or any movement at all by building or teaching – assuming [for the sake of the argument] that the builder or teacher is perfect so that he is not learning through practice because he is imperfect.

If the teacher is of this kind, and then teaches, he undergoes no alteration or any movement himself as a result of teaching. The movement that results from the teaching has taken place on the side of the pupil. He is the one who undergoes alteration and changes from not knowing to knowing. Similarly, if a mind skilled in building and [with] perfected skills, stirs a body to build, it does not become in any way different from its [former] self; the movement is seen among the building materials, namely, the stones and timber. It is they that undergo alteration; and the same applies in every case. Even though the activity in all these cases is not instantaneous, the alteration and movement take(s) place in the sphere of that which is acted upon rather than in the sphere of that which acts. For no different state of any kind arises in the mind that is skilled in teaching or skilled in building as a result of teaching or building. And even if the body moves, it is as an instrument, and its movement is different and not the kind that the things under discussion exhibit; for the movement of the body is local. And [anyway] God brings all things into existence by the very [act of] willing [them] and has no need of the assistance of an instrument.

We say further, as the Philosopher states in the book we have just named, that incomplete activity that takes place over time is not a movement of the agent, but a movement of the thing that is acted upon. In fact, the builder's mind when engaged in building and the teacher's mind when engaged in teaching, do not move in any way nor change their state in any way – and that is the case only when they possess perfect knowledge.

For the teacher, when he is perfect and has attained completeness in his knowledge, suffers no change in his condition because of his teaching. As to the movement occurring from the effect of the teaching, it only occurs in the one being taught: it is the pupil in effect who changes towards knowledge. The same is true of the builder when he is perfect and has attained completion [in his art] and then moves his body to build; he does not change his condition, the movement is only in what is being built, I mean in the stone and the wood. And movement occurs in the same way in the rest of things, I mean that movement happens in what is acted upon, not in what acts.

If someone objects: the builder's body moves, we say: even though the builder's body moves, it moves as the instrument of the intellect in which there is a knowledge of building. We further say: the movement of the builder's body is different from the movement of the stone or the wood: the builder's body moves with local movement, while the stone moves with qualitative movement. In fact it has shapes imposed on it, that is, the circle and the square, thus changing from its former state; as to the body of the builder, it will not change from its original state in any

6. Perhaps it will not be unprofitable to quote some passages in which Aristotle explicitly testifies to these very points.
In the third book of the *Physics*, soon after defining movement, he adds the following:

[67,3–68,2]

This is what he says:
The [solution to the] puzzle is clear; movement is in the moveable. It is its actualisation through the agency of that which is able to cause movement. And the actualisation of that which is able to cause movement is not something separate – for both must have an actualisation. It is 'able to cause movement' because it has the power to, and 'cause of movement' through its activity; but it is of its nature to activate the moveable.

What he is saying here is, to take an example, that even though one and the same thing, [the process of] building, is the actualisation of both the builder and of that which is being built, the movement is nevertheless not in the builder but [only] in that which is being built; for it is the fulfilment of that which is buildable that is being brought about through the agency of the builder. And the same applies to all movement.

It has, then, been shown by means of arguments drawn from Aristotle as well that production is a movement not of the producer but of that which is coming to be.

way. The Sage mentioned that also in his book that we have just named, saying: 'Movement is in the movable ; for movement is the actualisation of the movable which comes to it from the mover. Let us also summarise and say that the mover is the potentiality to [produce] movement, Movement is actualisation, and the actualisation is the actualisation of the mover in the movable.'[33] In explanation of the Philosopher's

[... 67,3–68,2 ...]

statement we say : he meant by this statement that even though the activity of building is single – and it is the actualisation of the builder and of that which is being built – the movement is not in the builder, but in that which is being built, for the movement is the fulfilment of the buildable which comes to it from the builder. And this holds good for all movements. It is now manifest that activity is not movement that belongs to the agent but to that which is acted upon.

If this is the case, it has become clear and is shown to be true that activity is more general than movement, according to the Philosopher's doctrine.

---

[33] 'Movement is in the movable; for movement is the actualisation of the movable which comes to it from the mover' (*Phys.* 3.3, 202a13–4). Should the phrase, 'the mover is the potentiality to [produce] movement', be taken as a translation of 202a16–17 with the reading ... *to dunasthai* (cf. Ross's apparatus)? The phrase, 'the actualisation is the actualisation of the mover in the movable,' might be a way of rendering 202b6–8. In that case, the adaptor would have gone beyond the limits of the text of Aristotle cited by Philoponus. But it is also possible that he is simply summarising Aristotle's teaching.

3

D.16 is entitled *Maqālatu al-Iskandari al-Afrūdīsī fī ibṭāli qawli man qāla innahu lā yakūnu šay'un illā min šay'in wa-iṯbāti anna kulla šay'in innamā yakūnu lā min šay'in* (Treatise of Alexander the Aphrodisian refuting the doctrine that states that something can only be generated from something and establishing that everything can only be generated out of non-being).[34] In fact it consists of an adapted version of the *Against Proclus* 9.11. More exactly, apart from an introductory passage borrowed from 9.8, the remainder of treatise D.16 corresponds, except for some lacunae, to *Against Proclus* 9.11, 345,4–355,27. At the end of D.16 in manuscript E, we find the following sentence: '*hāḏā āḫiru mā wuǧida min hāḏihi al-maqālati* ... (this is the end of what there is of this Treatise),' which tends to indicate that the copyist, at some stage in the transmission of the text was aware of the incomplete nature of the treatise he had just copied. The possibility that other manuscripts may give us a fuller version of it cannot thus be ruled out. The correspondences between Philoponus' Greek text and the Arabic translation are set out below, with a note of the passages of the Greek that are omitted in Arabic, which sometimes extend to several pages in Rabe's edition. Thereafter some specimens of the Arabic translation are set opposite the matching pieces of the Greek text, in the order in which they occur in the Greek.

Against Proclus 9		*D. 16*
• 338,21–5	≈	fol. 83a, 5–6
• 339,2–24 with an omission of about ten lines	≈	fol. 83a, 6–9
• 339,25–345,4: passage of more than five pages omitted in Arabic		[..................]
• 345,4–20	≈	fol. 83a, 9–16
• 345,20–346,11: passage of twenty or so lines omitted in Arabic, though the example in 346,2–5 is incorporated in the example in Arabic fol. 83a, 20–24		[..................]
• 346,11–355,27	≈	fol. 83a, 16–87a 4

In lines 5 to 9 at the start of fol. 83a are set out the theory that nothing comes from nothing and the argument supporting it from the evidence of the facts (these lines correspond to part of *Against Proclus* 9.8). The falsehood of the theory is about to be demonstrated in regard to *embodied forms* (*ta enula eidê* = *al-ṣuwaru al-hayūlāniyyatu*). It will be conceded that matter is incorruptible and that only form undergoes generation and decay, the hylomorphic compound being said to be generated and corrupted with respect to one of its parts, that is, with respect to the form. The gist of this line of

---

[34] This treatise is attributed to Alexander in the bibliographical notes provided on him by the Arab biobibliographers under the title: *Kitābu al-raddi* (in Ibn Abī Uṣaybiʻa: *Maqāla fī al-raddi) ʻalā man qāla innahu lā yakūnu šay'un illā min šay'in* (Refutation of the holder of the view that something is only generated from something): al-Nadīm, *al-Fihrist*, p. 313, 19; Ibn al-Qifṭī (d. 1248), *Ta'rīḫ al-ḥukamā'*, ed. A. Müller and J. Lippert (Leipzig, 1903), p. 54, 23; Ibn Abī Uṣaybiʻa (d. 1270), *ʻUyūn al-anbā' fī ṭabaqāt al-aṭibbā'*, ed. A. Müller, 2 vols (Cairo, Königsberg, 1882–84), vol. I, p. 70, 13–14. The manuscript source is Escorial² 798 (E).

argument is what is set out in the remainder of fol. 83a,[35] with, however, significant omissions to which attention will once again be drawn. My translation of the Arabic text (fol. 83a) is printed below opposite M. Share's translation of the extracts from the text of Philoponus[36]. The matching words or passages are underlined.

Philoponus, *Against Proclus* 338,21–346,26 Rabe	Extracts from *Treatise of Alexander the Aphrodisian refuting the doctrine of one who states that something can only be generated from something and establishing that everything can only be generated out of non-being.* (D.16: MS Escorial² 798, fol. 83a, 5–24)
8. Since Proclus next brings up <u>an argument</u> which is a commonplace <u>among the Hellenes</u> there being nothing, he says, from which it could come to be, nor would it come to be; for everything that comes to be must come to be from something and <u>it is impossible, he says, for anything to come to be from nothing.</u>	He says: <u>people among the Ancients have stated that it is impossible for something to be generated not from something.</u>
[338,25–339,2]	[...338,25–339,2...]
<u>One may, by observing everything that comes to be, convince oneself that each and every thing that comes to be comes to be from something</u> [already] in being. <u>A human being comes to be from</u> menses and sperm; the fig tree, for its part, from a planted seed and water which moistens it; <u>out of air, on the other hand, when it is thickened comes water and when it is thinned fire</u>: and the case is the same with everything else, whether natural or man-made.	They have argued on this subject stating that the things we see are generated one from another, for example a man from a man, a horse from a horse, <u>water from the air when the air condenses and fire from the air when the air becomes rarified.</u>

---

[35] – The hylomorphic composition of beings subject to generation and decay necessitates that if generation affects them as a whole, decay will affect them in the same way, lines 9–14.
 – But the ancients all agree that matter is incorruptible, lines 14–6.
 – Only the form is capable of being corrupted and therefore of being generated, lines 16–24.
[36] M. Share, *Philoponus, Against Proclus On the Eternity of the World 9–11* (London: Duckworth, 2010).

These, then, are the arguments by means of which one might support the view that everything that comes to be comes to be from something [already] in being and that nothing comes to be from absolute *non-being* and that the cosmos is therefore un-generated; the things that one might say in response to them follow.

[339,25–345,4]

11. ... Given that all things that are generated and not everlasting are composed of matter and form, and given, moreover, that generation is a change from non-being to being, just as perishing [is a change] from being to non-being, does the compound [of matter and form] come to be (i.e. change from non-being to being – for that is what generation is) as a whole (I mean both in respect of its matter and in respect of its form), or not as a whole?

Well, if that which comes to be comes to be as a whole (i.e. both in respect of its matter and in respect of its form), then clearly that which perishes also perishes as a whole. And so not only the form but the matter too must come to be and perish. But they believe that matter neither comes to be nor perishes and we shall hear Proclus say as much in what follows. And Aristotle too says the same thing towards the end of the first book of the *Physics*.

[345,20–346,11]

... if, then, [as I was saying,] the first substrate, or matter, neither comes to be in things that come to be nor perishes in things that perish, then it is neither the case that compound [things] perish as wholes (for matter remains unchanged in things that perish) nor that perishing occurs as far as matter is concerned.

It remains, then, that the form is what perishes, i.e. is what changes from being

If this is the case, it is impossible for something to be generated from non-being. We answer them by saying :

[... 339,25–345,4. ..]

Things that can be generated and are liable to corruption are composed of matter and form and generation is a change from non-being to being. It is then appropriate for us to examine whether it is the thing as a whole, that is, in its matter and its form, that admits of the change from not-being to being or whether it admits of generation in only one of its parts. For if the thing admits of generation in its matter and in its form then, necessarily when the thing perishes, its matter and its form perish together. But this is false, for matter does not perish. All the ancients recognized that and the Philosopher also demonstrated it in the first Treatise of his *Book of the Lectures on Physics*.

[... 345,20–346,11 ...]

If then the matter of the thing does not perish, we say that it is not the thing that can be generated as a whole that is subject to perishing, but that only the form of the thing perishes, ceases to be, and changes from being to non-being. Consequently, it is also form that is subject to generation and changes from non-being to being; for the form of flesh, for example, perishes and flesh does not remain flesh, but the

to non-being. Therefore it is to this too that generation, that is, the change from non-being to being, belongs; the body which is the substrate for bread, to take an example, has although it had not been flesh, become flesh, and when the flesh has once more perished, the form of the flesh disappears into non-being, but the body is still every bit as much body; for neither is the perishing of things into [something] incorporeal nor their generation out of incorporeal things; and so body remains absolutely unchanged.

form of flesh ceases to be in [the body] and its corporeality remains; and the form of flesh comes to be in the body without the body's changing, for the body does not change into a non-body nor into a different body; rather it remains stable and in continuing existence while attributes succeed one another in it and change without its changing itself or abandoning its state, I mean its corporeality.

In order to establish that *individual embodied forms* come from non-being and dissolve into it, Philoponus has recourse to a process of reasoning by elimination. As a preliminary, he sets out a *diairesis* involving the various possible cases whose exclusion – the purpose of the rest of 9.11 – will be bound to lead the reader to the conclusion sought.

Here are the parallel passages from Philoponus and the Arabic version devoted to this *diairesis*:

347,28–348,24 Rabe

And, speaking [more] generally, each of the enmattered forms or shapes (the form of flesh, for instance, or that of bone; or a particular triangle or a particular circle), and each of the qualities (I mean heat, coldness, whiteness, blackness, and the like), and, moreover, the irrational powers of the soul (I mean those of nourishment, growth, reproduction, sensation, appetition, and the rest) – there is every necessity that these and their like, since they have their existence in underlying bodies, will, when the particular bodies in which they exist cease to exist, either revert to matter and become, as it were, matter, or migrate into another substrate and [another] body and animate it and inform it in every way (as the Hellenes hold in the case of the rational soul), or be resolved into simpler elements

E, fol. 83b 21–84a 13

I say, speaking generally, that the embodied forms, the shapes, the qualities, the faculties of the animal soul: the nutritive faculty, the faculty of sensation and the faculty responsible for growth, all have bodies as substrates and that there is not one of them that is not in a body. Thus, it is necessary that, when particular bodies perish – the substrates of these attributes and these forms – either their forms change and they become the matter of something else; or they migrate into other bodies, thus endowing them with a form and a soul, just as in the case of rational souls the ancients maintained that they migrate from a body into a body; or these forms are resolved into other forms *…* simpler and less composite than they were – just as words break up into letters and a house into stones and wood; or these forms, when the bodies [which serve as

(as syllables are into letters and a house into stones and pieces of timber), or return to some totality of their own (as though the fiery [element] dispersed in us were to return to the totality of fire), or turn into another form (as if blackness, for instance, were to become whiteness when it perished, or sweetness, or something else), or exist on their own in separation from matter, like the intelligible forms; or, if it is shown that none of these [alternatives] is possible – *and*, as far as I know, it is not possible to even imagine any further mode of dissolution for them – it remains that they are dissolved into complete non-being when the underlying body ceases to exist.

their substrates] perish, are resolved by going into a different form, single, universal and common, which is appropriate to them – just as the innate heat that is in us is resolved and rises up and goes to the universal fire; or else the form changes into another form, as when we say whiteness mutates to blackness or into sweetness; or else [finally] the form abides, after its substrate perishes, stable, in an unchanged state, just as the intelligible form that is without matter remains stable. We can find no other way for their dissolution and breaking down apart from those we have mentioned. We shall now go on to show that it is impossible for the forms to change, after their substrates have perished, in any of the things we have mentioned. Once we have achieved that, have demonstrated it and made it clear by solid proofs, we shall be forced, after that, to say that forms pass into non-being and cease to be and that they are generated from non-being.

The first term of the diaeresis envisages the possibility that embodied forms return to matter when the individual bodies that serve as their substrates come to perish. It is excluded by Philoponus in two stages: 1) matter is not generative of forms (cf. Rabe 348,24–350,1); 2) matter does not turn into forms (Rabe 350,1–351,3). Both accounts as rendered in D.16 follow very closely the Greek text. The passage corresponding to the first is found in fols 84a13-b5, with some omissions, the most notable of which concerns Rabe 349,18–21, containing the examples of relatives (father/son, genus/species) of which one is prior by nature to the other. The passage corresponding to the second occurs in fols 84b5–85a3, once again with some omissions affecting particularly the following two passages: Rabe 350,14–18 and 350,26. In 351,3–27, Philoponus removes an objection upholding the view that matter is potentially forms. I quote this passage from Philoponus as a significant example, in M. Share's translation, with my own translation of the Arabic version opposite.

Against Proclus
351,3–27 Rabe

Maqālatu al-Iskandarī...
D.16: E, fol. 85a, 3–22

For even though matter is said to be potentially forms, this is not because [matter] itself gives birth to them or

If someone tried to answer our argument by saying that the Sage stated in one of his books that matter is potentially all the

changes itself into form (for it is unchanging in things that come to be), but because it is suited to accepting their existence within itself. For just as a blank writing surface is, as Aristotle says, potentially the letters that will be written on it not because the substance of the letters grows out of it, or indeed because the papyrus or wax changes into the substance of the letters (for the papyrus or wax remains unchanged when letters appear on it), but because it can accept the existence of letters on itself, and one would not say that the letters draw their existence from the existence of the papyrus or wax, in the same way, one assumes, even though the matter may be said to be the forms potentially, it is not on that account reasonable to say that the forms exist as a result of the matter existing, but that it is really, if anything, because they are not of a nature to exist by themselves apart from a substrate. [The manner of their] destruction makes the demonstration of this point clearer to us; for if, when letters are destroyed, their forms do not become matter, then clearly neither have they received their existence out of matter; for it is necessary for generation to take place out of that into which destruction takes place.

forms, we would retort that the Sage did not assert this in the sense that matter specifically becomes the various different forms, or that it propagates the forms, or that it changes into these forms, but he meant by this statement that matter is suited to accepting all the forms, capable of embracing the forms, one after another. As an example of this, the Sage tells us: we may perhaps say that there is writing potentially in a blank paper, not because the paper propagates the writing, nor because the paper changes and thus becomes writing, but rather in the sense that the writing appears on the paper without the paper's changing its state; for the paper is suited to accepting writing and capable of embracing it if it arrives on it. No one can say that the paper has changed and thus become writing, for that would be very unseemly and run counter to reason and the visible facts. It is in this way that we say that matter is potentially all the forms, not that it propagates the forms nor that it changes, but we meant by that that matter is suited to accepting each form; forms cannot exist by themselves, apart from a material substrate. If this is as we have described, we say: if the form does not become matter, when the things endowed with form perish, it is clear that it was not generated from matter either; for something only arises and is generated from the thing into which it is resolved and perishes. If then the form is not resolved into matter, neither is it generated from matter. Consequently, the assertion that forms change into matter and are resolved into it, rather than into non-being, is false.

Let us pursue the comparison of the Greek with the Arabic translation, restricting ourselves to the beginnings of the expositions in which the terms of the diaeresis are eliminated. The second term of the disjunction ruled out by Philoponus raises the possibility that embodied forms pass into a different substrate:

Against Proclus
351,27–352,2 Rabe

Maqālatu al-Iskandarī...
D. 16: E, fol. 85a, 22–5

But nor is it possible for any enmattered form or the powers of the soul (I mean the irrational ones) to migrate into another substrate.

If someone states that forms migrate into other substrates when they are separated from their substrates, we shall answer that it is impossible for any of the embodied forms or any of the powers of the soul to migrate into other substrates when they are separated from their substrates.

A notable feature of the rest of this exposition is that the examples mentioned are identical, despite the differences in the wording: the form of Socrates' body (≈ ṣūratu badani Suqrāṭ), the whiteness of the magpie (≈ bayāḍu al-ʿaqʿaq – where *kuknos* has become 'aqʿaq, so that the *swan* has turned into a *magpie*), the sphericity of the apple (≈ istidāratu al-tuffāḥati). Something else worth noting (fol. 85b, 18–86a, 8 ≈ 353,3–19) is the examination of the objection prompted by the case of fire heating up the surrounding air: the heat produced in the air is not a form transmitted from one substrate to another, for it is not numerically identical with the heat of the fire. The comparison with the transmission of ideas in the teaching situation (353,13–17) is also found in the Arabic version (fol. 86a, 2–4).

The third possibility excluded in the disjunction, is that embodied forms might break up into simpler elements when their substrate perishes. Here is the beginning of the section that deals with it:

Against Proclus
353,23–4 Rabe

Maqālatu al-Iskandarī...
D.16: E, fol. 86a, 9–10

But nor can they break up into anything simpler.

If someone asserts that the forms break up into simpler forms [...]

Finally, the fourth term excluded in the disjunction, at which point our manuscript of D.16 breaks off, is that the embodied forms might return, when their substrate perishes, to the whole to which they belong. Once again I quote only the beginning of the section that deals with it:

Against Proclus
354,13–16 Rabe

Maqālatu al-Iskandarī...
D.16: E, fol. 86b, 1–3

Can it then be the case that enmattered forms return to some totality of their own when their substrates perish? This too is manifestly impossible.

If someone asserts that the embodied forms, when they are separated from their substrates, return to another universal and common form, just as we see the heat generated with us return to the universal heat of fire, we shall answer that this is impossible.

As I said at the beginning of this account of D.16, it may be the case that the Escorial MS is incomplete. Of the seven excluded terms in Philoponus' disjunction,[37] only the four terms just set out survive in the Arabic translation, in the same order as Philoponus lists them. As with D.9, the epitomizer – whether or not it was the same person is at the moment uncertain – 'decontextualised' the arguments that he was adapting, and did it in two ways. First, all reference to Proclus is erased, and in parallel, everything to do with the problem of whether the cosmos, rather than just particulars, was or was not created, is eliminated. Proclus is mentioned twice by Philoponus in the course of the detailed accounts on which D.16 (or what we have left of it) draws. At the start of 9.8, Philoponus criticises him for adopting the doctrine so harped upon among the Greeks which states that nothing comes from nothing. The Arabic version mentions the Ancients, but does not name Proclus. The same procedure recurs further on, in 345,16–20, in an even more striking way: while Philoponus then brings in the Greeks, Proclus and Aristotle together, adding a 'precise' reference to the end of the first Book of Aristotle's *Physics*, the Arabic version, by contrast, keeps only the Ancients and the Philosopher (=Aristotle), preserving the reference to the *Physics* which yields in precision to that of Philoponus only by the omission of 'at the end'.

The elimination of the passages about the cosmos is every bit as significant, if not more so. In 9.8, Philoponus expounds how the partisans of the 'nothing comes from nothing' theory begin by observing 'composite' particulars (*ta merika*) and then go on to draw conclusions about the cosmos. D.16 includes the examples of generation revealed by observation, sometimes in adapted form, sometimes just as they are, but passes over the elevation of the argument to the cosmos in silence. Further omissions include section 9 in which the absolute incommensurability of divine *dêmiourgia* (creation) with natural *dêmiourgia* is deduced from the relative incommensurability of the latter with the *dêmiourgia* of art, and section 10 in which the idea that what holds good of its parts can be transposed to the whole of the cosmos is contested.[38]

If it is agreed that these modifications are deliberate, a question must arise as to the motive that lies behind the epitomizer's choice of material. In the two cases referred to, either a 'weak' or a 'strong' explanation can be offered. On the first interpretation, the erasure of Proclus' name and the removal of the passages about the cosmos[39] have a

---

[37] As listed in section 9.11, p. 316,7–12; actually only six on p. 348,9–20, which are summarised on p. 359,2–9; but seven possible cases are eliminated in the course of 9.11.

[38] Just as it is difficult to suppose that the suppression in D.9 of passages relating to God is accidental, so something similar does not seem wholly inconceivable in the case of D.16, when omission affects entire pages.

[39] Did both exclusions happen at the same time? It is more 'economical' to think that they did. Might the name of Proclus have been left out in the interest of 'chronological coherence', in that a treatise attributed to Alexander of Aphrodisias could not be attacking a Proclus born two centuries later? This presupposes two things: on the one hand that our treatise was attributed to Alexander from the outset (but account must be taken of the possibility that the attribution occurred later); on the other that the person responsible for the excisions was in a position to assign Alexander and Proclus their relative places on the time-line, which is not necessarily the case if he was a member of the philosophic circle in Baghdad in the ninth century. We may note that a gloss on al-Nadīm's *Fihrist* (p. 313, n. 1) places Proclus erroneously in the time of Diocletian; and that a detail added to the gloss ('at the beginning of the three-hundredth year of his [*sc.* Diocletian's] reign') is scarcely an improvement. The same *Fihrist* gives the wrong date for the composition of Philoponus' Commentary on the *Physics* (p. 315,8–10). Cf. Endress, *Proclus arabus*, p. 14 and n. 3.

didactic purpose where what matters are the theories and the arguments supporting them – in which case the reference to Proclus might appear to have little relevance; the allusion to Aristotle, called in D.16 simply 'the Philosopher' or 'the Sage' would, on the other hand, be kept because of the weight of his authority. In the same way, the inclusion of accounts relating to the cosmos might appear likely to distract attention from the principal subject, namely the creation *ex nihilo* of corporeal substances, more precisely the generation of the embodied forms.[40] The polemical content of these pages of *Against Proclus* would be spirited away to make room for an uncluttered didactic account.

On the second interpretation, the two omissions in question result from an intention to bring things unobtrusively into line. The epitomizer preserved from these pages only what he knew to be compatible with Proclus' professed opinions. He might know that Proclus also maintained that the embodied forms had their origin in non-being and dissolve into it, if he ever had access to the fragment of the *in Timaeum* accurately quoted by Philoponus at the end of *Against Proclus* 9.11.[41] This feeling may be reinforced by the observation that the passage in which Philoponus announces that he will discuss the status of primary matter, and in particular whether it is eternal or not, is omitted.[42]

The bringing to light of the 'contamination' of Alexander in Arabic by Philoponus certainly puts us in possession of a new key that I hope will enable us to solve certain problems, or at any rate to pay greater attention to certain facts.[43] At the same time it raises as many questions as it enables us to answer, if not more. First, at what level, Greek, Syriac, or Arabic did the epitomizer come in? Put another way, were the adapted Arabic versions known to us received just as they are in Baghdad philosophic circles in the first half of the ninth century, or are they the work of an adaptor belonging to that milieu? To provide a truthful answer to the question regarding the epitomizer's

---

[40] This interpretation requires us to consider that a classification by subjects, for example, entailed a grouping together of all the passages dealing with the creation of the cosmos. That is obviously pure hypothesis.

[41] *Aet.* 364,5–365,3. This fragment of the *in Tim.* is translated in *Proclus, Commentaire sur le Timée*, translation and notes by A. J. Festugière, 5 vols (Paris: Vrin, 1966–68), vol. 5, p. 239. See also M. Wolff, *Fallgesetz und Massebegriff* (Berlin: De Gruyter, 1971), p. 132, n. 7.

[42] *Aet.* 345,21–5. It had to be, given that the scope of the extract in question was too limited to allow for Philoponus' promise to be kept. It might however have left a trace in some form or other. Philoponus' provisional concession (345,16–18) that matter 'is neither generated nor destroyed' takes on, in the Arabic version, at least so it seems to me, the character of a thesis.

[43] I am not losing sight of the fact that there is a lot of Alexander in Philoponus. I have tried to demonstrate this above in my treatment of D.9. But there are features peculiar to Philoponus. From this point of view, particular attention will be paid to the appearance, in the early Arabic version of Alexander's *On Providence* (D.15) of Philoponus' argument for the finite duration of the world based on the Aristotelian principle that a finite body, such as the cosmos, cannot be endowed with an infinite force; *cf.* Ruland, *Über die Vorsehung*, p. 89,7–91,4, trans. pp. 90–2 and n. 3 on p. 90. Ruland prints in the body of the Arabic text the *Refutatio* of this passage which figures in the left-hand margin of fol.82a of MS E; that the passage has been integrated in this way is noted in the apparatus criticus and in the translation. *cf.* Preliminary remarks, p. viii; and pp. 143–4. S. Fazzo and H. Wiesner note a connection between the use of the Aristotelian principle by Philoponus and by D.15, but do not attach much significance to it; *cf.* 'Alexander of Aphrodisias in the Kindi-circle and in al-Kindi's cosmology,' *Arabic Sciences and Philosophy* 3 (1993), 119–53, on p. 134, n. 38.

intention, that is, to give the answer an historian would give, we must at least be able to place him in the milieu in which he moves. Another question to be considered concerns the attribution of these texts, and perhaps others, of this same Philoponus, to Alexander. There also, the first stage consists in determining at what point in history the attribution was made; then in asking ourselves whether it was an integral feature that was there from the start or due to the hazards of transmission.

Philoponus, the Christian author of polemical treatises against the eternity of the world strikes us as being anti-Aristotelian. But this anti-Aristotelian uses Aristotle against Aristotle and 'pagan' philosophers in general against themselves. All an epitomizer had to do was to carve up texts in which Philoponus claimed to expound Aristotle's teaching – as we have seen done by the epitomizer of D.9 and D.16 – in order to present them as a definitive account of Aristotle's views on this or that question. In that case, why not attribute them to the man who is known as *the* commentator on Aristotle, Alexander of Aphrodisias? Moreover, in their execution, some sections of *Against Proclus* show similarities to the *Problems and Solutions* by Alexander or members of his school and are sometimes introduced as such.[44] This aspect is accentuated in the Arabic versions. We have seen how D.9 gives Philoponus' text the canonical form of the pieces of Alexander issuing from the 'al-Kindī circle'; this is perhaps less visible in the case of D.16, which is from the outset presented as the refutation of an opinion held by certain people. Should we conclude, without further ado, that the epitomizer was active in the 'al-Kindī circle'? Attention has long since been drawn to the similarities between some of the positions espoused by Philoponus and by al-Kindī, in particular as regards creation *ex nihilo*, and the arguments in its favour, and likewise the difference between the activity of nature and divine activity.[45] Parallels have also been able to be established between certain elements of their noetics.[46] Moreover, the presence of Philoponus is to be observed not only in the works of al-Kindī but again in the adaptations of Aristotle's works attributed to members of 'al-Kindī's circle'. Parallels are in fact to be found in the Compendium of the *De Anima* edited by A. F. El Ahwani, between the interpretative additions and passages from Philoponus' *in De Anima*.[47] I have already referred in the introduction to how Philoponus' ideas found their way into the Arabic version of certain propositions in Proclus' *Elements of Theology*. We must also mention more generally how the subject

---

[44] See for example *Aet.* 4.9 and 11, pp. 57,27–58,5 and 58,12–18; 9.8, p. 315,13–15.

[45] R. Walzer, 'New studies on al-Kindī', *Oriens* 10 (1957), 203–32, repr. in *Greek into Arabic: Essays on Islamic Philosophy* (Oxford: Cassirer, 1962), pp. 190–6; H. A. Davidson, 'John Philoponus as a source of medieval Islamic and Jewish proofs of creation', *Journal of the American Oriental Society*, 89 (1969), 357–91, on pp. 370–3; id., *Proofs for Eternity, Creation and the Existence of God in Medieval Islamic and Jewish Philosophy* (New York: Oxford University Press, 1987), pp. 106–16.

[46] J. Jolivet, *L'Intellect selon Kindī* (Leiden: Brill, 1971), pp. 50–73.

[47] IBN ROCHD, *Talkhis al-nafs*, edited with commentary by Ahmed Fouad El Ahwani (Cairo, 1950). The text in question is No. 3, on pp. 128–75. The attribution of this version to Isḥāq does not figure in the MS (Escorial², 649). A. Hasnawi, 'Alexandre d'Aphrodise vs Jean Philopon,' p. 90, n. 52 should be corrected on this point. On this Compendium and the parallels with Philoponus' *in De Anima*, see Endress, *Proclus arabus*, pp. 71–3 and 199–200; see also now R. Arnzen, *Aristoteles' De anima: eine verlorene spätantike Paraphrase in arabischer und persicher Überlieferung* (Leiden: Brill, 1998).

of creation out of nothing figures in the Arabic versions of Neoplatonic works. We know that it occurs in the long recension of the *Theology of Aristotle* and that its presence in D.27g,[48] in *Proclus arabus* and in a passage in the *Letter on Divine Knowledge* by Pseudo-Fārābī, led F. W. Zimmermann to suppose that the subject should have been treated in the *Theology, by which he means the original *Theology* that he postulates as the matrix of the Neo-platonic texts in Arabic and also of certain of Alexander's treatises in that language.[49] Consequently we should no longer be surprised that Philoponus, perhaps under the assumed name of Alexander,[50] and shorn of his polemical aspects should fetch up in this original *Theology, or at any rate in its immediate vicinity. That would moreover explain why Proclus' name was excluded from D.16, assuming of course that it was known that he was the author of the *Elements of Theology* that they were in the process of adapting.[51] The excision of the passages about the cosmos would be explained both by the desire to make known the arguments of the supporters of the thesis that all that is created is created from non-being and by a reluctance to bring up a matter of dispute between the 'pagan' philosophers and the Christian philosophers, namely the question of whether the world was eternal, or had

---

[48] Under the title of *Fī al-Kawn* (*On generation*), D.27g forms part of a collection containing several treatises – some genuine, others not – attributed to Alexander, a collection preserved in the Carullah manuscript 1279 (C). On this collection and the details of its contents, see F. Zimmermann, 'Proclus arabus rides again,' pp 15–16. D. 27g is often confused with D. 16, no doubt because of their related subject-matter and the fact that there are parallels between some of their arguments; on these parallels and on the difference between the two treatises, see A. Hasnawi, 'Alexandre d'Aphrodise *vs* Jean Philopon', Appendix II, pp. 101–6.

[49] Here is how he describes the composition of this original *Theology*: 'In addition to *AP (an adapted version of *Enneads* 4–6 or of parts of them, produced in al-Kindī's circle and no longer preserved as such), it included (parts of?) Proclus's *Elements of Theology* and some metaphysical treatises of Alexander of Aphrodisias.' ('The Origins of the *Theology of Aristotle*', p. 134). The break-up of this *Theology must have been what led to the formation of the *Theology of Aristotle* as we know it (called K by the author), of the *Liber de causis* and of the **Extracts from the Theology* (*of Aristotle*) (a collection made by al-Dimašqī from the **Theology* comprising propositions from the *Elements of Theology*, no doubt more of them than were preserved in MS C and published by G. Endress under the title *Proclus arabus*, and some bits of Alexander originating from al-Kindī's circle). But see now 'Proclus arabus rides again', p. 37, n. 65. Further, *GS (of which all that is left to us are quotations assembled under the title of *Sayings of the Greek Sage*) and DS (*The letter on divine knowledge*) could have been extracts from the *Theology before it was broken up. The author is, of course, the first to stress the speculative nature of his conclusions.

The intention underlying the constitution of this original 'Theology' is described thus: 'The original *Theology would therefore appear to have been something of an anthology: a reader in classical theology – that is, for those around Kindi, the theology elaborated by philosophers in the succession of Aristotle', *ibid.*, p. 130.

On the subject of creation *ex nihilo*, see App. XIII (d), pp. 174–5; App. XIV (2), pp.177–8; App. XIX(a), pp. 198–200 where it is stated that the doctrine is implicit in *AP.

[50] If it is true that the pieces of Alexander figuring in MS Z go back to a copy in the possession of al-Dimašqī, should we then conclude that he did not recognise that 1) D.9 did not come from Alexander, and then again 2) that this was an indication that there was not yet a more complete version of *Against Proclus*? That would no doubt be precipitate, for D.9 could, with no great problem, be taken for a treatise by Alexander.

[51] See F. Zimmermann's remarks on this point, 'The origins of the *Theology of Aristotle*', App. XVI, p. 188 and App. XVII, pp. 188–9.

It is perhaps difficult to imagine that the name of Proclus was suppressed in a Greek environment.

a beginning in time. They were prompted, in short, by their wish to create an impression of unity in the Greek philosophic tradition.[52] All these elements[53] would tend to lend credibility to the hypothesis that the epitomizer was active in philosophic circles in Baghdad in the first half of the ninth century. We must however admit their essential fragility. In any event, one thing is certain, and that is the importance of Philoponus in those circles. It is not without some value to have uncovered hitherto unrecognised evidence that brings fresh proof of this.

---

[52] We know that there existed an early version of Proclus' eighteen arguments for the eternity of the world which preceded Isḥāq b. Ḥunayn's translation. The latter has come down to us in an incomplete form, including only the first nine arguments. The early version in question of which only eight arguments are preserved in two Istanbul manuscripts seems to be the one which al-Šahrastānī (d. 1153) used for the summary he gave of the 'sophisms' of Proclus in his *Kitāb al-Milal wa-al-niḥal*, composed in 1127–1128 (Book of religions and sects), ed. M. F. Badrān, 2 vols (Cairo, 1947–55), pp. 1025–32. This version was perhaps complete, in any case doubtless more complete than the one contained in the two Istanbul manuscripts. See for all this G. Endress, *Proclus arabus*, pp. 15–17. See also, pp. 106–7 for his remarks on a point of vocabulary. Mention should also be made of J. Jolivet's richly annotated French translation, *Shahrastani, Livre des religions et des sectes*, vol. II, Translation with introduction and notes by J. Jolivet and G. Monnot (Leuven, 1993), pp. 339–47. The existence of a version such as this, if it is contemporary with D.16, would show that the dispute, or at least the position of one of the parties to it, was known. What is more, if it was known that Proclus was the party in question, it would have become quite pointless for the epitomizer to keep his name quiet, when he was adapting a passage from a work of which Proclus was the target. We may add that al-Kindī had no hesitation in maintaining that the world was created *ex nihilo* and of finite duration.

[53] One element that some will no doubt judge to be significant for attributing the text to an epitomizer in the Muslim period cannot be passed over in silence, namely the fact that examples with a possible Christian resonance which figure in the passage of Philoponus covered by D.16 do not recur in D.16. On p. 346,20–1 of *Against Proclus* Philoponus takes the example of the bread that changes into flesh. This example is not repeated in D.16. Nothing can be said about the examples of the same type, of the bread that changes into flesh and of the wine that changes into blood, on pp. 356,16–17; 358,14–17. We do not know if they were affected by the adaptation for which D.16 provides our evidence. It must be appreciated that these examples could also be read as biological examples of the assimilation of nutriments; cf. p. 358,14–17: bread changes into flesh, but also into bone.

New Arabic Fragments of Philoponus and their Reinterpretation: Does the World Lack a Beginning in Time or Take no Time to Begin?[1]

Marwan Rashed

SUMMARY: Al-Nawbakhtī is shown already to have known Philoponus' *Against Proclus* as early as the ninth century CE, and some of the passages of Philoponus known in Arabic (two of them lost in Greek) explain how Philoponus could be attractive to opposite viewpoints because they record ambiguities exploited by earlier Greeks between the world being generated without a beginning in time and being generated (as Philoponus believed) with a beginning, and (according to a further ambiguity mentioned by Porphyry) generated without taking time to begin, i.e. instantaneously. The beginningless view suited eternalists: the Greek Neoplatonist supporters of Aristotle's eternalism and the Muslim Al-Fārābī (870–951 CE), who is recorded as an eternalist by Fakhr al-Din al Rāzī. The second view suited Fārābī's Christian successors in the Baghdad school, who followed Aristotle in other respects, but not on eternalism. The anti-eternalist *Harmonisation* was written not by Fārābī, as earlier thought, but by one of his Christian successors in the school who shared with ninth century Muslim theologians belief in an instantaneous beginning of the world.

Philoponus' two anti-Aristotelian treatises, the *De Aeternitate Mundi contra Aristotelem* and the *De Aeternitate Mundi contra Proclum* were both translated into Arabic. But neither version has survived. However, while the *Contra Aristotelem* did not survive in Greek or Arabic, the original text of the *Contra Proclum*, apart from twenty pages at the beginning and a few at the end, has come down to us in the *Marc. gr 236*, which is the archetype of the other witnesses, that I would date provisionally to about 850, when

---

This article first appeared in French as 'Nouveaux fragments antiprocliens de Philopon en version arabe et le problème des origines de la théorie de l'« instauration » (huduth)' by Marwan Rashed in *Études Philosophiques* 105(2) (2013), pp. 261–92 © Presses Universitaires de France 2013, reproduced with permission.

[1] Translated by Jennifer Barnes. I would like to thank also Jonathan Barnes for reading over the translation from French and for his help with the translation of Philoponus.

the emperor Bardas[2] was reorganising the Byzantine university. The survival of fragments in Arabic of this work is therefore of minimal interest to the Hellenist Quellenforscher,[3] but it does contribute to our understanding of the development of Peripatetic philosophy in ninth century Islam. For if the *Contra Proclum*, just like the *Contra Aristotelem*, is concerned with ideas to do with the eternity of the world, it adopts an approach that is, shall we say, less physical and more metaphysical: while the *Contra Aristotelem* focuses on the structure of matter and attacks the notion of physical eternity (the special problem of Aristotle's eternal fifth element), the *Contra Proclum* is more concerned with the relationship between the Creator and his creation, and tackles eternity in a way that may be described as theological, or at the very least quasi-theological.

This explains the historical aspect of the *Contra Proclum*, apparently absent from the *Contra Aristotelem*. It is no accident if the *Contra Proclum* contains one of the most authoritative accounts of Galen's *De demonstratione* (Book 4), and also a good deal of what we know of the theological cosmology of Middle Platonism.[4] So, in Book 6, we have a discussion of the possible meanings of the term generated/generable (*genêtos*) – that is, of whether it is possible to avoid the particular link between generability and a temporal beginning – which provides information of crucial importance for the teachings of the Middle Platonist Taurus (fl. *c.* 145 CE). Since Porphyry is quoted here, it seems likely that he was the source of all that Philoponus has to say on this point. And this gives rise to certain questions. The first concerns whether or not Arabic adherents of the various theories of instigation (*ḥudūth*) – the world's beginning without taking time to begin – via the *Contra Proclum*, had any acquaintance with Middle Platonism. Apart from general bibliographical references,

---

[2] Cf. Philoponus, *De Aeternitate Mundi contra Proclum*, ed. H. Rabe (Leipzig: Teubner, 1899). Unless otherwise indicated, the translations from the Arabic are mine. For the dating of the 'Collection philosophique', see M. Rashed, 'Nicolas d'Otrante, Guillaume de Moerbeke et la "Collection philosophique"', *Studi Medievali* 43 (2002), 693–717 (repr. in *L'héritage aristotélicien: Textes inédits de l'Antiquité* (Paris: Les Belles Lettres, 2007), pp. 513–41). It is generally agreed that the *Marc. 236* is one of the earliest copies of the collection.

[3] However I shall suggest that two Arabic quotations contain fragments of the lost first part. See below, pp. 505–10. For a bibliography of known Arabic fragments, see C. Scholten, *Johannes Philoponos: De opificio mundi, Über die Erschaffung der Welt*, 3 vols (Freiburg: Herder, 1997), vol. 1, pp. 39–40. For recent considerations of the *Contra Aristotelem* in Arabic and Greek tradition, see M. Rashed, 'The Problem of the Composition of the Heavens (529–1610): A New Fragment of Philoponus and Its Readers', in P. Adamson *et al.*, eds, *Philosophy, Science, and Exegesis in Greek, Arabic, and Latin Commentaries*, 2 vols (London: Institute of Classical Studies, 2004), vol. 2, p. 35–58 (reprinted in *L'Héritage aristotélicien*, pp. 269–92). Very likely other fragments lurk in unpublished treatises of theologians, both Muslim – the readers of the heresiographer al-Nawbakhtī, as we shall see below – and Christian. For the latter, see G. Graf, *Geschichte der christlichen arabischen Literatur*, 5 vols (Città del Vaticano: Biblioteca Apostolica Vaticana, 1944), vol. 1, pp. 417–18, for references to the *Contra Proclum* in Ibn al-'Assāl. However, this last may just be quotations from the *De contingentia mundi*.

[4] For Galen, see *Contra Proclum* 17.5, 599,17–601,20. Cf. I. von Mueller, 'Ueber Galens Werk vom wissenschaftlichen Beweis', *Abhandlungen der philosophisch-philologischen Classe der königlich bayerischen Akademie der Wissenschaften* 20 (1897), 405–78, at 461–3. For a study of Taurus' cosmological theories, see *Contra Proclum* 6.8, 144,16–149,26 and 13.15, 520,4–521,24. Cf. H. Dörrie and M. Baltes, *Der Platonismus in der Antike* (Stuttgart: Frommann-Holzboog, 1998), vol. 5, fr. 140.1, pp. 138–44, and the commentary, pp. 454–60.

attesting to a translation of Philoponus' immense work into Arabic,[5] do we have philological proof of this for Book 6 and, above all, reliable evidence that not only the translation itself but also its content were widespread?[6] And if so, can we therefore see a Middle Platonist *influence* on this content? These are the two questions I want to address here, with the help of texts overlooked till now.

I Two New Passages of the *Contra Proclum*

1) Preliminary Remarks on Aristotle's Historical Accuracy

In a treatise by Fakhr al-Dīn al-Rāzī, (*Al-Riyāḍ al-mu'niqa fī ārā' ahl al-'ilm*),[7] which has escaped modern notice, the doctrine of the eternity of the world is expressed like this:

> This doctrine derives from Aristotle and his followers, like Theophrastus, Themistius, Alexander of Aphrodisias, Proclus, Porphyry, and among the Moderns Abū Naṣr al-Fārābī and Abū 'Alī ibn Sīnā also take this view. John the Grammarian records, in his book *Contra Proclum*, that Aristotle was the first to uphold such a doctrine.[8]

So Philoponus would have claimed in the *Contra Proclum* that, historically, Aristotle was the first philosopher to maintain that the world is eternal. Rāzī, or his source, adds that this view was shared, among the Greeks, by orthodox Aristotelians and by Neoplatonists who thought to harmonise Plato and Aristotle, and subsequently by the Islamic philosophers Fārābī and Avicenna. Among such claims the comment on the Greeks is perhaps Philoponus' own idea, as we shall see in a moment, but this is neither incontrovertible nor, indeed, important, given that it has little intrinsic interest (except perhaps in the case of Themistius – for Porphyry and Proclus, see below).

---

[5] Cf. Al-Nadīm, *Al-Fihrist*, ed. R. Tajaddud (Tehran, 1971), p. 315, and above all Ibn al-Qifṭī, *Ta'rīkh al-ḥukamā'*, ed. J. Lippert (Leipzig, 1903), p. 89, who even says he owns a copy of this translation.

[6] A. Hasnawi, 'Alexandre d'Aphrodise vs Jean Philopon : notes sur quelques traités d'Alexandre "perdus" en grec, conservés en arabe', *Arabic Sciences and Philosophy* 4 (1994), 53–109, partly reprinted in ch. 19 above, has shown that two texts attributed to Alexander by Arab tradition are in fact reworkings, in Al-Kindī's time, of long passages of Books 4 and 9 of the *Contra Proclum*. On the relationship between these two texts and the complete Arabic version of the 18 books, see below, pp. 525–7.

[7] We owe the publication of this treatise, over 400 pages long, based on two Tunis manuscripts, to M. Al-As'ad Jum'a. Cf. Fakhr al-Dīn al-Rāzī, *Al-Riyāḍ al-mūniqa fī ārā' ahl al-'ilm*, ed. A. Jum'a (Qayrawān, 2004). The scholarly world owes a debt of gratitude to those who make it possible for us to consult these monuments of world heritage. The editor vocalises *mūniqa*, which unless I am much mistaken does not correspond to any recorded form. The root is '-*n-q* and not *w-n-q* ni *y-n-q*. The *ism al-fā'il* of the fourth form is therefore *mu'niq* and not *mūniq*. Cf. al-Fayrūzābādī, *Al-Qāmūs al-muḥīṭ*, 2 vols (Beyrouth, 1997), vol. 2, p. 1150: *'ānaqanī* [. . .] : *a'jabanī*'. Besides, it is in this form that it appears in a list of titles by Fakhr al-Dīn al-Rāzī that figures in the Istanbul manuscript Topkapi Saray 1461 (fol. 137r–v), cf. Fakhr al-Dīn al-Rāzī, *Kitāb al-muḥaṣṣal*, ed. H. Atay (Qom, 1999), p. 58, last line: *'Al-riyāḍ al-mu'niqa'*. We could translate the complete title thus: *'The Fascinating gardens of the opinions of scholars'*.

[8] Fakhr al-Dīn al-Rāzī, *Al-Riyāḍ al-mu'niqa*, p. 71 (reading *'alā Buruqlus* and not *'an Buruqlus*).

Any attempt to find this view of Philoponus' in the surviving Greek text of the *Contra Proclum* is doomed to failure. Of course, we might start by assuming that what we have has been deduced by some reader of the treatise, based on the contradiction that Philoponus sets up systematically between Aristotle and Plato. Every page of the *Contra Proclum* endorses the notion that, of Aristotle and Plato, only Aristotle believed in an eternal world. But on reflection this seems unlikely, because it makes mincemeat of the whole purpose of his message, that is, that the Presocratic fraternity unanimously adopted an explanation of the cosmos different from Aristotle's own. Of course, this isn't to say that natural philosophers before Plato opted for the belief he would later espouse. But they all, one way or another, accepted the hypothesis of a beginning of *our present* world. So I think that the Arab doxographers are accurate – and this is confirmed by the reliability of other accounts we have of the *Contra Proclum*.[9]

If this is so, we must assume that this passage of Philoponus comes from the beginning of the work, in the part that is lost,[10] or else from the end, in one of the few missing pages. The first alternative is the most plausible. It is hard to imagine that Philoponus spent nearly 700 pages discussing Plato's and Aristotle's cosmological theories and then decided that Aristotle was an innovator in this respect. Surely it is inappropriate to dress up a simple historical truth as the culmination of a doctrinal polemic. However, it does seem plausible that Philoponus made such a claim at the very start of his work. His introduction would thus flag up his intention to challenge Proclus when he attributed a thesis – the eternity of the world – to Plato when its first historical begetter was Aristotle. This comment, in other words, was not so much an interesting aside as a keynote statement setting the tone for the discussion that followed.

This is backed up by the great heresiographer al-Shahrastānī in his *Al-milal wa al-niḥal*.[11] Indeed, he devotes chapter 6 of Book 2 to Proclus. While he does quote, with reasonable accuracy, a selection of his arguments in favour of the eternal nature of the world, he considers them sophistic and refers the reader to another of his works, now unfortunately lost, where he refutes them.[12] Now this is how he begins the chapter:

> It was only after Aristotle that people began to say that the world was eternal and motions were without a beginning, whereas earlier the existence of the Demiurge had been asserted and the first cause described. Indeed, Aristotle made a clean break from the Ancients and thought up this doctrine by working from reasonings that seemed to him to construct a demonstrative argument. Then the people who

---

[9] Al-Rāzī also passes on to us a fragment of the commentary on Porphyry's *Isagôgê* by Philoponus, a work now lost and almost unknown (cf. Scholten (n. 2 above), p. 38). Cf. *Al-Riyāḍ al-muʾniqa*, p. 13: 'John the Grammarian has reported, in his commentary on the *Isagôgê*, that some people revoked science and knowledge'.

[10] See below, pp. 507–10.

[11] Cf. al-Shahrastānī, *Al-milal wa al-niḥal*, ed. M. F. Badrān, 2 vols (Cairo 1951–55).

[12] Cf. Al-Shahrastānī, *Al-milal wa al-niḥal*, vol. 2, p. 1029. On this point see J. Jolivet's note in *Shahrastani. Livre des Religions et des Sectes II*, translation with notes by J. Jolivet and G. Monnot (Paris : Peeters/ Unesco, 1993), p. 343.

were his disciples followed his example and explained what he was saying: like Alexander of Aphrodisias, Themistius, and Porphyry. Proclus the successor wrote a book on this question in which he set out the sophisms we shall quote; and the Ancients gave an account of it, reported above.[13]

Of course, this is by no means the same as al-Rāzī's fragment and cannot be considered a quotation from the *Contra Proclum*. Moreover, the last sentence proves that Shahrastānī was tailoring his source to fit his *own* needs. What follows in this chapter clearly indicates that he had before him a copy of Proclus' treatise. Still, since Shahrastānī had written a work in order to refute Aristotle and Proclus, it seems reasonable to assume that he was acquainted with Philoponus' refutation; Ibn al-Qifṭī, who died a century later, also owned a copy of it. So I am inclined to see this introduction to the chapter as an echo of the Prologue of the *Contra Proclum*. Yet again, Philoponus could be highlighting the specifically Aristotelian features, pretty much recent as they were, of the doctrine that our world is eternal. This thesis was dreamt up by Aristotle and his only subsequent adherents were his henchmen: Theophrastus (who only figures in Rāzī), Alexander, Porphyry, and Themistius.

2) A Fragment of the Missing Part of the Refutation of Proclus' First Argument

During his discussion of certain 'Theological Questions', Abū Ḥāmid al-Isfizārī (*c*. tenth century CE) considers the question of the temporal behaviour of certain qualities.[14] In this connection he quotes Proclus' first argument (which doesn't survive in Greek) and a passage from Philoponus' refutation:

> As for the qualities that may be not sempiternal in spite of His sempiternal nature, they are as if we said 'the Nourishing', 'the Indulgent', 'the Merciful', 'the Good'. Yet it is possible that He may be actually good although nothing exists. For from His <goodness> what Proclus said in his book does not follow[15]: 'If God is eternally good, then it follows that the world exists eternally in actuality, because otherwise He would have to undergo alteration when changing states'. Indeed, we say: 'So-and-so is an actual writer', even if he is not writing at this moment, as long as he has

---

[13] Al-Shahrastānī, *Al-milal wa al-niḥal*, vol. 2, p. 1025. I am using Jean Jolivet's translation, *Shahrastani*, pp. 339–40.

[14] These questions are edited by D. Gimaret, 'Un traité théologique du philosophe musulman Abū Ḥāmid al-Isfizārī', *Mélanges de l'Université Saint-Joseph* 50 (1984), 209–52 ; my thanks to E. Wakelnig for drawing my attention to this text. D. Gimaret only used the Istanbul manuscript, Ragıp Paşa 1463, which seems less than satisfactory. So I collate the paragraph of his edition which is of particular interest with the other evidence on record, the celebrated Damascus manuscript Ẓāhiriyya 4871, fol. 143v (l. 14 ab imo)-145r (l. 3). As I only offer a translation here, I omit the variants that have no bearing on the meaning (of which there are not a few). There is a detailed description of the relation between the two witnesses to al-Isfizārī's work which are stemmatically independent of one another in D. Reisman, 'Plato's *Republic* in Arabic: A Newly Discovered Passage', *Arabic Sciences and Philosophy* 14 (2004), 276–9.

[15] I read *lā yalzamu* with the Damascus manuscript. Gimaret : *lā yumna'u* ('is not forbidden').

the ability to write when he wants to. Furthermore, even if God is eternally good, it doesn't follow that the world exists eternally, because the good man is one who dispenses his goodness[16] as befits the time, the circumstances, and the recipient.[17] So we may say that goodness did not require Him to create the world at one specific moment, but to do so at another moment. And equally it doesn't follow, from our claim that God is eternally good in actuality, that the world exists eternally in actuality. This does not agree with Proclus' statement; nor does it follow what John the Grammarian says in his book[18] *Contra Proclum*, namely that his claim 'If God is eternally good, then the world exists eternally' implies that the world is the *cause* of the existence of God. John, in fact, said 'Given our declaration "If what is approaching is a man, then it is an animal", if by chance we say that it is not an animal, then it follows that it is not a man; similarly, if it followed[19] from our declaration "God is eternally good"[20] that the world existed eternally, as Proclus asserted, it would follow from this that if the world does not exist, then neither would God, †according to the first analogy, as when we say†:[21] "If God is eternally good[22], then the world exists eternally; but the world does not exist; it follows therefore that God is not good; but the goodness of God is his very essence. So if we claim that the world does not exist, it follows that God does not exist either"; from this we conclude that the world is the cause of the existence of God, may He be exalted.[23]

---

[16] Here I translate Gimaret's text, which seems preferable to me: *wa-al-jawād huwa al-ladhi yabdhulu al-jūda*. The Damascus manuscript offers the following variant, strangely jerky: *wa-al-jūdu huwa an yabdhula al-jawādu* ('goodness is when the good man makes a gift etc.').

[17] We could replace the reading of the three occurrences of *yajibu* (cf. 'necessary'), which also figure in the Damascus MS, with the almost identical written form *yaḥibbu* 'it pleases him'. This last verb appears in the Arabic version of Proclus' text (translated below) that Philoponus here refutes equipped, naturally, with a measure of eternity: 'It is always that it pleases Him...', *fa-abadan yaḥibbu*.

[18] The Damascus MS does have *fī kitābihi* before *fī al-radd*.

[19] Gimaret reads *inna Allāha abadan jawādan*, which is ungrammatical; the Damascus MS has, as one would expect: *inna Allāha abadan jawādun*.

[20] Reading *wa-ka-dhālika in kāna yalzamu qawlanā ... an yakūna al-'ālamu ...* with the Damascus MS (the vocalisations are of course my own – the sense would be the same if we vocalised *in kāna yulzimu qawlunā ... an* etc.).

[21] The words between daggers are almost meaningless, still more so in the Damascus MS (which replaces *'alā al-qiyās* by *'alā annahu t-y-ā-s*, a palaeographical error deriving from the other text, helped by its obscurity). It should probably be emended like this: *'alā al-qiyās ilā qawlinā al-awwal* ('by analogy with our first claim'). At a pinch it could be a mistake during transmission. Instead of 'according to the first syllogism', we would then have the verbal idiom familiar from the Greek commentators in general and Philoponus in particular (cf. Simplicius, *in Cael.* 28,14–21,6): *kata tēn sun antithesei antistrophēn*, 'according to contraposition' see, just for the *Contra Proclum*, 126,20; 150,14; 204,12; 225,28; 268,20; 592,17; 594,14.

[22] I reject Gimaret's *mawjūdan* ('existant') in favour of *jawādan* ('good') in the Damascus MS.

[23] Al-Isfizārī, *op. cit.*, pp. 247–8. A little earlier (p. 237), the writer refers jointly to 'John the Grammarian and Abū Bakr al-Rāzī' crediting them with the theory that production of existence by God could only be natural and not elected (*ṭabī'iyyan lā ikhtiyāriyyan*), which would contradict the theory of a God that chooses. This can only be an error. While we can well imagine Abū Bakr al-Rāzī, in his lost *Doubts against Proclus*, setting up this dilemma to Philoponus, al-Isfizārī would also have attributed this dialectical method to Philoponus, since the treatise was intended to attack Proclus. Perhaps al-Isfizārī only knew the *Contra Proclum* at second hand, via al-Rāzī's *Doubts against Proclus*? The latter would have quoted Proclus' first argument, certainly in order to demolish it – since Proclus makes Plato too Aristotelian – but he would also have taken issue with the logical mistake which al-Isfizārī criticises in Philoponus and, in general, with his Mosaic finitsm.

This is how Proclus reasoned in his first argument for the eternity of the world. Since God is eternal and must create for all time, the world must be eternal, even if in a weaker sense of the word 'eternity' – temporal and not transcendent. Here is a translation of one of the Arabic versions of this argument:

> First of Proclus' arguments demonstrating that the world is eternal.
>
> He said: The first of the arguments by which we show that the world is eternal derives from the Creator's goodness. There is no firmer conviction than that which this argument affords about the All, when it states that the All follows the model according to which the Creator[24] produced it and whence it exists. Indeed, since the generation of the All relies entirely on his goodness, He undertook it because it was impossible that it should be said that He created by reason of anything other than His goodness. Now, He isn't good at one moment and not good at another. So that He is always the cause of the existence of the world, as long as the being of the world is co-extensive with the being of the Creator. The fact is that we could never find anything that would be of a nature to produce the world by reason of its goodness alone, but that would not produce it in spite of being always good. Then, that He is always good is because it pleases Him that everything should be like Him. And since it has pleased Him that everything should be like him, He has the power to initiate everything in his likeness. For indeed, He is the Lord and Master of all. And since it has pleased Him that all things should be like Him, and since He had the power to instigate all things in His likeness, He always produces them. For everything that does not act, the fact that it eschews action is either because it does not *want* to or else because it *cannot* act – at least, supposing that we are dealing with someone who can be subject to one or other of these alternatives. Thus, since the Creator, may He be exalted, made the world by reason of His goodness, He made it eternally. From which it follows that the world was not generated a certain length of time ago and will not be destroyed in a certain length of time. In fact, the claim that He doesn't have the power to do what He wants deserves nothing but contempt, because it would imply, since He would sometimes be powerful and sometimes powerless, that it is false that He cannot be subject to change or passivity. Indeed, the loss of His power would involve His being subject to passivity, and what changes from powerlessness to power is altered, since power and powerlessness pertain to quality, and that alteration is a change according to quality. So since He has eternally the power to create and since He eternally wishes to create, it must necessarily follow that He creates eternally, that the All is eternally created, and that the world should be eternally existing, just as the Creator is eternally creating. Except just that the Creator is eternally existent, whereas the world is always engaged in a process of generation, because the meaning of 'eternally' is not the same in the two cases. Rather, its meaning as applied to the Creator is eternity and unchangeability, while its meaning as applied to the world

---

[24] I use *al-khāliq* ('the creator') instead of *al-ḥaqq* ('the true'), as Badawi himself does in his translation (cf. 'A. Badawi, *La transmission de la philosophie grecque au monde arabe* (Paris: Vrin, 1987), p. 133). Since Proclus is not Kindī, he has no reason to dub the Demiurge 'the True'.

is infinite time. For what is congruent to being is perpetuity and endurance, while what is congruent to what is generated is time.[25]

The text quoted by al-Isfizārī indubitably comes from the missing part of the refutation of this argument. Indeed, it is a response to the basic argument of radical emanation theorists who supported the eternity of the cosmos: there is no explanation for a change in the first principle of emanation. God being perfect, He always behaves in the same way, and the change which would enable nothingness to become a three-dimensional cosmos is inconceivable.

It is easy to understand Philoponus' reaction to this text of Proclus. The latter inflicts a heavy burden on God's shoulders: the notion that there is a necessary inference from God to the world automatically implies that the world determines the essence of God, at least in part. For this essence cannot be separated from the act of creating the cosmos. It is in this sense that the world 'causes' God. The world causes God from the moment we accept that God can't not cause the world.

So we have two new fragments that can be assigned to the initial, lost, part of Philoponus' work. They confirm, for the first time as far as I know, something that was until now evinced only in the manuscripts: the indisputable existence, at the beginning of the *Contra Proclum*, of a general introduction and of a first chapter.

II *Contra Proclum* 6 in Arabic

Al-Rāzī (c. 854–925), in *Al-riyāḍ al-muʾniqa*, made other references to Philoponus' *Contra Proclum*. A little further on, he has this to say:

> Philosophers differed about Plato's doctrine on this question. Aristotle and Alexander considered that he was in favour of initiation, a view shared by John the Grammarian, among the Moderns. Proclus and Porphyry claimed that he upheld eternity. Porphyry held this view, for he says that Plato states in the *Timaeus* that the world was incorruptible, in the *Phaedo* that everything that has been initiated is corruptible and that this implied that everything incorruptible has not been initiated, and that since [Plato] asserted that the world is incorruptible, it cannot therefore have been initiated. They then both tell us what Aristotle has to say about his approach to essential initiation, that is, that the world needs an initiator. And Al-Fārābī accepted this remark in his[26] book *On the agreement of the two Scholars*.

---

[25] Arabic text in 'A. Badawi, *Neoplatonici apud Arabes* (Cairo, 1955), pp. 34–5. French translation by G. C. Anawati, 'Un fragment perdu du *De aeternitate mundi* de Proclus', *Mélanges de philosophie grecque offerts à Mgr. Diès par ses élèves, ses collègues, ses amis* (Paris: Vrin, 1956), p. 21–5, and by Badawi, *La transmission de la philosophie grecque au monde arabe*, p. 133; English translation by J. McGinnis in H. S. Lang and A. D. Macro, *Proclus, On the Eternity of the World* (Berkeley: University of California Press, 2001), pp. 153–63. M. Maróth, 'Der erste Beweis des Proklos für die Ewigkeit der Welt', *Acta Antiqua Academiae Scientiarum Hungaricae* 30 (1982–84), 181–9, offers a partial reconstruction of the Greek, working from the Arabic translation.

[26] See warning below about this identification.

Al-Nawbakhtī said: The Grammarian [Philoponus], in his attack on the third of Proclus' arguments, said of Plato that he thought that the world had always turned in a disorganised way, devoid of harmony, until the Creator – may He be exalted – controlled it with His balanced rule and arranged it in this beneficent order, so that this world should result. As for Empedocles,[27] he is reported as saying that the world was initiated and corrupted infinitely many times in the past, under the alternating sway of Love and Discord.[28]

Let us begin with a comment on the avowed source of the second paragraph, which provides a clue to the probable origin of all of the translated passage. This is the great heresiographer of the end of the ninth century al-Nawbakhtī. And indeed, we know that he was well-versed in both *kalām* and philosophy proper – he bequeathed us a précis of the *De Generatione et Corruptione*.[29] It is highly likely that Al-Rāzī is here quoting his *magnum opus*, the book *On Opinions and Religions* (*Fī al-ārā' wa al-diyānāt*), which was certainly still available at that time. We know, for instance, that the Muʿtazilite al-Malāḥimī (d. 1141), whom Al-Rāzī knows and quotes, taking issue with some of his contemporary pupils, was still a source of direct information for him.[30] Further, at the beginning of *Al-Riyāḍ al-muʾniqa*[31] Al-Rāzī transcribes more than two pages from al-Nawbakhtī, most likely extracted from this treatise. Al-Nawbakhtī rubbed shoulders with the philosophers and translators from the second half of the ninth century and undoubtedly had a precise knowledge of the *Contra Proclum*.

So let us now turn to the beginning of Rāzī's doxography. As its first sentence suggests, the text focuses on a difference of opinion that is not philosophical – is the world created or not? – but historical, whether *Plato* thought the world was created or not. Rāzī's source mentions two camps: the first, the literalist readers of the *Timaeus*, numbering Aristotle, Alexander, and Philoponus in their ranks; the second Porphyry and Proclus. The doxography goes further and reports Porphyry's argument. Supposedly, he combined one theory from the *Timaeus* asserting the incorruptibility of the world and another deriving from the *Phaedo* asserting that we can argue from corruptibility to generability, and finally settling on a Platonic belief in eternity. It so happens that we have a parallel to this 'quotation' in the *Contra Proclum*. The sixth argument of Proclus in support of the eternity of the world does in fact combine the incorruptible nature of the world with a quotation from the Muses in Plato's *Republic* (8, 546A), which claims that 'for everything which has been generated there is corruption'. Here is the beginning of the second chapter of Philoponus, *Contra Proclum* 6.2:

---

[27] Greek Pre-Socratic philosopher, *c.* 495–35 BCE.
[28] *Al-Riyāḍal-muʾniqa*, pp. 81–2.
[29] See now M. Rashed, *Al-Ḥasan ibn Mūsā al-Nawbakhtī: Commentary on Aristotle De generatione et corruptione* (Berlin: De Gruyter, 2015).
[30] Cf. Ibn al-Malāḥimī, *Kitāb al-Muʿtamad fī Uṣūl al-Dīn*, ed. M. McDermott and W. Madelung (London: al-Hoda, 1991), pp. 29, 499, 552–6, 589. On Ibn al-Malāḥimi and al-Nawbakhtī, see the introduction, p. xiii; on Fakhr al-Dīn al-Rāzī and Ibn al-Malāḥimī, pp. v–vi.
[31] For an English translation, see Rashed (n. 29 above), pp. 372–81.

The sixth of Proclus' arguments is put together on the basis of this notion — or rather, here too he has transcribed Porphyry for us. For Porphyry clearly uses this argument too in his commentary on the *Timaeus* in order to show that Plato thought that the world is eternal. For he assumes that, according to Plato, the world is indestructible, and infers that it is also ingenerable — for if corruption necessarily holds of everything generated (as Plato himself says in the *Phaedrus*), then it certainly follows by contraposition that if something is not such as to be destroyed, then it has not been generated. So if Plato clearly says that the world is indestructible, it is perfectly plain that it is also ungenerated.[32]

Out of context, it might seem probable that the Arabic source was drawn directly from Porphyry's commentary on the *Timaeus*. However, since Philoponus and his onslaughts on Proclus figure in the same paragraph from Rāzī, it is obvious that the doxography here goes back to the *Contra Proclum*. The confusion between the *Phaedrus* (cf. 245C ff.) and the *Phaedo* must of course be interpreted as a copying slip at a given point in the work's transmission. Equally, it is the first evidence we have (philologically speaking) of the arrival of the crucial *Contra Proclum* 6 in the Islamic world. But before amplifying this point, we should continue with Rāzī's text.

Porphyry and Proclus – the dual form of the Arabic must refer to both of them – resolved the contradiction between their interpretation of the *Timaeus* and the reading of the Aristotelians by using the term 'essential initiation'. Rāzī's source is easy to detect, once we have identified the first reference to Porphyry. What we have is a brief summary of the long disquisition that occupies the eighth chapter of Philoponus' reply in his Book 6 to Proclus' sixth argument. Since it is so important, we shall translate and comment on the cardinal points. The text starts thus:

As for those who have done their best to force everything into agreement with their own opinions rather than to school their own thoughts into following the truth, if Plato seems to them in this point not to be correct, they should ask his pardon and recite to themselves that familiar phrase 'Plato is dear but truth is dearer' (as Plato's pupil Aristotle and others have done); but instead, caring little for their own consciences or for the truth, they leave no stone unturned (as the saying has it)[33] in their desire to have Plato's authority for their own error. For some of the earlier commentators on Plato (among them the Platonist Taurus and Porphyry the Phoenician, whom Proclus himself followed) agree that the world is said by Plato to be generated, but say nonetheless that it has not been generated in such a sense that it would have begun to exist from a certain beginning, but rather according to another sort of generation; they say in fact that 'generated' is said in several senses.[34]

---

[32] Philoponus, *Aet.* 126,10–23.
[33] Arabic 'shake every reef'.
[34] Philoponus, *Aet.* 144,16–145,8.

After a blast of rhetoric accusing his opponents of bad faith, Philoponus tells us how certain Platonist commentators on the *Timaeus* solved the question of the generation of the world. This they did by identifying different meanings of the term *genesis*, *genêtos*.[35] At this point we realise that there is nothing ambivalent in Rāzī's text when he links Proclus and Porphyry; they are there as a back-up. If Taurus doesn't figure, it will be because his name meant nothing in particular to ninth century Arabic readers. So the scholar responsible for this doxography, unquestionably al-Nawbakhtī, did not retain his name, even though it certainly cropped up in the translation of the *Contra Proclum* he had before him.

Philoponus then inserts a long quotation from Taurus; here is a translation of the central part:

> Since those who say that <the world> is generated invoke several passages, and in particular the phrase in which he says 'It was generated; for it is visible and tangible', we must distinguish among the ways in which things are called generated; and then we shall see that Plato does not say that it is generated in the sense in which we say that things which have come into existence at a certain starting-point in time are generated — for what has misled most people is that whenever the word 'generated' is used they refer it to this sense. Now 'generated' is also used of what has not been generated but belongs to the same class as generated things — just as we call 'visible' what has not been seen nor is being seen nor will be seen but belongs to the same class as visible things (for example, a body, if there were one, round the centre of the earth). 'Generated' is also used of what is composite in thought even if it has not been composed — in this sense the *mesê* note is a composite of the notes *nêtê* and *hypatê*; for although it has not been composed from them, you see in it the potency of the one with respect to the other. Similarly in the case of flowers and animals. And in the world itself we see composition and intermixture inasmuch as we can abstract and separate its qualities from it and reduce it to the primary substrate. The world is called generated insofar as it is always in the process of being generated, like Proteus changing into a thousand different forms. In the world, the earth and the parts below the moon are continuously changing into one another whereas the parts above the moon are pretty well the same in substrate, their changes being slight, but are changed as to their form (as a dancer who, remaining the same in substance, changes into many forms by this gesture or that). The heavenly bodies change and their relationships become different depending on the movement of the planets relative to the fixed stars and of the fixed stars relative to the planets. It is called generated because its being comes from elsewhere, namely from God, with respect to whom it has been ordered into a world. In this sense even according to those who hold that the world is in fact eternal the moon has its light generated from the sun, although there was no time when it was not illuminated by it.[36]

---

[35] On this question, see R. Sorabji, *Time, Creation and the Continuum* (London: Duckworth, 1983), esp. pp. 268–83.

[36] Philoponus, *Aet.* 145,26–147,9.

We can see that Taurus was distinguishing, in addition to the temporal meaning, four principal senses of the term 'generated'.[37] It can mean 1) what is of the same type as what has been generated; 2) what our thought considers to be composite; 3) what is involved in an eternal process of generation; 4) something whose existence is dependent on an external cause, in this instance, on God. So it is obvious why it is important that this passage is properly attested in Arabic. We now have proof that the Baghdad philosophers were familiar with Taurus' classification. They therefore knew perfectly well that one particular Greek tradition had tried to reconcile the cosmologies of Aristotle and Plato by identifying, in the *Timaeus*, a theory similar to the notion of eternally continuous creation.

We shouldn't be bothered by the fact that Philoponus expressly attributes this classification to Taurus, whereas our source mentions Proclus and Porphyry. Because Philoponus is also at pains to specify that Proclus recognised the validity of the two last meanings:

> Proclus allows the third sense and the fourth; for he himself says that Plato says that the world is generated not as having a beginning to its existence but as having its existence dependent on being generated, and also that it is generated insofar as it was generated by God and is not itself the cause of its own existence (that is to say, it is generated with respect to cause).[38]

Things are not as clear-cut where Porphyry is concerned. As a good teacher should, he added some more meanings of *genêtos* to those laid down by Taurus. According to Philoponus, Porphyry was describing 'that in which generation plays a rôle even if it has never been generated', in the same way as syllables and geometric shapes and what comes to be by a process of generation.[39] The first sense merges, Philoponus says, with Taurus' second sense.[40] That is no doubt what explains, he goes on, why Porphyry is the only one to refer to it.[41] As for the second sense, Porphyry must have mentioned it only to reject it: 'by thinking it, God gave everything its substance' (*hama ... noêmati eis ousiôsin ho theos ta panta parêgagen*).[42] So we are left with Taurus' four senses:

> So there remain the other four senses — I mean: belonging to the same class as generated things (even if it has not been generated), and being generated in the sense of being composed of matter and form (which Porphyry in particular insists upon), and of having its existence dependent on being generated and being generated with respect to cause.[43]

---

[37] Of course Taurus is consciously following a long tradition. Cf. Dörrie and Baltes, *Platonismus*, vol. 5, pp. 437–42 (on Proclus, *in Tim.* 1,277,8–17).
[38] Philoponus, *Aet.* 147,25–148,7.
[39] Ibid. 148,9–15 and 148,25–149,6.
[40] Ibid. 148,15–23.
[41] Ibid. 148,23–5.
[42] Ibid. 149,6–10.
[43] Ibid. 149,16–21.

We shall learn nothing more about Porphyry's position from Book 6, chapter 8. So there is no reason to suppose that he accepts Taurus' fourth sense, unlike the explicit remark about Proclus. It is not until 20 pages later, further on in Book 6, that we shall be able to confirm the reliability of the Arab doxography. Philoponus spent Book 6, chapters 9–16, on a refutation of the relevance of the three first senses of *genêtos* to the *Timaeus*, and then turned to the fourth in 6.17. Here is the beginning of this chapter:

> It remains to consider the fourth way of being generated, namely being generated with respect to cause. And to consider whether in saying that the world has been generated Plato means only that it has been generated in respect of cause. For that, as I have said, was the opinion of Proclus: he says that the universe is said by Plato to be generated inasmuch as it is not like what is always the cause of its own existence[44] but rather owes its subsistence to something else. So 'generated' is taken to be used in this way too by Plato insofar as the world is not cause of its own existence but found the cause of its existence in God. And Porphyry, who says that the world is called generated by Plato chiefly inasmuch as it is composite, nevertheless goes on to say that it is said to be generated with respect to cause. At any rate, when he comes to comment upon 'This, according to wise men is the chief cause, etc.', he says:
>
> But if this is the chief principle of the world, and if it began to be generated not spontaneously nor of its own accord but rather by proceeding from God and being generated from being, and if goodness is the being of God, then God is its chief principle. And when he wonders whether it was always without any starting-point of generation or rather started to be generated from some given starting-point, he should be understood to wonder whether it came to subsist spontaneously and without having any maker or rather was generated from something else and has the principle of its existence from something else.[45]

It is apparent that all the information relayed by Al-Rāzī in the first part of the doxography occurs, though sporadically, in Book 6 of the *Contra Proclum*. Before commenting briefly on Al-Fārābī's reference and the connection between Philoponus' text and the Arabic tradition, I should like to adduce one further piece of evidence to clinch it.

Our second paragraph claims to follow al-Nawbakhtī. I explained briefly why this scholar seems to me the source of the whole passage.[46] He certainly had a first-hand acquaintance with Philoponus' *Contra Proclum*. But if so, we run into a difficulty. The third of Proclus' arguments for the eternity of the world, founded on the correlativity, both temporal and other, of an actualised cause and what it causes, even though it is concerned with the question of world order before Plato's divine Creator, the demiurge, intervened, doesn't elicit any reference in Philoponus' reply to the doctrine in the *Timaeus*. This question will not be tackled until much later, in the reply to the fourteenth argument, where several remarks in the *Timaeus* 30A are attacked:

---

[44] I delete *oude monon* at 172,1.
[45] Philoponus, *Aet.* 171,21–172,20.
[46] See above, p. 511.

God wished everything to be good and nothing bad, so far as was possible, and so he took everything visible, which was not at rest but moving in an irregular and disorderly fashion, and brought it from disorder to order, thinking that the latter was certainly better than the former.

Exegesis is tricky here, because we are dealing with a section where Philoponus, elsewhere battening on the twin supports of the Bible and the *Timaeus* to combat Proclus, was perhaps forced to admit that there is a lack of consistency between a radical interpretation of Genesis – that is, where pre-existing 'water' is seen principally as an image – and the first part of the *Timaeus*' account, naively interpreted – that is, failing to see that time can only be properly so called after the Demiurge had introduced order and, especially, had instituted cosmic regularity. Here Porphyry and Proclus have an easier time of it than Philoponus, which probably explains why the refutation of the fourteenth argument is the shortest of all, and certainly far from the most trenchant.

However, he does attack the thesis in passing before Book 14. In view of what I have just proposed, it comes as no surprise that it is in Book 6, to be precise, in chapter 14. Philoponus adopts a strategy opposing the second sense, specifically Porphyrean, of the *genêton* – generable as 'composed of matter and form' – and also attacking Porphyry's theory that subsistence of bodies is characterised by the composition of matter and form, except for the world, whose subsistence is the ordering of bodies themselves. Whatever the underlying issues of the theory may be, I will confine myself here to pointing out that this passage of arms incites Philoponus to quote literally Plato's contentious phrase. Here is the most important part of his commentary, as far as this is concerned:

> For although he said that the world is generated as being composite of matter and form, when he goes on to explain 'God took everything visible, which was not at rest but moving in an irregular and disorderly fashion' he says (I quote) this: 'The making of a world and the construction of a body are not the same thing, nor do a world and a body have the same first principles: rather, whereas in order for a world to be generated there must exist bodies and there must exist God, in order for bodies to be generated there must be matter and God, and what is generated is one thing when matter becomes body and another when bodies are ordered.[47]

As early as Book 6, therefore, readers of the Arabic *Contra Proclum* had been provided with the quotation from the *Timaeus* where Plato is describing most vividly the situation before the Demiurge took action.

This quotation from al-Nawbakhtī by Al-Rāzī is to date, unless I am much mistaken, the only text in Arabic literature that refers to a specific book of the *Contra Proclum*. But how can we account for the incorrect reference to the 'third' argument instead of the 'sixth'? It seems unlikely that al-Nawbakhtī was using a version of the *Contra Proclum* in which our book came third. It is hard, too, to explain it away palaeographically (there is no room for confusion in the way either the words 'third' and 'sixth' or the

---

[47] Philoponus, *Aet.* 164,13–23.

figures 3 and 6 are written). Unless it is just plain carelessness, the mistake could have been caused by a mix-up when the manuscript was being dictated; whether it was a subconscious slip by the copyist or one made by the master to the pupil – *al-sādisa* ('sixth') could have been confused with *al-thālitha* ('third'). The two words do, indeed, have the same vowel pattern, as do all Arabic ordinal numbers from 'second' to 'tenth', but, crucially, they are the only ones whose root contains the sequence *sibilant-dental-sibilant*.

Rāzī's quotation therefore proves that al-Nawbakhtī was well acquainted with Book 6 of the *Contra Proclum*, and picked out the most important features in Book 6, chapters 2, 8, 14 and 17. This makes it practically certain that he was reading the book as a whole and not just extracts.[48]

III The Origins of the Islamic Theory of Instantaneous Initiation (*ḥudūth*)

The fragment of Porphyry relayed by Philoponus was known to a certain Arabic inheritance, and it is not hard to imagine what interest it aroused in its readers. Plato's *Timaeus*, at least in the versions of Porphyry and Proclus, became the forerunner of the Islamic doctrines of initiation.

1) *On The Harmonisation of the opinions of the Two Sages* Incorrectly Attributed to Al-Fārābī

We only have to read the last sentence of Al-Rāzī's first paragraph to realise that this is not just a modern reconstruction. After giving us his summary of Book 6 of the *Contra Proclum*, he adds off his own bat the following comment: 'And this argument [i.e. Proclus' and Porphyry's] is the one which al-Fārābī accepted (*irtaḍāhu*) in his book "On the harmonisation of the opinions of the two sages". Rāzī is here embarking on a tricky piece of exegesis. A few pages earlier, we recall, he had classed Fārābī among the eternalists.[49] Elsewhere, just like all the surviving body of manuscripts and following his predecessor Avicenna, Al-Rāzī attributes the *Harmonisation* to Fārābī. So he has to explain away the distinctly suspect claims on the subject that this treatise contains. This is the tricky passage:

> It is [...] evident that it is not possible, on the basis of the example that he gives in this book [i.e. the *Topics*] to attribute to him the belief that the world is eternal. What brought them also to this opinion is what he states in the book *Of the Heavens and the World*, namely that the universe has no beginning in time. They therefore think that he is asserting the eternity of the world. But this is not so, since he has already shown in this book, and others of those on natural science and theology, that time is only the numbering of the movement of the heavenly sphere

[48] The last chapter of the book, 6.29, also appeared in al-Bīrūnī. See below, n. 87.
[49] See the passage quoted above, pp. 511–12.

and its results. What results from a thing does not contain this thing. His statement that the world has no beginning in time means that it has not been generated gradually, bit by bit, as for example a plant is generated, or an animal, because among the parts of what is generated gradually, bit by bit, some come before others in time. Time results from the movement of the sphere, and so it is impossible that the creation of the sphere should have a starting-point in time. It therefore becomes certain that the sphere results from a creation *ex nihilo* by the Creator, at one single moment without duration in time, and that time results from its movement.[50]

Let us track this reasoning step by step. His starting-point is the clash – that he will have to 'harmonise' – between Plato and Aristotle à propos of the eternity of the world. Some claim that Plato considers the world created, while Aristotle considers it eternal. Our tactic must be to choose one of these two paths: either we must show that this reading of Plato is wrong and that he, just like Aristotle, thought the world was eternal, or we must show that this reading of Aristotle is wrong, and that he, just like Plato, thought the world was created. We have just seen how orthodox Middle Platonists and Neoplatonists took the first option. We misunderstand Plato if we attribute to him the notion of a point in time at which the universe began. What about the author of the *Harmonisation*?

He begins by adducing a text from the *Topics* in order to reject the attribution to Aristotle of the eternity of the world *on this basis*. Even if he probably reckoned that this thesis cannot *at all* be attributed to Aristotle, we could, if pushed, conceive of a subtle dialectical move based on a difference of status between the logical works and the important texts on eternalism in the works of natural science. However, the argument based on natural science under discussion makes this solution spurious. The writer builds his whole argument on a theory that his opponents, but also he himself, ascribe to Aristotle:

T_0 *The world has had no beginning in time*

This thesis, according to the writer, can be interpreted in two different ways. As his opponents interpret it:

T_1 *The world did not have a beginning at a certain point in time*
(whence we conclude: *the world is eternal*, i.e. *the duration of the world is infinite a parte ante*)

Or as he does:

T_2 *The world did not have a beginning lasting a certain length of time.*

T_2 moves from the idea of initiation to the idea of *instantaneous* initiation. The author of the *Harmonisation* thinks that the people he is refuting made the mistake of

[50] Abū Naṣr al-Fārābī, *L'Harmonie entre les opinions de Platon et d'Aristote*, Arabic text and translation by F. M. Najjar et D. Mallet (Damascus, 1999), §§ 54–5, p.128 (translation) and p.129 (Arabic text).

interpreting T_0 as T_1; they did so because they did not see that time, being a numbering of the motion of the heavenly sphere, was an integral part of the world. They therefore allowed themselves an infinite temporal axis, and they set the duration of the world on this infinite axis. If, however, they had realised that time is concomitant with the world, they couldn't even have *formulated* T_1, which embodies a category mistake.

We still have to explain the rejection of duration which is at the heart of theory T_2. T_2 characterizes divine creation which, unlike human artefacts, takes place instantaneously. In theory, there are two possible readings here, and they are not entirely at odds with each other. We may imagine either that the description of divine creation is equally and indiscriminately applicable to any moment when the world exists, or that the writer is here referring to the *first* moment when the divine decision to create the world was physically put into effect. This second reasoning is the most likely, but the text here is quite dense – maybe deliberately obscure. Now in the first case, since the argument never categorically excludes the eternity of the world – but only the eternity, or even the very existence, of time *before* the world – we can once again imagine a world that is infinite or infinite in time. This, however, would run counter to the impetus of the text, since its essentially disjunctive construction was from the outset intended to *reject* eternity as a logical consequence of the false theory T_1. Or else we must assume that eternity is not proven on the basis of T_1, but that it is none the less true, for some reason not revealed in the *Harmonisation*; and that, still more paradoxically, the *Harmonisation* was here discussing time just for the fun of it, without reconciling Aristotle to Plato or Plato to Aristotle.

So we are compelled to conclude that the *Harmonisation*, unlike the 'harmonising' Neoplatonists of antiquity, does not credit Plato with eternalist views, not even creationist ones. On the contrary, it whittles down Aristotle's teachings in natural science to the strictly temporal creationism that was so energetically rebuffed by Taurus, after Crantor[51] and before Porphyry and his followers. If Al-Rāzī does make a mistake of this kind, it must be because he is canny enough to see that Fārābī is fundamentally an eternalist. Comments of the instantaneous nature of creation, read carelessly and non-specifically, might lead us to believe that we are dabbling in Proclan waters, that is to say, merging the act of divine creation, with its essentially temporal nature, with a doctrine of continual creation in which the world needs its Creator *all the time*.[52]

In two recent articles I have tried to show that the authorship of the *Harmonisation* should be denied to Fārābī and assigned to a philosopher of the so-called 'School of Baghdad', who was active in the years immediately following Fārābī's death.[53] So I am

---

[51] Crantor, early Platonist. Cf. Dörrie and Baltes, *Platonismus*, vol. 5, p. 437: 'Wie Krantor die *genesis* des Kosmos gedeutet hat, sagt Proklos nicht; doch liegt es in der Logik der Sache, daß der immerwährenden Verursachung (*paragomenon*, Präsens !) ein immerwährendes Werden und Entstehen entspricht'.

[52] This is the interpretation of the second part of a text transmitted under the name of Ibn Suwār. See below.

[53] See M. Rashed, 'Al-Fārābī's Lost Treatise *On Changing Beings* and the Possibility of a Demonstration of the Eternity of the World', *Arabic Sciences and Philosophy* 18 (2008), 19–58 and 'On the Authorship of the Treatise *On the Harmonization of the opinions of the Two Sages* Attributed to al-Fārābī', *Arabic Sciences and Philosophy* 19 (2009), 43–82.

quite happy to credit the genuine Fārābī with a doctrine that is, on the whole, Proclan, similar to the one Rāzī believes he has identified in the *Harmonisation*. From an historical point of view, Al-Rāzī had no alternative to stretching the sense of this treatise. That he did so advisedly testifies to his good judgement.

2) About the Treatise of Ibn Suwār Called 'On the fact that the proof of John the Grammarian in support of the initiation of the world is basically more acceptable than the proof of the theologians'

Even though it has been published for half a century, *the treatise of Ibn Suwār* (942–1017 AD) called *On the fact that the proof of John the Grammarian in support of the initiation of the world is basically more acceptable than the proof of the theologians* has till not received the attention it deserves.[54] This text starts by reformulating the theologians' argument from the contingency of the world as syllogistically as possible and then by dismissing it; it then sets out Philoponus' argument based on the finitude of the world[55] and seems to accept it as valid, at least in so far as the author does not criticise it. He then concludes his account thus: 'John has shown by many proofs the initiation of the world; if they had studied them, they would have exchanged them for their own invalid proof'.[56] At this point, the title has achieved its goal: it has been shown that Philoponus' proof was 'more acceptable' (*awlā bi-al-qubūl*) than the theologians'.

What a surprise, then, for historians when they realised that there was another page to go in the treatise, in particular since it flies in the face of what has just been established. Here is what comes next in the manuscript:

> And you should know that 'initiated' (*muḥdath*) is a common noun used for something whose existence is within a time, like the shoots of this tree or the growth of this embryo. Indeed, the existence of both of them only comes to its end within a certain specified time. For natural things, that grow by nature, exist within a time and develop progressively. They start at the beginning and go on to their end, when after a specified time they reach their final perfection.
>
> We also say '<instantly> initiated' for what takes place not within a certain time, like the apprehension through sight of things seen, the apprehension through our understanding of things understood, the apprehension though feeling of things felt. All these things, in fact, do not happen in a set time.
>
> We also say 'initiated' for something that has a cause without which it cannot exist, but which runs in concert with this cause in time, i.e. without one preceding

---

[54] Notwithstanding the excellent *editio princeps* by Badawi, *Neoplatonici apud Arabes*, pp. 243–7. French translation and short introduction in B. Lewin, 'La notion de *muḥdaṯ* dans le kalām et dans la philosophie: *un petit traité inédit du philosophe chrétien Ibn Suwār*', in E. Gren, B. Lewin et al., *Donum Natalicum H. S. Nyberg Oblatum* (Uppsala: Universitetsbiblioteket, 1954), pp. 84–93.
[55] For references, see C. Wildberg's contribution in *Philoponus, Corollaries on Place and Void*, pp. 100–3, and Scholten (n. 2 above), p.35.
[56] Ibn Suwār, *op. cit.*, p. 246.

the other in time. This holds for daylight in relation to the sun, bringing a lamp into a dark house, the force of attraction for the object attracted. In all such cases, the causes do not precede in time what they cause, while they do precede them according to their nature, their rank, and their standing. Aristotle says that the world is 'initiated' in this sense of 'initiation',[57] that is to say, it has a cause – the Creator, may He be exalted – who made it exist, without one preceding the other in time; on the contrary, He made it exist all at one go, not as dictated by natural development. For seeing that the Creator, may He be exalted, is infinite, He does not need to generate his acts and to bring them to fruition in a certain time, but He has made them exist not within a time. He is the One of whom it is said 'He spoke and the thing was' and 'He commanded and the thing was created'.[58] Now since time is simply the numbering of the movement of the heavens according to before and after, time must therefore be subordinate to the heavens and existing after their existence; in which case it is not possible to say that the Creator, may He be exalted, precedes the world in time. If He does precede it, that is according to nature, standing, and rank.

This is how Proclus argued. He said: When we say of the world that it is perpetual and when we say of the Creator – may He be magnified and praised – that He is perpetual, we do not mean one and the same thing. Because when we speak of the Creator – may His names be hallowed – we mean to refer to eternity; but when we say of the world that it is perpetual, we are referring to time. So what is connected to the developing being is time, and what is connected to the Existing is eternity. So it follows that the meaning of perpetuity, in the case of the Creator, may He be exalted, is eternity, whereas in the case of the world, perpetuity is time. That is what Aristotle thinks about it.[59]

It is God who grants success; He is our measure; we trust in Him; we put our faith in him; to him be praise for all his blessings; may god give his protection to our lord Mohammed the Prophet, and to his people, the good and the pure, and His salvation.

We have here an argument expounded which is pretty close to what Philoponus attacked in Book 6 of the *Contra Proclum*. The distinction between time and eternity also derives from the last lines of Proclus' argument, lost in Greek, which I translated above,[60] rather than from the *Elements of Theology* or the *Timaeus* commentary referred to in a note by Lewin.[61] To return to Book 6: even if the three examples of *muḥdath* do not exactly tally with the four examples of *genêtos* – apart from the third sense of the former, identical with the fourth sense of the latter – the tactic is the same: to avoid the temporal beginning of the world by interpreting the word that designates it as simply a description of the relationship between the cause and what it causes. We are looking

---

[57] I suggest replacing *baḥth* in Badawi's version by *ḥadath*.
[58] Vocalising *khuliqa* (cf. Lewin (n. 54 above), p. 92: 'et ce fut créé'); Badawi: *khalaqa*.
[59] Ibn Suwār, *op. cit.*, pp. 246–7.
[60] See above, p. 710 and n. 25.
[61] Cf. Lewin (n. 54 above), p. 93.

at an intelligent reworking rather than a translation, however free. Hence the second sense of *muḥdath* – that of 'Aristotelian' instantaneous events – is explicitly excluded by Porphyry from the senses of *genêtos*.[62] The Arabic root *ḥ-d-th*, expressing instantaneous initiation rather than generation, in no way required the persistence of Porphyry's exclusion of a gradual coming into being. Ibn Suwār, if he is indeed the author of this text, was subtle enough to realise this. At any rate, in this intelligent reprise of the *eternalist* arguments of Book 1 and 6 of the *Contra Proclum*, Proclus and Aristotle were quoted approvingly.

In this predicament, where Proclus' ideas are accepted as blithely as Philoponus' objections, it would seem there are two solutions open to us.[63] The first is to posit two texts of different origins surviving under a single title. The treatise on the comparison of proofs of the instigation of the world would then stop at the sentence recapitulating the argument, and what follows in the manuscript would be another text, this time a variation on the *defence* of the thesis of eternity. The second solution would be simply to suggest either great carelessness, or some duplicity or perfunctoriness which first favours Philoponus over the theologians (an approval that is measured, see 'acceptable'), and then lumps them all together, implying that they failed to distinguish the different senses of *muḥdath*. The second solution may be more prudent – it is always risky to fiddle about with transmitted texts – but it lacks cohesion, since it boils down to accusing Philoponus of neglecting an argument that, as we have just seen, we owe entirely to him. In addition, the complete absence of a bridge between the two parts of the text remains troubling.

Without further evidence, no firm conclusion is possible. I would just like to point out, finally, that if Ibn Suwār is really the author of the contentious page defending the eternity of the world, this would support, if not the account of this centenarian scholar's conversion from Christianity to Islam, at least, and perhaps more reliably, Avicenna's admiration for this same Baghdad philosopher, who has no truck with the usual Oriental scorn of the pupils of Ibn ʿAdī.[64] For while Ibn ʿAdī and Ibn al-Ṭayyib, at least, are creationists,[65] being Christian theologians, Ibn Suwār, as a good philosopher, tended toward a belief in the eternity of the world.

3) Proclus out of Context: A Kindean Tradition

Even if a close reading of the *Harmonisation* makes it completely unambiguous, it was, as we have seen, nonetheless interpreted in an eternalist way by Fakhr al-Dīn al-Rāzī. This choice was dictated by the need to credit Fārābī with a minimum of consistency

---

[62] Cf. Philoponus, *Aet.* 148,25–149,10.
[63] At least if we do not accept the hypothesis that asserts: 'for Ibn Suwār, Philoponus, Proclus and Aristotle appear to be confused' (cf. Mallet, *op. cit.*, pp. 178–9). Surely it is inconceivable that a scholar of such standing could not distinguish the refuter from those refuted in the most famous polemic in all Antiquity? Are Arab philosophers really the idiots of the philosophical village?
[64] Cf. J. L. Kraemer, *Humanism in the Renaissance of Islam, The Cultural Revival during the Buyid Age* (Leiden: Brill, 1986), pp. 124–5.
[65] Cf. Rashed, 'Authorship' (n. 53 above).

in his cosmology. The attendant cause, not unimportant, derives from the way the metaphysicians of the ninth to the tenth centuries, no matter what their outlook, concentrated on the question of instantaneous creation. The criterion of 'generation' was superseded by that of 'initiation', and this brought with it a growing tendency to admit a form of instantaneous production of the world. Yet what are we rejecting if we exclude the notion of a 'temporal principle' to the world? Two things, as we have seen: the idea of a duration for God's creative act, and that of the existence of time before the creation of the world. But in neither case is either the infinity of the world or its temporal finitude excluded *a priori*, and this is why the texts, taken out of context, are ambiguous. It is clear that philosophers knew that they were divided on this question, crucial as it is, and their evasions can most likely be explained by the desire to present a united front to their opponents.

The historical development of this confusing state of affairs may, perhaps, be elucidated by a new text of al-Kindī's pupil Abū Zayd al-Balkhī (850–934), just unearthed by Elvira Wakelnig – it is appended to an unpublished recension of Miskawayh (932–1030).[66] True, it is only a fragment, two pages long, and we must be cautious in our conjectures. Nevertheless, in this text, unquestionably earlier than the *Harmonisation* according to my dating, al-Balkhī starts by attributing to Plato a contrast between temporal principle (*bad' zamānī*) and causal principle (*bad' 'illī*), and states explicitly that in this context the 'generated' must be understood as the 'initiated'. This twofold assertion marks the acceptance of Book 6 of the *Contra Proclum* in Arabic. Al-Balkhī clearly knows the *genêtos* in the sense of cause of Taurus, which he reformulates, as did al-Nawbakhtī, but explicitly as an Islamic 'initiated'. During the entire two pages of the fragment al-Balkhī manages not to commit himself about Plato's view of the eternity of the world. However, in just one passage he does assert that the world, according to Plato, 'has no temporal principle because it was initiated first' (*li-al-'ālam al-kullī laysa bad'un zamānī li-annahu awwal mubda'*). It seems hard not to interpret 'first' (*awwal*) here otherwise than indicating first in order. In which case, this interpretation of Plato is identical to the one in the *Harmonisation*. Al-Balkhī would have turned Taurus' argument round so as to defuse his eternalist artillery and reach a theory that agreed only formally with Proclus and actually with Philoponus and, of course, Al-Kindī.

As E. Wakelnig noted,[67] this distinction is taken up by Abū al-Ḥasan al-'Āmirī (died 992), pupil of Al-Balkhī and "grand-pupil" of Al-Kindī, in the following words:

> As for Plato, his doctrine provokes differences of opinion. He said in his book *Būlūṭīqūs* or *The Government of Cities* that the world is eternal, without generation, everlasting, and Proclus the eternalist espoused this belief, so that he wrote his book *On the Eternity of the World*, criticised by John the Grammarian. Then he [Plato] said, in his book that goes under the name of the *Timaeus*, that the world

---

[66] Cf. E. Wakelnig, 'A New Version of Miskawayh's *Book of Triumph*: An alternative Recession of *al-Fawz al-asghar* or the lost *Fawz al-akbar*?', *Arabic Sciences and Philosophy* 19 (2009), 83–119; see the Appendix, pp. 115–19.
[67] See ibid.

was generated and that the Creator made it out of chaos, that all the substance of the world is composed of matter and form, and that all that is composed is doomed to dissolution. And if his pupil Aristotle had not explained the underlying meaning of the two divergent expressions, he would have been accused of indecision. But he showed that the term 'generated' belongs to the class of equivocal words. So the meaning of the expression 'the world is eternal, without generation' is that no time preceded it and that it has not been initiated from something; whereas the meaning of the expression 'it is generated and the Creator transmuted it from chaos to order' is that its existence depends on the ordering disposition of form with matter, since nether of them of itself has an independent existence apart from its union with the other; their Creator therefore made them exist by enabling them to be unified and ordered. He is therefore, in his act of creation He who transmuted them from chaos to order, that is from void to existence. He asserted this in his book *Al-Nawāmīs*, where he said that the world had a causal principle but not a temporal principle, that is to say a producer who produced it not in time. And if anyone seeks the reason for this production, we shall answer that He was in himself equipped with a will to dispense His goodness and the power to put into effect what He wanted to achieve.[68]

So we are here witnessing a turning-point in Al-Kindī's School. Both al-Balkhī and Al-'Āmirī are faithful to their master's notion of a finite duration of the world, but in their hands it founders under a weight of conceptual apparatus quite foreign to Al-Kindī. Rather than supporting loud and clear the temporally finite nature of the world, they both echo Crantor's distinction between a causal and a temporal principle. But this is the whole irony of the thing: while the Greeks thought that the duty of this distinction was to reaffirm Platonist eternalism, our Kindians saw it as ringing down the curtain on a depraved view of temporal finiteness, which would either assign a certain length of time to god's creative act, or would position itself within an infinite duration. In this way we come back to our suggestion that the *Harmonisation* is an offshoot of tenth century Kindian finitism. We can now affirm that his pupils have shown us the way. It is undoubtedly with them, at any rate, that there begins a noticeable need in the Neoplatonist tradition, finitist though it has become, to tone down the strength of Kindian statements.[69]

We may assert that in the tenth century, and until Avicenna makes his entrance, Fārābī's eternalism was out on a limb. It was rather Kindian finitism that was the rule in schools of philosophy, in a radical or attenuated form: the cluster of Muslim Neoplatonists and the Christian school in Baghdad both adopt it. To the roster of finitists, we can indeed add the names of Miskawayh[70] and of al-Isfizārī.[71] This latter, in

---

[68] Al-'Āmirī, *Al-Amad 'alā al-Abad*, ed. E. K. Rowson (Beirut, 1979), pp. 82–4.
[69] The question of time and eternity is one of the rare instances where al-'Āmirī parts company with Proclus. Cf. E. Wakelnig, *Feder, Tafel, Mensch, al-'Āmirīs Kitāb al-fuṣūl fī l-ma'ālim al-ilāhīya und die arabische Proklos-Rezeption im 10. Jh.* (Leiden: Brill, 2006), pp. 151–4.
[70] Cf. P. Adamson, 'Miskawayh's Psychology', in his, ed., *Classical Arabic Philosophy: Sources and Reception* (London: The Warburg Institute, 2007), pp. 39–54, Appendix 2, pp. 52–4: 'Miskawayh and al-Kindī on the Eternal God and the Finite World'.
[71] cf. Gimaret (n. 14 above).

his *Theological Questions* edited by Gimaret, p. 234, arguing from the radical creation of forms to the creation of the world, is plainly adhering to the tradition of Al-Kindī and Philoponus (cf. *Contra Proclum* 9, and its reworking at the time of Al-Kindī into the format of an Alexandrian *Quaestio*).[72] Al-Isfizārī tells us here that he has written a treatise 'On the Initiation of the World'. Ancient sources, moreover, explicitly connect our author and al-Kindī.[73] His interest in mathematical philosophy – indeed, Avicenna criticises his remarks on curvilinear angles – is another feature linking him with the Kindian tradition.[74]

The question that now needs answering is this: what factors determined this historical phenomenon? There would seem to be two possible scenarios. Either the distinction between causal vs. temporal principle had already been employed by Al-Kindī, in a text now lost, or it was an innovation introduced by the next generation. In fact, al-Nawbakhtī was working on his *magnum opus* (which he never finished) between circa 880 and 910,[75] that's to say after Al-Kindī's heyday, when the great translations of the School of Ḥunayn and were either already completed or being worked on and circulated. Taken in conjunction with Al-Kindī's silence à propos of Book 6 of the *Contra Proclum*, this fact may be significant. Even though we should be cautious about arguing from silence, it is conceivable that the complete version of the *Contra Proclum* was only in use after Al-Kindī was active. But we might also think that the argument was already current in his time, maybe in the cluster of Neoplatonist 'reworked' texts that are attributed to Alexander. From this point of view, there is much to be learnt from A. Hasnawi's remarks about the two texts he identifies as originating in the *Contra Proclum*. One of these discusses the question of the relation between act and movement (*Contra Proclum* 4), the other the initiation of forms from nothing (*Contra Proclum* 9). These are both of them of an unusually technical nature. If we compare them to, for example, Al-Nawbakhtī's 'general public' style of cosmological doxography (*Contra Proclum* 6), these two other questions are really pretty abstruse, devoid of interest to all but the most hardened philosophers. Moreover, the extract from Book 9 deleted not only references to anti-Proclan polemic, but even all those to the question of the world. A. Hasnawi suggests two explanations for this which he calls 'weak' and 'strong'.[76] The first would ascribe a 'didactic purpose' to the textual emendations, on the grounds that 'accounts relating to the cosmos might appear likely to distract attention from the principal subject, namely the creation *ex nihilo* of corporeal substances, more precisely the generation of the embodied forms'. The second explanation is that 'the two omissions in question' reflect an attempt to camouflage conflation'. It seems to me that both these interpretations are justified and yet inadequate. For the first one, we can accept that the epitomator is redrafting the original, but the notion of a 'pedagogic' intent seems a bit convoluted: it is difficult to imagine a scholar using the *Contra Proclum* simply as a basic

---

[72] Cf. Hasnawi (n. 6 above), pp. 76–88 (see ch. 19 above, pp. 491–9).
[73] Cf. Reisman (n. 14 above), p. 271.
[74] Cf. Reisman, pp. 274–5.
[75] Cf. J. van Ess, *Theologie und Gesellschaft im 2. und 3. Jahrhundert Hidschra*, 6 vols (Berlin: De Gruyter, 1991–97), vol. 4, p. 92.
[76] Hasnawi (n. 6 above), pp. 87–8 (see ch. 19 above, pp. 498–9).

source for an Aristotelian text book, when the rest of his work is so intensely metaphysical. And if we are happy to allow that the second interpretation glosses over the discordances of the *Contra Proclum*, that still does not explain in fact what the epitomator *is aiming at* with his conflation: the 'strong' interpretation gives up the ghost just when the really important question arises.

The answer to these two questions may be linked to the precise role Al-Kindī played in the production of these translations. His *First Philosophy* – as, by the way, Al-Fārābī remarked with his usual acumen[77] – is not an ontology (*metaphysica generalis*) but a theology (*metaphysica specialis*). The surviving portion focuses on establishing the existence of the First Principle, along with its basic features, and what is lost must have dealt with the creation of the world. Several texts make it clear that the Kindian theory of creation relied on concepts of 'instantaneousness' that were very close to those Philoponus expresses in parts of Books 4 and 9 of the *Contra Proclum*.[78] Could this not then mean that Al-Kindī's vanished ontology, that *metaphysica generalis* whose loss so troubled Al-Fārābī, was simply this corpus of Greek texts 'excerpted'? These texts – the *Institutio theologica* by Proclus, the *Contra Proclum* by Philoponus and the *Quaestiones* by Alexander[79] – once they had been selected, lightly recast, and adapted to fit together, formed a sort of *ontological organon* which the user could turn to for a deductive method (based on mathematical reasoning) for philosophical *theology*. If this is so, we shall turn to reverse A. Hasnawi's two labels. The 'weak' interpretation, once amended – because we are now looking at a propaedeutic or analytical work, not a pedagogical one – becomes strong, because it implies a new metaphysical approach. The 'strong' interpretation, for its part, is weakened, since harmonisation is no longer an end in itself (as it is for the Porphyreans), but is rooted in and reliant on Kindian thought. In other words, the aim would be not to reconcile Proclus and Philoponus, but to preserve from the ancient corpora what would be of use in Al-Kindī's philosophical construct, while spurning the historical detritus that was, to ninth century eyes, the 'errors' of the ancient thinkers (Proclus or no Proclus).

It is not impossible, in this context, that Al-Kindī understood the distinction between temporal principle (*badʾ zamānī*) and causal principle (*badʾ ʿillī*) as a conceptual tool that was part of the proof of the instantaneousness of creation[80] – this,

---

[77] Al-Fārābī, *Sur les buts d'Aristote dans sa 'Métaphysique'*, in *Alfārābī's Philosophische Abhandlungen aus Londoner, Leidener und Berliner Handschriften*, ed. F. Dieterici (Leiden: Brill, 1890), pp. 34–8, on p. 34.

[78] Here too, it is al-Fārābī who was most perceptive about his predecessor, seeing clearly how his whole theological system made light of the possibility of an instantaneous act of creation (*ibdāʿ*), accepted by al-Kindī and rejected by al-Fārābī. Cf. Rashed, 'Al-Fārābī's Lost Treatise' (n. 53 above).

[79] Cf. Endress, *Proclus Arabus*, pp. 63–76. Even if they are to some extent connected, we must distinguish the *philological* question of the stylistic unity of this corpus from the *philosophical* question of the ontological *organon* of al-Kindī. Plainly, the latter is a subset of the former. Provisionally, I would include in it certain of Alexander's *Quaestiones* (the most ontological), the two texts of Philoponus identified by A. Hasnawi, the selection of propositions from Proclus' *Institutio theologica* and extracts from the beginning of Book 2 of his *Platonic Theology* (cf. J. Jolivet, 'Pour le dossier du Proclus arabe: Al-Kindī et la *Théologie platonicienne*', *Studia Islamica* 49 (1979), 55–75; repr. in *Philosophie médiévale arabe et latine* (Paris: Vrin, 1995), pp. 111–31).

[80] I am thinking in particular, of course, of the famous passage on creation *ex nihilo* in the epistle *De la quantité des livres d'Aristote*, ed. M. A. Abū Rīda, *Rasāʾil al-Kindī al-falsafiyya* (Cairo, 1950), vol. 1, p. 375.

once it had been reformulated in terms of 'initiation' (*ḥudūth*) and of 'creation' (*ibdāʿ*), and delicately 'Philoponised' to make it imply the opposite of what it said in Proclus' original.[81] If so, his followers would have transformed it by shifting, even elevating, it from the status of a tool to that of a *positive* concept in the discussion of the temporal finitude of the world, thus replacing their master's famous logical/mathematical proof. This, at least, is what seems to have happened with Balkhî, ʿĀmirî, and the author of the *Harmonisation*.

4) Some Considerations on Doctrine

This appearance, for the first time as far as we know, of Book 6 of the *Contra Proclum* in Arabic gives a clear perspective of the philosophical shifts of the ninth century. A cursory reading of the new information would come to the conclusion that Arabic theories of initiation were (only) a carbon copy of an exegetical point in the *Timaeus*. The Islamic philosophers would then have been content to dub Taurus' fourth sense of the generability of the world, explicitly linked by Proclus with Crantor,[82] with the proper noun *ḥudūth*. The doctrines of continuous creation, and the solution to the specific problems they raise, would themselves be no more than the final outcome of an avoidance strategy that the commentators on the *Timaeus* invented to defeat the Aristotelians' literal interpretation. Al-Rāzī himself would later back up this reading.

But we must beware the charms of hindsight. We are fortunate to be able to check up retrospectively on affinities in the *Contra Proclum*, something denied to Al-Rāzī. The later quotations of Al-Bīrūnī from Plato *Timaeus* 30A, prove beyond doubt that Al-Nawbakhtī had access to Philoponus' whole discussion of the *genêtos*. And yet he keeps mum about the three first senses, favouring instead a straightforward twofold contrast between generability in time and by cause (*kat' aitian*). Accordingly, I have a dual theory to suggest: that the notion of 'generability by cause' is indeed the ancestor of the concept of initiation; and that the gap between them is so great that it casts doubt on this genealogical schema.

To a certain degree, there can be no question that the generability by cause (*genêtos kat' aitian*) of Crantor and his followers was the origin of the Islamic *muḥdath*. In its own way, Ibn Suwār's text confirms this. Both expressions imply an ontological dependency of the world on a superior principle of the demiurge. At the very least, they are based on a shared intuition which connects them one to another. But a closer inspection reveals at once that this feeling is more honoured in the breach than in the observance. Before examining this phenomenon, I should just observe that such an intuitive apprehension of the ontological dependency of the world on a superior principle is hardly original. It may even be more Aristotelian than Platonist. Peeping out between the lines of Aristotle's *Metaphysics* 12.7, 1072b13–14 ('so on such an origin

---

[81] The decontextualisation here goes in the opposite direction from Philoponus' own arguments. However, they do share an aim: less an overlap of views between Philoponus and Proclus than a conformity to al-Kindī's cosmological system.

[82] Proclus, *in Tim.* 1,277,8–17.

(*arkhê*) the heavens and nature depend'), it is enhanced by Alexander of Aphrodisias' providentialism. It just goes to show that these ideas are not set or entrenched but rather shift their meanings according to where they figure in a system of thought. It so happens, however, that these systems seem to be diverse. I have four points to make.

The Greek philosophers' classification is above all *semantic*. We can determine several *senses* of the term 'generated', to prove that the Aristotelians are not necessarily correct when they see a temporal meaning in it. But a moment's thought will suffice to show that the generated by cause is not a *sense* of 'generated', for the simple reason that the only use is entirely *ad hoc*, and rooted in the point under discussion, namely the relationship between the world and its (external) cause. On the other hand, when the Islamic philosophers turn to the word 'initiated', (*muḥdath*), it is always in the context of a carefully laid-out contrast between *eternity* and an 'initiator' (*muḥdith*). So we have here an example of a doctrine that from the outset is robustly cosmological and theological – because it dares to speak its name.

For the Greek philosophers, the (semantic) classification that 'produces' the generated by cause is an integral part of an exegetical tactic. The 'immanent' reading of the *Timaeus* which sees in the generated a temporal feature of the world must be avoided. The reference therefore results from a build-up in the discussion, to some extent at least rhetorical in effect. In other words, we must not exaggerate the manifold senses of 'generated' that we find in Taurus and Porphyry. Piling up hypothetical explanations without being convinced of any of them is a gambit familiar to commentators in a pickle. But this doesn't hold of the supporters of 'initiation' (*ḥudūth*). They are dealing with a possible theory which will, it is true, involve them in a certain number of incidental adjustments, but which isn't one itself.[83]

Even when they venture to rise above simple exegetical enumeration and to plump for one of the solutions on offer, the Greek philosophers never voted for the fourth sense of 'generated': generated by cause. We know nothing about Taurus. Porphyry, on the other hand, as we have seen, had a distinct preference for the second sense ('composed of matter and form'):

> ... there remain the other four senses — I mean: belonging to the same class as generated things (even if it has not been generated), and being generated in the sense of being composed of matter and form (which Porphyry in particular insists upon), and of having its existence dependent on being generated and being generated with respect to cause.[84]

As for Proclus, although he allows that the third and fourth senses may properly be applied to the *Timaeus*, he seems to have a penchant for the third. Philoponus, when he was sharpening up his critical arrows against this interpretation, had this to say:

---

[83] We could, for example, claim that this theory is not without weight in the choice of atomism by Muslim theologians in their physics. But the theory itself is not imposed by any superior dictates. Perhaps, moreover, it is just one aspect of the latter.

[84] Philoponus, *Aet.* 149,16–21. See above, p. 514.

There was a third sense of 'generated', according to which the world is something dependent on being generated, and this is the sense which Proclus particularly accepts in his exegetical commentary on the passages in front of us.[85]

Even if the passage that I have quoted several times from Proclus' commentary (*in Tim.* 1,277,8–17) might seem to imply something else, inviting us to link Proclus more closely to Porphyry, the fact remains that Proclus has no brief for the fourth sense. At the very least, the Greek philosophers were not particularly seduced by the charms of the generated by cause. Porphyry and Proclus, who assign it explicitly to Crantor,[86] seem less than enthusiastic about it, no doubt because they suspect it may lure us into the coils of a naïve doctrine of divine activity. The different premise of generation by eternal composition is in any case there only as a safe-guard. Al-Nawbakhtī, when he sees in Neoplatonist tactics nothing more than a tug-of-war between instantaneous initiation and the temporal origin of the world, is engaged on a full-scale re-reading of the *Contra Proclum* in the light of Islamic discussions.

With the development of Greek neo-Platonism, the divine element is elaborated into triadic mediations, and the First Principle, above Being, tends to verge on Non-being. The root-and-branch simplifications embarked on by Islamic thinkers allow a fresh start. From now on, one point will be generally agreed on: There is just one First, different from all the rest and cause of all the rest. All mediations go by the board. Despite its plethora of schools, Islamic philosophy trumpets the arrival of a cosmological model in which a necessary being, God, confronts a cluster of contingent beings, the world. 'Initiation' is no more than the name for this novel arrangement, and at the same time reification of the modalities. It is just this new relationship which makes the world a metaphysical, not simply a cosmological, object. That is why Al-Nawbakhtī's, and then Al-Rāzī's, readings are purely retrospective.

Conclusion

The ancient bibliographers have nothing to tell us about the author of the translation of the *Contra Proclum*. Judging by the quality of the literal quotations of Al-Bīrūnī (eleventh century) and by the extent of the translated text, he must have been a matchless Greek scholar.[87] But the matter is too fragmentary for us to be certain about this. However, even if we assume that a complete translation of the treatise existed at

---

[85] Philoponus, *Aet.* 166,26–167,2.
[86] Though Crantor himself also accepted the 'pedagogical' interpretation of his master Xenocrates, we should not of course look for an elaborate cosmological theory in the view which Proclus ascribes to him. We might even wonder, given Philoponus' silence on this point, if Proclus' text does not come close to being an 'aporetic extrapolation' based on the slender doxographical material available to him. Cf. Plutarch, *De animae procreatione in Timaeo* 3, 1013A–B. Cf. Dörrie and Baltes, *Platonismus*, vol. 5, frag 138.1.
[87] Cf. E. Giannakis, 'The Quotations from John Philoponus' *De aeternitate mundi contra Proclum* in al-Bīrūnī's India', *Zeitschrift für Geschichte der arabisch-islamischen Wissenschaften* 15 (2002-3), 185–95, and M. Rashed, 'Nouveau fragment arabe du *De aeternitate mundi contra Aristotelem* de Jean Philopon', *Elenchos* 33 (2012), 291–300.

the time when Al-Kindī was at his most active (end of the first half of the ninth century), Book 6 of Philoponus' *Contra Proclum* is strikingly absent from his surviving corpus, whereas the argument appears to become a classic one, accepted even in the school of Al-Kindī, at the turn of the ninth-tenth centuries. So perhaps we can posit the following historical scenario. During the first stage (first half of the ninth century), the theology of the Muʿtazilite theologians, notably Abū al-Hudhayl, develop a theory of '*initiation*' that is so robust that it can be used to prove the existence of God. Al-Kindī, their coeval, both espouses and rejects it. He accepts the creation and the finitude of time but not Muʿtazilite atomism, which the theologians saw as an integral part.[88] Above all, he trawls the most technical Greek texts for conceptual weaponry aimed at analysing more closely the arguments for creation and for finitude. At the turn of the century, with the Basran Muʿtazilites on one side, Al-Fārābī and Al-Kindī's pupils on the other, the paths of theological *kalām* and Peripatetic philosophy diverge for at least a century.[89] The question of the eternity of the world becomes all the more pressing within philosophical circles. This is what accounts for Al-Fārābī's circumspection, despite his eternalist views, and also the caution of the Kindians, despite their devotion to the finitude of time. It is against this novel, hazy background that, paradoxically, the Middle Platonist argument about Book 6 of the *Contra Proclum* will be read, both from an eternalist viewpoint – Nawbakhtī, Ibn Suwār (?) – and from a finitist – Balkhī, ʿĀmirī, the author of the *Harmonisation*. Nonetheless, they will one and all detect in it not so much the old debate about the meaning of 'generated' in the *Timaeus* as the more recent one about the methods of divine creation. In this way, they would introduce into the Greek notion of becoming the occasionalist concept of instantaneous initiation, which had proved so elusive earlier, both in Proclus, of course, but also – for the worse, according to Ibn Suwār, in Philoponus.

---

[88] Cf. J. van Ess, *Theologie und Gesellschaft im 2. und 3. Jahrhundert Hidschra* (n. 75 above), vol. 3, pp. 230–1.

[89] Of course this is simplistic. But, taking into account the mutual influences of both camps, I am thinking here principally of the formal character of the debate (underlining scholarly qualifications, feigned ignorance of the opponent, etc.).

21

Simplicius' *Corollary on Place*: Method of Philosophising and Doctrines[1]

Philippe Hoffmann and Pantelis Golitsis

Simplicius' *Corollary on Place* (*Corollarium de loco*) is not a doxographic text but a strictly *Neoplatonic* philosophical work, with its own philosophical method. It takes the form of a *digression* interrupting the continuity of Simplicius' commentary on Aristotle's *Physics* (itself a *written* work intended for readers, *hoi entugkhanontes, hoi enteuxomenoi*),[2] and its literary genre is that of a monograph treatise using dialectic and exegesis as its principal methods. The *dialectical* method consists in discussing the opinions of Simplicius' predecessors, ancient and modern, mainly Aristotle and Proclus, to pave the way for the exposition of the truth, following the method inaugurated by Aristotle in the *Topics* and still very much alive.[3] It also proceeds by

---

This article first appeared in French as 'Simplicius et le "lieu". À propos d'une nouvelle édition du *Corollarium de loco*' by Philippe Hoffmann and Pantelis Golitsis in *Revue des études grecques* 127(1) (2014), pp. 119–175. Reproduced with permission.

[1] Translated by Christopher Strachan. The new critical edition of the *Corollarium de loco* by Philippe Hoffmann and Pantelis Golitsis, which will be published by Walter de Gruyter, is hereafter abbreviated to GH.
[2] On the use of digressions – as a framework providing the opportunity for philosophical innovation or personal reflexion – in the commentaries of Simplicius (and of Philoponus), see P. Golitsis, *Les Commentaires de Simplicius et de Jean Philopon à la 'Physique' d'Aristote* (Berlin: De Gruyter, 2008).
[3] Cf. Aristotle, *Topics* 1.2, 101a25–36: Of the three purposes for which dialectic is useful (training (*gumnasia*), direct encounters (*enteuxeis*), and the philosophical sciences (*tas kata philosophian epistêmas*)), it is the third, the acquisition of the philosophical sciences, that is involved here, in accordance with what Aristotle was saying already: 'For the study of the philosophical sciences [this treatise] is useful, because the ability to raise searching difficulties on both sides of a subject will make us detect more easily the truth and error about the several points that arise' (101a34–6, trans. Pickard-Cambridge). – The dialectical aspect of the *Corollarium* has recently been the subject of a special study by P. Hoffmann, 'Dialectical Strategies and the Construction of Truth: Simplicius and his Neoplatonic Predecessors on the subject of 'place' (*topos*)', a communication presented at the international colloquium organised by Naly Thaler and Sharon Weisser, '*Strategies of Polemics in Greek and Roman Philosophy*', The Van Leer Jerusalem Institute (Jerusalem, 14–16 January 2014), proceedings in preparation.

puzzles and solutions (*aporiai kai luseis*).[4] The *exegetic method* reappears even within a digression which breaks with the continuous commentary and Simplicius devotes sometimes long passages to quoting and commenting on texts from Aristotle, Theophrastus, Proclus, and Damascius, but also from the Chaldaean Oracles, Iamblichus, or Syrianus. Throughout this piece Simplicius maintains complete control over his material which includes the art of rhetoric, dialectical technique, and his philosophic intention[5]. In it, he replaces the Aristotelian definition of place ('the first unmoved boundary of the surrounding body' (*to tou periekhontos peras akinêton prôton*), *Phys.* 4.4, 212a20–1) with a new definition taken from his master Damascius (place is the measure of the intrinsic positioning (*metron tês theseôs*) of the parts of a body, and of its right *position* in a greater surrounding whole), and he departs from Aristotle's thought with a radical innovation which progressively works its way in.

The *Corollarium de loco* is in fact an exceptional document that enables us to measure the mixture of *respect* and *latitude* characterizing the mental attitude of a philosopher of late antiquity towards those who are, in his eyes, Authorities and Masters. That holds good also for the *Chaldaean Oracles*, whose revealed authority is absolute,[6] but whose obscurity of expression provides a pretext for an individual approach to the task of interpretation. But Aristotle is criticised about how he can allow for the heavens changing place if he allows them no place (that is the *magna quaestio*

---

[4] It may be supposed that Simplicius had practised this method with his master Damascius, an expert on puzzles and solutions, as is shown by his great work *On First Principles*. Damascius himself had studied dialectic with Isidore of Alexandria, according to Photius, *Bibliotheca* codex 181, 127a10–14: '[Damascius] contends that his lessons with Isidore were what gave him his strength in the practice of dialectic; he says that Isidore, such was his power in argument, even eclipsed all the men that time brought forth in that generation.'

[5] An extremely stimulating range of reading is offered by P. Hadot's article, 'Philosophie, dialectique, rhétorique dans l'Antiquité', *Studia Philosophica* 39 (1980), 139–66, repr. in *Études de Philosophie Ancienne* (Paris: Les Belles Lettres, 1998), pp. 159–93, and recently in X. Pavie, ed., *Pierre Hadot: Discours et mode de vie philosophique* (Paris: Les Belles Lettres, 2014), pp. 63–92. Equally worth reading are P. Soulier's perceptive and well-judged observations, *Simplicius et l'infini* (Paris: Les Belles Lettres, 2014), pp. 480–90, on the structure of the dialectical argument and scientific demonstration in Simplicius (see esp. pp. 488–90: 'In Simplicius' commentary, the Peripatetic dialectical method is used as an investigative method, designed to provide the solution to a puzzle raised by the text being commented on.').

[6] On the Chaldaean Oracles and the authority in which they were clothed in the Neoplatonic schools of late antiquity, see: H. Lewy, *Chaldaean Oracles and Theurgy: Mysticism, Magic and Platonism in the Later Roman Empire* (Cairo, 1956; 2nd edn by Michel Tardieu, Paris: Études Augustiniennes, 1978; 3rd edn 2011); Ruth Majercik, *The Chaldean Oracles: Text, Translation, and Commentary* (Leiden: Brill, 1989); H. Seng and M. Tardieu, eds, *Die Chaldaeischen Orakel: Kontext, Interpretation, Rezeption* (Heidelberg: Universitätsverlag Winter, 2011), and among the publications of H. Seng, *Un livre sacré de l'Antiquité tardive. Les Oracles Chaldaïques* (Turnhout: Brepols, 2016). Also to be recommended are H. D. Saffrey's important articles, 'La théurgie comme pénétration d'éléments extra-rationnels dans la philosophie grecque tardive', in *Wissenschaftliche und außerwissenschaftliche Rationalität* (Athens, 1981), pp. 153–69 (repr. in *Recherches sur le néoplatonisme après Plotin* (Paris: Vrin, 1990), pp. 33–49, and several other studies featured in the same volume, esp. 'La théurgie comme phénomène culturel chez les néoplatoniciens (IVe-Ve siècles)', pp. 51–61, and 'Les Néoplatoniciens et les Oracles Chaldaïques', pp. 63–79. On the authority of the Chaldean Oracles in Simplicius, see now, I. Hadot, 'Die Stellung des Neuplatonikers Simplikios zum Verhältnis der Philosophie zu Religion und Theurgie', in T. Kobusch and M. Erler (and Irmgard Männlein-Robert), eds, *Metaphysik und Religion: Zur Signatur des spätantiken Denkens* (Munich: Saur, 2002), pp. 323–42.

or great question) and Damascius himself becomes the subject of a discussion in the course of which Simplicius' own thinking emerges. Indeed he manages both to evince a profound respect for the Authorities, and a horror of both novelty and originality (*kainoprepeia*)[7] which is a feature of Neoplatonist psychology,[8] *and* at the same time a capacity for criticism that enables his philosophical ideas to diverge from the Masters. The divergence is certainly limited, since Simplicius makes only minor adjustments to Damascius' definition of 'place', substituting four measures for Damascius' three and also thinking of them – *in a very Platonic way* – as on the level of the Intelligible; but it is interesting to try to understand what it is in the Neoplatonist mentality that allows these innovations.

First of all, the spirit of criticism is an integral part of what might be called the 'professional ethics' of a good commentator on Aristotle: such a man, Simplicius says elsewhere, 'must possess unbiased judgement [...] which prevents him [...] if a point needs to be examined, from striving to prove that Aristotle is absolutely infallible in everything, as if the exegete were enrolled in the Philosopher's sect'.[9] Dialectical and critical examination seems, besides, to be, for the Neoplatonists, a way of activating and exercising the essential self-motion of the human soul (*to autokinêton*).[10] Consequently, following a route charted by Aristotle himself,[11] the exegete must abide

---

[7] The adjective *kainoprepês* (*-es*) is applied to Proclus' definitions (Simplicius, *in Phys.* 611,12 = p. 12,7 GH) and those of Damascius (*in Phys.* 625,2 = 27,24 GH). Simplicius is anxious to demonstrate that his Master's thought actually belongs firmly in the long tradition that goes back to Theophrastus and is exemplified by Iamblichus. See below, p. 535 and n. 18.

[8] Another word used is *kainotomia*. Cf. H. D. Saffrey and L. G. Westerink, *Proclus, Théologie Platonicienne: Livre II* (Paris: Les Belles Lettres, 1974), pp. 94–5, complementary note 7, (ad *Theol. Plat.* 2.4, p. 31,21–2, *kainotomiai*). Origen the Platonist is accused by Proclus of subscribing to the Peripatetic 'innovations'.

[9] Simplicius, *in Cat.* 7,26–9: eighth point in the general introduction to the study of the philosophy of Aristotle (the qualities required of the good exegete). See I. Hadot and P. Hoffmann, *Simplicius, Commentaire sur les 'Catégories': Fascicule I* (Leiden: Brill, 1990), pp. 14–15, and pp. 123–30.

[10] A very interesting sentence at the end of Philoponus' elucidation of the category of relation, explains that in Aristotle himself (*Cat.* 7, 8b21–4) there is an exhortation to exercise 'self-motion' by using one's initiative to raise difficulties: 'For an impasse is the beginning of finding a way through and a route to learning. He [Aristotle] says this because he wants us not to rest content with his words, but ourselves to seek out such things, and be propelled [by self] not others (*mê heterokinêtous*)' (Philoponus, *in Cat.* 133,1–4). On the doctrinal background (psychology and teaching method) to this conflict respect for authorities and independent philosophical initiative, see P. Hoffmann, 'La fonction des prologues exégétiques dans la pensée pédagogique néoplatonicienne', in B. Roussel and J.-D. Dubois, eds, *Entrer en matière* (Paris: Éditions du Cerf, 1998), pp. 209–45, at p. 231.

[11] Aristotle, *EN* 1.6, 1096a11–17, explains that it is necessary to submit Plato's theory of Forms to a critical examination (*episkepsasthai kai diaporêsai*), even if it has been introduced by 'friends' (*philoi andres*), for the sake of 'safeguarding the Truth' (*epi sôtêriai ge tês alêtheias*), 'especially if you are philosophers' (*allôs te kai philosophous ontas*): concern for the Truth is then preferable to friendship, 'for though both things are precious to us, it is a holy duty to give priority (*hosoin protiman*) to Truth'. As R. Bodéüs points out ((Paris: GF, 2004), p. 59, n. 3), 'the let-out granted to the Platonists echoes the form of words used by Plato himself (*Rep.* 10, 595B–C and 607C) before criticising Homer'. We may add that Aristotle seems to allude directly to Plato's very words (*Rep.* 10, 595C2–3: 'for a man is not to be given priority over (*pro ... timêteos*) the truth', and 607C7–8: 'it is not holy (*hosion*) to put first what is *thought* (*dokoun*) to be true'). The ethics of the Neoplatonist exegetes is planted in this venerable tradition, presided over by Plato and Aristotle, and Simplicius does no more than conform to it.

by the maxim 'Plato is a friend, but the truth is more so', a golden rule of Neoplatonist commentary.[12]

And thus, Simplicius, relying on his vast knowledge of the two major treatises (*Physics* and *De Caelo*) and of Aristotle's works as a whole,[13] has no hesitation in bringing up a basic difficulty affecting the consistency of the definition of place as 'the boundary of the surrounding body' and its cosmological consequences – can one say, on Aristotle's definition of place, that the heavens change their place, if they have no surroundings and so, on Aristotle's definition, no place? The difficulty is an *aporia* (impasse), or, as Simplicius calls it, a 'paralogism', which it is the precise purpose of the *Corollary* to resolve by showing that Damascius' definition of place as what causes right positioning can accommodate the conception of local movement of the Heavens.[14] He offers a step by step discussion of Proclus' exegesis of *Chaldaean Oracles* 51 (des Places), but also of Proclus' doctrine of place as the body of light, and he goes as far as adjusting and rounding off his own master's teaching, presenting it, however, as the perfect outcome of a long history of doctrines of 'place'. Likewise, the *Corollary on Time* (*Corollarium de tempore*) has the avowed purpose of resolving the Aristotelean *aporiai* concerning time, left without solution in *Physics* 4. As a result, the overall structure of the two 'corollaries' conforms to the 'difficulty – solution' (*aporia – lusis*) schema. In the *Corollary on Place*, he makes his rectification, not by adopting the method of dialectical discussion and controversy, the tactics he had used in refuting Proclus, but by engaging in a critical analysis of Damascius' treatise *On Number, Place, and Time* (which provides yet another illustration of Pierre Hadot's remarks on the role of exegesis in philosophical innovation),[15] and also conducting a closely argued discussion by 'puzzles and solutions' in which he must have been trained by the teaching of Damascius, whose virtuosity is illustrated by his great treatise *On First Principles*. Commentary and discussion by 'puzzles and solutions' enables Simplicius, as he goes along, to reformulate his Master's doctrine, to correct it and clarify it, while at the same time making clear that he had the greatest respect for it. It is only at the end that Simplicius ventures to offer two criticisms of Damascius in clarifying the list of *metra sunagôga*, 'uniting measures' (four instead of three) and in introducing a series of measures of the intelligible above the measures of the sensible.[16] To free Damascius from any suspicion of 'innovation' or 'originality',[17] he is very careful to appeal to passages of Theophrastus and Iamblichus and present them as precursors, and even as *holders* of the same doctrine, which

---

[12] L. Tarán, '*Amicus Plato sed magis amica veritas*: From Plato and Aristotle to Cervantes', *Antike und Abendland* 30 (1984), 93–124.

[13] A perfect knowledge of the whole of the corpus is one of the requisite qualifications of a good exegete of Aristotle's philosophy: cf. Simplicius, *in Cat.* 7,23–32; P. Hoffmann and I. Hadot, *Simplicius, Commentaire sur les 'Catégories': Fascicule I* (n. 9 above), pp. 14–15 and 123–30.

[14] P. Hoffmann, 'Simplicius: Corollarium de loco', in G. Aujac and J. Soubiran, eds, *L'Astronomie dans l'Antiquité classique* (Paris: Les Belles Lettres, 1979), pp. 143–61, at p. 161.

[15] Pierre Hadot, 'Philosophie, exégèse et contresens', in *Akten des XIV. Internationalen Kongress für Philosophie* (Vienna: Universität Wien, 1968), vol. 1, pp. 333–9; repr. in *Études de philosophie ancienne* (Paris: Les Belles Lettres, 1998), pp. 3–11.

[16] Simplicius, *in Phys.* (*Corollarium de loco*) 644,10–645,17 (= 48,32–50,10 GH).

[17] Simplicius, *in Phys.* (*Corollarium de loco*) 625,2–3 (= 27,24–5 GH), talks of 'the novelty (*to kainoprepes*) of the hypothesis that seeks to discover the essence of place from its usefulness'.

Simplicius' Corollary on Place: Method of Philosophising and Doctrines 535

Damascius, like Simplicius himself, had basically done no more than explain more clearly.[18] In the last analysis, the synoptic, bird's-eye view afforded by the Neoplatonist philosophic system as a whole (that is, by the doctrine of the Procession of all existents from the One-Good), allows Simplicius, once he has negotiated the rough ground of dialectical discussion and refutation, to orchestrate a final harmonisation (*sumphônia*) in which all the philosophers, now reconciled, find themselves assigned a place and a share of the truth.[19] In this way the audacity (*tolma*) of arguing against Aristotle is mitigated: moreover Simplicius immediately goes on to claim, 'And if I should myself prove able in some way to contribute to the articulation (*diarthrôsis*) of the notions about place, Aristotle would, I think, approve of my audacity (*tolma*), since he himself provided the principles I was following.[20] And Simplicius, by way of diminishing his 'audacity', takes care to quote the difficulties that had already been raised by Theophrastus against Aristotle's definition (*in Phys.* 604,5–11 = 4,8–14 GH = fr. 146 FHSG).

The *Corollarium de loco* offers a panoramic view[21] of Greek doctrines on space in the field of physics. The account is rigorously directed towards a definition that is, for Simplicius, the almost teleological outcome of a history that begins with Plato, and especially Aristotle's *Physics* and involves the successive efforts made to produce definitions expressing an 'aspect' of a subject 'with multiple forms', 'so that, if I give the impression that I am advancing outside the domain of exegetic commentary, my readers must put that down to the difficulty of the subject being studied and the multiplicity of aspects presented by it'.[22] The research is on-going, Simplicius even goes so far as to say that each philosopher has grasped one aspect of place, and does not rule out the possibility that another aspect might be discovered in the future: 'I shall then

---

[18] Simplicius, *in Phys.* (*Corollarium de loco*) 639,10–13 (= 43,17–20 GH): 'But now that I have explained this conception of place (*i.e that of Damascius*), as far as I could, and set out the puzzles that might be raised against it, and added the solutions to the puzzles, I want to show that this conception is not absolutely novel (*kainoprepês*), and that it was not unknown to some particularly distinguished philosophers.' There follows (639,13–640,9 = 43,20–44,20 GH) the evidence of Theophrastus (= fr. 149 FHSG) and of Iamblichus (*in Tim.* fr. 90 Dillon). Theophrastus, a close associate of Aristotle's, is both a *guarantor* when it comes to deploying *aporiai* against Aristotle (604,5–11 = 4,8–14 GH), and an *authority* when it is a matter of showing that Damascius' doctrine is neither new nor novel.

[19] The search for harmony (*sumphônia*) among the philosophers, among the Authorities, is a major feature of Neoplatonist commentary after Plotinus, and the harmonisation of Aristotle and Plato, for example, is the main task of a Neoplatonist teacher, especially after Ammonius of Alexandria. See for example P. Hoffmann, 'Sur quelques aspects de la polémique de Simplicius contre Jean Philopon: de l'invective à la réaffirmation de la transcendance du Ciel', in I. Hadot, ed., *Simplicius: Sa vie, son œuvre, sa survie* (Berlin: De Gruyter, 1987), pp. 183–221, at pp. 212–20; I. Hadot and P. Hoffmann, *Simplicius, Commentaire sur les 'Catégories': Fascicule I* (n. 9 above), pp. 7 and 15 (*in Cat.* 2,21–2 and 7,29–32), and pp. 123–30. This principle must have been theoretically framed in a lost treatise of Syrianus, entitled, according to the Suda, 'Agreement of Orpheus, Pythagoras, Plato with the Chaldaean Oracles in ten books': see H. D. Saffrey, 'Accorder entre elles les traditions théologiques: une caractéristique du néoplatonisme athénien', in E. P. Bos and P. A. Meijer, eds, *On Proclus and his Influence in Medieval Philosophy* (Leiden: Brill, 1992), pp. 35–50; repr. in *Le néoplatonisme après Plotin* (Paris: Vrin, 2000), pp. 143–58.

[20] Simplicius, *in Phys.* (*Corollarium de loco*) 601,10–12 (= 1,10–12 GH).

[21] But the panorama does not take in quite everything – for example it does not include a word on Stoic physics. It is the Atomists' definition of place as 'void' that is refuted – Simplicius responds to the great question (*magna quaestio*) about void.

[22] Simplicius, *in Phys.* (*Corollarium de loco*) 601,12–13 = 1,12–13 GH.

repeat now what I said at the beginning: each one of the philosophers who spoke about place had in view a concept of place that was true, and did not fail to appreciate its general character. And if all of them did not intuitively recognize all the species of place, there is nothing surprising in that; and it is not improbable either that there are also other species of place that have not yet come to light.'[23] The object of the digression is to show that with the philosopher Damascius, the last successor to Plato as head of the Neoplatonic Academy, the definition of place has attained a degree of completeness and generality that, like a sort of Hegelian sublation, simulataneously refutes, invalidates and assimilates the definitions advanced by a long tradition of philosophical enquiry. At the end of an account which is both historical and dialectical (in the Peripatetic sense that involves a critical examination of opinions that also leads to the extraction of their contribution to the truth so that it can be added to the sum of Knowledge), Simplicius sets out a definition which he uses to absolve himself of the sin of *novelty* by making it go back to Theophrastus and Iamblichus, which constitutes a perfect example of the 'theological' physics of late antiquity, the physics that, following the method of Plato himself (the Plato of the *Timaeus*), studies the phenomena of Nature in their relationship with the transcendent Principles that are above and beyond Nature. For Proclus, for example, these are, in ascending order, the Demiurge, the efficient cause, the Intelligible, the paradigmatic cause, and the Good, the final cause.[24] This is what is called 'doing physics like a theologian' or 'remaining a theologian even when doing physics' (thus Plato *aei phusiologôn theologei*).[25] In practice, this will come down to thinking of place, or space, as a transcendent principle whose function is to confer on the physical World and all bodies within it a type of *unity* and a disposition that is *good* (in the sense of the adverb *eu*) depending on the First Principle which is, as we know, both the One of the first Hypothesis of the *Parmenides* and the Good of Book 6 of the *Republic*. A passage from Simplicius, in the Prologue of his Commentary on the *Categories*, helps to throw some light on this thinking in general:

> Whereas the evidence (*enargeia*) which leads to conviction (*pistis*) is of two kinds – the one comes from intellectual insight, the other from sensation – Aristotle, since he is speaking to beings who live with sensation (*sc.* mankind), gives preference to evidence founded on sensation. That is why necessity is the characteristic of his demonstrations, so that even someone who, owing to certain unfortunate preconceptions, does not accept what he says, is nevertheless forced by necessity to shut his mouth. On every subject, Aristotle refuses to abandon nature, but on the contrary, he considers even the entities that are beyond nature from the point of view of their relationship with nature, just as the divine Plato,

---

[23] Simplicius, *in Phys.* (*Corollarium de loco*) 644,4–9 = 48,26–31 GH.
[24] Read A. Lernould, *Physique et théologie: Lecture du Timée de Platon par Proclus* (Villeneuve d'Ascq: Presses universitaires du Septentrion, 2001), pp. 12–15 (and n. 11, pp. 21–2, with bibliography – with cross-reference to the work of D. J. O'Meara and W. Beierwaltes), 34–5, 130–3, and 341.
[25] Cf. Elias, *in Cat.* 124,17–23, translated by I. Hadot, *Simplicius, Commentaire sur les 'Catégories': Fascicule I* (n. 9 above), p. 111 and n. 21, with cross-reference to K. Kremer, *Der Metaphysikbegriff in den Aristoteles-Kommentaren der Ammonius-Schule* (Münster: Aschendorffsche Verlagsbuchhandlung, 1960), pp. 189–95.

contrariwise, following the Pythagorean custom, examines even natural things in so far as they participate in the things that are beyond nature.[26]

In the midst of a commentary on Aristotle, Simplicius introduces a doctrine about place which is radically at variance with Aristotle's own findings. The *De Caelo* and the *Physics* offered a number of conflicting assertions: 1. the World is not 'somewhere' (that is, in a place), because there is no greater surrounding body outside it; 2. local movement is the movement of a body that is in a place, and 3. the World moves with local movement (uniform circular translation). Confronted by these contradictions Simplicius puts forward a definition of place capable of resolving this *paralogismos* (something shocking in an authoritative work that should be 'symphonic'), but at the cost of having to find fault with Aristotle's definition and replace it with Damascius' doctrine which is presented as general, inclusive and able, in the end, to encompass the theory of Aristotle himself. For him, 'place' (*topos*) is 'the first unmoved boundary of the surrounding body' (*to tou periekhontos peras akinêton prôton*, *Phys.* 4.4, 212a20–1), that is, a simple two-dimensional 'surface' (*epiphaneia*) that cannot be 'equal' to the body, which is a three-dimensional solid. This definition is included in a general view of the cosmos in which each body is surrounded by another and local movement is dependent on a process of reciprocal replacement (*antimetastasis*: for example 'Where water now is, there in turn, when the water has gone out as from a vessel, air is present', Aristotle, *Phys.* 4.1, 208b2–3, trans. Hardie and Gaye). In the thought of Damascius and Simplicius, place is an *internal power* of spatial organization, or more precisely a power of intrinsic '*spatialisation*', but also extrinsic *localisation*. Iamblichus, Damascius' and Simplicius' source, expresses this idea perfectly: place has an 'active power to accomplish things' (a *dunamis drastêrios*) which acts on the body itself, determines it and prevents its endless disintegration (*diastasis*).[27]

---

[26] Simplicius, *in Cat.* 6,22–30. See I. Hadot and P. Hoffmann, *Simplicius, Commentaire sur les 'Catégories': Fascicule I* (n. 9 above), p. 13 and pp. 108–12 (the type of expression in Aristotle's writing).

[27] This encapsulation is to be found in a passage of Iamblichus' commentary on Aristotle's *Categories* quoted by Simplicius. Place is a delimiting principle (*peras*) more powerful than bodies, and Iamblichus' insight will turn up again in the thought of Damascius: ' Iamblichus adds to all these considerations [i.e. the reasons given by Porphyry that 'where' (*pou*) should constitute a proper category] intellective contemplation (*noera theôria*, the intellective sense, that is, awareness of 'place' from the point of view of divine Knowledge), and he enquires first of all whether it is the entities themselves (*pragmata*) that, by being in a place, determine the place *around* them or *with* them (*peri heauta ê sun heautois*), or if it is the place that determines (*aphorizei*) the entities, by making them perfectly complete (*auta sumperainôn*). He says that if – as the Stoics maintain – place exists derivatively round the edge of bodies (*paruphistatai tois sômasin*), it only receives its determination (*horos*) from them in the exact measure in which it is filled up by the bodies (*kath' hoson sumplêroutai hupo tôn sômatôn*). On the other hand, if place in itself possesses substance (*ousia*), and if no body can actually exist if it is not in a place [...], then it is the place itself that determines the bodies and brings them to completion within itself (*autos ho topos aphorizei ta sômata kai en heautôi sumperainei*). For if place were without active power (*adranês*), and had its being, stripped of all substance, in an unbounded void extending without limit (*en apeirôi kenôi kai diastêmati aneu tinos hupostaseôs ekhôn to einai*), it would also receive its determination from outside (*kai ton horon an exôthen paredekheto*, it would have a purely extrinsic determination). But since it has an active power to accomplish (*drastêrios dunamis*) and a determinate incorporeal existence (*ousia asômatos hôrismenê*), and since it prevents the disintegration of bodies from going on more or less ad infinitum (*eis apeiron prokhôrein*), but on the contrary determines them within itself (*en heautôi horizei*), it is reasonable that it should also bestow their limit (*peras*) on bodies from itself.' (Simplicius, *in Cat.* 361,7–20)

In Damascius, this power is labelled 'measure' (*metron* meaning not a cognitive tool, but an ontological principle of unity and order) and its function is to *save*, that is to preserve bodies from catastrophic dispersion, and from draining away towards the unlimited (*hê eis apeiron ekkhusis*).[28] In a universe perceived as an *organic* whole (a particular body, the universal body of the Cosmos), place as 'measure' orders the relationship of the parts with each other, of the parts with respect to the whole and of the whole with respect to the parts. It is *metron tês theseôs*, 'the measure of the arrangement', the word *thesis* being understood as both the arrangement of the parts in a whole (the relative position of one part with respect to the other parts and in relation to the whole), and as the position of a body as a whole in respect of another, more inclusive, surrounding body. In order to ensure that every body is in the right position (*eutheton*), and that it is in the place that suits it, 'in its right place' – the place in which its essential nature is most properly realised, as in Aristotle's 'natural place' – 'place' strives actively and dynamically and is the cause of the right positioning (*euthetismos*, or *euthêmosunê*). In the human body, place contributes to its harmony and beauty, it ensures that each organ, each part of the body is in its place, and that we are not monsters. On a grander scale, in the Cosmos, it is responsible for the right positioning, the *euthetismos* of the parts of the All, from the disposition of the 'elementary wholes' (*hai holotêtes tôn stoikheiôn*) in the sublunary zone, to the ordering of the celestial bodies (the *taxis* of the planets, the arrangement of the spheres one within another, the way in which the last sphere of all surrounds the rest). Just as time is a principle of order regulating the progression of the ages of life, from embryo to old age in a fixed sequence (no one can be a baby, then an old man, then an adolescent ...), just as it separates the War of Troy from the Peloponnesian War, determining that one must succeed the other, and prevents all confusion of events, but above all just as it enables an event or a biological state to happen *exactly when it should* and to be *eukairon*, so place is the reason that a body is in the 'right position' and in the 'right' position for it (*eutheton*). Right positioning (*euthetismos*) corresponds to right time (*kairos*).[29] Late Neoplatonism seems, paradoxically, to remember what Aristotle had to say about the homonymy of the Good (the word 'Good' is used in as many senses as the word 'Being'),[30] and *euthetismos* (like *kairos* also) is a trace of the Good in the entities of the sublunary world, the ultimate 'participants' in it. The four 'measures' (number, *arithmos*; size, *megethos*; place, *topos*;

---

[28] Simplicius, *in Phys.* (*Corollarium de loco*) 640,33 (= 45,11 GH).
[29] On the origin of this notion see Moniqué Trédé's classic work, *Kairos, l'à propos et l'occasion: Le mot et la notion, d'Homère à la fin du IVe siècle avant J.-C.* (Paris: Klincksiek, 1992), and P. Aubenque's excellent book, *La Prudence chez Aristote* (Paris: PUF, 1963; 2nd edn 1976), pp. 95–105.
[30] Thus Aristotle, *EN* 1.6, 1096a23–9: '... since Good is used in as many senses as Being – for in the case of substance, it is applied, for example, to God and the intellect, in that of quality, to the virtues, in that of quantity, to just measure, in that of relation, to what is useful, in that of time, to the right moment (*kairos*), in that of place, to *the right (medically favourable) location*, and so on – it is clear that it cannot be something general, both universal and single, for if it were, it could not be used in all the categories but in one only.' In his commentary on this passage, P. Aubenque, *La Prudence chez Aristote* (see previous note), p. 101, n. 3, thinks that Aristotle is in fact making use of a *medical* idea (*diaita*, 'which means a mode of life, with particular reference to place') to illustrate the Good in the category of place. This interpretation is not shared by R. Bodéüs, *Aristote, Éthique à Nicomaque* (Paris: GF, 2004), p. 60, who translates *diaita* simply by 'habitat'. But the context (the plurality of meanings of *good*) here requires a beneficial notion.

time, *khronos*) that Simplicius substitutes for Damascius' three 'measures' (*arithmos, topos, khronos*), and to which there correspond four measures of the Intelligible realm[31] (including Eternity, *aiôn*, the paradigm of Time),[32] are the means of transmission, subordinate to the One-Good and the divine Henads, that communicate unity and goodness to physical phenomena, by unifying and ordering them. Neoplatonic participation (*methexis*) is also a generous sharing (*metadosis*) of 'goods' that the transcendent Principles bestow on the participating entities, and the right place granted to bodies is one of the gifts that come from the Principles. The doctrine of 'measures' is only understandable in the context of the Neoplatonic theory of Procession or emanation from the Good. Because phenomena, and in particular bodies, are beset by division (*diakrisis*) and distension (*diastasis*), that is, by dispersion coupled with descent towards matter and bad unlimitedness (*apeiron*), they are deficient, *needy* (*endeê*), and because of the threat of catastrophic dispersion, atomisation into the boundless, they stand in need (*deisthai*) of the benefits offered by the 'measures', that is, of the unity and order that guarantee both *being* (*einai*) and *well-being* (*eu einai*). The discovery of the essence (*ousia*) of place, presupposes the discovery of its 'utility' (*khreia*) in a reversal that strips the question of essence of the primacy established by classical philosophy. That is because the philosophers before Damascius did not understand that the question of utility (*khreia*) was primary, and must be asked within the overall perspective of the System governing what exists and that the history of attempts to define 'place', from Aristotle to Proclus, delivers only definitions that are partial and inadequate. The reversal of the order of the questions at last enables an overall definition that is entire and universal to emerge, and one which will, in turn, allow reconciliation and harmonisation by assigning each earlier doctrine its share of the truth (*partial* truth). This is a particularly striking example of the integrating power of Neoplatonism.

What is at stake in the enquiry into the nature of 'place' is a matter of major cosmological importance, and, what is more, the *Corollarium de loco* has a psychagogical and anagogical dimension to it. Simplicius invites us to contemplate a well-ordered World, *kosmos*, in which everything is in a good intrinsic position – illustrated by the perfection of the human body – and in the place that suits its essential nature. The right placement of bodies contributes to the beauty of a universe without a beginning or an end, which is itself the sempiternal (*aidios*) image of an eternal (*aiônios*) intelligible Paradigm.[33] The Cosmos, a visible god, an object of admiration and the still more

---

[31] Cf. Simplicius, *in Phys.* (*Corollarium de tempore*) 773,19–774,37, where Simplicius returns to and systematically expounds his own doctrine of the two series (intelligible and sensible) of *four* measures, that emerges from the discussion in the *Corollarium de loco*.

[32] Cf. Plato, *Timaeus* 37D5–7. It has been recognised that the background to this doctrine is to be found in the explanation Proclus gives in his commentary on the *Timaeus*, which was systematised in the *Elements of Theology*, Propositions 52–5, pp. 50–5 Dodds. This point was to give rise to prolonged detailed discussion and it could be shown that the doctrine of 'measures', as systematised in Simplicius, presupposes, as one of its sources, Proclus' thoughts on the relationship between Eternity and Time, which seems to have provided a model extended to cover other types of disintegration (numerical plurality, size, spatiality).

[33] In accordance with the teaching of the *Timaeus*, adopted by all the Neoplatonists, and especially by Proclus in his commentary on the *Timaeus*, and by Simplicius (e.g. *in Cael.* 95,16–30).

divine body of the Heaven that is part of it, by their very presence engender an exercise in universalization and assimilation by which the individual human being comes to understand the Principles. In Simplicius' commentary on the *Physics*, which, with his Commentary on the *De Caelo*, constitutes a long prayer to the demiurgic Intellect, the contemplation of the *good order* of the Universe and of the 'measures' that are its causes, has the appearance of a genuine spiritual exercise.[34] It is, in the end, through an understanding of what the 'measures' are, a step towards an awareness of the essentially dependent relationship between the sensible Universe and the unifying causes which all derive from the One-Good.[35] Physics is indeed, as Proclus calls it, a theology, and the study of it is leading upwards to the Good.

---

[34] Simplicius' commentaries are clearly consistent with the standpoints often described by Pierre Hadot in a number of his writings, for example *Qu'est-ce que la philosophie antique?* (Paris: Gallimard, 1995), pp. 309–22 (*What is Ancient Philosophy?*, trans. M. Chase (Cambridge, MA: Harvard University Press, 2002), pp. 202–11) on the relationship between the self and the Cosmos and physics as a spiritual exercise. The prologue of the Commentary on the *Physics* (4,17–5,26) proves that this was indeed how Simplicius thought of it: cf. P. Hoffmann, 'La triade chaldaïque *erôs, alêtheia, pistis*: de Proclus à Simplicius', in Alain-Philippe Segonds and Carlos Steel, eds, *Proclus et la Théologie Platonicienne* (Leuven: Leuven University Press, 2000), pp. 459–89, esp. pp. 476–80.

[35] P. Hoffmann, 'La triade chaldaïque *erôs, alêtheia, pistis*: de Proclus à Simplicius' (see previous note) and 'Science théologique et Foi selon le *Commentaire* de Simplicius au *De Caelo* d'Aristote', in E. Coda and C. Martini Bonadeo eds, *De l'Antiquité tardive au Moyen Âge: Études de logique aristotélicienne et de philosophie grecque, syriaque, arabe et latine offertes à Henri Hugonnard-Roche* (Paris: Vrin, 2014), pp. 277–364.

22

A Philosophical Portrait of Stephanus the Philosopher[1]

Mossman Roueché

Introduction

The role played by Stephanus the Philosopher in the history of philosophy in the sixth century has been poorly studied. The clearest indication of this is the absence of any entry for Stephanus in either the *Stanford Encyclopedia of Philosophy*[2] or the recent *Cambridge History of Philosophy in Late Antiquity*.[3] He is universally acknowledged to be the author of an extant commentary on Aristotle's *De Interpretatione* but beyond that, there has been considerable uncertainty concerning the identity, the date and the works attributed to someone who has been called 'a very shadowy figure'.[4] From the time of Hermann Usener's classic dissertation, *De Stephano Alexandrino*,[5] interest in Stephanus as a philosopher has been over-shadowed by interest in his non-philosophical activities. These include his supposed appointment as an 'ecumenical teacher' in Constantinople during the reign of Heraclius and his authorship of certain astrological, astronomical, alchemical and medical works that are attributed to 'Stephanus' in some manuscripts.[6] It has recently been shown that the arguments for ascribing to him these non-philosophical activities are based on anachronistic evidence and that the conclusions are no longer valid.[7] The removal of this

---

[1] I would like to thank Richard Sorabji for the opportunity to present some of this material at a Workshop in Oxford in 2014. I am grateful for his encouragement and comments and those of the other participants.
[2] Edward N. Zalta, ed., *The Stanford Encyclopedia of Philosophy*, URL <http:plato.stanford.edu>.
[3] Lloyd P. Gerson, ed., *The Cambridge History of Philosophy in Late Antiquity*, 2 vols (Cambridge: Cambridge University Press, 2010).
[4] N. G. Wilson, *Scholars of Byzantium* (London: Duckworth, 1983), p. 47.
[5] Hermann Usener, *Kleine Schriften*, 4 vols (Leipzig: Teubner, 1912–14), vol. 3, pp. 247–322.
[6] For the fullest presentation of this argument and the relevant references, see Wanda Wolska-Conus, 'Stéphanos d'Athènes et Stéphanos d'Alexandrie: Essai d'identification et de biographie', *Revue des études byzantines* 47 (1989), 5–89, and Maria Papathanassiou, 'Stephanus of Alexandria: a famous Byzantine scholar, alchemist and astrologer', in P. Magdalino and M. Mavroudi, eds, *The Occult Sciences in Byzantium* (Geneva: La Pomme d'or, 2006), pp. 163–203.
[7] Mossman Roueché, 'Stephanus the Philosopher and Ps. Elias: a case of mistaken identity', in *Byzantine and Modern Greek Studies* 36 (2012), 120–38, at 122–5, and 'Stephanus the Alexandrian Philosopher, the *Kanon* and a Seventh Century Millennium', *Journal of the Courtauld and Warburg Institutes* 74 (2011), 1–30.

'evidence' and the conclusions drawn from it provides a timely opportunity to examine afresh the genuine evidence that we have for his life and works as a philosopher and to draw some important conclusions regarding his influence. Far from being a shadowy figure, Stephanus was an important philosopher in sixth century Alexandria. He was a student of John Philoponus and, as one of the Christian successors of Olympiodorus, he continued the Christianisation of the introductory philosophical curriculum. His lectures covered the entire *Organon* and became the source of a philosophical vocabulary widely used by Christian theologians, including Maximus the Confessor and John Damascene, during the seventh and eighth centuries. Through translations into Syriac and Arabic, his commentaries continued to influence Syrian and Arabic philosophers well into the mediaeval period.

Ecumenical Teacher

One of the most frequently repeated statements made about Stephanus the Philosopher is that he was 'summoned from Alexandria' by the emperor Heraclius to take up the position of 'ecumenical teacher' in Constantinople at a new, imperially sponsored educational institution. This story has been universally accepted by historians of late antiquity for over a century and has provided a romantic narrative of the end of the teaching of philosophy in Alexandria, much in the way that Justinian's closure of the Academy in Athens and the departure of the seven philosophers to Persia has provided a romantic narrative of the end of the practice of Neoplatonism in Athens. Stephanus' supposed move to Constantinople has also been seen as a likely means whereby a large number of mainly philosophical manuscripts (known as the 'Collection Philosophique') were conveyed from Alexandria to Constantinople, thus ensuring their preservation prior to the Persian and Arab invasions of Egypt and conquest of Alexandria.[8] More importantly, this story has established as 'fact' the belief that the second half of Stephanus' professional career took place in Constantinople during the seventh century, under the reign of Heraclius. It is during this period, and in Constantinople, that the non-philosophical works attributed to Stephanus purport to have been composed.

The story owes its origin to Usener who based his hypothesis of Stephanus' move to Constantinople on two observations. The first and most important was his observation that the titles of 'ecumenical teacher' (*oikoumenikos didaskalos*), 'ecumenical philosopher' (*oikoumenikos philosophos*) and 'universal teacher' (*katholikos didaskalos*) are used to describe the author of three non-philosophical works attributed to 'Stephanus'. These are the so-called *Horoscope of Islam*, a fictitious horoscope of Mohammed and his successors supposedly cast on 1 September, 621 CE; an alchemical treatise *On the Making of Gold* that is in part addressed to Heraclius; and a handbook on the use of Ptolemy's *Handy Tables* and related computations of astronomical events

---

[8] Marwan Rashed, 'Nicolas d'Otrante, Guillaume de Moerbeke et la 'Collection Philosophique – Note complémentaire: sur l'origine et constitution de la 'Collection Philosophique'', *Studi Medievali* III, Ser. 43 (2002), 713–7.

that occurred in 617–19 CE.[9] Usener considered all three titles to be variants of the same thing, i.e., the title of a senior academic post in an imperially sponsored educational institution. He concluded from these titles that such an institution existed in Constantinople and that Stephanus, the author of the commentary on *De Interpretatione*, had held such a post.

Usener also observed that the rhetorical dialogue that serves as a *proem* to the seventh century *Universal History* of Theophylact Simocatta appears to be evidence of a revival of interest in learning under the reign of Heraclius.[10] In the *proem*, personifications of History and Philosophy rejoice at their return to favour in the court of the new emperor (Heraclius), having been banished by the previous emperor (Phocas). Usener saw this as confirmation of Heraclius' establishment of a new educational institution and the appointment of Stephanus as ecumenical teacher (or philosopher). Combining these two pieces of evidence, Usener set out his well-known conclusion as follows:

> If a reliable account of the event (*i.e., a resumption of higher education in the capital*), beyond the mere support of the emperor, is embellished by these flowery words (*i.e., the rhetorical proem to Theophylact Simocatta's Universal History*), which I truly believe to be the case, it means that the imperial chair of philosophy, disregarded by Phocas, was restored by Heraclius by the appointment of someone worthy of the title 'philosopher'. The one to whom the emperor will have conferred this office (*i.e., ecumenical teacher*) is now clear: Stephanus, summoned from Alexandria, the ancient citadel of learning.[11]

Despite the attraction of Usener's hypothesis, we now know that it was built on false foundations. A recent study[12] has shown that the titles 'ecumenical teacher', 'ecumenical philosopher', and 'universal teacher' are all anachronisms when used to describe a sixth or seventh century person. The title 'ecumenical teacher' is first attested in the ninth century and 'universal teacher' is first used in the fourteenth/fifteenth century. Consequently, these titles can provide no evidence for the establishment of an imperially sponsored educational institution in Constantinople at the time of Heraclius, or for Stephanus the Philosopher having held the position of 'ecumenical teacher' there, or indeed anywhere else. They provide no support for the suggestion that Stephanus moved from Alexandria to Constantinople (with or without the 'Collection Philosophique') and no grounds for locating Stephanus the Philosopher in the seventh century.[13] It follows

---

[9] Usener (n. 5 above), pp. 247–51.
[10] See *The History of Theophylact Simocatta*, trans. M. and M. Whitby (Oxford: Clarendon Press, 1986), pp. 3–5 and n. 7.
[11] Usener (n. 5 above), p. 251: 'His flosculis si praeter favorem imperatoris certa rei memoria exornatur, quod equidem existimo, significatur cathedram philosophiae imperialem a Phoca neglectam ab Heraclio instauratam esse inposito qui nomine dignus esset philosopho. Quod munus cui imperator dederit, iam liquet: Stephano Alexandria ab antiqua mathematon arce arcessito.'
[12] Mossman Rouché (n. 7 above), pp. 120–5.
[13] The further suggestion that Stephanus was the seventh century '*vardapet*' of Athens who, while in Constantinople, taught Tychikos, the teacher of the Armenian, Ananias of Shirak, will also have to be abandoned. See Wolska-Conus (n. 6 above), pp. 20–33.

that the titles provide no evidence that Stephanus the Philosopher was the author of the *Horoscope of Islam*, the treatise *On the Making of Gold*, or the astronomical handbook.

As for the *proem* to Theophylact's *Universal History*, this imaginary dialogue makes no mention of any philosopher, Stephanus or otherwise, or of the establishment of a new institution of education in Constantinople. The *proem* and its florid rhetorical style suggest nothing more than a literary *topos* for proclaiming the arrival of a golden age upon the accession of a new emperor.

With the non-philosophical evidence shown to be of no relevance, we are now able to consider the philosopher in the light of such evidence as we have for him as a philosopher, freed from the speculations regarding his association with astrology, alchemy, astronomy and seventh century Constantinople.[14] For Stephanus the Philosopher, the philosophical evidence is three-fold. First and foremost is his sole extant and undisputed commentary, the lectures on *De Interpretatione*. This is explicitly attributed to 'Stephanus the Philosopher' in *cod. Parisinus graecus 2064*, the unique tenth century manuscript that preserves it under the title: 'Notes with God's help from the voice (*apo phônês*) of Stephanus the philosopher on the *de Interpretatione* of Aristotle'.[15] To the evidence of this commentary, we can add the evidence of the fragments, mainly in the form of philosophical definitions that survive from his other works that are no longer extant. These have been preserved in *florilegia* and collections of definitions, principally in the seventh-eighth century anti-Monothelete *florilegium* known as the *Doctrina Patrum de Incarnatione Verbi*,[16] and also those recently published as *Horoi Kai Hypographai*.[17] Finally, there exist certain quotations and *testimonia* of Stephanus which give us information about the dissemination of his works and his influence in later centuries.

Identity

From the title preserved in cod. Paris gr. 2064 and the definitions attributed to him, his name was Stephanus and he was called simply 'philosopher' (*philosophos*). He is not given any toponymic such as 'of Alexandria' or 'of Athens', nor is he called 'sophist' or 'ecumenical teacher' or 'physician' or any other descriptive title such as the ones that we find associated with the non-philosophical texts that have been shown to be inauthentic. In the earliest references to him, a collection of definitions compiled by Maximus the Confessor (*ob*. 662 CE),[18] and the seventh-eighth century *Doctrina Patrum*, he is called

---

[14] Regarding the authorship of the medical commentaries that have been attributed to the philosopher, I remain agnostic other than to note that Adolf Lumpe's observations against such attributions continue to be pertinent and remain unaddressed. See Adolf Lumpe, 'Stephanos von Alexandrien', *Biographisch-Bibliographisches Kirchenlexikon* 10 (1995), 1406–9.

[15] Stephanus, *in Int.* (ed. Michael Hayduck, CAG 18.3), 1,1–2.

[16] Franz Diekamp, ed., *Doctrina Patrum de Incarnatione Verbi*, 2nd edn (Münster: Aschendorff, 1981), 249,12–266,5.

[17] Christiane Furrer-Pilliod, ed., *Horoi Kai Hypographai: Collections alphabétiques de définitions profanes et sacrées* (Città del Vaticano: Biblioteca Apostolica Vaticana, 2000).

[18] Mossman Roueché, 'The Definitions of Philosophy and a New Fragment of Stephanus the Philosopher', *Jahrbuch der Österreichischen Byzantinistik* 40 (1990), 107–28.

'Stephanus the Philosopher' (*Stephanos [ho] philosophos*). For this reason, and to distinguish him from the many others also called 'Stephanus', I propose that we should refer to him exclusively as 'Stephanus the Philosopher'.

This title, 'philosopher', and the evidence of his commentary on *De Interpretatione*, show that he was a teacher of philosophy and a commentator on Aristotle. His commentary was recorded in the form of notes (*scholia*) taken down by a *reportator* or student from oral lectures (*apo phônês*). It is presented in the highly structured format that characterises the commentaries of the later sixth century Alexandria, that is, of Olympiodorus and those usually referred to as his 'successors', Elias, David and Ps.-Elias. This format includes the formal division of the commentary into sections (*tmemata*), lectures (*praxeis*), continuous exposition (*theoria*), and detailed commentary (*lexis*).

From some of the remarks he makes in his commentary on *De Interpretatione* about the Egyptian language and alphabet, those lectures, and probably all his lectures, were delivered in Alexandria. For example, he says: 'There is one way of shaping letters with the Greeks and another with the Egyptians. And it is just the same way with words. The Greeks use one lot of words, say "horse" and "dog", the Egyptians and Romans another, and other nations other ones.' (*in Int.* 1,18–22).[19] And, again, 'And that thoughts and things are the same for everyone and on that account due to nature, is clear. An Egyptian does not have one thought concerning horses and a Greek another; they have the same.' (*in Int.* 1,25–7). Although these examples can trace their origin to Ammonius' commentary on *De Interpretatione*,[20] which Stephanus drew upon liberally,[21] it is unlikely that Stephanus would have repeated them unless they were of continued relevance to his own students, as well. There is nothing in the available evidence that suggests that he was, or had been, anywhere other than Alexandria.

His Teacher

Early in his commentary, Stephanus makes reference to 'our teacher' (*ho hêmeteros didaskalos* – *in Int.* 5,13 foll.) without revealing his identity. William Charlton suggested that this should be seen as a reference to Stephanus himself, taken down by the scribe who recorded the lectures *apo phônês*.[22]

The reference to 'our teacher' occurs in Stephanus' comments on *Int.* 16a4 (*in Int.* 5,1–19) where Aristotle speaks of the difference between 'spoken sounds' and 'things written', the latter being symbols of the former. There, Stephanus says, 'He (i.e., Aristotle) does well to say (*kalôs eipen*) "things written" (*ta graphomena*) as opposed to "letters" or "elements"'. Stephanus explains that what Aristotle said was *kalôs*

---

[19] William Charlton, *'Philoponus', On Aristotle On the Soul 3.9–13, with Stephanus, On Aristotle On Interpretation* (London: Duckworth, 2000), p. 117. I follow the translation of William Charlton, with occasional modifications.
[20] Ammonius, *in Int.* (ed. Adolf Busse, CAG 4.5), 19,9–15 and 30,32–5.
[21] Charlton (n. 19 above), p. 13.
[22] Ibid., p. 199, n. 16.

because it avoids the possible ambiguity (*anamphibolon*) that might arise from the primary and secondary senses in which 'letters' and 'elements' could be understood, had Aristotle used either of those terms instead. He concludes by ascribing this explanation to Ammonius: 'and so says the philosopher Ammonius' (*kai tauta men Ammonios ho philosophos*).

Stephanus goes on to report that his teacher raised two objections against Aristotle and Ammonius. The first objection is a pedantic, grammatical point concerning the way in which 'things written' is understood. He says, 'But our teacher says that Aristotle uses "things written" wrongly for "letters"'. Whereas Ammonius understood 'things written' as meaning 'things that have been written' or 'written things', i.e., 'words', Stephanus' teacher understood it as meaning 'things *being* written', in the sense of things in the process of coming to be but not yet in existence. If 'things written' do not yet exist, how can they be tokens of anything such as words? The teacher's second objection is an ill-tempered appeal to prior authority. He notes that a concern about possible ambiguities is not found in the commentaries of earlier philosophers and commentators. He asks, 'Whence can *they* demonstrate this (*pothen echousi deixai*) . . . ? None of the philosophers or interpreters of the past says this, nor does Alexander or Porphyry'.

The teacher's use of the third person plural, 'they', to describe those with whom he disagreed must be taken to mean Ammonius and his followers. It cannot include Stephanus because the teacher's rhetorical question is clearly addressed to his student, Stephanus. For Stephanus to have been intended as one of those with whom the teacher disagreed, the second person would have been used ('Whence can *you* demonstrate this . . . ?'). So, 'our teacher' cannot be a reference to Stephanus, as Charlton suggested, or Ammonius. The obvious candidate for 'our teacher' is the one who is well known to have regularly criticised Ammonius and for whom it would have been natural to raise a pedantic, grammatical objection: John Philoponus, the grammarian (*grammatikos*), is the one most likely to have been Stephanus' teacher. We know that Philoponus produced a commentary *In de Int.* that no longer survives. Ibn al-Nadīm gives a report of it in his *Kitāb al-Fihrist*[23] and Michael Psellos refers to it in his own *paraphrasis* of *De Interpretatione*.[24]

This is the only place in *in Int.* where Stephanus refers to 'our teacher' and strangely, he does so only to disagree with his pointless and deliberate misunderstanding of Aristotle's text. Why did he bother at all to record his teacher's views on what appears to be such an unimportant matter? And why did he refrain from revealing the identity of his teacher? Stephanus might have felt obliged to report his teacher's views at least once in the commentary out of respect for his teacher, but kept his teacher's identity hidden out of reluctance to publicise his disagreement with him. As we shall see, his disagreements with Philoponus undoubtedly extended beyond philosophical points to include the theological differences that Stephanus will have had with the Miaphysite

---

[23] F. E. Peters, *Aristoteles Arabus: The Oriental Translations and Commentaries on the Aristotelian Corpus* (Leiden: Brill, 1968), p. 12.
[24] Ammonius, *in Int.* (n. 20 above), xv–xvi.

(and, later, Tritheist) Philoponus.[25] In any case, his reticence also suggests that his teacher was still alive at the time the commentary was written.

The only other plausible candidate for Stephanus' 'teacher' is Olympiodorus, whose format of lecturing Stephanus follows. However he is unlikely to have been author of the sort of ill-tempered objections attributed by Stephanus to his teacher. Extracts from Olympiodorus' commentary *in Int.* are preserved as *scholia* in cod. Vat. Urb. gr. 35, but as Tarán observed, Stephanus' commentary exhibits no striking parallels, and at least one significant difference with these *scholia*. This would appear to rule out any student-teacher relationship.[26]

Religion and Philosophy

From his name it is generally assumed that he was a Christian, but there is not a great deal of evidence for this in his commentary on *De Interpretatione*. William Charlton observed some 'discreet de-paganising', particularly in Stephanus' treatment of theodicy and the problem of future contingents.[27] Henry Blumenthal suggested that the frequent use of the phrase 'with God's help' (*sun theôi*) to mark the end of sections in his lectures might be the sign that the author was a Christian.[28] This is not conclusive, however, because the pagan Olympiodorus also uses the same phrase to punctuate his lectures on the Platonic dialogues. There is more evidence of Christianity in the commentary *in De Anima 3*, a work that has frequently been claimed for Stephanus the Philosopher. However, Pantelis Golitsis[29] has shown that the commentary *in De Anima 3* is the work of John Philoponus, and not Stephanus, so the evidence of that commentary is irrelevant to the question of Stephanus' faith.

The strongest evidence of Stephanus' Christianity comes from the collection of definitions that forms Chapter 33 of the *Doctrina Patrum*. This collection bears the title: 'Definitions and descriptions (*horoi kai hypographai*) gathered from various writings' (*DP* 249,13-14) and begins with the statement: 'It is necessary to know that in the definitions that follow different symbols are used. They are the following:' (*DP* 249,15-6). What follows is a list of the names of various Church Fathers and philosophers from whose works the definitions were drawn (*DP* 249,17-24). Against each name is given a letter or combination of letters and these symbols are placed alongside many of the definitions in the collection to indicate their authorship. The Fathers so specified are: Gregory the Theologian, Basil, Gregory of Nyssa, Gregory the

---

[25] On Stephanus' Christianity, see below. He will have rejected both Philoponus' Miaphysite belief that Christ's nature was single, not double (human and divine), and his later Tritheist belief that the Christian Trinity was three godheads.

[26] Leonardo Tarán, ed., *Anonymous Commentary on Aristotle's De Interpretatione (Codex Parisinus Graecus 2064)* (Meisenheim am Glan: Hain, 1978), pp. xxv–xli (*scholia*), xiii and n. 20.

[27] Charlton (n. 19 above), p. 14, on Stephanus, *in Int.* 35,34–36,38.

[28] Henry Blumenthal, 'John Philoponus and Stephanus of Alexandria: Two Neoplatonic Christian Commentaries on Aristotle?', in D. J. O'Meara, ed., *Neoplatonism and Christian Thought* (Albany: State University of New York Press, 1982), pp. 54–63, at p. 61.

[29] See ch. 15 by Pantelis Golitsis in this volume.

Thumaturge, Anastasius of Antioch, Theodore of Raithu, Maximus ('the monk'), Leontius of Byzantium, Evagrius ('the accursed'), and Abba Mark ('the ascetic'). The final three in the list of authors are the following (*DP* 249,21–4):

ST (symbol) of Stephanus the philosopher (*Stephanou philosophou*)
EL (symbol) of Elias the philosopher (*Hêliou philosophou*)
I (symbol) of the pagan philosophers, such items as I found without attribution (*tôn exô philosophôn ta toiauta anepigrapha heuron*)

The inclusion of Stephanus and Elias in this list is highly significant. First, their presence shows that the compiler considered the names of Stephanus and Elias to be sufficiently important and well known to potential users of Chapter 33 for the authorship of their definitions to be identified. This also shows that the works from which their definitions were drawn were still available at the end of the seventh or the beginning of the eighth century when Chapter 33 of the *Doctrina Patrum* was compiled.[30] Secondly, the compiler categorises each of them as 'philosopher' (*philosophos*). This is in obvious and direct contrast to the category 'pagan philosophers' (*exô philosophoi*) which follows. It shows that the compiler, fully aware of the distinction between 'philosopher' and 'pagan philosopher', did not consider Stephanus and Elias to have been pagan philosophers. It follows that Stephanus and Elias were known to have been Christians. We can go further and observe that because their names and their definitions are preserved in an anti-Monothelete *florilegium*, and they are called 'philosophers' without qualification (e.g. not 'accursed' or 'pagan'), it follows that Stephanus and Elias were both considered to have been orthodox, that is, Chalcedonian Christians.[31] Final proof of Stephanus' acceptability to Chalcedonian theologians can be seen in the fact that Maximus, the most outstanding theologian of the seventh century, quotes one of his definitions of philosophy by name.[32]

The field of Christological debate in the sixth century was well populated with anti-Chalcedonian sophists named Stephanus and various attempts have been made to identify these with Stephanus the Philosopher.[33] There is a 'Stephanus the sophist' (*Stephanou tou sophistou*) who was visited by John Moschus and Sophronius, the future Chalcedonian Patriarch of Jerusalem, during a visit to Alexandria towards the end of the sixth century. In his *Pratum Spirituale*, John Moschus reports that the purpose of their visit was to debate with him (*hina praxômen*). This can only mean that

---

[30] I base this dating on the fact that the latest author to be included in Chapter 33 is Maximus the Confessor and that John Damascene is not included.
[31] The Council of Chalcedon orthodoxy opposed the concession that, although Christ's nature was double, his will was single. The inclusion of excerpts from Elias in the *Doctrina Patrum* provides independent evidence that Elias was a real person, and not just a Christian monastic name bestowed on an anonymous text, as suggested by Christian Wildberg in 'Three Neoplatonic Introductions to Philosophy: Ammonius, David and Elias', *Hermathena* 149 (1990), 33–51, at 42–5.
[32] See Roueché (n. 18 above), 110–13. This definition is discussed in detail below, pp. 550–51.
[33] For the most recent survey of these individuals, their theology and their possible relationships to one another, see Theresia Hainthaler, 'A Christological Controversy Among the Severans: IV: The Sophist Stephen of Alexandria', in *Christ in Christian Tradition 2.3: The Churches of Jerusalem and Antioch from 451 to 600* (Oxford: Oxford University Press, 2013), pp. 413–18.

they were seeking to convert him from his Miaphysitism.[34] There is another, sixth century 'Stephanus the sophist, also called Niobes' (*Stephanon ton sophistên, ton epiklên Niobên*) who is listed as the founder of a Miaphysite group, the Niobites, by Timothy of Constantinople in his *De Receptione Haereticorum*.[35] A third 'sophist of Alexandria named Stephanus' (*vir quidam sophista erat Alexandriae, Stephanus nomine*) is mentioned in the Chronicle of Dionysius of Tell-Mahre. He was an anti-Chalcedonian who was said to have debated with Probus and John Barbûr and to have temporarily converted them to his group.[36] Finally, there is a sixth century 'Stephanus surnamed Gobarus, a tritheist' whose *florilegium* Photius describes in his *Bibliotheca*.[37] The only thing that these Stephani have in common is their non-orthodoxy. However, as we have just seen, a defining feature of Stephanus the Philosopher was his Chalcedonian orthodoxy, so he cannot have been any of these other Stephani. Furthermore, in the philosophical evidence, he is never referred to as 'sophist' or 'tritheist' or anything other than 'philosopher'. As we shall see, Stephanus' philosophical commentaries were quarried by Chalcedonian Christian compilers of definitions (such as the compiler of Chapter 33 of the *Doctrina Patrum* and Maximus Confessor) for their useful definitions, but as Uthemann has argued, there is no evidence to suggest that his definitions derived from anything other than his philosophical works or that he participated in the Christological debate.[38]

Attitude to Suicide

An example of how Stephanus' Christian faith influenced his philosophy can be seen in the way he contributed to the debate regarding the acceptability of suicide. This is a topic that was regularly discussed in the *Prolegomena Philosophiae* when considering the definition of philosophy, 'practice of death' (*meletê thanatou*), in the context of Plato's ban on suicide. Olympiodorus, whose *Prolegomena Philosophiae* does not survive, believed that suicide could be justified in certain circumstances, whereas the Christian position (and that of Plato) was firmly against it. In his *Phaedo* commentary, Olympiodorus sets out the arguments for and against suicide and gives what is clearly his personal view on the matter in response to the rhetorical question 'what then is our own opinion?' (*ti oun hêmeis famen?*). His reply is: 'suicide is forbidden for the sake of the body and justified in certain cases for the sake of the soul.'[39] It is clear, however, that

---

[34] John Moschus, *Pratum Spirituale* (in *Patrologia Graeca* 87) 2929D.
[35] Timotheus Presbyter, *De Receptione Haereticorum* (in *Patrologia Graeca* 86) 65A.
[36] See the arguments of Theresia Hainthaler (n. 33 above), 414, in respect of his position as an anti-Chalcedonian.
[37] René Henry, ed., *Photius, Bibliothèque*, 9 vols (Paris: Les Belles Lettres, 1959–91), vol. 5, cod. 232, 67–79.
[38] So K. H. Uthemann, 'Stephanus von Alexandrien und die Konversion des Jakobiten Probos, des späteren Metropoliten von Chaklkedon: Ein Beitrag zur Rolle der Philosophie in der Kontroverstheologie des 6. Jahrhunderts', in C. Laga, J. A. Munitiz, and L. Van Rompay, eds, *After Chalcedon* (Leuven: Peeters, 1985), pp. 381–99, at pp. 389–99.
[39] L. G. Westerink, *The Greek Commentaries on Plato's Phaedo, Volume 1: Olympiodorus* (Amsterdam: North Holland Publishing, 1976), 1.9.

this personal view was not official school doctrine. What he considered to be the appropriate answer for beginning students is given in his discussion of the definition of philosophy, 'practice of death' in the *Prolegomena Philosophiae*.

David, expressing the Christian position, explains that the sort of death envisaged by the definition 'practice of death' is a voluntary death represented by virtuous living, and not the physical death that comes to us all. To illustrate this difference, he quotes Callimachus' epigram about a certain Cleombrotus who threw himself off the city walls in the mistaken belief that he was following Plato's words and 'practicing death'.[40] David reports Olympiodorus' response to this, also in the form of an epigram, rejecting this misinterpretation of Plato's words and affirming Plato's ban on suicide: 'Against this, Olympiodorus the philosopher said (*eipen*), "If the writing of Plato had not cut short my impulse, I would already have loosed the grievous baneful bond that binds my life".'[41] Here, Olympiodorus is expressing a school doctrine which he had no doubt developed out of concern for the sensitivities of his Christian students. Elias gives a virtually identical account, but attributes Olympiodorus' epigram to himself (Elias): 'But in reply to him I say (*phêmi*) these words, thus: "If the writing of Plato had not cut short my impulse, ... etc."'[42] Ps.-Elias is very similar to David and Elias but attributes Olympiodorus' epigram to philosophers in general: 'We say that (*phamen hoti*): "If the writing of Plato had not cut short my impulse, ... etc."'[43]

The differences between these passages confirm the likely chrononological order of these philosophers. The use of the first-person singular by Elias probably preserves the actual words of Olympiodorus, copied from the voice (*apo phônês*) of his *Prolegomena Philosophiae*, probably by Elias. David, writing in the third-person singular, represents a later version that preserves the attribution of the reply-epigram to Olympiodorus. Ps.-Elias, writing in the first-person plural, represents a yet later and more general report in which Olympiodorus' authorship of the epigram is no longer recalled. This is consistent with the original view of Westerink that Elias was a close pupil of Olympiodorus, David was later than Elias, whereas Ps.-Elias was the latest.[44]

David concludes his discussion of the suicide of Cleombrotus with the statement 'In order that there should not be many Cleombroti, let us add (*prosthômen*) to the definition something that preserves its meaning (*sêmasia*) and define it thus: philosophy is practice of death while the living being is preserved (*tou zôou sôzômenou*).' (David, 32,5–7). Ps.-Elias reports similarly: 'In order that there should not be many Cleombroti, it is necessary to add (*prostheinai*) something to the definition while preserving its intent (*ennoia*) and say it is thus: philosophy is practice of death while the living being is preserved (*tou zôou sunistamenou*)' (Ps.-Elias 12,38–9).

---

[40] This epigram is first used by Ammonius in his *Prolegomena Philosophiae* (ed. Adolph Busse, CAG 4.3), 4,18–28.
[41] David, *in Isag.* (ed. Adolf Busse, CAG 18.2), 31,23–32,8.
[42] Elias, *in Isag.* (ed. Adolf Busse, CAG 18.1), 14,1–14.
[43] L. G. Westerink, ed., *Pseudo Elias (Pseudo David) Lectures on Porphyry's Isagoge* (Amsterdam: North Holland Publishing, 1967), 12,1–39.
[44] L. G. Westerink, 'The Alexandrian Commentators and the Introductions to their Commentaries', in Richard Sorabji, ed., *Aristotle Transformed: The Ancient Commentators and Their Influence* (London: Duckworth, 1990), pp. 325–48, at pp. 336–40.

Stephanus' *Prolegomena Philosophiae* is no longer extant but we can be sure that he reported Olympiodorus' reply-epigram similarly. This is clear from a fragment from his *Prolegomena Philosophiae* preserved in the collection of definitions compiled by Maximus the Confessor. It shows that he too supplemented the definition, 'practice of death': 'Philosophy is practice of death. Stephanus the Philosopher added (*prosethêken*) to the definition, after the words "practice of death", "while the living being is still (*eti*) preserved (*eti tou zôou sunistamenou*)".'[45] What is most significant here is that Stephanus is explicitly remembered for having been the origin of this supplement to the definition. Clearly, this was his innovation, and David and Ps.-Elias followed him in their own versions. The purpose of the supplement was obviously to make Olympiodorus' prohibition of suicide yet more explicit for Christian students. This would ensure that 'practice of death' could not be misunderstood and remained an acceptable definition of philosophy, along with the other five definitions, for Christian students. It shows how the *Prolegomena Philosophiae* was subtly 'Christianised' by Stephanus, and it is no doubt for this reason that Stephanus' definition of philosophy was preserved by Maximus the Confessor.

Elias does not propose any supplement to the traditional definition, so the supplement must post-date him and his teacher, Olympiodorus. The supplements of David, Ps.-Elias and Stephanus are virtually identical, except for David's use of *sôzômenou* in place of the equivalent *sunistamenou* used by Stephanus and Ps.-Elias. It has been suggested that Stephanus and Ps.-Elias were the same person and that their common use of *sunistamenou* in the supplement was further evidence of this. However, it has recently been shown that they could not have been the same person.[46] One significant difference between the three can be seen in Stephanus' use of the adverb 'still' (*eti*) which the texts of Ps.-Elias and David both lack. Stephanus' version clearly preserves the *lectio difficilior* which shows that the supplement originated with him. It follows, therefore, that if Stephanus was the source of the supplement for Ps.-Elias and David, his discussion of 'practice of death' will have been very similar to those of Ps.-Elias and David, that is, it must have included the Cleombrotus epigram and Olympiodorus' reply-epigram. It is unlikely that Stephanus would have followed Elias or David in presenting the reply-epigram explicitly as the work of Olympiodorus. Like Ps.-Elias, he probably attributed it explicitly to philosophers (i.e. Christians) in general. Returning to the relative chronological order of Olympiodorus and his successors, Stephanus' supplement to the definition allows us to place him directly after Olympiodorus and Elias, who do not have the supplement, and ahead of David and Ps.-Elias who do.

Date

Following Usener, it has been customary to place the first half of Stephanus' life in Alexandria and the latter half of his life in Constantinople, during the reign of

---

[45] Roueché (n. 18 above), p. 112.
[46] Roueché (n. 7 above), pp. 125–38.

Heraclius. This made him one of the last, if not *the* last of the successors of Olympiodorus. We have now seen that Usener's dating must be abandoned. There are no grounds at all to locate Stephanus the Philosopher during the reign of Heraclius. We have also seen that John Philoponus is likely to have been Stephanus' teacher. By the way in which he dealt with the question of suicide, Stephanus came after Olympiodorus and Elias, and was the common source of Ps.-Elias and David. Therefore, we must necessarily locate him in the mainstream of philosophical activity in sixth century Alexandria.

Philoponus is thought to have commenced his career as a philosophical commentator as early as *c.* 515 CE and to have continued until *c.* 550 CE.[47] After that, he appears to have occupied himself exclusively with theological debate until his death sometime after 565 CE. It follows that Stephanus could have studied the *De Interpretatione* with Philoponus at any time prior to the middle of the sixth century. If we can make the plausible assumption that Stephanus was at least 20 years old when he studied with Philoponus, then his birth will have occurred before 530 CE and his death will have occurred towards the end of the sixth century. If we are correct in believing that Philoponus was still alive when Stephanus gave his lectures on *De Interpretatione*, then these lectures will have been delivered sometime during the period 550 CE and *c.* 565 CE. This period is consistent with Stephanus' adoption of the structured lecturing format that was developed by Olympiodorus, who is considered to have been the head of the school in Alexandria from *c.* 535 CE until his death in *c.* 570 CE.[48] It is also consistent with the evidence that Stephanus followed Olympiodorus and Elias and preceded David and Ps.-Elias.

Philosophical Commentaries

We can now turn to a consideration of the evidence of the definitions and citations relating to Stephanus' lost works to ascertain the scope of his philosophical teaching. By identifying the commentaries from which this evidence will have come, it is possible to determine which lectures Stephanus will have given. And by comparing his definitions with those in the commentaries of others, we can gain an idea of the other philosophers whom he influenced and by whom he was influenced. The majority of these fragments are preserved in the *Doctrina Patrum*, as described above. Others come from the related collections of definitions presented in Furrer-Pilliod's *Horoi Kai Hypographoi*. In addition, there is the definition of philosophy that we have just discussed from Maximus the Confessor's collection of definitions, an extract from his commentary *in De Caelo* and two extracts preserved in Oriental sources.

It is beyond the scope of this paper to study in detail all of this evidence. It will be sufficient for these purposes to identify the commentaries that are attributable to Stephanus on the basis of these definitions and citations. In some cases, where the

---

[47] So K. Verrycken, 'John Philoponus', in Lloyd P. Gerson, ed., *The Cambridge History of Philosophy in Late Antiquity*, 2 vols (Cambridge: Cambridge University Press, 2010), vol. 2, pp. 733–4.

[48] So Christian Wildberg, 'Olympiodorus', in E. Zalta, ed., *The Stanford Encyclopedia of Philosophy*, Fall 2008 Edition (n. 2 above).

similarities with other texts are of particular interest, textual parallels will be given. From the evidence we have examined thus far, we should expect to find that the majority of Stephanus' definitions have counterparts in the commentaries of Elias, David and Ps.-Elias. What is unexpected is to discover that some show that they were influenced by the commentaries of Simplicius and were re-used in the *Dialectica* of John Damascene.

Logic: *Prolegomena Philosophiae*

We have seen from the definition of philosophy preserved by Maximus the Confessor that Stephanus lectured on the *Prolegomena Philosophiae*. A discussion of the traditional definitions of philosophy was a regular part of the *Prolegomena Philosophiae*. Another topic that was regularly discussed in the *Prolegomena Philosophiae* was 'division' (*diairesis*) and its various types. An extract from Stephanus' *Prolegomena Philosophiae* discussing the types of division is preserved in the Syriac *Dialogues* of Severus bar Shakko, a Syrian monk active near Mosul during the thirteenth century. Severus presents six types (*tropoi*) of division, like Elias, but unlike David and Ps.-Elias who report eight types. Severus continues:

> But some also add to these a seventh *tropos* of division, namely from species to individual, and Stephanus the philosopher from Alexandria ruled this out, when he said, 'as a rule, every division, however comprehensive it may be, always divides into three subdivisions, and once in a while even up to four. But the division of species to individual is infinite (in subdivisions) – because the individuals are infinite and comprise the human species and are beyond comprehension – and instead we could call it a kind of enumeration rather than a division.'[49]

Where Stephanus was very similar to David and Ps.-Elias in his discussion of 'practice of death' he differs from them in the *tropoi* of division that he admits. Instead, he follows Elias in allowing just six *tropoi*. But Elias does not raise and reject the possibility of a seventh type of division so it would appear that this is another post-Elias innovation of Stephanus. The only other author to reject division 'from species to individuals' in this way is John Damascene. In his discussion of division in the *Dialectica*, he makes the same point using language that is very similar to that of Stephanus:

> But some rule out division from species to individuals saying rather that it is an enumeration. For every division results in two or three or very rarely in four [subdivisions]. But the species is divided into [things] infinite in number. For men taken severally are infinite in number.[50]

---

[49] Anton Baumstark, *Aristoteles bei den Syrern vom 5. bis 8. Jahrhundert* (Leipzig: Teubner, 1900), 196,35–41.
[50] Bonifatius Kotter, *Die Schriften des Johannes von Damaskos I* (Berlin: De Gruyter, 1969), *Recensio fusior* 6,125–32. For a detailed comparison of these texts and those of David and Ps.-Elias, see Mossman Roueché (n. 7 above), pp. 125–38.

The similarity between the two texts is remarkable but not surprising, given the way in which the *Dialectica* was composed. We know from John Damascene himself that the *Dialectica* was compiled from the works of others although nowhere does he reveal his sources.[51] Thanks to Severus, we can see that in this case, his source was the *Prolegomena Philosophiae* of Stephanus.

Severus' quotation of this one extract from Stephanus' *Prolegomena Philosophiae* does not, however, require us to conclude that he made use of a Syriac translation of the entire commentary, as Baumstark suggested.[52] This is the only place in the *Dialogues* where Stephanus is quoted, and it is more likely that Severus, like John Damascene, made use of a compilation of excerpts, drawn from a variety of sources and translated into Syriac, one of which included Stephanus' comments on the seventh *tropos* of division.[53] This quotation from Stephanus' *Prolegomena Philosophiae* is an example of the sort of text that was put into *florilegia* and compendia, and its use by both Severus and John Damascene shows the variety of uses to which they were put.

Logic: Porphyry's *Isagôgê*

The *Prolegomena philosophiae* was the standard introduction to a commentary on Porphyry's *Isagôgê* (*Introduction*). All extant commentaries on the *Isagôgê* (i.e. those of Ammonius, Elias, David, and Ps.-Elias) are preceded by a *Prolegomena philosophiae* and it would have been unusual for Stephanus not to have produced one. Direct evidence of such a commentary can be seen in the three definitions of 'difference' (*diaphora*) attributed to Stephanus in the *Horoi Kai Hypographai*.[54] *Diaphora* is one of the so-called 'quinque voces' (five terms) that are the subject of the *Isagôgê*.

Logic: *Categories*

That Stephanus gave lectures on the *Categories* has long been recognised from the cross-reference he makes to them in his commentary *in Int.*: 'Things are called "first" in five ways, as we have already learnt previously in the *Categories*' (*hôs êdê phthasantes en tais Katêgoriais memathêkamen*).[55] A commentary on the *Categories*, attributed to 'Stephanus the Alexandrian' (*Istifan al-Iskandarāni*), is also cited by Ibn al-Nadīm in his *Kitāb al-Fihrist*.[56]

The following definitions are taken from this commentary and preserved in Chapter 33 of the *Doctrina Patrum*: 'sect' (*hairesis*, DP 251,16–7), 'common notion'

---

[51] Ibid., *Prooemium* 60: 'I say nothing of my own, so to speak' (*erô de emon men, hôs ephên, ouden*).
[52] Baumstark (n. 49 above), pp. 186–7.
[53] Cf. Hans Daiber, 'Ein vergessener Syrischer Text: Bar Zo'bī über die Teile der Philosophie', *Oriens Christianus* 69 (1985), 73–80, who concludes that Baumstark overstated the influence of Stephanus (and John Philoponus) on Severus' *Dialogues*.
[54] *Horoi Kai Hypographoi* (n. 17 above), Collection A, *d*28.
[55] Stephanus, *in Int.* (n. 15 above) 2,11–12; see also 21,5–10.
[56] Peters (n. 23 above), p. 7.

(*koinê ennoia*, DP 251,18-9), 'supposition' (*thesis*, DP 251,19-22), 'state' (*hexis*, DP 259,7-8), 'condition' (*diathesis*, DP 259,8-9), and 'quality' (*poiotês*, DP 264,22-3). A definition of 'potential' or 'capacity' (*dunamis*, DP 202,8-16) is given separately in Chapter 28.vi of the *Doctrina Patrum* (202,8-16) and the definition of 'common' (*koinon*, HH Collection A, k40) is found in the Furrer-Pilliod's *Horoi Kai Hypographai*. This is the largest number of definitions attributed to Stephanus to come from a single source and that may be a sign of the importance that was attached to his commentary in the sixth and seventh centuries.

The first three of these definitions, which are given as a group in the *Doctrina Patrum*, are of particular interest because they demonstrate Stephanus' use of multiple sources for the same definition, and provide further evidence of subsequent re-use by John Damascene in his *Dialectica*.

> Stephanus' version:
> ST(ephanus). Sect (*hairesis*) is an opinion of many persons in agreement with one another but in disagreement with others. Common notion (*koinê ennoia*) is what is agreed by all. Thesis (*thesis*) is a paradoxical supposition of someone renowned in philosophy, such as the saying of Parmenides that what is is one, and such as the saying of Heraclitus that everything is in motion.[57]

In Elias' commentary on the *Categories*, we find this same trio of definitions in his discussion of the origins of the names of traditional schools (i.e. 'sects') of philosophy. This was traditionally the first topic covered in the standard introductions to Aristotle with which the commentaries on the *Categories* began.

> Elias' Version:
> A sect is an opinion of a group of men in agreement with one another but in disagreement with others. He spoke well saying 'men' and not 'a man' for the opinion of one man does not make a sect. Instead, a thesis then comes about, as that of Heraclitus who said that everything is in motion, or that of Parmenides who said what is is one and motionless (*akinêton*), or that of Antisthenes who said that contradiction is impossible. A thesis is a paradoxical supposition of someone renowned in philosophy ... if people are in agreement with one another and also with others that does not make a sect but the opposite of a sect, that is, a common notion.[58]

Stephanus' three definitions are very similar to those of Elias and certainly must have come from the analogous introductory section of his own commentary on the *Categories*. Elias is the only other commentator on the *Categories* to present this trio of definitions. They do not appear in the commentaries of Ammonius, John Philoponus or Olympiodorus or Simplicius. This suggests that the presentation of the three

---

[57] *Doctrina Patrum* (n. 16 above), ch. 33, 251,16-22.
[58] Elias, *in Cat.* (n. 42 above) 108,21-31.

definitions in this context was an innovation of Elias that Stephanus in turn took up. The differences between Elias and Stephanus principally lie in the order in which the three definitions are given and the examples given for a thesis. Elias clearly gives the fuller account, from which Stephanus' version is likely to have been derived.

In his commentary on *De Interpretatione*, Stephanus gives the same definition of a thesis, but with a different version of the example of Heraclitus. That example is derived not from his *Categories* commentary, but from the commentary *in Int.* of Ammonius, as the following comparison shows:

> Stephanus' *in Int.* Version:
> A paradoxical supposition of someone renowned in philosophy is called a *thesis*, like Heraclitus's saying that all things that are, are in motion and partake of no motionlessness (*kai staseôs mêdemias metechein*), or again, Parmenides' saying that what is is one.[59]

> Ammonius' *in Int.* Version:
> And we also call the paradoxical suppositions of someone renowned in philosophy about familiar things *theses*, for example, that everything is in motion and the things that are partake in no way of motionlessness (*kai staseôs mêdamôs ta onta metechein*) as Heraclitus said, or that what is is one, as Parmenides thought.[60]

We have seen that in his commentary on the *Categories*, Stephanus followed Elias as his general model for the trio of definitions and for two of Elias' three examples of thesis (Parmenides and Heraclitus, but not Antisthenes). We can now see that in his commentary on *De Interpretatione* he used a different version of Heraclius' thesis that derived from Ammonius. That he did not follow Ammonius in his commentary *in Cat.* shows that Stephanus composed his commentary *in Cat.* prior to composing his *in Int.* It also shows that in his commentary *in Int.*, Stephanus preferred to follow Ammonius rather than to re-use what he had previously taken from Elias.

Finally, we should note that Stephanus's version of the three definitions also reappears unattributed and virtually *verbatim* in the *Dialectica* of John Damascene. The definitions are given in the same order and with the same examples as in Stephanus' version and must have originated in Stephanus' *Categories* commentary.

> John Damascene's Version
> Sect (*hairesis*) is an opinion of many persons in agreement with one another but in disagreement with others. Common notion (*koinê ennoia*) is what is agreed by all, as, for example, that the sun exists. Thesis (*thesis*) is a paradoxical supposition of someone renowned in philosophy, that is, a strange notion, such as the saying of

---

[59] Stephanus, *in Int.* (n. 15 above) 2,17–20.
[60] Ammonius, *in Int.* (n. 20 above), 9,10–13. This definition of *thesis* can trace its origin to Aristotle (*Topics* 104b), who gives Heraclitus, Antisthenes, and Melissa as examples.

Parmenides that what is is one, and such as the saying of Heraclitus that everything is in motion.[61]

Another example of Stephanus' reliance on the commentary of a predecessor is his definition of 'common' (*koinon*). His definition is predictably similar to that given in Elias' commentary, and it also appears virtually *verbatim* in the *Dialectica* of John Damascene. Most importantly, however, it is virtually identical to one given by Simplicius in his commentary *in Cat.*.

Simplicius is generally considered to have lived from *c.* 480 to 560 CE.[62] His commentaries were probably written sometime before the middle of the sixth century, following his return from Persia in the 530s. Where he settled and where the commentaries were written is unknown but it is thought that he did not return to Athens or Alexandria. Stephanus will have made use of Simplicius' *in Cat.* and *in Cael.* (see below) in Alexandria during the second half of the sixth century, so copies of those commentaries must have been brought to Alexandria at that time and kept in a library or one of the schools. We have no evidence as to who requested the copies of Simplicius' commentaries; it may have been Stephanus himself as he seems to have been the only one to make use of Simplicius' commentaries. That Stephanus, a Christian, was confident to make use of Simplicius' commentaries shows the wide range of philosophical thinking that Alexandria was prepared to tolerate in the second half of the sixth century.

The versions of Stephanus, Simplicius, Elias, and John Damascene are given below:

Stephanus' version:
ST(ephanus). Common is spoken of in four ways: Either it refers to something that is divisible into parts, such as land that is divided into lots (*klêrouchoumenê gê*); or something that, being indivisible, is taken into common usage, but not simultaneously, such as one slave or one horse of two masters; or something that becomes private by prior reservation (*en prokatalêpsei idiopoioumenon*) but returns to common use, such as a seat in the theatre or a place at the baths; or something that, being indivisible, is proposed to the same common consideration, such as the voice of a herald.[63]

Simplicius' version:
Again, 'common' is also spoken of in many ways. For either it refers to something that is divisible into parts, such as land that is divided into lots (*klêrouchoumenê gê*); or something that, being indivisible, is available for common use but not simultaneously, such as a common slave or horse; or something that becomes

---

[61] John Damascene (n. 50 above), *Recensio fusior* 65,60–5.
[62] So Han Baltussen, 'Simplicius of Cilicia', in Lloyd P. Gerson, ed., *The Cambridge History of Philosophy in Late Antiquity*, 2 vols (Cambridge: Cambridge University Press, 2010), vol. 2, pp. 711–32, at pp. 711–2.
[63] *Horoi Kai Hypographai* (n. 17 above), Recension A *k*40, Recension C, *k*6. A seat in the theatre is originally a Stoic example of what can be (temporarily) mine, yet common, so Chrysippus *ap.* Cicero, *Fin.* 3.67 and many subsequent Stoics. See Richard Sorabji, *Gandhi and the Stoics* (Oxford: Oxford University Press, 2012), pp. 170–4.

private by prior reservation (*en prokatalêpsei idiopoioumenon*) but subsequently returns to common use such as a theatre (seat); or something that, being indivisible, is brought into the use of many, such as the voice.[64]

Elias' version:
Common is understood in four ways: Either something partaken of indivisibly, such as a common flute or slave, or something partaken of divisibly, such as a field or house, or something used personally from prior reservation, such as a common seat in a theatre that becomes personal as a result of prior reservation (*prokatalambanontos*), or something partaken of equally such as the word of a herald (for that is equally partaken of by all).[65]

John Damascene's version:
Common is spoken of in four ways: Either it refers to something that is divisible into parts, such as land that is divided into lots (*klêrouchoumenê gê*); or something that, being indivisible is taken into common usage, but not simultaneously, such as one slave or one horse of two masters now carrying out the orders at one time of one and at another time of the other; or something that becomes private by prior reservation (*en prokatalêpsei idiopoioumenon*) but returns to common use, such as a seat in the theatre or a place at the baths; or something that, being indivisible, is proposed to the same common consideration, such as the voice of the herald.[66]

Another instance in which Stephanus appears to have been influenced by Simplicius is his definition of 'potential' or 'capacity' (*dunamis*). Discussions of this term are regularly found in the extant commentaries on the *Categories* in connection with the various species of 'quality' (*poiotês*) but only Stephanus and Simplicius provide six different ways in which *dunamis* can be understood. Some of the examples that they use are unique to the two authors and show that, once again, Stephanus must have consulted a copy of Simplicius' commentary *in Cat.*.[67]

Logic: *De Interpretatione*

In his *Kitāb al-Fihrist*, Ibn al-Nadīm mentions a commentary (or possibly an 'epitome': *jawāmi'*) *in Int.* by 'Stephanus' (*Istifan*).[68] If this is a reference to the extant Greek version of his commentary, it is likely to be the one that Abū al-Faraj 'Abd Allāh Ibn al-Ṭayyib, the tenth/eleventh century Muslim philosopher, quotes in his commentary on Porphyry's *Isagôgê*. He writes: 'Stephanus (*Istifan*) says: the division of Existence is not like the

---

[64] Simplicius, *in Cat.* (ed. K. KalbFleisch, CAG 8) 26,11–15.
[65] Elias, *in Cat.* 138,12–18.
[66] John Damascene *Dialectica* (n. 50 above), *Recensio fusior* 65,67–73.
[67] On *dunamis*, compare Stephanus in *Doctrina Patrum*, Chapter 28.iv (p. 202) (n. 16 above) with Simplicius, *in Cat.* (n. 64 above) 225,1–14.
[68] Peters (n. 23 above), p. 12.

division of an equivocal name inasmuch as the meanings signified by an equivocal name are neither prior nor posterior. But substance is prior to accident.'[69] Kwame Gyekye observed that this is a reference to Stephanus in Int. 17,25–8: 'For thus Porphyry also in the Isagôgê says that 'being' (or existence) is predicated homonymously, although it has been demonstrated that "being" is not predicated homonymously – since there is in it priority and posteriority – but ambiguously.'[70] The significance of Ibn al-Tayyib's report of Stephanus' comment is that it shows that Stephanus' extant commentary in Int. must have been available in Arabic translation in the tenth/eleventh century.

Logic: *Analytics* and *Sophistical Refutations*

As noted by Hayduck, there is evidence that commentaries by Stephanus on the *Analytics* and *Sophistical Refutations* may have once existed but are now no longer extant.[71] A work described as: '*Scholia* of Stephanus the philosopher on the second book of the *Prior Analytics* – last part is missing (*ateles*)' is recorded in a list of Greek manuscripts compiled by John Lascaris, the sixteenth century collector.[72] In the catalogues of the Greek manuscripts that passed into the Escorial Library following the death of Diego Hurtado de Mendoza in 1575, there is mention of a 'Commentary of Stephanus the philosopher on the second book of the Prior Analytics' and also 'Commentaries on the *Prior* and *Posterior* (*Analytics*) and (*Sophistical*) *Refutations* of Stephanus the philosopher: a rare book'. The first of these would appear to be a copy of the text recorded by Lascaris; the Escorial manuscripts were destroyed in the fire of 1671.[73] For the present purposes, it is sufficient to see these references as an indication that Stephanus will have lectured on the final books of the *Organon*.

De Caelo

A final example of Simplicius' influence upon Stephanus can be seen in the excerpt from his commentary on *De Caelo*.[74] This exists in two copies. The first is found in cod.

---

[69] Kwame Gyekye, *Arabic Logic: Ibn al-Tayyib's Commentary on Porphyry's Eisagoge* (Albany: State University of New York Press, 1979), p. 82, and commentary n. 86.
[70] Both translations are by Gyekye; cf. Charlton (n. 19 above), p. 135.
[71] Stephanus, *in Int.* (n. 15 above), vi.
[72] K. Müller, 'Neue Mittheilungen über Janos Laskaris und die Mediceische Bibliothek', *Zentralblatt für Bibliothekswesen* 1 (1884), 395. This is reported as '*Scholia* of Stephanus the Philosopher of Alexandria on the first book of the *Second Analytics*' by E. Piccolomini, in 'Due Documenti relativi ad acquisiti di codici greci, fatti da Giovanni Lascaris per conto di Lorenzo de' Medici', *Rivista di filologia e d'instruzione classica* 2 (1874), 407.
[73] Gregorio de Andrés, 'La biblioteca de Don Diego Hurtado de Mendoza (1576)', in *Documentos para la historia del Monasterio de San Lorenzo el Real de El Escorial* 7 (Madrid: Sáez, 1964), p. 398 (MS no. 144; formerly Z-VI-26) and also, Gregorio de Andrés, *Catálogo de los códices griegos desaparecidos de la Real Biblioteca de El Escorial* (San Lorenzo de El Escorial: Imprenta del Monasterio, 1968), p. 59 (MS B.V.1). I am grateful to Peter Riedlberger for his kind assistance with these references. See his *Domninus of Larissa, Encheiridion and Spurious Works* (Pisa: Fabrizio Serra Editore, 2013), pp. 67–8.
[74] The existence of this text was originally reported by Usener, (n. 5 above), 253.

Vat. Ottobon. gr. 45 and was published by C.A. Brandis in 1836 in his *Scholia in Aristotelem*.[75] The second is quoted by Symeon Seth, the eleventh century Byzantine scholar, in his *Conspectus rerum naturalium*.[76] The excerpt concerns an *aporia* that is raised to argue that there is space beyond the finite limit of the heavens.

> Stephanus' version:
> The Alexandrian Stephanus interpreting the treatise *De Caelo* raised a new difficulty concerning 'place' saying, 'If we suppose someone ascends up to the highest part of the heavens and tries to extend his hand outside the heavens, then pushing, his hand will go out from below or it will be prevented from going out. And if we say that it goes out, then there will be some place there that is empty and capable of receiving a body. And if it does not go out, there will be at that place some body that is striking against it and preventing his hand from going out.'

The same *aporia*, this time attributed to the Stoics, is reported by Simplicius in his *De Caelo* commentary.

> Simplicius' version:
> The Stoics, however, wanted there to be a void outside the heavens, and they established this through the following supposition. Suppose, they say, someone stands at the extremity of the sphere of the fixed (stars) and extends his hand upwards. If he does extend it, they infer that there is something outside the heavens into which he extends it; but if he cannot extend it, there will be something outside in such a way as to prevent his hand's extension. And if he then stands at the limit of this and extends, then the same question (recurs). For something will be shown to exist outside this, as well.[77]

From the foregoing, we can be certain that Stephanus wrote commentaries on the entire *Organon* and *De Caelo*. In his *Prolegomena Philosophiae*, he followed the style and content of the commentaries of Olympiodorus and his successors. However, in the case of his commentary on the *Categories* and *De Caelo*, he appears to have made use of the commentaries of Simplicius, as well.

Influence

Stephanus' importance as a philosopher lies in three areas. The first is in the classroom in Alexandria from his position as a philosophical lecturer. He clearly had an active

---

[75] C. A. Brandis, *Scholia in Aristotelem* (Berlin: Reimer, 1836), 467,36–43.
[76] A. Delatte, *Anecdota Atheniensia et alia*, II (Liège and Paris: Faculté de Philosophie et Lettres de l'Université de Liège, 1939), 63,6–14 sq. The translation follows this text.
[77] Simplicius, *in Cael.* 284,28–285,2 (trans. R. J. Hankinson, *Simplicius, On Aristotle On the Heavens 1.5–9* (London: Duckworth, 2004), p. 108). Simplicius discusses the same problem, connecting it initially with the still earlier Pythagorean Archytas, in his commentary on Aristotle's *Physics*, 467,26–468,3. See Richard Sorabji, *Matter, Space, and Motion* (London: Duckworth, 1988), pp. 125–7.

teaching career. We have seen that at the very least, he lectured on virtually the entire *Organon* and the *De Caelo*. This is a considerably wider range of texts than is attested for Elias, David, or Ps.-Elias. It provides welcome confirmation that a full logic curriculum remained available in Alexandria in the second half of the sixth century and it shows that his contribution to philosophical teaching has been consistently underestimated. For the most part, it is impossible to assess the impact he had as a teacher because there is little in the way of contemporary reports of this activity. Charlton has remarked on Stephanus' particular liking for order and clarity and what has impressed that twentieth century commentator no doubt impressed students and compilers of definitions in the sixth century as well.[78] Clarity was no doubt a major factor when it came to choosing definitions for *florilegia*. Equally important was the influence that he had on David and Ps.-Elias in Christianising the school teaching concerning suicide. It had clearly become a matter of considerable contemporary interest whether 'practice of death' was an acceptable definition of philosophy for Christians.

Secondly, his importance lies in the influence that his various philosophical definitions, extracted from his commentaries and circulated in *florilegia* and collections of definitions, had upon seventh century and eighth century theologians. The circulation of these useful definitions ensured that the works of Stephanus the Philosopher probably reached a wider public, and for a longer period, than the bulky commentaries of his better-known contemporaries. They demonstrate that his influence reached the most outstanding theologians of the seventh and eighth centuries, Maximus the Confessor and John Damascene. The definitions of Stephanus are a prime example of how the philosophy of Alexandria became available to Christian theologians in the sixth and seventh centuries.

Thirdly, the influence of Stephanus' writings outside the Greek-speaking world can be readily seen in the translations that were made of them into Arabic and Syriac and their use by Arabic and Syriac scholars. In the Arabic tradition, two of his commentaries, *in Int.* and *in Cat.* were known to Ibn al-Nadīm in the tenth century, although it is not clear whether they had been completely translated. An Arabic translation of Stephanus' commentary *in Int.* was also known and used in the tenth/eleventh century by Ibn al-Ṭayyib who quotes him in his own *Categories* commentary.

In the Syriac tradition, there is evidence that Stephanus' commentary *in Int.* may have influenced Probus, the sixth century Syriac translator and commentator of Aristotle.[79] Elio Montanari has observed that Probus' commentary on *De Interpretatione* appears to follow the Alexandrian model and exhibits certain parallels with that of Stephanus.[80]

---

[78] Charlton (n. 19 above), pp. 6, 12–15. This may be one reason why his definitions were considered desirable.

[79] It has been suggested that this Probus might have been the companion of John Barbûr, who debated with the sophist named Stephanus (cf. pp. 548–9 above). See S. P. Brock, 'The Commentator Probus: Problems of Date and Identity', in Josef Lössl and J. W. Watt, eds, *Interpreting the Bible and Aristotle in Late Antiquity* (Farnham: Ashgate, 2011), pp. 195–206, at p. 206 and n. 41, and Daniel King, 'Why Were the Syrians Interested in Greek Philosophy?', in Philip Wood, ed., *History and Identity in the Late Antique Near East* (Oxford: Oxford University Press, 2013), pp. 61–82, at p. 63 and n. 9.

[80] Elio Montanari, *Le sezione linguistica del Peri Hermeneias di Aristotle* (Firenze: Università degli studi di Firenze, 1984), vol. 1, p. 90: 'Le coincidenze fra Probo e Stefano sono numerosissime ed assai significative.'

Henri Huggonnard-Roche has cautioned, however, that the parallels are not as numerous nor as significant as Montanari has suggested.[81] Nevertheless, such parallels as there are could be an indication of early Syriac interest in Stephanus and his commentary.

At the beginning of the ninth century, the East Syrian patriarch, Timothy I wrote (in Letter 19) to Sergius, the Metropolitan of Elam, asking him to provide him with a list of the books in the monastery of Mar Zina. He comments, 'perhaps you will find among them the commentary of Olympiodorus on the books of the logic or of Stephanus or of Sergius or of Alexander'.[82] At the very least, Timothy's words show that memory of Stephanus' commentaries on the *Organon* was still very much alive at that date in the Syrian world. That Timothy can refer to them in the same breath as the commentaries of Alexander and Olympiodorus suggests that it was Stephanus' quality as a philosopher, rather than merely his Christianity, that made those commentaries desirable to Timothy. Finally, in the thirteenth century, we have seen that Severus bar Shakko considered it worthwhile to quote Stephanus in his *Dialogues*. Although it is unlikely that a complete translation of Stephanus' *Prolegomena Philosophiae* was available to Severus, an excerpt was available to him probably via a compendium of extracts and definitions.

Conclusions

The evidence offered by Usener for the establishment of an imperial institution of education during the reign of Heraclius is now known to have been anachronistic and therefore of no value to his hypothesis. There is no evidence that Stephanus the Philosopher was called to Constantinople by Heraclius or that he took up a teaching post there. There is no evidence that Stephanus the Philosopher carried the 'Collection Philosophique' from Alexandria to Constantinople. Once we recognise that there is no evidence that ties Stephanus the Philosopher to Constantinople in the seventh century, it follows that he could not have been the polymath author of the non-philosophical works that have been attributed to him. When we consider him in this light and purely on the basis of the philosophical evidence, we see a totally different figure.

What emerges is a philosopher at the centre of philosophical teaching in late sixth century Alexandria. His teaching activity covered all of the *Organon*, including Porphyry's *Isagôgê*, and *De Caelo*. He influenced, or was influenced by, virtually every major philosopher of the period. Ammonius' commentary provided the basis for his own *in Int.*. John Philoponus was his teacher and he is the only student of John Philoponus that we know by name. He used the commentaries of Simplicius when composing his own commentaries *in Cat.* and *in Cael.*. That copies of these commentaries must have been available Alexandria during the second half of the sixth century is remarkable evidence of the degree of intellectual freedom that

---

[81] Henri Hugonnard-Roche, 'Probus (Proba)', in R. Goulet, ed., *Dictionnaire des philosophes antiques V* (Paris: CNRS Editions, 2012), pp. 1539–42, at pp. 1541–2.
[82] John W. Watt, 'Commentary and Translation in Syriac Aristotelian Scholarship: Sergius to Baghdad', *Journal for Late Antique Religion and Culture* 4 (2010), 28–42, at 40.

continued to prevail there at that time. His adoption of the structured lecturing format developed by Olympiodorus shows that he must have had a professional relationship with the school of which Olympiodorus was head. Elias was a source, and probably the model, for his *Prolegomena Philosophiae* and his commentary *in Cat.*. He was a common source for the *Prolegomena philosophiae* of David and Ps.-Elias, both of whom adopted his Christianised definition of philosophy. No other philosopher is so closely connected with the other philosophers of this period.

As the *Doctrina Patrum* makes clear, Stephanus was an Orthodox, Chalcedonian Christian. The most important example of the influence of his Christian faith upon his philosophy and teaching can be seen in the innovative amendment he proposed to Plato's definition of philosophy, 'practice of death'. By adding the words 'while the living being is still preserved', he strengthened the Christian opposition to suicide while preserving the traditional definition for Christian use. It clearly impressed Maximus the Confessor who included the definition and its attribution to Stephanus in his collection of definitions. His innovation is another example of the quiet Christianisation of a previously non-Christian curriculum that took place in the later sixth century. It was no doubt due as much to his clarity as a teacher of philosophy as to his Orthodoxy that so many of his definitions were included in Christian *florilegia* and collections of definitions and continued to circulate in Greek, Syriac and Arabic versions until the mediaeval period. John Damascene, in particular, appears to have made liberal use of his works in the compilation of the *Dialectica*. But what sets Stephanus apart from other philosophers of his period is the breadth of his influence. The circulation of his useful definitions in the convenient format of *florilegia* and collections of definitions will have ensured that the works of Stephanus the Philosopher may have reached a wider public in the medium term than the large commentaries of his better-known contemporary Simplicius.

23

Who Were the Real Authors of the *Metaphysics* Commentary Ascribed to Alexander and Ps.-Alexander?[1]

Pantelis Golitsis

In her learned entry devoted to the Greek commentaries on Aristotle's *Metaphysics*,[2] Concetta Luna fails to mention the text which one is used to refer to, since Michael Hayduck's edition published in Berlin in 1891, as the *recensio altera* (alternative recension) of the commentary by Alexander of Aphrodisias (second century CE) – *altera* as opposed to the *recensio vulgata* (received recension). The omission is not without logical basis: two *recensiones* of Alexander's commentary, it might be thought, stand for Alexander's sole commentary and, from this point of view, they do not deserve to be mentioned separately, let alone be published as two autonomous works. On the contrary, they must be examined equally, so that the true text of Alexander can be established.

As a matter of fact, this reasoning goes back, albeit unconsciously, to Hermann Bonitz who published the first complete and selfstanding edition of Alexander's commentary in Berlin in 1847.[3] In order to establish his edition, Bonitz used, alongside

---

This article first appeared in French as 'La *recensio altera du Commentaire* d'Alexandre d'Aphrodise à la *Métaphysique* d'Aristote et le témoignage des manuscrits byzantins Laurentianus plut. 87,12 et Ambrosianus F113 sup.' by Pantelis Golitsis in J. Signes Codoñer and I. Pérez Martin (eds), *Textual Transmission in Byzantum: Between Textual Criticism and Quellenforschung* (2014), pp. 199–230 © Brepols Publishers, Turnhout, Belgium 1999, reproduced with permission.

[1] I would like to thank Caroline Macé, Sten Ebbesen Stephen Menn, Marwan Rashed, Carlos Steel, and Richard Sorabji for their careful reading of this article, as well as for their valuable suggestions.
[2] C. Luna, 'Les commentaires grecs à la *Métaphysique*', in R. Goulet, ed., *Dictionnaire des philosophes antiques: Supplément* (Paris: CNRS, 2003), pp. 249–58.
[3] H. Bonitz, *Alexandri Aphrodisiensis Commentarius in libros metaphysicos Aristotelis* (Berlin: Reimer, 1847). Brandis had practically published earlier Alexander's genuine commentary (Books 1–5) in its entirety (see n. 5) but his edition, which aimed at providing a sort of 'hyper-commentary' uniting to Alexander's commentary several scholia coming from different sources, does not exhibit a continuous text.

the manuscripts which he had collated,[4] some excerpts published earlier by Christian August Brandis.[5] Although Brandis, who had transcribed these excerpts from the manuscript Florence, Biblioteca Medicea Laurenziana, plut. 87.12, carefully attributed them to a 'cod. Laur.', Bonitz, who relied on Angelo Maria Bandini's description of the contents of the manuscript,[6] thought that the Florentine manuscript included Alexander's commentary; thus, he believed he had restored the lost beginning of the commentary following the testimony of the Florentine manuscript.[7]

Faced with a manuscript that Bonitz's authority had already included in the recension of Alexander's text, Hayduck, who went on to collate the Laur. 87.12 integrally, had to resort to the concept of *recensio*: he classified under the heading of *recensio vulgata* most of the manuscripts that were consistent with the Latin translation of Alexander's commentary made by Juan Ginés de Sepúlveda (Rome, 1527; 2nd edn, Paris, 1536), while he classified under the heading of *recensio altera* the Laur. 87.12 and a second manuscript that he discovered, namely the Milano, Biblioteca Ambrosiana, F 113 sup.; these two manuscripts contained, according to Hayduck, a *species* of the commentary by Alexander, ascribable to an 'interpreter' posterior to Asclepius of Tralles (sixth century).[8] Despite his detailed analysis, Hayduck failed to report a fact of which Brandis, apparently, took heed: the fact that neither the manuscript of Florence nor the one of Milan attribute the text they contain to Alexander.

I should like to revisit the so-called *recensio altera* of Alexander of Aphrodisias' Commentary on the *Metaphysics*, part of which was published by Hayduck in the apparatus featured at the bottom of the page of his edition under the title 'the more serious discrepancy of the alternative recension' (*alterius recensionis gravior discrepantia*). To do this, I shall structure my thought around three questions which unfold in a decreasing chronological order, and which will all admit a negative answer: a) did the person who produced the so-called *recensio* want to produce an 'interpretation' of Alexander's commentary, in other words a text which, by means of its author's

---

[4] These are the manuscripts Paris, Bibliothèque nationale de France, gr. 1876 (A), collated in full, and München, Bayerische Staatsbibliothek, 81 (M), collated in part. Bonitz also used 'pro libro manuscripto' the Latin translation by Sepúlveda.

[5] See C. A. Brandis, *Scholia in Aristotelem*, Aristotelis Opera 4 (Berlin, 1836), pp. 521 sqq.; C. A. Brandis, *Scholia Graeca in Aristotelis Metaphysica* (Berlin, 1837).

[6] Cf. Bonitz (n. 3 above), p. xii: 'Laurentianus 87.12 [...] about which we read this in the catal. bibl. Laur. "Aristotle's Metaphysics with the commentary of Alexander of Aphrodisias, which surrounds the whole margin of the codex from every side [...] The commentary of Alexander begins *epeidê hê gnôsis* [...]"'; cf. A. M. Bandini, *Catalogus Codicum Manuscriptorum Bibliothecae Mediceae Laurentianae* (Florence, 1770; repr. Leipzig: Zentral-Antiquariat der Deutschen Demokratischen Republik, 1961), cols 392–3. Bandini, for his part, obviously relied on the fifteenth century inscription on f. II^v of the manuscript: 'Metaphysics of Aristotle with the commentary of Alexander in the margin, all in Greek' ('Metaphysica aristotelis cum comento Alexandri in margine o(mn)ia in greco').

[7] Bonitz (n. 3 above), 3,1–4,2 = Brandis 1837 (n. 5 above), 6,7–7,2 (= Brandis 1836 (n. 5 above), 521a14–b7). The prologue thus restored by Bonitz was then reproduced by Hayduck (CAG 1), 1,3–2,7. The first, however, to consider this prooemium as being identical to the lost prooemium of Alexander's commentary was Antonio Possevino (1533–1611), who supplied in the twelfth book of his *Biblotheca Selecta* (Rome, 1593) the missing beginning of Sepúlveda's translation by transcribing an additional folio of the ms. Milano, Biblioteca Ambrosiana, D 115 sup. (f. I^v).

[8] Cf. Hayduck (CAG 1), pp. viii–ix.

intention, maintains its relation to Alexander's commentary?[9] b) did the persons who thereafter reproduced and studied this text, i.e. Byzantine copyists or scholars, consider that they had before them a text by Alexander (whether it be a 'kind' of Alexander's text or not)? c) were the philologists of the modern era, who believed that they had detected a *recensio altera* of Alexander's commentary, judiciously helped in their critical work by an outlook which can be called alexandro-centric? At the end of this investigation, it will become apparent, I hope, that many elements of the exegetical history of the *Metaphysics* have disappeared because of a misapplication of the concept of *recensio*.

1. A Recensio of Alexander of Aphrodisias' Commentary on the *Metaphysics*?

I shall address the first question by means of a thought experiment. Let us imagine that Asclepius' commentary on the *Metaphysics*, based on the lessons given by Ammonius son of Hermias (*c.* 435/445–*c.* 515) in Alexandria, was handed down to us untitled. A thought experiment, as is well known, should not be arbitrary; that is the case, let us recall, with the commentary that we read in the two manuscripts of the so-called *recensio*. If, subsequently, we compared the text of this anonymized commentary with Alexander's commentary, the result we would obtain would be something like the following example:

Alexander of Aphrodisias, *in Metaph.* 2,22–3,2	(Asclepius [=Ammonius], *in Metaph.* 6,18-31)
{980a27} *By nature animals are born with sense perception.* Having said that man loves his senses too not only for the sake of their usefulness but also for the sake of knowing, since sense perception too contributes something to his knowledge, he is now teaching us that man does not have knowledge merely through sense perception, but that he possesses something more in relation to knowledge in comparison with other animals, namely reason, whose proper act is to know, and that on this account man is more perfect than the other animals, and that everyone	{980a27} *By nature animals are born with sense perception.* He said therefore that man loves his senses too not only for the sake of their usefulness but also for the sake of knowing, because sense perception too contributes to his knowledge. He says therefore that it is not mere sense perception that contributes to the knowledge of man, but reason as well, in virtue of which he has the advantage over other animals, and that man is more perfect than the other animals through reason, and that everyone thinks that wisdom, because of its existing in knowledge, is most

---

[9] Such texts are, e.g., the *recensiones pachymerianae* of Proclus' commentary on Plato's *Parmenides* and of Michael of Ephesus' commentary on Aristotle's *On the Parts of Animals*; see P. Golitsis, 'Copistes, élèves et érudits: la production de manuscrits philosophiques autour de Georges Pachymère', in A. Bravo García and I. Pérez Martín, eds, *The Legacy of Bernard de Montfaucon: Three Hundred Years of Studies on Greek Handwriting* (Turnhout: Brepols, 2010), pp. 157–70.

thinks that wisdom is knowledge and that it is most estimable, also confirming at the same time his previous assertion, [namely] that it has been said with probability that men love their senses for the sake of knowing as well. (trans. Dooley 1989, modified)

estimable; [this is what] he is now teaching us. But[10] he also confirms his previous assertion, [namely] that it is probable that men love their senses.

The differences that exist between the two texts are minimal. Would we not have, therefore, a specimen of another *recensio altera* of Alexander's commentary in the second column?

The example, one might legitimately object, is deliberately chosen; at other places, the two commentaries diverge considerably. But the so-called 'recensio', one might retort, diverges occasionally also from Alexander's commentary. What needs to be paid attention to is the fact that Hayduck, who had edited Asclepius' commentary in 1888, did not consider recognising retrospectivelly in this text another *recensio altera* of Alexander's commentary. Assuredly, he must have noticed – and now we are abandoning our thought experiment – the title transmitted by the manuscripts: *Scholia on book Alpha meizon [Book I] of Aristotle's [treatise] Metaphysics, recorded by Asclepius from the voice of Ammonius, son of Hermeias.*

Ammonius, in any case, made ample use of Alexander's commentary in preparing his lectures on the *Metaphysics*, published later by his pupil Asclepius; and in doing so, he certainly did not commit plagiarism, nor did he take an extraordinary approach. Quite on the contrary, he adopted the exegetical practice of his time, which was to make free use of the existing literature. In order to clearly understand this attitude, it is worth quoting a very illuminating passage of Porphyry's (*c.* 234 – *c.* 305) commentary on Ptolemy's *Harmonics*:[11]

> Wishing to explain the *Harmonics* by Ptolemy, we shall examine its largest part with the aim of symmetry. And if, for the purpose of our exegesis, we have overused certain remarks of our predecessors, let us not be accused of falsification! It is in order to save time [that we have acted in this way], in all cases where we have been able to make use of things well prepared in view of [their] usefulness. Indeed, I have always thought that it is very well said that 'Hermes is common', in the sense that discourses should be common to all, and I have always reproached for vain efforts those who wish to paraphrase or modify what others have said, lest they appear to say the same things. In doing so, they do not favour the things themselves, for which we really do need discourse, but rather they take advantage of things so as to speak. As for me, far from renouncing making use of what has been well said by somebody, I would wish that everyone said the same things about the same things and, as Socrates said, through the same [words]; in this way, the disagreement of men on reality would not be incontrovertible.

---

[10] Note, however, that 'but' (ΑΛΛΑ) is in all probability a later corruption of 'at the same time' (ΑΜΑ), due to a misreading of *mu* as double *lambda*, as is quite common in uncial script.

[11] I. Düring, *Porphyrius, Kommentar zur Harmonielehre des Ptolemaios* (Göteborg, 1932; repr. Hildesheim: Olms, 1978), 4,22–5,7.

Porphyry presents here the practice of exegesis in a philosophical perspective, and at the same time justifies the method that he adopted: this consists in reaching, via the exegesis, the truth of things, communicable through the single *logos*, i.e. Hermes, that is shared in principle by all men. It is by virtue of both this singularity and this commonness of *logos* (singular as to its essence, common from the point of view of those who participate in it) that men are likely to come one day to an agreement. That is why any thing well said, i.e. said truthfully, may be tacitly reproduced to the letter, according to an approach which favours the truth revealed by exegesis over the exegete who reveals the truth. Porphyry theorises here a way of proceeding which is found in almost all of the exegetical literature. To give just two examples, the commentary on Aristotle's *Physics* by John Philoponus (*c.* 490 – *c.* 570) tacitly draws over six hundred passages from Themistius' respective Paraphrase,[12] and the Neoplatonist Simplicius (born *c.* 485) composed his own commentary on the *Physics* by reproducing, without always reporting it, the respective exegeses of Alexander of Aphrodisias and Porphyry.[13] In accordance with an assessment of literary creation quite different from our own, the composition of a commentary in Late Antiquity is essentially *an act of recomposition*,[14] in which the opinions of previous exegetes are not in principle identified except when it comes to diverging from them – always in favour of truth.

It is as such an act of recomposition that we should also count the so-called *recensio altera* of Alexander of Aphrodisias' commentary on the *Metaphysics*. In all likelihood, we are dealing with the work of a professor who gives or, rather, prepares his lecture on the *Metaphysics* while using Alexander's commentary as a working tool. That this professor was aiming at producing not a *recensio* of Alexander's commentary but a new commentary, is prima facie obvious from the simple fact that before each piece of commentary he has drawn new lemmas, i.e. quotations, out of Aristotle's text; here is an example, among many:

Alexander of Aphrodisias, in Metaph. 22,20–23,8	'Recensio altera'
And this he himself made clear in the Ethics when he said, 'And for this reason people have rightly asserted that the good is that which all things desire'.	*And this he himself made clear in the Ethics when he said, 'And for this reason people have rightly asserted that the good is that which all things desire'.*
	{983a33} **'We have actually examined these things sufficiently in our [discourses] on nature'.**
Aristotle has now made the division of the causes, and intends to investigate what sort of cause it is that the wise men in particular should know. [But] since the causes [are	*Even if, he says, we have sufficiently treated of the natural principles in our discourses on nature, [i.e.] in the treatise that is entitled 'The Physics', we should*

---

[12] Cf. the Index nominum drawn up by Vitelli (CAG 16–17), *s.v. Themistios*.
[13] See P. Golitsis, *Les Commentaires de Simplicius et de Jean Philopon à la 'Physique' d'Aristote: Tradition et innovation* (Berlin: De Gruyter, 2008), pp. 66–70.
[14] See ibid., pp. 58–64.

spoken of] in various ways, it is reasonable that he first reviews the opinions of the others who preceded him [to learn] to what sort of cause or causes they had recourse. This procedure, he says, will also be advantageous [in enabling] us to confirm the causes of which we have spoken. For either we shall discover another type of cause as well, if it is obvious that what was said about the causes by the early [philosophers] does not fall under the division, or, if the causes of which they spoke do not exceed the causes we have enumerated, we shall then have greater confidence in the division as being sound.

{983b6} 'Most of the early philosophers, then'.
(trans. Dooley 1989)

nonetheless take over, in our discovery of causes, the opinions of those who philosophised before us. For this will contribute to our discovery of truth, as [something that] contributes to the accomplishment of something for those who prepare for it, e.g. as the arms and the horse do for those who prepare for war. It is agreed that the early [philosophers] presuppose principles and causes. From this point on, therefore, through discussing them, we shall either discover another genus of causes, different from those we have said, or, of course, if we do not discover anything, we shall have great confidence in the causes we have said.

{983b6} 'Most of the early philosophers, then'.

The professor therefore restructures Alexander's commentary according to his own exegetical 'rhythm'.[15] Some cases suggest even that he perhaps used as a manuscript of reference a different manuscript of the *Metaphysics* than the one on which Alexander's exegesis was primarily based. Here is what the two commentators say about the beginning of Book 2:

Alexander of Aphrodisias, *In Metaph.* 138,26–8

'Recensio altera'

There is a variant reading <u>without the hoti</u> [...]. It seems that it is rather this variant that makes a start [of a book], whereas the variant with the hoti is not a start but follows something that has been said before.

There is a variant reading in some manuscripts <u>with the hoti added</u> [...]. But in this way it is not a start of a book but follows something that has been said before, whereas without the hoti it makes a start [of a book].

It is possible, of course, that in this case the professor has reversed the textual explanations given by Alexander relying on Alexander's authority, but in another passage he clearly reports a textual variant of the *Metaphysics* (*sma*), which is transmitted unanimously by the Byzantine manuscript tradition, whereas it was, in all probability, unknown to Alexander:

---

[15] See also below, p. 573.

Alexander of Aphrodisias, *in Metaph.* 132,16–133,1	'Recensio altera'
But just as it is a subject of dispute whether the syllable za *should be analysed into* z *and* a *or into* s *and* d *and* a,	*But just as it is a subject of dispute whether the syllable* za *should be analysed into* z **(perhaps [Aristotle] named some other sound)** *or into* s *and* d **(for some of the manuscripts read** sma **instead of** za**; the reading** za**, however, is better)**,
there would also be in this way a dispute about the principles.	*there would also be in this way a dispute about the principles.*

Besides, Alexander's commentary is adapted to different educational methods. In the following case, we observe our professor in the process of reworking Alexander's text by adding examples of clarification as well as a development of the syllogism used by Aristotle, obviously for the benefit of students who were not yet familiar with Aristotle's elliptical syllogistic:

Alexander of Aphrodisias, *in Metaph.* 16,12–19	'Recensio altera'
'Even the lover of myth,' Aristotle adds, 'is in a sense a lover of wisdom,' for he is eager to learn the things that, because of his ignorance, he thinks wonders (for myths are composed of things wondrous and contrary to expectation);	*This is why he added 'Even the lover of myth is in a sense a lover of wisdom,' for he is eager to learn the things that he wonders because of his ignorance. For myths are composed of things wondrous and contrary to expectation.* **Indeed, [the myths] describe things that are beyond the assumptions of common people. To say, for instance, that human beings sprang from the earth, or that gods engaged in a battle for the city of Athens are beyond common conceptions. These are things that are object of wonder;**
and those who are eager to learn because they wonder at things are lovers of wisdom.	*and those who are eager to learn because they wonder at things are lovers of wisdom.* **The lover of myth [the 'philomyth'] and the lover of wisdom [the philosopher] have in common their wondering. The inference of the syllogism that the philomyth is a philosopher would be from two affirmative propositions in the third figure, their wondering being the middle term, in the following way: 'who wonders is a philosopher'; 'who wonders is philomyth'; therefore, 'the philomyth is a philosopher'.**

That men originally came to philosophize for the sake of knowledge rather than for the sake of some need or of performing some action Aristotle also establishes from history; for it was after the necessities and the things that make for comfort of life had been provided ... (trans. Dooley, modified)	That men originally came to philosophize for the sake of knowledge rather than for the sake of some need or of performing some action Aristotle also establishes from history; for it was after the necessities and the things that make for comfort of life had been provided ...

References to mythological scenes, like the following one which sheds more light to the previous example, also suggest an educational context:

Alexander of Aphrodisias, *in Metaph.* 167,14–19	'Recensio altera'
After this remark, Aristotle goes on to show how great is the force of customs. For lawgivers retain many legendary elements in their legislation because it is advantageous that [people] should believe the legends are true; [thus] the legislators keep those who are subject to the law obedient to it through tales familiar to them from their childhood.	*After this remark, Aristotle goes on to show how great is the force of customs. For lawgivers retain many legendary elements in their legislation because it is advantageous that [people]* **in the cities** *should believe the legends are true; [thus] the legislators keep those who are subject to the law obedient to it through tales familiar* **and habitual** *to them from their childhood.* **For they say many ridiculous things**, *e.g.*
Such, e.g., is the story that some people are indigenous to their native land, having sprung up from the earth itself, and that others originated from [the dragon's] teeth sown [in the ground].	*that some people are indigenous to their native land, having sprung up from the earth itself, and other [legislators] that* **giants** *originated from [the dragon's] teeth sown [in the ground].* **This is what lawgivers thought was for the benefit of the city**, *namely to fight for their homeland*
For this reason these people ought to fight for the earth as their mother, or because gods quarrelled over it. (trans. Dooley)	*as if they were fighting for their mother or* **nurse**.[16] *Or [they say] something else, [e.g.] that gods fought for it,* **as they say that Ares and Halirrothios quarrelled over the land of the Athenians.**

Those were some examples of reorganisation and of different aims compared to Alexander's commentary. As is hardly surpising in the exegetical literature, Alexander's commentary was not the only working tool of the anonymous professor. In the following passage, we see him combining (and expanding) Alexander's exegesis with that of Asclepius-Ammonius:

---

[16] Cf. Plato, *Republic* 3, 414E3: as of a mother or nurse.

Alexander of Aphrodisias, in Metaph. 33,27–34,6	'Recensio altera'
"He says, then, that these men, Empedocles and Anaxagoras, as well as Hermotimus, and Hesiod and Parmenides among the poets, made mention of an efficient cause in addition to the material. And these causes, he says, are the same as those we spoke about in our treatise On Nature, and do not fall outside them; however, [these men did not speak] clearly but vaguely, and made only limited use of the efficient cause. And to show that they did so, he adds, 'It is obvious that they made almost no use of these causes, or used them in only a limited way'. (Alexander, in Metaph. 33,27–34,6; trans. Dooley)	{985a18} Anaxagoras avails himself of Nous as an artificial device for producing order. Having mentioned those who accept in the generation of beings, besides the material cause, the efficient cause as well, he says that they too, even if they accepted the efficient cause in the generation of beings, do not accept it sufficiently, so that they use the efficient or making cause in as many ways as they use the material or affected cause, but mostly considered the material cause and posited rather that as the cause of the generation and the existence of beings. They mentioned the efficient cause vaguely and in impossible situations, in which they could not draw an explanation from the material cause.
He says that Anaxagoras employed Nous as a deus ex machina, just as in tragedies the gods are dragged in by a stage device [to resolve] an impossible situation. (Alexander, in Metaph. 35,1–3; trans. Dooley)	This is why he says that 'Anaxagoras employs Nous as a deus ex machina for producing order and drags it in whenever he is at a loss to explain'.
He says that Anaxagoras employed Nous as a deus ex machina, just as in tragedies the demons are dragged in by a stage device [to resolve] an impossible situation, e.g. as Artemis appeared to Hippolytus, when Theseus was in an impossible situation. It is actually in this way that Anaxagoras drags Nous in, when he is at a loss to explain for what cause order has been necessarily produced. On the contrary, he mentions as causes for the particular things everything except Nous. Empedocles has employed the efficient causes more than happens with Anaxagoras, but neither does he speak [of them] sufficiently.	He said that he employed [Nous] as a deus ex machina, just as those who drag in the gods in impossible situations of tragedies did, so that [the spectators] grasp the impossibility, e.g. as Artemis appeared to Hippolytus, when Theseus was in an impossible situation. It is actually in this way that Anaxagoras, when he is at a loss to explain for what cause order has been necessarily produced, drags Nous in, **saying that Nous is the cause of order**. On the contrary, he mentions as causes for the particular things everything except Nous. Empedocles employs the efficient causes more than happens with Anaxagoras, but neither does he [use them] **sufficiently, so as to attribute the attribution of causes to the efficient causes, nor does he respect the consequences of what he has admitted, but he changes the sequence**

	and attributes to strife what belongs to love, and to love what belongs to strife.
He says, in fact, that love is the cause of aggregation, whereas strife is the cause of separation, but many times we see the contrary, [namely] love [being the cause] of separation. For it is love that, according to Empedocles, separates the forms from matter and constitutes the sphere. In turn, strife aggregates the elements; for fire brings to a unity what is [dispersed] hither and thither and puts again the forms on matter. (Asclepius, in Metaph. 32,2–14)	He says, in fact, that love is the cause of aggregation, whereas strife is the cause of separation, but many times we see the contrary, [namely] love being the cause of separation. For it is love that, according to Empedocles, separates the forms from matter and constitutes the sphere. In turn, strife aggregates the elements; for fire brings to a unity what is **dispersed** hither and thither **in the** sphere and puts again the forms on matter. **It was actually Empedocles who first brought in, or conceived of, the contrary principles in the universe, which are opposed to each other: love, which is the cause of unity, and strife, which is the cause of separation; and love belongs to the good, since the good is the cause of union, whereas strife belongs to the bad; and love preserves, whereas strife destroys.**
But he does credit Empedocles with having been the first both to divide the efficient cause and to employ the four bodies as material principles and elements; he says, however, that Empedocles did not give equal status to these principles, but set three of them, as being a single nature, in opposition to fire, as is clear, he says, from his verses. (Alexander, in Metaph. 34,6–10; trans. Dooley)	But he does credit Empedocles with having been the first both to divide the efficient cause and to employ the four bodies as material principles and elements; he says, however, that Empedocles did not give equal status to these principles, but set three of them, as being a single nature, in opposition to fire, as is clear, he says, from his verses.

In the commentary on *Metaphysics* Book 5 (*Delta*), we encounter a lengthy explanation deriving from a combination of two passages by Asclepius separated by a transitional sentence:

Asclepius, in Metaph. 352,26–354,5	'Recensio altera'
This is why, [Aristotle] says, the person who infers syllogistically in the dialogue Hippias misleads us by fallacious reasoning. Indeed, Plato attempts to show there that the person who lies wittingly is better than the person who lies unwittingly, just as the person who is lame wittingly is better than the person who is lame	This is why, [Aristotle] says, the person who infers syllogistically in the dialogue Hippias misleads us by fallacious reasoning. Indeed, Plato attempts to show there that the person who lies wittingly is better than the person who lies unwittingly, just as the person who is lame wittingly is better than the person who is lame unwittingly. Therefore,

unwittingly. Therefore, according to this argument, the person who mutilated his legs wittingly is better than the person who has suffered this unwittingly – which, of course, is not true. We reply that Plato said this for a beneficial purpose, [meaning] the person who lies wittingly for the good, as happened with those who told the Phoenician lie and said that the citizens are sprung from the earth, so that they love more their city. For the person who lies for the harmful purpose is admittedly worse than the person who lies unwittingly.

Asclepius, in Metaph. 356,2–357,1 'false' means, in one way, false as a thing; and this is not or cannot be combined [in a proposition] (for 'false', when applied to things, denotes a simple nature). Such are the statements that the diagonal is commensurable [with the side], or that you are sitting. Of these one is false always, namely that referring to the diagonal, and the other sometimes, namely that referring to the sitting. It is in these senses that these things hold, without being [facts]. Others are said to be 'false'...

according to this argument, the person who mutilated his legs wittingly is better than the person who has suffered this unwittingly – which, of course, is not true. We reply that Plato said this for a beneficial purpose, [meaning] the person who lies wittingly for the good, as happened with those who told the Phoenician lie and said that the citizens are sprung from the earth, so that they love more their city. For the person who lies for the harmful purpose is admittedly worse than the person who lies unwittingly. **Such is the train of the general explanation of the passage. As for its expression, this is how it is**: 'false' means, in one way, false as a thing; and this is not or cannot be combined [in a proposition] (for 'false', when applied to things, denotes a simple nature). Such are the statements that the diagonal is commensurable [with the side], or that you are sitting. Of these one is false always, namely that referring to the diagonal, and the other sometimes, namely that referring to the sitting. It is in these senses that these things hold, without being [facts]. Others are said to be 'false'...

The composition of this passage provides a *terminus post quem* for the activity of our commentator, showing that it must be later than Asclepius' commentary which was written during the first decades of the sixth century. It is possible to specify even further the time and, perhaps, the place of his activity with the help of the two terms, *theôria* and *lexis*, which appear in the transitional sentence. These are technical terms indicating the twofold exegesis (*theôria* corresponding to the preliminary and general explanation of a passage, *lexis* to the examination of its letter) which was widely practiced in the Platonic school of Alexandria in the sixth and seventh centuries.[17] The Platonic orientation of our professor is also manifest in the following case, where he fills out Alexander's allusions by directly referring to the characters of Plato's homonymous dialogues:

---

[17] See Golitsis (n. 13 above), pp. 55–61.

Alexander of Aphrodisias, *in Metaph.* 49,20–50,3	'Recensio altera'
And he tells the source which led [Plato] to posit Ideas, and reports that from Cratylus, a Heraclitean, whose associate he was, he took [the belief] that all sensible things are in flux and never stand still, and that Plato continued to maintain this opinion as true. Socrates, however, occupied himself with ethical questions and in seeking the universal (for in dealing with beauty or anything else, he would ask in general what the beautiful is, not looking to the particular beautiful thing),	*And he tells the source which led Plato to posit Ideas, and reports that it was from Cratylus, who was a disciple of Heraclitus. Being an associate of Cratylus, he took [the belief] that all sensible things are in flux and never stand still, and that Plato continued to maintain this opinion as true. Socrates, however, occupied himself with ethical questions and in seeking the universal (for in dealing with beauty or anything else,* **for example justice**, *he would ask in general what the beautiful is* **and what the just is**, *not looking to the particular beautiful thing,* **say the beauty in Alcibiades, or to the particular just thing, say the justice in Euthyphro**)[18], *and was always trying to define the thing under discussion.*
and was always trying to define the thing under discussion. (trans. Dooley)	

But it is rather a case of a 'moderate Platonism' on our professor's part, who is in all probability a Christian. For one notices in the following passage the subtle suppression of the word 'divine' (*theios*) as an adjective characterising Plato, as well as the replacement of the word 'goodness' (*agathotês*) by the word with Christian overtones 'giving' (*dôrea*):[19]

Alexander of Aphrodisias, *in Metaph.* 18,2–5	'Recensio altera'
But 'the divine cannot be jealous' (for as the divine Plato says, 'jealousy is excluded from the divine choir'); it is rather that 'Bards tell many a lie', and this is one of them. Nor should any [of the particular sciences] be thought more estimable than one of this sort." (trans. Dooley)	*But the divine is not jealous; for jealousy, as Plato says, is far from the divine choir. Actually, jealousy is born [in us], because we see our neighbours doing better than us.*[20]

Asclepius, *in Metaph.* 21,18–27

| *How is it possible that god be jealous, since god is the source of goodness and that from* | *How is it possible that god be jealous, since god is the source of goodness and that from* |

---

[18] Cf. also Hayduck (CAG 1), ad 82,11–12: '... and whether the subjects of predication are equivocally said to be that or in the proper sense, e.g. Callias and Theaetetus said to be humans.'
[19] Cf., for instance, John Chrysostom, *In Joannem homiliae* 91,31–39 (*Patrologia Graeca* 59).
[20] Cf. Simplicius, *in Epict. Ench.* 56,45–8 Dübner: 'For this reason, those who lack intensity in their nature and don't have the power to make progress themselves want to equal or surpass their neighbours by pulling them down, and are grieved at their neighbours' doing well (*eupragiais*) – which is jealousy' (trans. Brittain and Brennan).

| which everything is supplied to anything else, as Plato too says, namely that god has produced everything for the sake of his goodness: 'He was good, and in him that is good no jealousy arises ever concerning anything'. Indeed, how would it be possible that the source of goodness be jealous? Nor should any [of the particular sciences] be thought more estimable than the primary science. For this science is most divine and most estimable in two ways: because god has this science and because it is [for us] possible through it, he says, to come to know god. This is why he says "divine among sciences is the science that god knows"; it is this science that god knows, because it has within it the principles of beings. | which everything is supplied to anything else, as Plato too says, namely that god has produced everything for the sake of his goodness: 'He was good, and in him that is good no jealousy arises ever concerning anything'. Indeed, how would it be possible that the source of giving be jealous?? Nor should any [of the particular sciences] be thought more estimable than the primary science. For this science is most divine and most estimable in two ways: because god has this science and because it is [for us] possible through it, he says, to come to know god. This is why he says "divine among sciences is the science that god knows"; it is this science that god knows, because it has within it the principles of beings. |

One could easily supply more examples, but that would be unnecessary.[21] Reorganisation of the text to be commented, simplification as well as clarification of the exegesis provided by Alexander, use of Asclepius' commentary toward a Platonist 'update' of the commentary by the Peripatetic Alexander, Christian adaptation of these two working tools: all these are features that plead in favour not of an 'interpretation' of Alexander's commentary but of a composition of a new commentary on the *Metaphysics*, which was probably carried out in the milieu of Christian Platonists coming from Alexandria at the very end of antiquity. This is further confirmed by the strictly Byzantine transmission of the commentary.

2. Adaptation and Reactualisation: A Persistent Attitude?

Thus composed,[22] the new commentary on the *Metaphysics*, misleadingly called 'recensio altera', subsequently found its way to the *scriptoria* of Constantinople, where

---

[21] Let us note, nevertheless, that when commenting 990b8–9 ('Further of the ways in which we prove that the Ideas exist none is convincing'), where Aristotle speaks as a Platonist, the anonymous professor adds to Alexander's remarks (78,2–4) 'For the sake of discovering the truth, [Aristotle] sets forth his objections not as opposing foreign arguments and doctrines, but as testing and examining a doctrine that is his own' the following clarification: 'this is why he appropriates this doctrine; he belonged to the Platonic school'. This 'Platonisation' of Aristotle confirms our professor's Neoplatonic origins.

[22] Of course, the question is raised of what was the extent of the commentary. Hayduck (CAG 1, p. xi) curiously thinks that from Book 3 onwards the Laur. 87,12 ceases to transmit the *recensio altera*; however, we find in Book 5 the apparatus which records the *alterius recensionis gravior discrepantia*. Be that as it may, the fact that the 'discrepancies' between the text transmitted by the Laur. 87,12 (and the Ambr. F 113 sup.) and the text transmitted by the other manuscripts are not, in the case of Books 3 (*Beta*) and 4 (*Gamma*), as 'serious' as they are in the case of Books 1 (*Alpha meizon*), 2 (*alpha*

the two manuscripts, i.e. the Laur. 87,12 and the Ambr. F 113 sup., were likely produced, the first towards the end of the eleventh century, the second towards the middle of the fourteenth century. Several separative readings suggest that the two Byzantine manuscripts are independent of one another.[23] I shall only mention here the incorporation in a slightly different position (cf. *ad* 313.2) of a marginal scholium of apparently ancient or protobyzantine origin (since the *thymele* is irrelevant to the Byzantine theatrical reality):

Laur. 87,12, fol. 142ᵛ–143ʳ

For of those who say these things, no one, if he is in Libya and a dream expresses [to him] that he is in Athens, presses on to the Athenian – 'music-hall' is the name of a certain part of the theatre, which is now

Ambr. F 113 sup., fol. 66ᵛ

For of those who say these things, no one, if he is in Libya and a dream expresses [to him] that he is in Athens, presses on to the Athenian music-hall; 'music-hall' was the name of a certain part of the theatre,

---

elatton), and 5 (*Delta*) does not mean that the 'recomposition' of Alexander's commentary by the anonymous professor was partial; it was selective, selectivity obviously not affecting the continuity of the new composition. A good number of the alternative readings for these books, recorded by Hayduck in the usual critical apparatus, are no doubt alterations by the anonymous professor (see e.g. ad 196,1–2; 202,11–12; 205,15–16; 222,12–13).

[23] This is also argued by Dieter Harlfinger (see W. Leszl and D. Harlfinger, *Il "De ideis" di Aristotele e la teoria platonica delle idee* (Florence: Olschki, 1975), pp. 18–19), and is further confirmed, with regard to the text of the *Metaphysics* that the two manuscripts transmit separately, by D. Harlfinger, 'Zur Überlieferungsgeschichte der *Metaphysik*', in P. Aubenque, ed., *Études sur la 'Métaphysique' d'Aristote* (Paris: Vrin, 1979), pp. 7–36. But we must carefully dissociate the text of the *Metaphysics* transmitted by the two manuscripts from the text of the *Metaphysics* on the basis of which the anonymous commentary was *originally* composed. Indeed, the two manuscripts are witnesses of the β-family of the *Metaphysics*, whereas the anonymous professor commented on a text belonging rather to the α-family. We see this clearly in 990b8–9 (see n. 21), where the professor explains the reading *deiknumen*, transmitted by the α-family, whereas the two manuscripts transmit the reading *deiknutai* of the β-family. Similarly, in 991b3, the professor comments on the text such as it is transmitted by the α-family (*en de tôi Phaidôni houtô legomen*; the β-family transmits the variant *en de tôi Phaidôni houtô legetai*): 'He again shares the doctrine (*koinopoieitai to dogma*), which is why he repeats 'we say', and not 'it is said'. Likewise, again, in 992a11 (*tithemen* α : *tithetai* β): 'evaluating the opinion as his own (*idian*), he said 'we posit', for, as has often been said, he shares (*koinopoieitai*) the doctrine'. The association of the anonymous commentary with the β-text of the *Metaphysics* is to be explained on the basis of its continuation (see below), which, in its turn, is partially grounded on the β-text. That the β-text was not originally associated with the anonymous commentary is also suggested by the fragment Y of the *Metaphysics* (Paris, Bibliothèque nationale de France, Suppl. gr. 687), copied towards the end of the ninth century, which transmits the β-text of the *Metaphysics* without a commentary. The same fragment also suggests that the β-text predates the continuation of the anonymous commentary. However, the α-text commented on by the anonymous professor (=α²) is also not identical to the α-text of the Byzantine manuscripts (=α³); cf., for instance, 985a10 *kai tôn kakôn to kakon* α³ Asclepius : non habent β α² Alexander Anonymus; 987b10 *sunônumôn homônuma* α³ : *sunônumôn* β α² Alexander Asclepius Anonymus). But it is not even identical to the text *a* used by Alexander (=α¹); cf. 984a32–3 *touto men gar arkhaion te kai pantes hômologêsan* α² Asclepius Anonymus : non habent β α¹ Alexander; 993a5 *za* α¹ Alexander Anonymus : *sma* α² α³ β Asclepius Anonymus⁽ᵛᵃʳⁱᵃ ˡᵉᶜᵗⁱᵒ⁾. We can deduce from the last example that, apart from α², α¹ was also known to the anonymous professor, perhaps through Alexander's commentary. On the two families, α and β, of the text of the *Metaphysics*, see now O. Primavesi, 'Aristotle, *Metaphysics* A: A New Critical Edition with Introduction', in C. Steel, ed., *Aristotle's Metaphysics A* (Oxford: Oxford University Press, 2012), pp. 387–458.

called thymele – music-hall; on the contrary, these people are convinced that the dream the man saw was false, but they posit that what appears to people while they are awake is true.

which is now called thymele;[24] *on the contrary, these people are convinced that the dream the man saw was false, but they posit that what appears to people while they are awake is true.*

Philological investigation may further confirm the protobyzantine origin of the anonymous commentary. Actually, a textual corruption suggests that the two Byzantine manuscripts originate from an archetype in majuscule script (which would therefore be produced in the sixth or seventh century), written in continuous script and damaged by time:

Alexander, 345,10–11: *kai autôi legomenôi pollakhôs· dio oukhi mathêmatikon ê ti tôn toioutôn*

Anonymus: *legomenôi kai autôi pollakhôs· dia touto kai oukhi mathêmatikon ê ti tôn toioutôn*

Uncial codex: *LEGOMENÔIKAIAUTÔIPOLLAKHÔSDIATOUTOKAIOYKH[...] TH[.]M[....]ONÊTITÔNTOIOUTÔN*

Miniscule codex (Laur., Ambr.): *legomenôi kai autôi pollakhôs dia touto· kai oukh ho monê ti tôn toioutôn*

Nonetheless, the two manuscripts are far from transmitting an identical text. On the contrary, they bear texts deriving from dynamic processes, which disappeared behind the stabilising concept of *recensio*. To describe these processes, we must now turn to the transmission of Alexander's own commentary.

In the two independent witnesses that transmit Alexander's text, i.e. the manuscripts Paris, Bibliothèque nationale de France, gr. 1876 and the Firenze, Biblioteca Medicea Laurenziana, plut. 85,1 (called the 'Ocean'), which date in my view from 1270–1290, Alexander's commentary is presented as follows: 'Commentary by Alexander of Aphrodisias on Aristotle's *Metaphysics*; of two volumes the first'; then, at the beginning of Book 4 (*Gamma*): 'By the same author, commentary on Book 4 (*Gamma*) of the *Metaphysics* by Aristotle; of two volumes the second'. These titles show straightaway an edition in two volumes, the first containing Alexander's commentary on Books 1, 2 and 3 (*Alpha meizon, alpha elatton*, and *Beta* of the *Metaphysics*), the second including the commentary on Books 4 (*Gamma*) and 5 (*Delta*), an edition which was the archetype of the two manuscripts of the thirteenth century.[25] Moreover, they reveal to us that at

---

[24] Cf. Phrynichus (second century CE), *Praeparatio sophistica* 74,9–10: 'Thymele; we nowadays call "thymele" the stage of the theatre. It seems that this part [of the theatre] was [originally] called that way from "sacrificing" (*thuein*)'.

[25] That the Par. gr. 1876 and the Laur. 85,1 are independent from one another is also suggested by Harlfinger (in Leszl and Harlfinger, n. 23 above), pp. 19–20.

the time of the production of this edition Alexander's commentary was not available in its entirety: only Books 1 to 5 (*Alpha* to *Delta*) were preserved. Hence the concern to produce in Byzantium a continuation of the mutilated commentary on the *Metaphysics*, usually associated with Anna Comnena and the two philosophers working under her command after 1118, i.e. Eustratius of Nicaea and Michael of Ephesus.[26] However, this is now contradicted by the new dating of the Laur. 87,12, proposed by Guglielmo Cavallo,[27] at the end of the eleventh century. Let me explain: from Book 6 (*Epsilon*) up to the end of the *Metaphysics*, the Laur. 87,12 contains the commentary that the Par. gr. 1876 attributes to Michael;[28] so if this attribution is correct, Michael produced his continuation of the commentary on the *Metaphysics* at least two decades before the Byzantine princess launched her own exegetical project.

We need not reopen the debate on the identity of the author of the commentary on Books 6 to 14 (*Epsilon* to *Nu*) of the *Metaphysics*. Called Pseudo-Alexander by Karl Praechter,[29] this author predated Syrianus (d. *c*. 437) according to Leonardo Tarán.[30] Tarán's arguments, however, have been refuted, once and for all, by Concetta Luna,[31] who sees in the person of pseudo-Alexander Michael of Ephesus, following the testimony of the Par. gr. 1876 and corroborating the suggestion made by Praechter. Besides, recording his commentaries at the end of his exegesis of the *Parva naturalia*, Michael himself *partly* confirms the testimony of the Par. gr. 1876:

> Thus I have explicated, to the best of my ability, the treatises *On the Parts of Animals* and *On the Progression of Animals*, the treatises *On Memory and Recollection* and *On the Movement of Animals*, the treatises *On the Generation of Animals* and *On Length and Shortness of Life*, and in addition to those the treatise *On Old Age and Youth*. I beg my readers to be grateful, if they acquired any benefit from my explications; if not, they should know that they will not be harmed by them. I have also written a commentary on the *Metaphysics*, precisely from Book 7 (*Zeta*) to

---

[26] See R. Browning, 'An Unpublished Funeral Oration on Anna Comnena', *Proceedings of the Cambridge Philological Society* 8 (1962), 1–12 (repr. in R. Sorabji, ed., *Aristotle Transformed: The Ancient Commentators and their Influence* (London: Duckworth 1990), pp. 393–406). The reconstruction proposed by Browning is based on the testimony of Georgios Tornikes (cf. J. Darrouzès, *Georges et Dèmètrios Tornikès, Lettres et Discours* (Paris: CNRS, 1970), p. 301,8–19), who actually says that Anna Comnena asked Michael of Ephesus to compose commentaries on aristotelian treatises for which no ancient commentary had survived. But we must pay attention to the fact that Tornikes does not specify which those treatises were.

[27] G. Cavallo, 'Scritture informali, cambio grafico e pratiche librarie a Bisanzio tra i secoli XI e XII', in G. Prato, ed., *I manoscritti greci tra riflessione e dibattito* (Florence: Gonnelli, 2000), pp. 219–38, at p. 233.

[28] The 'Ocean' contains only the commentary on Books 10 (*Iota*) to 14 (*Nu*), without attributing it to a specific author. This unexpected lacuna suggests the existence of the commentary on Books 6 (*Epsilon*) to 14 (*Nu*) in two volumes, the first of which, the one containing Books 6 (*Epsilon*) to 9 (*Theta*), was not accessible to the copyists of the 'Ocean'.

[29] K. Praechter, 'Commentaria in Aristotelem Graeca XXII 2', *Göttingische Gelehrte Anzeigen* 11 (1906), 861–907, at 882.

[30] L. Tarán, 'Syrianus and Pseudo-Alexander's commentary on *Metaph*. E-N', in J. Wiesner, ed., *Aristoteles, Werk und Wirkung*, 2 vols (Berlin: De Gruyter, 1987), vol. 2, pp. 215–32.

[31] C. Luna, *Trois études sur la tradition des commentaires anciens à la 'Métaphysique' d'Aristote* (Leiden: Brill, 2001).

Book 14 (*Nu*). It remains [to comment on] *On the Colours*, which we will explicate, God being willing, from another starting point.[32]

'I have also written', writes Michael, 'a commentary on the *Metaphysics*, precisely from Book 7 (*Zeta*) to Book 14 (*Nu*)'. Modern research has too hastily rejected this sentence as being an interpolation introduced by an intelligent copyist,[33] who nonetheless was not very well informed on Michael's exegetical output, granted that the latter continued the commentary on the *Metaphysics* starting not from Book 7 (*Zeta*) but from Book 6 (*Epsilon*). Henceforth, one should not doubt the authenticity of Michael's autobiographical testimony. The incongruity that some readers may feel in finding the *Metaphysics* mentioned among commentaries on Aristotle's biological treatises is to be explained, in light of the new dating proposed by Cavallo, by the fact that Michael is refering, for the sake of completeness, to an exegesis which he had written previously, i.e. *independently of* the project launched later by Anna Comnena. As for his affirmation that his commentary on the *Metaphysics* began at Book 7 and not at Book 6, it is not to be attributed to a memory lapse; it receives an indirect confirmation in two scholia recorded in the margins of a manuscript of Asclepius' commentary, Paris, Bibliothèque nationale de France, gr. 1901, fol. 342^r et 345^r,[34] to which not enough attention has been paid:

Disparaging Scholium no. 1

<By the Ephesian: The corrupted bodies> do not preexist as efficient causes, [...], but as material causes; so, [...] Alexander's text would have given you a most true conclusion. *But if only Alexander were here, he whom you have utterly destroyed!* For those disposed to laziness in the sciences rushed onto you, because you appeared to them more clear and more concise, and it is you whom they have saved. On the other hand, *Alexander*, Simplicius and all the rest of that golden generation who explained this treatise *have been completely done away with*, so that there is not even the iron generation left, but only your own race of straw.

Disparaging Scholium no. 2

By the Ephesian: From segments of bronze, wood, stone and others of this kind, the form of the circle can be separated. But how can it be separated from incorporeals – this is what you should tell us, you, most ignorant and most insolent of men! *So why did you not copy Alexander? We would be really grateful to you, had you copied him.* But, having set Alexander aside, you turned to nonsense of this sort.

---

[32] Wendland (CAG 22.1), 149,8–149,16.
[33] See e.g. Tarán (n. 30 above), p. 232; J. Dillon and D. O'Meara, *Syrianus, On Aristotle Metaphysics 13–14* (London: Duckworth, 2006), p. 10.
[34] On these scholia, highlighted by I. Hadot ('Recherches sur les fragments du commentaire de Simplicius sur la *Métaphysique* d'Aristote', in I. Hadot, ed., *Simplicius: Sa vie, son œuvre, sa survie* (Berlin: De Gruyter, 1987), pp. 225–45), see more recently P. Golitsis, 'Trois annotations de manuscrits aristotéliciens au XIIe siècle: les *Parisini gr.* 1901 et 1853 et l'*Oxoniensis Corp. Christi* 108', in D. Bianconi, ed., *Storia della scrittura e altre storie* (Rome: Accademia Nazionale dei Lincei, 2014), pp. 33–52.

These scholia, appearing in the margins of Asclepius' commentary on Book 7 of the *Metaphysics*, are very interesting in more than one respect. They suggest, first, that Michael resorted to Asclepius' commentary as a working tool while writing his own commentary on the *Metaphysics* from Book 7 onwards, and not from Book 6 (there is no scholium before Book 7); the arrangement of the two scholia is therefore consistent with the record drawn by Michael himself at the end of his commentary on the *Parva naturalia*. At first sight, they seem also to confirm the testimony of the Par. gr. 1876 and of the Laur. 85,1, which transmit only the first books of Alexander's commentary; indeed, Michael complains of not having Alexander's commentary at his disposal. But on a closer reading, one begins to see in these scholia that Michael had *no* knowledge of Alexander's commentary. Just as with the alleged commentary by Simplicius,[35] Alexander's commentary was known to him only by indirect means, in this case through the passages that Asclepius had incorporated by name in his own commentary. Therefore, if Michael undertook to write a commentary, it was in order to supplement a mutilated commentary,[36] but this mutilated commentary *was not* Alexander's commentary; it was, in all likelihood, the commentary of our anonymous professor. To this bear witness the Laur. 87,12 and the Ambr. F 113 sup., which contain from Book *Epsilon* onwards the commentary that the copyist of the Par. gr. 1876 attributes to Michael. But we should be henceforth wary of this last attribution[37] and pay attention to the fact that the Laur. 87,12 and the Ambr. F 113 sup. continue to transmit an anonymous commentary.[38] Indeed, it seems that Michael, following the example of the

---

[35] On the non-existence of such a commentary, see M. Rashed, 'Traces d'un commentaire de Simplicius sur la *Métaphysique* à Byzance?', *Revue des sciences philosophiques et théologiques* 84 (2000), 275–84.

[36] We may legitimately ask ourselves why did Michael wish to supplement this commentary, if it was not for Anna Comnena. It is possible that he got down to it at the instigation of his 'master', in view of his own education (and in view of the education of others), as the following references may suggest; cf. *in Metaph.* 610,11–15: 'A thing of ten cubits long is divided either according to its form or according to its quantity. [It is divided] according to its form when we divide it into [the elements] of which it is composed, [i.e.] fire, earth and their intermediaries, or into sizes of such and such form; [it is divided] according to [mere] size [i.e. quantity] when it is divided into ten cubits. This is actually the explication of our master (*houtô men oun ho hêmeteros kathêgemôn exêgêsato*). But perhaps [the truth is] . . .'); 716,24–7: 'All these contribute to the nature of all. For there is no sensible thing without size and shape. This is actually how our master explicated the present passage (*houtô men oun ho hêmeteros kathêgemôn toparon exêgeito chôrion*). But perhaps [the truth is] . . .').

[37] This copyist is Malachias, alias *Anonymus aristotelicus*, who completed the missing parts of the Par. gr. 1876 (identified by Harlfinger in Hadot (n. 34 above), p. 244). The attribution of the commentary on Book *Epsilon* to Michael is actually a post-scriptum made by him, which suggests that Malachias based this attribution on the authorship of the following books. On the identification of the *Anonymus aristotelicus* with Malachias, see B. Mondrain, 'Traces et mémoire de la lecture des textes: les marginalia dans les manuscrits scientifiques byzantins', in D. Jacquart, ed., *Scientia in margine: Études sur les 'marginalia' dans les manuscrits scientifiques du Moyen Âge à la Renaissance* (Geneva: Librairie Droz, 2005), pp. 1–25, at pp. 24–5. George Pachymeres also thought that Book E was by Michael; cf. S. Ebbesen, *Commentators and Commentaries on Aristotle's Sophistici elenchi: A Study of Post-Aristotelian Ancient and Medieval Writings on Fallacies* (Leiden: Brill, 1981), vol. 3, p. 87. In all probability, the first to attribute Book *Epsilon* to Michael was George of Cyprus (1241–1289) in his autograph manuscript Paris Supplement gr. 642.

[38] Note that, despite the appearances, this set of editions is not at all homogeneous: while the eleventh century edition (Laur. 87,12) contains an integral commentary on the *Metaphysics* which is wholly anonymous and appears therefore to be homogeneous, those of the thirteenth century contain either an anonymous commentary (Laur. 85,1) or a commentary attributed to Michel (Par. gr. 1876), which presents itself as a supplement to Alexander's commentary.

person whose commentary he was about to supplement, was not too keen on naming himself as an exegete. As for us, we now know that Michael started his work from Book 7 (*Zeta*). In sum, everything leads us to believe that, just as the commentary on Books 1–5 (*Alpha-Delta*), the commentary on Book 6 (*Epsilon*) is also the work of the anonymous professor.[39]

If this is true, we can even venture into the identification of this professor. Twice in the commentary on Book 6 (*Epsilon*) the professor mentions his exegesis of the treatise *On the Soul*.[40] Now, we know of three Alexandrian philosophers who dealt with this treatise: Ammonius, John Philoponus and Stephanus. A reference to the various sections (*tmêmata*) of the treatise *On Interpretation* which follows,[41] directs us to Stephanus: whereas Ammonius proceeds in his own exegesis according to chapters (*kephalaia*), Stephanus structured his commentary on sections. It is true, on the other hand, that this Stephanus' commentary on *On Interpretation*, unlike the commentary on the *Metaphysics*, is divided into *praxeis*, i.e. into lessons. We might account for this by saying that the commentary on the *Metaphysics* is not a commentary 'from the voice' of the master (*apo phônês*); it is rather the preparation, probably incomplete, of a series of lectures on the *Metaphysics* that Stephanus was preparing to give.

But let us return to the Laur. 87,12 and the Ambr. F 113 sup., classified under the same heading of alternative *recensio* by Hayduck. At a careful reading, we observe that various exegetical blocks present in the Laurentianus are not copied in the Ambrosianus. In folio 13ʳ, for example, the Ambrosianus exhibits a commentary which seems to be complete, both from the point of view of the layout and from the point of view of the numbering of scholia: 58, 59, 60. However, this is most likely a numbering made anew, and not a numbering picked up from a model. For, just before the scholium which is here numbered 60, there is in fol. 31ʳ of the Laurentianus an exegetical block (i.e. a lemma + commentary), titled 30, which spreads over approximately two pages of Hayduck's edition (55,17–57,34), and which is lacking from the Ambrosianus. This

---

[39] The similarities in vocabulary and method that we can detect between the commentary on Book 6 (*Epsilon*) and the commentary on Books 7–14 (*Zeta-Nu*) should not be a problem. Michael naturally adapted himself to the style of his predecessor. This can be seen in the expression 'in the *Ethics* called *Nicomachean*' found in the commentary on Book 6 (*Epsilon*) (443,35–6) and encountered again in the commentary on Book 11 (*Kappa*) (659,29). But we find the expression 'in what is called the *Physics*' already in the commentary on Book 1 (*Alpha*) (see Hayduck (CAG 1), ad 22,22), then in the *prooimion* to Book 4 (*Gamma*) (ad 238.1): 'the present book called Gamma'. The restitution of the commentary on Book 6 (*Epsilon*) to the anonymous professor has obviously important implications for our understanding of Alexander's genuine commentary. For it is most likely that, as in the case for Books 1–5 (*Alpha-Delta*), the anonymous professor largely based his own commentary on Book 6 (*Epsilon*) on the commentary by Alexander.

[40] *in Metaph.* 441,8–9: 'As has been said by us in [our commentary on] *On the Soul*'; *in Metaph.* 445,12–13: 'The reason has been stated by us in [our commentary on] *On the Soul*'. The references concern the first book of the treatise *On the Soul* and suggest use of the commentary by Ammonius (published by Philoponus). Such a commentary on Books 1–2 of *On the Soul* is preserved in the manuscript Venezia, Biblioteca Marciana, gr. 223, where it is wrongly attributed to Simplicius. It would be worthwhile considering whether 'Simplicius' is a corruption of 'Stephanus', generated by the fact that this commentary on *On the Soul* is preceded in the same manuscript by Simplicius' commentary on the *Categories*. Luna (n. 31 above), p. 67, considers these references as homogeneous to two other references to the treatise *On the Soul*, which we find precisely in Books 7 (*Zeta*) (505,2) and 9 (*Theta*) (589,23–5). But one should cautiously take into account the absence of the words 'by us' (*hêmin*) in these last references.

[41] *in Metaph.* 452,8–10.

happens too often to be due to mere chance or to the lack of attention of the copyist. In fol. 20^r, to give another example, two exegetical blocks, corresponding to 99,1–101,31 and 104,19–105,2 of Hayduck's edition, are missing between the blocks numbered 87 and 88. It seems that the copyist of the Ambrosianus deliberately dispensed with some exegetical blocks so as to preserve in his manuscript the parallel presence, i.e. on the same page, of the commentary and of the commented text. This is clear in fol. 13^v, where a block of only a few lines (58,27–31) is omitted, obviously because the lemma corresponding to the block which follows it (numbered 61 in the Ambr.) is located at the beginning of the page. Aesthetic result and reading practice seem to dominate over exegetical completeness.

But it is not only exegetical blocks that are concerned. A few lines appearing in folio 41^v of the Laurentianus, and testifying to a variant reading of Aristotle's text (*anikia* instead of *adikia*), are omitted in the Ambrosianus (folio 17^v), perhaps because the copyist (or, of course, the patron of this copy) did not deem it important enough to retain it. In folio 72^v, the commentary is heavily abridged and, in a way, rewritten: 'If the negation is true', one reads in the Ambrosianus, 'it is evident that the affirmation is necessarily false; it is, therefore, impossible that contradictory propositions are true at the same time'. This passage may well construct a hypothetical syllogism that gives perfect sense as far as the principle of contradiction is concerned, but actually it omits a long explication which, in the Laur. (fol. 156^v), intervenes between the phrases 'the affirmation is false' and 'it is impossible that contradictory propositions are true at the same time'; we should pay attention, of course, to the addition of 'therefore' (*oun*) in the text transmitted by the manuscrit of Milan.

So the copyist of the Ambrosianus opts for brevity, and we may relate this peculiarity to another observation. It has recently been pointed out that, beginning from Book 11 (*Kappa*), the Ambrosianus no longer contains Michael of Ephesus' commentary, but contains the (unpublished) commentary by George Pachymeres (1242 – *c*. 1315).[42] It has also been pointed out that Pachymeres' commentary, distinguished by its brevity and clarity (Pachymeres' exegeses are generally called *suntomoi* and *saphestatai*),[43] begins to be present in the Ambrosianus already from chapter 6 of Book 9 (*Theta*). In fact, we encounter in folio 151^v–152^r of the Ambrosianus two exegetical blocks[44] borrowed from Pachymeres, the second of which remedies the missing exegesis of Michael.[45] In

---

[42] S. Alexandru, 'A new manuscript of Pseudo-Philoponus' Commentary on Aristotle's *Metaphysics* containing a hitherto unknown ascription of the work', *Phronesis* 44 (1999), 347–52.

[43] On Pachymeres' Aristotelian exegeses, see P. Golitsis, 'Georges Pachymère comme didascale: Essai pour une reconstitution de sa carrière et de son enseignement philosophique', *Jahrbuch der Österreichischen Byzantinistik* 58 (2008), 53–68.

[44] Inc. *mnêstheis peri tou apeirou* and *touto to kephalaion en pollois leipei*.

[45] Cf. Città del Vaticano, Bibliotheca Apostolica Vaticana, Urb. gr. 49, f. 105^v–106^r. See M. Burnyeat, '*Kinêsis* vs. *Energeia*: A Much-Read Passage in (but not of) Aristotle's *Metaphysics*', *Oxford Studies in Ancient Philosophy* 34 (2008), 219–92, at 231–6, who refers, following W. D. Ross, *Aristotle's Metaphysics: A Revised Text with Introduction and Commentary*, 2 vols (Oxford: Clarendon Press, 1924), vol. 2, p. 253, to the exegetical block bearing on 1048b18–35, a passage not commented by Michael. But one must also pay attention to the first block borrowed from Pachymeres, which actually replaces Michael's commentary on 1048b9–17.

conclusion, we note that, in spite of the appearances, the two manuscripts Laur. 87,12 and Ambr. F 113 sup. are distinguished from each other by the very texts they contain.

3. Modern Editing and Textual Criticism: A Simplistic Approach?

We may now summarise the items that the concept of *recensio* has extracted from the exegetical history of the *Metaphysics*: a) a commentary probably written by Stephanus of Alexandria, which was seen as an 'interpretation' of Alexander's commentary; b) a book belonging to the same commentary by Stephanus, i.e. the commentary on Book 6 (*Epsilon*), which was wrongly attributed to Michael of Ephesus; c) the latter, named Pseudo-Alexander, was seen as someone who undertook to continue Alexander's mutilated commentary (Tarán, following Bonitz,[46] even characterised him as a forger), whereas he continued a commentary which was, to him as well, anonymous; and d) the integral commentary thus produced was then further elaborated with the help of George Pachymeres' commentary.

We realise that the Byzantine pluralism in the field of editions of commentaries on the *Metaphysics* disappeared in modern times because of the framework imposed by a monistic approach: to edit Alexander of Aphrodisias' commentary on the *Metaphysics*. No doubt Hayduck devoted himself to a work of criticism; thanks to his complete collation of the Laur. 87,12, he managed to restore passages omitted by a leap from similar to similar in the two manuscripts of the first branch,[47] as well as to correct quite a few blunders. In this, he seems to have been unwittingly the first to take into account derivative texts (the anonymous commentary) in order to restore source texts (Alexander's commentary) in the editing of ancient commentaries. I say 'unwittingly', because, although he acknowledged the existence of what he called *recensio altera* of Alexander's commentary, deep down he persisted (also under Bonitz's shadow) in treating the manuscripts containing this *recensio* as direct witnesses of Alexander's text.[48] It is indeed this paradox that is reflected in the editorial artifice which Hayduck devised so as to describe the situation: he relegated the important divergences of the 'alternative recension' from the 'received recension', i.e. the divergences which he considered as being due to a conscious intervention on Alexander's text, to a separate apparatus (the apparatus of 'the more serious discrepancy of the alternative recension'), whereas the small discrepancies, i.e. the discrepancies which according to him were merely copying mistakes,[49] were recorded in the usual critical apparatus, alongside readings coming from the 'received recension'. This method certainly obeys a rational principle – distinction between intended intervention and unconscious alteration –, but in practice it is rather unsafe. On p. 53 of his edition, for example, we encounter in

---

[46] Bonitz (n. 3 above), pp. xvi–xvii.
[47] See Hayduck (CAG 1), p. viii, n. 2.
[48] That Hayduck was not conscious of the application of such a principle in the ecdotics of ancient texts is also deduced by the fact that he was unable to restore the corrupted word *hê*** idôn* in Alexander's text (4,3) by means of Asclepius' commentary (7,13: *khelidôn*), which he had edited three years earlier. See Golitsis (n. 13 above), p. 63 and n. 84.
[49] Hayduck (CAG 1), p. ix.

the critical apparatus a series of readings which are considered 'mistakes', and which are for this reason separated from the 'serious discrepancies' of the *recensio altera*. But if we combine the reading of the two apparatuses, say, from line 14 onwards, we obtain the following text which gives perfect sense and actually reflects the professor's voice:

> He also says about the Pythagoreans that they did not posit a different kind of nature which would be the substratum of numbers, but that they said that numbers themselves are a substance; in fact, they did not predicate the One of another nature either, but they considered that it is a substance which has its being in its being one. This is what he also relates about Plato, i.e. that he said in the manner of the Pythagoreans that the One is a substance, and not that it is a different nature according to its substratum, which would then be affected by its being one. This is what Plato said in the manner of the Pythagoreans and also [the following, namely] that numbers are also principles of beings, even though he did not say it in quite the same way. For the Pythagoreans said that numbers are principles of beings qua immanent to them and qua their matter, because, according to them, all beings are constituted by numbers; according to Plato, on the other hand, numbers are separate from sensible forms and they are their causes qua paradigms. He said 'in the same way' not because Plato said that numbers are the causes of substance precisely as the Pythagoreans said [they are], but because he said like the Pythagoreans that numbers are the causes of beings.

Such cases can easily be multiplied as a detailed reading of Hayduck's two apparatuses progresses. Things are obviously more complicated, this time from the point of view of the establishment of Alexander's genuine text, whenever Hayduck prefers the reading transmitted by L (Laur. 87,12) and F (Ambr. F 113 sup.) against a reasonable reading of A (Par. gr. 1876). A flagrant case is the very beginning of the commentary, which Hayduck established, following Bonitz, on the sole testimony of the Laur. 87,12. I think that I have provided many arguments towards doubting that the text established by Hayduck corresponds to what Alexander had actually written.

In more recent times, Leonardo Tarán and Concetta Luna engaged in a polemic about the commentary on the *Metaphysics* attributed to Michael of Ephesus. Despite their disagreement, they both treated Michael as someone who consciously relied on Alexander of Aphrodisias, the former in order to show that this part of the commentary is not by Michael, the latter in order to show that this part of the commentary is by Michael. Neither of the two thought to consider the possibility that Michael undertook to supplement an anonymous commentary, nor did they take seriously Michael's own record of the commentaries that he wrote. This is perhaps a logical consequence of the fact that they both based their arguments on a, to some extent, artificial edition, which sought to stabilise texts that, by their very nature of being texts conceived for educational purposes, were destined to be subject to dynamic processes.

I believe that we have not recognised that an ancient or Byzantine work is not an autonomous work exclusively by virtue of the originality of its content or of its attribution to an author's name, but also by virtue of a new organisation of texts and inherited subject matters, designed to serve new goals different from those that had originally been served by the texts used as sources or as working tools. Only solid editions, thus defined, of Byzantine (or Proto-Byzantine) works will be able to, first, do historical justice to the diversity of the productions of the Byzantine genius, and, second, help us restore scientifically and prudently texts which are subject to various vicissitudes. I shall leave for later inquiry how Pachymeres comes to have statements in common with Syrianus, although the most plausible suggestion would be that he used selectively as sources for his commentary on *Metaphysics* 13–14 both Syrianus and Michael.

The Ancient Commentators on Aristotle Translations

This list records all translations published in the Ancient Commentators on Aristotle series, 1987–2015, arranged by author. These were published by Duckworth from 1987 to 2010 (and co-published in the USA by Cornell University Press). Since 2011, they have been published by Bloomsbury, initially under the Bristol Classical Press imprint, and since 2015 under Bloomsbury's own name. Bloomsbury now offers the entire series (102 volumes by 2015) in hardback, paperback, and ebook formats. Translations from languages other than Greek (i.e. Syriac, Arabic, Latin) are noted.

Aeneas of Gaza

Theophrastus, trans. J. Dillon and D. Russell, 2012 (part vol.)

Alexander of Aphrodisias

On Aristotle Metaphysics 1, trans. W. Dooley, 1989
On Aristotle Metaphysics 2–3, trans. W. Dooley and A. Madigan, 1992
On Aristotle Metaphysics 4, trans. A. Madigan, 1993
On Aristotle Metaphysics 5, trans. W. Dooley, 1993
On Aristotle Prior Analytics 1.1–7, trans. J. Barnes, S. Bobzien, K. Flannery, and K. Ierodiakonou, 1991
On Aristotle Prior Analytics 1.8–13, trans. I. Mueller with J. Gould, 1999
On Aristotle Prior Analytics 1.14–22, trans. I. Mueller with J. Gould, 1999
On Aristotle Prior Analytics 1.23–31, trans. I. Mueller, 2006
On Aristotle Prior Analytics 1.32–46, trans. I Mueller, 2006
On Aristotle Topics 1, trans. J. M. Van Ophuijsen, 2000
On Aristotle On Sense Perception, trans. A. Towey, 2000
On Aristotle Meteorology 4, trans. E. Lewis, 1996
On the Soul: Part I, trans. V. Caston, 2012
Supplement to On the Soul, trans. R. W. Sharples, 2004
Quaestiones 1.1–2.15, trans. R. W. Sharples, 1992
Quaestiones 2.16–3.15, trans. R. W. Sharples, 1994
Ethical Problems, trans. R. W. Sharples, 1990
On Aristotle On Coming-to-Be and Perishing 2.2–5, trans. E. Gannagé (from Arabic), 2005

Ammonius

On Aristotle Categories, trans. G. Matthews and M. Cohen, 1991
On Aristotle On Interpretation 1–8, trans. D. Blank, 1996
On Aristotle On Interpretation 9, trans. D. Blank, 1998 (part vol.)

Anonymous

On Aristotle Nicomachean Ethics 8–9, trans. D. Konstan, 2001 (part vol.)

Aspasius

On Aristotle Nicomachean Ethics 1–4, 7–8, trans. D. Konstan, 2006
On Aristotle Nicomachean Ethics 8–9, trans. D. Konstan, 2001 (part vol.)

Boethius

On Aristotle On Interpretation 1–3, trans. A. Smith (from Latin), 2010
On Aristotle On Interpretation 4–6, trans. A. Smith (from Latin), 2011
On Aristotle On Interpretation 9, trans. N. Kretzmann (from Latin), 1998 (part vol.)

Dexippus

On Aristotle Categories, trans. J. Dillon, 1990

Michael of Ephesus

On Aristotle Nicomachean Ethics 8–9, trans. D. Konstan, 2001 (part vol.)

Olympiodorus

Life of Plato and On Plato First Alcibiades 1–9, trans. M. Griffin, 2015

Philoponus

On Aristotle Categories 1–5, trans. R. Sirkel, M. Tweedale, and J. Harris, 2015 (part vol.)
On Aristotle Posterior Analytics 1.1–8, trans. R. McKirahan, 2008
On Aristotle Posterior Analytics 1.9–18, trans. R. McKirahan, 2012
On Aristotle Posterior Analytics 1.19–34, trans. O. Goldin and M. Martijn, 2012
(?) *On Aristotle Posterior Analytics 2*, trans. O. Goldin, 2009

On Aristotle Meteorology 1.1–3, trans. I. Kupreeva, 2011
On Aristotle Meteorology 1.4–9, 12, trans. I Kupreeva, 2012
On Aristotle On Coming-to-Be and Perishing 1.1–5, trans. C. J. F. Williams, 1999
On Aristotle On Coming-to-Be and Perishing 1.6–2.4, trans. C. J. F. Williams, 2000
On Aristotle On Coming-to-Be and Perishing 2.5–11, trans. I. Kupreeva, 2005
On Aristotle On the Soul 1.1–2, trans. P. van der Eijk, 2005
On Aristotle On the Soul 1.3–5, trans. P. van der Eijk, 2006
On Aristotle On the Soul 2.1–6, trans. W. Charlton, 2005
On Aristotle On the Soul 2.7–12, trans. W. Charlton, 2005
(?) *On Aristotle On the Soul 3.1–8*, trans. W. Charlton, 2000
(?) *On Aristotle On the Soul 3.9–13*, trans. W. Charlton, 2000 (part vol.)
On Aristotle On the Intellect, trans. W. Charlton with F. Bossier, 1991
On Aristotle Physics 1.1–3, trans. C. Osborne, 2006
On Aristotle Physics 1.4–9, trans. C. Osborne, 2009
On Aristotle Physics 2, trans. A. R. Lacey, 1993
On Aristotle Physics 3, trans. M. Edwards, 1994
On Aristotle Physics 4.1–5, trans. K. Algra and J. van Ophuijsen, 2012
On Aristotle Physics 4.6–9, trans. P. Huby, 2012
On Aristotle Physics 4.10–14, trans. S. Broadie, 2011
On Aristotle Physics 5–8, trans. P. Lettinck (from Arabic), 1994 (part vol.)
Corollaries on Place and Void, trans. D. Furley, 1991 (part vol.)
Against Aristotle on the Eternity of the World, trans. C. Wildberg, 1987
Against Proclus on the Eternity of the World 1–5, trans. M. Share, 2005
Against Proclus on the Eternity of the World 6–8, trans. M. Share, 2005
Against Proclus on the Eternity of the World 9–11, trans. M. Share, 2010
Against Proclus on the Eternity of the World 12–18, trans. J. Wilberding, 2006
A Treatise Concerning the Whole and the Parts, trans. D. King (from Syriac), 2015 (part vol.)

Porphyry

On Aristotle Categories, trans. S. Strange, 1992
On Abstinence from Killing Animals, trans. G. Clark, 2000
To Gaurus On How Embryos are Ensouled, trans. J. Wilberding, 2011 (part vol.)
On What is in Our Power, trans. J. Wilberding, 2011 (part vol.)

Priscian

On Theophrastus on Sense Perception, trans. P. Huby, 1997 (part vol.)

Proclus

On Plato Cratylus, trans. B. Duvick, 2007
On the Existence of Evils, trans. J. Opsomer and C. Steel, 2003
On Providence, trans. C. Steel, 2007
Ten Problems Concerning Providence, trans. J. Opsomer and C. Steel, 2012

Simplicius

On Aristotle On the Heavens 1.1–4, trans. R. J. Hankinson, 2002
On Aristotle On the Heavens 1.2–3, trans. I. Mueller, 2011
On Aristotle On the Heavens 1.3–4, trans. I. Mueller, 2011
On Aristotle On the Heavens 1.5–9, trans. R. J. Hankinson, 2004
On Aristotle On the Heavens 1.10–12, trans. R. J. Hankinson, 2006
On Aristotle On the Heavens 2.1–9, trans. I. Mueller, 2004
On Aristotle On the Heavens 2.10–14, trans. I. Mueller, 2005
On Aristotle On the Heavens 3.1–7, trans. I. Mueller, 2009
On Aristotle On the Heavens 3.7–4.6, trans. I. Mueller, 2009
On Aristotle Categories 1–4, trans. M. Chase, 2003
On Aristotle Categories 5–6, trans. F. de Haas and B. Fleet, 2001
On Aristotle Categories 7–8, trans. B. Fleet, 2002
On Aristotle Categories 9–15, trans. R. Gaskin, 2000
On Aristotle Physics 1.3–4, trans. P. Huby and C. C. W. Taylor, 2011
On Aristotle Physics 1.5–9, trans. H. Baltussen, M. Atkinson, M. Share, and I. Mueller, 2012
On Aristotle Physics 2, trans. B. Fleet, 1997
On Aristotle Physics 3, trans. J. O. Urmson with P. Lautner, 2001
On Aristotle Physics 4.1–5 and 10–14, trans. J. O. Urmson, 1992
On Aristotle Physics 5, trans. J. O. Urmson, 1997
On Aristotle Physics 6, trans. D. Konstan, 1989
On Aristotle Physics 7, trans. C. Hagen, 1994
On Aristotle Physics 8.1–5, trans. I. Bodnar, M. Chase, and M. Share, 2012
On Aristotle Physics 8.6–10, trans. R. McKirahan, 2001
Corollaries on Place and Time, trans. J. O. Urmson with L. Siorvanes, 1992
On Aristotle on the Void, trans. J. O. Urmson, 1994 (part vol.)
Against Philoponus On the Eternity of the World, trans. C. Wildberg, 1991 (part vol.)
On Aristotle On the Soul 1.1–2.4, trans. J. O. Urmson with P. Lautner, 1995
(?) On Aristotle On the Soul 2.5–12, trans. C. Steel, 1997 (part vol.)
(?) On Aristotle On the Soul 3.1–5, trans. H. Blumenthal, 2000
(?) On Aristotle On the Soul 3.6–13, trans. C. Steel (with A. Ritups), 2012
On Epictetus Handbook 1–26, trans. C. Brittain and T. Brennan, 2002
On Epictetus Handbook 27–53, trans. T. Brennan and C. Brittain, 2002

Stephanus

On Aristotle On Interpretation, trans. W. Charlton, 2000 (part vol.)

Syrianus

On Aristotle Metaphysics 3–4, trans. D. O'Meara and J. Dillon, 2008
On Aristotle Metaphysics 13–14, trans. J. Dillon and D. O'Meara, 2006

Themistius

On Aristotle Physics 1–3, trans. R. B. Todd, 2012
On Aristotle Physics 4, trans. R. B. Todd, 2003
On Aristotle Physics 5–8, trans. R. B. Todd, 2008
On Aristotle on the Soul, trans. R. B. Todd, 1996

Zacharias of Mytilene

Ammonius, trans. S. Gertz, 2012 (part vol.)

Bibliography

The following bibliography lists items referred to in this volume. Editions of Greek, Arabic, and Latin texts (including volumes in the CAG series [Commentaria in Aristotelem Graeca, 23 vols (Berlin: Reimer, 1882-1909)]) are in general not listed, unless they are referred to for their editorial material. Translations are listed under the translator's name.

For a bibliography of work on the commentators up to 1990 see R. Sorabji, ed., *Aristotle Transformed* (London: Duckworth 1990), pp. 485-524, and reprinted in the second edition published alongside this volume by Bloomsbury, 2016. In 2004 John Sellars prepared a guide to work on the commentators from 1990 to 2004, conceived as a supplement to that bibliography (listed below). A bibliography of material since 2004 is available online at <www.ancientcommentators.org.uk/bibliographies.html>. This was initially prepared in 2013 by Annie Hewitt, and later expanded and reorganised in 2015 by Malcolm Nicolson, drawing on work by Katherine O'Reilly. Readers new to the ancient commentators may benefit from an annotated guide to the literature, also available online: J. Sellars, 'Ancient Commentators on Aristotle', in D. Clayman, ed., *Oxford Bibliographies in Classics* (New York: Oxford University Press, 2014), DOI: 10.1093/OBO/9780195389661-0158.

Accatino, P., and Donini, P., *Alessandro di Afrodisia, L'anima* (Rome: Laterza, 1996)
Ackrill, J. L., *Aristotle: Categories and De Interpretatione* (Oxford: Clarendon Press, 1963)
Adamson, P., 'Correcting Plotinus: Soul's Relationship to Body in Avicenna's Commentary on the *Theology of Aristotle*', in P. Adamson, H. Baltussen, and M. W. F. Stone, eds, *Philosophy, Science, and Exegesis in Greek, Arabic, and Latin Commentaries*, 2 vols (London: Institute of Classical Studies, 2004), vol. 2, pp. 59-75
Adamson, P., 'On Knowledge of Particulars', *Proceedings of the Aristotelian Society* 105 (2005), 273-94
Adamson, P., *Al-Kindī* (New York: Oxford University Press, 2007)
Adamson, P., 'Knowledge of Universals and Particulars in the Baghdad School', *Documenti e Studi sulla Tradizione Filosofica Medievale* 18 (2007), 141-64
Adamson, P., 'Miskawayh's Psychology', in P. Adamson, ed., *Classical Arabic Philosophy: Sources and Reception* (London: The Warburg Institute, 2007), pp. 39-54
Adamson, P., 'The Kindian Tradition: The Structure of Philosophy in Arabic Neoplatonism', in C. D'Ancona, ed., *Libraries of the Neoplatonists* (Leiden: Brill, 2007), pp. 351-70
Adamson, P., '*Posterior Analytics* II.19: a Dialogue with Plato?', in V. Harte, M. M. McCabe, R. W. Sharples, and A. Sheppard, eds, *Aristotle and the Stoics Reading Plato* (London: Institute of Classical Studies, 2010), pp. 1-19
Adamson, P., 'Yaḥyā ibn ʿAdī and Averroes on *Metaphysics* Alpha Elatton', *Documenti e Studi sulla Tradizione Filosofica Medievale* 21 (2010), 343-74
Adamson, P., ed., *Ancient Philosophy in Memory of R. W. Sharples* = *Bulletin of the Institute of Classical Studies* 55/1 (2012)
Adamson, P., 'Arabic Philosophy: *Falsafa* and the *Kalām* Tradition before Avicenna', in J. Marenbon, ed., *The Oxford Handbook of Medieval Philosophy* (New York: Oxford University Press, 2012), pp. 58-82

Adamson, P., 'Galen and Al-Rāzī on Time', in Rotraud Hansberger, M. Afifi al-Akiti, and Charles Burnett, eds, *Medieval Arabic Thought: Essays in Honour of Fritz Zimmermann* (London: The Warburg Institute, 2012), pp. 1–14

Adamson, P., and Key, A., 'Philosophy of Language in the Medieval Arabic Tradition', in M. Cameron and R. Stainton, eds, *Linguistic Content: New Essays in the History of the Philosophy of Language* (Oxford: Oxford University Press, 2015), pp. 74–99

Adamson, P., and Pormann, P. E., *The Philosophical Works of al-Kindī* (Karachi: Oxford University Press, 2012)

Alberti, A., and Sharples, R. W., eds, *Aspasius: The Earliest Extant Commentary on Aristotle's Ethics* (Berlin: De Gruyter, 1999)

Alexandru, S., 'A new manuscript of Pseudo-Philoponus' Commentary on Aristotle's *Metaphysics* containing a hitherto unknown ascription of the work', *Phronesis* 44 (1999), 347–52

Algra, K., and van Ophuijsen, J., *Philoponus, On Aristotle Physics 4.1–5* (London: Bristol Classical Press, 2012)

Alline, H., *Histoire du Texte de Platon* (Paris: Librairie Ancienne Honoré Champion, 1915)

Anawati, G. C., 'Un fragment perdu du *De aeternitate mundi* de Proclus', *Mélanges de philosophie grecque offerts à Mgr. Diès par ses élèves, ses collègues, ses amis* (Paris: Vrin, 1956), pp. 21–5

Andrés, G., 'La biblioteca de Don Diego Hurtado de Mendoza (1576)', *Documentos para la historia di Monasterio de San Lorenzo el Real de El Escorial 7* (Madrid: Sáez, 1964)

Andrés, G., *Catálogo de los códices griegos desaparecidos de la Real Biblioteca de El Escorial* (San Lorenzo de El Escorial: Imprenta del Monasterio, 1968)

Annas, J., *Hellenistic Philosophy of Mind* (Berkeley: University of California Press, 1992)

Aouad, M., and Goulet, R., 'Alexandros d'Aphrodisias', in R. Goulet, ed., *Dictionnaire des philosophes antiques I* (Paris: CNRS, 1989), pp. 125–39

Arnzen, R., *Aristoteles' De anima: eine verlorene spätantike Paraphrase in arabischer und persicher Überlieferung* (Leiden: Brill, 1998)

Asztalos, M., 'Boethius as a Transmitter of Greek Logic to the Latin West: The *Categories*', *Harvard Studies in Classical Philology* 95 (1993), 367–407

Athanassiadi, P., *Damascius, the Philosophical History* (Athens: Apamea, 1999)

Aubenque, P., *La Prudence chez Aristote* (Paris: PUF, 1963; 2nd edn 1976)

Aubry, G., *Dieu sans la puissance: Dunamis et energeia chez Aristote et chez Plotin* (Paris: Vrin, 2006)

Avicenna, *Liber Tertius Naturalium De Generatione et Corruptione*, édition critique de la traduction latine médiévale par S. Van Riet, Introduction doctrinale par G. Verbeke (Leuven: Peeters, 1987)

Badawi, A., *La transmission de la philosophie grecque au monde arabe*, 2nd edn (Paris: Vrin, 1987)

Badawi, A., *Neoplatonici apud Arabes* (Cairo, 1955)

Balme, D. M., 'Development in Biology in Aristotle and Theophrastus: Theory of Spontaneous Generation', *Phronesis* 7 (1962), 91–104

Baltes, M., *Die Weltenstehung des Platonischen Timaios nach den antiken Interpreten*, 2 vols (Leiden: Brill, 1976–78)

Baltussen, H., 'Simplicius of Cilicia', in L. P. Gerson, ed., *The Cambridge History of Philosophy in Late Antiquity*, 2 vols (Cambridge: Cambridge University Press, 2010), vol. 2, pp. 711–32

Balty, J., 'Les mosaïques des maisons de Palmyre', *Bibliothèque archéologique et historique* 206 (2011), 1–70

Baltzly, D., 'What goes up: Proclus against Aristotle on the fifth element', *Australasian Journal of Philosophy* 80 (2002), 261–87
Bandini, A. M., *Catalogus Codicum Manuscriptorum Bibliothecae Mediceae Laurentianae* (Florence, 1770; repr. Leipzig: Zentral-Antiquariat der Deutschen Demokratischen Republik, 1961)
Barnes, J., ed., *The Complete Works of Aristotle: The Revised Oxford Translation*, 2 vols (Princeton: Princeton University Press, 1984)
Barnes, J., 'The Hellenistic Platos', *Apeiron* 24 (1991), 115–28
Barnes, J., 'Roman Aristotle', in M. Griffin and J. Barnes, eds, *Philosophia Togata II: Plato and Aristotle at Rome* (Oxford: Clarendon Press, 1997), pp. 1–69
Barnes, J., *Porphyry, Introduction* (Oxford: Clarendon Press, 2003)
Barnes, J., et al., *Alexander of Aphrodisias, On Aristotle Prior Analytics 1.1–7* (London: Duckworth, 1991)
Baumstark, A., *Aristoteles bei den Syrern vom 5. bis 8. Jahrhundert* (Leipzig: Teubner, 1900)
Bausani, A., *Un filosofo "laico" del medioevo musulmano: Abū Bakr Muḥammad ben Zakiryya Rāzī* (Rome: Istituto di studi islamici, 1981)
Bernard, W., 'Philoponus on Self-Awareness', in R. Sorabji, ed., *Philoponus and the Rejection of Aristotelian Science* (London: Duckworth, 1987), pp. 154–63
Berryman, S., '"It Makes No Difference": Optics and Natural Philosophy in Late Antiquity', *Apeiron* 45 (2012), 201–20
Bertolacci, A., 'Different Attitudes to Aristotle's Authority in the Arabic Medieval Commentaries on the *Metaphysics*', *Antiquorum Philosophia* 3 (2009), 145–63
Blank, D., *Ammonius, On Aristotle On Interpretation 1–8* (London: Duckworth, 1996)
Blank, D., 'Ammonius Hermeiou and his School', in L. P. Gerson, ed., *The Cambridge History of Philosophy in Late Antiquity*, 2 vols (Cambridge: Cambridge University Press, 2010), vol. 2, pp. 654–66
Blank, D., 'Ammonius', in E. N. Zalta, ed., *The Stanford Encyclopedia of Philosophy* (Fall 2014 Edition), <http://plato.stanford.edu/archives/fall2014/entries/ammonius/>
Blank, D., and Kretzmann, N., *Ammonius, On Aristotle On Interpretation 9, with Boethius, On Aristotle On Interpretation 9* (London: Duckworth, 1998)
Blum, R., *Kallimachos: The Alexandrian Library and the Origins of Bibliography* (Wisconsin: The University of Wisconsin Press, 1991)
Blumenthal, H. J., 'Neoplatonic Elements in the *De Anima* Commentaries', *Phronesis* 21 (1976), 64–87
Blumenthal, H. J., 'John Philoponus and Stephanus of Alexandria: Two Neoplatonic Christian Commentaries on Aristotle?', in D. J. O'Meara, ed., *Neoplatonism and Christian Thought* (Albany: State University of New York Press, 1982), pp. 54–63
Blumenthal, H. J., 'Alexandria as a Centre of Greek Philosophy in Later Classical Antiquity', *Illinois Classical Studies* 18 (1993), 307–25
Blumenthal, H. J. *Aristotle and Neoplatonism in Late Antiquity: Interpretations of the De Anima* (Ithaca: Cornell University Press, 1996)
Bobzien, S., 'Stoic Conceptions of Freedom and their Relation to Ethics', in R. Sorabji, ed., *Aristotle and After* (London: Institute of Classical Studies, 1997), pp. 71–89
Bobzien, S., *Determinism and Freedom in Stoic Philosophy* (Oxford: Clarendon Press, 1998)
Bobzien, S., 'Did Epicurus Discover the Free Will Problem?', *Oxford Studies in Ancient Philosophy* 19 (2000), 287–337
Bodéüs, R., *Porphyre, Commentaire aux Catégories d'Aristote* (Paris: Vrin, 2008)

Bodnar, I., 'Aristotle's Natural Philosophy', in E. N. Zalta, ed., *The Stanford Encyclopedia of Philosophy* (Spring 2012 Edition), <http://plato.stanford.edu/archives/spr2012/entries/aristotle-natphil/>

Böhm, W., *Johannes Philoponos, Grammatikos von Alexandrien: Ausgewählte Schriften* (Munich: Schöningh, 1967)

Bonazzi, M., 'Eudoro di Alessandria alle origini del Platonismo imperiale', in M. Bonazzi and V. Celluprica, eds, *L' Eredità Platonica: Studi sul Platonismo da Arcesilao a Proclo* (Naples: Bibliopolis, 2005), pp. 117–60

Bonitz, H., *Alexandri Aphrodisiensis Commentarius in libros metaphysicos Aristotelis* (Berlin: Reimer, 1847)

Bonitz, H., *Index Aristotelicus* (Berlin: Reimer, 1870)

Boudon-Millot, V., 'Un traité perdu de Galien miraculeusement retrouvé, le *Sur l'inutilité de se chagriner*', in V. Boudon-Millot, A. Guardasole, and C. Magdelain, eds, *La science médicale antique: Nouveaux regards* (Paris: Beauchesne, 2007), pp. 73–123

Boudon-Millot, V., Jouanna, J. and Pietrobelli, A., *Galien, Ne pas se chagriner* (Paris: Les Belles Lettres, 2010)

Boys-Stones, G., *Post-Hellenistic Philosophy: A Study of its Development from the Stoics to Origen* (Oxford: Oxford University Press, 2001)

Brague, R., *Themistius, Paraphrase de La* Métaphysique *D'Aristote (Livre Lamda)* (Paris: Vrin, 1999)

Brandis, C. A., *Scholia Graeca in Aristotelis Metaphysica* (Berlin: Typis Acadmicis, 1837)

Brandis, C. A., *Scholia in Aristotelem*, Aristotelis Opera 4 (Berlin: Reimer, 1836)

Brisson, L., '*Logos* et *logoi* chez Plotin, leur nature et leur rôle', *Les Cahiers Philosophiques de Strasbourg* 8 (1999), 87–108

Brisson, L., 'Le commentaire comme prière destinée à assurer le salut de l'âme', in M.-O. Goulet-Cazé, ed., *Le commentaire entre tradition et innovation* (Paris: Vrin, 2000), pp. 329–53

Brisson, L., ed., *Porphyre, Sentences*, 2 vols (Paris: Vrin, 2005)

Brisson, L., et al., *Porphyre, La Vie de Plotin*, 2 vols (Paris: Vrin, 1982–92)

Brisson, L., and Pradeau, J.-F., *Plotin, Traités*, 8 vols (Paris: GF-Flammarion, 2002–10)

Brittain, C., 'Non-Rational perception in the Stoics and Augustine', *Oxford Studies in Ancient Philosophy* 22 (2002), 253–308

Brittain, C., 'Common Sense: Concepts, Definition and Meaning in and Out of the Stoa', in D. Frede and B. Inwood, eds, *Language and Learning* (Cambridge: Cambridge University Press, 2005), pp. 164–209

Brittain, C., and Brennan, T., *Simplicius, On Epictetus Handbook*, 2 vols (London: Duckworth, 2002)

Brock, S., 'The Syriac Commentary Tradition' in C. Burnett, ed., *Glosses and Commentaries on Aristotelian Logical Texts* (London: The Warburg Institute, 1993), pp. 3–18

Brock, S., 'The Commentator Probus: Problems of Date and Identity', in J. Lössl and J. W. Watt, eds, *Interpreting the Bible and Aristotle in Late Antiquity* (Farnham: Ashgate, 2011), pp. 195–206

Browning, R., 'An Unpublished Funeral Oration on Anna Comnena', *Proceedings of the Cambridge Philological Society* 8 (1962), 1–12; repr. in R. Sorabji, ed., *Aristotle Transformed: The Ancient Commentators and their Influence* (London: Duckworth 1990), pp. 393–406

Brunschwig, J., 'La forme, prédicat de la matière ?', in P. Aubenque, ed., *Etudes sur la Métaphysique d'Aristote* (Paris : Vrin, 1979), pp. 131–66

Brunschwig, J., 'La théorie stoïcienne du genre suprême', in J. Barnes and M. Mignucci, eds, *Matter and Metaphysics* (Naples: Bibliopolis, 1988), pp. 19-127

Burnyeat, M. F., 'Is an Aristotelian Philosophy Of Mind Still Credible? (A Draft)', in M. C. Nussbaum and A. O. Rorty, eds, *Essays on Aristotle's De anima* (Oxford: Clarendon Press, 1992), pp. 15-26

Burnyeat, M. F., 'Aquinas on "Spiritual Change" in Perception', in D. Perler, ed., *Ancient and Medieval Theories of Intentionality* (Leiden: Brill, 2001), pp. 129-55

Burnyeat, M. F., 'What Was the 'Common Arrangement'? An Inquiry into John Stuart Mill's Boyhood Reading of Plato', *Apeiron* 34 (2001), 51-90

Burnyeat, M. F., '*De Anima* II 5', *Phronesis* 47 (2002), 28-91

Burnyeat, M. F., 'Aristotelian Revisions: The Case of the *De Sensu*', *Apeiron* 37 (2004), 177-80

Burnyeat, M. F., '*Kinêsis* vs. *Energeia*: A Much-Read Passage in (but not of) Aristotle's *Metaphysics*', *Oxford Studies in Ancient Philosophy* 34 (2008), 219-92

Caston, V., 'Something and Nothing: The Stoics on Concepts and Universals', *Oxford Studies in Ancient Philosophy* 17 (1999), 145-213

Caston, V., 'The Spirit and the Letter: Aristotle on Perception', in R. Salles, ed., *Metaphysics, Soul, and Ethics in Ancient Thought: Themes from the Work of Richard Sorabji* (Oxford: Clarendon Press, 2005), pp. 245-321

Cavallo, G., 'Scritture informali, cambio grafico e pratiche librarie a Bisanzio tra i secoli XI e XII', in G. Prato, ed., *I manoscritti greci tra riflessione e dibattito* (Florence: Gonnelli, 2000), pp. 219-38

Chaniotis, A., 'Epigraphic evidence for the philosopher Alexander of Aphrodisias', *Bulletin of the Institute of Classical Studies* 47 (2004), 78-81

Charlton, W., *Philoponus, On Aristotle on the Intellect* (London: Duckworth, 1991)

Charlton, W., '*Philoponus*', *On Aristotle On the Soul 3.1-8* (London: Duckworth, 2000)

Charlton, W., '*Philoponus*', *On Aristotle On the Soul 3.9-13, with Stephanus, On Aristotle On Interpretation* (London: Duckworth, 2000)

Charlton, W., *Philoponus, On Aristotle On the Soul 2.1-6* (London: Duckworth, 2005)

Charlton, W., *Philoponus, On Aristotle On the Soul 2.7-12* (London: Duckworth, 2005)

Chase, M., 'The Medieval Posterity of Simplicius' Commentary on the *Categories*: Thomas Aquinas and Al-Fārābī, in L. A. Newton, ed., *Medieval Commntaries on Aristotle's Categories* (Leiden: Brill, 2008), pp. 9-29

Chase, M., 'Philoponus' Cosmology in the Arabic tradition', *Recherches de Théologie et Philosophie médiévale* 79 (2012), 271-306

Cherniss, H., *Aristotle's Criticism of Plato and the Early Academy* (Baltimore: The Johns Hopkins Press, 1946)

Chiaradonna, R., 'La teoria dell'individuo in Porfirio e l'*idiôs poion* stoico', *Elenchos* 21 (2000), 303-31

Chiaradonna, R., 'Universali e intelligibili in Plotino', in V. Celluprica and C. D'Ancona, eds, *Aristotele e i suoi esegetici neoplatonici* (Naples: Elenchos, 2004), pp. 1-35

Chiaradonna, R., 'Porphyry and Iamblichus on Universals and Synonymous Predication', *Documenti e studi sulla tradizione filosofica medievale* 18 (2007), 123-40

Chiaradonna, R., 'Porphyry's Views on the Immanent Incorporeals', in G. Karamanolis and A. Sheppard, eds, *Studies on Porphyry* (London: Institute of Classical Studies, 2007), pp. 35-49

Chiaradonna, R., 'What is Porphyry's *Isagôgê*?', *Documenti e Studi sulla tradizione filosofica medievale* 19 (2008), 1-30

Chiaradonna, R., 'Alexander, Boethus and the other Peripatetics: The Theory of Universals in the Aristotelian Commentators', in R. Chiaradonna and G. Galuzzo, eds, *Universals in Ancient Philosophy* (Pisa: Edizioni della Normale, 2013), pp. 299–328

Chiaradonna, R., 'Platonist Approaches to Aristotle from Antiochus of Ascalon to Eudorus of Alexandria (and beyond)', in M. Schofield, ed., *Aristotle, Plato and Pythagoreanism in the First Century BC* (Cambridge: Cambridge University Press, 2013), pp. 28–52

Chiaradonna, R., 'Galen on What is Persuasive (*Pithanon*) and What Approximates to Truth', in P. Adamson, R. Hansberger, and J. Wilberding, eds, *Philosophical Themes in Galen* (London: Institute of Classical Studies, 2014), pp. 61–88

Chiaradonna, R., 'La *Lettera a Temistio* di Giuliano Imperatore e il dibattiyo filosofico nel IV secolo', in A. Marcone, ed., *L'imperatore Giuliano: Realtà storica e rappresentazione* (Florence: Le Monnier, 2015), pp. 149–71

Chiaradonna, R., 'Medioplatonismo e Aristotelismo', *Rivista di storia di filosofia* 2 (2015), 426–46

Chiaradonna, R., Rashed, M., and Sedley, D. N., 'A Rediscovered *Categories* Commentary', *Oxford Studies in Ancient Philosophy* 44 (2013), 129–94

Chiesa, C., 'Le problème du langage intérieur chez les Stoiciens', *Revue internationale de philosophie* 45, 178 (1991), 301–21

Christensen de Groot, J., 'Philoponus on *De Anima* II, 5, *Physics* III, 3 and the propagation of light', *Phronesis* 28 (1983), 177–96

Claghorn, G., *Aristotle's Criticism of Plato's Timaeus* (The Hague: Nijhoff, 1954)

Clark, G., 'Translate into Greek: Porphyry of Tyre on the New Barbarians', in M. Richard, ed., *Constructing Identities in Late Antiquity* (London: Routledge, 1999), pp. 112–32

Clark, G., 'Animal Passions', *Greece & Rome* 47 (2000), 88–93

Clark, G., 'Philosophic Lives and the Philosophic Life: Porphyry and Iamblichus', in T. Hägg and P. Rousseau, eds, *Greek Biography and Panegyric in Late Antiquity* (Berkeley: University of California Press, 2000), pp. 29–51

Clark, G., *Porphyry, On Abstinence from Killing Animals* (London: Duckworth, 2000)

Clark, G., 'Augustine's Porphyry and the Universal Way of Salvation', in G. Karamanolis and A. Sheppard, eds, *Studies on Porphyry* (London: Institute of Classical Studies, 2007), pp. 127–40

Clark, G., *Iamblichus, On the Pythagorean Life* (Liverpool: Liverpool University Press, 1989)

Clarke, E. C., Dillon, J. M., and Hershbell, J. P., *Iamblichus, De mysteriis* (Leiden: Brill, 2004)

Clavius, C., *In Sphaeram Ioannis de Sacro Bosco commentarius* (Geneva: Samuel Crispinus, 1608)

Coda, E., 'Un fragment du commentaire perdu au *De Caelo* d'Alexandre d'Aphrodise sur les different sens des termes "engendré" et "inengendré" Thémistius *In De Caelo* p. 43,3–44,17 Landauer', *Studia graeco-arabica* 5 (2015), 13–26

Code, A., 'Potentiality in Aristotle's Science and Metaphysics', in F. A. Lewis and R. Bolton, eds, *Form, Matter, and Mixture in Aristotle* (Oxford: Blackwell, 1996), pp. 217–30

Code, A., 'Some Remarks on Metaphysics Λ 5', in M. Frede and D. Charles, eds, *Aristotle's Metaphysics Lambda* (Oxford: Clarendon Press, 2000), pp. 161–79

Croese, I. *Simplicius on Continuous and Instantaneous Change* (Utrecht: Faculteit Wijsbegeerte, 1998)

D'Ancona, C., 'Commenting on Aristotle from Late Antiquity to the Arab Aristotelianism', in W. Geerlings and C. Schulze, eds, *Der Kommentar in Antike und Mittelalter* (Leiden: Brill, 2002), pp. 201–51

D'Ancona, C., 'Greek into Arabic: Neoplatonism in Translation', in P. Adamson and R. C. Taylor, eds, *The Cambridge Companion to Arabic Philosophy* (Cambridge: Cambridge University Press, 2005), pp. 10–31

D'Ancona, C., 'The Topic of the 'Harmony Between Plato and Aristotle': Some Examples in Early Arabic Philosophy', in A. Speer, ed., *Wissen über Grenzen. Arabisches Wissen und lateinisches Mittelalter* (Berlin: De Gruyter, 2006), pp. 379–405

D'Ancona, C., 'Greek Sources in Arabic and Islamic Philosophy', in E. N. Zalta, ed., *Stanford Encyclopedia of Philosophy*, <http://plato.stanford.edu/entries/arabic-islamic-greek>

Daiber, H., 'Ein vergessener Syrischer Text: Bar Zoʻbî über die Teile der Philosophie', *Oriens Christianus* 69 (1985), 73–80

Daiber, H., 'Die syrische Tradition in frühislamischer Zeit', in U. Rudolph, ed., *Grundriss der Geschichte der Philosophie: Philosophie in der islamischen Welt 1. 8.-10. Jahrhundert* (Basel: Schwabe, 2012), pp. 40–54

Dalsgaard Larsen, B., *Iamblique de Chalcis, Exégète et Philosophe* (Aarhus: Universitetsforlaget, 1972)

Daremberg, C., and Saglio, E., *Dictionnaire des Antiquités grecques et romaines*, vol. 2.2 (Paris: Hachette, 1896)

Darrouzès, J., *Georges et Dèmètrios Tornikès, Lettres et Discours* (Paris: CNRS, 1970)

Davidson, H. A., 'John Philoponus as a Source of Medieval Islamic and Jewish Proofs of Creation', *Journal of the American Oriental Society* 89 (1969), 357–91

Davidson, H. A., *Proofs for Eternity, Creation and the Existence of God in Medieval Islamic and Jewish Philosophy* (New York: Oxford University Press, 1987)

De Corte, M., ed., *Le Commentaire de Jean Philopon sur le Troisieme Livre du « Traité de l'Ame » d'Aristote* (Liège: Bibliothèque de la Faculté de Philosophie et Lettres de l'Université de Liège, 1934)

De Haas, F. A. J., *John Philoponus' New Definition of Prime Matter: Aspects of its Background in Neoplatonism and the Ancient Commentary Tradition* (Leiden: Brill, 1997)

De Haas, F. A. J., 'Mixture in Philoponus: An Encounter with a Third Kind of Potentiality', in J. M. M. H. Thijssen and H. A. G. Braakhuis, eds, *The Commentary Tradition on De Generatione et Corruptione* (Turnhout: Brepols, 1999), pp. 21–46

De Haas, F. A. J., 'Recollection and Potentiality in Philoponus', in M. Kardaun and J. Spruyt, eds, *The Winged Chariot* (Leiden: Brill, 2000), pp. 165–84

Delatte, A., *Anecdota Atheniensia et alia*, II (Liège and Paris: Faculté de Philosophie et Lettres de l'Université de Liège, 1939)

Den Boeft, J., *Calcidius on Fate: His Doctrines and Sources* (Leiden: Brill, 1970)

Diekamp, Franz ed., *Doctrina Patrum de Incarnatione Verbi*, 2nd edn (Münster: Aschendorff, 1981)

Dieterici, F., *Alfārābī's Philosophische Abhandlungen aus Londoner, Leidener und Berliner Handschriften* (Leiden: Brill, 1890)

Dietrich, A., 'Die arabische Version einer unbekannten Schrift des Alexander von Aphrodisias über die Differentia specifica', *Nachrichten der Akademie der Wissenschaften in Göttingen: Philologisch-historische Klasse* 2 (1964), 93–100

Dillon, J. M., *Iamblichi Chalcidensis: in Platonis Dialogos Commentariorum Fragmenta* (Leiden: Brill, 1973)

Dillon, J. M., *Alcinous, The Handbook of Platonism* (Oxford: Clarendon Press, 1993)

Dillon, J. M., *The Middle Platonists: A Study of Platonism 80 BC to AD 220*, 2nd edn (London: Duckworth, 1996)

Dillon, J. M., 'Iamblichus' *noera theôria* of Aristotle's *Categories*', *Syllecta Classica* 8 (1997), 65–77

Dillon, J. M., and O'Meara, D., *Syrianus, On Aristotle Metaphysics 13-14* (London: Duckworth, 2006)
Dillon, J. M., and Polleichtner, W., *Iamblichus of Chalcis, The Letters*, (Atlanta: Society of Biblical Literature, 2009)
Dinsmore, C. E., 'Premodern Theories of Generation', in Gary B. Ferngren, ed., *The History of Science and Religion in the Western Tradition* (New York: Garland, 2000), pp. 541-8
Dix, T. K., 'The library of Lucullus', *Athenaeum* 2 (2000), 441-64
Dodge, B., *The Fihrist of al-Nadīm: A Tenth-Century Survey of Muslim Culture*, 2 vols (New York: Columbia University Press, 1970)
Dombrowski, D. A., *Vegetarianism: The Philosophy Behind the Ethical Diet* (Amherst: University of Massachussetts Press, 1984)
Donini, P., 'Testi e commenti, manuali e insegnamento: la forma sistematica e i metodi della filosofia in eta postellenistica', in W. Haase, ed., *Aufstieg und Niedergang der römischen Welt* II 36.7 (Berlin: De Gruyter 1994), pp. 5027-5100
Donini, P., *Commentary and Tradition* (Berlin: De Gruyter, 2011)
Dooley, W. E., *Alexander of Aphrodisias, On Aristotle Metaphysics 1* (London: Duckworth, 1989)
Dooley, W. E., *Alexander of Aphrodisias, On Aristotle Metaphysics 2 & 3* (London: Duckworth, 1992)
Dorandi, T., '"Editori" antichi di Platone', *Antiquorum Philosophia* 4 (2010), 161-74
Dörrie, H., *Porphyrios' Symmikta Zetemata: Ihre Stellung in System und Geschichte des Neuplatonismus nebst einem Kommentar zu den Fragmenten* (Munich: Beck, 1959)
Dörrie, H., *Der Platonismus in der Antike II: Der hellenistische Rahmen des kaiserzeitlichen Platonismus* (Stuttgart: Frommann-Holzboog, 1990)
Dörrie, H., and Baltes, M., *Der Platonismus in der Antike V: Platonische Physik (im antiken Verständnis) II* (Stuttgart: Frommann-Holzboog, 1998)
Dörrie, H., and Baltes, M., *Der Platonismus in der Antike VI.1-2: Von der 'Seele' als der Ursache aller sinnvollen Abläufe* (Stuttgart: Frommann-Holzboog, 2002)
Dunlop, D. M., 'The Existence and Definition of Philosophy', *Iraq* 13 (1951), 76-94
Düring, I., *Porphyrius, Kommentar zur Harmonielehre des Ptolemaios* (Göteborg, 1932; repr. Hildesheim: Olms, 1978)
Düring, I., *Aristotle in the Ancient Biographical Tradition* (Göteborg: Elanders, 1957)
Düring, I., 'Ptolemy's Vita Aristotelis rediscovered', in R. B. Palmer and R. Hammerton-Kelly, eds, *Philomathes, In Memory of Philip Merlan* (The Hague: Nijhoff, 1971), pp. 264-9
Dyson, H., *Prolepsis and Ennoia in the Early Stoa* (Berlin: De Gruyter, 2009)
Ebbesen, S., 'Analyzing syllogisms or *Anonymous Aurelianensis III* - the (presumably) earliest extant Latin commentary on the *Prior Analytics*, and its Greek model', *Cahiers de l'Institut du Moyen-Âge Grec et Latin* 37 (1981), 9-11
Ebbesen, S., *Commentators and Commentaries on Aristotle's Sophistici Elenchi: A Study of Post-Aristotelian Ancient and Medieval Writings on Fallacies*, 3 vols (Leiden: Brill, 1981)
Ebbesen, S., 'Boethius as an Aristotelian Scholar', in J. Wiesner, ed., *Aristoteles: Werk und Wirkung*, 2 vols (Berlin: De Gruyter, 1986), vol. 2, pp. 286-311
Ebbesen, S., 'Boethius as an Aristotelian Commentator', in R. Sorabji, ed., *Aristotle Transformed* (London: Duckworth, 1990), pp. 373-91
Ebbesen, S., 'Philoponus, 'Alexander', and the Origins of Medieval Logic', in R. Sorabji, ed., *Aristotle Transformed* (London: Duckworth, 1990), pp. 445-61
Ebbesen, S., 'Porphyry's Legacy to Logic: A Reconstruction', in R. Sorabji, ed., *Aristotle Transformed* (London: Duckworth, 1990), pp. 141-71

Ebied, R. Y., Van Roey, A., and Wickham, L. R., *Peter of Callinicum, Anti-Tritheist Dossier* (Leuven: Peeters, 1981)
Edwards, G. F., 'Irrational Animals in Porphyry's Logical Works: A Problem for the Consensus Interpretation of *On Abstinence*', *Phronesis* 59 (2014), 22–43
Edwards, G. F., 'Food for Thought', in P. Adamson and G. F. Edwards, eds, *Animals* (Oxford: Oxford University Press, forthcoming)
Edwards, M., 'Two Images of Pythagoras: Iamblichus and Porphry', in H. J. Blumenthal and E. G. Clark, eds, *The Divine Iamblichus* (London: Duckworth, 1993), pp. 159–72
Edwards, M., 'Porphyry and the Christians', in G. Karamanolis and A. Sheppard, eds, *Studies on Porphyry* (London: Institute of Classical Studies, 2007), pp. 111–26
Elamrani-Jamal, A., 'Grammaire et logique d'après le philosophe arabe chrétien Yaḥyā b. ʿAdī (280–364 H/893–974)', *Arabica* 29 (1982), 1–15
Elamrani-Jamal, A., *Logique aristotélicienne et grammaire arabe: étude et documents* (Paris: Vrin, 1983)
Elders, L., *Aristotle's Theology* (Assen: Van Gorcum, 1972)
Ellis, J., 'The Trouble with Fragrance', *Phronesis* 35 (1990), 290–302
Elm, S., *Sons of Hellenism, Fathers of the Church* (Berkeley: University of California Press, 2012)
Emilsson, E. K., *Plotinus on Sense Perception* (Cambridge: Cambridge University Press, 1988)
Emilsson, E. K., *Plotinus on Intellect* (Oxford: Oxford University Press, 2007)
Emilsson, E. K., 'Plotinus and Plato on Soul and Action', in R. Barney, T. Brennan, and C. Brittain eds, *Plato and the Divided Self* (Cambridge: Cambridge University Press, 2012), pp. 350–67
Endress, G., *Proclus Arabus: Zwanzig Abschnitte aus der Institutio Theologica in arabischer Übersetzung* (Beirut: Orient-Institut der Deutschen, 1973)
Endress, G., 'La controverse entre la logique philosophique et la grammaire arabe au temps des khalifs', *Journal for the History of Arabic Science* 1 (1977), 339–51
Endress, G., *The Works of Yaḥyā ibn ʿAdī: An Analytical Inventory* (Weisbaden: Reichert, 1977)
Endress, G., 'Grammatik und Logik: Arabische Philologie und griechische Philosophie im Widerstreit', in B. Mojsisch, ed., *Sprachphilosophie in Antike und Mittelalter* (Amsterdam: Grüner, 1986), pp. 163–299
Endress, G., 'Die Wissenschaftliche Literatur', in H. Gätje, ed., *Grundriss der arabischen Philologie II* (Wiesbaden: Reichert, 1987), pp. 400–506; and W. Fischer, ed., *Grundriss der arabischen Philologie III* (Wiesbaden: Reichert, 1992), pp. 3–152
Endress, G., 'Alexander Arabus on the First Cause: Aristotle's First Mover in an Arabic Treatise attributed to Alexander of Aphrodisias', in C. D'Ancona and G. Serra, eds, *Aristotele e Alessandro di Afrodisia nella tradizione araba* (Padua: Il Poligrafo, 2002), pp. 19–74
Endress, G. ed., *Organizing Knowledge: Encyclopaedic Activities in the Pre-eighteenth Century Islamic World* (Leiden: Brill, 2006)
Erismann, C., *L'homme commun: La genèse du réalisme ontologique durant le haut Moyen Âge* (Paris: Vrin, 2011)
Erismann, C., 'John Philoponus on Individuality and Particularity', in J. Zachhuber and A. Torrance, eds, *Individuality in Late Antiquity* (Farnham: Ashgate, 2014), pp. 143–59
Everson, S., *Aristotle on Perception* (Oxford: Clarendon Press, 1997)
Evrard, E., 'Les convictions religieuses de Jean Philopon et la date de son commentaire aux Météorologiques', *Bulletin de l'Académie royale de Belgique* 39 (1953), 299–357

Fazzo, S., and Wiesner, H., 'Alexander of Aphrodisias in the Kindī Circle and in al-Kindī's Cosmology', *Arabic Sciences and Philosophy* 3 (1993), 119–53
Ferrari, C., *Die Kategorienkommentar von Abū l-Farāj ʿAbdallāh ibn aṭ-Ṭayyib* (Leiden: Brill, 2006)
Festugière, A. J., *La Révélation d'Hermès Trismégiste*, 4 vols (Paris: Gabalda, 1944–54)
Festugière, A. J., *Proclus, Commentaire sur le Timée*, 5 vols (Paris: Vrin, 1966–68)
Festugière, A. J., *Proclus, Commentaire sur la République*, 3 vols (Paris: Vrin, 1969–70)
Finamore, J. F., and Dillon, J. M., *Iamblichus, De Anima* (Leiden: Brill, 2002)
Fraenkel, C., 'Maimonides' God and Spinoza's Deus sive Natura', *Journal of the History of Philosophy* 44 (2006), 169–215
Frank, R. M., 'Some Textual Notes on the Oriental Versions of Themistius' Paraphrase of Book I [sic] of the *Metaphysics*', *Cahiers de Byrsa* 8 (1958–59), 215–30
Frede, D. 'The Sea-Battle Reconsidered', *Oxford Studies in Ancient Philosophy* 3 (1985), 31–87
Frede, M., 'The Stoic Conception of Reason', in K. Boudouris ed., *Hellenistic Philosophy* (Athens: International Association for Greek Philosophy, 1994), vol. 2, pp. 50–63
Frede, M., 'Epilogue', in K. Algra et al., eds, *The Cambridge History of Hellenistic Philosophy* (Cambridge: Cambridge University Press, 1999), pp. 771–97
Frede, M., *A Free Will* (Berkeley: University of California Press, 2011)
Freudenthal, G., *Aristotle's Theory of Material Substance* (Oxford: Clarendon Press, 1995)
Furley, D., and Wildberg, C., *Philoponus, Corollaries on Place and Void, with Simplicius, Against Philoponus on the Eternity of the World* (London: Duckworth, 1991)
Furrer-Pilliod, C., ed., *Horoi Kai Hypographai: Collections alphabétiques de définitions profanes et sacrées* (Vatican City: Biblioteca Apostolica Vaticana, 2000)
Gannagé, E., 'Alexandre d'Aphrodise In De generatione et corruptione apud Gabir b. Hayyan', *K. al-Tasrif*, *Documenti e studi sulla tradizione filosofica medievale* 9 (1998), 35–86
Gannagé, E., *Alexander of Aphrodisias, On Coming-to-Be and Perishing 2.2–5* (London: Duckworth, 2005)
Gätje, H., 'Zur arabischen Überlieferung des Alexander von Aphrodisias', *Zeitschrift der Deutschen Morgenländischen Gesellschaft* 116 (1966), 255–78
Gätje, H., *Studien zur Überlieferung der aristotelischen Psychologie im Islam* (Heidelberg: Winter, 1971)
Gaziel, A., 'Spontaneous Generation in Medieval Jewish Philosophy and Theology', *History and Philosophy of Life Sciences* 34 (2012), 461–80
Genequand, C., *Ibn Rushd's Metaphysics* (Leiden: Brill, 1984)
Genequand, C., *Alexander of Aphrodisias on the Cosmos* (Leiden: Brill, 2001)
Gerson, L. P. *Aristotle and Other Platonists* (Ithaca: Cornell University Press, 2005)
Gerson, L. P. ed., *The Cambridge History of Philosophy in Late Antiquity*, 2 vols (Cambridge: Cambridge University Press, 2010)
Gertz, S., *Death and Immortality in Late Neoplatonism* (Leiden: Brill, 2011)
Giannakis, E., *Philoponus in the Arabic Tradition of Aristotle's Physics*, D.Phil. Thesis (Oxford, 1992)
Giannakis, E., 'The Structure of Abū l-Ḥusayn al-Baṣrī's Copy of Aristotle's *Physics*', *Zeitschrift für Geschichte der arabisch-islamischen Wissenschaften* 8 (1993), 251–8
Giannakis, E., 'Fragments from Alexander's lost Commentary on Aristotle's *Physics*', *Zeitschrift für Geschichte der arabisch-islamischen Wissenschaften* 10 (1995–96), 157–87
Giannakis, E., 'The Quotations from John Philoponus' *De aeternitate mundi contra Proclum* in al-Bīrūnī's India', *Zeitschrift für Geschichte der arabisch-islamischen Wissenschaften* 15 (2002–3), 185–95

Gill, C., 'Particulars, Selves, and Individuals in Stoic Philosophy', in R. W. Sharples, ed., *Particulars in Greek Philosophy* (Leiden: Brill, 2009), pp. 127–46

Gimaret, D., 'Un traité théologique du philosophe musulman Abū Ḥāmid al-Isfizārī', *Mélanges de l'Université Saint-Joseph* 50 (1984), 209–52

Gioè, A., *Filosofi medioplatonici del II secolo d.c.: testimonianze e frammenti. Gaio, Albino, Lucio, Nicostrato, Tauro, Severo, Arpocrazione* (Naples: Bibliopolis, 2002)

Goichon, A.-M., *Ibn Sīnā (Avicenna) Livre des Directives et Remarques: Traduction avec Introduction et Notes* (Beruit: Commission internationale pour la traduction des chefs d'oeuvre / Paris: Vrin, 1951)

Goldin, O., *Philoponus (?), On Posterior Analytics 2* (London: Duckworth, 2009)

Golitsis, P., 'Georges Pachymère comme didascale: Essai pour une reconstitution de sa carrière et de son enseignement philosophique', *Jahrbuch der Österreichischen Byzantinistik* 58 (2008), 53–68

Golitsis, P., *Les Commentaries de Simplicius et de Jean Philopon à la Physique d'Aristote* (Berlin: De Gruyter, 2008)

Golitsis, P., 'Copistes, élèves et érudits: la production de manuscrits philosophiques autour de Georges Pachymère', in A. Bravo García and I. Pérez Martín, eds, *The Legacy of Bernard de Montfaucon: Three Hundred Years of Studies on Greek Handwriting* (Turnhout: Brepols, 2010), pp. 157–70

Golitsis, P., 'Trois annotations de manuscrits aristotéliciens au XIIe siècle: les *Parisini gr.* 1901 et 1853 et l'*Oxoniensis Corp. Christi* 108', in D. Bianconi, ed., *Storia della scrittura e altre storie* (Rome: Accademia Nazionale dei Lincei, 2014), pp. 33–52

Golitsis, P., '*Meta tinôn idiôn epistaseôn*: John Philoponus as an editor of Ammonius' lectures', in P. Golitsis and K. Ierodiakonou, eds, *Aristotle and His Commentators: Studies in Memory of Voula Kotzia* (Berlin: De Gruyter, forthcoming)

Golitsis, P., and Hoffmann, P., 'Simplicius et le 'lieu': À propos d'une nouvelle édition du Corollarium de loco', *Revue des Études Grecques* 127 (2014), 119–75

Göransson, T., *Albinus, Alcinous, Arius Didymus* (Göteborg: Acta Universitatis Gothoburgensis, 1995)

Gotthelf, A., 'Teleology and Spontaneous Generation in Aristotle: A Discussion', *Apeiron* 22 (1989), 181–93

Gotthelf, A. *Teleology, First Principles, and Scientific Method in Aristotle's Biology* (Oxford: Oxford University Press, 2012)

Gottschalk, H. B., 'Boethus' Psychology and the Neoplatonists', *Phronesis* 31 (1986), 243–57

Gottschalk, H. B., 'The Earliest Aristotelian Commentators', in R. Sorabji, ed., *Aristotle Transformed* (London: Duckworth, 1990), pp. 55–81

Gourinat, J.-B., *Le Stoïcisme* (Paris: Presses Universitaires de France, 2007)

Gourinat, J.-B., 'Le Platon de Panétius: à propos d'un témoignage inédit de Galien', *Philosophie Antique* 8 (2008), 139–51

Graf, G., *Geschichte der christlichen arabischen Literatur*, 5 vols (Vatican City: Biblioteca Apostolica Vaticana, 1944)

Grant, E., *Nicole Oresme and the Kinematics of Circular Motion* (Madison: University of Wisconsin Press, 1971)

Griffin, M., *The Reception of Aristotle's Categories c. 80 BC – AD 220*, D.Phil. thesis (Oxford, 2009)

Griffin, M., *Aristotle's Categories in the Early Roman Empire* (Oxford: Oxford University Press, 2015)

Guidi, M., and Walzer, R., *Uno Scritto Introduttivo allo Studio di Aristotele* (Rome: Bardi, 1940)

Guldentops, G., 'Plato's *Timaeus* in Simplicius *In De Caelo*', in T. Leinkauf and C. Steel, eds, *Plato's Timaeus and the Foundations of Cosmology in Late Antiquity, the Middle Ages and Renaissance* (Leuven: Leuven University Press, 2005), pp. 195-212

Gundert, B., 'Soma and Psyche in Hippocratic Medicine', in J. P. Wright and P. Potter, eds, *Psyche and Soma: Physicians and Metaphysicians on the Mind-Body Problem from Antiquity to the Enlightenment* (Oxford: Oxford University Press, 2000), pp. 13-35

Gutas, D., 'Paul the Persian on the Classification of the Parts of Aristotle's Philosophy: A Milestone Between Alexandria and Baghdad', *Der Islam* 60 (1983), 231-67

Gutas, D., 'The "Alexandria to Baghdad" Complex of Narratives: A Contribution to the Study of Philosophical and Medical Historiography among the Arabs', *Documenti e studi sulla tradizione filosofica medievale* 10 (1999), 155-93

Gutas, D., 'Greek Philosophical Works Translated into Arabic', in R. Pasnau, ed., *The Cambridge History of Medieval Philosophy*, 2 vols (Cambridge: Cambridge University Press, 2010), vol. 2, pp. 802-14

Gutas, D., *Theophrastus, On First Principles (known as his Metaphysics)* (Leiden: Brill, 2010)

Gyekye, K., *Arabic Logic: Ibn al-Ṭayyib's Commentary on Porphyry's Eisagoge* (Albany: State University of New York Press, 1979)

Gyekye, K., *Ibn al-Ṭayyib's Commentary on Porphyry's Eisagoge* (Beirut: Dar el-Machreq, 1975)

Hadot, I., *Le problème du néoplatonisme Alexandrin, Hiéroclès et Simplicius* (Paris: Études Augustiniennes, 1978)

Hadot, I., 'La vie et l'œuvre de Simplicius d'après des sources grecques et arabes', in I. Hadot, ed., *Simplicius: Sa vie, son œuvre, sa survie* (Berlin: De Gruyter, 1987), pp. 3-39; trans. as 'The Life and Work of Simplicius in Greek and Arabic Sources', in R. Sorabji, ed., *Aristotle Transformed* (London: Duckworth, 1990), pp. 275-303

Hadot, I., 'Recherches sur les fragments du commentaire de Simplicius sur la *Métaphysique* d'Aristote', in I. Hadot, ed., *Simplicius: Sa vie, son œuvre, sa survie* (Berlin: De Gruyter, 1987), pp. 225-45

Hadot, I., ed., *Simplicius: Sa vie, son œuvre, sa survie* (Berlin: De Gruyter, 1987)

Hadot, I., 'Le commentaire philosophique continu dans l'Antiquité', *Antiquité Tardive* 5 (1997), 169-76

Hadot, I., 'Die Stellung des Neuplatonikers Simplikios zum Verhältnis der Philosophie zu Religion und Theurgie', in T. Kobusch and M. Erler (and Irmgard Männlein-Robert), eds, *Metaphysik und Religion: Zur Signatur des spätantiken Denkens* (Munich: Saur, 2002), pp. 323-42

Hadot, I., *Le néoplatonicien Simplicius à la lumière des recherches contemporaine, Un bilan critique* (Sankt Augustin: Academia Verlag, 2014)

Hadot, I., *Athenian and Alexandrian Neoplatonism and the Harmonization of Aristotle and Plato* (Leiden: Brill, 2015)

Hadot, I., and Hoffmann, P., *Simplicius, Commentaire sur les 'Catégories': Fascicule I* (Leiden: Brill, 1990)

Hadot, P., 'Philosophie, exégèse et contresens', in *Akten des XIV. Internationalen Kongress für Philosophie* (Vienna: Universität Wien, 1968), vol. 1, pp. 333-9; repr. in his *Études de philosophie ancienne* (Paris: Les Belles Lettres, 1998), pp. 3-11

Hadot, P., *Porphyre et Victorinus* (Paris: Études Augustiniennes, 1968)

Hadot, P. 'Philosophie, dialectique, rhétorique dans l'Antiquité', *Studia Philosophica* 39 (1980), 139-66; repr. in his *Études de philosophie ancienne* (Paris: Les Belles Lettres, 1998), pp. 159-93

Hadot, P., 'La logique, partie ou instrument de la philosophie?', in I. Hadot, ed., *Simplicius, Commentaire sur les Catégories, fasc. 1: Introduction* (Leiden: Brill, 1990)

Hadot, P., 'The Harmony of Plotinus and Aristotle According to Porphyry', in R. Sorabji, ed., *Aristotle Transformed* (London: Duckworth, 1990), pp. 125–40

Hadot, P., *Qu'est-ce que la philosophie antique?* (Paris: Gallimard, 1995); trans. as *What is Ancient Philosophy?*, trans. M. Chase (Cambridge, MA: Harvard University Press, 2002)

Hadot, P. *Études de philosophie ancienne* (Paris: Les Belles Lettres, 1998)

Hahm, D. E., 'Critolaus and late Hellenistic Peripatetic philosophy', in A. M. Ioppolo and D. Sedley, eds, *Pyrrhonists, Patricians, Platonizers: Hellenistic Philosophy in the Period 155–86 BC* (Naples: Bibliopolis, 2007), pp. 47–101

Hainthaler, T., *Christ in Christian Tradition 2.3: The Churches of Jerusalem and Antioch from 451 to 600* (Oxford: Oxford University Press, 2013)

Halper, Y., 'Revision and Standardization of Hebrew Philosophical Terminology in the Fourteenth Century: The Example of Averroes's Long Commentary on Aristotle's Metaphysics Δ', *Aleph: Historical Studies in Science and Judaism* 13 (2013), 95–137

Hankinson, R. J., *Simplicius, On Aristotle On the Heavens 1.5–9* (London: Duckworth, 2004)

Harlfinger, D., 'Zur Überlieferungsgeschichte der *Metaphysik*', in P. Aubenque, ed., *Études sur la 'Métaphysique' d'Aristote* (Paris: Vrin, 1979), pp. 7–36

Hasnawi, A., 'Alexandre d'Aphrodise vs Jean Philopon: notes sur quelques traités d'Alexandre "perdus" en grec, conservés en arabe', *Arabic Sciences and Philosophy* 4 (1994), 53–109

Hasnawi, A., 'Le statut catégorial du mouvement chez Avicenne: contexte grec et postérité médiévale latine', in R. Morelon and A. Hasnawi, eds, *De Zénon d'Élée à Poincaré* (Louvain: Peeters, 2004), pp. 607–22

Hasnawi, A., 'Boèce, Averroès at Abū al-Barakāt al-Baghdādī, témoins des écrits de Thémistius sur les *Topiques* d'Aristote', *Arabic Sciences and Philosophy* 17 (2007), 203–65

Hasse, D. N., 'Spontaneous Generation and the Ontology of Forms in Greek, Arabic, and Medieval Latin Sources', in P. Adamson, ed., *Classical Arabic Philosophy: Sources and Reception* (London: The Warburg Institute, 2007), pp. 150–75

Haussleiter, J., *Der Vegetarismus in der Antike* (Berlin: Töpelmann, 1935)

Heiberg, J. L., 'Eine neue Archimedeshandschrift', *Hermes* 42 (1907), 235–303

Hein, C., *Definition und Einteilung der Philosophie: Von der Spätantike Einleitungsliteratur zür arabischen Enzyklopädie* (Frankfurt: Peter Lang, 1985)

Helmig, C., *Forms and Concepts: Concept Formation in the Platonic Tradition* (Berlin: De Gruyter, 2012)

Henry, D., 'Themistius and Spontaneous Generation in Aristotle's *Metaphysics*', *Oxford Studies in Ancient Philosophy* 24 (2003), 183–207

Henry, D., 'Understanding Aristotle's Reproductive Hylomorphism', *Apeiron* 39 (2006), 269–300

Henry, D., 'How Sexist is Aristotle's Developmental Biology?', *Phronesis* 52 (2007), 251–69

Henry, D., 'Generation of Animals', in G. Anagnostopoulos, ed., *A Companion to Aristotle* (Chichester: Wiley-Blackwell, 2009), pp. 368–83

Henry, R., ed., *Photius, Bibliothèque*, 9 vols (Paris: Les Belles Lettres, 1959–91)

Hirschle, M., *Sprachphilosophie und Namenmagie im Neuplatonismus: Mit einem Exkurs zu 'Demokrit' B 142* (Meisenheim am Glan: Hain, 1979)

Hoffmann, P., 'Simplicius: Corollarium de loco', in G. Aujac and J. Soubiran, eds, *L'Astronomie dans l'Antiquité classique* (Paris: Les Belles Lettres, 1979), pp. 143–61

Hoffmann, P., 'Jamblique, exégète du Pythagoricien Archytas: trois originalités d'une doctrine du temps', *Les Études philosophiques* 3 (1980), 307–23

Hoffmann, P., 'Catégories et language selon Simplicius – La question du «skopos» du traité aristotélicien des «Catégories»', in I. Hadot, ed., *Simplicius: sa vie, son œuvre, sa survie* (Berlin: De Gruyter, 1987), pp. 61–90

Hoffmann, P., 'Simplicius' Polemics', in R. Sorabji, ed., *Philoponus and the Rejection of the Aristotelian Science* (London: Duckworth, 1987), pp. 57–83

Hoffmann, P., 'Sur quelques aspects de la polémique de Simplicius contre Jean Philopon: de l'invective à la réaffirmation de la transcendance du Ciel', in I. Hadot, ed., *Simplicius: Sa vie, son œuvre, sa survie* (Berlin: De Gruyter, 1987), pp. 183–221

Hoffmann, P., 'La fonction des prologues exégétiques dans la pensée pédagogique néoplatonicienne', in B. Roussel and J.-D. Dubois, eds, *Entrer en matière* (Paris: Éditions du Cerf, 1998), pp. 209–45

Hoffmann, P., 'La triade chaldaïque *erôs, alêtheia, pistis*: de Proclus à Simplicius', in Alain-Philippe Segonds and Carlos Steel, eds, *Proclus et la Théologie Platonicienne* (Leuven: Leuven University Press, 2000), pp. 459–89

Hoffmann, P., 'Science théologique et Foi selon le *Commentaire* de Simplicius au *De Caelo* d'Aristote', in E. Coda and C. Martini Bonadeo eds, *De l'Antiquité tardive au Moyen Âge: Études de logique aristotélicienne et de philosophie grecque, syriaque, arabe et latine offertes à Henri Hugonnard-Roche* (Paris: Vrin, 2014), pp. 277–364

Huby, P. M., 'An Excerpt from Boethus of Sidon's Commentary on the *Categories*?', *Classical Quarterly* 31 (1981), 398–409

Hugonnard-Roche, H., 'Sergius de Resh'ayna commentaire sur les categories (à Théodore)', *Oriens-Occidens* 1 (1997), 126–35

Hugonnard-Roche, H., *La logique d'Aristote du grec au syriaque: études sur la transmission des texts de l'Organon et leur interpretation philosphique* (Paris: Vrin, 2004)

Hugonnard-Roche, H., 'Probus (Proba)', in R. Goulet, ed., *Dictionnaire des philosophes antiques V* (Paris: CNRS, 2012), pp. 1539–42

Hugonnard-Roche, H., 'Sur la lecture tardo-antique du *Peri Hermêneias* d'Aristote: Paul le Perse et la Tradition d'Ammonius', *Studia graeco-arabica* 3 (2013), 37–104

Hugonnard-Roche, H., 'Un organon court en syriaque: Paul le Perse vs. Boèce', in J. Brumberg-Chaumont, ed., *Ad notitiam ignoti* (Turnhout: Brepols, 2013), pp. 193–215

Ierodiakonou, K., 'Aristotle's Logic: An Instrument, Not a Part of Philosophy', in N. Avgelis and F. Peonidis, eds, *Aristotle on Logic, Language and Science* (Thessaloniki: Sakkoulas, 1997), pp. 33–53

Inwood, B., *Ethics and Human Action in Early Stoicism* (Oxford: Clarendon Press, 1985)

Ioppolo, A.-M., Review of A. A. Long, *From Epicurus to Epictetus: Studies in Hellenistic and Roman Philosophy*, *Elenchos* 27 (2006), 502–10

Ivry, A., *Al-Kindi's Metaphysics* (Albany: State University of New York Press, 1974)

Joachim, H. H., 'Aristotle's Conception of Chemical Combination', *Journal of Philology* 29 (1904), 72–86

Joachim, H. H., *Aristotle On Coming-to-Be and Passing-Away* (Oxford: Clarendon Press, 1922)

Johansen, T. K., *Aristotle on the Sense-Organs* (Cambridge: Cambridge University Press, 1998)

Johnson, A. P., *Religion and Identity in Porphyry of Tyre* (Cambridge: Cambridge University Press, 2013)

Jolivet, J., *L'Intellect selon Kindī* (Leiden: Brill, 1971)

Jolivet, J., 'Pour le dossier du Proclus arabe: Al-Kindī et la *Théologie platonicienne*', *Studia Islamica* 49 (1979), 55–75; repr. in his *Philosophie médiévale arabe et latine* (Paris: Vrin, 1995), pp. 111–31

Jolivet, J., and Monnot, G., *Shahrastani, Livre des religions et des sectes*, 2 vols (Paris: Peeters/Unesco, 1986–93)

Jones, C., 'Books and libraries in a newly-discovered treatise of Galen', *Journal of Roman Archaeology* 22 (2009), 390–7

Judson, L., 'God or Nature? Philoponus on Generability and Perishability', R. Sorabji, ed., *Philoponus and the Rejection of Aristotelian Science* (London: Duckworth, 1987), pp. 179–96

Judson, L., 'Metaphysics Λ 3', in M. Frede and D. Charles, eds, *Aristotle's Metaphysics Lambda* (Oxford: Clarendon Press, 2000), pp. 111–35

Kalligas, P., 'The Structure of Appearances: Plotinus on the Constitution of Sensible Objects', *Philosophical Quarterly* 61 (2011), 762–82

Karamanolis, G. E., *Plato and Aristotle in Agreement? Platonists on Aristotle from Antiochus to Porphyry* (Oxford: Clarendon Press, 2006)

Kendall, B., and Thompson, R. W., *Definitions and Divisions of Philosophy by David the Invincible Philosopher* (Chico: Scholars Press, 1983)

Kent Sprague, R., 'An Anonymous Argument against Mixture', *Mnemosyne* 26 (1973), 230–3

Khalifat, S., *Yaḥyā ibn 'Adī: The Philosophical Treatises* (Amman: Publications of University of Jordan, 1988)

King, D., 'Why Were the Syrians Interested in Greek Philosophy?', in Philip Wood, ed., *History and Identity in the Late Antique Near East* (Oxford: Oxford University Press, 2013), pp. 61–82

King, D., *Philoponus, A Treatise Concerning the Whole and the Parts* [publ. with R. Sirkel et al., *Philoponus, On Aristotle Categories 1–5*] (London: Bloomsbury, 2015)

King, H., *Hippocrates' Woman: Reading the Female Body in Ancient Greece* (London: Routledge, 1998)

Koetschet, P., 'Galien, al-Rāzī, et l'éternité du monde. Les fragment du traité *Sur la Démonstration* IV, dans les *Doutes sur Galien*', *Arabic Sciences and Philosophy* 25 (2015), 167–98

Kollesch, J., *Galen über das Riechorgan* (Berlin: Akademie-Verlag, 1964)

Kotter, B., *Die Schriften des Johannes von Damaskos I* (Berlin: De Gruyter, 1969)

Kraemer, J. L., *Humanism in the Renaissance of Islam, The Cultural Revival during the Buyid Age* (Leiden: Brill, 1986)

Kraemer, J. L., *Philosophy in the Renaissance of Islam: Abū Sulaymān al-Sijistānī and his Circle* (Leiden: Brill, 1986)

Kraus, P., *Jābir ibn Ḥayyān: Contribution à l'histoire des idées scientifiques dans l'Islam*, 2 vols (Cairo: n.p., 1941–42)

Kremer, K., Der Metaphysikbegriff in den Aristoteles-Kommentaren der Ammonius-Schule (Münster: Aschendorffsche Verlagsbuchhandlung, 1960)

Kruk, R., 'A Frothy Bubble: Spontaneous Generation in the Medieval Islamic Tradition', *Journal of Semitic Studies* 35 (1990), 265–82

Kupreeva, I., 'Alexander of Aphrodisias on Mixture and Growth', *Oxford Studies in Ancient Philosophy* 27 (2004), 297–334

Kupreeva, I., *Philoponus, On Aristotle On Coming-to-Be and Perishing 2.5–11* (London: Duckworth, 2005)

Kurland, S., *Averroes, On Aristotle's De Generatione et Corruptione Middle Commentary and Epitome* (Cambridge, MA: Mediaeval Academy of America, 1958)

Lamberz, E., 'Proklos und die Form des philosophischen Kommentars', in J. Pépin and H. D. Saffrey, eds, *Proclus, lecteur et interprète des anciens* (Paris: CNRS, 1987), pp. 1–20

Lameer, J., *Al-Fārābī and Aristotelian Syllogistics: Greek Theory and Islamic Practice* (Leiden: Brill, 1994)

Lang, H. S., and Macro, A. D., *Proclus, On the Eternity of the World* (Berkeley: University of California Press, 2001)

Lautner, P., 'Philoponus, in *De anima* 3: Quest for an author', *Classical Quarterly* 42 (1992), 510–22

Lee, T.-S., *Griechische Tradition der aristotelischen Syllogistik in der Spätantike* (Göttingen: Vandenhoeck & Ruprecht, 1984)

Lefebvre, D., 'Alexandre d'Aphrodise, Supplément au traité de l'âme (extrait)', in J. Laurent and C. Romano, eds, *Le néant: Contribution à l'histoire du non-être dans la philosophie occidentale* (Paris: Presses Universitaires de France, 2006), pp. 103–17

Leibniz, G. W., *De l'horizon de la doctrine humaine, Apokatastasis pantôn (La Restitution Universelle)*, Textes inédits, traduits et annotés par M. Fichant (Paris: Vrin, 1991)

Leibniz, G. W., *Recherches générales sur l'analyse des notions et des vérités* (Paris: Presses Universitaires de France, 1998)

Lennox, J. G., 'Teleology, Chance and Aristotle's Theory of Spontaneous Generation', *Journal of the History of Philosophy* 20 (1982), 219–38

Lennox, J. G., 'Commentary on Sorabji', *Proceedings of the Boston Area Colloquium in Ancient Philosophy* 4 (1988), 64–75

Lennox, J. G., ed., *Aristotle's Philosophy of Biology* (Cambridge: Cambrudge University Press, 2001)

Lennox, J. G. 'Are Aristotelian Species Eternal?', in J. Lennox, ed., *Aristotle's Philosophy of Biology* (Cambridge: Cambridge University Press, 2001), pp. 131–59

Lernould, A., *Physique et théologie: Lecture du Timée de Platon par Proclus* (Villeneuve d'Ascq: Presses universitaires du Septentrion, 2001)

Leszl, W., and Harlfinger, D., *Il 'De ideis' di Aristotele e la teoria platonica delle idee* (Florence: Olschki, 1975)

Lettinck, P., *Aristotle's Physics and its Reception in the Arabic World* (Leiden: Brill, 1994)

Lewin, B., 'La notion de *muḥdaṯ* dans le kalām et dans la philosophie: un petit traité inédit du philosophe chrétien Ibn Suwār', in E. Gren, B. Lewin et al., eds, *Donum Natalicum H. S. Nyberg Oblatum* (Uppsala: Universitetsbiblioteket, 1954), pp. 84–93

Lewis, E., *Alexander of Aphrodisias, On Aristotle Meteorology 4* (London: Duckworth, 1996)

Lewy, H., *Chaldaean Oracles and Theurgy: Mysticism, Magic and Platonism in the Later Roman Empire*, 2nd edn (Paris: Études Augustiniennes, 1978)

Lloyd, A. C., 'Neoplatonic and Aristotelian Logic', *Phronesis* 1 (1956), 146–60

Lloyd, A. C., 'The Principle that the Cause is Greater than its Effect', *Phronesis* 21 (1976), 146–56

Lloyd, A. C., *Form and Universal in Aristotle* (Liverpool: Francis Cairns, 1981)

Lloyd, A. C., 'The Aristotelianism of Eustratius of Nicaea', in J. Wiesner, ed., *Aristoteles Werk und Wirkung*, 2 vols (Berlin: De Gruyter, 1987), vol. 2, pp. 341–51

Lloyd, A. C., *The Anatomy of Neoplatonism* (Oxford: Clarendon Press, 1990)

Lloyd, G. E. R., *Aristotelian Explorations* (Cambridge: Cambridge University Press, 1996)

Lobel, D., *Between Mysticism and Philosophy: Sufi Language of Religious Experience in Judah Ha-Levi's Kuzari* (Albany: SUNY Press, 2000)

Long, A. A., 'Astrology: Arguments pro and contra', in J. Barnes, J. Brunschwig, et al., eds, *Science and Speculation: Studies in Hellenistic Theory and Practice* (Cambridge: Cambridge University Press, 1977), pp. 165–92

Long, A. A., *From Epicurus to Epictetus: Studies in Hellenistic and Roman Philosophy* (Oxford: Clarendon Press, 2006)

Long, A. A., and Sedley, D. N., *The Hellenistic Philosophers*, 2 vols (Cambridge: Cambridge University Press, 1987)
Lonie, I., *The Hippocratic Treatises 'On Generation', 'On the Nature of the Child,' and 'On Diseases IV'* (Berlin: De Gruyter, 1981)
Loredano Cardullo, R., 'Syrianus' lost commentaries on Aristotle', *Bulletin of the Institute of Classical Studies* 33 (1986), 112–24
Loredano Cardullo, R., *Siriano, Esegeta di Aristotele, I Frammenti e Testimonianze dei Commentari all' Organon* (Florence: La Nuova Italia, 1995)
Lorenz, H., 'The Assimilation of Sense to Sense-Object in Aristotle', *Oxford Studies in Ancient Philosophy* 33 (2007), 179–220
Lucchetta, G. A., *La natura e la sfera: la scienza antica e le sue metafore nella critica di Rāzī* (Lecce: Milella, 1987)
Lumpe, A., 'Stephanos von Alexandrien', *Biographisch-Bibliographisches Kirchenlexikon* 10 (1995), 1406–9
Luna, C., *Simplicius, Commentaire sur les Catégories: Fasc. III* (Leiden: Brill, 1990)
Luna, C., *Commentaire sur les Catégories d'Aristote: Chapitres 2–4* (Paris: Les Belles Lettres, 2001)
Luna, C., *Trois études sur la tradition des commentaries anciens à la* Métaphysique *d'Aristote* (Leiden: Brill, 2001)
Luna, C., 'Les commentaires grecs à la *Métaphysique*', in R. Goulet, ed., *Dictionnaire des philosophes antiques: Supplément* (Paris: CNRS, 2003), pp. 249–58
Luna, C. 'Boéthos de Sidon sur les rélatifs', *Studia graeco-arabica* 3 (2013), 1–31
Lyons, M. C., *An Arabic Translation of Themistius Commentary on Aristoteles De Anima* (Norfolk: Cassirer, 1973)
MacDonald, D. B., 'Ilhām', *Encyclopaedia of Islam*, 2nd edn, Brill Online, 2015. Accessed 31 March 2015 <http://referenceworks.brillonline.com/entries/encyclopaedia-of-islam-2/ilha-m-SIM_3533>
Madigan, A., 'Syrianus and Asclepius on Forms and Intermediates in Plato and Aristotle', *Journal of the History of Philosophy* 24 (1986), 149–71
Mahdi, M. 'Alfarabi against Philoponus', *Journal of Near Eastern Studies* 26 (1967), 233–60
Maier, A., *Die Vorläufer Galileis im 14. Jahrhundert* (Rome: Edizioni di Storia e Letteratura, 1949)
Maier, A., *An der Grenze von Scholastik und Naturwissenschaft: Die Struktur der materiellen Substanz, Das Problem der Gravitation, Die Mathematik der Formlatituden*, 2nd edn (Rome: Edizioni di Storia e Letteratura, 1952)
Maier, A., *Zwischen Philosophie und Mechanik* (Rome: Edizioni di Storia e Letteratura, 1958)
Majercik, R., *The Chaldean Oracles: Text, Translation, and Commentary* (Leiden: Brill, 1989)
Margouliath, D. S., 'The Discussion Between Abu Bishr Matta and Abu Saʿid al-Sirafi on the Merits of Logic and Grammar', *Journal of the Royal Asiatic Society* (1905), 79–129
Marmura, M. E., *Al-Ghazālī, The Incoherence of the Philosophers* (Provo: Brigham Young University Press, 1997)
Maróth, M., 'Der erste Beweis des Proklos für die Ewigkeit der Welt', *Acta Antiqua Academiae Scientiarum Hungaricae* 30 (1982–84), 181–9
Martijn, M., *Proclus on Nature* (Leiden: Brill, 2010)
Martin, A., *Grand commentaire de la Métaphysique d'Aristote: Tafsīr Mā baʿd aṭ-Ṭabīʿat. Livre lam-lambda* (Paris: Les Belles Lettres, 1984)
Martini Bonadeo, C., 'Un commento ad *alpha elatton* 'sicut litterae sonant' nella Baghdād del X secolo', *Medioevo* 28 (2003), 69–96

McGinnis, J., and Reisman, D. C., *Classical Arabic Philosophy: An Anthology of Sources* (Indianapolis: Hackett, 2007)
McMullin, E., 'Four Senses of Potency', in E. McMullin, ed., *The Concept of Matter* (Notre Dame: University of Notre Dame Press, 1965), pp. 295–315
McTaggart, J. E., 'The Unreality of Time', *Mind* 17 (1908), 457–74
Mercken, H. P. F., 'The Greek Commentators on Aristotle's *Ethics*', in R. Sorabji, ed., *Aristotle Transformed* (London: Duckworth, 1990), pp. 407–43
Mignucci, M., 'The Stoic Notion of Relatives', in J. Barnes and M. Mignucci, eds, *Matter and Metaphysics* (Naples: Bibliopolis, 1988), pp. 129–221
Mignucci, M., 'Sur la logique modale des Stoïciens', in J. Brunschwig, ed., *Les Stoïciens et leur logique*, 2nd edn (Paris: Vrin, 2006), pp. 303–32
Mondrain, B., 'Traces et mémoire de la lecture des textes: les *marginalia* dans les manuscrits scientifiques byzantins', in D. Jacquart, ed., *Scientia in margine: Études sur les 'marginalia' dans les manuscrits scientifiques du Moyen Âge à la Renaissance* (Geneva: Librairie Droz, 2005), pp. 1–25
Montanari, E., *Le sezione linguistica del Peri Hermeneias di Aristotle* (Florence: Università degli studi di Firenze, 1984)
Montanari, F., 'Zenodotus, Aristarchus and the *ekdosis* of Homer', in G. Most, ed., *Editing texts – Texte Edieren* (Göttingen: Vandenhoeck & Ruprecht, 1998), pp. 1–21
Moraux, P., *Alexandre d'Aphrodise: Exégète de la noétique d'Aristote* (Liège and Paris: Faculté de Philosophie et Lettres de l'Université de Liège, 1942)
Moraux, P., *Der Aristotelismus bei den Griechen von Andronikos bis Alexander von Aphrodisias I: Die Renaissance des Aristotelismus im I Jh. v. Chr.* (Berlin: De Gruyter, 1973)
Moraux, P., *Der Aristotelismus bei den Griechen von Andronikos bis Alexander von Aphrodisias II: Der Aristotelismus im I und II Jh. n. Chr.* (Berlin: De Gruyter, 1984)
Moraux, P., *Der Aristotelismus bei den Griechen von Andronikos bis Alexander von Aphrodisias III: Alexander von Aphrodisias* (Berlin: De Gruyter, 2001)
Morlet, S., *Le traité de Porphyre contre les Chrétiens: un siècle de recherches, nouvelles questions* (Paris: Études Augustiniennes, 2011)
Morrow, G., 'Qualitative Change in Aristotle's *Physics*', in I. Düring, ed., *Naturphilosophie bei Aristoteles und Theophrast* (Heidelberg: Lothar Stiehm Verlag, 1969), pp. 154–67
Mueller, I., *Simplicius, On Aristotle on the Heavens 3.1–7* (London: Duckworth, 2009)
Mueller, I., *Simplicius, On Aristotle on the Heavens 3.7–4.6* (London: Duckworth, 2009)
Mueller, I., 'Aristotelian Objections and Post-Aristotelian Responses to Plato's Elemental Theory', in J. Wilberding and C. Horn, eds, *Neoplatonism and the Philosophy of Nature* (Oxford: Oxford University Press, 2012), pp. 129–46
Müller, K. 'Neue Mittheilungen über Janos Laskaris und die Mediceische Bibliothek', *Zentralblatt für Bibliothekswesen* 1 (1884), 333–412
Netz, R., *The Works of Archimedes I* (Cambridge: Cambridge University Press, 2004)
Netz, R., Noel, W., Tchernetska, N., and Wilson, N., *The Archimedes Palimpsest*, 2 vols (Cambridge: Cambridge University Press, 2011)
Newmyer, S., *Animals in Greek and Roman Thought: A Sourcebook* (London: Routledge, 2011)
Noel, W., and Netz, R., *The Archimedes Codex* (London: Weidenfeld and Nicolson, 2007)
O'Meara, D., *Pythagoras Revived* (Oxford: Oxford University Press, 1989)
O'Meara, D., *Platonopolis* (Oxford: Oxford University Press, 2003)
O'Meara, D., 'A Neoplatonist Ethics for High-Level Officials; Sopatros' Letter to Himerios', in A. Smith, ed., *The Philosopher and Society in Late Antiquity* (Swansea: Classical Press of Wales, 2005), pp. 91–100

Opsomer, J., 'In Defence of Geometric Atomism: Explaining Elemental Properties', in J. Wilberding and C. Horn, eds, *Neoplatonism and the Philosophy of Nature* (Oxford: Oxford University Press, 2012), pp. 147–73

Opsomer, J., and Sharples, R. W., 'Alexander of Aphrodisias "De Intellectu" 110,4: "I heard this from Aristotle", A Modest Proposal', *Classical Quarterly* 50 (2000), 252–6

Osborne, C., *Philoponus, On Aristotle's Physics 1.1–3* (London: Duckworth, 2006)

Osborne, C., *Dumb Beasts and Dead Philosophers: Humanity and the Humane in Ancient Philosophy and Literature* (Oxford: Oxford University Press, 2007)

Osborne, C., *Philoponus, On Aristotle's Physics 1.4–9* (London: Duckworth, 2009)

Owen, G. E. L., 'Logic and Metaphysics in Some Early Works of Aristotle', in I. Düring and G. E. L. Owen, eds, *Aristotle and Plato in the Mid-Fourth Century* (Göteborg: Almqvist & Wiksell, 1960), pp. 163–90; repr. in his *Logic, Science, and Dialectic* (London: Duckworth, 1986), pp. 180–99

Papathanassiou, M., 'Stephanus of Alexandria: A Famous Byzantine Scholar, Alchemist and Astrologer', in P. Magdalino and M. Mavroudi, eds, *The Occult Sciences in Byzantium* (Geneva: La Pomme d'or, 2006), pp. 163–203

Passmore, J., 'Treatment of Animals', *Journal of History of Ideas* 36 (1975), 195–218

Pavie, X., ed., *Pierre Hadot: Discours et mode de vie philosophique* (Paris: Les Belles Lettres, 2014)

Penella, R. J., *The Private Orations of Themistius* (Berkeley: University of California Press, 1999)

Périer, A., 'Un traité de Yaḥyā ben ʿAdī. Défense du dogme de la Trinité contre les objections d'al-Kindi', *Revue de l'orient chrétien* 3rd ser. 22 (1920–1), 3–21

Perler, D., ed., *Ancient and Medieval Theories of Intentionality* (Leiden: Brill, 2001)

Peters, F. E., *Aristoteles Arabus: The Oriental Translations and Commentaries on the Aristotelian Corpus* (Leiden: Brill, 1968)

Pfeiffer, R., *History of Classical Scholarship* (Oxford: Clarendon Press, 1968)

Phillips, J. F., 'Neoplatonic Exegeses of Plato's Cosmogony (*Timaeus* 27C–28C)', *Journal of the History of Philosophy* 35 (1977), 173–97

Piccolomini, E., 'Due Documenti relativi ad acquisiti di codici greci, fatti da Giovanni Lascaris per conto di Lorenzo de' Medici', *Rivista di filologia e d'instruzione classica* 2 (1874), 401–23

Pines, S., 'A Tenth Century Philosophical Correspondence', *Proceedings of the American Society for Jewish Research* 23 (1954), 103–36

Pines, S., 'An Arabic Summary of a Lost Work of John Philoponus', *Israel Oriental Studies* 2 (1972), 320–52; repr. in vol. 2 of his *Studies in Arabic Versions of Greek Texts and in Medieval Science* (Jerusalem: The Magnes Press, 1986)

Pines, S., 'Some Distinctive Metaphysical Conceptions in Themistius' Commentary on Book *Lambda* and Their Place in the History of Philosophy', in J. Wiesner, ed., *Aristoteles: Werk und Wirkung*, 2 vols (Berlin: De Gruyter, 1987), vol. 2, pp. 177–204; repr. in *The Collected Works of Shlomo Pines III* (Jerusalem: The Magnes Press, 1996), pp. 267–304

Pines, S., *The Collected Works of Shlomo Pines III: Studies in the History of Arabic Philosophy*, ed. S. Stroumsa (Jerusalem: The Magnes Press, 1996)

Polemis, I., 'Philologikes paratêrêseis se anônumo upomnêma stis 'Katêgories' tou Aristotelê', *Parekbolai* [online journal] 2 (2012), 23–6

Praechter, K., 'Commentaria in Aristotelem Graeca XXII 2', *Göttingische Gelehrte Anzeigen* 11 (1906), 861–907

Praechter, K. 'Richtungen und Schulen im Neuplatonismus', in *Genethliakon für Carl Robert* (Berlin: Weidmann, 1910), pp. 105–56

Primavesi, O., 'Ein Blick in den Stollen von Skepsis: vier Kapitel zur frühen Überlieferung des *Corpus Aristotelicum*', *Philologus* 151 (2007), 51–77

Primavesi, O., 'Aristotle, *Metaphysics* A: A New Critical Edition with Introduction', in C. Steel, ed., *Aristotle's Metaphysics A* (Oxford: Oxford University Press, 2012), pp. 387–458

Rabe, H., *Ioannes Philoponus, De Aeternitate Mundi contra Proclum* (Leipzig: Teubner, 1899)

Rapp, C., 'Intentionalität und *Phantasia* bei Aristoteles', in D. Perler, ed., *Ancient and Medieval Theories of Intentionality* (Leiden: Brill, 2001), pp. 63–97

Rashed, M., 'Alexandre d'Aphrodise et la "Magna Quaestio"', *Les Études classiques* 63 (1995), 295–351; repr. in his *L'héritage aristotélicien: Textes inédits de l'Antiquité* (Paris: Les Belles Lettres, 2007)

Rashd, M., 'A "New" Text of Alexander on the Soul's Motion', in R. Sorabji, ed., *Aristotle and After* (London: Institute of Classical Studies, 1997), pp. 181–95; repr. in his *L'héritage aristotélicien: Textes inédits de l'Antiquité* (Paris: Les Belles Lettres, 2007)

Rashed, M., 'Théodicée et approximation: Avicenne', *Arabic Sciences and Philosophy* 10 (2000), 223–57

Rashed, M., 'Traces d'un commentaire de Simplicius sur la *Métaphysique* à Byzance?', *Revue des sciences philosophiques et théologiques* 84 (2000), 275–84

Rashed, M., 'Nicolas d'Otrante, Guillaume de Moerbeke et la "Collection philosophique"', *Studi Medievali* 43 (2002), 693–717; repr. in his *L'héritage aristotélicien: Textes inédits de l'Antiquité* (Paris: Les Belles Lettres, 2007)

Rashed, M., 'Entre Andronicos et Alexandre', *Arabic Sciences and Philosophy* 14 (2004), 29–30

Rashed, M., 'Priorité de l'*eidos* ou du *genos* entre Andronicos et Alexandre: vestiges arabes et grecs inedits', *Arabic Sciences and Philosophy* 14 (2004), 9–63; repr. in his *L'héritage aristotélicien: Textes inédits de l'Antiquité* (Paris: Les Belles Lettres, 2007)

Rashed, M., 'The Problem of the Composition of the Heavens (529–610): A New Fragment of Philoponus and its Readers', in P. Adamson, H. Baltussen, and M. Stone, eds, *Philosophy, Science, and Exegesis in Greek, Arabic, and Latin Commentaries*, 2 vols (London: Institute of Classical Studies, 2004), vol. 2, pp. 35–58; repr. in his *L'héritage aristotélicien: Textes inédits de l'Antiquité* (Paris: Les Belles Lettres, 2007)

Rashed, M., *Aristote, De la géneration et la corruption* (Paris: Les Belles Lettres, 2005)

Rashed, M., *Essentialisme: Alexandre d'Aphrodise entre logique, physique et cosmologie* (Berlin: De Gruyter, 2007)

Rashed, M., *L'héritage aristotélicien: Textes inédits de l'Antiquité* (Paris: Les Belles Lettres, 2007)

Rashed, M., 'Al-Fārābī's Lost Treatise *On Changing Beings* and the Possibility of a Demonstration of the Eternity of the World', *Arabic Sciences and Philosophy* 18 (2008), 19–58

Rashed, M., 'On the Authorship of the Treatise *On the Harmonization of the opinions of the Two Sages* Attributed to al-Fārābī', *Arabic Sciences and Philosophy* 19 (2009), 43–82

Rashed, M., 'Alexander of Aphrodisias on Particulars', in R. W. Sharples, ed., *Particulars in Greek Philosophy* (Leiden: Brill, 2010), pp. 157–79

Rashed, M., *Alexandre d'Aphrodise, Commentaire perdu à la Physique d'Aristote (Livres IV–VIII)* (Berlin: De Gruyter, 2011)

Rashed, M., 'Nouveau fragment arabe du *De aeternitate mundi contra Aristotelem* de Jean Philopon', *Elenchos* 33 (2012), 291–300

Rashed, M., 'Boethus' Aristotelian Ontology', in M. Schofield, ed., *Aristotle, Plato, and Pythagoreanism in the First Century BC* (Cambridge: Cambridge University Press, 2013), pp. 53–77

Rashed, M., *Al-Ḥasan ibn Mūsā al-Nawbakhtī: Commentary on Aristotle De generatione et corruptione* (Berlin: De Gruyter, 2015)

Rashed, R., 'Combinatoire et métaphysique: Ibn Sina, al-Tusi et al-Halabi', in R. Rashed, ed., *Les doctrines de la science de l'antiquité à l'âge classique* (Leuven: Peeters, 1999), pp. 61–86

Rashed, R., and Jolivet, J., *Oeuvres Philosophiques & Scientifiques d'al-Kindi: Volume 2, Métaphysique et cosmologie* (Leiden: Brill, 1998)

Reinhardt, T., 'Andronicus of Rhodes and Boethus of Sidon on Aristotle's *Categories*', in R. W. Sharples and R. Sorabji, eds, *Greek and Roman Philosophy 100 BC – 200 AD*, 2 vols (London: Institute of Classical Studies, 2007), vol. 2, pp. 513–29

Reisman, D. C., 'Plato's *Republic* in Arabic: A Newly Discovered Passage', *Arabic Sciences and Philosophy* 14 (2004), 276–9

Reisman, D. C., and Bertolacci, A., 'Thābit ibn Qurra's *Concise Exposition of Aristotle's Metaphysics*: Text, Translation and Commentary', in R. Rashed, ed., *Thābit ibn Qurra: Science and Philosophy in Ninth-Century Baghdad* (Berlin: De Gruyter, 2009), pp. 715–76

Rescher, N., 'A Tenth-Century Arab-Christian Apologia for Logic', *Islamic Studies* 2 (1963), 1–16

Rescher, N., and Marmura, M., *The Refutation by Alexander of Aphrodisias of Galen's Treatise on the Theory of Motion* (Islamabad: Islamic Research Institute, 1965)

Rescher, N., and Shehadi, F., 'Yaḥyā Ibn ʿAdī's Treatise "On the Four Scientific Questions Regarding the Art of Logic"', *Journal of the History of Ideas* 25 (1964), 572–8

Riedlberger, P., *Domninus of Larissa, Encheiridion and Spurious Works* (Pisa: Fabrizio Serra Editore, 2013)

Rist, J. M., 'Some Aspects of Aristotelian Teleology', *Transactions and Proceedings of the American Philological Association* 96 (1965), 337–49

Rist, J. M., 'Pseudo-Ammonius and the Soul/Body Problem in Some Platonic Texts of Late Antiquity', *American Journal of Philology* 109 (1988), 402–15

Ritups, A., *Aristotle De Anima III. 6: Essays in the History of its Interpretation*, PhD thesis (Leuven, 2010)

Ross, W. D., *Aristotle's Metaphysics: A Revised Text with Introduction and Commentary*, 2 vols (Oxford: Clarendon Press, 1924)

Roueché, M., 'The Definitions of Philosophy and a New Fragment of Stephanus the Philosopher', *Jahrbuch der Österreichischen Byzantistik* 40 (1990), 107–28

Roueché, M., 'Stephanus the Alexandrian Philosopher, the *Kanon* and a Seventh Century Millennium', *Journal of the Courtauld and Warburg Institutes* 74 (2011), 1–30

Roueché, M., 'Stephanus the Philosopher and Ps. Elias: A Case of Mistaken Identity', in *Byzantine and Modern Greek Studies* 36 (2012), 120–38

Ruland, H.-J., *Die arabischen Fassungen von zwei Schriften des Alexander von Aphrodisias: Über die Vorsehung und Über das liberum arbitrium*, PhD thesis (Universität des Saarlandes, 1976)

Rutten, C., 'La doctrine des deux actes dans la philosophie de Plotin', *Revue philosophique* 81 (1956), 100–6

Sabra, I. A., 'Simplicius' Proof of Euclid's Parallels Postulate', *Journal of the Courtauld and Warburg Institutes* 32 (1969), 1–24

Saffrey, H. D., 'Le chrétien Jean Philopon et la survivance de l'école d'Alexandrie au VIe siècle', *Revue des études grecques* 67 (1954), 396–410

Saffrey, H. D., 'Comment Syrianus, le maître de l'école néoplatonicienne d'Athènes, considerait-il Aristote?', in J. Wiesner, ed., *Aristoteles: Werk und Wirkung*, 2 vols (Berlin:

De Gruyter, 1987), vol. 2, pp. 205-14; repr. in his *Recherches sur le néoplatonisme après Plotin* (Paris: Vrin, 2000), pp. 131-40; trans. as 'How Did Syrianus Regard Aristotle?', in R. Sorabji, ed., *Aristotle Transformed* (London: Duckworth, 1990), pp. 173-9

Saffrey, H. D., 'Accorder entre elles les traditions théologiques: une caractéristique du néoplatonisme athénien', in E. P. Bos and P. A. Meijer, eds, *On Proclus and his Influence in Medieval Philosophy* (Leiden: Brill, 1992), pp. 35-50; repr. in *Le néoplatonisme après Plotin* (Paris: Vrin, 2000), pp. 143-58

Saffrey, H. D., 'Pourquoi Porphyre a-t-il edité Plotin?', in Luc Brisson et al., eds, *La vie de Plotin*, 2 vols (Paris: Vrin, 1982-92), vol. 2, pp. 31-64

Saffrey, H. D., *Recherches sur le néoplatonisme après Plotin* (Paris: Vrin, 2000)

Saffrey, H. D., and Westerink, L. G., *Proclus, Théologie Platonicienne: Livre I* (Paris: Les Belles Lettres, 1968)

Saffrey, H. D., and Westerink, L. G., *Proclus, Théologie Platonicienne: Livre II* (Paris: Les Belles Lettres, 1974)

Sambursky, S., 'On Some References to Experience in Stoic Physics', *Isis* 49 (1958), 331-5

Sambursky, S., *The Physical World of Late Antiquity* (London: Routledge & Kegan Paul, 1962)

Sambursky, S., and Pines, S., *The Concept of Time in Late Neoplatonism* (Jerusalem: Israel Academy of Sciences and Humanities, 1971)

Šanda, A., *Opuscula monophysitica Iohannis Philoponi* (Beirut: Typographia Catholica PP. Soc. Jesu., 1930)

Sandbach, F. H., *Aristotle and the Stoics* (Cambridge: Cambridge Philological Society, 1985)

Schibli, H., *Hierocles of Alexandria* (Oxford: Oxford University Press, 2002)

Schironi, F., 'Plato at Alexandria: Aristophanes, Aristarchus and the 'philological tradition' of a philosopher', *Classical Quarterly* 55 (2005), 423-34

Schmidt, E. G., 'Alexander von Aphrodisias in einem altarmenischen Kategorien-Kommentar', *Philologus* 110 (1966), 277-86

Schofield, M., ed., *Aristotle, Plato, and Pythagoreans in the First Century BC* (Cambridge: Cambridge University Press, 2013)

Scholten, C., *Antike Naturphilosophie und christliche Kosmologie in der Schrift "De Opificio Mundi" des Johannes Philoponos* (Berlin: De Gruyter, 1996)

Scholten, C., *Johannes Philoponos: De opificio mundi, Über die Erschaffung der Welt*, 3 vols (Freiburg: Herder, 1997)

Scholten, C., *Johannes Philoponos, De Aeternitate Mundi I* (Turnhout: Brepols, 2009)

Schroeder, F. M., and Todd, R. B., *Two Greek Aristotelian Commentators on the Intellect: The De Intellectu Attributed to Alexander of Aphrodisias, and Themistius' Paraphrase of Aristotle De Anima, 3.4-8* (Toronto: Pontifical Institute of Medieval Studies, 1990)

Sedley, D. N., 'The Etymologies in Plato's *Cratylus*', *Journal of Hellenic Studies* 118 (1998), 140-54

Sedley, D. N., 'Aristotelian Relativities', in M. Canto-Sperber and P. Pellegrin, eds, *Le style de la pensée* (Paris: Les Belles Lettres, 2002), pp. 324-52

Sedley, D. N., 'Philodemus and the Decentralisation of Philosophy', *Cronache Ercolanesi* 33 (2003), 31-41

Seeck, G. A., *Über die Elemente in der Kosmologie des Aristoteles: Untersuchungen zu 'de generatione et corruptione' und 'de caelo'* (Munich: Beck, 1964)

Sellars, J., 'The Aristotelian Commentators: A Bibliographical Guide', in P. Adamson, H. Baltussen, and M. Stone, eds, *Philosophy, Science, and Exegesis in Greek, Arabic, and Latin Commentaries*, 2 vols (London: Institute of Classical Studies, 2004), vol. 1, pp. 239-68

Seng, H., *Un livre sacré de l'Antiquité tardive: Les Oracles Chaldaïques* (Turnhout: Brepols, 2016)
Seng, H., and Tardieu, M., eds, *Die Chaldaeischen Orakel: Kontext, Interpretation, Rezeption* (Heidelberg: Universitätsverlag Winter, 2011)
Share, M., *Arethas of Caesarea's Scholia on Porphyry's Isagoge and Aristotle's Categories (Codex Vaticanus Urbinas Graecus 35): A Critical Edition* (Athens: Academy of Athens, 1994)
Share, M., *Philoponus, Against Proclus On the Eternity of the World 1-5* (London: Duckworth, 2004)
Share, M., *Philoponus, Against Proclus On the Eternity of the World 6-8* (London: Duckworth, 2005)
Share, M., *Philoponus, Against Proclus On the Eternity of the World 9-11* (London: Duckworth, 2010)
Sharif, M. M., ed., *A History of Muslim Philosophy* (Wiesbaden: Otto Harrassowitz, 1963)
Sharples, R. W., 'Responsibility, Chance, and Not-Being in Alexander of Aphrodisias *Mantissa* 169-172', *Bulletin of the Institute of Classical Studies* 22 (1975), 37-63
Sharples, R. W., 'Alexander of Aphrodisias, On Time', *Phronesis* 27 (1982), 58-81
Sharples, R. W., *Alexander of Aphrodisias On Fate* (London: Duckworth, 1983)
Sharples, R. W., 'Alexander of Aphrodisias: Scholasticism and Innovation', in W. Haase, ed., *Aufstieg und Niedergang der römischen Welt* II. 36.2 (Berlin: De Gruyter, 1987), pp. 1176-1243
Sharples, R. W., *Alexander of Aphrodisias, Ethical Problems* (London: Duckworth, 1990)
Sharples, R. W., *Alexander of Aphrodisias, Quaestiones 1.1-2.15* (London; Duckworth, 1992)
Sharples, R. W., 'Alexander of Aphrodisias on Universals: Two Problematic Texts', *Phronesis* 50 (2005), 43-55
Sharples, R. W., *Alexander Aphrodisiensis, De anima libri mantissa* (Berlin: De Gruyter, 2008)
Sharples, R. W., '*Habent sua fata libelli*: Aristotle's *Categories* in the First Century BC', *Acta Antiqua* 48 (2008), 273-87
Sharples, R. W., *Peripatetic Philosophy 200 BC to AD 200* (Cambridge: Cambridge University Press, 2010)
Sharples, R. W., 'Strato of Lampsacus: The Sources, Texts and Translations', in M.-L. Desclos and W. W. Fortenbaugh, eds, *Strato of Lampsacus: Text, Translation, and Discussion* (New Brunswick: Transaction Publishers, 2011), pp. 5-229
Sheppard, A. 'Proclus' Philosophical Method of Exegesis: The Use of Aristotle and the Stoics in the *Commentary on the Cratylus*', in J. Pépin and H. D. Saffrey, eds, *Proclus lecteur et interprète des anciens* (Paris: CNRS, 1987), pp. 137-51
Siorvanes, L., *Proclus: Neo-Platonic Philosophy and Science* (New Haven: Yale University Press, 1996)
Sirkel, R., 'Alexander of Aphrodisias' Account of Universals and its Problems', *Journal of the History of Philosophy* 49 (2011), 297-314
Sirkel, R., et al., *Philoponus, On Aristotle's Categories 1-5* (London: Bloomsbury, 2014)
Smith, A., *Porphyrii Philosophi Fragmenta* (Stuttgart: Teubner, 1993)
Smith, A., *Plotinus, Porphyry, and Iamblichus: Philosophy and Religion in Neoplatonism* (Aldershot: Ashgate, 2011)
Snyder, H. G., *Teachers and Texts in the Ancient World* (London: Routledge, 2000)
Sorabji, R., 'Body and Soul in Aristotle', *Philosophy* 49 (1974), 42-64

Sorabji, R., *Time, Creation and the Continuum* (London: Duckworth, 1983)
Sorabji, R., 'John Philoponus', in R. Sorabji, ed., ed., *Philoponus and the Rejection of Aristotelian Science* (London: Duckworth, 1987), pp. 1-40
Sorabji, R., ed., *Philoponus and the Rejection of Aristotelian Science* (London: Duckworth, 1987)
Sorabji, R., *Matter, Space, and Motion: Theories in Antiquity and Their Sequel* (London: Duckworth, 1988)
Sorabji, R., 'The Greek Origins of the Idea of Chemical Combination: Can Two Bodies be in the Same Place?', *Proceedings of the Boston Area Colloquium in Ancient Philosophy* 4 (1988), 35-63
Sorabji, R., ed., *Aristotle Transformed: The Ancient Commentators and Their Influence* (London: Duckworth 1990)
Sorabji, R., 'The Ancient Commentators on Aristotle', in R. Sorabji, ed., *Aristotle Transformed: The Ancient Commentators and Their Influence* (London: Duckworth, 1990), pp. 1-31
Sorabji, R., 'Perceptual Content in the Stoics', *Phronesis* 35 (1990), 307-14
Sorabji, R., 'From Aristotle to Brentano: The Development of the Concept of Intentionality', in H. Blumenthal and H. Robinson, eds, *Aristotle and the Later Tradition* (Oxford: Clarendon Press, 1991), pp. 227-60
Sorabji, R., *Animal Minds and Human Morals* (London: Duckworth, 1993)
Sorabji, R., 'Introduction', in A. R. Lacey, *Philoponus, On Aristotle Physics 2* (London: Duckworth, 1993), pp. 1-3
Sorabji, R., *Emotion and Peace of Mind* (Oxford: Oxford University Press, 2000)
Sorabji, R., 'Aristotle on Sensory Processes and Intentionality: A Reply to Myles Burnyeat', in D. Perler, ed., *Ancient and Medieval Theories of Intentionality* (Leiden: Brill, 2001), pp. 49-63
Sorabji, R., 'The Mind-Body Relation in the Wake of Plato's *Timaeus*', in G. Reydams-Schils, ed., *Plato's Timaeus as Cultural Icon* (Notre Dame: University of Notre Dame Press, 2003), pp. 152-62
Sorabji, R., *The Philosophy of the Commentators, 200-600 AD: A Sourcebook*, 3 vols (London: Duckworth, 2004)
Sorabji, R., 'Divine Names and Sordid Deals in Ammonius's Alexandria', in A. Smith, ed., *The Philosopher and Society in Late Antiquity* (Swansea: The Classical Press of Wales, 2005), pp. 203-13
Sorabji, R., *Self: Ancient and Modern Insights about Individuality, Life, and Death* (Oxford: Clarendon Press, 2006)
Sorabji, R., 'Universals Transformed: The First Thousand Years after Plato', in P. F. Strawson and A. Chakrabarti, eds, *Universals, Concepts and Qualities* (Aldershot: Ashgate, 2006), pp. 105-25
Sorabji, R., 'Adrastus: Modifications to Aristotle's Physics of the Heavens by Peripatetics and others, 100 BC to 200 AD', in R. Sorabji and R. W. Sharples, eds, *Greek and Roman Philosophy 100 BC-200 AD*, 2 vols (London: Institute of Classical Studies, 2007), vol. 2, pp. 575-94
Sorabji, R., 'Self-awareness', in M. M. McCabe and M. Textor, eds, *Perspectives on Perception* (Fankfurt: Ontos Verlag, 2007), pp. 131-42
Sorabji, R., 'Introduction', in R. Sorabji, ed., *Philoponus and the Rejection of Aristotelian Science*, 2nd edn (London: Institute of Classical Studies, 2010), pp. 1-40
Sorabji, R., *Gandhi and the Stoics* (Oxford: Oxford University Press, 2012)
Sorabji, R., *Perception, Conscience, and Will* (Aldershot: Ashgate, 2013)

Sorabji, R., 'The Alexandrian Classrooms Excavated and Sixth-Century Philosophy Teaching', in Pauliina Remes and Svetla Slaveva-Griffin, eds, *The Routledge Handbook of Neoplatonism* (Abingdon: Routledge, 2014), pp. 30–9

Sorabji, R., *Moral Conscience through the Ages* (Oxford: Oxford University Press 2014)

Sorabji, R., 'Introduction', in R. Sirkel, *et al.*, *Philoponus, On Aristotle Categories 1–5, with Philoponus, A Treatise Concerning the Whole and the Parts* (London: Bloomsbury, 2015), pp. 3–34

Soulier, P., *Simplicius et l'infini* (Paris: Les Belles Lettres, 2014)

Steel, C., 'Proclus et Aristote sur la causalité efficiente de l'intellect divin', in J. Pépin and H. D. Saffrey, eds, *Proclus, lecteur et interprète des anciens* (Paris: CNRS, 1987), pp. 213–25

Steel, C., 'Breathing Thought: Proclus on the Innate Knowledge of the Soul', in J. J. Cleary, ed., *The Perennial Tradition of Neoplatonism* (Leuven: Leuven University Press, 1997), pp. 293–309

Steel, C., 'Definitions and Ideas: Aristotle, Proclus and the Socrates of the *Parmenides*', *Proceedings of the Boston Area Colloquium in Ancient Philosophy* 19 (2003), 103–21

Steel, C., 'Why should we prefer Plato's *Timaeus* to Aristotle's *Physics*? Proclus' critique of Aristotle's causal explanation of the physical world', in R. W. Sharples and A. Sheppard, eds, *Ancient Approaches to Plato's Timaeus* (London: Institute of Classical Studies, 2003), pp. 175–87

Steel, C., 'Proclus' Defence of the *Timaeus* against Aristotle's Objections: A Reconstruction of a Lost Polemical Treatise', in T. Leinkauf and C. Steel, eds, *Plato's Timaeus and the Foundations of Cosmology in Late Antiquity, the Middle Ages and Renaissance* (Leuven: Leuven University Press, 2005), pp. 163–93

Steel, C., 'The Divine Earth: Proclus on *Timaeus* 40BC', in R. Chiaradonna and F. Trabatonni, eds, *Physics and Philosophy of Nature in Greek Neoplatonism* (Leiden: Brill, 2009), pp. 259–81

Steel, C., 'Plato's Geography: Damascius' Interpretation of the *Phaedo* Myth', in J. Wilberding and C. Horn, eds, *Neoplatonism and the Philosophy of Nature* (Oxford: Oxford University Press 2012), pp. 174–96

Steel, C., 'Surface Reading and Deeper Meaning: On Aristotle Reading Plato and Platonists Reading Aristotle', in M. Erler and J. E. Hessle, eds, *Argument und literarische Form in antiker Philosophie* (Berlin: De Gruyter, 2013), pp. 469–94

Steel, C., *'Simplicius', On Aristotle On the Soul 3.6–13* (London: Bristol Classical Press, 2013)

Steiner, G., *Anthropocentrism and Its Discontents: The Moral Status of Animals in the History of Western Philosophy* (Pittsburgh: University of Pittsburgh Press, 2005)

Steiner, G., 'Animal Rights and the Default of Postmodernism', in E. D. Protopapadakis, ed., *Animal Ethics* (Berlin: Logos Verlag, 2012), pp. 151–62

Stern, S. M., 'Ibn al-Tayyib's commentary on the Isagoge', *Bulletin of the School of Oriental and African Studies*, 19 (1957), 419–25

Stroumsa, S., 'Al-Farabi and Maimonides on the Christian philosophical tradition: a re-evaluation', *Der Islam* 68 (1991), 107–24

Stroumsa, S., *Freethinkers of Medieval Islam* (Leiden: Brill, 1999)

Swain, S., *Themistius, Julian, and Greek Political Theory under Rome* (Cambridge: Cambridge University Press, 2013)

Sylla, E. D., 'Medieval Concepts of the Latitude of Forms: The Oxford Calculators', *Archives d'Histoire doctrinale et littéraire du Moyen Age* 48 (1974), 223–83

Szlezák, T. A., *Pseudo-Archytas Über die Kategorien* (Berlin: De Gruyter, 1972)

Taormina, D. P., *Jamblique, critique de Plotin et de Porphyre* (Paris: Vrin, 1999)

Tarán, L., *Anonymous Commentary on Aristotle's De Interpretatione (Codex Parisinus Graecus 2064)* (Meisenheim am Glan: Hain, 1978)
Tarán, L., 'Aristotelianism in the First Century BC', *Gnomon* 53 (1981), 721–50; repr. in his *Collected Papers (1962–1999)* (Leiden: Brill, 2001), pp. 479–524
Tarán, L., '*Amicus Plato sed magis amica veritas*: From Plato and Aristotle to Cervantes', *Antike und Abendland* 30 (1984), 93–124
Tarán, L. 'Syrianus and Pseudo-Alexander's commentary on *Metaph.* E-N', in J. Wiesner, ed., *Aristoteles: Werk und Wirkung*, 2 vols (Berlin: De Gruyter, 1987), vol. 2, pp. 215–32
Tardieu, M., 'Chosroes', in R. Goulet, ed., *Dictionnaire des philosophes antiques II* (Paris: CNRS, 1994), pp. 309–18
Tarrant, H., *Thrasyllan Platonism* (Ithaca: Cornell University Press, 1993)
Taylor, A. E., *A Commentary on Plato's Timaeus* (Oxford: Clarendon Press, 1928)
Thesleff, H., *An Introduction to the Pythagorean Writings of the Hellenistic Period* (Abo: Abo Akedemi, 1961)
Thillet, P. *Alexandre d'Aphrodise, Traité de la providence = Peri pronoias* (Lagrasse: Verdier 2003)
Thomas Aquinas, *Commentary on the Metaphysics of Aristotle*, trans. J. P. Rowan, 2 vols (Chicago: Henry Regnery Company, 1961)
Todd, R. B., *Alexander of Aphrodisias on Stoic Physics: A Study of the De mixtione with Preliminary Essays, Text, Translation, and Commentary* (Leiden: Brill, 1976)
Todd, R. B., 'Galenic Medical Ideas in the Greek Aristotelian Commentators', *Symbolae Osloenses* 52 (1977), 117–34
Todd, R. B., 'Some Concepts in Physical Theory in John Philoponus' Aristotelian Commentaries', *Archiv für Begriffsgeschichte* 24 (1980), 151–70
Todd, R. B., 'Philosophy and Medicine in John Philoponus' Commentary on Aristotle's "De Anima"', *Dumbarton Oaks Papers* 38 (1984), 103–10
Todd, R. B., *Themistius, On Aristotle On the Soul* (London: Duckworth, 1996)
Topchyan, A., *David the Invincible, Commentary on Aristotle's Prior Analytics* (Leiden: Brill, 2010)
Tornau, C., 'Bemerkungen zu Stephanos von Alexandria, Plotin und Plutarch von Athen', *Elenchos* 28 (2007), 105–27
Trédé, M., *Kairos, l'à propos et l'occasion: Le mot et la notion, d'Homère à la fin du IVe siècle avant J.-C.* (Paris: Klincksiek, 1992)
Türker, M., 'Yaḥyā ibn ʿAdī ve Nesredilmemis, bir Risalesi', *Ankara Üniversitesi Dil ve Tarih-Cografya Fakültesi dergisi* 14 (1956), 87–102
Turner, E. G., *Greek Papyri: An Introduction* (Oxford: Clarendon Press, 1968)
Tweedale, M., 'Alexander of Aphrodisias' Views on Universals', *Phronesis* 29 (1984), 279–303
Ulacco, A., and Opsomer, J., 'Elements and elemental properties in Timaeus Locrus', *Rheinisches Museum für Philologie* 157 (2014), 154–206
Usener, H., *Kleine Schriften*, 4 vols (Leipzig: Teubner, 1912–14)
Uthemann, K. H., 'Stephanus von Alexandrien und die Konversion des Jakobiten Probos, des späteren Metropoliten von Chaklkedon: Ein Beitrag zur Rolle der Philosophie in der Kontroverstheologies des 6. Jahrhundert', in C. Laga, J. A. Munitiz, and L. Van Rompay, eds, *After Chalcedon* (Leuven: Peeters, 1985), pp. 381–99
Vallat, P., *Farabi et l'École d'Alexandrie* (Paris: Vrin, 2004)
Vallery-Radot, P., ed., *Oeuvres de Pasteur*, 2 vols (Paris: Masson, 1922)
van den Berg, R. M., 'Smoothing over the Differences', in P. Adamson, H. Baltussen, and M. Stone, eds, *Philosophy, Science, and Exegesis in Greek, Arabic, and Latin Commentaries*, 2 vols (London: Institute of Classical Studies, 2004), vol. 1, pp. 191–201

van den Berg, R. M. 'What's in a Divine Name? Proclus on Plato's *Cratylus*', in J. H. D. Scourfield, ed., *Texts & Cultures in Late Antiquity: Inheritance, Authority, and Change* (Swansea: The Classical Press of Wales, 2007), pp. 261–77

van der Eijk, P., *Philoponus, On Aristotle On the Soul 1.1-2* (London: Duckworth, 2005)

Van der Lugt, M., *Le ver, le démon et la vierge: Les théories médiévales de la génération extraordinaire* (Paris: Les Belles Lettres, 2004)

van Ess, J., *Theologie und Gesellschaft im 2. und 3. Jahrhundert Hidschra*, 6 vols (Berlin: De Gruyter, 1991–97)

van Riel, G., *Pleasure and the Good Life: Plato, Aristotle and the Neoplatonists* (Leiden: Brill, 2000)

Van Riet, S., 'Fragments de l'original grec du « De intellectu » de Philopon dans une compilation de Sophonias', *Revue philosophique de Louvain* 63 (1965), 5–40

van Roey, A., 'Les fragments trithéites de Jean Philopon', *Orientalia Lovaniensia Periodica* 11 (1980), 135–63

Verbeke, G., *Jean Philopon, Commentaire sur le De anima d'Aristote, Traduction de Guillaume de Moerbeke* (Louvain: Publications Universiatires de Louvain / Paris: Éditions Béatrice-Nauwelaerts, 1966)

Verbeke, G., 'Some Late Neoplatonic Views on Divine Creation and the Eternity of the World', in D. O'Meara, ed., *Neoplatonism and Christian Thought* (Albany: State University of New York Press, 1982), pp. 45–53

Verdenius, W. J., and Waszink, J. H., *Aristotle on Coming-to-Be and Passing-Away: Some Comments*, 2nd edn (Leiden: Brill, 1966)

Verrycken, K., *God en wereld in der wijsbegeerte van Ioannes Philoponus. De overgang van een Alexandrijns-Neoplatonische naar een christelijk scheppingsleer*, I–III, Ph.D. thesis (Leuven, 1985)

Verrycken, K., 'The Development of Philoponus' Thought and its Chronology', in R. Sorabji, ed., *Aristotle Transformed: The Ancient Commentators and Their Influence* (London: Duckworth, 1990), pp. 233–74

Verrycken, K., 'John Philoponus', in L. P. Gerson, ed., *The Cambridge History of Philosophy in Late Antiquity*, 2 vols (Cambridge: Cambridge University Press, 2010), vol. 2, pp. 733–55

Viltnioti, E., 'Divine statues in Makarios Magnes, Porphyry and Iamblichus', *Journal of Late Antiquity*, forthcoming

von Mueller, I., 'Ueber Galens Werk vom wissenschaftlichen Beweis', *Abhandlungen der philosophisch-philologischen Classe der königlich bayerischen Akademie der Wissenschaften* 20 (1897), 405–78

Vuillemin, J., 'Le carré chrysippéen des modalités', *Dialectica* 37 (1983), 235–47

Vuillemin, J., *Nécessité ou contingence: L' aporie de Diodore et les systèmes philosophiques* (Paris: Éditions de Minuit, 1984)

Vuillemin, J., 'Nouvelles réflexions sur l'argument dominateur: une double référence au temps dans la seconde prémisse', *Philosophie* 55 (1997), 14–30

Waitz, T., *Aristotelis Organon Graece*, 2 vols (Leipzig: Hahn, 1844–46)

Wakelnig, E., *Feder, Tafel, Mensch, al-'Āmirīs Kitāb al-fuṣūl fī l-ma'ālim al-ilāhīya und die arabische Proklos-Rezeption im 10. Jh.* (Leiden: Brill, 2006)

Wakelnig, E., 'A New Version of Miskawayh's *Book of Triumph*: An alternative Recession of *al-Fawz al-asghar* or the lost *Fawz al-akbar*?', *Arabic Sciences and Philosophy* 19 (2009), 83–119

Walker, J. T., 'The Limits of Late Antiquity: Philosophy between Rome and Iran', *The Ancient World* 33 (2002), 45–69

Walters, K., and Portmess, L., *Ethical Vegetarianism: From Pythagoras to Peter Singer* (Albany: State University of New York Press, 1999)
Walzer, R., 'New Studies on al-Kindi', *Oriens* 10 (1957), 203–32; repr. in his *Greek into Arabic: Essays on Islamic Philosophy* (Oxford: Cassirer, 1962)
Watt, J. W., 'Commentary and Translation in Syriac Aristotelian Scholarship: Sergius to Baghdad', *Journal for Late Antique Religion and Culture* 4 (2010), 28–42
Watt, J. W., 'The Syriac Aristotle between Alexandria and Baghdad', *Journal for Late Antique Religion and Culture* 7 (2013), 26–50
Watt, J. W., 'Sergius of Reshayna on the Prolegomena to Aristotle's Logic: The Commentary on the *Categories*, Chapter Two', in E. Coda and C. Martini Bonadeo eds, *De l'Antiquité tardive au Moyen Âge: Études de logique aristotélicienne et de philosophie grecque, syriaque, arabe et latine offertes à Henri Hugonnard-Roche* (Paris: Vrin, 2014), pp. 31–58
Westerink, L. G., 'Elias on the *Prior Analytics*', *Mnemosyne* 14 (1961), 126–39
Westerink, L. G., *Anonymous Prolegomena to Platonic Philosophy* (Amsterdam: North Holland Publishing, 1962)
Westerink, L. G., *Pseudo Elias (Pseudo David) Lectures on Porphyry's Isagoge* (Amsterdam: North Holland Publishing, 1967)
Westerink, L. G., *The Greek Commentaries on Plato's Phaedo, Volume 1: Olympiodorus* (Amsterdam: North Holland Publishing, 1976)
Westerink, L. G., 'The Alexandrian Commentators and the Introductions to their Commentaries', in R. Sorabji, ed., *Aristotle Transformed: The Ancient Commentators and Their Influence* (London: Duckworth, 1990), pp. 325–48
Westerink, L. G., *Texts and Studies in Neoplatonism and Byzantine Literature* (Amsterdam: Hakkert, 1980)
Whitby, M., and Whitby, M., *The History of Theophylact Simocatta* (Oxford: Clarendon Press, 1986)
Whittaker, J., and Louis, P., *Alcinoos, Enseignement des doctrines de Platon* (Paris: Les Belles Lettres, 1990)
Wilberding, J., *Plotinus' Cosmology: A Study of Ennead II.1 (40)* (Oxford: Oxford University Press, 2006)
Wilberding, J., 'Porphyry and Plotinus on the Seed', *Phronesis* 53 (2008), 406–32
Wilberding, J., *Porphyry, To Gaurus On How Embryos are Ensouled and On What is in Our Power* (London: Bristol Classical Press, 2011)
Wilberding, J., 'Neoplatonists on 'Spontaneous' Generation', in J. Wilberding and C. Horn, eds, *Neoplatonism and the Philosophy of Nature* (Oxford: Oxford University Press, 2012), pp. 197–213
Wilberding, J., 'The Myth of Er and the Problem of Constitutive Luck', in A. Sheppard, ed., *Ancient Approaches to Plato's Republic* (London: Institute of Classical Studies, 2013), pp. 87–105
Wilberding, J., 'Neoplatonists on the Causes of Vegetative Life', in A. Marmodoro and B. Prince, eds, *Causation and Creation in Late Antiquity* (Cambridge: Cambridge University Press, 2015), pp. 171–85
Wilberding, J., 'The Revolutionary Embryology of the Neoplatonists', *Oxford Studies in Ancient Philosophy* 49 (2015), 321–60
Wilberding, J., and Horn, C., eds, *Neoplatonism and the Philosophy of Nature* (Oxford: Oxford University Press, 2012)
Wildberg, C., *Philoponus, Against Aristotle on the Eternity of the World* (London: Duckworth, 1987)

Wildberg, C., 'Prolegomena to the study of Philoponus' *Contra Aristotelem*', in R. Sorabji, ed., *Philoponus and the Rejection of Aristotelian Science* (London: Duckworth, 1987), pp 197-209

Wildberg, C., *John Philoponus' Criticism of Aristotle's Theory of Aether* (Berlin: De Gruyter, 1988)

Wildberg, C., 'Three Neoplatonic Introductions to Philosophy: Ammonius, David and Elias', *Hermathena* 149 (1990), 33-51

Wildberg, C., 'Olympiodorus', in E. Zalta, ed., *The Stanford Encyclopedia of Philosophy*, Fall 2008 Edition

Williams, C. J. F., *Aristotle's De Generatione et Corruptione* (Oxford: Clarendon Press, 1982)

Wilson, N. G., *Scholars of Byzantium* (London: Duckworth, 1983)

Winsbury, R., *The Roman Book* (London: Duckworth, 2009)

Wolff, M., *Fallgesetz und Massebegriff* (Berlin: De Gruyter, 1971)

Wolska-Conus, W., 'Stéphanos d'Athènes et Stéphanos d'Alexandrie: Essai d'identification et de biographie', *Revue des études byzantines* 47 (1989), 5-89

Wurm, K., *Substanz und Qualität: Ein Beitrag zur Interpretation der plotinischen Traktate VI 1, 2, 3* (Berlin: De Gruyter, 1973)

Zghal, H., 'La relation chez Avicenne', *Arabic Sciences and Philosophy* 16 (2006), 237-86

Zimmermann, F., 'The Origins of the so-called *Theology of Aristotle*', in J. Kraye, W. Ryan, and C. Schmitt, eds, *Pseudo-Aristotle in the Middle Ages* (London: The Warburg Institute, 1986), pp. 110-240

Zimmermann, F., 'Proclus arabus rides again', *Arabic Sciences and Philosophy* 4 (1994), 9-51

Index Locorum

Compiled by David Robertson

Aetius
Plac.
4.11.4, 278 n.118
5.15.2, 171 n.23
Agathias
Hist.
2.28.2-4, 58
2.28.5, 58
2.29.7, 58
2.29.9, 58
2.29.11, 58
2.30.3-4, 58
2.31.2, 59
2.31.3, 58
2.32.2, 58
2.32.5, 58
3.31.1, 60
Albinus
Intr.
§ 4, 86 n.20
Alcinous
Didasc.
153,4-5, 157 n.67
179,8-13, 148
179,10-11, 142
179,20-3, 142
179,31-3, 142
§ 26, 136 n.14
Alexander of Aphrodisias
An. (Bruns)
6,2-6, 6 n.23, 112 n.24
25,4-9, 441 n.15
26,21-2, 441 n.15
66,6-8, 16
87,8-16, 297 n.33
87,13-14, 167 n.14
87,16, 299 n.40
89,9-13, 15 n.62
90,2-8, 299
90,2-11, 297 n.32
90,5-6, 299 n.42
in An. Pr. (CAG 2.1)
1,18-2,2, 457 n.15
15,4-11, 393 n.2
53-4, 457 n.17
162,31-2, 144
163,21-9, 139 n.28
169,6-9, 144
180,33-6, 168 n.16
180,36, 168
181,25-31, 168 n.16
270,23-5, 144
in Cael. ap. Simplicius *in Phys.*
278b1-3 ap. 279,7-8, 115
in Cat. (Schmidt)
280-2, 239 n.27, 300 n.44
281, 240 n.29
Diff. (Rashed)
I [1], 261
II [10/10']-[11/11'], 258
Fat. (Bruns)
169,12, 149
§ 6, 135, 154 n.63, 155
169,23-5, 13
§ 6, 171,11-16, 13 n.60
§ 6, 171,11-17, 130
174,30-175,4, 139 n.28
176,21-2, 129 n.3
177,7-14, 143 n.35
§ 11, 149 n.51
178,26-8, 151
179,3.11, 149 n.52
180, 136, 149
180,2, 146 n.41
§ 12, 147
§ 12, 180,8-12, 172 n.26
180,9-12, 151
180,26-8, 130, 146 n.42, 156 n.66
180,29-31, 155
181,5, 130, 146

181,5-6, 140, 146 n.42
§ 13, 153, 129 n.4
181,13-14, 146 n.42
181,14, 149 n.52
§ 13, 181,18-21, 133
181,21-5, 129 n.3
§ 13, 182,11-16, 133
182,22-4, 152
184,18-19, 146 n.42
§ 15, 12, 155
185,7-9, 129 n.3
§ 15, 185,7-11, 11 n.53
§ 15, 185,15-16, 12 n.57
§ 15, 185,21-8, 12 n.58
§ 16, 155 n.65
§ 17, 188,15, 12 n.56
§ 19, 155 n.65
189,9-11, 152
189,10-11, 149 n.52
§ 20, 155
191,30-192,14, 129
192,22, 129
192,22-4, 129
194-5, 149
§ 26, 146 n.41
§ 26, 196,24 ff., 145
§ 27, 155
§ 29, 155
§ 29, 199,27-200,7, 130
§ 29, 199,29-200,7, 145
206,16-18, 149
211,1-4, 137 n.17
212, 149
§ 39, 134 n.9
in GC
1.10, 424 n.43
2.2-5, 429 n.54
Mant. (Bruns)
§ 5, 120,33-121,7, 113 n.27
§ 5, 121,6, 115
141-7, 486 n.29
143,21, 486 n.29
143,26-7, 486 n.29
143,29-30, 486 n.29
144,36-145,3, 486 n.29
§ 22, 134 n.9, 144, 144 n.38, 146,
    146 n.41, 146 n.43, 147, 150 n.53,
    154, 156 n.66
§ 22, 169,38, 136

170,1, 146 n.41
171,14, 44
171,22-4, 146 n.43
171,24, 146 n.41
§ 22, 172,7-9, 153 n.60
172,10-12, 146 n.43
§ 23, 12, 134 n.9, 146, 146 n.41,
    146 n.43, 150
173,10-21, 155
174,2-7, 129 n.3
§ 23, 174,3-7, 11 n.53p174,4, 149 n.52+
§ 23, 174,9-10, 12 n.57
174,9-12, 146 n.43
§ 23, 174,13-24, 12 n.58
174,17-24, 155
174,32, 146 n.41
174,33-5, 155
§ 23, 174,35-9, 156
175,9-32, 155
175,23-5, 146 n.43
175,24-5, 149 n.52
§ 25, 136 n.14, 137 n.17, 183
180,28-31, 149 n.52
186, 135
in Metaph. Hayduck (CAG 1)
1,3-2,7, 566 n.7
2,22-3,2, 567
3,1-4,2, 566 n.7
4,3, 585 n.48
6,7-7,2, 566 n.7
7,13, 585 n.48
16,12-19, 571
18,2-5, 576
22,20-23,8, 569
22,22, 583 n.39
33,27-34,6, 573
34,6-10, 574
35,1-3, 573
49,20-50,3, 576
50,7-15, 293 n.11, 295 n.22
51,18, 294, 294 n.17
51,24-5, 294, 294 n.17
55,17-57,34, 583
58,27-31, 584
58,31-59,8, 94 n.51
78,2-4, 577 n.21
82,11-12, 576 n.18
83,12-17, 294 n.17
99,1-101,31, 584

103,4–104,18, 15 n.63
104,19–105,2, 584
132,16–133,1, 571
138,26–8, 570
167,14–19, 572
196,1–2, 578 n.22
202,11–12, 578 n.22
205,15–16, 578 n.22
206,12–207,6, 119 n.46
214,27–9, 301 n.48
215,16–18, 301 n.49
222,12–13, 578 n.22
238,1, 583 n.39
240,31–241,21, 294
263,25–36, 294
313,2, 578
345,10–11, 579
Mixt. (Bruns)
§ 1.11, 21,21–22,6, 249
§ 1.11, 21,22–9, 299 n.39
§ 1.11, 22,6–9, 299 n.39
§ 1.11, 23,22–24,8, 249
§ 1.11, 23,25–31, 298 n.38
§ 1.11, 24,8–16, 299 n.39
§ 1.11, 24,21–2, 302
§ 2, 214,18–28, 418 n.22
§ 2, 215,22–7, 430 n.60
§ 8, 204, 429 n.54
§ 13–15, 429
§ 13, 228,36–229,3, 429 n.54
§ 14, 230,34–231,4, 429 n.54
§ 14, 231,10–12, 432 n.67
§ 14, 231,12–13, 429 n.54
§ 15, 231,15–16, 432 n.66
§ 15, 231,16–22, 424 n.43, 429
§ 15, 231,22–9, 429 n.55
§ 15, 231,30–232,18, 429 n.55
§ 15, 232,18–20, 418 n.22
§ 15, 232,24–32, 429
§ 15, 232,25, 422 n.39
in Phys. (Rashed)
4.3, 210a20–1, 114
fr. 539, 256
in Phys. ap. Simplicius *in Phys.*, 16 n.64
2.1, 192b34 ff. ap. 270,32–3, 114
Prov. (Ruland)
77,12–79,9, 16 n.65
87,5–91,4, 14 n.61, 16 n.65
89,7–91,4

Quaest. (Bruns)
1.2, 7,3–4, 484 n.22
1.3, 301
1.3, 7,28–8,5, 299 n.42
1.3, 7,31–2, 301 n.52
1.3, 8,3–4, 297 n.32
1.3, 8,7–17, 299 n.40
1.3, 8,8–17, 299 n.39
1.3, 8,12–17, 249
1.3, 8,17–22, 297 n.32
1.3, 8,19–20, 297 n.34
1.3, 8,22–3, 301 n.53
1.11, 302
1.11a (= Badawi 279,16–28), 479 n.11
1.11, 21,21–22,6, 249
1.11, 21,22–9, 299 n.39
1.11, 22,6–9, 299 n.39
1.11, 23,22–24,8, 249
1.11, 23,25–31, 298 n.38
1.11, 24,8–16, 299 n.39
1.11, 24,21–2, 302
1.18, 467
1.18, 30,23–4, 467 n.47
1.18, 31,25–32,3, 467
1.18, 32,3–4, 467
1.21, 477, 479, 479 n.11, 481, 483 n.22, 483–4, 487
1.21 (= Badawi 279,5–16), 479 n.11
1.21, 34,30–35,15, 479
1.21, 34,31–3, 481 n.15
1.21, 35,3.4, 481
1.21, 35,4–5, 481 n.15
1.21, 35,6–7, 481
1.21, 35,10, 486 n.28
1.21, 35,10–11, 481
1.21, 35,11–12, 481
1.21, 35,13–14, 481
1.22 (= Badawi 278–279,5), 479 n.11
2.3, 49,29–50,7, 16 n.65
2.13, 58,1 ff., 346 n.79
2.28, 78,16–20, 300 n.43
2.28, 78,18–20, 297 n.32
3.7, 93,2–9, 487 n.30
3.13, 150
contr. Xenocr. (Pines)
vol. 2, p. 10, 299 n.39
Mund. (Genequand)
§ 4, 466
§ 23, 467 n.49

§ 46, 466
§ 49, 466
§ 52, 467
§ 57, 466
§ 66–9, 466
§ 70–1, 466
§ 89, 466
§§ 139–40, 466 n.45
Temp. (Sharples)
§ 11, 17 n.70
§§ 11–13, 466 n.44
§ 20, 17 n.70
§ 28, 17 n.70
in Top.
47,10–11, 258
112,14–24, 261
123,24–6, 258
177,19–27, 144
355,18–24, 249, 298 n.38
ap. Simplicius *in Cat.*
83,16–20, 302 n.56
ap. Simplicius *in Phys.*
310,25–311,21, 16 n.64

Ambr.
   F 113 sup., fol. 66, 566, 577 n.22, 578, 582–6

Ammonius
  in An. Pr. (CAG 4.6)
  10,38–11,3, 458 n.22
  22,34–23,8, 393 n.2
  23,8–9, 404 n.30
  31,7–32,7, 25 n.106
  31,18–21, 25 n.106
  in Cat. (CAG 4.4)
  4,22–7, 408 n.42
  21,9–15, 408
  26,3–10, 243 n.38
  30,2–5, 239 n.26
  31,9–12, 239 n.27
  31,25–30, 245 n.54
  40,19–21, 310 n.99, 381
  41,3–11, 308 n.85, 308 n.90
  41,5–6, 308 n.86
  41,6–11, 308 n.91
  41,7–12, 381
  in Int. Busse (CAG 4.5)
  1,6–11, 353 n.2, 372 n.13
  5,24–6,33, 398 n.17
  5,28, 4 n.14
  5,28–9, 93 n.49
  6,4–14, 357
  9,10–13, 556 n.60
  16,28–30, 356 n.11
  18,30–3, 362
  19,9–15, 545 n.20
  20,1–8, 359
  22,14, 305 n.75
  22,33–23,2, 356
  27,1–3, 393 n.2
  30,23, 285 n.171
  30,25–30, 286 n.173
  30,32–5, 545 n.20
  31,1–2, 286 n.174
  31,2, 285 n.170
  31,24, 286 n.172
  34,22–8, 360
  35,1–9, 360
  35,33–36,2, 362 n.24
  36,13 ff., 357 n.14
  37,1, 354
  37,15–27, 359 n.16
  38,23–8, 363
  39,6, 363
  88,17–23, 51 n.223
  130,23–33, 143
  130,30–2, 146
  130,32–3, 149
  131,25–32, 138 n.20
  143,1–7, 139 n.28
  148,14.23, 150
  242,24–5, 136
  242,24–7, 138
  242,27–8, 139
  in Isag. (CAG 4.3)
  41,2–42,26, 308 n.85
  41,10–42,26, 53 n.236
  41,20–42,7, 54 n.237
  41,21–42,7, 294, 308 n.88
  42,16–20, 54 n.237
  68,25–69,11, 295 n.23, 304 n.66, 308 n.85, 309 n.92, 310 n.95, 386 n.66
  69,2–11, 381
  104,28–31, 308 n.85
  Prol. Phil. Busse (CAG 4.3)
  4,15–5,27
  4,18–28, 550 n.40

Andronicus
  Pass.

§ 1 (LS 65B), 278 n.124
Anonymous
  in Cat. (Porphyry?)
  1,1–19, 247–8
  1,1–26, 247–8, 250
  1,1–6,8, 246
  1,1–7,2, 247
  1,1–7,8, 232, 235
  1,4–9, 238 n.20
  1,4–10, 248
  1,9–19, 238 n.20
  1,13–14, 248
  1,16–18, 248
  1,20–1, 248, 250
  1,20–6, 248
  1,21–2, 238 n.22
  1,21–4, 248
  1,26, 248
  1,26–2,13, 247–8
  1,27–2,14, 248
  2,3–4, 254
  2,4–13, 248–9, 254
  2,6–7, 236
  2,12–13, 236
  2,13–15, 249
  2,13–3,1, 239 n.26, 248–9
  2,13–14,12, 300 n.44
  2,24, 249
  3,1–5, 239 n.27
  3,1–16, 249
  3,1–4,17, 248
  3,5–16, 239 n.27
  3,7–8, 252
  3,8, 252
  3,8–10, 250
  3,9.13, 250
  3,11, 233 n.6
  3,12, 250
  3,12–16, 252
  3,13, 252
  3,16–19, 251
  3,16–22, 248, 250
  3,16–26, 6 n.26, 296 n.27
  3,18, 251
  3,19–22, 232
  3,23–6, 234, 251
  3,27–4,12, 240 n.29, 251
  4,12–14, 252
  4,12–21, 252
  4,13–14, 252
  4,16, 252
  4,17–21, 252
  4,20–1, 252
  4,21–5,2, 252
  4,24–6, 252
  4,28, 233 n.6
  5,1–2, 233 n.6
  5,2–30, 241 n.33
  5,2–6,8, 252, 259
  5,12–13, 253
  5,14–19, 234
  5,14–25, 237
  5,17–18, 253
  5,17–19, 253
  5,23, 253
  5,23–5, 253
  6,1–8, 253
  6,5–6, 253
  6,9–7,2, 241 n.34, 248, 254
  6,9–7,8, 5
  6,14–15, 254
  6,23–4, 254
  7,2–8, 254
  7,8–9,30, 232, 255
  7,8–13, 247, 255
  7,13–26, 255
  7,14–15, 255
  7,16–17, 255
  7,17, 255
  7,17–19, 232 n.4
  7,19–20, 235
  7,22–4, 255
  7,24–8,28, 235
  7,26–8,3, 255
  7,27–30, 241 n.36
  7,27–8,3, 255
  8,3–18, 255
  8,11–12, 235 n.12
  8,12–13, 256
  8,13–15, 234, 256
  8,18–20, 256
  8,20–7, 256
  8,28, 235 n.12
  8,28–9,11, 257
  9,11–22, 243 n.38, 257
  9,23–30, 243 n.42, 257
  9,24, 243 n.39
  9,24–5, 243 n.39

9,28–30, 243 n.41
9,30–10,12, 233, 257
9,30–14,30, 257
10,3, 257
10,13–18, 258
10,13–11,5, 244 n.45
10,18–23, 258
10,23–11,1, 258
11,1–7, 258
11,6–7, 244 n.45
11,7–11, 244 n.47
11,7–12, 258
11,12–17, 237, 244 n.48, 258
11,13, 258
11,17–12,6, 259
11,17–12,13, 244 n.50
12,1–13,3, 245 n.52
12,6–18, 257, 259
12,9–13, 259
12,12–13, 259
12,13–14, 235
12,13–15, 257
12,13–18, 259
12,18–22, 259
12,18–13,3, 245 n.52, 259
12,20–1, 245 n.51
12,22–13,5, 259
13,1, 233 n.6
13,3–19, 245 n.54, 260
13,3–14,4, 262
13,5, 257
13,12–19, 262
13,19, 260
13,20, 257
13,20–8, 261–2
13,20–14,4, 246 n.56, 260
13,28–14,4, 259–60
13,30, 260
14,2–6, 261
14,4–12, 232
14,4–15, 261
14,4–23, 262
14,4–15,7
14,6–7, 261
14,9–15, 261
14,10, 261
14,16, 234
14,16–17, 261
14,16–20, 246 n.59, 261

14,16–23, 260–1
14,18, 246 n.58
14,20–3, 262
14,20–6, 246 n.60
14,23–30, 235, 246 n.60, 262
Anonymous
  in EN
  150,1–4, 135 n.11
Anonymous
  in Int. (Tarán)
  pp. xxv–xli (*scholia*), xiii and n. 20,
    547 n.26
Anonymous
  Paraphr. Cat.
  8,4–10, 245 n.54
  8,10–22, 244 n.48
Anonymous
  Paraphr. NE
  52,25–7, 136, 146
Anonymous
  Prol. (Westerink)
  § 26, lines 16–44, 36 n.150
Anth. Pal.
  9.358, 88 n.25
Apuleius
  Plat.
  1.12, 136 n.14
Archytas
  ap. Simplicius *in Cat.*
  29,11 ff., 322
  352,24 ff., 322
Arethas
  Schol. in Isag. (Share)
  § 36, 20,29 ff., 50 n.220
Aristotle
  An. Post.
  1.5, 296
  1.22, 83a32, 402 n.26
  83a33, 336
  2.19, 100a13–14, 296, 422 n.35,
    463 n.37
  An. Pr.
  1.1–2, 46, 389
  32b8, 144
  Cael.
  1.2, 336
  1.3, 465
  1.9, 279a25–8, 333
  1.10, 333

1.11, 17
1.12, 291b25, 333
2.1, 284a27–35, 332
2.2, 285a3–4, 121 n.51
2.13, 293b30–2, 351 n.94
3, 330
3.1, 299a1–300a19, 345
3.7–8, 345, 348
3.7–8, 305b27 ff., 321 n.30
306a1–307b19, 345
306a1–307b24, 430
3.7, 306a12–16, 349 n.87
3.7, 306a17–21, 350 n.91
306b22–9, 430
Cat.
1a20, 246
1a20 ff., 243 n.40
1a20–b9, 104 n.5, 232, 255
1a20–b15, 232, 246
1a25–9, 249, 254
1b10, 240 n.31, 247
1b10–11, 238 n.21, 253
1b10–15, 232, 234–5, 247
1b11–12, 238 n.23
1b16, 244, 257–9
1b16–17, 245
1b16–20, 8 n.39, 28 n.116, 259, 261
1b16–24, 233, 243, 257
1b17, 260, 262
1b20–4, 262
2a11–13, 5
2a19–27, 240 n.32
2a36–b6, 308
2b17–21, 239 n.25
3a7–9, 5
3a13–14, 239 n.25
3b13–16, 118 n.40
3b18–23, 119 n.43
4a10, 317
4b32, 356 n.11
8b21–4, 533 n.10
10a11–26, 321
11b10, 322
11b15, 304
12a9–25, 420 n.28
15b18–19, 109 n.18
DA
1.1, 402a7–10, 398 n.17
1.1, 402a9, 398 n.17

1.1, 402b5–8, 296 n.25
1.1, 402b5–9, 310 n.94, 386 n.65
1.1, 403a3–5, 398 n.17
1.1, 403a5–10, 398 n.17
1.1, 403a8, 398 n.17
1.3, 406b25–407b25, 331
1.3, 407a2, 332
1.3, 407a10, 332
1.3, 407a31, 332
1.3, 407b2–3, 332 n.18
1.3, 407b22, 342
1.3, 407b22–5, 342
1.5, 410b22–3, 344 n.70
2.1, 6
2.1, 412a27–8, 213 n.11
2.2, 413b24–7, 399 n.19
2.3, 414b3–6, 283 n.159
2.3, 414b18–19, 264 n.10
2.3, 415a7–12, 264 n.10
2.3, 415a11, 399
2.5, 73, 387, 422
2.5, 417a11, 422
2.5, 417a14, 487 n.30
2.5, 417b2–7, 443 n.22
2.5, 417b12–16, 443
2.11, 424a2–7, 420 n.29
2.11, 424a4, 451
2.12, 424a32–b3, 344 n.70
3.2, 442 n.18
3.2, 425b26–426a19, 442 n.18
3.3, 10, 487, 487 n.32
3.3, 427b7–8, 284 n.161
3.3, 427b7–9, 264 n.10
3.3, 427b13, 264 n.10
3.3, 428a23–4, 264 n.10, 283 n.159
3.3, 429a5–8, 264 n.10
3.4–8, 55, 72, 384–6, 388, 391, 395, 446
3.4, 429a27–8, 402–3
3.4, 429b30–430a2, 54, 386
3.5, 15, 21
3.5, 430a14–15, 403
3.8, 209
3.8, 431b28–432a3, 209 n.35
3.8, 432a2, 402
3.9. 432b6–7, 283 n.159
3.10, 433a11–12, 264 n.10
3.10, 433b27–30, 284 n.161
3.12, 434a30–b1, 284 n.161

Insomn.
461b11, 444 n.27
Int.
16a3–4, 305
16a3–9, 356
16a4, 275 n.104, 545
16a5–7, 246 n.11
16a10, 7, 305
16a28, 286 n.178
16b33 ff., 356
ch. 7, 240 n.28
17a39–40, 298
ch. 9, 11, 146
18a39–b9, 139
18b9, 139
18b31, 139
19a9, 139
19a18, 139
ch. 12, 138
22b36 ff., 137
22b36–23a6, 138
23a3–4, 138, 140–1, 141 n.31
ch. 13, 138, 150
23a15–16, 137
EE
1218b34, 102 n.84
2.10, 134
1223a1–9, 134
1223a7–8, 141
1224a27, 264 n.10
1226a27–8, 134
1226b30–1, 141, 142
EN
1096a11–17, 533 n.11
1096a11–1097a14, 336
1096a23–9, 538 n.30
1102a26, 102 n.84
3.1, 155 n.65
3.2, 134
1111b23–4, 153 n.61
1111b26, 153 n.61
3.3, 134, 136, 138
1112a21–33, 134
1112a30–b4, 153 n.61
1112a31–3, 137
1112a31.34, 134
1112b27, 153 n.61
1113a10, 172 n.26
1113a10–11, 134

1113b3–1115a3, 134
1113b7–8, 134
1114a3–1114b25, 128 n.2
5.10, 24
1137b8–11, 24 n.102
1137b24, 24 n.102
1137b33–4, 24 n.102
1170a31–2, 66 n.286
GA
716a11–13, 188 n.23
724a14–726a25, 344
724b14–18, 188 n.23
724b18, 185
725a18–26, 179
726b31–727a2, 188 n.23
727a26–30, 188 n.23
727b6–7, 188 n.23
727b34, 188 n.23
728a26–7, 188 n.23
728a27–31, 188 n.23
728b23, 188 n.23
728b34–5, 188 n.23
729a9–13, 185, 189
729b5–7, 184
730a14–15, 184
730b12–19, 191
731a2–4, 188 n.23
734b34–735a4, 182, 191
734b37–735a4, 184
737a1–4, 190
737a4–5, 190
738a12–15, 188 n.23
738a34–b2, 188 n.23
739b20–33, 185, 189
740b25–9, 191
740b29–741a3, 184
743a26–36, 184
743a27–36, 182
743a35–6, 188–9
750b4–5, 188 n.23
759a8–763b16, 213 n.7
761a14–762a7, 191
761a16–18, 184 n.16
761a16–32, 215 n.16
761b24–762a8, 184 n.16
761b33–5, 184 n.16
762a8–18, 188
762a8–26, 184 n.16
762a8–31, 179

Index Locorum

762a9–13, 189
762a12–13, 186 n.18, 189
762a12–14, 186 n.19, 189 n.25
762a13–15, 189
762a18–27, 186
762a27–32, 187, 191
762a35–b6, 185
762b6–8, 186 n.18
762b6–9, 189
762b6–18, 186
762b14–16, 189
763a33–b4, 222 n.43
765b10–14, 182
765b16, 190 n.29
765b16–35, 188 n.23
766b12–14, 184
767b16–17, 188 n.23
767b20–768a2, 184
768a5–21, 182
771b20, 188 n.23
771b22–3, 188 n.23
771b22–4, 185, 189
777b16–778a9, 193
778b4–11, 194
783a18–29, 187
GC
317a23–7, 418 n.24
1.4, 418
323a15–20, 485
1.7, 419 n.27
1.10, 388, 417–8, 419 n.27, 420–1,
   423–6, 428, 428 n.50, 430–1
327a34–b6, 416
327b6–10, 416
327b10–31, 417
327b15–17, 417 n.21
327b22–31, 413, 417, 417 n.18, 419 n.27
327b25, 417 n.17, 417 n.19
327b25–6, 417 n.19
327b27 ff., 417 n.19
327b29–30, 417 n.17
327b30–1, 417 n.17
328a33–b5, 429 n.54
2.1–6, 419
2.2–6, 429 n.54
332b5–10, 388
2.7, 387, 417, 419, 421, 423–5, 428,
   428 n.50
334b8–16, 419 n.27

334b7–30, 420
334b16–18, 413 n.2
334b18, 419 n.26
2.7, 334b18–19, 426
2.7, 334b18 ff., 426
2.8, 413 n.2, 416 n.16
334b28, 423 n.42
2.8, 335a3–6, 114 n.31
335b9–24, 336
2.9, 335b20–4, 183 n.15
2.10, 336a33–b16, 193
2.11, 14
2.11, 338b3–5, 193
2.11, 338b5–19, 164
HA
536a14, 275 n.105
539a21–5, 213 n.7
546b15–548a24, 213 n.7
550b32–551a13, 213 n.7, 213 n.9,
   221 n.38
569a10–15, 188
569a10–570a24, 213 n.7
570a7–12, 188
587a27, 285 n.165
602a30–b5, 264 n.11
618a5, 285 n.165
631b19–632a14, 264 n.11
632b17, 285 n.165
Mem.
450a13–14, 283 n.159
Metaph.
980a27, 283 n.159, 284 n.161, 567
983a33, 569
984a32–3, 578 n.23
985a10, 578 n.23
985a18, 573
987a29–b10, 357
987b10, 578 n.23
1.6, 988a10–11, 94
1.9, 402
990b8–9, 577 n.21, 578 n.22
991a20–2, 336
991b3, 578 n.23
1.9, 991b3–7, 291 n.2, 291 n.4
992a11, 578 n.23
993a5, 578 n.23
3.3, 998b22, 257
4.2, 1003a33, 294
4.14, 1020a33 ff., 320

6.1, 1026a5–6, 399
6.3, 44
7.6, 1031a31–b3, 408
7.7, 180, 183
7.7–9, 180, 191, 198
1032a12–15, 182–3
1032b11–14, 191
1032b31–3, 191
1032b32–1033a1, 191
7.7, 1033b26–1034a8, 16 n.66
7.8, 183
7.8, 1033b26–1034a5, 180
1034a4–6, 182
7.9, 182–4, 189–90
1034a14–19, 183
1034a22, 191
1034a23, 191
1034a33–b7, 184
1034b4–7, 191
1034b5–6, 221, 213 n.10
7.11, 1037a5–7, 119 n.42
7.13, 1038b34–1039a2, 118 n.41
7.13, 1038b34–1039a3, 296
7.13, 1039a17–20, 296
7.15, 295
7.17, 6
8, 1042a3–4, 6 n.22
8.1, 1042a15, 291 n.3
8.1, 1042a31, 296
8, 1043a2–4, 6 n.22
8, 1043b13–14, 6 n.22
9, 150
9, 1046b1–2, 138
9, 1046b4–7, 138
9, 1048a2–3, 138
9, 1048a8–9, 138
9, 1048a10–15, 138 n.23
9.6, 482 n.16
9.6, 1048a25–35, 417 n.17
9, 1048b9–17, 584 n.45
9, 1048b18–35, 584 n.45
9, 1050b30–4, 138
10.3, 402
10.4–5, 402
10.7, 420 n.28
11.3, 1061a5–7, 403
11.8, 179 n.3
12.3, 197–8
1070a4–5, 198 n.9

1070a26–8, 198, 222 n.40, 226
12.3, 1070a27–30, 180 n.4
12.4, 208
12.5, 1071a13–17, 205 n.27
12.5, 1071a20–3, 182
12.7, 1072b13–14, 527
12.8, 1073b32 ff., 341
12.10, 1075a14–15, 402–3
13.9, 1086a32–3, 291 n.3
13.10, 1087a16, 417 n.17
Meteor.
1.3, 340a1, 426 n.48
4.1, 418 n.23
379a8–9, 188
379a22–3, 188
379a23–4, 188
379a25–6, 188
379b7–9, 189
382a6–9, 215 n.16
PA
640a19–27, 194
640a23–6, 182
640a23–33, 184
640a27–34, 213 n.7
641a32–b10, 399
641b7, 264 n.10
641b23–8, 194
645a7–10, 203 n.22
645a15–17, 203 n.22
677b21–8, 194
679b15–31, 187
Phys.
2.2, 194b14, 193
2.3, 194b26, 180 n.5
2.4–6, 179 n.3
196b10–22, 179 n.3
197a8–24, 179 n.3
197b14–37, 213 n.6
2.8, 198b34–6, 214 n.12
3.1, 483
3.1, 200b32–201a3, 483
3.1, 201a10–11, 482
3.2, 202a7 ff., 482
3.3, 202a13–14, 490 n.33
3.3, 202a14, 95 n.56
3.3, 202a16–17, 490 n.33
3.3, 202b6–8, 490 n.33
3.6, 206a21–8, 63
4.1–5, 374 n.18, 375–6

Index Locorum

4.1–9, 375
4.1–10, 376, 378–80, 392
4.1, 208b2–3, 537
4.2, 384
4.3, 106, 118
4.3, 210a14–24, 105
4.4, 212a20–1, 532, 537
4.4, 212a24–8, 401
4.5, 373
4.6–9, 374–5
4.10, 37, 62, 373, 375
4.10–14, 374 n.18, 374–6, 378, 380, 391
4.10, 217b29–218a30, 63 n.265
4.11, 219b1–2, 334
4.11, 219b5–8, 375
4.13, 376–7
4.14, 20
4.14, 223a21–9, 374
5, 418 n.24
5.4, 14
5.4, 228b11–15, 481 n.16
5.6, 298
7.3, 424 n.44
7.3, 247b13–16, 422 n.36
7.3, 247b13–248a6, 388 n.74
8.1, 19, 69, 75, 375–7, 380, 467 n.50, 468, 474
8.1, 251a9–b10, 464
8.1, 251b10–28, 377 n.29, 465
8.1, 251b19–26, 377
8.1, 251b28–252a6, 464
8.2, 253a7–20, 172
8.6, 259a6–7, 466
8.8, 264b9–265a12, 465
Pol.
1253a10–14, 286 n.177
1253a14–19, 287 n.180
1253a15, 271 n.61
1332b4–5, 264 n.10
Post. An.
72b18–25, 462
92b14, 257
99b15–17, 462
99b35–6, 283 n.159
Rhet.
1374a27, 24 n.102
1375a29, 24 n.102
Sens.
436a7–10, 283 n.159
436b11–13, 284 n.161
439b17–440b24, 433 n.71
441a26–30
441b24–442a10, 186 n.18
442a26–30, 186 n.18
447b24–448a1, 447 n.41
Somn.
454a11–19, 344 n.70
Top.
101a25–36, 531 n.3
101a34–6, 531 n.3
102a31–2, 243 n.44, 258
104b, 556 n.60
1.15, 260
1.15, 106a9–13, 245 n.53
112b1, 144
6.6, 114b20–5, 260
144b20–5, 261
Arius Didymus
Epit.
fr. phys. 4 (= *Dox. Gr.* 449,1–3 = Stobaeus *Ecl.* 1.17.2,1–4), 430 n.58
Asclepius
in Metaph. (CAG 6.2)
4,4–15, 92 n.44
6,18–31, 567
21,18–27, 576
32,2–14, 574
87,25–32, 54 n.240
92,29–31, 404 n.30
166,30–168,18, 54 n.239, 308 n.89
352,26–354,5, 574
356,2–357,1, 575
389,26–33, 409
408,2 ff., 225 n.47
408,7–10, 221 n.39
408,14–15, 19 n.75
411,9–12, 221 n.39
433,9–436,8, 41 n.175
Aspasius
in EN
71,25–7, 135
74,10–13, 135
74,10–14, 135 n.11
76,11–14, 135
149,34–5, 135
Athenaeus
5.214D–E (= Posidonius fr. 253 Edelstein–Kidd), 84

Atticus
    fr. 9, pp. 67-9 (des Places),
        336 n.29
Augustine
    Civ.
    8.7 (= LS 32F), 277 n.115
    10.9, 31 n.128
    10.32, 32 n.129
    19.22, 33 n.135
    Ep.
    166, 551,7-12 (CSEL 44), 35
    Gen. Litt.
    3.12 (19), 215 n.15
    Lib. Arb.
    201-5, 154 n.62
    Quaest. in Hept.
    vii, q. 2, 215 n.15
    Trin.
    3.8 [13], 214
    9, 35
Aulius Gellius
    NA
    14.1.23, 148 n.50
    20.5.11-12, 102 n.83
Averroes
    Epit. GC
    35,10-36,9, 165 n.10
    35,11, 168
    36,3-6, 174 n.29
    36,9, 168

Boethius
    in Cat. (Brandt)
    162A, 20 n.81
    176D-177A, 300 n.45
    178B-C, 245 n.52
    Cons.
    § 1.4,5, 18 n.74
    § 5, 45, 57
    Div. (PL 64)
    879B-880A, 27 n.112
    891-2, 5 n.17
    in Int.
    7,5-6, 287 n.179
    54,1-2, 286 n.172
    54,16-21, 286 n.172
    54,21-5, 285 n.169
    56,18-20, 286 n.174
    59,14, 285 n.169

    in Int.[2] (Meiser)
    29,29-30,10
    40,9-28, 305 n.76
    203, 146
    208,1-3, 143 n.35
    in Isag.[2] (PL 64)
    84B-85A, 298 n.35

Calcidius
    Tim.
    142-87, 136 n.14
    151, 146, 148
    154, 148 n.47
    155-6, 137 n.16
    156, 139 n.25
    160-1, 138 n.21, 145 n.39
Chaldean Oracles
    § 51 (des Places), 534
    fr. 58 (Majercik), 341 n.54
    fr. 200 (Majercik), 341 n.53
Cicero
    Acad.
    2.21 (= LS 39C), 277 n.115
    2.30 (= LS 40N), 277 n.115
    Att.
    1.7, 83
    4.4a, 93
    4.8, 93
    4.16.2, 102 n.84
    Fat.
    7-8, 169
    7-9, 156
    11, 154 n.63
    13, 138 n.22
    15, 169
    18, 154 n.62
    41-3, 156
    Fin.
    3.67, 557 n.63
    3.7-10, 83
    5.12, 100, 102 n.84
    5.16, 256
    5.21-2, 256
    Leg.
    1.30, 277 n.115
    Luc.
    11-12, 94 n.50
    Off.
    1.109, 170 n.19

Or.
2.160, 99
3.182, 100 n.74
Orat.
114, 99
172, 100 n.74
192–3, 100 n.74
214, 100 n.74
228, 100 n.74
Claudianus Mamertus
Stat. An.
§ 1.15, 59,20–60,16, 35
Clement
Strom. (Stählin)
6.135.4, 500,20–1, 150 n.54

Damascius
in Parm. (Westerink–Combès)
§ 2, 241,29–242,15, 63 n.266
§ 3, 43,7–9, 345 n.73
in Phaed. (Westerink)
I 3, 221 n.36
I 144, 38 n.158
I 172, 61 n.257
II 36,9–16, 66 n.284
in Phil.
§ 6, 6,5–6, 345 n.73
§ 6, 35,3–4, 345 n.73
87,1–4, 62 n.262
§ 6, 163,4–5, 345 n.73
190, 62 n.262
Princ.
§ 2, 154,2, 345 n.73
§ 79, 450 n.46
Vit. Isid. (Athanassiadi)
fr. 4A, 61 n.258
fr. 34D (= fr. 79 Zintzen), 55 n.243
fr. 56–7, 46 n.202
fr. 57B, 61 n.253, 61 n.254
fr. 57C, 55 n.243, 385 n.62
fr. 88A, 62 n.259
fr. 117–9, 47 n.203
fr. 145A, 62 n.260
fr. 146, 67 n.288
fr. 150, 62 n.261
ap. Simplicius *in Phys.*
775,31–4, 64 n.271, 65 n.280
796,27–797,13, 63 n.266
797,29–36, 64 n.272
797,36–798,4, 63 n.268, 65
798,4, 64 n.269, 65 n.275
799,14–18, 63 n.268, 64 n.271
799,18–30, 64 n.270
799,35–800,16, 64 n.273
David
in An. Pr.
3.1
11.1, 25 n.106
in Cat.
107,24–6, 48 n.208
in Isag.
113,11–116,2, 54 n.238
Prol. Phil. Busse (CAG 18.2)
31,23–32,8, 550 n.41
31,34, 49 n.210
32,5–7, 550
32,7, 49 n.214
Dexippus
in Cat. (CAG 4.2)
5,20 ff., 318 n.18
7,1–2, 305 n.72
7,4–9,24, 316 n.13
9,22–10,10, 305 n.72
22,32–3, 6 n.25, 296 n.26
26,13–16, 239 n.26
26,13–27,2, 300 n.44
26,23–8, 240 n.29
26,23–27,2, 300 n.45
26,27–31, 239 n.27
28,6–29,15, 246 n.60
28,16–27, 245 n.52
29,31–30,2, 245 nn.53–4
30,20–6, 162
30,26–30, 163
45,19–22, 299 n.39
57,18–59,8, 318
58,24 ff., 318 n.19
Didymus Caecus
Comm. in Eccl.
80,2, 240 n.28
Diogenes Laertius
Vit. Phil.
2.64, 88 n.25
2.85, 88 n.25
3.37, 88 n.25
3.56, 86
3.57–8, 89
3.61–2, 85

3.63-4, 87
3.65-6, 87
3.66, 85 n.15, 94
4.22-7, 91
5.28-34, 99
5.29, 99
5.73, 94
7.25, 138 n.20
7.40-1, 97
7.51, 278 n.120
7.54, 277 n.116
7.102, 267 n.39
7.103, 267 n.39
7.121-2, 267 n.40
7.163, 88 n.25
9.4, 89 n.33
10.150, 269 n.50
10.150-1, 269 n.48

Elias (David)
  in Cat. Busse (CAG 18.1)
  107,11-13, 98 n.67
  108,21-31, 555 n.58
  113,17-20, 98 n.67
  115,3-13, 102 n.85
  117,17-118,31, 4 n.16
  117,21-2, 106 n.11
  123,1-3, 36 n.151
  123,2-3, 251
  124,17-23, 536 n.25
  129,10-130,13, 303 n.65
  130,14 ff., 317 n.14
  130,14-131,14, 7 n.31, 303 n.62
  133, 88 n.25
  138,12-18, 558 n.65
  144,20-1, 409 n.43
  144,31-145,4, 257
  158,10-11, 260
  158,11-14, 245 n.52
  167,1-2, 299 n.39
  in Isag. Busse (CAG 18.1)
  12,1-39, 49 n.214, 550 n.43
  12,38-9, 550
  14,1-14, 550 n.42
  48,15-30, 54 n.238
Epictetus
  Diss.
  1.12.34, 147

1.25.2, 152 n.57
2.19, 138 n.20
2.23, 150
4.1.62, 152 n.57
4.1.68, 152 n.57
4.7.16, 152 n.57
4.12.8, 152 n.57
Epicurus
  Kur. Dox.
  § 32, 269 n.50
  § 32-3, 269 n.48
Eusebius
  Eccl. Hist.
  6.19.1-12, 33 n.141
  Praep. Ev.
  3.7 (= Porphyry fr. 352F Smith), 33 n.138
  3.9 (= Porphyry fr. 354F Smith), 33 n.139
  9.10.1-5 (= Porphyry fr. 323F, 324F Smith), 32 n.131
Eustathius
  ad Od. (Stallbaum)
  23.220, II.305.31-4, 88 n.25
Eustratius
  in An. Post.
  195,5-196,16, 312
  195,16-18, 312
  195,26-8, 79
  195,34-6, 312
  196,3-12, 312
  196,9, 312
  in NE
  40,22 ff., 79
Exodus 7:12, 214

Galen
  Peri alup(ês)ias
  § 13, 87
  Diff. Puls. (Kühn)
  8,626, 121 n.50
  in Hipp. Nat. Hom. (Kühn)
  15, 32,1-11 (= *SVF* 2.463), 430 n.58
  Instr. Odorat. (Kollesch)
  30,13-14, 440 n.13
  36,4-5, 440 n.13
  Lib. Prop. (Kühn)
  19,42.47, 236 n.18

Loc. Affect.
6.5, 344
6.5, 425,4–14, 344 n.66
PHP
2.5.11–13 (= LS 53U), 278 n.121
2.5.85, 261
2.5.91, 261
4.2.10–18 (= LS 65D), 278 n.124
4.3.2–5 (= LS 65K), 277 n.114
5.3.1 (= LS 53V), 278 n.118
5.6.34–7 (= LS 65I), 277 n.114
5.6.37 (= LS 65I4), 278 n.120, 279 n.127
7.1.12–15 (= LS 29E), 277 n.114
Quod An. Mor. (Müller)
§ 3, 32,1–13, 441 n.15
§ 3, 37,16–24, 441 n.15
Sem.
525,13–17, 344 n.66
in Tim. (Schröder)
fr. II.107–9, 88 n.31
fr. 19, 343 n.63
Usu Part. (Helmreich)
8.6–7, 440 n.13
8.6, i. 463,25–464,1, 440 n.13
12.7, ii. 198,11.14–15, 440 n.13
12.7, ii. 199,10, 440 n.13
12.7, ii. 201,16.20.28, 440 n.13
Ps.-Galen
Ei zôon to kata gastros
175,6 ff., 225 n.47
Gregory of Nyssa
In illud: 'tunc et ipse filius'
12.17–18, 261
Vit. Mos.
2.65.10, 261

Herodianus
Reliq. GG (Lentz)
3.1.108, 9–16, 277 n.111
Hesiod
Op.
188, 407 n.35
Hierocles
ap. Photius
173a, 328 n.7
Prov. ap. Photius
cod. 251, 461a, 328 n.6

Hippocrates
Morb.
4 § 34, 212 n.4
4 § 54, 212 n.4
Hippolytus
Ref.
19.19 (= *Dox. Gr.* 569,19–22), 148 n.47
Homer
Od.
18.131, 228
23.296, 98 n.69
23.310–43, 98 n.69
Hor. Hyp. (Furrer-Pilliod)
coll. A, d28, 554 n.54
rec. A, k40, 557 n.63
rec. C, k6, 557 n.63

Iamblichus
An.
28.379, 38 n.161
in An. Pr.
fr. 137–45, 316 n.10
DA ap. Stobaeus *Ecl.*
13 ap. 1,369,20–3, 282 n.154
15 ap. 1,317,20, 279 n.128
Ep.
8, fr. 2, 38 n.162
219.1–2, 40 n.170
219.6–7, 40 n.170
223.14–24, 40 n.170
Myst.
2.11, 38 n.159
5.3, 38 n.160
5.23, 38 n.157
8.7, 38 n.163
10.1, 32 n.130
in Phaedr.
fr. 1, 316 n.12
in Tim.
1,204,24 ff., 316 n.11
fr. 1, 316 n.12
fr. 63, 324
fr. 64, 323 n.40
fr. 90, 324 n.41, 535 n.18
ap. Ammonius *in Int.*
135,14, 40 n.172
ap. Proclus *in Tim.*
3,33,1–30 (= fr. 64), 323 n.40

ap. Simplicius *in Cat.*
25,1–3, 319
53,8–18, 253
116,25 ff. (= fr. 33), 318
117,27–30, 318
118,2, 319
128,16–129,7 (= fr. 36), 319
129,1, 314 n.4
135,8–28 (= fr. 37), 319
135,10–17, 319
155,15, 314 n.4
160,10–11, 314 n.4
216,6–219,35 (= fr. 65), 320
218,5 ff., 320
218,8–9, 321
219,10, 321
271,6 ff., 321
271,23 ff., 321
302,25–6, 314 n.4
353,19 ff. (= fr. 110), 322
354,9–26, 37 n.153
361,7, 324
361,7–362,33, 36 n.152
364,3, 324
ap. Simplicius *in Phys.*
639,22–640,12, 36 n.152
639,23–640,11, 324 n.41
787,17–20 (= fr. 107,37–43), 323
ap. Stobaeus *Ecl.*
1,318,1–4 (= *SVF* 1.149), 278 n.118, 279 n.129
4,223,24–224,17, 24 n.101
Isidore
Etym.
6.5, 83
Isocrates
Archid.
108,1, 407 n.36

John 14:6, 22 n.95
John Chrysostom
in Jo. (PG 59)
91,31–9, 576 n.19
John Damascene
Dial. (Kotter)
prooem. 60, 554 n.51
prooem. 61,25–32
prooem. 65,60–5, 557 n.61

prooem. 65,67–74, 558 n.66
6,125–32, 553 n.50
Her. (Kotter)
83.52–5, 311 n.102
83.59–68, 311 n.103
748A (PG 94), 311 n.101
744C (PG 94), 311 n.101
John Moschus
Prat. Spirit.
PG 87, 2929D, 549 n.34
Josephus
Ant.
13.172, 135 n.11
Julian
Ep. (Bidez)
ad Themist. 10, 24 n.103
12, 39 n.166
Mis.
356, 24
Or.
§ 6, 23
§ 6, 184C–185A, 22 n.96
§ 7, 23
Justin
Apol.
§ 44, 148 n.47

Laur.
71.32, 106, 107, 110
87.12, 566, 566 n.6, 577 n.22, 578, 580, 582–6
Libanius
Or. 12, 80–2, 25 n.104
Lucretius
Rer. Nat.
5.1011–27, 269 n.48
Lysias
Epitaph.
70,5, 407 n.36

Macrobius
in Somn. Scip.
1.19, §§ 14–17, 341 n.51
Makarios Magnes
Apokr. (Goulet)
4.28, 33 n.140
Marinus
Vit. Procl. (Saffrey–Segonds)
§ 11, 45 n.197

§ 12, 372 n.14, 376 n.28
§§ 12–14, 43 n.186
§ 13, 329, 375 n.24
§§ 13–14, 41
§ 15, 45 n.198
§ 18, 45 n.197
§ 22, 353 n.1
§§ 24–6, 45 n.197
§ 26, 42 n.185
§ 28, 45 n.197
§§ 29–37, 353 n.1

Maximus of Tyre
  Or.
  41.5a, 148 n.47, 151
  41.5g, 151

Michael of Ephesus
  in Metaph.
  441,8–9, 583 n.40
  443,35–6, 583 n.39
  445,12–13, 583 n.40
  452,8–10, 583 n.41
  501,1–10, 221 n.39
  505,2, 583 n.40
  589,23–5, 583 n.40
  610,11–15, 582 n.36
  659,29, 583 n.39
  716,24–7, 582 n.36
  in PN Wendland
    (CAG 22.1)
  149,8–149,16, 581 n.32

Michael Psellus
  Opusc. (O'Meara)
  142,13–16, 215 n.18
  Or. Min.
  28,27 ff., 225 n.47
  Paraphr. Int. ap. Ammonius in Int.
    (Busse)
  xv–xvi, 546 n.24

Nemesius
  Nat. Hom. (Morani)
  39c, 418 n.22
  40–1, 34
  83,2, 343 n.62
  102, 153 n.59
  103–4, 137 n.16, 144
  103,20–1, 137 n.18
  104,1–2, 139 n.25
  104,2–4, 139 n.26

104,4–5, 139 n.27
104,6–7, 140
104,18–21, 148 n.50
105–6, 129 n.4, 133
105,18–21, 129 n.3
109, 148
110, 136 n.14
110,5–9, 148
110,7–9, 148 n.47
112,10, 150
112,13–15, 137 n.17
114,15–16, 153 n.59
114,19–22, 139 n.27
114,21–2, 140
114,21–4, 137 n.19
114,24–115,2, 140
115,22–7, 146
115,22–8, 149
115,25, 150
116,3–5, 149
119,4–5, 150 n.54
119,11, 150, 150 n.54
125–6, 136 n.14
174,3–27, 12 n.55

Olympiodorus
  in Alc. I (Westerink)
  22,4–23,13, 47 n.206
  in Cat.
  18,23–20,12, 7 n.31, 303 n.62,
    303 n.65
  19,36 ff., 317
  44,1–22, 243 n.38
  50,12–22, 239 n.26
  51,25–36, 245 n.54
  in Meteor.
  5,19–23, 407 n.39
  175,14–15, 407
  239,14–28, 407 n.39
  278,9–10, 225 n.47
  310,16–25, 215 n.16
  321,26–9, 344 n.64
  in Phaed.
    (Westerink)
  1.9, 549 n.39
Origen
  Cels.
  1.24, 287 n.182
  4.68, 169 n.17

P. Hib.
    § 228, 85
P. Petr.
    II.5–8, 85
    II.50, 85
Pal. Anth.
    7.553, 61 n.255
Paris. Suppl. Gr.
    643, 113
Philo
    Anim.
    83, 279 n.127
    98, 276 n.108
    98–99, 277 n.111
    Opif.
    § 99, 232 n.4
    § 148, 287 n.182
    Quaest. in Gen.
    1.20, 287 n.182
Philodemus
    Po.
    5.16, 121 n.50
    Synt. Phil.
    Index Ac. XXXV 10–16, 94 n.52
Philoponus
    Aet. (Rabe)
    29,2–13, 402 n.27
    29,3–8, 336 n.28
    29,5–6, 411 n.48
    31,7–32,10, 335
    32,5–8, 336 n.30
    32,8–13, 336 n.31
    55,25–56,26, 485 n.27
    4.1–3, 485
    61,23–62,11, 486 n.28
    4.4–6, 485
    4.4 (= Badawi 293,7–15), 487 n.30
    65,1–68,17, 487
    65,5–6, 486 n.28
    65,7–8 (= Badawi 293,8–9), 486 n.28
    65,8–10, 486 n.28
    65,10 (= Badawi 293,10), 486 n.28
    65,18–19, 487 n.30
    65,20–2, 486 n.28
    65,22–4, 487 n.30
    65,24–6, 486
    66,1 (= Badawi 293,18), 487 n.32
    66,2 (= Badawi 293,19), 487 n.32
    66,19 (= Badawi 294,3), 487 n.32
    66,20 (= Badawi 294,4), 487 n.32
    66,25–7, 486
    67,2 (= Badawi 294,8), 486 n.28
    67,3–68,2, 490
    67,3–68,3, 486
    68,15 (= Badawi 294,14), 486 n.28
    68,16 (= Badawi 294,15), 487 n.32
    68,20–3, 486
    4.9, 57,27–58,5, 500 n.44
    4.11, 58,12–18, 500 n.44
    82,12–25, 335
    95,2–12, 335
    95,27–96,18, 335
    96,6–14, 335
    96,7–11, 335
    99,1–8, 335
    6.2, 511, 517
    126,10–23, 512 n.32
    126,20, 508 n.21
    138,19–28, 333 n.22
    138,19–139,3, 335
    6.8, 515, 517
    144,16–145,8, 512 n.34
    144,16–149,26, 504 n.4
    145,26–147,9, 513 n.36
    147,25–148,7, 514 n.38
    148,1–7, 335
    148,9–15, 514 n.39 148,25–149,10, 522 n.62
    148,15–23, 514 n.40
    148,23–5, 514 n.41
    148,25–149,6, 514 n.39
    148,25–149,10, 522 n.62
    149,6–10, 514 n.42
    149,16–21, 514 n.43, 528 n.84
    6.9–16, 515
    150,14, 508 n.21
    6.14, 517
    164,13–23, 516 n.47
    166,26–167,2, 529 n.85
    166,26–168,2, 335
    167,17–20, 335
    6.17, 515, 517
    171,21–172,20, 515 n.45
    172,1, 515 n.44
    204,12, 508 n.21
    224,18–225,10, 335
    225,28, 508 n.21
    6.29, 517 n.48

Index Locorum 643

238,3 ff., 335
238,3–240,9, 335
238,3–242,15, 335
239,25–240,4, 335
240,19–23, 471
268,20, 508 n.21
297,5 ff., 335
297,5–300,2, 335
300,22–6, 335
9.8, 491, 498
9.8, 315,13–15, 500 n.44
318,5–12, 340 n.48
318,13–18, 340 n.50
318,13–319,14, 339
318,19–319,2, 335, 342 n.55
319,2–5, 343 n.60
319,5–8, 344 n.65
319,9–10, 344 n.68
319,10–15, 340 n.49
9.11, 491, 494, 498 n.37, 499
338,21–5, 491
338,21–346,26, 492
338,25–339,2, 492
339,2–24, 491
339,25–345,4, 491, 493
345,4–20, 491
9.11, 345,4–355,27, 491
345,16–18, 499 n.42
345,16–20, 498
345,20–346,11, 491, 493
345,21–5, 499 n.42
346,11–355,27, 491
346,20–1, 502 n.53
347,28–348,24, 494
348,24–350,1, 495
349,18–21, 495
350,1–351,3, 495
350,14–18, 495
350,26, 495
351,3–27, 495
351,27–352,2, 497
353,3–19, 497
353,13–17, 497
353,23–4, 497
354,13–16, 497
356,16–17, 502 n.53
358,14–17, 502 n.53
364,5–365,3, 499 n.41
426,22, 348 n.85

445,7–14, 412
11.14, 389 n.75, 427
462,9–15, 427
482,21–483,6, 335
483,1, 338
13.14, 518,17–18, 426 n.48
520,4–521,24, 504 n.4
523,1–7, 338 n.35
523,5, 338
523,11–18, 338 n.38
523,12–524,8, 335
524,2–8, 338 n.39
524,9, 338
526,20, 338
531,13, 339 n.45
532,15–20, 339 n.46
532,20–537,21, 339 n.47
533,21, 347 n.81
534,15, 347 n.81
581,26–582,5, 335
592,17, 508 n.21
594,14, 508 n.21
599,17–601,20, 504 n.4
626,1–627,20, 335
in An. Post.
111,31–112,1, 400 n.22
242,14–243,25, 389 n.77
242,26–243,21, 402
243,16–19, 336 n.28
in An. Pr.
1,5, 383
273,1, 383
325,27–33, 252
contr. Arist. (Wildberg)
fr. II.49, 470 n.62
fr. VI.115, 470 n.63
in Cat. (Busse)
1,2, 368 n.5, 390
1,2–6, 49 n.216
4,15–22, 408 n.42
5,15–20, 3 n.12
5,15–24, 97
5,16–18, 106 n.11
6,30–5, 374, 406
7,26–9, 99 n.73, 533 n.9
8,23–7, 383
9,3–12, 304 n.67, 381
9,12–15, 7 n.31, 303 n.62
12,19, 50, 390

15,13–14, 383
23,8–13, 409
25,27–27,9, 382
27,11–27, 382
27,27–31, 382
29,14–27, 382
29,22–30,24, 382
30,1–24, 243 n.38
31,19–26, 382
32,32, 50, 390
33,20–31, 382
33,32–34,7, 382
34,16–35,8, 382
36,6–11, 382
38,28–39,15, 382
41,22–42,9, 245 n.54
43,3–9, 382
43,17–44,2, 382
46,14–48,27, 382
53,11–13, 310 n.98
53,28–9, 310 n.98
58,7–59,2, 71, 310 n.100, 381
58,13–21, 381 n.52
65,18, 348 n.85
83,17, 348 n.85
133,1–4, 383, 533 n.10
169,19, 381
in DA
12,18, 445 n.33
15,11, 445 n.33
17,9–19, 224 n.46, 229 n.55
18,26–8, 445 n.33
18,35, 445 n.33
19,21–3, 445 n.33
19,27–8, 445
19,35, 449 n.45
19,35–6, 444
20,31–21,7, 400 n.21
27,21–8, 97
27,21–9, 397 n.17
37,18, 451 n.50
37,18–32, 399 n.18, 403
38,13–15, 294, 309 n.93, 390 n.80
38,13–17, 294, 310 n.94, 386 n.65
45,8–14, 398 n.17
47,20–6, 445 n.31
51,13–52,1, 441 n.15
52,4–21, 222 n.40

52,13–25, 220 n.34
55,22–4, 451 n.52
58,9, 294, 309 n.93, 390 n.80
63,4.12, 451 n.50
70,19–25, 395 n.9
77,6, 451 n.50
78,27, 451 n.50
79,16, 451 n.50
80,23, 451 n.50
95,7–12, 398
95,22–6, 399
98,47–99,50, 446 n.36
99,50, 446 n.38
99,51.52.54, 446 n.38
114,24–8, 399 n.18
116,26–8, 399 n.18
140,25, 449 n.45
158,11–12, 447 n.39
158,12–24, 439 n.8
161,20–1, 445 n.28, 447 n.39
161,25–6, 446 n.35 161,25–6, 446 n.35
162,2–15, 439 n.8
164,4, 445 n.33
165,28–32, 399 n.18
187,25, 449
198,10–12, 220 n.34
239,5–15, 445
246,24–7, 395 n.9
255,10–11, 451 n.54
261,10–18, 399 n.20
261,27–35, 400
266,4–6, 395 n.9
268,9–14, 220 n.33
268,14–31, 220 n.33
268,31–6, 220 n.33
268,31–7, 220 n.33
268,36–8, 220 n.33
282,23–5, 440
292,15–18, 449 n.45
293,7, 449 n.45
296,25–6, 487 n.30
297,1–3, 487 n.30
304,24–6, 444
304,29–305,2, 443
307,33–4, 310 n.96
309,15–29, 438, 449
309,19, 450, 450 n.48
309,24–9, 450 n.49

Index Locorum

309,25.29, 450
309,28–9, 449 n.45
316,35–317,2, 449 n.44
326,30–1, 449
326,30–2, 449 n.45
329,14–20, 451 n.55
331,13–15, 445 n.30
334,30–335,12, 405
334,30–355,11, 405
334,38, 371 n.10
334,40, 385
335,7, 371 n.10
335,12–30, 405 n.32
336,17.20.33.37, 445 n.29
336,33–7, 439
336,34–6, 446 n.35
337,6.14.32, 445 n.29
338,31, 449 n.45
340,33–6, 442 n.19
341,6–7, 442 n.19
348,37, 445 n.29
350,25.31, 445 n.29
350,25–6, 447 n.39, 448 n.42
350,31–2, 448 n.42
350,31–3, 447 n.39
353,12–13, 440 n.11, 442 n.19
353,20–1, 440 n.11, 442 n.19
353,29–30, 440 n.13
354,10, 440 n.11, 442 n.19
357,15–16, 442 n.19
357,19.22, 442 n.19
358,3, 442 n.19
364,15, 445 n.29
364,16–17, 445
364,16–365,2, 443 n.20
364,19–20, 445 n.29
364,20, 445 n.34
364,22, 442 n.19
364,35–365,2, 446 n.35
364,36, 445 n.29
365,30, 445 n.29
365,33, 446 n.35
366,11–13, 439
366,13, 445 n.29
368,1–3, 445 n.32
368,5–7, 443 n.20
369,4–6, 450 n.47
369,13, 451 n.52
388,23–8, 440 n.12

390,30, 440 n.11
391,4–6, 440 n.11
391,32, 383
391,32 ff., 383
392,1, 443 n.21
392,32, 440 n.13
393,13.26, 440 n.11
394,12, 440 n.11
395,13–14, 443 n.21
395,15–16, 440 n.13
396,15–16, 446
397,10, 451 n.52
416,23, 441 n.14
416,30, 449
417,37, 441
418,13, 441
418,20–2, 446
423,15–19, 445 n.32
433,1–4, 441
433,7–11, 441 n.17
433,25–30, 444
433,33, 440 n.13
433,33–4, 444 n.26
433,35, 444, 447
433,36–434,1, 441 n.16
435,25–7, 451 n.54
435,27–8, 451
435,34–436,6, 451 n.54
437,8–11, 450 n.48
437,11, 450
438,6–15, 439
438,10, 449 n.45
439,5–10, 451 n.54
439,9–10, 451
439,18–20, 446 n.37
439,31, 451 n.54
439,33–440,3, 444
440,1–2, 451 n.53
440,9, 451 n.54
440,17–18, 451 n.54
450,20, 406
464,13–14, 411
464,30–4, 410
464,30–465,17, 66 n.285
464,30–465,31, 385 n.59
465,10–16, 450 n.46
465,31–4, 411
466,27–35, 406
467,4–5, 406

473,10, 407 n.40
486,22.23, 411
495,5–27, 276 n.108
527,30–1, 407 n.37
528,34–529,4, 385, 408
543,29–31, 412 n.49
544,26–31, 407 n.41
547,8–14, 407 n.37
Diait.
§ 7, 311 nn.102–3
in GC
1,1–5, 426 n.47
84,8–12, 221 n.39, 222 n.40
169,4–27, 444 n.24
169,6 ff., 220 nn.34–5
169,7, 387
170,12, 423 n.40
188,14–15, 421
188,16–26, 388, 422
188,17–25, 428 n.51
188,21–3, 423
188,23–6, 423
188,30–3, 423
189,10–17, 421
190,15–21, 424 n.44
191,16–17, 417 n.19
191,26–7, 428 n.51
191,26–8, 422 n.39
191,29–31, 418 n.22
191,31–192,4, 418 n.22
192,4–8, 424 n.44
192,11–14, 422 n.39
198,21–3, 422 n.37
198,22–3, 424
198,24–30, 428 n.51
198, 26–7, 422 n.37
200,19–23, 429 n.54
200,25–7, 429 n.54
200,30–201,5, 429 n.54
202,12–13, 422 n.37, 424
202,16–18, 429 n.54
202,21–5, 424
203,8, 424
203,10–16, 424
203,11, 424
245,18–25, 427
245,18–246,1, 388, 427
245,25–246,1, 427
270,16–18, 425

270,18–271,2, 425
271,1–24, 422 n.34
271,2–24, 425
271,7–10, 422 n.36
271,11–14, 423
271,14.16, 422 n.38
271,14–24, 423
271,16–272,24, 387
271,18, 422 n.38
271,25–6, 370 n.8
271,25–272,10, 425, 427
271,25–272,12, 388
271,26 ff., 426 n.47
272,12–33, 423 n.42
274,21 ff., 423 n.42
275,31 ff., 419 n.26
276,11–23, 427
276,18–23, 388, 430
277,27–278,2, 425 n.45
283,27–284,7, 220 n.34
313,16–22, 311 n.104
314,9–16, 164 n.7
314,16–22, 165 n.8,
    298 n.36
319,5 ff. (= 2.7), 427
Intell. (Verbeke)
2,27–31, 395 n.9
15,50, 451 n.51
18,2–3, 447
20,3–4, 447
23,28, 409
38,99–39,3, 395 n.9
39,1–20, 423 n.41
39,27–40,43, 386 n.68
53,62–6, 395 n.9
62,6–63,18, 386 n.68
99,48, 445 n.32
99,49, 445 n.29
99,49–57, 446
99,63–5, 447 n.41
119,62–4, 395
in Meteor.
16,31, 390 n.83
24,38–25,2, 390 n.83
35,18–19, 397 n.15
91,18–20, 390 n.83
97,16, 390 n.83
in Nicom. Intr. Arith.
2.7.19–20, 376 n.28

Part. (Šanda)
§ 4, 389 n.75
§ 4, 130–1, 427 n.49, 429 n.55
§ 7, 134–5, 428 n.49
in Phys.
1.1, 12,2, 379 n.39
14,3–17, 310 n.97
15,20–4, 310 n.97
1.2, 39,7–8, 379 n.40
1.3, 55,22–4, 379 n.41
1.3, 86,12, 379 n.39
105,14 ff., 225 n.47
119,14–120,18, 379 n.37
1.6, 133,27–8, 294, 379 n.38, 390 n.81
156,16, 348 n.85
179,5 ff., 225 n.47
191,1–33, 387 n.71
1.9, 191,9–29, 220 nn.34–5
1.9, 191,10–25, 379 n.42
1.9, 191,11–16, 444 n.24
1.9, 191,24–5, 216 n.22
1.9, 193,1–4, 294, 379 n.38, 390 n.81
197,30–198,1, 379 n.43
236,29–237,4, 380 n.44
241,20–3, 294, 449
2.3, 250,28, 49 n.215, 368 n.5, 390
298,6–12, 380 n.44
303,1–5, 380 n.44
303,18–25, 380 n.44
309,9–310,15, 379 n.43
342,17–343,12, 483 n.20
343,22–344,7, 484 n.23
349,5–6, 484 n.24
403,19–31, 220 nn.34–5
405,3–7, 380 n.47
410,21–4, 380 n.47
414,20–7, 385, 409
428,23–430,10, 380 n.45
438,5–6, 380 n.47
440,16–17, 380 n.48
444,5–6, 380 n.49
447,18–20, 380 n.49
448,20–1, 380 n.49
456,17–458,31, 380 n.46
3.5, 458,30, 377 n.30, 410 n.45
463,3–4, 380 n.49
464,23–4, 380 n.49
467,1–468,4, 380 n.45
484,15–19, 380 n.47
541,6–7, 374 n.18
552,10–14, 374 n.18
583,13–14, 371 n.9, 376 n.26
583,13–15, 374 n.18
583,30–585,4, 401 n.23
584,1–4, 401 n.23
587,22–30, 374 n.18
592,16–17, 401
597,32–598,2, 374 n.18
600,6, 374 n.18
4.8, 639,7–9, 377 n.30, 410 n.45
650,27–651,4, 411
703,16–20, 375
705,20–4, 408 n.42
762,2–3, 377
762,2–5, 377 n.29
762,7–9, 376, 410 n.45
770,19–21, 374
contr. Themist. (Ebied–van Roey–
    Wickham)
51,5–9, 311 n.105
51,31–2, 311 n.105
ap. Ammonius *in Cat.*
58,13–59,1, 53 n.236, 308 n.85
67,19–24, 53 n.236, 308 n.85
Philoponus (?)
in An. Post.
2,435,25–30, 390 n.79
in DA
3,546,1–6, 393 n.2
Photius
Bibl. (Henry)
cod. 181, 126b40–127a14, 60 n.251,
    61 n.252
cod. 181, 127a10–14, 532 n.4
cod. 232, 67–79, 549 n.37
cod. 400a, 225 n.47
Phrynichus
Praep. Sophist.
74,9–10, 579 n.24
Plato
Alc. I
114E7–9, 412
Crat.
389A2, 362
390A, 356
393A–B, 360
426C–427D, 355 n.7
428E6–7, 361

439A–440D, 357
Euth.
7B–C, 319 n.26
Leg.
684E1, 349 n.89
752D ff., 24
757E, 24
913B9, 349 n.89
Parm.
132B–C, 308 n.87
Phaed.
64A4–6, 48
79C1–8, 387 n.69
81E–82B, 342
108C–110B, 350
109B, 350
Phaedr.
245C ff., 512
249B, 287 n.180, 342
Phil.
22B5, 344 n.69
55E, 319 n.26
Pol.
270C–272B, 179
271A ff., 182 n.10
Prot.
322C, 271 n.61
323C–D, 271 n.61
324A, 271 n.61
325A, 271 n.61
351B, 271 n.61
Rep.
327B7, 85 n.17
327C6, 85 n.17
335D–E, 270 n.57
373C, 271 n.67
404A–D, 271 n.67
414E3, 572 n.16
414E7, 85 n.17
441E, 270 n.57
546A, 511
568A8, 85 n.17
10, 44
10, 595B–C, 533 n.11
10, 595C2–3, 533 n.11
602D, 319 n.26
10, 607C, 533 n.11
10, 607C7–8, 533 n.11
611C7–D7, 395 n.9

617D–620D, 342
617E, 148
617E2–5, 34
618A, 342
618A3, 34
618B2, 34
Theaet.
167B–C, 344 n.69
176B, 29, 273 n.85
176B1–2, 48
209C
Tim.
27C–28C, 468 n.54
27D–28A, 469
27D5–28B4, 180, 181 n.7
28B, 469
30A, 515, 527
36E, 332
37D, 323
37D5–7, 539 n.32
38D1–2, 340
39E, 53
39E–40B, 215 n.16
40A2–4, 337
40B–C, 350–1
40C, 205 n.26
40C2–3, 19
42C, 342
42E–43A, 432 n.65
42E8–43A2, 427
43A2, 432 n.65
43A6–44C2, 43
50B10–C6, 351
52C, 251
53C–57D, 345, 347
54B1–D2, 427
54C, 349
55C, 339
55D ff., 321
55D–57D, 321 n.29
56D, 349
77A3–C5, 19, 205 n.26
77B, 345
77B–C, 205 n.26
77B6–7, 344 n.69
77C4, 88
80B–C, 343
91C1–2, 344
91D–92C, 342

Plotinus
 Enn. (Henry-Schwyzer)
 1.1.4.1–13, 282 n.149
 1.1.4.3–4, 281 n.147
 1.1.11.9–15, 43 n.193
 1.1.11.13–15, 223 n.44
 1.1.12.28–9, 220 n.31
 1.2, 272 n.72
 1.2.3, 29
 1.2.3.28, 293
 1.2.3.30, 293
 1.3, 458 n.21
 1.4.7.31–3, 30 n.124
 1.9.1–19, 30 n.124
 1.9.1.6–7, 220 n.31
 2.1.6.54, 215 n.16
 2.3.8.6–8, 223 n.44
 2.3.10.7–10, 223 n.44
 2.3.12.1–11, 223 n.44
 2.3.14.4–7, 223 n.44
 2.3.14.15–17, 223 n.44
 2.3.14.16, 223 n.44
 2.3.15.13, 223 n.44
 2.3.18.9, 223 n.44
 2.7.1.8–9, 430 n.58
 2.7.1.15–20, 432 n.63
 2.7.2.22–5, 430 n.56
 2.9.7.5, 223 n.44
 2.9.13.14–18, 223 n.44
 2.10–11, 430 n.58
 3.1.5.21–2, 223 n.44
 3.1.5, 24–7, 223 n.44
 3.1.6.1–4, 223 n.44
 3.1.6.3–5, 223 n.44
 3.1.8.5, 223 n.44
 3.1.8.7–8, 215 n.18
 3.1.9–10, 153
 3.2.2.34, 281 n.147
 3.2.10, 153
 3.3.4.37–41, 220 n.31
 3.4.6, 224
 3.6.1.2, 284 n.164
 3.7.11, 323
 3.8.5.24–5, 216 n.22
 3.8.8.16, 19, 293
 4–6, 501 n.49
 4.3.1.26, 223 n.44
 4.3.3.23, 284 n.164
 4.3.8.49–50, 220 n.31

4.3.10.39, 293
 4.3.12.35–9, 220 n.31
 4.3.13.8–10, 220 n.31
 4.3.13.23–5, 220 n.31
 4.3.26.8, 284 n.164
 4.3.27, 282 n.150
 4.3.27.1–3, 223 n.44
 4.4.6.14, 284 n.164
 4.4.6.15–16, 223 n.44
 4.4.17.22, 281 n.144
 4.4.22, 205 n.26
 4.4.22.1–46, 19, 293
 4.4.22.30–3, 284 n.164
 4.4.22.33, 344
 4.4.23.37–43, 284 n.164
 4.4.27.1–17, 19, 293
 4.4.28.64, 281 n.147
 4.4.29.1–8, 224
 4.4.30.1–16, 223 n.44
 4.4.31.3 ff., 223 n.44
 4.4.31.8–12, 223 n.44
 4.4.37.13, 223 n.44
 4.4.38.22–3, 223 n.44
 4.4.43.7, 281 n.147
 4.6.2.17, 284 n.164
 4.7.8.9–11, 216 n.22
 4.9.2.28–33, 223 n.44
 4.9.3.21, 344
 4.9.3.23, 223 n.44
 4.9.3.26–7, 284 n.164
 5.1.5.11–13, 216 nn.20–1
 5.1.6.37–9, 216 n.22
 5.1.7.47–8, 216 n.22
 5.5.13.37–8, 216 n.22
 5.7, 220 n.31
 5.8.1.19–21, 216 n.22
 5.8.1.32–40, 360 n.17
 5.9.6.15–20, 216 n.20
 6.1, 7
 6.1–3, 233 n.8, 314
 6.1.2.15–18, 318, 318 n.17
 6.1.3.1–5, 8 n.37
 6.1.10.54 ff., 320
 6.2, 318
 6.3.5.3, 8 n.37
 6.3.5.18–23, 253
 6.4.15.6–8, 220 n.31
 6.5.3.5–8, 251
 6.7.3.26–8, 282 n.149

6.7.17.4–6, 216 n.22
6.8.7, 153
Plutarch
  Aem.
  28.11, 83
  Agis
  60.5, 225 n.47
  Alex.
  7.6–8, 102 n.83
  An. Procr. in Tim.
  § 3, 1013A–B, 529 n.86
  Ant.
  § 58, 84
  contr. Colot.
  1115B–C, 336 n.30
  Comm. Not.
  1058E–F, 278 n.118
  Luc.
  19.7, 92 n.48
  42.1–2, 84
  Mor.
  78D, 24 n.103
  446F (= LS 65G1), 278 n.120
  446F–447A (= LS 65G), 277 n.114, 278 n.124
  Quaest. Conv.
  740C, 148 n.48
  Stoic. Rep.
  1038B, 268 n.44
  1055E, 138 n.22
  Sull.
  § 26, 83, 93
Plutarch (?)
  Fat.
  570F–572F, 137 n.16
  571B, 137 n.18
  571B–D, 144
  571C, 139 nn.25–6, 139 n.28
  571C–D, 137 n.19, 139 n.27
  571D, 147
  571D–E, 153 n.58
  574E, 138 n.21
  574E–F, 145 n.39
Porphyry
  Abst.
  1.4–6, 266–7
  1.4.1–2, 266 n.32
  1.4.2, 266 n.34, 267 n.36, 267 nn.39–40
  1.4.3, 267 nn.37–8, 268 n.43
  1.4.4, 267 n.42
  1.5.2, 267 n.38, 267 nn.40–1
  1.5.3, 267 n.42
  1.6.1, 268 n.45
  1.6.2, 267 n.40
  1.6.3, 266 n.31, 274 n.89
  1.7–12, 269
  1.10.3, 269 n.50
  1.11.2–3, 269 n.49
  1.12.5, 269 n.48
  1.12.6, 269 nn.49–50
  1.21.1, 269 n.49, 271 n.69
  1.26.3, 271 n.67
  1.27, 32
  1.27–8, 264 n.14
  1.27.1, 271 n.67
  1.29–30, 280 n.136
  1.30, 281 n.145
  1.30.1, 282 n.151
  1.30.6, 281 n.146
  1.30.7, 281 n.147, 282 n.149, 282 n.155
  1.31.1, 282 n.149, 282 n.151
  1.31.2, 281 n.147
  1.32.3, 282 n.150
  1.33.2, 282 nn.152–3
  1.33.3, 281 n.147, 282 n.149, 282 n.155
  1.33.4, 282 n.151
  1.34.1, 281 n.147
  1.34.3, 281 n.147
  1.34.4, 282 n.151
  1.34.7, 282 n.150, 282 n.154
  1.36.2, 282 n.151
  1.37.3, 265 n.14
  1.38.2, 30 n.123
  1.38.4, 282 n.149, 282 n.155
  1.39.2, 282 n.149
  1.41.5, 282 n.149
  1.43.2–3, 281 n.147
  1.43.3, 272 n.81
  1.44.1, 273 n.83, 281 n.147
  1.45.2, 281 n.147
  1.48.1–2, 265 n.14
  1.52.2, 265 n.14
  1.56.2, 265 n.14
  2.3.1, 265 n.14
  2.3.2, 271 n.69
  2.4.2, 264 n.12
  2.4.3, 271 n.67

2.4.3–4, 265 n.14
2.12.3, 270 n.55, 273 n.84
2.24.2, 273 n.84
2.34, 31
2.34.2, 275 n.103
2.37, 31
2.42, 31
2.47.1, 30 n.123
2.61, 31
3.1.4, 264 nn.2–3, 265 n.24, 266 n.28, 267 n.35, 269 n.51, 275 n.95, 287 n.185
3.2, 32
3.2.1–4, 276 n.110
3.2.2, 264 n.11
3.2.4, 265 n.25, 287 n.186
3.3–6, 264 n.7
3.3.1, 277 n.112
3.3.2, 275 n.103
3.3.6–7, 276 n.108
3.3.7, 285 n.165
3.4.1, 276 n.108
3.4.2, 275 n.105, 285 n.165
3.4.2.12, 344
3.4.4–5, 276 n.108
3.4.5, 285 n.165
3.4.7, 26 n.108
3.5.1–2, 285 n.168
3.5.6, 275 n.106
3.5.7, 276 n.107
3.6.1, 276 n.108
3.6.5, 264 n.11
3.6.7, 264 n.11
3.7.1, 264 n.9, 264 n.11, 265 n.24, 265 nn.26–7, 277 n.112, 287 n.185, 287 n.187
3.7.2, 275 n.98
3.7.3–7, 275 n.99
3.7.4–5, 264 n.11
3.8, 264 n.2
3.8.1, 264 n.6, 275 nn.96–7
3.8.6, 264 n.11, 275 n.96
3.8.6–7, 274 n.93, 275 n.100
3.8.7, 264 n.9, 265 n.27
3.8.8, 265 n.26, 275 n.96, 287 n.187
3.9.1, 265 n.24, 287 n.185
3.9.5, 264 n.11
3.10–13, 264 n.7
3.10.3, 264 n.3, 277 n.115

3.12.1, 266 n.32
3.12.4, 264 n.11
3.12.5, 270 n.55
3.13.1, 266 n.28, 266 n.32, 269 n.50
3.15, 264 n.7
3.18.1, 265 n.23, 266 n.28, 266 n.32, 269 n.52, 287 n.184
3.18.2, 265 n.13, 266 n.30, 273 n.84, 274 n.89
3.18.3, 273 n.84
3.19.2, 264 n.2, 264 n.6, 268 n.44, 274 n.92
3.21.3–4, 284 n.160
3.21.4, 264 n.2
3.21.6, 264 n.3
3.21.6–7, 275 n.101
3.21.7, 264 n.5
3.21.8–9, 284 n.163
3.22.1, 284 n.163
3.22.2, 264 n.3, 278 n.123, 284 n.162
3.22.3, 264 n.5, 278 n.124
3.22.3–5, 264 n.6, 274 n.92, 275 n.101, 284
3.22.4–5, 264 n.4
3.22.5, 274 n.93, 279 nn.126–7
3.22.6–7, 268 n.44
3.22.7, 266 n.32
3.22.8, 264 n.7
3.23.2, 265 n.24, 287 n.185
3.23.3, 265 n.26, 287 n.187
3.23.3–4, 264 n.7
3.23.7–8, 265 n.26, 287 n.187
3.24.5, 264 n.3
3.24.6, 266 n.31
3.25.3, 264 n.2, 275 n.98
3.26, 29
3.26.1, 265 n.26, 287 n.187
3.26.3, 264 n.12
3.26.4, 265 n.13, 270 n.55
3.26.4–5, 266 n.29
3.26.9, 30, 268 n.44
3.26.9–11, 270 n.53
3.26.10, 273 n.84
3.26.11, 273 n.82, 273 nn.86
3.27.2, 272 n.80, 273 n.84, 281 n.147
3.27.3, 273 n.84
3.27.3–4, 273 n.86
3.27.7, 281 n.147
4.6.1, 265 n.14

4.18.8, 265 n.14
AG (Kalbfleisch)
1.1, 218 n.27
1.1–2,4, 217 n.24
2.2, 215 n.18
4.9.4–5, 284 n.164
6.2.9, 281 n.147
6.2.9–3.1, 282 n.148
6.3, 227 n.50
6.3.1, 281 n.147
6.3.5–7, 285 n.168
10.6, 227 n.50
11.4, 219
12.1.3–3.2, 279 n.130
12.2.3–3.2, 281 n.143
12.3, 219
12.3.12–4.1, 282 n.154
12.4.7–10, 285 n.167
12.5.1–4, 280 n.133
12.5.2–4, 279 n.130
12.7.1–8, 282 n.154
13, 217 n.24
14.1, 216
14.2–4, 217 n.24
14.3, 216 n.23
14.3.1–7, 280 n.134
14.3.8, 280 n.135
14.4, 170, 219 n.29
16.4, 227 n.50
16.4.7, 281 n.147
16.4.7–5.1, 282 n.148
Antr.
35, 272 n.70
contr. Boeth. ap. Eusebius *Praep.*
11.28.2–3 (= fr. 242F Smith),
    280 n.131
31,7, 31 n.127
32.107, 282 n.154
32.113, 282 n.154
32.115, 282 n.154
32.117, 282 n.154
32.120, 282 n.154
32.124, 282 n.154
in Cat.
56,31, 255
57,5, 96 n.61
57,35–58,7, 8 n.35
58,4–7, 27 n.114, 303 n.59
58,12–15, 303 n.59

59,17–18, 7 n.34
59,21–2, 3 n.11
59,34–60,10, 258
71,16–26, 255
71,28–9, 255
75,25–9, 304 n.69
79,35–80,2, 247
80,29–81,2, 239 n.26
81,3–14, 239 n.27
81,3–22, 249, 300 n.44
81,9–16, 252
81,14–22, 239 n.27
81,16.20, 250
81,26, 257
82,5–10, 258
82,5–22, 244 n.45
82,10–11, 258
82,14–15, 258
82,17–22, 258
82,23–4, 244 n.45
82,23–8, 244 n.47
82,25–9, 258
82,29–32, 244 n.48, 258
83,4–10, 260
83,7, 257
83,14–24, 244 n.50
83,35–84,4, 259
83,35–84,20, 245 n.52
84,4, 257
84,4–9, 259
86,7–13, 243 n.42
90,12–91,12, 306
90,33–91,3, 304 n.71
91,16, 256
91,24–5, 306
99,1–100,8, 318 n.19
contr. Christ. (Harnack)
fr. 39, 33 n.141
Ep. ad Aneb. ap. Iamblichus *Myst.*
7.5.1–6, 287 n.181
Ep. ad Marc.
14, 29
16, 29
25.1–6, 272 n.70
Plot.
11, 30 n.122
14.7, 96 n.61
14.19–20, 215 n.18
16, 32 n.134

17, 26 n.107
18, 26 n.110
24, 3 n.10, 26 n.109, 96
24.2, 95
48.1, 96 n.61
in Ptol. Harm. (Düring)
13,21–14,6, 307
14,6–30, 307
14,10, 282 n.156
14,24–7, 287 n.180
14,31–15,5, 280 n.137
15,10–20, 280 n.137
16,16–19, 284 n.164
Pyth.
§ 15, 271 n.6
Sent. (Lamberz)
§ 8, 30
§ 9, 30
§ 13, 216 n.22
§ 13.1–2, 280 n.135
§ 32.6, 272 n.74
§ 32.7–9, 272 n.77
§ 32.13–14, 270 n.58, 272 n.73
§ 32.15, 272 n.79
§ 32.28–9, 270 n.58, 272 n.73
§ 32.29, 272 n.72
§ 32.29–30, 272 n.74
§ 32.32–3, 272 n.78
§ 32.75, 272 n.75
§ 32.77, 272 n.74, 281 n.147, 282 n.154
§ 32.84–5, 272 n.76
§ 32.95–7, 272 n.72
§ 32.129, 281 n.147
§ 32.138–9, 273 n.83
§ 37.33–41, 216 n.21
§ 40.75–7, 270 n.58
§ 41,6–8, 35
§ 41,17, 35
§ 41,19–20, 35
§ 42.18–20, 287 n.183
§ 43.14–45, 281 n.140
§ 43.36–40, 282 n.157
§ 52,7–53,5, 35
ap. Boethius *in Int.*[2] (Meiser)
29,29–30,10, 28 n.118, 305 n.74
ap. Simplicius *in Cat.*
53,6–9 (= fr. 56F Smith), 253
57,22–58,14 (= fr. 57F Smith), 262

79,24–30 (= fr. 59F Smith), 253
213,8–28, 296 n.24, 305
213,10 ff. (= fr. 70 Smith), 320
ap. Stobaeus *Ecl.*
2,164, 148 n.47
fr. 273F–275F (Smith), 37 n.156
Priscian
Sol. ad Khos. (Bywater)
51,18, 34
51,25, 34
51,30, 34
52,2–3, 34
Theoph. de Sens.
21,32–22,23, 66 n.287
Proclus
in Crat.
§ 2, 354 n.6
§ 4, 354 n.6
§ 9, 3,17–24, 362 n.22
§ 10, 4,12, 354
§ 10, 4,16–18, 356
§ 16, 5,25–6,19, 357 n.13
§ 16, 5,28, 354 n.5
§ 17, 7,18–8,4, 361
§ 35, 35,25–6, 356 n.10
§ 36, 354 n.6
§ 47, 354 n.6
§ 49, 354 n.6
§ 51, 19,12–17, 358
§ 51, 19,22–20,21, 362 n.23
§ 51, 29,21–32,4, 356 n.8
§ 53, 23,24–5, 357 n.13
§ 58, 354 n.6
§ 77, 37,3–5, 356 n.9
§ 81, 37,26–7, 357 n.12
§ 135, 178,13–22, 362 n.22
in Parm. (Steel)
513,32–3 (Latin), 295 n.20
792,7–8, 216 n.23
792,9–15, 228
793,4 ff., 222 n.40
793,4–11, 228 n.52
880,3–11, 45 n.200
883,37–885,3, 301 n.55
896,23–7, 294
896,25, 294
897,15–16, 294
897,22–3, 294
939,10–22, 295 n.20

980,6–981,3, 295 n.21
980,29–33, 295 n.21
982,4–9, 294
986,10–14, 295 n.20
in Tim. (Diehl)
1,1,17–18, 469 n.56
1,2,19–26, 222 n.40
1,2,19–31, 222 n.41
1,6,21–4, 354 n.4
1,6,21–7,16, 354 n.4
1,6,30–7,2, 339 n.43
1,77,24 ff. 318 n.22
1,223–264,3, 333 n.22
1,251,11–254,18, 333 n.21
1,262,5–12, 222 n.41
1,267,16–268,6, 46 n.201
1,276,8–296,12, 468 n.5
1,277,8–17, 514 n.37, 527 n.82, 529
1,277,11–14, 469
1,278,19–21, 470
1,279,9–29, 333 n.21
1,279,23–5, 469
1,279,24 ff., 470 n.58
1,288,14 ff., 469
1,288,16–17, 469
1,289,14–15, 469
1,290,2–3, 469
1,293,6–296,12, 333 n.21
1,294,28–295,19, 334 n.24
1,295,20–7, 334 n.27
1,295,22–7, 470
1,395,1–10, 333 n.21
1,404,7–21, 332 n.17
1,404,20–1, 431 n.61
1,446,1–7, 221 n.36
2,43,21–6, 338 n.36
2,49,19–29, 338 n.37, 339 n.42
2,63,20–1, 341
2,82,20–3, 345 n.71
2,83,15 ff., 345
2,83,30–84, 5, 345 n.72
2,85,5–7, 345 n.71
2,250,8–14, 332 n.16
2,278,27–279,16, 331 n.15, 332 n.16
2,278,29–30, 346 n.77
2,278,32–279,1, 330 n.14
2,279,2–4, 431 n.61
2,279,3–4, 43 n.190

3,30,30–32,6, 323 n.40
3,33,1–30, 323 n.40
3,53,6–13, 221 n.36
3,60,31–63,30, 341
3,141,1–144,22, 351 n.93
3,196,3–4, 345 n.71
3,329,2–6, 345 n.71
3,330,9–331,1, 43 n.191
3,332,24–6, 215 n.18
3,341,4–342,2, 43 n.191
ET (Dodds)
§ 7, 216 n.22
§ 39, 450 n.46
§ 52–5, 539 n.32
§ 194, 294
in Eucl.
I 50,15–51,9, 292 n.8, 307 n.84
I 50,16–51,9, 45 n.199
I 51,3, 292 n.8
I 141,2–9, 357
Prov.
39,4–9, 44
63–5, 45 n.196
in Remp.
1,232,25, 345 n.71
2,12,13–15, 345 n.71
2,219,20–221,26, 341
2,220,11–18, 341 n.54
2,334,11–13, 343 n.59
2,334,14, 43 n.192
2,335,19–20, 342 n.58
2,339,15–16, 342 n.58
Theol. Plat. (Saffrey–Westerink)
19,6–8, 469 n.57
24,17, 469 n.57
25,8–11, 469 n.57
§ 1.5, 25,18–23, 362 n.22
27,17–18, 469 n.57
29,24–30,3, 469 n.57
§ 2.4, 31,21–2, 533 n.8
1,75,16 ff., 332 n.19
§ 1.29, 124,9–11, 358
§ 1.29, 124,12–20, 362 n.23
3,24,9, 345 n.71
§ 5.15–20, 469 n.57
ap. Philoponus *Aet.*
238,3–240,9, 46 n.201
297,21–300,2, 46 n.201
626,1–627,20, 46 n.201

Schol. *Od.*
  ad 23.296, 98 n.69
  ad 23.310-43, 98 n.69
Seneca
  Ep.
  58.16, 293 n.13
  124.16, 279 n.127
  Ir.
  1.3.6-7, 279 n.125
  1.3.8, 277 n.111
Sextus Empiricus
  Math.
  8.70 (= LS 33C), 278 n.121
  8.274, 276 n.108
  8.274-6, 277 n.111
  9.210, 232 n.4
  11.14.2, 330 n.14
Simplicius
  in Cael.
  12,16-28, 339 n.44
  13,22-14,29, 166 n.12
  13,31, 167
  26,21-3, 373 n.16
  28,6, 508 n.21
  28,14-21, 508 n.21
  79,2-8, 470 n.62
  87,1-21, 339 n.44
  90,21-5, 338 n.41
  95,16-30, 539 n.33
  98,6 ff., 225 n.47
  134,10, 348 n.85
  159,3.7, 373 n.16
  279,5-9, 113 n.27
  284,28-285,2, 560 n.77
  296,16-18, 328 n.3
  297,1-5, 329 n.11
  306,1-16, 433 n.72
  376,28 ff., 332 n.20
  379,16-18, 328 n.3
  444,11, 334 n.25
  462,12-31, 385 n.63
  462,20-31, 55 n.244
  517,1-519,11, 351 n.94
  562,1-2, 346 n.75
  563,26-566,20, 347 n.83
  564,10-14, 347 n.80
  565,3.6, 348 n.85
  578,20-6, 346 n.78
  599,5, 348 n.85

640,20-672,23, 431
640,21-7, 346 n.76
640,24-5, 330 n.12
640,27-641,5, 347 n.82
643,13-27, 350 n.90
644,7-13, 351 n.95
645,15-28, 350
645,28-646,3, 351 n.96
657,2-9, 432
659,11-661,14, 431
659,33-660,3, 430 n.60
660,4-14, 431
660,7-8, 431
660,19 ff., 431
660,26-661,14, 431
661,13-14, 432 n.68
in Cat. (Kalbfleisch)
1,9-2,29, 233
1,13-14, 236
1,18-2,2, 248
2,5-9, 236, 314
2,8-9, 235
2,9 ff., 314, 315 n.7
2,9-15, 236
2,9-25, 27 n.115, 36, 303 n.61
2,13, 251
2,13-25, 236
2,21-2, 535 n.19
3,10-17, 315
6,22-30, 537 n.26
7,23-32, 534 n.13
7,26-9, 401
7,29-32, 535 n.19
9,4-10,8, 316 n.13
9,7, 303 n.64
10,20 ff., 317
12,16-25, 294
12,16-13,32, 364 n.30
13,4 ff., 315
13,11-18, 7 n.30, 303 n.63
13,13-16, 317
13,15 ff., 317
13,20, 303 n.64
15,35-16,16, 97 n.64
16,2, 101
18,16-21, 98 n.70
24,19, 322 n.32
26,11-15, 558 n.64
26,17-20, 4

27,23–33, 253
30,2, 5 n.19
30,3–5, 4
41,28–42,2, 303 n.65
44,3–11, 256
44,26–45,7, 257
45,8–18, 256
45,30–2, 243 n.42
50,5–8, 6 n.25, 296 n.26
50,6–9, 250, 310 n.98
51,26–54,21, 235
52,11–13, 240 n.29
52,11–18, 239 n.27
53,4–18, 241 n.33
53,6–14, 237
53,7–9, 234
54,8–16, 119 n.44, 254
54,8–21, 241 n.34
54,24–5, 258
55,8–20, 254
55,24–56,15, 163 n.6
56,6–8, 237, 244 n.48
56,6–10, 258
56,16–18, 244 n.47
56,18–57,1, 244 n.50
57,11–13, 245 n.52
57,13–21, 245 n.54
57,21–2, 257
57,22–58,1, 260
57,22–58,12, 246 n.56
57,26–7, 245 n.55
58,7–12, 235, 246 n.60
58,19–21, 246 n.59
59,13–19, 245 n.52, 259
63,22, 5 n.18
69,19–71,2, 53 n.236, 308 n.85
73,15–76,16, 7 n.33
73,27–8, 7 n.32
78,4–5, 7 n.33
78,5–20, 6 n.21, 104 n.7
78,17–20, 116 n.32
79,28–9, 234
82,26–8, 299 n.39
82,35–83,20, 53 n.236, 292 n.6, 308 n.85
85,13–17, 299 n.39
114,21 ff., 318 n.16
115,24–116,10, 318
116,11–24, 318 n.21
116,29, 318 n.23

128,8, 319 n.26
134,5, 5 n.18
140,27, 348 n.85
146,22 ff., 322 n.33
157,18–21, 5 n.18
159,31–2, 94 n.50
159,32, 233 n.8
165,32–166,29, 120 n.47
167,2–18, 121 n.50, 122
167,15–16, 121 n.50
188,3–7, 109 n.20
217,24 ff., 320 n.28
225,1–14, 558 n.67
281,2–31, 433
281,4–6, 432 n.64
281,7–15, 433 n.71
327,7 ff., 322 n.33
347,19–21, 5 n.18
350,10–19, 20 n.81
350,11–12, 37 n.154
361,7–20, 537 n.27
373,7–18, 108 nn.15–16
373,18–32, 108 n.17
374,7 ff., 322 n.33
379,9–12, 97
in Ench. (Dübner)
20, 150
56,45–8, 576 n.20
99,50–100,45, 433 n.70
in Phys. (CAG 9–10)
4,8–16, 100 n.78
4,17–5,26, 540 n.34
8,6–9, 400
8,16–39, 102 n.83
100,1–22, 433 n.69
100,15–18, 433 n.69
162,29–31, 221 n.39
186,32–4, 238 n.22
192,22–3, 381 n.51
193,4–5, 381 n.51
211,15–18, 109 n.19
228 ff., 347 n.83
234,13–19, 298 n.37
234,17–18, 301 n.47
239,18 ff., 225 n.47
270,26–34, 113 n.27
311,12–17, 301 n.51
313,11–13, 227 n.51
402,9–406,16, 484 n.23

Index Locorum

403,13-19, 484 n.24
403,13-23, 484 n.24
440,14-17, 95 n.56
467,26-468,3, 560 n.77
473,11-24, 410 n.44
514,9, 348 n.85
530,9-531,10, 432 n.62
531,5-7, 433 n.70
552,18-24, 113 n.27
583,13-29, 400
601,10-12, 535 n.20
601,12-13, 535 n.22
604,5-11, 535, 535 n.18
611,12, 533 n.7
625,2, 533 n.7
625,2-3, 534 n.17
625,29, 62 n.263
626,7-9, 62 n.263
626,13-16, 62 n.263
639,10-13, 535 n.18
639,13-640,9, 535 n.18
640,33, 538 n.28
644,4-9, 536 n.23
644,10-645,17, 534 n.16
644,33-4, 62 n.263
663,6, 343 n.61
759,18-20, 106 n.12
773,19-774,37, 539 n.31
777,4-33, 65 n.282
777,8-12, 65 n.276
777,13, 65 n.277
777,15-16, 65 n.278
777,27-31, 65 n.279
777,28-31, 65 n.283
784,2-8, 65 n.281
786,11-13, 37 n.154
791,32-3, 401 n.25
792,20-793,23, 323 n.36
792,20-795,3, 323 n.40
793, 323
795,15-17, 401 n.25
821,20-1, 399 n.18
871,2, 334 n.25
886,12-16, 168 n.16
923,3-7, 90 n.38
923,3-925,2, 100
923,10, 98
923,18-924,13, 100
1130,7-1131,7, 378 n.34
1133,10, 373 n.16
1133,17-1135,15, 378 n.34
1141,12-16, 470 n.63
1147,10-1149,4, 378 n.34
1157,6-1159,4, 378 n.34
1164,11-30, 378 n.34
1165,28-33, 339 n.44
1166,37-1167,16, 378 n.34
1171,30-1175,26, 378 n.34
1190,21 ff., 343 n.62
1293,3-5, 221 n.39
1326-36, 470 n.61
1363,4-12, 53 n.234

Simplicius (?)
in DA
52,19-22, 433 n.72
63,15-17, 222 n.40
109,25-7, 442 n.18
161,11-12, 450 n.46
162,28, 450 n.46
173,3-7, 66 n.287
187,27-188,35, 66 n.287
317,12-14, 345 n.73

Socrates
Eccl. Hist.
4.32.2-4, 22 n.94

Sopater
Ep. ad Him. ap. Stobaeus *Ecl.*
4,215,12-218,9, 40 n.171

Sophonias
in DA
57,4-9, 220 n.33
57,9-14, 220 n.33
57,14-17, 220 n.33, 221 n.37

Stephanus
in Int. Hayduck (CAG 18.3)
1,1-2, 544 n.15
1,18-22, 545
1,25-7, 545
2,11-12, 554 n.55
2,17-20, 556 n.59
5,1-19, 545
5,13 ff., 545
6,23-5, 393 n.2
17,25-8, 559
21,5-10, 554 n.55
35,34-36,38, 547 n.27
Schol. in Hipp.
1,328,5-8, 344 n.67

ap. *Doctr. Patr.* (Diekamp)
§ 28.iv, 202, 558 n.67
§ 28.vi, 202,8–16, 555
§ 28.vi, 202,9–16, 555
§ 33, 249,13–14, 547
§ 33, 249,15–16, 547
§ 33, 249,17–24, 547
§ 33, 249,21–4, 548
§ 33, 251,16–17, 554
§ 33, 251,16–22, 555 n.57
§ 33, 251,18–19, 555
§ 33, 251,19–22, 555
§ 33, 259,7–8, 555
§ 33, 259,8–9, 555
§ 33, 264,22–3, 555
Stobaeus
  Ecl. (Wachsmuth)
  1,54,8–11, 418 n.22
  1,89,2–5, 135 n.11
  2,86,17 (= *SVF* 3.169), 278 n.120
  2,173,21, 150
Strabo
  Geogr.
  2.3.8, 92 n.42
  10.2.21, 83 n.9
  12.5.3, 83 n.9
  13.1.19, 83 n.9
  13.1.54, 83, 84, 91
  14.1.37, 84
  14.2.19, 83 n.9
  16.2.24, 92 n.43
  17.1.5, 92 n.45, 94 n.50
St. Vet. Frag. (von Arnim)
  2.695, 171
  2.804–8, 170
Syrianus
  in Metaph.
  54,12–15, 41 n.178
  56,13–57,21, 294
  57,22 ff., 41 n.179
  80,4–81,14, 41 n.176, 329 n.10
  81,32–5, 450 n.46
  85,38–86,2, 347 n.81
  95,29–38, 42 n.182
  101–2, 41 n.177
  105,36–106,2, 293 n.10
  106,5–7, 251
  114,35–115,3, 292 n.5
  115,19–26, 295 n.18
  117,25–118,11, 42 n.183
  186,4, 222 n.41
  186,4–5, 221 n.39
  186,7, 222 n.42
  186,12–14, 222 n.41
  194,9–13, 44
  195, 41 n.177
  233,36–40, 398

Tacitus
  Ann.
  6.20–1, 84
  6.22, 148 nn.47–8
Themistius
  in DA
  15,9, 206 n.29
  26,7–11, 206 n.28
  26,15–18, 206 n.28
  26,25–9, 220 n.35 26,25–9, 220 n.35
  26,25–30, 19 n.76
  26,27–30, 206 n.28
  26,28–9, 206 n.29
  30,37, 241 n.35
  61,24, 200 n.12
  68,28, 241 n.35
  98,35–99,10, 21 n.87
  100,18–20, 21 n.86
  100,37–101,1, 21 n.86
  101,4–37, 21 n.89
  101,5–9, 21 n.88
  101,9–10, 21 n.86
  101,13–20, 21 n.90
  102,16–24, 21 n.89
  102,36–103,19, 21 n.91
  103,16–17, 21 n.86
  103,22–36, 22 n.92
  103,36–8, 21 n.86, 21 n.90
  105,18–27, 21 n.89
  105,22–30, 21 n.88
  in Metaph.
  5,9, 201 n.18
  7,17–21, 198
  7,20–3, 199
  7,23–7, 199
  7,27–8.2, 200
  10,32–11,4, 206 n.27
  12,6, 21 n.85
  17,10–13, 209

17,14–15, 209 n.34
20,17–22,26, 209
20,25–6, 209 n.34
in Metaph. 12 ap. Averroes *in Metaph.*
   12 (Bouyges)
III, 1292–4, 293 n.14
III, 1492,3–9, 200
III, 1492,3–1494,14, 197 n.6
III, 1492,9–12, 201
III, 1492,13–1493,2, 202
III, 1492–4, 54 n.241, 181
III, 1493,2–6, 203
III, 1493,6–1494,1, 204
III, 1494,1–9, 206
III, 1494,9–14, 208
III, 1494,11–13, 208 n.32
Orat.
§ 5, 22
§ 13.165D6–166A1, 207 n.29
§ 20.235, 24 n.100
§ 20.235C8–D3, 210 n.36
§ 21, 23
§ 21.244, 20 n.80
§ 21.255, 23 n.97
§ 22, 23
§ 22.265, 23 n.97
§ 23, 20
§ 23.294D1–3, 210 n.36
§ 26, 23
§ 26.313, 23 n.97
§ 26.320, 24 n.100
§ 26.320–1, 23 n.97
§ 26.327–8, 23 n.97
§ 31, 18 n.73
§ 31.352, 25
§ 34, 18 n.73, 23, 25
§ 34.13, 18 n.73
in Phys.
12,13 ff., 468

13,5, 468
26,20 ff., 109 n.19
68,16–30, 484 n.23
69,9–20, 483 n.20
114,7–21, 21 n.82
120,17–21, 21 n.84
149,4–19, 21 n.83
160,26–8, 106 n.12
163,1–7, 21 n.84
210,3 ff., 467 n.50
211,34 ff., 467 n.50
212,8, 467 n.50
212,10 ff., 467 n.50
233,14–17, 467 n.50
Theophrastus
   Princ.
   7b6, 208 n.31
   ap. Stobaeus *Ecl.*
   1,89,2–5, 137 n.17
   fr. 149 (FHSG), 535 n.18
Thomas Aquinas
   in Metaph.
   7.12.8, § 1402, 192
   7.12.8, § 1403, 192–3
   7.12.8, § 1455, 192
   7.12.8, § 1457, 193
Timotheus Presbyter
   Recept. Haer. (PG 87)
   65A, 549 n.35

Varro
   Ling. Lat.
   6.56, 277 n.111, 279 n.127
   7.37, 86

Zacharias of Mytilene
   Ammonius (Colonna)
   362–5, 386 n.64

Index

Accusative case, 407–10
Actuality. *See* Mixtures
Ad Gaurum, 218–20, 236
Against Proclus on the Eternity of the World
    Arabic translation of 4.4–6, 485–90
    Arabic translation of 9.11, 491–502
Agathias, 58, 59–60
Alcinous, 142–3
Alexander of Aphrodisias. *See also* Alexander of Aphrodisias (Arabic translations); Alexander of Aphrodisias (particulars)
    Boethus of Sidon, 6
    Categories (rediscovered commentary), 234–6, 249–50
    choice, 149
    commentaries on Aristotle, 10–17
    determinism, 11, 13–14
    eph' hêmin, 143–6
    freedom and determinism, 129–32
    introduction, 10
    mixtures, 428–30
    new theory of inherence, 112–15
    'the parts of the substance are substances', 110–12
    Philopator, 12–13
    Stoic philosophy, 10–14
    substantiality, 110–15
    universals, 297–303
    world's eternity, 466–7
Alexander of Aphrodisias (Arabic translations)
    Against Proclus 4.4–6, 485–90
    Against Proclus 9.11, 491–502
    forms, 494–9
    introduction, 477–8
    movement, 478–84
    Philoponus, John, 500–1
    Quaest. 1.21, 478–84
    world's eternity, 485–502

Alexander of Aphrodisias (particulars)
    astral and cosmic configurations, 168–73
    Avicenna, 173–5
    Chrysippus of Soli, 169, 171–2
    Dexippus, 161–4
    divination, 169
    eternal return, 164–7
    individuals, 161–2
    introduction, 161
    Leibniz, 175–7
    matter, 167–8, 173
    Philoponus, John, 170–1
    Porphyry's *Introduction (Isagôgê)*, 161–3
    Socrates, 165, 168
Al-Fārābī, 461
Al-Kindī
    Arab world, 456
    world's eternity, 471–2
Al-Rāzī, Abū Bakr
    Islamic doctrines of initiation, 517–18
    On The Harmonisation of the opinions of the Two Sages, 517–20
    world's eternity, 473–6
Amelius, 26
Ammonius of Alexandria
    Aristotle's Creator God, 53
    astronomy, 55–6
    blank mind, 54–5
    Categories, 49–50
    commentaries and works, 46
    curriculum and other cultures, 50–3
    curriculum of six introductions, 48–50
    David the Invincible, 52–3
    De Anima, 397–401, 405
    determinism, 56–7
    geometry and mathematics, 55–6
    mind as a blank writing tablet, 54–5
    names, 356–63
    natural names, 55
    Neoplatonist teacher, 48

Paul the Persian, 50–1
Phaedo, 48–9
Philoponus' divergence, 392
philosophy definitions, 48–9
re-harmonisation, 53–5
riots, 47
school, 47
seminars, 71
Sergius of Resh, 51
Stephanus, 52
teacher of leading Neoplatonists, 48
Timaeus, 328–9
training, 46
universals, 53–4, 307–9
what depends on us, 143
Analytics, 559
Andronicus of Rhodes
    Andronicus' canon, 90–1, 95, 97, 99–102
    Aristotle's books, 93–5, 95–9
    Categories, 4–5
    commentaries on Aristotle, 3–5
Animals. *See* Spontaneous generation; Vegetarianism
Anonymi in Aristotelis Categorias Commentarium, 238–46
Apellicon of Teos, 91–2
Aquinas, Thomas
    spontaneous generation, 192–3
Arab world. *See also* Alexander of Aphrodisias (Arabic translations); *Contra Proclum* in Arabic
    Alexander of Aphrodisias, 466–7
    al-Fārābī, 461
    al-Kindī, 456, 471–2
    al-Rāzī, Abū Bakr, 473–6
    Arabic commentaries, 454–7
    Bishr, Abū, 459–60
    conclusion, 476
    corruption, 467, 471
    grammar, 459
    Greek commentators, 454–6
    Ibn ʿAdī, Yahya, 461–3
    introduction, 453
    logic's use in philosophy, 457–64
    Organon, 457, 463–4
    Philoponus, John, 470–1
    Proclus, 468–70
    Thābit Ibn Qurra, 472–3

Themistius, 467–8
    world's eternity, 464–76
Aristophanes of Byzantium, 85–6
Aristotelianism, 19–20
Aristotle. *See also* Commentaries on Aristotle
    choice, 147
    Metaphysics, 180–4, 190–2
    mixtures, 416–21
    names, 355–6
    Porphyry of Tyre's commentaries, 35
    Timaeus criticism, 327–30
Aristotle's books. *See also* Commentaries on Aristotle
    Andronicus' canon, 90–1, 95, 97, 99–102
    Andronicus of Rhodes, 93–5, 95–9
    Apellicon of Teos, 91–2
    arrangement, 96–8
    authenticity, 97–8
    Cicero, 93
    circulation and publication, 90–4
    history, 90–3
    introduction, 89–91
    Strabo, 91–2
    Sulla, 91–4
    summary, 94–5
    Theophrastus, 91
    Tyrannio, 93
Astral configurations
    Alexander of Aphrodisias, 168–73
    Chrysippus of Soli, 169, 171–2
    Philoponus, John, 170–1
    Socrates, 168
Astronomy, 55–6
Athenian philosophers, 58–9
Augustine
    Porphyry of Tyre, 32
    spontaneous generation, 214–15
Avicenna, 173–5

Bishr, Abū, 459–60
Blank mind, 54–5
Boethus of Sidon
    Alexander of Aphrodisias, 6
    Categories, 5–8
    Categories (rediscovered commentary), 250–1
    commentaries on Aristotle, 5–8

concepts, 7
forms, 5–6
Boethus of Sidon (substance)
   Alexander of Aphrodisias, 110–15
   categories of form, 116–19
   definitions and terminology, 109–10
   having, 107–8
   having vs. Stoic sayable, 122–3
   health, 107–8
   inherence, 105–9
   introduction, 103–4
   non-substantiality, 115–16
   Physics, 106–7
   Stoic relatively, 119–22
   theory of substance and predication, 104–5
Books. *See* Texts in First Century BCE

Categories. *See also Categories* (Iamblichus); *Categories* (rediscovered commentary)
   Ammonius of Alexandria, 49–50
   Andronicus, 4–5
   Boethus of Sidon, 5–8
   dating of Philoponus' commentaries, 380–4
   Elias' commentary, 555–6
   Porphyry of Tyre, 27
   Simplicius' commentary, 557–8
   Stephanus the Philosopher, 554–8
   universals, 303–6
Categories (Iamblichus)
   introduction, 313–16
   Plato, 36–7
   Porphyry of Tyre, 314–15
   Quality, 320–2
   Quantity, 319–20
   Simplicius, 314–15
   skopos, 316–17
   substance, 317–18
   summary, 324–5
   time, 322–4
Categories (rediscovered commentary)
   Alexander of Aphrodisias, 234–6, 249–50
   Anonymi in Aristotelis Categorias Commentarium, 238–46
   Boethus of Sidon, 250–1
   differentia, 257–62
   fourfold division, 255–7
   genus, 257–62
   Iamblichus, 236–7
   introduction, 231–3
   length of commentary, 235–6
   Nicostratus, 248–9, 254
   parallel passages, 237
   Porphyry of Tyre, 234–7, 253
   species, 257–62
   subaltern genera, 259–60
   text presentation, 237–8
   transitivity principle, 246–54
Causational synonymy, 182, 191
Choice
   Alexander of Aphrodisias, 149
   Aristotle, 147
   Epictetus, 147
   generally, 146–50
   Middle-Platonists, 148
   Plato, 147–8
   what depends on us, 146–50
Christianity
   freedom of religion, 22
   Philoponus, John, 71
   Porphyry of Tyre, 32
   Stephanus the Philosopher, 547
Chrysippus of Soli, 169, 171–2
Cicero, 93
Cleombrotus, 550
Cognition of senses. *See* Sense-perception
Commentaries on Aristotle. *See also specific commentators*
   Adrastus, 9
   Agathias, 58, 59–60
   Alexander of Aphrodisias, 6, 10–17
   Ammonius of Alexandria, 46–57, 71
   Andronicus, 3–5
   Aristotelianism, 19–20
   Athenian philosophers, 58–9
   Boethus of Sidon, 5–8
   Categories, 4–5, 5–8, 9, 49–50
   commentators, 8–9
   Damascius, 60–7
   David the Invincible, 52–3
   determinism, 11, 13–14, 56–7
   Eustratius, 79–81
   freedom of religion, 22
   freedom of speech, 22–3
   Iamblichus, 36–40

infinite power in a finite body, 45–6, 66
intellect and immortality, 21–2
intellective theory, 36–7
introduction, 1–3
Julian (emperor), 23–5
Khosroes I, 57–9
knowledge advancements and fragments, 1–3
Maximus of Ephesus, 25
Michael of Ephesus, 79–81
mind as a blank writing tablet, 54–5
natural names, 55
Neoplatonism, 19–20
Paul the Persian, 50–1
Philopator, 12–13
Philoponus, John, 70–8
Porphyry of Tyre, 2, 6–7, 9, 26–38
Priscian of Lydia, 57–60
Proclus, 42–6
self-knowledge and conscience, 66–7
Sergius of Resh, 51
Simplicius, 64–5, 67–70
spontaneous generation, 18–19
Stephanus, 52, 78–9
Stoic philosophy, 10–14
syllogism, 25
Syrianus, 40–2
Themistius, 17–25
theology, 61–2
theurgy, 38, 61–2
time, 36–7, 62–5
world's eternity, 19
'Common sense', 447–8
Communication, 285–7
Concepts
    Boethus of Sidon, 7
    universals, 303–7, 309, 310–11
Conscience, 66–7
Contra Proclum in Arabic
    al-Rāzī, Abū Bakr, 517–18
    conclusion, 529–30
    considerations on doctrine, 527–9
    Contra Proclum 6, 510–17
    historical accuracy, 505–7
    Ibn Suwār, 520–2
    introduction, 503–5
    Islamic doctrines of initiation, 517–29
    Kindean tradition, 522–7

On The Harmonisation of the opinions of the Two Sages, 517–20
    Philoponus' refutation, 507–10
    Proclus' first argument, 509–10
    Taurus, 513–15
    world's eternity, 503, 505–9, 517–18
Corollary on Place
    cosmos, 534, 537–40
    Damascius, 534–8
    definitions, 537, 539
    'measures', 538–9
    Simplicius, 531–40
Corruption, 416–21, 423–4, 467, 471
Cosmos
    Alexander of Aphrodisias, 168–73
    Chrysippus of Soli, 169, 171–2
    Corollary on Place, 534, 537–40
    Philoponus, John, 170–1
    Socrates, 168
Cratylus
    Ammonius, 356–63
    Aristotle, 355–6
    conclusions, 363–5
    definitions, 356–7
    function, 361–3
    introduction, 353–5
    name-givers, 357–8
    object resemblance, 358–61
    Plato, 355–6
    Proclus, 356–63
    Socrates, 354–5
Creator God, 53

Damascius
    commentaries and works, 60
    infinite power in a finite body, 66
    life, 60–1
    Phaedo, 61, 66
    place, 534–8
    Plato, 60–2
    school, 60–1
    self-knowledge and conscience, 66–7
    Simplicius on time, 64–5
    theology and theurgy, 61–2
    time, 62–5
Dative case, 407–10
David the Invincible
    Ammonius of Alexandria, 52–3
    Stephanus the Philosopher, 550–1

De Anima
  Ammonius, 397–401, 405
  authenticity, 396
  commentary on third book, 393–7
  dating of Philoponus' commentaries, 385–7
  dative and accusative cases, 407–10
  epistaseis, 401
  intellect, 396, 399
  Latin commentary, 395
  manuscripts, 394
  Philoponus' commentary on third book, 406–13
  Philoponus on Ammonius' commentary, 401–6
  Stephanus, 394–5
De Caelo, 559–60
De Generatione et Corruptione, 387–9
De Interpretatione. *See also* Names
  Alcinous, 142–3
  Ammonius of Alexandria, 143
  link with *Nicomachean Ethics*, 140–2
  Stephanus the Philosopher, 558–9
  what depends on us, 138–9
De mistione, 414–15
Deceased organisms, 225
Determinism. *See also* Freedom and determinism
  Alexander of Aphrodisias, 11, 13–14
  Ammonius of Alexandria, 56–7
Dexippus, 161–4
Differentia, 257–62
Divination, 169
Division, 553–4

Elias, 548, 550–1, 555–6
Embryos, 185–8
Eph' hêmin
  Alexander of Aphrodisias, 143–6
  Middle-Platonists, 143–6
  what depends on us, 134–5
Epictetus, 147
Epistaseis, 401
Eternal return, 164–7
Eternity of the world. *See* World's eternity
Ethics, 28–31
Eustratius
  commentaries on Aristotle, 79–81
  universals, 312

Evil, 44
Extraordinary generation. *See* Spontaneous generation

Fifth element, 337–9
Force of attraction in bodies, 343–4
Forms. *See also* Mixtures; Substance; Universals
  Alexander of Aphrodisias, 494–9
  Boethus of Sidon, 5–6
  form-principles, 221–2
  spontaneous generation, 212–18
Fourfold division, 255–7
Freedom and determinism
  Alcinous, 142–3
  Alexander of Aphrodisias, 129–32, 143–6, 149
  Ammonius of Alexandria, 143
  Aristotle, 147
  choice, 146–9
  De Interpretatione, 138–43
  eph' hêmin, 134–5, 143–6
  Epictetus, 147
  exousia, 150–2
  freedom to do otherwise, 152–8
  introduction, 125–8
  Middle-Platonists, 136–40, 143–6, 148
  Nicomachean Ethics, 135–6, 140–2
  On Fate, 129
  one-sided causative concept, 132–3
  Plato, 147–8
  results, 158–61
  two-sided indeterminist concept, 134–5
  what depends on us, 132–43, 146–52
Freedom of religion, 22
Freedom of speech, 22–3

Generation & corruption, 416–21, 423–4
Generation of Animals. *See* Spontaneous generation
Genus, 257–62
Geometry
  Ammonius of Alexandria, 55–6
  geometrical elements, 327, 345–52, 430
Gnôstikôs, 449–51
God
  Creator God, 53
  Proclus, 45
  world's eternity, 467, 470–6

Index

Harmonisation, 517–20
Having
    Boethus' having vs. Stoic sayable, 122–3
    substance, 107–8
Health, 107–8
Hearing, 442–3
Hermeneutical tradition, 328–9
Heterogenesis, 211, 222, 225–8
Hierocles, 328–9
Homogenetic biogenesis, 218–20
Homonymy, 291–2, 294

Iamblichus. *See also* Iamblichus (*Categories*)
    Categories (rediscovered commentary), 236–7
    commentaries on Aristotle, 36–40
    intellective theory, 36–7
    Julian (emperor), 39–40
    Pythagoreans, 38–9
    relationship with Porphyry, 37–8
    school, 39
    souls and reincarnation, 38
    theurgy, 38
    time, 36–7
Iamblichus (*Categories*)
    introduction, 313–16
    Plato, 36–7
    Porphyry of Tyre, 314
    Quality, 320–2
    Quantity, 319–20
    Simplicius, 314–15
    skopos, 316–17
    substance, 317–18
    summary, 324–5
    time, 322–4
Ibn 'Adī, Yaḥyā, 461–3
Ibn Suwār, 520–2
Ideas
    definitions, 295–6
    paraphrase of *Metaphysics* 12, 198–201, 208–10
    Timaeus, 336–7
    universals, 291–5
Immortality, 332
Individuals, 161–2
Infinite power in a finite body
    Damascius, 66

Proclus, 45–6
Ingredient qualities, 424–6
Inherence
    new theory of inherence, 112–15
    substance, 105–9
Initiation. *See* Islamic doctrines of initiation
Intellect
    De Anima, 396, 399
    Proclus' defence of *Timaeus*, 21–2
    Themistius, 332
Intellective theory, 36–7
Islam. *See* Arab world
Islamic doctrines of initiation
    al-Rāzī, Abū Bakr, 517–18
    casual principle, 523–6
    considerations on doctrine, 527–9
    Ibn Suwār, 520–2
    introduction, 517
    Kindean tradition, 522–7
    On The Harmonisation of the opinions of the Two Sages, 517–20
    temporal principle, 523–6

Julian (emperor)
    Iamblichus, 39–40
    Themistius, 23–5
Justice
    conclusions, 274
    introduction, 266
    Porphyry's theory of justice, 269–73
    Stoic theory of justice, 266–8

Khosroes I, 57–9
Kindean tradition, 522–7
Knowledge potentiality, 422–3

Leibniz, 175–7
Logic
    al-Fārābī, 461
    Arab world, 457–64
    Bishr, Abū, 459–60
    definitions, 461–2
    grammar, 459
    Ibn 'Adī, Yaḥyā, 461–3
    Porphyry of Tyre, 27–8
    Stephanus the Philosopher, 553–9
    Stoic philosophy, 457

Logoi
   names, 55, 357, 361
   paraphrase of *Metaphysics* 12, 200–8
   quality, 321
   spontaneous generation, 18–19, 182, 216, 218, 221–2, 225–8
   souls, 34
   universals, 54, 293–6, 307–8

Mathematics, 55–6
Matter, 167–8, 173
Maximus of Ephesus, 25
'Measures', 538–9
Metaphysics. *See also* Paraphrase of *Metaphysics* 12
   adaptation and reactualisation, 577–81
   Alexander of Aphrodisias' commentary, 567–77
   Ammonius, 567–8
   authors of commentary, 565–7, 585–7
   Michael of Ephesus, 580–3, 586
   modern editing and textual criticism, 585–7
   Porphyry of Tyre, 569
   scholiums, 581–5
   spontaneous generation, 180–4, 190–2
Meteorologica, 189
Meteorology, 390
Michael of Ephesus, 79–81
Middle-Platonists
   choice, 148
   eph' hêmin, 143–6
   what depends on us, 136–40
Mind as a blank writing tablet, 54–5
Mixtures
   actuality, 413–15, 422–4, 428
   Alexander of Aphrodisias, 428–30
   Aristotle, 416–21
   conclusion, 434–5
   De mistione, 414–15
   generation & corruption, 416–21, 423–4
   ingredient qualities, 424–6
   introduction, 413–15
   knowledge potentiality, 422–3

Philoponus, John, 421–8, 433–4
potentiality, 413, 416–28, 433
Proclus, 430–1
Renaissance study, 414
Simplicius, 431–3
Zabarella, Jacopo, 414–15, 428
Movement, 478–84
Multigrade genera, 307–9
Multigrade universals, 297–303, 303–7, 309–11
Myth of Er, 34, 147–8, 341

Names
   Ammonius, 356–63
   Aristotle, 355–6
   conclusions, 363–5
   definitions, 356–7
   function, 361–3
   introduction, 353–5
   logoi, 55, 357, 361
   name-givers, 357–8
   natural names, 55
   object resemblance, 358–61
   Plato, 355–6
   Proclus, 356–63
   Socrates, 354–5
Natural generation, 182–4, 191, 193
Natural names, 55
Neoplatonism
   Aristotle's Creator God, 53
   Porphyry of Tyre, 26
   spontaneous generation, 211–25, 225–8, 228–9
   Themistius, 19–20
Nicomachean Ethics, 140–2
Nicostratus, 248–9, 254

Objects. *See* Names
Olympiodorus, 547, 549–51
On Abstinence from Animal Food. *See* Vegetarianism
On Fate, 129
On the Eternity of the World. *See Against Proclus on the Eternity of the World*; World's eternity
On The Harmonisation of the opinions of the Two Sages, 517–20
On the Soul. *See De Anima*
Organon, 457, 463–4

Paraphrase of *Metaphysics* 12
  ideas, 198–201, 208–10
  introduction, 195–8
  logoi, 200–8
Particulars
  astral and cosmic configurations, 168–73
  Avicenna, 173–5
  Chrysippus of Soli, 169, 171–2
  Dexippus, 161–4
  divination, 169
  eternal return, 164–7
  individuals, 161–2
  introduction, 161
  Leibniz, 175–7
  matter, 167–8, 173
  Philoponus, John, 170–1
  Porphyry's *Introduction (Isagôgê)*, 161–3
  Socrates, 165, 168
'The parts of the substance are substances', 110–12
Paul the Persian, 50–1
Perception. *See* Sense-perception
Phaedo
  Ammonius of Alexandria, 48–9
  Damascius, 61, 66
  Proclus, 42, 350–1
  Stephanus the Philosopher, 549
  Varro, 86
Philopator, 12–13
Philoponus, John. *See also Contra Proclum* in Arabic; Philoponus, John (dating of commentaries); Philoponus, John (*Timaeus*)
  Alexander of Aphrodisias, 500–1
  Ammonius' *De Anima* commentary, 401–6
  Ammonius' seminars, 71
  Arabic tradition, 74–8
  Arabic translation of *Against Proclus* 4.4–6, 485–90
  Arabic translation of *Against Proclus* 9.11, 491–502
  Christianity, 71
  commentaries, 71–4
  De Anima commentary, 406–13
  introduction, 70
  mixtures, 421–8, 433–4
  particulars, 170–1
  refutation of Proclus' first argument, 507–10
  sense-perception, 440–4, 450–1
  spontaneous generation, 220–1
  universals, 309–11
  world's eternity, 470–1
Philoponus, John (dating of commentaries)
  Categories, 380–4
  De Anima, 385–7
  De Generatione et Corruptione, 387–9
  divergence from Ammonius, 392
  evidence from titles, 369–73
  hypotheses on dating, 367–9
  Introduction (Isagôgê), 390–1
  Meteorology, 390
  order of commentaries, 391–2
  Physics 4.1–10, 378
  Physics 4.10–14, 373–6
  Physics 8.1, 376–8
  Physics books 1–3, 378–80
  Posterior Analytics, 389–90
  Prior Analytics, 389
Philoponus, John (*Timaeus*)
  errors, 339–45
  eternity of the world, 337
  fifth element, 337–9
  force of attraction in bodies, 343–4
  ideas, 336–7
  plants' perception, 344–5
  quotations from Proclus' lost treatise, 334–6
  sun's position, 340–2
  transmigration of souls, 342–3
  wombs, 344
Philosophy definitions, 48–9
Physics
  Andronicus' canon, 100
  dating of Philoponus' commentaries, 373–80
  substance, 106–7
Place
  Damascius, 534–8
  'measures', 538–9
  Simplicius, 531–40
Plants' perception, 344–5
Plato. *See also* Ideas; *Phaedo*; *Timaeus*
  Ammonius of Alexandria, 48–9
  choice, 147–8

Damascius, 60–2
Iamblichus' commentaries, 36–7, 39
ideas, 198–201, 208–10, 291–6
Myth of Er, 34, 147–8, 341
names, 355–6
Neoplatonism, 19–20, 26, 53
Porphyry of Tyre's commentaries, 35
Proclus' commentaries, 42–5
schools, 39–40, 42, 60–1, 68
Syrianus, 40–1
Plato's text
Aristophanes of Byzantium, 85–6
arrangement, 85–7
circulation, 85
editions and copies, 87–9
introduction, 84
summary, 89
Thrasyllus, 84–5
Plotinus
Porphyry of Tyre, 30
spontaneous generation, 222–4
Pneuma, 444–9
Porphyry of Tyre. *See also* Vegetarianism
achievements, 26
Ad Gaurum, 218–20, 236
Augustine, 32
Categories, 27, 314–15
Categories (rediscovered commentary), 234–7, 253
Christianity, 32–3
commentaries on Aristotle, Pythagoras, and Plato, 35
ethics, 28–31
Iamblichus (*Categories*), 314
introduction, 26–7
Introduction (Isagôgê), 161–3, 390–1, 554
logic, 27–8
Plato, 35
Plotinus, 30
reincarnation, 34
relationship with Iamblichus, 37–8
religion, 31–3
skopos, 317
souls, 33–5
spontaneous generation, 218–20, 236
universals, 303–7
Posterior Analytics, 389–90
Potentiality. *See* Mixtures

Principle of causational synonymy, 182, 191
Principles. *See* Logoi
Prior Analytics, 389
Priscian of Lydia
Agathias, 58, 59–60
Athenian philosophers, 58–9
commentaries on Aristotle, 57–60
Khosroes I, 57–9
Proclus. *See also Timaeus*
commentaries, 42–6
God, 45
infinite power in a finite body, 45–6
introduction, 42–3
lost treatise quotations, 334–6
mixtures, 430–1
Myth of Er, 341
names, 356–63
Phaedo, 42, 350–1
Plato, 42–5
providence and evil, 44
school, 42
souls and reincarnation, 43–4
world's eternity, 468–70, 509–10
Prolegomena Philosophiae, 553–4
Providence and evil, 44
Putrefaction, 188–9
Pythagoras
Porphyry of Tyre's commentaries, 35
texts, 82
Pythagoreans, 38–9

Quadrilaterals, 246, 261–2
Quality, 320–2
Quantity, 319–20

Rationality
communication, 285–7
conclusions, 288
introduction, 274
Porphyry's evidence, 274–6, 283–8
Porphyry's theory of rationality, 279–83
Stoic theory of rationality, 276–9
Reincarnation. *See also* Spontaneous generation
Iamblichus, 38
Myth of Er, 34

Porphyry of Tyre, 34
Proclus, 43–4
transmigration of souls, 342–3
Religion. *See also* Theurgy
   Christianity, 22, 32, 71, 547
   Creator God, 53
   freedom of religion, 22
   God, 45
   Philoponus, John, 71
   Porphyry of Tyre, 31–3
   Stephanus the Philosopher, 547–9
   theology, 61–2
Renaissance study, 414
Riots, 47
Roman acquisition of texts, 83

Seeds, 216–17
Self-knowledge and conscience, 66–7
Sense-perception
   'common sense', 447–8
   gnôstikôs, 449–51
   hearing, 442–3
   introduction, 437–9
   Philoponus, John, 440–4, 450–1
   pneuma, 444–9
   sight, 445–7
   smell, 440, 442, 443
   summary, 452
   touch, 441–2
   zôtikôs, 449–51
Sergius of Resh, 51
Sexual organs, 344
Sight, 445–7
Simplicius
   commentaries, 67–70
   Corollary on Place, 531–40
   Damascius on place, 534–8
   Iamblichus (*Categories*), 314–15
   introduction, 67–8
   'measures', 538–9
   mixtures, 431–3
   schools, 68
   Stephanus the Philosopher, 557–8, 559–60
   substance, 104–5, 116
   Timaeus defence, 345–52
   time, 64–5
Skopos, 316–17
Smell, 440, 442, 443

Socrates
   names, 354–5, 360
   particulars, 165, 168
Sophistical Refutations, 559
Souls. *See also De Anima*; Spontaneous generation; *Timaeus*
   Iamblichus, 38
   logoi, 34
   Myth of Er, 34
   Porphyry of Tyre, 33–5
   Proclus, 43–4
   transmigration, 342–3
Species, 257–62
Spontaneous generation. *See also* Spontaneous generation (Neoplatonic perspective)
   Aquinas, Thomas, 192–3
   embryos, 185–8
   ideas, 198–201, 208–10
   logoi, 18–19, 182, 200–8
   Metaphysics, 180–4, 190–2
   Meteorologica, 189
   natural generation, 182–4, 191, 193
   paraphrase of *Metaphysics* 12, 195–8
   principle of causational synonymy, 182, 191
   putrefaction, 188–9
   Themistius, 18–19, 179–94
Spontaneous generation (Neoplatonic perspective)
   Augustine, 214–15
   conclusion, 228–9
   deceased organisms, 225
   form-principles, 221–2
   forms, 212–18
   heterogenesis, 211, 222, 225–8
   homogenetic biogenesis, 218–20
   logoi, 216, 218, 221–2, 225–8
   generally, 211–25
   summary, 225–8
   Philoponus, John, 220–1
   Plotinus, 222–4
   Porphyry's *Ad Gaurum*, 218–20
   seeds, 216–17
   teleology, 213–14
   Themistius, 227
   types of spontaneous generation, 211–12

Stephanus
  commentaries, 78–9
  De Anima, 394–5
  influence in Ammonian school, 52
  introduction, 78
Stephanus the Philosopher
  Analytics, 559
  Categories, 554–8
  Christianity, 547–9
  Cleombrotus' suicide, 550
  commentaries, 552–3
  conclusions, 562–3
  dates, 551–2
  David the Invincible, 550–1
  De Caelo, 559–60
  De Interpretatione, 558–9
  division, 553–4
  ecumenical teacher, 542–4
  Elias, 548, 550–1, 555–6
  identity, 544–5
  influence, 560–2
  introduction, 541–2
  Introduction (Isagôgê), 554
  logic, 553–9
  Olympiodorus, 547, 549–51
  Phaedo, 549
  Prolegomena Philosophiae, 553–4
  religion and philosophy, 547–9
  Simplicius, 557–8, 559–60
  Sophistical Refutations, 559
  Stephanus' teacher, 545–7
  suicide, attitude to, 549–51
Stoic philosophy
  Alexander of Aphrodisias, 10–14
  downgrade of universals, 297
  justice, 266–8
  logic, 457
  rationality, 276–9
  relatively, 119–22
  sayable vs. Boethus' having, 122–3
Strabo, 91–2
Subaltern genera, 259–60
Substance
  Alexander of Aphrodisias, 110–15
  Boethus of Sidon, 103–23
  categories of form, 116–19
  conclusion, 123
  definitions and terminology, 109–10
  having, 107–8

  having vs. Stoic sayable, 122–3
  health, 107–8
  Iamblichus (*Categories*), 317–18
  inherence, 105–9
  new theory of inherence, 112–15
  non-substantiality, 115–16
  'the parts of the substance are substances', 110–12
  Physics, 106–7
  Simplicius, 104–5, 116
  Stoic relatively, 119–22
  Stoic sayable vs. Boethus' having, 122–3
  theory of substance and predication, 104–5
Suicide
  Cleombrotus, 550
  Stephanus the Philosopher, 549–51
Sulla, 91–4
Sun's position, 340–2
Syllogism, 25
Synonymy, 291–2, 294–5
Syrianus
  commentaries on Aristotle, 40–2
  universals, 291–5

Taurus, 513–15
Teleology, 213–14
Texts in first century BCE. *See also* Plato's text
  conclusion, 102
  introduction, 81
  Pythagoras, 82
  Roman acquisition of texts, 83
  text-based philosophy, 81–4
Thābit Ibn Qurra, 472–3
That which depends on us. *See* What depends on us
Themistius. *See also* Paraphrase of *Metaphysics* 12
  Aristotelianism, 19–20
  civil servant, 17–18
  commentaries on Aristotle, 17–18, 20–1
  freedom of religion, 22
  freedom of speech, 22–3
  harmonisation, 18–19
  ideas, 198–201, 208–10
  intellect and immortality, 21–2

introduction, 17–18
Julian (emperor), 23–5
logoi, 200–8
Maximus of Ephesus, 25
Neoplatonism, 19–20
paraphrase of *Metaphysics* 12, 195–8
philosopher king, 24–5
public life, 22–5
spontaneous generation, 18–19, 179–94, 227
syllogism, 25
world's eternity, 19, 467–8
Theology
    Damascius, 61–2
    Philoponus' downgrading of universals, 309–11
Theophrastus, 91
Theurgy
    Damascius, 61–2
    Iamblichus, 38
Thrasyllus, 84–5
Timaeus
    Ammonius of Alexandria, 328–9
    Aristotle's criticism, 327–30
    conclusion, 352
    errors, 339–45
    eternity of the world, 337
    fifth element, 337–9
    force of attraction in bodies, 343–4
    geometrical elements, 345–52
    harmonising Plato and Aristotle, 347–8
    hermeneutical tradition, 328–9
    Hierocles, 328–9
    ideas, 336–7
    intellect, 332
    Philoponus, John, 334–45
    plants' perception, 344–5
    Proclus' defence, 329–34, 345–52
    quotations from Proclus' lost treatise, 334–6
    sexual organs, 344
    Simplicius' defence, 345–52
    sun's position, 340–2
    transmigration of souls, 342–3
    wombs, 344
    world's eternity, 337
Time
    Damascius, 62–5
    Iamblichus, 36–7

Iamblichus (*Categories*), 322–4
Simplicius, 64–5
Touch, 441–2
Transformations, 312
Transitivity principle, 246–54
Transmigration of souls, 342–3
Triangles, 246, 261–2, 327, 345–52, 430
Tyrannio, 93

Universals
    Alexander of Aphrodisias, 297–303
    Ammonius of Alexandria, 53–4, 307–9
    Categories, 303–6
    concepts, 303–7, 309, 310–11
    downgraded by Aristotle, Boethus and Stoics, 296–7
    Eustratius, 312
    homonymy, 291–2, 294
    ideas as universals, 291–5
    ideas defined, 295–6
    logoi, 54, 293–6, 307–8
    multigrade genera, 307–9
    multigrade universals, 297–303, 303–7, 309–11
    Philoponus, John, 309–10, 310–11
    Porphyry of Tyre, 303–7
    synonymy, 291–2, 294–5
    Syrianus, 291–5
    theology, 309–11
    transformations, 312

Varro, 86
Vegetarianism
    communication, 285–7
    conclusion, 288–9
    consensus interpretation, 264–6
    introduction, 263
    justice, 266–74
    Porphyry's evidence, 274–6, 283–8
    Porphyry's theory of justice, 269–73
    Porphyry's theory of rationality, 279–83
    rationality, 274–88
    Stoic theory of justice, 266–8
    Stoic theory of rationality, 276–9

What depends on us
    Alcinous, 142–3
    Ammonius of Alexandria, 143

choice, 146–50
De Interpretatione, 138–9, 140–2
eph' hêmin, 134–5
exousia, 150–2
Middle-Platonists, 136–40
Nicomachean Ethics, 135–6, 140–2
one-sided causative concept, 132–3
two-sided indeterminist concept, 134–5
Wombs, 344
World's eternity. *See also Against Proclus on the Eternity of the World*
Alexander of Aphrodisias (Arabic translations), 485–502
Alexander of Aphrodisias, 466–7
al-kindī, 471–2
al-Rāzī, Abū Bakr, 473–6, 517–18
approaches, 465
casual principle, 523–6
Contra Proclum in Arabic, 503, 505–9, 517–18
corruptibility, 467, 471
God, 467, 470–6
Ibn Suwār, 520–2
introduction, 464–5
Islamic doctrines of initiation, 517–29
Kindean tradition, 522–7
On The Harmonisation of the opinions of the Two Sages, 517–20
Philoponus, John, 470–1
physical approach, 465–6, 468–71
Proclus, 468–70, 509–10
temporal principle, 523–6
Thābit Ibn Qurra, 472–3
Themistius, 19, 467–8
theological approach, 465, 470–1, 473
Timaeus, 337

Zabarella, Jacopo, 414–15, 428
Zôtikôs, 449–51

Made in the USA
Columbia, SC
22 December 2024